HAMILTON COUNTY OHIO

CITIZENSHIP RECORD ABSTRACTS

1837–1916

Prepared by

Archives & Rare Books Department
University Libraries
University of Cincinnati

Compiled by
Lois E. Hughes

HERITAGE BOOKS
2009

HERITAGE BOOKS
AN IMPRINT OF HERITAGE BOOKS, INC.

Books, CDs, and more—Worldwide

For our listing of thousands of titles see our website
at
www.HeritageBooks.com

Published 2009 by
HERITAGE BOOKS, INC.
Publishing Division
100 Railroad Ave. #104
Westminster, Maryland 21157

Copyright © 1991 Lois E. Hughes

Other books by the author:
Hamilton County, Ohio Birth Records, 1874–1875
Hamilton County, Ohio Death Records, Volume I, 1865–1869
Hamilton County, Ohio Death Records, Volume II, 1870–1873
Hamilton County, Ohio Death Records, 1874–1877
Hamilton County, Ohio Marriage Index, Volume 1, 1817–1845
Wills Filed in Probate Court, Hamilton County, Ohio, 1791–1901

All rights reserved. No part of this book may be reproduced or transmitted in any form or by any means, electronic or mechanical, including photocopying, recording or by any information storage and retrieval system without written permission from the author, except for the inclusion of brief quotations in a review.

International Standard Book Numbers
Paperbound: 978-1-55613-421-0
Clothbound: 978-0-7884-8243-4

INTRODUCTION

Immigration to America, the land of opportunity, was realized by millions of people during the middle to late 19th Century. Famine, civil uprising, persecution, and the spirit of adventure, among other reasons, drove these immigrants to leave their homelands and travel thousands of miles to America to seek their fortunes and a better way of life.

This collection of immigration records includes original and restored Declarations of Intention to Naturalize and Naturalization papers filed in Hamilton County approximately between 1837 and 1916. During a riot in 1884 the courthouse was burned and many records series were destroyed. A great number of the citizenship documents were lost forever but a significant number that survived were "restored". Many of the 25, 517 records on the database are records from other states and counties that were filed in Hamilton County.

The data abstracted from these records by the staff of the Archives & Rare Books Department of the University of Cincinnati Libraries have been entered in a database using dBase IV. This database can be manipulated in many ways for purposes of demographic, statistical, historical and genealogical research. For example, a list could be compiled of all those persons arriving in a specified year, at a specified port, from a specified country. Further data compilations and correlations can be generated from this database upon written request. The Archives & Rare Books Department will also provide full copies of any documents at a small charge per page.

The data abstracted contain the following elements: APPLICANT NAME; AGE; COUNTRY OF ORIGIN; DEPARTURE PORT AND DATE; ARRIVAL PORT AND DATE; DECLARATION DATE; NATURALIZATION DATE; AND RESTORED DATE.

Four headings in the text require explanation. DEC is a logical field indicating whether the record is that of a declaration of intention (T) or a naturalization (F). Some of the original records are in volumes and some are individual documents. VOL and PG numbers locate documents in volumes. FLD is a logical field indicating if an item is in a folder (T) or a volume (F).

Archives & Rare Books staff members who worked on this project were Lois Hughes, Juli Peters, Kevin Grace, Anne J. Gilliland and Alice M. Cornell.

The citizenship records are a small part of the Department's Ohio Network Collection. The University of Cincinnati is a depository of government records from the eight counties of southwestern Ohio (Adams, Brown, Butler, Clermont, Clinton, Hamilton, Highland, and Warren). The Archives & Rare Books Department is open Monday-Friday from 8am-5pm and Wednesday from 8am-8pm. Mail inquiries to Archives & Rare Books Department, Eighth Floor - Carl Blegen Library, University of Cincinnati, Cincinnati, Ohio 45221-0113. Phone: 513-556-1959.

Lois E. Hughes
Compiler

CITIZENSHIP RECORDS

APPLICANT	AGE	COUNTRY OF ORIGIN	DEC	DEPART PORT	ENTRY PORT	ARRIVE DATE	DEC DATE	VOL	PG.	FLD	NAT DATE
Aarnink, Geert	33	Hanover	Y	Bremen	New Orleans	05/19/1852	11/07/1855	13	190	N	
Aaron, Louis	37	Russia	Y	Hamburg	New York	09/26/1886	04/17/1891			Y	
Abbato, Frank	30	Italy	Y	Havre	New York	05/12/1891	08/31/1894	21	71	N	
Abel, Frederick	27	Brunswick	Y	Bremen	New Orleans	11/21/1854	04/19/1860	27	169	N	
Abel, Jacob	38	England	Y	Liverpool	New York	11/27/1868	10/11/1882			Y	
Abel, Jacob	30	England	Y	Antwerp	New York	04/18/1886	10/14/1895			Y	
Abel, Joseph	38	Germany	Y	Havre	New York	03/01/1882	01/10/1883			N	
Abel, Michael	25	Prussia	Y	Hamburg	New York	08/01/1855	07/02/1857	15	122	N	
Abeling, Henry	24	Oldenburg	Y	Bremen	Baltimore	10/15/1848	09/13/1852	25	460	N	
Abeling, John Bernard	24	Germany	Y	Amsterdam	New York	05/15/1887	12/27/1888			Y	
Abeling, John Clement	22	Germany	Y	Amsterdam	New York	05/15/1887	12/27/1888			Y	
Abelowitz, Harris	41	Russia	Y	Hamburg	New York	07/17/1889	10/12/1892			Y	
Abig, Philipp	28	Russia	Y	Hamburg	New York	08/25/1892	10/29/1900			Y	
Abraham, Albert	41	Germany	N	Hamburg	New York	01/01/1862	?			Y	
Abraham, David	74	Germany	N	Havre	New Orleans	07/??/1849	??/??/1852	28	370	N	09/??/1854
Abraham, Emanuel	6	England	N	?	New York	00/00/1873				Y	10/11/1888
Abraham, Isidor	30	Germany	Y	Hamburg	New York	06/16/1878	10/26/1889			Y	
Abraham, John	17	England	N	?	New York	00/00/1880				Y	10/12/1888
Abraham, Joseph	24	Syria	Y	Bayruth	New York	06/23/1889	07/16/1892			Y	
Abraham, Morris	47	Germany	Y	Bremen	New York	10/28/1891	03/06/1897			Y	
Abraham, Samuel	8	England	N	?	New York	00/00/1873				Y	10/23/1886
Abrahart, William	50	England	Y	Liverpool	New York	10/24/1880	03/02/1886			Y	
Abrams, Evan	23	Wales	Y	Liverpool	Philadelphia	08/25/1848	02/24/1853	7	230	N	
Abrams, Jacob	57	Poland	Y	London	New York	10/13/1873	10/20/1888			Y	
Abromovicz, Jacob	??	Romania	Y	?	?	01/19/1901	08/24/1903			Y	
Abt, Christoph	44	Prussia	Y	?	New York	09/02/1884	11/16/1887			Y	
Achtzehn, Chas.	47	Germany	Y	Hamburg	New York	10/31/1867	09/28/1885			Y	
Ackemann, Valentine	30	Bavaria	Y	Havre	New York	11/20/1850	10/07/1854	10	526	N	
Ackemann, Valentine	30	Bavaria	Y	Havre	New York	11/20/1850	10/07/1854	12	465	N	
Ackenhausen, Henry	48	Germany	N	Bremen	New York	09/15/1866	?			Y	
Acker, Leopold	28	Germany	Y	Bremen	New York	10/07/1882	10/13/1884			Y	
Acker, Philip	62	Bavaria	N	Havre	New York	06/11/1872	?			Y	
Ackerman, C.M.	26	Germany	Y	Bremen	New York	03/??/1872	11/07/1882			Y	
Ackerman, S. Joseph	36	Germany	Y	Havre	New York	10/03/1877	11/26/1886			Y	
Ackermann, Bernard	24	Germany	Y	Rotterdam	New York	09/04/1880	10/18/1883			Y	
Ackermann, Charles	32	Germany	Y	Havre	New York	11/02/1880	12/13/1887			Y	
Ackermann, John	24	Bavaria	Y	Havre	New Orleans	10/17/1852	03/23/1858	16	440	N	
Ackermann, Joseph	21	Germany	Y	Havre	New York	02/14/1884	08/18/1886			Y	
Ackermann, Peter	39	Germany	Y	Antwerp	New York	10/07/1882	09/11/1889			Y	
Ackerstaff, John L.	27	Hanover	Y	Bremen	New Orleans	12/29/1847	11/13/1848	1	258	N	
Ackmal, Francis	29	Belgium	Y	?	New York	??/08/1841	10/??/1849	23	270	N	
Acton, Patrick	24	Ireland	Y	Liverpool	New Orleans	12/23/1850	12/29/1852	5	470	N	
Acuntius, Adam	31	Bavaria	Y	Havre	New York	08/16/1850	10/27/1851	4	415	N	
Adam, Charles	22	Hanover	Y	?	New York	05/11/1882	01/14/1884			Y	
Adam, Matthias	38	Germany	Y	Bremen	New York	06/29/1880	10/06/1883			Y	
Adam, Thomas	34	Bavaria	Y	Havre	New Orleans	12/07/1848	01/07/1851	2	470	N	
Adamczak, Adalbert	49	Germany	Y	Bremen	New York	05/06/1881	10/30/1891			Y	
Adamek, John	39	Bohemia	Y	Bremen	New York	03/21/1884	06/11/1890			Y	
Adams, Geo.	38	Germany	Y	Germany	New York	03/17/1882	11/15/1885			Y	
Adams, George	30	England	Y	Liverpool	New York	04/26/1884	07/16/1888			Y	
Adams, George	38	Germany	N	Havre	New York	03/17/1882	?			Y	
Adams, Jacob	??	Germany	Y	?	?	?	10/08/1888			Y	
Adams, Wm.	41	Ireland	Y	Liverpool	New York	10/01/1868	03/01/1887			Y	
Adamsky, John	23	Russia	Y	Bremen	New York	05/30/1890	02/21/1894			Y	
Addis, William	36	England	Y	Liverpool	New York	12/??/1847	03/27/1851	3	359	N	
Addy, Matthew	27	Canada	Y	Montreal	Cincinnati	03/07/1857	04/12/1862	18	316	N	
Adelhardt, Carl	35	Germany	Y	Antwerp	New York	08/06/1878	11/01/1881			Y	
Adelman, William	58	Germany	N	Havre	New York	??/??/1849	?			Y	
Adelmann, August C.	??	Germany	N	?	?	08/15/1883				Y	10/27/1892

CITIZENSHIP RECORDS

APPLICANT	AGE	COUNTRY OF ORIGIN	DEC	DEPART PORT	ENTRY PORT	ARRIVE DATE	DEC DATE	VOL	PG.	FLD	NAT DATE
Ader, Anton	44	Bavaria	Y	Rotterdam	New Orleans	12/??/1846	10/13/1857	15	412	N	
Adler, Bernard	45	Wurttemberg	Y	Havre	New York	07/04/1854	10/17/1857	15	441	N	
Adler, Eduard	22	Russia	Y	Rotterdam	New York	05/29/1896	10/18/1897			Y	
Adler, Gustav	41	Germany	Y	Hamburg	New York	09/??/1866	06/26/1886			Y	
Adler, H.	44	Germany	N	Hamburg	New York	05/??/1880	?			Y	
Adler, Henry	37	Germany	Y	Hamburg	New York	01/15/1877	03/31/1887			Y	
Adler, Leonhard	25	Bavaria	Y	Havre	New Orleans	04/20/1854	07/23/1855	11	424	N	
Adler, Theodore	27	Germany	Y	Bremen	New York	07/06/1892	01/16/1900			Y	
Adrion, Andreas	24	Germany	Y	Havre	New York	09/21/1881	11/23/1885			Y	
Adrion, Ernst	28	Germany	Y	?	?	?	01/18/1894			Y	
Adrion, F.G.	33	Germany	Y	Bremen	New York	10/14/1890	10/27/1892			Y	
Adrion, Gotfried	23	Germany	Y	Bremen	New York	09/03/1880	10/05/1883			Y	
Aebersold, Christian	30	Switzerland	Y	?	?	?	09/18/1884			Y	
Aebi, Carl J.	26	Switzerland	Y	Havre	New York	03/17/1881	12/27/1886			Y	
Aeckerle, Philip	26	Bavaria	Y	Havre	New Orleans	11/12/1854	03/24/1856	26	280	N	
Aeh, Frederick	48	Bavaria	Y	Bremen	New York	08/18/1853	04/12/1858	16	464	N	
Aekermann, Jacob	49	Switzerland	Y	Havre	New York	12/14/1883	09/15/1896			Y	
Aeschbach, John Gotfrid	??	Switzerland	Y	?	New York	?	05/08/1884			Y	
Affelhoy, William E.	17	Denmark	N	?	Boston	00/00/1877				Y	10/26/1888
Agen, Christ	42	Ireland	Y	Liverpool	New York	05/16/1883	09/27/1890			Y	
Aghone, Mariano	45	Italy	Y	Palermo	New York	03/01/1883	10/31/1900			Y	
Agin, Michael	40	Ireland	Y	Galway	New York	10/20/1846	03/01/1853	7	251	N	
Agostino, Capiano	40	Italy	Y	Palermo	New York	08/19/1891	10/21/1895	21	82	N	
Agricola, Peter H.	32	Germany	Y	Bremen	Baltimore	07/30/1884	10/12/1885			Y	
Ahaus, Joseph	29	Prussia	Y	Bremen	New Orleans	06/04/1848	05/01/1854	8	316	N	
Ahaus, Joseph	29	Prussia	Y	Bremen	New Orleans	06/04/1848	05/01/1854	9	189	N	
Ahern, John	??	Ireland	N	?	?	04/22/1882	?			Y	03/26/1892
Ahlenstorf, Herman H. C.	44	Holland	Y	Liverpool	New York	02/07/1857	10/10/1860	27	481	N	
Ahlenstorf, John Henry	31	Hanover	Y	Amsterdam	New York	08/02/1846	12/13/1851	4	516	N	
Ahlers, Albert	26	Brunswick	Y	Bremen	Baltimore	06/15/1847	10/02/1848	1	28	N	
Ahlers, Ben	27	Germany	N	Bremen	Baltimore	05/17/1873	?			Y	
Ahlers, Carl	27	Oldenburg	Y	Bremen	Baltimore	05/08/1848	10/10/1854	6	231	N	
Ahlers, Charles	27	Oldenburg	Y	Bremen	Baltimore	05/08/1848	10/10/1854	11	234	N	
Ahlers, H.F.	47	Germany	Y	Bremen	New York	06/?/1865	06/20/1884			Y	
Ahlers, Henry	30	Hanover	Y	Bremen	New York	07/10/1843	11/22/1848	1	375	N	
Ahlers, Henry	4	Germany	N	?	Baltimore	00/00/1870				Y	10/27/1888
Ahlers, John Bernhard	31	Oldenburg	Y	Bremen	Baltimore	06/12/1848	01/04/1851	2	447	N	
Ahlers, John Fredericks	25	Hanover	Y	Bremen	New Orleans	12/16/1845	01/17/1850	23	517	N	
Ahlert, Louis H.	26	Germany	Y	Bremen	New York	03/21/1882	09/19/1888			Y	
Ahlert, William	30	Prussia	Y	Hamburg	New York	08/28/1852	05/06/1854	8	389	N	
Ahlert, William	30	Prussia	Y	Hamburg	New York	08/28/1852	05/06/1854	9	263	N	
Ahles, Christian Ludwig	24	Wurttemberg	Y	Antwerp	New York	02/01/1853	12/31/1855	13	411	N	
Ahlfeld, William	48	Prussia	Y	Bremen	New York	12/12/1846	01/27/1849	1	524	N	
Ahmann, Mathew	??	Germany	Y	?	?	06/14/1894	02/28/1895			Y	
Ahr, Mathew	??	Germany	Y	?	?	?	12/14/1889			Y	
Ahrens, August	45	Hanover	Y	Bremen	New Orleans	12/12/1854	07/20/1858	16	514	N	
Ahrens, Charles	29	Germany	Y	Hamburg	New York	09/17/1881	05/07/1883			Y	
Ahrens, Ferdinand	32	Germany	Y	Bremen	New York	04/18/1888	02/15/1893			Y	
Ahrens, Fred	25	Germany	Y	Bremen	New York	10/14/1881	03/10/1885			Y	
Ahrens, John Christoph	21	Hanover	Y	Bremen	New York	11/15/1853	03/11/1856	26	184	N	
Ahrens, John Henry	28	Oldenburg	Y	Bremen	New Orleans	11/23/1845	10/11/1848	1	129	N	
Ahrens, Louis	40	Germany	N	Hamburg	New York	02/21/1867	?			Y	
Ahrens, Louis	52	Germany	N	Hamburg	New York	02/27/1868	?			Y	
Ahrman, Chrisitan	51	Switzerland	Y	?	New York	??/??/1863	09/28/1880			Y	
Ahus, Henry	28	Prussia	Y	Havre	New York	06/26/1849	03/28/1853	7	447	N	
Aichholz, Jacob	31	Wuertemberg	Y	Rotterdam	New York	08/26/1853	03/29/1856	26	376	N	
Aignes, Mathes	35	Austira	Y	Havre	New York	08/02/1894	03/11/1897			Y	
Aker, Ferdinand	29	Germany	Y	Antwerp	New York	09/09/1885	01/08/1887			Y	
Aker, Gaudenz	32	Germany	Y	Antwerp	New York	05/28/1882	05/01/1886			Y	

CITIZENSHIP RECORDS

APPLICANT	AGE	COUNTRY OF ORIGIN	DEC	DEPART PORT	ENTRY PORT	ARRIVE DATE	DEC DATE	VOL	PG.	FLD	NAT DATE
Aksban, Moses	56	Russia	Y	Hamburg	New York	07/11/1894	11/19/1902			Y	
Alban, John	26	Germany	Y	Hamburg	New York	09/19/1885	04/23/1890			Y	
Albanese, Salvatore	40	Italy	Y	Palermo	New York	04/30/1889	12/18/1900			Y	
Albanesius, Wilhelm Augu	??	Germany	Y	?	?	?	03/15/1893			Y	
Albauck, George	28	Oldenburg	Y	Bremen	New Orleans	04/15/1846	04/19/1850	3	1	N	
Albers, August	22	Germany	Y	Bremen	Baltimore	04/18/1883	11/06/1887			Y	
Albers, Bernard Henry	23	Oldenburg	Y	Bremen	Baltimore	04/30/1848	06/19/1851	3	432	N	
Albers, Frederick	23	Germany	Y	Bremen	Baltimore	09/11/1884	08/24/1888			Y	
Albers, Henry	35	Germany	Y	Bremen	New York	12/23/1883	07/06/1895			Y	
Albers, John	30	Oldenburg	Y	Bremen	New Orleans	12/23/1845	10/16/1848	1	239	N	
Albers, John B.	49	Germany	Y	Bremen	Baltimore	10/12/1884	11/03/1888			Y	
Albers, John Joseph	51	Germany	Y	Bremen	Baltimore	11/01/1857	10/27/1888	19	192	N	
Albers, John Joseph	51	Germany	Y	Bremen	Baltimore	11/07/1857	10/27/1888			Y	
Albers, Joseph	30	Germany	Y	Rotterdam	New York	09/15/1882	02/01/1892			Y	
Albers, Ludwig	??	Hamburg	Y	?	New Orleans	??/13/18??	10/24/1850	2	291	N	
Albersmann, Theodore	21	Prussia	Y	Bremen	New Orleans	10/25/1850	05/21/1856	26	516	N	
Albert, Andrew	32	Germany	Y	Hamburg	New York	07/15/1872	11/03/1882			Y	
Albert, Charles	49	Switzerland	Y	?	New York	??/??/1864	01/17/1887			Y	
Albert, Charles	23	Russia	Y	Hamburg	Boston	11/??/1886	10/23/1888			Y	
Albert, Frederick	27	Germany	Y	Havre	New York	11/13/1891	10/27/1894			Y	
Albert, George	30	Germany	Y	Liverpool	New York	06/12/1880	12/09/1889			Y	
Albert, John	30	Bavaria	Y	Bremen	New Orleans	08/12/1853	10/10/1854	6	228	N	
Albert, John	30	Bavaria	Y	Bremen	New York	08/12/1853	10/10/1854	11	231	N	
Albert, Nathan	29	Russia	Y	Hamburg	New York	12/??/1885	10/12/1888			Y	
Albertz, Henry	??	Germany	Y	?	?	?	10/17/1882			Y	
Albertzahrt, John Herman	30	Oldenburg	Y	Bremen	New York	08/25/1853	10/09/1854	6	174	N	
Albes, Conrad H.	21	Hanover	Y	Bremen	New York	11/20/1854	02/09/1857	15	5	N	
Albink, B.	28	Germany	Y	Rotterdam	New York	04/25/1874	10/08/1880			Y	
Albiz, Edward	43	Germany	Y	Rotterdam	New York	07/04/1885	11/11/1893			Y	
Albrecht, Carl	37	Prussia	Y	Hamburg	New York	12/24/1854	03/31/1858	16	454	N	
Albrecht, Carl	22	Prussia	Y	Bremen	New York	02/08/1869	01/03/1872	18	447	N	
Albrecht, David	36	Baden	Y	Havre	New Orleans	04/17/1849	04/12/1852	24	450	N	
Albrecht, George A.	24	Hamburg	Y	Carocas	Baltimore	05/20/1848	03/20/1851	3	297	N	
Albrecht, Ignatz	29	Switzerland	Y	Havre	New Orleans	11/26/1845	11/01/1852	5	96	N	
Albrecht, John	25	Germany	Y	?	?	08/01/1886	09/28/1893			Y	
Albrecht, John George	45	Bavaria	Y	Bremen	Baltimore	??/01/1847	03/19/1851	3	237	N	
Albrecht, Max	49	Germany	N	Bremen	New York	01/??/1873	?			Y	
Albrecht, Michael	24	Baden	Y	Havre	New Orleans	06/01/1847	08/15/1848	22	112	N	
Albrecht, Paul	30	Prussia	Y	Bremen	Baltimore	05/04/1869	05/30/1872	18	495	N	
Albrecht, Paul	23	Switzerland	Y	Havre	New York	03/15/1891	07/27/1893			Y	
Albrecht, Wm.	32	Germany	Y	Hamburg	New York	05/17/1882	10/26/1888			Y	
Albring, Charles	44	Germany	N	Bremen	New York	07/25/1873	?			Y	
Album, Mayer	33	Russia	Y	Hamburg	Philadelphia	06/05/1882	06/06/1889			Y	
Aldendorff, John Henry	21	Prussia	Y	Bremen	New Orleans	06/10/1853	10/10/1854	6	205	N	
Aldendorff, John Henry	21	Prussia	Y	Bremen	New Orleans	06/10/1853	10/10/1854	11	208	N	
Alderson, Thomas	46	England	Y	Liverpool	Philadelphia	07/??/1880	03/24/1890			Y	
Alegier, Charles	17	Germany	N	?	New York	00/00/1876	10/27/1888			Y	
Alering, H.H.	34	Germany	Y	Bremen	New York	04/28/1881	01/09/1884			Y	
Alex, Richard	34	Germany	Y	Bremen	Baltimore	08/27/1883	01/17/1887			Y	
Alexander, George	28	Bavaria	Y	Havre	New Orleans	01/20/1848	06/12/1854	10	118	N	
Alexander, George	28	Bavaria	Y	Havre	New Orleans	01/20/1848	06/12/1854	12	55	N	
Alexander, George	40	Germany	N	Bremen	Baltimore	04/??/1871	?			Y	
Alexander, Henry	22	Ireland	Y	Belfast	New York	09/04/1889	06/23/1892			Y	
Alexander, John	40	Ireland	Y	Liverpool	New York	11/27/1873	09/22/1885			Y	
Alexander, Moses Meyers	38	England	Y	Glasgow	New York	03/05/1854	05/12/1854	8	430	N	
Alexander, Moses Meyers	38	England	Y	Glasgow	New York	03/05/1854	05/12/1854	9	303	N	
Alexander, Robert	29	Ireland	Y	London	New York	06/01/1847	03/11/1852	24	286	N	
Alexander, Samuel	25	Poland (Russi	Y	Liverpool	New York	??/25/1854	04/17/1855	11	262	N	
Alexander, William	23	Scotland	Y	Glasgow	New York	12/??/1852	04/24/1855	11	291	N	

CITIZENSHIP RECORDS

APPLICANT	AGE	COUNTRY OF ORIGIN	DEC	DEPART PORT	ENTRY PORT	ARRIVE DATE	DEC DATE	VOL	PG.	FLD	NAT DATE
Alexander, William	26	Scotland	Y	?	?	?	08/21/1889			Y	
Alfisi, Andrew	??	Italy	N	?	?	??/??/1874	?			Y	
Alge, John	26	Austria	Y	Hamburg	New York	10/06/1880	02/26/1881			Y	
Alig, Adam	14	Germany	N	?	Baltimore	00/00/1879				Y	03/23/1888
Alig, Peter	48	Bavaria	Y	London	New York	07/18/1857	09/25/1857	15	316	N	
Allan, Louis	25	Hanover	Y	Bremen	Baltimore	08/15/1842	10/13/1848	1	209	N	
Allan, William A.	60	Ireland	N	Liverpool	New York	05/28/1857	?			Y	
Alldoesfer, George	54	Germany	Y	Havre	New York	06/06/1880	09/11/1884			Y	
Alle, Henry	37	Switzerland	Y	Havre	New York	02/16/1882	10/26/1896			Y	
Allen, Edward	29	Scotland	Y	Glasgow	New York	04/20/1839	08/11/1848	22	92	N	
Allen, Henry	26	Ireland	Y	Londonderry	Buffalo	09/??/1848	05/17/1854	8	460	N	
Allen, Henry	26	Ireland	Y	Londonderry	Buffalo	09/??/1848	05/17/1854	9	333	N	
Allen, Samuel Edson	22	England	Y	Liverpool	Philadelphia	04/02/1855	01/14/1856	13	465	N	
Allendorf, August	22	Germany	Y	Bremen	New York	02/14/1882	07/25/1884			Y	
Allering, Aloysius	54	Germany	Y	Bremen	New York	09/27/1866	04/04/1896			Y	
Allf, Hermann	45	Hanover	Y	Bremen	New Orleans	11/26/1841	10/06/1854	10	472	N	
Allf, Hermann	45	Hanover	Y	Bremen	New Orleans	11/26/1841	10/06/1854	12	411	N	
Allgeyer, Clemens	25	Baden	Y	Havre	New Orleans	04/10/1852	09/22/1854	10	158	N	
Allgeyer, Clemens	25	Baden	Y	Havre	New Orleans	04/10/1852	09/22/1854	12	97	N	
Allgoever, Phillip	48	Germany	Y	Hamburg	New York	10/01/1857	11/03/1883			Y	
Allingham, William	42	Ireland	Y	Sligo	Buffalo	11/??/1836	10/03/1854	10	396	N	
Allingham, William	42	Ireland	Y	Sligo	Buffalo	11/??/1836	10/03/1854	12	335	N	
Allman, John	30	Ireland	Y	Cork	New York	05/30/1848	04/21/1853	8	92	N	
Allsop, Samuel	26	England	Y	Liverpool	New York	06/12/1885	08/16/1889			Y	
Allsteadt, Aldolph	27	Germany	Y	Bremen	Baltimore	11/18/1891	05/18/1892			Y	
Almenrader, Robert	33	Germany	Y	Amsterdam	New York	07/14/1889	06/19/1894			Y	
Alphonso, Gabriel	48	Italy	Y	Naples	New York	05/30/1884	11/27/1793			Y	
Alpiner, Morris	26	Cracow	Y	Hamburg	New York	09/12/1853	09/13/1855	13	24	N	
Alpiner, Solomon	21	Cracow	Y	Liverpool	New York	09/09/1853	??/??/18??	13	25	N	
Alsentzer, Henry	55	Germany	Y	Hamburg	New York	05/28/1885	11/21/1902			Y	
Alt, Christian	48	Wuertemberg	Y	Havre	New York	05/17/1850	02/18/1856	26	101	N	
Alt, Gerhard	30	Prussia	Y	Rotterdam	New York	06/08/1845	01/19/1849	1	462	N	
Altegelbers, Henry	55	Germany	Y	Rotterdam	New York	06/12/1869	10/12/1896			Y	
Altehulsing, Wenzelaus	40	Germany	Y	Bremen	New York	09/28/1871	09/24/1880			Y	
Alteman, William	32	Prussia	Y	Bremen	New York	04/14/1847	10/09/1854	6	147	N	
Altemeyer, Heinrich	38	Hanover	Y	Bremen	New Orleans	11/01/1849	05/29/1854	10	21	N	
Altenau, Joseph	21	Prussia	Y	Bremen	Baltimore	11/10/1854	07/06/1855	11	343	N	
Altenau, William	32	Prussia	Y	Bremen	New York	04/14/1847	10/09/1854	11	150	N	
Altenburg, Franz	42	Prussia	Y	Havre	New York	08/30/1849	04/16/1860	27	156	N	
Altendorn, Nicolaus	27	Germany	Y	Hamburg	New York	05/09/1883	08/10/1889			Y	
Altenhoff, Herman Henry	??	Hanover	Y	Bremen	Baltimore	11/01/1845	10/12/1848	1	168	N	
Altenshulten, John Berna	28	Hanover	Y	Bremen	New Orleans	12/01/1848	11/04/1858	17	277	N	
Alteoogt, Rudolph	23	Prussia	Y	Bremen	New York	07/20/1854	07/31/1858	16	543	N	
Altevers, John Herman	40	Hanover	Y	Bremen	New Orleans	12/12/1845	02/25/1856	26	122	N	
Altgibbers, Bernard	55	Germany	Y	Rotterdam	New York	06/12/1869	10/12/1896			Y	
Althammer, William	33	Wurttemberg	Y	Bremen	New York	11/10/1852	04/03/1858	16	488	N	
Althaus, Bernard	31	Germany	N	Bremen	New York	08/22/1874	?			Y	
Althoefer, Henry	50	Germany	N	Bremen	New York	10/13/1866	10/15/1869	28	344	N	11/01/1876
Althoefer, Henry	50	Germany	N	Bremen	New York	10/13/1866	10/15/1869			Y	11/01/1876
Althoff, Bernard	31	Prussia	Y	New Diep	Baltimore	10/21/1853	03/14/1856	26	199	N	
Altman, Antoni	33	Russia	Y	Bremen	Baltimore	09/07/1887	10/11/1887			Y	
Altman, Moritz	34	Austria	Y	Bremen	New York	06/11/1888	02/06/1894			Y	
Altmeyer, Heinrich	38	Hanover	Y	Bremen	New Orleans	11/01/1849	05/29/1854	9	438	N	
Altnorthoff, Herman	26	Germany	Y	Rotterdam	New York	10/14/1882	11/14/1884			Y	
Altwegger, Andreas	42	Germany	Y	Bremen	New York	02/05/1882	01/21/1885			Y	
Aman, Martin	54	Bavaria	Y	Bremen	Baltimore	08/18/1845	08/17/1848	22	195	N	
Amann, August	24	Germany	Y	Bremen	New York	03/20/1890	07/05/1890			Y	
Amann, Engelbert	25	Prussia	Y	Havre	New York	03/30/1851	09/17/1755	13	59	N	
Amann, Fridolin	24	Baden	Y	Havre	New Orleans	02/02/1856	09/22/1857	15	300	N	

CITIZENSHIP RECORDS

APPLICANT	AGE	COUNTRY OF ORIGIN	DEC	DEPART PORT	ENTRY PORT	ARRIVE DATE	DEC DATE	VOL	PG.	FLD	NAT DATE
Amann, Leon	28	Germany	Y	Havre	New York	05/09/1886	01/23/1890			Y	
Amann, Leopold	30	Germany	Y	Havre	New York	08/05/1881	08/28/1885			Y	
Amann, Magnus	32	Baden	Y	Havre	New Orleans	04/07/1852	09/30/1854	10	322	N	
Amann, Magnus	32	Baden	Y	Havre	New Orleans	04/07/1852	09/30/1854	12	261	N	
Amann, Martin	30	Baden	Y	Havre	New York	06/28/1854	10/29/1858	17	167	N	
Amann, Victor	21	Germany	Y	Havre	New York	06/17/1895	03/08/1898			Y	
Ambas, Moses	14	Russia	N	?	Philadelphia	00/00/1881				Y	10/23/1888
Ambaum, Jacob	30	Germany	Y	Bremen	New York	04/11/1893	10/26/1895			Y	
Amberg, Adolf	33	Switzerland	Y	Havre	New York	06/28/1883	10/21/1889			Y	
Amberg, Joshua	??	Bavaria	Y	Sulzdorf	New York	??/27/1846	08/??/1851	4	181	N	
Amberger, Joseph	31	Bavaria	Y	Bremen	Baltimore	08/10/1854	09/28/1854	10	289	N	
Amberger, Joseph	31	Bavaria	Y	Bremen	Baltimore	08/10/1854	09/28/1854	12	228	N	
Ambler, Perry Troughton	21	England	Y	Liverpool	Philadelphia	07/05/1885	08/11/1888			Y	
Ambrose, Robert	45	Ireland	Y	Liverpool	New Orleans	02/10/1849	02/16/1852	24	121	N	
Ambrosius, Gustav	34	Germany	Y	Bremen	Baltimore	01/28/1891	10/20/1897			Y	
Ameer, Babilla Y.	30	Persia	Y	Bremen	New York	09/15/1895	01/09/1889			Y	
Ameringer, Edward	28	Germany	Y	Antwerp	New York	09/03/1884	08/15/1889			Y	
Amirkanian, John	27	Turkey	Y	?	New York	07/23/1893	11/18/1895			Y	
Ammann, Herny	25	Switzerland	Y	?	?	04/17/1884	03/04/1890			Y	
Ammann, John	45	Germany	N	Bremen	New York	12/27/1869	?			Y	
Ammon, John	30	Germany	Y	Bremen	New York	04/28/1882	10/14/1887			Y	
Amon, Lorenz	25	Austria	Y	Hamburg	New York	05/03/1880	02/11/1886	19	30	N	
Amon, Lorenz	25	Austria	Y	Hamburg	New York	05/03/1880	02/11/1880			Y	
Amon, Peter	??	Austria	Y	?	?	?	11/01/1893			Y	
Amrhein, Anthony	16	Germany	N	?	Philadelphia	00/00/1882				Y	11/06/1888
Amrhein, Barthel	30	Bavaria	Y	Rotterdam	New York	06/??/1847	12/??/1850	2	404	N	
Ams, Henry	31	Germany	Y	Amsterdam	New York	07/18/1881	10/28/1886	19	93	N	
Amschler, John	33	Bavaria	Y	Bremen	New York	09/07/1853	11/05/1855	13	169	N	
Amshoff, Bernard	28	Germany	Y	Bremen	Baltimore	06/11/1881	05/11/1887			Y	
Amsler, Samuel	32	Switzerland	Y	Havre	New Orleans	12/24/1854	10/13/1860	27	489	N	
Anarino, Giavanni	27	Italy	Y	Palermo	New York	04/27/18??	10/18/1893			Y	
Anbrey, John	25	England	Y	Liverpool	Boston	04/13/1891	05/20/1896			Y	
Ande, Jacob	34	Prussia	Y	Bremen	Baltimore	07/12/1857	07/05/1860	27	205	N	
Anderhalder, John	32	Switzerland	Y	Havre	New York	04/11/1883	08/18/1888			Y	
Anders, G.	35	Germany	Y	Hamburg	New York	10/03/1881	12/28/1886			Y	
Anders, Otto	31	Germany	Y	?	New York	??/??/1890	09/14/1895			Y	
Anderson, Axel A.	23	Sweden	Y	?	New York	04/??/1892	10/27/1894			Y	
Anderson, Charles	51	Sweden	Y	Goteborg	Boston	07/03/1861	10/23/1886			Y	
Anderson, Gust.	24	Sweden	Y	Guerney	New york	04/24/1879	11/06/1882			Y	
Anderson, James	30	Scotland	Y	Glasgow	New York	06/13/1879	07/24/1884			Y	
Anderson, John	14	Sweden	N	?	Boston	00/00/1873				Y	10/27/1888
Anderson, John A.	71	Scotland	N	Leith	New York	05/24/1831	?	28	36	N	08/25/1850
Anderson, John A.	14	Scotland	N	Leith	New York	04/24/1831				Y	08/25/1850
Anderson, John M.	??	Sweden	Y	?	?	?	10/27/1890			Y	
Anderson, Martin	48	Denmark	N	Copenhagen	New York	06/??/1862	09/??/1865	28	323	N	11/??/1868
Anderson, Martin	18	Denmark	N	Copenhagen	New York	06/00/1862	09/00/1865			Y	11/01/1868
Anderson, Pelle	??	Denmark	Y	?	?	?	09/27/1884			Y	
Anderson, Thomas MacDona	26	Scotland	Y	London	New York	08/01/1885	11/12/1891			Y	
Anderson, William	25	Ireland	N	Liverpool	New York	03/??/1881	?			Y	
Andler, Adam	21	Germany	Y	Bremen	New York	05/15/1881	05/19/1893			Y	
Andler, Adam	29	Germany	N	Bremen	New York	05/15/1881	?			Y	
Andre, Gustavus	24	Baden	Y	Havre	New York	06/28/1854	02/04/1857	14	538	N	
Andreacio, Sebastino	32	Italy	Y	Naples	New York	06/01/1888	10/07/1896			Y	
Andree, Adolph	34	Germany	Y	Bremen	Baltimore	03/27/1888	11/19/1892			Y	
Andree, Ernst	23	Germany	Y	Bremen	Baltimore	12/02/1889	09/10/1892			Y	
Andreson, Fedder	??	Germany	Y	?	New York	?	02/24/1885			Y	
Andrew, Hugh	21	Scotland	Y	Greenock	New York	07/10/1851	09/26/1854	10	251	N	
Andrew, Hugh	21	Scotland	Y	Greenock	New York	07/10/1851	09/26/1854	12	190	N	
Andrew, John Sinclair	27	Scotland	Y	Glasgow	Boston	04/04/1882	08/21/1888			Y	

CITIZENSHIP RECORDS

APPLICANT	AGE	COUNTRY OF ORIGIN	DEC	DEPART PORT	ENTRY PORT	ARRIVE DATE	DEC DATE	VOL	PG.	FLD	NAT DATE
Andrew, William	29	Scotland	Y	Glasgow	Philadelphia	05/25/1885	08/21/1888			Y	
Andrews, Charles	21	England	Y	Liverpool	Buffalo	07/04/1857	10/08/1860	27	461	N	
Andrews, Rupert R.	84	England	N	Liverpool	New York	09/05/1827	?	28	122	N	09/18/1838
Andrews, Rupert R.	23	England	N	Liverpool	New York	09/05/1827	?			Y	09/18/1838
Anetzberger, Max	24	Germany	Y	Antwerp	Philadelphia	04/28/1894	09/19/1896			Y	
Angelbeck, Joseph	31	Oldenburg	Y	Bremen	Baltimore	07/05/1855	12/05/1859	17	490	N	
Angelhaus, Henry	33	Hanover	Y	Bremen	New York	11/25/1853	10/12/1857	15	403	N	
Angler, Caspar	40	Germany	Y	Bremen	Baltimore	03/29/1890	03/06/1890			Y	
Angne, Jacob	24	Germany	Y	Rotterdam	New York	09/01/1879	05/06/1882			Y	
Anhalt, August	32	Prussia	Y	Bremen	New York	11/01/1853	12/23/1857	16	242	N	
Ankenbauer, John	33	Bavaria	Y	Bavaria	New York	07/10/1851	05/30/1854	9	451	N	
Ankenbauer, John	33	Bavaria	Y	Bremen	New York	07/10/1851	05/30/1854	10	34	N	
Ankeubauer, Burkhard	31	Germany	Y	Bremen	Baltimore	10/27/1881	01/15/1889			Y	
Annink, Jan William	28	Holland	Y	Antwerp	New York	07/15/1857	05/19/1859	17	417	N	
Ansbro, James C.	23	Ireland	Y	Liverpool	New York	08/26/1848	04/15/1852	24	509	N	
Ansbury, James	50	Ireland	Y	Liverpool	New Orleans	05/10/1847	11/11/1852	5	270	N	
Ansbury, James	50	Ireland	Y	Liverpool	New Orleans	05/10/1847	11/11/1852	6	394	N	
Anschuetz, Ferdinand	53	Prussia	Y	Bremen	Baltimore	11/09/1853	03/31/1856	26	382	N	
Anschutz, Charles	30	Prussia	Y	Havre	New York	06/??/1847	??/??/1851	3	226	N	
Anselm, Landolin	30	Germany	Y	Havre	New York	07/04/1883	08/25/1885			Y	
Anshutz, Christian	23	Prussia	Y	Havre	New York	04/06/1849	03/15/1853	7	328	N	
Ante, Antoni	42	Germany	Y	?	New York	??/??/1864	01/12/1881			Y	
Ante, Jacob	61	Germany	N	Bremen	Baltimore	07/04/1855	?			Y	
Anter, Peter	52	Germany	N	Bremen	New York	06/04/1853	?	28	156	N	03/29/1860
Anter, Peter	17	Germany	N	Bremen	New York	06/04/1853	?			Y	03/29/1860
Anthe, Fritz	28	Germany	Y	Bremen	Baltimore	03/29/1886	10/08/1889			Y	
Anthony, Andrew	36	Germany	Y	Antwerp	New York	09/29/1881	10/16/1893			Y	
Anthony, Patrick	34	Ireland	Y	Liverpool	New York	07/05/1842	10/03/1854	10	389	N	
Anthony, Patrick	34	Ireland	Y	Liverpool	New York	07/05/1842	10/03/1854	12	328	N	
Anton, Adam	31	Bavaria	Y	Havre	New York	07/26/1850	09/08/1852	25	413	N	
Anton, Laugel	29	France	Y	Havre	New York	07/07/1848	09/29/1856	14	32	N	
Antoni, Henry	28	Austria	Y	Hamburg	New York	03/24/1893	04/22/1893			Y	
Antonie, Francis	34	Germany	Y	Antwerp	New York	12/24/1879	11/19/1892			Y	
Antreck, Herman	41	Germany	N	Bremen	New York	09/08/1880	?			Y	
Anyan, George	38	England	Y	Liverpool	New York	07/??/1848	10/12/1858	17	65	N	
Apfel, Jacob	31	Bavaria	Y	Havre	New Orleans	11/26/1848	03/30/1853	7	466	N	
Apfel, John	35	Germany	Y	Bremen	New York	02/12/1880	12/02/1885			Y	
Apke, Joseph	24	Germany	Y	Rotterdam	New York	12/14/1892	04/18/1895			Y	
Appel, Abe	14	Germany	Y	Bremen	New York	07/26/1889	08/24/1891			Y	
Appel, Carl	27	Germany	Y	Bremen	Baltimore	05/14/1881	05/08/1886			Y	
Appel, Ferdinand	22	Baden	Y	Rotterdam	New Orleans	03/17/1845	01/22/1849	1	486	N	
Appel, Frank	36	Baden	Y	Havre	New Orleans	07/22/1848	11/08/1852	5	251	N	
Appel, Frank	36	Baden	Y	Havre	New Orleans	07/22/1848	11/08/1852	6	375	N	
Appel, Jacob	24	Bavaria	Y	Havre	New York	04/03/1867	09/24/8172	18	523	N	
Appel, Joseph	33	Bavaria	Y	Havre	New York	05/01/1853	10/07/1854	11	47	N	
Appel, Louis	22	Germany	Y	Antwerp	New York	02/17/1885	02/04/1888			Y	
Appelmann, George	23	Germany	Y	Bremen	Baltimore	06/15/1887	12/29/1887			Y	
Appelmann, George	21	Bavaria	Y	Havre	New Orleans	07/02/1852	03/10/1856	26	178	N	
Appelmann, John	35	Bavaria	Y	Bremen	New Orleans	??/10/1844	06/14/1851	3	376	N	
Appermann, George	25	Hanover	Y	Bremen	New Orleans	10/25/1854	10/12/1858	17	64	N	
Apple, Joseph	23	Bavaria	Y	Havre	New York	04/??/18??	10/07/1854	6	46	N	
Apt, Henry	32	Prussia	Y	Liverpool	New York	09/23/1850	04/02/1853	7	497	N	
Aram, Arnold	33	Germany	Y	Hamburg	New York	08/02/1881	10/17/1884			Y	
Aram, B.	29	Germany	Y	Hamburg	New York	09/02/1881	09/21/1883			Y	
Arand, Albin	21	Prussia	Y	Bremen	New York	05/25/1854	12/11/1857	16	216	N	
Arand, Frank Frederick	21	Prussia	Y	Bremen	Baltimore	05/26/1854	03/28/1856	26	369	N	
Arata, James	45	Italy	N	Genoa	New York	08/20/1866	?			Y	
Arata, John	30	Sardinia	Y	Genoa	New Orleans	03/05/1853	10/20/1858	17	74	N	
Arata, Joseph	43	Sardinia	Y	Havre	New York	06/15/1850	10/30/1858	17	13	N	

CITIZENSHIP RECORDS

APPLICANT	AGE	COUNTRY OF ORIGIN	DEC	DEPART PORT	ENTRY PORT	ARRIVE DATE	DEC DATE	VOL	PG.	FLD	NAT DATE
Arata, Louis D.	36	Italy	N	Genoa	New York	??/??/1855	?			Y	
Arate, Bartholomeo	26	Italy (Sardin	Y	Genoa	New York	07/06/1850	02/15/1853	7	166	N	
Arbegust, John George	31	Baden	Y	Bremen	New York	04/??/1852	03/15/1853	7	331	N	
Arbenz, John	36	Switzerland	Y	Havre	New York	05/18/1873	10/28/1886			Y	
Arbino, Joseph	??	Italy	Y	?	?	11/13/1881	10/27/1888			Y	
Arbogars, Lorentz Peter	??	France	Y	Havre	New Orleans	03/01/1847	01/11/1849	1	395	N	
Arbogast, Carl	29	Germany	Y	Antwerp	New York	04/21/1883	11/07/1889			Y	
Arbogast, Wilhelm	27	Germany	Y	Havre	New York	05/19/1880	10/03/1881			Y	
Archbold, James	17	Ireland	N	?	?	00/00/1850	?			Y	10/23/1886
Arend, Diederich	29	Prussia	Y	Bremen	New York	10/09/1854	11/03/1857	15	525	N	
Arend, Herman	39	Germany	N	Bremen	New York	09/20/1872	?			Y	
Arend, John William	27	Hanover	Y	Bremen	Buffalo	07/??/1847	07/09/1855	11	352	N	
Arenel, Franz	27	Italy	Y	?	?	04/09/1889	10/18/1895			Y	
Arens, Bernhard	24	Hanover	Y	Bremen	Baltimore	05/??/1847	11/08/1851	4	505	N	
Arens, Christian	27	Prussia	Y	Bremen	Baltimore	10/05/1866	10/17/1872	18	535	N	
Arens, John Henry	40	Oldenburg	Y	Bremen	New Orleans	01/31/1853	03/03/1858	16	363	N	
Arenstan, Sam	37	Germany	Y	Hamburg	New York	07/08/1892	07/31/1895			Y	
Argast, Charles	21	Germany	Y	Havre	New York	04/27/1892	10/25/1894			Y	
Ariolo, Nicholas	22	Genoa	Y	Genoa	New York	06/09/1849	04/06/1852	24	402	N	
Ark, Christopher	31	Oldenburg	Y	Bremen	Baltimore	04/27/1857	10/01/1860	27	393	N	
Arkenau, Henry	35	Oldenburg	Y	Bremen	New Orleans	12/04/1845	06/19/1851	3	417	N	
Arlt, Louis	27	Germany	Y	Hamburg	New York	04/29/1880	03/20/1883			Y	
Arman, Aims	38	Germany	Y	Havre	New York	10/14/1872	01/04/1875			Y	
Armanino, John	55	Italy	Y	Havre	New York	03/15/1878	10/18/1892			Y	
Armannino, John	55	Italy	Y	Havre	New York	03/15/1878	10/18/1892	19	369	N	
Armarrono, Antonio	??	Italy	Y	?	?	?	09/23/1896			Y	
Armbruester, Henry	24	Bavaria	Y	Havre	New York	09/02/1847	02/19/1849	23	167	N	
Armbrust, John	52	Germany	Y	Rottterdam	New York	11/01/1881	08/03/1885			Y	
Armbruster, Andrew	27	Germany	Y	Antwerp	New York	05/22/1885	04/01/1887			Y	
Armbruster, Ignatz	46	Baden	Y	Havre	New York	09/15/1846	10/04/1848	22	416	N	
Armbruster, John	25	Germany	Y	Havre	New York	12/02/1888	06/29/1892			Y	
Armstroff, Gustavius	27	Saxony	Y	Bremen	New York	06/15/1851	05/17/1854	8	463	N	
Armstrong, Bolten S.	30	Canada	Y	Windsor	Detroit	09/30/1892	07/31/1900			Y	
Armstrong, Charles L.	??	England	Y	Liverpool	Buffalo	07/03/1889	03/20/1895			Y	
Armstrong, Edward	26	Canada	Y	London, Ont.	Detroit	05/12/1879	01/19/1885			Y	
Armstrong, James	38	Ireland	Y	Belfast	New York	11/08/1851	10/05/1854	10	447	N	
Armstrong, James	28	Ireland	Y	Belfast	New York	11/08/1851	10/05/1854	12	386	N	
Armstrong, James	27	Ireland	Y	Liverpool	New Orleans	01/02/1854	10/28/1858	17	157	N	
Armstrong, John	30	Ireland	Y	Liverpool	New Orleans	07/??/1850	12/17/1857	16	229	N	
Armstrong, John F.	41	Sweden	Y	Goteborg	New York	11/??/1854	10/10/1879			Y	
Armstruff, Gustavius	27	Saxony	Y	Bremen	New York	06/15/1851	05/17/1854	9	337	N	
Arndt, Carl	32	Germany	Y	Hamburg	New York	07/17/1882	03/05/1885			Y	
Arndt, Frederick	48	Hesse Darmsta	Y	Bremen	New York	06/01/1841	01/17/1849	1	448	N	
Arnesen, Bernhard	39	Norway	Y	Frederikstad	New York	08/21/1886	10/14/1886			Y	
Arnetz, Peter	34	France	Y	Havre	New Orleans	01/21/1849	05/25/1854	8	521	N	
Arnetz, Peter	34	France	Y	Havre	New Orleans	01/21/1849	05/25/1854	9	395	N	
Arning, Henry	24	Hanover	Y	Bremen	New Orleans	11/29/1852	03/30/1857	15	100	N	
Arning, William	27	Hanover	Y	Bremen	Baltimore	05/23/1848	01/23/1849	1	504	N	
Arnink, Arnold	35	Holland	N	Rotterdam	Baltimore	02/??/1870	?			Y	
Arnold, Carl	23	Germany	Y	Havre	New York	11/10/1888	05/17/1890			Y	
Arnold, Christian	27	Bavaria	Y	Bremen	Baltimore	??/04/1846	02/21/1850	2	112	N	
Arnold, Christoph	35	Wuerttemberg	Y	Havre	New York	09/25/1847	09/04/1852	25	353	N	
Arnold, Emil	24	Germany	Y	Bremen	New York	10/04/1881	10/20/1883			Y	
Arnold, Frank	28	Switzerland	Y	Antwerp	New York	09/28/1852	04/17/1854	8	178	N	
Arnold, Franz	28	Switzerland	Y	Antwerp	New York	09/28/1852	04/17/1854	9	49	N	
Arnold, George	37	Germany	Y	Bremen	Baltimore	09/25/1888	10/27/1782			Y	
Arnold, Henry	52	Hanover	Y	Hamburg	New York	07/19/1860	10/08/1860	27	443	N	
Arnold, Johannes	27	Germany	Y	Antwerp	New York	05/22/1882	09/19/1889			Y	
Arnold, John	43	Germany	Y	Antwerp	New York	02/05/1882	01/14/1886			Y	

CITIZENSHIP RECORDS

APPLICANT	AGE	COUNTRY OF ORIGIN	DEC	DEPART PORT	ENTRY PORT	ARRIVE DATE	DEC DATE	VOL	PG.	FLD	NAT DATE
Arnold, Ludwig	31	Germany	Y	Bremen	New York	06/14/1882	03/30/1886			Y	
Arnold, Montgomery	34	Ireland	Y	Belfast	New York	12/21/1847	02/25/1850	2	125	N	
Arnold, Peter	29	Germany	Y	Antwerp	New York	10/12/1890	12/13/1894			Y	
Arnold, Simon	??	Bavaria	Y	Havre	New Orleans	07/29/18??	10/11/1848	1	109	N	
Arnold, William	29	Hesse Darmsta	Y	Havre	New York	05/26/1853	09/16/1857	15	275	N	
Arnolds, Rudolph	24	Hanover	Y	Hamburg	New York	08/28/1857	12/26/1857	16	247	N	
Arnoldt, Otto	25	Germany	Y	Hamburg	New York	07/27/1880	06/26/1883			Y	
Arns, Gerhard	22	Germany	Y	Amsterdam	New York	01/01/1883	12/26/1883			Y	
Arns, Henry	31	Germany	Y	Amsterdam	New York	07/28/1881	10/28/1886			Y	
Arnschtam, Esekiel	??	Russia	Y	?	?	??/??/1861	12/16/1881			Y	
Arnstam, A.	28	Russia	Y	Hamburg	New York	10/??/1878	12/02/1886			Y	
Aronovitz, Max	32	Russia	Y	Hamburg	New York	05/15/1894	05/30/1898			Y	
Arrighi, Giovanni	32	Italy	Y	?	New York	04/29/1887	10/24/1890			Y	
Arrigo, Salvatore	43	Itlay	Y	Palermo	New York	11/27/1880	02/28/1888			Y	
Arshak, Moses	33	Russia	Y	Bremen	New York	11/16/1890	06/15/1891			Y	
Arsitti, Giovanni	??	Italy	Y	?	?	?	10/19/1892			Y	
Arthon, Anthony	29	Germany	Y	Bremen	New York	01/01/1894	06/06/1898			Y	
Artz, Julius	29	Germany	Y	Antwerp	New York	11/19/1882	02/27/1883			Y	
Artz, Julius	47	Germany	N	Antwerp	New York	02/??/1882	?			Y	
Arundel, John	30	England	Y	Liverpool	New York	12/??/1848	09/21/1855	13	92	N	
Arus, Anthony	35	Prussia	Y	Bremen	Richmond	07/12/1838	09/30/1848	22	366	N	
Asalage, Henry	25	Oldenburg	Y	Bremen	New Orleans	11/01/1851	06/13/1854	10	127	N	
Asalege, Henry	25	Oldenburg	Y	Bremen	New Orleans	11/01/1851	06/13/1854	12	64	N	
Asbre, John Henry	44	Germany	Y	Bremen	Baltimore	08/16/1867	10/22/1884			Y	
Asch, Edward	32	Hesse Cassel	Y	Bremen	Baltimore	07/03/1867	12/23/8172	18	543	N	
Asch, Edward	49	Germany	N	Bremen	Baltimore	07/??/1867	?			Y	
Asche, Bernard	32	Prussia	Y	Bremen	New Orleans	12/04/1850	?	26	164	N	
Aschemoor, Charles	22	Hanover	Y	Bremen	New Orleans	11/22/1848	07/14/1851	3	531	N	
Aschemor, Frederick Henr	23	Hanover	Y	Bremen	New Orleans	12/22/1848	01/23/1849	1	505	N	
Aschenbach, Joseph	28	Prussia	Y	Bremen	Baltimore	09/27/1857	06/28/1861	18	199	N	
Aschendorf, William	22	Hanover	Y	Bremen	New York	09/??/1854	11/03/1856	14	441	N	
Ascherenka, Mendel	33	Russia	Y	Rotterdam	New York	04/15/1891	03/14/1892			Y	
Asfinwall, John George	45	England	Y	Liverpool	New York	02/11/1868	10/05/1891	19	331	N	
Ash, Thomas	24	Ireland	Y	Cork	Boston	05/04/1847	08/23/1852	25	329	N	
Asharn, John Bernard	22	Oldenburg	Y	Bremen	New Orleans	01/02/1856	10/01/1856	14	112	N	
Ashe, Thomas Powys	37	England	Y	Liverpool	New York	12/15/1840	03/03/1853	7	261	N	
Asheim, Joseph	29	Prussia	Y	Bremen	New York	09/23/1857	07/14/1860	27	220	N	
Ashforth, Thomas W.	30	England	Y	London	New York	09/07/1884	04/06/1895			Y	
Ashton, George	48	England	Y	Liverpool	New York	10/19/1875	11/02/1891			Y	
Ashton, Joseph	42	England	Y	Liverpool	New York	04/01/1882	10/13/1888	19	145	N	
Ashton, Joseph	42	England	Y	Liverpool	New York	04/01/1882	10/13/1888			Y	
Ashworth, John	??	England	Y	?	?	?	07/09/1889			Y	
Asira, Deefs	26	Turkey	Y	Tripoli	New York	02/05/1892	09/17/1896			Y	
Askew, Robert	33	England	Y	Liverpool	New York	04/20/1855	01/29/1861	18	76	N	
Askew, Robert	59	England	N	Liverpool	New York	04/??/1855	?			Y	
Asmus, Charles	23	Germany	Y	?	New York	05/17/1886	04/05/1890			Y	
Asmus, Louis	36	Brunswick	Y	Bremen	Baltimore	10/03/1846	01/30/1849	1	543	N	
Asmus, Wilhelm	30	Germany	N	Havre	New York	08/28/1880	?			Y	
Aspenleiter, Nicholaus	31	Bavaria	Y	Havre	New York	06/18/1857	06/25/1862	18	359	N	
Assebrock, Henry	??	Germany	Y	Bremen	Baltimore	09/21/1881	01/29/1886			Y	
Assel, Valentine	21	Bavaria	Y	Bremen	New York	04/20/1850	01/17/1851	2	504	N	
Assheton, Walter	23	England	Y	?	?	09/01/1869	04/04/1873			Y	
Assion, John H.	31	Germany	Y	Antwerp	New York	07/13/1878	06/02/1884			Y	
Assmann, Charles	25	Hesse Cassel	Y	Liverpool	Philadelphia	10/15/1854	01/30/1857	14	520	N	
Assmann, Peter	34	Nassau	Y	Antwerp	Galveston	12/21/1848	01/??/1850	23	505	N	
Assmus, Frederick	54	Brunswick	Y	Bremen	New Orleans	09/26/1849	10/07/1854	6	11	N	
Assmus, William Ludwig	24	Baden	Y	Havre	New York	11/03/1848	01/23/1849	1	496	N	
Assur, Alexander	32	Prussia	Y	London	New York	12/03/1845	08/20/1855	11	464	N	
Ast, John Adam	24	Bavaria	Y	Havre	New Orleans	11/??/1846	10/29/1850	2	328	N	

CITIZENSHIP RECORDS

APPLICANT	AGE	COUNTRY OF ORIGIN	DEC	DEPART PORT	ENTRY PORT	ARRIVE DATE	DEC DATE	VOL	PG.	FLD	NAT DATE
Astbury, John	34	England	Y	Liverpool	New York	02/05/1844	03/18/1850	2	216	N	
Astbury, John Joshua	28	England	Y	Liverpool	New York	08/29/1886	10/20/1891			Y	
Aszmann, Henry F.	63	Germany	N	Bremen	New Orleans	10/23/1823	10/??/1846	28	205	N	10/??/1851
Aszmann, Henry J.	63	Germany	N	Bremen	New Orleans	11/23/1823	10/00/1846			Y	10/00/1851
Aszmus, Frederick	54	Brunswick	Y	Bremen	New Orleans	09/26/1849	10/07/1854	10	12	N	
Atecheson, James G.	37	Canada	Y	Toronto	Detroit	07/30/1895	06/23/1897			Y	
Atkins, Abraham J.	25	Ireland	Y	Cork	Baltimore	??/??/1849	04/18/1855	11	267	N	
Atkins, Robert	36	Ireland	Y	Cork	New Orleans	07/11/1848	02/07/1850	2	46	N	
Atkinson, Edward	35	Ireland	Y	Liverpool	New York	04/??/1851	02/02/1856	26	2	N	
Atkinson, Samuel	42	Canada	Y	Windsor	Detroit	09/15/1869	07/15/1893			Y	
Atkinson, Thompson	??	England	Y	?	?	?	09/06/1888			Y	
Atter, Thomas	29	England	Y	Liverpool	New Orleans	12/24/1849	11/11/1852	5	271	N	
Atter, Thomas W.	29	England	Y	Liverpool	New Orleans	12/24/1849	11/11/1852	6	395	N	
Attlesey, James	27	England	Y	London	New York	11/08/1836	03/31/1849			Y	
Auberger, Peter	22	Bavaria	Y	Rotterdam	New York	12/09/1843	10/03/1854	10	375	N	
Auberger, Peter	22	Bavaria	Y	Rotterdam	New York	12/09/1843	10/03/1854	12	314	N	
Aubin, Simon John Louis	48	Switzerland	Y	Havre	New York	12/13/1852	03/31/1858	16	453	N	
Aubky, Henry	27	Hanover	Y	Bremen	New Orleans	10/16/1852	09/29/1856	14	1	N	
Auchter, Nicolaus	34	Wurttemberg	Y	Antwerp	New York	??/02/18?4	04/16/1855	11	254	N	
Auckland, William	37	England	Y	Liverpool	New York	11/10/1879	09/10/1883			Y	
Auel, Adam	26	Germany	Y	Bremen	New York	08/09/1881	01/30/1888			Y	
Auer, Janh	27	Hungary	Y	Rotterdam	New York	12/18/1895	09/24/1896			Y	
Auerbach, Joseph	32	Austria	Y	Hamburg	New York	01/17/1887	04/13/1893			Y	
Aufdemberge, Henry	26	Germany	Y	Bremen	Baltimore	07/31/1883	09/07/1887			Y	
Aufderhaar, William	25	Prussia	Y	Bremen	Baltimore	06/29/1860	09/12/1860	27	369	N	
Aufderhar, Adolph	26	Germany	Y	Bremen	New York	07/28/1881	03/08/1886			Y	
Aufderheide, Ernst	42	Germany	Y	Bremen	Batlimore	06/11/1881	10/28/1886			Y	
Aufderheide, Rudolph	48	Prussia	Y	Bremen	New York	07/17/1845	06/12/1854	10	124	N	
Aufderheide, Rudolph	48	Prussia	Y	Bremen	New York	07/17/1845	06/12/1854	12	61	N	
Augenbauer, Andrew	29	Bavaria	Y	Bremen	New York	07/01/1847	10/11/1848	1	114	N	
Augenthaler, Michael	35	Austria	Y	Bremen	New York	06/28/1887	05/18/1897			Y	
Auglund, John P.	??	Sweden	Y	?	?	07/19/1889	10/21/1890			Y	
Augsberger, Alsonso	24	Germany	Y	Havre	New York	12/11/1892	11/25/1895			Y	
Augsel, Alfons	??	Germany	Y	?	?	?	08/25/1894			Y	
August, Reinhardt	30	Switzerland	Y	Havre	New York	09/26/1883	10/22/1892			Y	
Auguste, Vogt	24	Germany	Y	Havre	New York	05/02/1886	11/10/1886			Y	
Augustin, Joseph	33	Germany	Y	Bremen	New York	03/29/1881	02/21/1891			Y	
Augusting, Vincent	30	Russia	Y	Hamburg	New York	03/21/1884	06/20/1892			Y	
Augustus, Edward	27	England	Y	Liverpool	Boston	11/04/1888	03/12/1892			Y	
Aujeski, John	48	Austria	Y	Antwerp	New York	02/11/1883	10/21/1889			Y	
Aulkmeier, Martin	22	Prussia	Y	Bremen	Baltimore	04/23/1846	08/15/1848	22	175	N	
Aultenbuk, Henry	37	Prussia	Y	Bremen	New Orleans	12/06/1848	07/28/1851	4	56	N	
Aultmeyer, Peter	??	Germany	Y	?	?	09/04/1891	11/02/1892			Y	
Aumiller, Paulis	40	Bavaria	Y	Bremen	Baltimore	09/30/1846	04/13/1852	24	494	N	
Aupke, Frederick	25	Hanover	Y	Bremen	New Orleans	06/04/1845	08/15/1848	22	115	N	
Aureden, John Henry	25	Prussia	Y	Bremen	New York	07/22/1854	12/28/1857	16	273	N	
Austermann, Franz	25	Germany	Y	Bremen	New York	05/22/1881	05/26/1881			Y	
Austin, James	32	England	Y	?	New York	??/??/1870	10/08/1880			Y	
Austing, Clemens	43	Germany	Y	Bremen	Baltimore	10/03/1888	10/26/1895			Y	
Autenrieth, Louis	22	Wurttemberg	Y	London	New York	05/28/1849	11/06/1852	5	248	N	
Autenrieth, Louis	22	Wurttemberg	Y	London	New York	05/28/1849	11/06/1852	6	372	N	
Averbeck, Anthony	26	Germany	Y	Bremen	Baltimore	11/01/1884	01/30/1889			Y	
Avert, John	33	Germany	N	Havre	New York	10/??/1872	?			Y	
Avril, John Anton	26	Germany	Y	Antwerp	New Yoork	04/13/1887	02/14/1889			Y	
Awothe, Charles	25	Germany	Y	?	Philadelphia	??/??/1877	11/01/1884			Y	
Ax, Joseph	26	Germany	Y	Rotterdam	New York	07/11/1886	06/13/1893			Y	
Axen, Anton Gerhard	24	Oldenburg	Y	Hamburg	New York	07/19/1860	08/20/1860	27	303	N	
Axford, Herbert	31	England	Y	?	New York	06/??/1888	04/24/1895			Y	
Axmann, Herman A.	31	Germany	Y	Antwerp	New York	11/30/1886	04/06/1894			Y	

CITIZENSHIP RECORDS

APPLICANT	AGE	COUNTRY OF ORIGIN	DEC	DEPART PORT	ENTRY PORT	ARRIVE DATE	DEC DATE	VOL	PG.	FLD	NAT DATE
Axtmann, Carl	50	Germany	Y	Hamburg	New York	08/28/1879	04/03/1888			Y	
Ayers, George Fred	23	Germany	Y	?	?	?	10/??/1884			Y	
Aylward, Michael	30	Ireland	Y	Waterford	New York	05/03/1852	05/25/1854	8	525	N	
Aylward, Michael	30	Ireland	Y	Waterford	New York	05/03/1852	05/25/1854	9	399	N	
Aylward, Thomas	29	Ireland	Y	Liverpool	New York	01/18/1845	12/30/1852	5	475	N	
Baarsch, J.	46	Germany	Y	Hamburg	New York	06/28/1883	01/04/1887			Y	
Baas, David	27	Germany	Y	Havre	New York	03/17/1882	02/24/1883			Y	
Baas, John Frederick	32	Bavaria	Y	Dover	Burlington	12/??/1856	09/17/1860	27	380	N	
Baath, Charles	40	Germany	Y	Bremen	Baltimore	12/21/1881	07/12/1886			Y	
Baatz, Christian	51	Germany	Y	Antwerp	New York	07/14/1883	10/24/1888			Y	
Babros, John	22	Hungary	Y	Hamburg	New York	05/15/1881	04/07/1884			Y	
Babst, Carl	59	Germany	Y	?	Philadelphia	??/??/1860	10/31/1887			Y	
Babst, Henry	52	Hanover	Y	Bremen	Baltimore	??/12/1845	10/09/1848	1	60	N	
Bacciocco, John	36	Italy	Y	Genoa	New York	01/20/1838	03/16/1858	16	416	N	
Bach, Adam	72	Germany	N	Bremen	New Orleans	07/??/1848	?			Y	
Bach, Casper	22	Hanover	Y	Bremen	Baltimore	10/20/1857	09/10/1860	27	354	N	
Bach, Francis	45	Germany	Y	Havre	New York	04/29/1872	10/23/1882			Y	
Bach, Fritz	25	Switzerland	Y	Havre	New York	03/23/1887	12/05/1892			Y	
Bach, John Sebastian	16	Germany	N	?	Baltimore	00/00/1882				Y	10/13/1888
Bach, Joseph Henry	??	Germany	Y	Antwerp	New York	06/19/1885	04/28/1890			Y	
Bach, Louis	25	France	Y	Havre	New York	11/??/1848	12/19/1850	2	377	N	
Bach, Morand	30	Germany	Y	Havre	New York	07/23/1891	08/03/1896			Y	
Bach, Nicholas	40	Germany	Y	Rotterdam	Jersey City	10/22/1877	08/25/1885			Y	
Bacharach, Theodore	31	Germany	Y	Bremen	New York	05/20/1882	11/08/1887			Y	
Bacher, Henry	28	Germany	Y	Hamburg	Baltimore	05/23/1884	03/25/1893			Y	
Bachmann, Edward	46	Switzerland	Y	Antwerp	New York	04/09/1881	03/22/1894			Y	
Bachmann, Emil	29	Switzerland	Y	Havre	New York	08/23/1885	07/05/1889			Y	
Bachmann, Frank	39	Germany	Y	Bremen	Baltimore	05/18/1873	05/22/1882			Y	
Bachmann, Franz	55	Bavaria	Y	Havre	New York	11/05/1854	08/10/1860	27	259	N	
Bachmann, Isidor	35	Russia	Y	?	New York	03/01/1881	04/01/1890			Y	
Bachmann, John	46	Germany	Y	Hamburg	New York	03/30/1886	12/27/1890			Y	
Bachmann, John	17	Germany	N	?	Baltimore	00/00/1869				Y	10/29/1886
Bachmann, Michael	29	Baden	Y	Havre	New Orleans	03/26/1857	02/01/1858	16	71	N	
Bachmann, Nicholas	40	Bavaria	Y	Bremen	New York	08/19/1859	04/11/1860	27	143	N	
Bachmann, Nickolaus	20	Germany	Y	Hamburg	New York	04/19/1887	06/14/1889			Y	
Bachmann, William	45	Germany	Y	Hamburg	New York	08/27/1880	12/27/1884			Y	
Bachrach, Davis	28	Russia	Y	?	?	?	06/21/1894			Y	
Bachrach, Hayman	60	Russia	Y	Bremen	New York	07/15/1891	10/18/1894			Y	
Bachrach, Martin	52	Austria	Y	Bremen	Philadelphia	08/28/1884	08/28/1888	19	136	N	
Bachrach, Max	38	Russia	Y	Hamburg	New York	12/25/1891	11/04/1895			Y	
Back, Anthony	29	Oldenburg	Y	Bremen	Baltimore	04/26/1857	05/16/1859	17	413	N	
Back, George	24	Bavaria	Y	Havre	New York	05/16/1850	08/27/1855	11	508	N	
Backer, Peter	36	Bavaria	Y	Havre	New Orleans	10/15/1859	08/20/1862	18	427	N	
Backes, Michael (Baeckes	25	Prussia	Y	Antwerp	New York	05/08/1849	05/19/1852	25	48	N	
Backes, Peter	32	Bavaria	Y	Havre	New York	05/28/1857	09/21/1857	15	291	N	
Backhaus, Frederick	42	Hanover	Y	Bremen	New Orleans	11/25/1848	06/18/1852	25	289	N	
Backhaus, Joseph	27	Germany	Y	Bremen	Baltimore	11/07/1883	12/??/1883			Y	
Backhaus, Joseph	38	Germany	N	Bremen	Baltimore	11/09/1883	?			Y	
Backhaus, Wm.	45	Germany	Y	Bremen	New York	04/08/1881	12/16/1886			Y	
Backmann, Bernard	28	Prussia	Y	Bremen	Baltimore	05/10/1856	10/01/1856	14	87	N	
Backmeier, Charles	5	Germany	N	?	Baltimore	00/00/1848				Y	10/15/1888
Backmeier, Henry William	??	Hanover	Y	Bremen	New Orleans	??/31/1847	04/16/1855	11	253	N	
Backs, H.	29	Germany	Y	Bremen	Baltimore	05/17/1881	10/01/1884			Y	
Backs, Henry	21	Germany	Y	Bremen	Baltimore	04/30/1885	03/11/1887			Y	
Backscheider, Pierre	56	Germany	Y	Havre	New York	04/??/1866	11/07/1887			Y	
Bacon, James	37	England	Y	London	New York	09/07/1847	02/18/1852	24	133	N	
Badde, Joseph	32	Prussia	Y	Bremen	Philadelphia	12/26/1858	12/19/1861	18	235	N	
Badelt, Florian	40	Germany	Y	Bremen	New York	10/??/1882	04/11/1887			Y	
Badenhop, F.	36	Hanover	Y	Bremen	Baltimore	11/03/1850	04/10/1861	18	106	N	

CITIZENSHIP RECORDS

APPLICANT	AGE	COUNTRY OF ORIGIN	DEC	DEPART PORT	ENTRY PORT	ARRIVE DATE	DEC DATE	VOL	PG.	FLD	NAT DATE
Bader, Alois	26	Germany	Y	Havre	New York	07/01/1891	11/02/1896			Y	
Bader, Bernard	25	Hanover	Y	Bremen	Baltimore	07/18/1850	01/29/1853	7	85	N	
Bader, Chas	41	Germany	Y	Bremen	New York	05/02/1882	11/01/1888			Y	
Bader, Frederick	32	Switzerland	Y	Havre	New York	02/01/1883	10/20/1890			Y	
Badraun, Josias	34	Switzerland	Y	Bremen	New York	06/??/1868	05/08/1882			Y	
Baechmann, Anton	45	Germany	Y	Bremen	Batlimore	05/28/1888	01/30/1893			Y	
Baechtold, William M.	26	Switzerland	Y	Bremen	Baltimore	09/21/1881	02/15/1886			Y	
Baehner, August	51	Germany	Y	Hamburg	New York	05/19/1893	08/28/1900			Y	
Baehner, Herman	28	Germany	Y	Rotterdam	New York	05/22/1882	07/27/1885			Y	
Baehr, William	38	Bavaria	Y	Havre	New Orleans	04/15/1843	08/02/1848	22	45	N	
Baer, Abraham	41	Russia	Y	Liverpool	Philadelphia	09/??/1879	08/20/1891			Y	
Baer, Felix	25	Hesse Darmsta	Y	Liverpool	New York	01/08/1852	03/02/1852	24	211	N	
Baer, Heinrich	29	Germany	Y	Bremen	New York	09/14/1880	10/14/1880			Y	
Baer, John	26	Hesse Darmsta	Y	Havre	New Orleans	06/12/1849	01/16/1851	2	502	N	
Baer, Karl	24	Bavaria	Y	Havre	New York	07/26/1850	09/04/1852	25	357	N	
Baer, Konrad	22	Bavaria	Y	Bremen	New York	05/03/1852	02/08/1853	7	128	N	
Baer, Robert	41	Germany	Y	Bremen	New York	03/09/1881	10/26/1886			Y	
Baerle, Leonhard Jacob	33	Wuertenberg	Y	Antwerp	New York	07/20/1847	07/??/1848	22	3	N	
Baermann, Armand	??	?	N	?	?	?				Y	03/19/1888
Baerthlein, Albrecht	23	Bavaria	Y	Bremen	New York	09/18/1852	12/20/1852	5	431	N	
Baeuml, John	38	Germany	Y	Hamburg	New York	09/18/1881	12/19/1882			Y	
Baeumler, Nicholas	29	Germany	Y	Antwerp	New York	07/21/1888	10/03/1891			Y	
Baffinger, John	30	Hesse Darmsta	Y	Antwerp	New York	08/23/1848	05/31/1852			Y	03/26/1853
Bagne, Henry	37	Bavaria	Y	Havre	New York	07/01/1853	11/12/1857	16	11	N	
Bahan, Cornelius	36	Ireland	Y	Liverpool	New York	11/28/1850	11/08/1852	5	255	N	
Bahan, Cornelius	36	Ireland	Y	Liverpool	New York	11/28/1850	11/08/1852	6	379	N	
Bahlmann, Francis	25	Oldenburg	Y	Bremen	New Orleans	11/15/1854	09/23/1858	16	149	N	
Bahlmann, Henry	34	Germany	Y	Bremen	New York	05/23/1888	05/07/1891			Y	
Bahlmann, Hermann A.	36	Germany	Y	Bremen	Baltimore	05/22/1884	04/24/1890			Y	
Bahmann, John Gottfried	31	Saxony	Y	Bremen	New Orleans	05/03/1849	04/12/1852	24	447	N	
Bahmann, Joseph	38	Oldenburg	Y	Bremen	New Orleans	02/22/1846	04/04/1853	7	508	N	
Bahnfeck, Frederick	28	Bavaria	Y	Havre	New Orleans	10/01/1853	10/02/1854	12	297	N	
Bahnfick, Frederick	28	Bavaria	Y	Havre	New Orleans	10/01/1853	10/02/1854	10	358	N	
Bahr, Johann	31	Germany	Y	Hamburg	Philadelphia	05/13/1881	01/08/1883			Y	
Bahr, Joseph	25	Baden	Y	Havre	New Orleans	05/??/1846	12/??/1849	23	435	N	
Bahrmeister, Henry	36	Prussia	Y	Bremen	New York	05/??/1854	11/05/1856	14	469	N	
Bahrs, Fred	16	Germany	N	?	New York	00/00/1882				Y	10/22/1888
Baier, Albert	23	Germany	Y	Bremen	New York	05/21/1892	02/18/1896			Y	
Baier, George	39	Germany	Y	Bremen	Baltimore	05/31/1884	10/17/1889			Y	
Baier, John	23	Germany	Y	Bremen	New York	06/06/1887	07/05/1892			Y	
Bailer, Fred	55	Germany	Y	Havre	New York	04/21/1867	10/24/1896			Y	
Bailer, Kasper	26	Prussia	Y	Liverpool	New York	05/30/1853	10/06/1856	14	195	N	
Bailer, Martin	26	Wurttemberg	Y	Havre	New York	06/22/1849	11/01/1851	4	464	N	
Bailey, James	23	Ireland	Y	Belfast	New York	06/10/1847	01/??/1850	23	511	N	
Bailey, John	28	Ireland	Y	Liverpool	New York	10/07/1841	03/28/1850	2	275	N	
Bailey, Samuel	35	Ireland	Y	Belfast	New York	05/21/1847	03/04/1853	7	271	N	
Bain, George S.	40	Scotland	Y	Glasgow	Philadelphia	05/13/1884	12/18/1888			Y	
Bain, John	32	Ireland	Y	Queenstown	New York	04/02/1874	10/02/1883			Y	
Bainker, Frederick	39	Prussia	Y	Bremen	Baltimore	10/26/1856	10/06/1860	27	409	N	
Baiter, Jacob	29	Wurttemberg	Y	Havre	New York	11/16/1848	01/29/1851	1	536	N	
Baitz, Valentine	22	Hesse Darmsta	Y	Bremen	Baltimore	08/06/1846	10/03/1848	22	406	N	
Baizer, Louis	27	Wurtemberg	Y	Havre	New Orleans	05/??/1848	01/03/1853	5	504	N	
Bakan, Andreas	26	Austria	Y	Bremen	New York	05/31/1885	04/25/1888			Y	
Baker, Christopher	40	Oldenburg	Y	Bremen	New Orleans	03/??/1844	09/10/1852	25	446	N	
Baker, Eugenius	27	Prussia	Y	Bremen	Baltimore	05/04/1854	10/01/1856	14	95	N	
Baker, George	28	Bavaria	Y	Havre	New York	05/24/1842	09/09/1848	22	315	N	
Baker, Robert	35	Ireland	Y	Liverpool	New York	07/17/1851	02/04/1856	26	15	N	
Baker, Robert P.	37	Ireland	Y	Queenstown	New York	12/19/1885	07/05/1888			Y	
Baker, William J.	36	Ireland	Y	Liverpool	New York	08/28/1857	12/14/1857	16	220	N	

CITIZENSHIP RECORDS

APPLICANT	AGE	COUNTRY OF ORIGIN	DEC	DEPART PORT	ENTRY PORT	ARRIVE DATE	DEC DATE	VOL	PG.	FLD	NAT DATE
Balard, Nicholas	25	Ireland	Y	Liverpool	New Orleans	04/20/1850	11/29/1852	5	358	N	
Balas, John	50	Hungary	Y	Antwerp	New York	04/13/1891	09/24/1896			Y	
Balbach, Wilhelm	??	Germany	Y	?	?	?	09/11/1890			Y	
Baldauf, Louis	28	Germany	Y	Havre	New York	06/12/1883	06/18/1887			Y	
Baldauf, Philipp	27	Germany	Y	?	?	?	09/11/1891			Y	
Baldinger, Frederick	22	Germany	Y	Havre	New York	08/26/1880	04/10/1882			Y	
Balhauser, Joseph	22	Prussia	Y	Bremen	New York	10/??/1845	10/??/1849	23	291	N	
Balitzer, Maritz	40	Austria	N	Bremen	Baltimore	??/??/1870	?			Y	
Balkenhohl, Ferdinand	49	Germany	Y	Bremen	Hoboken	08/15/1874	03/31/1881			Y	
Ball, Henry	20	Germany	Y	?	?	?	10/07/1887			Y	
Ball, Joseph	40	Baden	Y	Havre	New Orleans	02/02/1852	04/05/1856	26	441	N	
Ballbach, John	??	Germany	N	?	New York	10/16/1872	?			Y	
Ballenweg, Peter	30	Hesse Darmsta	Y	Bremen	New York	07/16/1851	07/10/1855	11	372	N	
Ballmann, Andreas	64	Russia	Y	Bremen	New York	08/26/1893	03/04/1901			Y	
Ballmann, Henry	27	Hanover	Y	Bremen	Baltimore	10/09/1848	01/06/1851	2	453	N	
Balme, George	25	England	Y	Liverpool	New York	08/01/1883	05/03/1886			Y	
Balmer, Peter	42	Switzerland	Y	Havre	New York	11/??/1879	01/22/1893			Y	
Balsinger, Henry	57	Bavaria	Y	Havre	New York	01/25/1855	04/17/1860	27	163	N	
Balster, Henry Rudolph	23	Hanover	Y	Bremen	New Orleans	11/12/1847	01/19/1849	1	465	N	
Baltauf, Adam	34	Germany	Y	Antwerp	New York	10/10/1883	10/31/1894			Y	
Balton, George	45	England	Y	?	New York	??/??/1872	11/01/1884			Y	
Balz, Jacob	36	Hesse Darmsta	Y	Antwerp	New York	05/25/1856	11/30/1857	16	59	N	
Balzer, George	59	Germany	Y	Rotterdam	New York	07/16/1883	04/09/1891			Y	
Balzer, Henry	30	Germany	Y	Bremen	New York	10/14/1892	10/13/1894			Y	
Balzer, William	45	Germany	Y	Rotterdam	New York	03/18/1867	02/23/1892			Y	
Balzheisser, Jacob	55	Hesse Darmsta	Y	Havre	New Orleans	12/??/1854	06/26/1860	27	8	N	
Balzil, Karl	31	Germany	Y	Bremen	Baltimore	06/11/1880	10/24/1882			Y	
Bambeck, Balthaser	35	Bavaria	Y	Bremen	New York	05/24/1847	09/15/1852	25	518	N	
Bamberger, Emanuel	36	Germany	N	Bremen	New York	09/10/1865	?			Y	
Bamburger, Joseph	50	Germany	N	Havre	New York	11/11/1854	?			Y	
Bamford, Thomas	28	England	Y	Liverpool	Philadelphia	08/13/1883	06/04/1888			Y	
Bamler, John H.	24	Oldenburg	Y	Bremen	New Orleans	12/28/1846	02/12/1849	23	60	N	
Bammbeck, Sebastian	26	Bavaria	Y	Havre	New York	07/05/1851	09/23/1857	15	306	N	
Bamrasch, Fred	27	Prussia	Y	Bremerhafen	New York	09/??/1857	02/02/1861	18	83	N	
Bamrick, John (Baumrick?)	23	Ireland	Y	Dublin	New Orleans	11/20/1849	09/15/1852	25	530	N	
Banahan, Cornelius A.	28	Ireland	Y	Queenstown	New York	07/23/1888	10/27/1893			Y	
Banahan, John	22	Ireland	Y	Liverpool	New York	10/20/1853	10/25/1855	13	140	N	
Banash, Albert	??	Russia	Y	?	?	?	05/08/1888			Y	
Bande, Emil	24	Germany	Y	Bremen	New York	05/19/1882	06/28/1883			Y	
Bandet, Samuel Johann	37	Austria	Y	Bremen	Baltimore	12/20/1889	05/20/1893			Y	
Bandmann, George	19	Germany	Y	Bremen	New York	07/06/1881	03/13/1882			Y	
Banfield, Thomas	35	Canada	Y	Canada	Detroit	11/15/1876	05/12/1894			Y	
Banholzer, Christ	35	Germany	Y	Rotterdam	New York	08/15/1880	07/25/1885			Y	
Bannan, John	30	Ireland	Y	Liverpool	New Orleans	05/??/1849	11/01/1851	4	452	N	
Banner, Patrick	25	Ireland	Y	Liverpool	New York	04/10/1849	01/02/1851	2	438	N	
Bannkucken, Frederick	25	Hanover	Y	Bremen	New York	09/25/1858	10/08/1860	27	430	N	
Bannon, Richard	28	Ireland	Y	Liverpool	New Orleans	04/10/1849	02/19/1850	2	103	N	
Bans, John Herman	31	Hanover	Y	Bremen	New Orleans	06/07/1860	05/13/1861	18	167	N	
Bansman, Frederick	25	Hanover	Y	Bremen	Baltimore	11/22/1844	10/12/1848	1	180	N	
Bansshuf, Frederick	40	Germany	Y	Rotterdam	New York	03/29/1881	10/06/1890			Y	
Bantel, Friedrich	30	Germany	Y	Havre	New York	08/03/1882	10/24/1882			Y	
Bantlin, Julius	25	Germany	N	Wurtenberg	New York	06/06/1850	01/29/1851			Y	02/02/1858
Bantlin, Julius J.	25	Wurttemberg	Y	Liverpool	New York	06/11/1850	01/30/1851	2	543	N	
Bantlin, Julius J.	67	Germany	N	Wuerttemberg	New York	06/06/1850	01/29/1851	28	318	N	02/02/1858
Bantz, Adam	24	Germany	Y	Bremen	New York	12/03/1880	01/06/1881			Y	
Banzhof, Friedrich	31	Germany	Y	Bremen	Baltimore	11/11/1871	04/05/1882			Y	
Banzhof, John	25	Germany	Y	Antwerp	New York	06/25/1880	06/16/1884			Y	
Banzhof, Michael	33	Germany	Y	Hamburg	New York	07/01/1888	03/05/1894			Y	
Bar, Anton	23	France	Y	Havre	New Orleans	01/26/1853	11/16/1857	16	28	N	

CITIZENSHIP RECORDS

APPLICANT	AGE	COUNTRY OF ORIGIN	DEC	DEPART PORT	ENTRY PORT	ARRIVE DATE	DEC DATE	VOL	PG.	FLD	NAT DATE
Baram, Abe	21	Russia	Y	Bremen	Baltimore	11/20/1890	04/01/1893			Y	
Barber, Joseph	42	Canada	Y	Montreal	Detroit	12/15/1836	11/01/1852	5	127	N	
Barber, Joseph	42	Canada	Y	Montreal	Detroit	12/15/1836	11/01/1852	6	255	N	
Barclay, William R.	23	Canada	Y	?	Brookfield	06/02/187?	10/15/1891			Y	
Bardes, Christian	26	Bavaria	Y	Havre	New York	05/06/1852	05/09/1854	8	404	N	
Bardey, John Frederick	25	Hanover	Y	Bremen	Baltimore	11/10/1851	01/12/1856	13	453	N	
Bardie, Henry	59	Germany	N	Bremen	Baltimore	07/08/1848	?			Y	
Bardsley, Sidney	47	England	Y	Liverpool	New York	04/21/1848	06/08/1852	25	205	N	
Bardua, Charles	24	Germany	Y	Amsterdam	New York	06/??/1882	10/29/1887			Y	
Bardua, Daniel	24	Germany	Y	Amsterdam	New York	09/01/1882	08/26/1885			Y	
Bardua, John	28	Germany	Y	Antwerp	New York	05/07/1882	06/12/1884			Y	
Barfknecht, Karl	23	Germany	Y	Hamburg	New York	05/17/1896	10/31/1900			Y	
Barg, Frederick	24	Hanover	Y	Bremen	Baltimore	05/28/1854	09/03/1857	15	222	N	
Barge, Karl	22	Germany	Y	Hamburg	New York	10/26/1884	02/21/1888			Y	
Bargen, Leonard	21	Hanover	Y	Bremen	New York	06/17/1849	05/02/1850	3	41	N	
Bargreve, John	40	Holland	Y	Bremen	New Orleans	06/01/1843	09/30/1856	14	62	N	
Barie, Jacob	30	Germany	Y	Antwerp	New York	03/31/1884	01/21/1895			Y	
Barkau, Fritz	27	Germany	Y	Bremen	Baltimore	03/25/1883	10/31/1887			Y	
Barlag, Frank George	44	Germany	Y	Bremen	New York	05/20/1865	10/23/1888			Y	
Barlage, Bernd Henry	41	Oldenburg	Y	Bremen	New Orleans	11/18/1849	03/13/1856	26	193	N	
Barland, Jake	33	Russia	Y	Hamburg	Philadelphia	07/15/1881	03/??/1883	28	174	N	
Barland, Jake	28	Russia	Y	Hamburg	Philadelphia	07/15/1881	03/00/1883			N	
Barling, Theodore	26	Germany	Y	Amsterdam	New York	10/02/1890	10/13/1896			Y	
Barloesius, Louis	37	Mecklenburg	Y	Hamburg	New York	09/01/1852	10/09/1854	6	111	N	
Barloesius, Louis	37	Mecklenburg	Y	Hamburg	New York	09/01/1852	10/09/1854	11	114	N	
Barn, Patrick	24	Ireland	Y	Liverpool	New Orleans	12/14/1853	09/22/1858	16	153	N	
Barnan, Lawrence	25	Ireland	Y	Liverpool	New York	05/25/1847	09/14/1848	22	345	N	
Barnel, John	35	England	Y	Liverpool	New York	08/15/1853	02/23/1857	15	55	N	
Barnet, Anton	63	Switzerland	Y	Havre	New York	03/24/1882	09/08/1893			Y	
Barnett, James	54	Ireland	Y	Londonderry	New Orleans	01/??/1850	10/10/1885			Y	
Barnett, Louis	35	Poland	Y	Hamburg	New York	??/??/1879	10/10/1884			Y	
Barnin, Terns	25	Ireland	Y	Liverpool	New York	02/26/1847	01/??/1850	23	487	N	
Barniss, John	42	Wuerttenberg	Y	Bremen	Baltimore	05/15/1845	02/12/1849	23	49	N	
Barns, George	27	Hanover	Y	Bremen	New Orleans	05/01/1849	05/20/1852	25	64	N	
Baron, Jacob	28	Bavaria	Y	Havre	New Orleans	12/17/1853	02/09/1857	15	7	N	
Baron, John	24	Germany	Y	Hamburg	New York	10/21/1881	01/31/1887			Y	
Baron, John B.	30	Bavaria	Y	Havre	New Orleans	04/18/1846	03/24/1856	26	281	N	
Baron, Sheye	50	Russia	Y	Hamburg	New York	03/20/1888	04/04/1893			Y	
Barone, Guiseppe	36	Italy	Y	Naples	New York	06/28/1889	05/23/1894			Y	
Barot, Joseph	21	France	Y	Havre	New York	06/03/1853	11/30/1855	13	266	N	
Barrasch, Joseph	35	Russia	Y	Hamburg	New York	12/30/1891	01/02/1894			Y	
Barrath, Oscar Edward	??	Affidavit Onl	N							N	
Barrett, David	25	Ireland	Y	Cork	New York	05/26/1854	04/03/1858	16	490	N	
Barrett, John	26	Ireland	Y	Liverpool	New York	05/15/1851	01/03/1851	5	498	N	
Barrett, John	25	Ireland	Y	Liverpool	New Orleans	12/15/1848	05/20/1852	25	74	N	
Barrington, William	37	Ireland	Y	Liverpool	Philadelphia	07/03/1847	09/16/1858	16	165	N	
Barron, Robert James	43	Ireland	Y	Londonderry	Portland	??/??/1866	10/31/8172	18	537	N	
Barrow, David	22	Ireland	Y	Limerick	Burlington	06/??/1850	05/30/1854	9	461	N	
Barrow, David	22	Ireland	Y	Liverpool	Burlington	06/??/1850	05/31/1854	10	44	N	
Barrow, John	29	Ireland	Y	Liverpool	New York	05/01/1848	12/26/1850	2	394	N	
Barrow, Richard	36	Ireland	Y	Queenstown	New York	04/27/1894	10/26/1900			Y	
Barry, Denis	27	Ireland	Y	Liverpool	Boston	??/24/1848	12/12/1849	23	394	N	
Barry, John	65	Ireland	Y	London	New York	04/19/1851	08/18/1862	18	392	N	
Barry, Michael	40	Ireland	Y	Liverpool	New York	09/??/1865	10/16/1880			Y	
Barry, Thomas Albert	??	England	Y	?	?	?	02/15/1888			Y	
Barsen, Peter	27	Prussia	Y	Bremen	New York	09/17/1846	03/14/1850	2	197	N	
Bartel, August	25	Germany	Y	Havre	New York	12/11/1881	08/29/1887			Y	
Bartel, John	52	Hanover	Y	Bremen	Baltimore	10/27/1854	11/01/1858	17	232	N	
Bartell, Frank	26	Oldenburg	Y	Bremen	New Orleans	11/25/1849	11/01/1852	5	120	N	

CITIZENSHIP RECORDS

APPLICANT	AGE	COUNTRY OF ORIGIN	DEC	DEPART PORT	ENTRY PORT	ARRIVE DATE	DEC DATE	VOL	PG.	FLD	NAT DATE
Bartell, Isaac	45	Austria	Y	Hamburg	New York	03/15/1893	04/03/1894			Y	
Bartell, Julius	16	Germany	N	?	New York	00/00/1872				Y	10/29/1888
Bartels, August	22	Bavaria	Y	London	New York	07/04/1849	01/03/1852			Y	03/26/1855
Bartels, Jacob Henry	35	Hanover	Y	Bremen	New York	03/15/1850	04/07/1856	26	455	N	
Bartels, John Henry	25	Prussia	Y	Bremen	New York	07/03/1846	10/13/1848	1	187	N	
Bartels, Rudolph	37	Germany	N	Hamburg	New York	09/01/1880	?			Y	
Bartelt, Mathias	27	Hanover	Y	Bremen	Baltimore	11/30/1856	12/26/1857	16	261	N	
Bartenschlager, Wilhelm	26	Bavaria	Y	Antwerp	New York	10/28/1849	11/01/1852	6	285	N	
Bartes, Christian	26	Bavaria	Y	Havre	New York	05/06/1852	05/09/1854	9	277	N	
Bartetzke, August	37	Germany	Y	Hamburg	Boston	05/21/1882	12/24/1886			Y	
Barth, John	32	Germany	Y	Varendorf	New York	05/05/1882	04/11/1882			Y	
Barth, John Henry	29	Bavaria	Y	Havre	New Orleans	06/06/1848	05/17/1854	8	464	N	
Barth, John Henry	29	Bavaria	Y	Havre	New Orleans	06/06/1848	05/17/1854	9	338	N	
Barth, Paul	30	Germany	Y	Bremen	New York	10/27/1881	12/29/1883			Y	
Bartling, Christian L.	25	Germany	Y	Bremen	Baltimore	03/30/1880	11/16/1885			Y	
Bartling, Ernst A.	40	Germany	Y	Bremen	New York	05/01/1870	12/05/1882			Y	
Bartling, Henry	46	Germany	N	Bremen	New Orleans	07/??/1854	?			Y	
Bartman, Simon	24	Baden	Y	Havre	New York	07/15/1850	01/31/1853	7	95	N	
Barton, Edward	37	England	Y	Manchester	New York	12/09/1872	10/10/1881			Y	
Barton, Robert S.	25	England	Y	Liverpool	Phila(?)	09/21/1847	03/13/1851	3	273	N	
Bartruff, Charles	23	Wurttemberg	Y	Havre	New York	09/29/1848	08/07/1851	4	95	N	
Bartsch, Karl W.	33	Germany	Y	Hamburg	New York	05/08/1881	06/02/1884			Y	
Bartsch, Ludwig	32	Germany	Y	Bremen	New York	11/22/1881	06/12/1882			Y	
Bartsh, Edward	28	Prussia	Y	Hamburg	New Orleans	10/28/1852	04/17/1854	8	182	N	
Bartsh, Edward	28	Prussia	Y	Hamburg	New Orleans	10/28/1852	04/17/1854	9	53	N	
Bartz, Eugene	32	Germany	Y	Bremen	New York	03/15/1887	04/06/1900			Y	
Bartz, Friedrich	27	Prussia	Y	Bremen	Baltimore	09/19/1850	06/08/1852	25	208	N	
Bartz, Henry	27	Leipzig	Y	Bremen	New York	05/09/1850	06/30/1851	3	468	N	
Bartz, Max	29	Germany	Y	Hamburg	New York	02/03/1888	12/27/1893			Y	
Barwe, Bernard Henry	31	Prussia	Y	Bremen	New York	07/11/1857	05/03/1860	27	177	N	
Barwick, Conrad	79	Bavaria	Y	Antwerp	New Orleans	01/02/1847	01/31/1860	27	82	N	
Barwinkel, Barney	17	Germany	N	?	Baltimore	00/00/1882				Y	10/29/1888
Barz, Jacob	41	Germany	Y	Bremen	New York	10/01/1881	11/09/1891			Y	
Baschang, George	23	Baden	Y	Antwerp	New York	11/30/1853	10/06/1856	14	217	N	
Basche, Joseph	41	Germany	N	Bremen	New Orleans	07/??/1852	?			Y	
Baschert, Bernhard	31	Baden	Y	Havre	New Orleans	05/10/1846	02/01/1850	2	26	N	
Basele, E.	25	Oldenburg	Y	Bremen	Baltimore	09/27/1858	11/01/1860	27	522	N	
Basenach, John	21	Prussia	Y	Havre	New York	06/29/1858	06/14/1861	18	192	N	
Baskerville, Robert	34	Ireland	Y	Dublin	New Orleans	02/??/1849	01/16/1851	2	500	N	
Basket, Bernard	??	Prussia	Y	Bremen	New Orleans	12/15/18??	10/09/1848	1	64	N	
Basler, Philipp	26	Switzerland	Y	Bremen	Baltimore	05/24/1888	05/17/1890			Y	
Basshartt, Rudolph	24	Switzerland	Y	?	New York	04/01/1880	03/17/1881			Y	
Bassit, Jason	32	Canada	Y	Canada	Buffalo	10/??/1846	09/10/1855	11	529	N	
Bast, John	23	Bavaria	Y	Havre	New York	05/03/1854	03/24/1856	26	266	N	
Bastian, John	29	Germany	Y	Liverpool	New York	02/22/1886	05/10/1890			Y	
Batchovchin, Stephen	33	Austria	Y	Hamburg	New York	01/16/1883	04/28/1894			Y	
Bate, James	??	England	Y	?	?	?	02/08/1886			Y	
Bate, Samuel	32	England	Y	Liverpool	New York	03/28/1840	07/25/1851	4	40	N	
Bateman, George W.	??	England	Y	?	?	?	11/22/1879			Y	
Bates, Stephan	34	England	Y	Liverpool	New York	10/24/1849	10/22/1851	5	47	N	
Bath, Franz	51	France	Y	Havre	New York	06/21/1853	03/03/1856	26	154	N	
Bath, John Nicholas	21	France	Y	Havre	New York	06/21/18??	03/03/1856	26	155	N	
Batisti, Franaucina	40	France	Y	Havre	New York	06/21/1881	06/10/1895			Y	
Batman, Nicholas	21	Bavaria	Y	Havre	New Orleans	06/15/1845	10/02/1848	1	15	N	
Batsche, William	63	Germany	N	Bremen	New York	06/21/1872	?			Y	
Batscher, John	24	Baden	Y	London	New York	05/10/1849	10/13/1851	4	230	N	
Batsner, Daniel	40	England	Y	Canada	Detroit	12/19/1894	10/25/1900			Y	
Batzsch, Charles	38	Prussia	Y	Hamburg	Buffalo	08/01/1847	11/15/1852	5	292	N	
Batzsch, Charles	38	Prussia	Y	Hamburg	Buffalo	08/01/1847	11/15/1852	6	417	N	

CITIZENSHIP RECORDS

APPLICANT	AGE	COUNTRY OF ORIGIN	DEC	DEPART PORT	ENTRY PORT	ARRIVE DATE	DEC DATE	VOL	PG.	FLD	NAT DATE
Bauduin, Gottfried	31	Holland	Y	Liverpool	New York	07/20/1859	07/29/1861	18	209	N	
Bauer, Adam	48	Germany	Y	Bremen	New York	03/22/1882	04/11/1887			Y	
Bauer, Alois	25	Hesse Darmsta	Y	Bremen	New Orleans	05/08/1852	10/05/1854	10	435	N	
Bauer, Alois	25	Hesse Darmsta	Y	Bremen	New Orleans	03/08/1852	10/05/1843	12	374	N	
Bauer, Andrew	34	Hanover	Y	Bremen	New Orleans	11/28/1855	05/20/1861	18	173	N	
Bauer, Anton	40	Germany	Y	Hamburg	New York	11/??/1869	10/09/1888			Y	
Bauer, Carl Fred	36	Germany	Y	Havre	New York	05/20/1880	05/29/1882			Y	
Bauer, Christ	29	Germany	Y	Hamburg	New York	08/24/1880	05/19/1887			Y	
Bauer, Dominick	31	Austria	Y	Havre	New York	09/01/1850	05/13/1852	25	15	N	
Bauer, Frank	34	Hanover	Y	Bremen	Philadelphia	01/04/1848	01/11/1849	1	387	N	
Bauer, Frank	33	Bavaria	Y	Bremen	New Orleans	05/26/1850	03/03/1852	24	231	N	
Bauer, Franz	25	Germany	Y	Hamburg	New York	12/06/1878	07/15/1882			Y	
Bauer, Frederick	34	Wurttemberg	Y	Antwerp	New York	??/10/1847	02/14/1850	2	77	N	
Bauer, Frederick	40	Germany	Y	Bremen	New York	08/21/1882	03/05/1885			Y	
Bauer, George	25	Bavaria	Y	London	New York	05/18/1852	01/31/1856	13	525	N	
Bauer, George	26	Germany	Y	Bremen	New York	06/17/1882	04/06/1885			Y	
Bauer, George Adam	43	Bavaria	Y	Bremen	New York	05/??/1848	10/??/1849	23	293	N	
Bauer, Goswin	33	Baden	Y	Havre	New York	09/02/1866	07/31/8172	18	509	N	
Bauer, Gottfried	31	Germany	Y	Antwerp	New York	10/29/1885	10/15/1892			Y	
Bauer, Gottlieb	25	Gotha	Y	Hamburg	New York	06/10/1847	08/21/1848	22	221	N	
Bauer, Herman	47	Hanover	Y	Bremen	New Orleans	12/30/1848	02/01/1849	23	2	N	
Bauer, Jacob	28	Wurttemberg	Y	Havre	New York	05/??/1854	11/16/1857	16	29	N	
Bauer, Jacob	30	Germany	Y	Bremen	New York	03/??/1883	03/??/1883				
Bauer, John	32	Hanover	Y	Bremen	Baltimore	10/25/1846	01/11/1849	1	392	N	
Bauer, John	38	Germany	Y	Bremen	New York	03/18/1870	12/19/1881			Y	
Bauer, John	43	Germany	Y	Hamburg	Boston	06/14/1882	10/03/1885			Y	
Bauer, John Baptist	34	Bavaria	Y	Hamburg	New York	10/04/1844	08/17/1848	22	201	N	
Bauer, John Henry	23	Saxony	Y	Bremen	New York	??/30/1849	01/02/1850	23	455	N	
Bauer, John L.	??	Germany	Y	?	?	?	04/02/1879			Y	
Bauer, Joseph	45	Wurttemberg	Y	Hamburg	Galveston	08/04/1847	11/20/1848	1	326	N	
Bauer, Joseph	31	Wurttemberg	Y	Havre	New York	05/16/1850	09/27/1854	10	261	N	
Bauer, Joseph	31	Wurttemberg	Y	Havre	New York	05/16/1850	09/27/1854	12	200	N	
Bauer, Martin	17	Germany	N	?	New York	00/00/1881				Y	10/23/1886
Bauer, Michael	28	Wurttemberg	Y	Havre	New York	05/06/1857	04/06/1858	16	502	N	
Bauer, Peter	36	Bavaria	Y	Bremen	Baltimore	09/01/1847	10/04/1854	10	407	N	
Bauer, Peter	23	Prussia	Y	London	New York	06/12/1852	10/05/1854	10	466	N	
Bauer, Peter	36	Bavaria	Y	Bremen	Baltimore	09/01/1847	10/04/1854	12	346	N	
Bauer, Peter	23	Prussia	Y	London	New York	06/12/1852	10/05/1854	12	405	N	
Bauer, Philipp	21	Hesse Darmsta	Y	Havre	New Orleans	05/12/1852	10/05/1854	10	434	N	
Bauer, Philipp	21	Hesse Darmsta	Y	Havre	New Orleans	05/12/1852	10/05/1854	12	373	N	
Bauer, William	21	Germany	Y	Antwerp	New York	09/17/1887	04/11/1891			Y	
Bauereiss, George	28	Bavaria	Y	Hamburg	New York	08/01/1854	03/24/1856	26	269	N	
Bauerlin, Carl	29	Wurttemberg	Y	Havre	New York	09/28/1851	10/09/1854	6	127	N	
Bauersachs, Otto	36	Bavaria	Y	Bremen	New York	11/11/1852	10/04/1854	10	416	N	
Bauersachs, Otto	36	Bavaria	Y	Bremen	New York	11/11/1852	10/04/1854	12	355	N	
Bauge, Adolph	35	Germany	Y	Bremen	Baltimore	11/09/1890	09/10/1896			Y	
Baukemper, Henry	34	Prussia	Y	Bremen	New York	09/15/1858	05/08/1861	18	164	N	
Baum, George	29	?	Y	Havre	New York	04/04/1834	10/07/1848	22	491	N	
Baum, John	43	Germany	Y	Bremen	New York	03/06/1885	07/09/1897			Y	
Baum, Leon	39	Austira	Y	Hamburg	New York	11/17/1887	10/16/1894			Y	
Baum, Sam	??	Poland	Y	?	?	?	11/15/1897			Y	
Baumann, August	29	Oldenburg	Y	Bremen	Baltimore	05/22/1870	03/29/1872	18	479	N	
Baumann, Charles	25	Germany	Y	Hamburg	New York	08/23/1884	06/14/1887			Y	
Baumann, Charles L.	??	Germany	Y	?	?	04/07/1895	05/07/1895			Y	
Baumann, Daniel	34	Bavaria	Y	Havre	New Orleans	10/07/1846	10/07/1848	22	493	N	
Baumann, Fred	52	Germany	N	Baden	New York	05/04/1866	?			Y	
Baumann, Friedrich	43	Switzerland	Y	Havre	New York	11/??/1887	12/02/1887			Y	
Baumann, George	39	Germany	Y	Havre	New York	03/02/1875	10/24/1895			Y	
Baumann, Herman	32	Germany	Y	Bremen	Baltimore	11/10/1889	12/26/1896			Y	

15

CITIZENSHIP RECORDS

APPLICANT	AGE	COUNTRY OF ORIGIN	DEC	DEPART PORT	ENTRY PORT	ARRIVE DATE	DEC DATE	VOL	PG.	FLD	NAT DATE
Baumann, Jacob	31	Germany	Y	Havre	New York	02/06/1882	09/22/1892			Y	
Baumann, John	21	Bavaria	Y	Havre	New York	06/10/1847	10/12/1848	1	164	N	
Baumann, John	38	Germany	Y	Bremen	New York	09/07/1872	05/23/1883			Y	
Baumann, John	17	Germany	N	?	New York	05/00/1883				Y	10/27/1888
Baumann, Joseph A.	53	Switzerland	Y	Antwerp	New York	05/12/1886	12/18/1890			Y	
Baumann, Karl	26	Germany	Y	Bremen	New York	08/27/1887	09/01/1888			Y	
Baumann, Leo	34	Germany	Y	Antwerp	New York	10/08/1896	01/03/1903			Y	
Baumann, Robert	38	Switzerland	Y	Havre	New York	04/27/1883	01/28/1887			Y	
Baumblatt, Max	19	Germany	Y	Antwerp	Philadelphia	05/22/1888	10/02/1888			Y	
Baumeister, Benjamin	17	Germany	N	?	New York	00/00/1877				Y	10/29/1886
Baumeister, Bernard	31	Prussia	Y	Havre	New York	05/29/1847	06/21/1851	3	434	N	
Baumeister, Willie	17	Germany	N	?	New York	00/00/1881				Y	10/18/1886
Baumer, Xavier	31	Baden	Y	Havre	New Orleans	04/23/1847	10/07/1851	4	215	N	
Baumgaertner, John	38	Wurttemberg	Y	Havre	New York	09/10/1854	03/02/1858	16	481	N	
Baumgardner, Farsulli	27	Switzerland	Y	Havre	New Orleans	06/02/1848	10/02/1848	1	14	N	
Baumgardner, John	28	Switzerland	Y	Havre	New Orleans	06/02/1848	10/02/1848	1	32	N	
Baumgardner, Lawrence	64	Bavaria	Y	Bremen	New York	12/24/1836	10/06/1848	22	461	N	
Baumgart, Jacob	71	Bavaria	N	Havre	New York	02/03/1852	?	28	400	N	08/15/1858
Baumgarten, Fred	29	Germany	Y	Antwerp	New York	05/15/1881	02/19/1887			Y	
Baumgarten, Henry	25	Hanover	Y	Bremen	New Orleans	11/??/1848	10/29/1851	4	432	N	
Baumgarten, Moses	22	Austria	Y	Liverpool	New York	08/28/1852	04/22/1854	9	110	N	
Baumgartner, Anthony	27	Switzerland	Y	Havre	New York	12/04/1882	06/??/1883			Y	
Baumgartner, Anthony	37	Switzerland	N	Havre	New York	12/04/1882	?			Y	
Baumgartner, Joseph	37	Switzerland	Y	Havre	New York	12/15/1853	09/26/1857	15	327	N	
Baumgartner, Joseph	32	Switzerland	Y	Havre	New York	03/10/1881	10/22/1889			Y	
Baumgartner, Kaspar	43	Germany	Y	Bremen	New York	04/01/1872	10/22/1886	19	70	N	
Baumgartner, Kaspar	43	Germany	Y	Bremen	New York	04/01/1872	10/22/1886			Y	
Baumgartner, Theophile	25	Germany	Y	Havre	New York	08/31/1891	10/24/1896			Y	
Baumgartner, Thomas	31	Switzerland	Y	Rotterdam	New York	05/18/1889	06/11/1895			Y	
Baumgarton, Moses	22	Austria	Y	Liverpool	New York	08/28/1852	04/22/1854	8	239	N	
Baunach, Ignatz	31	Germany	Y	Bremen	Baltimore	09/05/1888	12/03/1891			Y	
Baur, Ernst V.	32	Germany	Y	Bremen	New York	05/13/1884	03/01/1887			Y	
Baur, Gabhard	37	Germany	Y	Havre	New York	08/25/1879	03/25/1885			Y	
Baurheun, Charles	23	Hesse Cassel	Y	Bremen	New York	??/10/1845	10/09/1848	1	79	N	
Bausch, Charles	32	Germany	Y	?	New York	??/??/1871	10/01/1880			Y	
Bauscher, Conrad	29	Hesse Darmsta	Y	Havre	New Orleans	06/17/1851	04/04/1853	8	50	N	
Bauscher, Ludwig	28	Hesse Darmsta	Y	Havre	New Orleans	05/20/1847	11/16/1848	1	283	N	
Bautheim, Ludwig	23	Germany	Y	Hamburg	New York	09/11/1881	07/08/1883			Y	
Bax, Henry	35	Lippe Detmold	Y	Bremen	New Orleans	06/20/1849	01/25/1853	7	68	N	
Baxter, John	31	England	Y	London	New York	09/14/1882	01/04/1892			Y	
Bay, Christian	24	Wuerttemberg	Y	Havre	New York	10/23/1854	05/08/1860	27	187	N	
Bayer, Andrew	46	Bavaria	N	Havre	New York	06/01/1867	?			Y	
Bayer, Anton	27	Germany	Y	Havre	New York	10/12/1891	02/07/1893			Y	
Bayer, Ernst	27	Germany	Y	Bremen	New York	05/28/1890	10/29/1892			Y	
Bayer, George	23	Germany	Y	Antwerp	New York	12/09/1880	10/04/1883			Y	
Bayer, Gottlieb	23	Wuertemberg	Y	Havre	New York	08/23/1853	02/28/1856	26	139	N	
Bayer, Jacob	21	Germany	Y	Bremen	New York	05/25/1880	11/03/1884			Y	
Bayer, John	21	Germany	Y	Boulogna	New York	07/08/1892	02/07/1893			Y	
Bayer, John Adam	33	Baden	Y	Havre	New Orleans	12/24/1847	03/05/1852	24	235	N	
Bayer, Philip	22	Bavaria	Y	Havre	New York	04/20/1854	03/22/1856	26	249	N	
Bayerdoerfer,Charles Fre	??	Wurttemberg	Y	Havre	New Orleans	05/23/18??	10/09/1848	1	80	N	
Bayersdorfer, John	45	Bavaria	Y	Havre	New Orleans	11/28/1854	11/26/1855	13	258	N	
Bazzanello, George	??	Austria	Y	?	?	?	02/08/1889			Y	
Beaker, Bernard	41	Oldenburg	Y	Bremen	New Orleans	05/01/1849	04/04/1853	8	29	N	
Beamer, Joseph	33	Prussia	Y	Bremen	New Orleans	11/28/1848	06/12/1852	25	240	N	
Bean, Thomas	35	Ireland	Y	Queenstown	New York	03/24/1879	11/10/1891			Y	
Beanchino, Raffaele	40	Italy	Y	Naples	New York	03/30/1890	03/22/1894			Y	
Bear, Henry	35	Hesse Darmsta	Y	Bremen	New York	07/15/1850	09/21/1855	13	93	N	
Bearan, James	31	Wales	Y	Liverpool	New York	04/04/1883	11/22/1889			Y	

CITIZENSHIP RECORDS

APPLICANT	AGE	COUNTRY OF ORIGIN	DEC	DEPART PORT	ENTRY PORT	ARRIVE DATE	DEC DATE	VOL	PG.	FLD	NAT DATE
Beauerlein, Carl	29	Wurttemberg	Y	Havre	New York	09/28/1851	10/09/1854	11	130	N	
Beaumer, John Henry	??	Oldenburg	Y	Bremen	Baltimore	08/08/1846	10/09/1848	22	504	N	
Beaupre, Charles	27	Canada	Y	?	?	11/06/1882	04/02/1888			Y	
Bebb, Robert E.	27	Wales	Y	Liverpool	Philadelphia	06/02/1848	05/08/1854	8	399	N	
Bebb, Robert E.	27	Wales	Y	Liverpool	Philadelphia	06/02/1848	05/08/1854	9	272	N	
Bech, Henry	36	Denmark	Y	Hamburg	New York	04/17/1887	10/14/1890			Y	
Bechem, Emanuel Florian	26	Prussia	Y	Havre	New Orleans	01/21/1854	05/29/1854	9	447	N	
Bechem, Emanuel Florian	26	Prussia	Y	Havre	New Orleans	01/21/1854	05/29/1854	10	30	N	
Bechener, John Gottlob	??	Germany	Y	?	?	01/??/1881	04/16/1883			Y	
Becher, Fred	52	Germany	Y	Antwerp	New York	06/07/1889	06/09/1891			Y	
Becher, Gus	20	Germany	Y	Antwerp	New York	06/07/1889	06/09/1891			Y	
Becher, John	23	Prussia	Y	Rotterdam	Baltimore	06/16/1849	03/01/1852	24	204	N	
Becherer, William	30	Saxe Weimar	Y	Delfseal	New York	08/25/1849	10/16/1851	4	314	N	
Bechman, John	29	Germany	Y	?	?	?	10/31/1866			Y	
Bechmann, Albert	23	Baden	Y	Havre	New York	04/11/1854	09/21/1857	15	294	N	
Bechmann, Henry	35	Germany	Y	Hamburg	New York	11/10/1893	10/03/1895			Y	
Bechmann, Nathan Henry	22	Germany	Y	Bremen	New York	10/13/1880	10/27/1882			Y	
Bechmann, Robert	25	Baden	Y	Havre	New York	04/07/1850	04/12/1852	24	456	N	
Becht, John Philip	26	Germany	Y	Bremen	New York	06/09/1878	03/26/1883			Y	
Becht, Peter	24	Bavaria	Y	Havre	New York	07/01/1848	02/21/1849	23	245	N	
Becht, Philip	33	Germany	Y	Bremen	Baltimore	11/10/1881	11/02/1886			Y	
Bechtel, Justus	32	Hesse Cassel	Y	Bremen	New York	08/22/1849	05/13/1852	25	12	N	
Bechtel, Justus	25	Baden	Y	Havre	New York	10/??/1849	09/09/1852	25	432	N	
Bechtel, Ludwig	22	Hesse Cassel	Y	Bremen	New York	10/10/1849	10/06/1851	4	193	N	
Bechtold, Fred	24	Germany	Y	Baden	New York	03/17/1882	04/27/1885			Y	
Bechtold, John	43	Germany	Y	ANtwerp	New York	09/13/1883	10/14/1893			Y	
Bechtold, Joseph	14	Germany	N	?	New York	00/00/1877				Y	10/23/1886
Bechtold, Leopold	25	Baden	Y	Havre	New York	04/20/1854	09/26/1856	14	398	N	
Bechtolt, Joseph	37	Baden	Y	Havre	New York	07/15/1852	12/13/1855	13	310	N	
Bechtolt, Raimunt	26	Germany	Y	Bremen	New York	05/20/1878	11/06/1882			Y	
Beck, Bernard	36	Germany	Y	Hamburg	New York	04/03/1888	06/15/1895			Y	
Beck, Ferdinand	36	Germany	Y	Havre	New York	01/28/1883	03/16/1891			Y	
Beck, Frank	40	Germany	N	Bremen	New York	03/27/1866	?			Y	
Beck, Fred	25	Germany	Y	Havre	New York	03/16/1892	06/03/1895			Y	
Beck, Frederick	23	Prussia	Y	Bremen	Baltimore	05/03/1849	11/01/1852	5	92	N	
Beck, George	30	Bavaria	Y	Antwerp	New York	11/23/1849	09/30/1856	14	64	N	
Beck, George	59	Germany	N	Havre	New York	11/??/1854	?			Y	
Beck, George Peter	24	Baden	Y	Rotterdam	New York	05/26/1848	10/27/1851	4	421	N	
Beck, Heinrich	34	Wurttemberg	Y	Havre	New Orleans	12/29/1852	02/19/1853	7	184	N	
Beck, Henry	??	Oldenburg	Y	Bremen	New Orleans	05/03/1849	03/24/1851	3	312	N	
Beck, Henry	28	Germany	Y	Havre	New York	09/13/1882	09/19/1885			Y	
Beck, Herman	29	Germany	Y	Antwerp	New York	08/28/1881	01/31/1887			Y	
Beck, Jacob	22	Wurttemberg	Y	Havre	New York	08/15/1853	09/28/1854	10	293	N	
Beck, Jacob	22	Wurttemberg	Y	Havre	New York	08/15/1853	09/28/1854	12	232	N	
Beck, John	30	Germany	Y	Rotterdam	New York	07/29/1891	10/18/1896			Y	
Beck, Joseph	??	Germany	Y	?	?	?	10/18/1881			Y	
Beck, Michael	24	Baden	Y	Rotterdam	New York	11/18/1845	11/20/1848	1	336	N	
Beck, Peter	45	France	Y	Havre	New Orleans	03/03/1847	08/05/1856	14	342	N	
Beck, Philip	41	Germany	Y	Havre	Baltimore	12/12/1870	01/03/1891			Y	
Beck, Romuald	25	Baden	Y	Havre	New Orleans	??/26/1854	04/24/1855	11	290	N	
Beck, Sylvester	30	Wurttemberg	Y	Havre	New York	09/28/1851	02/21/1853	7	192	N	
Beck, Valentine	26	Bavaria	Y	Havre	New York	06/18/1851	10/05/1854	10	454	N	
Beck, Valentine	26	Bavaria	Y	Havre	New York	06/18/1851	10/05/1854	12	393	N	
Beck, William	32	England	Y	London	New York	04/13/1884	10/14/1891			Y	
Beck, William	43	Germany	Y	?	New York	06/??/1866	11/15/1880			Y	
Beckel, August	35	Germany	N	Bremen	New York	12/??/1867	?			Y	
Beckel, Herman	54	Germany	Y	Bremen	Baltimore	05/01/1890	06/19/1896			Y	
Beckel, Jacob	38	Germany	N	Hamburg	New York	09/27/1871	?			Y	
Beckemeyer, Joseph	25	Germany	Y	Amsterdam	New York	10/22/1888	10/03/1892			Y	

CITIZENSHIP RECORDS

APPLICANT	AGE	COUNTRY OF ORIGIN	DEC	DEPART PORT	ENTRY PORT	ARRIVE DATE	DEC DATE	VOL	PG.	FLD	NAT DATE
Beckemeyer, Joseph	50	Germany	N	Bremen	New York	07/30/1866	?			Y	
Becker, Adam	38	Germany	Y	Hamburg	New York	05/20/1873	09/09/1885			Y	
Becker, Adam	54	Germany	Y	Amsterdam	New York	04/10/1882	10/31/1896			Y	
Becker, August	24	Hesse Darmsta	Y	Liverpool	New York	12/20/1856	05/11/1859	17	408	N	
Becker, August	38	Germany	Y	Antwerp	New York	04/01/1883	09/03/1886			Y	
Becker, Bernard	25	Oldenburg	Y	Bremen	New Orleans	11/05/1854	09/17/1857	15	280	N	
Becker, Carl	26	Germany	Y	Antwerp	New York	09/18/1884	11/02/1886			Y	
Becker, Carl	22	Germany	Y	Hamburg	New York	09/11/1882	12/29/1885			Y	
Becker, Charles	28	Luxembourg	Y	Havre	Philadelphia	08/15/1882	11/05/1889			Y	
Becker, Charles G.	??	Germany	Y	?	?	?	05/07/1889			Y	
Becker, Chris	26	Germany	Y	Bremen	Baltimore	04/16/1891	09/06/1891			Y	
Becker, Christian	28	Baden	Y	Hamburg	New York	06/28/1850	05/31/1852	25	142	N	
Becker, Conrad	37	Bavaria	Y	Rotterdam	New York	10/01/1854	11/07/1860	18	30	N	
Becker, Francis	24	Bavaria	Y	Liverpool	New York	09/25/1852	12/29/1857	16	279	N	
Becker, Frank	28	Germany	Y	Antwerp	New York	04/03/1889	11/22/1892			Y	
Becker, Fred	30	Germany	Y	Bremen	Baltimore	05/22/1881	07/03/1883			Y	
Becker, Friedrich	42	Switzerland	Y	Havre	New York	05/15/1878	10/16/1891			Y	
Becker, George	29	Germany	Y	Havre	New York	06/21/1881	02/27/1890			Y	
Becker, Gerhard	23	Germany	Y	Bremen	New York	01/09/1893	06/20/1896			Y	
Becker, Henry	22	Hanover	Y	Amsterdam	New York	12/08/1849	02/03/1851	3	82	N	
Becker, Henry	30	Hesse Darmsta	Y	Havre	New York	10/06/1858	04/21/1862	18	323	N	
Becker, Henry	28	Germany	Y	Antwerp	Philadelphia	07/15/1888	06/20/1891			Y	
Becker, Henry	48	Germany	Y	Hamburg	New York	10/??/1873	10/10/1887			Y	
Becker, Henry	??	Germany	N	Bremen	Baltimore	??/??/1852	?			Y	
Becker, Henry J.	49	Germany	Y	Rotterdam	Jersey City	10/21/1877	05/22/1885			Y	
Becker, Herman	28	Germany	Y	Bremen	Baltimore	07/20/1872	05/10/1882			Y	
Becker, Jacob	??	Germany	Y	?	?	?	06/20/1882			Y	
Becker, Jacob	27	Germany	Y	Rotterdam	New York	03/01/1883	02/12/1887			Y	
Becker, Jacob	48	Russia	Y	Hamburg	New York	02/14/1886	02/05/1894			Y	
Becker, Jacob	33	Germany	N	Havre	New York	07/??/1869	?			Y	
Becker, James	30	Ireland	Y	Glasgow	New York	08/22/1851	01/04/1858	16	299	N	
Becker, Johann	21	Germany	Y	Antwerp	Philadelphia	05/18/1886	03/31/1888			Y	
Becker, John	32	Germany	Y	Bremen	New York	06/12/1880	10/19/1893			Y	
Becker, John	28	Germany	Y	Bremen	New York	03/04/1882	10/27/1887			Y	
Becker, John	27	Bavaria	Y	Havre	New Orleans	01/03/1848	04/07/1852	24	410	N	
Becker, John	32	Bavaria	Y	London	New York	05/01/1852	09/06/1852	25	367	N	
Becker, John Rudolph	24	Germany	Y	Bremen	New York	07/04/1885	05/21/1888			Y	
Becker, John W.	28	Germany	Y	Havre	New York	09/12/1879	04/10/1882			Y	
Becker, Joseph	25	Prussia	Y	Antwerp	New York	08/16/1854	03/25/1856	26	345	N	
Becker, Louis	29	Prussia	Y	Antwerp	New York	06/02/1851	05/13/1854	8	434	N	
Becker, Louis	29	Prussia	Y	Antwerp	New York	06/22/1851	05/13/1854	9	307	N	
Becker, Louis	52	Germany	N	Havre	New York	06/??/1857	?			Y	
Becker, Mathias	28	Bavaria	Y	Havre	New York	08/28/1851	10/02/1856	14	147	N	
Becker, Michael	28	Germany	Y	Bremen	New York	05/01/1880	05/15/1883			Y	
Becker, Michael	50	Germany	Y	?	New York	04/30/1866	10/16/1890			Y	
Becker, Moritz Heinrich	33	Germany	N	Antwerp	New York	06/13/1883	?			Y	
Becker, Peter	28	Germany	Y	Antwerp	New York	08/04/1887	06/09/1891			Y	
Becker, Peter Joseph	31	Bavaria	Y	London	New York	12/02/1854	09/23/1858	16	146	N	
Becker, Robert	31	Germany	Y	Bremen	New York	07/04/1885	01/22/1887			Y	
Becker, Samuel	28	Hesse Darmsta	Y	Havre	New York	11/25/1852	12/29/1855	13	392	N	
Becker, Thomas C.	57	Ireland	Y	Liverpool	New York	05/25/1866	06/26/1891			Y	
Becker, William	??	Germany	Y	?	?	?	10/12/1886			Y	
Beckers, Joseph	35	Germany	Y	Antwerp	New York	02/26/1883	10/29/1887			Y	
Beckett, Thomas Sothern	27	England	Y	Liverpool	New York	09/18/1850	11/08/1858	17	290	N	
Beckhaus, Bernard	24	Hanover	Y	Bremen	Baltimore	07/14/1848	04/12/1852	24	461	N	
Beckman, Gerhard	31	Hanover	Y	Bremen	Baltimore	07/06/1845	08/15/1848	22	151	N	
Beckmann, Barney	29	Germany	Y	?	?	?	12/20/1880			Y	
Beckmann, Barney	40	Germany	Y	Rotterdam	New York	06/16/1881	10/24/1892			Y	
Beckmann, Casper Henry	32	Hanover	Y	Bremen	New Orleans	12/25/1845	01/17/1853	7	37	N	

CITIZENSHIP RECORDS

APPLICANT	AGE	COUNTRY OF ORIGIN	DEC	DEPART PORT	ENTRY PORT	ARRIVE DATE	DEC DATE	VOL	PG.	FLD	NAT DATE
Beckmann, Fred	58	Germany	Y	Bremen	New York	08/12/1885	01/08/1892			Y	
Beckmann, Frederick Will	32	Prussia	Y	Bremen	New Orleans	10/27/18??	10/09/1854	6	114	N	
Beckmann, Frederick Will	32	Prussia	Y	Bremen	New Orleans	10/27/1848	10/09/1854	11	117	N	
Beckmann, George	29	Oldenburg	Y	Bremen	New Orleans	??/01/1846	10/09/1848	1	73	N	
Beckmann, Henry William	35	Hanover	Y	Bremen	Baltimore	08/06/1846	01/25/1849	1	511	N	
Beckmann, John	26	Prussia	Y	Bremen	Baltimore	??/17/1847	10/09/1848	1	75	N	
Beckmann, John	27	Germany	Y	Rotterdam	New York	09/15/1881	03/31/1888			Y	
Beckmann, John Henry	28	Oldenburg	Y	Bremen	New Orleans	05/07/1849	05/10/1852	24	529	N	
Beckmann, Rudolph	32	Prussia	Y	Bremen	New York	10/25/1857	01/18/1860			Y	
Beckmann, Th.	25	Germany	Y	Bremen	Baltimore	11/13/1882	11/01/1884			Y	
Beckmann, William	30	Prussia	Y	Bremen	Baltimore	05/??/1854	09/24/1855	13	127	N	
Beckmann, William	35	Prussia	Y	Bremen	New York	06/05/1852	02/06/1857	14	541	N	
Becksmith, Frank	57	Germany	N	Hamburg	Baltimore	??/??/1836	?			Y	
Beckstedde, Bernard	23	Oldenburg	Y	Bremen	New Orleans	11/20/1854	05/22/1856	26	539	N	
Beckstedt, Casper	28	Oldenburg	Y	Bremen	New Orleans	06/??/1853	09/17/1855	13	62	N	
Beckwermert, William	22	Prussia	Y	Rotterdam	New York	08/17/1846	11/22/1848	1	379	N	
Becky, Charles	16	Germany	N	?	New York	00/00/1883				Y	10/30/1888
Becky, Henry	37	Germany	Y	Havre	New York	10/28/1883	10/11/1886			Y	
Bedacht, George	42	Bavaria	Y	Havre	New York	11/01/1852	03/20/1860	27	134	N	
Beddinghaus, Benjamin	??	Germany	N	?	?	08/26/1881				Y	10/28/1892
Beddoe, Albert	26	England	Y	Liverpool	Boston	12/01/1880	12/20/1889			Y	
Bedinghaus, Joseph	50	Germany	Y	Bremen	Baltimore	08/28/1882	09/26/1892			Y	
Bedinglaus, Joseph	50	Germany	Y	Bremen	Baltimore	08/28/1882	09/26/1892	19	353	N	
Beehler, John	39	Germany	Y	Bremen	New York	04/24/1880	11/01/1893			Y	
Beeken, Arnold H. (Wichl	27	Germany	Y	?	?	?	02/??/1886			Y	
Beeker, William	31	Prussia	Y	Liverpool	New York	11/30/1852	04/05/1858	16	496	N	
Beeker, William	46	England	Y	Liverpool	New York	09/25/1841	06/12/1852	25	241	N	
Beel, Herman	37	Germany	Y	Rotterdam	New York	12/??/1867	05/18/1882			Y	
Beer, George	31	Germany	Y	Bremen	New York	01/21/1892	02/20/1892			Y	
Beerle, Alfred	39	Switzerland	Y	Antwerp	New York	02/27/1886	01/02/1889			Y	
Beerman, August	54	Germany	N	Bremen	New York	11/01/1863	?			Y	
Beermann, Adolf	29	Germany	Y	Bremen	Baltimore	11/19/1882	11/20/1885			Y	
Beermann, Henry	29	Germany	Y	Bremen	Baltimore	04/07/1878	05/04/1881			Y	
Beermann, Henry	53	Germany	Y	Bremen	New York	10/12/1881	04/06/1882			Y	
Beermann, John	24	Germany	Y	Bremen	Baltimore	10/12/1881	04/06/1882			Y	
Beese, Charles	34	Germany	Y	Hamburg	New York	11/01/1883	05/27/1896			Y	
Beesten, F.	24	Germany	Y	Rotterdam	New York	10/18/1880	12/31/1883			Y	
Beesten, Herman	25	Prussia	Y	Bremen	New Orleans	12/16/1844	02/04/1850	2	33	N	
Beesten, Joseph	27	Prussia	Y	Bremen	New Orleans	11/18/1846	02/04/1850	2	34	N	
Beetz, Adeldard	33	Germany	Y	Amsterdam	New York	09/10/1881	09/05/1887			Y	
Beetz, John	44	Germany	Y	Bremen	New York	04/11/1881	04/01/1903			Y	
Beetz, Louis	31	Germany	Y	Bremen	Baltimore	09/22/1881	08/01/1888			Y	
Beez, Ignatz	41	Bavaria	Y	Bremen	Baltimore	06/15/1847	10/09/1854	6	104	N	
Beez, Ignatz	41	Bavaria	Y	Bremen	Baltimore	06/15/1847	10/09/1854	11	107	N	
Begino, Antonio	??	Italy	N	Genoa	New York	??/??/1857	?			Y	
Begler, John	30	Bavaria	Y	Havre	New Orleans	05/07/1846	02/08/1853	7	125	N	
Behan, Patrick	64	Ireland	Y	Liverpool	New Orleans	02/09/1850	04/01/1853	7	477	N	
Behenna, William Henry	46	England	Y	Liverpool	New York	03/01/1892	09/11/1903			Y	
Behl, ?	??	Prussia	Y	?	New York	??/02/18??	10/26/1850	2	310	N	
Behm, Lorentz	36	Bavaria	Y	Bremen	Baltimore	08/17/1845	01/26/1849	1	519	N	
Behne, Joseph	22	Germany	Y	Bremen	Baltimore	10/02/1889	10/29/1892			Y	
Behner, Charles A.	33	Germany	Y	Antwerp	New York	03/00/1873	06/25/1886			Y	
Behr, August	53	Germany	N	Hamburg	New York	07/??/1859	?			Y	
Behr, George Henry Willi	29	Hanover	Y	Bremen	New Orleans	01/09/1850	12/18/1855	13	325	N	
Behr, John Louis	45	Germany	Y	Antwerp	New York	09/11/1885	10/12/1893			Y	
Behr, Karl	25	Germany	Y	Bremen	New York	09/15/1883	10/12/1886	19	47	N	
Behr, Karl	25	Germany	Y	Bremen	New York	09/15/1883	10/12/1886			Y	
Behr, Nicholas	39	Bavaria	Y	Bremen	Baltimore	07/20/1849	08/04/1851	4	79	N	
Behrens, B.	27	Germany	Y	Bremen	New York	06/05/1885	07/05/1887			Y	

CITIZENSHIP RECORDS

APPLICANT	AGE	COUNTRY OF ORIGIN	DEC	DEPART PORT	ENTRY PORT	ARRIVE DATE	DEC DATE	VOL	PG.	FLD	NAT DATE
Behrens, Bernard	24	Germany	Y	Rotterdam	New York	09/15/1887	08/21/1890			Y	
Behrens, H.G.F.	29	Germany	Y	Hamburg	New York	10/05/1881	01/22/1884			Y	
Behrens, Henry	45	Hanover	Y	Bremen	New Orleans	01/10/1854	11/06/1855	13	172	N	
Behrens, Henry	50	Germany	Y	Hamburg	New York	07/28/1883	10/27/1889			Y	
Behrens, John	30	Germany	Y	Bremen	Baltimore	05/10/1882	10/26/1886			Y	
Behrens, John Henry	28	Hanover	Y	Bremen	New Orleans	05/22/1848	06/12/1851	3	368	N	
Behrens, John Martin	27	Germany	Y	Bremen	New York	10/08/1888	10/18/1892			Y	
Behring, Frederick	28	Prussia	Y	Bremen	Baltimore	05/13/1849	01/15/1851	2	497	N	
Behringer, Stephen	34	Bavaria	Y	Bremen	New York	06/12/1848	09/07/1852	25	406	N	
Behrle, Anton	42	Germany	Y	Havre	New York	06/22/1865	04/11/1882			Y	
Behrle, Peter	??	Baden	Y	Havre	New York	08/01/1847	12/14/1850	2	364	N	
Behrman, Max	23	Russia	Y	Hamburg	New York	01/07/1888	11/23/1892			Y	
Behrmann, Henry	23	Hanover	Y	Bremen	New Orleans	11/13/1854	11/06/1857	15	537	N	
Behrmann, John Henry	32	Hanover	Y	Bremen	Baltimore	09/22/1857	11/06/1857	15	538	N	
Beier, Henry	38	Hesse Darmsta	Y	Bremen	New York	06/20/1849	12/29/1855	13	384	N	
Beier, Jacob	27	France	Y	Havre	New Orleans	07/04/1849	02/18/1853	7	181	N	
Beierbach, J. Henry	58	Germany	Y	Antwerp	New York	04/13/1891	04/16/1891			Y	
Beierlein, Frank	28	Baden	Y	Havre	New York	05/30/1849	01/??/1850	23	501	N	
Beierlein, George F.	40	Bavaria	Y	Bremen	New York	08/24/1844	01/27/1851	2	529	N	
Beierlein, Peter	22	Baden	Y	Havre	New York	05/26/1849	01/14/1850	23	502	N	
Beigel, George	29	Bavaria	Y	Bremen	New York	06/??/1843	12/29/1852	5	464	N	
Beiger, Nicholas	36	France	Y	Havre	New Orleans	07/04/1848	02/23/1853	7	220	N	
Beilmann, Eberhard	39	Baden	Y	Havre	New Orleans	10/03/1853	12/28/1855	13	368	N	
Beinecke, E.	??	Germany	Y	?	?	06/01/1885	09/10/1886			Y	
Beinecke, Ernst	46	Germany	Y	Bremen	Baltimore	11/26/1864	02/08/1881			Y	
Beinecke, Wilhelm	25	Germany	Y	Bremen	New York	02/13/1891	08/11/1894			Y	
Beineke, Herman	47	Germany	Y	Bremen	New York	08/20/1878	12/18/1882			Y	
Beinesche, John G.A.	22	Germany	Y	Bremen	Baltimore	11/11/1886	12/20/1886			Y	
Beirck, John	30	Bavaria	Y	Havre	New York	??/04/1846	10/??/1849	23	286	N	
Beiring, Henry	38	Hanover	Y	Bremen	New Orleans	06/30/1854	11/09/1858	17	313	N	
Beis, G.H. Fritz	33	Hanover	Y	Bremen	New Orleans	06/20/1851	11/08/1858	17	294	N	
Beisel, Charles	27	Germany	Y	Antwerp	New York	08/03/1892	05/22/1893			Y	
Beiser, Andreas	30	Baden	Y	Havre	New Orleans	05/17/1846	10/06/1848	22	462	N	
Beising, Conrad	26	Hanover	Y	Bremen	New Orleans	09/15/1843	03/08/1851	3	213	N	
Beisner, Chas August	46	Germany	Y	Amsterdam	New York	08/31/1891	09/02/1893			Y	
Beiumscheyper, Bernard	27	Prussia	Y	Bremen	New Orleans	11/15/1849	04/27/1853	8	129	N	
Beland, George	45	Bavaria	Y	Bremen	New Orleans	09/16/1846	02/16/1853	7	168	N	
Belbronan, Bernhard	26	Prussia	Y	Bremen	Baltimore	01/24/1849	11/01/1852	6	308	N	
Belcher, John R.	23	England	Y	Liverpool	New York	05/24/1859	10/08/1860	27	460	N	
Belcher, William	25	Ireland	Y	Waterford	New York	07/??/1853	01/27/1857	14	510	N	
Beler, Charles	40	Austria	Y	Bremen	Baltimore	08/23/1853	10/09/1854	11	200	N	
Belgard, Allen	32	Canada	Y	Prescott	Ogdensburg	04/01/1869	09/17/1881			Y	
Bell, August	34	Germany	Y	Antwerp	New York	10/09/1886	03/17/1888			Y	
Bell, Edward G.	37	Ireland	Y	?	?	?	11/24/1884			Y	
Bell, James	28	Ireland	Y	Liverpool	Baltimore	09/29/1882	01/10/1884			Y	
Bell, John	21	Ireland	Y	Liverpool	New York	11/12/1849	12/20/1851	4	535	N	
Bell, John	22	Ireland	Y	Liverpool	New York	12/10/1847	06/09/1852	25	217	N	
Bell, Thomas	28	Ireland	Y	Liverpool	New York	10/11/1850	04/28/1854	8	279	N	
Bell, Thomas	28	Ireland	Y	Liverpool	New York	10/11/1850	04/28/1854	9	150	N	
Bell, Thomas	??	England	Y	?	?	?	08/29/1881			Y	
Bell, William C.	??	England	Y	?	?	?	04/01/1892			Y	
Bellamy, Joseph	44	England	Y	Liverpool	New York	07/25/1887	10/29/1888			Y	
Bellamy, William	30	England	Y	Liverpool	Philadelphia	04/19/1855	01/17/1860	27	58	N	
Beller, George	57	Germany	N	Havre	New York	07/02/1849	??/??/1851	28	234	N	10/11/1854
Beller, Michael	30	Germany	Y	Hamburg	New York	04/15/1881	01/25/1886			Y	
Bellhorn, John	46	Germany	Y	Hamburg	New York	05/17/1873	03/03/1894			Y	
Belli, Fermo	45	Italy	Y	Hamburg	New York	10/16/1887	08/09/1894			Y	
Bellmann, Ernst	29	Hamburg	Y	Hamburg	New York	08/03/1854	03/31/1856	26	388	N	
Bellon, John	31	Austria	Y	Bremen	Baltimore	01/28/1884	04/09/1887			Y	

CITIZENSHIP RECORDS

APPLICANT	AGE	COUNTRY OF ORIGIN	DEC	DEPART PORT	ENTRY PORT	ARRIVE DATE	DEC DATE	VOL	PG.	FLD	NAT DATE
Bellonby, Thomas	31	England	Y	Liverpool	New York	08/04/1849	05/23/1854	8	497	N	
Bellonby, Thomas	31	England	Y	Liverpool	New York	08/04/1849	05/23/1854	9	371	N	
Bellow, Lawrence	27	Ireland	Y	Drogheda	New York	06/??/1851	05/22/1852	25	91	N	
Belman, Barney	34	Hanover	Y	Bremen	New Orleans	06/24/1845	01/29/1849	1	533	N	
Belmont, Louis A.	32	France	Y	Havre	New York	03/31/1870	05/26/1885			Y	
Bemauer, George	26	Germany	Y	Antwerp	New York	04/15/1886	11/13/1888			Y	
Bencken, Bernard Theodor	??	Hanover	Y	Bremen	New Orleans	??/09/1848	03/25/1851	3	342	N	
Bencsik, Charles	27	Hungary	Y	?	?	?	08/08/1883			Y	
Bendale, Mathaus	25	Bavaria	Y	Liverpool	New York	05/20/1854	10/05/1854	10	443	N	
Bender, Adam	34	Nassau	Y	Liverpool	New York	10/18/1852	11/05/1855	13	165	N	
Bender, C. Charles	2	Germany	N	?	New York	00/00/1868				Y	10/27/1888
Bender, Daniel	??	Germany	Y	Havre	New York	03/28/1884	05/14/1885			Y	
Bender, Fred	32	Germany	Y	?	Baltimore	08/29/1879	04/27/1885			Y	
Bender, Frederick Willia	67	Prussia	N	Prussia	New York	08/18/1853	09/14/1854	28	236	N	09/09/1858
Bender, George	21	Bavaria	Y	Havre	New Orleans	11/14/1853	02/10/1857	15	12	N	
Bender, Jacob	27	Prussia	Y	Havre	New York	05/03/1849	10/06/1856	14	215	N	
Bender, Jacob	21	Germany	Y	Antwerp	Philadelphia	11/21/1892	10/25/1894			Y	
Bender, Mathaus	??	Germany	Y	?	?	?	07/17/1885			Y	
Bender, William	35	Baden	Y	Havre	New York	05/22/1854	03/15/1858	16	401	N	
Bendorf, Andreas	50	Germany	Y	Bremen	New York	04/20/1863	10/08/1880			Y	
Bene, H.	25	Germany	Y	Bremen	New York	09/??/1881	03/21/1887			Y	
Benedde, Johann H.	34	Germany	Y	Bremen	Baltimore	06/02/1872	01/10/1883			Y	
Benedict, Frank	29	Germany	Y	Bremen	New York	08/25/1890	05/03/1895			Y	
Benedie, Joseph	29	Germany	Y	Havre	New York	06/22/1893	11/05/1900			Y	
Benesch, Anton	29	Austria	Y	Hamburg	New York	10/28/1881	10/25/1886	19	87	N	
Benesch, Anton	29	Austria	Y	Hamburg	New York	10/28/1881	10/25/1886			Y	
Benesch, Ignatz	32	Austria	Y	Bremen	Baltimore	08/12/1887	11/18/1890			Y	
Beness, Frank	29	Canada	Y	Winnipeg	Detroit	09/??/1890	10/04/1895			Y	
Bengel, Philip	29	Bavaria	Y	London	New York	07/10/1852	07/09/1855	11	364	N	
Bengel, William	23	Baden	Y	London	New York	05/21/1848	01/14/1850	23	504	N	
Bengert, Jacob	38	Germany	Y	Antwerp	New York	10/19/1883	10/24/1896			Y	
Beni, Jules		no additional	Y					9	156	N	
Benjamin, Max	45	Russia	Y	Hamburg	New York	12/20/1887	11/06/1891			Y	
Benjamin, Michael	43	England	Y	Liverpool	New York	11/??/1842	03/19/1853	7	352	N	
Benjamin, Raphael	38	England	Y	Plymouth	San Francisc	09/06/1881	06/06/1885			Y	
Benjamin, Salomon	38	Germany	Y	Rotterdam	New York	01/13/1883	09/07/1887			Y	
Benjamin, Samuel	54	England	Y	Paris	New York	11/??/1883	10/13/1893	21	2	N	
Benkart, Severin	29	Germany	Y	Havre	New York	03/02/1892	04/05/1897			Y	
Benke, Albert	30	Germany	Y	Bremen	Baltimore	10/16/1881	11/20/1883			Y	
Benken, Bernhard	30	Germany	Y	Bremen	Baltimore	03/20/1883	02/04/1889			Y	
Benken, Gustav	23	Germany	Y	Bremen	New York	03/03/1890	03/06/1894			Y	
Benken, Henry	24	Germany	Y	Bremen	New York	05/11/1885	10/16/1889			Y	
Benken, William	34	Germany	Y	Amsterdam	New York	01/30/1879	03/07/1894			Y	
Benneckenstein, Otto	30	Germany	N	Hamburg	Philadelphia	05/21/1880	?			Y	
Benner, Christian	44	Prussia	N	Bremen	New York	03/28/1866	?			Y	
Benner, Herman	24	Prussia	Y	Bremen	New York	11/07/1847	01/25/1849	1	520	N	
Bennet, W.M.	25	Ireland	Y	Queenstown	New York	08/20/1881	10/08/1884			Y	
Bennett, George E.	24	Scotland	Y	Liverpool	Philadelphia	08/03/1849	06/10/1854	10	113	N	
Bennett, George E.	24	Scotland	Y	Liverpool	Philadelphia	08/03/1849	06/10/1854	12	50	N	
Bennett, Irwin	22	Ireland	Y	Sligo	Niagra	06/13/1851	01/17/1856	13	478	N	
Bennett, James	46	Ireland	Y	Liverpool	New Orleans	08/01/1848	12/26/1850	2	396	N	
Bennett, James	38	Ireland	Y	Liverpool	New York	08/??/1848	12/??/1849	23	397	N	
Bennett, Lawrence	44	Ireland	N	Liverpool	New York	??/??/1850	?			Y	
Bennie, John	24	Scotland	Y	Glasgow	New Orleans	10/07/1848	09/06/1852	25	377	N	
Benning, John	40	Hanover	Y	Bremen	Baltimore	12/12/1857	09/12/1860	27	366	N	
Benold, Fred H.	30	Germany	Y	?	New York	??/??/1880	11/01/1884			Y	
Bens, John	64	Baden	Y	Havre	New York	02/09/1854	04/05/1856	26	443	N	
Benson, John	??	England	Y	?	?	?	11/07/1891			Y	
Benson, Patrick	17	Ireland	N	?	New York	00/00/1866				Y	10/20/1887

CITIZENSHIP RECORDS

APPLICANT	AGE	COUNTRY OF ORIGIN	DEC	DEPART PORT	ENTRY PORT	ARRIVE DATE	DEC DATE	VOL	PG.	FLD	NAT DATE
Bent, Fred W.	50	Canada	Y	Winnipeg	St. Paul	09/10/1880	04/02/1890			Y	
Bentel, John Adam	31	Wurttemberg	Y	Rotterdam	New York	01/29/1851	08/04/1856	14	321	N	
Benton, Daniel	31	England	Y	Liverpool	New Orleans	07/31/1847	02/13/1851	3	128	N	
Bentsinger, Abraham	28	Bavaria	Y	London	New York	07/15/1847	04/13/1853	8	60	N	
Bentz, Theodor	30	Germany	Y	Bremen	New York	06/02/1891	10/16/1897			Y	
Bentzler, Henry	48	Prussia	Y	Bremen	Baltimore	09/19/1851	01/11/1853	7	7	N	
Benvie, William H.	42	Scotland	Y	Glasgow	New York	06/25/1888	04/03/1894			Y	
Benz, Franz	31	Bavaria	Y	Havre	New York	04/19/1848	02/13/1849	23	87	N	
Benz, Fred	30	Germany	Y	Antwerp	New York	08/06/1882	10/27/1886			Y	
Benz, Frederick	38	Germany	N	Bavaria	New York	04/??/1871	?			Y	
Benz, George	26	Baden	Y	Havre	New York	08/19/1854	03/21/1856	26	243	N	
Benz, George	17	Germany	N	?	New York	00/00/1881				Y	11/03/1888
Benz, George Anton	35	Bavaria	Y	Havre	New York	07/04/1852	01/31/1856	13	528	N	
Benz, John	29	Switzerland	Y	Havre	New York	08/18/1881	09/22/1885			Y	
Benz, John	45	Germany	N	Liverpool	New York	03/04/1871	?			Y	
Benz, Leonhard	23	Baden	Y	Havre	New York	06/01/1856	04/24/1860	27	170	N	
Benzer, John	30	Bavaria	Y	Bremen	Baltimore	05/05/1847	04/04/1853	7	527	N	
Benzinger, Jacob	26	Germany	Y	Havre	New York	01/16/1881	04/14/1885			Y	
Benzinger, Wm.	25	Germany	Y	Antwerp	New York	05/18/1880	09/03/1887			Y	
Berberich, Jacob	26	Baden	Y	Havre	New York	??/05/1855	04/26/1855	11	310	N	
Berberich, Joseph Anton	27	Baden	Y	Havre	New Orleans	04/13/1852	09/17/1855	13	42	N	
Berberich, William	26	Germany	Y	Antwerp	New York	10/11/1881	01/15/1885			Y	
Berbericht, Peter Chas	24	Canada	Y	Hamilton	Buffalo	08/15/1875	10/11/1880			Y	
Berchieb, Theodore	33	Germany	Y	Bremen	Baltimore	04/30/1885	06/16/1890			Y	
Berchiet, Walentz	??	Germany	Y	?	?	?	03/27/1884			Y	
Bercker, Charles	33	Germany	Y	Antwerp	New York	05/24/1882	02/23/1884			Y	
Berding, Peter	23	Oldenburg	Y	Bremen	New Orleans	05/03/1849	03/24/1851	3	311	N	
Bere, Eugene	34	Germany	Y	Bremen	New York	05/14/1892	12/07/1894			Y	
Beren, Christ	25	Prussia	Y	Bremen	New York	06/18/1856	04/16/1860	27	158	N	
Berendsen, H. Th.	20	Germany	Y	Hamburg	?	08/16/1881	10/06/1883			Y	
Berendt, Isadore	37	Russia	Y	Hamburg	New York	10/04/1885	10/26/1895			Y	
Berenheimer, Zachariah	45	Bavaria	Y	Liverpool	New York	11/01/1849	09/29/1854	10	311	N	
Berenheimer, Zachariah	45	Bavaria	Y	Liverpool	New York	11/01/1849	09/29/1854	12	250	N	
Berens, August	16	Germany	N	?	Baltimore	00/00/1880				Y	10/19/1886
Berens, Lambertus	24	Germany	Y	Rotterdam	New York	09/01/1885	10/04/1888			Y	
Berezin, Alexander	27	Russia	Y	Moscow	New York	10/24/1892	10/20/1894			Y	
Berg, Abraham	43	Russia	Y	Hamburg	New York	03/11/1889	07/09/1892			Y	
Berg, Frederick	28	Wurttemberg	Y	Havre	New Orleans	10/27/1847	02/20/1850	2	107	N	
Berg, Richard	29	Germany	Y	Hamburg	New York	06/04/1881	02/26/1887			Y	
Berga, Michele	??	Italy	Y	?	?	?	04/12/1892			Y	
Bergan, John	41	Ireland	Y	Liverpool	New York	04/21/1845	03/10/1852	24	281	N	
Bergdolt, Emile	28	Germany	Y	Havre	New York	03/15/1892	09/22/1896			Y	
Bergefeld, Herman Henry	22	Oldenburg	Y	Bremen	Baltimore	10/06/1846	02/05/1849	23	25	N	
Bergel, John B.	44	Germany	Y	Bremen	Baltimore	11/00/1859	11/27/1883			Y	
Bergen, Michael	26	Ireland	Y	Dublin	New Orleans	04/20/1848	10/07/1854	11	26	N	
Berger, August	25	Hanover	Y	Bremen	New Orleans	05/09/1852	06/05/1854	10	81	N	
Berger, August	25	Hanover	Y	Bremen	New Orleans	05/09/1852	06/05/1854	12	18	N	
Berger, Charles	22	Germany	Y	Bremen	Baltimore	08/27/1890	03/10/1891			Y	
Berger, Charles	34	Switzerland	Y	Havre	New York	07/14/1878	10/08/1884			Y	
Berger, Charles August	23	Saxony	Y	Bremen	New Orleans	11/12/1856	03/40/1858	16	369	N	
Berger, Charles P.	26	Sweden	Y	?	New York	06/13/1878	09/29/1884			Y	
Berger, F. J.	64	Germany	N	Antwerp	New York	09/??/1852	?			Y	
Berger, Frederick	26	Prussia	Y	Bremen	New York	12/16/1854	12/26/1855	13	366	N	
Berger, George	37	Germany	Y	Bremen	New York	05/28/1884	09/13/1895			Y	
Berger, Gerhard Henry	30	Hanover	Y	Bremen	New ?	12/01/1850	03/22/1858	16	432	N	
Berger, Henry	22	Hanover	Y	Bremen	Baltimore	05/02/1849	02/13/1852	24	105	N	
Berger, Jae R.	??	Hungary	Y	?	?	?	02/20/1889			Y	
Berger, John Theodore	26	Hanover	Y	Bremen	New York	05/26/1846	09/12/1848	22	334	N	
Berger, Joseph	28	Prussia	Y	Bremen	Baltimore	10/09/18??	10/12/1848	1	154	N	

CITIZENSHIP RECORDS

APPLICANT	AGE	COUNTRY OF ORIGIN	DEC	DEPART PORT	ENTRY PORT	ARRIVE DATE	DEC DATE	VOL	PG.	FLD	NAT DATE
Berger, Joseph	35	Germany	Y	Bremen	New York	03/12/1883	09/09/1887			Y	
Berger, Leo	45	Baden	Y	Havre	New Orleans	03/18/1847	04/20/1854	8	227	N	
Berger, Leo	45	Baden	Y	Havre	New Orleans	03/18/1847	04/20/1854	9	98	N	
Berger, Matheus	23	Baden	Y	Havre	New York	03/02/1852	09/25/1856	14	368	N	
Berger, Mathew	54	Germany	N	Havre	New Orleans	03/10/1853	?			Y	
Berger, Michael	26	Ireland	Y	Dublin	New Orleans	04/20/1848	10/07/1854	6	25	N	
Berger, Saul	38	Austria	Y	Hamburg	New York	03/25/1881	09/28/1891			Y	
Berger, W.	45	Austria	Y	Hamburg	New York	07/18/1869	08/28/1884			Y	
Bergers, William	27	Baden	Y	Rotterdam	Boston	12/29/1847	02/09/1852	24	79	N	
Bergfeld, Dietrich	25	Germany	Y	Bremen	New York	05/29/1881	07/05/1884			Y	
Berghaus, Bernard	27	Prussia	Y	Antwerp	New York	07/02/1849	04/08/1852	24	414	N	
Berghausen, Charles	30	Germany	Y	Hamburg	New York	05/03/1883	04/17/1889			Y	
Bergin, James	50	Ireland	Y	Liverpool	New Orleans	12/01/1852	10/03/1856	14	181	N	
Bergin, Thomas	27	Ireland	Y	Queenstown	New York	10/27/1888	11/23/1893			Y	
Bergin, Thomas	30	Ireland	Y	Queenstown	New York	06/29/1880	08/30/1887			Y	
Bergjohann, Henry	28	Prussia	Y	Bremen	New Orleans	12/??/1848	09/18/1855	13	63	N	
Bergmann, Aaron	36	Wurttemberg	Y	Bremen	New York	07/30/1834	02/02/1850	2	29	N	
Bergmann, Christopher	28	Germany	Y	Antwerp	New York	04/03/1880	08/22/1885			Y	
Bergmann, David	24	Hanover	Y	Bremen	New York	05/25/1849	08/04/1851	4	77	N	
Bergmann, George	31	Bavaria	Y	Rotterdam	New York	12/08/1853	10/28/1858	17	137	N	
Bergmann, George	30	Germany	Y	Amsterdam	New York	04/03/1880	08/22/1885			Y	
Bergmann, George Adam	??	Germany	Y	?	?	?	10/30/1884			Y	
Bergmann, Henry	33	Hanover	Y	Bremen	New York	11/07/1851	10/09/1854	6	191	N	
Bergmann, Henry	33	Hanover	Y	Bremen	New York	11/07/1851	10/09/1854	11	194	N	
Bergmann, Hermann	??	Hanover	Y	?	Baltimore	06/13/18??	11/03/1856	14	442	N	
Bergmann, John Henry	32	Hanover	Y	Bremen	New Orleans	01/04/1844	10/06/1854	10	520	N	
Bergmann, John Henry	32	Hanover	Y	Bremen	New Orleans	01/04/1844	10/07/1854	12	459	N	
Bergmann, Louis	22	Hanover	Y	Bremen	New York	09/01/1859	12/30/1859	17	537	N	
Bergmann, Wolfgang	65	Germany	N	Bremen	New York	04/01/1853	?			Y	
Bergmeier, John Frederic	25	Prussia	Y	Bremen	New Orleans	05/06/1849	10/25/1851			Y	03/26/1855
Bergold, Joseph	50	Germany	N	Havre	Quebec	06/??/1857	?			Y	
Bergsch, Franz J.	36	Germany	Y	Rotterdam	Jersey City	10/22/1877	05/25/1885			Y	
Beringer, Daniel	24	Bavaria	Y	Havre	New York	06/??/1859	01/14/1861	18	56	N	
Beringer, Johann Michael	33	Germany	Y	Antwerp	New York	06/10/1884	11/07/1887	19	129	N	
Berinne, Carl	37	Austria	Y	Bremen	New York	05/29/1852	10/09/1854	6	108	N	
Berinne, Charles	37	Austria	Y	Bremen	New York	05/29/1852	10/09/1854	11	111	N	
Berk, John Theodore	37	Hanover	Y	Bremen	Baltimore	07/04/1845	11/18/1848	1	318	N	
Berkemeier, William	25	Germany	Y	Bremen	Baltimore	06/25/1881	02/15/1884			Y	
Berkemeyer, Gerhard	29	Prussia	Y	Bremen	New Orleans	11/29/1853	12/31/1855	13	401	N	
Berkemeyer, Joseph Alexa	46	Prussia	Y	Bremen	Baltimore	06/21/1852	01/03/1856	13	421	N	
Berkes, George	30	Hesse Darmsta	Y	Antwerp	New York	11/??/1847	10/29/1858	17	3	N	
Berkle, Anthony	30	Bavaria	Y	Havre	New York	04/26/1854	10/09/1857	15	383	N	
Berkman, Hermann	25	Russia	Y	Hamburg	New York	06/01/1884	10/15/1888			Y	
Berlier, Michael	30	France	Y	Havre	New Orleans	05/18/1848	08/15/1851	4	137	N	
Berliner, Martin	29	Wurttemberg	Y	Havre	New York	10/16/1856	09/26/1857	15	323	N	
Berling, August	32	Germany	Y	Bremen	Baltimore	05/23/1887	11/17/1893			Y	
Berling, George	30	Germany	Y	Amsterdam	New York	11/01/1884	10/17/1893			Y	
Berling, H. Gerrad	37	Hanover	Y	Bremen	New Orleans	05/01/1846	04/01/1852	24	348	N	
Berling, Henry	23	Germany	Y	Antwerp	New York	05/11/1889	01/26/1893			Y	
Berling, Herman Henry	31	Hanover	Y	Bremen	New Orleans	06/11/1847	10/21/1852	5	34	N	
Berling, Jacques	31	Germany	Y	Havre	New York	06/17/1884	05/15/1888			Y	
Berlyn, Adolph	35	Germany	Y	Amsterdam	New York	08/11/1882	04/26/1889			Y	
Berman, Hyman	45	Russia	Y	Hamburg	New York	06/18/1889	09/24/1891			Y	
Berman, Max	??	Russia	Y	?	?	09/17/1889	11/08/1889			Y	
Berman, Max	24	Russia	Y	Rotterdam	New York	02/15/1900	12/28/1903			Y	
Berman, Meyer	52	Russia	Y	Hamburg	New York	06/18/1890	04/04/1893			Y	
Bermann, Frederick	22	Hanover	Y	Bremen	Baltimore	10/09/1848	11/08/1852	5	259	N	
Bermann, Frederick	22	Hanover	Y	Bremen	Baltimore	10/09/1848	11/08/1852	6	383	N	
Bermann, Simon	37	Austria	Y	Liverpool	New York	07/13/1853	08/21/1857	15	164	N	

CITIZENSHIP RECORDS

APPLICANT	AGE	COUNTRY OF ORIGIN	DEC	DEPART PORT	ENTRY PORT	ARRIVE DATE	DEC DATE	VOL	PG.	FLD	NAT DATE
Bermingham, James	43	Ireland	Y	Queenstown	New York	12/09/1882	03/13/1888			Y	
Bermingham, Thomas	31	Ireland	Y	Liverpool	New Orleans	03/16/1848	02/24/1851	3	164	N	
Bernanaug, Fedal	34	Baden	Y	Havre	New York	09/18/1854	10/10/1854	11	211	N	
Bernard, Christian	27	Nassau	Y	Canada	Cleveland	07/21/1847	09/04/1848	22	297	N	
Bernard, John Joseph	25	Belgium	Y	Antwerp	New York	03/??/1848	12/01/1855	13	268	N	
Bernard, Joseph	21	Switzerland	Y	?	?	08/10/1884	11/04/1890			Y	
Bernauer, Fidel	34	Baden	Y	Antwerp	New York	05/18/1854	10/10/1854	6	208	N	
Bernbeck, Frederick	24	Hesse Darmsta	Y	London	New York	08/10/1849	04/04/1853	8	33	N	
Berndsen, Bernard Heinri	27	Germany	Y	Rotterdam	New York	10/19/1881	11/01/1888	19	212	N	
Berndsen, Bernhard Heinr	27	Germany	Y	Rotterdam	New York	10/19/1881	11/01/1888			Y	
Berndt, Albert	35	Germany	Y	Amsterdam	New York	07/03/1889	10/31/1889			Y	
Berndt, August	40	Prussia	Y	Bremen	New York	04/28/1849	03/01/1852	24	184	N	
Berndt, Ernst	43	Prussia	Y	Bremen	Philadelphia	05/09/1860	02/19/1861	18	113	N	
Berndt, John Gottlieb	51	Prussia	Y	Hamburg	New Orleans	11/24/1857	06/02/1859	17	445	N	
Berndt, Reinhold	23	Prussia	Y	Hamburg	New Orleans	11/30/1858	12/31/1858	17	392	N	
Berndt, Reinhold	23	Prussia	Y	Hamburg	New Orleans	11/30/1858	12/30/1859	17	539	N	
Berner, Aug	23	Germany	Y	Bremen	New York	01/22/1882	10/08/1885			Y	
Berner, Henry	38	Wurttemberg	Y	Bremen	New York	10/27/1875	10/09/1882			Y	
Berner, Hubert	31	Wurttemberg	Y	Havre	New York	03/04/1853	02/04/1861	18	87	N	
Bernges, Christian	49	Germany	N	Hamburg	New York	05/17/1864	?			Y	
Bernhard, Franz Joseph	26	Wurttemberg	Y	Havre	New York	04/18/1852	11/01/1852	6	275	N	
Bernhard, Johann	35	Germany	Y	Havre	New York	07/02/1882	01/23/1890			Y	
Bernhard, John	29	Germany	Y	Antwerp	New York	04/24/1879	08/06/1879			Y	
Bernhard, Joseph	37	Germany	Y	Hamburg	New York	09/12/1880	09/28/1887			Y	
Bernhard, Peter	23	Bavaria	Y	Havre	New Orleans	03/12/1854	10/06/1857	15	361	N	
Bernhard, Peter	41	Bavaria	Y	Havre	New Orleans	11/24/1852	10/04/1858	17	53	N	
Bernhard, William	29	Germany	Y	Bremen	Baltimore	05/08/1880	05/14/1883			Y	
Bernhardt, Jacob	??	?	Y	?	?	?	?			Y	?
Bernhardt, Simon	37	Austira	Y	Hamburg	Philadelphia	07/11/1882	08/20/1889			Y	
Bernhart, Frank Joseph	26	Wurttemberg	Y	Havre	New York	04/01/1852	11/01/1852	5	149	N	
Bernhart, John Philip	29	Bavaria	Y	Havre	New Orleans	01/14/1850	05/30/1854	9	458	N	
Bernhart, John Philip	29	Bavaria	Y	Havre	New Orleans	01/14/1850	05/31/1854	10	41	N	
Bernheimer, Herman	??	Germany	N	?	?	?	?	28	435	N	?
Bernig, Franl	27	Germany	Y	?	?	?	12/22/1891			Y	
Berning, Anthony	28	Russia	Y	Bremen	New Orleans	01/01/1846	08/23/1848	22	245	N	
Berning, Henry	22	Germany	Y	Rotterdam	New York	05/02/1882	08/12/1884			Y	
Berninger, Adam	38	Bavaria	Y	London	New York	06/08/1850	10/01/1856	14	128	N	
Bernst, Charles	22	Germany	Y	Rotterdam	New York	01/03/1887	01/03/1888			Y	
Bernstein, Benjamin	23	Russia	Y	Hamburg	Philadelphia	10/03/1887	10/04/1889			Y	
Bernstein, Hugo	34	Germany	Y	?	?	?	03/21/1894			Y	
Bernstein, Joseph	??	Russia	Y	?	?	?	06/06/1889			Y	
Berringer, Johann Michae	33	Germany	Y	Antwerp	New York	06/10/1884	11/07/1887			Y	
Berritt, Lue	32	Russia	Y	Rotterdam	New York	03/02/1891	10/02/1893			Y	
Berry, Anthony	22	Ireland	Y	Liverpool	Buffalo	10/20/1850	02/27/1852	24	176	N	
Berry, Augustus	40	Fort Mahone	Y	Fort Mahone	Charleston	??/??/1832	03/30/1857	15	105	N	
Berry, James	23	England	Y	Liverpool	New Orleans	11/20/1847	09/09/1852	25	433	N	
Berry, James	23	Ireland	Y	Liverpool	New Orleans	11/20/1847	09/09/1852			Y	03/26/1855
Berry, John	38	Ireland	Y	St. Johns	Baltimore	05/06/1848	09/14/1850	25	495	N	
Berry, Michael	32	Ireland	Y	Liverpool	New Orleans	05/19/1849	03/11/1858	16	390	N	
Berry, Theodore Louis	??	Germany	Y	?	?	?	03/09/1896			Y	
Berssler, George	25	Bavaria	Y	Havre	New Orleans	03/27/1854	10/01/1856	14	92	N	
Bertele, John	24	Germany	Y	Havre	New York	11/02/1881	09/04/1884			Y	
Berteling, Bernhard Jose	34	Prussia	Y	Rotterdam	New York	05/05/1854	10/02/1854	10	337	N	
Berteling, Bernhard Jose	34	Prussia	Y	Rotterdam	New York	05/05/1854	10/02/1854	12	276	N	
Bertelsen, Peter	44	Germany	N	Hamburg	New York	04/20/1870	?			Y	
Bertelt, Frank	26	Oldenburg	Y	Bremen	New Orleans	11/25/1849	11/01/1852	6	246	N	
Berthal, Michael	36	Bavaria	Y	Antwerp	New York	11/20/1857	01/04/1860	27	26	N	
Berthel, Peter	30	France	Y	Havre	New York	06/22/1869	04/25/1872	18	490	N	
Berthlein, John	28	Bavaria	Y	Bremen	New York	09/18/1852	11/26/1855	13	257	N	

CITIZENSHIP RECORDS

APPLICANT	AGE	COUNTRY OF ORIGIN	DEC	DEPART PORT	ENTRY PORT	ARRIVE DATE	DEC DATE	VOL	PG.	FLD	NAT DATE
Berthold, Joseph	23	Baden	Y	London	New York	07/04/1849	09/14/1852	25	505	N	
Berthold, Stephen	28	Germany	Y	Havre	New York	04/04/1882	08/22/1888			Y	
Bertke, Bernhardt	26	Germany	Y	Rotterdam	New York	10/10/1883	03/08/1886			Y	
Bertke, Henry	28	Hanover	Y	Bremen	New Orleans	12/03/1853	11/15/1858	17	331	N	
Bertke, Herman	31	Germany	Y	Bremen	Baltimore	11/02/1883	03/10/1886			Y	
Bertram, Adolph G.	??	Germany	Y	?	?	?	08/06/1889			Y	
Bertram, Jacob	41	Germany	Y	Bremen	New York	10/19/1879	04/04/1888			Y	
Bertrand, George	30	Germany	Y	Amsterdam	New York	04/18/1882	01/28/1884			Y	
Bertsch, Frederick	22	Wuerttenberg	Y	Havre	New York	03/09/1852	04/12/1852	24	459	N	
Bertsch, Jacob Michael	26	Wurttemberg	Y	Rotterdam	New York	04/27/1849	03/01/1851	3	183	N	
Bertsch, Xaver	34	Germany	N	Bremen	New York	10/27/1871	?			Y	
Bertsche, John	29	Germany	Y	Hamburg	New York	07/15/1889	10/20/1892			Y	
Bertsinger, Charles	24	Switzerland	Y	Havre	New York	11/25/1854	12/01/1858	17	370	N	
Berty, Benny	24	Oldenburg	Y	Bremen	New Orleans	02/02/1848	07/23/1851	4	30	N	
Berwanger, Jacob	34	Germany	Y	Antwerp	New York	06/18/1884	10/24/1889	19	254	N	
Berwanger, Louis	22	Germany	Y	?	New York	??/??/1882	05/12/1884			Y	
Berzinger, Fred	33	Germany	Y	Antwerp	New York	04/27/1887	10/29/1892			Y	
Berzoll, Valentine	58	Wurttemberg	Y	Antwerp	New York	05/15/1848	10/07/1854	12	479	N	
Besel, Rudolph	45	Germany	Y	Bremen	Baltimore	10/20/1880	05/17/1886			Y	
Besimer, Sam	24	Russia	Y	Bremen	Baltimore	08/02/1893	04/28/1896			Y	
Besl, Franz	29	Germany	Y	Havre	New York	11/16/1889	04/15/1897			Y	
Bessen, Martin	52	Germany	Y	Bremen	New York	07/03/1881	03/05/1894			Y	
Bessenbacher, Conrad	57	Germany	Y	Bremen	New York	05/19/1864	03/04/1891			Y	
Bessenger, David	36	Germany	Y	Antwerp	New York	06/10/1883	10/24/1896			Y	
Bessler, Friedrich	36	Germany	Y	Bremen	New York	10/04/1885	06/04/1890			Y	
Bessler, George	25	Germany	Y	Antwerp	New York	80/25/1888	10/12/1891	19	334	N	
Best, Jacob	35	Germany	Y	?	New York	??/??/1881	04/28/1884			Y	
Beste, J.C.	40	Holland	Y	Rotterdam	New York	08/29/1854	09/30/1858	17	25	N	
Besuden, Louis	36	Oldenburg	Y	Bremen	Baltimore	11/07/1842	04/04/1853	8	23	N	
Besuner, Lewis	26	Russia	Y	Blozk	Jersey City	08/12/1885	08/26/1886			Y	
Besuner, Meyer	28	Russia	Y	Hamburg	New York	11/02/1885	10/30/1886			Y	
Beter, Carl	40	Austria	Y	Bremen	Baltimore	08/23/1853	10/09/1854	6	197	N	
Bethge, Ferdinand	26	?	Y	?	Baltimore	07/??/1888	04/02/1889			Y	
Bethge, Gustav	21	Brandenburg	Y	Bremen	New York	08/05/1852	10/09/1954	6	72	N	
Bethge, Gustav	21	Brandenburg	Y	Bremen	New York	08/05/1852	10/09/1854	11	73	N	
Bethge, Gustav	24	Anhalt Bernbu	Y	Bremen	New York	08/04/1854	11/03/1857	15	523	N	
Bethke, Louis	48	Germany	Y	?	Baltimore	??/??/1871	03/27/1885			Y	
Betigheimer, Frank	22	Bavaria	Y	Havre	New Orleans	12/24/1852	01/08/1856	13	433	N	
Betmann, Moses	35	Russia	Y	Hamburg	New York	06/26/1882	02/15/1883			Y	
Betscher, Joseph	25	Baden	Y	London	New York	05/10/1849	10/13/1851	4	231	N	
Betscher, Michael	60	Baden	Y	London	New York	05/10/1849	10/13/1851	4	232	N	
Bettels, Clemens	39	Germany	Y	Bremen	New York	05/28/1871	08/12/1889			Y	
Betting, Joseph	49	Germany	Y	Bremen	New York	05/12/1869	10/28/1898			Y	
Bettinger, Mathias	30	Wuerttenberg	Y	Rotterdam	New York	01/30/1848	04/07/1852	24	412	N	
Bettinger, Peter	30	Wurttemberg	Y	Rotterdam	New York	06/??/1845	03/27/1851	3	363	N	
Betty, William	60	Ireland	Y	Liverpool	New York	09/28/1851	03/31/1853	7	474	N	
Betvon, Vaclav	??	Austria	Y	?	?	?	10/29/1880			Y	
Betz, Charles	31	Wurttemberg	Y	Liverpool	New York	??/??/1848	05/01/1855	11	340	N	
Betz, Fred	22	Germany	Y	Antwerp	New York	10/18/1893	06/11/1895			Y	
Betz, Gustav	24	Germany	Y	Antwerp	New York	04/14/1881	10/09/1883			Y	
Betz, John	38	Germany	Y	Bremen	New York	09/20/1889	10/20/1899			Y	
Betz, John	26	Bavaria	Y	Bremen	New Orleans	11/01/1846	10/02/1848	22	385	N	
Betz, Joseph	36	Germany	Y	Bremen	Baltimore	11/29/1880	02/09/1885			Y	
Betz, Pankratz	29	Bavaria	Y	Bremen	Baltimore	07/19/1846	08/30/1848	22	283	N	
Betz, Peter	28	Bavaria	Y	Havre	New Orleans	05/01/1854	10/03/1856	14	182	N	
Betz, William	33	Germany	Y	Hamburg	New York	12/22/1881	06/15/1883			Y	
Beudale, Mathias	25	Bavaria	Y	Liverpool	New York	05/20/1854	10/04/1854	12	382	N	
Beukhart, Joseph	??	Germany	N	Bremen	Baltimore	07/04/1860	?			Y	
Beumer, Franz	28	Germany	Y	Amsterdam	New York	05/12/1884	01/14/1888			Y	

CITIZENSHIP RECORDS

APPLICANT	AGE	COUNTRY OF ORIGIN	DEC	DEPART PORT	ENTRY PORT	ARRIVE DATE	DEC DATE	VOL	PG.	FLD	NAT DATE
Beumer, Joseph	40	Prussia	Y	Bremen	Baltimore	10/20/1842	08/15/1848	22	109	N	
Beumer, Theodore Wm.	29	Prussia	Y	Bremen	New York	10/29/1848	11/05/1851	4	489	N	
Beus, Heinrich	??	Germany	Y	?	?	?	09/14/1885			Y	
Beuse, John Henry	21	Bremen	Y	Bremen	New York	02/11/1853	02/04/1856	26	24	N	
Beuse, John Henry Ludwig	28	Bremen	Y	Bremen	Baltimore	05/16/1854	09/27/1854	10	263	N	
Beuse, John Henry Ludwig	28	Bremen	Y	Bremen	Baltimore	05/16/1854	09/27/1854	12	202	N	
Beuse, Lewis	22	Germany	Y	Bremen	New York	06/07/1884	01/10/1893	19	416	N	
Beushauser, Andreas	39	Hanover	Y	Bremen	New Orleans	11/26/1854	10/06/1856	14	238	N	
Beushof, John George	46	Wurttemberg	Y	Havre	New York	04/23/1855	05/15/1861	18	109	N	
Beuss, Veit	29	Germany	Y	Hamburg	New York	07/18/1882	09/24/1885			Y	
Beusterien, Gottfried	28	Germany	Y	Bremen	New York	05/01/1882	11/30/1886			Y	
Beutelschiesz, Adam	25	Wurttemberg	Y	Havre	New York	05/15/1857	08/22/1862	18	395	N	
Beuter, Fidel	27	Germany	Y	Antwerp	New York	07/02/1882	04/29/1885			Y	
Beuting, B.	35	Germany	Y	Bremen	New York	10/06/1888	09/25/1896			Y	
Beuttenmueller, Charles	30	Wurttemberg	Y	Havre	New Orleans	04/01/1851	10/30/1858	17	213	N	
Beuttermuller, John	39	Wurttemberg	Y	Bremen	New York	07/27/1871	10/07/1880			Y	
Bevermann, August	32	Hanover	Y	Bremen	Baltimore	08/08/1845	10/06/1851	4	204	N	
Bevermann, Conrad	40	Hanover	Y	Bremen	New Orleans	11/20/1855	04/22/1861	18	140	N	
Bex, Frank	26	France	Y	Havre	New York	07/03/1849	04/31/1852	25	144	N	
Bexell, John	27	Sweden	Y	Denmark	New York	11/30/1851	02/21/1853	7	194	N	
Beyer, Bernard	36	Prussia	Y	Bremen	New Orleans	01/23/1857	10/04/1858	17	54	N	
Beyer, Ignatz	39	France	Y	Havre	New York	08/26/1853	09/07/1857	15	239	N	
Beyer, Karl	27	Germany	Y	Antwerp	New York	01/26/1889	05/10/1892			Y	
Beyer, Lorenz	27	Bavaria	Y	Hamburg	New York	08/12/1854	10/20/1858	17	70	N	
Beyer, Louis Daniel	24	Bavaria	Y	Havre	New York	04/05/1852	07/09/1855	11	359	N	
Beyer, Philip	30	Germany	Y	Havre	New York	04/22/1880	10/27/1886			Y	
Beyer, Richard	29	Germany	Y	Bremen	New York	03/16/1884	12/17/1889			Y	
Beyer, Valentine	26	Wurttemberg	Y	Havre	New York	04/13/1852	07/10/1855	11	369	N	
Beyer, William	15	Germany	N	?	Baltimore	00/00/1882				Y	08/27/1888
Beyerlein, Henry	29	Germany	Y	Bremen	New York	08/29/1882	03/12/1884			Y	
Beyland, Charles F.	40	Wuerttemberg	Y	Hamburg	New Orleans	10/30/1850	05/31/1852	25	158	N	
Beyland, Daniel Gottlieb	38	Wuerttemberg	Y	Hamburg	New Orleans	10/30/1850	05/31/1852	25	133	N	
Bezold, Clemens Benedict	34	Wuerttemberg	Y	Rotterdam	New York	07/25/1845	08/17/1848	22	191	N	
Bezold, Franz Michael	29	Wurttemberg	Y	Rotterdam	Baltimore	06/12/1846	10/02/1848	1	10	N	
Bezold, Valentine	27	Wuerttemberg	Y	Antwerp	New York	07/25/1847	08/17/1848	22	192	N	
Bezoll, Valentine	58	Wurttemberg	Y	Antwerp	New York	05/15/1848	10/07/1854	10	540	N	
Bialing, John	35	Hanover	Y	Bremen	New York	09/14/1843	10/28/1858	17	149	N	
Bianchi, Andreas	25	Tuscany	Y	Leghorn	New York	09/22/1851	11/20/1857	16	37	N	
Bibus, Franz	38	Germany	Y	Antwerp	New York	09/21/1887	11/23/1887			Y	
Bichard, Peter	51	Germany	N	Antwerp	New York	07/04/1849	?			Y	
Bick, August	23	Germany	Y	Bremen	New York	10/11/1882	11/301/886			Y	
Bickel, Charles	24	Germany	Y	Havre	New York	06/16/1882	02/23/1884			Y	
Bickel, Fred	27	Germany	Y	Antwerp	New York	04/18/1881	10/05/1883			Y	
Bickel, John George	27	Baden	Y	Havre	New Orleans	11/01/1852	10/09/1854	6	131	N	
Bickel, John George	27	Baden	Y	Havre	New Orleans	11/01/1852	10/09/1854	11	134	N	
Bickers, John	24	Hanover	Y	Bremen	New Orleans	12/??/1852	11/07/1856	14	501	N	
Bickmann, Rudolph	32	Westphalia	Y	Bremen	New York	10/25/1857	01/18/1860	27	60	N	
Biecker, Frank Ludwig	24	Hesse Cassel	Y	Bremen	Baltimore	06/17/1852	05/22/1856	26	537	N	
Biedenbach, John George	33	Wuerttemberg	Y	Bremen	New York	06/14/1854	02/23/1856	26	119	N	
Biedenhenn, Henry	34	Oldenburg	Y	Bremen	New Orleans	11/??/1845	09/11/1855	11	534	N	
Biedenhorn, Bernard	30	Oldenburg	Y	Bremen	Baltimore	11/11/1852	10/08/1860	27	402	N	
Biedermann, August	26	Germany	Y	Antwerp	Philadelphia	06/01/1893	07/27/1896			Y	
Biedermann, Nicklas	33	Baden	Y	London	New York	10/??/1851	09/15/1852	25	531	N	
Biederwolf, John	65	Bavaria	Y	Havre	New York	11/28/1853	10/21/1857	15	469	N	
Biedinghaus, Barney	33	Germany	Y	Hanover	New York	04/27/1884	10/26/1893			Y	
Biefand, Bernard	25	Germany	Y	Bremen	New York	09/19/1881	10/19/1886			Y	
Biefang, Bernard	25	Germany	Y	Bremen	New York	09/19/1881	10/19/1886	19	52	N	
Biefang, Frank Jr.	16	Germany	N	?	New York	00/00/1881				Y	10/19/1886
Biegesser, Charles	36	Switzerland	Y	Havre	New York	05/03/1854	02/10/1858	16	97	N	

CITIZENSHIP RECORDS

APPLICANT	AGE	COUNTRY OF ORIGIN	DEC	DEPART PORT	ENTRY PORT	ARRIVE DATE	DEC DATE	VOL	PG.	FLD	NAT DATE
Biegner, Anthony	25	Bavaria	Y	Havre	New Orleans	11/26/1848	02/14/1849	23	90	N	
Biehler, Charles	??	Germany	Y	Bremen	New York	05/12/1882	03/23/1897			Y	
Biehler, Jacob	32	Germany	Y	Havre	New York	03/18/1885	11/03/1890			Y	
Biel, Joseph	26	Prussia	Y	Antwerp	New York	12/17/1854	11/14/1855	13	225	N	
Bielafald, John Henry	??	Prussia	Y	Bremen	New Orleans	01/04/18??	10/09/1848	1	76	N	
Bielenberg, John H. A.	30	Holstein	Y	Hamburg	New York	05/01/1849	05/28/1852	25	123	N	
Bielfeld, Diedrich	45	Brunswick	Y	Bremen	New York	09/27/1853	05/20/1861	18	174	N	
Bielinger, George	22	Bavaria	Y	Havre	New York	05/??/1860	02/06/1862	18	255	N	
Bielstein, Christian	??	Prussia	Y	?	?	?	02/16/1882			Y	
Biendl, Anton	??	Germany	Y	?	?	11/20/1882	05/01/1883			Y	
Bierbaum, Frank	21	Germany	Y	Bremen	Baltimore	08/26/1883	01/26/1886			Y	
Bierbaum, Henry	24	Prussia	Y	Bremen	New Orleans	11/29/1849	10/10/1854	6	210	N	
Bierbaum, Henry	24	Prussia	Y	Bremen	New Orleans	11/29/1849	10/10/1854	11	213	N	
Bierbaum, Peter	72	Germany	N	Bremen	New York	09/01/1838	?	28	314	N	10/??/1843
Bierbaum, Peter	18	Germany	N	Bremen	New York	09/01/1838				Y	10/00/1843
Biere, Wilhelm	30	Lippe Detmold	Y	Bremen	New Orleans	11/06/1852	09/24/1856	14	362	N	
Bierhorst, Henry	35	Germany	Y	Bremen	New York	04/07/1882	10/31/1891			Y	
Biermann, John	42	Mecklenburg	Y	Liverpool	New Orleans	11/28/1851	09/06/1852	25	368	N	
Biermann, Lazarus	25	Baden	Y	Bremen	Baltimore	09/01/1844	10/02/1848	1	31	N	
Bierwirth, Frank	29	Hanover	Y	Bremen	New Orleans	05/24/1852	10/09/1854	11	175	N	
Bierwirth, Franz	29	Hanover	Y	Bremen	New Orleans	05/24/1852	10/09/1854	6	172	N	
Bietighoefer, John	26	Germany	Y	Bremen	New York	12/14/1884	08/08/1888			Y	
Bifulci, Rolitio	33	Italy	Y	Naples	New York	04/07/1881	03/22/1894			Y	
Bigger, Peter	21	Wurttemberg	Y	Havre	New York	07/04/1847	03/19/1850	2	221	N	
Bihl, Paul	??	Germany	Y	?	?	?	04/17/1896			Y	
Bihn, Moritz	24	Saxony	Y	London	New York	04/19/1852	06/05/1854	10	90	N	
Bihn, Moritz	24	Saxony	Y	London	New York	04/19/1852	06/05/1854	12	27	N	
Bijach, Herman	??	Germany	Y	?	?	09/??/1886	03/30/1888			Y	
Bilger, Jakob	29	Switzerland	Y	?	?	?	03/17/1893			Y	
Bilger, Matthias	32	Germany	Y	Antwerp	New York	05/28/1882	04/15/1889			Y	
Bill, Henry	35	Hanover	Y	Bremen	Baltimore	04/16/1847	11/13/1855	13	217	N	
Billam, Joseph	31	Nova Scotia	Y	Liverpool	Boston	08/31/1850	12/08/1855	13	295	N	
Billet, John	37	Bavaria	Y	Bremen	New York	06/24/1845	09/30/1848	22	374	N	
Billet, Joseph	41	Baden	Y	Havre	New York	09/01/1854	02/23/1858	16	338	N	
Billiau, Charles	27	Germany	Y	?	Philadelphia	??/??/1880	07/08/1884			Y	
Billilof, Joseph	48	Russia	Y	Kiev	New York	10/14/1881	10/26/1887			Y	
Billing, David	25	Hanover	Y	Bremen	New Orleans	11/03/1857	10/15/1860	27	497	N	
Billing, Herman	57	Germany	Y	Bremen	New York	05/14/1893	10/22/1900			Y	
Billinger, Frank	43	Germany	Y	?	New York	04/28/1882	11/01/1887			Y	
Billingham, Benjamin	42	England	Y	Liverpool	New York	11/12/1842	10/14/1851	4	279	N	
Billington, Andrew	23	England	Y	Liverpool	New York	07/30/1890	07/11/1893			Y	
Billiods, Peter	58	France	Y	Havre	Baltimore	08/10/1840	03/22/1850	2	231	N	
Biltz, Charles	32	Bavaria	Y	Havre	New York	08/??/1833	03/09/1857	15	75	N	
Bilz, Lorenz	??	Bavaria	Y	Liverpool	New York	05/31/1856	12/31/1860	18	35	N	
Bilz, Valentine	32	Bavaria	Y	Liverpool	New York	04/18/1854	04/08/1856	26	464	N	
Binder, Caspar	32	Hohenzollern	Y	Havre	New York	11/19/1865	09/12/1872	18	519	N	
Binder, Christoph	40	Germany	Y	Bremen	New York	12/??/1866	12/28/1883			Y	
Binder, Franz H.	26	Prussia	Y	Liverpool	New York	07/28/1852	11/01/1852	5	109	N	
Binder, Frederick	34	Germany	Y	Bremen	New York	04/18/1881	08/08/1884			Y	
Binder, Haver	39	Germany	N	Havre	New York	07/??/1874	?			Y	
Binder, John	30	Prussia	Y	Rotterdam	New York	06/01/1851	11/01/1852	5	108	N	
Binder, John	36	Hungary	Y	Halofax	Toledo	04/19/1893	05/04/1897			Y	
Binder, Joseph	21	Prussia	Y	Rotterdam	New York	06/01/1851	11/01/1852	5	112	N	
Binder, Louis	23	Heckingen	Y	Bremen	Baltimore	06/13/1847	03/28/1849	23	261	N	
Binder, Maritz	30	Russia	Y	?	New York	06/01/1882	12/15/1882			Y	
Binder, Melchius	24	Prussia	Y	Rottérdam	New York	06/01/1851	11/01/1852	5	111	N	
Binder, Stephen	17	Germany	N	Baden	New York	04/05/1866	?			Y	
Bing, David	23	Hesse Darmsta	Y	Liverpool	New York	06/11/1852	09/21/1855	13	95	N	
Bingham, Thomas	54	England	Y	Liverpool	New Orleans	11/16/1842	09/29/1856	14	429	N	

CITIZENSHIP RECORDS

APPLICANT	AGE	COUNTRY OF ORIGIN	DEC	DEPART PORT	ENTRY PORT	ARRIVE DATE	DEC DATE	VOL	PG.	FLD	NAT DATE
Binghammer, Paul	30	Bavaria	Y	Antwerp	New York	11/30/1846	09/04/1848	22	294	N	
Binkert, Joseph	35	Baden	Y	Hamburg	New York	03/12/1866	04/01/1872	18	482	N	
Binning, John	43	Prussia	Y	Rotterdam	New York	09/25/1851	11/18/1857	16	32	N	
Binstadt, Anthony	44	Germany	Y	Bremen	Baltimore	07/??/1880	08/??/1881			Y	
Binte, Henry	29	Hanover	Y	Bremen	New Orleans	11/24/1848	11/29/1852	5	256	N	
Bippus, Mathaus	39	Germany	Y	Hamburg	New York	02/02/1879	03/15/1882			Y	
Birch, Peter	36	England	Y	Liverpool	Philadelphia	09/21/1847	03/23/1853	7	380	N	
Birch, Peter	30	England	N	Liverpool	Philadelphia	09/21/1847	03/23/1853			Y	03/27/1855
Bird, Michael	17	Ireland	N	?	New York	00/00/1858				Y	10/24/1888
Bird, Richard	46	Ireland	N	Liverpool	New York	07/04/1844	?			Y	
Bird, Thomas	2	Ireland	N	?	New Orleans	00/00/1858				Y	10/31/1888
Birick, Charles	38	Baden	Y	Havre	New Orleans	02/15/1859	08/23/1862	18	397	N	
Birk, Frank	37	Germany	Y	Havre	New York	10/21/1887	11/05/1892	19	412	N	
Birk, Martin	25	Wurttemberg	Y	Havre	New York	09/28/1854	07/30/1858	16	542	N	
Birke, Andreas	28	Germany	Y	Hamburg	New York	04/11/1881	08/22/1883			Y	
Birkehnhauer, Friederick	25	Germany	Y	Antwerp	New York	02/14/1886	11/01/1886	19	102	N	
Birmingham, James	23	Ireland	Y	Liverpool	New York	06/15/1855	10/19/1857	15	452	N	
Birmingham, James	35	Ireland	N	Liverpool	New York	04/??/1867	?			Y	
Birmmelhaus, Bernard Hen	24	Prussia	Y	Havre	New Orleans	11/??/1846	12/31/1849	23	447	N	
Birnbrauer, Aloise	44	Baden	Y	Havre	New York	09/12/1849	02/23/1853	7	216	N	
Birnbrauer, Aloys	44	Baden	N	Havre	New York	09/12/1849	02/23/1853			Y	03/26/1855
Biro, Peter P.	60	Hungary	Y	Antwerp	New York	02/04/1882	10/20/1897			Y	
Birrell, Wm. H.	??	England	Y	?	?	?	10/11/1884			Y	
Birsinger, Michael	33	Switzerland	Y	Havre	New Orleans	04/??/1847	12/??/1849	23	391	N	
Birt, William	59	England	N	Liverpool	New York	08/??/1849	?			Y	
Birtsch, Friedrich	??	Germany	Y	?	?	?	03/02/1883			Y	
Bischof, Friedrich Wilhe	44	Germany	Y	Bremen	New York	10/05/1881	02/23/1900			Y	
Bischof, John	25	Germany	Y	Bremen	New York	05/24/1886	10/07/1892			Y	
Bischoff, George	42	Germany	Y	Antwerp	New York	10/19/1887	09/18/1890			Y	
Bischoff, Hermann	26	Oldenburg	Y	Bremen	New Orleans	12/05/1854	05/29/1862	18	342	N	
Bischoff, William	??	Switzerland	Y	?	?	?	03/11/1882			Y	
Biser, Loui	34	Prussia	Y	Antwerp	New York	12/25/1891	09/20/1893			Y	
Bishoprick, Henry	40	England	Y	?	Buffalo	11/??/1848	02/03/1853	7	111	N	
Bisig, Casper	35	Switzerland	Y	Bremen	New York	09/21/1853	09/29/1856	14	13	N	
Bisig, Gustav	45	Switzerland	Y	Havre	New YOrk	10/07/1879	10/04/1888			Y	
Bisinger, Alois	44	Wurttemberg	Y	Havre	New Orleans	01/20/1854	09/21/1855	13	104	N	
Bisliop, William Henry	32	England	Y	?	?	?	10/23/1905			Y	
Bismark, George Frederic	33	Prussia	Y	Bremen	Baltimore	05/04/1861	04/04/1862	18	299	N	
Bittel, Michael	50	Bavaria	Y	Rotterdam	New Orleans	09/20/1846	10/09/1854	6	68	N	
Bittel, Michael	50	Bavaria	Y	Rotterdam	New York	09/20/1846	10/09/1854	11	69	N	
Bitter, Frederick	30	Hesse Darmsta	Y	Havre	New York	05/11/1852	12/16/1859	17	520	N	
Bitter, George	33	Germany	Y	Bremen	New York	12/16/1885	08/23/1890			Y	
Bitter, Peter	30	Kour Hessen	Y	Havre	New York	07/15/1848	09/14/1852	25	493	N	
Bitterle, Edward	38	Germany	Y	Bremen	New York	04/09/1873	10/08/1883			Y	
Bittig, Nicholas	24	Germany	Y	Antwerp	Philadelphia	09/12/1892	03/27/1897			Y	
Bittinger, Jacob	36	Baden	Y	Havre	New Orleans	03/01/1846	10/14/1848	1	235	N	
Bittinger, Peter	23	Bavaria	Y	London	New York	04/12/1852	10/03/1856	14	180	N	
Bittner, John	34	Germany	N	Bremen	Baltimore	05/??/1869	?			Y	
Bittner, Peter	33	Germany	Y	?	New York	??/??/1879	10/06/1886			Y	
Bitzer, Andreas	22	Bavaria	Y	Havre	New Orleans	04/24/1852	11/15/1852	5	283	N	
Bitzer, Andrew	22	Bavaria	Y	Havre	New Orleans	04/24/1852	11/15/1852	6	407	N	
Bitzer, George	21	Bavaria	Y	Havre	New Orleans	11/18/1849	11/15/1852	5	282	N	
Bitzer, George	21	Bavaria	Y	Havre	New Orleans	11/18/1849	11/15/1852	6	406	N	
Bizer, John	27	Wurttemberg	Y	Havre	New York	06/02/1852	04/23/1853	8	97	N	
Black, Edward	55	Ireland	Y	Sligo	New Orleans	04/13/1848	04/25/1854	8	265	N	
Black, Edward	55	Ireland	Y	Sligo	New Orleans	04/13/1848	04/25/1854	9	136	N	
Black, Frank	24	Germany	Y	Antwerp	New York	09/22/1883	05/12/1886			Y	
Black, James	23	Ireland	Y	Liverpool	New Orleans	12/18/1849	02/18/1852	24	134	N	
Black, John	25	Ireland	Y	Liverpool	New Orleans	10/??/1850	10/25/1855	13	142	N	

CITIZENSHIP RECORDS

APPLICANT	AGE	COUNTRY OF ORIGIN	DEC	DEPART PORT	ENTRY PORT	ARRIVE DATE	DEC DATE	VOL	PG.	FLD	NAT DATE
Black, Thomas	21	Ireland	Y	Liverpool	New Orleans	04/28/1849	11/05/1852	5	235	N	
Black, Thomas	21	Ireland	Y	Liverpool	New Orleans	04/28/1849	11/05/1852	6	359	N	
Blackburn, Thomas	30	Ireland	Y	Canada	Rochester	11/??/1844	11/17/1852	5	300	N	
Blackburn, Thomas	30	Ireland	Y	Canada	Rochester	11/??/1844	11/17/1852	6	424	N	
Blacker, Joseph S.	64	England	N	Cornwell	New Orleans	04/01/1852	?			Y	
Blacker, Thomas John	31	England	Y	Liverpool	New Orleans	03/10/1851	02/25/1853	7	233	N	
Blackmann, Michael	29	Russia	Y	Hamburg	New York	07/04/1882	10/08/1889			Y	
Blackschleger, Abe	29	Russia	Y	Hamburg	Philadelphia	07/00/1881	05/00/1883			Y	
Blackschleger, Abe (Alex	29	Russia	Y	Hamburg	Philadelphia	07/??/1881	05/??/1883	28	162	N	?
Blacksmith, Joseph	40	Italy	Y	Naples	New York	05/10/1871	05/18/1894			Y	
Blackwell, Charles	48	England	Y	?	Buffalo	??/??/1882	11/05/1891			Y	
Blackwell, William Antho	??	England	Y	?	?	?	04/06/1885			Y	
Blackwood, Thomas	41	Ireland	Y	Belfast	Philadelphia	07/04/1847	12/04/1852	5	376	N	
Blaeser, John Peter	31	Prussia	Y	Antwerp	New York	08/??/1852	12/27/1855	13	373	N	
Blaeser, Peter	26	Prussia	Y	Rotterdam	Baltimore	08/12/1849	02/04/1850	3	94	N	
Blah, John	48	Germany	Y	Amsterdam	New York	07/24/1880	10/26/1893			Y	
Blair, Isidor	26	Rumania	Y	?	New York	11/18/1900	07/23/1904			Y	
Blair, Thomas	45	Germany	Y	Bremen	Baltimore	11/08/1873	08/02/1893			Y	
Blaising, Rami	22	Germany	Y	Havre	New York	05/01/1887	10/23/1890	19	295	N	
Blaising, Rami	22	Germany	Y	Havre	New York	05/01/1884	10/23/1890			Y	
Blaizer, John Henry	63	Prussia	Y	Rotterdam	New York	09/16/1851	10/29/1851	4	431	N	
Blake, John	15	Canada	N	?	Detroit	00/00/1845				Y	10/29/1888
Blake, Patrick	22	Ireland	Y	Liverpool	Boston	10/30/1854	02/04/1858	16	78	N	
Blamer, Bernard	24	Oldenburg	Y	Bremen	New Orleans	11/10/1847	02/03/1851	3	85	N	
Blanchart, Ferdinand	31	Prussia	Y	Bremen	New York	05/08/1870	01/02/1871	18	445	N	
Blanckardt, Theodore Aug	35	Hanover	Y	Bremen	New York	08/10/1852	11/03/1852	5	214	N	
Blanckardt, Theodore Aug	35	Hanover	Y	Bremen	New York	08/10/1852	11/03/1852	6	340	N	
Bland, Michael	14	Ireland	N	?	New York	00/00/1880				Y	10/25/1887
Blank, Charles	25	Germany	Y	Hamburg	New York	06/20/1883	06/20/1889			Y	
Blank, Gregor	27	Baden	Y	Havre	New Orleans	05/18/1848	10/06/1854	10	489	N	
Blank, Gregor	27	Baden	Y	Havre	New Orleans	05/18/1848	10/06/1854	12	428	N	
Blank, John	23	Germany	Y	Antwerp	New York	05/20/1881	03/07/1884			Y	
Blank, John	35	Bavaria	Y	Havre	New Orleans	07/10/1843	02/12/1849	23	67	N	
Blank, Mathias	29	Baden	Y	Havre	New York	04/16/1847	10/05/1854	10	465	N	
Blank, Mathias	29	Baden	Y	Havre	New York	04/16/1847	10/05/1854	12	404	N	
Blank, Philip	44	Russia	Y	Bremen	Baltimore	09/15/1889	10/30/1896			Y	
Blank, Selig	31	Germany	Y	Bremen	New York	10/02/1880	10/07/1882			Y	
Blanke, Frank	35	Germany	Y	Bremen	New York	05/31/1880	10/17/1887			Y	
Blanken, J. Henry	29	Germany	Y	Amsterdam	New York	05/21/1881	10/24/1882			Y	
Blanken, John A.	30	Holland	Y	Rotterdam	New York	04/23/1884	10/27/1890			Y	
Blankenbiler, John	27	Bavaria	Y	Bremen	Baltimore	07/12/1845	10/11/1848	1	138	N	
Blanz, Heinrich	52	Germany	Y	Hamburg	New York	10/02/1872	10/10/1887			Y	
Blas, John	38	Wuertemberg	Y	Havre	New York	04/10/1854	05/22/1856	26	524	N	
Blasch, Franz	56	Austria	Y	Bremen	New York	04/28/1882	10/29/1888			Y	
Blasdorfer, Andy	25	Germany	Y	Bremen	New York	06/05/1882	11/03/1885			Y	
Blasir, Aug	50	Switzerland	Y	Havre	New York	09/23/1882	06/08/1886			Y	
Blasse, Henry	30	Hanover	Y	Bremen	Baltimore	11/02/1845	08/21/1855	11	471	N	
Blatt, Max	48	Austria	Y	Hamburg	New York	07/01/1880	10/30/1895			Y	
Blattmann, Edward	35	Switzerland	Y	Bremen	Baltimore	05/10/1872	04/13/1880			Y	
Blattner, Michael	23	Bavaria	Y	Havre	New Orleans	04/20/1850	03/22/1853	7	366	N	
Blattner, Peter Paul	??	Germany	Y	?	?	?	11/29/1884			Y	
Blau, Edward	37	Switzerland	Y	Havre	New York	03/27/1880	09/02/1890			Y	
Blau, Meyer	26	Saxe Weimar E	Y	Bremen	New York	09/08/1853	12/03/1855	13	278	N	
Blaustein, James	17	Hungary/Austr	N	?	New York	00/00/1883				Y	10/25/1888
Blecchliger, Moses	43	Russia	Y	Hamburg	Philadelphia	07/04/1881	05/07/1883			Y	
Blechschmied, John	30	Germany	Y	Antwerp	New York	01/14/1893	06/09/1897			Y	
Bleh, Martin	23	Bavaria	Y	Rotterdam	New York	04/??/1883	??/??/1884			Y	
Bleh, Martin	31	Bavaria	N	Rotterdam	New York	03/??/1883	?			Y	
Bleher, Christoph	28	Wurttemberg	Y	Havre	New Orleans	01/25/1848	01/02/1851	2	437	N	

CITIZENSHIP RECORDS

APPLICANT	AGE	COUNTRY OF ORIGIN	DEC	DEPART PORT	ENTRY PORT	ARRIVE DATE	DEC DATE	VOL	PG.	FLD	NAT DATE
Blei, Heinrich	22	Oldenburg	Y	Bremen	New Orleans	11/08/1856	06/02/1859	17	450	N	
Bleibel, Charles	38	Baden	Y	Bremen	New York	04/22/1852	02/13/1856	26	79	N	
Bleier, Robert	34	Germany	Y	Bremen	New York	06/16/1879	10/13/1885			Y	
Bleile, Charles	33	Germany	Y	Havre	New York	03/04/1887	09/24/1892			Y	
Bleile, Joseph	26	Germany	Y	Havre	New York	06/04/1890	04/21/1894			Y	
Bleir, William	33	Ireland	Y	Liverpool	Philadelphia	06/22/1839	03/24/1851	3	315	N	
Bleisch, Ernest	67	Wuerttemberg	N	Antwerp	New York	09/03/1851	?	28	440	N	09/27/1857
Bleiwein, Solomon	27	Russia	Y	Bremen	New York	08/28/1900	06/08/1903			Y	
Blenckhamer, Frederick	21	Hanover	Y	Bremen	New Orleans	10/09/1850	10/07/1854	5	24	N	
Blendinger, John	30	Bavaria	Y	Bremen	New York	07/11/1851	05/18/1854	8	468	N	
Blendinger, John	30	Bavaria	Y	Bremen	New York	07/11/1851	05/18/1854	9	342	N	
Blesch, Blasius	32	Baden	Y	Liverpool	New York	06/01/1853	04/03/1856	26	424	N	
Blesi, Peter	54	Switzerland	Y	Havre	New York	01/25/1891	02/10/1894			Y	
Blesi, Samuel	28	Switzerland	Y	Havre	New Orleans	06/02/1845	09/11/1855	13	2	N	
Blessing, William	33	Germany	Y	Hamburg	New York	10/06/1882	03/12/1884			Y	
Bleuler, Adolph	37	Switzerland	Y	Havre	New York	04/04/1848	03/18/1850	2	211	N	
Bley, Henry	32	Germany	Y	Bremen	New York	06/21/1888	03/10/1894			Y	
Bley, Henry	57	Germany	N	Bremen	New Orleans	10/??/1852	?			Y	
Bley, John	22	Germany	Y	Bremen	Baltimore	05/28/1883	10/13/1885			Y	
Bley, Joseph	25	Germany	Y	Antwerp	New York	08/23/1885	02/02/1891			Y	
Bley, William Charles Fr	21	Oldenburg	Y	Bremen	Baltimore	12/14/1847	02/22/1850	2	114	N	
Blicke, Francis	23	Prussia	Y	Bremen	New York	06/01/1856	10/28/1858	17	164	N	
Blight, William	35	England	Y	Plymouth	New York	05/23/1850	09/06/1852	25	372	N	
Blinzinger, Charles	44	Wuerttemberg	Y	Antwerp	New York	05/10/1847	02/19/1849	23	194	N	
Bloch, Alexis	41	Bavaria	Y	Antwerp	New Orleans	12/??/1842	09/10/1855	11	527	N	
Bloch, Ben	34	Germany	Y	Bremen	New York	05/17/1881	11/08/1889			Y	
Bloch, Emil	26	Baden	Y	London	New York	04/05/1849	03/24/1853	7	386	N	
Bloch, Emil	32	Germany	Y	Havre	New York	06/22/1882	12/04/1890			Y	
Bloch, H.	35	Russia	Y	Bremen	New York	06/??/1885	12/17/1886			Y	
Bloch, John	38	Russia	Y	Hamburg	New York	07/05/1882	12/17/1886			Y	
Bloch, M.	18	Russia	Y	Hamburg	New York	04/??/1885	12/17/1886			Y	
Bloch, Mayer	45	France	Y	Havre	New York	10/20/1867	09/22/1888			Y	
Bloch, Solomon	50	Germany	Y	Hamburg	New York	02/06/1875	03/07/1890			Y	
Blochlinger, Albert	27	Switzerland	Y	Havre	New York	05/07/1881	05/25/1885			Y	
Block, Aram	31	France	Y	Havre	New Orleans	12/07/1842	03/16/1850	2	201	N	
Block, Henry	24	Hesse Cassel	Y	Bremen	New York	06/17/1852	03/21/1856	26	246	N	
Block, Jacob	24	Germany	N	Antwerp	New York	11/01/1881	?			Y	
Block, Lion	22	Bavaria	Y	London	New York	10/01/1852	01/12/1856	13	455	N	
Block, W.	27	Germany	Y	Amsterdam	New York	11/14/1883	11/05/1888			Y	
Bloechle, John	31	Germany	Y	Bremen	Baltimore	06/27/1883	10/25/1888			Y	
Bloemer, Heinrich	44	Germany	Y	Bremen	New York	05/14/1884	10/27/1899			Y	
Blom, William	21	Hanover	Y	Bremen	New Orleans	11/27/1848	04/12/1852	24	486	N	
Blomberg, Wm. Theodore	58	Denmark	Y	Hamburg	New York	09/23/1860	03/22/1887			Y	
Blome, Arnold	30	Germany	Y	Bremen	Baltimore	09/04/1889	08/20/1891			Y	
Blome, Friedrich	41	Germany	N	Bremen	New York	09/06/1872	?			Y	
Blome, Herman	29	Germany	N	Bremen	Baltimore	05/??/1875	?			Y	
Blome, Louis	27	Germany	Y	?	New York	00/00/1882	04/16/1884			Y	
Blome, Robert	54	Poland	N	Liverpool	New York	??/??/1853	?			Y	
Blome, William	52	Prussia	Y	Bremen	Baltimore	06/05/1854	11/03/1857	15	526	N	
Blomer, Clemens August	28	Oldenburg	Y	Bremen	Baltimore	09/01/1858	10/18/1860	27	509	N	
Blomer, Joseph	29	Germany	Y	?	Baltimore	05/29/1875	06/23/1877			Y	
Blomeyer, Jobst Henry	40	Hanover	Y	Bremen	Bremen?	09/01/1853	04/07/1856	26	457	N	
Blommer, Bernard (Blomme	55	Prussia	Y	Rotterdam	New Orleans	01/06/1846	08/15/1848	22	124	N	
Bloom, Harris	48	Russia	Y	Hamburg	New York	09/15/1878	07/21/1894			Y	
Bloom, Harry	22	Russia	Y	?	?	?	09/03/1894			Y	
Bloom, Philip	38	Russia	Y	Hamburg	New York	08/06/1879	12/27/1889			Y	
Bloom, Simon	44	Russia	Y	Hamburg	New York	07/31/1878	11/02/1891			Y	
Bluatt, Matthew	25	Ireland	Y	Liverpool	New York	06/15/1853	03/24/1856	26	287	N	
Bludan, August	28	Germany	N	Bremen	Baltimore	04/??/1872	?			Y	

CITIZENSHIP RECORDS

APPLICANT	AGE	COUNTRY OF ORIGIN	DEC	DEPART PORT	ENTRY PORT	ARRIVE DATE	DEC DATE	VOL	PG.	FLD	NAT DATE
Bluemal, Michael	26	Germany	Y	Bremen	New York	04/02/1889	06/11/1892			Y	
Bluett, Charles	27	Ireland	Y	Quebec	Buffalo	08/??/1852	10/28/1857	15	499	N	
Blum, Abraham	50	Bavaria	Y	Antwerp	New York	08/06/1845	09/21/1855	13	89	N	
Blum, Albert	26	Switzerland	Y	?	New York	??/??/1879	10/17/1887			Y	
Blum, George	24	Germany	Y	Havre	New York	05/22/1882	08/28/1884			Y	
Blum, George	23	Bavaria	Y	Bremen	Baltimore	04/26/1849	01/20/1852	24	35	N	
Blum, John	27	Bavaria	Y	Bremen	Baltimore	11/01/1854	11/24/1855	13	249	N	
Blum, Joseph	46	Baden	Y	Havre	New York	06/20/1848	08/10/1848	22	85	N	
Blum, Michael	26	Bavaria	Y	Havre	New York	04/17/1852	11/06/1858	17	285	N	
Blum, Peter	25	Bavaria	Y	Bremerhafen	Baltimore	01/16/1860	01/15/1861	18	59	N	
Blum, Peter	50	Germany	Y	Havre	New York	10/15/1881	12/08/1884			Y	
Blum, Peter	44	Baden	Y	Havre	New York	06/29/1849	05/24/1856	26	544	N	
Blume, Adam	??	Germany	Y	?	?	?	04/20/1884			Y	
Blume, Adolph	51	Germany	Y	Bremen	New York	06/18/1888	06/21/1893	19	423	N	
Blume, Adolph	51	Germany	Y	Bremen	New York	06/18/1888	06/21/1893			Y	
Blume, Albert	38	Germany	Y	Antwerp	Philadelphia	03/24/1882	10/25/1886			Y	
Blume, Hugo	22	Germany	Y	Bremen	New York	10/30/1888	02/05/1892	19	374	N	
Blume, Hugo	22	Germany	Y	Bremen	New York	10/30/1888	02/05/1892			Y	
Blume, Robert B.	28	Germany	Y	Antwerp	New York	02/14/1885	11/07/1892			Y	
Blume, Theodore	22	Prussia	Y	Bremen	New Orleans	05/11/1848	02/12/1851	3	125	N	
Blumenthal, Abraham	29	Russia	Y	Hamburg	New York	03/28/1888	04/05/1890			Y	
Bluminthal, Walter V.	33	England	Y	London	New York	09/23/1883	03/23/1891	19	318	N	
Blust, Wilhelm	26	Germany	Y	Bremen	New York	06/25/1882	04/23/1886			Y	
Blustein, Moses	??	Russia	N	?	?	06/25/1883				Y	10/27/1892
Blyth, John	43	England	Y	Liverpool	New York	03/24/1887	03/29/1894			Y	
Blyttersdorf, Charles	21	Prussia	Y	Havre	New York	08/03/1848	05/24/1852	25	96	N	
Boak, Henry	27	Denmark	Y	Hamburg	New York	04/13/1851	03/19/1853	7	350	N	
Bobe, Otto	34	Germany	Y	Hamburg	New York	10/01/1887	09/19/1893			Y	
Boberg, Henry	23	Hanover	Y	Bremen	Baltimore	06/04/1846	02/05/1849	23	27	N	
Bobery, Anton	29	Hanover	Y	Bremen	Baltimore	08/15/1852	09/10/1855	11	519	N	
Boccuti, Antonio	37	Italy	Y	Naples	New York	12/??/1870	11/??/1882			Y	
Bochmann, Oscar	25	Germany	Y	Hamburg	Baltimore	07/16/1892	04/22/1895			Y	
Bock, Bartholomew	29	Wurttemberg	Y	Havre	New Orleans	03/07/1840	01/18/1849	1	455	N	
Bock, Gottfried	28	Germany	Y	Rotterdam	New York	07/15/1879	01/13/1888			Y	
Bock, Henry	24	Germany	Y	Antwerp	Philadelphia	07/29/1892	08/29/1894			Y	
Bockelman, Henry	49	Germany	Y	Bremen	Baltimore	08/17/1888	10/05/1891			Y	
Bockelmann, Louis	30	Germany	Y	Bremen	New York	03/05/1875	02/11/1878			Y	
Bockerstette, Ferdinand	30	Germany	Y	Bremen	New York	03/16/1891	10/27/1899			Y	
Bockerstette, Henry	25	Germany	Y	Bremen	Baltimore	09/28/1876	05/05/1880			Y	
Bockhold, Theodore	25	Germany	Y	Rotterdam	New York	10/14/1884	03/16/1889			Y	
Bockholt, John	28	Hanover	Y	Bremen	Baltimore	06/04/1848	03/06/1852	24	248	N	
Bockholt, Theodore	33	Prussia	Y	Bremen	Baltimore	12/21/1854	02/02/1857	14	526	N	
Bockhorst, Herm	22	Germany	Y	Amsterdam	New York	08/14/1881	06/29/1884			Y	
Bockhorst, Herman	26	Germany	N	Amsterdam	New York	09/14/1881	?			Y	
Bockhorst, T.	26	Germany	Y	Hanover	Baltimore	11/02/1870	10/12/1880			Y	
Bocklage, Henry	27	Hanover	Y	Bremen	New Orleans	05/28/1851	09/25/1854	10	218	N	
Bocklage, Henry	27	Hanover	Y	Bremen	New Orleans	05/28/1851	09/25/1854	12	157	N	
Bockman, Anton	46	Germany	N	Bremen	New York	06/09/1866	?			Y	
Bockman, Herman	17	Germany	N	?	Baltimore	00/00/1881				Y	04/05/1886
Bockmann, Frank	16	Germany	N	?	Baltimore	00/00/1880				Y	10/19/1886
Bockstiegel, Heinrich	24	Germany	Y	Amsterdam	New York	10/22/1883	07/20/1887			Y	
Bockstieger, Diedrich	34	Germany	Y	Bremen	Baltmore	11/13/1882	08/18/1891			Y	
Bockway, John	30	Hanover	Y	Bremen	Baltimore	11/01/1857	09/28/1860	27	384	N	
Bodan, Phillip	37	Bavaria	Y	Havre	New York	09/14/1854	03/19/1858	16	425	N	
Bodda, John	29	Prussia	Y	Bremen	New Orleans	12/??/1845	11/??/1849	23	330	N	
Bode, August H.	41	Germany	N	Hamburg	New York	03/17/1867	?			Y	
Bode, Gustavus	27	Hesse Cassel	Y	Hamburg	New York	11/01/1858	05/07/1861	18	161	N	
Bode, Henry	33	Germany	Y	Amsterdam	New York	06/??/1870	10/25/1883			Y	
Bode, Herman Henry Charl	23	Germany	Y	Rotterdam	New York	12/17/1889	04/23/1892			Y	

CITIZENSHIP RECORDS

APPLICANT	AGE	COUNTRY OF ORIGIN	DEC	DEPART PORT	ENTRY PORT	ARRIVE DATE	DEC DATE	VOL	PG.	FLD	NAT DATE
Bode, William	21	Brunswick	Y	Bremen	New York	11/20/1853	02/02/1856	13	537	N	
Bodecke, Anton Henry	33	Bremen	Y	Bremen	New York	01/12/1847	02/09/1853	7	135	N	
Boden, James	28	Ireland	Y	Drogheda	New York	04/15/1883	04/10/1888				Y
Boden, William	29	England	Y	Liverpool	New Orleans	04/05/1851	12/22/1852	5	440	N	
Bodenkirch, William	37	Prussia	Y	Antwerp	Galveston	09/11/1846	08/23/1848	22	231	N	
Bodenstein, William Fred	29	Hanover	Y	Bremen	New York	04/05/1866	11/01/1871	18	436	N	
Boebinger, Jacob	23	Bavaria	Y	Havre	New York	07/02/1848	02/12/1849	23	68	N	
Boeckelmann, Fred	20	Germany	Y	Bremen	Baltimore	08/17/1888	04/07/1890				Y
Boeckenholt, George	35	Oldenburg	Y	Bremen	New York	11/15/1846	09/12/1848	22	332	N	
Boecker, Henry	28	Germany	Y	Bremen	Baltimore	09/01/1882	01/07/1885				Y
Boeckerstette, John Frie	35	Germany	Y	Bremen	Baltimore	10/08/1891	10/30/1894				Y
Boeckle, Andreas	24	Austria	Y	Havre	New York	09/24/1852	01/27/1853	7	75	N	
Boeckmann, Bernard	??	Oldenburg	Y	Bremen	New Orleans	11/26/18??	10/09/1848	1	98	N	
Boedekker, Fritz	35	Germany	N	Bremen	New York	04/??/1865	?				Y
Boedker, William	31	Prussia	Y	Bremen	New Orleans	02/18/1847	12/21/1850	2	382	N	
Boeffinger, Charles Rein	22	Hesse Darmsta	Y	Antwerp	New York	08/23/1848	05/31/1852	25	136	N	
Boeffinger, John	30	Hesse Darmsta	Y	Antwerp	New York	08/23/1848	05/31/1852	25	137	N	
Boegel, John Philip	46	Bavaria	Y	Havre	New Orleans	12/27/1852	03/24/1856	26	261	N	
Boeglin, John	??	Germany	Y	?	?	03/00/1883	04/19/1884				Y
Boeglin, Peter	28	Germany	Y	Antwerp	New York	09/27/1891	08/15/1892				Y
Boeh, William	24	Germany	Y	Bremen	New York	01/01/1881	05/19/1884				Y
Boehle, J.	34	Germany	Y	Bremen	Baltimore	04/??/1874	10/08/1880				Y
Boehler, Jacob	24	Bavaria	Y	Havre	New York	04/22/1856	11/19/1858	17	342	N	
Boehm, Adam	48	Germany	Y	Havre	New Orleans	12/??/1859	05/08/1885				Y
Boehm, Anthony	32	Austria	Y	Bremen	New York	03/28/1854	10/27/1858	17	135	N	
Boehm, Christian	32	Wurttemberg	Y	Hamburg	New York	12/??/1848	08/??/1851	4	152	N	
Boehm, Conrad	34	Bavaria	Y	Bremen	Baltimore	11/11/1854	09/30/1856	14	56	N	
Boehm, Frederick	34	Bavaria	Y	Bremen	Philadelphia	09/03/1848	02/23/1852	24	151	N	
Boehm, Frederick	38	Bavaria	Y	Amsterdam	New York	07/04/1849	03/11/1852	24	290	N	
Boehm, Geo.	33	Germany	Y	Bremen	New York	03/15/1882	05/14/1885				Y
Boehm, Hugo	23	Germany	Y	Hamburg	New York	05/??/1872	05/??/1873				Y
Boehm, Jacob	29	Switzerland	Y	Havre	New York	09/07/1880	04/17/1889				Y
Boehm, John Gottleib	37	Prussia	Y	Bremen	New York	07/14/1856	10/07/1856	14	247	N	
Boehm, Michael	38	France	Y	Havre	New York	03/03/1848	11/15/1852	5	291	N	
Boehmann, Casper	28	Germany	Y	Amsterdam	New York	08/21/1893	01/02/1896				Y
Boehme, Frederick	47	Prussia	Y	Bremen	New York	09/01/1850	05/12/1854	8	429	N	
Boehme, Frederick	47	Prussia	Y	Bremen	New York	09/01/1850	05/12/1854	9	302	N	
Boehme, Frederick	36	Germany	Y	Hamburg	New York	02/25/1882	06/04/1885				Y
Boehme, Frederick	32	Saxe Weimar	Y	Bremen	Galveston	10/01/1846	09/05/1848	22	305	N	
Boehme, Louis	28	Germany	Y	Hamburg	New York	02/23/1882	06/15/1886				Y
Boehmer, Gerhard Henry	35	Hanover	Y	Bremen	Baltimore	07/01/18??	04/06/1852	24	406	N	
Boehmer, Herman	28	Germany	Y	Rotterdam	New York	06/17/1881	01/06/1886				Y
Boehmer, Peter	58	Germany	Y	Bremen	New York	10/23/1871	11/03/1900				Y
Boehmler, John	26	Wurttemberg	Y	Havre	New York	02/02/1853	09/29/1856	14	35	N	
Boehner, Andrew	25	Germany	Y	Bremen	New York	02/21/1884	01/30/1889				Y
Boehner, Joseph	27	Bavaria	Y	Hamburg	New York	04/25/1852	05/10/1852	24	531	N	
Boehner, Michael	26	Germany	Y	Antwerp	New York	04/04/1880	09/30/1887				Y
Boehnlein, Joseph	43	Germany	Y	Antwerp	New York	11/13/1879	12/30/1882				Y
Boehrer, Joseph	21	Baden	Y	London	New York	04/01/1852	04/04/1853	8	24	N	
Boehringer, Adam Wolfgan	??	?	Y	?	New York	06/16/18??	11/03/1856	14	445	N	
Boekhacker, William E.	??	Germany	Y	?	New York	02/20/1900	02/10/1904				Y
Boekler, John Ernst	21	Wurttemberg	Y	Havre	New Orleans	05/10/1848	10/17/1851	4	318	N	
Boekweg, John Henry	26	Hanover	Y	Bremen	New York	02/22/1849	03/08/1852	24	260	N	
Boelger, John	33	Bavaria	Y	Amsterdam	New York	06/01/1848	02/27/1850	2	143	N	
Boelhauer, John	30	Germany	Y	Bremen	Baltimore	03/03/1881	04/02/1888				Y
Boelike, Otto	38	Germany	Y	Bremen	Baltimore	08/27/1882	10/01/1888				Y
Boelke, Julius	37	Germany	Y	Hamburg	New York	09/17/1885	12/29/1887				Y
Boellmann, Joseph	34	Germany	Y	Hamburg	New York	11/24/1882	08/13/1886				Y
Boelscher, Johann Bernha	26	Germany	Y	Bremen	New York	08/29/1885	02/26/1889				Y

CITIZENSHIP RECORDS

APPLICANT	AGE	COUNTRY OF ORIGIN	DEC	DEPART PORT	ENTRY PORT	ARRIVE DATE	DEC DATE	VOL	PG.	FLD	NAT DATE
Boelz, Adam	26	Wurttemberg	Y	Bremen	New Orleans	??/04/1852	04/24/1855	11	299	N	
Boelzner, William	27	Baden	Y	London	New York	06/04/1848	04/17/1854	8	146	N	
Boelzner, William	27	Baden	Y	London	New York	06/04/1848	04/17/1854	9	17	N	
Boemer, Bernard	26	Prussia	Y	Rotterdam	New Orleans	10/27/1846	03/04/1850	2	151	N	
Boenitsch, Val	30	Germany	Y	Bremen	New York	05/21/1882	08/06/1885			Y	
Boenke, Joseph	36	Germany	Y	Hamburg	New York	01/19/1880	08/25/1886			Y	
Boer, John	30	Bavaria	Y	Bremen	New Orleans	06/16/1850	06/07/1852	25	194	N	
Boeras, Henry	25	Prussia	Y	Antwerp	New York	05/05/1848	08/12/1851	4	119	N	
Boerger Henry	26	Germany	Y	Rotterdam	New York	09/24/1891	12/15/1897			Y	
Boerger, John	71	Germany	Y	Bremen	Baltimore	04/23/1869	10/20/1884			Y	
Boerger, John	31	Germany	Y	Bremen	New York	05/20/1884	02/15/1897			Y	
Boering, Bernard	32	Holland	Y	Bremen	Baltimore	05/17/1853	09/24/1856	14	366	N	
Boerman, George	14	Germany	N	?	New York	00/00/1881				Y	11/03/1888
Boerner, Edmund	31	Germany	Y	Bremen	New York	05/26/1892	11/04/1895			Y	
Boernes (Barnes), John W	??	Hanover	Y	Bremen	New Orleans	07/28/1847	03/25/1851	3	340	N	
Boertzel, Frederick	32	Germany	Y	Hamburg	New York	03/13/1876	07/20/1886			Y	
Boesch, Frank	35	France	Y	Havre	New York	12/28/1853	10/07/1854	6	32	N	
Boesch, Frank	35	France	Y	Havre	New York	12/28/1853	10/07/1854	11	33	N	
Boesch, John	48	Germany	Y	Havre	New York	03/13/1881	10/22/1897			Y	
Boesch, Werner	25	Switzerland	Y	Havre	New York	05/22/1854	09/23/1854	10	178	N	
Boeschlin, Theophile	30	Germany	Y	Havre	New York	12/29/1891	06/12/1897			Y	
Boesck, Frederick Willia	23	Baden	Y	Liverpool	New York	03/27/1851	10/09/1854	11	135	N	
Boeshens, John	50	Bavaria	Y	London	New York	10/22/1852	10/30/1858	17	11	N	
Boesk, Frederick William	23	Baden	Y	Liverpool	New York	03/27/1851	10/09/1854	6	132	N	
Boettcher, Frederick	30	Mecklenburg S	Y	Hamburg	New York	09/02/1852	04/12/1856	26	495	N	
Boettcher, Martin	48	Germany	Y	Bremen	New York	03/??/1869	10/11/1884			Y	
Boettger, William	38	Hanover	Y	Bremen	New York	??/13/1849	11/??/1849	23	347	N	
Boetticher, Gustav	??	Germany	Y	Bremen	?	06/??/1867	07/??/1870			Y	
Boewer, Jonh T.	59	Germany	Y	Bremen	Baltimore	04/30/1881	12/06/1884			Y	
Boewer, Th. H.	25	Germany	Y	Bremen	Baltimore	04/30/1881	07/07/1884			Y	
Boewiker, Christian	54	Germany	N	Bremen	New York	10/26/1857	?			Y	
Bofsmann, Henry Fred Wil	27	Germany	Y	Hamburg	New York	04/23/1881	04/02/1883			Y	
Bogel, Henry	24	Prussia	Y	Bremen	Baltimore	07/20/1857	04/11/1860	27	149	N	
Bogenreif, John	26	Germany	Y	Antwerp	New York	03/04/1881	08/25/1887			Y	
Bogenschuetz, Christian	30	Germany	Y	Bremen	New York	05/01/1880	03/27/1891			Y	
Bogenschuetz, Michael	23	Heckingen	Y	Havre	New Orleans	05/14/1847	03/28/1849	23	258	N	
Bogenschutz, Joseph	27	Germany	Y	Antwerp	New York	10/03/1880	02/12/1883			Y	
Boggiano, Dominick	37	Italy	N	Bremen	New York	11/??/1864	?			Y	
Boggiano, John	26	Sardina	Y	Havre	New York	08/01/1842	03/29/1850	2	278	N	
Bogner, John	46	Bavaria	Y	Bremen	New York	07/30/1851	04/16/1853	8	68	N	
Bogner, Leonard	25	Bavaria	Y	Bremen	Baltimore	07/21/1846	08/24/1848	22	250	N	
Bogner, Nathan	25	Austira	Y	Hamburg	New York	02/01/1900	04/12/1904			Y	
Bogus, Vandal	27	Bavaria	Y	Havre	New Orleans	05/??/1847	03/16/1853	7	333	N	
Bohan, James	??	Ireland	N	?	?	09/00/1849				Y	10/29/1892
Bohen, Jacob	28	Prussia	Y	Havre	New York	08/28/1858	01/13/1862	18	243	N	
Bohlamnn, Theodor F.	33	Germany	Y	Bremen	New York	08/18/1890	06/09/1898			Y	
Bohlander, George	26	Bayerm	N	Havre	New York	07/13/1835	10/08/1842			Y	10/30/1844
Bohlander, John	74	Germany	N	Ellenbach	New Orleans	11/??/1838	?	28	392	N	??/??/1844
Bohle, Franz	33	Prussia	Y	Bremen	New Orleans	11/24/1849	06/05/1854	10	91	N	
Bohle, Franz	33	Prussia	Y	Bremen	New Orleans	11/24/1849	06/05/1854	12	28	N	
Bohleber, George	23	Baden	Y	Havre	New Orleans	03/01/1851	01/22/1856	13	496	N	
Bohlen, Michael	38	Prussia	Y	Havre	New York	03/01/1852	02/23/1853	7	219	N	
Bohlender, Alexander	34	Prussia	Y	Liverpool	New York	04/15/1855	02/22/1858	16	327	N	
Bohlender, Daniel	??	Bavaria	Y	Havre	New Orleans	??/10/1853	04/16/1855	11	244	N	
Bohling, Henry	??	Hanover	Y	Bremen	Baltimore	??/18/1846	12/??/1850	2	408	N	
Bohlinger, Christian	30	Bavaria	Y	Havre	New York	06/12/1848	02/22/1851	3	155	N	
Bohlke, Herman	27	Oldenburg	Y	Bremen	New Orleans	05/24/1851	02/01/1853	7	104	N	
Bohm, Joseph	31	Germany	Y	Nassau	New York	11/07/1881	02/18/1885			Y	
Bohm, Mathias	26	Germany	Y	Antwerp	New York	02/02/1880	12/26/1882			Y	

CITIZENSHIP RECORDS

APPLICANT	AGE	COUNTRY OF ORIGIN	DEC	DEPART PORT	ENTRY PORT	ARRIVE DATE	DEC DATE	VOL	PG.	FLD	NAT DATE
Bohm, Michael	38	France	Y	Havre	New York	03/03/1848	11/15/1852	6	415	N	
Bohm, Sam	35	Russia	Y	Hamburg	New York	11/25/1885	11/06/1891			Y	
Bohmann, B.	36	Germany	Y	Rotterdam	Baltimore	05/01/1872	10/20/1886			Y	
Bohmrich, Louis G.	28	Germany	Y	Antwerp	New York	07/10/1880	08/08/1883			Y	
Bohn, John	28	Baden	Y	Havre	New Orleans	05/05/1852	03/28/1857	15	95	N	
Bohn, Lawrence	23	Germany	Y	Rotterdam	New York	03/28/1880	12/04/1884			Y	
Bohn, Lorenz	48	France	Y	Havre	New Orleans	02/??/1849	05/08/1854	8	398	N	
Bohn, Lorenz	48	France	Y	Havre	New Orleans	?	05/08/1854	9	271	N	
Bohn, Nicholas	25	Germany	Y	Baden	New York	01/28/1879	09/24/1880			Y	
Bohne, Ferdinand	32	Prussia	Y	Bremen	New York	08/31/1854	02/18/1857	15	32	N	
Bohne, Henry	26	Prussia	Y	Bremen	New Orleans	05/23/1852	10/07/1856	14	248	N	
Bohnen, Leonard	35	Germany	Y	Bremen	Baltimore	10/20/1883	10/24/1889	19	257	N	
Bohnen, Leonard	35	Germany	Y	Bremen	Baltimore	10/20/1883	10/24/1889			Y	
Bohnert, Anton	32	Baden	Y	Havre	New Orleans	05/01/1847	01/29/1849	1	535	N	
Bohnesack, John	38	Mecklenburg	Y	Hamburg	New York	12/01/1854	07/29/1862	18	381	N	
Bohnlein, Andrie	25	Germany	Y	Rotterdam	New York	05/28/1890	09/21/1895			Y	
Bohnstengel, Albert	33	Germany	Y	Hamburg	New York	11/04/1882	11/14/1888			Y	
Bohnstengel, Gustav Adol	32	Germany	Y	Rotterdam	New York	02/08/1884	02/01/1889			Y	
Bohrer, Friedrich	38	Bavaria	Y	Havre	New York	02/28/1854	10/06/1856	14	203	N	
Bohrer, Heinrich	45	Switzerland	Y	Antwerp	New York	03/20/1890	02/06/1897			Y	
Bohrer, Herman	27	Switzerland	Y	Havre	New York	09/01/1879	10/30/1888			Y	
Bohrmann, George	24	Germany	Y	Antwerp	New York	10/27/1883	12/10/1886			Y	
Bohsdorf, Robert	30	Germany	Y	Hamburg	New York	03/08/1882	04/27/1882			Y	
Boimann, Gerhard	28	Germany	Y	Amsterdam	New York	10/03/1882	09/17/1888			Y	
Boing, Herman	33	Germany	Y	Bremen	New York	07/29/1883	10/27/1890			Y	
Bojmann, Bernhardt	39	Germany	Y	?	New York	??/??/1881	10/12/1888			Y	
Bokelmann, Hermann	27	Germany	Y	Bremen	New York	05/03/1892	07/06/1895			Y	
Boknecht, Henry	36	Prussia	Y	Bremen	New Orleans	05/01/1849	07/23/1855	11	416	N	
Boland, James	24	Ireland	Y	Limerick	Buffalo	11/??/1852	03/16/1858	16	410	N	
Boland, Matthew	27	Ireland	Y	Liverpool	New York	09/23/1847	01/19/1852	24	32	N	
Boland, Thomas	41	Ireland	N	Queenstown	New York	05/29/1867	?			Y	
Boland, William	28	Ireland	Y	Queenstown	Philadelphia	05/08/1892	04/08/1901			Y	
Bolen, John	32	Ireland	Y	Liverpool	New Orleans	02/25/1848	03/03/1857	15	57	N	
Bolge, Henry	32	Prussia	Y	Bremen	New Orleans	06/16/1845	01/29/1853	7	81	N	
Bolger, James	29	Ireland	Y	Liverpool	New York	08/01/18??	03/10/1851	3	229	N	
Bolger, John	25	Ireland	Y	Liverpool	New York	10/31/1849	03/10/1851	3	230	N	
Bolin, Patrick	27	Ireland	Y	Liverpool	New York	06/26/1851	10/03/1856	14	183	N	
Bollard, James	37	England	Y	Liverpool	New Orleans	10/28/1850	09/26/1854	10	228	N	
Bollard, James	37	England	Y	Liverpool	New Orleans	10/28/1850	09/26/1854	12	167	N	
Boller, Edward	22	Baden	Y	Bremen	New York	08/01/1868	12/13/1871	18	443	N	
Bollers, Bernard	24	Oldenburg	Y	Bremen	Baltimore	07/08/1858	11/18/1860	27	531	N	
Bollhauer, Frank	24	Germany	Y	Rotterdam	New York	10/11/1881	07/11/1884			Y	
Bollin, Baselius	29	Baden	Y	Havre	New York	05/02/1853	09/30/1857	15	335	N	
Bolling, Christoph	33	Bavaria	Y	Bremen	New York	05/15/1857	01/16/1860	27	56	N	
Bollinger, Bernhard	36	Wurttemberg	Y	Havre	New Orleans	05/31/1849	04/18/1854	8	194	N	
Bollinger, Bernhard	36	Wurttemberg	Y	Havre	New Orleans	05/31/1849	04/18/1854	9	65	N	
Bollinger, John	25	Germany	Y	Bremen	New York	06/20/1890	10/20/1893			Y	
Bollinger, Melchoir	27	Switzerland	Y	Havre	New York	08/12/1840	02/17/1849	23	157	N	
Bollmann, Theodore	24	Hanover	Y	Bremen	New Orleans	12/03/1851	10/12/1857	15	393	N	
Bollmann, William	54	Prussia	Y	Bremen	New York	11/04/1852	05/03/1859	17	395	N	
Bolmer, Frank	51	Germany	N	Bremen	Baltimore	11/??/1859	?			Y	
Bolster, Henry	22	Prussia	Y	Rotterdam	Baltimore	??/04/1848	11/22/1849	23	365	N	
Bolte, John F.	45	Germany	N	Bremen	New York	09/??/1865	?			Y	
Bolten, William	30	Ireland	Y	Liverpool	New Orleans	03/25/1850	03/07/1853	7	288	N	
Bolton, Edward	40	Germany	Y	Liverpool	New York	01/01/1865	07/20/1872	18	508	N	
Boltz, George	41	Bavaria	Y	Havre	New York	05/10/1848	06/18/1851	3	403	N	
Bolwerk, William	24	Prussia	Y	Antwerp	New York	10/50/1856	05/05/1859	17	399	N	
Bolz, Bruno	36	Germany	Y	Havre	New York	08/28/1873	09/12/1883			Y	
Bolzer, Peter	17	Germany	N	?	New York	00/00/1883				Y	10/25/1888

34

CITIZENSHIP RECORDS

APPLICANT	AGE	COUNTRY OF ORIGIN	DEC	DEPART PORT	ENTRY PORT	ARRIVE DATE	DEC DATE	VOL	PG.	FLD	NAT DATE
Bomash, Maks	??	Russia	Y	?	?	?	10/08/1878			Y	
Bomberger, John	48	Bavaria	Y	Antwerp	New York	12/07/1851	06/10/1872			Y	
Bomschein, William Frede	40	Saxony	Y	Hamburg	New York	09/11/1852	07/30/1858	16	539	N	
Bonapfel, Emil	34	Germany	Y	Havre	New York	02/15/1883	10/26/1893			Y	
Bond, John	17	Ireland	N	?	New York	00/00/1876				Y	10/27/1888
Bonde, Gerhard	35	Hanover	Y	Hamburg	New York	09/15/1855	12/26/1857	16	246	N	
Bondi, Lorenzo	??	Italy	Y	?	?	?	03/21/1892			Y	
Boner, John	38	Poland	Y	Hamburg	New York	09/14/1848	10/12/1848	1	171	N	
Bonert, Moritz	20	Baden	Y	Havre	New York	10/06/1854	04/18/1860	27	165	N	
Bonfield, Thomas	17	Ireland	N	?	New York	00/00/1882				Y	10/24/1888
Bongartz, Theodore	??	Germany	Y	?	?	?	06/23/1882				
Bonn, Adam	21	Bavaria	Y	Havre	New Orleans	12/??/1857	01/16/1861	18	64	N	
Bonn, Henry	24	Kurhessen	Y	Bremen	New York	12/19/1853	02/25/1858	16	342	N	
Bonn, William	24	Prussia	Y	Hamburg	Baltimore	02/05/1852	08/05/1856	14	343	N	
Bonnekessel, Heinrich	34	Germany	Y	Bremen	New York	07/26/1893	10/19/1895			Y	
Bonnes, John	27	Germany	Y	Marseilles	New York	01/26/1888	12/20/1890			Y	
Bonnick, Robert	46	England	Y	Liverpool	New York	04/07/1883	10/25/1886	19	84	N	
Bonnick, Robert	46	England	Y	Liverpool	New York	04/07/1873	10/25/1886			Y	
Bonnlander, Sigmund	42	Germany	Y	Antwerp	New York	10/09/1887	05/29/1890			Y	
Boogaart, Cornelius	30	Holland	Y	Rotterdam	New Orleans	07/28/1852	09/17/1858	16	166	N	
Boogard, James	36	Holland	Y	Rotterdam	New York	04/26/1890	09/28/1896			Y	
Bookhart, Valentine	??	Germany	Y	?	?	03/??/1881	10/17/1884			Y	
Booth, William H.	35	England	Y	Liverpool	Philadelphia	01/13/1896	01/14/1901			Y	
Booth, William J.	24	Ireland	Y	Liverpool	Philadelphia	04/27/1857	11/05/1860	18	12	N	
Boots, Christian	30	Bavaria	Y	Havre	New York	10/27/1826	11/16/1848	1	281	N	
Bootz, Jacob	38	Germany	Y	Rotterdam	New York	10/08/1882	06/02/1887			Y	
Bootz, Mathias	54	France	Y	Havre	New York	04/22/1854	03/25/1858	16	449	N	
Bootz, Peter Hubert	22	Germany	Y	Bremen	Jersey City	04/29/1887	05/26/1890			Y	
Bopert, John Ferdinand	32	Wurttemberg	Y	Havre	New York	10/24/1852	10/01/1856	14	130	N	
Bople, Frederick William	28	Hanover	Y	Bremen	Baltimore	10/10/1857	06/28/1860	27	14	N	
Bopp, Jacob	??	Switzerland	Y	Havre	New Orleans	05/16/1848	??/??/1851	3	221	N	
Borchard, Henry	61	Germany	N	Bremen	New York	08/12/1866	?			Y	
Borchers, Eduard	44	Germany	Y	Bremen	Baltimore	04/10/1882	12/22/1882			Y	
Borchert, Peter Hermann	28	Germany	Y	Bremen	New York	06/08/1885	04/26/1888			Y	
Borchertmeyer, Clem	33	Germany	Y	Bremen	New York	10/13/1883	06/12/1884			Y	
Borckenhagen, William	43	Mecklenburg S	Y	Hamburg	New York	11/17/1856	12/26/1859	17	525	N	
Bordanora, Agostino	34	Italy	Y	Palermo	New York	10/03/1885	10/17/1893			Y	
Bordonaro, Agostino	34	Italy	Y	Palermo	New York	10/03/1885	10/17/1893	21	17	N	
Borgelt, Caspar	22	Germany	Y	Amsterdam	New York	07/29/1882	12/01/1884			Y	
Borgelt, Frederick	30	Hanover	Y	Bremen	New York	11/02/1846	09/13/1848	22	341	N	
Borgemenke, Bernard	23	Oldenburg	Y	Bremen	New Orleans	11/20/1854	12/28/1857	16	268	N	
Borger, George	25	Germany	Y	Amsterdam	New York	10/18/1885	03/21/1889			Y	
Borger, J.	25	Germany	Y	Hamburg	New York	09/05/1881	09/17/1884			Y	
Borger, Jacob	33	Bavaria	Y	Havre	New York	07/03/1845	11/16/1848	1	304	N	
Borger, Wendel	26	Bavaria	Y	Havre	New York	07/03/1845	10/07/1848	22	487	N	
Borgerding, Frank	23	Germany	Y	Bremen	New York	09/08/1882	12/05/1884			Y	
Borgerding, Henry	28	Germany	Y	Bremen	New York	08/22/1891	10/27/1900			Y	
Borgerding, Herman	37	Germany	Y	Bremen	Baltimore	08/20/1892	09/21/1904			Y	
Borgert, Johann	42	Germany	N	Bremen	New York	03/23/1881	?			Y	
Borgert, Johann Bernard	32	Germany	Y	Bremen	New York	03/23/1881	03/??/1882			Y	
Borges, Johann	50	Germany	Y	Bremen	New York	12/25/1876	03/14/1898			Y	
Borges, John Henry	57	Germany	Y	Bremen	Baltimore	04/31/1891	12/20/1892			Y	
Borgmann, Albert	53	Germany	Y	Antwerp	New York	09/24/1891	10/27/1897			Y	
Borgmann, George	39	Germany	Y	Rotterdam	New York	10/13/1881	10/28/1897			Y	
Borgmann, Henry	26	Germany	Y	Rotterdam	New York	08/13/1881	10/10/1887			Y	
Borgmann, Joseph	28	Germany	Y	?	?	?	10/21/1874			Y	
Borgrefe, Frederick	20	Germany	Y	Bremen	New York	10/04/1880	12/24/1880			Y	
Borhorst, Henry	23	Oldenburg	Y	Bremen	Baltimore	12/06/1845	02/16/1849	23	141	N	
Bork, Alexander	31	Prussia	Y	Hamburg	New York	07/??/1851	02/14/1853	7	156	N	

CITIZENSHIP RECORDS

APPLICANT	AGE	COUNTRY OF ORIGIN	DEC	DEPART PORT	ENTRY PORT	ARRIVE DATE	DEC DATE	VOL	PG.	FLD	NAT DATE
Bork, Patrick	37	Ireland	Y	Liverpool	New Orleans	02/13/1852	10/01/1856	14	104	N	
Bormann, Frederick	23	Germany	Y	Bremen	Baltimore	05/17/1890	07/06/1891			Y	
Bormann, Henry	22	Germany	Y	Bremen	Baltimore	05/28/1891	04/10/1894			Y	
Bormann, Valentine	25	Bavaria	Y	Havre	New York	09/15/1850	12/03/1857	16	66	N	
Born, Carl August	22	Bavaria	Y	Havre	New York	12/04/18??	05/19/1854	9	446	N	
Born, Charles August	22	Bavaria	Y	Havre	New York	12/04/1851	05/19/1854	8	472	N	
Born, Henry	24	Bavaria	Y	Havre	New York	09/20/1848	10/21/1851	4	356	N	
Born, Jacob	29	Bavaria	Y	Havre	New York	05/13/1846	10/17/1851	4	321	N	
Bornemann, Herman	35	Germany	Y	Bremen	Baltimore	04/25/1884	07/14/1886			Y	
Bornhausen, Frank	60	Germany	N	Havre	Philadelphia	06/??/1863	?			Y	
Bornhorst, Heinrich	22	Germany	Y	Bremen	New York	05/10/1885	01/14/1889			Y	
Bornschein, Edward	62	Germany	N	Hamburg	New York	10/22/1853	?			Y	
Bornstein, Frederick	30	Saxony	Y	Hamburg	New York	??/19/1846	02/12/1850	2	67	N	
Borosch, Johann	??	Germany	Y	?	?	?	05/22/1893			Y	
Borr, Vincent	27	Italy	Y	Genoa	New York	05/14/1846	10/09/1854	6	129	N	
Borr, Vincent	27	Italy	Y	Genoa	New York	05/14/1846	10/09/1854	11	132	N	
Borreson, Olaf C.	??	Norway	Y	?	?	10/15/1893	01/20/1899			Y	
Borsodi, Morris	??	Austria	Y	?	?	?	05/28/1892			Y	
Borsody, Moritz	48	Austria	Y	Bremen	New York	07/28/1891	08/07/1896			Y	
Bortoli, Constanti	??	Italy	Y	?	New York	?	01/04/1893			Y	
Bortoli, Louis	38	Italy	Y	Liverpool	New York	02/16/1890	10/24/1896			Y	
Borucki, Teofil	32	Germany	Y	Hamburg	Philadelphia	03/28/180	09/03/1888			Y	
Borwick, Joseph	49	England	Y	Glasgow	New York	02/21/1876	10/30/1896			Y	
Borzer, August	32	Germany	Y	Bremen	Baltimore	02/01/1890	10/18/1894			Y	
Bos, George Bernhardt	38	Holland	Y	Amsterdam	New York	06/03/1887	09/28/1887			Y	
Bosch, Joseph Anton	32	Baden	Y	Havre	New York	09/18/1854	10/10/1854	6	199	N	
Bosch, Joseph Anton	32	Baden	Y	Havre	New York	09/18/1854	10/09/1854	11	201	N	
Bosch, Werner	25	Switzerland	Y	Havre	New York	05/22/1854	09/23/1854	12	117	N	
Bosch, William	38	Germany	Y	?	New York	??/??/1883	04/30/1884			Y	
Bosche, Henry	48	Germany	N	Bremen	New Orleans	12/??/1853	?			Y	
Boscher, Robert	32	England	Y	Liverpool	New Orleans	08/01/1850	09/18/1858	16	170	N	
Boschker, John Berend	30	Holland	Y	Rotterdam	New York	09/20/1852	05/22/1856	26	540	N	
Bosma, John M.	38	Holland	Y	Amsterdam	New York	04/18/1882	11/06/1893			Y	
Bosmhart, John (Bosmarth	39	Prussia	Y	Bremen	Galveston	07/06/1844	02/17/1849	23	149	N	
Boss, August	32	Germany	N	Hamburg	New York	06/01/1877	?			Y	
Bosse, Barney	11	Germany	N	?	Baltimore	00/00/1875				Y	10/23/1888
Bosse, George	30	Germany	Y	Bremen	New York	10/15/1897	01/28/1903			Y	
Bosse, George	38	Germany	N	Bremen	Baltimore	06/20/1868	?			Y	
Bosse, George Henry	40	Germany	Y	Bremen	Baltimore	10/28/1874	10/11/1880			Y	
Bosse, Henry	??	Germany	N	?	?	08/15/1880				Y	11/07/1892
Bosse, William	24	Hanover	Y	London	New York	11/06/1851	09/28/1854	10	297	N	
Bosse, William	24	Hanover	Y	London	New York	11/06/1851	09/28/1854	12	236	N	
Bossenberger, Joseph	50	Germany	N	Bremen	New York	08/04/1866	?			Y	
Bossenmeyer, Alois	23	Germany	Y	Havre	New York	05/03/1880	10/08/1883			Y	
Bossert, Charles	36	Germany	Y	Havre	New York	12/16/1881	03/25/1896			Y	
Boswell, William	23	Ireland	Y	?	?	06/??/1885	07/25/1885			Y	
Bosz, Paul	25	Bavaria	Y	Bremen	New York	10/04/1850	06/09/1854	10	106	N	
Bosz, Paul	25	Bavaria	Y	Bremen	New York	10/04/1850	06/09/1854	12	43	N	
Both, Robert	31	Germany	Y	Bremen	Philadelphia	05/03/1882	10/24/1892			Y	
Bothe, Bernard	27	Prussia	Y	Rotterdam	New York	11/05/1855	09/01/1857	15	210	N	
Bothwell, William	??	Ireland	Y	?	?	11/??/1880	03/22/1887			Y	
Botker, Bernard	32	Prussia	Y	Bremen	New Orleans	02/10/1856	09/14/1860	27	373	N	
Bott, Charles	25	Germany	Y	Bremen	New York	04/07/1882	11/30/1886			Y	
Bott, Charles	17	Germany	N	?	New York	00/00/1881				Y	10/16/1888
Bott, Fritz	25	Germany	Y	Antwerp	New York	01/17/1880	11/11/1885			Y	
Bott, Herman	26	germany	Y	Havre	New York	07/27/1880	09/05/1887			Y	
Bottenhorn, John Adam	22	Hesse Cassel	Y	Bremen	New York	08/26/1853	04/07/1856	26	452	N	
Botter, Henry	22	Hanover	Y	Bremen	New Orleans	01/02/1854	09/24/1858	16	141	N	
Bottle, Joseph	33	France	Y	Havre	New Orleans	11/26/1848	05/28/1852	25	125	N	

CITIZENSHIP RECORDS

APPLICANT	AGE	COUNTRY OF ORIGIN	DEC	DEPART PORT	ENTRY PORT	ARRIVE DATE	DEC DATE	VOL	PG.	FLD	NAT DATE
Bottler, Charles	32	Prussia	Y	Havre	New York	08/09/1849	02/16/1852	24	124	N	
Botzuen, Andreas	49	Bavaria	Y	Bremen	Buffalo	07/04/1847	02/01/1851	3	77	N	
Bouchonnet, Charles	39	Germany	Y	Havre	New York	08/13/1892	08/06/1900			Y	
Boucke, Henry	21	Prussia	Y	Bremen	Baltimore	10/05/1855	01/19/1856	13	486	N	
Boudel, Frank	43	Bavaria	Y	Kigland	New York	12/01/1858	12/17/1589	17	508	N	
Boudot, Louis	51	Germany	Y	Havre	New York	05/10/1880	08/30/1884			Y	
Boulger, Thomas I.	28	Ireland	Y	Liverpool	New York	07/18/1842	10/20/1852	5	28	N	
Boulter, William H.	??	England	Y	?	?	?	09/26/1889			Y	
Bouma, Sipke	48	Holland	Y	Amsterdam	New York	06/18/1881	08/23/1883			Y	
Bouquet, Fred	23	Germany	Y	Bremen	New York	05/08/1888	10/27/1893			Y	
Bouquet, Fred	40	Germany	Y	Bremen	New York	02/05/1881	01/28/1884			Y	
Bour, Franz	24	France	Y	Havre	New York	06/27/1858	03/24/1850	27	138	N	
Bourgmgnon, Joseph	45	Prussia	Y	Havre	New Orleans	12/??/1847	??/??/1851	3	224	N	
Bourke, Dennis	23	Ireland	Y	Liverpool	Boston	09/02/1854	09/01/1857	15	216	N	
Bourke, John	21	Ireland	Y	Liverpool	New Orleans	12/25/1849	03/22/1850	2	235	N	
Bourke, Michael	26	Ireland	Y	Galway	Boston	06/07/1846	03/18/1851	3	302	N	
Bourke, Thomas	26	Ireland	Y	Liverpool	New York	05/19/1849	03/22/1850	2	236	N	
Bovare, Valentine	28	Bavaria	Y	Havre	New York	06/01/1846	08/02/1848	22	37	N	
Bowers, Frederick	23	Hanover	Y	Bremen	New Orleans	12/23/1845	10/14/1848	1	227	N	
Bowers, Robert	26	Ireland	Y	London	New York	01/04/1854	01/11/1856	13	447	N	
Bowes, James	36	Ireland	Y	Liverpool	New York	05/28/1843	10/02/1848	1	23	N	
Bowie, David	??	England	Y	?	?	?	11/10/1888			Y	
Bowie, Donald	29	Scotland	Y	Liverpool	Philadelphia	07/15/1851	08/24/1855	11	489	N	
Bowing, Herman Henry	26	Hanover	Y	Bremen	Baltimore	??/24/1844	01/09/1850	23	486	N	
Bowley, Charles George	40	England	Y	Portsmouth	New York	09/??/1841	04/23/1855	11	285	N	
Bowmann, Meron	26	France	Y	Havre	New York	12/18/1882	10/28/1886			Y	
Box, William	25	Ireland	Y	Dublin	Philadelphia	05/24/1855	11/08/1858	17	305	N	
Boxleiter, Ludwig F.	52	Germany	N	Bremen	Baltimore	08/??/1850	?			Y	
Boyd, Benjamin	21	Ireland	Y	Liverpool	New York	07/09/1854	03/04/1857	15	60	N	
Boyd, Edward	32	Ireland	Y	Belfast	New York	07/17/1850	10/29/1858	17	186	N	
Boyd, Leonard	35	Germany	N	Bremen	New York	08/18/1867	?			Y	
Boyd, M. William	22	Ireland	Y	Cork	New York	04/13/1860	05/07/1860	27	185	N	
Boyd, William	65	Scotland	N	Glasgow	Philadelphia	??/??/1856	?			Y	
Boylan, William	21	Ireland	Y	Liverpool	New York	09/15/1853	03/07/1853	7	297	N	
Boyle, Alexander	57	Ireland	N	Liverpool	New York	12/??/1848	?			Y	
Boyle, Charles	26	Ireland	Y	Liverpool	Boston	01/30/1852	07/29/1862	18	380	N	
Boyle, Charles	43	England	Y	Liverpool	New York	03/10/1866	03/25/1889			Y	
Boyle, Daniel	27	Ireland	Y	Liverpool	New York	05/29/1847	11/29/1852	5	360	N	
Boyle, Francis	22	Ireland	Y	Liverpool	New York	09/15/1851	05/25/1854	8	535	N	
Boyle, Francis	22	Ireland	Y	Liverpool	New York	09/15/1851	05/25/1854	9	409	N	
Boyle, John J.	23	Ireland	Y	Queenstown	New York	03/31/1880	10/19/1887			Y	
Boyle, Patrick	27	Ireland	Y	Westport	New York	10/10/1848	05/01/1854	8	296	N	
Boyle, Patrick	27	Ireland	Y	Westport	New York	10/10/1848	05/01/1854	9	168	N	
Boyle, Robert	21	Ireland	Y	Belfast	Charleston	10/20/1845	06/24/1851	3	449	N	
Boyus, Gottlob	37	Wurttemberg	Y	Amsterdam	New York	01/06/1850	01/08/1853	5	534	N	
Brabant, Herman	42	Germany	Y	Hamburg	New York	05/00/1873	10/29/1888			Y	
Bracewell, John	21	England	Y	Liverpool	Philadelphia	02/22/1894	05/18/1895			Y	
Brach, Ludwig	28	Germany	Y	?	New York	08/27/1880	05/24/1883			Y	
Brach, Theodore	37	Germany	Y	Bremen	New York	10/30/1871	10/02/1884			Y	
Brackemeyer, Arnold	27	Prussia	Y	Bremen	Baltimore	12/10/1848	10/05/1854	10	450	N	
Brackemeyer, Arnold	27	Prussia	Y	Bremen	Baltimore	12/10/1848	10/05/1854	12	389	N	
Brackland, Arnold Henry	26	Hanover	Y	Bremen	New Orleans	01/08/1854	03/04/1856	26	158	N	
Brackmann, Joseph J.	??	Prussia	Y	?	?	?	10/11/1880			Y	
Brackmann, Ludwig	22	Germany	Y	Rotterdam	New York	11/01/1882	06/29/1884			Y	
Brackmann, Otto	22	Germany	Y	Amsterdam	New York	05/20/1891	02/16/1892			Y	
Brackmann, Theodore	23	Germany	Y	Bremen	New York	06/02/1881	01/06/1883			Y	
Brackmann, William	35	Germany	Y	Antwerp	New York	04/16/1885	07/05/1898			Y	
Brackrogge, Carl	29	Prussia	Y	Hamburg	New York	12/05/1853	10/09/1854	6	83	N	
Brackrogge, Charles	29	Prussia	Y	Hamburg	New York	12/05/1853	10/09/1854	11	86	N	

CITIZENSHIP RECORDS

APPLICANT	AGE	COUNTRY OF ORIGIN	DEC	DEPART PORT	ENTRY PORT	ARRIVE DATE	DEC DATE	VOL	PG.	FLD	NAT DATE
Bradburry, Vincent C.	28	England	Y	Liverpool	New Orleans	06/05/1848	10/09/1854	6	130	N	
Bradbury, Vincent C.	28	England	Y	Liverpool	New Orleans	06/05/1848	10/09/1854	11	133	N	
Brademeier, Frederick	62	Germany	N	Bremen	New Orleans	12/??/1851	?			Y	
Bradford, Alexander	44	Ireland	Y	Liverpool	New York	03/01/1848	04/02/1853	7	501	N	
Bradford, John	26	Ireland	Y	Belfast	Philadelphia	??/12/1847	11/??/1849	23	317	N	
Bradford, Robert	48	Ireland	Y	Liverpool	New York	08/??/1845	09/23/1854	10	179	N	
Bradford, Robert	48	Ireland	Y	Liverpool	New York	08/??/1845	09/23/1854	12	118	N	
Bradke, Charles	27	Germany	Y	?	New York	04/??/1893	03/12/1894			Y	
Bradley, Michael	30	Ireland	Y	London	New York	12/30/1847	11/02/1852	5	190	N	
Bradley, Michael	30	Ireland	Y	London	New York	12/30/1847	11/02/1852	6	316	N	
Bradley, Patrick	25	Ireland	Y	Liverpool	New Orleans	12/05/1849	09/29/1856	14	437	N	
Bradley, Thomas	28	Ireland	Y	London	Boston	05/28/1846	05/26/1852	25	117	N	
Bradley, Timothy	26	Ireland	Y	London	New York	07/04/1847	04/05/1852	24	393	N	
Bradshan, Martin C.	25	Ireland	Y	Liverpool	New York	07/09/1847	02/10/1851	3	108	N	
Brady, G. W.	47	Ireland	N	Liverpool	New York	07/16/1853	?			Y	
Brady, Hugh	26	Ireland	Y	Liverpool	New York	05/13/1846	08/19/1848	22	209	N	
Brady, Matt	60	Ireland	N	?	New Orleans	05/??/1850				Y	
Brady, Michael	35	Ireland	Y	Liverpool	New York	06/05/1851	02/02/1856	26	5	N	
Brady, Patrick	17	Ireland	N	New Rossau	Burlington,	00/00/1842				Y	10/20/1892
Brady, Peter	31	Ireland	Y	Liverpool	New Orleans	04/??/1851	04/24/1855	11	288	N	
Brady, Philip	47	Ireland	Y	Liverpool	Oswego	09/??/1849	05/17/1854	8	466	N	
Brady, Philip	47	Ireland	Y	Liverpool	Oswego	09/??/1849	05/17/1854	9	340	N	
Brady, Simon	30	Ireland	Y	Liverpool	New Orleans	??/14/1851	04/24/1855	11	289	N	
Braehmann, Henry	26	Prussia	Y	Bremen	Baltimore	12/03/1847	06/15/1852	25	272	N	
Braemer, Henry Christ	32	Brunswick	Y	Bremen	Baltimore	04/25/1849	03/13/1851	3	263	N	
Braemming, Gottlieb	33	Germany	Y	Antwerp	Philadelphia	09/26/1886	10/05/1896			Y	
Braeninger, Michael	30	Baden	Y	New York	New York	08/02/1853	10/29/1858	17	182	N	
Braeuer, Ernst Moritz	43	Germany	Y	Rotterdam	New York	07/24/1882	09/21/1887			Y	
Braeunning, Martin	40	Germany	Y	Bremen	New York	??/??/1872	04/25/1888			Y	
Brahm, Bernard	54	Hanover	Y	Bremen	New Orleans	01/01/1847	10/01/1856	14	123	N	
Brahm, Henry	58	Hanover	Y	Bremen	New Orleans	12/24/1852	11/01/1858	17	214	N	
Brahm, John Bernard	28	Hanover	Y	Bremen	New Orleans	12/24/1852	09/11/1855	13	4	N	
Braidmeyer, Jacob	23	Bavaria	Y	Havre	New York	01/01/1860	10/08/1860	27	431	N	
Brake, William	41	Germany	N	Liverpool	New York	01/??/1867	?			Y	
Brakenmann, Henry	30	Prussia	Y	Bremen	New Orleans	12/23/1846	09/10/1852	25	444	N	
Brakensieck, Fred Willia	30	Hanover	Y	Bremen	New Orleans	12/28/1842	02/17/1849	23	162	N	
Bramkamp, Bernard	56	Germany	Y	Bremen	Baltimore	09/30/1872	10/25/1899			Y	
Bramkamp, William	23	Hanover	Y	Bremen	New Orleans	11/11/1847	02/27/1852	24	177	N	
Bramsche, Frederick Ferd	31	Hanover	Y	Bremen	Buffalo	07/02/1847	06/26/1851	3	458	N	
Bramscher, Henry	22	Hanover	Y	Bremen	New Orleans	11/26/1853	10/06/1854	10	503	N	
Bramscher, Henry	22	Hanover	Y	Bremen	New Orleans	11/26/1853	10/06/1854	12	442	N	
Branch, William	28	Germany	Y	Bremen	Baltimore	07/24/1881	04/06/1885			Y	
Brand, Franz Huge	31	Germany	Y	Hamburg	New York	09/05/1890	08/21/1893			Y	
Brand, George Ambrose	??	England	Y	?	?	?	09/06/1876			Y	
Brand, Henry	28	Germany	Y	Hanover	New York	06/05/1890	08/29/1890			Y	
Brand, Hermann Frederick	22	Hanover	Y	Bremen	New York	09/27/1853	01/18/1856	13	484	N	
Brand, John D.	59	Germany	N	Bremen	Baltimore	06/29/1845	?			Y	
Brand, John Henry	23	Oldenburg	Y	Bremen	Baltimore	12/??/1848	12/14/1850	2	365	N	
Brand, Peter	34	Bavaria	Y	Havre	New York	10/21/1858	11/01/1860	27	526	N	
Brandburger, Adolf	23	Germany	Y	Bremen	Baltimore	01/06/1882	10/13/1885			Y	
Branden, Jeffries Robert	48	Holland	N	Bremen	New York	09/03/1863	10/18/1876	28	421	N	10/??/1876
Brandenburg, Cornelius	71	Holland	Y	Rotterdam	New York	03/25/1872	09/26/1894			Y	
Branderhoff, John	31	Holland	Y	Bremen	New Orleans	12/16/1845	08/15/1848	22	152	N	
Brandert, Leon	??	Rumania	Y	?	?	?	05/11/1902			Y	
Brandes, Louis	28	Germany	Y	Hamburg	New York	11/14/1883	02/07/1889			Y	
Brandhorst, William	26	Germany	Y	Bremen	New York	04/10/1884	04/25/1892			Y	
Brandhorst, William	26	Germany	Y	Bremen	New York	11/01/1878	06/26/1886			Y	
Brandhuber, Sebastian	33	Wurttemberg	Y	Havre	New Orleans	12/20/1853	10/09/1854	6	59	N	
Brandhuber, Sebastian	33	Wurttemberg	Y	Havre	New Orleans	12/20/1853	10/09/1854	11	60	N	

CITIZENSHIP RECORDS

APPLICANT	AGE	COUNTRY OF ORIGIN	DEC	DEPART PORT	ENTRY PORT	ARRIVE DATE	DEC DATE	VOL	PG.	FLD	NAT DATE
Brandis, Wm	24	Germany	Y	Antwerp	New York	07/03/1884	05/02/1887			Y	
Brandner, Anton	33	Prussia	Y	Bremen	New Orleans	05/22/1852	02/10/1857	15	13	N	
Brandner, Anton	25	Austria	Y	Bremen	Baltimore	09/14/1881	12/04/1884			Y	
Brandner, John	26	Bavaria	Y	Hamburg	Buffalo	08/01/1847	12/16/1851	4	527	N	
Brandner, Vincenze	56	Austira	Y	Bremen	Baltimore	09/16/1881	09/09/1891			Y	
Brandstatler, Ignatz	23	Baden	Y	Havre	New York	06/26/1847	07/14/1851	3	533	N	
Brandstatter, Isidore	31	Baden	Y	Havre	New York	11/18/1849	08/11/1860	27	262	N	
Brandt, Carl F.	67	Germany	N	Bremen	Baltimore	06/31/1839	??/??/1840	28	13	N	10/??/1844
Brandt, Carl J.	19	Germany	N	Bremen	Baltimore	06/31/1839	00/00/1840			Y	10/00/1844
Brandt, George	23	Germany	Y	Havre	New York	02/05/1884	04/14/1887			Y	
Brandt, John	29	Germany	Y	Rotterdam	New York	05/06/1884	05/24/1889			Y	
Brandt, Jules	24	Germany	Y	Havre	New York	02/05/1884	11/03/1886			Y	
Brandt, Richard	??	Prussia	Y	?	?	?	03/17/1885			Y	
Brangan, George H.	17	Ireland	N	?	New York	00/00/1882				Y	10/27/1888
Brangan, Robert C.	30	Ireland	Y	Queenstown	New York	05/11/1883	01/31/1889			Y	
Brangel, Adam	34	Bavaria	Y	Bremen	New York	10/14/1847	06/25/1851	3	451	N	
Brangenberg, Joseph	27	Prussia	Y	Antwerp	New York	07/01/1852	10/22/1857	15	473	N	
Branigan, Patrick	28	England	Y	Liverpool	New York	11/27/1881	10/22/1889	19	247	N	
Branigan, Patrick	28	England	Y	Liverpool	New York	12/27/1881	10/22/1889			Y	
Branitz, Frederick	23	Prussia	Y	Bremen	New York	09/04/1854	09/29/1856	14	11	N	
Brank, Frank	22	Bavaria	Y	Havre	New Orleans	02/02/1852	10/09/1854	6	75	N	
Brank, Frank	22	Bavaria	Y	Havre	New Orleans	02/02/1852	10/09/1854	11	76	N	
Brankamp, Joseph	43	Germany	Y	Amsterdam	New York	05/19/1890	02/29/1896			Y	
Brankensieck, Henry	41	Germany	Y	Bremen	New York	05/10/1868	09/29/1884			Y	
Branksick, Henry	33	Germany	Y	Bremen	Baltimore	08/11/1881	04/29/1885			Y	
Brann, Charles	23	Germany	Y	Bremen	Baltimore	08/28/1886	09/16/1889			Y	
Brannan, Pat	16	Ireland	N	?	Boston	00/00/1855				Y	10/26/1888
Brannan, Patrick	29	Ireland	Y	Liverpool	New York	07/28/1886	03/24/1890			Y	
Brannard, John	32	Wurttemberg	Y	Havre	New York	05/25/1849	03/13/1851	3	265	N	
Branno, Louis	53	Italy	Y	?	New York	??/??/1873	04/06/1887			Y	
Brannon, John	32	England	Y	Liverpool	New York	09/08/1848	06/03/1854	9	479	N	
Brannon, John	32	England	Y	Liverpool	New York	09/08/1848	06/03/1854	10	62	N	
Brass, Edward	36	Prussia	Y	?	?	02/??/1872	03/02/1882			Y	
Brater, John Frederick	29	Bavaria	Y	Bremen	Baltimore	05/16/1850	04/12/1852	24	479	N	
Braudy, L.	34	Russia	Y	Hamburg	New York	07/??/1886	10/31/1892			Y	
Brauer, A.G.	28	Germany	Y	?	New York	12/??/1890	03/05/1896			Y	
Brauer, Emil	37	Germany	Y	?	New York	04/??/1894	05/15/1895			Y	
Brauer, Frank J.	63	Germany	Y	Rotterdam	New Orleans	??/??/1858	10/12/1885			Y	
Braum August	??	Germany	Y	?	?	?	11/04/1891			Y	
Braum, Bernard	26	Prussia	Y	Bremen	Baltimore	01/24/1849	11/01/1852	6	308	N	
Braun, Adam	33	Germany	Y	Bremen	New York	10/01/1881	11/22/1884			Y	
Braun, Albert	25	Baden	Y	Havre	New Orleans	07/??/1848	12/20/1852	5	429	N	
Braun, Alexander	33	Germany	Y	Bremen	New York	11/30/1870	01/06/1883			Y	
Braun, Andrew A.	28	Canada	Y	Toronto	Port Huron	04/02/1891	04/23/1896			Y	
Braun, Anthony	30	Baden	Y	Havre	New Orleans	04/10/1850	03/01/1858	16	348	N	
Braun, Apolonia	68	Germany	Y	Havre	New York	05/??/1870	03/13/1884			Y	
Braun, August	27	Germany	Y	Havre	New York	12/07/1890	10/19/1894			Y	
Braun, Bernard	26	Prussia	Y	Bremen	Baltimore	01/24/1849	11/01/1852	5	182	N	
Braun, Charles Eduard	27	Canada	Y	?	Port Huron	02/26/1891	03/02/1897			Y	
Braun, Charles F.	28	Germany	Y	Hamburg	Baltimore	12/21/1882	10/13/1886			Y	
Braun, Conrad	29	Bavaria	Y	Rotterdam	New York	08/21/1854	12/27/1855	13	376	N	
Braun, Francis Anthony	56	France	Y	Havre	New York	06/19/1853	03/25/1858	16	448	N	
Braun, Frederick	25	Lippe Detmol	Y	Bremen	New Orleans	??/31/1847	12/03/1849	23	388	N	
Braun, Friederich	24	Germany	Y	Antwerp	New York	03/21/1891	03/31/1894			Y	
Braun, George	24	Bavaria	Y	Havre	New York	06/22/1852	05/29/1854	9	446	N	
Braun, George	24	Bavaria	Y	Havre	New York	06/23/1852	05/29/1854	10	29	N	
Braun, George	33	Baden	Y	Antwerp	New York	08/11/1853	09/16/1857	15	278	N	
Braun, George	38	Baden	Y	Havre	New Orleans	01/05/1856	05/08/1862	18	309	N	
Braun, Guegorius	45	Germany	N	Havre	New Orleans	12/??/1868	?			Y	

CITIZENSHIP RECORDS

APPLICANT	AGE	COUNTRY OF ORIGIN	DEC	DEPART PORT	ENTRY PORT	ARRIVE DATE	DEC DATE	VOL	PG.	FLD	NAT DATE
Braun, Herman	30	Lippe Detmol	Y	Bremen	New Orleans	12/??/1847	12/??/1849	23	377	N	
Braun, Jacob	26	Bavaria	Y	Havre	New Orleans	04/14/1858	03/20/1862	18	275	N	
Braun, Jacob	30	Germany	Y	Bremen	New York	08/03/1888	03/28/1892			Y	
Braun, Jacob	32	Germany	Y	Antwerp	New York	12/02/1888	10/24/1896			Y	
Braun, John	36	Wurttemberg	Y	Bremerhafen	New Orleans	01/28/1853	01/02/1861	18	42	N	
Braun, John E.	??	Germany	Y	?	?	03/20/1883	11/07/1887			Y	
Braun, Joseph	26	Hungary	Y	Bremen	Baltimore	04/01/1886	04/08/1890			Y	
Braun, Karl	27	Germany	Y	Havre	New York	09/29/1880	02/28/1882			Y	
Braun, Karl	31	Germany	Y	Havre	New York	05/08/1887	08/22/1892			Y	
Braun, M.	31	Germany	Y	Bremen	Baltimore	01/26/1884	10/28/1886			Y	
Braun, Richard	41	Germany	Y	Havre	New York	06/25/1879	09/24/1890			Y	
Braun, Urban	22	Baden	Y	Antwerp	New York	08/16/1852	09/27/1854	10	253	N	
Braun, Urban	22	Baden	Y	Antwerp	New York	08/16/1852	09/27/1854	12	192	N	
Braun, Valentine	36	Baden	Y	Havre	New Orleans	08/20/1847	06/15/1852	25	273	N	
Braun, William	59	Germany	Y	London	New York	09/07/1854	10/06/1884			Y	
Braunling, Frank	??	Bavaria	Y	Havre	New Orleans	05/12/18??	10/09/1848	1	66	N	
Braunschweiger, A.	21	Germany	Y	Havre	Boston	09/02/1882	12/17/1884			Y	
Brausch, Peter	51	Prussia	Y	Antwerp	New York	08/03/1846	08/16/1855	11	442	N	
Braymeyer, Bernhard	27	Baden	Y	Havre	New York	05/25/1847	03/14/1850	2	196	N	
Brazil, John	26	Ireland	Y	Waterford	Burlington	06/??/1848	06/02/1854	9	478	N	
Brazil, John	26	Ireland	Y	Waterford	Burlington	06/??/1848	06/02/1854	10	61	N	
Brechtel, George	35	Germany	Y	Bremen	New York	11/21/1889	10/15/1895			Y	
Breck, Nicholas	21	France	Y	Havre	New York	05/06/1852	08/23/1852	25	336	N	
Breckheimer, Paul	45	Germany	Y	Havre	New Orleans	11/01/1871	06/02/1883			Y	
Bredel, William	33	England	Y	London	New York	09/20/1843	01/08/1851	2	476	N	
Bredemeier, Ferdinand	33	Prussia	Y	Bremen	New Orleans	12/20/1853	09/10/1860	27	352	N	
Bredemeier, Gottlieb	35	Prussia	Y	Bremen	New Orleans	07/12/1851	07/11/1855	11	377	N	
Bredenberg, Frederick	32	Hanover	Y	Bremen	New Orleans	11/27/1852	02/12/1856	26	75	N	
Bredenberg, Henry	23	Hanover	Y	Bremen	New Orleans	10/22/1854	10/05/1857	15	349	N	
Bredenforder, Charles	21	Germany	Y	Bremen	New York	10/10/1880	09/29/1882			Y	
Bredestege, Joseph	38	Prussia	Y	Bremen	Baltimore	01/03/1854	12/16/1857	16	225	N	
Bredinger, John	74	Germany	N	Germany	New Orleans	06/10/1840	??/??/1843	28	292	N	10/12/1846
Breeck, John Conrad	41	Germany	Y	Bremen	Baltimore	05/17/1873	08/15/1891			Y	
Breen, James	48	Ireland	Y	Londonderry	New York	08/14/1869	10/11/1886			Y	
Breen, Patrick	33	Ireland	Y	Queenstown	New York	05/21/1892	10/13/1899			Y	
Breen, Patrick	66	Ireland	N	Liverpool	Boston	01/04/1853	?			Y	
Breen, Peter	45	Ireland	N	Queenstown	New York	03/??/1861	?			Y	
Breen, William	44	Ireland	Y	New Ross	Buffalo	07/??/1844	02/06/1860	27	91	N	
Breese, David	29	Wales	Y	Liverpool	New York	07/07/1847	06/14/1851	3	378	N	
Bregear, Christoph	44	France	Y	Havre	New Orleans	01/14/1846	05/16/1854	8	448	N	
Bregenzer, Marcus	23	Wurttemberg	Y	Havre	New York	05/07/1854	08/17/1857	15	143	N	
Bregier, Christoph	44	France	Y	Havre	New Orleans	01/14/1846	05/16/1854	9	321	N	
Brehm, Charles	27	Bavaria	Y	Havre	New York	07/07/1848	09/20/1852			Y	03/27/1855
Brehm, George	21	Hesse Darmsta	Y	Havre	New York	10/21/1851	05/26/1854	9	424	N	
Brehm, George	21	Hesse Darmsta	Y	Havre	New York	10/21/1851	05/26/1854	10	6	N	
Brehme, Rudolf	33	Germany	Y	Hamburg	Philadelphia	07/16/1881	12/31/1889			Y	
Breibach, Robert	25	Prussia	Y	Bremen	New York	08/06/1852	11/08/1852	5	253	N	
Breidenstein, Henry	31	Hesse Cassel	Y	Bremen	New York	06/04/1846	07/02/1851	3	477	N	
Breier, John	24	Germany	Y	Bremen	Baltimore	06/07/1892	08/21/1893			Y	
Breig, Joseph	43	Germany	Y	Havre	New York	07/06/1883	11/02/1886			Y	
Breiling, Arnold	25	Prussia	Y	Rotterdam	New York	08/01/1850	03/01/1852	24	188	N	
Breisacher, William	27	Germany	Y	Antwerp	New York	02/05/1882	03/07/1885			Y	
Breitenbach, John	53	Hesse Cassel	Y	Bremen	New York	09/15/1837	02/12/1849	23	59	N	
Breitenback, Frederick	40	Hesse Cassel	Y	Bremen	New York	06/09/1847	?	23	58	N	
Breitenbucher, Gottfried	??	Germany	Y	?	?	?	05/03/1884			Y	
Breitenbuecher, Charles	45	Germany	Y	Rotterdam	New York	07/09/1882	12/24/1888			Y	
Breitenfeldt, Carl	28	Germany	Y	Bremen	New York	07/19/1893	04/23/1898			Y	
Breiter, Gustav	29	Germany	Y	Bremen	Baltimore	06/17/1882	12/02/1885			Y	
Breitholle, William	33	Germany	Y	Bremen	Baltimore	09/04/1884	04/14/1893			Y	

CITIZENSHIP RECORDS

APPLICANT	AGE	COUNTRY OF ORIGIN	DEC	DEPART PORT	ENTRY PORT	ARRIVE DATE	DEC DATE	VOL	PG.	FLD	NAT DATE
Breiting, F.E.	30	Germany	Y	Havre	New York	07/06/1881	11/26/1883			Y	
Breius, Charles	23	Germany	Y	?	New York	??/??/1886	10/26/1888			Y	
Brekelhaus, Jake	37	Russia	Y	Hamburg	Philadelphia	07/10/1881	05/??/1883	28	102	N	
Brekelhous, Jake	32	Russia	Y	Hamburg	Philadelphia	07/10/1881	05/00/1883			Y	
Brekerbohm, Wilhelm	33	Germany	Y	Bremen	New York	06/07/1881	11/01/1886			Y	
Brelage, Lucas Anton	35	Hanover	Y	Bremen	Boston	01/??/1845	09/19/1855	13	72	N	
Brellert, Fritz	26	Germany	Y	Rotterdam	New York	10/03/1881	10/25/1889			Y	
Brem, Jacob	30	Prussia	Y	Antwerp	New York	??/18/1847	02/05/1851	3	98	N	
Bremen, Edward	28	Ireland	Y	Liverpool	New York	05/28/1851	12/23/1852	5	442	N	
Bremen, Herman Henry	29	Prussia	Y	Bremen	Baltimore	07/03/1848	02/21/1849	23	239	N	
Bremer, Fred	24	Germany	Y	Bremen	New York	10/??/1881	01/16/1886			Y	
Bremer, Frederick	30	Prussia	Y	Antwerp	New York	05/04/1849	01/13/1851	2	484	N	
Bremer, Henry	35	Germany	Y	Bremen	New York	06/06/1883	12/28/1887			Y	
Bremer, Peter John	40	Holland	Y	Amsterdam	New York	04/28/1881	05/05/1885			Y	
Bremer, Philipp Adam	25	Baden	Y	Havre	New York	12/04/1857	12/26/1857	16	264	N	
Bremer, Stephan Henry	25	Prussia	Y	Bremen	Baltimore	??/25/1848	02/21/1849	23	238	N	
Bremke, Diederick	34	Hanover	Y	Bremen	New Orleans	01/01/1856	12/26/1859	17	524	N	
Bremmer, Charles	??	Germany	Y	?	?	?	11/19/1888			Y	
Brendamour, Francis	30	Bavaria	Y	Havre	New York	02/08/1853	12/07/1858	17	383	N	
Brendel, John	39	Germany	Y	Bremen	New York	04/21/1883	10/05/1886			Y	
Brender, Ernst Raymond	29	Bohemia, Aust	Y	Bremen	New York	10/18/1868	01/04/1872	18	449	N	
Brennan, James	26	Ireland	Y	Liverpool	New Orleans	02/28/1852	10/06/1856	14	240	N	
Brennan, John	31	England	Y	Liverpool	New York	04/05/1850	10/12/1857	15	405	N	
Brennan, Lawrence	42	Ireland	Y	Londonderry	New York	04/19/1868	11/07/1890			Y	
Brennan, Pat	??	?	Y	?	New York	03/??/1882	01/22/1890			Y	
Brennan, Timothy	27	Ireland	Y	Tralle	Buffalo	09/15/1853	10/12/1860	27	487	N	
Brenneman, Jacob	16	Germany	N	?	Baltimore	00/00/1881				Y	10/20/1886
Brennemann, Chris	30	Germany	Y	Bremen	New York	07/27/1892	08/31/1899			Y	
Brennen, George John	27	England	Y	Liverpool	New York	03/??/1852	04/23/1855	11	281	N	
Brenner, Bernhard	30	Germany	Y	Bremen	New York	08/05/1887	10/23/1893			Y	
Brenner, Charles John	25	Wurttemberg	Y	Antwerp	New York	10/01/1849	10/18/1852	5	13	N	
Brenner, John	26	Germany	Y	Bremen	New York	07/03/1883	11/26/1883			Y	
Brenner, John	68	Germany	N	Rotterdam	New York	08/07/1852	?			Y	
Brenner, John Christoph	27	Baden	Y	Havre	New York	12/10/1853	01/31/1856	13	529	N	
Brenner, Ludwig	33	Germany	Y	Bremen	Baltimore	10/29/1883	06/09/1894			Y	
Brent, John	32	Bavaria	Y	Bremen	Baltimore	06/25/1847	04/04/1853	7	526	N	
Brenzikhofer, Emil	34	Switzerland	Y	Antwerp	New York	10/17/1893	12/06/1902			Y	
Breslauer, Berthold	35	Germany	Y	Hamburg	New York	07/22/1886	03/29/1894			Y	
Bresnan, Daniel	24	Ireland	Y	Tralee	New York	05/01/1852	05/22/1854	8	484	N	
Bresnan, Daniel	24	Ireland	Y	Tralee	New York	05/01/1852	05/20/1854	9	358	N	
Brester, John	28	Hanover	Y	Bremen	New York	12/06/1857	07/10/1862	18	373	N	
Brester, Philipp	39	Russia	Y	Bremen	New York	04/21/1892	10/29/1900			Y	
Bretthauer, Fred Wm	??	Germany	Y	?	?	?	02/10/1891			Y	
Brettmann, William	28	Hanover	Y	Bremen	New York	08/15/1850	05/10/1852	25	2	N	
Bretz, William	28	Kurhessen	Y	Bremen	New York	06/05/1846	09/30/1856	14	65	N	
Breuer, Frederick	30	Prussia	Y	Bremen	Baltimore	05/26/1853	08/04/1856	14	319	N	
Breuer, Wm	26	Germany	Y	Antwerp	New York	11/19/1881	10/26/1886			Y	
Breuleux, Philip	28	France	Y	Havre	New York	06/15/1850	12/02/1858	17	371	N	
Breving, John	27	Germany	Y	Bremen	Baltimore	06/03/1891	02/06/1894			Y	
Breving, William	27	Germany	Y	Bremen	New York	02/20/1893	08/14/1894			Y	
Brewer, James	26	Ireland	Y	Liverpool	New York	07/15/1852	01/08/1856	13	432	N	
Brewer, Philip	25	Ireland	Y	Liverpool	New Orleans	12/??/1850	03/17/1853	7	340	N	
Brewer., Philip	62	Ireland	N	Liverpool	New Orleans	12/??/1849	?			Y	
Brian, August	46	Germany	Y	Hamburg	New York	11/11/1885	09/06/1890			Y	
Bribeck, Harbert	25	Prussia	Y	Bremen	New York	08/06/1852	11/08/1852	6	377	N	
Brichta, Michael	42	Germany	Y	Amsterdam	New York	05/02/1877	02/02/1903			Y	
Brickler, Andrew	44	France	Y	Havre	Baltimore	07/27/1846	08/23/1848	22	234	N	
Brickley, James	??	?	N	?	?	?	?			Y	
Brickwedde, Henry	33	Hanover	Y	Bremen	Baltimore	10/28/1855	10/28/1858	17	165	N	

CITIZENSHIP RECORDS

APPLICANT	AGE	COUNTRY OF ORIGIN	DEC	DEPART PORT	ENTRY PORT	ARRIVE DATE	DEC DATE	VOL	PG.	FLD	NAT DATE
Brickwede, John B,	33	Germany	Y	Bremen	New York	09/05/1882	09/22/1886			Y	
Brickweg, Bernard	27	Germany	Y	Bremen	Baltimore	08/27/1884	10/18/1887			Y	
Brickweg, Henry	38	Germany	Y	Bremen	New York	03/28/1867	03/11/1882			Y	
Brickweg, Joseph	37	Germany	Y	Amsterdam	New York	04/??/1871	10/19/1888			Y	
Bridgeland, Daniel	27	England	Y	London	New York	05/04/1849	04/18/1854	8	197	N	
Bridgeland, Daniel	27	England	Y	London	New York	05/04/1849	??/??/1854	9	68	N	
Bridgeland, James W.	29	England	Y	London	New York	11/25/1848	04/18/1854	8	198	N	
Bridgeland, James W.	29	England	Y	London	New York	11/25/1848	04/18/1854	9	69	N	
Briegel, Charles	40	Germany	Y	Bremen	New York	05/15/1867	02/16/1882			Y	
Briehler, Joseph	35	France	Y	Havre	New Orleans	05/02/1847	04/20/1850	3	3	N	
Briel, Charles	22	Germany	Y	Rotterdam	New York	10/11/1881	10/13/1883			Y	
Briel, Fridolin	29	Germany	Y	Rotterdam	New York	10/11/1883	02/12/1887			Y	
Brielmayer, Leonidas	35	Baden	Y	Havre	New Orleans	12/20/1852	09/26/1857	15	322	N	
Briese, Fried.	??	Germany	Y	?	?	?	05/21/1891			Y	
Brigel, Jacob	28	Wurttemberg	Y	Havre	New York	08/15/1856	11/11/1858	17	319	N	
Brill, Andreas	32	Bavaria	Y	Havre	New York	06/14/1843	04/06/1852	24	405	N	
Brill, John Claus	28	Hesse Cassel	Y	Bremen	Philadelphia	05/??/1848	01/02/1851	2	440	N	
Brill, Louis	41	Germany	Y	Havre	New York	05/02/1880	03/06/1899			Y	
Brill, Samuel	31	France	Y	Havre	New Orleans	08/22/1847	01/21/1860	27	66	N	
Brill, Simon	34	Germany	Y	Hamburg	New York	09/14/1883	10/03/1892			Y	
Brillert, John	24	Germany	Y	Antwerp	New York	10/04/1882	07/26/1889			Y	
Brillmaeyer, Rudolf	29	Germany	Y	Antwerp	New York	03/22/1880	08/10/1887			Y	
Brimick, Wenzel	57	Germany	Y	Hamburg	New York	10/22/1872	10/22/1891	19	339	N	
Brinck, H.	41	Germany	Y	Bremen	New York	09/27/1866	10/08/1880			Y	
Brinckmann, Henry	32	Bremen	Y	Bremen	Baltimore	09/06/1854	09/22/1854	10	157	N	
Brinckmann, Henry	32	Bremen	Y	Bremen	Baltimore	09/06/1854	09/22/1854	12	96	N	
Brinckmann, Henry	36	Germany	Y	Bremen	New York	03/27/1880	02/05/1885			Y	
Brinckmann, Wilhelm	24	Hanover	Y	Bremen	Baltimore	09/18/1852	10/01/1856	14	133	N	
Brinckmeier, Henry	28	Hanover	Y	Bremen	Baltimore	??/04/1846	12/19/1850	2	376	N	
Brindasso, John B.	51	Italy	Y	?	New York	12/??/1868	10/04/1889			Y	
Brine, Frank M.	??	England	Y	?	?	05/03/1886	05/01/1889			Y	
Bringelman, John	21	Oldenburg	Y	Bremen	New York	11/19/1846	01/??/1850	23	460	N	
Brinick, Wenzel	57	Austria	Y	Hamburg	New York	10/22/1872	10/22/1891			Y	
Brink, Hermann Edward	30	Hanover	Y	Bremen	Baltimore	05/27/1857	08/15/1860	27	276	N	
Brink, John Hermann	21	Hanover	Y	Bremen	Baltimore	11/18/1857	01/06/1860	27	36	N	
Brink, William	29	Hanover	Y	Bremen	Baltimore	10/24/1847	09/15/1852	25	515	N	
Brinker, ?	35	Germany	Y	Bremen	Baltimore	11/01/1879	11/01/1884			Y	
Brinker, August	36	Germany	Y	Bremen	Baltimore	10/01/1881	02/25/1886			Y	
Brinker, Bernard H. J.	27	Hanover	Y	Bremen	New Orleans	12/24/1852	03/25/1856	26	315	N	
Brinker, George	29	Germany	Y	Bremen	Baltimore	04/07/1880	06/08/1882			Y	
Brinker, John H.	44	Germany	N	Bremen	Baltimore	06/13/1861	?			Y	
Brinker, Tony	23	Germany	Y	Hanover	New York	10/??/1876	10/12/1880			N	
Brinker, William	38	Germany	N	Bremen	Baltimore	09/27/1872	?			Y	
Brinkers, Bernhard Heinr	22	Hanover	Y	Bremen	New Orleans	05/28/1849	05/20/1852	25	60	N	
Brinkhaus, Lambert	25	Oldenburg	Y	Bremen	New Orleans	11/12/1857	08/15/1860	27	279	N	
Brinkhoff, Bernard	27	Prussia	Y	Bremen	New York	06/20/1847	02/21/1849	23	247	N	
Brinkkroeger, Frederick	30	Prussia	Y	Bremen	New Orleans	11/01/1848	10/07/1854	10	538	N	
Brinkkroeger, Frederick	30	Prussia	Y	Bremen	New Orleans	11/01/1848	10/07/1854	12	477	N	
Brinkley, James	40	Ireland	N	Queenstown	New York	06/??/1866	?			Y	
Brinkman, Frederick	49	Mecklenburg S	Y	Hamburg	New York	08/13/1851	03/28/1853	7	426	N	
Brinkman, Henry	37	Prussia	Y	Amsterdam	New York	06/09/1848	02/20/1849	23	224	N	
Brinkman, Jacob Fred	27	Wurttemberg	Y	Bremen	New York	12/??/1845	??/??/1851	3	222	N	
Brinkmann, Barnard	33	Germany	Y	Bremen	Baltimore	05/26/1870	10/08/1883			Y	
Brinkmann, Christian	22	Oldenburg	Y	Bremen	New Orleans	10/28/1851	10/10/1854	6	233	N	
Brinkmann, Christian	22	Oldenburg	Y	Bremen	New Orleans	10/28/1851	10/10/1854	11	236	N	
Brinkmann, Christian	50	Hanover	Y	Bremen	Baltimore	10/30/1853	09/18/1858	16	175	N	
Brinkmann, Christian Fre	22	Hanover	Y	Bremen	Baltimore	09/18/1855	04/02/1858	16	478	N	
Brinkmann, Clemens	27	Germany	Y	Bremen	Baltimore	09/??/1876	10/20/1884			Y	
Brinkmann, Friedrich Aug	46	Germany	Y	Bremen	New York	10/06/1888	09/09/1889			Y	

CITIZENSHIP RECORDS

APPLICANT	AGE	COUNTRY OF ORIGIN	DEC	DEPART PORT	ENTRY PORT	ARRIVE DATE	DEC DATE	VOL	PG.	FLD	NAT DATE
Brinkmann, Henry	26	Prussia	Y	Bremen	New Orleans	12/??/1846	03/18/1853	7	347	N	
Brinkmann, Henry	26	Germany	Y	Bremen	Baltimore	05/24/1884	10/13/1892			Y	
Brinkmann, Henry	32	Germany	Y	Hamburg	New York	05/20/1884	02/24/1888			Y	
Brinkmann, J. H.	53	Germany	Y	Bremen	New York	09/01/1865	10/20/1884			Y	
Brinkmann, Jacob	22	Germany	Y	Bremen	Baltimore	05/19/1886	04/03/1890			Y	
Brinkmann, John Fred	41	Germany	N	Bremen	Baltimore	09/15/1860	?			Y	
Brinkmann, John Henry	31	Oldenburg	Y	Bremen	New Orleans	11/09/1852	12/31/1855	13	404	N	
Brinkmann, John Henry	22	Hanover	Y	Bremen	New Orleans	11/28/1848	02/25/1852	24	164	N	
Brinkmann, Joseph	40	Germany	Y	Bremen	New York	06/20/1880	12/08/1887			Y	
Brinkmeier, Bernhard	45	Hanover	Y	Bremen	Baltimore	04/15/1847	02/22/1853	7	215	N	
Brinkmeier, William	??	Hanover	Y	?	New York	06/??/18??	11/08/1856	14	481	N	
Brinkmeyer, Casper	49	Prussia	Y	Bremen	New Orleans	01/01/1849	10/12/1858	17	58	N	
Brinkmeyer, Ernst	23	Germany	Y	Bremen	Baltimore	10/07/1880	12/05/1885			Y	
Brinstadt, Anthony	51	Germany	N	Bremen	Baltimore	07/??/1880	?			Y	
Bristh, Gottlieb W. (Bri	27	Wuerttemberg	Y	Bremen	New Orleans	02/06/1848	04/14/1852	24	499	N	
Britscher, Jean	46	Germany	Y	Antwerp	New York	09/??/1873	09/??/1881			Y	
Britting, John	36	Germany	Y	Bremen	New York	05/12/1884	04/21/1888			Y	
Britton, James	??	?	Y	?	New York	??/20/18??	10/29/1850	2	327	N	
Britton, Matthew	??	?	N	?	?	?	?	28	283	N	?
Britton, Matthew	14	Ireland	N	Liverpool	New York	07/??/1856	?	28	444	N	09/??/1863
Britton, Matthew	??	?	N	?	?	?					
Britz, George	??	Germany	Y	?	?	10/08/1883				Y	10/22/1892
Britz, John	??	Germany	N	?	?	10/08/1883				Y	10/22/1892
Brockamp, Henry	38	Germany	Y	Bremen	New York	03/15/1866	02/11/1880			Y	
Brockbank, Henry	35	England	Y	Liverpool	New York	05/19/1883	06/10/1890			Y	
Brocker, Henry	24	Germany	Y	Bremen	Baltimore	09/01/1882	09/14/1885			Y	
Brockhaus, Alfred	40	Prussia	Y	Antwerp	New York	07/??/1887	11/22/1895			Y	
Brockhaus, John	26	Hanover	Y	Bremen	Baltimore	10/??/1848	11/01/1851	4	462	N	
Brockhoff, Henry	25	Hanover	Y	Bremen	New York	08/01/1845	09/01/1848	22	288	N	
Brockhoff, John A.	70	Germany	N	Bremen	New Orleans	02/28/1846	??/??/1849	28	364	N	09/??/1851
Brockhoff, Julius	28	Prussia	Y	Bremen	New Orleans	12/18/1851	09/29/1854	10	315	N	
Brockhoff, Julius	28	Prussia	Y	Bremen	New Orleans	12/18/1851	09/29/1854	12	254	N	
Brocking, Joseph	40	Prussia	Y	Bremen	New Orleans	01/01/1845	09/17/1855	13	49	N	
Brockman, Herman	24	Hanover	Y	Bremen	New Orleans	11/20/1846	01/24/1851	2	525	N	
Brockman, Joseph Henry	32	Hanover	Y	Bremen	New Orleans	07/20/1844	03/17/1851	3	289	N	
Brockmann, George H.	21	Germany	Y	Bremen	Baltimore	08/26/1882	03/21/1884			Y	
Brockmann, John	27	Prussia	Y	Bremen	New Orleans	05/06/1854	03/25/1856	26	347	N	
Brockmann, John H.	25	Hanover	Y	Bremen	New Orleans	12/25/1849	11/01/1852	5	148	N	
Brockmann, John H.	25	Hanover	Y	Bremen	New Orleans	12/25/1849	11/01/1852	6	274	N	
Brockmans, John Henry	25	Holland	Y	Rotterdam	New York	09/17/1851	11/23/1855	13	243	N	
Brockmeyer, Henry	30	Germany	Y	Bremen	New York	11/25/1892	04/06/1896			Y	
Brocks, Franz	35	Prussia	Y	Rotterdam	New York	09/08/1849	09/17/1855	13	48	N	
Brockschmidt, John Henry	32	Hanover	Y	Bremen	Baltimore	12/02/1846	04/18/1853	8	82	N	
Brodbeck, Charles	21	Germany	Y	?	?	?	05/31/1884			Y	
Brodbeck, Gabriel	30	Baden	Y	Havre	New York	05/03/1854	02/16/1857	15	21	N	
Brodbeck, Isadore	21	Switzerland	Y	Havre	New Orleans	05/26/1845	02/01/1849	23	11	N	
Brodenstein, Bartholomau	35	Bavaria	Y	?	New York	??/15/1849	10/25/1852			Y	03/26/1855
Broderick, Dennis	25	Ireland	Y	Limerick	Buffalo	06/14/1847	09/28/1858	16	115	N	
Broderick, James	25	Ireland	Y	Limerick	Buffalo	05/??/1845	10/02/1856	14	156	N	
Broderick, Martin	??	England	Y	?	?	?	07/31/1871			Y	
Broderick, Michael	27	Ireland	Y	Liverpool	New Orleans	05/23/1851	08/04/1856	14	316	N	
Brodhagen, John Edward	25	Holstein	Y	Hamburg	New York	02/13/1854	10/20/1857	15	464	N	
Brodstine, Christian	39	Germany	Y	?	?	?	10/11/1851			Y	03/26/1855
Brody, Michael	27	Ireland	Y	Limerick	New Orleans	03/04/1848	03/17/1851	3	291	N	
Brody, William	28	Ireland	Y	Galway	Boston	07/05/1847	03/18/1851	3	300	N	
Broeckelmann, H.	45	Germany	Y	Hamburg	New York	03/08/1883	09/08/1885			Y	
Broeker, Gerhard	22	Hanover	Y	Bremen	Baltimore	06/02/1854	11/02/1857	15	512	N	
Broemer, Conrad	28	Bavaria	Y	Liverpool	New York	06/02/1853	04/08/1856	26	468	N	
Broemer, Gottfried Georg	34	Saxe Weimar	Y	Bremen	New Orleans	10/28/1849	02/25/1851	3	170	N	

CITIZENSHIP RECORDS

APPLICANT	AGE	COUNTRY OF ORIGIN	DEC	DEPART PORT	ENTRY PORT	ARRIVE DATE	DEC DATE	VOL	PG.	FLD	NAT DATE
Broermann, Bernard	23	Germany	Y	Rotterdam	New York	09/14/1888	04/18/1892			Y	
Broermann, Werner	22	Germany	Y	Bremen	New York	09/06/1886	10/26/1889			Y	
Broesamle, John Martin	22	Wuertemberg	Y	Bremen	New York	10/14/1853	02/05/1856	26	48	N	
Broesecke, Emil	??	Germany	Y	?	?	?	05/31/1889			Y	
Broestter, Adam (Boerstt	30	Bavaria	Y	Havre	New York	??/13/1849	12/19/1849	23	414	N	
Brogan, Peter	33	Ireland	Y	Liverpool	New York	07/01/1846	02/19/1852	24	143	N	
Brogen, Patrick	28	Ireland	Y	Liverpool	New York	06/??/1847	12/15/1855	13	318	N	
Broh, Adam	41	Bavaria	Y	Havre	New York	09/26/1857	08/30/1862	18	423	N	
Brokamp, Henry	21	Hanover	Y	Bremen	Baltimore	06/01/1846	10/13/1848	1	192	N	
Brokamp, John Frederick	29	Oldenburg	Y	Bremen	Baltimore	09/30/1846	08/15/1848	22	133	N	
Brokamp, Joseph	25	Hanover	Y	Bremen	Baltimore	05/19/1844	10/13/1848	1	202	N	
Brokenshire, Benjamin	26	England	Y	Padslow	Ogdens...?	10/??/1847	10/13/1849			Y	03/26/1855
Brokerede, Joseph	59	Germany	N	Bremen	Baltimore	08/20/1868	?			Y	
Bromkamp, Wm.	33	Hanover	Y	Bremen	Baltimore	06/??/1847	03/17/1853	7	343	N	
Bronner, Edwar	28	Germany	Y	Havre	Hew York	09/01/1881	02/20/1883			Y	
Bronner, George	45	Germany	Y	Havre	New York	06/10/1880	05/09/1887			Y	
Bronner, Joseph Jr.	??	France	N	?	?	10/14/1878				Y	10/28/1892
Bronnert, John Jacob	44	Germany	N	Havre	New York	06/05/1867	?			Y	
Brooke, Charles	42	England	Y	Liverpool	Philadelphia	07/05/1841	05/21/1852	25	86	N	
Brookmeier, Barney	24	Hanover	Y	Bremen	Baltimore	10/05/1858	11/01/1860	27	548	N	
Brooks, George	35	England	Y	Liverpool	New York	07/06/1849	09/24/1858	16	144	N	
Brooks, George Henry	27	England	Y	Liverpool	New York	04/24/1854	11/10/1858	17	315	N	
Brooks, Xavier	42	Germany	Y	Bremen	New York	08/11/1887	07/17/1781			Y	
Brooksbank, George	36	England	Y	Liverpool	New York	05/26/1849	09/25/1854	10	205	N	
Brooksbank, George	36	England	Y	Liverpool	New York	05/26/1849	09/25/1854	12	144	N	
Brophy, James J.	31	Ireland	Y	Queenstown	New York	05/09/1883	03/25/1889			Y	
Brornig, Henry	51	Germany	N	Bremen	New York	08/25/1866	?			Y	
Bros, Ferdinand	26	Baden	Y	Havre	New Orleans	03/??/1854	09/22/1855	13	111	N	
Brosart, Jacob	42	Bavaria	Y	Havre	New Orleans	01/25/1854	08/24/1857	15	182	N	
Brose, Diedrich	50	Hanover	Y	Bremen	New Orleans	12/21/1845	03/01/1853	7	247	N	
Brose, Jacob	38	Germany	Y	Hamburg	New York	06/28/1882	11/13/1889			Y	
Brosnau, Maurice	21	Ireland	Y	?	New York	07/??/1881	10/25/1882			Y	
Brossard, Miachael	24	Germany	Y	Antwerp	Philadelphia	06/11/1881	09/22/1883			Y	
Brossenne, Charles	27	Germany	Y	Hamburg	New York	10/20/1881	12/18/1882			Y	
Brotherton, John Goulden	33	England	Y	Liverpool	New York	05/25/1849	01/24/1856	13	502	N	
Brotsky, Jacob	26	Russia	Y	Hamburg	New York	06/??/1882	03/19/1887			Y	
Broughton, William	40	England	Y	Hull	New York	07/??/1830	11/??/1849	23	360	N	
Brouner, Joseph	44	France	Y	Havre	New York	04/28/1874	02/03/1883			Y	
Brouwer, Linius	35	Holland	Y	Rotterdam	New York	03/25/1891	04/06/1891			Y	
Brown, Andrew A.	26	Canada	Y	Windsor	Detroit	07/03/1880	07/19/1888			Y	
Brown, Francis	33	France	Y	Havre	New York	09/20/1847	02/15/1851	3	134	N	
Brown, George	30	Bavaria	Y	Bremen	Baltimore	05/20/1848	09/05/1848	22	300	N	
Brown, Henry	??	Ireland	Y	?	?	?	01/30/1882			Y	
Brown, Henry	28	Prussia	Y	Havre	New Orleans	01/06/1849	03/15/1852	24	299	N	
Brown, Henry	22	Ireland	Y	Liverpool	New York	08/10/1849	09/11/1852	25	453	N	
Brown, Hieronimus	30	Baden	Y	Havre	New Orleans	04/03/1852	03/24/1858	16	443	N	
Brown, James	48	Ireland	Y	Liverpool	New Orleans	04/16/1850	03/26/1853	7	414	N	
Brown, James	37	Ireland	Y	Cork	New York	04/07/1849	03/24/1856	26	264	N	
Brown, John	40	Ireland	Y	Dublin	New York	06/28/1828	02/15/1853	7	165	N	
Brown, John	28	Scotland	Y	Glasgow	New York	05/15/1851	10/14/1857	15	419	N	
Brown, John	23	Ireland	Y	Liverpool	New York	??/07/1848	11/??/1849	23	320	N	
Brown, John	50	Ireland	Y	Belfast	New York	09/01/1846	02/10/1852	24	89	N	
Brown, Joseph	35	Ireland	Y	Liverpool	New York	04/27/1848	04/01/1853	7	478	N	
Brown, Joseph	50	Hungary	Y	Bremen	New York	05/17/1873	07/06/1873	28	416	N	
Brown, Julius	31	Germany	Y	?	New York	05/23/1882	05/05/1885			Y	
Brown, Leopold	23	Baden	Y	Havre	New Orleans	03/21/1849	04/07/1852	24	408	N	
Brown, Maier	37	REussia	Y	Hamburg	New York	07/20/1887	10/30/1891			Y	
Brown, Michael	30	Ireland	Y	Liverpool	New Orleans	01/01/1852	03/28/1856	26	365	N	
Brown, Patrick	22	Ireland	Y	Dublin	New Orleans	01/01/1851	11/01/1852	5	162	N	

CITIZENSHIP RECORDS

APPLICANT	AGE	COUNTRY OF ORIGIN	DEC	DEPART PORT	ENTRY PORT	ARRIVE DATE	DEC DATE	VOL	PG.	FLD	NAT DATE
Brown, Patrick	22	Ireland	Y	Dublin	New Orleans	01/01/1851	11/01/1852	6	288	N	
Brown, Patrick	??	Ireland	Y	?	?	?	10/10/1872			Y	
Brown, Peter	40	Ireland	Y	Liverpool	New York	00/00/1868	10/26/1886			Y	
Brown, Samuel	26	Denmark	Y	Heslrn Nove	Boston	08/15/1842	02/27/1851	3	173	N	
Brown, Samuel	25	Ireland	Y	Liverpool	New Orleans	02/23/1850	04/01/1853	7	479	N	
Brown, Theodore	22	Russia	Y	Hamburg	New York	05/13/1886	09/06/1889			Y	
Brown, Thomas	24	Ireland	Y	New Ross	Savannah	12/25/1852	06/03/1854	9	480	N	
Brown, Thomas	24	Ireland	Y	New Ross	Savannah	12/25/1852	06/03/1854	10	63	N	
Brown, Thomas	42	Ireland	Y	Liverpool	New Orleans	05/07/1854	09/30/1856	14	69	N	
Brown, Thomas	48	England	Y	Liverpool	New Orleans	??/??/1856	11/03/1884			Y	
Brown, Thomas	40	Ireland	N	Queenstown	New York	11/09/1864	?				
Brown, Thomas	35	Ireland	Y	Canada	Buffalo	04/28/1848	02/12/1849	23	66	N	
Brown, William	35	Ireland	Y	Liverpool	New York	09/01/1848	03/31/1853	7	472	N	
Brown, William	79	Germany	Y	Bremen	Baltimore	01/01/1871	10/26/1900			Y	
Browne, James S.	76	Ireland	N	Ireland	New York	05/08/1849	06/11/1849	28	217	N	06/15/1854
Browne, Peter	27	Ireland	Y	Liverpool	New York	11/02/1865	10/17/1872			Y	
Browne, Richard	??	Ireland	N	?	?	02/26/1883				Y	10/28/1892
Brownell, Geo. S.	29	Canada	Y	Windsor	Detroit	12/01/1882	06/23/1891			Y	
Bruce, Alexander	29	Scotland	Y	Canada	Whitehall	10/21/1843	03/12/1850	2	187	N	
Bruch, Conrad	54	Germany	Y	Amsterdam	New York	05/15/1882	09/05/1887			Y	
Bruck, Ignatz	27	Baden	Y	Havre	New York	09/09/1846	03/29/1850	2	284	N	
Bruck, Jacob	30	Baden	Y	Havre	New York	04/28/1846	08/17/1848	22	197	N	
Brucker, Anton	22	Baden	Y	Havre	New Orleans	05/25/1854	10/09/1854	6	62	N	
Brucker, Anton	22	Baden	Y	Havre	New Orleans	05/25/1854	10/09/1854	11	63	N	
Brucker, Emil	??	Germany	Y	?	?	?	10/06/1894			Y	
Brucker, John S.	26	Germany	Y	Antwerp	New York	04/14/1881	02/25/1884			Y	
Bruckert, Peter	32	Bavaria	Y	?	New York	05/15/1849	10/29/1852			Y	03/26/1855
Bruckner Jacob	28	Germany	Y	Hamburg	New York	03/28/1883	05/10/1886			Y	
Bruder, L.	24	Germany	Y	Bremen	New York	03/29/1881	08/15/1883			Y	
Bruderlein, Adolf	??	Germany	Y	?	?	?	06/20/1882			Y	
Brudermiller, Adolf	29	Germany	Y	Antwerp	New York	12/13/1883	03/26/1885			Y	
Brueckerhoff, Anton	50	Prussia	Y	Bremen	Baltimore	10/12/1846	01/16/1850	23	516	N	
Brueckmann, Frank	32	Bavaria	Y	Havre	New Orleans	06/20/1851	04/09/1852	24	427	N	
Brueckmann, Frederick	26	Saxony	Y	Bremen	New York	06/22/1853	08/31/1857	15	203	N	
Brueckmann, Henry	42	Germany	N	Bremen	New York	06/14/1861	?			Y	
Brueggemann, Adam	24	Lippe Detmold	Y	Bremen	Baltimore	09/30/1849	04/18/1853	8	71	N	
Brueggemann, Heinrich	21	Germany	Y	Bremen	Baltimore	08/25/1882	01/02/1886			Y	
Brueggemann, Henry	26	Hanover	Y	Bremen	New Orleans	01/27/1851	11/01/1852	5	141	N	
Brueggemann, William H.	22	Germany	Y	Bremen	Baltimore	09/30/1881	03/27/1886			Y	
Bruegmann, Peter	36	Germany	Y	Hamburg	New York	11/01/1891	03/08/1894			Y	
Bruehl, Charles	38	Prussia	Y	Antwerp	New York	08/23/1848	02/03/1849	23	20	N	
Bruehl, Gustav	23	Prussia	Y	Antwerp	New York	08/??/1849	11/??/1849	23	312	N	
Bruehl, R.A.W.	28	Prussia	Y	London	New York	07/07/1851	09/18/1858	16	177	N	
Bruell, Adolph	22	Germany	Y	Amsterdam	New York	05/15/1882	10/12/1885			Y	
Bruemmer, Bernard	24	Hanover	Y	Bremen	New Orleans	07/04/1854	10/06/1857	15	359	N	
Bruen, John	40	Ireland	Y	Liverpool	New Orleans	12/23/1848	05/15/1852	25	24	N	
Bruene, Henry	23	Hanover	Y	Bremen	New Orleans	11/??/1853	11/07/1856	14	500	N	
Bruengger, Henry	19	Switzerland	Y	Havre	New York	09/08/1883	09/??/1883			Y	
Bruengger, Henry	29	Switzerland	N	Havre	New York	09/08/1883	?			Y	
Bruening, Diedrich	27	Germany	Y	Hamburg	New York	09/16/1892	09/28/1896			Y	
Bruening, Frank	47	Prussia	Y	Bremen	New York	10/27/1850	09/23/1857	15	304	N	
Bruening, Joseph	??	Germany	N	?	?	05/29/1864				Y	10/18/1892
Bruening, William	64	Germany	N	Bremen	New York	04/??/1849	?			Y	
Bruenisholz, Anton	39	Switzerland	Y	Havre	New York	03/??/1852	12/26/1857	16	260	N	
Bruermann, Christ	21	Hanover	Y	Bremen	Baltimore	09/20/1852	10/10/1854	11	239	N	
Bruesehaber, Albert	45	Germany	Y	Bremen	Baltimore	04/29/1888	09/15/1895			Y	
Bruestle, Joseph	32	Germany	Y	Havre	New York	09/11/1874	10/11/1884			Y	
Bruewer, Heinrich	26	Germany	Y	Rotterdam	New York	08/08/1884	05/17/1886			Y	
Bruewer, Henry	37	Germany	Y	Bremen	Baltimore	08/27/1881	02/26/1889			Y	

CITIZENSHIP RECORDS

APPLICANT	AGE	COUNTRY OF ORIGIN	DEC	DEPART PORT	ENTRY PORT	ARRIVE DATE	DEC DATE	VOL	PG.	FLD	NAT DATE
Bruewer, Theodor	27	Germany	Y	Rotterdam	New York	05/22/1890	05/22/1893			Y	
Brug, Jacob	37	Germany	Y	Bremen	Baltimore	09/23/1882	10/19/1899			Y	
Brugemann, John Henry	50	Hanover	Y	Bremen	New Orleans	11/01/1846	10/04/1848	1	50	N	
Bruggemann, Francis	37	Prussia	Y	Bremen	New York	04/19/1857	03/25/1862	18	280	N	
Bruggemann, Fritz	23	Hanover	Y	Bremen	New Orleans	11/29/1852	09/17/1855	13	44	N	
Bruggemann, Heinrich	26	Hanover	Y	Bremen	New Orleans	01/27/1851	11/01/1852	6	267	N	
Bruggemann, Herman	27	Germany	Y	Bremen	Baltimore	10/09/1880	10/22/1887			Y	
Bruggemann, Joseph	55	Germany	N	Bremen	Baltimore	08/28/1882	09/28/1885			Y	
Bruggemann, Theodor	56	Germany	Y	Bremen	New York	09/15/1882	03/27/1886			Y	
Brugger, Henry	66	Germany	N	Bremen	New York	11/03/1865	?			Y	
Bruggmann, John	30	Switzerland	Y	Havre	New York	04/13/1880	01/02/1883			Y	
Bruhne, Frederick	22	Prussia	Y	Havre	New Orleans	04/30/1848	10/09/1854	6	189	N	
Bruker, Carl	26	Germany	Y	Bremen	New York	07/23/1880	09/19/1882			Y	
Brum, Christ	53	France	Y	Havre	New York	02/13/1890	10/14/1890	19	287	N	
Brum, Christ	53	France	Y	Havre	New York	02/13/1870	10/14/1890			Y	
Brummer, Henry	49	Germany	N	Bremen	Baltimore	10/08/1865	?			Y	
Brummer, Herman	??	Prussia	Y	?	New York	04/20/1881	03/31/1888			Y	
Brummer, Klaus	39	Hanover	Y	Bremen	New Orleans	12/14/1849	05/25/1852	25	107	N	
Brun, Achille	31	Germany	Y	Havre	New York	08/14/1873	03/??/1881			Y	
Brun, Peter	38	Ireland	Y	Havre	New Orleans	04/??/1848	05/24/1852	25	104	N	
Brunch, Frank	32	France	Y	Havre	New York	05/04/1872	11/01/1886	19	107	N	
Brunck, Michael	63	Germany	Y	Antwerp	New York	11/25/1873	10/10/1884			Y	
Brune, Frederick	25	Prussia	Y	Havre	New Orleans	04/30/1848	10/09/1854	11	192	N	
Brune, Henry	21	Oldenburg	Y	Bremen	Baltimore	08/14/1858	11/02/1860	27	558	N	
Brunemann, Heinrich	50	Germany	N	Bremen	New Orleans	05/18/1856	?			Y	
Brunemann, John Adolph	21	Hanover	Y	Bremen	Baltimore	07/17/1850	06/10/1852	25	313	N	
Bruner, Emanuel	39	Switzerland	Y	?	?	02/16/1883	11/06/1888			Y	
Bruner, John	22	Baden	Y	Havre	New York	06/26/1852	07/10/1855	11	371	N	
Bruning, Bernhard Jacob	26	Oldenburg	Y	Bremen	New York	08/08/1848	01/28/1853	7	78	N	
Bruning, Heinrich	27	Prussia	Y	Bremen	New York	05/20/1867	05/25/1872	18	475	N	
Bruning, Henry	29	Hanover	Y	Bremen	New Orleans	12/29/1847	02/23/1852	24	159	N	
Bruning, Sigmund	32	Hanover	Y	Bremen	New Orleans	11/13/1847	11/20/1848	1	333	N	
Brunk, Frank	32	France	Y	Havre	New York	05/04/1872	11/01/1886			Y	
Brunnen, Owen	23	Ireland	Y	Liverpool	New Orleans	12/23/1849	01/06/1853	5	530	N	
Brunner, Chris	16	Germany	N	?	Philadelphia	00/00/1882				Y	10/19/1888
Brunner, Frank	43	Germany	N	Havre	New York	07/21/1866	?			Y	
Brunner, George	43	Switzerland	Y	?	New York	??/??/1881	11/03/1884			Y	
Brunner, George Jacob	47	Bavaria	Y	Havre	New Orleans	05/03/1851	10/07/1854	6	35	N	
Brunner, George Jacob	47	Bavaria	Y	Havre	New Orleans	05/03/1851	10/07/1854	11	36	N	
Brunner, Jacob	43	Germany	Y	Hamburg	New York	01/11/1863	08/21/1888			Y	
Brunner, John	35	Baden	Y	Liverpool	New Orleans	02/20/1852	10/02/1856	14	163	N	
Brunner, Josef	37	Austira	Y	Antwerp	New York	06/15/1874	10/17/1889			Y	
Bruns, Bernhard	24	Germany	Y	Rotterdam	Baltimore	12/01/1882	10/21/1886			Y	
Bruns, Caspar	44	Prussia	Y	Bremen	Baltimore	09/15/1860	02/10/1872	18	553	N	
Bruns, Frederick J.	24	Germany	Y	Bremen	New York	01/30/1878	01/14/1882			Y	
Bruns, H. John	29	Hanover	Y	Bremerhafen	New Orleans	09/27/1857	01/26/1861	18	73	N	
Bruns, Herman H.	21	Hanover	Y	Bremen	New Orleans	12/14/1845	10/12/1848	1	179	N	
Bruns, John	24	Hanover	Y	Bremen	New Orleans	02/28/1845	01/29/1849	1	531	N	
Bruns, John	32	Hanover	Y	London	New York	06/01/1852	05/24/1859	17	428	N	
Brunsbach, Joseph	21	Germany	Y	Antwerp	New York	10/22/1879	01/06/1882			Y	
Brunsen, William John	??	Germany	Y	?	?	06/??/1882	11/26/1884			Y	
Brunsewick, Frederick	31	Germany	Y	Bremen	New York	09/01/1882	12/22/1892			Y	
Brunsmann, Eberth	32	Prussia	Y	Bremen	Baltimore	10/08/1857	10/19/1860	27	512	N	
Brunsmann, William	33	Prussia	Y	Bremen	Buffalo	08/15/1847	10/04/1854	10	431	N	
Brunsmann, William	33	Prussia	Y	Bremen	Buffalo	08/15/1847	10/04/1854	12	370	N	
Brunz, Fritz	28	Germany	Y	Bremen	Baltimore	08/11/1881	04/29/1885			Y	
Brunz, H.	32	Germany	Y	Bremen	Baltimore	07/06/1882	04/29/1885			Y	
Brup, Thomas	??	Germany	Y	?	New York	04/01/1882	03/03/1883			Y	
Brurmann, Christ.	21	Hanover	Y	Bremen	Baltimore	09/20/1852	10/10/1854	6	236	N	

CITIZENSHIP RECORDS

APPLICANT	AGE	COUNTRY OF ORIGIN	DEC	DEPART PORT	ENTRY PORT	ARRIVE DATE	DEC DATE	VOL	PG.	FLD	NAT DATE
Bruser, Fritz	39	Germany	Y	Bremen	Baltimore	10/18/1872	11/22/1886			Y	
Brustle, Conrad	64	Germany	N	Havre	New York	09/??/1854	?			Y	
Brutschin, Emil	28	Germany	Y	?	New York	??/??/1881	10/30/1886			Y	
Brutschin, William	31	Germany	Y	Havre	New York	10/03/1881	10/08/1890			Y	
Bruwer, Bernhard	17	Germany	N	?	Baltimore	00/00/1881				Y	10/11/1888
Bruwer, Henry	34	Germany	Y	Rotterdam	New York	11/??/1865	10/07/1882			Y	
Bruwer, Herman	25	Germany	Y	Rotterdam	New York	05/25/1889	09/07/1897			Y	
Bruwer, John	21	Germany	Y	Rotterdam	New York	07/27/1883	04/13/1885			Y	
Brwon, Elise	42	Russia	Y	Bremen	New York	05/06/1889	04/11/1899			Y	
Brwon, Picton C.	38	Canada	Y	Hamilton	Buffalo	11/24/1890	10/06/1896			Y	
Brwon, Robert	22	Germany	Y	?	?	?	04/23/1879			Y	
Bryan, Bernard	29	Germany	Y	Bremen	Baltimore	09/18/1890	10/12/1898			Y	
Bryan, Patrick	43	Ireland	Y	Liverpool	New Orleans	12/24/1848	03/08/1850	2	173	N	
Bryan, Patrick	21	Ireland	Y	Liverpool	New Orleans	05/23/1849	08/21/1850			Y	03/26/1855
Bryan, William	29	Ireland	Y	Waterford	New York	05/27/1849	03/31/1852	24	347	N	
Bryer, Duncan	39	Scotland	Y	Greenock	Buffalo	08/??/1854	10/08/1857	15	371	N	
Bub, Nicholaus	25	Bavaria	Y	Antwerp	New Orleans	11/02/1848	10/24/1851	4	389	N	
Buch, Albion J.	50	Germany	Y	Hamburg	New York	06/18/1882	05/14/1885			Y	
Buch, Francis	22	Nassau	Y	London	New York	05/03/1854	10/26/1857	15	491	N	
Buch, Franz	60	Germany	Y	Antwerp	New York	10/26/1886	08/27/1892			Y	
Buch, George	31	Germany	Y	Bremen	Baltimore	09/??/1881	10/13/1884			Y	
Buchanan, James	25	Ireland	Y	Liverpool	New York	04/15/1847	01/13/1853	7	19	N	
Buchanan, John	27	Ireland	Y	Belfast	New York	03/01/1849	01/01/1853	5	486	N	
Buchanan, John	58	Scotland	Y	Liverpool	Philadelphia	08/03/1879	10/31/1885			Y	
Buchanan, Wm.	32	Scotland	Y	Glasgow	Detroit	06/24/1879	10/12/1889			Y	
Buchdrucker, Charles	31	Bavaria	Y	Bremen	New Orleans	01/20/1849	02/24/1851	3	161	N	
Bucher, Joseph	23	Switzerland	Y	Havre	New Orleans	04/22/1851	10/19/1852	5	19	N	
Bucher, Martias	22	Wuertemberg	Y	Havre	New York	04/04/1854	03/27/1856	26	354	N	
Buchert, John	??	Germany	Y	?	?	03/??/1890	06/28/1894			Y	
Buchholz, Charles	66	Germany	Y	Bremen	New York	09/20/1882	11/01/1887			Y	
Buchholz, Conrad	24	Hanover	Y	Bremen	Baltimore	05/10/1844	08/07/1848	22	66	N	
Buchholz, George	30	Hanover	Y	Bremen	Baltimore	09/28/1849	01/24/1853	7	56	N	
Buchholz, Jacob	24	Prussia	Y	Havre	New Orleans	12/28/1847	10/14/1848	1	234	N	
Buchholz, Mathias	29	Baden	Y	Havre	New York	05/31/1850	12/07/1852	5	396	N	
Buchler, Jacob	30	Wurttemberg	Y	London	New York	05/15/1854	09/25/1854	12	135	N	
Buchler, Jacob	34	Switzerland	Y	Havre	New York	06/20/1896	10/26/1903			Y	
Buchmann, Nicolaus	30	Prussia	Y	Liverpool	New York	06/01/1852	05/30/1854	9	465	N	
Buchmann, Nicolaus	30	Prussia	Y	Liverpool	New York	06/01/1852	05/31/1854	10	48	N	
Buchmann, Peter	30	Prussia	Y	Antwerp	New York	12/??/1852	08/27/1855	11	494	N	
Buchner, Andrew	25	Germany	Y	Antwerp	New York	10/04/1884	04/23/1888			Y	
Buchner, George	27	Bavaria	Y	Havre	New York	05/07/1856	05/03/1859	17	394	N	
Buchner, John B. H.	30	Prussia	Y	Bremen	Baltimore	04/29/1846	10/03/1848	22	413	N	
Buchwald, Andreas	21	Wurttemberg	Y	Antwerp	New York	04/18/1848	01/13/1849	1	406	N	
Buck, Edward George	20	England	Y	London	New York	04/06/1888	02/12/1889			Y	
Buck, Frederick	27	Germany	Y	Antwerp	New York	03/20/1888	11/01/1893			Y	
Buck, Henry	69	Germany	N	Bremen	New Orleans	06/??/1848	?			Y	
Buck, Henry	28	Prussia	Y	Bremen	New Orleans	06/10/1847	04/03/1852	24	364	N	
Buck, Herman	38	Hanover	Y	Bremen	Baltimore	09/25/1850	11/01/1852	6	253	N	
Buck, Herman	27	Germany	Y	?	Baltimore	??/??/1881	04/14/1884			Y	
Buck, John Henry	32	Hanover	Y	Bremen	New York	10/19/1850	10/26/1858	17	116	N	
Buck, John Herman	38	Hanover	Y	Bremen	Baltimore	09/25/1850	11/01/1852	5	129	N	
Buck, William	29	Prussia	Y	Bremen	New Orleans	12/05/1849	04/05/1858	16	495	N	
Bucker, Fritz	36	Germany	Y	Bremen	Baltimore	08/29/1881	10/18/1886	19	51	N	
Bucker, Fritz	36	Germany	Y	Bremen	Baltimore	08/29/1881	10/18/1886			Y	
Buckhart, Nicholas	25	Bavaria	Y	Havre	New York	07/04/1851	06/01/1854	9	472	N	
Buckhart, Nicholas	25	Bavaria	Y	Havre	New York	07/04/1851	06/01/1854	10	55	N	
Buckholt, Henry	32	Germany	Y	?	?	??/??/1880	07/14/1886			Y	
Buckholz, Fritz	53	Germany	N	Bremen	New York	03/??/1866	?			Y	
Buckler, Jacob	30	Wurttemberg	Y	London	New York	05/15/1854	09/25/1854	10	196	N	

47

CITIZENSHIP RECORDS

APPLICANT	AGE	COUNTRY OF ORIGIN	DEC	DEPART PORT	ENTRY PORT	ARRIVE DATE	DEC DATE	VOL	PG.	FLD	NAT DATE
Buckley, Andrew	24	Baden	Y	Havre	New Orleans	05/15/1848	07/05/1851	3	490	N	
Buckley, Daniel	30	Ireland	Y	Liverpool	New York	06/14/1852	12/29/1857	16	281	N	
Buckley, Denis	29	Ireland	Y	Liverpool	Portland	07/01/1851	10/06/1856	14	200	N	
Buckley, Eugene	28	Ireland	Y	Liverpool	New York	12/07/1847	05/04/1854	8	372	N	
Buckley, Eugene	28	Ireland	Y	Liverpool	New York	12/07/1847	05/04/1854	9	245	N	
Buckley, Eugene	62	Ireland	N	Liverpool	New York	11/??/1848	10/??/1853	28	55	N	10/??/1856
Buckley, Eugene	22	Ireland	N	Liverpool	New York	11/00/1848	10/00/1853			Y	10/00/1856
Buckley, Frank	28	England	Y	Liverpool	New York	04/30/1844	09/15/1851			Y	03/27/1855
Buckley, James	28	Ireland	Y	Cork	New York	06/20/1848	07/07/1851	3	501	N	
Buckley, Jerry	56	Ireland	Y	Liverpool	New Orleans	12/07/1850	02/15/1853	7	167	N	
Buckley, Jerry	24	Ireland	Y	Liverpool	New Orleans	11/01/1851	03/07/1853	7	301	N	
Buckley, John	30	Ireland	Y	Baltimore	Eastport	08/01/1845	04/04/1853	8	12	N	
Buckley, Michael	28	Ireland	Y	Liverpool	New Orleans	01/??/1847	12/??/1849	23	441	N	
Buckley, Patrick	23	Ireland	Y	Cork	Boston	08/07/1850	05/04/1854	8	373	N	
Buckley, Patrick	23	Ireland	Y	Cork	Boston	08/07/1850	11/04/1854	9	246	N	
Buckley, Stephan	30	Ireland	Y	Liverpool	New Orleans	06/04/1848	04/16/1852	24	514	N	
Buckley, Timothy	38	Ireland	Y	Liverpool	Boston	10/08/1847	10/06/1854	10	519	N	
Buckley, Timothy	38	Ireland	Y	Liverpool	Boston	10/08/1847	10/06/1854	12	458	N	
Buckney, Henry D.	55	Germany	N	Hamburg	New York	10/25/1860	?			Y	
Budd, Alfred	34	England	Y	Liverpool	New York	08/09/1889	07/13/1891			Y	
Budde, F.W.	27	Prussia	Y	Hamburg	New York	07/19/1860	02/14/1861	18	100	N	
Budde, Franz	22	Germany	Y	Amsterdam	New York	10/09/1881	07/30/1883			Y	
Budde, Heinrich	22	Germany	Y	Amsterdam	New York	12/22/1883	01/25/1886			Y	
Budde, Herman	27	Germany	Y	Amsterdam	New York	07/21/1886	09/27/1894			Y	
Budde, Ludwig	28	Hanover	Y	Bremen	New Orleans	05/04/1848	02/19/1849	23	179	N	
Buddemeier, Henry Willia	36	Prussia	Y	Bremen	Baltimore	11/09/1858	08/27/1862	18	406	N	
Buddendick, Herman	30	Germany	Y	Amsterdam	New York	04/18/1882	10/06/1884			Y	
Budelmann, Herman	22	Hanover	Y	Bremen	New York	04/28/1849	04/06/1852	24	401	N	
Budenbender, August	51	Germany	Y	Rotterdam	New York	06/09/1882	06/16/1882			Y	
Budenbender, Wilhelm	27	Germany	Y	Rotterdam	New York	03/24/1881	06/16/1882			Y	
Budke, Eberhard	24	Germany	Y	Bremen	Baltimore	08/04/1881	10/01/1885			Y	
Budke, William	25	Prussia	Y	Bremen	Baltimore	05/25/1848	02/21/1852	24	146	N	
Buechel, Blasius	46	Germany	Y	?	New York	06/??/1868	04/03/1876			Y	
Buecker, Bernard	27	Prussia	Y	Bremen	New Orleans	11/26/1852	08/16/1855	11	441	N	
Buecker, Christoph	27	Prussia	Y	Bremen	New Orleans	12/17/1851	10/12/1857	15	404	N	
Bueckmann, John	32	Hanover	Y	Bremen	New Orleans	06/29/1845	09/20/1852			Y	03/27/1855
Bueher, John G.	22	Hanover	Y	Bremen	New Orleans	11/??/1848	10/27/1851	4	410	N	
Buehl, Xaver	45	Wuertemberg	Y	Havre	New York	01/12/1854	03/24/1856	26	253	N	
Buehle, John	21	Bavaria	Y	Bremen	Baltimore	07/05/1852	05/22/1854	8	486	N	
Buehler, Charles	40	Germany	Y	Havre	New York	04/12/1866	01/14/1885			Y	
Buehler, Daniel	28	Wurttemberg	Y	Antwerp	New York	07/28/1847	04/04/1853	8	3	N	
Buehler, Edward	45	Prussia	Y	Bremen	New York	06/30/1849	05/17/1852	25	25	N	
Buehler, Frederick	38	Baden	Y	Havre	New York	03/14/1853	09/16/1858	16	162	N	
Buehler, Johannes	28	Germany	Y	Bremen	New York	10/02/1892	03/24/1898			Y	
Buehler, John Andrew	28	Wurttemberg	Y	Havre	New York	06/17/1852	08/22/1855	11	477	N	
Buehner, Cornelius	43	Germany	Y	Bremen	New York	03/23/1871	10/27/1888			Y	
Buehning, Fred.	29	Germany	Y	Bremen	New York	05/25/1883	11/03/1887			Y	
Bueltel, Herman	56	Hanover	Y	Bremen	New Orleans	12/22/1852	10/02/1856	14	145	N	
Bueltel, John (Beltar)	32	Hanover	Y	Bremen	New Orleans	11/16/1845	08/15/1848	22	155	N	
Buendert, Julius	44	Germany	Y	Havre	New York	01/19/1886	11/06/1888			Y	
Buenger, Henry	24	Hanover	Y	Bremen	Baltimore	10/15/1854	11/22/1858	17	345	N	
Buenning, Herman	26	Germany	N	Rotterdam	New York	11/10/1880	?			Y	
Buenning, Herman	26	Germany	Y	Rotterdam	New York	11/10/1880	04/00/1883			Y	
Buergenmeister, Charles?	14	Germany	Y	?	New York	00/00/1865				Y	10/20/1888
Buerger, Joseph	35	Germany	Y	Bremen	New York	08/31/1880	10/25/1889			Y	
Buerghoffer, George	37	France	Y	Havre	New York	08/04/1854	10/07/1856	14	245	N	
Buergler, John	37	Switzerland	Y	Antwerp	New York	09/28/1851	06/14/1852	25	251	N	
Buerglin, Andrew	37	France	Y	Havre	New York	06/22/1852	07/18/1855	11	406	N	
Buerk, Charles	34	Germany	Y	Havre	New York	10/01/1880	09/28/1886			Y	

CITIZENSHIP RECORDS

APPLICANT	AGE	COUNTRY OF ORIGIN	DEC	DEPART PORT	ENTRY PORT	ARRIVE DATE	DEC DATE	VOL	PG.	FLD	NAT DATE
Buerk, John	32	Germany	Y	Havre	New York	08/01/1882	03/13/1884			Y	
Buerkle, Pius	28	Baden	Y	Rotterdam	New York	12/25/1846	08/02/1848	22	42	N	
Buerkle, Sigmund	43	Germany	Y	Havre	New York	05/??/1868	12/09/1884			Y	
Buerkles, Richard	22	Germany	Y	Bremen	New York	07/02/1891	04/04/1892			Y	
Buerling, Charles	24	Germany	Y	Antwerp	New York	09/17/1883	04/05/1887			Y	
Buescher, Fred	64	Prussia	N	Bremen	New York	10/08/1852	?			Y	
Buete, Henry	32	Hanover	Y	Bremen	Baltimore	06/08/1847	01/19/1849	1	475	N	
Bueter, Heinrich	36	Germany	Y	Bremen	Baltimore	06/10/1883	10/28/1896			Y	
Bueter, William	28	Germany	Y	Bremen	Baltimore	10/05/1883	10/22/1888			Y	
Buetler, Victor	37	Switzerland	Y	Antwerp	New York	07/16/1857	12/06/1858	17	378	N	
Buetschi, Adolph	34	Switzerland	Y	Havre	New York	05/14/1884	05/18/1896			Y	
Buettel, Ludwig	??	Baden	Y	Havre	New York	??/07/18??	04/16/1855	11	255	N	
Buettner, John	36	Germany	Y	Hamburg	New York	02/02/1884	02/14/1895			Y	
Buhl, John	21	Bavaria	Y	Bremen	Baltimore	07/05/1852	05/22/1854	9	360	N	
Buhler, Charles	??	Germany	Y	?	?	?	10/31/1893			Y	
Buhler, Nicholas	30	Germany	N	Bremen	New York	07/??/1873	?			Y	
Buhlheller, John	36	Germany	Y	Antwerp	New York	05/31/1883	02/09/1887			Y	
Buhning, Joseph	24	Oldenburg	Y	Hamburg	New York	07/16/1858	10/28/1858	17	150	N	
Buhr, Henry	22	Germany	Y	Hamburg	New York	02/24/1884	10/10/1885			Y	
Buhr, Philipp	26	Germany	Y	Amsterdam	New York	08/29/1882	09/11/1886			Y	
Buhrmester, Christian	32	Prussia	Y	Bremen	New York	06/02/1854	05/22/1856	26	521	N	
Buiano, Raffaele	42	Italy	Y	Naples	New York	04/10/1885	03/23/1894			Y	
Buicke, Albert A.	28	Germany	Y	Bremen	New York	09/05/1884	06/04/1886	19	38	N	
Buken, Anthony T.	4	Germany	N	?	Baltimore	00/00/1870				Y	11/01/1888
Buker, Gerhard F.A.	49	Germany	Y	Bremen	Baltimore	09/01/1884	01/09/1892			Y	
Buller, Edward	31	Germany	Y	Bremen	New York	10/18/1882	08/12/1891			Y	
Buller, Leopold	54	Germany	Y	Bremen	New York	03/08/1866	11/04/1889	19	276	N	
Buller, Leopold	54	Germany	Y	Bremen	New York	03/08/1866	11/04/1889			Y	
Bullinger, George	24	Wurttemberg	Y	Bremen	New York	06/05/1851	09/25/1858	16	128	N	
Bullio, John	45	Italy	Y	?	New York	??/??/1872	01/04/1893			Y	
Bullio, Robert	29	Itlay	Y	Havre	New York	06/05/1888	10/26/1892			Y	
Bullock, Thomas	36	England	Y	Liverpool	New York	12/30/1867	11/18/1881			Y	
Bultel, Herman	26	Germany	Y	Bremen	Baltimore	04/19/1882	04/22/1885			Y	
Bultmann, John Henry	28	Hanover	Y	Bremen	Baltimore	07/10/1845	08/03/1848	22	55	N	
Bumb, Jacob	35	Hesse Darmsta	Y	Antwerp	New York	05/15/1850	05/30/1854	9	450	N	
Bumb, Jacob	35	Hesse Darmsta	Y	Antwerp	New York	05/15/1850	05/30/1854	10	33	N	
Bumster, John	29	Ireland	Y	Liverpool	New York	?	04/10/1852	24	436	N	
Bundschuh, Joseph	24	Baden	Y	Havre	New York	11/02/1854	02/17/1857	15	26	N	
Bungarten, John	28	Germany	Y	Antwerp	Boston	07/16/1887	05/23/1889			Y	
Bungenstock, August	27	Germany	Y	Bremen	New York	07/20/1881	02/08/1884			Y	
Bungenstock, C.	28	Germany	Y	Bremen	New York	07/20/1881	02/08/1884			Y	
Bunger, Clemens	29	Germany	Y	Bremen	Baltimore	12/05/1878	12/28/1882			Y	
Bunger, Frank	29	Germany	Y	Bremen	New York	10/22/1892	04/09/1896			Y	
Bungers, Franz	22	Germany	Y	Rotterdam	New York	07/14/1880	08/15/1883			Y	
Buning, Gerhard	30	Germany	Y	Bremen	New York	04/26/1881	05/03/1883			Y	
Buning, Henry	21	Hanover	Y	Bremen	New Orleans	06/20/1850	01/06/1853	5	528	N	
Buning, John Fred	21	Hanover	Y	Bremen	Baltimore	05/06/1848	02/24/1851	3	166	N	
Bunjes, August	??	Germany	Y	?	?	04/??/1884	09/22/1884			Y	
Bunker, H.	42	Germany	Y	Bremen	New York	04/17/1872	04/14/1885			Y	
Bunker, Johan Gerhard	35	Germany	Y	Bremen	New York	05/02/1888	05/29/1895	21	79	N	
Bunnemeyer, Clemens	22	Oldenburg	Y	Bremen	Baltimore	06/25/1848	10/14/1851	4	274	N	
Buns, Bernard Henry	24	Hanover	Y	Bremen	New Orleans	12/16/1845	10/05/1848	22	434	N	
Buns, Henry	47	Germany	Y	Bremen	Baltimore	10/13/1859	11/15/1886			Y	
Bunselmeier, William	27	Hanover	Y	Bremen	New Orleans	01/01/1846	10/30/1852	5	68	N	
Bunte, John B,	22	Germany	Y	Bremen	New York	11/08/1883	06/16/1885			Y	
Bunyan, John	23	Ireland	Y	Cork	Buffalo	10/10/1848	07/21/1851	4	13	N	
Bunyan, Morris	21	Ireland	Y	Liverpool	New Orleans	12/01/1849	07/21/1851	4	12	N	
Buob, Joseph	??	Germany	Y	?	?	?	05/15/1893			Y	
Buob, Louis	30	Wurttemberg	Y	Havre	New York	05/08/1857	04/20/1861	18	138	N	

CITIZENSHIP RECORDS

APPLICANT	AGE	COUNTRY OF ORIGIN	DEC	DEPART PORT	ENTRY PORT	ARRIVE DATE	DEC DATE	VOL	PG.	FLD	NAT DATE
Buob, Louis	30	Wurttemberg	Y	Havre	New York	05/08/1851	04/20/1861			Y	
Burbach, August	24	Baden	Y	Liverpool	New York	06/02/1852	12/13/1852	5	409	N	
Burck, Patrick	50	Ireland	N	Liverpool	New York	06/??/1865	?			Y	
Burckard, Henry Julius B	31	Hanover	Y	Bremen	New York	10/01/1854	02/18/1858	16	318	N	
Burckhardt, Christian Lu	59	Baden	Y	Liverpool	Philadelphia	05/01/1851	03/11/1852	24	289	N	
Burckle, John Frederick	42	Wurttemberg	Y	Havre	New York	10/12/1853	09/30/1854	10	329	N	
Burckle, John Frederick	42	Wurttemberg	Y	Havre	New York	10/12/1853	09/30/1854	12	268	N	
Burd, Gerhard	50	Oldenburg	Y	Bremen	Baltimore	10/20/1859	04/10/1860	27	141	N	
Burg, Ignatz	22	Hesse Darmsta	Y	Havre	New York	01/22/1855	03/04/1858	16	367	N	
Burg, Jacob	33	Germany	Y	Amsterdam	New York	07/14/1883	10/28/1887			Y	
Burg, John Nichols	39	Bavaria	Y	Havre	New Orleans	05/02/1851	04/08/1858	16	505	N	
Burg, Ludwig	44	Bavaria	Y	Havre	New Orleans	02/20/1855	11/03/1860	18	5	N	
Burgading, Henry	26	Oldenburg	Y	Bremen	Baltimore	05/20/1844	01/27/1849	1	529	N	
Burgand, Henry (Hugh)	26	Prussia	Y	Antwerp	New York	08/31/1849	03/20/1851			Y	03/26/1855
Burge, Nicholas	25	Prussia	Y	Antwerp	New York	07/01/1849	03/07/1853	7	308	N	
Burger, Alois	25	Germany	Y	Havre	New York	03/08/1881	12/22/1887			Y	
Burger, Basilius	29	Germany	Y	Havre	New York	05/28/1881	11/20/1887			Y	
Burger, Casper	37	Prussia	Y	Bremen	New Orleans	06/09/1859	03/25/1862	18	281	N	
Burger, Charles	??	Germany	Y	?	?	?	10/13/1891			Y	
Burger, Frank	43	Germany	N	Bremen	New York	01/01/1853	?			Y	
Burger, Henry G.	??	Germany	Y	?	?	05/01/1889	03/01/1893			Y	
Burger, Joseph	23	Prussia	Y	Bremen	New Orleans	06/09/1859	03/25/1862	18	279	N	
Burger, Joseph	21	Germany	Y	Havre	New York	03/11/1881	07/23/1884			Y	
Burger, Ludwig	40	Bavaria	Y	Havre	New York	09/20/1853	01/09/1856	13	434	N	
Burger, Mathias	26	Germany	Y	Antwerp	New York	06/01/1882	03/21/1887			Y	
Burger, Max	22	Baden	Y	Havre	New Orleans	12/27/1854	09/05/1857	15	228	N	
Burger, Nicholas	30	Wuerttenberg	Y	Antwerp	New York	12/12/1847	01/??/1850	23	489	N	
Burger, William	28	Germany	N	Havre	New York	08/01/1880	?			Y	
Burgermeister, Ludwig	37	Baden	Y	Havre	New York	11/22/1854	07/26/1858	16	528	N	
Burgert, John	27	Baden	Y	Havre	New Orleans	10/15/1849	12/21/1852	5	435	N	
Burgert, Lucas	33	Baden	Y	Havre	New York	06/04/1857	10/08/1860	27	437	N	
Burgess, Henry	34	England	Y	London	New York	06/03/1848	09/30/1854	10	325	N	
Burgess, Henry	34	England	Y	London	New York	06/03/1848	09/30/1854	12	264	N	
Burgess, Samuel	24	England	Y	Bristol	New York	05/??/1852	12/18/1855	13	327	N	
Burgess, William	40	Ireland	Y	Liverpool	Buffalo	??/20/1840	10/02/1854	10	349	N	
Burgess, William	40	Ireland	Y	Liverpool	Buffalo	??/20/1840	10/02/1854	12	288	N	
Burggraf, William	32	Germany	Y	Hamburg	New York	06/01/1881	10/20/1886			Y	
Burghardt, William	21	Germany	Y	Antwerp	New York	07/28/1887	11/24/1888			Y	
Burgheim, Max	43	Germany	N	Hamburg	New York	11/??/1863	?			Y	
Burgmann, David	23	Baden	Y	Havre	New York	05/12/1846	03/02/1850	2	148	N	
Burgmann, Henry	26	Prussia	Y	Antwerp	New York	08/31/18??	?	22	514	N	
Burgtorf, George	27	Hanover	Y	Bremen	Baltimore	10/10/1846	01/13/1849	1	411	N	
Burhmann, August	26	Hanover	Y	Bremen	Baltimore	10/18/1869	01/22/1872	18	458	N	
Burhoff, Barney	29	Prussia	Y	Rotterdam	New York	05/06/1849	10/09/1854	6	166	N	
Burk, Christ	27	Germany	Y	Bremen	New York	02/26/1881	04/28/1882			Y	
Burk, Christopher	35	Ireland	Y	Liverpool	New Orleans	12/08/1848	06/07/1852	25	191	N	
Burk, Edmond	24	Ireland	Y	Galway	Boston	06/07/1846	03/18/1851	3	299	N	
Burk, John	31	Ireland	Y	Liverpool	New Orleans	04/12/1846	10/16/1851	4	301	N	
Burk, John	37	Ireland	Y	Waterford	Boston	06/22/1847	10/28/1858	17	154	N	
Burk, Michael	28	Ireland	Y	Cork	New York	05/01/1845	01/13/1853	7	20	N	
Burk, Otto	28	Germany	Y	Rotterdam	New York	05/17/1880	10/25/1887			Y	
Burk, William	17	Ireland	N	?	New York	00/00/1864				Y	10/22/1888
Burkamp, William Henry	26	Hanover	Y	Bremen	Baltimore	11/06/1851	04/23/1853	8	131	N	
Burkart, Herman	35	Germany	Y	Havre	New York	06/07/1882	02/11/1889			Y	
Burkart, Joseph	34	Germany	Y	Antwerp	Philadelphia	06/22/1875	10/27/1884			Y	
Burkart, Michael	47	Germany	Y	Hamburg	New York	05/16/1886	01/15/1894			Y	
Burke, Edmund	35	Ireland	Y	Liverpool	New Orleans	02/02/1848	11/09/1858	17	308	N	
Burke, Francis N.	24	Ireland	Y	Liverpool	New York	??/01/1852	04/16/1855	11	260	N	
Burke, Henry	23	Hanover	Y	Bremen	New Orleans	10/10/1845	11/15/1848	1	297	N	

CITIZENSHIP RECORDS

APPLICANT	AGE	COUNTRY OF ORIGIN	DEC	DEPART PORT	ENTRY PORT	ARRIVE DATE	DEC DATE	VOL	PG.	FLD	NAT DATE
Burke, James F.	54	Ireland	Y	Dublin	Philadelphia	09/??/1850	10/07/1882			Y	
Burke, John	21	Ireland	Y	Liverpool	New Orleans	12/28/1849	10/14/1851	4	271	N	
Burke, Joseph W.	21	Ireland	Y	Liverpool	New York	07/26/1851	08/04/1856	14	324	N	
Burke, Michael	43	Ireland	Y	Liverpool	New York	04/??/1880	10/08/1884			Y	
Burke, Miles	27	Ireland	Y	Tipperary	New York	05/29/1851	11/24/1858	17	353	N	
Burke, Patrick	30	Ireland	Y	Liverpool	New Orleans	04/18/1850	12/28/1852	5	462	N	
Burke, Patrick	26	Ireland	Y	Liverpool	New York	09/28/1848	09/29/1856	14	427	N	
Burke, Patrick	55	Ireland	N	Liverpool	New Orleans	04/??/1849	?			Y	
Burke, Peter	17	Ireland	N	?	New York	00/00/1874				Y	10/27/1888
Burke, Stanislas	35	Ireland	Y	Queenstown	New York	05/23/1895	10/19/1895			Y	
Burke, Stephen	32	Ireland	Y	Liverpool	New Orleans	11/29/1851	04/04/1853	7	520	N	
Burke, Thomas	32	Ireland	Y	Queenstown	New York	12/??/1874	10/23/1888	19	166	N	
Burke, Thomas	32	Irleand	Y	Queenstown	New York	12/??/1877	10/23/1888			Y	
Burke, Thomas	??	Ireland	Y	?	?	?	10/22/1872			Y	
Burke, Thomas D.	66	Ireland	N	Liverpool	Rochester	04/??/1849	??/??/1849	28	11	N	10/??/1854
Burke, Thomas D.	28	Ireland	N	Liverpool	Rochester NY	04/00/1849	00/00/1849			Y	10/00/1854
Burke, William	26	Ireland	Y	Limerick	Buffalo	10/??/1848	10/29/1851	4	434	N	
Burke, William	23	Ireland	Y	Queenstown	New York	08/16/1885	12/30/1887			Y	
Burkhard, Joseph F.	36	Switzerland	Y	Havre	New York	06/08/1881	08/23/1894			Y	
Burkhardt, Charles	26	Germany	Y	Bremen	Baltimore	07/21/1886	02/01/1890			Y	
Burkhardt, Ernst	27	Germany	Y	Hamburg	New York	04/20/1884	05/02/1887			Y	
Burkhardt, George	28	Wuerttenberg	Y	Antwerp	New York	09/11/1847	02/19/1849	23	204	N	
Burkhardt, Gustav	30	Germany	Y	Hamburg	New York	02/01/1893	09/25/1895			Y	
Burkhardt, Henry Ernst	29	Germany	Y	Antwerp	New York	07/22/1892	05/25/1898			Y	
Burkhardt, Joseph	??	Germany	N	?	?	08/07/1884				Y	10/19/1892
Burkhardt, Julius	25	Oldenburg	Y	Bremen	Baltimore	06/26/1860	07/06/1860	27	207	N	
Burkhardt, Michael	40	Russia	Y	Oesse	New York	10/10/1849	03/06/1852	24	252	N	
Burkhardt, Mike	24	Germany	Y	Antwerp	New York	08/16/1889	11/29/1892			Y	
Burkle, George Fred	25	Germany	Y	Havre	New York	08/15/1886	09/21/1889			Y	
Burling, George	22	Bavaria	Y	Havre	New York	05/10/1860	09/17/1860	27	379	N	
Burmann, Frank	37	Germany	N	Bremen	Baltimore	09/25/1875	?			Y	
Burn, John	40	Ireland	Y	Liverpool	Boston	05/17/1850	11/01/1860	27	550	N	
Burn, Lawrence	27	Ireland	Y	Ross	Detroit	11/??/1854	09/03/1867			Y	
Burnes, Henry	28	Ireland	Y	Liverpool	New Orleans	12/23/1850	12/29/1852	5	469	N	
Burnhoff, Barney	29	Prussia	Y	Rotterdam	New York	05/06/1849	10/09/1854	11	169	N	
Burns, Arthur	51	Ireland	Y	Londonderry	New York	09/09/1886	04/04/1893			Y	
Burns, Daniel	23	Ireland	Y	Liverpool	New Orleans	12/24/1852	03/30/1857	15	102	N	
Burns, James	21	Ireland	Y	Liverpool	New York	01/11/1855	09/11/1855	11	535	N	
Burns, John	28	Ireland	Y	Liverpool	Boston	08/01/1847	11/08/1852	5	241	N	
Burns, John	23	Ireland	Y	Liverpool	New York	08/24/1851	10/03/1854	10	382	N	
Burns, John	23	Ireland	Y	Liverpool	New York	08/20/1851	10/03/1854	12	321	N	
Burns, John	25	Ireland	Y	Liverpool	New Orleans	04/01/1854	02/02/1857	14	527	N	
Burns, John	32	Ireland	Y	Liverpool	Philadelphia	05/18/1878	10/19/1891			Y	
Burns, John	50	Ireland	Y	Queenstown	New York	04/30/1872	11/05/1873			Y	
Burns, Johnathon	26	Ireland	Y	St. Johns	Boston	01/24/1850	10/05/1854	10	438	N	
Burns, Jonathon	26	Ireland	Y	Saint Johns	Boston	01/24/1850	10/05/1854	12	377	N	
Burns, Joseph	22	Ireland	Y	Liverpool	New York	07/04/1847	02/27/1851	3	174	N	
Burns, Joseph	28	Ireland	Y	Liverpool	Boston	08/01/1847	?	6	365	N	
Burns, Michael	27	Ireland	Y	Liverpool	New Orleans	01/01/1848	02/03/1851	3	86	N	
Burns, Michael	29	Ireland	Y	Liverpool	New York	01/17/1850	10/21/1858	17	88	N	
Burns, Michael	47	Ireland	N	Limeriok	Detroit	??/??/1843	?			Y	
Burns, Nicholas	24	Ireland	Y	Liverpool	New Orleans	01/16/1850	03/24/1853	7	384	N	
Burns, Thomas	40	Ireland	Y	Liverpool	New York	03/16/1882	04/04/1894	21	69	N	
Burns, Thomas	40	Ireland	Y	Liverpool	New York	03/16/1882	04/04/1894			Y	
Burns, Thomas	29	Ireland	N	Liverpool	New York	03/15/1887	?			Y	
Burns, Thomas	56	Ireland	N	Ireland	New York	06/??/1850	??/??/1850	28	140	N	??/??/1856
Burns, Thomas	14	England	N	?	New York	00/00/1872				Y	10/26/1888
Burns, Thomas	18	Ireland	N	?	New York	06/00/1850	00/00/1850			Y	00/00/1856
Burns, Timothy	22	Ireland	Y	Liverpool	New Orleans	03/15/1851	10/02/1854	10	340	N	

CITIZENSHIP RECORDS

APPLICANT	AGE	COUNTRY OF ORIGIN	DEC	DEPART PORT	ENTRY PORT	ARRIVE DATE	DEC DATE	VOL	PG.	FLD	NAT DATE
Burns, Timothy	22	Ireland	Y	Liverpool	New Orleans	03/15/1851	10/02/1854	12	279	N	
Burns, Wm M.	40	Scotland	Y	Glasgow	Boston	08/??/1871	10/26/1886			Y	
Burrichter, Joseph H.	42	Germany	N	Bremen	New York	09/??/1867	?			Y	
Burridge, John	27	England	Y	Liverpool	Philadelphia	03/22/1853	07/17/1855	11	404	N	
Burriss, George	29	France	Y	Havre	New York	06/05/1852	01/14/1853	7	23	N	
Burrow, Robert	??	England	N	?	?	?	?			Y	03/26/1855
Burrus, Edward	38	Germany	Y	Havre	New York	02/05/1881	10/13/1884			Y	
Burski, William	29	Germany	Y	Bremen	Baltimore	09/18/1889	10/18/1895			Y	
Burt, John	37	Scotland	Y	Liverpool	Philadelphia	04/05/1852	01/02/1856	13	416	N	
Bury, August	31	Germany	Y	Havre	New York	04/30/1881	11/01/1883			Y	
Burz, John	27	Wuerttenberg	Y	Havre	New York	05/18/1847	09/08/1848	22	311	N	
Busam, Joseph	24	Baden	Y	Havre	New York	07/08/1854	02/04/1856	26	20	N	
Busch, Anton	26	Germany	Y	Bremen	New York	10/20/1881	11/01/1889			Y	
Busch, August	30	Germany	Y	Antwerp	Philadelphia	06/27/1881	04/??/1882			Y	
Busch, August	30	Germany	N	Antwerp	Philadelphia	06/27/1881	?			Y	
Busch, August	50	Germany	N	Bremen	New Orleans	01/??/1854	?			Y	
Busch, Charles	22	Hanover	Y	Bremen	Baltimore	08/18/1849	11/06/1852	5	249	N	
Busch, Charles	24	Baden	Y	Rotterdam	Baltimore	09/15/1846	05/11/1852	25	4	N	
Busch, Christian	23	Germany	Y	Hamburg	New York	12/02/1880	12/26/1885			Y	
Busch, Daniel	??	Germany	N	?	?	03/16/1886				Y	10/27/1892
Busch, Frederick	27	Germany	Y	Hamburg	New York	03/15/1883	10/28/1886			Y	
Busch, H.	27	Germany	Y	Hamburg	New York	07/27/1882	07/13/1885			Y	
Busch, Heironimus	58	Germany	Y	Bremen	New York	10/20/1881	11/04/1889			Y	
Busch, Henry	43	Germany	Y	Bremen	New York	12/??/1865	10/23/1879			Y	
Busch, Herman	29	Germany	Y	Hamburg	New York	07/26/1882	05/25/1885			Y	
Busch, John B.E.	32	Germany	Y	Bremen	Baltimore	02/01/1880	04/07/1886			Y	
Busch, John Frederick	35	Hanover	Y	Bremen	Baltimore	06/??/1845	03/26/1853	7	404	N	
Busch, John Frederick	35	Hanover	Y	Bremen	Baltimore	06/??/1845	03/26/1853			Y	03/26/1855
Busch, Konrad	26	Germany	Y	Antwerp	Philadelphia	03/19/1887	10/12/1889			Y	
Busch, Wilhelm	59	Germany	N	Bremen	Baltimore	03/03/1875	?			Y	
Buschelmann, B.	16	Germany	N	?	Baltimore	00/00/1873				Y	10/26/1882
Buscher, Andrew Clements	23	Prussia	Y	Bremen	New Orleans	12/25/1852	02/12/1856	26	72	N	
Buscher, Ernst	28	Prussia	Y	Bremen	Baltimore	05/01/1857	07/23/1860	27	234	N	
Buscher, Herman	16	Germany	N	?	New York	00/00/1881				Y	10/23/1886
Buscher, Joseph	23	Hanover	Y	Bremen	Baltimore	05/08/1848	11/22/1848	1	370	N	
Buscherfeld, Joseph	32	Germany	Y	Bremen	Baltimore	06/03/1891	02/23/1900			Y	
Buschermoehle, Gerhard	34	Hanover	Y	Bremen	New York	05/22/1854	03/05/1858	16	374	N	
Buschermuehle, Diederich	33	Hanover	Y	Bremen	New Orleans	05/01/1849	10/09/1854	11	61	N	
Buschermuehle, Diederick	33	Hanover	Y	Bremen	New Orleans	05/01/1849	10/09/1854	6	60	N	
Buschmann, Frederick	28	Prussia	Y	Antwerp	New Orleans	03/15/1851	09/21/18??	10	141	N	
Buschmann, Frederick	28	Prussia	Y	Antwerp	New Orleans	03/15/1851	09/21/1852	12	80	N	
Buschmann, William	27	Germany	Y	Bremen	New York	04/25/1882	05/25/1885			Y	
Buschmeier, Frank	50	Germany	Y	Bremen	New York	11/03/1865	11/11/1892			Y	
Buschorn, Diedrich	30	Hanover	Y	Bremen	New Orleans	11/12/1847	01/19/1849	1	463	N	
Buschow, Carl Ludwig	43	Hamburg	Y	Hamburg	New York	01/10/1854	05/01/1854	9	310	N	
Buschow, Charles Ludwig	43	Hamburg	Y	Hamburg	New York	01/10/1854	05/01/1854	8	337	N	
Busemeyer, Joseph	28	Germany	Y	Bremen	Baltimore	06/09/1881	11/01/1890			Y	
Buser, Henry	41	Germany	Y	Havre	New York	11/10/1891	01/12/1892			Y	
Bush, Charles	22	Hanover	Y	Bremen	Baltimore	08/18/1849	11/06/1852	6	373	N	
Bush, John Gerhard	27	Prussia	Y	Antwerp	New York	09/15/1857	01/02/1860	27	19	N	
Bush, John L.	47	Germany	Y	Sagnitz	New York	05/23/1880	08/28/1883			Y	
Bushell, Patrick	63	Ireland	N	Liverpool	New York	12/??/1856	?			Y	
Busiger, Joseph	25	Switzerland	Y	Havre	New Orleans	07/27/1847	02/17/1849	23	160	N	
Buske, Bernard	32	Oldenburg	Y	Bremen	New York	12/??/1847	05/08/1854	8	402	N	
Buske, Bernard	32	Oldenburg	Y	Bremen	New York	12/??/1847	05/08/1854	9	274	N	
Buske, John	27	Oldenburg	Y	Bremen	Baltimore	09/10/1847	11/01/1852	5	97	N	
Buske, William Rudolph	24	Prussia	Y	Bremen	New Orleans	10/05/1847	02/08/1849	23	123	N	
Busken, Henry	30	Prussia	Y	Bremen	Baltimore	04/25/1846	02/14/1849	23	94	N	
Busken, John Herman	??	Hanover	N	?	?	?	?			Y	03/27/1855

CITIZENSHIP RECORDS

APPLICANT	AGE	COUNTRY OF ORIGIN	DEC	DEPART PORT	ENTRY PORT	ARRIVE DATE	DEC DATE	VOL	PG.	FLD	NAT DATE
Busmann, Joseph	23	Prussia	Y	Bremen	Baltimore	05/01/1856	12/06/1859	17	493	N	
Busmeier, Christ	40	Hanover	Y	Bremen	New York	05/01/1857	04/05/1861	18	134	N	
Busmeyer, Aug. (Busemeye	17	Germany	N	?	Baltimore	04/00/1883				Y	10/27/1888
Busse, Charles	24	Germany	N	Antwerp	New York	09/27/1885	11/29/1889			Y	
Busse, Frederick	24	Prussia	Y	Bremen	Baltimore	12/16/1849	10/07/1854	6	40	N	
Busse, Frederick	24	Prussia	Y	Bremen	Baltimore	12/16/1849	10/07/1854	11	41	N	
Busser, Adolph	31	Germany	Y	Bremen	New York	10/25/1890	11/23/1894			Y	
Bussing, George Henry	41	Oldenburg	Y	Bremen	Baltimore	06/??/1832	03/23/1853	7	373	N	
Bussmann, Frank	22	Germany	Y	Rotterdam	New York	10/09/1881	04/09/1883			Y	
Bussmann, Henry	29	Germany	Y	Bremen	New York	11/22/1882	09/05/1885			Y	
Bussmann, J.F.	24	Germany	Y	Bremen	Baltimore	07/24/1881	02/03/1883			Y	
Bussmann, Joseph	36	Germany	Y	Bremen	New York	08/??/1874	07/03/1888			Y	
Busz, Jacob	26	Prussia	Y	?	?	06/07/1895	10/23/1896			Y	
Butel, Antoine Victor Re	27	France	Y	Havre	New York	12/20/1868	01/25/1872	18	459	N	
Buter, Henrich	23	Hanover	Y	Bremen	New Orleans	11/15/1857	08/03/1860	27	247	N	
Butke, George W.	65	Germany	N	Bremen	Baltimore	10/11/1857	?			Y	
Butke, John Henry	29	Hanover	Y	Bremen	New Orleans	11/10/1845	08/03/1848	22	54	N	
Butler, Colum	28	Ireland	Y	Liverpool	New York	09/21/1849	11/01/18??	5	165	N	
Butler, Colum	28	Ireland	Y	Liverpool	New York	09/21/1849	11/01/1852	6	291	N	
Butler, James	22	Ireland	Y	Liverpool	New York	09/15/1850	05/25/1854	8	529	N	
Butler, James	22	Ireland	Y	Liverpool	New York	09/25/1850	05/25/1854	9	403	N	
Butler, James	??	?	N	?	?	?	?			Y	10/29/1844
Butler, John	24	Ireland	Y	Liverpool	New Orleans	12/01/1850	11/16/1857	16	21	N	
Butler, John	30	Ireland	Y	Liverpool	Boston	04/05/1851	12/14/1857	16	221	N	
Butler, John Gerhard	23	Hanover	Y	Bremen	Baltimore	05/01/1849	06/01/1852	25	170	N	
Butler, Michael	26	Ireland	Y	Liverpool	New Orleans	04/29/1852	04/04/1853	7	523	N	
Butler, Michael	38	Ireland	Y	Liverpool	New York	08/10/1854	02/06/1858	16	80	N	
Butler, Morris	22	Ireland	Y	Liverpool	New York	08/18/1842	08/25/1857	15	185	N	
Butler, Patrick C.	48	Canada	Y	Quebec	Buffalo	09/01/1862	11/03/1892	19	408	N	
Butler, Patrick C.	48	Canada	Y	Quebec	Buffalo	09/01/1862	11/03/1892			Y	
Butler, Thomas A.	50	Newfoundland	N	St. John	Detroit	??/??/1859	?			Y	
Butler, William	25	Ireland	Y	Liverpool	Boston	05/25/1848	01/23/1851	2	522	N	
Butler, William	24	Ireland	Y	Liverpool	New Orleans	04/29/1852	04/04/1853	7	522	N	
Butralik, Frank	23	Russia	Y	Hamburg	Philadelphia	04/06/1890	04/11/1891			Y	
Butscha, Frederick	28	Baden	Y	Havre	New York	05/10/1851	12/13/1851	4	512	N	
Butschi, Albert	55	Switzerland	N	Hamburg	New York	04/07/1867	?			Y	
Buttel, Barney	??	Hanover	Y	?	New Orleans	??/20/18??	10/28/1850	2	316	N	
Buttenwieser, Moses	41	Germany	Y	Amsterdam	New York	06/06/1897	08/18/1903			Y	
Butter, Conrad	22	Hesse Darmsta	Y	London	New York	11/26/1854	10/08/1857	15	380	N	
Butterhoff, John	??	Bavaria	Y	Bremen	New York	??/06/1853	04/18/1855	11	272	N	
Butterley, Thomas	36	Ireland	Y	Liverpool	New Orleans	11/12/1847	10/21/1851	4	364	N	
Buttker, John	33	Mecklenburg S	Y	Hamburg	New York	07/12/1857	02/14/1860	27	106	N	
Buttland, John	26	Wales	Y	?	New York	02/17/1883	10/05/1888			Y	
Buttner, Adam G.	43	Germany	Y	Antwerp	New York	01/22/1882	09/08/1887			Y	
Buttner, Adolf	20	Germany	Y	Antwerp	New York	06/11/1881	01/30/1882			Y	
Buttner, Christian	28	Germany	Y	Antwerp	New York	09/19/1877	11/02/1882			Y	
Buttner, Frank	27	Germany	Y	Havre	New York	10/10/1882	08/02/1889			Y	
Buttner, George	46	Germany	Y	Bremen	New York	08/19/1882	08/05/1889			Y	
Butz, Andreas	28	Baden	Y	Havre	New Orleans	09/13/1847	10/29/1852	5	59	N	
Butz, Christian Henry	25	Wurttemberg	Y	Havre	New York	04/29/1847	02/18/1850	2	95	N	
Buxbaum, Aaron	33	Bavaria	Y	Havre	New York	08/13/1847	04/21/1854	8	233	N	
Buxbaum, Aaron	33	Bavaria	Y	Havre	New York	08/13/1847	04/21/1854	9	104	N	
Buxe, John Theodore	31	Hanover	Y	Bremen	New Orleans	05/13/1849	03/25/1856	26	334	N	
Byard, Nathaniel	31	England	Y	Liverpool	New York	05/26/1849	03/13/1858	16	398	N	
Byarsky, Ike	28	Russia	Y	Hamburg	Philadelphia	07/23/1881	05/07/1883	28	168	N	
Byarsky, Ike	23	Russia	Y	Hamburg	Philadelphia	07/23/1881	05/07/1883			Y	
Byrane, John	27	Ireland	Y	Liverpool	New Orleans	12/17/1849	01/29/1851	2	541	N	
Byrne, Eugene	26	Ireland	Y	New Ross	Lewiston	10/20/1852	03/25/1856	26	313	N	
Byrne, Hugh	29	Ireland	Y	Liverpool	New York	04/??/1870	04/07/1879			Y	

CITIZENSHIP RECORDS

APPLICANT	AGE	COUNTRY OF ORIGIN	DEC	DEPART PORT	ENTRY PORT	ARRIVE DATE	DEC DATE	VOL	PG.	FLD	NAT DATE
Byrne, James	24	Ireland	Y	Canada	Rochester	06/02/1842	11/21/1848	1	357	N	
Byrne, James	21	Ireland	Y	Liverpool	New York	05/20/1849	05/14/1852	25	19	N	
Byrne, John	40	Ireland	Y	Liverpool	New York	08/07/1849	08/04/1851	4	88	N	
Byrne, John	23	Ireland	Y	Liverpool	New Orleans	01/03/1848	03/17/1853	7	339	N	
Byrne, John	21	Ireland	Y	Liverpool	New Orleans	01/01/1851	10/04/1858	17	39	N	
Byrne, Joseph	30	Ireland	Y	New Ross	Buffalo	06/09/1850	12/27/1852	5	451	N	
Byrne, Michael	29	Ireland	Y	Liverpool	New Orleans	11/19/1847	11/20/1848	1	339	N	
Byrne, Michael	32	Ireland	Y	Liverpool	New Orleans	06/15/1847	11/21/1848	1	361	N	
Byrne, Michael	32	Ireland	Y	Liverpool	New York	05/08/1848	05/18/1852	25	35	N	
Byrne, Michael	28	Ireland	Y	New Ross	Oswego	05/17/1851	03/14/1856	26	196	N	
Byrne, Patrick	28	Ireland	Y	Dublin	New Orleans	12/03/1848	08/??/1851	4	158	N	
Byrne, Patrick	27	Ireland	Y	Liverpool	New York	11/02/1852	02/07/1857	14	543	N	
Byrne, Thomas	35	Ireland	N	Liverpool	New York	09/??/1867	?			Y	
Byrnes, John	29	Ireland	Y	Liverpool	New York	06/22/1844	05/17/1852	25	26	N	
Byrnes, Michael	21	Ireland	Y	Dublin	New Orleans	12/30/1850	11/03/1851	4	471	N	
Byrnes, William	30	Ireland	Y	Liverpool	New York	06/07/1847	04/17/1852	24	522	N	
Byrns, James J.	39	Ireland	N	Canada	Detroit	11/??/1865	?			Y	
Byrns, John	30	Ireland	Y	Dublin	New York	07/03/1849	10/06/1854	10	475	N	
Byrns, John	30	Ireland	Y	Dublin	New York	07/03/1849	10/06/1854	12	414	N	
Byrns, Laurence	24	Ireland	Y	Liverpool	New Orleans	11/19/1852	04/17/1854	9	24	N	
Byrns, Lawrence	24	Ireland	Y	Liverpool	New Orleans	11/19/1852	04/17/1854	8	153	N	
Byrns, Maurice	24	Ireland	Y	Dublin	New Orleans	03/20/1844	10/06/1854	10	480	N	
Byrns, Maurice	24	Ireland	Y	Dublin	New Orleans	03/20/1844	10/06/1854	12	419	N	
Byrns, Thomas	28	Ireland	Y	Liverpool	New Orleans	01/06/1852	10/01/1856	14	121	N	
Bywaters, Edward	36	Ireland	Y	Waterford	New Orleans	04/23/1848	07/09/1851	3	516	N	
Cabry, John	41	Ireland	Y	Dublin	New York	04/24/1852	09/30/1854	10	321	N	
Cabry, John	41	Ireland	Y	Dublin	New York	04/24/1852	09/30/1854	12	260	N	
Caburet, Peter F.	45	France	Y	Havre	New York	09/12/1849	11/27/1852	5	348	N	
Cadot, Joseph	40	France	Y	Havre	New York	11/09/1890	11/02/1892			Y	
Caffery, Patrick	38	Ireland	Y	Liverpool	New York	07/03/1848	01/16/1851	2	499	N	
Caffrey, Michael	29	Ireland	Y	Canada	Cleveland	??/20/1847	11/??/1849	23	319	N	
Cahill, Patrick	32	Ireland	Y	Liverpool	New Orleans	06/??/1845	12/??/1849	23	439	N	
Cahn, Berthold	27	Germany	Y	Hamburg	New York	11/22/1883	01/25/1888			Y	
Cahn, John	27	Ireland	Y	Liverpool	New Orleans	05/19/1849	09/13/1852	25	491	N	
Caie, Thomas J.	??	England	Y	?	?	?	10/09/1886			Y	
Cain, John	25	Ireland	Y	Glasgow	New York	10/24/1852	09/25/1854	10	208	N	
Cain, John	25	Ireland	Y	Glasgow	New York	10/24/1852	09/25/1854	12	147	N	
Cain, John F.	41	Canada	Y	Toronto	Detroit	08/20/1891	08/14/1893			Y	
Cain, Patrick	30	Ireland	Y	Cork	New Orleans	02/04/1848	08/02/1851	4	75	N	
Cain, Peter	28	Ireland	Y	Liverpool	New York	06/??/1841	08/23/1852	25	326	N	
Cairncross, Alex	50	Scotland	Y	Glasgow	New York	04/12/1847	01/06/1853	5	526	N	
Caito, G. Battista	48	Italy	Y	Palermo	New York	04/20/1882	10/17/1893	21	18	N	
Caito, G. Battista	48	Italy	Y	Palermo	New York	04/20/1882	10/17/1893			Y	
Caito, Leonardo	39	Itlay	Y	Palermo	New York	10/10/1881	01/24/1890			Y	
Calabrese, Salvatore	28	Italy	Y	Naples	New York	05/09/1889	06/05/1894			Y	
Calacoff, Naten	??	Russia	Y	?	?	?	04/21/1896			Y	
Calder, George S.	??	England	Y	?	?	?	08/23/1894			Y	
Caldwell, John	50	Ireland	Y	Liverpool	New York	07/??/1841	12/09/1850	2	353	N	
Calin, James	25	Ireland	Y	Dublin	New York	05/01/1849	11/03/1851	4	468	N	
Callaghan, Jeremiah	23	Ireland	Y	Cork	New York	04/10/1849	12/15/1851	4	518	N	
Callahan, Daniel	24	Ireland	Y	Londonderry	New York	04/15/1893	10/17/1889			Y	
Callahan, Daniel	29	Ireland	Y	Gallway	Detroit	??/??/1857	10/01/1858			Y	
Callahan, Eugene	23	Ireland	Y	Liverpool	New York	06/01/1847	03/17/1851	3	284	N	
Callahan, John	29	Ireland	Y	Liverpool	New Orleans	05/04/1849	12/28/1852	5	457	N	
Callahan, Owen	38	Ireland	Y	Cork	Boston	06/28/1840	02/15/1851	3	131	N	
Callahan, Owen Francis	33	Ireland	Y	Liverpool	New Orleans	11/07/1848	12/27/1851	24	21	N	
Callahan, Patrick	26	Ireland	Y	Liverpool	New Orleans	03/07/1852	04/07/1858	16	503	N	
Callanan, Michael	26	Ireland	Y	Galway	New York	04/01/1850	10/13/1857	15	413	N	
Callander, Thomas	38	Scotland	Y	Liverpool	New York	??/16/1842	02/07/1850	2	45	N	

CITIZENSHIP RECORDS

APPLICANT	AGE	COUNTRY OF ORIGIN	DEC	DEPART PORT	ENTRY PORT	ARRIVE DATE	DEC DATE	VOL	PG.	FLD	NAT DATE
Calmbach, Ch.	21	Wurttemburg	Y	Bremen	New York	09/07/1872	10/06/1873			Y	
Calnan, Michael	30	Ireland	Y	Liverpool	New York	11/15/1847	11/02/1858	17	261	N	
Cambeis, John	24	Bavaria	Y	Havre	New Orleans	12/24/1846	03/25/1850	2	253	N	
Campbell, Benjamin	53	England	Y	Liverpool	New York	08/14/1882	04/03/1890			Y	
Campbell, Daniel	35	Ireland	Y	Galway	New York	06/19/1842	07/15/1851	3	538	N	
Campbell, Francis	22	Ireland	Y	Liverpool	New Orleans	12/13/1851	11/23/1852	5	333	N	
Campbell, George U.	45	Canada	Y	Bradford	Cincinnati	05/08/1865	10/31/1889			Y	
Campbell, James	49	Ireland	Y	Liverpool	New Orleans	10/29/1849	04/04/1853	8	39	N	
Campbell, James	31	Italy	Y	Naples	New York	04/15/1880	10/13/1893	21	4	N	
Campbell, James Morley	??	England	Y	?	?	?	10/06/1894			Y	
Campbell, John	28	Scotland	Y	Glasgow	New York	08/01/1843	07/09/1851	3	513	N	
Campbell, John	44	Scotland	Y	Glasgow	Boston	01/22/1884	08/02/1889			Y	
Campbell, Joseph	??	England	Y	?	?	?	02/26/1884			Y	
Campbell, Martin	25	Canada	Y	Windsor	Detroit	09/20/1887	10/29/1889			Y	
Campbell, Patrick	26	Ireland	Y	Londonderry	New York	11/11/1884	07/10/1889			Y	
Campbell, William	??	England	Y	?	?	?	04/26/1892			Y	
Campion, Martin	??	Ireland	Y	Canada	Oswego	??/18/1848	03/25/1851	3	339	N	
Cancelliere, Mariano	??	Italy	Y	?	?	?	05/15/1884			Y	
Canda, Leo	??	Austria	Y	?	?	?	05/28/1892			Y	
Canfield, John	26	Ireland	Y	Canada	Buffalo	06/01/1848	11/13/1848	1	271	N	
Cannon, Michael	17	Ireland	N	?	New York	00/00/1882				Y	10/13/1888
Canolopy, Timothy	23	Ireland	Y	Limerick	Philadelphia	04/18/1847	10/02/1848	1	8	N	
Canon, James	45	Ireland	N	Dunndock	?	?	?			Y	
Cantelon, Samuel A.	30	Canada	Y	Windsor	Detroit	10/21/1892	03/16/1895			Y	
Cantner, John Christian	29	Wurttemberg	Y	Havre	New Orleans	?	07/12/1851	3	524	N	
Cantrup, Henry	23	Hanover	Y	Bremen	Baltimore	06/30/1855	04/02/1858	16	471	N	
Canty, Jeremiah	50	Ireland	Y	London	Oswego	05/01/1877	01/31/1883			Y	
Cantzler, Andrew	26	Austria	Y	Hamburg	New York	??/15/1850	06/12/1854	10	115	N	
Cantzler, Andrew	26	Austria	Y	Hamburg	New York	??/15/1850	06/12/1854	12	52	N	
Capell, Peter	30	Prussia	Y	Antwerp	New York	09/26/1852	10/30/1858	17	210	N	
Caplan, Rubi	22	Russia	Y	?	New York	04/??/1890	10/17/1892			Y	
Capone, John	24	Italy	Y	?	?	?	10/09/1903			Y	
Cappaca, Solomon	23	Italy	Y	Naples	New York	04/02/1891	10/30/1896			Y	
Cappay, Thomas	29	Italy	Y	Naples	New York	04/15/1894	11/02/1896			Y	
Cappel, Peter S.	36	Germany	N	Bremen	New York	05/16/1863	?			Y	
Caproni, Enrico	17	Italy	N	?	New York	00/00/1882				Y	10/26/1888
Caproni, Joe	11	Italy	N	?	New York	00/00/1870				Y	10/20/1888
Carbade, Nicolaus	33	Germany	Y	Bremen	Baltimore	10/08/1892	01/02/1896			Y	
Carderone, Salvatore	48	Italy	Y	?	New York	05/27/1883	10/26/1900			Y	
Care, Timothy	31	Ireland	Y	Liverpool	Boston	04/29/1845	04/20/1853	8	89	N	
Carey, Daniel	23	Ireland	Y	Queenstown	New York	08/10/1888	06/05/1889	19	228	N	
Carey, Dennis	36	Ireland	Y	Liverpool	New Orleans	04/01/1851	05/15/1854	8	444	N	
Carey, Dennis	36	Ireland	Y	Liverpool	New Orleans	04/01/1851	05/15/1854	9	317	N	
Carey, James W.	25	Ireland	Y	Queenstown	New York	11/???/1878	09/30/1881			Y	
Carey, William	35	Scotland	Y	Glasgow	New York	05/30/1881	10/26/1896			Y	
Carfagna, Luigi	60	Italy	Y	Naples	New York	11/16/1882	02/11/1895			Y	
Cariotti, Joseph	32	Italy	Y	Naples	New York	03/15/1890	10/26/1900			Y	
Carl, Carl August	22	Prussia	Y	Liverpool	New York	10/28/1852	09/26/1854	10	229	N	
Carl, Carl August	22	Prussia	Y	Liverpool	New York	10/28/1852	09/26/1854	12	168	N	
Carl, Joseph	29	Germany	Y	Antwerp	New York	06/20/1889	02/03/1894			Y	
Carl, Samuel	35	Baden	Y	Havre	New York	?	03/??/1850	2	229	N	
Carlsson, Algot	??	Norway	Y	?	?	?	03/20/1891			Y	
Carmaco, Gaetano	25	Italy	Y	Naples	New York	05/01/1896	12/05/1898			Y	
Carmal, Henry Philip	34	Oldenburg	Y	Bremen	Baltimore	09/01/1845	10/28/1858	17	142	N	
Carmichael, Robert	27	Ireland	Y	Liverpool	New York	03/23/1850	04/02/1853	7	488	N	
Carney, Austin	23	Ireland	Y	Queenstown	New York	05/19/1888	09/20/1889			Y	
Carney, Edward	36	Ireland	Y	Liverpool	New Orleans	03/31/1852	05/22/1856	26	527	N	
Carney, James	30	Ireland	Y	Liverpool	New Orleans	05/04/1849	06/07/1854	10	100	N	
Carney, James	30	Ireland	Y	Liverpool	New Orleans	05/04/1849	06/06/1854	12	37	N	

CITIZENSHIP RECORDS

APPLICANT	AGE	COUNTRY OF ORIGIN	DEC	DEPART PORT	ENTRY PORT	ARRIVE DATE	DEC DATE	VOL	PG.	FLD	NAT DATE
Carney, John	43	Ireland	Y	Cork	Baltimore	04/10/1851	11/05/1858	17	282	N	
Carney, John	64	Ireland	Y	Liverpool	New York	11/??/1856	10/12/1885	19	22	N	
Carney, John	35	Ireland	Y	Liverpool	New York	04/26/1857	07/09/1860	27	214	N	
Carney, John	64	Ireland	Y	Liverpool	New York	10/00/1856	10/12/1885			Y	
Carney, John	14	England	N	?	New York	00/00/1879				Y	04/03/1886
Carney, Michael	27	Ireland	Y	Liverpool	New York	04/27/1858	07/09/1860	27	213	N	
Carney, Patrick	26	Ireland	Y	Westport	New York	06/25/1885	04/10/1891			Y	
Carney, Patrick	47	Ireland	N	Liverpool	New York	12/14/1855	?			Y	
Carney, William	37	Ireland	Y	Liverpool	New York	04/22/1842	09/11/1848	22	328	N	
Carr, Edward	23	Ireland	Y	Liverpool	New York	05/04/1857	10/16/1857	15	434	N	
Carr, John	47	Ireland	Y	Liverpool	New York	01/06/1850	10/21/1858	17	84	N	
Carr, Michael	29	Ireland	Y	Liverpool	New Orleans	01/07/1848	03/15/1852	24	302	N	
Carrigan, James	29	Ireland	Y	Liverpool	New York	05/20/1880	08/16/1886			Y	
Carrigan, John	35	Ireland	Y	Queenstown	New York	05/01/1882	10/27/1892	19	386	N	
Carrigan, John	35	Ireland	Y	Queenstown	New York	05/01/1882	10/27/1892			Y	
Carrino, Angelo	??	Italy	Y	?	?	?	04/01/1891			Y	
Carrol, James	24	Ireland	Y	Liverpool	New Orleans	08/12/1847	10/15/1851	4	299	N	
Carrol, John	45	Ireland	Y	Waterford	Lowell	08/??/1835	04/15/1853	8	66	N	
Carroll, Bernard	31	Ireland	Y	Liverpool	New York	06/22/1849	01/18/1850	23	523	N	
Carroll, Cornelius	23	Ireland	Y	Liverpool	New York	05/13/1846	10/14/1851	4	268	N	
Carroll, John	45	Ireland	Y	Queenstown	New York	07/??/1869	10/25/1892	19	382	N	
Carroll, John	22	Ireland	Y	Queenstown	New York	05/19/1882	12/17/1883			Y	
Carroll, John	45	Ireland	Y	Queenstown	New York	07/??/1869	10/25/1892			Y	
Carroll, John Charles	24	Ireland	Y	Queenstown	New York	06/04/1897	04/04/1903			Y	
Carroll, Michael	66	Ireland	N	Queenstown	New York	06/??/1861	?			Y	
Carroll, Patrick	24	Ireland	Y	Liverpool	New York	06/22/1848	01/11/1851	2	482	N	
Carroll, Patrick	23	Ireland	Y	Queenstown	New York	06/20/1893	09/03/1897			Y	
Carroll, Patrick	41	Ireland	N	Queenstown	New York	11/17/1862	?			Y	
Carroll, Patrick	4	Ireland	N	?	New York	00/00/1845				Y	10/16/1888
Carroll, Philip L.	??	Ireland	N	?	?	?				Y	03/15/1855
Carroll, William	24	Ireland	Y	Dublin	New Orleans	04/10/1847	09/26/1854	10	250	N	
Carroll, William	24	Ireland	Y	Dublin	New Orleans	04/10/1847	09/26/1854	12	189	N	
Carstens, Julius	29	Germany	Y	Hamburg	New York	10/27/1879	03/29/1881			Y	
Cartan, Michael	27	Ireland	Y	Cork	Boston	08/22/1845	08/??/1851	4	168	N	
Carter, John	24	Ireland	Y	Liverpool	New York	04/04/1849	09/20/1854	10	327	N	
Carter, John	24	Ireland	Y	Liverpool	New York	04/04/1849	09/30/1854	12	266	N	
Carter, Sydney F.	26	England	Y	Liverpool	Detroit	08/09/1888	10/28/1893			Y	
Cartwright, James	23	England	Y	Liverpool	New York	03/05/1849	02/24/1851	3	167	N	
Cartwright, Mark	50	England	Y	Liverpool	New York	03/05/1849	02/24/1851	3	168	N	
Cartwright, William T.	22	Ireland	Y	Liverpool	New Orleans	05/02/1849	04/05/1852	24	388	N	
Carty, John	25	Ireland	Y	London	New York	04/05/1849	10/20/1851	4	350	N	
Carty, Thomas	25	Ireland	Y	St. Johns	Boston	10/30/1846	02/16/1852	24	125	N	
Caruso, Antonio	24	Italy	Y	Naples	New York	21/19/1886	09/23/1890			Y	
Caruso, Zilomeno	28	Italy	Y	Naples	New York	07/19/1890	10/27/1900			Y	
Carvill, William	27	Ireland	Y	Liverpool	Detroit	05/20/1882	10/28/1886	19	123	N	
Carvill, William	27	Ireland	Y	Liverpool	Detroit	05/20/1882	10/28/1884			Y	
Carvill, William	46	Ireland	Y	Liverpool	New York	06/24/1867	10/30/1882			Y	
Cary, Michael	23	Ireland	Y	Liverpool	New York	04/13/1849	05/01/1854	8	312	N	
Cary, Michael	23	Ireland	Y	Liverpool	New York	04/13/1849	05/01/1854	9	185	N	
Casey, John	60	Ireland	Y	Liverpool	New Orleans	03/09/1850	03/01/1853	7	249	N	
Casey, John	25	Ireland	Y	Liverpool	New Orleans	03/10/1850	03/07/1853	7	287	N	
Casey, John	28	Ireland	Y	Queenstown	New York	06/21/1885	10/06/1887			Y	
Casey, Luke	55	Ireland	N	Limerick	Buffalo	??/??/1847	?			Y	
Casey, Patrick	32	Ireland	Y	Liverpool	New York	06/10/1846	03/05/1850	2	160	N	
Casey, Patrick	30	Ireland	Y	Liverpool	Boston	05/06/1848	03/31/1852	24	343	N	
Casey, Peter	23	Ireland	Y	Liverpool	New York	05/10/1853	10/20/1858	17	81	N	
Casey, Thomas John	25	Ireland	Y	Dublin	New York	06/06/1849	07/25/1851	4	39	N	
Cash, Tony	31	Italy	Y	Naples	New York	03/17/1889	10/13/1896			Y	
Caslin, Martin	28	Ireland	Y	Dublin	New York	05/10/1847	04/17/1852	24	524	N	

CITIZENSHIP RECORDS

APPLICANT	AGE	COUNTRY OF ORIGIN	DEC	DEPART PORT	ENTRY PORT	ARRIVE DATE	DEC DATE	VOL	PG.	FLD	NAT DATE
Casper, Ludwig	40	Germany	Y	Havre	New York	03/01/1873	10/09/1882			Y	
Casper, Meinrad	31	Switzerland	Y	Bremen	New York	10/22/1880	10/10/1888			Y	
Casperson, Hans Peter	??	Denmark	Y	?	?	?	05/06/1892			Y	
Cass, John Joseph	??	England	Y	?	?	?	01/04/1893			Y	
Cassani, John	24	Switzerland	Y	?	New York	??/??/1890	07/20/1891			Y	
Cassedy, John	6	Ireland	N	?	New York	00/00/1856				Y	10/23/1888
Cassedy, Michael	32	Ireland	N	Queenstown	New York	06/06/1871	?			Y	
Casselley, Patrick	30	Ireland	Y	Liverpool	New York	08/15/1852	05/04/1854	9	249	N	
Casselmann, Thomas	36	Prussia	Y	Bremen	New Orleans	11/25/1850	09/27/1856	14	402	N	
Casserly, John	30	Ireland	N	Liverpool	New York	08/??/1869	?			Y	
Cassidy, Barney	33	Ireland	Y	Liverpool	New Orleans	04/??/1852	04/29/1854	8	285	N	
Cassidy, Barney	33	Ireland	Y	Liverpool	New Orleans	04/??/1852	04/29/1854	9	157	N	
Cassidy, James H.	28	Ireland	Y	Liverpool	New York	10/15/1847	10/20/1852	5	65	N	
Cassidy, John	24	Ireland	Y	Liverpool	New York	04/08/1847	11/24/1848	1	381	N	
Cassidy, John	29	Ireland	Y	Liverpool	New York	12/25/1850	02/09/1853	7	132	N	
Cassidy, John	22	Ireland	Y	Liverpool	New Orleans	04/14/1848	04/24/1854	8	248	N	
Cassidy, John	22	Ireland	Y	Liverpool	New Orleans	04/14/1848	04/24/1854	9	119	N	
Cassidy, Patrick	28	Ireland	Y	Liverpool	New York	05/01/1849	03/01/1853	7	252	N	
Cassilly, Patrick	30	Ireland	Y	Liverpool	New York	08/15/1852	05/05/1854	8	376	N	
Cassilly, William	40	Ireland	N	Queenstown	New York	06/10/1870	?			Y	
Cassini, Oswaldo	??	Italy	Y	?	?	?	12/24/1892			Y	
Cassini, Pietro	??	Italy	Y	?	?	?	03/28/1892			Y	
Cassini, Remigio	??	Italy	Y	?	?	?	12/19/1892			Y	
Cassini, Sante	??	Italy	Y	?	?	?	12/27/1892			Y	
Castellini, Luigi	37	Italy	Y	Genoa	New York	04/12/1881	06/16/1892			Y	
Castello, William	55	Ireland	Y	Liverpool	New York	03/01/1863	10/21/1896			Y	
Caston, George	27	Greece	Y	Athens	New York	05/05/1885	02/04/1891			Y	
Castrucci, Giustino	??	Italy	Y	?	?	?	01/07/1897			Y	
Catazano, Petro	32	Italy	Y	Palermo	New York	02/21/1887	10/18/1893			Y	
Cattani, John	32	Switzerland	Y	Havre	New York	10/27/1879	03/12/1886			Y	
Caulfield, John	24	Ireland	Y	Dublin	New York	10/30/1849	12/20/1852	5	430	N	
Caulfield, John	40	Ireland	Y	Waterford	New York	01/15/1883	03/05/1888			Y	
Caulfield, Robert	??	Ireland	N	?	?	01/18/1886				Y	10/27/1892
Caunnan, Timothy	??	Ireland	Y	Liverpool	New York	??/18/1846	03/10/1851	3	271	N	
Cavanagh, Michael	28	Ireland	Y	Limerick	Buffalo	06/27/1848	11/17/1852	5	302	N	
Cavanagh, Thomas	25	Ireland	Y	Dublin	New York	09/20/1851	10/04/1854	10	420	N	
Cavanagh, Thomas	25	Ireland	Y	Dublin	New York	09/20/1850	10/04/1854	12	359	N	
Cavanagh, Thomas	17	Ireland	N	?	New York	00/00/1849				Y	10/23/1888
Cavanaugh, Hugh	37	Ireland	N	Liverpool	Boston	06/?/1850	?			Y	
Cavanaugh, James	23	Ireland	Y	Liverpool	New Orleans	05/04/1850	06/10/1852	25	306	N	
Cavanaugh, John	30	Ireland	Y	Liverpool	Philadelphia	05/16/1880	11/22/1886			Y	
Cavanaugh, Joseph	27	Ireland	Y	Liverpool	Philadelphia	07/31/1900	03/31/1902			Y	
Cavanaugh, Michael	36	Ireland	Y	Liverpool	New York	07/27/1852	02/01/1861	18	82	N	
Cavanaugh, Michael	41	Ireland	Y	Londonderry	New York	09/10/1890	09/13/1893			Y	
Cavanaugh, Thomas	24	Ireland	Y	Londonderry	Buffalo	05/??/1881	10/22/1886	19	65	N	
Cavanaugh, Thomas	27	Ireland	Y	Liverpool	New Orleans	12/25/1849	04/05/1852	24	387	N	
Cavanaugh, Thomas	24	Ireland	Y	Londonderry	Buffalo	05/00/1881	10/22/1886			Y	
Cavenah, Michael	28	Ireland	Y	Limerick	Buffalo	06/27/1848	11/17/1852	6	425	N	
Cavenah, Patrick	25	Ireland	Y	New Foundlan	Baltimore	05/??/1849	10/24/1851	4	396	N	
Cawelty, John	27	Wuertemberg	Y	Bremen	New York	05/28/1848	03/25/1856	26	321	N	
Cawley, Thomas	21	Ireland	Y	Liverpool	New York	04/07/1850	10/07/1854	11	28	N	
Cawley, Thomas A.	25	England	Y	Liverpool	Boston	11/12/1887	01/09/1892			Y	
Cayden, Michael	33	Ireland	Y	Liverpool	New York	08/15/1863	05/30/1878			Y	
Ceasey, Luke	26	Ireland	Y	Limerick	Buffalo	05/??/1847	10/02/1856	14	155	N	
Ceberek, Casmier	32	Russia	Y	Hamburg	New York	03/15/1886	10/22/1897			Y	
Cebernick, Chas	29	Germany	Y	Bremen	Baltimore	01/30/1880	07/23/1883			Y	
Cedilote, John B.	57	Canada	Y	Montreal	Rochester	09/??/1847	05/11/1882			Y	
Cerace, Salvatore	41	Italy	Y	Palermo	New York	03/30/1889	10/26/1900			Y	
Cerf, Charles	39	Germany	Y	Havre	Boston	09/01/1873	08/29/1882			Y	

CITIZENSHIP RECORDS

APPLICANT	AGE	COUNTRY OF ORIGIN	DEC	DEPART PORT	ENTRY PORT	ARRIVE DATE	DEC DATE	VOL	PG.	FLD	NAT DATE
Cerio, Antonio	??	Italy	Y	?	?	?	07/20/1900			Y	
Cerkowsky, Meyer	28	Poland	Y	Hamburg	New York	07/04/1848	11/13/1857	16	15	N	
Chairsell, T. F. H.	21	Hanover	Y	Hamburg	New York	09/19/1858	06/25/1860	27	2	N	
Chale, David	??	Germany	Y	?	?	?	05/10/1890			Y	
Chaliff, David	30	Russia	Y	Hamburg	Buffalo	06/10/1886	12/26/1891			Y	
Chambers, Patrick	32	Ireland	Y	Liverpool	New York	09/30/1853	01/02/1862	18	239	N	
Chamozo, Nicholo	28	Italy	Y	Naples	New York	03/10/1881	05/21/1894			Y	
Champ, Charles	31	England	Y	London	New York	07/01/1849	02/17/1852	24	131	N	
Champier, Pierre	30	France	Y	Havre	New York	08/06/1854	11/04/1857	15	530	N	
Chancholi, Jim	30	Italy	Y	Palermo	New York	03/10/1883	10/20/1893			Y	
Chaplin, Richard Roberts	21	England	Y	Liverpool	New York	08/22/1881	05/16/1882			Y	
Charek, Israel	??	Russia	Y	Hamburg	New York	03/15/1891	03/22/1897			Y	
Charles, Christian	42	Prussia	Y	Rotterdam	Baltimore	06/30/1846	08/29/1848	22	274	N	
Charles, John	25	Ireland	Y	Liverpool	New Orleans	03/07/1750	10/07/1856	14	256	N	
Charles, William	23	Ireland	Y	Liverpool	New Orleans	02/20/1848	09/11/1852	25	457	N	
Charlesworth, Darius	??	England	Y	?	Philadelphia	??/??/1887	10/27/1890			Y	
Charlesworth, Sidney Joh	29	England	Y	Sarina	Port Huron	09/28/1890	11/22/1888			Y	
Cheevers, Frank	45	Ireland	Y	Queenstown	New York	11/29/1873	06/26/1893			Y	
Chellino, Carlo	37	Italy	Y	Naples	New York	05/07/1883	12/11/1888			Y	
Cherlein, Messior	66	France	Y	Havre	New Orleans	05/??/1850	11/10/1857	16	3	N	
Chernen, Moritz	30	Russia	Y	Hamburg	New York	09/??/1886	09/06/1888			Y	
Cherrington, Henry	29	England	Y	Liverpool	New York	10/01/1853	05/16/1859	17	416	N	
Chevre, Emile	28	France	Y	?	New York	10/??/1891	10/06/1894			Y	
Chiappe, Andrew	34	Sardinia	Y	London	New York	09/21/1848	10/21/1858	17	90	N	
Childs, John	30	England	Y	Liverpool	New York	10/08/1852	03/29/1856	26	373	N	
Chine, Mathew	28	Ireland	Y	Liverpool	New York	01/14/1847	??/??/1851	4	419	N	
Chirinosky, Wolf	24	Russia	Y	Hamburg	Philadelphia	07/11/1882	04/20/1886			Y	
Chors, John Henry	32	Germany	Y	Bremen	Baltimore	06/09/1883	03/??/1884			Y	
Chrisman, Henry	23	Germany	Y	Hamburg	New York	03/??/1879	11/01/1886	19	106	N	
Christ, Peter	43	Prussia	Y	Havre	New Orleans	06/??/1852	07/02/1860	27	194	N	
Christ, William	32	Germany	Y	Bremen	?	04/17/1876	11/02/1882			Y	
Christel, George	54	Germany	N	Havre	New York	07/??/1848	?			Y	
Christen, Albert	??	?	Y	?	?	?	07/??/1882			Y	
Christian, Christian	32	Prussia	Y	Bremen	New York	06/23/1850	08/22/1857	15	168	N	
Christiany, John	30	Prussia	Y	Havre	New York	05/01/1851	11/06/1855	13	175	N	
Christin, John Conrad	34	Switzerland	Y	Havre	New Orleans	01/10/1846	02/02/1857	14	528	N	
Christjan, John	27	Hanover	Y	Bremen	New York	09/30/1853	02/04/1856	26	26	N	
Christmann, Heinrich	37	Germany	Y	Rotterdam	New York	08/27/1881	11/12/1889			Y	
Christmann, Jacob	34	Bavaria	Y	Bremen	New York	05/26/1852	05/04/1861	18	157	N	
Christmann, Nicholas	30	Germany	Y	Antwerp	New York	02/??/1879	10/29/1884			Y	
Christmann, Peter	35	Bavaria	Y	Havre	New Orleans	04/01/1851	12/26/1857	16	254	N	
Christophal, John Valent	54	Bavaria	Y	Havre	New York	10/26/1852	10/07/1854	6	6	N	
Christophel, John Valent	54	Bavaria	Y	Havre	New York	10/26/1852	10/07/1854	11	7	N	
Chrnschwender, Christoph	??	Bavaria	Y	Bremen	New York	??/28/18??	04/16/1855	11	248	N	
Churchill, Charles J.	23	Ireland	Y	Queenstwon	New York	05/30/1890	04/22/1892			Y	
Chytraeus, Bruno	35	Germany	Y	Hamburg	New York	07/08/1882	10/17/1889			Y	
Chytraeus, Charles	17	Germany	N	?	New York	00/00/1880				Y	10/23/1888
Cianciola, Frank	38	Italy	Y	Palermo	New York	02/01/1887	10/18/1893			Y	
Cianciolo, Girolamo	32	Italy	Y	Palermo	New York	06/17/1883	01/24/1890			Y	
Cianciolo, Joseph	59	Italy	Y	Palermo	New York	12/22/1883	10/11/1893	19	429	N	
Cianciolo, Joseph	50	Italy	Y	Palermo	New York	12/22/1883	10/11/1893			Y	
Cianguilli, Guitano	35	Italy	Y	Naples	New York	05/15/1885	05/10/1892			Y	
Cimet, Herman	16	Austria	N	?	Baltimore	00/00/1882				Y	10/18/1888
Cinnamon, John	21	Ireland	Y	Southhampton	New York	01/17/1851	02/11/18??	3	121	N	
Cischeck, Oscar	24	Germany	Y	Bremen	Baltimore	09/03/1877	06/14/1881			Y	
Clabby, James	21	Ireland	Y	Toronto	Rochester	10/04/1848	11/01/1852	5	172	N	
Clabby, James	21	Ireland	Y	Toronto	Rochester	10/04/1848	11/01/1852	6	298	N	
Claden, Worand	55	France	N	Havre	New York	12/08/1857	?			Y	
Clampett, William G.	29	Ireland	Y	Waterford	New York	06/01/1854	06/11/1859	17	454	N	

CITIZENSHIP RECORDS

APPLICANT	AGE	COUNTRY OF ORIGIN	DEC	DEPART PORT	ENTRY PORT	ARRIVE DATE	DEC DATE	VOL	PG.	FLD	NAT DATE
Clancy, D. J.	-1	Canada	N	?	New York	00/00/1861				Y	11/06/1888
Clancy, James	26	Ireland	Y	Limerick	New York	07/06/1848	04/22/1854	8	237	N	
Clancy, James	26	Ireland	Y	Limerick	New York	07/06/1848	04/23/1854	9	108	N	
Clancy, John	31	Ireland	Y	Limerick	New York	04/15/1847	05/08/1854	8	392	N	
Clancy, John	31	Ireland	Y	Limerick	New York	04/15/1847	05/08/1854	9	265	N	
Clancy, Martin	45	Ireland	Y	Liverpool	New Orleans	01/12/1848	02/14/1850	2	71	N	
Clancy, Michael	26	Ireland	Y	Liverpool	New Orleans	04/02/1849	10/20/1851	4	345	N	
Clancy, Peter	22	Ireland	Y	Liverpool	New Orleans	11/29/1850	01/05/1853	5	518	N	
Clare, James	35	Ireland	Y	Dublin	New York	05/30/1848	08/15/1851	4	132	N	
Clark, Bryne	28	Ireland	Y	Liverpool	Philadelphia	07/04/1852	09/26/1854	10	234	N	
Clark, Bryne	28	Ireland	Y	Liverpool	Philadelphia	07/04/1852	09/26/1854	12	173	N	
Clark, Charles	59	England	Y	Liverpool	New York	06/06/1881	03/21/1887			Y	
Clark, Ezekiel	35	England	Y	London	New York	04/01/1880	10/25/1886	19	86	N	
Clark, Ezekiel	35	England	Y	London	New York	04/01/1880	10/25/1886			Y	
Clark, Henry	24	Scotland	Y	Liverpool	New York	?	05/27/1852	25	118	N	
Clark, James	35	Ireland	Y	Liverpool	New York	09/08/1847	01/11/1849	1	391	N	
Clark, James	21	England	Y	Portsmouth	New York	07/??/1848	11/??/1849	23	346	N	
Clark, John	28	Scotland	Y	Glasgow	New York	??/03/1844	10/09/1848	1	89	N	
Clark, John	26	Scotland	Y	Glasgow	New York	08/11/1851	02/07/1857	14	545	N	
Clark, John	36	England	Y	London	New York	08/29/1887	10/31/1894			Y	
Clark, John	25	Ireland	Y	Liverpool	New York	03/01/1847	09/06/1852	25	378	N	
Clark, Lawrence	34	Ireland	Y	Liverpool	New York	07/01/1846	03/26/1853	7	407	N	
Clark, Patrick	34	Ireland	Y	Liverpool	New York	05/30/1847	09/27/1854	10	283	N	
Clark, Patrick	34	Ireland	Y	Liverpool	New York	05/30/1847	09/28/1854	12	222	N	
Clarke, Eric Vance	28	Australia	Y	Melbourne	New York	09/11/1886	01/21/1887			Y	
Clarke, Ernest Albert Fr	??	England	Y	?	?	?	09/09/1890			Y	
Clarke, Felix	37	Ireland	Y	Liverpool	New York	02/10/1851	08/21/1857	15	165	N	
Clarke, Frederick	24	England	Y	Liverpool	New York	10/04/1852	05/01/1854	8	305	N	
Clarke, Frederick	24	England	Y	Liverpool	New York	10/04/1852	05/01/1854	9	178	N	
Clarke, James G.	35	Ireland	Y	?	Philadelphia	?	06/28/1897			Y	
Clarke, Patrick	35	Ireland	Y	Liverpool	New York	08/15/1881	08/16/1886			Y	
Clarke, Thomas	33	Ireland	Y	Liverpool	New York	05/23/1871	10/12/1881			Y	
Clary, Daniel	30	Ireland	Y	Liverpool	New Orleans	02/12/1849	02/10/1852	24	86	N	
Clary, John	55	Ireland	Y	Liverpool	New York	07/00/1860	10/07/1876			Y	
Clary, Patrick	34	Ireland	Y	Liverpool	New Orleans	05/18/1846	02/22/1851	3	154	N	
Class, Jacob	28	Wurttemberg	Y	Liverpool	New York	04/20/1855	09/01/1862	18	432	N	
Classen, Wolbert	24	Hanover	Y	Bremen	New Orleans	09/20/1848	05/02/1850	3	42	N	
Clauder, Arthur	20	Germany	Y	Antwerp	New York	04/08/1882	04/12/1882			Y	
Clauder, Carl H.	28	Germany	Y	Rotterdam	Boston	10/??/1872	04/25/1881			Y	
Clauder, Robert	21	Germany	Y	Bremen	Baltimore	08/10/1883	10/05/1885	19	11	N	
Claus, John	52	Germany	Y	Bremen	New York	11/15/1866	10/13/1885			Y	
Clausing, George	32	Germany	Y	Bremen	Baltimore	09/16/1880	12/20/1888			Y	
Clauss, Theodor	53	Germany	N	Bremen	New York	07/??/1865	?			Y	
Claver, Henry	48	Germany	N	Havre	New York	08/25/1864	?			Y	
Clayborn, Solomon	43	Russia	Y	Bremen	New York	04/11/1889	09/17/1894			Y	
Clayton, Frank	17	Canada	N	?	Port Huron	00/00/1871				Y	03/21/1887
Clayton, Frederick	29	England	Y	?	New York	??/??/1880	09/27/1883			Y	
Cleary, Edmund	25	Ireland	Y	Liverpool	New Orleans	02/01/1849	05/29/1854	9	442	N	
Cleary, Edmund	25	Ireland	Y	Liverpool	New Orleans	02/10/1849	05/29/1854	10	25	N	
Cleary, John	25	Ireland	Y	Liverpool	New York	05/22/1878	10/08/1882			Y	
Cleary, Robert	58	Ireland	N	Liverpool	New Orleans	10/30/1847	?			Y	
Cleasby, F.W.	25	England	Y	Liverpool	Philadelphia	05/??/1882	04/02/1886			Y	
Clegg, James	39	England	Y	Liverpool	New York	05/03/1848	11/11/1852	5	269	N	
Clegg, James	29	England	Y	Liverpool	New York	05/03/1848	11/11/1852	6	393	N	
Clemen, Theodor C.	43	Germany	Y	Bremen	New York	09/??/1866	06/10/1889			Y	
Clement, Arthur D.	39	Canada	Y	Queenstwon	Cleveland	08/27/1876	11/02/1888			Y	
Clenckhamer, Frederick	21	Hanover	Y	Bremen	New Orleans	10/09/1850	10/07/1854	11	25	N	
Clephas, John Baptist	25	Holland	Y	Antwerp	New York	05/10/1857	12/19/1859	17	510	N	
Cliffe, George	34	England	N	Liverpool	New York	07/15/1883	?			Y	

CITIZENSHIP RECORDS

APPLICANT	AGE	COUNTRY OF ORIGIN	DEC	DEPART PORT	ENTRY PORT	ARRIVE DATE	DEC DATE	VOL	PG.	FLD	NAT DATE
Clifford, John	37	Ireland	Y	Dublin	New Orleans	12/20/1849	10/30/1852	5	80	N	
Clifford, John	42	Ireland	Y	Cork	Buffalo	??/??/1862	09/23/1885			Y	
Clifford, Michael	44	Ireland	Y	Queenstown	New York	05/22/1885	10/14/1896			Y	
Clifford, Samuel	25	Ireland	Y	Dublin	New Orleans	01/24/1851	04/04/1853	8	46	N	
Clifford, William	35	Ireland	Y	Liverpool	Boston	12/??/1849	03/16/1853	7	336	N	
Clifford, William	25	Ireland	Y	Liverpool	New Orleans	??/12/1847	12/15/1849	23	404	N	
Clo, Mathias	42	France	Y	Havre	New York	10/13/1853	04/12/1858	16	462	N	
Clodts, Theodore	22	Hanover	Y	Bremen	Philadelphia	05/30/1848	03/13/1852	24	295	N	
Cloke, John F.	25	England	Y	Liverpool	New York	05/04/1880	10/09/1886			Y	
Cloney, John	32	Ireland	Y	Liverpool	Philadelphia	02/01/1851	01/23/1860	27	67	N	
Clott, John	25	Germany	Y	?	New York	??/??/1872	10/11/1880			Y	
Clough, Wm	??	England	Y	?	?	?	10/03/1881			Y	
Clouth, Joseph	37	Prussia	Y	Rotterdam	New York	09/19/1846	10/14/1848	1	230	N	
Clucas, John G.	32	The Isle of M	Y	Liverpool	New York	03/25/1858	11/05/1860	18	22	N	
Coakley, Thomas	36	Ireland	Y	Liverpool	New Orleans	12/26/1851	10/07/1854	6	28	N	
Coakley, Thomas	36	Ireland	Y	Liverpool	New Orleans	12/26/1851	10/07/1854	11	29	N	
Coates, Joseph M.	21	Ireland	Y	Liverpool	New York	09/29/1857	09/12/1860	27	362	N	
Coch, Ziprian	25	Baden	Y	Rotterdam	New Orleans	01/04/1847	09/04/1848	22	298	N	
Cochian, James	24	Greece	Y	Athens	New York	06/02/1886	02/04/1891			Y	
Cochran, Thomas	31	Ireland	Y	Liverpool	New Orleans	12/21/1848	10/07/1854	6	15	N	
Cochran, Thomas	31	Ireland	Y	Liverpool	New Orleans	12/21/1848	10/07/1854	11	16	N	
Cody, Daniel	28	Ireland	Y	Liverpool	New York	06/16/1855	10/10/1860	27	478	N	
Cody, William	25	Ireland	Y	Queenstown	Boston	04/??/1880	10/09/1886			Y	
Coffee, Darby	22	Ireland	Y	Liverpool	New Orleans	04/??/1851	03/18/1852	24	327	N	
Coffey, James	35	Ireland	Y	Liverpool	New Orleans	04/19/1851	10/06/1854	10	479	N	
Coffey, James	35	Ireland	Y	Liverpool	New Orleans	04/19/1851	10/06/1854	12	418	N	
Coffey, John	28	Ireland	Y	Liverpool	New York	02/22/1851	11/15/1852	5	285	N	
Coffy, James	23	Ireland	Y	Liverpool	New Orleans	01/01/1848	01/19/1852	24	33	N	
Coffy, John	28	Ireland	Y	Liverpool	New York	02/22/1851	11/15/1852	6	409	N	
Cogan, Patrick	35	Ireland	Y	Dublin	New York	07/04/1846	07/19/1851	4	3	N	
Coghlan, John	27	Ireland	Y	Queenstown	New York	06/25/1882	11/19/1888			Y	
Coghlan, Matthew J.	30	England	Y	?	?	?	10/16/1896			Y	
Coghlan, William	22	Ireland	Y	Liverpool	Boston	05/07/1857	07/22/1858	16	520	N	
Cohen, Alexander	27	Russia	Y	Hamburg	New York	07/15/1881	10/24/1888			Y	
Cohen, Bennett	43	Russia	N	Hamburg	New York	09/13/1869	?			Y	
Cohen, Harry	??	Rumania	Y	?	?	05/16/1900	07/09/1901			Y	
Cohen, Henry	47	England	Y	Liverpool	New York	09/10/1893	11/03/1897			Y	
Cohen, Henry	24	Hanover	Y	Bremen	New Orleans	10/19/1846	01/??/1850	23	524	N	
Cohen, Isidore	27	Prussia	Y	Hamburg	New York	09/04/1851	02/02/1856	26	13	N	
Cohen, Israel	49	Russia	Y	Bremen	New York	05/20/1889	04/06/1893			Y	
Cohen, John M.H.	36	England	N	Liverpool	Niagara Fall	06/18/1868	?			Y	
Cohen, Julius	22	Prussia	Y	London	New York	05/28/1855	09/30/1856	14	50	N	
Cohen, Lewis	35	Hanover	Y	Bremen	New York	01/??/1850	03/17/1853	7	348	N	
Cohen, Louis	63	Russia	Y	Hamburg	New York	08/14/1884	11/22/1894			Y	
Cohen, Moses L.	48	Russia	Y	?	?	?	06/03/1892			Y	
Cohen, Nathan	38	Russia	Y	Hamburg	New York	07/23/1881	02/15/1883	28	44	N	
Cohen, Nathan	31	Russia	Y	Hamburg	New York	07/23/1881	02/15/1883			Y	
Cohen, Nathan	33	Russia	Y	Hamburg	New York	07/23/1881	02/15/1883			Y	
Cohen, Samuel	40	Poland	Y	Liverpool	New York	09/20/1850	02/26/1853	7	236	N	
Cohn, David	26	Russia	Y	Hamburg	New York	10/07/1887	10/26/1892			Y	
Cohn, Frank	21	Rumania	Y	?	New York	10/27/1899	10/02/1900			Y	
Cohn, Harry	22	Germany	Y	Bremen	New York	05/31/1888	03/28/1891			Y	
Cohn, Henry	45	Germany	N	Liverpool	New York	05/10/1864	?			Y	
Cohn, Isaac	25	Prussia	Y	Hamburg	New York	07/09/1847	03/09/1850	2	178	N	
Cohn, Julius	32	Germany	N	Bremen	New York	11/11/1876	?			Y	
Cohn, Louis	24	Russia	Y	Liverpool	New York	06/14/1882	10/19/1885			Y	
Cohn, Marx	21	Bavaria	Y	Havre	New York	08/26/1852	04/12/1856	26	492	N	
Cohn, Sam	21	Russia	Y	Hamburg	New York	11/11/1890	10/13/1892			Y	
Cohn, Sam	28	Rumania	Y	Hamburg	New York	08/30/1899	09/23/1903			Y	

CITIZENSHIP RECORDS

APPLICANT	AGE	COUNTRY OF ORIGIN	DEC	DEPART PORT	ENTRY PORT	ARRIVE DATE	DEC DATE	VOL	PG.	FLD	NAT DATE
Cohn, Samuel	28	Poland	Y	Hamburg	New York	12/22/1879	01/??/1883			Y	
Cohn, Samuel	28	Poland	N	Hamburg	New York	12/22/1879	?			Y	
Cohn, Wolf	49	Russia	Y	Bremen	Baltimore	02/28/1891	05/11/1893			Y	
Cohrs, Christian	28	Hanover	Y	Bremen	Baltimore	05/05/1847	01/14/1850	23	500	N	
Cohrs, John Henry	40	Germany	N	Bremen	Baltimore	06/09/1883	?			Y	
Coin, Francis	23	Ireland	Y	Liverpool	New Orleans	04/20/1848	09/22/1855	13	118	N	
Coin, Michael	28	Ireland	Y	Liverpool	New Orleans	02/08/1848	08/23/1855	11	487	N	
Colanna, Angela	35	Tuscany	Y	Leghorn	New York	01/01/1844	11/18/1852	5	306	N	
Colary, Patrick	50	Ireland	Y	Liverpool	New Orleans	07/29/1851	10/07/1854	6	26	N	
Colborn, Charles L.	33	Canada	Y	Montreal	New York	05/20/1845	10/09/1854	11	202	N	
Colburn, Charles L.	33	Canada	Y	Montreal	New York	05/20/1845	10/09/1854	6	198	N	
Colchinsky, Elly	33	Russia	Y	Bremen	New York	06/30/1888	12/08/1893			Y	
Coldnick, Edward	44	England	N	England	New Orleans	09/12/1872	?			Y	
Cole, G.P.	30	Ireland	Y	Liverpool	New Orleans	03/06/1852	10/26/1858	17	112	N	
Cole, Richard	39	England	Y	Liverpool	New York	05/13/1869	09/14/1887			Y	
Coleman, Dominick	22	Ireland	Y	Liverpool	New York	05/28/1849	10/06/1851	4	203	N	
Coleman, John	23	Ireland	Y	Liverpool	New York	05/04/1850	11/16/1852	5	296	N	
Coleman, John	23	Ireland	Y	Liverpool	New York	05/04/1850	11/16/1852	6	420	N	
Coleman, John	39	Ireland	Y	Liverpool	Boston	09/16/1850	09/02/1852	25	343	N	
Coleman, Michael	22	Ireland	Y	Liverpool	New York	05/03/1849	06/24/1851	3	446	N	
Coleman, Patrick	34	Ireland	Y	Liverpool	New York	09/28/1848	06/13/1854	10	131	N	
Coleman, Patrick	34	Ireland	Y	Liverpool	New York	09/28/1848	06/13/1854	12	68	N	
Coleman, Patrick	40	Ireland	Y	Quebec	Utica	07/28/1835	10/07/1848	22	490	N	
Coleman, Samuel	60	England	N	England	New York	05/05/1849	?			Y	
Coleman, Thomas	56	Ireland	N	Liverpool	New Orleans	04/??/1851	?			Y	
Colery, Patrick	50	Ireland	Y	Liverpool	New Orleans	01/29/1851	10/07/1854	11	27	N	
Coletta, Michele	38	Italy	Y	Naples	New York	05/15/1890	03/10/1894			Y	
Coletto, Antonio	26	Italy	Y	Naples	New York	04/19/1887	05/07/1892			Y	
Colgin, Patrick	23	Ireland	Y	Liverpool	Philadelphia	03/??/1852	04/23/1854	11	282	N	
Colina, Patrick	21	Ireland	Y	Liverpool	New York	05/01/1854	09/25/1856	14	373	N	
Colina, Thomas	30	Ireland	Y	Liverpool	New Orleans	05/05/1846	??/??/18??	14	375	N	
Colleran, Ned	30	Ireland	Y	Liverpool	New York	04/14/1852	09/25/1854	10	221	N	
Colleran, Ned	30	Ireland	Y	Liverpool	New York	04/14/1852	09/25/1854	12	160	N	
Colligan, Patrick	26	Ireland	Y	Liverpool	New York	08/16/1885	10/03/1890			Y	
Collins, Andrew	38	Ireland	N	Belfast	Detroit	03/17/1870	?			Y	
Collins, Con	28	Ireland	Y	Cork	New York	05/??/1854	12/24/1855	13	343	N	
Collins, Daniel	27	Ireland	Y	Canada	Oswego	??/22/1846	12/20/1849	23	420	N	
Collins, Edward	60	Ireland	N	Liverpool	New York	03/??/1855	?			Y	
Collins, James	23	Ireland	Y	Liverpool	New York	03/09/1849	06/12/1852	25	246	N	
Collins, John	21	Ireland	Y	Cork	New York	05/06/1853	12/24/1855	14	344	N	
Collins, John	29	Ireland	N	Queenstown	New York	07/02/1881	?			Y	
Collins, Michael	??	Ireland	Y	?	?	?	10/13/1891			Y	
Collins, Michael	27	Ireland	Y	Belfast	New York	06/07/1882	10/24/1892			Y	
Collins, Michael H.	37	Ireland	Y	Liverpool	Buffalo	03/20/1848	10/13/1851	4	229	N	
Collins, Morris	44	Ireland	Y	Limerick	New York	04/12/1847	04/25/1853	8	108	N	
Collins, Thomas	23	Ireland	Y	Canada	Oswego	09/??/1846	12/??/1849	23	423	N	
Collins, Timothy	28	Ireland	Y	Cork	New Orleans	08/04/1847	01/30/1849	1	546	N	
Colman, Michael	22	Ireland	Y	Liverpool	New Orleans	10/28/1851	02/01/1853	7	105	N	
Colonel, Boniface	30	Bavaria	Y	Bremen	New York	09/12/1855	02/08/1860	27	92	N	
Columbus, John	35	France	N	Havre	New Orleans	03/??/1869	?			Y	
Colvenbach, John	33	Germany	Y	Amsterdam	New York	07/24/1891	10/16/1897			Y	
Comay, Michael	??	England	Y	?	?	04/03/1853	01/12/1859			Y	
Comella, Joseph	34	Italy	Y	Palermo	New York	08/01/1886	10/19/1893			Y	
Comer, John	25	Ireland	Y	Queenstown	New York	04/17/1885	10/24/1890	19	297	N	
Commins, Patrick	25	Ireland	Y	Liverpool	New Orleans	01/01/1847	07/21/1847	22	11	N	
Concannon, John	38	Ireland	Y	Liverpool	New Orleans	05/04/1848	10/13/1851	4	248	N	
Concannon, Patrick	30	Ireland	Y	Liverpool	New Orleans	05/04/1848	10/13/1851	4	247	N	
Condron, John	27	Ireland	Y	Liverpool	New Orleans	11/15/1848	03/11/1858	16	391	N	
Conighton, Michael	24	Ireland	Y	Liverpool	New York	12/25/1845	10/13/1848	1	204	N	

CITIZENSHIP RECORDS

APPLICANT	AGE	COUNTRY OF ORIGIN	DEC	DEPART PORT	ENTRY PORT	ARRIVE DATE	DEC DATE	VOL	PG.	FLD	NAT DATE
Conlan, Denis	26	Ireland	Y	Liverpool	New Orleans	12/20/1849	12/28/1852	5	455	N	
Conlon, Charles	45	Ireland	Y	Liverpool	New Orleans	02/05/1848	03/15/1851	3	281	N	
Connally, William	26	Ireland	Y	Queenstown	New York	08/03/1895	10/11/1901			Y	
Connaughty, James	??	?	N	?	?	?	?			Y	
Connel, James	48	Ireland	Y	Liverpool	New York	09/22/1866	11/17/1886			Y	
Connell, Cornelius	29	Ireland	Y	Liverpool	New York	12/25/1850	06/05/1854	10	72	N	
Connell, Cornelius	29	Ireland	Y	Liverpool	New York	12/25/1850	06/05/1854	12	9	N	
Connell, Daniel	34	Ireland	Y	Galway	New York	06/09/1851	10/28/1858	17	156	N	
Connell, James	62	Ireland	N	Liverpool	Boston	06/01/1850	??/??/1854	28	124	N	12/01/1856
Connell, James	24	Ireland	N	Liverpool	Boston	06/01/1850	00/00/1854			Y	12/01/1856
Connell, John	27	Ireland	Y	Liverpool	New Orleans	03/12/1849	11/01/1858	17	253	N	
Connell, John	38	Ireland	N	Liverpool	New York	05/01/1866	?			Y	
Connell, Michael	25	Ireland	Y	Queenstown	New York	07/18/1890	01/05/1894			Y	
Connell, Morris	35	Ireland	Y	Liverpool	New York	03/25/1854	08/29/1857	15	199	N	
Connell, Patrick	28	Ireland	Y	Liverpool	New York	05/07/1848	10/03/1854	10	384	N	
Connell, Patrick	28	Ireland	Y	Liverpool	New York	05/07/1848	10/03/1854	12	323	N	
Connell, Phillip	58	Ireland	Y	Liverpool	New York	05/12/1863	10/19/1897			Y	
Connell, William	26	Ireland	Y	Liverpool	New York	03/21/1885	11/03/1890			Y	
Connelly, James	30	Ireland	Y	Liverpool	New Orleans	06/18/1851	02/15/1853	7	162	N	
Connelly, John	40	Ireland	Y	Queenstown	New York	03/12/1882	10/15/1890			Y	
Connelly, John	??	Ireland	N	?	?	04/00/1882				Y	10/17/1892
Connelly, Martin	25	Ireland	Y	Queenstown	Philadelphia	04/19/1883	02/05/1887			Y	
Connelly, Owen	33	Ireland	Y	Liverpool	New Orleans	01/06/1852	12/30/1857	16	285	N	
Connelly, Peter	30	Ireland	Y	Liverpool	New York	10/15/1850	04/07/1856	26	456	N	
Connelly, Thomas	29	Ireland	Y	Liverpool	New York	11/??/1850	10/30/1858	17	204	N	
Conner, Francis	26	Ireland	Y	Dublin	New Orleans	12/12/1848	11/01/1852	5	158	N	
Conner, John	25	Ireland	Y	Liverpool	New Orleans	03/03/1849	10/14/1851	4	270	N	
Conner, John	38	Ireland	Y	Liverpool	New York	07/17/1852	11/15/1852	5	284	N	
Conner, John	38	Ireland	Y	Liverpool	New York	07/17/1852	11/15/1852	6	408	N	
Conner, John	30	Ireland	Y	Liverpool	New Orleans	01/01/1850	02/18/1853	7	182	N	
Conner, John	28	Ireland	Y	Liverpool	New Orleans	12/11/1848	09/18/1858	16	176	N	
Conner, John	25	Ireland	Y	Glasgow	New Orleans	01/19/1854	05/22/1856	26	523	N	
Conner, Michael	21	Ireland	Y	Liverpool	New Orleans	12/15/1853	11/02/1858	17	266	N	
Conner, William	41	Ireland	Y	Limerick	Philadelphia	07/10/1847	10/31/1851	4	445	N	
Conners, Maurice	23	Ireland	Y	Cork	Boston	??/29/1849	02/07/1850	2	47	N	
Conners, Patrick	8	Ireland	N	Liverpool	New York	06/00/1866				Y	04/00/1879
Conneughton, Andrew	22	Ireland	Y	Liverpool	Boston	04/25/1847	05/06/1850	3	49	N	
Connolly, Lawrence	25	Ireland	Y	Liverpool	New Orleans	03/08/1851	09/23/1854	10	176	N	
Connolly, Lawrence	25	Ireland	Y	Liverpool	New Orleans	03/08/1851	09/23/1854	12	115	N	
Connolly, Thomas	21	Ireland	Y	Queenstown	New York	09/26/1880	03/12/1881			Y	
Connoly, Hugh	29	Ireland	Y	Liverpool	New York	03/13/1871	09/27/1876			Y	
Connor, Francis	26	Ireland	Y	Dublin	New Orleans	12/12/1848	11/01/1852	6	284	N	
Connor, James	30	Ireland	Y	Glasgow	New Orleans	02/13/1849	06/30/1851	3	463	N	
Connor, Martin	28	Ireland	Y	Liverpool	New Orleans	12/10/1850	09/27/1854	10	281	N	
Connor, Martin	28	Ireland	Y	Liverpool	New Orleans	12/10/1850	09/27/1854	12	220	N	
Connor, Michael	27	Ireland	Y	Liverpool	New Orleans	04/27/1852	01/05/1854	10	445	N	
Connor, Michael	27	Ireland	Y	Liverpool	New Orleans	04/27/1852	10/05/1854	12	384	N	
Connor, Patrick	28	Ireland	Y	Liverpool	New Orleans	03/01/1849	03/03/1851	3	193	N	
Connor, Thomas	26	Ireland	Y	Liverpool	New York	01/01/1869	01/??/1872	18	455	N	
Connor, Thomas	40	Ireland	N	Liverpool	New York	06/??/1870	?			Y	
Connor, Timothy	28	Ireland	Y	Queenstown	New York	05/06/1868	01/??/1872	18	456	N	
Connors, Michael	45	Ireland	N	?	Pittsburgh	??/??/1861	?			Y	
Connors, Patrick	28	Ireland	N	Liverpool	New York	06/??/1866	?	28	203	N	04/??/1879
Connot, Maurice	22	Ireland	Y	Liverpool	Boston	06/10/1844	10/20/1851	4	338	N	
Connoughton, Patrick	18	Ireland	Y	Liverpool	New York	12/10/1850	10/04/1858	17	34	N	
Conrad, Anton	31	Hesse Darmsta	Y	Havre	New York	01/17/1852	11/08/1858	17	300	N	
Conrad, Casper	26	Bavaria	Y	Havre	New York	07/28/1853	04/02/1856	26	403	N	
Conrad, Charles	26	Prussia	Y	Rotterdam	New Orleans	12/15/1849	04/17/1854	8	150	N	
Conrad, Charles	26	Prussia	Y	Rotterdam	New Orleans	12/15/1849	04/17/1854	9	21	N	

CITIZENSHIP RECORDS

APPLICANT	AGE	COUNTRY OF ORIGIN	DEC	DEPART PORT	ENTRY PORT	ARRIVE DATE	DEC DATE	VOL	PG.	FLD	NAT DATE
Conrad, George	22	Germany	Y	Antwerp	New York	05/27/1897	05/12/1899			Y	
Conrad, John	42	France	Y	?	Cleveland	??/??/1869	10/11/1884			Y	
Conrad, Julius	22	Germany	Y	Bremen	New York	05/12/1883	11/07/1887			Y	
Conradi, Henry	33	Hanover	Y	Bremen	New Orleans	10/21/1847	10/30/1852	5	82	N	
Conraedy, Nicholas	22	Prussia	Y	Antwerp	New York	07/04/1854	09/29/1856	14	34	N	
Conray, Matthew	28	Ireland	Y	Liverpool	New York	05/30/1864	10/24/1898			Y	
Conron, Fenton	34	Ireland	Y	Liverpool	New York	02/05/1850	11/09/1852	5	264	N	
Conron, Fenton	34	Ireland	Y	Liverpool	New York	02/05/1849	11/09/1852	6	388	N	
Conroy, Andy	15	Ireland	N	?	Boston	00/00/1881				Y	10/17/1888
Conroy, James	38	Ireland	Y	Liverpool	New York	08/04/1840	05/25/1854	8	513	N	
Conroy, John	36	Ireland	Y	Liverpool	New Orleans	01/14/1848	01/19/1849	1	471	N	
Conroy, John	60	Ireland	N	Liverpool	New York	11/??/1851	?			Y	
Conroy, Martin	25	Ireland	Y	Liverpool	New Orleans	05/??/1847	09/06/1852	25	363	N	
Conroy, Martin B.	36	Ireland	Y	Queenstown	Boston	07/02/1885	04/03/1891			Y	
Conroy, Michael	50	Ireland	Y	Glaway	Boston	05/29/1883	03/26/1890			Y	
Conroy, Thomas	24	Ireland	Y	Queenstown	New York	04/19/1891	06/23/1894			Y	
Conschaky, David	33	Prussia	Y	Bremen	New York	11/22/1854	10/19/1857	15	448	N	
Constance, John	50	Germany	N	Bremen	New York	??/??/1867	?			Y	
Constantine, Phillip	30	Baden	Y	Havre	New York	06/05/1846	10/03/1848	22	402	N	
Contadino, Guiseppe	31	Italy	Y	Palermo	New Orleans	03/20/1881	11/21/1888			Y	
Conway, James	38	Ireland	Y	Liverpool	New York	08/04/1840	05/25/1854	9	387	N	
Conway, John	24	Ireland	Y	Liverpool	New Orleans	05/04/1848	07/28/1851	4	49	N	
Conway, Lawrence	36	Ireland	Y	Canada	Rochester	08/12/1837	09/11/1848	22	327	N	
Conway, Michael	68	Ireland	N	Liverpool	New York	07/??/1835	??/??/1852	28	128	N	??/??/1855
Conway, Michael	15	Ireland	N	Liverpool	New York	07/00/1835				Y	00/00/1855
Conway, Myles H.	??	England	Y	?	?	?	08/01/1887			Y	
Conway, Neal	30	Ireland	Y	Westport	Rochester	07/??/1840	09/13/1852	25	490	N	
Conway, Patrick	27	Ireland	Y	Queenstown	New York	05/27/1870	01/17/1877			Y	
Conway, Patrick	??	Ireland	Y	?	?	06/00/1860	?			Y	
Conzetti, Martin	51	Switzerland	Y	Havre	New York	06/??/1872	10/??/1882			Y	
Conzetti, Martin	51	Switzerland	N	Havre	New York	06/??/1872	?			Y	
Coogan, Patrick	60	Ireland	Y	Liverpool	New York	05/??/1825	05/01/1854	8	331	N	
Coogan, Patrick	60	Ireland	Y	Liverpool	New York	05/??/1825	05/01/1854	9	204	N	
Cook, Andrew	35	Ireland	Y	Liverpool	New Orleans	10/30/1849	01/24/1851	2	527	N	
Cook, Bernard	38	Ireland	Y	Liverpool	New Orleans	04/27/1844	02/09/1853	7	134	N	
Cook, Charles Edward	26	Ireland	Y	Liverpool	Philadelphia	04/??/1847	10/??/1850	2	303	N	
Cook, Frank	13	Germany	N	?	New York	00/00/1870				Y	10/31/1888
Cook, Hugh	34	Scotland	Y	Trinidad	Baltimore	11/15/1843	11/23/1852	5	335	N	
Cook, Ignatz	23	Bavaria	Y	Rotterdam	New York	09/01/1851	08/15/1857	15	139	N	
Cook, Jacob C.	30	Bavaria	Y	Havre	New York	07/03/1849	09/05/1860	27	337	N	
Cook, James	40	Ireland	Y	Liverpool	New York	06/30/1850	10/25/1858	17	108	N	
Cook, Jesse	52	England	N	Liverpool	New Orleans	02/25/1851	?			Y	
Cook, John	22	Ireland	Y	Liverpool	New York	05/16/1853	10/03/1854	10	399	N	
Cook, John	22	Ireland	Y	Liverpool	New York	05/16/1853	10/03/1854	12	338	N	
Cook, Thomas	23	Ireland	Y	Liverpool	New York	08/17/1852	09/27/1854	10	273	N	
Cook, Thomas	23	Ireland	Y	Liverpool	New York	08/17/1852	09/27/1854	12	212	N	
Cooke, Edward	17	Ireland	N	?	New York	00/00/1875				Y	10/26/1888
Cooke, Matthew William	42	England	Y	Liverpool	New York	03/02/1850	10/13/1865			Y	
Cooney, James	22	Ireland	Y	Canada	Burlington	07/15/1849	12/26/1851	24	16	Y	
Cooney, Patrick	14	Ireland	N	?	New York	00/00/1864				Y	10/25/1886
Coors, William	33	Hanover	Y	Bremen	Baltimore	06/10/1860	02/12/1862	18	259	N	
Cope, Thomas	??	England	Y	Liverpool	Philadelphia	??/24/1829	12/??/1850	2	400	N	
Coppa, Frank	50	Italy	Y	Naples	New York	04/08/1891	10/29/1896			Y	
Coppell, Michael	24	Prussia	Y	Liverpool	Boston	06/10/1844	10/13/1851	4	223	N	
Coppinger, Thomas J.J.	25	Ireland	Y	Liverpool	New Orleans	12/25/1851	10/06/1857	15	357	N	
Coppola, Charles	37	Italy	Y	Messina	New York	05/27/1887	03/04/1901			Y	
Coppola, J. V.	28	Italy	N	Milazzo	Baltimore	11/??/1859	?			Y	
Corbett, David	22	Ireland	Y	Queenstown	New York	06/01/1887	04/11/1890			Y	
Corbett, James	51	Ireland	N	Queenstown	New York	06/??/1859	?			Y	

CITIZENSHIP RECORDS

APPLICANT	AGE	COUNTRY OF ORIGIN	DEC	DEPART PORT	ENTRY PORT	ARRIVE DATE	DEC DATE	VOL	PG.	FLD	NAT DATE
Corbett, John	34	Ireland	Y	Liverpool	New York	05/??/1848	03/25/1851	3	334	N	
Corbett, Timothy	45	Ireland	N	Liverpool	New York	07/17/1862	?			Y	
Corchoran, Michael	38	Ireland	Y	Liverpool	New York	06/19/1837	01/??/1850	23	481	N	
Corcin, Michael	22	Ireland	Y	Liverpool	New York	10/09/1849	02/05/1853	7	119	N	
Corcoran, Edward	25	Ireland	Y	Canada	Oswego	05/??/1842	03/07/1853	7	300	N	
Corcoran, Henry	30	Ireland	Y	Liverpool	New Orleans	02/21/1849	06/12/1854	10	123	N	
Corcoran, Henry	30	Ireland	Y	Liverpool	New Orleans	02/02/1849	06/12/1854	12	60	N	
Corcoran, James	23	Ireland	Y	Liverpool	Ogdensburg	08/16/1857	11/05/1860	18	20	N	
Corcoran, James	40	Ireland	Y	Waterford	New York	06/27/1848	06/10/1852	25	231	N	
Corcoran, John	40	Ireland	Y	Liverpool	New York	08/20/1835	03/07/1853	7	305	N	
Corcoran, John	50	Ireland	Y	Liverpool	New Orleans	05/??/1850	05/02/1854	8	343	N	
Corcoran, John	50	Ireland	Y	Liverpool	New Orleans	05/??/1850	05/02/1854	9	216	N	
Corcoran, John	30	Ireland	Y	Galway	Burlington	06/??/1849	04/27/1855	11	311	N	
Corcoran, John	23	Ireland	Y	Canada	Burlington	??/18/18??	10/??/1849	23	272	N	
Corcoran, Martin	30	Ireland	Y	Liverpool	New Orleans	07/??/1849	10/??/1849	23	273	N	
Corcoran, Patrick	37	Ireland	Y	Queenstown	New York	11/00/1875	09/17/1890			Y	
Corcoran, Paul	32	Ireland	Y	Liverpool	New Orleans	05/27/1848	10/15/1851	4	296	N	
Corcoran, Thomas	30	Ireland	Y	Quebec	Vermont	05/25/1838	11/06/1852	5	239	N	
Corcoran, Thomas	43	Ireland	Y	Liverpool	New York	02/20/1846	11/23/1852	5	334	N	
Corcoran, Thomas	30	Ireland	Y	Quebec	Vermont	05/25/1838	11/06/1852	6	363	N	
Corcoran, Thomas	25	Ireland	Y	Liverpool	New Orleans	03/05/1849	02/14/1853	7	150	N	
Corcran, Martin	27	Ireland	Y	Liverpool	New Orleans	11/20/1849	12/28/1852	5	458	N	
Cordemeyer, Justus	39	Germany	Y	Rotterdam	New York	05/23/1891	10/22/1897			Y	
Cordes, Henry	22	Prussia	Y	Bremen	Baltimore	07/09/1850	10/05/1854	10	461	N	
Cordes, Henry	22	Prussia	Y	Bremen	Baltimore	07/09/1850	10/05/1854	12	400	N	
Cordes, John Herman	??	Germany	Y	?	?	?	10/28/1870			Y	
Cordes, Theodore	31	Prussia	Y	Bremen	New York	11/13/1856	03/20/1858	16	428	N	
Cordesman, H. J.	48	Oldenburg	Y	Bremen	Baltimore	06/06/1832	10/08/1860	27	455	N	
Corley, John	??	Ireland	N	?	?	10/03/1885				Y	10/28/1892
Corley, Michael	22	Ireland	Y	Liverpool	New York	07/14/1881	11/06/1882			Y	
Corly, Thomas	28	Ireland	Y	Liverpool	New York	03/16/1849	10/24/1851	4	391	N	
Corner, John	40	England	Y	Liverpool	New York	02/16/1887	05/19/1890			Y	
Correvont, Ferdinand	43	Bavaria	Y	Bremen	Baltimore	04/28/1854	05/25/1859	17	429	N	
Correvont, Rudolph	38	Bavaria	Y	London	New York	01/15/1854	05/25/1859	17	430	N	
Corrigan, James	29	Ireland	Y	Dublin	New York	08/05/1853	08/21/1857	15	166	N	
Corrigan, Pat	17	Ireland	N	?	New York	00/00/1877				Y	11/05/1888
Corrigan, Thomas	23	Ireland	Y	Liverpool	New York	04/08/1847	10/30/1852	5	83	N	
Corry, Patrick	28	Ireland	Y	Liverpool	New York	10/??/1851	08/02/1856	14	314	N	
Cors, Diederick	40	Oldenburg	Y	Bremen	Baltimore	06/21/1841	11/01/1852	6	294	N	
Corsmeier, Bernard	30	Prussia	Y	Bremen	Baltimore	04/29/1848	05/31/1852	25	164	N	
Corso, Antonio	32	Itlay	Y	Palermo	New York	04/09/1883	10/17/1893	21	14	N	
Corso, Antonio	32	Italy	Y	Palermo	New York	04/09/1883	10/17/1893			Y	
Corter, John	38	Italy	Y	Naples	New York	12/23/1881	11/03/1891			Y	
Corter, William	35	Italy	Y	Naples	New York	12/23/1881	11/03/1891			Y	
Corvers, Chas	34	Germany	Y	Rotterdam	New York	11/10/1879	10/13/1893			Y	
Cosgrove, Daniel	33	Ireland	Y	Londonderry	?	04/23/1871	03/23/1882			Y	
Cosgrove, John	25	Ireland	Y	Liverpool	New York	03/25/1845	11/13/1848	1	259	N	
Cosgrove, John	30	Ireland	Y	Maath	New York	??/??/1878	10/07/1885	19	19	N	
Cosgrove, John	30	Ireland	Y	Maarh	New York	00/00/1878	10/07/1885			Y	
Cosgrove, Peter	30	Ireland	Y	Liverpool	New York	06/30/1844	01/??/1853	7	70	N	
Cosgrove, Thomas	23	Ireland	Y	Liverpool	New Orleans	04/18/1850	04/04/1853	8	27	N	
Cosgrove, Thomas	25	Ireland	Y	Queenstown	New York	11/21/1887	06/22/1889			Y	
Costa, James	43	Italy	Y	Palermo	New York	01/10/1884	10/16/1893	21	13	N	
Costa, James	43	Italy	Y	Palermo	New York	01/10/1884	10/16/1893			Y	
Costa, Joseph	35	Italy	Y	Palermo	New York	05/03/1883	02/06/1889			Y	
Costello, Alexander	44	Italy	Y	Genoa	New York	04/17/1870	10/15/1896			Y	
Costello, John	23	Ireland	Y	Queenstown	New York	06/05/1888	10/25/1889	19	260	N	
Costello, John	23	Ireland	Y	Queenstown	New York	06/04/1888	10/25/1889			Y	
Costello, Martin	25	Ireland	Y	Queenstown	New York	09/12/1880	12/15/1884			Y	

CITIZENSHIP RECORDS

APPLICANT	AGE	COUNTRY OF ORIGIN	DEC	DEPART PORT	ENTRY PORT	ARRIVE DATE	DEC DATE	VOL	PG.	FLD	NAT DATE
Costello, Michael	50	Ireland	Y	Liverpool	New Orleans	12/01/1849	06/05/1854	10	71	N	
Costello, Michael	50	Ireland	Y	Liverpool	New Orleans	12/01/1849	06/05/1854	12	8	N	
Costello, Michael	23	Ireland	Y	Queenstown	Boston	09/29/1891	10/19/1896			Y	
Costello, Michael	47	Ireland	N	Queenstown	New York	05/08/1867	?			Y	
Costello, Michael	40	Ireland	Y	Liverpool	New Orleans	03/17/1850	11/02/1860	27	555	N	
Costello, Patrick	27	Ireland	N	Queenstown	Philadelphia	02/17/1865	?			Y	10/24/1892
Costigan, Patrick J.	29	Ireland	N	Liverpool	New York	07/05/1865	?			Y	
Costigan, William	40	Ireland	Y	Liverpool	New York	12/08/1852	10/11/1858	17	62	N	
Cotter, John	44	Ireland	Y	Queenstown	New York	05/16/1864	10/06/1882			Y	
Cotters, Barney	38	Germany	Y	Rotterdam	New York	09/00/1868	10/13/1884			Y	
Coudts, James	31	Scotland	Y	Glasgow	New York	07/05/1847	02/05/1856	26	44	N	
Coulan, Michael	23	Ireland	Y	Liverpool	New York	01/01/1845	09/20/1854	12	71	N	
Coumell, John	32	Ireland	Y	Liverpool	New Orleans	09/25/1849	04/27/1853	8	128	N	
Counrette, Alex McG.	15	Canada	N	?	Ogdensberg,	00/00/1868				Y	10/09/1888
Courtis, John	34	France	Y	London	New York	07/28/1854	03/03/1858	16	365	N	
Courtney, George	24	Ireland	Y	Cork	New York	05/26/1848	03/25/1850	2	244	N	
Courtney, Michael	45	Ireland	Y	Cork	New York	??/??/1855	10/06/1885	19	14	N	
Cousley, Andrew	24	Ireland	Y	Belfast	New York	11/07/1848	10/09/1854	6	74	N	
Cousley, Andrew	24	Ireland	Y	Belfast	New York	11/07/1848	10/09/1854	11	75	N	
Couton, Peter	27	France	Y	Havre	New York	12/14/1858	03/08/1862	18	270	N	
Cowhay, Thomas	23	Ireland	Y	Liverpool	New Orleans	03/29/1848	04/02/8153	7	500	N	
Cowpland, Samuel	25	England	Y	Hull	New York	05/31/1853	05/02/1859	17	419	N	
Cox, John	24	Prussia	Y	Bremen	New Orleans	12/01/1853	12/08/1857	16	207	N	
Cox, Thomas	36	England	Y	Liverpool	New York	05/01/1851	06/26/1851	3	454	N	
Coyle, Anthony	17	Ireland	N	?	New York	00/00/1875				Y	10/23/1888
Coyle, James	39	Ireland	Y	Bermuda	New York	11/03/1883	04/04/1890	19	281	N	
Coyle, James	39	Ireland	Y	Bermuda	New York	11/03/1883	04/04/1890			Y	
Coyle, John	??	England	Y	?	?	?	11/01/1886			Y	
Coyne, Daniel	37	Ireland	Y	Queenstown	New York	04/23/1873	10/15/1890			Y	
Coyne, Michael	28	Ireland	Y	Liverpool	Toledo	05/28/1882	02/09/1891			Y	
Coyne, Michael	24	Ireland	N	Liverpool	New Orleans	02/00/1848	00/00/1850			Y	10/00/1854
Coyne, Owen	39	Ireland	Y	Liverpool	Whitehall	08/??/1847	03/25/1851	3	345	N	
Coyne, Thomas	??	Ireland	N	Queenstown	New York	??/??/1854	?			Y	
Cozens, William Joseph	24	England	Y	?	?	?	04/13/1888			Y	
Crabey, James	4?	Ireland	Y	Dublin	Philadelphia	??/??/1832	01/29/1849	1	540	N	
Cracknell, Charles	25	England	Y	Newcastle	New York	??/23/1848	12/10/1849	23	398	N	
Craddick, Martin	59	Ireland	N	Liverpool	New York	02/??/1854	?			Y	
Crahy, William	50	Ireland	Y	Liverpool	New Orleans	12/20/1847	01/28/1850	2	6	N	
Craig, David	??	Great Britain	Y	?	?	?	03/05/1883			Y	
Craig, William	30	Ireland	Y	Liverpool	New York	04/??/1848	05/01/1854	8	308	N	
Craig, William	30	Ireland	Y	Liverpool	New York	04/??/1848	05/01/1854	9	181	N	
Crain, Thomas	36	Ireland	Y	Liverpool	New Orleans	02/09/1849	09/21/1854	10	138	N	
Crain, Thomas	36	Ireland	Y	Liverpool	New Orleans	02/09/1849	09/21/1854	12	77	N	
Cramer, George	25	Wurttemberg	Y	Havre	New York	09/12/1856	09/28/1858	16	106	N	
Cramer, William	25	Prussia	Y	Bremen	New York	01/14/1847	03/31/1853	7	469	N	
Cramer, William	33	Germany	Y	Antwerp	New York	12/24/1881	10/05/1885			Y	
Crampton, James	32	Ireland	Y	Dublin	New York	06/08/1887	10/27/1890			Y	
Crance, August	25	France	Y	Havre	New York	02/10/1852	06/27/1857	15	113	N	
Crane, Barney	66	Ireland	N	Liverpool	New Orleans	01/15/1850	?			Y	
Crane, Edmond	30	Ireland	Y	Liverpool	Sandusky	11/24/1849	03/07/1853	7	291	N	
Crane, Michael	30	Ireland	Y	Liverpool	New York	09/27/1851	09/27/1856	14	401	N	
Craus, William	29	Prussia	Y	Bremen	Baltimore	??/22/1846	02/19/1850	2	98	N	
Crauser, Michael	51	Germany	Y	Havre	New York	12/09/1879	01/30/1882			Y	
Craven, John	16	Ireland	N	?	Philadelphia	00/00/1882				Y	10/27/1888
Craven, Thomas	23	Ireland	Y	Liverpool	New York	12/03/1849	03/05/1853	7	282	N	
Crawford, Robert	26	Ireland	Y	Liverpool	New Orleans	12/12/1850	10/12/1858	17	61	N	
Crawford, William	30	Ireland	Y	Sligo	New York	07/08/1840	07/28/1851	4	54	N	
Crawley, Dan	26	Ireland	Y	Queenstown	New York	07/25/1887	10/22/1889	19	249	N	
Crawley, Michael	27	Ireland	Y	Liverpool	New Orleans	03/01/1849	09/21/1854	10	148	N	

CITIZENSHIP RECORDS

APPLICANT	AGE	COUNTRY OF ORIGIN	DEC	DEPART PORT	ENTRY PORT	ARRIVE DATE	DEC DATE	VOL	PG.	FLD	NAT DATE
Crawley, Michael	27	Ireland	Y	Liverpool	New Orleans	03/01/1849	09/21/1854	12	87	N	
Crawley, Patrick	29	Ireland	Y	Liverpool	New York	06/12/1848	03/25/1851	3	323	N	
Crawley, Thomas	20	Ireland	Y	Liverpool	New York	04/07/1850	10/07/1854	6	27	N	
Crawley, Thomas	25	Ireland	Y	?	Baltimore	??/??/1880	07/09/1886			Y	
Crawly, Dan	26	Ireland	Y	Queenstown	New York	07/25/1887	10/22/1889			Y	
Creahan, Patrick	43	Ireland	Y	Queenstown	New York	05/20/1871	03/24/1887	19	114	N	
Crean, Michael	28	Ireland	Y	Canada	Oswego	08/29/1847	03/01/1851	3	189	N	
Creaton, Francis	35	Ireland	Y	Liverpool	New York	06/10/1853	10/19/1857	15	453	N	
Creaven, Martin	34	Ireland	Y	Galway	New Orleans	04/15/1849	11/01/1858	17	231	N	
Creed, Dennis	24	Ireland	Y	Cork	Buffalo	09/28/1848	08/13/1851	4	235	N	
Creedon, Daniel	??	Ireland	Y	?	?	?	02/02/1889			Y	
Creedon, Timothy	38	Ireland	Y	Liverpool	New York	10/14/1852	10/05/1854	10	453	N	
Creedon, Timothy	38	Ireland	Y	Liverpool	New York	10/14/1852	10/05/1854	12	392	N	
Cremering, Bernard	31	Hanover	Y	Bremen	New Orleans	11/19/1852	03/25/1856	26	304	N	
Creysson, August	50	France	Y	Havre	New York	12/??/1869	10/15/1887			Y	
Cribbet, Samuel	36	England	Y	Plymouth	New York	08/01/1849	11/03/1852	5	199	N	
Cribbet, Samuel	36	England	Y	Plymouth	New York	08/01/1849	11/03/1852	6	323	N	
Cribbin, Peter	46	Ireland	Y	Queenstown	New York	04/20/1884	06/04/1890			Y	
Cridlaw, William	27	Canada	Y	Port Huron	Cass City	03/19/1891	11/16/1896			Y	
Crilley, Thomas	28	Ireland	Y	Liverpool	New York	09/??/1843	09/03/1852	25	345	N	
Crimmon, Charles	42	Prussia	Y	Hamburg	New York	07/25/1852	04/27/1854	9	148	N	
Crisanti, Gaspare	36	Italy	Y	Naples	New York	09/14/1892	07/07/1896			Y	
Crist, John	35	Bavaria	Y	Havre	New York	06/18/1848	02/15/1856	26	85	N	
Crock, Patrick	30	Ireland	Y	Liverpool	Boston	06/20/1848	10/22/1852	5	45	N	
Croester, Peter	42	France	Y	Havre	New Orleans	12/26/1846	08/16/1848	22	186	N	
Cronagh, Cornelius	33	Ireland	Y	Cork	Oswego	07/01/1834	03/25/1850	2	254	N	
Crone, John Joseph	21	Hanover	Y	Bremen	New Orleans	11/29/1854	03/02/1858	16	359	N	
Crone, Peter	28	Hanover	Y	Bremen	New York	09/12/1854	10/06/1854	10	510	N	
Crone, Peter	28	Hanover	Y	Bremen	New York	09/12/1854	10/06/1854	12	449	N	
Cronen, James	25	Ireland	Y	Cork	New York	08/28/1850	10/25/1858	17	106	N	
Cronin, Denis	22	England	Y	Liverpool	New York	11/27/1847	?	22	513	N	
Cronin, Dennis J.	57	Ireland	N	Liverpool	New York	11/30/1847	?			Y	
Cronin, Jeremiah C.	23	Ireland	Y	Queenstown	New York	04/00/1878	01/30/1883			Y	
Cronin, John	25	Ireland	Y	Queenstown	New York	11/02/1887	10/28/1893			Y	
Cronin, Philip	24	Ireland	Y	Liverpool	New York	12/10/1850	03/30/1853	7	464	N	
Cronin, William	40	Ireland	Y	Youghal	Uttica	06/01/1847	05/25/1854	8	520	N	
Cronin, William	40	Ireland	Y	Youghal	Uttica	06/01/1848	05/25/1854	9	394	N	
Crooks, William	25	Scotland	Y	Glasgow	New York	05/04/1849	03/02/1852	24	216	N	
Crosby, James	32	England	Y	Liverpool	New York	02/15/1845	10/22/1852	5	49	N	
Cross, Charles Abbot	25	Prussia	Y	Hamburg	New York	06/10/1852	03/21/1853	7	361	N	
Cross, Henry	29	England	Y	Liverpool	New Orleans	03/20/1849	03/05/1852	24	239	N	
Cross, William	49	Nassau	Y	Rotterdam	New York	11/06/1856	09/09/1857	15	250	N	
Crothy, Edmund	41	Ireland	Y	Liverpool	New Orleans	01/21/1850	09/03/1852	25	346	N	
Crotty, Michael	66	Ireland	N	Limerick	New York	04/19/1851	?	28	449	N	10/01/1856
Crouch, James	23	England	Y	Liverpool	New Orleans	05/03/1849	06/28/1851	3	462	N	
Croucher, William G.	34	England	Y	?	?	?	04/01/1885			Y	
Crow, James	26	Ireland	Y	Limerick	New York	04/26/1852	04/18/1853	8	77	N	
Crowley, Cornelius	32	Ireland	Y	Bristol	New Orleans	12/10/1852	01/30/1856	13	522	N	
Crowley, Cornelius	49	Ireland	N	Liverpool	New York	04/14/1851	?			Y	
Crowley, Daniel	23	Ireland	Y	Liverpool	New Orleans	04/??/1848	10/25/1848	2	301	N	
Crowley, Jeremiah	49	Ireland	Y	Liverpool	New Orleans	04/16/1852	05/04/1854	8	374	N	
Crowley, Jeremiah	49	Ireland	Y	Liverpool	New Orleans	04/16/1852	05/04/1854	9	247	N	
Crowley, Timothy	30	Ireland	Y	Cork	New York	06/29/1846	04/23/1852	8	99	N	
Crowther, George H.	26	England	Y	Liverpool	New York	07/27/1849	03/28/1853	7	431	N	
Cruden, Timothy	30	Ireland	Y	Liverpool	New Orleans	01/28/1851	10/30/1852	5	64	N	
Crumley, William	23	Ireland	Y	Liverpool	Buffalo	06/25/1847	11/24/1848	1	385	N	
Cruse, Engelbert	31	Germany	Y	Bremen	New York	09/21/1880	08/25/1885	19	8	N	
Cruse, Engelbert	31	Germany	Y	Bremen	New York	09/21/1880	08/25/1885			Y	
Cryan, John	21	Ireland	Y	Queenstown	Philadelphia	09/25/1882	04/03/1885			Y	

CITIZENSHIP RECORDS

APPLICANT	AGE	COUNTRY OF ORIGIN	DEC	DEPART PORT	ENTRY PORT	ARRIVE DATE	DEC DATE	VOL	PG.	FLD	NAT DATE
Cryans, John	??	Ireland	Y	?	New York	04/??/1862	10/01/1878			Y	
Csach, Andreas	40	Hungary	Y	Bremen	New York	05/04/1890	10/12/1900			Y	
Cucack, Michael	63	Ireland	N	Hamilton Can	Detroit	03/09/1857	?	28	342	N	10/??/1864
Cucack, Michael	18	Ireland	N	Canada	Detroit	03/09/1857				Y	10/00/1864
Cucinotta, Pietro	38	Italy	Y	Naples	New York	04/13/1887	05/19/1894			Y	
Cueni, Ferdinand	28	Switzerland	Y	Havre	New Orleans	05/10/1848	06/25/1851	3	452	N	
Cullaney, Patrick	31	Ireland	Y	Southampton	New Orleans	09/??/1850	06/12/1854	12	54	N	
Cullany, Patrick	31	Ireland	Y	Southampton	New Orleans	09/??/1850	06/12/1854	10	117	N	
Cullen, Francis	24	Ireland	Y	Dublin	New Orleans	02/??/1849	08/??/1851	4	188	N	
Cullen, John J.	27	Ireland	Y	Liverpool	New York	12/29/1877	04/02/1887	19	118	N	
Cullen, Joseph	9	Ireland	N	?	New York	00/00/1861				Y	10/23/1886
Cullen, Michael	46	Ireland	Y	Liverpool	New York	11/15/1852	12/19/1857	16	236	N	
Cullen, Patrick	30	Ireland	Y	Liverpool	New York	03/31/1849	03/09/1857	15	83	N	
Cullen, Thomas	35	Ireland	Y	Liverpool	New York	04/05/1851	04/15/1852	24	507	N	
Cullinan, Dennis	22	Ireland	Y	London	New York	02/22/1850	03/20/1850	2	225	N	
Cullinan, William	50	Ireland	Y	Liverpool	New York	05/31/1851	05/25/1854	9	417	N	
Cullinane, William	50	Ireland	Y	Liverpool	New York	05/31/1851	05/25/1854	8	1	N	
Cultry, Martin	30	Ireland	Y	Liverpool	New Orleans	05/12/1848	10/10/1854	6	229	N	
Cultry, Martin	30	Ireland	Y	Liverpool	New Orleans	05/12/1848	10/10/1854	11	232	N	
Cummings, Richard O.D.	51	Ireland	Y	London	New York	07/16/1849	06/25/1851	3	453	N	
Cummings, Thomas	40	Ireland	Y	Liverpool	New York	08/??/1871	05/28/1888			Y	
Cummins, James	28	Ireland	Y	Liverpool	New York	03/??/1880	05/27/1882			Y	
Cummins, John	36	Ireland	Y	Queenstown	New York	07/11/1866	03/31/1881			Y	
Cummins, John	26	Ireland	Y	Liverpool	New York	07/16/1846	08/15/1848	22	137	N	
Cundy, Richard	47	England	N	Liverpool	New York	06/02/1868	?			Y	
Cuni, Ferdinand	64	Switzerland	N	Havre	New Orleans	05/09/1848	?			Y	
Cunniff, Thomas	30	Ireland	Y	Liverpool	New York	04/07/1884	05/04/1889			Y	
Cunningham, Daniel	35	Ireland	Y	Liverpool	New York	10/01/1853	11/30/1857	16	57	N	
Cunningham, Henry	26	Ireland	Y	Liverpool	New Orleans	11/26/1848	08/23/1852	25	339	N	
Cunningham, James	28	Ireland	Y	Liverpool	New Orleans	05/16/1849	04/25/1853	8	102	N	
Cunningham, James	2?	Ireland	Y	Queenstwon	New York	05/10/1887	11/03/1890			Y	
Cunningham, James	51	Ireland	Y	Liverpool	New Orleans	02/??/1849	09/27/1880			Y	
Cunningham, James	24	Ireland	Y	Dublin	New York	08/16/1847	01/02/1850	23	459	N	
Cunningham, James	24	Ireland	Y	Canada	Whitehall	06/14/1850	04/12/1852	24	457	N	
Cunningham, John	29	Ireland	Y	Cork	Boston	05/30/1844	03/27/1850	2	273	N	
Cunningham, Martin	22	Ireland	Y	Liverpool	New Orleans	01/16/1850	01/12/1853	7	15	N	
Cunningham, Patrick	21	Great Britain	Y	Liverpool	New York	12/02/1857	09/15/1860	27	378	N	
Cunningham, Peter	40	Ireland	N	Queenstown	New York	12/24/1864	?			Y	
Cunningham, Peter	46	Ireland	Y	Queenstown	New York	12/24/1864	04/00/1875			Y	
Cunningham, Robert Henry	24	Ireland	Y	Liverpool	New York	05/01/1848	02/19/1853	7	189	N	
Cunningham, Thomas	17	Ireland	N	?	New York	00/00/1883				Y	03/30/1888
Cunningham, William	25	Ireland	Y	Liverpool	New York	06/14/1848	02/22/1851	3	156	N	
Cuppo, Valentine	36	Italy	Y	Havre	New York	12/10/1873	04/02/1885			Y	
Curey, Patrick	35	Ireland	Y	Liverpool	New Orleans	05/07/1848	10/29/1852	5	62	N	
Curio, Friederick	24	Germany	Y	Amsterdam	New York	12/00/1882	11/12/1884			Y	
Curley, Michael	28	Ireland	Y	Liverpool	Lewiston	??/??/1847	10/14/1850	2	294	N	
Curley, Patrick	42	Ireland	N	Liverpool	New York	05/08/1861	?			Y	
Curley, Peter	54	Ireland	N	Liverpool	New York	04/??/1853	?			Y	
Curme, Job.	39	England	Y	Liverpool	New Orleans	04/02/1848	02/20/1850	2	111	N	
Curnes, Joseph	23	Baden	Y	Bremen	New York	05/15/1871	10/10/1876			Y	
Curran, John	24	Ireland	Y	Queenstown	New York	08/22/1886	07/02/1888			Y	
Curran, John	46	Ireland	Y	Ireland	New York	06/19/1874	11/01/1874	28	372	N	
Curran, John	15	Ireland	N	?	New York	00/00/1875				Y	10/20/1886
Curran, Joseph	27	Ireland	Y	Whernspoint	New York	06/01/1846	05/19/1854	8	474	N	
Curran, Joseph	27	Ireland	Y	Whrens Point	New York	06/01/1846	05/19/1854	9	348	N	
Curran, Martin	23	Ireland	Y	?	?	04/16/1882	10/18/1884			Y	
Curran, Matthew	??	England	Y	?	?	?	03/21/1889			Y	
Curran, Michael	25	Ireland	Y	Liverpool	New Orleans	11/25/1849	03/17/1852	24	324	N	
Currin, Edward	25	Ireland	Y	Liverpool	New Orleans	03/29/1849	02/14/1852	24	106	N	

CITIZENSHIP RECORDS

APPLICANT	AGE	COUNTRY OF ORIGIN	DEC	DEPART PORT	ENTRY PORT	ARRIVE DATE	DEC DATE	VOL	PG.	FLD	NAT DATE
Curry, Luke	50	England	Y	Liverpool	New York	08/31/1884	07/16/1888			Y	
Cusack, Farrell	24	Ireland	Y	Liverpool	New York	11/29/1847	03/03/1851	3	190	N	
Cusher, Louis	??	Russia	N	?	?	09/15/1887				Y	10/20/1892
Cusher, Noh	30	Russia	Y	Hamburg	New York	01/18/1882	07/19/1889			Y	
Cushing, Robert	38	Ireland	Y	Limerick	Whitehall	06/21/1848	05/25/1854	9	418	N	
Cushing, Robert	38	Ireland	Y	Limerick	Whitehall	06/21/1848	05/25/1854	10	1	N	
Cushing, Thomas	28	Ireland	Y	Liverpool	New York	06/01/1843	04/25/1853	8	105	N	
Cusick, James	25	Ireland	Y	Liverpool	New York	08/31/1892	10/29/1897			Y	
Cusick, Michael	50	Ireland	Y	Liverpool	New Orleans	04/19/1849	11/21/1855	13	239	N	
Cymann, Charles	23	Hanover	Y	Bremen	New York	08/24/1848	11/04/1851	4	487	N	
Czajka, Franz	34	Germany	Y	Hamburg	New York	04/26/1883	04/02/1888			Y	
Czezok, Florian	47	Germany	Y	Bremen	New York	03/04/1882	01/10/1885			Y	
Czoppelt, Julius	26	Hungary	Y	?	?	?	07/03/1892			Y	
D'Amico, August	??	Italy	Y	?	?	?	01/03/1893			Y	
D'Arcy, Michael	36	Ireland	Y	Dublin	San Francisc	09/04/1892	04/07/1896			Y	
D'Elia, Eugenio	35	Italy	Y	?	?	?	07/09/1883			Y	
D'Onofria, Nicondro	30	Italy	Y	Naples	New York	11/29/1891	10/11/1900			Y	
Da Costa, Moses P.	37	England	Y	Liverpool	New York	08/??/1869	04/03/1885			Y	
DaCosta, Moses P.	37	England	Y	Liverpool	New York	08/??/1869	04/03/1885			Y	
Daber, Nicholas	36	Bavaria	Y	Havre	New Orleans	10/15/1836	12/26/1851	24	6	N	
Dabinski, Casper	32	Prussia	Y	Bremen	New York	06/17/1852	03/21/1856	26	240	N	
Dabry, John	??	Austria	Y	?	?	?	05/05/1890			Y	
Dacey, Daniel	21	Ireland	Y	London	New York	05/19/1850	05/01/1854	8	319	N	
Dacey, Daniel	21	Ireland	Y	London	New York	05/19/1850	05/01/1854	9	193	N	
Dacy, Cornelius	25	Ireland	Y	Liverpool	Boston	04/14/1845	07/29/1851	4	58	N	
Dacy, Luke	??	Ireland	N	?	?	07/13/1881				Y	10/14/1892
Dacy, Timothy	25	Ireland	Y	Liverpool	New Orleans	08/10/1847	07/29/1851	4	59	N	
Daey, Jacob	26	Bavaria	Y	Antwerp	New York	12/27/1849	08/04/1856	14	337	N	
Dagenbach, Joseph A.	34	Germany	Y	Rotterdam	New York	08/23/1881	03/19/1887			Y	
Dagenbach, Martin	22	Germany	Y	Rotterdam	New York	09/25/1881	05/22/1882			Y	
Dahling, John	28	Mecklenburg S	Y	Hamburg	New York	07/16/1855	10/06/1856	14	207	N	
Dahlman, W.	25	Germany	Y	Antwerp	New York	10/03/1882	12/08/1883			Y	
Dahlmann, David	37	Germany	Y	Havre	New York	10/02/1872	10/14/1886			Y	
Dahlmans, Christian	??	Germany	Y	Antwerp	New York	04/11/1884	04/11/1887			Y	
Dahman, Peter Joseph	52	Prussia	Y	Liverpool	New York	?	12/??/1849	23	422	N	
Dahmann, Henry	46	Hanover	Y	Bremen	New Orleans	10/05/1853	10/01/1856	14	134	N	
Dahms, Otto	35	Germany	Y	Rotterdam	New York	11/04/1891	12/15/1893			Y	
Dahringer, Joseph	33	Germany	Y	Havre	New York	07/06/1880	05/17/1884			Y	
Daigger, Anton	??	Germany	Y	?	?	?	03/18/1878			Y	
Dailey, Con	16	Ireland	N	?	New York	00/00/1881				Y	10/20/1887
Dailey, Eugene	25	Ireland	Y	Queenstown	Baltimore	10/28/1880	08/03/1886			Y	
Daily, ?	??	?	Y	?	?	??/29/18??	10/28/1850	2	320	N	
Daily, Carrell	34	Ireland	Y	Liverpool	New York	05/07/1856	01/06/1860	27	32	N	
Daily, Martin	50	Ireland	Y	Liverpool	Buffalo	08/??/1851	09/27/1856	14	406	N	
Dake, John	23	France	Y	Havre	New Orleans	01/08/1851	03/11/1853	7	324	N	
Dakin, Francis	26	Ireland	Y	Liverpool	New Orleans	12/??/1850	12/27/1852	5	448	N	
Dalberg, Albert M.	??	Germany	N	Dusseldorf	New York	09/15/1872	?			Y	
Daley, Michael	21	Ireland	Y	Liverpool	New Orleans	01/10/1850	04/19/1854	8	209	N	
Daley, Michael	21	Ireland	Y	Liverpool	New Orleans	01/10/1850	04/19/1854	9	80	N	
Daley, Michael	??	England	Y	?	?	?	02/20/1891			Y	
Dalle, Philip	24	Prussia	Y	Liverpool	New York	04/10/1854	02/06/1858	16	81	N	
Dallmann, Henry	23	Hanover	Y	Bremen	Baltimore	10/08/1854	10/07/1857	15	364	N	
Dallmann, Herman Henry	38	Hanover	Y	Bremen	New Orleans	11/28/1853	09/29/1856	14	43	N	
Dallwig, Valentine	34	Kurhessen	Y	Bremen	New York	08/10/1852	07/09/1861	18	204	N	
Dalton, Arthur	24	Ireland	Y	Liverpool	New Orleans	04/??/1849	10/28/1851	4	426	N	
Dalton, Jeremiah	49	Ireland	Y	London	New York	04/27/1871	10/15/1889	19	238	N	
Dalton, Jeremiah	49	Ireland	Y	London	New York	04/22/1871	10/15/1889			Y	
Daly, Dennis	63	Ireland	Y	Queenstown	Boston	05/??/1851	07/??/1857	28	191	N	03/??/1862
Daly, Eugen	30	Ireland	Y	Queenstown	New York	04/29/1882	12/06/1890	19	311	N	

CITIZENSHIP RECORDS

APPLICANT	AGE	COUNTRY OF ORIGIN	DEC	DEPART PORT	ENTRY PORT	ARRIVE DATE	DEC DATE	VOL	PG.	FLD	NAT DATE
Daly, Eugene	30	Ireland	Y	Queenstown	New York	04/29/1882	12/06/1890			Y	
Daly, James	37	Ireland	Y	Cork	New York	10/20/1853	04/03/1858	16	491	N	
Daly, John	25	Ireland	Y	Liverpool	New York	03/09/1852	03/03/1853	7	268	N	
Daly, John	24	Ireland	Y	Liverpool	New York	10/16/1879	09/30/1885			Y	
Daly, John K.	33	Ireland	Y	Liverpool	New York	08/02/1845	08/08/1848	22	77	N	
Daly, Michael	24	Ireland	Y	?	?	?	02/14/1885			Y	
Daly, Michael Victor	28	Ireland	Y	Liverpool	New Orleans	??/04/1849	02/25/1850	2	124	N	
Daly, Patrick	30	Ireland	Y	Limerick	Burlington	06/15/1848	05/30/1854	9	462	N	
Daly, Patrick	30	Ireland	Y	Limerick	Burlington	06/15/1848	05/31/1854	10	45	N	
Daly, Patrick	48	Ireland	N	Liverpool	New York	02/??/1858	?			Y	
Daly, Peter	26	Ireland	Y	Galway	Boston	05/30/1887	10/18/1892	19	368	N	
Damal, Martin	26	Baden	Y	Antwerp	New York	08/28/1851	10/07/1856	14	302	N	
Damann, William	??	Prussia	Y	Havre	New York	05/09/1850	06/10/1854	10	114	N	
Damann, William	28	Prussia	Y	Havre	New York	05/09/1850	06/10/1854	12	51	N	
Damberg, Johannes	28	Germany	Y	Hamburg	Philadelphia	05/13/1881	01/08/1883			Y	
Dames, August (Damer?)	17	Germany	N	?	Baltimore	00/00/1881				Y	10/23/1886
Dames, H.	??	Prussia	Y	?	?	?	09/19/1882			Y	
Damm, Ernst Frederick	36	Wurttemberg	Y	Rotterdam	New York	08/01/1850	07/23/1855	11	417	N	
Dammann, Charles	29	Germany	Y	Bremen	Baltimore	08/16/1887	10/15/1895			Y	
Dammann, Ernst	25	Germany	Y	Hamburg	New York	08/17/1887	03/28/1890			Y	
Dammann, Louis	31	Germany	Y	Hamburg	New York	09/05/1883	12/13/1890			Y	
Dammel, Philip	27	Germany	Y	Rotterdam	New York	10/21/1881	11/11/1885			Y	
Dammert, William	52	Germany	Y	Antwerp	New York	04/02/1888	10/30/1893	21	45	N	
Dammhus, John	26	Germany	Y	Bremen	Baltimore	06/19.1880	09/??/1881			Y	
Dammhus, John	36	Germany	N	Bremen	Baltimore	06/19/1880	?			Y	
Danbach, Frederick	22	Bavaria	Y	Havre	New Orleans	11/??/1853	09/22/18??	10	155	N	
Danbach, Frederick	22	Bavaria	Y	Havre	New Orleans	11/04/1853	09/22/1854	12	94	N	
Danby, Joseph	24	England	Y	Liverpool	New York	09/27/1848	03/16/1852	24	316	N	
Danenmaier, Philip	??	Germany	Y	?	?	?	02/18/1889			Y	
Dangelmeier, Lucas	??	Germany	Y	?	?	?	06/13/1892			Y	
Dangelzer, Joseph	33	France	Y	Havre	New York	08/16/1853	10/07/1854	6	38	N	
Dangelzer, Joseph	33	Havre	Y	Havre	New York	08/16/1853	10/07/1854	11	39	N	
Danger, Ferdinand	32	Bavaria	Y	Havre	New Orleans	03/13/1850	02/10/1862	18	258	N	
Dangers, Herman	48	Germany	Y	Bremen	Baltimore	02/06/1883	09/13/1898			Y	
Daniel, Alois	40	Germany	Y	Hamburg	New York	10/18/1874	11/01/1882			Y	
Daniel, Conde	27	Ireland	Y	Liverpool	New York	07/01/1844	01/21/1850	23	531	N	
Daniel, Franz	22	Germany	Y	Bremen	New York	05/??/1882	02/12/1883			Y	
Daniel, Henry	30	Prussia	Y	Bremen	Baltimore	05/14/1849	10/07/1854	6	21	N	
Daniel, Henry	30	Prussia	Y	Bremen	Baltimore	05/14/1849	10/07/1854	11	22	N	
Daniel, Henry	38	Germany	Y	Bremen	New York	10/??/1869	06/28/1883			Y	
Daniel, Julius	30	Germany	Y	Hamburg	New York	05/06/1879	06/21/1884			Y	
Dankelmann, Heinrich Geo	34	Prussia	Y	Bremen	New York	05/01/1849	01/25/1853	7	66	N	
Danker, Charles	24	Germany	Y	Bremen	Baltimore	07/26/1883	07/22/1889			Y	
Danker, Charles	59	Germany	Y	Bremen	Baltimore	03/19/1883	10/27/1893			Y	
Danmiller, George	37	Bavaria	Y	Bremen	New York	06/15/1851	05/31/1852	25	145	N	
Dannacher, Etienne	41	France	Y	Havre	New York	12/22/1881	10/16/1888	19	151	N	
Dannenfelser, L.P.A.	??	Germany	Y	?	?	08/10/1879	03/08/1883			Y	
Dantzenberg, Leonhard	??	Germany	Y	?	?	?	06/29/1882			Y	
Dappes, John B.	24	Germany	Y	Amsterdam	New York	07/24/1881	02/26/1886			Y	
Darby, James	74	Ireland	N	London	New York	06/04/1848	07/??/1849	28	27	N	??/??/1856
Darby, James	35	Ireland	N	London	New York	06/04/1848	07/00/1849			Y	00/00/1856
Darcy, Edward	22	Ireland	Y	Liverpool	New York	07/22/1881	04/19/1882			Y	
Dardis, John	11	Ireland	N	?	New York	00/00/1859				Y	11/03/1887
Darlington, William Henr	56	England	Y	Liverpool	New Orleans	06/06/1850	02/08/1851	3	105	N	
Darmoty, Philip	27	Ireland	Y	Liverpool	New Orleans	04/21/1849	10/02/1854	10	363	N	
Darmoty, Philip	27	Ireland	Y	Liverpool	New Orleans	04/02/1849	10/02/1854	12	302	N	
Darpel, Bernard	33	Hanover	Y	Bremen	Baltimore	07/06/1845	08/15/1848	22	181	N	
Darpel, Henry (Duepel?)	24	Hanover	Y	Bremen	Baltimore	07/06/1845	08/22/1848	22	222	N	
Darpel, John	26	Hanover	Y	Bremen	Baltimore	05/01/1843	08/15/1848	22	178	N	

CITIZENSHIP RECORDS

APPLICANT	AGE	COUNTRY OF ORIGIN	DEC	DEPART PORT	ENTRY PORT	ARRIVE DATE	DEC DATE	VOL	PG.	FLD	NAT DATE
Darvey, James	34	Ireland	Y	Liverpool	New Orleans	01/10/1840	04/29/1850	3	22	N	
Dasch, Frank	32	Germany	Y	Hamburg	New York	07/10/1879	11/01/1886	19	105	N	
Dasen, Jacob	35	Switzerland	Y	Bremen	Baltimore	04/07/1876	09/06/1883			Y	
Dash, Samuel	46	England	Y	Liverpool	Port Huron	05/21/1867	10/17/1890			Y	
Dastillung, Joseph	29	Germany	Y	Havre	New York	09/12/1892	06/24/1895			Y	
Dattila, Geroloma	54	Italy	Y	Palermo	New York	09/02/1883	10/17/1900			Y	
Datz, John Michael	22	Bavaria	Y	Bremen	New York	06/19/1852	03/02/1853	7	258	N	
Daub, Joseph	46	Germany	Y	Rotterdam	New York	05/26/1882	06/14/1886	19	39	N	
Daub, Joseph	46	Germany	Y	Rotterdam	New York	05/26/1882	06/14/1886			Y	
Daubach, John	30	Prussia	Y	Havre	New York	08/15/1850	12/04/1852	5	378	N	
Daubalk, Henry Adam	36	Bavaria	Y	Hamburg	New York	09/??/1844	03/28/1853	7	417	N	
Daubenneicke, George	37	Germany	Y	Bremen	New York	06/18/1881	05/09/1888			Y	
Daubenthal, John	55	Germany	Y	Bremen	Baltimore	10/09/1858	10/02/1884			Y	
Dauce, Edward	30	England	N	Liverpool	New York	06/25/1876	?			Y	
Daudistel, Fred	39	Germany	Y	Antwerp	New York	05/02/1882	12/30/1885			Y	
Daum, Christ	23	Germany	Y	Bremen	New York	10/20/1883	03/13/1884			Y	
Daum, Daniel	??	Germany	Y	?	?	?	06/19/1895			Y	
Daum, George	26	Wurttemberg	Y	Havre	New York	04/25/1851	04/04/1853	8	45	N	
Daum, George	39	Bavaria	Y	Havre	New York	07/04/1846	03/29/1849	23	265	N	
Daum, John	23	Bavaria	Y	Bremen	New York	07/20/1871	04/01/1872	18	486	N	
Daum, Michael	25	Bavaria	Y	Havre	New York	07/31/1846	02/19/1849	23	205	N	
Daumm, Conrad	25	Hesse Darmsta	Y	Havre	New York	05/25/1853	10/27/1858	17	133	N	
Daumm, John	64	Hesse Darmsta	Y	Havre	New York	05/25/1853	10/27/1858	17	134	N	
Daumm, Peter	35	Hesse Darmsta	Y	Havre	New York	05/25/1853	10/27/1858	17	125	N	
Daunt, Robert	25	Ireland	Y	Liverpool	New Orleans	01/10/1849	07/19/1858	16	511	N	
Dauwalter, William	28	Baden	Y	Havre	New York	06/20/1851	11/23/1855	13	244	N	
Dauwe, August	27	Germany	Y	Bremen	Baltimore	08/18/1882	01/12/1885			Y	
Dauwe, Gerhard	24	Germany	Y	?	?	?	11/01/1886			Y	
Davaillon, Victor	21	France	Y	Havre	New York	05/17/1897	12/13/1897			Y	
Davan, Patrick	60	Ireland	N	Liverpool	?	12/22/1853	?			Y	
Davey, Matt	27	Ireland	Y	Queenstown	Philadelphia	05/23/1883	10/18/1888	19	154	N	
Davey, Matt	27	Ireland	Y	Queenstown	New York	05/23/1883	10/18/1888			Y	
David, Charles	43	France	Y	Brest	New York	09/24/1871	03/26/1872	18	476	N	
David, Daniel R.	31	Ireland	Y	Dublin	New Orleans	03/10/1849	01/22/1852	24	56	N	
David, Frank	23	Germany	Y	Hamburg	New York	03/20/1885	03/01/1887			Y	
Davidorff, Bernard	41	Russia	Y	Hamburg	New York	10/30/1881	01/02/1891			Y	
Davidson, David	??	Germany	Y	?	?	?	07/13/1885			Y	
Davidson, Samuel L.	??	Germany	Y	?	?	?	11/20/1893			Y	
Davies, Daniel	30	England	Y	Liverpool	Newport News	08/12/1887	11/02/1889			Y	
Davies, Evan	29	Wales	Y	Carmarthiu	New York	06/??/1842	10/28/1851	4	430	N	
Davies, Evan	54	Wales	Y	Liverpool	New York	10/10/1880	10/30/1896			Y	
Davies, G.T.	24	Wales	Y	Liverpool	New York	03/14/1880	09/04/1884			Y	
Davies, George	23	England	Y	Liverpool	Boston	09/26/1848	02/10/1851	3	116	N	
Davies, John Ebenezer	53	England	Y	Liverpool	Philadelphia	09/30/1888	11/02/1889			Y	
Davies, John T.	??	England	Y	?	?	?	09/20/1880			Y	
Davies, John W.	25	Wales	Y	Liverpool	New York	07/15/1857	04/10/1860	27	140	N	
Davies, Joseph	51	England	Y	Canada	Lewiston	06/10/1850	06/02/1852	25	174	N	
Davies, Morgan J.	24	Wales	Y	Liverpool	Philadelphia	12/23/1887	10/03/1891			Y	
Davies, Richard	40	England	Y	Liverpool	New Orleans	02/??/1849	12/16/1850	2	367	N	
Davies, Richard	24	Wales	Y	Liverpool	New York	04/22/1886	11/07/1888			Y	
Davis, Charles Henry	35	England	Y	Liverpool	New York	10/13/1883	10/24/1887			Y	
Davis, David	30	Wales	Y	Liverpool	New York	08/03/1859	01/07/1860	27	41	N	
Davis, Edward	25	Wales	Y	Liverpool	?	10/24/1889	11/07/1892			Y	
Davis, George	41	England	Y	Liverpool	New York	01/22/1859	06/03/1862	18	346	N	
Davis, John	26	Wales	Y	Liverpool	New York	04/01/1851	04/04/1853	7	532	N	
Davis, John M.	35	Wales	Y	Liverpool	New York	10/04/1847	10/20/1851	4	342	N	
Davis, John P.	23	England	Y	Liverpool	New Orleans	12/??/1849	12/??/1850	2	407	N	
Davis, Joseph	28	Ireland	Y	Liverpool	New Orleans	12/25/1854	03/08/1858	16	386	N	
Davis, Louis	40	Russia	Y	Bremen	Baltimore	05/29/1891	10/19/1898			Y	

CITIZENSHIP RECORDS

APPLICANT	AGE	COUNTRY OF ORIGIN	DEC	DEPART PORT	ENTRY PORT	ARRIVE DATE	DEC DATE	VOL	PG.	FLD	NAT DATE
Davis, Nicholas	38	England	Y	London	New York	07/18/1848	09/06/1852	25	370	N	
Davis, William	27	England	Y	London	New York	05/14/1855	06/04/1861	18	183	N	
Davishewski, Simon	26	Poland	Y	Hamburg	New York	02/15/1887	04/24/1894			Y	
Davison, Ben	47	Russia	Y	Hamburg	New York	09/14/1890	09/12/1893			Y	
Davison, George	??	England	Y	?	?	?	10/07/1878			Y	
Davy, Thomas	30	Ireland	Y	Liverpool	New Orleans	04/15/1850	01/24/1853	7	57	N	
Daw, Walter	47	Ireland	Y	Liverpool	New York	06/10/1863	08/29/1887			Y	
Dawes, James	37	Ireland	Y	Liverpool	New York	??/11/1847	12/26/1849	23	434	N	
Dawidoff, Max	29	Russia	Y	Glasgow	New York	10/01/1885	10/29/1888	19	194	N	
Dawson, George	28	Ireland	Y	Belfast	New York	06/01/1848	09/22/1855	13	116	N	
De Crignis, Louis	25	Germany	Y	Bremen	New York	05/28/1882	04/09/1887			Y	
De George Lewis	40	France	Y	Havre	New York	05/01/1883	10/24/1894			Y	
De Gisbert, Leon	??	France	Y	?	?	?	05/17/1887			Y	
De Heff, Paul	30	Switzerland	Y	Havre	New York	03/12/1892	04/15/1895			Y	
De Laurian, Benjamin	??	Canada	Y	?	?	05/??/1883	10/14/1884			Y	
De Lio, Vincenzo	37	Italy	Y	Naples	Philadelphia	12/12/1883	10/04/1897			Y	
De Luche, Peter	34	Italy	Y	Naples	New York	05/10/1888	01/09/1895			Y	
De Vries, Ruegenier	27	Holland	Y	?	New York	03/20/1900	05/20/1901			Y	
De Yong, Leendertd	39	Holland	Y	Amsterdam	New York	04/26/1886	10/31/1892			Y	
DeCourcie, Charles Henry	31	Prussia	Y	Liverpool	New York	05/29/1855	02/22/1858	16	325	N	
DeRomo, Anthony	33	Italy	Y	Naples	New York	01/20/1882	03/30/1891			Y	
DeRoo, Cornelius	38	Holland	Y	Rotterdam	New York	01/26/1852	09/25/1858	16	130	N	
DeRoo, James	28	Holland	Y	Rotterdam	New York	01/12/1855	09/25/1858	16	132	N	
DeRoo, Leonard	25	Holland	Y	Antwerp	New York	02/21/1856	09/25/1858	16	131	N	
DeRoy, John	34	Holland	Y	Rotterdam	New Orleans	10/19/1846	08/21/1848	22	211	N	
DeSilver, Frank (Silvers	73	Portuguese Ma	N	?	Charleston	03/??/1835	07/??/1837	28	40	N	06/??/1840
DeWaay, Henry	36	Holland	N	Rotterdam	New York	03/17/1873	?			Y	
Deal, Henry	25	Bavaria	Y	Havre	New Orleans	11/26/1848	10/14/1851	4	278	N	
Dean, Barnabas	36	Ireland	Y	Londerry	Portland	03/04/1873	80/30/1883			Y	
Dean, Patrick	6	Ireland	N	?	New York	00/00/1867				Y	10/29/1888
Deans, John	38	Scotland	Y	Glasgow	New York	06/30/1873	04/05/1889			Y	
Deasy, John	29	Ireland	Y	Cork	New York	04/22/1845	03/18/1850	2	203	N	
Deasy, John	36	Ireland	Y	Liverpool	New Orleans	01/22/1848	08/11/1851	4	108	N	
Debler, John	44	Wurttemberg	Y	Antwerp	New York	07/20/1852	08/22/1862	18	394	N	
Debre, Nicholas	27	France	Y	Havre	New Orleans	03/16/1853	12/27/1859	17	531	N	
Debrunner, Konrad	26	Switzerland	Y	?	?	?	09/02/1891			Y	
Debunda, Ferdinand	31	Austria	Y	?	New York	03/27/1883	10/16/1884			Y	
Deck, George	60	Bavaria	Y	Havre	New Orleans	06/30/1844	02/14/1849	23	104	N	
Deck, Jacob	24	Bavaria	Y	Havre	New York	05/03/1858	07/14/1862	18	374	N	
Deck, John	28	Germany	Y	Antwerp	New York	06/01/1883	09/08/1886			Y	
Deck, John	28	Bavaria	Y	Havre	New Orleans	06/17/1842	07/27/1848	22	5	N	
Decker, Andrew	24	Baden	Y	Havre	New York	09/16/1854	09/16/1857	15	273	N	
Decker, Charles	39	Hesse Darmsta	Y	London	New York	02/21/1852	02/23/1857	15	50	N	
Decker, Frederick	25	Hanover	Y	Bremen	Baltimore	09/20/1852	09/10/1855	11	516	N	
Decker, George	23	Germany	Y	Antwerp	New York	08/01/1879	01/20/1884			Y	
Decker, Joseph	47	Baden	Y	Liverpool	New Orleans	12/28/1853	11/06/1857	15	533	N	
Decker, Joseph	34	Wuerttemberg	Y	London	New York	05/01/1846	08/30/1848	22	285	N	
Decker, Peter	28	Germany	Y	Antwerp	New York	08/22/1885	10/18/1893	21	24	N	
Decker, Peter	28	Germany	Y	Antwerp	New York	08/22/1885	10/18/1893			Y	
Deckert, Jos.	24	Germany	Y	Bremen	New York	11/12/1881	03/11/1884			Y	
Deckmann, Hermann	41	Germany	Y	Holland	New York	06/02/1872	10/19/1886			Y	
Dee, Michael	30	Ireland	Y	Liverpool	New Orleans	12/25/1851	11/30/1858	17	366	N	
Dee, Patrick	17	Ireland	N	?	Baltimore	00/00/1879				Y	10/20/1886
Dee, Richard	38	Ireland	Y	Liverpool	New York	06/29/1847	09/26/1854	10	237	N	
Dee, Richard	38	Ireland	Y	Liverpool	New York	06/29/1847	09/26/1854	12	176	N	
Deegan, Thomas	27	Ireland	Y	Liverpool	New York	06/29/1846	09/26/1854	10	241	N	
Deegan, Thomas	27	Ireland	Y	Liverpool	New York	06/29/1846	09/26/1854	12	180	N	
Deery, Patrick	17	Ireland	N	?	New York	00/00/1873				Y	10/26/1888
Deffren, George	56	Germany	N	Havre	New York	04/??/1861	?			Y	

CITIZENSHIP RECORDS

APPLICANT	AGE	COUNTRY OF ORIGIN	DEC	DEPART PORT	ENTRY PORT	ARRIVE DATE	DEC DATE	VOL	PG.	FLD	NAT DATE
Deffren, George	56	Germany	Y	Havre	New York	04/00/1861	03/00/1881			Y	
Degel, George	36	Bavaria	Y	Bremen	Baltimore	07/24/1857	11/07/1860	18	27	N	
Degen, George Adam	17	Germany	N	?	New York	00/00/1881				Y	11/02/1888
Degen, John	28	Bavaria	Y	Bremen	Baltimore	11/04/1847	10/16/1851	4	204	N	
Degenhart, August	32	Prussia	Y	Bremen	New York	09/08/1849	10/06/1854	10	490	N	
Degenhart, August	22	Prussia	Y	Bremen	New York	09/08/1849	10/06/1854	12	429	N	
Degenhart, Philipp	25	Prussia	Y	Bremen	Baltimore	06/01/1857	03/19/1860	27	130	N	
Degermann, Gadfrey	48	Germany	N	Havre	New York	12/15/1877	?			Y	
Degidio, Michele	??	Italy	Y	?	?	?	05/11/1895			Y	
Degischer, Christoph	22	Wuertemberg	Y	Havre	New York	02/27/1854	05/20/1856	26	509	N	
Degischer, Ernst	25	Wuertemberg	Y	Liverpool	New York	05/20/1853	05/20/1856	26	508	N	
Degmann, Frank	27	Prussia	Y	Bremen	New Orleans	07/04/1849	07/16/1851	3	541	N	
Dehler, Ferdinand	33	Prussia	Y	Bremen	Baltimore	06/10/1872	10/12/1880			Y	
Dehls, Frederick	34	Prussia	Y	Bremen	Baltimore	02/20/1852	09/27/1856	14	418	N	
Dehls, Martin	33	Bremen	Y	Hamburg	New York	08/06/1853	09/29/1856	14	40	N	
Dehmel, Henry	38	Holstein	Y	Hamburg	New York	09/06/1855	09/22/1855	13	122	N	
Dehmen, August	25	Germany	Y	Rotterdam	New York	08/13/1884	10/29/1887			Y	
Dehmen, Peter J. F. X.	52	Prussia	Y	Liverpool	New York	??/27/1849	12/21/1849	23	418	N	
Dehn, L. D.	44	France	Y	Havre	New York	09/22/1873	10/07/1884			Y	
Dehne, Charles Christoph	29	Hanover	N	Havre	Baltimore	12/21/1842	08/15/1848	22	132	N	
Dehner, Daniel	70	Germany	N	Bremen	New York	06/17/1842	??/??/1845	28	60	N	09/??/1850
Dehner, Daniel	24	Germany	N	Bremen	New York	06/17/1842	00/00/1845			Y	98/00/1859
Dehner, Hilarias	27	Hohenzollen H	Y	Havre	New Orleans	06/27/1846	10/02/1848	1	3	N	
Dehof, Nicholas	38	Germany	N	Havre	New York	10/20/1867	?			Y	
Deichmann, Henry L.	28	Hanover	Y	Hamburg	New York	05/14/1847	01/16/1849	1	443	N	
Deickmann, Gustav	46	Germany	Y	Hamburg	New York	12/21/1880	10/19/1886	19	54	N	
Deidesheimer, Philip	??	Germany	Y	?	?	?	04/05/1886			Y	
Deie, John	29	Oldenburg	Y	Bremen	New Orleans	12/17/1845	04/04/1853	7	509	N	
Deimel, Franz Joseph	28	Prussia	Y	Antwerp	New York	08/08/1853	10/03/1854	10	385	N	
Deimel, Franz Joseph	48	Prussia	Y	Antwerp	New York	08/08/1853	10/03/1854	12	324	N	
Deimel, George	32	Bavaria	Y	London	New York	03/08/1853	11/01/1858	17	227	N	
Deininger, Lorenz	27	Wurtemberg	Y	Rotterdam	New York	07/01/1847	09/14/1852	25	498	N	
Deinlein, Bankrog	30	Bavaria	Y	Hamburg	New York	07/14/1845	01/20/1851	2	510	N	
Deinlein, Frederick	30	Bavaria	Y	Havre	New York	??/16/1847	11/17/1849	23	345	N	
Deinlein, George	65	Germany	N	Bremen	New York	12/23/1847	?			Y	
Deirner, Henry	36	Germany	N	Bremen	New York	11/??/1864	?			Y	
Deisler, Conrad	27	Baden	Y	Rotterdam	New York	03/02/1849	10/18/1852	5	3	N	
Deiss, August	26	Germany	Y	Antwerp	Philadelphia	02/11/1893	02/26/1896			Y	
Deitemann, John	29	Prussia	Y	Bremen	New Orleans	07/10/1854	08/04/1856	14	318	N	
Deitmann, Ollig	34	Hanover	Y	Bremen	New Orleans	07/07/1847	02/17/1849	23	148	N	
Deitz, Valentine	21	Hesse Cassel	Y	Antwerp	New York	05/??/1850	10/25/1850	2	304	N	
Del Corso, Guiseppa	39	Italy	Y	Naples	New York	02/02/1887	05/17/1894			Y	
Del Plato, Michele	32	Italy	Y	Naples	New York	07/02/1890	01/10/1898			Y	
Del Vecchio, Domenico	31	Italy	Y	Naples	New York	09/23/1888	10/16/1893	21	8		
Del Vecchio, Dominico	31	Italy	Y	Naples	New York	09/23/1888	10/16/1893			Y	
Delahunty, Dennis	??	England	Y	?	?	?	08/15/1874			Y	
Delahunty, James	36	Ireland	Y	Waterford	New York	09/29/1848	06/10/1852	25	232	N	
Delaney, Edward	17	England	N		Baltimore	00/00/1878				Y	10/23/1888
Delaney, James H.	35	Canada	Y	Halifax	Portland	10/??/1868	10/03/1885			Y	
Delaney, John	41	Ireland	Y	Liverpool	New York	03/??/1867	08/31/1880			Y	
Delaney, Joseph	35	Ireland	Y	Liverpool	New York	03/15/1881	06/07/1895			Y	
Delaney, Martin	36	Ireland	Y	Liverpool	New York	05/??/1842	05/18/1854	9	345	N	
Delaney, Michael	25	Ireland	Y	Dublin	New York	06/12/1851	08/02/1851	4	73	N	
Delany, Martin	36	Ireland	Y	Liverpool	New York	05/??/1842	05/18/1854	8	471	N	
Delapo, August	51	Italy	Y	Naples	New YOrk	04/02/1875	10/17/1900			Y	
Delb, John	57	Hesse Darmsta	Y	Antwerp	New York	03/29/1852	04/24/1854	8	247	N	
Delb, John	57	Hesse Darmsta	Y	Antwerp	New York	03/29/1852	04/24/1854	9	118	N	
Delehant, John	48	Ireland	Y	Dublin	New Orleans	03/09/1849	03/06/1852	24	250	N	
Delfendahl, John	42	Hanover	Y	Bremen	New Orleans	11/??/1848	10/31/1853	4	444	N	

CITIZENSHIP RECORDS

APPLICANT	AGE	COUNTRY OF ORIGIN	DEC	DEPART PORT	ENTRY PORT	ARRIVE DATE	DEC DATE	VOL	PG.	FLD	NAT DATE
Delfendahl, John Henry	27	Hanover	Y	Bremen	New Orleans	11/12/1848	08/??/1851	4	165	N	
Delin, George	5	Belgium	N	?	New York	00/00/1856				Y	10/23/1886
Delitsch, Bernard	25	Saxony	Y	London	New York	05/19/1855	02/18/1856	26	96	N	
Dellahauty, Michael	34	Ireland	Y	Liverpool	New Orleans	02/10/1848	10/28/1858	17	155	N	
Dellanty, James	36	Ireland	Y	Liverpool	New Orleans	10/14/1850	06/06/1854	10	98	N	
Dellbrugge, Frederick Wi	45	Prussia	Y	Bremerhafen	New Orleans	12/??/1849	01/21/1861	18	67	N	
Delle, Emil	??	Germany	Y	?	?	?	10/17/1884			Y	
Dellem, Jacob (Bellem?)	39	Germany	Y	Antwerp	Philadelphia	08/18/1881	03/26/1894			Y	
Deller, Adam Peter	47	Bavaria	Y	Havre	New York	05/24/1854	09/26/1854	10	231	N	
Deller, Adam Peter	47	Bavaria	Y	Havre	New York	05/24/1854	09/26/1854	12	170	N	
Deller, Frederick	43	Nassau	Y	Bremen	New York	07/03/1853	10/01/1856	14	99	N	
Deller, Henry	42	Bavaria	Y	Havre	New York	04/13/1852	10/18/1852	5	12	N	
Dellmann, Julius	32	Germany	Y	Rotterdam	New York	09/12/1880	08/14/1882			Y	
Delmarco, Guiseppa	36	Switzerland	Y	Havre	New York	02/21/1883	10/14/1885			Y	
Delmonaco, Andrew	20	Italy	Y	Naples	New York	04/10/1882	09/21/1891			Y	
Delor, Emile	30	France	Y	Havre	New York	08/27/1883	10/17/1888			Y	
Delor, Lucian	36	France	Y	Havre	New York	07/20/1872	01/18/1888			Y	
Deluse, Jacob	29	Germany	Y	Rotterdam	New York	09/27/1881	06/05/1889			Y	
Demankovski, John	56	Germany	Y	Bremen	New York	12/20/1890	03/29/1894			Y	
Deml, John	49	Germany	Y	Bremen	New York	06/25/1881	05/04/1891			Y	
Demler, Xaver	28	Bavaria	Y	Bremen	New York	04/13/1854	05/15/1854	8	445	N	
Demme, Herman	30	Prussia	Y	Bremen	New York	06/20/1855	09/27/1858	16	122	N	
Demme, Joseph	25	Germany	Y	Rotterdam	New York	04/29/1888	05/05/1891			Y	
Demming, Joseph A.	38	Germany	N	Glasgow	New York	09/??/1871	?			Y	
Demmler, Xaver	28	Bavaria	Y	Bremen	New York	04/13/1854	05/15/1854	9	318	N	
Demonowski, Martin	24	Germany	Y	Rotterdam	Baltimore	10/05/1891	10/24/1896			Y	
Dempsey, Christopher	23	Ireland	Y	Dublin	New Orleans	12/27/1849	02/25/1856	26	123	N	
Dempsey, John	20	Ireland	Y	Dublin	New Orleans	11/26/1850	10/21/1852	5	40	N	
Dempsey, John	31	Ireland	Y	Queenstown	New York	07/04/1884	11/21/1893			Y	
Dempsey, Lewis	29	Ireland	Y	Liverpool	New Orleans	11/05/1851	10/14/1857	15	423	N	
Demuth, Frank	36	Bavaria	Y	Havre	New Orleans	11/27/1846	09/15/1852	25	533	N	
Denahy, John	22	Ireland	Y	Liverpool	Boston	05/??/1854	12/29/1857	16	280	N	
Denedy, Patrick	24	Ireland	Y	Liverpool	New York	03/??/1851	11/10/1856	14	477	N	
Denert, Franz	30	Hanover	Y	London	New York	12/01/1856	08/05/1862	18	388	N	
Dengler, Philip	23	Bavaria	Y	Havre	New York	06/01/1853	04/12/1856	26	493	N	
Denholm, John	42	Scotland	Y	Liverpool	New York	04/19/1882	11/06/1885			Y	
Denig, Simon	29	Germany	Y	Havre	New York	04/??/1884	03/09/1886			Y	
Denis, Louis	33	Oldenburg	Y	Bremen	New York	10/09/1847	11/04/1851	4	486	N	
Denk, John	39	Bavaria	Y	Bremen	Baltimore	09/08/1845	10/24/1851	4	395	N	
Denkelacher, Frederick	21	Wurttemberg	Y	London	New York	04/20/1853	10/23/1855	13	147	N	
Denn, John	26	Prussia	Y	Rotterdam	New York	02/26/1852	10/04/1854	10	429	N	
Denn, John	26	Prussia	Y	Rotterdam	New York	02/26/1852	10/04/1854	12	368	N	
Dennedy, Michael	29	Ireland	Y	Queenstown	New York	03/29/1873	02/14/1882			Y	
Denney, Morris	28	Canada	N	Canada	Cincinnati?	??/??/1861	?			Y	
Denney, Thomas	??	Ireland	Y	Liverpool	New Orleans	??/23/1848	04/16/1855	11	246	N	
Denngg, Rudolff	42	Germany	Y	Bremen	New York	04/13/1884	10/03/1899			Y	
Dennig, Barney	??	Hanover	Y	Bremen	New York	05/01/1849	03/25/1851	3	326	N	
Dennigan, John	38	Ireland	Y	Liverpool	New Orleans	01/04/1848	03/08/1851	3	208	N	
Denninger, Joseph	29	Wurttemberg	Y	London	New York	11/01/1853	10/07/1854	6	31	N	
Denninger, Joseph	29	Wurttemberg	Y	London	New York	11/01/1853	10/07/1854	11	32	N	
Dennis, Joseph	21	Ireland	Y	Liverpool	Boston	11/04/1848	12/06/1852	5	385	N	
Dennis, Thomas	24	England	Y	Liverpool	New York	03/23/1889	10/09/1893	19	428	N	
Dennis, Thomas	24	England	Y	Liverpool	New York	03/23/1889	10/09/1893			Y	
Dennisten, John F.	??	England	Y	?	?	?	03/05/1897			Y	
Denterlein, Lorenz	42	Bavaria	Y	London	New York	09/10/1852	12/20/1852	5	432	N	
Dentsch, Anton	17	Germany	N	?	New York	00/00/1883				Y	10/23/1888
Denugg, Rudolff	42	Germany	Y	Bremen	New York	04/13/1884	10/03/1899			Y	
Denusch, Eberhard	45	Prussia	Y	Bremen	Baltimore	08/28/1856	09/26/1856	14	395	N	
Denzler, John	40	Bavaria	Y	Bremen	New York	08/01/1847	02/27/1850	2	136	N	

CITIZENSHIP RECORDS

APPLICANT	AGE	COUNTRY OF ORIGIN	DEC	DEPART PORT	ENTRY PORT	ARRIVE DATE	DEC DATE	VOL	PG.	FLD	NAT DATE
Depenbrock, B.	41	Germany	Y	Bremen	Baltimore	09/21/1871	06/12/1884			Y	
Deppe, August	34	Lippe Detmold	Y	Bremen	New Orleans	05/25/1851	12/17/1855	13	322	N	
Deppe, August	32	Germany	Y	Bremen	New York	09/19/1883	08/23/1889	19	230	N	
Deppermann, Herman	34	Hamburg	Y	Hamburg	New York	12/05/1852	10/30/1858	17	199	N	
Deprez, Fred J.	27	Germany	Y	Bremen	New York	10/09/1882	06/11/1885			Y	
Derflinger, Anton	??	Austria	Y	?	?	?	10/10/1887			Y	
Derfman, Hiller	??	Germany	Y	?	?	?	06/03/1884			Y	
Derge, William	32	Prussia	Y	Hamburg	New Orleans	01/12/1842	10/13/1848	1	208	N	
Derham, Samuel G.	46	England	Y	Antwerp	New York	03/22/1882	01/05/1891			Y	
Derie, Frank	26	Germany	Y	Antwerp	Boston	03/24/1887	01/23/1894			Y	
Derksen, Johannes	??	Holland	Y	?	?	?	07/11/1882			Y	
Derlin, Edward	24	Ireland	Y	Liverpool	New Orleans	12/??/1848	10/30/1851	4	428	N	
Derman, Henry	35	Hanover	Y	Bremen	Baltimore	05/01/1849	12/23/1851	4	548	N	
Dermody, William	41	Ireland	Y	Waterford	New York	05/07/1849	04/12/1852	24	477	N	
Dermoff, Luke	30	Ireland	N	Liverpool	New York	05/??/1874	?			Y	
Dermott, Patrick	47	Ireland	Y	Liverpool	New Orleans	02/01/1851	08/22/1855	11	476	FLD	
Derr, Johannes	49	Bavaria	Y	Bremen	New York	??/??/1870	10/13/1885			Y	
Derrelli, John	??	Italy	Y	?	?	10/??/1883	04/21/1892			Y	
Derrin, Peter (Deerin?)	23	Ireland	Y	Canada	New York	06/??/1847	12/??/1849	23	405	N	
Desch, Amant	31	Germany	Y	Antwerp	New York	08/27/1880	10/26/1888			Y	
Desch, Joseph	37	Germany	Y	Bremen	Baltimore	02/09/1873	10/17/1888			Y	
Desch, Lawrence	31	Bavaria	Y	Hamburg	New York	10/10/1861	11/04/1861	18	219	N	
Deschler, August	30	Germany	N	Antwerp	New York	06/??/1878	?			Y	
Deschner, Andrew	29	Germany	Y	Amsterdam	New York	07/22/1883	12/28/1887			Y	
Deschner, August	24	Germany	Y	Antwerp	New York	05/30/1883	06/20/1888			Y	
Desenberg, Moses	34	Prussia	Y	Liverpool	New Orleans	11/??/1851	11/26/1855	13	251	N	
Desmond, Humphrey	27	Ireland	Y	Cork	Boston	06/??/1846	09/15/1852	25	529	N	
Despa, Ernst	34	Prussia	Y	Bremen	New York	??/26/1848	11/??/1849	23	301	N	
Desserick, Joseph	34	Germany	Y	Havre	New York	12/12/1882	10/28/1893			Y	
Dessirich, Joseph	34	Germany	Y	Havre	New York	12/12/1882	10/28/1893	21	42	N	
Deterding, Henry	37	Germany	Y	Bremen	Baltimore	08/08/1872	01/10/1882			Y	
Determann, Joseph	23	Germany	Y	Rotterdam	New York	07/19/1888	06/26/1889			Y	
Deters, Ferdinand	24	Oldenburg	Y	Bremen	Baltimore	09/18/1853	09/26/1857	15	320	N	
Deters, Henry Arnold	26	Oldenburg	Y	Bremen	New Orleans	05/15/1848	09/22/1854	10	167	N	
Deters, Henry Arnold	26	Oldenburg	Y	Bremen	New Orleans	05/15/1848	09/22/1854	12	106	N	
Deters, John Bernard	21	Hanover	Y	Bremen	New Orleans	12/21/1853	10/07/1854	10	534	N	
Detert, Henry	22	Hanover	Y	Bremen	Baltimore	10/29/1854	10/22/1857	15	476	N	
Detling, George	28	Wurttemberg	Y	Havre	New York	04/11/1854	09/10/1855	11	528	N	
Detmers, Frederick W. A.	??	Germany	Y	?	?	10/00/1883	06/02/1886			Y	
Dette, Frank W.	25	Germany	Y	Amsterdam	New York	07/02/1882	04/09/1888			Y	
Dette, Henry	25	Germany	Y	Hamburg	New York	06/30/1882	01/27/1888			Y	
Detters, John Bernard	21	Hanover	Y	Bremen	New Orleans	12/21/1853	10/07/1854	12	473	N	
Dettlaff, Franz Michael	36	Germany	Y	Bremen	Baltimore	09/19/1880	04/02/1888			Y	
Dettlefsen, Waldmar	32	Germany	Y	Hamburg	New York	01/14/1882	11/14/1893			Y	
Dettmer, Henry	26	Germany	Y	Bremen	Baltimore	12/23/1887	08/02/1893			Y	
Detzauer, Andrew	24	Bavaria	Y	Bremen	New York	08/24/1852	02/01/1855	13	270	N	
Detzel, Jacob	24	Germany	Y	Havre	New York	10/29/1880	12/16/1880			Y	
Detzel, John George	22	Germany	Y	Bremen	Baltimore	09/15/1887	11/07/1889			Y	
Detzel, Paul	25	Germany	Y	Bremen	Baltimore	08/08/1883	10/31/1884			Y	
Detzer, Adam	25	Bavaria	Y	Havre	New Orleans	02/??/1847	10/24/1850	2	295	N	
Deubach, Nicholas	28	Saxony	Y	Antwerp	Galveston	08/??/1846	02/12/1850	2	68	N	
Deuber, Charles	31	Wuertemberg	Y	Havre	New York	05/10/1853	05/20/1856	26	501	N	
Deuerlein, Paul	29	Germany	Y	Antwerp	New York	03/02/1892	11/09/1892			Y	
Deuschle, George	19	Germany	Y	Antwerp	New York	04/30/1880	09/23/1880			Y	
Deuszer, Christian Matha	45	Germany	Y	Rotterdam	New York	08/04/1874	03/16/1880			Y	
Deutemeier, H.	30	Germany	Y	Bremen	New York	05/13/1883	07/17/1885			Y	
Deutenberg, Joseph	47	Germany	Y	Antwerp	New York	10/01/1881	12/29/1883			Y	
Deutsch, Frank	24	Germany	Y	Bremen	Baltimore	08/20/1881	05/22/1885			Y	
Deutsch, Gotthard	35	Austira	Y	Hamburg	New York	11/28/1891	10/23/1894			Y	

CITIZENSHIP RECORDS

APPLICANT	AGE	COUNTRY OF ORIGIN	DEC	DEPART PORT	ENTRY PORT	ARRIVE DATE	DEC DATE	VOL	PG.	FLD	NAT DATE
Deutsch, Jacob	39	Germany	Y	Bremen	New York	04/10/1887	05/14/1892			Y	
Devalin, Laurence	26	Ireland	Y	Liverpool	New Orleans	12/24/1849	04/04/1853	7	517	N	
Devaney, David	25	Ireland	Y	Queenstown	New York	06/15/1889	10/19/1891			Y	
Devaney, John	19	Ireland	Y	?	New York	10/23/1883	10/03/1884			Y	
Devang, Thomas	28	Ireland	Y	Liverpool	New Orleans	12/24/1851	11/06/1852	5	245	N	
Devang, Thomas	28	Ireland	Y	Liverpool	New Orleans	12/24/1851	11/06/1852	6	369	N	
Devany, Daniel	25	Ireland	Y	Liverpool	New York	08/11/1845	02/17/1853	7	171	N	
Devenish, Robert J.	23	Ireland	Y	Londonderry	Baltimore	02/02/1888	05/25/1888			Y	
Devine, Arthur	27	Ireland	Y	Liverpool	New York	04/13/1843	01/03/1853	5	496	N	
Devine, Felix	22	Ireland	Y	Liverpool	New York	09/??/1852	10/02/1856	14	164	N	
Devine, John	49	Ireland	Y	?	?	?	10/15/1884			Y	
Devine, Luke	26	Ireland	Y	Liverpool	New York	09/09/1888	09/22/1896			Y	
Devitt, Anthony	40	Ireland	Y	Slago	New York	07/??/1868	04/02/1887			Y	
Devitt, Thomas	50	Ireland	N	Liverpool	New York	04/??/1873	?			Y	
Devlin, James	23	Ireland	Y	Londonderry	New York	07/01/1848	01/23/1850	23	545	N	
Devoy, Patrick	23	Ireland	Y	Liverpool	New York	05/29/1847	04/17/1852	24	521	N	
Dewald, Henry	33	Germany	Y	Bremen	New York	03/26/1876	10/25/1888			Y	
Dewald, Jacob	24	Bavaria	Y	Havre	New York	02/20/1851	04/27/1854	8	278	N	
Dewald, Jacob	24	Bavaria	Y	Havre	New York	02/20/1851	04/27/1854	9	149	N	
Dewald, Mathias	24	Prussia	Y	Havre	New York	07/08/1855	09/12/1857	15	261	N	
Dewar, David	57	Scotland	Y	Glasgow	New York	09/??/1854	09/21/1855	13	101	N	
Dewar, David	27	Scotland	Y	Liverpool	New York	08/12/1848	03/08/1852	24	262	N	
Dewein, Christian	30	Bavaria	Y	Havre	New York	07/??/1847	06/16/1852	25	281	N	
Dewelius, Henry	31	Germany	Y	Bremen	Baltimore	07/30/1880	06/14/1884			Y	
Dewerth, John Peter	33	Baden	Y	Havre	New York	08/05/1848	08/29/1848	22	277	N	
Dewhorst, Richard	24	England	Y	Liverpool	New York	08/??/1847	08/??/1851	4	169	N	
Dexheimer, John	37	Hesse Darmsta	Y	Havre	New Orleans	03/13/1857	06/26/1860	27	7	N	
Dey, John Casper	35	Oldenburg	Y	Bremen	New York	06/04/1845	10/15/1851	4	293	N	
Deye, Casper	43	Germany	Y	Bremen	New York	05/12/1873	10/22/1892	19	375	N	
Deye, Casper	43	Germany	Y	Bremen	New York	05/12/1873	10/22/1892			Y	
Deye, Joseph	38	Oldenburg	Y	Bremen	New York	11/03/1856	12/05/1859	17	491	N	
Di Circa, Francesci	36	Italy	Y	Naples	New York	05/15/1890	03/10/1894			Y	
Di Cunzolo, Donato	30	Italy	Y	Naples	New York	02/23/1889	10/05/1896			Y	
Di Gregoria, Pasquale	30	Italy	Y	Naples	New York	05/01/1893	07/07/1896			Y	
Di Lapa, Pasquale	33	Italy	Y	Naples	New York	03/29/1884	09/28/1896			Y	
Di Puccio, Luigi	42	Italy	Y	Naples	New York	03/01/1894	01/13/1897			Y	
Diamant, A.L.	39	Germany	Y	Hamburg	New York	09/??/1869	08/19/1884			Y	
Diamont, Henry	44	Russia	Y	Stettin	New York	05/15/1889	11/04/1892			Y	
Diandrea, Vincenzo	25	Italy	Y	Naples	New York	05/02/1888	03/09/1894			Y	
Dibarbero, Gim	35	Italy	Y	Naples	New York	11/22/1883	11/08/1888			Y	
Dicesere, Gioseppe	21	Italy	Y	Naples	New York	07/03/1888	11/16/1891			Y	
Dick, Augustus	27	Wurttemberg	Y	Antwerp	New York	08/26/1848	03/25/1853	7	389	N	
Dick, Henry	28	Reuss	Y	Bremen	Baltimore	06/28/1854	12/06/1858	17	380	N	
Dickan, Bernard	47	Germany	N	Liverpool	New York	06/26/1870	?			Y	
Dicken, Herman	32	Germany	Y	Bremen	Baltimore	10/17/1883	10/22/1891			Y	
Dickens, Henry	36	England	Y	Liverpool	New York	09/10/1883	10/03/1891			Y	
Dickhaus, Bernard	32	Oldenburg	Y	Bremen	New Orleans	12/??/1843	12/??/1850	2	420	N	
Dickhaus, Frederick	26	Oldenburg	Y	Bremen	Baltimore	10/30/1846	02/11/1852	24	93	N	
Dickhausen, Henry	26	Nassau	Y	Antwerp	New York	04/28/1848	03/01/1852	24	200	N	
Dickhoff, Edward	33	Germany	Y	Hamburg	New York	12/27/1878	03/26/1883			Y	
Dickore, William	42	Germany	N	Bremen	New York	02/??/1876	?			Y	
Dickow, August	26	Germany	Y	Bremen	Baltimore	03/11/1887	05/02/1888			Y	
Dickow, Wm.	31	Germany	Y	Antwerp	New York	11/27/1882	10/14/1889			Y	
Dickschen, Ferdinand	28	Germany	Y	?	?	04/14/1888	08/31/1894			Y	
Dickten, Rudolf	34	Germany	Y	Rotterdam	New York	01/26/1891	12/07/1893			Y	
Diddie, Frederick	??	Germany	Y	?	?	?	10/26/1888			Y	
Didie, Christ	??	Germany	Y	?	?	?	04/04/1887			Y	
Diebold, John	29	Germany	Y	Havre	New York	08/25/1880	05/04/1886			Y	
Dieckhaus, Henry	33	Prussia	Y	Bremen	New York	08/??/1847	12/??/1850	2	432	N	

CITIZENSHIP RECORDS

APPLICANT	AGE	COUNTRY OF ORIGIN	DEC	DEPART PORT	ENTRY PORT	ARRIVE DATE	DEC DATE	VOL	PG.	FLD	NAT DATE
Dieckmann, Bernard	32	Hanover	Y	Bremen	New York	??/28/1849	05/01/1855	11	338	N	
Dieckmann, Gerhard	43	Germany	Y	Bremen	Baltimore	03/28/1886	10/24/1889			Y	
Dieckmann, Gustav	46	Germany	Y	Hamburg	New York	12/21/1880	10/19/1886			Y	
Dieckmann, Henry	27	Prussia	Y	Bremen	Baltimore	09/21/1850	10/07/1857	15	369	N	
Dieckmann, Herman	27	Hanover	Y	Bremen	Baltimore	10/15/1854	10/19/1857	15	450	N	
Dieckmann, Herman	41	Germany	Y	Holland	New York	06/02/1872	10/19/1886	19	53	N	
Dieckmann, Herman	57	Germany	N	Bremen	Baltimore	11/??/1854	?			Y	
Dieckmann, Herman	37	Prussia	Y	Bremen	Baltimore	10/09/1857	10/09/1860	27	467	N	
Dieckmann, Herman Fred.	24	Hanover	Y	Bremen	Baltimore	10/29/1856	09/25/1857	15	317	N	
Dieckmann, Hermann	47	Germany	N	Bremen	Baltimore	06/28/1854	?			Y	
Dieckmann, John H. L.	33	Hanover	Y	Bremen	New Orleans	06/01/1852	02/15/1856	26	89	N	
Diedenhoefer, Adam	24	Germany	Y	Antwerp	New York	10/25/1882	04/23/1885			Y	
Diedenhoefer, Adam	53	Germany	N	Antwerp	New York	08/16/1881	?			Y	
Diedenhofer, Adam	50	Germany	Y	Antwerp	New York	09/16/1881	08/16/1883			Y	
Diedling, Henry	25	Luxembourg	Y	Antwerp	New York	06/26/1854	03/06/1857	15	68	N	
Diedricks, G.	28	Germany	Y	Bremen	Baltimore	05/18/1881	09/06/1885			Y	
Diedschy, Michael	56	Switzerland	Y	Havre	New York	03/26/1866	09/17/1896			Y	
Diefenborn, Anton	44	Germany	Y	Antwerp	New York	11/14/1888	03/06/1893			Y	
Diegedio, Giavania	32	Italy	Y	Naples	New York	05/05/1890	07/02/1900			Y	
Diegers, John Henry	30	Oldenburg	Y	Bremen	New Orleans	11/30/1845	01/07/1851	2	469	N	
Diehl, Conrad	33	Nassau	Y	Bremen	New York	08/15/1853	09/20/1858	16	186	N	
Diehl, Gottlieb	38	Germany	Y	Bremen	New York	02/02/1884	10/17/1892			Y	
Diehl, Henry	53	Germany	Y	?	New York	??/??/1866	10/09/1883			Y	
Diehl, John	37	Nassau	Y	Liverpool	New York	09/15/1840	04/16/1852	24	518	N	
Diehl, Valentine	26	Bavaria	Y	Havre	New York	09/29/1846	01/23/1850	23	539	N	
Diehl, Wilhelm	??	India	Y	?	?	?	04/02/1867			Y	
Diehm, John	32	Bavaria	Y	Havre	New York	08/03/1854	01/04/1858	16	301	N	
Diehm, John	45	Baden	Y	Havre	New York	05/10/1851	03/24/1856	26	278	N	
Diehm, Michael	30	Bavaria	Y	Havre	New York	09/03/1857	12/26/1859	17	521	N	
Diekamp, John Herman	26	Germany	Y	Bremen	Baltimore	05/24/1888	01/29/1890			Y	
Diekemper, J. Henry	26	Hanover	Y	Bremen	Baltimore	11/04/1848	03/18/1852	24	332	N	
Dieker, Gerhard Henry	29	Prussia	Y	Bremen	Baltimore	05/01/1856	10/01/1856	14	114	N	
Dieker, Herman Henry	32	Prussia	Y	Bremen	Buffalo	08/11/1854	10/01/1856	14	115	N	
Diekhoff, John	28	Hanover	Y	Bremen	Baltimore	10/??/1846	12/30/1852	5	472	N	
Diekhone, August	29	Prussia	Y	Bremen	New Orleans	01/27/1854	08/28/1862	18	411	N	
Diekman, Henry	29	Hanover	Y	Bremen	New York	05/21/1851	03/25/1853	7	388	N	
Diekmann, Barney	48	Germany	N	?	Baltimore	10/21/1866	?			Y	
Diekmann, Frank	23	Hanover	Y	Bremen	New York	08/11/1849	09/09/1852	25	435	N	
Diekmann, Gerhard Henry	31	Hanover	Y	Bremen	New Orleans	12/30/1852	08/15/1855	11	439	N	
Diekmann, Henry	23	Germany	Y	Bremen	New York	06/22/1881	05/09/1882			Y	
Diekmann, John Henry	28	Hanover	Y	Bremen	New York	08/21/1846	02/02/1850	2	30	N	
Diekmann, Stephan Henry	26	Prussia	Y	Bremen	Baltimore	05/01/1846	10/30/1852	5	78	N	
Diekmeier, Gottlieb	44	Germany	Y	Bremen	New York	06/07/1882	08/09/1892			Y	
Diekmeyer, Henry	27	Germany	N	Borninghause	New York	09/00/1871	10/00/1871			Y	10/00/1876
Dielmann, John Bernard	23	Hanover	Y	Bremen	New Orleans	05/24/1853	01/18/1856	13	482	N	
Diemer, Henry	21	Germany	Y	Antwerp	New York	06/02/1884	07/24/1888			Y	
Diener, Augustine	30	Germany	Y	Antwerp	New York	07/01/1879	05/25/1885			Y	
Dienger, Ferdinand	??	Germany	Y	?	?	03/??/1890	11/15/1892			Y	
Dier, Herman Henry	33	Hanover	Y	Bremen	New Orleans	12/11/1847	11/01/1852	5	121	N	
Dierckes, Hermann Bernad	27	Prussia	Y	Bremen	Baltimore	05/06/1849	10/05/1854	12	376	N	
Dierckes, Hermann Bernar	27	Prussia	Y	Bremen	Baltimore	05/06/1849	10/05/1854	10	437	N	
Diere, Frank	27	Germany	Y	Bremen	New York	07/22/1879	10/22/1886	19	68	N	
Dierig, Hermann	24	Germany	Y	Bremen	Baltimore	05/04/1887	03/01/1888			Y	
Dieringer, Charles	29	Germany	Y	Antwerp	New York	10/18/1882	11/28/1888			Y	
Dieringer, Severin	??	Prussia	Y	?	?	?	03/02/1886			Y	
Dierken, Bernard	28	Germany	Y	Bremen	Baltimore	05/26/1889	10/04/1894			Y	
Dierken, John Bernard	42	Oldenburg	Y	Bremen	Baltimore	10/03/1859	07/07/1862	18	371	N	
Dierker, Henry	17	Germany	N	?	Baltimore	00/00/1883				Y	08/17/1888
Dierkes, August	48	Germany	Y	Antwerp	New York	12/04/1880	02/15/1892			Y	

CITIZENSHIP RECORDS

APPLICANT	AGE	COUNTRY OF ORIGIN	DEC	DEPART PORT	ENTRY PORT	ARRIVE DATE	DEC DATE	VOL	PG.	FLD	NAT DATE
Dierkes, Bernhard	37	Germany	Y	Bremen	Baltimore	09/06/1873	10/05/1880			Y	
Dierkes, Clement	25	Germany	Y	Amsterdam	New York	10/21/1889	10/31/1894			Y	
Dierking, Frederick	??	Hanover	Y	Bremen	New York	07/30/1846	10/09/1848	22	506	N	
Dierking, John	26	Hanover	Y	Bremen	New York	07/31/1846	10/12/1848	1	181	N	
Dierks, Henry	30	Germany	Y	Bremen	Baltimore	04/19/1883	06/04/1885			Y	
Dierling, August	34	France	Y	Havre	New Orleans	06/08/1854	10/29/1858	17	184	N	
Diers, Henry	23	Hanover	Y	Bremen	New York	01/03/1847	10/12/1848	1	177	N	
Diers, Herman	30	Hanover	Y	Bremen	New Orleans	12/??/1848	05/01/1855	11	339	N	
Diers, Herman Heinrich	33	Hanover	Y	Bremen	New Orleans	12/11/1847	11/01/1852	6	247	N	
Diesel, August	23	Bavaria	Y	Bremen	New York	05/01/1845	05/31/1852	25	147	N	
Diesel, Gustav	21	Bavaria	Y	Bremen	New York	06/15/1851	05/31/1852	25	151	N	
Diesenberg, Ludolf	38	Hanover	Y	Bremen	Baltimore	06/23/1855	08/22/1860	27	306	N	
Diessle, Louis	27	Germany	Y	Bremen	New York	04/??/1890	10/19/1896			Y	
Dietenhoffer, Jo.	17	Germany	N	?	New York	00/00/1881				Y	10/18/1886
Dieter, John	42	Germany	N	Bremen	New York	06/01/1863	?			Y	
Dieter, Karl	28	Germany	Y	Havre	New York	05/10/1883	03/26/1889			Y	
Dieterich, Gottlieb	27	Kurhessen	Y	Bremen	New York	07/23/1858	11/04/1858	17	273	N	
Dieterich, Lawrence F. B	26	Germany	Y	Amsterdam	New York	09/12/1888	02/27/1894			Y	
Dieterle, Gregor	25	Germany	Y	Havre	New York	10/19/1882	05/14/1885			Y	
Dieterle, John	32	Germany	Y	Antwerp	New York	10/30/1884	06/15/1887			Y	
Dieterle, Mathias	43	Germany	Y	Antwerp	New York	06/05/1890	02/19/1894			Y	
Dietermann, George	35	Hanover	Y	Hamburg	New York	04/??/1879	09/??/1880			Y	
Dietermann, George	46	Germany	N	Hamburg	New York	04/??/1879	?			Y	
Diether, Sebastian	26	Germany	Y	Antwerp	Philadelphia	04/08/1881	10/05/1883			Y	
Dietrich, Anton	52	Germany	Y	Bremen	Baltimore	03/26/1881	10/26/1888			Y	
Dietrich, Engelbert	28	Austria	Y	Havre	New York	04/11/1879	11/28/1881			Y	
Dietrich, Fred	25	Hesse Darmsta	Y	Havre	New York	05/22/1851	05/31/1852	25	138	N	
Dietrich, John	24	Bavaria	Y	Havre	New Orleans	11/30/1855	11/10/1857	16	5	N	
Dietrich, Peter	40	Germany	Y	Antwerp	New York	01/06/1886	06/16/1890			Y	
Dietrichs, Charles Ludwi	38	Prussia	Y	Bremen	Baltimore	06/13/1854	12/14/1855	13	312	N	
Dietsch, Emil	22	Germany	Y	Havre	New York	02/28/1892	10/10/1895			Y	
Dietsch, Adam Christian	24	Bavaria	Y	Bremen	New York	08/09/1854	05/19/1856	26	496	N	
Dietz, August	??	Prussia	Y	?	?	07/??/1881	08/23/1884			Y	
Dietz, Caspar	37	Germany	Y	Bremen	Baltimore	10/20/1879	09/03/1888			Y	
Dietz, Charles	21	Hesse Cassel	Y	Antwerp	New York	05/17/1850	05/25/1852	25	110	N	
Dietz, Ernst	46	Germany	N	Bremen	New York	08/??/1862	?			Y	
Dietz, Frederick William	30	Saxony	Y	Rotterdam	Boston	06/17/1846	10/03/1848	22	398	N	
Dietz, Henry	36	Prussia	Y	Bremen	Baltimore	05/27/1849	03/27/1850	2	272	N	
Dietz, John	28	Bavaria	Y	Bremen	Baltimore	06/05/1848	04/04/1853	7	525	N	
Dietz, Louis	23	Wurttemberg	Y	Havre	New York	10/28/1852	08/17/1857	15	147	N	
Dietz, Valentine	26	Germany	Y	Rotterdam	New York	05/30/1881	09/24/1887			Y	
Dietzel, Henry	25	Prussia	Y	Hamburg	New York	06/01/1849	01/06/1851	2	456	N	
Dievers, Henry	41	Waldeck	Y	Hamburg	New Orleans	11/13/1847	10/02/1848	1	9	N	
Digman, Patrick	23	Ireland	Y	Liverpool	New York	12/15/1854	03/23/1858	16	438	N	
Dignan, ?	??	?	Y	?	?	??/20/18??	10/24/1850	2	293	N	
Dignan, John	31	Ireland	Y	Liverpool	New Orleans	12/14/1849	12/04/1852	5	379	N	
Dignan, Michael	41	Ireland	Y	Liverpool	New York	05/25/1836	11/08/1851	4	506	N	
Dignen, Patrick	36	Ireland	Y	Liverpool	New Orleans	06/19/1843	05/26/1852	25	113	N	
Dignin, Hugh	30	Ireland	Y	Greenock	New York	04/28/1849	07/21/1851	4	17	N	
Dilapo, Nicola	34	Italy	Y	Naples	New York	12/02/1886	11/08/1888			Y	
Dilg, Adam (Delk?)	32	Hasse Darmsta	Y	Rotterdam	New York	10/20/1847	08/14/1848	22	104	N	
Dilg, Philig	64	Germany	N	Havre	New Orleans	02/??/1850	?			Y	
Dilger, Henry	35	Germany	Y	Bremen	Baltimore	06/03/1883	12/26/1885			Y	
Dillanty, James	36	Ireland	Y	Liverpool	New Orelans	10/11/1850	06/06/1854	12	35	N	
Dillenburger, Georg	??	Germany	Y	?	?	?	07/20/1885			Y	
Dillhoff, J. H.	21	Hanover	Y	Bremen	New Orleans	12/21/1856	01/16/1860	27	55	N	
Dilling, Joseph	33	Germany	Y	Bremen	New York	09/13/1883	02/03/1890			Y	
Dillinger, John	49	Bavaria	Y	Havre	New York	07/18/1848	02/13/1849	23	82	N	
Dillinger, Martin	56	Bavaria	Y	Havre	New York	08/15/1853	10/30/1858	17	191	N	

CITIZENSHIP RECORDS

APPLICANT	AGE	COUNTRY OF ORIGIN	DEC	DEPART PORT	ENTRY PORT	ARRIVE DATE	DEC DATE	VOL	PG.	FLD	NAT DATE
Dillman, Henry	26	Hanover	Y	Bremen	New Orleans	07/01/1849	06/16/1852	25	275	N	
Dillmann, Henry	30	Darmstadt	Y	Havre	New York	08/30/1845	02/27/1850	2	133	N	
Dillon, Jeremiah	23	Ireland	Y	Limerick	Buffalo	08/??/1851	11/03/1851	4	476	N	
Dillon, Joseph	58	Ireland	N	Liverpool	New York	05/26/1857	?			Y	
Dillon, Matthew	50	Ireland	Y	Queenstown	New York	08/05/1884	10/25/1890	19	299	N	
Dillon, Matthew	50	Ireland	Y	Queenstown	New York	08/05/1884	10/25/1890			Y	
Dillon, Michael	30	Ireland	Y	Liverpool	New York	07/01/1847	04/20/1850	3	6	N	
Dillon, Michael	29	Ireland	Y	Limerick	Cleveland	07/26/1851	03/15/1852	24	307	N	
Dillon, Patrick	29	Ireland	Y	Liverpool	New Orleans	02/01/1850	06/30/1851	3	464	N	
Dillon, Patrick	40	Ireland	Y	Liverpool	New Orleans	12/25/1844	05/15/1852	25	23	N	
Dillon, William	17	Ireland	N	?	New York	00/00/1873				Y	10/15/1888
Dillonburger, Philipp	27	Germany	Y	Bremen	New York	06/13/1893	08/29/1896			Y	
Diltey, Jacques	36	Germany	Y	Havre	New York	06/28/1890	09/10/1896			Y	
Dilz, Fred	28	Germany	Y	Antwerp	New York	04/25/1889	05/26/1890			Y	
Dimant, Hyman	23	Russia	Y	Hamburg	New York	05/31/1888	01/09/1893			Y	
Dimber, Peter	27	Bavaria	Y	Bremen	New Orleans	10/23/1853	02/02/1860	27	85	N	
Dindinger, Emil	24	Germany	Y	?	Baltimore	08/??/1887	10/29/1888			Y	
Dindorf, Carl M.	??	Germany	Y	?	?	?	10/13/1884			Y	
Dinger, August (Staenger	35	Germany	Y	?	New York	??/??/1872	10/11/1884			Y	
Dinger, Joseph	29	Germany	Y	Havre	New York	07/10/1884	10/06/1888			Y	
Dinger, Joseph	40	Baden	Y	Havre	New York	07/03/1845	09/15/1852	25	514	N	
Dinger, Konstantine	48	Germany	Y	Havre	New York	04/10/1881	05/12/1890			Y	
Dinger, Leopold	30	Germany	Y	Havre	New York	02/18/1881	11/01/1886			Y	
Dingfelder, John	32	Bavaria	Y	Bremen	New Orleans	12/12/1846	05/06/1850	3	51	N	
Dinkel, Mathias	??	Bavaria	Y	Wirtsburg	New York	05/28/1847	10/05/1848	22	435	N	
Dinkel, Simon	23	Germany	Y	Rotterdam	New York	09/07/1881	05/26/1885			Y	
Dinkel, Stephen	21	Bavaria	Y	Bremen	Baltimore	07/04/1852	10/02/1856	14	166	N	
Dinkelacker, Christian	20	Germany	Y	Bremen	New York	05/31/1882	08/07/1886			Y	
Dinkelacker, Henry	22	Wurttemberg	Y	Havre	New York	11/08/1858	03/26/1862	18	284	N	
Dinkelman, Henry	24	Germany	Y	Bremen	New York	10/10/1884	09/02/1885			Y	
Dinkelmann, Fred	28	Germany	Y	Bremen	New York	03/05/1889	09/06/1892			Y	
Dinkels, William	38	Germany	Y	Bremen	Baltimore	07/23/1882	01/15/1892			Y	
Dinsmore, Matthew	17	Ireland	N	?	Philadelphia	00/00/1876				Y	11/07/1887
Dinwiddie, James	??	Scotland	Y	?	?	?	11/05/1888			Y	
Diorio, Amanzo	31	Italy	Y	Naples	New York	02/12/1893	02/07/1896			Y	
Dipentie, Antonio	38	Italy	Y	Naples	New York	06/06/1883	05/21/1894			Y	
Dippel, Andrew	38	Hesse Cassel	Y	Bremen	New York	12/10/1847	01/??/1850	23	515	N	
Dippel, George	36	Germany	Y	Bremen	New York	09/09/1883	03/10/1890			Y	
Dirkes, Herman	35	Germany	Y	Bremen	Baltimore	07/26/1881	01/18/1886			Y	
Dirnbach, Joseph	46	Austira	Y	Bremen	New York	03/01/1882	11/02/1895			Y	
Dirr, Balser	46	Germany	Y	Havre	New York	02/22/1889	10/26/1893			Y	
Dirr, Herman	54	Germany	Y	Havre	New York	05/08/1881	10/25/1893	21	32	N	
Dirr, Paul	33	Germany	Y	Havre	New York	03/17/1890	08/15/1898			Y	
Diselkamper, Geo.	21	Germany	Y	Bremen	Baltimore	05/18/1882	05/14/1885			Y	
Diskin, John	31	Ireland	Y	Queenstown	New York	05/05/1879	10/22/1886	19	66	N	
Disqua, Valentine	32	Germany	Y	Havre	New York	09/13/1880	10/28/1893			Y	
Diss, Eugene	??	France	Y	?	?	04/01/1899	09/05/1900			Y	
Dissau, Ernst	47	Germany	Y	?	Baltimore	05/16/1883	07/03/1893			Y	
Distel, C. Karuben	23	Germany	Y	Havre	New York	03/02/1886	04/21/1891			Y	
Distiller, Nathan	28	Russia	Y	Bremen	Baltimore	12/14/1890	01/02/1895			Y	
Distler, John	28	Bavaria	Y	Hamburg	New York	10/05/1848	11/20/1848	1	337	N	
Distler, John	29	Germany	Y	Bremen	New York	06/07/1879	06/02/1884			Y	
Distler, John George	42	Bavaria	Y	Bremen	Baltimore	11/04/1849	04/05/1856	26	444	N	
Dittly, Joseph	32	Germany	Y	Havre	New York	06/05/1892	09/09/1896			Y	
Dittmann, Christian Lore	33	Prussia	Y	Bremen	New York	06/03/1848	02/11/1853	7	142	N	
Dittmann, Johann	40	Wurttemberg	Y	Havre	New York	05/28/1844	10/06/1856	14	241	N	
Dittmer, Christian	??	Germany	Y	?	?	?	10/20/1884			Y	
Dittrich, Alois	21	Germany	Y	Antwerp	New York	05/25/1885	04/25/1887			Y	
Dittrich, Edmund	30	Germany	Y	Bremen	Baltimore	08/05/1881	12/28/1893			Y	

CITIZENSHIP RECORDS

APPLICANT	AGE	COUNTRY OF ORIGIN	DEC	DEPART PORT	ENTRY PORT	ARRIVE DATE	DEC DATE	VOL	PG.	FLD	NAT DATE
Dittrich, Ernest	??	Germany	Y	?	?	?	11/22/1884			Y	
Dittrich, Joseph	26	Germany	Y	Hamburg	New York	04/16/1880	03/12/1884			Y	
Dittus, Ada,	32	Germany	Y	Liverpool	New York	05/08/1882	05/23/1888			Y	
Dittus, John	25	Wurttemberg	Y	Havre	New York	05/10/1857	04/17/1862	18	318	N	
Diver, Anthony	27	Ireland	Y	Liverpool	Philadelphia	04/05/1848	07/17/1851	3	549	N	
Diviny, Michael	35	Ireland	Y	Canada	Whitehall	04/26/1847	03/07/1853	7	298	N	
Dixon, Daniel	45	Ireland	Y	Canada	Portland	08/??/1849	06/04/1852	25	183	N	
Dixon, James	43	Ireland	Y	Canada	Cleveland	10/??/1844	05/31/1852	25	135	N	
Dixon, James M.	30	Ireland	Y	Liverpool	New York	08/04/1842	08/??/1851	4	173	N	
Dixon, Thomas W.	35	England	Y	Liverpool	New York	04/09/1886	03/04/1891			Y	
Dlugokinsky, Adam	35	Germany	Y	Bremen	New York	05/24/1885	03/19/1888			Y	
Dobert, Phil A.	25	Germany	Y	Bremen	Baltimore	05/00/1882	03/13/1886			Y	
Doblander, Joseph	34	Germany	Y	Bremen	Baltimore	03/29/1880	10/11/1886			Y	
Doble, Richard	38	England	Y	Liverpool	New York	04/01/1850	04/08/1858	16	508	N	
Dobner, Isidor	42	Germany	N	Hamburg	New York	08/15/1864	?			Y	
Dobrovsky, Asar	23	Russia	Y	Hamburg	New York	07/29/1886	01/20/1891			Y	
Dobson, George H.	56	England	N	Liverpool	New York	10/??/1854	?			Y	
Dockenberg, Ernst Henry	44	Hanover	Y	Bremen	Baltimore	01/12/1846	02/07/1849	23	128	N	
Dodd, Peter	27	Ireland	Y	Liverpool	New York	05/05/1848	02/14/1852	24	107	N	
Dodds, James	33	England	Y	London	New York	08/??/1851	02/09/1857	15	2	N	
Doddy, James	56	Ireland	N	Liverpool	New York	03/??/1856	?			Y	
Dods, John	54	Scotland	Y	?	?	02/??/1880	08/22/1883			Y	
Dodsmouth, Martin	30	England	Y	London	Galveston	12/29/1841	04/02/1853	7	487	N	
Doebele, Frank	25	Baden	Y	Havre	New Orleans	04/23/1854	04/04/1856	26	440	N	
Doebler, Hugo	28	Germany	Y	?	?	10/11/1891	02/02/1892			Y	
Doecker, G.	27	Germany	Y	Bremen	Baltimore	06/10/1881	10/04/1883			Y	
Doefler, John	26	Bavaria	Y	Bremen	Buffalo	08/04/1847	02/21/1851	3	148	N	
Doehler, Peter	33	Bavaria	Y	Bremen	Baltimore	06/27/1852	11/14/1857	16	17	N	
Doeksen, John	25	Holland	Y	Rotterdam	Baltimore	04/17/1847	02/03/1851	3	87	N	
Doelker, Frederick	26	Wurttemberg	Y	Havre	New York	08/27/1853	10/10/1854	11	216	N	
Doelker, Jacob	54	Germany	N	Havre	New York	10/??/1854	?			Y	
Doell, Charles	23	Hesse Darmsta	Y	Bremen	New York	09/25/1869	12/21/1871	18	444	N	
Doellmann, Theodore	28	Germany	Y	Bremen	Baltimore	04/26/1882	12/29/1884			Y	
Doench, Frederick	22	Kurhessen	Y	Bremen	Baltimore	06/28/1848	02/01/1851	3	76	N	
Doepke, Frederick Henry	29	Hanover	Y	Bremen	Baltimore	10/21/1854	02/04/1856	26	28	N	
Doepke, John Henry Phill	21	Hanover	Y	Bremen	Baltimore	08/06/1846	09/13/1848	22	339	N	
Doepke, Theodore	28	Hanover	Y	Bremen	New Orleans	12/01/1854	03/07/1857	15	73	N	
Doepke, Wilhelm	26	Germany	Y	Bremen	Baltimore	10/28/1886	11/01/1888	19	208	N	
Doepke, Wilhelm	26	Germany	Y	Bremen	Baltimore	10/28/1886	11/01/1888			Y	
Doerfler, George	??	Germany	N	?	?	10/01/1887				Y	10/27/1892
Doerger, Bernard	43	Germany	N	Bremen	Baltimore	06/06/1866	?			Y	
Doering, Christ G.	64	Germany	Y	Bremen	New York	05/18/1881	10/14/1889			Y	
Doering, Christoph	33	Germany	Y	Bremen	Baltimore	07/10/1885	05/26/1891			Y	
Doering, Heinrich	??	Prussia	Y	?	?	?	12/04/1882			Y	
Doering, John	30	Germany	Y	Bremen	Baltimore	05/16/1883	08/03/1885			Y	
Doering, Otto	??	Germany	Y	?	?	?	04/09/1888			Y	
Doering, Paul	36	Germany	Y	?	New York	??/??/1886	04/22/1898			Y	
Doerly, Mathias	38	Baden	Y	Havre	New Orleans	04/28/1854	03/31/1857	15	110	N	
Doerner, Bernard J.	44	Germany	Y	Bremen	New York	04/28/1866	06/10/1884			Y	
Doerner, Charles	36	Germany	Y	Antwerp	Detroit	05/22/1872	09/19/1883			Y	
Doernhoefer, Moritz	26	Bavaria	Y	Bremen	Buffalo	08/09/1847	02/15/1849	23	136	N	
Doerr, Ferdinand	47	Germany	N	Rotterdam	New Orleans	02/??/1853	?			Y	
Doerr, Francis Joseph	22	Bavaria	Y	Havre	New York	08/15/1855	12/05/1857	16	196	N	
Doerr, George	33	Bavaria	Y	Havre	New Orleans	05/22/1854	04/03/1858	16	485	N	
Doerr, John	23	Bavaria	Y	London	New York	12/15/1853	09/04/1856			Y	
Doerr, John	25	Germany	Y	Liverpool	New York	08/16/1880	04/30/1883			Y	
Doerr, Louis	26	Baden	Y	Antwerp	New York	09/27/1849	04/18/1853	8	74	N	
Doescher, John	39	Germany	N	Hamburg	New York	09/24/1866	?			Y	
Doetkert, Herman Henry	25	Hanover	Y	Bremen	New York	08/15/1845	02/05/1849	23	28	N	

CITIZENSHIP RECORDS

APPLICANT	AGE	COUNTRY OF ORIGIN	DEC	DEPART PORT	ENTRY PORT	ARRIVE DATE	DEC DATE	VOL	PG.	FLD	NAT DATE
Doetterl, John	29	Bavaria	Y	Hamburg	New York	06/07/1846	01/20/1849	1	477	N	
Doettker, Henry	26	Hanover	Y	Bremen	Buffalo	07/??/1848	11/29/1852	5	355	N	
Doherty, Denis	30	Ireland	Y	Limerick	Buffalo	06/23/1842	10/06/1851	4	210	N	
Doherty, Edward	38	Ireland	Y	Canada	Boston	03/15/1840	01/14/1851	2	496	N	
Doherty, Edward	26	Ireland	Y	Liverpool	New York	04/24/1852	09/30/1856	14	49	N	
Doherty, James	24	Ireland	Y	?	?	?	03/15/1858			Y	
Doherty, James H.	34	Ireland	Y	Glasgow	New York	08/04/1885	11/01/1886	19	103	N	
Doherty, Thomas	44	Ireland	Y	Liverpool	New Orleans	06/29/1848	03/22/1850	2	232	N	
Doherty, William	28	Ireland	Y	Liverpool	New York	09/21/1851	05/25/1854	8	537	N	
Dohnan, Jacob	21	Prussia	Y	Liverpool	New Orleans	12/02/1851	09/25/1854	10	198	N	
Dohnau, Jacob	21	Prussia	Y	Liverpool	New Orleans	12/02/1851	09/25/1854	12	137	N	
Dohrmann, August	43	Germany	N	Bremen	New York	04/01/1871	?			Y	
Dolan, Dominick	23	Ireland	Y	Liverpool	New York	02/26/1893	03/11/1896			Y	
Dolan, John	25	Ireland	Y	Quebec	Buffalo	10/??/1854	03/18/1858	16	422	N	
Dolan, John	23	Ireland	Y	Liverpool	New York	09/15/1848	04/12/1852	24	452	N	
Dolan, Michael	25	Ireland	Y	Liverpool	New York	06/17/1844	03/25/1850	2	263	N	
Dolan, Michael	28	Ireland	Y	Liverpool	New Orleans	12/16/1848	03/17/1851	3	292	N	
Dolan, Pat	23	Ireland	Y	Queenstown	New York	09/29/1885	11/07/1889			Y	
Dolan, Patrick	26	Ireland	Y	Liverpool	New York	05/??/1845	09/26/1856	14	396	N	
Dolan, Patrick	27	Ireland	Y	Queenstown	New York	05/09/1885	05/21/1891			Y	
Dolan, Peter K.	25	Ireland	Y	Liverpool	New York	09/15/1848	11/03/1851	4	472	N	
Dolan, Thomas	32	Ireland	N	Queenstown	New York	04/29/1878	?	28	368	N	10/06/1883
Dolan, Thomas M.	27	England	Y	Liverpool	New York	05/04/1854	05/04/1860	27	178	N	
Dolan, Timothy	23	Ireland	N	Queenstown	New York	11/09/1878	?			Y	
Dold, Charles	67	Germany	N	Havre	New York	08/18/1854	?			Y	
Dolenske, Michael	50	Austria	Y	Hamburg	New York	12/20/1880	09/22/1891			Y	
Dolf, Peter	31	Prussia	Y	Bremen	Baltimore	12/15/1859	03/25/1862	18	282	N	
Dolfinger, Charles	22	Wuertemberg	Y	Havre	New York	08/18/1853	03/25/1856	26	310	N	
Dolka, Frederick	26	Wurttemberg	Y	Havre	New York	08/27/1853	10/10/1854	6	213	N	
Dolkote, Franz	21	Prussia	Y	Amsterdam	Baltimore	10/16/1853	10/07/1856	14	249	N	
Doll, Jacob	28	Bavaria	Y	Havre	New York	05/20/1846	11/13/1848	1	260	N	
Doll, John	32	Germany	Y	Havre	New York	03/23/1881	11/03/1881			Y	
Doll, Joseph	22	Baden	Y	Havre	New York	03/03/1855	11/01/1858	17	235	N	
Doll, Joseph	37	Germany	Y	Amsterdam	New York	04/19/1885	10/19/1903			Y	
Doll, Phillip	40	Germany	N	Rotterdam	New York	07/??/1869	?			Y	
Dollard, Martin	52	Ireland	Y	Liverpool	New Orleans	04/24/1849	08/15/1851	4	136	N	
Dollenmeyer, August	35	Germany	Y	Hamburg	New York	09/15/1883	11/26/1889			Y	
Dollenmeyer, Jacob	38	Germany	Y	Antwerp	New York	10/01/1880	08/??/1883			Y	
Dollenmeyer, Jacob	38	Germany	N	Antwerp	New York	10/01/1880	?			Y	
Doller, George	27	Bavaria	Y	Havre	New York	11/08/1848	12/04/1855	13	281	N	
Doller, Max	36	Austria	Y	Hamburg	New York	05/28/1879	10/17/1889			Y	
Dollinger, John Frederic	31	Wurttemberg	Y	Liverpool	New York	04/26/1852	11/24/1855	13	247	N	
Dollmann, F.F. August	28	Germany	Y	Bremen	Baltimore	10/01/1881	12/30/1884			Y	
Dollrichs, Joseph	22	Germany	Y	?	New York	??/??/1882	03/17/1885			Y	
Dollriechs, Sebastian	25	Germany	Y	Bremen	Baltimore	03/04/1887	10/23/1891	19	340	N	
Dollries, Alois	??	Germany	N	?	?	06/15/1887				Y	10/22/1892
Dolmeier, John	43	Bavaria	Y	Havre	New York	10/13/1846	10/03/1848	1	47	N	
Dolting, Friedrich	27	Germany	Y	Bremen	Batlimore	06/03/1883	10/09/1883			Y	
Dolweber, Henry	41	Hanover	Y	Bremen	New York	12/10/1847	11/03/1852	6	338	N	
Domagalski, Constantine	51	Austria	Y	Bremen	New York	03/09/1884	03/14/1888			Y	
Dome, Nicholas	40	Bavaria	Y	Havre	New York	08/13/1854	10/03/1856	14	178	N	
Domeier, Henry	28	Hanover	Y	Bremen	New Orleans	11/30/1845	09/09/1848	22	313	N	
Domhoff, John Henry	25	Hanover	Y	Bremen	Baltimore	10/18/1845	10/05/1848	22	422	N	
Domhoff, John William	24	Hanover	Y	Bremen	Baltimore	10/18/1845	10/05/1848	22	421	N	
Dominski, Martin	27	Germany	Y	Hamburg	New York	03/08/1881	11/28/1885			Y	
Domis, John	29	Germany	Y	Hamburg	New York	12/25/1882	11/01/1888			Y	
Domis, Joseph	21	Germany	Y	Hamburg	Baltimore	12/29/1884	04/22/1889			Y	
Domis, Joseph	65	Germany	Y	Bremen	Batlimore	12/28/1884	10/12/1896			Y	
Domis, Theodore	25	Germany	Y	?	Baltimore	??/??/1884	03/06/1894			Y	

CITIZENSHIP RECORDS

APPLICANT	AGE	COUNTRY OF ORIGIN	DEC	DEPART PORT	ENTRY PORT	ARRIVE DATE	DEC DATE	VOL	PG.	FLD	NAT DATE
Dommermann, Henry	62	Germany	N	Bremen	Baltimore	10/??/1847	??/??/1851	28	142	N	??/??/1854
Dommermann, Henry	21	Germany	N	Bremen	Baltimore	10/00/1847	00/00/1851			Y	00/00/1854
Dommis, Bernard	32	Germany	Y	?	New York	05/??/1883	03/08/1892			Y	
Don, Peter	39	Holland	Y	Seeland	New York	12/07/1857	01/22/1862	18	246	N	
Donafria, Nicola	36	Italy	Y	Naples	New York	11/11/1891	10/11/1900			Y	
Donagan, Eugene	42	Ireland	N	Queenstown	New York	09/01/1863	?			Y	
Donahoe, John	33	Ireland	Y	Dublin	New York	05/01/1848	10/21/1852	5	42	N	
Donahue, James	25	Ireland	Y	Liverpool	New Orleans	12/14/1851	04/19/1854	8	475	N	
Donahue, James	25	Ireland	Y	Liverpool	New Orleans	12/14/1851	05/19/1854	9	349	N	
Donahue, John	21	Ireland	Y	Canada	New York	07/20/1847	02/19/1849	23	185	N	
Donahy, Denis	35	Ireland	Y	Cork	New York	06/12/1847	02/14/1852	24	109	N	
Donan, William	37	Ireland	Y	Cork	New Orleans	01/25/1849	03/02/1852	24	212	N	
Donat, Carl	27	Germany	Y	Hamburg	New York	05/21/1881	06/09/1884			Y	
Donath, Ernst H.	24	Germany	Y	Antwerp	New York	09/23/1881	08/18/1885			Y	
Donati, Pietro	21	Italy	Y	Naples	New York	04/01/1884	11/03/1891			Y	
Donato, Frank	29	Italy	Y	Naples	New York	05/01/1885	06/26/1894			Y	
Donavan, Daniel	24	Ireland	Y	Cork	Philadelphia	11/??/1853	02/20/1856	26	109	N	
Donceel, Ferdinand	17	Belgium	N	?	New York	03/00/1883				Y	10/27/1888
Done, Joseph	27	Ireland	Y	Liverpool	New York	08/20/1845	10/14/1848	1	225	N	
Donelly, Thomas	34	Ireland	Y	Liverpool	New York	04/12/1879	10/26/1888	19	185	N	
Donlan, John	22	Ireland	Y	Liverpool	New York	04/03/1864	09/20/1866			Y	
Donnelley, John	50	Ireland	N	Surierick	Detroit	07/??/1863	?			Y	
Donnellon, Edward	25	Ireland	Y	Queenstown	New York	03/00/1880	10/13/1884			Y	
Donnelly, John	30	Ireland	Y	Queenstown	New York	06/11/1881	11/01/1884			Y	
Donnelly, Thomas	34	Ireland	Y	Liverpool	New York	04/12/1879	10/26/1888			Y	
Donnerberg, August	23	Prussia	Y	Bremen	Baltimore	10/25/1849	11/18/1852	5	303	N	
Donnerberg, Henry	27	Hanover	Y	Bremen	New York	01/01/1849	06/25/1851	3	450	N	
Donnerling, John	30	Bavaria	Y	Bremen	New Orleans	07/08/1847	07/07/1852	25	192	N	
Donnewald, Christoph	30	Prussia	Y	Bremen	Philadelphia	06/20/1847	01/30/1850	2	16	N	
Donnoly, Michael	30	Ireland	Y	Liverpool	New Orleans	11/10/1952	10/12/1858	17	63	N	
Donoghue, Timothy	21	Ireland	Y	London	New York	01/07/1850	03/05/1853	7	281	N	
Donohue, Bartholemew	37	Canada	N	Canada	Cincinnati?	07/??/1860	?			Y	
Donohue, John	27	Ireland	Y	Liverpool	Boston	08/06/1857	07/29/1861	18	210	N	
Donohue, John J.	55	Ireland	N	Dublin	New Orleans	01/??/1849	??/??/1865	28	433	N	??/??/1865
Donohue, Owen G.	44	Ireland	Y	Liverpool	New York	10/04/1870	08/??/1882			Y	
Donovan, Cornelius	40	Ireland	Y	Cork	Boston	06/01/1846	07/02/1860	27	196	N	
Donovan, Daniel	49	Ireland	Y	Queenstown	Philadelphia	05/20/1887	10/26/1898			Y	
Donovan, Denis	??	Ireland	Y	Queenstown	New York	05/20/1891	08/20/1895			Y	
Donovan, James	24	Ireland	Y	Liverpool	New York	07/17/1853	04/02/1856	26	415	N	
Donovan, John	24	Ireland	Y	Queenstwon	Philadelphia	05/21/1882	06/11/1885			Y	
Donovan, Michael	23	Ireland	Y	Liverpool	New York	10/??/1854	02/02/1857	14	530	N	
Donovan, Michael	32	Ireland	Y	Liverpool	New York	06/03/1849	02/10/1852	24	83	N	
Donttenthauer, Andreas	26	Austria	Y	Bremen	Baltimore	09/08/1892	01/02/1893			Y	
Doob, Leo	39	Austria	Y	?	New York	??/??/1871	10/17/1892			Y	
Doodeward, Henry Isaac	25	England	Y	?	?	?	03/31/1873			Y	
Doolan, John	21	Ireland	Y	Liverpool	New York	03/06/1853	09/29/1856	14	10	N	
Dooley, Edward	30	Ireland	Y	Liverpool	Boston	05/??/1850	08/18/1855	11	457	N	
Dooley, James	25	Ireland	Y	Liverpool	New York	03/03/1848	03/05/1853	7	278	N	
Dooley, Patrick	27	Ireland	Y	Liverpool	New Orleans	05/27/1852	11/01/1852	5	137	N	
Dooly, James	23	Ireland	Y	Liverpool	New Orleans	02/01/1851	09/07/1852	25	390	N	
Dooly, Patrick	27	Ireland	Y	Liverpool	New Orleans	05/27/1852	11/01/1852	6	263	N	
Dooly, Timothy	27	Ireland	Y	Liverpool	New York	??/22/1845	12/18/1849	23	410	N	
Doorley, John	38	Ireland	Y	Limerick	New York	06/27/1851	04/05/1853	7	273	N	
Doorly, James	28	Ireland	Y	Liverpool	New Orleans	10/21/1852	12/28/1857	16	274	N	
Dopke, Henry	21	Germany	Y	Bremen	New York	11/05/1882	08/31/1883			Y	
Dopper, Bernard	25	Hanover	Y	Bremen	New Orleans	??/15/1847	02/19/1850	2	96	N	
Doran, Daniel	29	Ireland	Y	Donegal	New York	07/05/1847	07/17/1851	3	548	N	
Doran, David C.	27	Ireland	Y	Belfast	New York	05/09/1850	09/24/1857	15	312	N	
Doran, James	22	Ireland	Y	Liverpool	New York	08/24/1850	03/07/1853	7	294	N	

CITIZENSHIP RECORDS

APPLICANT	AGE	COUNTRY OF ORIGIN	DEC	DEPART PORT	ENTRY PORT	ARRIVE DATE	DEC DATE	VOL	PG.	FLD	NAT DATE
Doran, James E.	27	Ireland	Y	Queenstown	New York	08/22/1886	10/23/1886	19	76	N	
Doran, John	28	Ireland	Y	Liverpool	New Orleans	10/10/1848	10/10/1854	6	219	N	
Doran, John	28	Ireland	Y	Liverpool	New Orleans	10/10/1848	10/10/1854	11	223	N	
Doran, John	21	Ireland	Y	?	New York	??/??/1891	08/18/1893			Y	
Doran, Matthew	40	Ireland	Y	Liverpool	New York	08/24/1850	03/07/1853	7	293	N	
Doran, Michael	??	Ireland	Y	Liverpool	New York	??/30/1847	12/05/1850	2	341	N	
Doran, Michael	26	Ireland	Y	Liverpool	New Orleans	01/05/1851	11/01/1858	17	233	N	
Doran, Patrick C.	24	Ireland	Y	Liverpool	New York	10/26/1850	11/09/1852	5	262	N	
Doran, Patrick C.	24	Ireland	Y	Liverpool	New York	10/26/1850	11/09/1852	6	386	N	
Doran, William	28	Ireland	Y	Queenstown	New York	04/13/1873	10/07/1880			Y	
Dorander, Salvador	18	Italy	Y	?	?	??/??/1893	02/27/1893			Y	
Doren, Adolph	25	Mecklenburg S	Y	Hamburg	New York	01/27/1857	08/31/1857	15	204	N	
Dorenbus, Adolph	38	Prussia	Y	London	New York	11/10/1845	10/09/1854	11	173	N	
Dorenbush, Adolph	38	Prussia	Y	London	New York	11/10/1845	10/09/1854	6	170	N	
Dorer, Charles	32	Hohenzollern	Y	Havre	New York	01/12/1853	07/25/1857	15	133	N	
Dorfler, John	23	Bavaria	Y	Bremen	Baltimore	08/04/1845	01/17/1849	1	447	N	
Dorgeloh, Louis	24	Prussia	Y	Bremen	New York	07/??/1856	11/03/1856	14	455	N	
Doring, Henry	21	Hesse Darmsta	Y	Bremen	New York	04/23/1852	09/29/1854	10	314	N	
Doring, Henry	21	Hesse Darmsta	Y	Bremen	New York	04/23/1852	09/29/1854	12	253	N	
Doriott, William	26	Bavaria	Y	Hamburg	New York	08/25/1855	07/23/1858	16	521	N	
Dormady, Edward	29	Ireland	N	Liverpool	New York	05/01/1863	?			Y	
Dorman, Christ.	31	Prussia	Y	Bremen	Philadelphia	07/??/1845	01/20/1851	2	512	N	
Dormann, Henry	37	Hanover	Y	Bremen	New York	05/??/1847	09/17/1855	13	60	N	
Dormayer, John	43	Germany	Y	Antwerp	New York	01/15/1878	03/03/1903			Y	
Dormer, Max	42	Germany	Y	Naples	San Francisc	07/15/1881	11/27/1883			Y	
Dormey, Pierre	28	Germany	Y	Havre	New York	05/20/1888	07/31/1889			Y	
Dorn, Eli	50	Russia	Y	Hamburg	New York	10/24/1883	10/16/1900			Y	
Dorn, Frederick	23	Germany	Y	?	?	?	01/14/1888			Y	
Dorn, Jacob	30	Wuerttemberg	Y	Havre	New York	10/13/1858	05/14/1860	27	188	N	
Dorn, William	53	Hesse Darmsta	Y	Havre	New York	09/06/1850	12/26/1851	24	11	N	
Dornan, Patrick	26	Ireland	Y	Belfast	New York	06/10/1852	10/19/1857	15	451	N	
Dornberger, Andrew	23	France	Y	Havre	New York	02/??/1854	08/21/1855	11	470	N	
Dornbusch, Frederick	27	Hanover	Y	Bremen	Baltimore	05/28/1856	10/15/1860	27	496	N	
Dornbush, Charles	??	Prussia	Y	?	?	04/01/1884	08/23/1890			Y	
Dornhagen, Phillipp	57	Germany	N	Bremen	Baltimore	09/??/1856	?			Y	
Dornlacher, John	35	France	Y	Havre	New Orleans	04/13/1852	04/02/1856	26	402	N	
Dorr, Henry	??	Germany	Y	?	?	?	03/03/1885			Y	
Dorsch, John	24	Bavaria	Y	Bremen	Buffalo	08/09/1847	02/19/1849	23	188	N	
Dorticos, Juan P.	33	Cuba	Y	Havanna	New York	10/25/1874	03/26/1892			Y	
Dosie, Franklin	22	France	Y	Havre	New Orleans	07/18/1846	08/17/1848	22	200	N	
Dost, George	31	Germany	Y	Bremen	New York	10/01/1889	03/31/1893			Y	
Dotzauer, Anton	24	Austria	Y	Bremen	New York	08/30/1884	07/07/1888			Y	
Dougherty, Bernard	25	Ireland	Y	Liverpool	New York	02/23/1847	09/03/1852	25	350	N	
Dougherty, Cornelius	30	Ireland	Y	Liverpool	New York	05/27/1848	06/20/1851	3	470	N	
Dougherty, Michael	35	Ireland	Y	Londonderry	Philadelphia	05/20/1848	04/27/1861	18	151	N	
Dougherty, William	28	Ireland	Y	Liverpool	New York	09/21/1851	05/25/1854	9	411	N	
Douglass, Meyers	35	England	Y	Liverpool	New Orleans	12/31/1849	05/29/1854	9	440	N	
Douglass, Myers	35	England	Y	Liverpool	New Orleans	12/31/1849	05/29/1854	10	23	N	
Dovid, Ernest	??	Austira	Y	?	?	06/07/1885	08/01/1887			Y	
Dowd, Michael	30	Ireland	Y	Liverpool	New Orleans	01/01/1852	01/17/1856	13	474	N	
Dowd, Thomas	47	Ireland	N	Queenstown	New York	05/27/1871	?			Y	
Dowgialo, Alex	27	Poland	Y	Bremen	New York	07/15/1890	09/15/1893			Y	
Dowling, James	24	Ireland	Y	Liverpool	New York	06/02/1846	06/05/1854	10	87	N	
Dowling, James	24	Ireland	Y	Liverpool	New York	06/02/1846	06/05/1854	12	24	N	
Dowling, John	45	Ireland	Y	Liverpool	New York	07/15/1853	04/06/1858	16	501	N	
Dowling, Joseph	24	Ireland	Y	Liverpool	New York	08/01/1848	10/09/1854	6	119	N	
Dowling, Joseph	24	Ireland	Y	Liverpool	New York	08/01/1848	10/09/1854	11	122	N	
Dowling, William	31	Ireland	N	Liverpool	New York	06/04/1862	?			Y	
Downer, John	23	England	Y	Liverpool	Middletown	07/03/1886	11/04/1889			Y	

CITIZENSHIP RECORDS

APPLICANT	AGE	COUNTRY OF ORIGIN	DEC	DEPART PORT	ENTRY PORT	ARRIVE DATE	DEC DATE	VOL	PG.	FLD	NAT DATE
Downes, Peter	33	Ireland	Y	Canada	Lewistown	04/20/1849	08/??/1851	4	159	N	
Downey, John	35	Ireland	Y	Liverpool	New Orleans	04/23/1849	05/20/1852	25	72	N	
Downey, Michael	25	Ireland	Y	Liverpool	New Orleans	05/28/1849	02/21/1853	7	202	N	
Downey, Patrick	40	Ireland	Y	Liverpool	New Orleans	04/29/1849	02/18/1851	3	143	N	
Downey, William	42	Ireland	Y	Canada	Boston	08/??/1834	10/??/1850	2	306	N	
Downs, James	30	Ireland	Y	Queenstown	New York	07/29/1880	04/18/1883				Y
Downs, John	27	Ireland	Y	Liverpool	New York	07/29/1847	09/21/18??	10	153	N	
Downs, John	27	Ireland	Y	Liverpool	New York	07/29/1847	09/21/1854	12	92	N	
Doyen, Joseph	42	France	Y	Havre	New York	10/13/1885	03/26/1889				Y
Doyle, Bernard J.	27	Canada	Y	Windsor	Detroit	12/05/1882	10/09/1888				Y
Doyle, Edward	35	Ireland	Y	Liverpool	New Orleans	12/23/1848	01/12/1853	7	13	N	
Doyle, Garrett	35	Ireland	Y	Liverpool	New York	09/02/1850	11/03/1851	4	481	N	
Doyle, Henry	30	Ireland	Y	Liverpool	New Orleans	12/23/1848	03/06/1852	24	241	N	
Doyle, James	27	Ireland	Y	Liverpool	New Orleans	04/15/1849	03/12/1852	24	293	N	
Doyle, John	40	Ireland	Y	Liverpool	New Orleans	10/??/1848	06/15/1854	10	130	N	
Doyle, John	40	Ireland	Y	Liverpool	New Orleans	10/??/1848	06/13/1854	12	67	N	
Doyle, John	25	Great Britain	Y	Dublin	New York	01/07/1868	10/03/1872				Y
Doyle, Martin	37	Ireland	Y	Liverpool	New York	11/05/1856	09/18/1858	16	173	N	
Doyle, Patrick	28	Ireland	Y	Liverpool	New York	??/31/1852	04/30/1855	11	331	N	
Doyle, Patrick	??	Ireland	Y	?	?	?	10/22/1880				Y
Doyle, Patrick	??	Ireland	N	?	?	09/13/1879	?				Y
Doyle, Thomas	46	Ireland	Y	Liverpool	New York	04/02/1854	10/15/1857	15	432	N	
Doyle, Thomas	39	Ireland	Y	Queenstown	New York	05/10/1887	10/18/1895				Y
Doys, August	24	Prussia	Y	Hamburg	New York	06/19/1855	01/22/1856	13	492	N	
Drach, Isaac	65	Germany	N	Havre	New York	05/08/1852	?				Y
Drachenburg, David	28	Russia	Y	Bremen	Boston	10/01/1897	09/24/1900				Y
Draebing, John	30	Kurhessen	Y	Bremen	Baltimore	05/23/1857	11/16/1858	17	335	N	
Drager, Andreas	35	Bavaria	Y	Bremen	Baltimore	05/15/1851	10/09/1854	6	156	N	
Dragesen, John	47	Germany	N	Bremen	New York	06/??/1857	?				Y
Drahmann, John Henry	27	Oldenburg	Y	Bremen	Baltimore	02/02/1850	09/23/18??	10	173	N	
Drahmann, John Henry	27	Oldenburg	Y	Bremen	Baltimore	02/02/1850	09/23/1854	12	112	N	
Draller, Louis	28	Germany	Y	Bremen	New York	04/01/1873	10/10/1874				Y
Drapp, Joseph	22	Germany	Y	Hamburg	New York	09/??/1870	10/03/1872				Y
Drapp, Joseph	44	Germany	N	Havre	New York	01/??/1871	?				Y
Drautz, Rudolf	27	Germany	Y	?	?	?	01/06/1890				Y
Drave, Friedrich	26	Germany	Y	Bremen	Baltimore	06/18/1891	04/05/1894				Y
Drave, William	28	Germany	Y	Bremen	Baltimore	06/14/1891	04/06/1894				Y
Drees, George	53	Germany	Y	Bremen	Baltimore	10/??/1857	09/21/1888				Y
Drees, Gerhard	32	Hanover	Y	Bremen	New Orleans	12/01/1853	10/24/1855	13	144	N	
Drees, Herman	23	Oldenburg	Y	Bremen	Baltimore	10/23/1854	11/12/1857	16	10	N	
Drees, Rudolph	33	Prussia	Y	Bremen	New York	11/28/1856	06/02/1859	17	446	N	
Drees, William	36	Prussia	Y	Bremen	Baltimore	10/12/1846	11/01/1852	5	156	N	
Drees, William	36	Prussia	Y	Bremen	Baltimore	10/12/1846	11/01/1852	6	282	N	
Dreher, Baptist	21	Bavaria	Y	Havre	?	?	04/12/1852	24	474	N	
Dreher, Frederick	27	Bavaria	Y	Havre	New York	07/23/1851	01/15/1853	7	31	N	
Dreher, George	22	Bavaria	Y	Havre	New York	12/26/1854	03/31/1856	26	377	N	
Dreher, Gottfired	35	Germany	Y	Bremen	Baltimore	04/20/1891	02/04/1896				Y
Dreher, Louis	23	Bavaria	Y	London	New York	07/02/1849	04/12/1852	24	473	N	
Dreher, Valentine Rein	47	Bavaria	Y	Rotterdam	New Orleans	12/10/1851	04/12/1852	24	466	N	
Dreher, Victorin	40	Germany	Y	Havre	New York	10/28/1880	09/22/1888				Y
Dreidel, Theodore	35	Hesse Darmsta	Y	Liverpool	New York	08/01/1854	03/11/1858	16	393	N	
Dreier, August	47	Germany	Y	Bremen	Baltimore	08/18/1882	08/18/1888				Y
Dreier, Christopher	35	Germany	Y	Bremen	New York	09/29/1865	06/29/1872				Y
Dreier, Gerhard	24	Hanover	Y	Bremen	Buffalo	08/??/1849	11/??/1849	23	298	N	
Dreier, William	23	Germany	Y	Bremen	New York	09/11/1883	10/08/1884				Y
Dreiling, Henry	29	Prussia	Y	Bremen	New Orleans	06/11/1858	04/21/1862	18	324	N	
Dreiling, Joseph	25	Germany	N	Hamburg	New York	04/25/1872	?				Y
Dreiling, Sebastian	41	Germany	Y	Bremen	New York	04/13/1878	02/14/1884				Y
Dreman, Henry	56	Germany	N	Bremen	Quebec	06/??/1852	?				Y

CITIZENSHIP RECORDS

APPLICANT	AGE	COUNTRY OF ORIGIN	DEC	DEPART PORT	ENTRY PORT	ARRIVE DATE	DEC DATE	VOL	PG.	FLD	NAT DATE
Drennan, James	34	Ireland	Y	Liverpool	New York	08/16/1852	05/07/1859	17	403	N	
Dreschel, O.F. Henry	36	Germany	Y	Antwerp	New York	10/01/1886	04/08/1891			Y	
Drescher, Casper	25	Prussia	Y	Antwerp	New York	07/01/1846	10/02/1848	22	393	N	
Drescher, Philip	28	Germany	Y	Bremen	New York	05/28/1874	10/06/1883			Y	
Dreser, Chris	27	Germany	Y	?	Baltimore	??/??/1879	10/11/1880			Y	
Dreses, Henry	29	Germany	Y	Antwerp	New York	08/27/1881	10/04/1882			Y	
Dressel, Edmund	44	Germany	Y	Bremen	New York	02/02/1892	10/23/1897			Y	
Dressel, Louis	33	Saxony	Y	Bremen	New York	07/24/1846	02/25/1852	24	173	N	
Dressler, Albert	25	Germany	Y	Havre	New York	03/20/1883	01/30/1888			Y	
Dressler, Henri	24	Germany	Y	London	New York	03/01/1882	05/01/1883			Y	
Dretel, Ludwig	35	France	Y	Havre	New Orleans	12/??/1854	01/03/1856	14	446	N	
Drewer, Henry	22	Prussia	Y	Bremen	New Orleans	12/19/1849	10/06/1851	4	195	N	
Drewes, William	26	Prussia	Y	Bremen	New Orleans	05/12/1849	10/09/1854	6	50	N	
Drewes, William	26	Prussia	Y	Bremen	New Orleans	05/12/1849	10/09/1854	11	51	N	
Drexler, Nicholas	27	France	Y	Havre	New York	02/15/1855	09/25/1858	16	138	N	
Dreyer, Charles	25	Hanover	Y	Bremen	New York	10/17/1854	12/07/1857	16	200	N	
Dreyer, Henry	33	Hanover	Y	Bremen	New Orleans	12/17/1852	07/16/1855	11	397	N	
Dreyer, Henry	24	Hanover	Y	Bremen	New York	08/??/1846	10/??/1849	23	283	N	
Dreyer, William	38	Hanover	Y	Bremen	New York	10/17/1851	12/07/1857	16	199	N	
Driemeier, Frederick	24	Prussia	Y	Bremen	New Orleans	11/24/1849	01/??/1850	23	497	N	
Driemeier, Henry	27	Prussia	Y	Bremen	Baltimore	11/15/1854	09/30/1856	14	75	N	
Dries, John	33	Germany	Y	Bremen	New York	11/05/1881	02/25/1892			Y	
Driesner, Christoph	29	Germany	Y	Bremen	New York	07/10/1887	10/14/1887			Y	
Drigoul, Nathan	40	Austria	Y	Hamburg	New York	07/16/1881	05/10/1883	28	186	N	
Drigoul, Nathan	35	Austria	Y	Hamburg	New York	07/16/1881	05/10/1883			Y	
Driscal, John	28	Ireland	Y	Quebec	Albany	09/06/1843	08/??/1851	4	184	N	
Drischel, Daniel	27	Germany	Y	Havre	New York	08/14/1882	12/28/1886			Y	
Drischel, George	33	Germany	Y	Havre	New York	10/04/1882	10/18/1887			Y	
Driscoll, Cornelius	31	Ireland	Y	Queenstown	New York	05/19/1881	06/04/1883			Y	
Driscoll, Jerry	23	Ireland	Y	Queenstown	New York	03/25/1889	09/23/1892			Y	
Driscoll, John	23	Ireland	Y	Liverpool	Ashtabula	08/01/1886	01/18/1890			Y	
Driscoll, John	29	Ireland	Y	Queenstown	New York	06/23/1888	09/17/1896			Y	
Driscoll, Michael Henry	27	England	Y	Liverpool	New York	08/01/1857	08/24/1857	15	180	N	
Drodtloff, Daniel	??	Austria	Y	?	?	?	05/18/1891			Y	
Droege, Charles Frederic	30	Prussia	Y	Bremen	New York	05/27/1854	05/26/1856	26	548	N	
Droeger, Anton	22	Prussia	Y	Antwerp	New York	05/03/1850	01/01/1853	5	495	N	
Droppelmann, Ferdinand	22	Germany	Y	Rotterdam	New York	10/12/1892	06/07/1895			Y	
Droscher, August	21	Hanover	Y	Bremen	New York	11/19/1847	02/15/1850	2	81	N	
Droste, Henry	54	Hanover	Y	Bremen	New Orleans	12/20/1845	10/02/1854	10	364	N	
Droste, Henry	54	Hanover	Y	Bremen	New Orleans	12/20/1849	10/02/1854	12	303	N	
Droste, John Diederich	28	Hanover	Y	Bremen	Baltimore	06/03/1845	01/23/1852	24	61	N	
Droste, John Gerhard Hen	22	Hanover	Y	Bremen	Baltimore	06/08/1855	03/06/1855	15	70	N	
Drought, Edward	31	Ireland	Y	Liverpool	New York	04/??/1846	10/18/1851	4	329	N	
Drube, Adolph	37	Germany	N	Hamburg	New York	05/??/1871	?			Y	
Druhe, Bernard	26	Germany	Y	Bremen	New York	05/08/1888	09/16/1891			Y	
Drummond, James	58	Canada	N	Canada	New York	12/17/1850	?			Y	
Drury, Thomas	35	Ireland	Y	Canada	Buffalo	07/15/1845	05/06/1850	3	56	N	
Drutsch, Leon	33	Germany	Y	Havre	New York	09/11/1881	10/26/1896			Y	
DuBrul, Napoleon	42	Canada	N	Windsor	Detroit	06/06/1866	12/31/1869	28	240	N	04/05/1880
Duane, John	27	Ireland	Y	Liverpool	Vermont	07/25/1847	02/12/1852	24	101	N	
Dubar, Joseph	43	Belgium	Y	Antwerp	New York	07/11/1870	05/29/1882			Y	
Dubber, Wilhelm	34	Germany	Y	Bremen	Baltimore	05/24/1884	03/11/1890			Y	
Dubelirer, Isaac	40	Austria	Y	Liverpool	New York	07/12/1890	10/02/1893			Y	
Dubois, Peter	57	France	Y	Havre	New York	06/19/1834	05/29/1854	9	441	N	
Dubois, Peter	57	France	Y	Havre	New York	06/19/1854	05/29/1854	10	24	N	
Duboski, John	39	Ireland	N	Hamburg	New York	??/??/1864	?			Y	
Ducart, Robert	25	Switzerland	Y	Havre	New York	11/06/1883	01/25/1889			Y	
Duchen, Isaac	34	Russia	Y	Hamburg	New York	07/01/1886	03/14/1893			Y	
Duchscher, Andrew	40	France	Y	Antwerp	New York	07/10/1896	09/26/1896			Y	

CITIZENSHIP RECORDS

APPLICANT	AGE	COUNTRY OF ORIGIN	DEC	DEPART PORT	ENTRY PORT	ARRIVE DATE	DEC DATE	VOL	PG.	FLD	NAT DATE
Duchscher, Nicholas	32	Luxemburg	Y	Havre	New Orleans	01/18/1849	05/22/1856	26	532	N	
Duchscher, Peter	31	France	Y	Antwerp	New York	12/??/1851	08/23/1852	25	332	N	
Duckett, Anselm	53	England	Y	Liverpool	New York	02/21/1872	04/10/1893			Y	
Duckson, John	23	Ireland	Y	Liverpool	New York	08/10/1848	01/18/1849	1	456	N	
Dudderidge, James Edward	38	England	Y	Montreal	Ogdensburg	06/10/1852	06/08/1854	10	102	N	
Dudderidge, James Edward	38	England	Y	Montreal	Ogdensburg	06/10/1852	06/08/1854	12	39	N	
Dudenhoeffer, Joseph	28	Bavaria	Y	Havre	New Orleans	??/06/1849	12/10/1849	23	400	N	
Dudkiewicz, Jacob	32	Germany	Y	Hamburg	New York	05/06/1882	03/19/1889			Y	
Due, Adolph Lauritz	42	Denmark	Y	Copenhagen	Detroit	11/15/1878	11/02/1891			Y	
Dueing, William	51	Germany	Y	Bremen	Baltimore	11/??/1863	10/08/1884			Y	
Duenken, Henry	30	Oldenburg	Y	Bremen	New Orleans	12/06/1848	06/30/1851	3	465	N	
Duennes, August	25	Germany	Y	Antwerp	New York	05/14/1886	04/04/1889			Y	
Duensdorf, Joseph	28	Oldenburg	Y	Bremen	New Orleans	05/23/1855	10/30/1858	17	8	N	
Duenser, Joseph R.	22	Austria	Y	?	?	?	12/26/1887			Y	
Duepner, Chas.	29	Germany	Y	Havre	New York	04/07/1880	09/25/1885			Y	
Duerbeck, Gottfried	25	Hesse Cassel	Y	Liverpool	New York	05/05/1852	04/17/1854	8	133	N	
Duerbeck, William	22	Hesse Cassel	Y	Bremen	New York	09/25/1851	04/17/1854	8	167	N	
Duerck, Martin	23	Hesse Darmsta	Y	London	New York	12/28/1846	02/22/1849	23	255	N	
Duerholder, Gottfried	31	Baden	Y	Havre	New Orleans	11/06/1853	02/05/1856	26	49	N	
Duerr, George	50	Wurttemberg	Y	Havre	New York	06/02/1852	04/23/1853	8	98	N	
Duerstock, Joseph	24	Germany	Y	Rotterdam	New York	09/10/1893	01/03/1899			Y	
Duff, William J.	25	Ireland	Y	Londonderry	New York	12/08/1889	03/19/1895			Y	
Duffey, Michael	21	Ireland	Y	Liverpool	New Orleans	02/??/1849	04/17/1854	9	36	N	
Duffin, Felix	??	Ireland	Y	Liverpool	New Orleans	??/18/1848	03/25/1851	3	337	N	
Duffner, Joseph	25	Germany	Y	Antwerp	New York	05/02/1876	11/04/1882			Y	
Duffy, Isaac	56	Ireland	Y	Liverpool	New York	10/25/1852	10/25/1889	19	264	N	
Duffy, James	25	Ireland	Y	Queenstown	New York	04/14/1881	10/08/1883			Y	
Duffy, James J.	37	Canada	Y	Niagara	Niagara	11/17/1888	10/13/1898			Y	
Duffy, John	24	Ireland	Y	Liverpool	New Orleans	04/14/1850	08/02/1851	4	76	N	
Duffy, John	26	Ireland	Y	Dublin	New York	06/17/1885	11/28/1888			Y	
Duffy, John	30	Ireland	Y	Galway	New York	04/26/1849	03/18/1852	24	331	N	
Duffy, John	24	Ireland	Y	Liverpool	New York	04/01/1844	05/13/1852	25	14	N	
Duffy, John P.	24	Ireland	Y	Queenstown	New York	03/11/1892	04/27/1897			Y	
Duffy, Martin	24	Ireland	Y	Liverpool	New York	04/08/1847	11/24/1848	1	380	N	
Duffy, Martin	25	Ireland	Y	Queenstown	New York	09/??/1881	09/15/1888			Y	
Duffy, Michael	23	Ireland	Y	Liverpool	New York	04/08/1847	01/12/1849	1	404	N	
Duffy, Michael	21	Ireland	Y	Liverpool	New Orleans	02/??/1849	04/17/1854	8	165	N	
Duffy, Patrick	25	Ireland	Y	Liverpool	New York	04/08/1847	11/24/1848	1	382	N	
Duffy, Roger	25	Ireland	Y	Queenstown	New York	05/05/1882	10/22/1889	19	250	N	
Duffy, Roger	25	Ireland	Y	Queenstown	New York	05/05/1882	10/22/1889			Y	
Duffy, Thomas	28	Ireland	Y	Liverpool	New Orleans	02/26/1850	02/21/1853	7	209	N	
Dufner, Frederick	17	Germany	N	?	New York	03/00/1883				Y	10/27/1888
Dugan, James	17	Ireland	N	?	New York	00/00/1874				Y	10/26/1888
Dugan, James F.	36	Ireland	N	Liverpool	New York	05/??/1870	?			Y	
Dugan, John	34	Ireland	Y	Liverpool	New Orleans	02/23/1849	01/08/1851	2	478	N	
Dugan, John	22	Ireland	Y	Londonderry	Lewiston	05/??/1851	04/30/1855	11	330	N	
Dugan, Richard	44	Ireland	Y	Londonderry	New York	05/30/1868	11/08/1880			Y	
Dugan, Richard	44	Ireland	N	Londonderry	New York	05/30/1868	?			Y	
Dugan, Thomas	32	Ireland	Y	Dublin	Boston	07/28/1847	10/30/1852	5	69	N	
Duggan, Anthony	27	Ireland	Y	Sligo	Eastport	06/25/1846	10/03/1854	10	400	N	
Duggan, Anthony	27	Ireland	Y	Sligo	Eastport	06/25/1846	10/03/1854	12	339	N	
Duggan, James	27	Ireland	Y	Liverpool	New Orleans	11/??/1850	06/10/1852	25	307	N	
Duggan, John	22	Ireland	Y	Queenstown	New York	04/26/1886	09/22/1888	19	139	N	
Duhamel, Gaston	??	France	Y	?	?	11/??/1898	09/13/1900			Y	
Duhig, John	21	Ireland	Y	Liverpool	Boston	03/01/1850	02/23/1853	7	224	N	
Duhlmeier, H. William	??	Prussia	Y	?	?	?	04/05/1858			Y	
Duis, Hero	29	Hanover	Y	Bremen	New York	09/17/1849	10/12/1858	17	59	N	
Duke, Jephson P.	26	Ireland	Y	Canada	Sandusky	11/01/1847	09/10/1852	25	443	N	
Duke, John	23	Ireland	Y	Liverpool	New York	04/04/1849	03/03/1852	24	227	N	

CITIZENSHIP RECORDS

APPLICANT	AGE	COUNTRY OF ORIGIN	DEC	DEPART PORT	ENTRY PORT	ARRIVE DATE	DEC DATE	VOL	PG.	FLD	NAT DATE
Duke, John P.	28	Ireland	Y	Liverpool	Philadelphia	04/23/1846	03/03/1851	3	195	N	
Duke, Joseph	32	Ireland	Y	Liverpool	New York	06/16/1849	09/06/1852	25	359	N	
Duke, Patrick	27	Ireland	Y	Liverpool	New York	05/14/1845	11/06/1852	5	247	N	
Duke, Patrick	27	Ireland	Y	Liverpool	New York	05/14/1845	11/06/1852	6	371	N	
Dukenhoffer, John Adam	24	Bavaria	Y	Havre	New Orleans	05/28/1849	03/15/1852	24	311	N	
Dukering, Hermann F.	19	Germany	Y	Bremen	Baltimore	11/02/1880	02/25/1882			Y	
Dulle, George	60	Germany	N	Bremen	New Orleans	12/??/1858	?			Y	
Dulle, Gerhard Henry	39	Hanover	Y	Bremen	New Orleans	05/18/1848	10/09/1857	15	384	N	
Dullweber, Henry	29	Germany	Y	Bremen	Baltimore	04/16/1891	10/06/1894			Y	
Dultmeier, Henry Arnd	29	Oldenburg	Y	Bremen	Baltimore	??/29/1846	12/31/1849	23	442	N	
Dulweber, Henry	41	Hanover	Y	Bremen	New York	12/10/1847	11/03/1852	5	212	N	
Dumler, John	26	Bavaria	Y	Bremen	New York	07/25/1852	10/15/1857	15	430	N	
Dumler, Joseph	42	Bavaria	Y	Bremen	New York	07/10/1852	05/10/1854	8	416	N	
Dumler, Joseph	42	Bavaria	Y	Bremen	New York	07/10/1852	05/10/1854	9	289	N	
Dumler, Joseph	43	Bavaria	Y	Havre	Baltimore	09/24/1853	10/15/1857	15	429	N	
Dumperth, Anton	28	Germany	Y	Bremen	New York	12/29/1886	05/01/1890			Y	
Dunahoe, Patrick	30	Ireland	Y	Londonderry	Philadelphia	05/03/1850	12/23/1851	4	551	N	
Duncan, John	24	Scotland	Y	Liverpool	New York	04/01/1852	10/29/1858	17	176	N	
Duncan, Thomas	26	Ireland	Y	Liverpool	New York	09/16/1856	07/08/1859	17	464	N	
Duncan, Thomas	45	Ireland	Y	Londonderry	Detroit	05/20/1868	12/16/1885			Y	
Duncan, Thomas	56	Ireland	N	Liverpool	New York	10/02/1856	?			Y	
Duncan, William	22	Ireland	Y	Liverpool	New York	10/01/1857	02/14/1860	27	109	N	
Dungey, Charles	??	England	Y	?	?	?	03/04/1893			Y	
Dunhoft, Frank	49	Germany	N	Bremen	New York	05/15/1872	?			Y	
Dunhoft, John B.	34	Germany	Y	Bremen	New York	05/19/1882	05/12/1891			Y	
Dunken, Joseph Gottfried	26	Oldenburg	Y	Bremen	Baltimore	10/13/1846	11/09/1852	5	261	N	
Dunken, Joseph Gottfried	26	Oldenburg	Y	Bremen	Baltimore	10/13/1846	11/09/1852	6	385	N	
Dunker, Adolphus Frederi	34	Hesse Cassel	Y	Bremen	Galveston TX	10/24/1846	08/11/1848	22	94	N	
Dunker, August	23	Germany	Y	Bremen	New York	03/15/1880	10/31/1882			Y	
Dunker, Frederick Willia	40	Hanover	Y	Rotterdam	New York	09/25/1847	04/29/1850	3	20	N	
Dunker, Henry F. W.	34	Hanover	Y	Bremen	New York	09/28/1847	04/09/1852	24	425	N	
Dunker, William	28	Hanover	Y	Bremen	New Orleans	11/07/1849	12/18/1852	5	423	N	
Dunkmann, William	22	Hanover	Y	Bremen	Baltimore	10/22/1853	06/02/1856	14	285	N	
Dunlavy, James	28	Ireland	Y	Donegal	Portland	05/??/1849	02/21/1857	15	45	N	
Dunlop, Joseph	31	Ireland	Y	Belfast	New York	05/31/1847	10/23/1858	17	97	N	
Dunn, Cornelius	27	Ireland	Y	Cork	Buffalo	06/??/1842	11/09/1858	17	311	N	
Dunn, Edward	45	Ireland	N	Liverpool	New Orleans	??/??/1851	?			Y	
Dunn, Henry	28	Prussia	Y	Rotterdam	Baltimore	05/04/1848	04/04/1853	7	535	N	
Dunn, John	28	Ireland	Y	Liverpool	New Orleans	02/04/1851	02/09/1853	7	133	N	
Dunn, Joseph	35	Ireland	Y	Glasgow	New York	11/01/1850	10/09/1854	6	167	N	
Dunn, Joseph	35	Ireland	Y	Glasgow	New York	11/01/1850	10/09/1854	11	170	N	
Dunn, Luke	15	Ireland	N	?	New York	00/00/1877				Y	10/26/1888
Dunn, Mike	25	Ireland	Y	Waterford	New York	05/16/1849	12/06/1852	5	382	N	
Dunn, Owen	35	Ireland	Y	Liverpool	Phila(?)	09/10/1846	03/10/1851	3	272	N	
Dunn, Patrick	54	Ireland	Y	Queenstown	New York	11/30/1862	10/04/1899			Y	
Dunn, Thomas	30	Ireland	Y	Liverpool	New Orleans	07/04/1852	09/22/1855	13	115	N	
Dunne, Herman	31	Germany	Y	Antwerp	New York	05/21/1881	07/07/1882			Y	
Dunne, William	23	Ireland	Y	Liverpool	New Orleans	04/04/1848	03/07/1850	2	167	N	
Dunnigan, Michael	35	Ireland	Y	Liverpool	New Orleans	01/06/1847	02/10/1851	3	113	N	
Dunniman, Bartholomew	36	Ireland	Y	Cork	Eastport	08/??/1841	03/09/1853	7	316	N	
Dunphy, Edward	23	Ireland	Y	Liverpool	New Orleans	12/17/1848	10/18/1851	4	334	N	
Dunphy, Henry	22	Ireland	Y	Liverpool	New Orleans	05/10/1851	04/04/1853	8	31	N	
Dunphy, Michael	23	Ireland	Y	Liverpool	New Orleans	05/10/1851	04/04/1853	8	32	N	
Dunseith, Benjamin	21	Ireland	Y	Liverpool	New York	10/31/1851	04/19/1854	8	211	N	
Dunseith, Benjamin	21	Ireland	Y	Liverpool	New York	10/31/1851	04/19/1854	9	83	N	
Dunseith, Joseph	25	Ireland	Y	Belfast	New York	12/04/1850	04/19/1854	8	212	N	
Dunseith, Joseph	25	Ireland	Y	Belfast	New York	12/04/1850	04/19/1854	9	83	N	
Dunstorf, W.	34	Germany	Y	Bremen	New York	07/02/1872	11/01/1884			Y	
Duntemann, Henry Ludwig	67	Germany	Y	?	New York	??/??/1880	04/21/1885			Y	

CITIZENSHIP RECORDS

APPLICANT	AGE	COUNTRY OF ORIGIN	DEC	DEPART PORT	ENTRY PORT	ARRIVE DATE	DEC DATE	VOL	PG.	FLD	NAT DATE
Dunworth, John	27	Ireland	Y	Canada	Buffalo	07/12/1847	03/25/1850	2	255	N	
Dupner, Joseph	22	Germany	Y	Havre	New York	02/28/1879	09/20/1881			Y	
Duppernell, John	28	Bavaria	Y	Havre	New Orleans	02/08/1848	08/28/1848	22	269	N	
Dupps, Wm.	31	Germany	Y	Havre	New York	09/26/1883	03/01/1890			Y	
Dupre, Joseph	31	Ireland	Y	Liverpool	Philadelphia	04/23/1886	04/21/1891			Y	
Dur, Alphonse	24	Luxembourg	Y	Rotterdam	New York	02/07/1891	02/08/1893			Y	
Durack, Michael R.	??	Ireland	Y	Queenstown	New York	10/28/1891	10/20/1896			Y	
Durand, John A.	32	Germany	Y	Bremen	New York	07/19/1872	10/13/1886			Y	
Durant, Peter	5	Germany	N	?	New York	00/00/1872				Y	10/27/1888
Durant, William	49	England	Y	London	New York	09/27/1850	01/03/1853	5	501	N	
Durban, David	28	Germany	Y	Bremen	New York	07/30/1883	02/04/1886			Y	
Durban, David	34	Germany	Y	Amsterdam	New York	04/09/1882	10/26/1888			Y	
Durbeck, Gottfried	25	Hesse Cassel	Y	Liverpool	New York	05/05/1852	04/17/1854	9	3	N	
Durbeck, William	22	Hesse Cassel	Y	Bremen	New York	09/25/1851	04/17/1854	9	38	N	
Durfarth, Frederick	30	Hanover	Y	Bremen	Baltimore	10/01/1845	01/19/1849	1	473	N	
Durig, Albert	24	Switzerland	Y	Havre	New York	04/09/1881	07/06/1885			Y	
Durin, Mathew	27	Ireland	Y	Liverpool	New Orleans	12/24/1849	10/02/1856	14	153	N	
Durkan, Patrick	34	Ireland	Y	Liverpool	New Orleans	01/01/1852	??/??/1852	25	323	N	
Durmeyer, Henry	21	France	Y	Havre	New Orleans	??/14/1847	02/08/1850	2	53	N	
Durnin, Bryan	28	Ireland	Y	Liverpool	New Orleans	11/07/1847	06/15/1852	25	268	N	
Durr, Peter	34	Prussia	Y	Bremen	Baltimore	08/??/1844	12/??/1849	23	385	N	
Durszewicz, Jacob	44	Germany	Y	Hamburg	New York	08/04/1883	10/11/1886			Y	
Dusing, Henry	34	Hanover	Y	Bremen	Baltimore	05/28/1845	01/23/1849	1	508	N	
Dust, Gerd Henry	56	Hanover	Y	Bremen	New Orleans	01/15/1846	10/01/1856	14	122	N	
Dutt, Nicklous	??	Germany	Y	?	?	?	10/30/1872			Y	
Duttlinger, Gustav	38	Germany	Y	Havre	New York	11/??/1872	03/03/1887			Y	
Dutz, Joseph	57	Austria	Y	Bremen	Baltimore	08/19/1872	04/02/1883			Y	
Dutzer, Henry	28	Hanover	Y	Bremen	Baltimore	07/04/1857	09/08/1857	15	242	N	
Dutzi, Bernhard	34	Germany	Y	Havre	New York	08/24/1889	03/27/1891			Y	
Duval, E.C.	46	France	Y	?	New York	??/??/1884	09/08/1892			Y	
Duve, Adolph	30	Germany	Y	Bremen	New York	05/15/1885	05/07/1888			Y	
Duveline, Barney	21	Hanover	Y	Bremen	New York	07/16/1850	09/09/1852	25	437	N	
Duvernoy, Emile	27	France	Y	?	?	04/04/1887	03/08/1890			Y	
Duwelius, Charles	27	Hanover	Y	Bremen	New York	07/14/1859	08/03/1860	27	246	N	
Dwir, Hugh	40	Ireland	Y	Liverpool	Philadelphia	04/29/1851	11/08/1851	4	502	N	
Dworak, Johann	52	Austria	Y	Bremen	Baltimore	05/20/1888	05/26/1890			Y	
Dworsky, Louis	44	Russia	Y	Hamburg	Philadelphia	06/10/1888	12/29/1892			Y	
Dwoyer, Patrick	47	Ireland	Y	Dublin	New Orleans	03/09/1849	11/01/1858	17	220	N	
Dwyer, Alexander	25	Ireland	Y	Liverpool	New Orleans	01/08/1851	04/04/1853	8	11	N	
Dwyer, Andrew	21	Ireland	Y	Dublin	New York	04/16/1852	09/15/1855	13	41	N	
Dwyer, James	24	Ireland	Y	Dublin	New York	06/21/1848	02/05/1850	2	37	N	
Dwyer, James	51	Ireland	N	Liverpool	New Orleans	01/??/1848	?			Y	
Dwyer, John	24	Ireland	Y	Limerick	Buffalo	09/03/1850	04/04/1853	8	26	N	
Dwyer, Patrick Francis	28	Ireland	Y	Waterford	New York	05/16/1849	04/25/1853	8	113	N	
Dwyer, William	23	Ireland	Y	Liverpool	New Orleans	01/03/1853	02/10/1857	15	10	N	
Dwyer, William	23	Ireland	Y	Liverpool	New Orleans	01/01/1850	05/18/1852	25	36	N	
Dyer, James	22	Ireland	Y	Liverpool	New York	05/10/1847	06/18/1851	3	399	N	
Dyer, James	46	Ireland	Y	Liverpool	New York	06/05/1842	07/05/1851	3	492	N	
Dyer, Thomas	25	England	Y	Liverpool	New York	04/13/1857	08/28/1862	18	412	N	
Dyer, Thomas	57	Ireland	N	Liverpool	New Orleans	05/??/1849	?			Y	
Dykema, Jeremias	43	Holland	Y	Rotterdam	New York	07/02/1853	04/02/1856	26	408	N	
Dziech, Johann	43	Austria	Y	Hamburg	New York	07/01/1886	09/11/1888			Y	
Eaers, Frederick	25	Hanover	Y	Bremen	New York	03/30/1857	04/05/1862	18	301	N	
Eagan, Jeremiah	46	Ireland	Y	Liverpool	New Orleans	12/23/1848	10/07/1854	11	3	N	
Eagen, Jeremiah	46	Ireland	Y	Liverpool	New Orleans	12/23/1848	10/07/1854	6	2	N	
Earl, Edward Patrick	40	Canada	N	Canada	Illinois	11/??/1862	?			Y	
Earley, John	48	Ireland	N	Liverpool	New York	08/??/1852	?			Y	
Early, Bernard	29	Ireland	Y	Liverpool	New York	04/09/1848	03/17/1851	3	287	N	
Early, John	28	Ireland	Y	Liverpool	New York	08/17/1847	03/17/1851	3	283	N	

CITIZENSHIP RECORDS

APPLICANT	AGE	COUNTRY OF ORIGIN	DEC	DEPART PORT	ENTRY PORT	ARRIVE DATE	DEC DATE	VOL	PG.	FLD	NAT DATE
Early, John	45	Ireland	Y	Liverpool	New York	06/27/1846	10/12/1858	17	60	N	
Easthope, Fred H.	28	England	Y	Liverpool	New York	11/11/1882	07/15/1889			Y	
Ebann, Benjamin	43	Germany	Y	Bremen	Baltimore	09/01/1882	03/14/1887			Y	
Ebbers, Herman Henry	24	Hanover	Y	Bremen	New Orleans	12/23/1853	02/13/1856	26	82	N	
Ebbers, John	35	Germany	Y	Bremen	Baltimore	05/26/1883	03/12/1890			Y	
Ebbing, Anthony	21	Prussia	Y	?	?	08/02/1882	01/05/1885			Y	
Ebe, Peter	46	Germany	Y	Bremen	New York	07/29/1860	12/15/1881			Y	
Ebel, Ferd.	30	Germany	Y	Hamburg	New YOrk	05/08/1882	04/16/1886			Y	
Ebel, Jacob	66	Germany	Y	Hamburg	New York	05/08/1882	04/16/1886			Y	
Ebeling, Frank	21	Oldenburg	Y	Bremen	Baltimore	11/??/1848	11/01/1851	4	454	N	
Ebenhack, John	39	Germany	Y	Bremen	New York	05/17/1873	10/05/1883			Y	
Eberhard, Christoph	??	Hanover	Y	Bremen	Baltimore	11/05/18??	10/11/1848	1	111	N	
Eberhardt, Otto	27	Germany	Y	Hamburg	New York	05/18/1882	09/19/1885			Y	
Eberhardt, Valentine	26	Bavaria	Y	Havre	New Orleans	03/23/1853	03/30/1857	15	103	N	
Eberhart, G.	38	Germany	Y	Havre	New York	08/??/1857	03/04/1860	28	38	N	
Eberhart, Peter	23	Bavaria	Y	Havre	New Orleans	11/06/1853	11/16/1857	16	26	N	
Eberle, Henry	30	Bavaria	Y	Antwerp	New York	09/10/1851	03/12/1856	26	189	N	
Eberle, Jacob	21	Baden	Y	Havre	New York	10/20/1850	04/16/1852	24	516	N	
Eberle, John	22	Wurttemberg	Y	Havre	New York	08/16/1854	09/07/8157	15	233	N	
Eberle, John	30	Germany	Y	Rotterdam	New York	10/02/1885	05/01/1890			Y	
Eberle, Michael	28	Germany	Y	Havre	New York	05/24/1882	02/28/1889			Y	
Eberle, Valentine	26	Bavaria	Y	Rotterdam	New York	09/12/1850	01/19/1853	7	44	N	
Eberlin, John	36	Germany	N	Bremen	New York	06/01/1871	?			Y	
Eberling, Conrad	22	Hanover	Y	Bremen	New Orleans	12/23/1852	12/31/1852	5	485	N	
Eberspacher, Frederick	22	Wurttemberg	Y	Antwerp	New York	05/01/1853	09/20/1854	12	74	N	
Eberspaecher, Fred	51	Germany	Y	Amsterdam	New York	07/17/1882	12/01/1887			Y	
Eberspaecher, Frederick	22	Wurttemberg	Y	Antwerp	New York	05/??/1853	09/20/1854	10	135	N	
Ebert, A.	33	Germany	Y	Bremen	New York	09/17/1881	07/29/1885			Y	
Ebert, Leo	24	Bavaria	Y	Bremen	New York	07/18/1859	08/02/1861	18	214	N	
Ebert, Max	36	Germany	Y	Bremen	New York	09/19/1881	09/27/1883			Y	
Ebert, Peter	31	Baden	Y	Havre	New York	08/28/1854	01/11/1856	13	450	N	
Ebinger, Adam	21	Wurttemberg	Y	Havre	New York	09/19/1849	10/16/1851	4	303	N	
Ebke, Henry	26	Germany	Y	Bremen	New York	05/29/1889	11/03/1891			Y	
Eble, Anton	29	Wurttemberg	Y	Liverpool	New York	05/06/1852	05/24/1854	8	508	N	
Ebner, Conrad	28	Germany	Y	Antwerp	Philadelphia	04/09/1881	09/08/1885			Y	
Ebner, Frank	24	Germany	Y	Havre	New York	04/01/1869	10/01/1871			Y	
Ebnet, George	35	Germany	Y	Bremen	Baltimore	08/22/1887	10/11/1892			Y	
Ebruy, Ludwig F.	50	Prussia	Y	Hamburg	New York	09/14/18??	10/11/1848	1	142	N	
Echelmaier, Joseph	32	Bavaria	Y	Bremen	New York	05/19/1849	01/31/1853	7	88	N	
Echtekamp, Dick	34	Prussia	Y	Bremen	New Orleans	11/12/1845	07/31/1848	22	19	N	
Eck, George	45	Bavaria	Y	Havre	New York	03/??/1848	03/16/1853	7	334	N	
Eck, George Jacob	24	Bavaria	Y	Havre	New Orleans	10/19/1851	09/13/1855	13	26	N	
Eck, Peter	21	Bavaria	Y	Havre	New York	10/17/1855	11/08/1858	17	295	N	
Eck, Valentine	39	Germany	Y	Hamburg	New York	10/??/1873	03/01/1887			Y	
Eckart, William	28	Germany	Y	Hamburg	New York	03/13/1879	03/26/1885			Y	
Eckelkang, George	34	Hanover	Y	Bremen	New Orleans	11/30/1858	06/03/1862	18	347	N	
Eckent, George	35	Germany	N	Rotterdam	New York	10/04/1873	?			Y	
Eckerle, Adolf	39	Germany	Y	Antwerp	Philadelphia	03/??/1880	07/26/1888			Y	
Eckerle, Balthasar	32	Germany	Y	Antwerp	New York	07/03/1882	07/24/1888			Y	
Eckerle, Florentin	22	Baden	Y	Havre	New York	08/16/1854	03/19/1856	26	231	N	
Eckerle, Henry	27	Germany	Y	Havre	New York	10/29/1880	01/24/1884			Y	
Eckerle, Jacob	31	Germany	Y	Bremen	Baltimore	06/28/1884	08/12/1889			Y	
Eckerle, John	29	Germany	Y	Havre	New York	09/16/1866	04/16/1873			Y	
Eckerle, John	??	Germany	N	?	?	06/30/1886				Y	10/12/1892
Eckerle, Michael	52	Baden	Y	Havre	New York	08/16/1854	03/19/1856	26	230	N	
Eckerle, Valentine	24	Germany	Y	Antwerp	New York	09/08/1879	02/28/1882			Y	
Eckerlin, Albert	32	Germany	Y	Havre	New York	12/15/1890	01/12/1897			Y	
Eckerlin, Nikolaus	26	Germany	Y	Antwerp	New York	05/12/1883	09/30/1887			Y	
Eckert, Charles	25	Germany	Y	Bremen	Baltimore	05/26/1888	10/22/1889			Y	

CITIZENSHIP RECORDS

APPLICANT	AGE	COUNTRY OF ORIGIN	DEC	DEPART PORT	ENTRY PORT	ARRIVE DATE	DEC DATE	VOL	PG.	FLD	NAT DATE
Eckert, Charles	37	Germany	Y	Havre	New York	05/05/1888	03/03/1892			Y	
Eckert, Christian	21	Wuerttenberg	Y	Bremen	New Orleans	12/31/1847	02/19/1849	23	193	N	
Eckert, Gottfried	30	Bavaria	Y	Bremen	New York	07/??/1847	12/03/1850	2	334	N	
Eckert, Gottfried	29	Wurttemberg	Y	Havre	New York	04/19/1854	10/07/1856	14	461	N	
Eckert, John	53	Baden	Y	Havre	New York	05/19/1847	08/15/1848	22	113	N	
Eckert, Joseph Urban	??	Germany	Y	?	?	?	04/23/1886			Y	
Eckert, Peter	40	Germany	Y	?	New York	??/??/1880	11/10/1884			Y	
Eckhardt, John	40	Germany	N	Bremen	New York	05/29/1871	?			Y	
Eckhardt, William	34	Bavaria	Y	Havre	New York	01/09/1853	09/25/1856	14	382	N	
Eckhof, Henry	28	Hanover	Y	Bremen	New York	07/25/1846	01/23/1849	1	507	N	
Eckhoff, John W.	25	Bremen	Y	Bremen	New Orleans	07/01/1848	07/22/1851	4	27	N	
Eckl, Anton	55	Austria	Y	Bremen	New York	12/??/1866	10/07/1882			Y	
Eckstein, Conrad	32	Germany	N	Havre	New York	12/10/1865	?			Y	
Eckstein, Conrad	36	Germany	N	Bremen	Baltimore	12/27/1867	?			Y	
Eckstein, Joseph	13	Germany	N	?	New York	00/00/1862				Y	10/21/1886
Eckstein, Morris	??	Austria	Y	?	?	?	10/15/1896			Y	
Eckstein, Roman	63	Germany	N	Havre	New Orleans	01/??/1852	?			Y	
Edel, Charles	31	Germany	Y	Hamburg	New York	06/10/1881	10/04/1887			Y	
Edeler, Charles	35	Germany	Y	Bremen	New York	01/10/1880	10/24/1885			Y	
Edelmann, Charles	??	Germany	Y	?	?	?	03/16/1891			Y	
Edelmann, John	27	Germany	Y	Antwerp	New York	09/19/1881	09/24/1886			Y	
Edelmann, Michael	36	Bavaria	Y	Antwerp	New York	09/01/1854	10/28/1858	17	147	N	
Eden, Mark	27	Ireland	Y	Belfast	Burlington	11/15\6?/1	01/29/1849	1	542	N	
Eder, Benno	30	Germany	Y	Havre	New York	06/11/1884	01/10/1887			Y	
Ederich, Francis	33	Bavaria	Y	Havre	New Orleans	05/15/1852	05/29/1856	14	257	N	
Edgar, Frederick	24	England	Y	Toronto	Cincinnati	09/15/1886	10/15/1890			Y	
Edge, Enoch	46	England	Y	Liverpool	Boston	07/08/1881	07/14/1883			Y	
Edighoffer, George	29	Germany	Y	Antwerp	Philadelphia	05/19/1881	11/25/1884			Y	
Edler, Jacob J. D.	40	Luebeck	Y	Hamburg	New York	01/04/1841	08/12/1848	22	96	N	
Edman, Justus L.	??	Sweden	Y	?	?	?	04/24/1882			Y	
Edmeads, Thomas	28	England	Y	London	New York	04/25/1851	04/18/1854	8	206	N	
Edmeides, Thomas	28	England	Y	London	New York	04/25/1851	04/18/1854	9	77	N	
Edmunds, Edmund H.	??	England	Y	?	?	?	05/02/1888			Y	
Edson, Alfred	31	England	Y	London	New York	03/05/1849	02/10/1851	3	112	N	
Edwards, Edwin	26	England	Y	Portsmouth	New York	04/01/1840	10/06/1848	22	454	N	
Edwards, Harry W.	23	Wales	Y	Liverpool	Philadelphia	05/10/1886	11/10/1888			Y	
Edwards, Henry	56	England	Y	Portsmouth	New York	04/01/1840	10/07/1848	22	467	N	
Edwards, Peter H.	??	England	Y	?	?	?	02/07/1874			Y	
Edwards, Roland Lewis	26	Wales	Y	Liverpool	New York	??/10/1842	10/09/1848	1	99	N	
Effkemann, John	30	Prussia	Y	Bremen	New York	05/20/1848	04/05/1852	24	372	N	
Effron, Elias	53	Russia	Y	Hamburg	New York	02/28/1890	10/31/1898			Y	
Efker, John	30	Prussia	Y	Bremen	Philadelphia	06/23/1847	07/05/1851	3	487	N	
Egan, Dominick	??	Ireland	Y	Queenstown	New York	05/07/1891	04/10/1895			Y	
Egan, John	58	Ireland	Y	Liverpool	New Orleans	03/01/1847	03/09/1850	2	177	N	
Egan, John	48	Ireland	Y	Liverpool	Boston	06/15/1848	11/29/1858	17	363	N	
Egan, Michael	22	Ireland	Y	Queenstown	New York	04/28/1884	10/27/1886			Y	
Egan, Peter	22	Ireland	Y	Queenstown	New York	08/22/1880	12/15/1882			Y	
Egan, Simon P.	32	Canada	Y	Windsor	Detroit	09/06/1887	10/20/1891			Y	
Egan, Thomas P.	??	Ireland	N	?	?	??/??/1869	?			Y	
Egbers, Bernard	28	Germany	Y	Bremen	Baltimore	05/27/1886	12/24/1888			Y	
Egbers, John Gerhard	29	Hanover	Y	Bremen	Baltimore	12/02/1843	03/17/1853	7	341	N	
Egbert, Christian Freder	34	Hanover	Y	Bremen	Baltimore	10/03/1850	03/06/1852	24	246	N	
Egbert, Herman	30	Hanover	Y	Bremen	Baltimore	10/20/1847	02/20/1851	3	146	N	
Egbring, Arnold	26	Hanover	Y	Bremen	New Orleans	06/01/1855	11/01/1860	27	547	N	
Ege, Anton	26	Germany	Y	Hamburg	New York	11/09/1889	10/28/1892			Y	
Ege, Konrad	23	Germany	Y	?	?	?	05/25/1893			Y	
Egel, Frederick William	44	Prussia	Y	Liverpool	New York	04/06/1852	04/17/1854	8	145	N	
Egel, John	28	Bavaria	Y	Bremen	New York	09/25/1849	04/13/1852	24	490	N	
Egen, Michael	22	Ireland	Y	Queenstown	New York	04/28/1884	10/24/1886	19	91	N	

CITIZENSHIP RECORDS

APPLICANT	AGE	COUNTRY OF ORIGIN	DEC	DEPART PORT	ENTRY PORT	ARRIVE DATE	DEC DATE	VOL	PG.	FLD	NAT DATE
Eger, Alfred	24	Germany	Y	Antwerp	New York	11/14/1882	06/23/1886			Y	
Eger, John	33	Germany	Y	Antwerp	Boston	03/??/1881	08/07/1886			Y	
Eger, Max	27	Germany	Y	Antwerp	New York	02/??/1881	02/03/1885			Y	
Eger, Reinhart	??	Germany	Y	?	?	?	10/09/1856			Y	
Eggemeyer, Mathias	27	Hanover	Y	Bremen	Baltimore	09/25/1850	11/05/1852	5	236	N	
Eggemeyer, Mathias	27	Hanover	Y	Bremen	Baltimore	09/25/1850	11/05/1852	6	360	N	
Egger, Jacob	27	Switzerland	Y	Havre	New York	03/??/1882	09/22/1888			Y	
Eggers, John	36	Germany	Y	Hamburg	New York	05/07/1883	08/25/1892			Y	
Eggloff, George	25	Germany	Y	Bremen	New York	07/??/1880	07/14/1884			Y	
Eggstein, Frederick	27	Bavaria	Y	Havre	New York	09/07/1853	10/27/1858	17	123	Y	
Egle, Charles	??	Germany	N	?	?	08/20/1886				Y	10/27/1892
Eglea, August	70	Prussia	N	Havre	New Orleans	07/31/1846	?				
Egli, John Anton (Egly?)	24	Switzerland	Y	Havre	New York	06/16/1849	04/13/1852	24	496	N	
Egloff, Daniel	42	Switzerland	Y	Havre	New York	10/10/1851	06/14/1852	25	253	N	
Egloff, Edward	44	Switzerland	N	Bremen	?	??/??/1851	?			Y	
Egly, Jacob A.	28	Switzerland	Y	Havre	New York	11/20/1856	03/02/1860	27	117	N	
Egly, Joseph Urs	34	Switzerland	Y	Havre	New York	06/12/1852	05/26/1856	26	550	N	
Egner, Charles	30	Germany	Y	Antwerp	New York	05/13/1889	03/01/1899			Y	
Egner, Franz	21	Hesse Darmsta	Y	Antwerp	New York	06/18/1853	01/17/1856	13	480	N	
Egner, Heinrich	56	Germany	Y	Antwerp	New York	07/09/1889	10/27/1900			Y	
Egner, John	21	Prussia	Y	Antwerp	New Orleans	11/11/1852	04/17/1854	8	186	N	
Egner, Nicholas	30	Prussia	Y	Liverpool	New York	05/12/1854	10/09/1854	6	162	N	
Egner, Nicholas	30	Prussia	Y	Liverpool	New York	05/12/1854	10/09/1854	11	165	N	
Egner, Nicolaus	25	Prussia	Y	Liverpool	Boston	11/30/1853	09/25/1854	20	226	N	
Egner, Nicolaus	25	Prussia	Y	Liverpool	Boston	11/30/1853	09/25/1854	12	165	N	
Ehalt, Abraham	25	France	Y	Havre	New York	10/12/1848	?	24	426	N	
Ehebauer, Jacob	36	Bavaria	Y	Bremen	Baltimore	08/08/1846	10/09/1854	6	135	N	
Ehebauer, Jacob	36	Bavaria	Y	Bremen	Baltimore	08/08/1846	10/09/1854	11	138	N	
Ehl, John B,	27	Germany	Y	Antwerp	New York	06/16/1881	12/12/1885			Y	
Ehl, Peter	24	Germany	Y	Antwerp	New York	04/28/1887	03/28/1888			Y	
Ehle, Otto	??	Germany	Y	?	?	?	06/22/1885			Y	
Ehlers, Christ	39	Germany	Y	Bremen	Baltimore	10/29/1883	06/20/1889			Y	
Ehlers, Henry	31	Mecklenburg S	Y	Hamburg	New York	06/01/1857	05/15/1860	27	190	N	
Ehlman, Barney	27	Hanover	Y	Bremen	New York	02/20/1847	07/25/1851	4	36	N	
Ehlmann, William	51	Germany	N	?	?	??/??/1849	?			Y	
Ehman, August	35	Prussia	Y	Bremen	New Orleans	10/26/1849	10/20/1851	4	344	N	
Ehmann, George	31	Baden	Y	Havre	New Orleans	05/11/1847	08/23/1848	22	244	N	
Ehorst, George	39	Germany	Y	Bremen	Baltimore	07/??/1866	10/08/1880			Y	
Ehrensberger, John Leonh	31	Bavaria	Y	Bremen	New York	04/29/1854	02/21/1856	26	114	N	
Ehrentraut, Ernst	34	Prussia	Y	Bremen	Baltimore	12/06/1853	10/05/1854	10	441	N	
Ehrentraut, Ernst	34	Prussia	Y	Bremen	Baltimore	12/06/1853	10/05/1854	12	380	N	
Ehrentreich, Karl August	26	Germany	Y	Bremen	New York	05/02/1888	11/21/1890			Y	
Ehrgott, Martin	27	Bavaria	Y	Havre	New Orleans	12/25/1849	09/07/1857	15	236	N	
Ehrhardt, Frederick Jaco	46	Bavaria	Y	Havre	New York	07/01/1857	03/04/1858	16	360	N	
Ehrhardt, George	43	Germany	Y	Antwerp	New York	07/22/1883	09/15/1887			Y	
Ehrhardt, Joseph	21	Baden	Y	Havre	New Orleans	01/07/1858	10/08/1860	27	428	N	
Ehrhardt, William	24	Hanover	Y	Bremen	New York	07/03/1854	09/30/1854	10	331	N	
Ehrhardt, William	24	Hanover	Y	Bremen	New York	07/03/1854	09/30/1854	12	270	N	
Ehrhart, George	31	Wurttemberg	Y	Havre	New York	07/06/1849	11/01/1852	5	160	N	
Ehrhart, George	31	Wurttemberg	Y	Havre	New York	07/06/1849	11/01/1852	6	286	N	
Ehrlich, Enil	28	Germany	Y	Hamburg	New York	07/21/1881	03/29/1887			Y	
Ehrmannstrant, Michael	24	Bavaria	Y	Havre	Baltimore	08/04/1846	08/03/1848	22	51	N	
Ehrsam, Jacob	33	Germany	Y	Hamburg	New York	10/10/1895	02/29/1896			Y	
Ehser, A. Joseph	??	Germany	Y	?	?	?	03/03/1891			Y	
Eiberl, Joseph	34	Germany	Y	Havre	New York	05/??/1870	04/24/1882			Y	
Eibes, Louis	26	Germany	Y	Bremen	New York	04/18/1881	10/18/1884			Y	
Eich, George Franz	26	Germany	Y	Bremen	New York	05/12/1887	10/25/1889			Y	
Eich, Joseph	39	Bavaria	Y	Bremen	New York	08/19/1859	04/11/1860	27	144	N	
Eich, Peter	27	Bavaria	Y	Bremen	Baltimore	11/04/1852	10/02/1854	10	342	N	

CITIZENSHIP RECORDS

APPLICANT	AGE	COUNTRY OF ORIGIN	DEC	DEPART PORT	ENTRY PORT	ARRIVE DATE	DEC DATE	VOL	PG.	FLD	NAT DATE
Eich, Peter	27	Bavaria	Y	Bremen	Baltimore	11/04/1852	10/02/1854	12	281	N	
Eich, Reinhard	22	Saxony	Y	Hamburg	New York	09/20/1848	09/13/1852	25	459	N	
Eichbaum, Fred	48	Germany	N	?	?	??/??/1849	?			Y	
Eichberg, Frederick	26	Wurttemberg	Y	Havre	New York	07/29/1851	04/24/1854	8	249	N	
Eichberg, Frederick	26	Wurttemberg	Y	Havre	New York	07/29/1851	04/24/1854	9	120	N	
Eichborn, Gerhard Frank	62	Germany	N	Havre	New Orleans	12/05/1850	??/??/1854	28	408	N	09/??/1856
Eiche, Frederick	29	Prussia	Y	Antwerp	New York	05/04/1848	04/04/1853	8	7	N	
Eichel, Julius	21	Germany	Y	Havre	New York	03/07/1890	12/05/1892			Y	
Eichel, Michael	38	Germany	N	Havre	New York	10/??/1872	?			Y	
Eichelsbacher, Michael	32	Bavaria	Y	Havre	New Orleans	03/13/1852	09/16/1857	15	279	N	
Eichenberger, Rudolf	24	Switzerland	Y	Antwerp	New York	04/04/1884	09/03/1888			N	
Eichenlaub, George	28	Bavaria	Y	Havre	New Orleans	10/29/1845	09/13/1852	25	478	N	
Eichenlaub, Martin	21	Bavaria	Y	Havre	New York	06/13/1853	01/22/1856	13	490	N	
Eichert, Geroge	25	Bavaria	Y	London	New York	07/15/1846	04/04/1853	8	2	N	
Eichert, Henry	35	Bavaria	Y	Havre	New York	06/10/1849	09/13/1852	25	485	N	
Eichhorn, George	30	Bavaria	Y	Bremen	New Orleans	06/10/1853	12/24/1855	13	350	N	
Eichler, Charles	26	Saxony	Y	Hamburg	New York	10/22/1853	10/05/1854	10	444	N	
Eichler, Charles	26	Saxony	Y	Hamburg	New York	10/22/1853	10/05/1854	12	383	N	
Eichler, Emil W.	26	Germany	Y	Rotterdam	New York	10/??/1879	02/17/1887			Y	
Eichler, Friedrich	26	Germany	Y	Hamburg	New York	03/31/1885	03/11/1889			Y	
Eichler, Hugo Richard	29	Germany	Y	Bremen	New York	11/13/1880	09/21/1882			Y	
Eichler, John	37	Germany	Y	Bremen	New York	09/02/1882	10/12/1896			Y	
Eichmann, Michael	28	Germany	Y	Bremen	New York	03/11/1892	09/15/1897			Y	
Eichner, Ernst	28	Germany	Y	Hamburg	Philadelphia	05/05/1887	11/16/1889			Y	
Eichner, Michael	36	Bavaria	Y	Bremen	Baltimore	07/04/1845	02/15/1849	23	110	N	
Eichoff, H. H.	70	Germany	N	Hanover	New Orleans	06/11/1847	10/??/1849	28	402	N	06/20/1852
Eichstaedt, Peter Albert	32	Germany	Y	Hamburg	New York	10/02/1887	11/05/1890			Y	
Eick, Frederick	28	Prussia	Y	Havre	New York	12/25/1857	09/10/1860	27	350	N	
Eickershoff, John	30	Germany	Y	Hamburg	New York	10/24/1880	03/24/1881			Y	
Eickhoff, Henry	40	Germany	N	Bremen	Baltimore	07/02/1859	?			Y	
Eickhold, Heinrich	33	Germany	Y	Bremen	Baltimore	04/??/1876	10/08/1888			Y	
Eickrush, Frederick Henr	32	Hanover	Y	Bremen	New Orleans	12/09/1844	03/04/1857	15	59	N	
Eiden, Mathias	52	Prussia	Y	Liverpool	New York	05/12/1852	09/20/1858	16	188	N	
Eigner, John	31	France	Y	Havre	New York	03/30/1854	04/12/1858	16	461	N	
Eikens, William	51	Germany	N	Rotterdam	New York	04/07/1867	10/01/1875	28	346	N	10/07/1878
Eikens, William	26	Germany	N	Rotterdam	New York	04/07/1867	10/01/1875			Y	10/07/1878
Eilermann, Geo.	29	Germany	Y	Bremen	Batlimore	01/21/1884	10/25/1889	19	263	N	
Eilers, Barney	39	Germany	Y	Bremen	Baltimore	04/20/1884	03/23/1893			Y	
Eilers, Bernard	24	Hanover	Y	Bremen	New Orleans	12/29/1847	01/06/1851	2	466	N	
Eilers, Christoph	24	Hanover	Y	Bremen	New Orleans	12/20/1859	04/07/1862	18	305	N	
Eilers, Fred	42	Germany	Y	Bremen	New York	06/29/1881	03/14/1890			Y	
Eilers, Friederick	49	Germany	N	Bremen	New Orleans	12/??/1860	?			Y	
Eilers, John Gerhard	23	Hanover	Y	Bremen	New Orleans	11/22/1848	??/??/1852	25	319	N	
Eilers, John Jacob	33	Oldenburg	Y	Bremen	New Orleans	11/15/1850	09/29/1854	10	310	N	
Eilers, John Jacob	33	Oldenburg	Y	Bremen	New Orleans	11/15/1850	09/29/1854	12	249	N	
Eilersen, Ludwig K. N.	??	Denmark	Y	?	?	?	07/12/1892			Y	
Eimer, Pius	22	Hesse Cassel	Y	Bremen	New York	10/14/1854	12/08/1857	16	209	N	
Einhard, Christian Henry	23	Oldenburg	Y	Bremen	New Orleans	12/14/1849	01/10/1853	7	6	N	
Einhaus, Frederick	32	Germany	Y	Bremen	New York	05/19/1884	03/02/1892			Y	
Einhaus, Nicolaus G. E.	31	Oldenburg	Y	Bremen	Baltimore	10/30/1855	02/05/1856	26	47	N	
Eisele, Francis Anton	22	Baden	Y	Havre	New York	09/09/1853	03/25/1856	26	301	N	
Eisele, John Baptist	42	Wurttemberg	Y	Antwerp	New Orleans	02/06/1848	03/??/1851	3	319	N	
Eisele, Joseph	29	Germany	Y	Antwerp	Philadelphia	01/15/1888	11/07/1894			Y	
Eisele, Wm.	30	Germany	Y	Amsterdam	New York	10/28/1883	05/14/1887			Y	
Eisemann, Xavier	44	Baden	Y	Antwerp	New York	08/16/1851	10/09/1854	6	58	N	
Eisen, Wilhelm	28	Germany	Y	Bremen	New York	12/22/1882	08/11/1886			Y	
Eisenaecher, Christian	26	Germany	Y	Antwerp	New York	03/10/1881	04/02/1883			Y	
Eisenbarth, John	24	Germany	Y	Antwerp	New York	04/24/1881	05/08/1883			Y	
Eisenbauer, Henry	29	Hanover	Y	Bremen	New York	05/25/1867	03/07/1872	18	469	N	

CITIZENSHIP RECORDS

APPLICANT	AGE	COUNTRY OF ORIGIN	DEC	DEPART PORT	ENTRY PORT	ARRIVE DATE	DEC DATE	VOL	PG.	FLD	NAT DATE
Eisenberg, Abraham	57	Russia	Y	Hamburg	New York	02/04/1887	10/12/1896			Y	
Eisenhardt, Charles	31	France	Y	Havre	New Orleans	12/13/1848	05/01/1854	8	300	N	
Eisenhardt, Charles	37	France	Y	Havre	New Orleans	12/13/1848	05/01/1854	9	172	N	
Eisenhardt, John	23	Wurttemberg	Y	Havre	New York	06/02/1849	08/04/1851	4	87	N	
Eisenlohr, Gustav Willia	39	Baden	Y	Havre	New York	??/13/1850	12/17/1850	2	370	N	
Eisenmann, Jacob	24	Baden	Y	Havre	New Orleans	05/??/1854	12/24/1855	13	349	N	
Eisenschmidt, Charles	30	Saxe Auldenbu	Y	Bremen	New York	05/03/1849	04/07/1852	24	409	N	
Eiser, Jacob	24	Germany	Y	?	?	?	10/31/1893			Y	
Eiser, John	26	Baden	Y	Havre	New York	04/24/1855	12/07/1857	16	203	N	
Eisermann, Xaver	44	Baden	Y	Antwerp	New York	08/16/1851	10/09/1854	11	59	N	
Eisert, Carl	29	Germany	Y	Bremen	New York	09/07/1882	12/26/1885			Y	
Eisert, Henry	28	Germany	Y	Antwerp	New York	05/02/1882	03/30/1889			Y	
Eisinmann, Wolf	36	Russia	Y	Hamburg	New York	08/05/1891	11/01/1894			Y	
Eismann, A. Henry	22	Germany	Y	Bremen	Baltimore	08/20/1884	02/26/1887			Y	
Eissing, William	30	Prussia	Y	Bremen	Baltimore	05/01/1856	12/22/1859	17	512	N	
Eith, John	27	Wuertemberg	Y	Havre	New York	11/12/1851	02/27/1856	26	134	N	
Ekberg, Charles	28	Sweden	Y	Goteborg	Philadelphia	05/05/1888	04/03/1893			Y	
Ekeln, George	58	Germany	Y	Rotterdam	New York	07/29/1869	03/14/1881			Y	
Ekemeyer, Carl	26	Germany	Y	Bremen	New York	09/12/1880	06/18/1885			Y	
Ekerle, Henry	55	Germany	N	Bremen	New Orleans	03/??/1854	?			Y	
Ekhoff, Herman Henry	25	Hanover	Y	Bremen	New Orleans	06/28/1848	06/16/1851	3	384	N	
Elbe, Anton	29	Wurttemberg	Y	Liverpool	New York	05/06/1852	05/24/1854	9	382	N	
Elbe, Henry	22	Wuertemberg	Y	London	New York	05/22/1854	05/26/1856	26	552	N	
Elbeisser, Joseph	30	Germany	Y	Havre	New York	08/13/1888	04/12/1892			Y	
Elbershardt, Henry	22	Hanover	Y	Bremen	Baltimore	06/22/1854	06/30/1857	15	119	N	
Elbert, George	35	Hesse Darmsta	Y	Havre	New York	04/03/1848	11/23/1857	16	46	N	
Elbertzahrt, John Herman	30	Oldenburg	Y	Bremen	New York	08/25/1853	10/09/1854	11	177	N	
Elbrecht, Heinrich	35	Prussia	Y	Bremen	Baltimore	06/21/1858	09/14/1872	18	520	N	
Elckmann, John Bernard	41	Prussia	Y	Bremen	New York	04/07/1850	02/18/1858	16	314	N	
Eldrich, Joseph	33	Portugal	Y	Liverpool	New Orleans	05/04/1847	03/05/1851	3	216	N	
Elenhorst, Francis Henry	27	Hanover	Y	Bremen	New Orleans	12/18/1845	01/23/1850	23	535	N	
Eletio, Henry	22	Hanover	Y	Bremen	Baltimore	08/25/1857	12/08/1859	17	498	N	
Elfers, Franz Anton	27	Prussia	Y	Bremen	New York	12/27/1854	03/11/1856	26	183	N	
Elfers, John	29	Hanover	Y	Bremen	New York	10/03/1846	11/24/1848	1	397	N	
Elfers, Joseph	31	Westphalen	Y	Bremen	New Orleans	02/02/1849	01/01/1853	5	491	N	
Elff, Jacob	26	Bavaria	Y	Havre	New York	09/17/1852	01/15/1856	13	471	N	
Elg, Anton	30	Wurttemberg	Y	Havre	New York	11/10/1849	08/04/1851	4	84	N	
Elias, David	25	Russia	Y	Hamburg	Detroit	07/02/1891	07/05/1892			Y	
Elias, Louis	40	Russia	Y	Hamburg	New York	01/19/1888	02/28/1896			Y	
Elias, Selim Joseph	25	Germany	Y	Havre	New York	01/23/1897	03/14/1903			Y	
Elias, Theophilus	28	Germany	Y	Hamburg	New York	09/09/1881	09/17/1888			Y	
Elias, Walter	24	Germany	Y	Hamburg	Baltimore	04/06/1887	10/24/1892			Y	
Elias, Wladislaus	24	Germany	Y	Hamburg	Baltimore	04/06/1887	10/24/1892			Y	
Elkemann, Hermann	36	Germany	Y	Bremen	Baltimore	04/24/1868	09/29/1880			Y	
Elkus, Philip	35	Russia	Y	Hamburg	New York	03/20/1889	07/13/1895			Y	
Ell, George J.	35	Germany	Y	Hamburg	New York	01/04/1873	10/05/1888			Y	
Elleas, Mike	24	Syria	Y	Beirut	New York	05/15/1889	05/26/1894			Y	
Ellebrecht, Henry	26	Germany	Y	Bremen	Baltimore	11/03/1877	10/27/1888			Y	
Ellerbrock, Heinrich	35	Prussia	Y	Bremen	New Orleans	11/17/1851	06/05/1854	10	69	N	
Ellerbrock, Heinrich	35	Prussia	Y	Bremen	New Orleans	11/17/1851	06/05/1854	12	6	N	
Ellerbrock, Hermann	24	Germany	Y	Bremen	New York	09/??/1876	03/17/1881			Y	
Ellerhorst, Casper	27	Hanover	Y	Bremen	New Orleans	11/07/1851	10/09/1854	6	152	N	
Ellerhorst, Casper	27	Hanover	Y	Bremen	New Orleans	11/07/1851	10/09/1854	11	155	N	
Ellerhorst, Louis	37	Hanover	Y	Bremen	New Orleans	11/28/1845	01/??/1850	23	499	N	
Ellermann, H.W.	40	Germany	Y	Bremen	New York	03/31/1881	07/07/1884			Y	
Ellermann, Henry	46	Germany	Y	Bremen	Baltimore	06/20/1881	08/21/1884			Y	
Ellermann, John Henry	29	Hanover	Y	Bremen	Baltimore	08/06/1846	10/05/1848	22	431	N	
Ellermann, Joseph	28	Oldenburg	Y	Bremen	Baltimore	07/??/1846	12/03/1857	16	64	N	
Ellermann, Nicholas	21	Bavaria	Y	Havre	New York	06/02/1853	12/20/1855	13	335	N	

CITIZENSHIP RECORDS

APPLICANT	AGE	COUNTRY OF ORIGIN	DEC	DEPART PORT	ENTRY PORT	ARRIVE DATE	DEC DATE	VOL	PG.	FLD	NAT DATE
Ellers, Theodore	27	Oldenburg	Y	Bremen	Baltimore	11/02/1857	11/01/1858	17	245	N	
Ellert, Hermann	26	Germany	Y	Amsterdam	New York	10/20/1882	03/26/1888				Y
Elles, John George	27	Baden	Y	Havre	New Orleans	01/28/1852	09/08/1852	25	412	N	
Ellinger, William	30	Germany	Y	Hamburg	New York	06/29/1880	10/27/1887				Y
Ellinghaus, Mathias	28	Hanover	Y	Bremen	New York	11/05/1854	12/26/1857	16	248	N	
Ellinghausen, Henry	26	Hanover	Y	Bremen	New Orleans	09/12/1846	03/31/1852	24	345	N	
Elliot, Henry	24	Scotland	Y	Liverpool	New York	06/27/1849	03/08/1852	24	261	N	
Elliott, John H.	31	England	Y	Liverpool	New York	07/15/1885	01/24/1887				Y
Ellis, George	59	Scotland	N	Edinburough	New York	09/12/1847	?				Y
Ellis, Samuel	70	England	N	London	Canada	?	?				Y
Ellmann, Bernard	33	Oldenburg	Y	Bremen	Buffalo	12/01/1852	09/20/1858	16	190	N	
Ellmann, Moses	33	Turkey	Y	Hamburg	New York	06/29/1886	10/22/1894				Y
Elmes, Henry	27	England	Y	Liverpool	Baltimore	10/24/1854	07/10/1860	27	216	N	
Elmiger, Robert	??	Switzerland	Y	?	?	?	10/22/1884				Y
Elmrich, Anton	29	Germany	Y	Havre	New York	01/08/1890	10/27/1892				Y
Elsaeser, Severin	??	Germany	Y	?	?	?	01/07/1893				Y
Elsaesser, Charles	31	Germany	Y	Hamburg	New York	01/28/1891	10/19/1897				Y
Elsaesser, Hermann	25	Germany	Y	Havre	New York	10/22/1883	03/25/1889				Y
Elsbroek, George	46	Holland	Y	Amsterdam	New York	06/24/1881	02/05/1897				Y
Elsen, Gerhard	39	Germany	Y	Bremen	Baltimore	05/26/1883	02/04/1891				Y
Elsenheimer, John George	68	Germany	N	Hamburg	New York	10/18/1845	?				Y
Elsenheimer, Nicholas Jo	26	Germany	Y	?	?	10/10/1890	10/12/1892				Y
Elshoff, Anton	58	Germany	Y	Rotterdam	New York	05/06/1886	10/27/1891				Y
Elshoff, Henry S.	24	Germany	Y	Rotterdam	New York	05/01/1886	10/24/1891				Y
Elskofer, Frederick	27	Baden	Y	Havre	New York	01/01/1854	12/26/1857	16	245	N	
Elsner, Franz	29	Germany	Y	Hamburg	New York	11/28/1887	03/10/1896				Y
Elsner, George	32	Germany	Y	Bremen	New York	09/12/1885	09/09/1892	19	351	N	
Elstro, John Francis	27	Hanover	Y	Bremen	New Orleans	01/04/1846	11/05/1852	5	237	N	
Elstro, John Francis	27	Hanover	Y	Bremen	New Orleans	01/04/1846	11/05/1852	6	361	N	
Elzenhoefer, George	50	Germany	N	Havre	New Orleans	06/??/1852	?				Y
Emann, John	30	Germany	Y	Bremen	New York	03/26/1880	10/19/1887				Y
Emanuel, Philipp	24	Bavaria	Y	Havre	New York	07/08/1859	11/01/1860	27	541	N	
Emery, Joseph	31	England	Y	London	New York	08/31/1848	05/01/1850	3	38	N	
Emlich, George	35	Germany	Y	Bremen	New York	08/08/1880	08/21/1882				Y
Emmel, George	23	Hanover	Y	Bremen	New York	06/24/1856	03/15/1858	16	402	N	
Emmenhort, William	22	Germany	Y	Bremen	New York	09/09/1881	01/30/1886				Y
Emmerick, Frank Jos.	28	Germany	Y	Rotterdam	New York	11/01/1881	04/01/1889				Y
Emmerling, Frank	32	Germany	Y	Bremen	New York	06/13/1879	02/10/1882				Y
Emmert, John Todocus	31	Bavaria	Y	Havre	New York	07/26/1850	06/07/1852	25	200	N	
Emmet, Michael	38	Ireland	Y	Liverpool	New York	07/04/1852	??/??/1852	25	467	N	
Emming, John	36	Hanover	Y	Bremen	Baltimore	05/30/1846	02/07/1852	24	70	N	
Emminger, Joseph	26	Germany	Y	Bremen	Baltimore	12/03/1884	08/20/1889				Y
Emrich, Henry	31	Prussia	Y	Havre	New Orleans	05/19/1853	04/17/1854	8	139	N	
Emrich, Henry	31	Prussia	Y	Havre	New Orleans	05/19/1853	04/17/1854	9	10	N	
Endebrook, Henry	22	Hanover	Y	Bremen	Philadelphia	10/05/1845	02/14/1849	23	96	N	
Endebrook, Hermann	32	Germany	Y	Bremen	Baltimore	07/28/1884	02/07/1887				Y
Endejann, Bernard	24	Germany	Y	Amsterdam	New York	10/12/1884	07/10/1888				Y
Ender, George R.	24	Germany	Y	Bremen	New York	06/04/1884	11/15/1886				Y
Enderlin, Charles	23	Germany	Y	Havre	New York	10/01/1880	10/12/1882				Y
Enders, Frank Louis	38	Prussia	Y	Bremen	New York	06/04/1853	05/26/1856	26	551	N	
Enders, Frederick	??	Germany	Y	?	?	?	09/18/1888				Y
Enders, Nicholas	25	Prussia	Y	Antwerp	New York	05/29/1849	03/10/1851	3	266	N	
Enders, Phillip	33	Bavaria	Y	Bremen	New Orleans	01/05/1845	02/12/1849	23	48	N	
Endres, John	34	Prussia	Y	Havre	New Orleans	01/03/1854	08/18/1857	15	156	N	
Endress, John Adam	22	Bavaria	Y	Bremen	New York	11/17/1853	09/24/1856	14	365	N	
Endrichs, John George	47	Bavaria	Y	Bremen	Baltimore	??/??/1846	10/09/1848	1	93	N	
Endter, Franz	30	Germany	Y	Hamburg	New York	08/10/1887	12/18/1893				Y
Engbring, Henry	32	Prussia	Y	Bremen	New Orleans	11/23/1847	11/24/1858	17	350	N	
Engbringhoff, George	32	Prussia	Y	Bremen	Baltimore	10/28/1855	11/06/1858	17	286	N	

CITIZENSHIP RECORDS

APPLICANT	AGE	COUNTRY OF ORIGIN	DEC	DEPART PORT	ENTRY PORT	ARRIVE DATE	DEC DATE	VOL	PG.	FLD	NAT DATE
Engel, Henry	29	Hanover	Y	Bremen	New York	10/??/1850	04/25/1855	11	304	N	
Engel, John	32	France	Y	Havre	New York	10/04/1852	09/17/1855	13	55	N	
Engel, Konrad	33	Bavaria	Y	Bremen	Baltimore	07/13/1845	11/13/1848	1	252	N	
Engel, Moritz	29	Saxony	Y	Hamburg	New York	06/02/1853	02/09/1857	15	4	N	
Engel, Theodore	23	Saxe Weimar	Y	Hamburg	New York	11/24/1854	02/08/1858	16	83	N	
Engelau, Frederick Willi	33	Germany	Y	Bremen	Baltimore	04/22/1881	09/11/1890			Y	
Engelbert, Schapker	26	Prussia	Y	Bremen	New York	11/??/1843	02/17/1847	23	152	N	
Engelhard, Ludwig	41	Germany	Y	Bremen	New York	10/28/1879	09/24/1883			Y	
Engelhardt, Carl Friedri	42	Hanover	Y	Bremen	New York	09/??/1848	10/24/1851	4	386	N	
Engelhardt, Franz Joseph	33	France	Y	Havre	New Orleans	07/30/1849	10/29/1852	5	61	N	
Engelhardt, George	33	Hanover	Y	Bremen	New York	08/01/1847	11/01/1852	5	177	N	
Engelhardt, George	33	Hanover	Y	Bremen	New York	08/01/1847	11/01/1852	6	303	N	
Engelhardt, Johann	28	Germany	Y	Bremen	Baltimore	10/31/1884	04/02/1888			Y	
Engelhardt, Lorenz	50	Hanover	Y	Bremen	New Orleans	12/31/1847	06/05/1854	10	64	N	
Engelhardt, Peter	43	Germany	N	?	?	06/??/1862	?			Y	
Engelhart, Ignatz	46	Hanover	Y	Bremen	Baltimore	07/16/1846	08/15/1848	22	157	N	
Engelhorn, Lawrence	26	Bavaria	Y	Havre	New York	??/26/1849	12/??/1850	2	410	N	
Engelke, George	24	Hanover	Y	Bremen	Baltimore	07/03/1859	11/26/1859	17	481	N	
Engelke, Hermann	??	Germany	N	?	?	09/09/1884				Y	10/28/1892
Engelmann, Gerhard	22	Oldenberg	Y	Bremen	New York	08/01/1854	03/25/1856	26	323	N	
Engelmann, Herman Arnold	22	Oldenburg	Y	Bremen	Baltimore	07/02/1854	03/31/1856	26	385	N	
Engeln, Johann Hermann	27	Germany	Y	Bremen	Baltimore	09/09/1892	12/15/1893			Y	
Engeln, John	26	Germany	Y	Bremen	Baltimore	05/22/1891	12/08/1892			Y	
Engelr, Herman	28	Germany	Y	Bremen	Baltimore	04/16/1882	10/03/1884			Y	
Engels, C.	35	Prussia	Y	Bremerhafen	New York	06/??/1849	01/28 1861	18	74	N	
Engels, Herman	22	Germany	Y	Hamburg	?	05/25/1888	11/06/1888			Y	
Engemann, John Gottfried	58	Saxony	Y	Hamburg	New York	01/03/1849	06/09/1852	25	220	N	
Enghauser, Andrew	26	Baden	Y	Havre	New York	02/30/1851	10/06/1854	12	433	N	
Enghauser, Anselm	26	Baden	Y	Havre	New York	02/30/1851	10/06/1854	10	494	N	
Englander, Max	50	Austria	Y	Hamburg	New York	05/23/1880	08/31/1892			Y	
Englehardt, Lorenz	50	Hanover	Y	Bremen	New Orleans	12/31/1847	06/05/1854	12	1	N	
Engleka, Conrad	40	Hanover	Y	Bremen	New Orleans	01/12/1845	10/03/1848	22	412	N	
Enler, Peter	46	Bavaria	Y	Havre	New York	04/24/1851	07/19/1851	4	4	N	
Enneking, Bernard	29	Oldenburg	Y	Bremen	Baltimore	09/08/1844	07/31/1848	22	22	N	
Ennen, Gerhard	43	Germany	N	Bremen	Baltimore	03/23/1868	?			Y	
Ennis, James	26	Ireland	Y	Liverpool	New York	04/10/1847	12/26/1850	2	397	N	
Ennis, Lawrence	45	Ireland	N	Liverpool	New York	04/??/1864	?			Y	
Ennis, Thomas	25	Ireland	Y	Canada	Buffalo	??/14/1848	12/23/1850	2	384	N	
Enright, John	24	Ireland	Y	Liverpool	New Orleans	05/28/1851	05/04/1854	8	371	N	
Enright, John	24	Ireland	Y	Liverpool	New Orleans	05/28/1851	05/04/1854	9	244	N	
Enright, Thomas	21	Ireland	Y	Liverpool	New Orleans	11/06/1853	10/31/1857	15	506	N	
Enrirt, John Peter	39	Prussia	Y	Antwerp	New Orleans	08/25/1848	10/07/1848	22	465	N	
Ens, Frank	24	Wurttemberg	Y	Havre	New York	04/24/1851	12/31/1855	13	406	N	
Ensfelder, Carl	23	Prussia	Y	Bremen	New York	08/30/1858	08/15/1860	27	270	N	
Ensfelder, Joseph	25	Prussia	Y	Hamburg	New York	01/02/1859	08/15/1860	27	271	N	
Ensler, John	25	Bavaria	Y	Bremen	New Orleans	12/05/1846	01/03/1851	2	446	N	
Enslin, Adolph	28	Baden	Y	Antwerp	New York	08/18/1854	04/11/1856	26	489	N	
Enslin, Frederick Jr.	29	Baden	Y	Antwerp	New York	08/18/1854	04/11/1856	26	490	N	
Enslin, Frederick Sr.	57	Baden	Y	Antwerp	New York	08/18/1854	04/11/1856	26	488	N	
Ensslin, John	21	Wurttemberg	Y	Havre	New York	06/03/1854	08/17/1855	11	447	N	
Enz, Edward	25	Baden	Y	Antwerp	New York	07/24/1849	09/02/1852	25	342	N	
Eppel, Frank Joseph	22	Baden	Y	Havre	New York	05/21/1852	07/09/1856	14	300	N	
Eppens, Bernhard	37	Hanover	Y	Bremen	New Orleans	12/04/1854	09/24/1856	14	364	N	
Epping, John	35	Prussia	Y	Rotterdam	Philadelphia	06/24/1849	11/16/1857	16	19	N	
Eppinger, Joel	54	Bavaria	Y	Bremen	New York	07/19/1853	11/05/1858	17	279	N	
Epple, John Stephen	44	Germany	Y	?	?	?	10/21/1896			Y	
Eppler, Christian	28	Germany	Y	Havre	New York	04/15/1888	10/08/1889			Y	
Epstein, Hermann	28	Prussia	Y	Hamburg	New York	07/12/1859	08/05/1859	17	467	N	
Epstein, Jacob	27	Prussia	Y	London	New York	07/04/1848	01/24/1853	7	59	N	

CITIZENSHIP RECORDS

APPLICANT	AGE	COUNTRY OF ORIGIN	DEC	DEPART PORT	ENTRY PORT	ARRIVE DATE	DEC DATE	VOL	PG.	FLD	NAT DATE
Epstein, Jacob	29	Russia	Y	Hamburg	New York	09/30/1881	10/23/1883			Y	
Epstein, Levi	31	Germany	Y	Antwerp	New York	11/16/1881	12/01/1890			Y	
Epstein, Mac	31	Russia	Y	Hamburg	New York	03/??/1882	04/26/1886			Y	
Epstein, Samuel	41	Prussia	Y	Liverpool	New York	07/28/1856	11/13/1858	17	327	N	
Equer, John	21	Prussia	Y	Antwerp	New Orleans	11/11/1852	04/17/1854	9	57	N	
Erb, John	25	Wurttemberg	Y	Havre	New York	04/26/1853	10/09/1854	6	65	N	
Erb, John	25	Wurttemberg	Y	Havre	New York	04/26/1853	10/09/1854	11	66	N	
Erbersdobler, Joseph	40	Germany	Y	Bremen	New York	06/22/1881	09/10/1884			Y	
Erchinger, Christian	25	Wurttemberg	Y	Havre	New York	11/30/1850	03/28/1862	18	285	N	
Erchinger, Simon	29	Wuerttenberg	Y	Havre	New Orleans	12/04/1847	02/07/1849	23	130	N	
Erck, Nicholas Heinrich	19	Germany	Y	?	?	09/23/1882	08/02/1886			Y	
Erd, Louis	26	Germany	Y	Antwerp	New York	03/23/1883	03/16/1885			Y	
Erdelmeier, Charles	27	Hesse Darmsta	Y	Worms	New York	06/19/1852	09/18/1858	16	172	N	
Erdmann, Ferdinand	40	Prussia	Y	Hamburg	New York	10/08/1856	03/08/1858	16	382	N	
Erdmann, Joseph	31	Germany	Y	Bremen	New York	11/09/1887	06/30/1892			Y	
Erdmann, Joseph	32	Prussia	Y	Bremen	New York	12/07/1877	06/20/1882			Y	
Erfft, George Gotthold	30	Prussia	Y	Hamburg	New York	08/04/1849	06/13/1851	3	372	N	
Erfkamp, Simon	39	Lippe Detmold	Y	Bremen	Philadelphia	05/26/1850	04/08/1856	26	471	N	
Erhard, Peter	27	Baden	Y	Antwerp	New York	08/10/1854	11/01/1860	27	518	N	
Erhardt, John	42	Germany	Y	Bremen	New York	04/23/1880	04/03/1890			Y	
Erk, Christopher	35	Hanover	Y	Bremen	New York	10/28/1847	02/??/1852	24	161	N	
Erk, John Frederick	31	Hanover	Y	Bremen	New York	10/28/1847	02/24/1852	24	160	N	
Erk, Martin	31	Bavaria	Y	Bremen	Buffalo	08/20/1846	02/19/1849	23	197	N	
Erke, Peter	23	Prussia	Y	Bremen	New York	10/05/1857	04/14/1860	27	154	N	
Erkenbrecker, Frederick	26	Saxe Meininge	Y	Hamburg	New York	08/26/1846	09/14/1855	13	29	N	
Erlebach, Robert	??	Austria	Y	?	?	?	11/25/1891			Y	
Erlenwein, Peter	29	Bavaria	Y	Havre	New Orleans	06/22/1852	09/30/1854	10	323	N	
Erlenwein, Peter	29	Bavaria	Y	Havre	New Orleans	06/22/1852	09/30/1854	12	262	N	
Erler, David	30	Germany	Y	Bremen	New York	03/18/1890	12/06/1895			Y	
Erlewein, Leo	31	Germany	Y	Antwerp	New York	07/14/1881	10/16/1884			Y	
Erlewein, Peter	64	Bavaria	N	Havre	New Orleans	06/12/1852	?			Y	
Erls, William	35	Ireland	Y	Liverpool	New Orleans	05/??/1844	11/23/1852	5	332	N	
Erlwein, John	24	Germany	Y	Bremen	New York	06/28/1879	10/07/1882			Y	
Erlwein, Lorenz	26	Germany	Y	Bremen	New York	06/27/1880	10/03/1882			Y	
Ermer, Michael	52	Bavaria	Y	Rotterdam	New York	09/15/1844	10/09/1854	6	150	N	
Ermer, Michael	52	Bavaria	Y	Rotterdam	New York	09/15/1844	10/09/1854	11	153	N	
Ernest, Sigmund	43	Germany	Y	Bremen	New York	10/22/1882	10/22/1886	19	63	N	
Ernst, Anton	23	Austria	Y	Bremen	New York	06/30/1854	01/14/1856	13	467	N	
Ernst, Basil	40	Baden	Y	Havre	New York	02/03/1857	12/12/1857	16	217	N	
Ernst, Carl	29	Germany	Y	Bremen	Baltimore	08/29/1883	03/02/1887			Y	
Ernst, Charles	44	Germany	Y	Bremen	?	05/28/1871	03/03/1894	21	68	N	
Ernst, Charles	19	Germany	Y	Havre	New York	10/24/1887	05/23/1888			Y	
Ernst, Charles	44	Germany	Y	Bremen	New York	05/28/1871	03/31/1894			Y	
Ernst, Conrad	38	Prussia	Y	Bremen	Baltimore	06/14/1853	02/08/1856	26	65	N	
Ernst, Frank	50	Germany	Y	Havre	New York	04/11/1880	10/08/1883			Y	
Ernst, Fred	??	Germany	Y	?	?	11/01/1886	02/20/1890			Y	
Ernst, Heinrich	24	Baden	Y	Havre	New York	07/09/1852	02/23/1853	9	217	N	
Ernst, Henry	40	Prussia	Y	Bremen	New Orleans	12/16/1848	05/16/1854	8	449	N	
Ernst, Henry	40	Prussia	Y	Bremen	New Orleans	12/16/1848	05/16/1854	9	322	N	
Ernst, Henry	38	Germany	Y	Bremen	New York	10/05/1871	08/29/1883			Y	
Ernst, John	57	Prussia	Y	Bremen	Baltimore	06/22/1853	11/19/1857	16	35	N	
Ernst, Joseph	46	Germany	Y	Havre	New York	02/28/1892	01/15/1898			Y	
Ernst, Louis	??	Germany	N	?	?	09/01/1887				Y	10/24/1892
Ernst, Martin	42	Germany	Y	Bremen	New York	09/14/1880	11/22/1893			Y	
Ernst, Martin	32	Wuerttemberg	Y	London	New York	05/19/1848	02/08/1849	23	125	N	
Ernst, Philipp	45	Germany	Y	Bremen	New York	08/27/1890	10/26/1900			Y	
Ernst, Sigmund	43	Germany	Y	Bremen	New York	10/22/1882	10/22/1886			Y	
Ernst, William	39	Germany	Y	Hamburg	New York	04/17/1865	04/12/1880			Y	
Ernst, William Albert	33	Prussia	Y	Hamburg	New York	09/04/1857	11/27/1858	17	360	N	

CITIZENSHIP RECORDS

APPLICANT	AGE	COUNTRY OF ORIGIN	DEC	DEPART PORT	ENTRY PORT	ARRIVE DATE	DEC DATE	VOL	PG.	FLD	NAT DATE
Ernste, Christ	39	Germany	Y	Havre	New York	09/28/1880	10/27/1880			Y	
Erp, Henry	24	Germany	Y	Bremen	New York	11/01/1881	02/03/1885			Y	
Erpenbeck, August	24	Germany	Y	Hamburg	Hoboken	10/12/1882	05/17/1888			Y	
Errgang, Louis	27	Germany	Y	Hamburg	New York	10/06/1876	04/02/1887			Y	
Ertel, John	55	Austria	Y	Bremen	New York	??/??/1882	06/04/1888			Y	
Ertes, Edward	27	Poland	Y	Hamburg	New York	05/01/1849	06/19/1851	3	409	N	
Ertmann, Ernst	22	Saxe Meininge	Y	Hamburg	New York	08/12/1854	11/16/1857	16	22	N	
Erwin, John	30	Ireland	Y	Liverpool	New York	04/03/1854	03/03/1857	15	56	N	
Esberger, Jacob	35	Bavaria	Y	Havre	New York	07/10/1855	03/26/1857	15	86	N	
Escales, Moritz	35	Bavaria	Y	Havre	New York	11/20/1850	01/04/1853	5	513	N	
Eschbach, John	23	Baden	Y	Antwerp	New York	05/21/1854	09/01/1857	15	218	N	
Eschbach, Wendelin	41	Dutschland	N	Havre	New York	06/28/1881	?			Y	
Eschbacher, Anton	36	Baden	Y	Havre	New York	06/28/1853	08/02/1856	14	311	N	
Esche, Bvorden	43	Germany	Y	?	?	07/28/1883	10/09/1884			Y	
Eschen, Joseph	38	Germany	N	Bremen	Baltimore	??/??/1861	?			Y	
Eschenbach, John	33	Bavaria	Y	London	New York	04/29/1852	03/05/1853	7	279	N	
Eschenbach, Philip	26	Bavaria	Y	Havre	New York	06/05/1849	03/05/1853	7	280	N	
Eschenbrenner, Charles	22	France	Y	Havre	New Orleans	01/22/1854	03/28/1857	15	96	N	
Eschenbrenner, Frederick	30	France	Y	Havre	New Orleans	04/??/1853	04/24/1855	11	294	N	
Eschenbrenner, George	33	France	Y	Havre	New Orleans	01/22/1853	03/28/1857	15	97	N	
Eschenbrenner, George	25	Germany	Y	Havre	New York	02/18/1889	02/27/1892			Y	
Eschenick, Erhard	40	Bavaria	Y	Hamburg	New York	06/25/1853	09/29/1856	14	432	N	
Eschler, Jacob	45	Switzerland	Y	Havre	New York	03/27/1868	12/22/1887			Y	
Eschmann, Ernst	23	Prussia	Y	Bremen	Baltimore	05/28/1850	01/22/1853	7	53	N	
Eschmann, George	25	Germany	Y	Bremen	New York	11/23/1887	11/21/1890			Y	
Eschmann, George	47	Germany	Y	Hamburg	New York	05/31/1880	10/10/1889			Y	
Eschmeier, Heinrich	48	Germany	Y	Bremen	New York	09/28/1867	01/16/1889			Y	
Eschmeier, William	26	Prussia	Y	Bremen	Baltimore	11/08/1859	10/19/1860	27	510	N	
Eschrich, Anton	??	Austria	Y	?	?	?	10/16/1876			Y	
Eschrich, Christel	50	Hanover	Y	Bremen	Baltimore	06/14/1834	08/10/1848	22	90	N	
Esel, Earhardt	28	Bavaria	Y	Bremen	New Orleans	07/20/1846	05/03/1854	9	231	N	
Esel, Leonhardt	27	Bavaria	Y	Bremen	New Orleans	07/20/1846	05/03/1854	8	358	N	
Eselbach, Jacob	32	Germany	Y	Bremen	Baltimore	07/09/1881	10/27/1884			Y	
Esert, Martin	24	Bavaria	Y	Rotterdam	New York	06/22/1845	03/19/1850	2	219	N	
Eshlanche, Jacob	23	France	Y	Havre	New Orleans	05/01/1846	05/01/1850	3	39	N	
Eshman, Gustav	30	Switzerland	Y	Havre	New York	03/02/1885	10/21/1896			Y	
Espach, Nicholas	24	Bavaria	Y	Havre	New York	09/19/1854	10/20/1857	15	462	N	
Espel, August	23	Germany	Y	Bremen	Baltimore	10/29/1880	04/02/1883			Y	
Espel, Joseph	32	Germany	Y	Bremen	Baltimore	07/09/1881	08/18/1881			Y	
Espel, William	26	Germany	Y	Bremen	Baltimore	10/29/1880	04/02/1883			Y	
Espenleider, John	61	Germany	N	Havre	New York	01/06/1854	?			Y	
Espensheid, Peter	28	Hesse Darmsta	Y	Antwerp	New York	11/04/1848	02/26/1852	24	174	N	
Esplage, Bernard	29	Oldenburg	Y	Bremen	Baltimore	08/04/1839	01/20/1849	1	478	N	
Espohl, Heinrich	26	Germany	Y	Bremen	Baltimore	04/03/1881	10/11/1884			Y	
Ess, John	25	Bavaria	Y	Havre	New York	06/22/1852	04/17/1854	9	60	N	
Essel, Henry	49	Germany	Y	Hamburg	Philadelphia	07/24/1888	04/07/1892			Y	
Essel, Joseph	25	Germany	Y	Havre	New York	05/24/1882	11/13/1884			Y	
Essighe, Richard	21	Prussia	Y	Bremen	New York	08/07/1857	03/19/1860	27	131	N	
Essling, Herman Henry	??	Hanover	Y	Bremen	New York	06/28/1845	10/09/1848	22	510	N	
Esslinger, Adolph	22	Germany	Y	Havre	New York	01/02/1894	09/15/1897			Y	
Esslinger, Frederick	52	Germany	Y	Havre	New York	09/10/1860	05/25/1892			Y	
Esslinger, John	33	Wurttemberg	Y	Havre	New York	09/20/1852	10/20/1852	5	33	N	
Esslinger, John	32	Wurttemberg	Y	Havre	New York	10/05/1853	09/27/1856	14	413	N	
Esslinger, John	29	Germany	Y	Hamburg	New York	12/19/1886	11/04/1891			Y	
Estermann, Herman Bernar	24	Hanover	Y	Bremen	Baltimore	10/08/1854	11/07/1857	15	543	N	
Estermann, J. Bernard	22	Hanover	Y	Bremen	Baltimore	10/08/1854	08/31/1857	15	202	N	
Esz, John	25	Bavaria	Y	Havre	New York	06/22/1852	04/17/1854	8	189	N	
Etli, Frank	37	Switzerland	Y	Havre	New York	02/05/1884	03/18/1897			Y	
Ettlin, Simon	32	Switzerland	Y	Havre	New York	07/24/1871	10/26/1876			Y	

CITIZENSHIP RECORDS

APPLICANT	AGE	COUNTRY OF ORIGIN	DEC	DEPART PORT	ENTRY PORT	ARRIVE DATE	DEC DATE	VOL	PG.	FLD	NAT DATE
Etz, Franz	45	Germany	Y	Bremen	Baltimore	12/09/1893	11/16/1896			Y	
Etzel, Christian	27	Saxe Weimar	Y	Liverpool	New York	06/01/1853	05/27/1854	9	430	N	
Etzel, Christian	27	Saxe Weimar	Y	Liverpool	New York	06/01/1853	05/27/1854	10	13	N	
Etzel, George A.	32	Germany	Y	Bremen	Baltimore	09/15/1882	04/11/1887			Y	
Etzel, Michael	33	Bavaria	Y	London	Philadelphia	10/26/1857	02/14/1861	18	98	N	
Eucker, John	23	Hesse Cassel	Y	Bremen	Baltimore	02/22/1855	12/24/1855	13	360	N	
Eugler, Adolph	33	Germany	Y	Bremen	New York	05/28/1882	09/17/1889			Y	
Eukhoff, George Henry	30	Hanover	Y	Bremen	Philadelphia	09/11/1842	03/25/1850	2	243	N	
Eulen, Valentine	37	Germany	Y	?	New York	08/28/1881	01/31/1885			Y	
Euler, Conrad	35	Prussia	Y	Havre	New Orleans	05/24/1847	07/28/1851	4	51	N	
Euter, Justus	25	Kurhassen	Y	Bremen	Baltimore	06/25/1847	12/31/1849	23	446	N	
Evans, Alexander	16	Ireland	N	?	Philadelphia	00/00/1880				Y	10/23/1888
Evans, Daniel	24	Wales	Y	Liverpool	New York	06/26/1847	01/31/1851	3	70	N	
Evans, David	32	England	Y	London	New Orleans	12/15/1851	09/25/1858	16	139	N	
Evans, David R.	29	Wales	Y	Liverpool	New York	08/01/1846	04/02/1853	7	495	N	
Evans, Evan	42	Wales	Y	Liverpool	New York	08/01/1851	02/23/1858	16	335	N	
Evans, George Day	71	Ireland	N	Cork	New Orleans	01/??/1848	?			Y	
Evans, Guilym Posthumous	39	Wales	Y	Liverpool	New York	04/22/1883	09/20/1887			Y	
Evans, Job	21	England	Y	Liverpool	New York	09/25/18??	04/12/1852	24	487	N	
Evans, John	29	Wales	Y	Liverpool	New York	09/09/1858	01/18/1862	18	245	N	
Evans, John Ash	32	England	Y	Liverpool	New Orleans	01/16/1851	05/25/1854	8	524	N	
Evans, John Ash	32	England	Y	Liverpool	New Orleans	01/16/1851	05/25/1854	9	298	N	
Evans, Morris	45	Wales	Y	Liveprool	New York	04/14/1880	06/09/1885			Y	
Evans, Rees C.	34	England	Y	Liverpool	New York	02/03/1852	09/13/1852	25	473	N	
Evans, Richard	35	Wales	Y	Liverpool	New York	04/14/1871	04/20/1882			Y	
Evans, Thomas	32	Wales	Y	Liverpool	New York	04/23/1855	09/29/1856	14	431	N	
Evans, Thomas	28	Wales	Y	Liverpool	New York	09/09/1881	08/06/1885			Y	
Evans, Thomas	34	Canada	Y	Bramford	Buffalo	04/23/1880	01/23/1891			Y	
Evelt, Joseph	26	Hanover	Y	Bremen	New York	09/11/1846	10/02/1848	1	18	N	
Even, Albert Bernard	47	Holland	Y	Amsterdam	New York	04/12/1881	10/29/1892			Y	
Everding, John	66	Germany	N	Bremen	Philadelphia	06/01/1845	12/20/1845	28	248	N	10/07/1850
Everdink, John Matthias	24	Hanover	Y	Bremen	New Orleans	06/11/1849	04/04/1853	8	13	N	
Everhardy, Mathias	49	Germany	Y	Antwerp	New York	10/12/1878	10/21/1899			Y	
Evers, Anthony	37	Prussia	Y	Bremen	New York	10/15/1855	10/28/1858	17	162	N	
Evers, Gerhard	28	Hanover	Y	Bremen	New Orleans	05/16/1849	08/02/1851	4	71	N	
Evers, Wm. Ernst	30	Germany	Y	Rotterdam	New York	02/24/1883	11/05/1888			Y	
Eversmann, Geo. E.A.	??	Holland	Y	?	?	?	05/28/1895			Y	
Ewald, J.	36	Germany	Y	Antwerp	New York	11/04/1880	12/08/1883			Y	
Ewert, Henry	56	Germany	Y	Bremen	New York	03/15/1877	12/26/1889			Y	
Ewins, Joseph	30	England	Y	Liverpool	New York	01/24/1888	10/26/1894			Y	
Exeler, Gerhard Heinrich	25	Prussia	Y	Bremen	Baltimore	05/01/1849	05/20/1852	25	82	N	
Exterkamp, Barney	34	Germany	Y	Bremen	Baltimore	04/20/1884	10/12/1888			Y	
Exterkamp, Henry	26	Holland	Y	Antwerp	New York	06/28/1858	02/19/1861	18	114	N	
Exterkamp, John G.	35	Holland	Y	Amsterdam	Baltimore	12/17/1880	11/20/1884			Y	
Ey, John	30	Bavaria	Y	Havre	New York	08/27/1853	01/17/1856	13	475	N	
Eyer, Leopold	30	Switzerland	Y	Havre	New York	01/14/1892	08/11/1899			Y	
Eyer, Victor	26	Switzerland	Y	Havre	New York	12/25/1896	03/13/1900			Y	
Eyrich, George Frederick	23	Wurttemberg	Y	London	New York	10/16/1854	08/16/1855	11	444	N	
Fabb, George	31	England	Y	Liverpool	Detroit	07/01/1893	09/07/1900			Y	
Faber, Charles	35	Hesse Darmsta	Y	Liverpool	New York	09/23/1857	03/01/1858	16	353	N	
Faber, H.	29	Germany	Y	Amsterdam	New York	06/17/1882	04/18/1883			Y	
Fabing, John	23	France	Y	Havre	New York	01/01/1854	03/13/1856	26	192	N	
Fabronius, Dominick	30	Belgium	Y	Liverpool	New York	07/15/1854	09/24/1858	16	142	N	
Fackler, Anthony	36	Bavaria	Y	Liverpool	New York	08/01/1853	07/23/1858	16	522	N	
Fadley, John	38	Ireland	Y	Liverpool	New Orleans	01/01/1851	04/04/1853	8	10	N	
Faeger, John	26	Wuerttenberg	Y	Antwerp	New York	05/02/1849	05/24/1852	25	95	N	
Faellhardt, Jacob	??	Bavaria	N	?	?	?	05/20/1842			Y	10/15/1844
Faesler, Jacob	21	Baden	Y	Havre	New York	11/16/1850	04/14/1853	8	63	N	
Faessler, Jerome	26	Bavaria	Y	Havre	New Orleans	06/??/1849	12/26/1850	2	398	N	

CITIZENSHIP RECORDS

APPLICANT	AGE	COUNTRY OF ORIGIN	DEC	DEPART PORT	ENTRY PORT	ARRIVE DATE	DEC DATE	VOL	PG.	FLD	NAT DATE
Faeth, Adam	40	Germany	Y	Bremen	Baltimore	09/16/1883	03/17/1887			Y	
Fagan, Michael	27	Ireland	Y	Dublin	New York	05/19/1848	03/02/1853	7	256	N	
Fagan, Patrick	25	Ireland	Y	Dublin	New York	06/03/1849	08/15/1851	4	140	N	
Fagin, Thomas	22	Ireland	Y	Dublin	New York	09/??/1852	09/26/1856	14	394	N	
Fagon, John	45	Ireland	Y	Canada	Rochester	06/22/1836	03/07/1850	2	165	N	
Faherty, Patrick	27	Ireland	Y	Queenstown	New York	05/11/1884	03/27/1891			Y	
Fahey, Frank	24	Ireland	Y	Queenstown	Philadelphia	05/01/1888	01/09/1889			Y	
Fahey, John	35	Ireland	Y	Liverpool	New York	06/01/1879	10/18/1889	19	242	N	
Fahey, John	28	Ireland	Y	Queenstown	Philadelphia	04/19/1890	10/16/1894			Y	
Fahey, John	35	Ireland	Y	Liverpool	New York	06/01/1879	10/18/1889			Y	
Fahey, Pat	24	Ireland	Y	Queenstown	New York	02/02/1887	10/18/1889	19	240	N	
Fahey, Patrick	42	Ireland	Y	Liverpool	New York	04/??/1860	09/10/1880			Y	
Fahrbach, Gottfried	56	Germany	N	Antwerp	New York	07/??/1849	?			Y	
Fahrenhorst, Charles Lud	37	Prussia	Y	Bremen	New York	08/28/1854	02/20/1858	16	323	N	
Fahrholz, Henry	32	Prussia	Y	Bremen	Galveston	01/02/1847	03/01/1851	3	186	N	
Fahrian, John	27	Germany	Y	?	New York	03/18/1883	07/23/1883			Y	
Fahrlemder, Joseph	25	Baden	Y	Havre	New York	04/04/1848	10/09/1854	6	159	N	
Fahrlender, Joseph	25	Baden	Y	Havre	New York	04/04/1848	10/09/1854	11	162	N	
Fahy, Michael	28	Ireland	Y	Galway	Baltimore	04/15/1849	03/01/1853	7	250	N	
Faighle, Gotthilf	24	Germany	Y	Havre	New oOrk	07/21/1895	10/25/1895			Y	
Faigle, John F.	35	Germany	Y	Hamburg	New York	07/11/1887	10/28/1893			Y	
Failler, Benedict	29	Baden	Y	Havre	New York	04/18/1854	08/03/1860	27	244	N	
Fainstain, Samuel	30	Russia	Y	Hamburg	New York	11/??/1881	01/04/1888			Y	
Fairbank, Arthur	26	England	Y	Belfast	New York	03/13/1893	01/08/1898			Y	
Fairbank, Herbert	27	England	Y	Liverpool	New York	07/17/1891	02/25/1897			Y	
Fairfax, Charles	44	Ireland	Y	Liverpool	New Orleans	??/14/1850	04/23/1855	11	280	N	
Faitz, Charles	25	Germany	Y	Havre	New York	07/17/1887	10/28/1890	19	308	N	
Falch, Hermann Robert	28	Germany	Y	Bremen	Baltimore	09/24/1884	04/02/1888			Y	
Falco, Raffaele	36	Italy	Y	Naples	New York	05/03/1882	03/10/1894			Y	
Falk, Fidel	38	Baden	Y	Havre	New Orleans	11/18/1846	08/15/1848	22	162	N	
Falk, Herman	26	Prussia	Y	Havre	New York	08/17/1849	11/01/1852	5	102	N	
Falke, Francis H.	24	Prussia	Y	Bremen	New Orleans	11/??/1852	11/05/1856	14	467	N	
Falkenstein, Bela	25	Austria	Y	Bremen	New York	12/12/1888	10/27/1892			Y	
Falkenstein, Ignatz	52	Austria	Y	Bremen	New York	06/12/1888	10/27/1892			Y	
Faller, Anton	25	Baden	Y	Havre	New York	12/15/1852	04/17/1854	8	183	N	
Faller, Anton	25	Baden	Y	Havre	New York	12/15/1852	04/17/1854	9	54	N	
Faller, Karl	32	Germany	Y	Havre	New York	03/15/1880	04/07/1890			Y	
Fallon, John	??	Ireland	Y	Liverpool	New Orleans	04/15/18??	10/11/1848	1	107	N	
Fallon, John	25	Ireland	Y	Liverpool	New Orleans	05/??/1848	03/25/1851	3	338	N	
Fallon, Owen	21	Ireland	Y	Liverpool	New Orleans	06/01/1852	02/26/1853	7	239	N	
Fallon, Patrick	23	Ireland	Y	Liverpool	New Orleans	12/04/1850	04/04/1853	8	6	N	
Fallon, Thomas	16	Ireland	N	?	Boston	00/00/1877				Y	10/29/1887
Falls, John	61	Ireland	N	Liverpool	New York	05/??/1847	?			Y	
Falls, John	25	Ireland	Y	Liverpool	New York	05/20/1847	03/30/1852	24	340	N	
Falls, Rudolph	31	Germany	Y	Hamburg	New York	06/02/1882	03/04/1884			Y	
Falstrom, Oscar F.	44	Sweden	Y	Gotheborg	New York	06/04/1866	10/25/1894			Y	
Falz, Simon	39	Baden	Y	Havre	New Orleans	01/29/1856	09/10/1860	27	353	N	
Fambrij, Louis	36	Germany	Y	Antwerp	Philadelphia	04/19/1893	03/21/1894			Y	
Fand, Frederick	30	France	Y	Havre	New York	03/10/1857	09/08/1860	27	348	N	
Fanger, John H.	58	Germany	N	Bremen	New York	06/29/1840	?	28	213	N	06/25/1851
Fangman, B.	33	Germany	Y	Bremen	Baltimore	06/28/1873	06/19/1883			Y	
Fangman, Henry	21	Germany	Y	Bremen	Baltimore	05/02/1892	08/04/1894			Y	
Fangmann, August	24	Germany	Y	Bremen	New York	08/13/1880	10/13/1886	19	48	N	
Fangmann, Ferd	33	Germany	Y	Bremen	Baltimore	06/28/1873	08/03/1885			Y	
Fangmann, John Frederick	22	Oldenburg	Y	Bremen	New Orleans	01/21/1847	02/21/1849	23	242	N	
Fangmann, Theodore	29	Germany	Y	Bremen	New York	09/23/1889	03/05/1894			Y	
Fangmeyer, Christian	33	Prussia	Y	Bremen	Baltimore	11/02/1857	05/10/1859	17	407	N	
Fanning, John P.	30	Ireland	Y	Liverpool	New York	09/07/1849	07/30/1858	16	536	N	
Fanning, Michael	26	Ireland	Y	Liverpool	New York	06/04/1838	03/28/1850	2	277	N	

CITIZENSHIP RECORDS

APPLICANT	AGE	COUNTRY OF ORIGIN	DEC	DEPART PORT	ENTRY PORT	ARRIVE DATE	DEC DATE	VOL	PG.	FLD	NAT DATE
Fansy, Michael	38	Ireland	Y	Liverpool	New Orleans	06/11/1850	09/23/1854	12	114	N	
Faragher, Patrick	26	Ireland	Y	?	?	07/07/1881	12/11/1889			Y	
Farber, Harris	34	Russia	Y	?	?	?	10/27/1890			Y	
Farber, Harris	??	Russia	N	?	?	10/05/1878				Y	10/17/1892
Farber, Herman	57	Germany	Y	Bremen	New York	10/08/1866	08/31/1896			Y	
Farber, Jake	29	Russia	Y	?	?	?	12/12/1891			Y	
Farber, Nathan	35	Russia	Y	Hamburg	New York	05/15/1891	12/19/1893			Y	
Fardy, John	24	Ireland	Y	Queenstown	Philadelphia	06/18/1891	11/04/1896			Y	
Farenkopf, William (Fern	34	Germany	Y	Hamburg	New York	10/04/1874	11/26/1884			Y	
Farley, John F.	29	Ireland	Y	Liverpool	New Orleans	04/??/1849	12/??/1849	23	429	N	
Farly, John	24	Ireland	Y	Liverpool	New Orleans	11/??/1848	10/24/1850	2	292	N	
Farmer, Peter	35	Ireland	Y	Liverpool	New Orleans	05/08/1848	05/11/1854	8	423	N	
Farnen, Owen	50	Ireland	Y	Drogheda	New York	06/22/1832	05/22/1852	25	90	N	
Farnich, Henry	21	Oldenburg	Y	Bremen	New Orleans	10/09/1851	03/31/1856	26	383	N	
Farragher, Anthony	23	Ireland	Y	Queenstown	New York	01/25/1888	10/24/1891			Y	
Farrel, John	21	Ireland	Y	Liverpool	New York	04/03/1848	08/12/1851	4	114	N	
Farrel, Martin	29	Ireland	Y	Galway	New York	05/26/1843	08/??/1851	4	166	N	
Farrel, Patrick	22	Ireland	Y	Liverpool	New Orleans	04/13/1851	09/09/1852	25	429	N	
Farrell, Dominick	25	Ireland	Y	Liverpool	New York	05/10/1854	12/08/1858	17	384	N	
Farrell, Fergus	25	Ireland	Y	Liverpool	New York	02/??/1847	09/19/1855	13	71	N	
Farrell, Francis	27	Ireland	Y	Queenstown	New York	04/25/1886	10/16/1893	21	7	N	
Farrell, Francis	24	Ireland	Y	Queenstown	New York	04/25/1886	10/16/1893			Y	
Farrell, Henry	25	Ireland	Y	Liverpool	New Orleans	12/05/1849	10/13/1851	4	250	N	
Farrell, James	53	Ireland	N	Liverpool	New Orleans	05/??/1848	?			Y	
Farrell, John	30	Ireland	Y	Liverpool	New York	06/13/1848	01/12/1853	7	14	N	
Farrell, John	23	Ireland	Y	Galway	New York	??/??/1879	10/07/1885	19	18	N	
Farrell, John	35	Ireland	N	Dublin	New York	11/30/1867	?			Y	
Farrell, Michael	25	Ireland	Y	Glasgow	New York	05/11/1851	05/03/1854	8	353	N	
Farrell, Michael	25	Ireland	Y	Glasgow	New York	05/11/1851	05/03/1854	9	226	N	
Farrell, Patick	28	Ireland	Y	Liverpool	New York	04/28/1888	11/06/1893	21	54	N	
Farrell, Patrick	29	Ireland	Y	Cork	New York	05/10/1847	05/01/1854	8	293	N	
Farrell, Patrick	29	Ireland	Y	Cork	New York	05/10/1847	05/01/1854	9	165	N	
Farrell, Patrick	30	Ireland	Y	Liverpool	New York	05/09/1847	10/05/1854	10	455	N	
Farrell, Patrick	30	Ireland	Y	Liverpool	New York	05/09/1847	10/05/1843	12	394	N	
Farrell, Patrick	24	Ireland	Y	Liverpool	New York	??/07/1847	12/29/1849	23	438	N	
Farrell, Thomas	28	Ireland	Y	Liverpool	New York	12/05/1849	10/13/1851	4	251	N	
Farrell, William	27	Ireland	Y	Liverpool	New Orleans	04/30/1848	10/07/1848	22	485	N	
Farrelly, Charles	39	Ireland	Y	Dublin	New York	04/??/1852	04/20/1855	11	277	N	
Farrelly, James	22	Ireland	Y	Liverpool	New York	04/22/1857	11/23/1857	16	42	N	
Farrington, Peter	23	Ireland	Y	Liverpool	New York	05/20/1851	06/08/1854	10	104	N	
Farrington, Peter	23	Ireland	Y	Liverpool	New York	05/20/1851	06/08/1854	12	41	N	
Farwick, John	42	Hanover	Y	Bremen	Baltimore	06/10/1846	10/27/1858	17	129	N	
Farwig, William	55	Germany	N	Bremen	Baltimore	04/??/1857	?			Y	
Fasel, Charles	33	Prussia	Y	Hamburg	New York	05/03/1853	10/02/1854	10	343	N	
Fasel, Charles	33	Prussia	Y	Hamburg	New York	05/03/1853	10/02/1854	12	282	N	
Faske, Barney	34	Germany	Y	Bremen	Baltimore	12/22/1892	03/01/1892			Y	
Faske, Hermann	32	Oldenburg	Y	Bremen	Baltimore	12/14/1852	09/17/1855	13	46	N	
Fasnacht, Frederick Gott	27	Heckingen	Y	Havre	New Orleans	06/21/1846	02/15/1849	23	109	N	
Fasoro, Antonio	31	Italy	Y	Naples	New York	11/21/1891	07/07/1896			Y	
Fasser, Hieronimas	27	Bavaria	Y	Havre	New York	03/05/1849	12/19/1851	4	531	N	
Fasshauer, Ferdinand	26	Prussia	Y	Bremen	New York	07/27/1860	04/05/1862	18	302	N	
Fast, Otto	28	Germany	Y	Hamburg	New York	08/13/1883	05/02/1885			Y	
Fasznaehl, Carl J.	37	Germany	Y	Amsterdam	New York	07/16/1882	12/10/1883			Y	
Fath, John Adam	42	Bavaria	Y	Liverpool	New York	06/10/1854	09/18/1855	13	67	N	
Fathmann, Gerhard	40	Germany	Y	Amsterdam	New York	01/??/1894	03/07/1884			Y	
Fatt, Nicholas	33	Germany	Y	Bremen	New York	10/29/1877	04/03/1882			Y	
Fatthauer, William	33	Germany	Y	Bremen	New York	05/21/1882	10/01/1883			Y	
Faughuey, Martin	32	Ireland	Y	Liverpool	New Orleans	05/02/1851	10/01/1856	14	113	N	
Faul, Adam	28	Germany	Y	Antwerp	New York	07/20/1887	11/05/1894			Y	

CITIZENSHIP RECORDS

APPLICANT	AGE	COUNTRY OF ORIGIN	DEC	DEPART PORT	ENTRY PORT	ARRIVE DATE	DEC DATE	VOL	PG.	FLD	NAT DATE
Faulhaber, Hubert	22	Germany	Y	Havre	New York	05/26/1892	08/07/1895			Y	
Faulhaber, John	29	Germany	Y	Havre	New York	05/10/1883	08/18/1884			Y	
Faulhaber, Xavier	24	Germany	Y	Havre	New YOrk	05/07/1883	08/19/1889			Y	
Faulk, Leopold	24	Baden	Y	Havre	New Orleans	12/01/1846	10/16/1848	1	240	N	
Faulkerber, Michael	??	Wurttemberg	Y	Antwerp	New York	01/03/18??	?	1	92	N	
Faulkner, John	28	Ireland	Y	Liverpool	New York	06/16/1851	10/05/1854	10	446	N	
Faulkner, John	25	Ireland	Y	Liverpool	New York	06/16/1851	10/05/1854	12	385	N	
Faulstich, John	46	Hesse Cassel	Y	Liverpool	New York	09/25/1852	12/28/1852	5	456	N	
Faulwetter, C. H.	43	Bremen	Y	Bremen	Baltimore	09/18/1856	01/16/1860	27	53	N	
Faust, John Henry	43	Germany	N	Hamburg	New York	04/05/1864	?			Y	
Fautz, Joseph	29	Baden	Y	Havre	New York	10/04/1848	10/22/1851	4	373	N	
Fax, Frank	27	France	Y	Havre	New Orleans	05/11/1837	10/06/1854	12	435	N	
Fay, Francis Gustav	31	Baden	Y	Bremen	New York	06/19/1854	02/15/1856	26	93	N	
Fay, Thomas	21	Ireland	Y	Queenstown	New York	05/20/1887	02/06/1889			Y	
Fazio, Gosi	28	Italy	Y	Naples	New York	05/18/1883	08/15/1888			Y	
Fazio, Peter	32	Italy	Y	Naples	New York	05/24/1883	08/13/1888			Y	
Fealen, Thomas	31	Ireland	Y	Liverpool	New York	07/16/1851	09/28/1854	10	296	N	
Fealen, Thomas	31	Ireland	Y	Liverpool	New York	07/16/1851	09/28/1854	12	235	N	
Febel, George	34	Baden	Y	Havre	New York	07/01/1849	04/12/1852	24	449	N	
Fechheimer, Simon	21	Germany	Y	Bremen	New York	09/27/1886	02/25/1890			Y	
Fechter, George	34	Prussia	Y	London	New York	04/20/1848	08/12/1851	4	117	N	
Fedders, John Henry	26	Hanover	Y	Bremen	Baltimore	06/24/1859	04/01/1861	18	125	N	
Feder, John	29	Germany	Y	Bremen	New York	01/??/1884	10/22/1889			Y	
Feder, Louis	30	Germany	Y	Havre	New York	05/10/1888	01/15/1891			Y	
Feder, Stephan	43	Germany	Y	Havre	New York	10/??/1881	11/30/1887			Y	
Federle, Joseph	23	Germany	Y	Havre	New York	06/15/1882	02/25/1885			Y	
Federle, Joseph	25	Germany	Y	Havre	New York	09/01/1890	12/15/1893			Y	
Federle, Nickolaus	30	Germany	Y	Antwerp	New Ork	02/05/1891	01/06/1893			Y	
Federle, Valentine	50	Germany	Y	Havre	New York	05/13/1879	05/10/1892			Y	
Federle, William	56	Germany	Y	Havre	New York	04/30/1865	03/23/1900			Y	
Federmann, Gottfried	45	Germany	N	Havre	New York	03/??/1867	?			Y	
Federmann, Gottlieb	27	Germany	Y	Rotterdam	New York	03/??/1879	10/02/1884			Y	
Fedschan, Constantin	37	Germany	Y	Hamburg	Philadelphia	05/14/1889	11/01/1897			Y	
Feely, Patrick J.	30	Ireland	Y	?	?	?	09/29/1876			Y	
Feely, Thomas	22	Ireland	Y	Liverpool	Baltimore	09/05/1851	09/14/1852	25	502	N	
Feen, Barnert	31	Russia	Y	?	?	?	10/16/1891			Y	
Feenway, John	50	Saxony	Y	Bremen	Philadelphia	12/27/1839	10/09/1854	6	70	N	
Feeny, Dominick	23	Ireland	Y	Queenstown	New York	10/10/1887	10/27/1887			Y	
Feeway, John	50	Saxony	Y	Bremen	Philadelphia	12/27/1839	10/09/1854	11	71	N	
Fegen, Joseph	53	France	N	Havre	New York	03/28/1866	?			Y	
Fehr, Frank	37	Germany	Y	Havre	New York	08/12/1887	08/20/1889			Y	
Fehr, John Bernard	44	Hanover	Y	Bremen	New Orleans	11/01/1852	08/02/1858	16	546	N	
Fehren, G.	26	Hanover	Y	Bremen	Baltimore	06/24/1858	01/09/1860	27	43	N	
Fehrenbach, August	32	Germany	Y	Antwerp	New York	02/27/1883	10/15/1896			Y	
Fehrenbach, Wnedelin	28	Germany	Y	Havre	New York	03/23/1881	03/01/1889			Y	
Fehrler, Frank	28	Germany	Y	Havre	New York	05/30/1881	10/21/1886	19	59	N	
Fehrmann, Bernard Henry	22	Hanover	Y	Bremen	New Orleans	06/02/1849	04/12/1852	24	485	N	
Fehrmann, Henry	34	Germany	N	Bremen	New York	04/??/1856	?			Y	
Fei, Joseph (John?)	32	Hanover	Y	Bremen	New Orleans	01/10/1854	02/02/1856	26	10	N	
Feibelman, Julius	31	Germany	Y	Havre	New York	08/15/1881	10/28/1893			Y	
Feichtner, Jacob	21	Germany	Y	Antwerp	New York	07/12/1889	10/31/1892	19	406	N	
Feichtner, Jacob	21	Germany	Y	Atwerp	New York	07/12/1889	10/03/1892			Y	
Feig, Henry	28	Germany	Y	Hamburg	New York	07/17/1866	01/23/1873	18	551	N	
Feigazzi, Alex	49	Italy	Y	Genoa	New Orleans	01/15/1869	08/09/1889			Y	
Feige, Carl Gustav	30	Russia	Y	Bremen	New York	05/23/1883	01/10/1888			Y	
Feigert, ?	??	Bavaria	Y	Bremen	New York	??/19/1849	03/27/1851	3	362	N	
Feik, John	24	Bavaria	Y	Rotterdam	New York	12/01/1849	11/05/1852	5	223	N	
Feik, John	24	Bavaria	Y	Rotterdam	New York	12/01/1849	11/05/1852	6	349	N	
Feiler, Adam	51	Baden	Y	Rotterdam	New York	02/01/1855	01/22/1856	13	491	N	

CITIZENSHIP RECORDS

APPLICANT	AGE	COUNTRY OF ORIGIN	DEC	DEPART PORT	ENTRY PORT	ARRIVE DATE	DEC DATE	VOL	PG.	FLD	NAT DATE
Feilhauer, Edmund	43	Austria	Y	Bremen	New York	07/21/1886	05/02/1894			Y	
Feinberg, Siegmund	25	Russia	Y	Hamburg	New York	05/04/1848	07/15/1851	3	536	N	
Feinthel, Frederick Jaco	52	Bavaria	Y	Antwerp	New Orleans	12/24/1849	05/22/1854	8	483	N	
Feinthel, Frederick Jaco	52	Bavaria	Y	Antwerp	New Orleans	12/24/1849	05/22/1854	9	357	N	
Feinthel, John	25	Bavaria	Y	Havre	New Orleans	07/03/1848	04/05/1852	24	381	N	
Feiss, Pius	54	Germany	N	Liverpool	New York	05/??/1853	?			Y	
Feistner, William	??	Germany	Y	?	?	?	09/19/1885			Y	
Feitzer, George	31	Wurtemberg	Y	Bremen	New York	06/17/1854	10/03/1854	10	403	N	
Feitzer, George	32	Wurtemberg	Y	Bremen	New York	06/17/1854	10/03/1854	12	342	N	
Feld, Johann Heinrich	24	Hanover	Y	Bremerhafen	New Orleans	11/??/1857	02/26/1861	18	119	N	
Felden, M.	35	Germany	Y	Havre	New York	02/26/1881	09/30/1885			Y	
Feldhake, Henry	32	Hanover	Y	Bremen	New Orleans	11/01/1848	03/30/1852	24	338	N	
Feldhaker, Fred	32	Hanover	Y	Bremen	New York	07/??/1845	08/??/1851	4	156	N	
Feldhaus, Fred	27	Germany	Y	Bremen	Baltimore	10/28/1880	03/12/1888			Y	
Feldhaus, Henry	31	Germany	Y	Bremen	Baltimore	02/17/1874	10/11/1882			Y	
Feldhaus, Henry	39	Germany	Y	Bremen	Baltimore	07/28/1880	11/05/1889			Y	
Feldhaus, John Henry	35	Germany	Y	Bremen	Baltimore	09/28/1872	07/29/1881			Y	
Feldhaus, Joseph	39	Germany	Y	Bremen	New York	07/10/1875	11/27/1882			Y	
Feldkamp, Bernard	21	Hanover	Y	Bremen	New Orleans	12/30/1852	04/02/1856	26	420	N	
Feldkamp, Frank Heinrich	30	Germany	Y	Amsterdam	New York	09/25/1887	03/18/1889			Y	
Feldkamp, George	48	Germany	N	Bremen	New Orleans	12/??/1849	?			Y	
Feldkamp, Herman	24	Hanover	Y	Bremen	Baltimore	11/29/1850	04/22/1853	8	94	N	
Feldkamp, Herman Diedric	30	Hanover	Y	Bremen	New Orleans	06/04/1845	01/22/1851	2	520	N	
Feldkamp, J. H. Henry	29	Germany	Y	Bremen	New York	03/20/1880	11/05/1888			Y	
Feldkamp, J.H. Henry	29	Germany	Y	Bremen	New York	03/20/1880	11/05/1888	19	220	N	
Feldkamp, Joseph	29	Germany	Y	Bremen	Baltimore	05/05/1880	10/13/1880			Y	
Feldkamp, Joseph	33	Germany	Y	Bremen	Baltimore	05/23/1887	02/01/1892			Y	
Feldman, Barney	29	Oldenburg	Y	Bremen	Baltimore	??/24/1844	10/30/1849	23	294	N	
Feldman, Diedrich	25	Hanover	Y	Bremen	Baltimore	08/03/1845	11/18/1848	1	324	N	
Feldman, Meyer	21	Russia	Y	Hamburg	New York	08/02/1882	04/??/1883			Y	
Feldman, Victor	29	Prussia	Y	Bremen	Baltimore	11/01/1850	05/25/1854	8	514	N	
Feldman, Victor	29	Prussia	Y	Bremen	Baltimore	11/01/1850	05/25/1854	9	358	N	
Feldmann, Abe	??	Russia	Y	?	Detroit	04/??/1861	03/21/1892			Y	
Feldmann, Anton	31	Germany	N	Bremen	New York	03/??/1870	?			Y	
Feldmann, Charles	38	Germany	Y	?	?	05/06/1881	05/28/1890			Y	
Feldmann, D.	35	Austria	N	Hamburg	New York	09/??/1873	?			Y	
Feldmann, David	35	Austria	Y	Hamburg	New York	09/??/1873	11/03/1888			Y	
Feldmann, Henry	21	Hanover	Y	Bremen	New Orleans	06/28/1849	11/01/1852	5	89	N	
Feldmann, Henry	41	Germany	Y	Bremen	Baltimore	09/16/1882	09/18/1889			Y	
Feldmann, John	32	Prussia	Y	Rotterdam	New York	09/22/1851	10/02/1856	14	138	N	
Feldmann, John	25	Germany	Y	?	?	06/??/1884	12/31/1884			Y	
Feldmann, John	24	Germany	Y	?	?	11/03/1883	11/14/1887			Y	
Feldmann, Meyer	32	Russia	N	Hamburg	New York	08/02/1882	?			Y	
Feldmeyer, Herman	23	Germany	Y	Bremen	Baltimore	06/29/1882	02/11/1884			Y	
Feldschnieders, John	30	Germany	Y	Rotterdam	New York	07/19/1882	12/08/1892			Y	
Feldthart, Michael	25	Hanover	Y	Bremen	New Orleans	11/05/1847	?	24	96	N	
Felix, Frederick	28	Baden	Y	Bremen	New Orleans	05/19/1852	11/07/1855	13	186	N	
Felix, Herman	29	Germany	Y	Bremen	New York	04/28/1884	05/10/1888			Y	
Felix, John Adam	61	Bavaria	Y	Havre	New Orleans	11/02/1849	03/25/1856	26	297	N	
Felix, Mike	33	Austria	Y	Bremen	New York	03/15/1885	10/09/1896			Y	
Feliz, F.W.C.	26	Mecklenburg S	Y	Hamburg	New York	08/14/1854	07/21/1858	16	519	N	
Fell, Nicolaus	25	Prussia	Y	Antwerp	New York	05/16/1854	01/30/1856	13	523	N	
Feller, Nicholas	35	Bavaria	Y	Havre	New Orleans	12/25/1849	11/01/1852	5	103	N	
Fellerman, John A.	22	Hanover	Y	Bremen	New York	07/03/1846	03/29/1850	2	280	N	
Fellermann, John	29	Hanover	Y	Bremen	New York	07/04/1846	10/14/1851	4	290	N	
Fellheimer, Joseph	30	Wurtemberg	Y	Havre	New York	08/25/1848	08/18/1857	15	154	N	
Fellner, Adolf	43	Germany	Y	Liverpool	Boston	06/25/1880	12/16/1885			Y	
Fels, John	32	Bavaria	Y	Havre	New Orleans	05/25/1846	10/07/1848	22	492	N	
Fels, Mathias	55	Germany	N	Havre	New Orleans	12/25/1849	?			Y	

CITIZENSHIP RECORDS

APPLICANT	AGE	COUNTRY OF ORIGIN	DEC	DEPART PORT	ENTRY PORT	ARRIVE DATE	DEC DATE	VOL	PG.	FLD	NAT DATE
Felten, Mathias	42	Prussia	Y	Antwerp	New York	12/15/1853	08/25/1862	18	398	N	
Feltenpohe, Herman	40	Germany	Y	Bremen	New York	03/17/1867	10/12/1880			Y	
Felthart, Bernard	23	Hanover	Y	Bremen	New Orleans	11/04/1849	02/11/1852	24	95	N	
Felthaus, Peter	24	Prussia	Y	Bremen	New York	05/29/1846	11/24/1848	1	398	N	
Felthoster, Henry	33	Hanover	Y	Bremen	Baltimore	07/07/1848	11/01/1852	5	161	N	
Felthoster, Henry	33	Hanover	Y	Bremen	Baltimore	07/07/1848	11/01/1852	6	287	N	
Feltmann, Henry	22	Prussia	Y	Bremen	New Orleans	10/23/1853	11/16/1857	16	24	N	
Femme, Henry	30	Hanover	Y	Bremen	New Orleans	06/24/1855	05/30/1856	14	269	N	
Fender, Mortiz	38	France	N	Havre	New York	05/??/1854	?			Y	
Fendt, Casimere	29	Hesse Darmsta	Y	Bremen	Baltimore	??/01/1847	04/28/1855	11	324	N	
Fenger, John Henry	28	Hanover	Y	Bremen	New Orleans	08/12/1845	09/13/1852	25	482	N	
Fening, Henry	24	Germany	Y	Bremen	Baltimore	03/12/1882	05/14/1883			Y	
Fening, John	22	Germany	Y	Amsterdam	New York	10/10/1881	12/27/1883			Y	
Fening, Michael	25	Ireland	Y	Liverpool	New Orleans	06/??/1846	05/26/1854	9	427	N	
Fening, Michael	26	Ireland	Y	Liverpool	New Orleans	06/??/1846	05/26/1854	10	10	N	
Fenkelstein, Mayer	55	Russia	Y	Hamburg	New York	07/15/1879	10/25/1890	19	301	N	
Fenkelstein, Mayer	55	Russia	Y	Hamburg	New York	07/15/1879	10/25/1890			Y	
Fenker, Frederick Henry	34	Prussia	Y	Bremen	Baltimore	10/01/1854	09/19/1857	15	285	N	
Fenker, William	23	Hanover	Y	Bremen	Baltimore	12/18/1853	10/07/1854	10	528	N	
Fenker, William	23	Hanover	Y	Bremen	Baltimore	12/18/1853	10/07/1854	12	467	N	
Fenkler, George	34	Bavaria	Y	Havre	New Orleans	12/29/1849	03/02/1852	24	214	N	
Fennel, Adolph	30	Hesse Cassel	Y	Hamburg	New York	06/20/1852	09/21/1854	10	154	N	
Fennel, Adolph	30	Hesse Cassel	Y	Hamburg	New York	06/20/1852	09/21/1854	12	93	N	
Fennell, John	35	England	Y	London	New York	03/10/1851	12/27/1852	5	450	N	
Fennelly, John	25	Ireland	Y	Liverpool	New York	06/27/1854	10/13/1857	15	411	N	
Fenneman, Dirck	29	Hanover	Y	Bremen	Baltimore	07/04/1848	02/17/1853	7	174	N	
Fennen, Gerhard	56	Germany	Y	Bremen	New York	05/10/1868	03/17/1894			Y	
Fennerty, William	36	Ireland	Y	Liverpool	Charleston	03/03/1847	01/19/1849	1	470	N	
Fenster, Adolphe	36	Rumania	Y	Bucharest	New York	07/10/1900	09/20/1901			Y	
Fenszlein, John	28	Saxe Coburg G	Y	Bremen	New York	09/23/1852	10/04/1854	10	426	N	
Fenszlein, John	28	Saxe Coburg G	Y	Bremen	New York	09/23/1852	10/04/1854	12	365	N	
Fenz, Andrew	31	Germany	N	Antwerp	Philadelphia	09/22/1879	?			Y	
Fenzel, Casper	36	Hesse Darmsta	Y	London	New York	09/22/1854	10/06/1856	14	229	N	
Ferber, Gerhard	32	Prussia	Y	Havre	New York	05/10/1850	01/10/1853	5	537	N	
Ferdinand, Rothier Ludov	38	France	Y	Havre	New York	09/21/1855	03/03/1858	16	364	N	
Ferguson, James	67	Ireland	N	Dublin	New Orleans	10/??/1850	?			Y	
Ferhenholz, Ferdinand	33	Prussia	Y	Bremen	New York	12/14/1848	03/08/1852	24	267	N	
Ferlan, Joseph	??	Austira	Y	?	?	?	05/19/1893			Y	
Fern, Thomas	38	England	Y	?	?	??/??/1874	02/02/1886			Y	
Ferntheil, Julis	31	Germany	Y	Bremen	New York	06/26/1880	11/08/1887			Y	
Ferry, Neil	24	Ireland	Y	Londonderry	New York	05/26/1888	09/25/1894			Y	
Fetjohn, Thomas	27	Austria	Y	Bremen	New York	04/11/1888	12/17/1892			Y	
Fetler, Christian	22	Wurtemberg	Y	Havre	New York	06/18/1854	10/04/1858	17	43	N	
Fette, B.	38	Germany	Y	Bremen	New York	05/02/1883	09/05/1887			Y	
Fette, Christian	23	Oldenburg	Y	Bremen	New York	10/28/1853	09/25/1854	10	215	N	
Fette, Christian	23	Oldenburg	Y	Bremen	New York	10/28/1853	09/25/1854	12	154	N	
Fette, J. B.	24	Germany	Y	Bremen	New York	09/01/1881	10/10/1883			Y	
Fetter, Joseph	21	Bavaria	Y	Bremen	New York	07/15/1852	12/31/1852	5	484	N	
Fettig, Nicholas	23	France	Y	Havre	New York	03/30/1857	10/19/1857	15	454	N	
Feucht, Charles	58	Germany	Y	Amsterdam	New York	08/05/1883	08/24/1891			Y	
Feucht, Simon	34	Bavaria	Y	Havre	New Orleans	08/28/1849	08/17/1861	18	217	N	
Feuchtinger, Otto	34	Germany	Y	Amsterdam	New York	02/26/1886	03/13/1890			Y	
Feucker, Paul	27	Germany	Y	Hamburg	New York	09/14/1880	10/25/1887			Y	
Feuersinger, Joseph	33	Bavaria	N	Pheinpflaz	New York	09/27/1867	?			Y	
Feuerstein, Albert	24	Germany	Y	Havre	New York	04/08/1881	01/11/1884			Y	
Feuerstein, Francis	40	Baden	Y	Havre	New Orleans	12/30/1854	09/29/1856	14	36	N	
Feuerstein, Valentine	26	Baden	Y	Havre	New York	09/20/1851	10/09/1854	6	154	N	
Feuerstein, Valentine	26	Baden	Y	Havre	New York	09/20/1851	10/09/1854	11	157	N	
Feuser, Anton	??	Germany	Y	?	?	?	04/28/1886			Y	

CITIZENSHIP RECORDS

APPLICANT	AGE	COUNTRY OF ORIGIN	DEC	DEPART PORT	ENTRY PORT	ARRIVE DATE	DEC DATE	VOL	PG.	FLD	NAT DATE
Feuss, Henry	28	Germany	Y	Bremen	Baltimore	08/31/1884	10/29.1892			Y	
Feust, H. W.	67	Germany	N	Bremen	New York	09/??/1849	?			Y	
Feust, Herman Wolfgang	53	Bavaria	Y	Liverpool	New York	03/02/1867	11/04/1872	18	538	N	
Feusterbusch, Henry Brun	31	Germany	Y	Bremen	New York	09/03/1890	02/08/1892			Y	
Fey, Ferdinand	30	Germany	Y	Bremen	New York	03/11/1881	09/16/1889			Y	
Fey, Frank	39	Germany	N	Bremen	New York	05/29/1870	?			Y	
Fey, Michael	33	Bavaria	Y	Rotterdam	New York	07/04/1849	01/05/1853	5	519	N	
Fey, Peter	26	Germany	Y	Bremen	New York	03/09/1881	03/22/1884			Y	
Fezer, Ullrich	32	Wurttemberg	Y	Bremen	New York	05/20/1854	10/03/1854	12	341	N	
Fezer, Ulrich	32	Wurttemberg	Y	Bremen	New York	05/20/1854	10/03/1854	10	402	N	
Fflum, Dominick	30	Prussia	Y	Antwerp	New York	05/04/1851	01/20/1853	7	45	N	
Fialkowski, Victor	36	Austria	Y	Bremen	New York	09/??/1886	02/13/1889			Y	
Fibbe, John Henry	40	Hanover	Y	Bremen	New Orleans	05/01/1849	09/26/1854	10	235	N	
Fibbe, John Henry	40	Hanover	Y	Bremen	New Orleans	05/01/1849	09/26/1854	12	174	N	
Ficher, Barnardus	22	Baden	Y	Havre	New York	08/20/1847	03/26/1850	2	269	N	
Ficher, Charles	26	Hanover	Y	Bremen	New York	07/26/1846	11/20/1848	1	327	N	
Fichtenkoetter, Henry	27	Prussia	Y	Bremen	New York	10/13/1853	10/28/1858	17	160	N	
Fichter, Emil	23	Germany	Y	Havre	New York	08/20/1885	09/02/1889			Y	
Fichter, Nicholas	44	France	Y	Havre	New Orleans	12/29/1854	10/19/1857	15	449	N	
Fichtl, Moritz	43	Austria	N	Bremen	Baltimore	04/??/1871	?			Y	
Fick, Michael	48	Germany	Y	Bremen	New York	05/19/1888	12/27/1890			Y	
Ficke, P.	36	Hanover	Y	Bremen	Baltimore	11/28/1855	01/12/1860	27	51	N	
Fickers, B.H.	29	Hanover	Y	Bremen	New Orleans	12/28/1853	04/04/1861	18	129	N	
Fiebermann, Richard	26	Prussia	Y	Hamburg	New York	05/01/1845	07/05/1851	3	495	N	
Fiedler, George	27	Germany	Y	Rotterdam	New York	06/01/1889	07/28/1891			Y	
Fiedtke, Ernest Ludwig	44	Germany	Y	?	New York	??/??/1882	07/27/1886			Y	
Fiefhaus, Heinrich	31	Prussia	Y	Bremen	Baltimore	06/29/1860	07/01/1862	18	367	N	
Fiege, Christian Frederi	21	Bremen	Y	Bremen	New York	08/01/1855	02/04/1856	26	25	N	
Field, Michael	16	Ireland	N	?	New York	00/00/1846				Y	11/01/1886
Fielder, Richard	23	Germany	Y	Rotterdam	New York	09/10/1881	08/15/1883			Y	
Fieler, Herman	48	Germany	Y	Rotterdam	New York	09/08/1881	10/11/1888			Y	
Filacoro, Benjamin	40	Prussia	Y	Bremen	Baltimore	08/20/1885	03/29/1897			Y	
Filbin, Julius	38	Germany	Y	Boulogna	New York	04/13/1893	10/18/1897			Y	
Filgis, F. Xavier	??	Germany	Y	?	New York	??/??/1882	10/13/1884			Y	
Fillmer, Henry	26	Germany	Y	Hamburg	New York	08/27/1880	09/30/1881			Y	
Fillmor, William	28	Hanover	Y	Oustler	Baltmiore	09/15/1858	12/02/1858	17	372	N	
Filusch, Florian	46	Germany	Y	Bremen	Baltimore	06/16/1866	03/31/1880			Y	
Filz, George	18	Hungary	Y	?	New York	00/00/1875	08/19/1878			Y	
Fimmer, John Gerd.	29	Hanover	Y	Bremen	New Orleans	01/??/1843	11/22/1852	5	325	N	
Finch, Edward	37	England	Y	London	New York	09/13/1857	10/09/1860	27	463	N	
Finck, Moritz	30	Russia	Y	Hamburg	New York	07/15/1885	04/09/1890			Y	
Finder, Emil	30	Germany	Y	Berlin	New York	08/20/1881	12/19/1881			Y	
Findley, Peter	28	Ireland	Y	Liverpool	New Orleans	02/21/1851	05/04/1854	8	365	N	
Findley, Peter	28	Ireland	Y	Liverpool	New Orleans	02/21/1851	05/04/1854	9	238	N	
Fine, Peter	26	Russia	Y	Glasgow	New York	10/20/1886	08/15/1898			Y	
Finen, Mathew	25	Ireland	Y	Canada	New York	07/30/1847	02/20/1849	23	229	N	
Fingerhut, Franz	22	Prussia	Y	Bremen	Baltimore	09/03/1858	08/30/1862	18	425	N	
Fingernagel, George	28	Hesse Darmsta	Y	Bremen	Baltimore	09/03/1841	05/06/1850	3	50	N	
Fink, John	29	Wurttemberg	Y	Havre	New York	03/30/1852	09/13/1855	13	17	N	
Fink, John	42	Germany	Y	Antwerp	New York	05/23/1882	09/25/1883			Y	
Fink, Karl	33	Germany	Y	Antwerp	New York	03/26/1886	03/18/1890			Y	
Finkbeiner, George	25	Germany	Y	?	?	?	03/30/1887			Y	
Finkbeiner, Jacob F.	22	Germany	Y	Hamburg	New York	09/01/1882	05/01/1885			Y	
Finke, Frank William	24	Hanover	Y	Bremen	New Orleans	05/13/1851	05/19/1854	8	478	N	
Finke, Franz William	24	Hanover	Y	Bremen	New Orleans	05/13/1851	05/19/1854	9	352	N	
Finke, Jacob	28	Wurttemberg	Y	Havre	New York	11/09/1845	10/29/1851	4	435	N	
Finkelman, Moses	??	Russia	Y	?	?	?	12/28/1887			Y	
Finkelstein, Abraham	35	Russia	Y	Hamburg	Philadelphia	07/15/1882	09/??/1884			Y	
Finkelstein, Abraham	45	Russia	N	Hamburg	Philadelphia	07/15/1882	?			Y	

CITIZENSHIP RECORDS

APPLICANT	AGE	COUNTRY OF ORIGIN	DEC	DEPART PORT	ENTRY PORT	ARRIVE DATE	DEC DATE	VOL	PG.	FLD	NAT DATE
Finkelstein, Simon J.	28	Russia	Y	Bremen	New York	10/??/1885	05/14/1891			Y	
Finkilston, Arin	24	Russia	Y	Liverpool	New York	10/28/1853	09/30/1856	14	51	N	
Finley, Philip	??	Ireland	N	?	?	12/28/1881				Y	10/25/1892
Finn, Patrick	32	Ireland	Y	Liverpool	New York	05/28/1846	06/18/1851	3	398	N	
Finn, Edmund	52	Ireland	Y	Cork	New Orleans	05/12/1849	10/17/1851	4	319	N	
Finn, James	26	Ireland	Y	Queenstown	New York	04/02/1891	01/12/1897			Y	
Finn, Lawrence	44	Ireland	Y	Liverpool	New Orleans	01/12/1850	08/04/1856	14	336	N	
Finn, Mathias	30	Ireland	Y	Liverpool	New York	04/11/1883	10/26/1888	19	184	N	
Finn, Matthew	30	Ireland	Y	Liverpool	New York	04/01/1883	10/26/1888			Y	
Finn, Patrick	30	Ireland	Y	Liverpool	New Orleans	??/24/1847	02/06/1850	2	41	N	
Finn, Patrick	53	Ireland	Y	Liverpool	New Orleans	02/03/1849	11/27/1858	17	362	N	
Finn, Patrick	26	Ireland	Y	Liverpool	New York	09/17/1886	10/14/1890			Y	
Finn, Timothy	24	Ireland	Y	Liverpool	New York	04/29/1887	10/14/1890			Y	
Finn, William A.	40	England	Y	Liverpool	Philadelphia	03/15/1881	11/04/1895			Y	
Finnegan, John	22	Ireland	Y	Dublin	Thomastown	08/??/1846	12/??/1849	23	413	N	
Finnegan, Michael	25	Ireland	Y	Liverpool	New Orleans	01/??/1847	12/??/1849	23	415	N	
Finnegan, Patrick	33	Ireland	Y	Liverpool	New York	09/20/1850	09/25/1854	10	219	N	
Finnegan, Patrick	33	Ireland	Y	Liverpool	New York	09/20/1850	09/25/1854	12	158	N	
Finner, Benedict	26	Germany	Y	Antwerp	Philadelphia	04/16/1891	03/28/1894			Y	
Finneran, Michael	38	Ireland	Y	Liverpool	New York	06/10/1882	05/05/1890			Y	
Finneran, Peter	52	Ireland	N	Liverpool	Boston	04/??/1845	?	28	152	N	04/??/1856
Finnerty, Thomas	??	Ireland	Y	?	?	?	12/08/1884			Y	
Finnigan, James	44	Ireland	N	Cork	New York	06/??/1867	?			Y	
Finnigan, John	44	Ireland	Y	Liverpool	New Orleans	02/05/1849	02/18/1857	15	28	N	
Finster, Anton	40	Germany	Y	Hamburg	Boston	06/15/1894	07/03/1894			Y	
Finsterle, Gottlieb	28	Wurttemberg	Y	Liverpool	New York	08/26/1852	11/02/1857	15	511	N	
Firner, Joseph	22	Baden	Y	Havre	New York	09/14/1848	02/12/1850	2	66	N	
Firner, Theodore	25	Baden	Y	Havre	New York	08/??/1849	12/??/1849	23	437	N	
Firohy, Dennis	23	Ireland	Y	Dublin	New York	05/??/1848	01/??/1850	23	483	N	
Fisch, Fritz	58	Germany	Y	?	New York	06/??/1884	10/09/1886			Y	
Fischang, Joseph	27	Germany	Y	?	Baltimore	03/??/1885	10/27/1888			Y	
Fischbach, Kilian	23	Baden	Y	Havre	New York	09/16/1854	10/02/1856	14	141	N	
Fischer, Andreas	40	Germany	Y	Antwerp	New York	06/14/1885	04/28/1891			Y	
Fischer, Anton	42	Germany	Y	Havre	New York	05/25/1872	11/01/1882			Y	
Fischer, Anton	52	Germany	Y	Bremen	New York	05/25/1881	10/05/1885			Y	
Fischer, August	23	Bavaria	Y	Bremen	New Orleans	06/16/1849	11/01/1852	5	135	N	
Fischer, August	23	Bavaria	Y	Bremen	New Orleans	06/16/1849	11/01/1852	6	261	N	
Fischer, August	55	Germany	Y	Havre	New York	10/20/1891	02/10/1893			Y	
Fischer, Bernard	30	Oldenburg	Y	Bremen	New Orleans	12/29/1845	01/??/1850	23	536	N	
Fischer, Carl	31	Germany	Y	Bremen	Baltimore	08/30/1886	10/16/1893			Y	
Fischer, Charles	21	Germany	Y	Bremen	New York	05/25/1891	10/28/1893			Y	
Fischer, Chas	21	Germany	Y	Hamburg	New York	05/01/1881	06/02/1884			Y	
Fischer, Christian	31	Baden	Y	Havre	New Orleans	06/02/1854	01/17/1856	13	479	N	
Fischer, Christoph	??	Austria	Y	?	?	?	09/22/1873			Y	
Fischer, Daniel	39	Germany	Y	?	New York	00/00/1871	10/10/1884			Y	
Fischer, Edward	24	Germany	Y	?	?	10/03/1886	06/01/1886			Y	
Fischer, Edward	22	Germany	Y	Havre	New York	02/27/1887	04/24/1888			Y	
Fischer, Ferdinand	20	Germany	Y	Rotterdam	New York	06/28/1880	10/21/1881			Y	
Fischer, Florain	48	Wurttemberg	Y	Havre	New York	10/26/1848	04/21/1854	9	106	N	
Fischer, Florian	48	Wurttemberg	Y	Havre	New York	10/26/1848	04/21/1854	8	235	N	
Fischer, Francis	29	Baden	Y	Havre	New York	09/02/1851	11/12/1857	16	12	N	
Fischer, Frank	27	Austria	Y	Bremen	Baltimore	02/28/1890	09/07/1898			Y	
Fischer, Frank	27	Germany	Y	Havre	New York	06/12/1888	11/08/1889			Y	
Fischer, Frank	30	Germany	Y	Antwerp	New York	03/19/1883	07/23/1888			Y	
Fischer, Fred	24	Germany	Y	Havre	New York	10/15/1879	10/10/1884			Y	
Fischer, Frederick	36	Saxony	Y	Bremen	New York	12/06/1853	05/06/1854	8	391	N	
Fischer, Frederick	36	Saxony	Y	Bremen	New York	12/06/1853	05/06/1854	9	264	N	
Fischer, Frederick	37	Hanover	Y	Bremen	Baltimore	08/04/1847	07/19/1855	11	410	N	
Fischer, Frederick	58	Germany	N	Hamburg	New York	06/30/1851	?			Y	

CITIZENSHIP RECORDS

APPLICANT	AGE	COUNTRY OF ORIGIN	DEC	DEPART PORT	ENTRY PORT	ARRIVE DATE	DEC DATE	VOL	PG.	FLD	NAT DATE
Fischer, Frederick C.	??	?	N	?	?	?	?	28	294	N	10/07/1878
Fischer, Frederick Engel	25	Baden	Y	Havre	New York	06/06/1853	10/26/1857	15	490	N	
Fischer, Frederick Willi	27	Oldenburg	Y	Hamburg	New York	06/17/1856	07/21/1858	16	518	N	
Fischer, George	26	Wurttemberg	Y	Antwerp	New York	09/27/1849	02/27/1850	2	132	N	
Fischer, Gerhard	28	Prussia	Y	Bremen	New Orleans	06/18/1850	06/05/1854	10	82	N	
Fischer, Gerhard	28	Prussia	Y	Bremen	New Orleans	06/18/1850	06/05/1854	12	19	N	
Fischer, Gerhard Lucas	32	Hanover	Y	Bremen	New Orleans	05/28/1849	05/29/1854	9	436	N	
Fischer, Gerhard Lucas	32	Hanover	Y	Bremen	New Orleans	05/28/1849	05/29/1854	10	19	N	
Fischer, Henry	34	Germany	Y	?	New York	09/13/1880	04/05/1882			Y	
Fischer, Henry	39	Germany	Y	Bremen	Baltimore	04/30/1868	03/07/1881			Y	
Fischer, Henry Fredderic	23	Prussia	Y	Bremen	New York	05/20/1857	10/26/1857	15	492	N	
Fischer, Henry Frederick	??	Brunswick	Y	Bremen	Baltimore	09/17/18??	10/11/1848	1	143	N	
Fischer, Herman Henry	31	Hanover	Y	Bremen	New Orleans	12/23/1851	11/01/1858	17	237	N	
Fischer, Hermann Heinric	61	Germany	N	Bremen	New Orleans	12/??/1851	?			Y	
Fischer, John	37	Germany	Y	?	New York	12/17/1869	07/16/1873			Y	
Fischer, John	26	Germany	Y	Bremen	Baltimore	09/22/1880	12/08/1883			Y	
Fischer, John	28	Germany	Y	Bremen	Baltimore	02/20/1889	04/05/1894			Y	
Fischer, John	28	Germany	N	Antwerp	New York	10/19/1882	?			Y	
Fischer, John	42	Prussia	Y	Bremen	New York	04/19/1857	01/06/1860	27	37	N	
Fischer, John	23	Bavaria	Y	Havre	New Orleans	05/17/1857	08/23/1860	27	309	N	
Fischer, John	14	Austria	N	?	Baltimore	00/00/1879				Y	04/05/1886
Fischer, John George	22	Bavaria	Y	Bremen	New York	07/18/1853	11/16/1857	16	25	N	
Fischer, John M.	38	Germany	N	Bremen	New Orleans	??/??/1855	?			Y	
Fischer, Josef	28	Austria	Y	Bremen	Baltimore	05/29/1884	07/21/1887			Y	
Fischer, Joseph	28	Prussia	Y	Bremen	Baltimore	11/01/1854	05/16/1859	17	412	N	
Fischer, Joseph	??	Germany	Y	?	?	?	11/01/1882			Y	
Fischer, Joseph	26	Germany	Y	Bremen	Baltimore	05/25/1879	10/11/1884			Y	
Fischer, Karl C.	27	Germany	Y	Havre	New York	10/23/1884	07/11/1885			Y	
Fischer, Lambert	38	Germany	Y	Bremen	New York	06/02/1880	04/02/1894			Y	
Fischer, Leonard	24	France	Y	Havre	New Orleans	12/01/1851	07/21/1855	11	414	N	
Fischer, Louis C.	36	Germany	N	Hamburg	New York	03/??/1869	?			Y	
Fischer, Ludwig	29	Germany	Y	Bremen	Baltimore	05/20/1892	08/20/1896			Y	
Fischer, Michael	52	Germany	Y	Bremen	New York	11/14/1879	10/26/1888	19	177	N	
Fischer, Michael	25	Germany	Y	Rotterdam	New York	08/06/1880	05/29/1882			Y	
Fischer, Michael	52	Germany	Y	Bremen	New York	11/14/1879	10/26/1888			Y	
Fischer, Philip	43	Germany	Y	Havre	New York	03/26/1867	11/07/1887	19	128	N	
Fischer, Sebastian	28	Saxe Weimar	Y	Hamburg	Buffalo	09/05/1847	01/04/1853	5	510	N	
Fischer, Thomas	??	Germany	Y	?	?	?	04/01/1879			Y	
Fischer, Wendelin	31	Bavaria	Y	Havre	New York	07/10/1854	02/06/1856	26	58	N	
Fischer, William	??	Germany	Y	?	?	?	10/29/1892			Y	
Fischer, William	??	Austria	N	?	?	05/15/1884				Y	10/07/1892
Fischer, William Imisson	26	England	Y	Liverpool	New York	09/26/1844	10/03/1848	22	408	N	
Fischer, Xaver	35	France	Y	Havre	New Orleans	01/18/1854	03/15/1856	26	203	N	
Fischeresser, Edward	35	Germany	Y	Havre	New York	??/??/1892	10/23/1896			Y	
Fischersser, Frank	32	Germany	Y	Havre	New York	06/17/1888	10/24/1896			Y	
Fischersser, Tony	25	Germany	Y	Havre	New York	03/17/1891	10/24/1896			Y	
Fischmann, Abraham	48	Russia	Y	Hamburg	New York	11/20/1889	12/30/1891			Y	
Fischmann, August	30	Prussia	Y	Bremen	New York	07/04/1855	10/06/1856	14	235	N	
Fischmann, Morris	24	Russia	Y	Hamburg	New York	03/12/1887	07/14/1891			Y	
Fischmann, Samuel	25	Russia	Y	Antwerp	New York	12/17/1887	07/08/1889			Y	
Fischvogt, John Henry	30	Hanover	Y	Bremen	New Orleans	11/25/1848	02/05/1849	23	32	N	
Fish, James	34	England	Y	Hull	New Orleans	06/12/1846	01/23/1849	1	500	N	
Fisher, Anthony H.	44	Holland	Y	Rotterdam	Boston	04/15/1866	04/14/1892			Y	
Fisher, Anton	27	Bavaria	Y	Bremen	New York	05/24/1852	10/10/1860	27	479	N	
Fisher, Charles Frederic	24	Saxe Meininge	Y	Hamburg	New York	07/14/1851	09/21/1855	13	91	N	
Fisher, George	??	Baden	Y	?	New Orleans	02/12/18??	11/10/1856	14	478	N	
Fisher, George	??	Bavaria	Y	?	?	?	09/14/1856			Y	
Fisher, Jacob	54	Bavaria	Y	Havre	New York	03/19/1849	10/16/1851	4	300	N	
Fisher, John (Fischer?)	26	Bavaria	Y	Havre	New York	08/20/1846	09/04/1848	22	295	N	

CITIZENSHIP RECORDS

APPLICANT	AGE	COUNTRY OF ORIGIN	DEC	DEPART PORT	ENTRY PORT	ARRIVE DATE	DEC DATE	VOL	PG.	FLD	NAT DATE
Fisher, Michael	30	Baden	Y	Havre	New York	06/16/1845	08/08/1851	4	101	N	
Fisher, Philipp	34	Hesse	Y	Bremen	Baltimore	07/04/1855	09/20/1858	16	189	N	
Fisher, Richard	30	England	Y	Liverpool	New York	12/06/1879	09/22/1885			Y	
Fisher, Thomas	33	England	Y	Liverpool	New York	12/??/1879	10/11/1890	19	286	N	
Fisher, Thomas	33	England	Y	Liverpool	New York	12/00/1879	10/11/1890			Y	
Fishmar, J.S.	34	Germany	Y	Hamburg	New York	06/??/1878	01/26/1884			Y	
Fisler, Louis	25	Hanover	Y	Bremen	New York	05/01/1852	10/02/1854	10	338	N	
Fisler, Louis	25	Hanover	Y	Bremen	New York	05/01/1852	10/02/1854	12	277	N	
Fisse, August	30	Germany	Y	Bremen	Baltimore	02/05/1881	12/26/1885			Y	
Fissel, Peter	25	Germany	Y	Hamburg	New York	07/20/1881	03/29/1884			Y	
Fisson, John	35	Prussia	Y	Bremen	New York	06/15/1845	08/15/1848	22	119	N	
Fiszler, John	27	Wuerttenberg	Y	Antwerp	New Orleans	12/20/1846	01/??/1850	23	526	N	
Fiszler, Severus	34	Wuerttenberg	Y	Antwerp	New Orleans	12/20/1846	01/26/1850	23	527	N	
Fitzenriter, Herman	28	Prussia	Y	Bremen	New York	02/27/1866	03/29/1867			Y	
Fitzer, E.A.	45	Germany	Y	Bremen	Baltimore	03/24/1879	07/07/1883			Y	
Fitzetamm, Heinrich	26	Mecklenburg S	Y	Bremen	New York	12/29/1859	01/04/1860	27	30	N	
Fitzgerald, Dennis	33	Ireland	Y	Canada	Buffalo	06/05/1848	03/25/1850	2	265	N	
Fitzgerald, Francis	32	Ireland	Y	London	New York	02/22/1850	03/20/1850	2	224	N	
Fitzgerald, James	25	Ireland	Y	Liverpool	Philadelphia	04/15/1848	04/02/1856	26	416	N	
Fitzgerald, James	50	Ireland	Y	Ireland	Cincinnati	05/25/1864	09/12/1864	28	398	N	
Fitzgerald, John	24	Ireland	Y	Liverpool	New York	??/15/1838	10/09/1848	1	77	N	
Fitzgerald, John	28	Ireland	Y	New Ross	Buffalo	08/05/1849	10/06/1851	4	202	N	
Fitzgerald, Oliver	27	Ireland	Y	Liverpool	New York	09/15/1851	03/30/1858	16	460	N	
Fitzgerald, Patrick	28	Ireland	Y	Cork	Boston	07/19/1848	11/01/1852	5	166	N	
Fitzgerald, Patrick	28	Ireland	Y	Cork	Boston	07/19/1848	11/01/1852	6	292	N	
Fitzgerald, Richard	39	Ireland	N	Liembick	Quebec	05/??/1862	?			Y	
Fitzgerald, Thomas	24	Ireland	Y	Limerick	Burlington	07/02/1847	03/09/1852	24	277	N	
Fitzgerald, William	26	Ireland	Y	Liverpool	New Orleans	04/19/1848	02/17/1849	23	145	N	
Fitzgibbon, Maurice	26	Canada	Y	Toronto	Detroit	07/13/1859	09/05/1860	27	339	N	
Fitzgibbon, Thomas	30	Ireland	Y	Liverpool	New Orleans	12/19/1849	06/04/1852	25	184	N	
Fitzgibbon, William	30	Ireland	Y	Waterford	New York	11/10/1854	03/24/1860	27	136	N	
Fitzgibbons, John	22	Ireland	Y	Cork	New Orleans	01/13/1852	04/25/1853	8	114	N	
Fitzmorris, John	49	Ireland	Y	Queenstown	New York	05/??/1864	03/20/1889	19	226	N	
Fitzmorris, John	49	Ireland	Y	Queenstown	New York	05/??/1864	03/20/1889			Y	
Fitzpatrick, Dennis	51	Ireland	Y	Dublin	New York	11/??/1849	08/18/1855	11	456	N	
Fitzpatrick, James	23	Ireland	Y	Dublin	New Orleans	09/08/1847	10/04/1854	10	421	N	
Fitzpatrick, James	23	Ireland	Y	Dublin	New Orleans	09/08/1847	10/04/1843	12	360	N	
Fitzpatrick, James	26	Ireland	Y	Liverpool	New York	07/12/1857	01/03/1860	27	24	N	
Fitzpatrick, John	30	England	Y	?	New York	??/??/1873	10/11/1880			Y	
Fitzpatrick, Martin	27	Ireland	Y	Liverpool	New York	08/??/1847	05/22/1854	8	490	N	
Fitzpatrick, Martin	27	Ireland	Y	Liverpool	New York	08/??/1847	05/22/1854	9	364	N	
Fitzpatrick, Michael	60	Ireland	N	Liverpool	New York	11/??/1845	?			Y	
Fitzpatrick, Moses	22	Ireland	Y	Liverpool	New Orleans	05/06/1851	10/07/1854	6	13	N	
Fitzpatrick, Moses	22	Ireland	Y	Liverpool	New Orleans	05/06/1851	10/07/1854	11	14	N	
Fitzpatrick, Patrick	25	Ireland	Y	Liverpool	New Orleans	02/??/1849	04/21/1854	8	231	N	
Fitzpatrick, Patrick	25	Ireland	Y	Liverpool	New Orleans	02/??/1849	04/21/1854	9	102	N	
Fitzpatrick, Patrick B.	23	Ireland	Y	Kilrush	St. Johns N.	??/10/1849	02/05/1850	2	38	N	
Fitzpatrick, Thomas	27	Ireland	Y	Dublin	New Orleans	03/09/1849	02/24/1851	3	165	N	
Fitzpatrick, Thomas	22	Ireland	Y	Liverpool	New York	06/07/1852	05/22/1854	8	494	N	
Fitzpatrick, Thomas	22	Ireland	Y	Liverpool	New York	06/07/1852	05/22/1854	9	368	N	
Fitzpatrick, Thomas	30	Ireland	Y	Liverpool	New Orleans	02/25/1849	10/17/1857	15	440	N	
Fitzsimmons, Henry	26	Ireland	Y	Liverpool	New York	10/15/1851	09/23/1854	12	116	N	
Fitzsimmons, Henry	26	Ireland	Y	Liverpool	New York	10/15/1851	09/23/18??	10	177	N	
Fitzsimons, Peter	30	Ireland	Y	Liverpool	New York	02/20/1848	03/11/1851	3	248	N	
Flach, Hermann Robert	28	Germany	Y	Bremen	Baltimore	09/24/1884	04/02/1888			Y	
Flacke, August	35	Lippe Detmold	Y	Bremen	New York	10/02/1851	10/02/1856	14	169	N	
Flad, John	40	Heckingen	Y	Havre	New Orleans	03/12/1849	07/29/1851	4	61	N	
Fladdermann, Herman	59	Germany	N	Bremen	New Orleans	12/22/1850	?			Y	
Fladung, Ferdinand	57	Germany	N	Bremen	New York	02/29/1867	?			Y	

CITIZENSHIP RECORDS

APPLICANT	AGE	COUNTRY OF ORIGIN	DEC	DEPART PORT	ENTRY PORT	ARRIVE DATE	DEC DATE	VOL	PG.	FLD	NAT DATE
Flaharty, Thomas	17	Ireland	N	Dublin	New York	04/??/1868	?			Y	
Flaherty, James	43	Ireland	N	Queenstown	New York	05/??/1873	?			Y	
Flaherty, James	23	Ireland	Y	Canada	Boston	07/20/1847	02/16/1852	24	126	N	
Flaherty, Michael	26	Ireland	Y	Canada	Cleveland	06/16/1848	05/11/1852	25	5	N	
Flaherty, Patrick	27	Ireland	Y	Liverpool	Baltimore	05/10/1852	10/06/1856	14	196	N	
Flaig, Oscar	29	Germany	Y	Havre	New York	05/16/1881	01/16/1884			Y	
Flake, John	24	Hanover	Y	Hamburg	Buffalo	09/07/1859	08/27/1860	27	314	N	
Flake, William	38	Germany	N	Bremen	New York	05/??/1869	?			Y	
Flamm, Joseph	21	Germany	Y	Havre	New York	05/09/1881	03/25/1884			Y	
Flamm, Paul	21	Germany	Y	Havre	New York	11/23/1889	01/06/1892			Y	
Flanagan, Michael	70	Ireland	N	Sligo	Canada	06/??/1844	?			Y	
Flanagan, Michael	17	Ireland	N	?	New York	00/00/1876				Y	04/09/1886
Flanagan, Peter	27	Ireland	Y	Liverpool	New York	05/28/1843	11/22/1848	1	377	N	
Flanagan, Thomas	25	Ireland	Y	Liverpool	New York	05/05/1851	04/17/1854	8	152	N	
Flanagan, Thomas	25	Ireland	Y	Liverpool	New York	05/05/1851	04/17/1854	9	23	N	
Flanary, James	43	Ireland	N	Liverpool	New York	07/??/1861	?			Y	
Flannagan, Joseph	35	Ireland	Y	Canada	Ogdensburg	03/17/1835	01/??/1850	23	520	N	
Flannagan, Nicolas	27	Ireland	Y	Liverpool	New York	03/06/1849	02/18/1853	7	177	N	
Flannagin, Michael	40	Ireland	Y	Liverpool	New York	12/15/1847	01/??/1850	23	534	N	
Flannery, Denis	21	IReland	Y	Queenstwon	New York	05/14/1892	07/22/1892			Y	
Flannery, Lawrence	35	Ireland	Y	Liverpool	New York	01/??/1852	02/15/1858	16	307	N	
Flannery, M.	38	Ireland	Y	Queenstown	New York	04/00/1880	10/08/1884			Y	
Flannery, Michael	36	Ireland	Y	Liverpool	New York	08/??/1851	12/30/1857	16	286	N	
Flannery, Michael	22	Ireland	Y	Queenstown	New York	09/19/1881	10/27/1884			Y	
Flannery, Thomas	29	Ireland	Y	Liverpool	New York	01/12/1852	04/08/1858	16	507	N	
Flaspeher, Henry	24	Hanover	Y	Bremen	Galveston	01/01/1845	07/31/1851	4	64	N	
Flaspoehler, Gerhard H.	52	Hanover	Y	Bremen	New Orleans	05/19/1848	11/01/1852	5	173	N	
Flaspohler, Gerhard H.	52	Hanover	Y	Bremen	New Orleans	05/19/1848	11/01/1852	6	299	N	
Flaspoll, Barney	52	Hanover	Y	Bremen	New Orleans	12/29/1847	04/05/1852	24	365	N	
Flatt, Karl	35	Germany	Y	Bremen	New York	09/26/1872	06/12/1889			Y	
Flatt, Leopold	29	Germany	Y	Bremen	New York	11/30/1881	11/05/1888			Y	
Flatt, Wm.	31	Germany	Y	Bremen	New York	12/13/1881	10/18/1888			Y	
Flautz, Friedrich	25	Germany	Y	Bremen	New York	08/31/1886	09/20/1890			Y	
Fleck, Ernst Emil	31	Germany	Y	Hamburg	New York	10/15/1879	09/29/1887			Y	
Fleckenstein, Christ	??	Germany	Y	?	?	?	11/19/1884			Y	
Fleckenstein, Edward	24	Germany	Y	Bremen	Baltimore	11/16/1889	05/10/1892			Y	
Fledderjohn, Frederick	36	Prussia	Y	Bremen	New Orleans	12/25/1851	08/21/1855	11	474	N	
Fleddermann, Heinrich	27	Hanover	Y	Bremen	Baltimore	06/17/1856	07/27/1858	16	532	N	
Flege, Bernhard	22	Germany	Y	Rotterdam	New York	11/12/1881	11/01/1883			Y	
Flei, John H.	44	Prussia	Y	Bremen	New York	07/03/1842	09/30/1848	22	365	N	
Fleig, Anastasius	31	Baden	Y	Havre	New York	08/06/1849	09/27/1854	10	258	N	
Fleig, Anastasius	30	Baden	Y	Havre	New York	08/06/1849	09/27/1854	12	197	N	
Fleig, Benjamin	25	Baden	Y	Havre	New Orleans	05/16/1848	10/18/1851	4	331	N	
Fleischer, Emil	25	Prussia	Y	Hamburg	New York	06/20/1852	02/12/1856	26	77	N	
Fleischer, Ernst Robert	??	Germany	Y	?	?	?	10/29/1880			Y	
Fleischer, Jacob	22	Austria	Y	Hamburg	New York	01/13/1854	05/28/1856	14	264	N	
Fleischmann, Charles	21	Bavaria	Y	Havre	New York	07/01/1849	12/09/1852	5	404	N	
Fleischmann, Charles	56	Austria	N	Hamburg	New York	08/14/1867	?			Y	
Fleischmann, Christian	27	Wuerttenberg	Y	Bremen	New York	04/18/1849	03/11/1852	24	283	N	
Fleischmann, Frank	??	Austria	N	?	?	?		28	484	N	10/05/1878
Fleischmann, Martin	25	Germany	Y	Bremen	New York	09/30/1885	06/20/1888			Y	
Fleischmann, Maxamilian	40	Austria	N	Austria	New York	05/??/1866	?			Y	
Fleiss, Julius Albert	33	Germany	Y	Bremen	Baltimore	07/01/1886	03/21/1893			Y	
Fleitz, Heinrich	??	Germany	N	?	?	03/09/1884				Y	10/27/1892
Fleitz, Valentine	38	Baden	Y	Havre	New York	09/04/1853	03/24/1856	26	260	N	
Fleming, Bartley	28	Ireland	Y	Liverpool	New York	06/24/1844	12/28/1852	5	460	N	
Fleming, James	33	Ireland	Y	Liverpool	New York	04/27/1884	07/07/1890			Y	
Fleming, John	35	Ireland	Y	Queenstown	New York	05/03/1882	03/08/1894			Y	
Fleming, John	35	Ireland	Y	Canada	Burlington	06/26/1842	08/28/1848	22	259	N	

CITIZENSHIP RECORDS

APPLICANT	AGE	COUNTRY OF ORIGIN	DEC	DEPART PORT	ENTRY PORT	ARRIVE DATE	DEC DATE	VOL	PG.	FLD	NAT DATE
Fleming, Richard	23	Ireland	Y	Liverpool	New York	??/28/1848	12/26/1850	2	392	N	
Flemmer, August Herman	23	Saxony	Y	Bremen	Philadelphia	05/10/1848	02/19/1849	23	171	N	
Flemming, John	43	Ireland	Y	Queenstown	New York	08/28/1880	10/09/1902			Y	
Flemming, John	16	Ireland	N	?	New York	00/00/1863				Y	10/23/1886
Flemming, Michael	27	Ireland	Y	Queenstown	New York	05/16/1882	07/07/1887			Y	
Flerloge, Geor.	??	Germany	Y	?	?	?	03/20/1882			Y	
Flessner, William	26	Germany	Y	Bremen	Baltimore	07/26/1888	10/22/1891			Y	
Fletcher, Charles	23	Poland	Y	Liverpool	New York	05/24/1853	10/01/1856	14	85	N	
Fletcher, James	49	England	Y	London	New Orleans	06/28/1849	11/07/1857	15	540	N	
Fletcher, Louis	25	Russia	Y	Hamburg	New York	02/25/1890	02/28/1893			Y	
Fletcher, Thomas	52	England	N	London	Detroit	??/??/1858	?			Y	
Fletcher, William	??	England	Y	?	?	?	04/30/1894			Y	
Fletcher, William	24	England	Y	?	?	?	12/20/1890			Y	
Fletcher, William	51	England	Y	Liverpool	New York	05/25/1873	10/30/1891			Y	
Fletcher, William	??	England	Y	?	?	11/13/1884	11/19/1889			Y	
Fletemeyer, Frederick	24	Prussia	Y	Bremen	New Orleans	11/15/1849	06/14/1852	25	265	N	
Flick, Albert	30	Nassau	Y	Bremen	Baltimore	08/20/1857	11/15/1858	17	328	N	
Flick, Daniel	56	Germany	N	Havre	New Orleans	10/24/1852	?			Y	
Flick, Frederick	58	Germany	Y	Bremen	New York	05/20/1883	04/07/1891			Y	
Flick, Jacob	26	Germany	Y	Hamburg	New York	06/??/1880	02/29/1883			Y	
Flick, Jacob Frederick	45	Nassau	Y	Rotterdam	New York	06/16/1849	04/12/1852	24	445	N	
Flick, Mathias	24	Bavaria	Y	Havre	New York	10/04/1849	03/31/1856	26	379	N	
Flickinger, Theodore	45	France	N	Havre	New York	10/30/1865	?			Y	
Fliehman, Jacob	25	Bavaria	Y	Havre	New Orleans	02/19/1847	10/20/1851	4	347	N	
Flierl, Leonhard	28	Bavaria	Y	Bremen	Buffalo	08/??/1847	03/26/1851	3	357	N	
Flinn, Edward	23	Ireland	Y	Youghal	New York	05/??/1847	10/27/1851	4	420	N	
Flinn, James	35	Ireland	Y	Liverpool	New Orleans	05/01/1852	11/02/1860	18	4	N	
Flinn, John	44	Ireland	Y	Liverpool	New York	06/10/1852	10/01/1856	14	105	N	
Flinn, John	31	Baden	Y	Antwerp	New York	07/21/1854	12/06/1858	17	379	N	
Flinn, John	35	Ireland	Y	Liverpool	New York	09/??/1862	10/08/1872	18	528	N	
Flinn, Lawrence	26	Ireland	Y	Liverpool	Philadelphia	04/10/1847	01/08/1850	23	478	N	
Flinn, Michael	??	Ireland	Y	Cork	New York	??/16/1848	03/27/1851	3	358	N	
Flinn, Michael	23	Ireland	Y	Liverpool	Philadelphia	04/10/1847	01/??/1850	23	465	N	
Flinn, Patrick	24	Ireland	Y	Liverpool	New Orleans	05/04/1846	01/17/1849	1	446	N	
Flinspach, William	28	Wuertemberg	Y	Havre	New York	04/18/1852	02/26/1856	26	131	N	
Fliszik, John	35	Germany	Y	Hamburg	Boston	04/09/1882	09/15/1894			Y	
Flizykowski, Edmund	28	Germany	Y	Bremen	Baltimore	03/28/1885	04/22/1891			Y	
Flock, Solomon	52	Bavaria	Y	Havre	New Orleans	04/26/1854	09/27/1856	14	408	N	
Flocken, Jacob F.	34	Bavaria	N	Bremen	New York	07/04/1865	?			Y	
Flocker, Conrad	26	Bavaria	Y	Havre	New Orleans	05/03/1855	02/07/1857	14	542	N	
Floeter, Heinrich	31	Germany	Y	Antwerp	Philadelphia	04/20/1893	10/21/1897			Y	
Floherty, James	32	Ireland	Y	Liverpool	New York	06/09/1853	08/26/1857	15	188	N	
Flohn, Daniel	30	Germany	Y	Rotterdam	New York	07/??/1879	09/29/1885			Y	
Flohr, Frederick	31	Prussia	Y	Rotterdam	Baltimore	07/02/1845	02/01/1849	23	8	N	
Flohr, Oscar	34	Germany	Y	Bremen	Baltimore	05/20/1888	12/30/1893			Y	
Flood, James	25	Ireland	Y	Liverpool	New York	10/22/1849	09/27/1854	10	270	N	
Flood, James	25	Ireland	Y	Liverpool	New York	10/22/1849	09/27/1854	12	209	N	
Flood, James	33	Ireland	Y	Liverpool	New York	08/??/1848	06/10/1852	25	233	N	
Flood, John	21	Ireland	Y	Limerick	Buffalo	06/05/1849	02/01/1853	7	101	N	
Flood, Michael	28	Ireland	Y	Liverpool	New York	08/08/1858	04/08/1861	18	136	N	
Flood, William	30	Ireland	Y	Galway	New York	06/14/1859	07/21/1860	27	230	N	
Flooger, Abraham	32	Holland	Y	Rotterdam	New York	01/06/1847	08/17/1848	22	199	N	
Florence, Philip	36	France	Y	Antwerp	New York	08/25/1847	12/15/1852	5	416	N	
Floro, George	??	Italy	Y	?	?	10/18/1892	10/12/1897			Y	
Flory, Frank	31	Germany	N	Hamburg	New York	08/30/1879	?			Y	
Floth, John	40	Austria	Y	Bremen	New Orleans	11/04/1853	05/22/1856	26	529	N	
Flottmann, Henry	24	Hanover	Y	Bremen	Baltimore	12/24/1860	07/31/1862	18	382	N	
Fluck, Bernhard	29	Germany	N	Rotterdam	New York	03/29/1883	?			Y	
Fluck, Michael	26	Germany	Y	Antwerp	Philadelphia	12/23/1884	04/21/1892			Y	

CITIZENSHIP RECORDS

APPLICANT	AGE	COUNTRY OF ORIGIN	DEC	DEPART PORT	ENTRY PORT	ARRIVE DATE	DEC DATE	VOL	PG.	FLD	NAT DATE
Fluckiger, Emil	32	Switzerland	Y	?	?	04/14/1893	10/22/1898			Y	
Flueck, Bernhard	23	Germany	Y	Rotterdam	New York	03/29/1883	09/10/1883			Y	
Flueck, Hubert	27	Germany	Y	Amsterdam	New York	03/18/1883	10/27/1886			Y	
Flueck, Theodore	39	Germany	Y	Bremen	New York	09/04/1887	09/05/1890			Y	
Flueh, Francis	27	Baden	Y	Havre	New Orleans	??/14/1845	11/13/1849	23	343	N	
Flugemann, Ludwig	28	Germany	Y	Bremen	New York	11/05/1881	02/12/1883			Y	
Fluhmann, Phillip	24	Bavaria	Y	Antwerp	New Orleans	03/??/1851	05/26/1854	9	428	N	
Fluhmann, Phillip	24	Bavaria	Y	Antwerp	New Orleans	03/??/1851	05/26/1854	10	11	N	
Fluhrer, Christian	48	Wurttemberg	Y	Antwerp	New Orleans	11/19/1850	10/18/1852	5	4	N	
Flurenberg, Joseph	30	Hanover	Y	Bremen	New Orleans	01/14/1845	10/16/1848	1	244	N	
Flynn, Daniel	23	Ireland	Y	Liverpool	New Orleans	05/12/1851	05/04/1854	8	361	N	
Flynn, Daniel	23	Ireland	Y	Liverpool	New Orleans	05/12/1851	05/04/1854	9	234	N	
Flynn, Dennis	30	Ireland	Y	Liverpool	New Orleans	04/27/1850	07/07/1860	27	209	N	
Flynn, Edward	22	Ireland	Y	Liverpool	New York	05/29/1853	03/26/1856	26	352	N	
Flynn, John	30	Ireland	Y	Liverpool	New York	07/08/1855	10/08/1860	27	440	N	
Flynn, Martin	39	Ireland	N	Liverpool	New York	07/22/1866	?			Y	
Flynn, Michael	23	Ireland	Y	Liverpool	New York	11/01/1854	04/??/1867			Y	
Flynn, Michael	56	Ireland	Y	Liverpool	New York	11/01/1857	04/??/1867	28	258	N	?
Flynn, Patrick	24	Ireland	Y	Queenstown	New York	11/11/1899	03/24/1903			Y	
Flynn, Thomas	37	Ireland	Y	Cork	Boston	06/??/1843	05/01/1854	8	325	N	
Flynn, Thomas	37	Ireland	Y	Cork	Boston	06/??/1843	05/01/1854	9	198	N	
Flynn, William	30	Ireland	Y	Liverpool	New Orleans	12/15/1848	09/26/1854	10	243	N	
Flynn, William	30	Ireland	Y	Liverpool	New Orleans	12/15/1848	09/26/1854	12	182	N	
Fobbe, Anton	29	Prussia	Y	Bremen	New Orleans	11/20/1852	03/25/1856	26	330	N	
Fobbe, Henry	21	Prussia	Y	Bremen	New Orleans	12/22/1853	03/25/1856	26	331	N	
Fobker, Herman	22	Hanover	Y	Bremen	Baltimore	11/01/1856	10/15/1860	27	493	N	
Fock, Frank	24	Prussia	Y	Bremen	New York	05/05/1849	10/14/1851	4	286	N	
Fock, Joseph	22	Prussia	Y	Rotterdam	New York	10/04/1848	02/02/1849	23	16	N	
Focke, Anton	42	Germany	N	?	?	??/??/1865	?			Y	
Focks, Bernard H.	32	Germany	Y	Rotterdam	New York	10/22/1885	05/14/1891			Y	
Focks, Herman John	31	Hanover	Y	Bremerhafen	New Orleans	12/??/1856	01/15/1861	18	60	N	
Foehr, Edward	21	Baden	Y	Havre	New York	05/15/1855	03/09/1858	16	388	N	
Foehr, Valentine	42	Baden	Y	Havre	New Orleans	05/??/1846	01/01/1853	5	492	N	
Foeller, Ludwig	26	Hanover	Y	Bremen	Baltimore	10/22/1851	10/07/1854	11	23	N	
Foelsch, John Frederick	39	Mecklenburg S	Y	Havre	New Orleans	04/20/1853	03/24/1856	26	284	N	
Foerster, John	41	Germany	Y	Hamburg	New York	10/26/1883	10/23/1891			Y	
Foertsch, Andreas	33	Germany	Y	Bremen	New York	11/09/1881	10/19/1888			Y	
Foertsch, John	39	Germany	Y	Bremen	Baltimore	04/15/1881	09/17/1888			Y	
Foester, Henry	26	Germany	Y	Hamburg	New York	07/28/1880	04/14/1882			Y	
Fogarty, John	28	Ireland	Y	Queenstown	New York	06/14/1890	04/20/1897			Y	
Fogarty, Patrick	30	Ireland	Y	Limerick	Oswego	??/20/1842	02/26/1850	2	130	N	
Fogarty, Thomas	28	Ireland	Y	Liverpool	New York	07/03/1857	10/10/1860	27	483	N	
Fogel, Henry	40	Hanover	Y	Bremen	Baltimore	11/??/1841	03/07/1853	7	309	N	
Fogel, Louis	28	Russia	Y	Hamburg	New York	10/15/1889	09/14/1892			Y	
Fogerty, Isaac	40	Ireland	Y	Dublin	New York	06/29/1846	05/01/1854	8	304	N	
Fogerty, Isaac	40	Ireland	Y	Dublin	New York	06/29/1846	05/01/1854	9	177	N	
Fohrmann, Charles	47	Germany	N	Hamburg	New York	08/??/1867	?			Y	
Fohy, Dennis	36	Ireland	Y	Cork	New Orleans	12/25/1849	08/09/1851	4	105	N	
Foith, Adolph	50	Germany	Y	Havre	New York	05/22/1888	05/05/1892			Y	
Foith, William	22	Germany	Y	Havre	New York	06/29/1889	05/05/1892			Y	
Foken, Gerhard	29	Germany	Y	Amsterdam	New York	11/12/1883	06/18/1889			Y	
Foley, Daniel	29	Ireland	Y	Cork	Boston	07/??/1843	12/18/1857	16	233	N	
Foley, Daniel	27	Ireland	Y	Cork	Buffalo	06/20/1848	11/29/1859	17	487	N	
Foley, George J.	??	Ireland	Y	Londonderry	New York	05/20/1888	10/27/1900			Y	
Foley, Michael	35	Ireland	Y	Waterford	New York	06/20/1851	11/25/1858	17	354	N	
Foley, Patrick	30	Ireland	Y	Liverpool	New York	09/20/1843	11/12/1855	13	214	N	
Foley, Patrick	28	Ireland	Y	Galway	New York	11/20/1848	03/18/1852	24	333	N	
Foley, William	50	Ireland	Y	Liverpool	New Orleans	01/01/1851	11/06/1852	5	243	N	
Foley, William	50	Ireland	Y	Liverpool	New Orleans	01/01/1851	11/06/1852	6	367	N	

CITIZENSHIP RECORDS

APPLICANT	AGE	COUNTRY OF ORIGIN	DEC	DEPART PORT	ENTRY PORT	ARRIVE DATE	DEC DATE	VOL	PG.	FLD	NAT DATE
Folgmann, Charles Ferdin	28	Prussia	Y	Hamburg	New York	07/09/1848	10/07/1848	22	471	N	
Folgmann, Frederick Gott	24	Prussia	Y	Hamburg	New York	01/05/1848	10/07/1848	22	474	N	
Folk, Gottfried	??	?	Y	?	?	06/00/1880	10/12/1883			Y	
Foller, Ludwig	26	Hanover	Y	Bremen	Baltimore	10/22/1851	10/07/1854	6	22	N	
Folley, Edward	22	Ireland	Y	Liverpool	New York	05/03/1845	08/13/1851	4	234	N	
Follmer, Anton	62	Germany	Y	?	Philadelphia	??/??/1891	03/16/1894			Y	
Follnar, Gerhard Frank	60	Germany	N	Bremen	New Orleans	12/??/1843	??/??/1845	28	81	N	10/??/1849
Foltz, Frederick	58	Bavaria	Y	Havre	New York	02/14/1851	10/04/1858	17	44	N	
Foltzer, Theodore	26	Germany	Y	Havre	New York	04/28/1890	04/18/1892			Y	
Fondenbaum, Clemens Augu	30	Prussia	Y	Bremen	New York	06/04/1847	02/12/1849	23	55	N	
Fontaine, Friedrich	34	Germany	Y	Bremen	New York	09/15/1880	10/28/1886			Y	
Foot, Clemens	31	Oldenburg	Y	Amsterdam	New York	06/01/1848	10/09/1854	6	168	N	
Foot, Clemens	31	Oldenburg	Y	Amsterdam	New York	06/01/1848	10/09/1854	11	171	N	
Foote, Henry	30	Hanover	Y	Liverpool	New York	09/17/1846	09/28/1854	10	287	N	
Foote, Henry	30	Hanover	Y	Liverpool	New York	09/17/1846	09/28/1854	12	226	N	
Fopmar, John	43	Holland	Y	Rotterdam	New York	02/23/1881	02/27/1884			Y	
Foppe, Gerhard	21	Germany	Y	Amsterdam	New York	09/25/1887	12/29/1887			Y	
Foppe, Gerhard John	21	Germany	Y	Rotterdam	New York	07/17/1878	08/13/1879			Y	
Foran, Denis	28	Ireland	Y	Liverpool	New York	06/10/1847	12/19/1851	4	530	N	
Foran, James	59	Ireland	N	Liverpool	New Orleans	10/??/1848	?			Y	
Forbes, James	44	Scotland	Y	Glasgow	New York	05/01/1849	04/22/1853	8	95	N	
Forbes, James	??	England	Y	?	?	?	05/03/1856			Y	
Forbes, Jeremiah	35	Ireland	Y	Queenstown	New York	06/02/1888	10/16/1889			Y	
Forbes, John	21	Ireland	Y	Queenstown	New York	04/23/1890	04/16/1892			Y	
Forch, Joseph	38	Spain	Y	Buenos Aires	New York	03/01/1883	07/30/1897			Y	
Ford, Bernard J.	26	Ireland	Y	Queenstown	New York	05/15/1893	11/06/1902			Y	
Ford, Charles W.	26	Ireland	Y	Queenstown	New York	04/22/1879	01/10/1884			Y	
Ford, James	28	Ireland	Y	Liverpool	Philadelphia	05/07/1849	09/10/1857	15	254	N	
Ford, John	30	Ireland	Y	Queenstown	New York	06/19/1883	10/09/1891	19	333	N	
Ford, Michael	30	Ireland	Y	Galway	Boston	07/10/1846	01/28/1850	2	538	N	
Ford, Patrick	27	Ireland	Y	Queenstown	Philadelphia	04/26/1887	10/22/1889	19	245	N	
Ford, Starr	32	Canada	Y	Halifax	Boston	10/29/1894	01/09/1899			Y	
Forde, Michael	27	Ireland	Y	Liverpool	New York	03/27/1848	08/??/1851	4	170	N	
Forhske, John Henry	23	Hanover	Y	Bremen	Baltimore	09/01/1845	09/12/1848	22	338	N	
Formes, Jacob	48	Germany	Y	Antwerp	New York	08/20/1886	11/06/1895			Y	
Formichella, Guiseppa	32	Italy	Y	Naples	New York	04/27/1883	08/04/1892			Y	
Forrest, Henry	29	England	Y	?	New York	??/??/1882	11/14/1889			Y	
Forrester, John	48	Ireland	N	Liverpool	New York	??/??/1861	?			Y	
Forst, Frederick	26	Prussia	Y	Bremen	New York	08/05/1856	01/31/1860	27	81	N	
Forstel, Adam	35	Germany	Y	Bremen	New York	11/31/1888	10/24/1895			Y	
Forster, August	23	Germany	Y	?	?	?	05/26/1890			Y	
Forster, John	46	Austria	Y	Bremen	New York	06/26/1867	03/21/1883			Y	
Forte, Cosmo	??	Italy	Y	?	?	03/29/1888	07/12/1895			Y	
Forte, John A.	26	Germany	Y	Bremen	Baltimore	06/27/1830	05/11/1836			Y	08/10/1842
Fortlage, Christ	24	Germany	Y	Bremen	New York	09/01/1885	04/09/1890	19	285	N	
Fortmann, Anton	25	Oldenburg	Y	Bremen	New Orleans	12/25/1849	10/06/1854	10	505	N	
Fortmann, Anton	25	Oldenburg	Y	Bremen	New Orleans	12/25/1849	10/06/1854	12	444	N	
Fortmann, August	30	Germany	Y	Bremen	New York	03/24/1879	09/05/1884			Y	
Fortmann, Herman	23	Germany	Y	Bremen	Baltimore	09/30/1882	10/15/1886			Y	
Fortmann, John Henry	37	Oldenburg	Y	Bremen	New Orleans	12/28/1854	09/17/1855	13	61	N	
Fortunato, Giorgio	27	Italy	Y	Naples	New York	05/20/1888	04/10/1894			Y	
Forwerg, Paul J.	??	Germany	Y	?	?	?	11/14/1881			Y	
Fosgroene, John Henry	25	Hanover	Y	Bremen	Baltimore	08/25/1856	09/29/1856	14	421	N	
Foss, Bernard	23	Prussia	Y	Bremen	New Orleans	11/30/1853	09/29/1856	14	28	N	
Foss, Joseph (Fusz?)	31	Bavaria	Y	Havre	New York	06/22/1847	08/14/1848	22	103	N	
Foster, Jacob	22	Bavaria	Y	Havre	New Orleans	12/12/1847	10/28/1851	4	428	N	
Foster, Lewis	??	Great Britain	Y	Nova Scotia	?	?	09/12/1888			Y	
Foster, Stephen	35	England	Y	Liverpool	New York	08/09/1849	08/02/1858	16	548	N	
Foster, Thomas	44	Ireland	Y	Liverpool	New York	06/15/1888	10/28/1896			Y	

CITIZENSHIP RECORDS

APPLICANT	AGE	COUNTRY OF ORIGIN	DEC	DEPART PORT	ENTRY PORT	ARRIVE DATE	DEC DATE	VOL	PG.	FLD	NAT DATE
Foth, Henry	23	Germany	Y	Bremen	New York	05/10/1880	02/15/1883			Y	
Fournelle, Jean Pierre M	32	Luxembourg	Y	Antwerp	New York	11/30/1884	12/24/1888			Y	
Fox, Barney	30	Ireland	Y	Liverpool	New Orleans	05/03/1847	02/28/1850	2	145	N	
Fox, Francis	36	Ireland	Y	Liverpool	New York	04/20/1848	02/28/1850	2	146	N	
Fox, Frank	27	France	Y	Havre	New Orleans	05/11/1837	10/06/1854	10	496	N	
Fox, George	45	Austria	N	Austria	New York	11/09/1867	?			Y	
Fox, James	24	England	Y	Liverpool	New York	07/14/1849	12/18/1855	13	326	N	
Fox, John	28	Bavaria	Y	Bremen	New York	10/01/1845	10/02/1848	1	26	N	
Fox, John	47	Ireland	Y	Liverpool	New York	07/05/1847	12/17/1852	5	422	N	
Fox, John	29	Ireland	Y	Liverpool	New York	05/15/1849	02/21/1853	7	201	N	
Fox, John	32	Ireland	N	Liverpool	New York	05/??/1871	?			Y	
Fox, Neil	33	Ireland	Y	Canada	Whitehall	06/18/1848	03/28/1853	7	419	N	
Fox, Thomas	42	Ireland	Y	Liverpool	New York	04/19/1855	08/28/1860	27	318	N	
Foy, John	26	Ireland	Y	Liverpool	New Orleans	10/29/1851	05/20/1854	8	482	N	
Foy, John	36	Ireland	Y	Liverpool	New Orleans	10/29/1851	05/20/1854	9	356	N	
Fraenzle, Damas	30	Baden	Y	Havre	New York	10/28/1854	10/07/1856	14	254	N	
Fraessle, George	25	Baden	Y	Havre	New Orleans	04/08/1855	12/26/1857	16	259	N	
Fraisanz, John	28	Hesse Darmsta	Y	London	New Orleans	01/01/1848	08/28/1848	22	256	N	
Framme, Herman Henry	39	Oldenburg	Y	Bremen	New Orleans	12/13/1845	03/04/1850	2	156	N	
Francis, Frank	42	Germany	N	Bremen	New York	04/01/1864	?			Y	
Francis, James	31	Ireland	Y	Liverpool	New York	02/20/1836	08/23/1848	22	242	N	
Francis, Peter	40	Ireland	Y	Galway	New York	04/24/1840	10/07/1856	14	255	N	
Francis, Richard	22	Ireland	Y	Queenstown	New York	05/27/1891	10/12/1891			Y	
Franck, Eugene	??	?	Y	?	?	?	05/20/1895			Y	
Frand, Lazarus	60	Bavaria	Y	Havre	New Orleans	07/02/1847	06/12/1852	25	248	N	
Franger, Michael	??	Bavaria	Y	Rotterdam	New Orleans	04/13/18??	10/11/1848	1	120	N	
Frank, Abraham	28	Prussia	Y	London	New York	10/09/1866	04/01/1872	18	481	N	
Frank, Abraham	27	Poland	Y	?	New York	??/??/1885	08/03/1891			Y	
Frank, Adolf	40	Germany	Y	Havre	New York	10/26/1880	08/13/1886			Y	
Frank, Andreas	22	Austria	Y	Bremen	Baltimore	06/21/1879	05/29/1882			Y	
Frank, Anton	27	Wuertemberg	Y	Bremen	New York	06/01/1853	03/31/1856	26	386	N	
Frank, August	29	Germany	Y	Hamburg	New York	04/01/1881	03/31/1887	19	117	N	
Frank, August	21	Germany	Y	Antwerp	Philadelphia	06/18/1889	11/05/1891			Y	
Frank, C. Friedrich	31	Germany	Y	Havre	New York	12/18/1879	05/31/1880			Y	
Frank, Clemens	24	Prussia	Y	Rotterdam	New York	04/15/1856	03/10/1858	16	389	N	
Frank, Daniel	38	Russia	Y	Hamburg	New York	12/24/1887	07/13/1896			Y	
Frank, Eugene	36	Germany	Y	Hamburg	New York	06/27/1891	12/14/1898			Y	
Frank, Franz	29	Wurttemberg	Y	Antwerp	New York	05/05/1849	10/07/1854	6	36	N	
Frank, Franz	32	Germany	Y	Havre	New York	08/09/1883	10/14/1887			Y	
Frank, Gustav	42	Germany	Y	Hamburg	Boston	11/27/1872	12/20/1888			Y	
Frank, Henry	??	Germany	Y	?	?	?	11/27/1883			Y	
Frank, Herman	30	Germany	Y	Havre	New York	05/13/1884	10/07/1884			Y	
Frank, Isaac Nathan	39	Prussia	Y	Rotterdam	New York	12/03/1844	09/16/1848	22	353	N	
Frank, John	27	Germany	Y	Bremen	New York	08/09/1893	05/14/1896			Y	
Frank, John Bernard	34	Prussia	Y	Bremen	New Orleans	01/01/1850	12/17/1852	5	424	N	
Frank, Joseph	??	Darmstadt	Y	Bremen	Baltimore	?	04/14/1855	11	242	N	
Frank, Joseph	22	Germany	Y	Bremen	Baltimore	05/16/1888	10/18/1892			Y	
Frank, Mathew	21	Bavaria	Y	Bremen	Baltimore	09/06/1849	09/13/1852	25	480	N	
Frank, Otto	28	Germany	Y	Hamburg	New York	10/21/1888	02/27/1893			Y	
Frank, Phillipp	27	Germany	Y	Antwerp	Philadelphia	03/06/1889	04/06/1893			Y	
Frank, Samuel Morris	25	Prussia	Y	Hamburg	New York	05/02/1852	03/11/1856	26	186	N	
Frank, Sebastian	44	Baden	Y	Havre	New Orleans	04/27/1854	09/15/1855	13	39	N	
Frank, Ulrich	40	Wurttemberg	Y	Liverpool	New York	05/06/1853	09/24/1855	13	132	N	
Frank, Zacharias	31	Bavaria	Y	Havre	New Orleans	11/20/1847	03/05/1850	2	159	N	
Franke, George	33	Germany	Y	Bremen	New York	10/14/1891	10/24/1896			Y	
Franke, Heinrich	31	Hanover	Y	Bremen	New York	08/20/1867	02/17/1873	18	555	N	
Franke, Herman	29	Germany	Y	Hamburg	New York	05/07/1881	01/28/1886			Y	
Franke, Leopold	23	Anhalt Bernbu	Y	Havre	New York	08/04/1849	01/26/1853	7	71	N	
Franke, Wilhelm Gustave	55	Germany	Y	Bremen	Baltimore	11/17/1870	08/30/1880			Y	

CITIZENSHIP RECORDS

APPLICANT	AGE	COUNTRY OF ORIGIN	DEC	DEPART PORT	ENTRY PORT	ARRIVE DATE	DEC DATE	VOL	PG.	FLD	NAT DATE
Frankel, Louis	60	Germany	N	Liverpool	New York	01/18/1862	?			Y	
Frankel, Marcus	25	Prussia	Y	Bremen	Baltimore	08/??/1845	10/28/1850	2	324	N	
Frankel, Samuel	??	Russia	Y	?	?	?	02/25/1884			Y	
Franken, Solomon	25	Germany	Y	Antwerp	New York	10/28/1885	06/03/1886			Y	
Franken, Theodore	44	Germany	Y	Antwerp	New York	05/09/1882	05/21/1890			Y	
Frankenbach, Valentine	33	Baden	Y	Bremen	New York	07/19/1847	10/04/1848	1	52	N	
Frankenberg, Isaak	26	Hanover	Y	Bremen	New York	11/24/1857	11/07/1860	18	28	N	
Frankenstein, Jacob	50	Germany	N	Havre	New York	12/??/1853	?			Y	
Frankenstein, Michael	67	Bavaria	Y	Havre	New Orleans	01/01/1855	10/30/1858	17	15	N	
Frankl, Mathias	24	Germany	Y	Hamburg	New York	08/23/1881	10/14/1882			Y	
Frankle, William	36	Germany	Y	?	?	?	02/09/1885			Y	
Franklin, Marcus	28	Russia	Y	Bremen	New York	10/28/1890	08/24/1896			Y	
Franklin, Michael H.	57	Germany	N	Hamburg	New York	01/??/1855	?			Y	
Franklin, Ralf	30	Russia	Y	Bremen	New York	07/20/1891	03/03/1894			Y	
Franndorf, Robert	34	Germany	Y	Hamburg	New York	05/23/1891	03/11/1895			Y	
Franz, August	29	Germany	Y	Rotterdam	New York	05/06/1884	10/14/1891			Y	
Franz, Charles	22	Wurttemberg	Y	Havre	New York	04/22/1854	12/21/1857	16	238	N	
Franz, Engelbert	16	Germany	N	?	New York	00/00/1882				Y	10/24/1887
Franz, Henry	41	Bavaria	Y	Bremen	New York	09/17/1854	10/27/1858	17	127	N	
Franz, Henry	??	Germany	N	?	?	11/02/1886				Y	11/07/1892
Franz, Joseph	61	Germany	Y	Havre	New York	08/23/1872	05/28/1897			Y	
Franz, Karl	31	Germany	Y	Rotterdam	New York	10/01/1893	03/12/1903			Y	
Franz, Karl	58	Germany	Y	Liverpool	New York	05/10/1887	11/02/1903			Y	
Franzel, Friedrich	47	Germany	N	Havre	New York	04/24/1869	?			Y	
Franzmeier, Frederick	56	Germany	N	Bremen	Baltimore	07/??/1852	?			Y	
Franzmeier, Friedrich	21	Prussia	Y	Bremen	New York	07/04/1849	06/07/1852	25	193	N	
Franzreb, Friedrich	30	Germany	Y	Antwerp	New York	09/18/1883	04/30/1891			Y	
Fraser, James Alexander	??	England	Y	?	?	?	04/03/1886			Y	
Fratz, Joseph	35	Bavaria	Y	Havre	New York	07/08/1852	11/28/1855	13	262	N	
Frauley, John	60	Ireland	Y	Liverpool	New Orleans	02/03/1853	11/09/1858	17	307	N	
Frawley, John	23	Ireland	Y	Liverpool	New York	12/??/1851	09/28/1854	10	291	N	
Frawley, John	23	Ireland	Y	Liverpool	New York	12/??/1851	09/28/1854	12	230	N	
Frawley, John	50	Ireland	Y	Liverpool	New York	12/??/1852	03/16/1858	16	414	N	
Frayne, John	26	Ireland	Y	Liverpool	New York	06/01/1846	10/03/1848	22	397	N	
Frazer, Phillip	24	Ireland	Y	Liverpool	New Orleans	02/18/1849	01/18/1853	7	40	N	
Frazer, Wesley	??	England	Y	?	?	?	04/13/1888			Y	
Frazer, William J.	36	Canada	Y	Windsor	Detroit	03/31/1897	03/31/1900			Y	
Frech, Jacob	30	Germany	Y	Rotterdam	New York	11/20/1881	11/08/1887			Y	
Frech, Nicholas	27	Germany	Y	?	New York	??/??/1881	10/08/1884			Y	
Freckert, Joseph	23	Baden	Y	Antwerp	New Orleans	07/15/1848	02/05/1851	3	100	N	
Frecking, Hermann Heinri	26	Germany	Y	?	?	?	06/08/1883			Y	
Frede, August	32	Hanover	Y	Bremen	New York	06/08/1852	10/06/1854	10	498	N	
Frede, August	32	Hanover	Y	Bremen	New York	06/08/1852	10/06/1854	12	437	N	
Fredelake, Frederick	24	Hanover	Y	Bremen	Baltimore	06/02/1848	11/05/1851	4	490	N	
Frederick, Frank	34	Bavaria	Y	Bremen	New York	08/07/1857	08/06/1860	27	249	N	
Frederick, Henry Christo	22	Bavaria	Y	Bremen	Baltimore	??/04/1852	04/30/1855	11	336	N	
Frederick, Simon	??	Germany	Y	?	?	07/10/1873	07/??/1880			Y	
Frederick, William	33	Prussia	Y	Hamburg	New York	12/08/1848	01/10/1850	23	492	N	
Freedlob, Louis	34	Russia	Y	Hamburg	New York	02/06/1880	10/15/1894			Y	
Freely, Andrew	24	Ireland	Y	Liverpool	New York	04/12/1849	10/06/1851	4	207	N	
Freeman, Francis	28	England	Y	London	Lewiston	06/15/1846	02/03/1851	3	90	N	
Freericks, Charles	52	Germany	Y	Bremen	New York	10/08/1881	10/30/1888			Y	
Freese, Charles	31	Prussia	Y	Hamburg	New York	??/03/1849	02/19/1850	2	104	N	
Freese, Joseph	31	Oldenburg	Y	Bremen	New Orleans	12/21/1848	04/04/1853	7	511	N	
Freese, Louis	39	Germany	N	Bremen	Baltimore	06/??/1864	?	28	154	N	10/05/1878
Freeze, Clemens	32	Oldenburg	Y	Bremen	New Orleans	11/02/1851	10/06/1853	10	493	N	
Freeze, Clemens	32	Oldenburg	Y	Bremen	New Orleans	11/02/1851	10/06/1854	12	432	N	
Frehse, John	64	Germany	N	Hamburg	New York	07/??/1865	?			Y	
Frei, Charles	42	Switzerland	Y	Havre	New York	07/27/1886	10/26/1899			Y	

CITIZENSHIP RECORDS

APPLICANT	AGE	COUNTRY OF ORIGIN	DEC	DEPART PORT	ENTRY PORT	ARRIVE DATE	DEC DATE	VOL	PG.	FLD	NAT DATE
Frei, Franz Xavier	40	Germany	Y	Bremen	Baltimore	08/22/1892	10/05/1898			Y	
Frei, John	48	Germany	Y	Antwerp	New York	11/??/1868	10/05/1880			Y	
Freiberger, George	40	Germany	Y	Hamburg	New York	05/16/1882	02/24/1885			Y	
Freiberger, Peter	47	Germany	Y	Bremen	New York	06/26/1878	10/24/1892			Y	
Freidel, Jacob	39	Baden	Y	Bremen	Baltimore	08/12/1856	12/28/1860	18	31	N	
Freidman, Adolph	22	Russia	Y	Liverpool	New York	09/12/1851	04/19/1854	9	88	N	
Freidman, Jacob	??	Russia	Y	?	?	?	04/05/1889			Y	
Freidrichs, Wm.	31	Germany	Y	Bremen	New York	06/09/1892	04/21/1897			Y	
Freiheit, Andreas	33	Prussia	Y	Havre	New York	12/01/1855	07/05/1862	18	270	N	
Freihofer, Jacob	26	Switzerland	Y	Havre	New York	06/04/1848	05/25/1854	8	523	N	
Freihoffer, Jacob	26	Switzerland	Y	Havre	New York	06/04/1848	05/25/1854	9	397	N	
Freinz, George	54	Hesse Cassel	Y	Bremen	Baltimore	08/09/1853	12/28/1857	16	270	N	
Freise, George	??	Germany	Y	?	?	?	03/17/1884			Y	
Freisz, John	60	France	Y	Havre	New Orleans	?	10/09/1854	10	85	N	
Freitag, Andreas	54	Germany	Y	Bremen	New York	12/23/1894	03/16/1903			Y	
Freitag, Friedrich	42	Germany	Y	Bremen	New York	11/22/1883	01/18/1886			Y	
Freitag, Friedrich Wilhl	36	Germany	Y	Rotterdam	New York	11/15/1881	01/18/1886			Y	
Freitag, Henry Frederick	33	Wuerttenberg	Y	Antwerp	New Orleans	11/24/1849	03/06/1852	24	242	N	
Freitag, Lorenz	43	Bavaria	Y	Havre	New Orleans	05/27/1847	02/19/1849	23	211	N	
Frendergast, James	42	Ireland	Y	Liverpool	New Orleans	05/04/1847	01/24/1853	7	63	N	
Frensel, Wilhelm	26	Germany	Y	Rotterdam	New York	04/16/1888	11/23/1895			Y	
Frenser, Wilhelm	26	Germany	Y	Rotterdam	New York	04/16/1888	11/23/1895			Y	
Frerichs, Enne	23	Hanover	Y	Bremen	New Orleans	09/04/1853	03/31/1856	26	393	N	
Frericks, Gerhard Henry	28	Prussia	Y	New Diep	Baltimore	10/21/1853	03/14/1856	26	200	N	
Freriks, John	25	Holland	Y	Rotterdam	New York	12/28/1846	02/19/1849	23	165	N	
Frerking, Henry	30	Germany	Y	Bremen	New York	06/01/1872	10/08/1880			Y	
Frers, Frederick Henry	30	Hanover	Y	Bremen	New Orleans	11/02/1853	02/06/1856	26	52	N	
Frers, William	22	Hanover	Y	Bremen	Baltimore	11/01/1854	12/26/1857	16	263	N	
Frese, Ben	25	Germany	Y	Rotterdam	New York	09/07/1891	10/10/1896			Y	
Frese, Heinrich	60	Germany	Y	Bremen	New York	04/02/1852	11/02/1895			Y	
Frese, Henry	22	Oldenburg	Y	Bremen	New Orleans	10/01/1852	07/13/1855	11	381	N	
Frese, Henry	29	Prussia	Y	Bremen	New Orleans	02/19/1854	10/11/1860	27	486	N	
Frese, Johann Diedr	22	Germany	Y	Rotterdam	New York	05/25/1891	11/13/1891			Y	
Freshman, Edward N.	25	Hungary-Austr	Y	Hamilton	Detroit	09/??/1867	10/08/1872	18	529	N	
Freshman, Julius	34	Hungary	Y	?	?	??/??/1875	10/11/1880			Y	
Freudenberg, August	25	Germany	Y	Bremen	Baltimore	04/28/1885	10/26/1892	19	384	N	
Freudenberg, August	25	Germany	Y	Bremen	Baltimore	04/28/1885	10/26/1892			Y	
Freudenberg, Clemens	28	Germany	Y	Bremen	Baltimore	08/10/1872	02/15/1882			Y	
Freudenberg, Henry	20	Germany	Y	Bremen	Baltimore	11/12/1881	02/25/1882			Y	
Freudiger, John	34	Switzerland	Y	Havre	New York	03/21/1882	06/23/1885			Y	
Freund, Adolf	32	Germany	Y	Bremen	Baltimore	07/12/1888	07/05/1890			Y	
Freund, Christian	35	Bavaria	Y	Havre	New Orleans	02/20/1851	09/27/1856	14	416	N	
Freund, Frank (Friend?)	25	Baden	Y	Antwerp	New York	07/04/1849	05/08/1852	24	416	N	
Freund, George C.	34	Germany	Y	Hamburg	New York	10/23/1882	04/08/1887			Y	
Freund, Herman	46	Prussia	Y	Hamburg	New York	??/31/1848	08/07/1851	4	94	N	
Freund, Valentine	25	Hesse Cassel	Y	Bremen	New York	11/25/1856	05/20/1861	18	171	N	
Frewer, John Anton	32	Prussia	Y	Bremen	Baltimore	08/08/1849	06/10/1852	25	305	N	
Frey, Baldus	30	Baden	Y	Havre	New York	08/20/1852	10/09/1854	6	164	N	
Frey, Baldus	30	Baden	Y	Havre	New York	06/20/1852	10/09/1854	11	167	N	
Frey, Christ	25	Germany	Y	Antwerp	New York	03/26/1881	07/06/1886			Y	
Frey, Erhardt	30	Germany	Y	Havre	New York	10/18/1882	05/27/1885			Y	
Frey, Eugene	35	Germany	Y	Antwerp	New York	07/08/1884	10/11/1895			Y	
Frey, Fridolin	53	Germany	Y	Havre	New York	06/04/1881	06/03/1887			Y	
Frey, Henry	27	Switzerland	Y	Havre	New York	03/09/1881	12/24/1884			Y	
Frey, Herman	40	Germany	Y	Boulogna	New York	03/03/1890	03/08/1895			Y	
Frey, Jacob	23	Germany	Y	Antwerp	New York	03/09/1881	07/19/1884			Y	
Frey, John	36	Switzerland	Y	Havre	New York	01/05/1848	11/20/1852	5	317	N	
Frey, John	32	Germany	Y	Bremen	New York	05/26/1871	05/05/1885			Y	
Frey, John Robert	29	Switzerland	Y	Havre	New Orleans	12/23/1849	04/17/1854	8	157	N	

CITIZENSHIP RECORDS

APPLICANT	AGE	COUNTRY OF ORIGIN	DEC	DEPART PORT	ENTRY PORT	ARRIVE DATE	DEC DATE	VOL	PG.	FLD	NAT DATE
Frey, John Rubert	29	Switzerland	Y	Havre	New Orleans	12/23/1849	04/17/1854	9	28	N	
Frey, Samuel	32	Switzerland	Y	Havre	New York	03/28/1884	09/30/1889			Y	
Frey, Sigmund	29	Austria	Y	Havre	New York	08/21/1878	06/17/1881			Y	
Freyberg, Julius	29	Bavaria	Y	Havre	New York	09/01/1847	04/02/1853	7	499	N	
Freyburger, Paul	23	Wuertemberg	Y	Havre	New York	10/04/1854	05/19/1856	26	498	N	
Freytag, Henry	30	Germany	Y	Antwerp	New York	04/23/1881	03/23/1886			Y	
Friatch, Segmund	24	Baden	Y	Havre	New York	09/17/1852	10/09/1854	6	194	N	
Fricha, Charles	38	Germany	Y	Bremen	Baltimore	11/??/1861	06/28/1873			Y	
Frick, Charles	36	Prussia	Y	Liverpool	Philadelphia	05/07/1852	12/22/1855	13	339	N	
Frick, Constantin	31	Baden	Y	Havre	New York	11/20/1854	10/07/1856	14	258	N	
Frick, Karl	23	Germany	Y	Glasgow	New York	05/16/1893	01/28/1895			Y	
Fricke, August	24	Hanover	Y	Bremen	Baltimore	08/08/1846	08/29/1848	22	272	N	
Fricke, Charles	22	Hanover	Y	Bremen	Baltimore	08/??/1846	02/04/1850	2	36	N	
Fricke, Francis	28	Prussia	Y	Bremen	New Orleans	05/12/1848	06/16/1851	3	385	N	
Fricke, Frederick	32	Prussia	Y	Bremen	New York	05/28/1849	03/04/1853	7	269	N	
Fricke, Henry	25	Prussia	Y	Bremen	Baltimore	11/29/1847	06/21/1851	3	435	N	
Fricker, Casper	34	Switzerland	Y	Havre	New Orleans	01/30/1845	02/14/1849	23	108	N	
Fricker, Daniel	??	Switzerland	Y	?	?	?	07/29/1884			Y	
Fricker, Lawrent	25	Germany	Y	Havre	New York	07/29/1889	02/09/1892			Y	
Frickers, John	23	Hanover	Y	Bremen	New Orleans	04/28/1846	01/23/1849	1	509	N	
Friday, Conrad	26	Bavaria	Y	Havre	New Orleans	07/23/1847	02/19/1849	23	175	N	
Friday, James Richie	??	England	N	?	?	08/00/1869				Y	10/27/1892
Frie, Barney	26	Oldenburg	Y	Bremen	New Orleans	04/21/1849	02/22/1853	7	213	N	
Frie, Franz	24	Prussia	Y	Bremen	New Orleans	12/28/1848	01/07/1853	5	532	N	
Friedel, Andreas	41	Germany	Y	Bremen	New York	05/18/1882	04/04/1890			Y	
Friedemann, Richard	34	Germany	Y	Bremen	Baltimore	04/20/1892	06/06/1892			Y	
Friederich, Franz P.	26	Germany	Y	Rotterdam	New York	01/06/1882	05/16/1885			Y	
Friederich, Leonard	32	Germany	Y	Bremen	New York	10/06/1882	04/23/1886			Y	
Friederich, Theodor	33	Germany	Y	Rotterdam	New York	04/20/1881	03/04/1884			Y	
Friedlander, Abraham	22	Bavaria	Y	Rotterdam	New York	09/22/1850	09/14/1852	25	504	N	
Friedler, Heinrich	32	Germany	Y	Bremen	New York	08/22/1889	09/10/1896			Y	
Friedman, Adolph	22	Russia	Y	Liverpool	New York	09/12/1851	04/19/1854	8	217	N	
Friedman, Anton	61	Germany	N	Havre	New York	05/05/1848	?			Y	
Friedman, Bernhardt	28	Russia	Y	Hamburg	New York	06/01/1891	12/26/1893			Y	
Friedman, Frank	??	Russia	Y	Hamburg	New York	11/27/1881	04/28/1891			Y	
Friedman, Heinrich	35	Hungary	Y	Antwerp	Philadelphia	10/06/1895	12/31/1900			Y	
Friedman, Jacob	38	Russia	Y	?	?	??/??/1887	10/15/1892			Y	
Friedman, Jacob	38	Austria	Y	Bremen	New York	05/31/1888	12/24/1891			Y	
Friedman, Jacob	38	Russia	N	Bremen	New York	04/??/1865	?			Y	
Friedman, Joseph	24	Baden	Y	Havre	New York	11/17/1853	07/10/1856	14	306	N	
Friedman, Julius	24	Poland	Y	?	?	05/??/1887	06/24/1891			Y	
Friedman, Markus	24	Hungary	Y	Bremen	New York	06/15/1888	04/23/1891			Y	
Friedman, Nathan	25	Russia	Y	Bremen	New York	12/24/1888	05/19/1894			Y	
Friedman, Samuel	25	Russia	Y	Hamburg	New York	12/28/1886	04/22/1892			Y	
Friedmann, A.	42	Austria	Y	Bremen	Baltimore	05/24/1877	09/30/1888			Y	
Friedmann, Aron	??	Germany	Y	?	?	?	09/06/1888			Y	
Friedmann, Edw. W.	26	Germany	Y	?	New York	??/??/1888	11/14/1890			Y	
Friedmann, Fajwel	42	Russia	Y	Bremen	Baltimore	09/12/1886	07/12/1889			Y	
Friedmann, William	??	Bavaria	Y	Hamburg	New York	06/01/1847	10/07/1848	22	466	N	
Friedrich, Adam	??	Bavaria	Y	Bremen	Baltimore	07/06/1848	12/03/1850	2	333	N	
Friedrich, Albert	38	Germany	N	Bremen	New York	03/??/1871	?			Y	
Friedrich, Anton	28	Prussia	Y	Antwerp	New York	07/03/1851	08/15/1851	4	151	N	
Friedrich, Christ	32	Germany	Y	Bremen	New York	05/24/1892	05/19/1898			Y	
Friedrich, Conrad	26	Hesse Darmsta	Y	Antwerp	New Orleans	05/05/1849	10/17/1851	4	320	N	
Friedrich, Gustav	30	Germany	Y	Bremen	New York	05/14/1888	03/31/1893			Y	
Friedrich, Johann	28	Germany	Y	Hamburg	New York	08/08/1891	02/10/1893			Y	
Friedrich, John	34	Switzerland	Y	Havre	New York	04/10/1893	05/02/1893			Y	
Friedrich, Melchior	41	Germany	Y	Hamburg	New York	12/21/1880	08/15/1889			Y	
Friedrick, William	29	Germany	Y	Bremen	Baltimore	05/26/1882	10/27/1885			Y	

CITIZENSHIP RECORDS

APPLICANT	AGE	COUNTRY OF ORIGIN	DEC	DEPART PORT	ENTRY PORT	ARRIVE DATE	DEC DATE	VOL	PG.	FLD	NAT DATE
Friedriechsdorf, August	27	Germany	Y	?	?	?	08/02/1888			Y	
Friel, Patrick	30	Ireland	Y	Londonderry	Philadelphia	06/22/1848	02/??/1850	2	90	N	
Friend, John	3	Germany	N	?	New York	00/00/1851				Y	10/30/1886
Frierdick, Ignatz	70	Germany	N	Havre	New Orleans	01/18/1850	?			Y	
Friericks, Charles	52	Germany	Y	Bremen	New York	10/08/1884	10/30/1888	19	203	N	
Fries, Ferdinand	23	Baden	Y	Havre	New Orleans	03/??/1853	09/18/1855	13	68	N	
Fries, George	34	Bavaria	Y	Havre	New York	06/24/1845	10/03/1848	22	395	N	
Fries, John	24	Bavaria	Y	Havre	New Orleans	01/20/1854	03/11/1856	26	188	N	
Fries, Michael	27	Bavaria	Y	Havre	New York	06/24/1845	10/03/1848	22	399	N	
Fries, Michael A.	69	Germany	N	Havre	Boston	08/??/1837	?			Y	
Fries, Nicholas	27	France	Y	Havre	New Orleans	01/08/1848	10/09/1854	11	93	N	
Fries, Nicolas	27	France	Y	Havre	New Orleans	01/07/1848	10/09/1854	6	88	N	
Friess, John	23	France	Y	Havre	New York	11/29/1845	04/29/1850	3	21	N	
Friesz, John	60	France	Y	Havre	New Orleans	01/07/1848	10/09/1854	6	82	N	
Friling, John Henry	27	Oldenburg	Y	Bremen	New Orleans	12/20/1845	02/13/1849	23	79	N	
Frillmann, Charles Henry	41	Prussia	Y	Bremen	New York	12/14/1853	11/09/1855	13	201	N	
Frimming, Henry	29	Germany	Y	Rotterdam	New York	11/07/1882	10/22/1889			Y	
Frimming, Herman	24	Germany	Y	Amsterdam	New York	11/17/1886	10/22/1889			Y	
Frisbee, Mark	25	Ireland	Y	Liverpool	New Orleans	03/??/1850	03/28/1853	7	450	N	
Frisch, Christian	??	Germany	Y	?	?	?	09/19/1884			Y	
Frisch, Hieronymus	29	Bavaria	Y	Havre	New Orleans	12/??/1852	09/24/1855	13	133	N	
Frisch, John Joseph	35	Bavaria	Y	Havre	New York	04/08/1852	09/30/1856	14	66	N	
Frisch, Sol	33	Russia	Y	Hamburg	New York	09/04/1883	05/16/1893			Y	
Frishknecht, Rudolf	34	Switzerland	Y	Havre	New York	04/06/1858	09/14/1860	27	374	N	
Fritch, Rudolph	40	Germany	N	Bremen	New York	12/03/1871	?			Y	
Fritsch, Eugene	22	Germany	Y	Havre	New York	09/29/1887	04/17/1890			Y	
Fritsch, Francis	27	France	Y	Havre	New Orleans	05/19/1849	03/25/1853	7	396	N	
Fritsch, Martin	??	Prussia	Y	Bremerhafen	Baltimore	07/27/1859	12/31/1860	18	33	N	
Fritsch, Nicholas	28	Baden	Y	Havre	New Orleans	11/29/1849	04/12/1852	24	458	N	
Fritsch, Sigmund	24	Baden	Y	Havre	New York	09/17/1852	10/09/1854	11	197	N	
Fritsch, William	??	Germany	Y	?	?	?	06/01/1898			Y	
Fritsh, Bernhard	??	Baden	Y	Havre	New Orleans	11/24/1845	10/07/1848	22	469	N	
Fritz, Adam	21	Germany	Y	Antwerp	New York	10/20/1893	10/28/1896			Y	
Fritz, Andrew	35	Germany	Y	Antwerp	New York	06/24/1888	12/03/1896			Y	
Fritz, Anton	34	Austria	Y	Hamburg	New York	05/04/1881	08/31/1881			Y	
Fritz, Charles	25	Germany	Y	Havre	New York	07/17/1887	10/28/1890			Y	
Fritz, Fred	29	Germany	Y	Antwerp	New York	11/05/1885	02/21/1887			Y	
Fritz, Frederick	23	Baden	Y	Havre	New York	05/01/1851	05/25/1854	8	517	N	
Fritz, Frederick	23	Baden	Y	Havre	New York	05/01/1851	05/25/1854	9	391	N	
Fritz, Friedrich	57	Germany	N	Havre	New York	05/01/1852	?			Y	
Fritz, George	25	Germany	Y	Havre	New York	09/19/1883	11/09/1886			Y	
Fritz, Herman	26	Germany	Y	Stettin	New York	09/24/1892	08/22/1894			Y	
Fritz, Joe	26	Germany	Y	Havre	New York	04/27/1891	03/27/1894			Y	
Fritz, Joseph	37	Austria	Y	Hamburg	New York	05/05/1881	08/11/1888			Y	
Fritz, Mathias	22	Baden	Y	Havre	New Orleans	01/13/1854	12/24/1855	13	342	N	
Fritzsch, Bernhard	34	Germany	Y	Bremen	New York	08/12/1889	10/16/1896			Y	
Frizzle, Martin	21	Ireland	Y	Liverpool	New York	05/01/1860	06/25/1860	27	1	N	
Frobitten, Heinrich	30	Germany	Y	Bremen	New York	05/23/1881	11/19/1885			Y	
Frodermann, August	30	Germany	Y	Bremen	Baltimore	04/??/1885	06/25/1889			Y	
Froehle, Herman Henry	34	Oldenburg	Y	Bremen	New Orleans	05/15/1849	04/25/1853	8	121	N	
Froehlich, Charles	26	Bavaria	Y	Bremen	Baltimore	08/27/1846	11/20/1852	5	320	N	
Froehlich, Gregor	22	Germany	Y	Bremen	Baltimore	04/10/1880	09/08/1881			Y	
Froehlich, Jacob	27	Hesse Cassel	Y	Bremen	Baltimore	05/17/1854	03/24/1856	26	255	N	
Froehlich, Theodore	42	Switzerland	Y	Havre	New York	01/29/1879	10/16/1793			Y	
Froehlich, Wilhelm	??	Germany	Y	Bremen	New York	04/21/1892	02/06/1897			Y	
Froelich, Alexander Loui	28	Prussia	Y	Hamburg	New York	10/17/1854	12/31/1855	13	409	N	
Froelking, Frederick Aug	24	Hanover	Y	Bremen	New York	06/28/1848	09/13/1852	25	471	N	
Froesch, John	59	Germany	Y	Havre	New York	04/30/1885	10/24/1896			Y	
Froeschle, Jacob Frederi	36	Wurttemberg	Y	Liverpool	New York	05/01/1852	12/30/1852	5	477	N	

CITIZENSHIP RECORDS

APPLICANT	AGE	COUNTRY OF ORIGIN	DEC	DEPART PORT	ENTRY PORT	ARRIVE DATE	DEC DATE	VOL	PG.	FLD	NAT DATE
Froger, Victor	47	France	Y	Havre	New York	05/17/1876	10/29/1886	19	98	N	
Froh, Henry	27	Germany	Y	Bremen	Wilmington	08/15/1883	02/28/1888			Y	
Frolich, William	41	Hanover	Y	Bremen	Baltimore	06/02/1848	11/13/1848	1	249	N	
From, Conrad	28	Wurttemberg	Y	Havre	New York	07/22/1852	11/22/1852	5	323	N	
Fromholt, Martin	30	Baden	Y	Havre	New Orleans	07/01/1846	08/15/1848	22	165	N	
Fromme, Bernard	32	Prussia	Y	Bremen	New York	11/03/1857	10/25/1858	17	103	N	
Frommeyer, Herman Henry	31	Hanover	Y	Bremen	Baltimore	10/04/1845	10/16/1848	1	245	N	
Frommeyer, Joseph M.	57	Germany	N	Bremen	Baltimore	11/??/1853	?			Y	
Frost, William	32	Mecklenburg S	Y	Hamburg	New York	09/12/1853	05/18/1854	8	467	N	
Frost, William	32	Mecklenburg S	Y	Hamburg	New York	09/12/1853	05/18/1854	9	341	N	
Frotscher, Herman	27	Germany	Y	Bremen	New York	05/18/1882	05/17/1884			Y	
Frotz, Israel S.	??	Austria	Y	?	?	?	12/29/1894			Y	
Froug, August	22	Russia	Y	Hamburg	New York	09/??/1885	11/08/1886			Y	
Froy, Denis	30	Ireland	Y	Liverpool	New Orleans	05/09/1848	11/24/1852	5	342	N	
Frtisch, Wendelin	27	Germany	Y	Havre	New York	03/10/1889	05/19/1892			Y	
Frucht, Valentine	32	Baden	Y	Havre	New York	12/31/1847	04/10/1852	24	433	N	
Fruechtemeyer, George	40	Germany	Y	Bremen	Baltimore	08/04/1892	12/27/1894			Y	
Fruechtemeyer, William	31	Germany	Y	Hamburg	New York	09/23/1880	02/13/1892			Y	
Frueh, Ferdinand	39	Germany	N	Hamburg	New York	07/??/1873	?			Y	
Frueh, John	24	Baden	Y	Havre	New York	03/23/1856	10/29/1858	17	171	N	
Fruehe, Norbert	22	Germany	Y	Antwerp	New York	03/04/1884	09/22/1887			Y	
Fruehwein, Joseph	28	Germany	Y	Bremen	New York	12/22/1884	10/12/1887			Y	
Fry, Henry	45	England	Y	London	New Orleans	11/21/1849	05/26/1852	25	112	N	
Fry, William Henry	22	England	Y	London	New Orleans	11/21/1849	05/26/1852	25	114	N	
Frye, Anton	??	Germany	Y	?	?	?	04/06/1886			Y	
Frye, John B.	30	Germany	Y	Bremen	Baltimore	08/11/1882	05/09/1887			Y	
Frye, John Henry	34	Oldenburg	Y	Bremen	Baltimore	06/12/1848	11/17/1848	1	309	N	
Fuchs, Bruno	32	Germany	Y	Bremen	Baltimore	06/10/1896	10/19/1903			Y	
Fuchs, Charles	48	Baden	Y	Havre	New York	06/20/1852	04/25/1854	8	264	N	
Fuchs, Charles	48	Baden	Y	Havre	New York	06/20/1852	04/25/1854	9	135	N	
Fuchs, Edward	31	Germany	Y	Antwerp	New York	12/04/1873	06/21/1880			Y	
Fuchs, Emil	28	Germany	Y	Bremen	New York	10/17/1881	10/13/1884			Y	
Fuchs, Frederick	43	Prussia	Y	Havre	New York	06/12/1842	09/11/1848	22	320	N	
Fuchs, Gerhard	54	Germany	N	Bremen	New York	07/17/1857	?			Y	
Fuchs, Gottlieb	30	Wurttemberg	Y	Havre	New York	04/22/1854	04/02/1858	16	479	N	
Fuchs, Henry	41	Germany	N	Germany	New York	09/04/1865	?			Y	
Fuchs, Ignatz	??	Germany	Y	?	?	?	11/13/1882			Y	
Fuchs, John	33	Nassau	Y	Havre	New Orleans	05/17/1849	03/29/1856	26	374	N	
Fuchs, Joseph	22	Bavaria	Y	Havre	New York	06/12/1852	09/28/1854	10	312	N	
Fuchs, Joseph	22	Bavaria	Y	Havre	New York	06/12/1852	09/29/1854	12	251	N	
Fuchs, Ludwig	31	Germany	Y	Antwerp	New York	11/01/1888	09/08/1892			Y	
Fuchs, Max	30	Austria	Y	Antwerp	New York	11/01/1892	06/25/1896			Y	
Fuchs, Michael	24	Switzerland	Y	Havre	New Orleans	03/10/1848	03/17/1856	26	219	N	
Fuchs, Phillip	24	Prussia	Y	Antwerp	New York	12/04/1846	09/11/1848	22	322	N	
Fuchs, Phillip	48	Hesse Homberg	Y	Antwerp	New Orleans	02/15/184?	02/07/1852	24	67	N	
Fuchs, Simon	23	Baden	Y	Antwerp	New York	10/05/1857	06/30/1862	18	365	N	
Fuchs, Valentine	31	Bavaria	Y	Bremen	New Orleans	12/23/1848	02/09/1849	23	126	N	
Fuchs, William Hugo	??	Germany	Y	?	?	?	04/18/1887			Y	
Fuchsberger, Robert	50	Austria	Y	Bremen	Indianola TX	12/16/1852	09/10/1860	27	351	N	
Fuchshuber, Carl	22	Germany	Y	Havre	New York	07/23/1883	10/01/1883			Y	
Fuegli, Hans Casper	41	Switzerland	Y	Hamburg	New York	05/21/1850	11/20/1852	5	318	N	
Fueller, Philip Joseph	23	Bavaria	Y	Liverpool	New York	06/09/1854	09/18/1857	15	284	N	
Fuellhardt, Christian	41	Bavaria	Y	Havre	New York	11/19/1849	04/08/1856	26	467	N	
Fuerchtenicht, Ernst	37	Brunswick	Y	Bremen	New Orleans	11/11/1849	04/24/1854	8	251	N	
Fuergens, John Frederick	28	Hanover	Y	Bremen	New York	08/09/1845	08/21/1848	22	212	N	
Fuersattle, John Simon	??	Bavaria	Y	Bremen	New York	06/10/1848	03/24/1851	3	310	N	
Fuerst, Ferdinand	51	Bavaria	Y	Hamburg	New York	10/01/1844	11/20/1848	1	330	N	
Fuerste, Herman Henry	23	Hanover	Y	Bremen	Baltimore	11/05/1854	02/22/1858	16	331	N	
Fuerste, John Henry	27	Hanover	Y	Bremen	Baltimore	05/01/1850	05/01/1854	8	297	N	

CITIZENSHIP RECORDS

APPLICANT	AGE	COUNTRY OF ORIGIN	DEC	DEPART PORT	ENTRY PORT	ARRIVE DATE	DEC DATE	VOL	PG.	FLD	NAT DATE
Fuerster, John George	33	Bavaria	Y	Hamburg	New York	11/01/1854	08/20/1858	16	547	N	
Fuesser, John	54	Germany	Y	Havre	New York	05/07/1865	12/18/1888			Y	
Fugazzi, J. B.	1	Italy	N	?	New Orleans	00/00/1864				Y	10/20/1886
Fuger, Henry	??	Bavaria	Y	Bremen	Baltimore	09/18/18??	10/12/1848	1	158	N	
Fuhr, John Anton	27	Nassau	Y	Antwerp	New York	05/17/1850	01/03/1853	5	497	N	
Fuhrmann, Jacob	52	Germany	N	Hamburg	Boston	07/17/1874	?			Y	
Fuhrmann, Michael	40	Bavaria	Y	Antwerp	New York	03/30/1851	05/10/1854	8	418	N	
Fuhrmann, Michael	40	Bavaria	Y	Antwerp	New York	03/30/1851	05/10/1854	9	291	N	
Fuhsner, John	24	Bavaria	Y	Antwerp	New York	08/05/1848	02/15/1849	23	111	N	
Fuke, Gerhard F.	16	Germany	N	?	New York	00/00/1881				Y	10/23/1886
Fuldner, Andreas	24	Bavaria	Y	?	New York	09/27/1846	10/02/1848	1	2	N	
Full, Kaspar	36	Germany	Y	Bremen	New York	01/25/1888	06/18/1896			Y	
Fuller, James	56	Ireland	N	Queenstown	New York	12/19/1862	?			Y	
Fullriede, Louis	66	Germany	N	Bremen	Baltimore	05/??/1845	??/??/1846	28	112	N	??/??/1850
Fuls, Otto	44	Germany	N	Hamburg	New York	05/15/1866	?			Y	
Fummers, Bernard	21	Prussia	Y	Bremen	Baltimore	11/01/1854	09/14/1855	13	28	N	
Funck, Adam	38	Germany	Y	Antwerp	New York	11/22/1889	10/25/1895			Y	
Funk, Frank	29	Wurttemberg	Y	Antwerp	New York	05/05/1849	10/07/1854	11	37	N	
Funke, John Henry	??	Hanover	Y	Bremen	Baltimore	06/02/18??	10/09/1848	1	78	N	
Funke, Tony	33	Germany	Y	Rotterdam	New York	01/02/1885	10/16/1891			Y	
Fupman, Jacob	44	Holland	Y	Liverpool	Philadelphia	04/14/1892	01/21/1896			Y	
Furchtenicht, Ernst	37	Brunswick	Y	Bremen	New Orleans	11/11/1849	04/24/1854	9	122	N	
Furer, Edward	35	Switzerland	Y	Havre	New York	08/30/1891	01/12/1894			Y	
Furgeus, Joseph	28	Prussia	Y	Bremen	New York	04/22/1850	10/10/1854	6	201	N	
Furio, Gus	30	Italy	Y	Palermo	New York	05/21/1885	10/23/1893			Y	
Furrer, John Rudolph	38	Switzerland	Y	Havre	New York	01/29/1859	05/26/1859	17	433	N	
Furschutte, Louis	27	Germany	Y	Bremen	Baltimore	05/26/1882	09/22/1884			Y	
Furst, Lyon	48	Bavaria	Y	Havre	New Orleans	04/13/1848	03/11/1856	26	185	N	
Furst, Mathias	25	Wurttemberg	Y	Rotterdam	Philadelphia	01/08/1845	01/16/1849	1	439	N	
Furste, August	27	Prussia	Y	Liverpool	New York	07/20/1847	07/07/1851	3	506	N	
Furster, John Henry	27	Hanover	Y	Bremen	Baltimore	05/01/1850	05/01/1854	9	169	N	
Furtwengler, Ferdinand	24	Baden	Y	Havre	New York	08/12/1856	11/16/1857	16	27	N	
Furtwengler, Lorenz	39	Germany	Y	Antwerp	New York	11/20/1869	10/16/1888			Y	
Fuss, John	40	Baden	Y	Havre	New York	07/01/1856	12/10/1859	17	500	N	
Fussenegger, Franz Josep	??	Austria	Y	Havre	New York	03/10/1889	12/26/1894			Y	
Fust, John	30	Holland	Y	Rotterdam	New York	02/28/1848	04/03/1852	24	362	N	
Futterer, Charles	32	Hohenzollern	Y	Havre	New York	09/01/1853	07/16/1855	11	400	N	
Fye, Henry	46	Germany	Y	Bremen	Baltimore	08/25/1882	12/08/1885			Y	
Fyfe, John	37	Scotland	Y	Glasgow	Philadelphia	07/09/1888	10/27/1900			Y	
Gaab, Paul	33	Germany	Y	Bremen	New York	03/17/1893	11/02/1894			Y	
Gabel, Max	28	Russia	Y	Hamburg	New York	04/10/1882	11/20/1889			Y	
Gable, Sebastian	27	Germany	Y	Bremen	Baltimore	10/04/1883	05/07/1887			Y	
Gable, Sebastian	27	Germany	Y	Bremen	Baltimore	10/04/1883	05/07/1887			Y	
Gabriel, Leonhard	??	Germany	Y	?	?	?	04/25/1889			Y	
Gabriel, William	25	Ireland	Y	Cork	New Orleans	04/10/1852	04/10/1858	16	467	N	
Gaddum, Leonhard	26	Prussia	Y	London	New York	11/??/1848	11/??/1849	23	381	N	
Gadzinski, Michael	59	Germany	Y	Bremen	New York	05/01/1891	11/08/1893			Y	
Gaebke, Theodore	32	Hanover	Y	Bremen	New York	09/29/1853	03/28/1856	26	366	N	
Gaeckemeyer, Henry	33	Hanover	Y	Bremen	New York	10/20/1853	09/19/1857	15	287	N	
Gaeckle, Andrew	27	Hohlenzollern	Y	Havre	New York	04/??/1854	09/22/1855	13	123	N	
Gaelhard, Joseph	35	France	Y	Havre	New York	02/15/1856	12/07/1858	17	381	N	
Gaelter, Christian	28	Bavaria	Y	Havre	New Orleans	06/23/1854	09/29/1857	15	334	N	
Gaenger, Philip	29	Baden	Y	Havre	New York	05/02/1847	06/15/1852	25	271	N	
Gaerthoeffner, Gottlob	70	Germany	Y	Bremen	Baltimore	03/08/1887	02/28/1891			Y	
Gaertlein, John	29	Bavaria	Y	Bremen	New Orleans	06/28/1853	10/19/1857	15	447	N	
Gaertner, Ernst Edward	36	Germany	Y	Bremen	New York	03/31/1883	05/03/1887			Y	
Gaerttner, John	38	Germany	Y	Bremen	New York	02/26/1880	10/20/1887			Y	
Gaerttner, John G.	26	Germany	Y	Antwerp	New York	04/15/1882	07/26/1883			Y	
Gaeser, John	21	France	Y	Havre	New York	10/28/1854	13/14/1855	13	311	N	

CITIZENSHIP RECORDS

APPLICANT	AGE	COUNTRY OF ORIGIN	DEC	DEPART PORT	ENTRY PORT	ARRIVE DATE	DEC DATE	VOL	PG.	FLD	NAT DATE
Gaesler, Matthias	30	Hohenzollern	Y	Havre	New York	08/01/1858	05/29/1862	18	343	N	
Gaettel, Charles	27	Bavaria	Y	Havre	New York	05/19/1849	06/21/1851	3	438	N	
Gaffiny, William	23	Ireland	Y	Liverpool	New York	06/??/1851	03/07/1853	7	310	N	
Gaffney, John	22	Ireland	Y	Liverpool	New York	04/16/1889	07/11/1890			Y	
Gaffney, Michael	24	Ireland	Y	Liverpool	New York	04/01/1883	10/26/1888	19	183	N	
Gaffney, Michael	24	Ireland	Y	Liverpool	New York	04/01/1883	10/26/1888			Y	
Gaffny, Phillip	24	Ireland	Y	Liverpool	New York	04/25/1846	01/28/1850	2	10	N	
Gage, Thomas	23	Ireland	Y	Liverpool	New York	10/20/1845	02/15/1850	2	82	N	
Gahan, William	??	Ireland	N	?	?	07/17/1886				Y	10/17/1892
Gaherty, Thomas	25	Ireland	Y	Liverpool	New Orleans	05/26/1851	03/20/1856	26	238	N	
Gahlmann, Joseph	33	Prussia	Y	Antwerp	New York	09/15/1856	12/06/1859	17	496	N	
Gahner, John Martin	26	Wurtemberg	Y	Antwerp	New York	07/24/1848	09/13/1852	25	479	N	
Gaide, Joseph	40	Germany	Y	Hamburg	New York	05/01/1876	06/18/1883			Y	
Gaiser, Henry	42	Germany	Y	Bremen	Baltimore	03/27/1872	10/05/1883			Y	
Gaiser, John	25	Wurttemberg	Y	Havre	New Orleans	05/28/1849	10/04/1854	10	408	N	
Gaiser, John	25	Wurttemberg	Y	Havre	New Orleans	05/28/1849	10/04/1854	12	347	N	
Gaiser, William	25	Baden	Y	Rotterdam	New York	06/10/1849	03/06/1852	24	245	N	
Gaisle, Mike	42	Wurttemberg	Y	Rotterdam	New York	08/03/1849	11/30/1852	5	364	N	
Gaking, Gerhard John	24	Prussia	Y	Bremen	New Orleans	03/04/1844	11/14/1848	1	291	N	
Galen, Theodore	36	Prussia	Y	Bremen	New York	06/04/1852	09/25/1854	10	206	N	
Galen, Theodore	26	Prussia	Y	Bremen	New York	06/04/1852	09/25/1854	12	145	N	
Galigar, Patrick	29	Ireland	Y	Liverpool	New York	04/??/1853	11/03/1856	14	443	N	
Galione, Francisco	36	Italy	Y	Palermo	New York	01/27/1890	10/26/1900			Y	
Gall, Frederick	59	Germany	N	Havre	New York	06/??/1849	?			Y	
Gall, George	26	Germany	Y	Bremen	Baltimore	11/27/1889	07/27/1891			Y	
Gallagher, Andrew	50	Ireland	Y	Liverpool	New York	10/20/1854	10/12/1857	15	398	N	
Gallagher, Francis	21	Ireland	Y	Liverpool	Philadelphia	05/01/1853	06/09/1854	10	110	N	
Gallagher, Francis	21	Ireland	Y	Liverpool	Philadelphia	05/01/1853	06/09/1854	12	47	N	
Gallagher, James	28	Ireland	Y	Londonderry	Philadelphia	04/01/1849	06/09/1854	10	111	N	
Gallagher, James	28	Ireland	Y	Londonderry	Philadelphia	04/06/1849	06/09/1854	12	48	N	
Gallagher, James	65	Ireland	Y	Queenstown	New York	04/19/1881	10/03/1883			N	
Gallagher, James	27	Ireland	Y	Liverpool	New York	03/01/1849	02/17/1852	24	127	N	
Gallagher, John	27	Ireland	Y	Liverpool	New York	04/02/1847	12/06/1852	5	387	N	
Gallagher, John	24	Ireland	Y	Liverpool	New York	03/21/1853	06/09/1854	10	109	N	
Gallagher, John	24	Ireland	Y	Liverpool	New York	03/21/1853	06/09/1854	12	46	N	
Gallagher, John	22	Ireland	Y	Liverpool	New York	06/03/1854	03/04/1857	15	62	N	
Gallagher, John	40	Ireland	N	Queenstown	New York	05/??/1864	?			Y	
Gallagher, John	33	Ireland	N	Liverpool	New York	05/??/1876	?			Y	
Gallagher, Manas	25	Ireland	Y	London	New York	05/07/1849	11/29/1852	5	361	N	
Gallagher, Manus	27	Ireland	Y	Glasgow	New York	03/25/1853	03/15/1852	24	310	N	
Gallagher, Michael	21	Ireland	Y	Liverpool	New Orleans	12/25/1851	10/07/1854	6	7	N	
Gallagher, Michael	21	Ireland	Y	Liverpool	New Orleans	12/25/1851	10/07/1854	11	8	N	
Gallagher, Patrick	31	Ireland	Y	Liverpool	New Orleans	12/21/1851	10/18/1852	5	7	N	
Gallagher, Patrick	28	Ireland	Y	Liverpool	New York	03/12/1880	10/12/1882			Y	
Gallagher, Patrick	26	Ireland	Y	Liverpool	New York	05/09/1845	10/03/1848	22	396	N	
Gallagher, Thomas	30	Ireland	Y	Liverpool	New York	05/01/1846	01/06/1853	5	520	N	
Gallard, Louis H.	??	Germany	N	?	?	10/15/1887				Y	10/27/1892
Galle, John Henry	29	Prussia	Y	Bremen	New York	10/??/1845	10/25/1851	4	405	N	
Gallenkamp, Ernst	30	Germany	Y	Hamburg	New York	09/16/1880	09/22/1883			Y	
Gallieo, Abraham	??	Syria	Y	?	?	?	05/01/1893			Y	
Gallion, Christian	28	Baden	Y	Havre	New York	09/??/1847	10/05/1848	22	447	N	
Gallitzendorfer, John	49	Germany	Y	Bremen	Baltimore	06/11/1882	10/18/1892			Y	
Gallivein, Richard	32	Ireland	Y	Liverpool	Boston	05/??/1844	03/09/1857	15	81	N	
Gallo, Agusto	??	Italy	N	?	?	07/13/1877				Y	10/18/1892
Gallo, Ferdinand	31	Nassau	Y	Bremen	New York	09/01/1852	09/14/1855	13	35	N	
Gallop, Mayer	33	Russia	Y	Hamburg	New York	08/01/1887	02/24/1891			Y	
Gallum, Henry	30	Prussia	Y	Bremen	New York	01/26/1856	03/28/1857	15	99	N	
Galluzzo, Antonio	42	Italy	Y	Palermo	New York	05/22/1886	12/19/1895			Y	
Galogly, Patrick	35	Ireland	Y	Liverpool	New Orleans	10/01/1848	12/23/1851	4	546	N	

CITIZENSHIP RECORDS

APPLICANT	AGE	COUNTRY OF ORIGIN	DEC	DEPART PORT	ENTRY PORT	ARRIVE DATE	DEC DATE	VOL	PG.	FLD	NAT DATE
Galster, John	24	Germany	Y	Antwerp	New York	05/25/1883	06/17/1886			Y	
Galvin, Roderick	25	Ireland	Y	Queenstown	New York	04/11/1880	11/19/1882			Y	
Gambert, George	48	Bavaria	Y	Havre	New York	04/06/1854	10/07/1854	6	47	N	
Gambert, George	48	Bavaria	Y	Havre	New York	04/06/1854	10/07/1854	11	48	N	
Gamble, Andrew	25	Ireland	Y	Belfast	New York	05/07/1849	01/29/1851	2	540	N	
Gamble, Hubert Harvey	??	England	Y	?	?	?	06/12/1894			Y	
Gamble, James	30	Ireland	Y	Belfast	Cleveland	09/14/1848	03/12/1851	3	254	N	
Gambs, Jacob	39	Germany	Y	Havre	New York	09/19/1865	09/29/1880			Y	
Gamel, John	37	France	Y	Havre	New York	09/12/1846	11/01/1842	5	183	N	
Gamm, Bernhard	25	Germany	Y	Bremen	New York	04/02/1882	04/07/1886			Y	
Gammel, John	37	France	Y	Havre	New York	09/12/1846	11/01/1852	6	309	N	
Gammelein, Christian	45	Mecklenburg S	Y	Hamburg	New York	09/04/1858	02/14/1860	27	105	N	
Gammon, John	30	Ireland	Y	Liverpool	New York	04/04/1845	10/06/1856	14	210	N	
Gams, Casper	23	Bavaria	Y	Bremen	Baltimore	04/29/1847	11/15/1848	1	302	N	
Gander, Aloys	28	Germany	Y	Havre	New York	07/12/1882	10/07/1892			Y	
Gander, George	27	Baden	Y	Havre	New York	08/23/1854	09/19/1855	13	75	N	
Gandmann, Henry	28	Prussia	Y	Bremen	New Orleans	11/17/1855	12/24/1857	16	243	N	
Gang, George	34	Austria	Y	Bremen	New York	06/06/1896	10/13/1903			Y	
Gangloff, Antonie	32	Germany	Y	Havre	New York	09/07/1892	06/04/1904			Y	
Ganley, Thomas	43	Ireland	Y	Liverpool	New York	03/22/1886	03/28/1891	19	321	N	
Ganley, Thomas	43	Ireland	Y	Liverpool	New York	03/22/1886	03/28/1891				
Gannon, Gilbert	27	Ireland	Y	Canada	Troy	07/02/1840	02/15/1849	23	140	N	
Gannon, Thomas	43	England	Y	Liverpool	Philadelphia	06/23/1884	03/13/1889	19	225	N	
Gannon, Thomas H.	25	England	Y	Liverpool	New York	11/09/1886	10/19/1891			Y	
Gannon, Thomas Hy	25	England	Y	Liverpool	New York	11/09/1886	10/19/1891	19	336	N	
Gans, August	40	Sax Weimar	Y	Bremen	New York	01/12/1848	03/08/1852	24	257	N	
Gansel, Fred	21	Germany	Y	Hamburg	New York	09/15/1885	10/05/1885			Y	
Gansing, John Herman	30	Hanover	Y	Bremen	New Orleans	05/11/1848	10/09/1854	11	137	N	
Gansing, John Hermann	30	Hanover	Y	Bremen	New Orleans	05/11/1848	10/09/1954	6	134	N	
Ganster, George	36	Germany	Y	Antwerp	New York	07/21/1883	07/07/1887			Y	
Ganter, John	32	Baden	Y	Havre	New Orleans	05/15/1847	05/07/1850	3	61	N	
Ganter, Leopold	24	Germany	Y	Havre	New York	09/01/1891	01/18/1892			Y	
Ganz, Henry	29	Prussia	Y	Hamburg	New York	08/09/1850	03/03/1852	24	232	N	
Ganzenmueller, Frederick	34	Wurtemberg	Y	Havre	New York	07/13/1851	10/30/1858	17	207	N	
Gardiner, Michael	27	Ireland	Y	Liverpool	New York	12/05/1846	02/23/1853	7	222	N	
Gareis, John	50	Germany	N	Hamburg	New York	06/15/1867	?			Y	
Garive, John	24	Hanover	Y	Bremen	New Orleans	10/25/1845	08/07/1848	22	59	N	
Garland, Frederick	33	Hanover	Y	Bremen	New Orleans	12/28/1849	09/26/1857	15	325	N	
Garland, Henry John	26	Hanover	Y	Bremen	Baltimore	??/20/1846	11/??/1849	23	333	N	
Garlich, Henry	34	Germany	Y	Bremen	Baltimore	06/22/1882	01/15/1890			Y	
Garlichs, George Henry	29	Bremen	Y	Bremen	New York	11/??/1847	11/21/1855	13	242	N	
Garling, Heinrich	29	Germany	Y	Bremen	New York	07/26/1884	07/17/1888			Y	
Garney, Louis Edward	??	Canada	Y	?	?	??/??/1863	??/??/1871			Y	
Garns, Ludeke	48	Oldenburg	Y	Bremen	Baltimore	08/02/1867	06/26/1872	18	502	N	
Garratt, Oscar Edward	??	Sweden/Norway	Y	?	?	?	03/01/1883			Y	
Garraty, Thomas	22	Ireland	Y	Belfast	New York	07/14/1851	04/01/1853	7	481	N	
Garraty, William	23	Ireland	Y	Liverpool	New Orleans	01/01/1848	10/13/1848	1	200	N	
Garraughty, Bernard	30	Ireland	Y	Liverpool	New York	10/10/1840	02/11/1850	2	58	N	
Garrett, Patrick	54	Ireland	N	Liverpool	New York	04/??/1858	?			Y	
Garrigan, John	31	Ireland	Y	Liverpool	New York	03/20/1851	03/26/1856	26	348	N	
Gars, William	33	Germany	Y	Rotterdam	New York	09/07/1878	03/24/1886			Y	
Gartner, Nicholaus	51	Germany	N	Hamburg	New York	08/??/1862	?			Y	
Gartner, Valentine	32	Bavaria	Y	Liverpool	New York	06/04/1858	08/22/1872	18	513	N	
Gasahl, Jacob	32	Switzerland	Y	Havre	New York	05/23/1856	04/17/1860	27	164	N	
Gasche, Jacob	25	Bavaria	Y	Havre	New York	06/02/1851	10/30/1858	17	9	N	
Gasner, Andrew	25	Germany	Y	?	?	08/03/1891	11/07/1892			Y	
Gasner, Lorenz	??	Germany	Y	?	?	10/??/1893	05/16/1896			Y	
Gass, William	??	Germany	Y	?	?	06/11/1881	07/11/1881			Y	
Gasser, Anthony	31	Switzerland	Y	Havre	New Orleans	05/04/1843	10/14/1848	1	217	N	

CITIZENSHIP RECORDS

APPLICANT	AGE	COUNTRY OF ORIGIN	DEC	DEPART PORT	ENTRY PORT	ARRIVE DATE	DEC DATE	VOL	PG.	FLD	NAT DATE
Gassmann, Johann	26	Germany	Y	Hamburg	Philadelphia	07/01/1881	01/25/1883			Y	
Gastdorf, Paul Joseph	21	Prussia	Y	Bremen	New York	06/01/1857	02/23/1858	16	337	N	
Gastl, David	48	Austria	Y	Havre	New York	05/25/1884	02/05/1901			Y	
Gastner, John George	40	Bavaria	Y	Havre	Baltimore	10/01/1842	10/20/1851	4	348	N	
Gasz, John	28	Baden	Y	Havre	New Orleans	01/16/1847	03/03/1853	7	266	N	
Gatens, Charles	24	Ireland	Y	Liverpool	New York	08/01/1853	06/04/1856	14	294	N	
Gatter, Jacob	30	Wuerttemberg	Y	Antwerp	New York	10/08/1851	07/03/1860	27	201	N	
Gattmann, Franz Henry	32	Hanover	Y	Bremen	New Orleans	12/31/1852	10/07/1854	12	472	N	
Gatze, William	28	Oldenburg	Y	Bremen	Baltimore	05/10/1846	03/01/1852	24	202	N	
Gauggel, Theodore	27	Germany	Y	Antwerp	Philadelphia	09/10/1890	11/14/1891			Y	
Gaughan, John	??	Ireland	Y	Liverpool	New Orleans	04/12/18??	10/12/1848	1	178	N	
Gaup, Michael	33	Wurttemberg	Y	Havre	New York	07/??/1854	02/11/1861	18	95	N	
Gausmann, G.	35	Hanover	Y	Bremen	Baltimore	06/28/1845	11/03/1859	18	9	N	
Gausmann, Herman	23	Prussia	Y	Bremen	New Orleans	11/17/1856	04/02/1858	16	473	N	
Gauwatz, Henry	32	Prussia	Y	Hamburg	New York	12/10/1854	12/26/1857	16	253	N	
Gavin, John	25	Ireland	Y	Liverpool	New York	08/01/1854	06/03/1856	14	286	N	
Gavin, Martin	21	Ireland	Y	Queenstown	New York	10/19/1881	10/08/1883			Y	
Gavin, Thomas	32	Ireland	Y	Queenstown	New York	05/30/1886	11/20/1895			Y	
Gawe, John	23	Germany	Y	Bremen	Baltimore	07/25/1883	07/09/1884			Y	
Gayner, William	25	Hanover	Y	Bremen	Baltimore	10/04/1847	11/18/1848	1	323	N	
Gaynor, Con.	33	Ireland	Y	Liverpool	Philadelphia	04/28/1848	12/20/1851	4	532	N	
Geary, John	23	Ireland	Y	London	New York	05/??/1849	08/??/1851	4	154	N	
Geary, Thomas	46	Ireland	Y	Queenstown	New York	??/??/1872	05/26/1886			Y	
Gebauer, Geo.	??	Germany	Y	?	?	?	10/30/1881			Y	
Gebauer, Gustave	24	Germany	Y	Hamburg	New York	07/07/1885	97/25/1885			Y	
Gebel, Wilhelm	32	Germany	Y	Bremen	New Orleans	11/15/1879	10/29/1889			Y	
Geber, Christian	31	Hesse Darmsta	Y	London	New York	06/04/1848	05/03/1854	8	354	N	
Geber, Christian	31	Hesse Darmsta	Y	London	New York	06/04/1848	05/03/1854	9	227	N	
Gebert, John	23	Germany	Y	Hamburg	New York	08/12/1883	11/02/1886			Y	
Gebert, Philip	42	Prussia	Y	Liverpool	Boston	05/17/1852	02/19/1856	26	105	N	
Gebert, William	28	Mecklenburg S	Y	Hamburg	New York	01/11/1854	03/26/1857	15	87	N	
Gebhardt, August	25	Prussia	Y	Bremen	Baltimore	06/29/1860	07/03/1860	27	198	N	
Gebhardt, Christian	22	Germany	Y	?	Baltimore	??/??/1881	11/04/1887			Y	
Gebhardt, George	28	Germany	Y	Hamburg	New York	04/06/1890	03/21/1892			Y	
Gebhardt, John	27	Germany	Y	Antwerp	New York	02/06/1893	02/06/1900			Y	
Gebhauer, Andreas	22	Bavaria	Y	Havre	New Orleans	05/31/1852	05/29/1854	10	27	N	
Gecks, Anthony	29	Nassau	Y	Antwerp	New York	11/16/1851	09/30/1854	12	271	N	
Gecks, Antony	29	Nassau	Y	Antwerp	New York	11/16/1851	09/30/1854	10	332	N	
Gecks, John	42	Nassau	Y	Bremen	New York	06/05/1866	10/08/1872	18	526	N	
Gedeun, Joseph	28	Prussia	Y	Antwerp	New York	05/28/1850	04/02/1853	7	498	N	
Gedike, Ernst	37	Germany	Y	Bremen	New York	10/28/1888	03/28/1900			Y	
Geering, William A.	??	Germany	Y	?	?	?	11/04/1899			Y	
Geerken, Henry	28	Oldenburg	Y	Bremen	New York	03/04/1849	07/28/1851	4	44	N	
Geers, Anton	44	Germany	Y	Bremen	New York	08/16/1877	09/29/1893	19	425	N	
Geers, Anton	47	Germany	Y	Bremen	New York	08/16/1877	09/29/1893			Y	
Geers, Bernard	29	Germany	Y	Bremen	Baltimore	07/01/1895	07/26/1897			Y	
Geers, Clemens	53	Germany	Y	Bremen	New York	08/10/1885	09/29/1893	19	426	N	
Geers, George H.	26	Germany	Y	Bremen	New York	08/28/1881	09/02/1886			Y	
Geers, Gerhard	25	Germany	Y	Bremen	New York	10/01/1880	12/26/1885			Y	
Geesen, Henry	21	Germany	Y	Bremen	Baltimore	06/06/1881	03/25/1884			Y	
Geesen, Henry	28	Germany	Y	Bremen	New York	11/20/1892	02/16/1899			Y	
Gefruhrer, John	52	Prussia	Y	Rotterdam	New York	05/01/1848	11/01/1854	6	248	N	
Gegauff, Gustav	??	Germany	Y	?	?	?	05/09/1890			Y	
Gegel, Jacob	24	Germany	Y	Rotterdam	New York	06/01/1891	03/13/1893			Y	
Gegenhenner, Martin	26	Germany	Y	Antwerp	New York	11/05/1870	09/21/1883			Y	
Geghan, John J.	45	Ireland	N	Liverpool	New Orleans	03/03/1852	?			Y	
Geglein, Andreas	28	Bavaria	Y	Bremen	Baltimore	10/06/1849	11/08/1851	4	500	N	
Gegner, George	30	Bavaria	Y	Bremen	Baltimore	08/06/1845	02/14/1849	23	113	N	
Gehbauer, Andreas	22	Bavaria	Y	Havre	New Orleans	05/31/1852	05/29/1854	9	444	N	

CITIZENSHIP RECORDS

APPLICANT	AGE	COUNTRY OF ORIGIN	DEC	DEPART PORT	ENTRY PORT	ARRIVE DATE	DEC DATE	VOL	PG.	FLD	NAT DATE
Gehefer, Cornelius	21	Hesse Darmsta	Y	Havre	New York	05/19/1847	03/28/1850	2	276	N	
Gehle, Heinrich	49	Germany	Y	Hamburg	New York	07/07/1881	11/13/1885			Y	
Gehlker, Christian	22	Germany	Y	Bremen	New York	09/18/1881	08/02/1884			Y	
Gehlker, Wm.	25	Germany	Y	Bremen	New York	08/07/1880	08/06/1883			Y	
Gehmerge, Joseph	26	Prussia	Y	Bremen	Baltimore	11/08/1847	02/17/1849	23	163	N	
Gehr, John	26	Baden	Y	London	New York	07/26/1852	10/02/1857	15	343	N	
Gehring, Anton	31	Prussia	Y	Bremen	New York	04/25/1850	08/20/1855	11	458	N	
Gehring, Basilus	35	Baden	Y	Havre	New York	08/03/1853	01/09/1856	13	437	N	
Gehring, Joseph	27	Baden	Y	Havre	New Orleans	05/15/1852	11/05/1852	5	225	N	
Gehring, Joseph	27	Baden	Y	Havre	New Orleans	05/15/1852	11/05/1852	6	351	N	
Gehring, Nicholas	28	Bavaria	Y	Havre	New York	08/18/1846	01/??/1850	23	518	N	
Gehringer, George	31	Germany	Y	Hamburg	New York	05/11/1871	10/10/1881			Y	
Gehringer, George	31	Germany	Y	Bremen	New York	11/12/1881	10/22/1889			Y	
Gehrum, John	??	Bavaria	Y	Havre	New York	05/??/1858	12/31/1860	18	32	N	
Gehrum, Michael	23	Bavaria	Y	Havre	New York	07/23/1853	05/10/1854	8	414	N	
Gehrum, Michael	23	Bavaria	Y	Havre	New York	07/23/1853	05/10/1854	9	287	N	
Geier, Charles Joseph	23	Baden	Y	Liverpool	New York	06/01/1853	04/03/1856	26	425	N	
Geier, Karl	33	Germany	Y	Rotterdam	New York	04/12/1881	11/01/1886			Y	
Geier, Louis	35	Baden	Y	Havre	New York	06/26/1846	10/07/1851	4	217	N	
Geier, Martin	39	Germany	Y	Bremen	Baltimore	06/01/1870	10/04/1880			Y	
Geiffert, Alfred	??	Germany	Y	?	?	?	02/24/1884			Y	
Geiger, Charles	??	Germany	Y	?	?	?	04/06/1891			Y	
Geiger, Friedrich	42	Germany	Y	Hamburg	New York	06/14/1871	03/30/1883			Y	
Geiger, George Frederick	56	Baden	Y	Havre	New York	05/31/1846	10/03/1848	1	43	N	
Geiger, Henry	27	Bavaria	Y	Havre	New Orleans	01/23/1847	03/08/1851	3	211	N	
Geiger, Jacob	25	Wurttemberg	Y	London	New York	08/02/1854	10/06/1856	14	204	N	
Geiger, John	22	Bavaria	Y	Havre	New Orleans	05/05/1852	04/04/1853	7	538	N	
Geiger, John	35	Wuerttemberg	Y	Rotterdam	New York	07/15/1845	08/15/1848	22	170	N	
Geiger, John	22	Wuerttemberg	Y	Havre	New York	11/25/1856	10/09/1860	27	464	N	
Geiger, John George	32	Wurttemberg	Y	Havre	New York	05/29/1850	09/20/1854	10	319	N	
Geiger, John George	32	Wuerttemberg	Y	Havre	New York	05/29/1850	09/30/1854	12	258	N	
Geiger, Julius	31	Germany	Y	Bremen	New York	11/02/1884	10/18/1893	21	23	N	
Geiger, Julius	31	Germany	Y	Bremen	New York	11/15/1884	10/18/1893			Y	
Geiger, Lambert	22	Germany	Y	Bremen	New York	08/03/1881	10/27/1884			Y	
Geiger, Ludwig	41	Germany	Y	Bremen	New York	01/19/1880	09/30/1889			Y	
Geiger, Wm.	35	Germany	Y	Havre	New York	10/27/1880	03/28/1892			Y	
Geigle, Louis	24	Germany	Y	Antwerp	New York	02/28/1880	10/13/1884			Y	
Geile, Gerhard H.	23	Germany	Y	Bremen	Baltimore	11/20/1882	06/12/1884			Y	
Geilpus, Wm. Chas. Zach.	30	Saxe Darmstad	Y	Havre	New York	11/06/1847	04/01/1853	7	480	N	
Geimeiner, Hyronimus	31	Baden	Y	Havre	New Orleans	12/30/1846	08/15/1848	22	163	N	
Geir, John Hennich	32	Oldenburg	Y	Bremen	Baltimore	09/03/1845	08/15/1848	22	156	N	
Geise, Bernard	52	Germany	N	Bremen	Baltimore	07/03/1857	?			Y	
Geise, Davis	28	Hanover	Y	Bremen	New York	11/02/18??	10/11/1848	1	134	N	
Geisel, Heinrich	28	Germany	Y	Rotterdam	New York	07/14/1881	10/14/1887			Y	
Geiselmann, Henry	25	Germany	Y	Bremen	New York	05/01/1881	10/08/1883			Y	
Geiselmann, John	57	Germany	N	Hamburg	New York	05/06/1864	?			Y	
Geiser, Christian	28	Wurttemberg	Y	Havre	New York	03/01/1853	10/09/1854	6	118	N	
Geiser, Christian	28	Wurttemberg	Y	Havre	New York	03/01/1853	10/09/1854	11	121	N	
Geiske, Henry	22	Germany	Y	Amsterdam	New York	06/??/1882	08/04/1884			Y	
Geisler, August	25	Germany	Y	Hamburg	New York	08/30/1884	04/05/1888			Y	
Geisler, Henry	22	Germany	Y	Antwerp	New York	10/01/1881	06/06/1884			Y	
Geisler, Leonard	30	Wuerttemberg	Y	Havre	New York	07/25/1845	02/13/1849	23	84	N	
Geisman, Louis	26	Russia	Y	Hamburg	Philadelphia	??/??/1880	11/28/1884			Y	
Geismann, Bernard	27	Hanover	Y	Bremen	New York	11/17/1850	09/25/1854	10	227	N	
Geismann, Bernard	27	Hanover	Y	Bremen	New York	11/17/1850	09/25/1854	12	166	N	
Geismar, Louis	57	Germany	Y	Hamburg	New York	05/28/1893	10/28/1899			Y	
Geiss, A.	42	Germany	Y	Havre	New York	03/12/1881	01/22/1884			Y	
Geiss, Conrad	26	Germany	Y	Bremen	New York	05/21/1889	08/24/1892			Y	
Geissler, Herman	24	Prussia	Y	Hamburg	New York	06/??/1849	12/20/1850	2	381	N	

CITIZENSHIP RECORDS

APPLICANT	AGE	COUNTRY OF ORIGIN	DEC	DEPART PORT	ENTRY PORT	ARRIVE DATE	DEC DATE	VOL	PG.	FLD	NAT DATE
Geist, August	44	Germany	Y	Rotterdam	New York	09/12/1893	10/23/1895	21	84	N	
Geist, August	44	Germany	Y	Rotterdam	New York	09/12/1893	10/23/1895			Y	
Geiszler, Wilhelm	38	Germany	Y	Havre	New York	03/01/1882	01/10/1883			Y	
Geithausen, Anthony	??	Prussia	Y	?	New Orleans	06/16/18??	11/06/1856	14	491	N	
Gelan, Louis	23	Hesse Cassel	Y	Bremen	New Orleans	11/01/1844	08/21/1848	22	219	N	
Gelbke, Curt	25	Germany	Y	Bremen	New York	03/09/1892	06/08/1894			Y	
Gelbke, Gustav A.	24	Germany	Y	Bremen	Baltimore	06/29/1882	06/18/1884			Y	
Gelbricht, Julius	45	Germany	Y	Bremen	Baltimore	06/17/1882	10/31/1887			Y	
Geldreich, Charles	29	Germany	Y	Hamburg	New York	05/14/1881	09/21/1889			Y	
Geldreich, Joseph	24	Baden	Y	Havre	New Orleans	10/06/1853	09/29/1856	14	22	N	
Gell, Peter	25	Oldenburg	Y	Bremen	New York	05/??/1853	11/06/1856	14	490	N	
Gellenbeck, George	25	Hanover	Y	Bremen	New Orleans	12/10/1848	03/16/1852	24	320	N	
Gellenbeck, William	25	Germany	Y	Antwerp	New York	07/03/1884	07/22/1886			Y	
Gellman, Moses	31	Russia	Y	?	?	?	11/28/1891			Y	
Gelting, Samuel	25	Germany	Y	Bremen	Baltimore	09/25/1882	10/18/1888			Y	
Geltz, George	55	Bavaria	Y	Havre	New York	06/04/1845	05/16/1854	8	452	N	
Geltz, George	55	Bavaria	Y	Havre	New York	06/04/1845	05/16/1854	9	325	N	
Gemmell, Alfred	39	Scotland	Y	Glasgow	Buffalo	03/18/1880	07/24/1888			Y	
Gempp, Ernst	38	Germany	Y	Havre	New York	12/22/1881	10/09/1886			Y	
Genau, Bernard	35	Germany	Y	Amsterdam	New York	10/29/1883	04/07/1890			Y	
Genau, George	21	Germany	Y	Rotterdam	New York	12/09/1885	01/02/1886			Y	
Gendy, Louis	23	Russia	Y	Hamburg	New York	05/15/1889	10/25/1890	19	302	N	
Gendy, Louis	23	Russia	Y	Hamburg	New York	05/15/1889	10/25/1890			Y	
Geng, George	24	Germany	Y	Hamburg	New York	09/13/1886	07/09/1889			Y	
Genge, Ferdinand	??	Prussia	Y	?	?	?	02/18/1873			Y	
Genge, Robert	37	Prussia	Y	Bremen	New Orleans	06/03/1857	12/26/1859	17	523	N	
Genkinger, Jacob	34	Germany	Y	Rotterdam	New York	07/19/1888	04/20/1891			Y	
Gensheimer, Adam	58	Germany	Y	Havre	New York	11/10/1859	09/16/1889			Y	
Gensheimer, Christopher	25	Bavaria	Y	Havre	New York	09/04/1844	08/15/1848	22	129	N	
Gensheimer, Henry	21	Germany	Y	Bremen	Baltimore	01/28/1884	11/09/1886			Y	
Gentile, Joseph	33	Italy	Y	?	New York	??/??/1877	05/15/1884			Y	
Gentner, George	22	Wurttemberg	Y	Havre	New York	08/23/1853	02/02/1856	13	540	N	
Gentner, Jacob	33	Wuertemberg	Y	Havre	New York	08/28/1853	02/02/1856	26	1	N	
Gentner, Martin	24	Germany	Y	Amsterdam	New York	06/01/1882	09/22/1883			Y	
Gentrup, Henry Andrew Wi	??	Prussia	Y	Bremen	Baltimore	09/02/1845	10/04/1848	1	48	N	
Gentsch, Max	27	Germany	Y	Hamburg	New York	07/02/1878	03/01/1884			Y	
Gentsch, Wm.	43	Germany	Y	Hamburg	New York	04/??/1869	03/04/1887			Y	
Gentsheimer, Philipp	25	Germany	Y	Bremen	Baltimore	06/21/1884	08/15/1889			Y	
Gentz, Louis	21	Prussia	Y	Hamburg	New York	11/22/1855	11/08/1860	18	29	N	
Gentzheimer, Henry	21	Germany	Y	Bremen	Baltimore	01/28/1884	11/09/1886			Y	
Genzlinger, Michael	32	Bavaria	Y	Havre	New York	11/27/1854	10/06/1856	14	214	N	
Genzlinger, Stephen	34	Bavaria	Y	Havre	New Orleans	12/16/1856	11/25/1861	18	229	N	
Geoghagen, John	23	Ireland	Y	Limerick	Buffalo	09/01/1850	06/08/1854	12	42	N	
Geoghegan, John	23	Ireland	Y	Limerick	Buffalo	09/01/1850	06/08/1854	10	105	N	
Georg, Wm.	24	Germany	Y	Antwerp	New York	09/18/1884	10/25/1889			Y	
George, Adam	72	Germany	N	Havre	New York	08/01/1851	?			Y	
George, F. Moritz	34	Saxony	Y	Canada	Buffalo	07/??/1855	10/27/1858	17	136	N	
George, Gaab	27	Bavaria	Y	London	New York	03/06/1854	10/09/1854	6	126	N	
George, Gaab	27	Bavaria	Y	London	New York	03/06/1853	10/09/1854	11	129	N	
George, Isaac	25	Syria	Y	Beruit	New York	07/15/1891	03/29/1897			Y	
George, John	29	Wales	Y	Liverpool	New York	07/??/1852	05/31/1859	17	443	N	
George, Nicholas	25	Syria	Y	Tripoli	New Orleans	12/25/1889	10/29/1892			Y	
George, Thomas Benjamin	24	England	Y	Liverpool	New York	11/12/1883	12/07/1888			Y	
Georgeson, James	46	Scotland	Y	Glasgow	Philadelphia	05/31/1892	09/12/1900			Y	
Geowe, H.B.	42	Hanover	Y	Bremerhafen	Baltimore	11/??/1856	01/10/1861	18	54	N	
Geppert, Anton	26	Baden	Y	Havre	New Orleans	04/06/1852	05/26/1856	26	557	N	
Ger, David	32	Baden	Y	Havre	New Orleans	05/??/1851	03/28/1853	7	435	N	
Geraci, Joseph	30	Italy	Y	Palermo	New York	02/01/1884	10/16/1893	21	6	N	
Geraci, Joseph	30	Italy	Y	Palermo	New York	02/01/1884	10/16/1893			Y	

CITIZENSHIP RECORDS

APPLICANT	AGE	COUNTRY OF ORIGIN	DEC	DEPART PORT	ENTRY PORT	ARRIVE DATE	DEC DATE	VOL	PG.	FLD	NAT DATE
Geraci, Salvatore	46	Italy	Y	Palermo	New York	01/24/1886	10/31/1900			Y	
Geraghty, Patrick	26	Ireland	Y	Liverpool	New York	05/14/1882	10/19/1883			Y	
Geraghty, Peter	25	Ireland	Y	Londonderry	New York	03/20/1888	10/28/1891	19	244	N	
Geraghty, Peter J.	25	Ireland	Y	Londonderry	New York	03/20/1888	10/28/1891			Y	
Geraughty, Patrick	35	Ireland	Y	Liverpool	New Orleans	04/25/1847	02/24/1852	24	162	N	
Gerber, George	62	Germany	N	Liverpool	Boston	05/25/1852	?			Y	
Gerber, John	33	Prussia	Y	Antwerp	New York	06/02/1851	09/25/1854	10	225	N	
Gerber, John	33	Prussia	Y	Antwerp	New York	06/02/1851	09/25/1854	12	164	N	
Gerbus, George	38	Germany	N	Rotterdam	New York	03/13/1868	?			Y	
Gerder, William	29	Oldenburg	Y	Rotterdam	New York	09/25/1865	02/12/1872	18	463	N	
Gerdes, Arnold	40	Germany	Y	Bremen	Baltimore	11/01/1871	03/27/1879			Y	
Gerdes, F. G.	30	Oldenburg	Y	Bremen	New York	09/29/1856	01/10/1860	27	48	N	
Gerdes, George	27	Germany	Y	Amsterdam	New York	12/12/1891	10/24/1896			Y	
Gerdes, Henry	47	Germany	Y	Bremen	Baltimore	09/08/1866	03/29/1887	19	115	N	
Gerdes, Henry	31	Germany	Y	Bremen	New York	01/18/1889	08/15/1896			Y	
Gerdes, Henry	47	Germany	Y	Bremen	Baltimore	09/05/1866	03/29/1884			Y	
Gerdes, John	31	Oldenburg	Y	Bremen	New Orleans	12/18/1850	03/07/1853	7	299	N	
Gerdes, John	27	Germany	Y	Bremen	New York	09/12/1894	10/25/1900			Y	
Gerdes, Klassemius	32	Germany	Y	Bremen	New York	04/01/1892	03/25/1899			Y	
Gerding, Bernard	33	Prussia	Y	Bremen	Baltimore	05/25/1845	01/29/1849	1	534	N	
Gerdt, Ernst	25	Prussia	Y	Bremen	Baltimore	??/14/18?8	04/16/1855	11	247	N	
Gereis, John	23	Bavaria	Y	Bremen	New York	05/??/1851	02/29/1856	26	140	N	
Gerhard, Conrad	27	Hesse Darmsta	Y	Antwerp	New York	04/02/1849	05/10/1854	8	410	N	
Gerhard, Conrad	27	Hesse Darmsta	Y	Antwerp	New York	04/02/1849	05/10/1854	9	283	N	
Gerhard, Erasmus	30	Bavaria	Y	Hamburg	New York	06/10/1856	10/04/1858	17	33	N	
Gerhard, Henry	30	Germany	Y	Antwerp	New York	06/10/1888	10/28/1891			Y	
Gerhard, Joseph	30	Austria	Y	Bremen	New York	12/16/1854	09/12/1857	15	262	N	
Gerhardt, Ernst W.	42	Germany	Y	Hamburg	New York	10/08/1880	05/14/1883			Y	
Gerhardt, Herman	26	Germany	Y	Bremen	New York	08/02/1885	07/09/1888			Y	
Gerhardt, John	29	Germany	N	?	?	06/29/1887				Y	10/14/1892
Gerhardt, Louis	28	Reuss	Y	Bremen	New Orleans	09/13/1854	09/28/1858	16	104	N	
Gerick, Bernard	32	Germany	Y	Bremen	New York	09/15/1883	06/12/1884			Y	
Gerick, William	35	Prussia	Y	Bremen	Baltimore	05/12/1858	06/19/1862	18	353	N	
Gericke, Gustav	26	Germany	Y	Hamburg	New York	05/27/1881	04/06/1883			Y	
Gering, Charles	30	Prussia	Y	Bremen	New York	12/18/1853	12/08/1857	16	206	N	
Gering, Frank	23	France	Y	Havre	New York	08/??/1879	09/22/1883			Y	
Gering, Frank	54	France	Y	Havre	New York	08/12/1878	09/17/1884			Y	
Gering, George	26	France	Y	Antwerp	New York	07/??/1878	09/27/1884			Y	
Gerke, Fred	31	Hanover	Y	Bremen	New York	10/??/1845	01/??/1850	23	464	N	
Gerke, Henry	27	Hanover	Y	Bremen	New Orleans	05/02/1849	10/30/1852	5	71	N	
Gerke, Henry	44	Germany	Y	Rotterdam	New York	07/12/1881	11/28/1887			Y	
Gerke, Richard	21	Hanover	Y	Bremen	Baltimore	01/03/1847	01/15/1850	23	512	N	
Gerken, Gustav	??	Germany	Y	?	?	?	09/16/1889			Y	
Gerlach, George Frederic	38	Hesse Darmsta	Y	Havre	New York	01/11/1849	10/21/1858	17	82	N	
Gerlach, John Frederick	36	Prussia	Y	Bremen	New York	01/14/1850	02/22/1850	2	117	N	
Gerlach, Otto F.	44	Prussia	N	Bremen	New York	05/??/1868	?			Y	
Gerlacher, John	25	Germany	Y	Bremen	Baltimore	09/06/1887	10/22/1888			Y	
Gerland, Herman	21	Hanover	Y	Bremen	New York	05/31/1852	07/23/1855	11	418	N	
Gerlemann, H.	33	Hanover	Y	Bremen	New York	04/28/1857	11/03/1860	18	7	N	
Gerling, Joseph	27	Prussia	Y	Bremen	New York	03/12/1869	04/11/1872	18	489	N	
Germ, Christian	27	Germany	Y	Antwerp	Philadelphia	05/29/1879	11/01/1886			Y	
Germau, John A.	45	Germany	Y	Hamburg	Baltimore	04/16/1883	01/23/1884			Y	
Germbal, Gottfried	30	Bavaria	Y	Antwerp	New York	10/06/1849	01/13/1851	2	487	N	
Gerner, Simon	37	Bavaria	Y	Bremen	New York	05/17/1847	03/03/1853	7	265	N	
Gerngross, Sebastian	34	Germany	Y	Hamburg	New York	09/17/1883	10/02/1888			Y	
Geroisle, Magnus	24	Wuerttenberg	Y	Liverpool	New York	08/04/1845	02/19/1849	23	191	N	
Gerold, Joseph	24	Germany	Y	Bremen	New York	06/21/1884	03/32/1889			Y	
Gerrard, George	36	England	Y	Liverpool	New York	06/11/1880	04/26/1888			Y	
Gerrien, Daniel	17	Ireland	N	Liverpool	New York	08/05/1867				Y	10/01/1877

CITIZENSHIP RECORDS

APPLICANT	AGE	COUNTRY OF ORIGIN	DEC	DEPART PORT	ENTRY PORT	ARRIVE DATE	DEC DATE	VOL	PG.	FLD	NAT DATE
Gerritsey, Abraham	29	Holland	Y	Rotterdam	New York	08/04/1849	05/25/1852	25	109	N	
Gerrity, James	26	Ireland	Y	Liverpool	New York	03/15/1849	10/27/1858	17	124	N	
Gerrity, John	39	Ireland	N	Liverpool	New York	??/??/1863	?			Y	
Gershung, Louis	??	Russia	N	?	?	07/15/1882				Y	10/26/1892
Gersmann, George	54	Germany	Y	Bremen	New York	09/11/1863	05/18/1882			Y	
Gerson, Joseph	20	Prussia	Y	Bremen	New York	06/24/1866	06/10/1872	18	499	N	
Gerst, Anton	22	Oldenburg	Y	Bremen	New York	07/26/1857	10/08/1860	27	458	N	
Gerst, August	27	Germany	Y	Bremen	New York	10/18/1879	10/25/1883			Y	
Gerst, Fritz	51	Germany	Y	Bremen	New York	10/14/1890	06/27/1894			Y	
Gerst, Martin	24	Germany	Y	Bremen	Baltimore	08/11/1882	05/06/1887			Y	
Gerstacker, Conrad	25	Bavaria	Y	Bremen	New York	12/01/1855	03/06/1856	26	167	N	
Gerstner, Nicholas	33	Baden	Y	Havre	New York	06/01/1854	10/30/1858	17	205	N	
Gerstner, Nicolaus	64	Germany	N	Havre	New York	06/??/1854	?			Y	
Gerstner, Simon	26	Baden	Y	Havre	New York	03/05/1854	11/06/1860	18	24	N	
Gert, Jacob	23	Prussia	Y	Bremen	Baltimore	12/13/1853	02/09/1856	26	66	N	
Gerth, Charles	??	Mexico	N	?	?	05/00/1886				Y	10/20/1892
Gerth, Fred	47	Germany	Y	Antwerp	New York	05/22/1887	09/30/1890			Y	
Gerth, Valentine	60	Baden	Y	Havre	New Orleans	12/20/1853	03/11/1858	16	392	N	
Gerther, George	28	Bavaria	Y	?	New Orleans	??/07/1848	10/??/1849	23	274	N	
Gertig, Charles	30	Prussia	Y	Hamburg	?	03/19/1869	03/10/1870			Y	
Gertis, Frank	27	Germany	Y	Bremen	New York	10/05/1889	04/27/1891			Y	
Gertkin, Henry	20	Hanover	Y	Bremen	New York	04/28/1842	01/20/1849	1	482	N	
Gertz, Henry	32	Mecklenburg S	Y	Hamburg	Buffalo	06/15/1850	02/17/1853	7	175	N	
Gertzen, Arnold	36	Germany	Y	Bremen	Baltimore	05/11/1891	02/12/1894	21	60	N	
Gertzen, Arnold	36	Germany	Y	Bremen	Baltimore	05/11/1891	01/12/1894			Y	
Gerve, Christian	25	Hanover	Y	Bremen	New York	11/04/1852	03/25/1856	26	344	N	
Gervelmeier, Barney	32	Hanover	Y	Bremen	Baltimore	10/27/1858	08/16/1860	27	292	N	
Gerversmann, Albert	37	Germany	Y	Bremen	New York	07/16/1868	11/01/1871	18	435	N	
Gerwe, Henry	33	Hanover	Y	Bremen	New Orleans	11/03/1855	03/30/1857	15	104	N	
Gerwing, John	30	Germany	Y	Rotterdam	New York	08/13/1885	08/15/1888			Y	
Geschwind, John	33	Switzerland	Y	Havre	New Orleans	05/26/1845	02/01/1849	23	12	N	
Gesse, Max A.	35	Germany	Y	Bremen	New York	03/24/1893	06/29/1896			Y	
Gessing, Gerhard	49	Germany	Y	Bremen	Baltimore	10/07/1890	09/18/1893			Y	
Gessner, John	23	Germany	Y	Rotterdam	New York	04/08/1885	06/05/1889			Y	
Gesterkamp, Anton	36	Prussia	Y	Bremen	New York	05/12/1852	04/02/1856	26	412	N	
Gesting, Louis	29	Germany	Y	Antwerp	Philadelphia	11/17/1889	10/25/1897			Y	
Geszner, Nicholas	30	Bavaria	Y	London	New York	10/02/1857	10/08/1860	27	422	N	
Gettey, Bernard	??	Ireland	Y	Liverpool	New York	07/07/1832	10/07/1848	22	484	N	
Getzug, Hermann	32	Russia	Y	?	New York	??/??/1892	06/11/1892			Y	
Geuer, Michael	30	Baden	Y	Havre	New York	10/20/1854	03/25/1856	26	314	N	
Geyer, Albert	31	Germany	Y	Bremen	New York	04/24/1880	09/26/1883			Y	
Geyer, Ferdinand	26	Austria	Y	Bremen	New York	03/15/1880	10/03/1882			Y	
Geyer, George	30	Germany	Y	Bremen	Baltimore	07/??/1876	07/22/1884			Y	
Geyer, John	27	Germany	Y	Bremen	New York	05/31/1880	08/19/1882			Y	
Geyer, Philip	21	Bavaria	Y	Bremen	New Orleans	05/05/1853	08/23/1855	11	486	N	
Gezendorfer, Sebastian	35	Bavaria	Y	Bremen	New York	07/05/1857	09/12/1860	27	368	N	
Gfroer, John	52	Prussia	Y	Rotterdam	New York	05/01/1848	11/01/1852	5	122	N	
Ghenzi, Jakob	51	Switzerland	Y	Bremen	New York	12/13/1883	10/26/1889			Y	
Ghenzis, Jakob	51	Switzerland	Y	Bremen	New York	12/13/1883	10/26/1889	19	267	N	
Ghio, A.J.	19	Sardinia	Y	Havre	New York	07/08/1854	11/20/1857	16	38	N	
Ghirlande, Bernard	32	Sardinia	Y	Genoa	New York	06/28/1852	10/30/1858	17	73	N	
Giacin, Tomaso	??	Italy	Y	?	?	?	01/08/1895			Y	
Giambruni, Angelo	23	Italy	Y	Genoa	New York	05/17/1878	11/15/1888			Y	
Gianciolo, Fabbiano	44	Italy	Y	Palermo	New York	03/30/1883	03/12/1903			Y	
Giancola, Angelo	37	Italy	Y	Naples	New York	03/14/1896	10/19/1896			Y	
Gianella, Henry	33	Switzerland	Y	Havre	New York	06/08/1882	06/13/1890			Y	
Giangiolli, Guiseppe	27	Italy	Y	Naples	New York	01/07/1887	08/24/1894			Y	
Gibbon, William	32	Ireland	Y	Liverpool	New York	05/13/1880	10/13/1892	19	359	N	
Gibbons, John	24	England	Y	Liverpool	New York	04/04/1849	02/24/1851	3	169	N	

CITIZENSHIP RECORDS

APPLICANT	AGE	COUNTRY OF ORIGIN	DEC	DEPART PORT	ENTRY PORT	ARRIVE DATE	DEC DATE	VOL	PG.	FLD	NAT DATE
Gibbons, John	34	Ireland	Y	Liverpool	Philadelphia	05/05/1883	10/28/1892	19	397	N	
Gibbons, John	34	Ireland	Y	Liverpool	Philadelphia	05/05/1883	10/28/1892			Y	
Gibbons, John	38	Ireland	Y	Liverpool	New Orleans	03/19/1844	04/13/1852	24	489	N	
Gibbons, Miles	52	Ireland	N	Liverpool	New York	07/??/1864	?			Y	
Gibson, George	45	England	Y	Hull	New York	05/22/1850	03/11/1852	24	287	N	
Gibson, John W.	31	England	Y	London	New York	03/??/1882	04/03/1889			Y	
Gibson, Stephan	24	England	Y	Liverpool	Philadelphia	08/31/1851	03/11/1852	24	288	N	
Gibson, Willis	30	Ireland	Y	Liverpool	Philadelphia	05/??/1848	11/07/1856	14	485	N	
Gibson, Wm.	35	Scotland	Y	Liverpool	New York	11/30/1882	08/03/1891			Y	
Giebelmeier, Rudolph	25	Prussia	Y	Bremen	Baltimore	11/05/1854	12/22/1857	16	241	N	
Giebing, Herman	39	Germany	Y	Bremen	New York	01/27/1868	04/01/1882			Y	
Gieck, Gottfried	36	Bavaria	Y	Bremen	New York	09/01/1846	03/31/1853	7	470	N	
Gieck, John	29	Bavaria	Y	Bremen	New Orleans	05/13/1856	05/26/1856	26	547	N	
Giedraitys, Jacob	30	Russia	Y	Hamburg	New York	11/??/1873	06/04/1883			Y	
Giegel, Frederick	26	Prussia	Y	Bremen	New York	05/01/1854	09/15/1855	13	38	N	
Giering, Daniel	36	Waldeck	Y	Bremen	New York	10/24/1847	01/19/1849	1	476	N	
Giering, Leonhard	25	Germany	Y	Bremen	New York	12/06/1879	10/06/1882			Y	
Gierse, Fred	24	Germany	Y	Antwerp	Philadelphia	06/06/1888	08/30/1889			Y	
Giese, Frank	29	Germany	Y	Bremen	Baltimore	05/27/1881	10/02/1886	19	58	N	
Giese, Frank	26	Germany	Y	Bremen	New York	04/15/1886	11/12/1888			Y	
Giesecki, Carl	30	Hanover	Y	Bremen	New York	10/02/1857	07/18/1860	27	224	N	
Gieseke, Frederick	28	Germany	Y	?	New York	??/??/1882	03/09/1885			Y	
Giesendorfer, Frederick	24	Bavaria	Y	Bremen	New Orleans	07/05/1847	08/15/1848	22	143	N	
Gieske, Henry	22	Germany	Y	Amsterdam	New York	06/??/1882	08/04/1884			Y	
Giesken, Gerd Bernard	28	Hanover	Y	Bremen	Baltimore	05/30/1848	12/10/1855	13	299	N	
Giesker, William	33	Germany	Y	Bremen	New York	03/05/1887	09/15/1896			Y	
Giesmann, William	41	Germany	Y	Amsterdam	New York	08/13/1882	10/17/1890			Y	
Gigliotte, Salvatore	42	Italy	Y	Naples	New York	04/11/1882	12/11/1888			Y	
Gilb, Franz	52	Germany	Y	Havre	New York	06/10/1880	08/25/1884			Y	
Gilday, Edward		Pages missing	N				9/21/1854?	10	140	N	
Gilday, Edward	29	Ireland	Y	Liverpool	New Orleans	03/10/1848	09/21/1854	12	79	N	
Gilday, James	33	Ireland	Y	Queenstown	New York	05/03/1882	07/07/1894			Y	
Gildehaus, Henry	21	Hanover	Y	Bremen	New York	10/20/1853	10/06/1856	14	208	N	
Gildehaus, Herman	28	Germany	Y	Bremen	Hoboken	06/21/1886	01/03/1889			Y	
Gildehaus, William	36	Germany	N	Bremen	Baltimore	09/01/1864	?			Y	
Gilgin, Michael	25	Ireland	Y	Liverpool	New York	04/12/1856	01/03/1862	18	240	N	
Gill, Charles	30	Ireland	Y	Liverpool	New Orleans	05/01/1848	02/18/1853	7	183	N	
Gill, George	49	Ireland	N	Liverpool	New York	??/??/1862	?			Y	
Gill, James	23	Ireland	Y	Liverpool	New York	09/??/1858	09/01/1862	18	428	N	
Gill, John	25	Ireland	Y	Liverpool	New York	06/19/1853	10/14/1857	15	425	N	
Gilleece, Patrick	30	Ireland	Y	Liverpool	New York	11/10/1851	09/30/1858	17	21	N	
Gillespie, Christopher	31	Ireland	Y	Liverpool	New York	08/25/1858	11/03/1860	18	6	N	
Gilleth, W.H.	35	England	Y	Liverpool	New York	05/??/1867	10/08/1883			Y	
Gilligan, A. C.	31	Ireland	N	?	New York	03/27/1876	?			Y	
Gilligan, Bartley	27	Ireland	Y	Liverpool	New York	07/29/1848	04/12/1852	24	439	N	
Gilligan, Dominick	21	Ireland	Y	Sligo	New Orleans	04/17/1849	07/19/1851	4	9	N	
Gilligan, Edward	24	Ireland	Y	Liverpool	New York	12/10/1848	07/19/1851	4	7	N	
Gilligan, James	26	Ireland	Y	Sligo	New Orleans	01/01/1849	07/19/1851	4	8	N	
Gilligan, Michael	36	Ireland	Y	Dublin	New Orleans	05/??/1847	01/07/1856	13	429	N	
Gilligan, Patrick	26	Ireland	Y	Liverpool	New York	06/01/18??	03/10/1851	3	270	N	
Gilligan, Patrick	41	Ireland	Y	Liverpool	New York	12/18/1869	01/22/1873	18	549	N	
Gilligan, Patrick	??	Ireland	N	?	?	04/12/1887				Y	10/17/1892
Gilligan, Thomas	26	Ireland	Y	Liverpool	New York	03/30/1888	03/07/1894	21	62	N	
Gilligan, Thomas	26	Ireland	Y	Liverpool	New York	03/30/1888	03/07/1894			Y	
Gillmen, Bernard	31	Austria	Y	Havre	New York	01/09/1888	10/26/1893			Y	
Gillott, Joab	26	England	Y	Liverpool	New York	10/15/1851	11/03/1855	13	155	N	
Gilmartin, Owen	32	Ireland	Y	Dublin	New York	07/??/1881	10/18/1886	19	152	N	
Gilmartin, Owen	32	Ireland	Y	Dublin	New York	07/??/1881	10/18/1888			Y	
Gilmurray, James	25	Ireland	Y	Liverpool	New York	03/09/1849	?	14	98	N	

CITIZENSHIP RECORDS

APPLICANT	AGE	COUNTRY OF ORIGIN	DEC	DEPART PORT	ENTRY PORT	ARRIVE DATE	DEC DATE	VOL	PG.	FLD	NAT DATE
Gilroy, James	33	Ireland	Y	Liverpool	New Orleans	??/16/1847	03/22/1851	3	308	N	
Gimbel, Michael	28	Hesse Darmsta	Y	Maintz	New York	08/07/1846	04/15/1852	24	510	N	
Gimkel, Ernst	70	Germany	N	Bremen	New York	01/??/1854	?			Y	
Gimpel, William	35	Baden	Y	Havre	New Orleans	12/25/1848	11/16/1858	17	338	N	
Ginandt, George	25	Bavaria	Y	Havre	New York	07/29/1848	03/11/1853	7	325	N	
Ginandt, William	37	Bavaria	Y	Havre	New Orleans	11/??/1838	09/20/1855	13	86	N	
Gindele, Anthony	37	Wurttemberg	Y	Liverpool	New York	05/03/1855	07/28/1857	15	136	N	
Ginder, Francis	23	Hesse Cassel	Y	Bremen	Baltimore	10/08/1854	10/14/1857	15	421	N	
Ging, William	23	Ireland	Y	Liverpool	New York	04/16/1850	09/29/1856	14	436	N	
Gingench, Christian	61	Germany	N	Hesse Darmst	New York	08/??/1850	??/??/1854	28	376	N	09/??/1856
Gingl, Andrew	25	Austria	Y	?	?	04/29/1901	08/25/1903			Y	
Gininder, Eberhard	40	Wurttemberg	Y	Havre	New Orleans	09/15/1853	10/30/1858	17	211	N	
Ginn, William	46	Ireland	Y	Dublin	New Orleans	04/30/1849	01/10/1853	7	5	N	
Ginsburg, Aaron	25	Russia	Y	?	New York	??/??/1890	07/16/1894			Y	
Ginsonie, William Franci	24	Switzerland	Y	?	?	?	09/16/1899			Y	
Ginty, James	27	Ireland	Y	Liverpool	New York	07/01/1847	04/18/1853	8	85	N	
Gioglardi, Carlo	38	Italy	Y	?	New York	??/??/1885	05/21/1894			Y	
Giovanni, Russo	31	Italy	Y	Palermo	New York	03/19/1894	10/26/1900			Y	
Giringer, George	35	Baden	Y	Havre	New York	08/18/1843	11/14/1855	13	224	N	
Given, James	23	Ireland	Y	Londonderry	New York	08/04/1851	04/20/1854	8	225	N	
Given, James	23	Ireland	Y	Londonderry	New York	08/04/1851	04/20/1854	9	76	N	
Given, Patrick	28	Ireland	Y	Liverpool	New York	03/06/1849	04/26/1853	8	124	N	
Giver, J. M.	48	Prussia	N	Rotterdam	New York	08/05/1864	?			Y	
Glaab, George	??	Bavaria	Y	?	?	?	04/03/1868			Y	
Glacken, Charles	29	Ireland	Y	Liverpool	New York	03/31/1883	04/25/1888			Y	
Glahsl, Adam	26	Germany	Y	Bremen	New York	05/13/1887	11/04/1893			Y	
Glancy, Patrick	38	Ireland	Y	Liverpool	New Orleans	01/21/1848	02/28/1850	2	144	N	
Glannan, Michael	24	Ireland	Y	Liverpool	New Orleans	05/22/1848	09/09/1848	22	312	N	
Glanzberg, Isaak	21	Austria	Y	Hamburg	New York	10/19/1898	09/13/1900			Y	
Glanzman, Martin	26	Baden	Y	Havre	New Orleans	01/27/1848	05/07/1850	3	59	N	
Glas, Moses	44	Germany	N	Bavaria	New York	04/??/1863	?			Y	
Glasbrener, Adam	58	Baden	Y	Havre	New Orleans	12/10/1846	09/07/1852	25	393	N	
Glascher, Frederick	30	Prussia	Y	Bremen	New York	09/18/1852	06/05/1854	10	93	N	
Glascher, Frederick	30	Prussia	Y	Bremen	New York	09/18/1852	06/05/1854	12	30	N	
Glascow, John	23	Ireland	Y	Liverpool	New Orleans	07/04/1848	03/10/1851	3	214	N	
Glaser, Adam	22	Bavaria	Y	Antwerp	New York	05/18/1850	05/31/1852	25	140	N	
Glaser, Baltser	68	France	N	Havre	New York	03/28/1851	11/??/1854	28	246	N	10/??/1857
Glaser, Emile Frederick	35	Switzerland	Y	Antwerp	Philadelphia	12/14/1892	08/16/1894			Y	
Glaser, Friederich Augus	36	Germany	Y	Bremen	Baltimore	05/24/1888	01/07/1890			Y	
Glaser, Jacob	40	Germany	Y	Bremen	New York	03/23/1880	10/14/1886			Y	
Glaser, John	28	Bavaria	Y	Havre	New York	08/06/1849	10/02/1856	14	158	N	
Glaser, Joseph	28	Bavaria	Y	Bremen	New York	08/08/1853	01/01/1856	14	76	N	
Glaser, Lawrence	28	Germany	Y	Havre	New York	03/10/1881	03/05/1889			Y	
Glaser, Lewis	23	Bavaria	Y	Havre	New York	09/15/1847	01/13/1851	2	483	N	
Glaser, Martin	28	Bavaria	Y	Antwerp	New York	05/18/1850	05/31/1852	25	157	N	
Glaser, Mathias	27	Bavaria	Y	Antwerp	New Orleans	01/06/1849	04/09/1852	24	423	N	
Glaser, Max	22	Bavaria	Y	London	New York	08/08/1848	09/14/1852	25	503	N	
Glaser, William	31	Baden	Y	Havre	New York	12/02/1854	12/18/1855	13	329	N	
Glasmeier, Henry	30	Germany	Y	Bremen	New York	10/12/1872	05/03/1883			Y	
Glasmeyer, Friedrich	28	Germany	Y	Bremen	New York	04/18/1885	12/31/1888			Y	
Glass, Alexander	??	England	Y	?	?	?	04/17/1893			Y	
Glasser, Frank	34	Germany	Y	Havre	New York	06/25/1887	03/20/1900			Y	
Glassmeyer, Gerhard Henr	73	Germany	N	Bremen	New York	06/??/1844	??/??/1847	28	78	N	09/??/1851
Glaszer, John	27	Germany	Y	Bremen	Baltimore	12/18/1879	07/12/1885			Y	
Glatt, John	35	Baden	Y	Antwerp	New Orleans	12/07/1853	09/26/1856	14	385	N	
Glatter, Franz	29	Austria	Y	Hamburg	New York	08/25/1852	05/25/1854	9	420	N	
Glatter, Franz	29	Austria	Y	Hamburg	New York	08/25/1852	05/25/1854	10	3	N	
Glattus, Joseph	36	France	Y	Havre	New Orleans	04/27/1848	10/07/1856	14	424	N	
Glatz, Henry A.	28	Prussia	Y	Bremen	New York	07/29/1850	06/19/1851	3	408	N	

CITIZENSHIP RECORDS

APPLICANT	AGE	COUNTRY OF ORIGIN	DEC	DEPART PORT	ENTRY PORT	ARRIVE DATE	DEC DATE	VOL	PG.	FLD	NAT DATE
Glaub, George	??	Bavaria	Y	?	?	?	04/03/1868			Y	
Glauck, Edmond	23	Germany	Y	Bremen	Baltimore	09/22/1880	07/30/1883			Y	
Glawe, Charles	26	Germany	Y	Hamburg	New York	12/14/1868	10/19/1875			Y	
Gleascher, Christian G.W	24	Prussia	Y	Bremen	New Orleans	05/01/1849	03/30/1852	24	335	N	
Gleeson, James	28	Ireland	Y	Liverpool	New York	07/26/1847	02/20/1852	24	144	N	
Gleeson, Michael	38	Ireland	Y	Liverpool	New Orleans	03/02/1850	02/21/1853	7	208	N	
Gleeson, Patrick	28	Ireland	Y	Liverpool	New Orleans	02/14/1848	03/03/1851	3	197	N	
Gleeson, Patrick	32	Ireland	Y	Liverpool	New York	06/01/1849	06/21/1851	3	436	N	
Gleich, Balthazan	75	Germany	N	Havre	New York	07/01/1850	?			Y	
Gleim, Ernst C.	37	Germany	Y	Rotterdam	New York	02/03/1883	11/30/1886			Y	
Glen, William H.	26	Canada	Y	Toronto	Detroit	06/18/1882	09/24/1885			Y	
Glenn, Patrick	49	Ireland	Y	Liverpool	New York	10/20/1861	03/15/1893			Y	
Glennon, James	40	Ireland	Y	Liverpool	New York	05/04/1848	11/16/1852	5	299	N	
Glennon, James	40	Ireland	Y	Liverpool	New York	05/04/1848	11/16/1852	6	423	N	
Glick, Harry	21	Russia	Y	Hamburg	Baltimore	07/12/1890	12/17/1872			Y	
Glingmeier, Fred	54	Germany	Y	Bremen	Baltimore	11/15/1854	03/27/1889			Y	
Glissen, William G.	29	Ireland	Y	Liverpool	New York	04/22/1849	01/07/1851	2	473	N	
Glockhof, Alexander	25	Mecklenburg	Y	Hamburg	New Orleans	12/11/1848	07/05/1851	3	486	N	
Glogenbeigh, Joseph Henr	28	Hanover	Y	Bremen	New Orleans	12/28/1844	04/02/1852	24	357	N	
Gloor, John	28	Switzerland	Y	Havre	New York	05/01/1883	04/08/1887			Y	
Gloss, George	57	Wurttemberg	Y	Havre	New York	06/06/1853	10/08/1857	15	375	N	
Glotz, Oscar	29	Germany	Y	Bremen	New York	01/25/1885	11/17/1891			Y	
Glover, Henry	61	England	N	New Castle	New York	09/19/1855	?			Y	
Glover, Joseph	34	England	Y	Liverpool	Philadelphia	06/20/1842	05/03/1850	3	44	N	
Gluck, John George	28	Bavaria	Y	Hamburg	New York	08/01/1854	10/03/1854	12	325	N	
Gluck, Morris	20	Russia	Y	Hamburg	New York	05/17/1888	07/25/1891			Y	
Gluckmann, Joseph	22	Russia	Y	Antwerp	New York	10/12/1881	01/09/1882			Y	
Glueck, Jacob	22	Bavaria	Y	Havre	New York	09/01/1846	02/06/1851	3	102	N	
Glueck, John George	28	Bavaria	Y	Hamburg	New York	08/01/1854	10/03/1854	10	386	N	
Glueck, Nicholas	24	Bavaria	Y	Havre	New York	06/04/1859	05/01/1860	27	176	N	
Glunz, Jacob	40	Germany	Y	Antwerp	New York	04/14/1870	10/26/1893	21	36	N	
Glunz, Jacob	40	Germany	Y	Antwerp	New York	04/14/1870	10/26/1893			Y	
Glunz, John	27	Baden	Y	Havre	New York	03/07/1854	04/05/1858	16	492	N	
Glynn, Michael	25	Ireland	Y	Liverpool	New York	03/12/1882	04/04/1883			Y	
Glynn, Patrick	26	Ireland	Y	Dublin	New York	04/08/1850	01/31/1853	7	92	N	
Gnaedinger, John	23	Baden	Y	Havre	New York	08/27/1853	03/10/1856	26	176	N	
Gnau, Gustav	??	Germany	Y	?	?	?	08/01/1893			Y	
Gnecco, Antonio	31	Italy	Y	Genoa	New York	10/30/1879	01/14/1890			Y	
Gnecco, John	42	Italy	N	Hamburg	New York	??/??/1868	?			Y	
Gnecco, Paul	26	Italy	Y	Geneva	New York	11/28/1886	09/06/1893			Y	
Gneiting, Adam	42	Wurtemberg	Y	Rotterdam	New Orleans	04/01/1848	09/07/1852	25	394	N	
Gnoelk, Dionis	45	Germany	Y	Havre	New York	12/09/1881	03/10/1888			Y	
Gnoeth, John	26	Germany	Y	Havre	New York	07/01/1890	10/29/1892			Y	
Gobrecht, Christ G.	??	Germany	N	?	?	06/14/1875				Y	10/27/1892
Gobrecht, William	37	Germany	Y	Bremen	New York	09/26/1866	03/26/1883			Y	
Gocke, John Henry	35	Prussia	Y	Bremen	New York	07/08/1852	09/18/1855	13	64	N	
Gocke, Peter	29	Prussia	Y	Antwerp	New York	06/20/1852	06/12/1854	10	120	N	
Gocke, Peter	29	Prussia	Y	Antwerp	New York	06/20/1852	06/12/1854	12	57	N	
Gockemeyer, Henry	24	Germany	Y	Bremen	Baltimore	07/06/1882	05/09/1887			Y	
Godeke, Henry	42	Hanover	Y	Bremen	Philadelphia	09/04/1845	10/02/1848	22	382	N	
Godemann, Joseph	29	Germany	Y	Bremen	Baltimore	09/01/1882	06/30/1886			Y	
Goderwis, John	22	Hanover	Y	Bremen	New Orleans	11/05/1853	03/25/1856	26	339	N	
Godfrey, Charles H.	31	Canada	Y	?	Portland	04/10/1869	09/25/1878			Y	
Godfrey, Patrick	23	Ireland	Y	Queenstown	New York	05/01/1888	11/02/1891			Y	
Goebel, Frederick	??	Waldeck	Y	?	New York	07/17/18??	11/03/1856	14	457	N	
Goebel, Frederick	22	Wurttemberg	Y	Havre	New ?	06/13/1857	11/22/1858	17	347	N	
Goebel, George Anthony	??	Germany	Y	?	?	?	10/06/1897			Y	
Goebel, Henry	26	Waldeck	Y	Bremen	New York	08/17/1854	04/05/1858	16	494	N	
Goebel, John	26	Hesse Darmsta	Y	London	New York	10/02/1854	10/01/1856	14	97	N	

CITIZENSHIP RECORDS

APPLICANT	AGE	COUNTRY OF ORIGIN	DEC	DEPART PORT	ENTRY PORT	ARRIVE DATE	DEC DATE	VOL	PG.	FLD	NAT DATE
Goebel, Julius	26	Prussia	Y	Hamburg	New York	08/08/1873	11/19/1885			Y	
Goebele, John Michael	33	Bavaria	Y	Havre	New York	05/15/1854	02/11/1856	26	68	N	
Goedhart, Abraham	35	Holland	Y	Rotterdam	New York	05/01/1878	09/08/1888			Y	
Goees, Frederick	36	Hanover	Y	Bremen	Baltimore	08/13/1844	05/01/1854	8	315	N	
Goees, Frederick	36	Hanover	Y	Bremen	Baltimore	08/13/1844	05/01/1854	9	188	N	
Goefft, Lawrent	38	Germany	Y	Havre	New York	07/10/1890	03/18/1898			Y	
Goegal, Leonard	36	Bavaria	Y	Havre	New York	06/02/1852	10/07/1854	6	19	N	
Goegal, Leonhard	36	Bavaria	Y	Havre	New York	06/02/8152	10/07/1854	11	19	N	
Goehl, Anthony	28	Bavaria	Y	Havre	New York	05/21/1856	09/26/1856	14	391	N	
Goehlamnn, August	45	Germany	Y	Bremen	New York	03/20/1879	04/02/1888			Y	
Goehring, Martin	22	Germany	Y	Antwerp	Philadelphia	05/17/1892	03/14/1894			Y	
Goeldner, Adolph	37	Germany	Y	Bremen	Baltimore	04/17/1891	12/26/1896			Y	
Goeldner, Charles	38	Germany	Y	Bremen	Baltimore	03/24/1887	10/25/1893			Y	
Goelkel, Adam	32	Bavaria	Y	Bremen	New York	09/15/1849	09/01/1852	18	429	N	
Goeltz, Peter	28	Germany	Y	Antwerp	Philadelphia	10/04/1882	12/14/1887			Y	
Goemann, John Henry	50	Hanover	Y	Bremen	Baltimore	08/29/1860	07/08/1861	18	203	N	
Goemann, W.	25	Germany	Y	Bremen	New York	06/18/1882	08/11/1884			Y	
Goennenwein, Frederick	??	Germany	Y	?	?	?	03/25/1889			Y	
Goepfert, John	28	Bavaria	Y	Hamburg	New York	07/15/1859	04/29/1861	18	152	N	
Goepfert, John	51	Germany	N	Havre	New York	09/??/1872	?			Y	
Goepfert, Mathias	44	Baden	Y	Havre	New Orleans	11/25/1845	10/13/1851	4	238	N	
Goepp, Charles	22	Germany	Y	Havre	New York	04/15/1891	09/18/1893			Y	
Goeppinger, Karl	24	Germany	Y	Bremen	Baltimore	08/24/1890	11/01/1892			Y	
Goergen, Peter	26	Germany	Y	Antwerp	New York	08/21/1891	03/04/1895			Y	
Goering, August	29	Bavaria	Y	Havre	New York	11/21/1854	02/19/1857	15	27	N	
Goering, Marcus	21	Baden	Y	Havre	New Orleans	04/14/1854	08/24/1857	15	179	N	
Goerl, John	31	Germany	Y	Bremen	New York	03/28/1873	03/31/1883			Y	
Goeser, August	34	Wuerttenberg	Y	Bremen	New York	02/03/1849	11/12/1852	25	9	N	
Goesker, Clamor Leopold	22	Hanover	Y	Bremen	New Orleans	11/30/1855	09/26/1856	14	388	N	
Goesling, Eduard	29	Germany	Y	Bremen	Baltimore	11/01/1892	10/26/1900			Y	
Goesling, Francis Arnold	24	Oldenburg	Y	Bremen	Baltimore	11/01/1855	03/31/1858	16	456	N	
Goesling, William	29	Germany	Y	Bremen	Baltimore	02/21/1889	08/02/1892			Y	
Goess, Henry	45	Bavaria	Y	Bremen	Baltimore	06/24/1844	08/02/1848	22	38	N	
Goesslen, John	30	Wuerttenberg	Y	Bremen	New York	10/17/1842	01/19/1842	24	29	N	
Goettke, Johann B.	31	Germany	Y	Bremen	Baltimore	12/??/1879	10/15/1884			Y	
Goettke, Ludwig	30	Germany	Y	Bremen	New York	06/25/1881	11/01/1883			Y	
Goetz, August	??	Germany	N	?	?	06/17/1887				Y	10/13/1892
Goetz, Christian	55	Baden	Y	Liverpool	New York	07/12/1852	02/15/1856	26	84	N	
Goetz, Friedrich	35	Germany	Y	Bremen	New York	11/04/1881	02/23/1898			Y	
Goetz, George	??	Germany	Y	?	Baltimore	??/??/1870	10/08/1880			Y	
Goetz, Gottlieb	23	Wuertemberg	Y	Havre	New York	04/01/1854	04/07/1856	26	458	N	
Goetz, Jacob	32	Baden	Y	Havre	New York	??/15/18??	02/21/1853	7	196	N	
Goetz, Jacob	38	Hesse Darmsta	Y	Havre	New York	10/06/1858	04/21/1862	18	322	N	
Goetz, Jacob	47	Germany	N	Havre	New Orleans	12/23/1851	?			Y	
Goetz, John	25	Bavaria	Y	Bremen	New York	05/01/1849	10/16/1851	4	310	N	
Goetz, John	27	Bavaria	Y	Bremen	New Orleans	05/24/1852	11/01/1852	5	142	N	
Goetz, John	31	Germany	Y	Bremen	New York	03/14/1885	03/18/1885			Y	
Goetz, Leonhard	43	Bavaria	Y	Bremen	Baltimore	08/29/1852	05/27/1856	26	558	N	
Goetz, Peter	28	Bavaria	Y	Havre	New York	08/10/1848	03/05/1852	24	236	N	
Goetze, Ernst	34	Germany	Y	Hamburg	New York	05/29/1887	03/07/1891			Y	
Goetze, Gustav	29	Germany	Y	Bremen	New York	07/12/1887	09/17/1889			Y	
Goetze, William	35	Prussia	Y	Hamburg	New York	06/24/1853	10/20/1858	17	80	N	
Goetze, William	34	Hanover	Y	Bremen	Baltimore	06/23/1855	10/30/1858	17	198	N	
Goffny, Peter	23	Ireland	Y	Liverpool	New York	12/13/1851	12/24/1852	5	444	N	
Gogoll, Frederick	??	Germany	Y	?	?	?	02/16/1893			Y	
Gogrene, Christ. Henry	29	Hanover	Y	Bremen	New Orleans	??/14/1845	01/31/1850	2	19	N	
Gogreve, Henry William	33	Hanover	Y	Bremen	New Orleans	03/02/1849	09/28/1854	10	288	N	
Gogreve, Henry William	33	Hanover	Y	Bremen	New Orleans	05/20/1849	09/28/1854	12	227	N	
Gohman, Bernard	47	Hanover	Y	Bremen	New York	07/??/1837	02/28/1856	26	136	N	

CITIZENSHIP RECORDS

APPLICANT	AGE	COUNTRY OF ORIGIN	DEC	DEPART PORT	ENTRY PORT	ARRIVE DATE	DEC DATE	VOL	PG.	FLD	NAT DATE
Gohmann, Clem	??	Germany	N	?	?	11/01/1882				Y	10/28/1892
Gohmann, Henry	33	Germany	Y	Amsterdam	New York	01/01/1882	04/01/1893			Y	
Gohn, Eduard	??	Germany	Y	?	?	?	07/15/1890			Y	
Goken, Bernard	21	Hanover	Y	Bremen	New Orleans	11/04/1853	09/27/1854	10	262	N	
Goken, Bernard	21	Hanover	Y	Bremen	New Orleans	11/04/1853	09/27/1865	12	201	N	
Golatzki, Anton	27	Prussia	Y	Hamburg	New York	05/28/1854	10/01/1856	14	117	N	
Gold, Meier	33	Russia	Y	Hamburg	Philadelphia	04/04/1891	01/24/1894			Y	
Gold, Woolf	27	Russia	Y	Hamburg	Boston	07/04/1894	06/27/1904			Y	
Goldammer, Wilhelm	38	Germany	Y	Hamburg	New York	02/27/1883	10/02/1889			Y	
Goldate, John	27	Bavaria	Y	Havre	New York	07/27/1848	01/21/1853	7	49	N	
Goldate, Theobald	28	Germany	Y	Anterp	New York	08/30/1883	10/19/1888			Y	
Goldbach, John	30	Bavaria	Y	Bremen	New York	06/05/1850	04/30/1852	24	528	N	
Goldberg, Jacob	49	Roumania	Y	Bremen	New York	08/28/1900	01/25/1904			Y	
Goldberg, Joe	45	Austria	Y	Hamburg	New York	07/16/1881	05/10/1883	28	176	N	
Goldberg, Maier	25	Russia	Y	Hamburg	New York	05/09/1886	05/20/1889			Y	
Goldberg, Moritz	29	Austria	Y	Antwerp	New York	10/04/1881	09/19/1887			Y	
Goldberg, Morris	32	Russia	Y	London	New York	05/18/1852	04/19/1854	8	216	N	
Goldberg, Morris	32	Russia	Y	London	New York	05/18/1852	04/19/1854	9	87	N	
Goldberg, Sammuel	35	Turkey	Y	Hamburg	New York	09/15/1887	10/01/1894			Y	
Goldberg, Solomon	40	Russia	Y	Hamburg	Philadelphia	05/??/1882	06/10/1886			Y	
Goldberger, Henry	??	Austria	Y	?	?	?	09/27/1887			Y	
Goldblatt, Moses	35	Russia	Y	Hamburg	New York	06/30/1889	06/25/1895			Y	
Golde, Charles	25	Reuss	Y	Bremen	New York	05/01/1854	08/17/1857	15	151	N	
Golden, James	26	Ireland	Y	Cork	Bangor	05/04/1845	10/14/1851	4	285	N	
Goldenberg, Abraham	39	Russia	Y	Hamburg	New York	12/29/1891	11/04/1893			Y	
Goldenberg, Benjamin	??	Roumania	Y	?	?	01/??/1900	08/12/1902			Y	
Goldenberger, John	33	Switzerland	Y	Havre	New York	11/11/1845	10/06/1851	4	198	N	
Goldenburg, Myron	40	Russia	Y	Hamburg	Philadelphia	05/18/1882	09/27/1888	19	141	N	
Goldenstede, John	32	Germany	Y	Bremen	New York	04/15/1881	10/19/1888	19	156	N	
Goldenstede, John	32	Germany	Y	Bremen	New York	04/15/1881	10/19/1888			Y	
Golder, Gotllob	??	Germany	Y	?	?	?	02/09/1889			Y	
Goldfarb, Wolf	22	Russia	Y	Bremen	Baltimore	11/20/1891	09/07/1894			Y	
Goldfus, John	28	Germany	Y	Bremen	New York	05/27/1879	10/03/1882			Y	
Goldfuss, John	30	Germany	Y	Bremen	Baltimore	05/26/1883	03/28/1891			Y	
Goldkuehler, Gerhard	39	Germany	Y	Bremen	Baltimore	08/01/1882	09/16/1884			Y	
Goldman, Adolph	??	Austria	Y	?	?	?	10/04/1880			Y	
Goldman, Charles	??	Russia	Y	?	?	10/20/1891	07/07/1896			Y	
Goldman, Joseph	32	Austria	Y	Vienna	New York	01/15/1882	01/23/1886			Y	
Goldoff, Abraham	38	Russia	Y	Bremen	Baltimore	03/20/1888	10/03/1895			Y	
Goldsch, Charles	21	Braunschweig	Y	Bremen	New York	09/15/1854	10/12/1857	15	406	N	
Goldschmidt, Abraham	27	Oldenburg	Y	Bremen	Baltimore	09/??/1848	08/??/1851	4	162	N	
Goldschmidt, Bernhard	35	Hanover	Y	Bremen	New Orleans	11/30/1852	08/29/1862	18	420	N	
Goldschmidt, Conrad	35	Baden	Y	Hamburg	New York	06/02/1860	06/01/1872	18	496	N	
Goldstein, Albert	35	Russia	Y	Hamburg	New York	09/17/1884	05/12/1898			Y	
Goldstein, Barnett	30	Russia	Y	Hamburg	New York	07/??/1885	09/14/1888			Y	
Goldstein, Isaac (Israel	28	Russia	Y	?	?	03/01/1881	09/19/1887			Y	
Goldstein, John Davis	31	Russia	Y	Constantinop	New York	12/31/1849	05/27/1859	17	434	N	
Goldstein, Joseph	25	Russia	Y	Hamburg	New York	??/??/1883	07/30/1888			Y	
Goldstein, Morris	32	Russia	Y	Antwerp	New York	04/01/1887	04/07/1890			Y	
Goldstein, Samuel	30	Russia	Y	Hamburg	New York	10/24/1890	10/10/1900			Y	
Goldstein, Sol	26	Russia	Y	Kijow	New York	10/12/1882	01/15/1884			Y	
Goldstein, Sol	38	Russia	N	Kijour	New York	10/12/1821	?			Y	
Golembiewski, John	27	Russia	Y	Bremen	Baltimore	05/19/1892	10/09/1896			Y	
Gollenstine, Philip	25	Bavaria	Y	Havre	New York	03/12/1857	07/10/1860	27	218	N	
Gollins, Jacob H.	23	Hesse Darmsta	Y	Havre	New York	10/25/1857	10/13/1860	27	491	N	
Gollmer, John Frederick	51	Wurttemberg	Y	Rotterdam	New York	09/13/1847	10/11/1848	1	119	N	
Golsch, Fred	36	Germany	N	Hamburg	New York	05/22/1870	?			Y	
Golter, John Conrad	54	Wurttemberg	Y	Rotterdam	New York	06/04/1847	04/07/1855	11	346	N	
Golz, Michael	46	Prussia	Y	Bremen	Baltimore	06/15/1855	10/30/1857	15	502	N	

CITIZENSHIP RECORDS

APPLICANT	AGE	COUNTRY OF ORIGIN	DEC	DEPART PORT	ENTRY PORT	ARRIVE DATE	DEC DATE	VOL	PG.	FLD	NAT DATE
Goman, John	31	Hanover	Y	Bremen	New Orleans	01/01/1847	04/18/1853	8	80	N	
Gomann, Diedrich	35	Hanover	Y	Bremen	New Orleans	01/02/1844	05/08/1852	24	417	N	
Gommel, August	35	Germany	Y	Hamburg	New York	06/15/1888	10/21/1896			Y	
Gondzwaard, Aart	30	Holland	Y	Antwerp	New York	04/25/1857	03/01/1860	27	116	N	
Gontermann, John Charles	29	Kurhassen	Y	Bremen	New York	??/07/1848	12/24/1849	23	428	N	
Gooder, Edwin	38	Canada	Y	Fort Erie	Buffalo	05/15/1879	07/01/1892			Y	
Goodfellow, S.A.	37	England	Y	Rotterdam	New York	04/17/1881	01/21/1892	19	346	N	
Goodfellow, S.A.	37	Ireland	Y	Rotterdam	New York	04/17/1881	01/21/1892			Y	
Goodman, Adolph	30	Wurttemberg	Y	London	New York	08/20/1847	10/18/1851	4	328	N	
Goodman, Bernard	30	Poland	Y	?	New York	??/??/1871	07/15/1882			Y	
Goodman, Harris	29	Russia	Y	Liverpool	New York	11/28/1888	02/11/1893			Y	
Goodman, Jacob	41	Russia	Y	Hamburg	New York	08/14/1888	05/22/1893			Y	
Goodman, Marcus	49	Germany	Y	Liverpool	New York	04/30/1887	10/19/1888			Y	
Goodwin, John	36	Ireland	Y	Liverpool	New York	05/23/1850	02/24/1853	7	229	N	
Goosmann, Bernard	23	Germany	Y	Bremen	Baltimore	06/16/1880	04/03/1882			Y	
Goosmann, Fred	21	Germany	Y	Amsterdam	New York	09/28/1881	09/13/1884			Y	
Goosmann, Hermann	24	Germany	Y	Amsterdam	New York	08/27/1884	06/08/1887			Y	
Goosmann, Richard	29	Germany	N	Bremen	New York	10/??/1872	?			Y	
Goothas, Gerhard	30	Hanover	Y	Havre	New Orleans	05/11/1849	05/20/1852	25	83	N	
Goppus, Jacob	30	Russia	Y	Hamburg	New York	06/15/1892	01/24/1894			Y	
Gorbach, Albert	??	Austria	Y	?	?	?	03/25/1891			Y	
Gorbach, Carl	56	Austria	Y	Havre	New York	12/20/1887	01/27/1897			Y	
Gordes, Joseph	30	Germany	Y	Bremen	Baltimore	03/24/1888	10/28/1890	19	307	N	
Gordon, Franklin	64	Scotland	Y	?	New York	??/??/1856	10/11/1892			Y	
Gordon, James	23	Ireland	Y	Liverpool	New Orleans	11/26/1847	11/21/1848	1	358	N	
Gordon, James	22	Ireland	Y	Liverpool	New York	06/15/1851	05/01/1854	8	292	N	
Gordon, James	22	Ireland	Y	Liverpool	New York	06/15/1851	05/01/1855	9	164	N	
Gordon, James	39	England	Y	Liverpool	New Orleans	11/??/1847	11/??/1849	23	352	N	
Gordon, Morris	24	Russia	Y	?	New York	06/16/1889	10/22/1892			Y	
Gorean, Henry	28	Ireland	Y	Liverpool	Philadelphia	08/16/1852	07/20/1855	11	412	N	
Gorian, Daniel	49	Ireland	N	Liverpool	Philadelphia	08/??/1855	?			Y	
Gorigfer, George	28	Bavaria	Y	Antwerp	New Orleans	02/01/1848	05/31/1852	25	165	N	
Gorman, Patrick	30	Ireland	Y	Liverpool	New York	08/01/1851	02/21/1853	7	205	N	
Gorman, William	24	Ireland	Y	?	?	?	04/25/1885			Y	
Gormann, Theodore	33	Prussia	Y	Antwerp	New York	07/16/1857	03/14/1860	27	126	N	
Gormley, Edward	20	Ireland	Y	Liverpool	New York	08/02/1844	11/17/1848	1	315	N	
Gormly, John	22	Ireland	Y	Liverpool	New Orleans	02/01/1850	04/05/1852	24	386	N	
Gornersall, Bruce	40	England	N	Liverpool	New York	03/??/1864	?			Y	
Gorrian, Daniel	42	Ireland	N	Liverpool	New York	08/15/1867	?	28	340	N	10/01/1877
Gorrian, Patrick	58	Ireland	N	Liverpool	New York	09/??/1854	?			Y	
Gorsler, Albert	23	Germany	Y	Rotterdam	New York	06/01/1879	08/15/1882			Y	
Gorterweis, Leonard	??	Hanover	Y	Bremen	New Orleans	05/30/1848	10/09/1848	22	507	N	
Gosemeyer, Henry	30	Hanover	Y	Bremen	New Orleans	??/27/1844	02/19/1849	23	218	N	
Gosker, John Heinrich	21	Hanover	Y	Bremen	Baltimore	05/03/1857	07/30/1860	27	239	N	
Gosker, Joseph	23	Hanover	Y	Havre	New York	05/27/1849	01/24/1853	7	58	N	
Gosker, Max	50	Germany	Y	Bremen	New York	03/27/1867	10/08/1883			Y	
Goslin, Thomas	24	Ireland	Y	Liverpool	New York	05/24/1848	04/01/1853	7	484	N	
Gosling, Herman	26	Germany	Y	Bremen	New York	08/26/1881	11/22/1888			Y	
Gossling, Joseph	33	Prussia	Y	Antwerp	New York	09/21/1847	11/22/1848	1	368	N	
Gossmann, Henry	23	Hesse Cassel	Y	Bremen	New York	03/03/1852	05/22/1856	26	520	N	
Gothsprich, Andrew	24	Baden	Y	Rotterdam	New York	12/25/1846	10/11/1848	1	103	N	
Gotlieb, Jidel	31	Austria	Y	Bremen	New York	07/01/1884	04/27/1893			Y	
Gottlieb, Gottlieb	53	Germany	N	Bavaria	New York	11/??/1856	?			Y	
Gottlieb, Joseph	55	Germany	N	Havre	New York	05/??/1853	?			Y	
Gottlieb, Simon	26	Bavaria	Y	London	New York	06/06/1848	03/17/1852	24	325	N	
Gottlieb, Zieskind	28	Russia	Y	Hamburg	New York	11/28/1886	10/09/1890			Y	
Gottlob, David	48	Germany	N	Havre	New York	11/??/1856	?			Y	
Gottlob, Lorenz	38	Saxe Weimar	Y	Bremen	New York	06/26/1850	11/08/1851	4	503	N	
Gottmann, Franz Heinrich	22	Hanover	Y	Bremen	New Orleans	12/31/1852	10/07/1854	10	533	N	

CITIZENSHIP RECORDS

APPLICANT	AGE	COUNTRY OF ORIGIN	DEC	DEPART PORT	ENTRY PORT	ARRIVE DATE	DEC DATE	VOL	PG.	FLD	NAT DATE
Gottmann, Henry	25	Baden	Y	London	New York	01/03/1848	06/19/1851	3	425	N	
Gottmann, Henry	30	Hanover	Y	Bremen	New Orleans	05/30/1852	10/06/1854	10	501	N	
Gottmann, Henry	30	Hanover	Y	Bremen	New Orleans	05/30/1852	10/06/1854	12	440	N	
Gottschalg, Hermann	32	Germany	Y	Hamburg	New York	01/26/1886	08/10/1889			Y	
Gottschalk, Chas. A	24	Germany	Y	Bremen	Baltimore	09/13/1878	01/14/1884			Y	
Gottschalk, Frederick	27	Prussia	Y	Bremen	New York	07/01/1853	08/24/1857	15	175	N	
Gottschalk, Henry	28	Germany	Y	Rotterdam	New York	05/19/1881	10/29/1883			Y	
Gottschalk, Robert	25	Prussia	Y	Hamburg	New York	09/13/1857	08/27/1862	18	407	N	
Gottschall, Henry	27	Germany	Y	Hamburg	New York	08/06/1898	03/03/1903			Y	
Gottschlich, Paul	42	Germany	Y	Hamburg	New York	05/26/1880	10/23/1886	19	77	N	
Gottschol, Frank	39	Germany	Y	Bremen	Baltimore	06/20/1883	12/31/1891			N	
Gotz, John	29	Bavaria	Y	Bremen	New Orleans	05/24/1852	11/01/1852	6	268	N	
Gough, Patrick	31	Ireland	Y	Liverpool	New York	06/03/1839	02/21/1851	3	151	N	
Gough, Thomas	25	Ireland	Y	Liverpool	New York	06/12/1849	07/05/1851	3	484	N	
Gould, William	??	Scotland	N	?	?	04/28/1875				Y	10/24/1892
Goulet, Joseph	55	Canada	N	Montreal	Chicago	06/??/1857	?			Y	
Goulet, Joseph	54	Canada	N	Montreal	Chicago	09/??/1857	?			Y	
Gousey, John	34	Germany	N	Havre	?	?	??/??/1877	28	114	N	??/??/1884
Gousy, John	24	Germany	Y	Havre	New York	07/31/1873	09/19/1877			Y	
Gouy, Dominick	40	Germany	Y	Havre	New York	09/27/1871	07/03/1876			Y	
Gow, Walter	26	Scotland	Y	Glasgow	New York	07/27/1854	12/14/1857	16	223	N	
Gownan, Michael	29	Ireland	Y	Liverpool	New Orleans	03/10/1851	10/03/1857	15	346	N	
Goyan, William	30	Ireland	Y	Liverpool	New Orleans	11/27/1850	11/01/1852	6	266	N	
Grabau, Walther	??	Germany	Y	?	?	?	09/01/1872			Y	
Grabe, Gerhard	34	Hanover	Y	Bremen	Baltimore	08/03/1851	02/29/1856	26	142	N	
Grabe, John J.	25	Russia	Y	?	Boston	07/15/1893	07/11/1895			Y	
Grabenstetter, Fred	50	Germany	N	Havre	New York	05/??/1854	?			Y	
Graber, Frederick	42	Germany	Y	Bremen	Baltimore	08/18/1868	10/18/1884			Y	
Grabol, Herman	29	Prussia	Y	Bremen	New York	??/10/1848	12/03/1849	23	382	N	
Grabosch, Mathias	34	Prussia	Y	Hamburg	New York	10/20/1847	10/02/1848	1	36	N	
Grace, Gerald	27	Ireland	N	Queenstown	Boston	05/29/1876	?			Y	
Grace, Gerold C.	36	Ireland	Y	Queenstown	New York	09/07/1873	09/25/1884			Y	
Grace, John C.	33	England	Y	Liverpool	Vermont	09/10/1847	11/18/1852	5	304	N	
Grace, Michael	30	Ireland	N	Queenstown	Boston	05/29/1876	?			Y	
Grace, Patrick	36	Ireland	Y	Queenstown	New York	05/12/1894	10/26/1900			Y	
Grace, Richard Evans	23	Ireland	Y	Liverpool	San Francisc	02/15/1854	09/23/1857	15	308	N	
Grace, William	34	England	Y	Bristol	New York	08/23/1852	05/11/1854	8	426	N	
Grace, William	34	England	Y	Bristol	New York	08/23/1852	05/11/1854	9	299	N	
Grad, Bennet	27	Russia	Y	Hamburg	Philadelphia	09/22/1886	04/06/1893			Y	
Grad, Edward	22	Russia	Y	Hamburg	New York	05/24/1893	03/22/1897			Y	
Grad, Julius	45	Russia	Y	Hamburg	New York	06/15/1882	10/30/1888			Y	
Grad, Samuel	50	Russia	Y	Rotterdam	Detroit	08/25/1898	10/16/1903			Y	
Gradolph, John	36	Germany	N	Havre	New York	06/02/1865	?			Y	
Gradvohl, Emmanuel	29	Germany	Y	Havre	New York	08/28/1877	10/22/1889			Y	
Grady, John	21	Ireland	Y	Liverpool	New York	04/28/1856	10/27/1857	15	496	N	
Grady, John	30	Ireland	Y	Liverpool	New Orleans	11/12/1849	12/01/1857	16	62	N	
Grady, John	??	Ireland	Y	?	?	03/01/1893	11/06/1894			Y	
Grady, Martin	21	Ireland	Y	Liverpool	New Orleans	04/01/1853	10/04/1854	10	419	N	
Grady, Martin	21	Ireland	Y	Liverpool	New Orleans	04/01/1853	10/04/1854	12	358	N	
Grady, Michael	??	Ireland	N	?	?	05/20/1897				Y	09/27/1892
Grady, Patrick	30	Ireland	Y	Liverpool	New Orleans	03/19/1851	12/29/1852	5	468	N	
Grady, Patrick	26	Ireland	Y	Liverpool	Buffalo	09/??/1849	12/18/1857	16	234	N	
Grady, Thomas J.	22	Ireland	Y	Queenstown	New York	09/10/1882	10/22/1886			Y	
Grady, Timothy	35	Ireland	Y	Liverpool	New York	05/03/1849	04/13/1852	24	492	N	
Graeber, Henry Frederick	28	Prussia	Y	Bremen	New Orleans	12/16/1850	11/05/1852	5	230	N	
Graef, Frederick	24	Germany	Y	Bremen	New York	11/26/1882	02/09/1883			Y	
Graef, Nicholas	32	Bavaria	Y	Havre	New York	07/20/1859	11/04/1858	17	276	N	
Graefe, Ludwig	32	Saxony	Y	Bremen	New York	08/22/1852	05/25/1854	9	422	N	
Graefe, Ludwig	32	Saxony	Y	Bremen	New York	08/22/1852	05/25/1854	10	5	N	

CITIZENSHIP RECORDS

APPLICANT	AGE	COUNTRY OF ORIGIN	DEC	DEPART PORT	ENTRY PORT	ARRIVE DATE	DEC DATE	VOL	PG.	FLD	NAT DATE
Graefe, Robert	25	Germany	Y	Bremen	New York	09/19/1882	01/16/1886			Y	
Graefenhan, Julius Rober	24	Saxe Coburg G	Y	Hamburg	New York	08/05/1852	07/26/1855	11	431	N	
Graeff, Charles	30	Bavaria	Y	Liverpool	Philadelphia	07/16/1854	11/25/1857	16	53	N	
Graeler, William	33	Germany	Y	Bremen	Baltimore	04/26/1877	11/26/1883			Y	
Graeser, Hanibald	28	Wurttemberg	Y	Antwerp	New York	08/24/1848	11/14/1848	1	286	N	
Graeser, Michael Joseph	33	Bavaria	Y	Liverpool	New York	06/02/1853	?	14	239	N	
Graesslie, Frederick	23	Germany	Y	Bremen	New York	10/16/1888	05/24/1889			Y	
Graeter, Jacob	42	Wurttemberg	Y	Havre	New York	07/15/1853	12/18/1857	16	235	N	
Graf, Daniel	22	Baden	Y	Havre	New ?	03/24/1853	11/09/1855	13	197	N	
Graf, Ferdinand	25	Baden	Y	Havre	New Orleans	03/24/1853	10/09/1854	6	97	N	
Graf, Ferdinand	25	Baden	Y	Havre	New Orleans	03/24/1852	10/09/1854	11	100	N	
Graf, Frank A.	66	Germany	Y	Havre	New York	12/24/1854	08/02/1888			Y	
Graf, Frederick	34	Germany	Y	Havre	New York	01/21/1888	11/06/1891			Y	
Graf, Fritz	29	Germany	Y	Hamburg	New York	09/12/1882	11/09/1886			Y	
Graf, John	26	Germany	Y	Antwerp	New York	06/12/1880	09/30/1887			Y	
Graf, John	55	Prussia	N	Havre	New York	05/??/1839	?			Y	
Graf, Ludwig	21	Germany	Y	Havre	New York	05/19/1880	04/07/1881			Y	
Graf, Martin	31	Germany	Y	Havre	New York	04/14/1866	06/28/1876			Y	
Graf, Nicholas	23	Prussia	Y	Havre	New York	05/24/1854	01/02/1856	13	418	N	
Graf, Norbert	33	Baden	Y	Havre	New Orleans	11/04/1849	04/18/18??	8	84	N	
Grafe, Theodore	33	Germany	Y	Bremen	Baltimore	09/03/1884	11/29/1893			Y	
Graff, Frederick	30	Bavaria	Y	Havre	New Orleans	01/24/1844	10/02/1848	1	13	N	
Graff, Harris	29	Russia	Y	Hamburg	Philadelphia	08/??/1882	02/20/1888			Y	
Graff, Lorenz	27	Germany	Y	Havre	New York	05/17/1879	07/03/1882			Y	
Graft, Anton	29	Baden	Y	Havre	New York	09/18/1854	11/15/1858	17	333	N	
Grah, Albert	??	Germany	Y	?	?	?	10/10/1887			Y	
Graham, Adam	26	Scotland	Y	Glasgow	New York	10/25/1854	01/10/1856	13	443	N	
Graham, C. T.	34	England	Y	Liverpool	New York	07/29/1882	07/02/1883			Y	
Graham, Charles	36	Scotland	Y	Liverpool	New York	??/01/1845	04/23/1855	11	287	N	
Graham, James	46	Ireland	Y	Liverpool	New Orleans	05/07/1848	01/01/1853	5	493	N	
Graham, Robert	29	Scotland	Y	Glasgow	New York	09/04/1852	02/05/1856	26	45	N	
Graham, William P.	26	Ireland	Y	Belfast	New York	04/14/1847	10/11/1848	1	144	N	
Grahn, Peter	36	Nassau	Y	Antwerp	New York	08/17/1854	04/08/1861	18	135	N	
Grahn, Peter	63	Germany	N	Antwerp	New York	09/20/1852	?			Y	
Grahs, Henry	26	Hanover	Y	Bremen	New York	07/01/1844	02/15/1850	2	80	N	
Gramer, Gottlieb	24	Wuertemberg	Y	Havre	New York	04/12/1854	04/07/1856	26	460	N	
Gramke, William	25	Germany	Y	Bremen	New York	09/18/1890	06/11/1892			Y	
Gramlich, Henry	31	Baden	Y	Havre	New York	06/27/1852	10/09/1854	6	99	N	
Gramlich, Henry	31	Baden	Y	Havre	New York	06/27/1852	10/09/1854	11	102	N	
Grandfield, John	66	Ireland	N	Queenstown	New York	09/15/1854	?			Y	
Grandjean, John	31	Switzerland	Y	Havre	New York	05/13/1884	08/30/1897			Y	
Grane, William	54	Hanover	Y	Bremen	New York	10/09/1837	10/14/1848	1	220	N	
Graney, Thomas	42	Ireland	N	Queenstown	New York	??/??/1861	?	28	244	N	10/??/1868
Grant, Martin	33	Russia	Y	Bremen	New York	04/22/1884	12/17/1894			Y	
Grasman, Andreas	28	Bavaria	Y	Hamburg	New York	09/??/1846	11/24/1852	5	338	N	
Grasmuch, John	22	Austria	Y	Bremen	Baltimore	08/10/1855	10/06/1856	14	219	N	
Grasmuck, Alois	45	Austria	Y	Bremen	New Orleans	11/20/1854	01/14/1856	13	466	N	
Grass, Donart	39	Baden	Y	Havre	New York	05/05/1848	05/27/1854	9	431	N	
Grass, Donart	39	Baden	Y	Havre	New York	05/05/1848	05/27/1854	10	14	N	
Grass, Edward	24	Ireland	Y	Quebec	New York	08/??/1847	12/26/1851	24	14	N	
Grassel, Raimund	25	Germany	Y	Antwerp	Philadelphia	11/14/1880	12/11/1880			Y	
Grasser, George	34	Bavaria	Y	Liverpool	New York	06/03/1853	09/25/1854	10	204	N	
Grasser, George	34	Bavaria	Y	Liverpool	New York	06/03/1853	09/25/1854	12	143	N	
Grasshaber, John	22	Wurttemberg	Y	Antwerp	New York	07/04/1849	03/14/1850	2	191	N	
Grassman, Jacob	66	Germany	Y	Bremen	Baltimore	09/23/1885	08/04/1891			Y	
Grasteit, August	51	Germany	Y	?	?	05/05/1882	11/03/1890			Y	
Grathwohl, George	25	Germany	Y	Bremen	New York	08/13/1882	02/16/1886			Y	
Grau, Leo	23	Germany	Y	Rotterdam	New York	09/19/1878	12/11/1882			Y	
Grau, Otto	23	Germany	Y	Hamburg	New York	02/03/1883	12/14/1886			Y	

CITIZENSHIP RECORDS

APPLICANT	AGE	COUNTRY OF ORIGIN	DEC	DEPART PORT	ENTRY PORT	ARRIVE DATE	DEC DATE	VOL	PG.	FLD	NAT DATE
Graudt, Heinrich	58	Germany	N	Bremen	Baltimore	09/26/1862	?			Y	
Grauert, Clemens August	21	Prussia	Y	Bremen	New York	08/27/1856	10/04/1858	17	51	N	
Grauf, Gottlieb	28	Germany	Y	Antwerp	New York	06/05/1880	09/19/1885			Y	
Graus, John	39	Bavaria	Y	Bremen	New York	06/??/1846	02/21/1853	7	197	N	
Graus, Wendellin	26	France	Y	Havre	New York	06/07/1847	08/10/1848	22	91	N	
Grauvogel, Nicholas	30	Germany	Y	Hamburg	New York	01/02/1882	06/05/1889			Y	
Grave, Joseph	25	Oldenburg	Y	Bremen	New York	06/26/1849	10/07/1854	6	39	N	
Grave, Joseph	25	Oldenburg	Y	Bremen	New York	06/26/1849	10/07/1854	11	40	N	
Gravel, Herman	35	Germany	Y	Bremen	New York	04/28/1881	03/13/1889			Y	
Graver, Gustav	42	Germany	N	Bremen	New York	08/15/1864	?			Y	
Graves, Ernst	27	England	Y	Southampton	New York	04/26/1893	09/28/1893			Y	
Graveson, William	44	England	Y	Liverpool	New Orleans	10/29/1851	09/29/1854	10	305	N	
Graveson, William	44	England	Y	Liverpool	New Orleans	10/29/1851	09/29/1854	12	244	N	
Grawe, Bernhard	21	Oldenburg	Y	Bremen	New Orleans	05/07/1849	10/29/1852	5	60	N	
Grawe, Herman	31	Prussia	Y	Bremen	New Orleans	01/03/1847	02/02/1849	23	17	N	
Gray, Alexander C.	33	Canada	Y	Windsor	Detroit	09/08/1896	08/30/1898			Y	
Gray, David	23	Ireland	Y	Liverpool	New York	04/21/1849	02/23/1852	24	149	N	
Gray, Frank Eugene	25	Germany	Y	Antwerp	New York	09/26/1889	03/16/1895			Y	
Gray, James	25	Ireland	Y	Liverpool	New Orleans	10/28/1847	10/13/1851	4	246	N	
Gray, Walter J.	36	England	Y	Liverpool	New York	10/12/1878	11/06/1891			Y	
Gray, William	24	Ireland	Y	Toronto	Buffalo	08/??/1849	08/15/1851	4	148	N	
Gready, John	26	Ireland	Y	Liverpool	New York	06/01/1849	11/01/1852	5	131	N	
Gready, John	26	Ireland	Y	Liverpool	New York	06/01/1849	11/01/1852	6	257	N	
Greaham, Michael	21	Ireland	Y	Liverpool	New York	08/06/1886	10/29/1888			Y	
Greaney, James D.	52	Ireland	Y	Liverpool	New York	05/03/1865	03/11/1893			Y	
Grebenstein, Charles	26	Prussia	Y	Antwerp	New York	07/03/1849	09/15/1852	25	527	N	
Grebner, William	27	Prussia	Y	Hamburg	New York	03/10/1849	09/06/1852	25	373	N	
Green, David	35	Roumania	Y	Hamburg	New York	03/23/1899	10/12/1901			Y	
Green, George	39	Germany	Y	Hamburg	New York	08/25/1880	08/30/1892			Y	
Green, Harry Bear	26	Russia	Y	Bremen	New York	01/11/1888	07/29/1891			Y	
Green, John	24	Ireland	Y	Liverpool	New Orleans	01/14/1850	09/10/1852	25	439	N	
Green, Peter	49	Ireland	N	Liverpool	New York	09/29/1869	??/??/1871	28	378	N	10/??/1876
Green, Peter	26	Ireland	N	Liverpool	New York	09/29/1869	00/00/1871			Y	10/00/1876
Green, Sam	36	Germany	Y	Hamburg	New York	10/15/1894	09/10/1904			Y	
Green, William	29	England	Y	Hull	New York	10/15/1850	01/04/1853	5	514	N	
Greenbaum, Solomon	21	Saxe Weimar E	Y	Bremen	Baltimore	08/12/1853	09/13/1855	13	19	N	
Greenberg, Isaac	31	Russia	Y	Hamburg	New York	12/29/1885	10/24/1888			Y	
Greenberg, Leezer	31	Russia	Y	Antwerp	New York	09/17/1886	01/26/1889			Y	
Greenberg, Moses	??	Russia	Y	?	?	?	06/26/1893			Y	
Greene, James	27	Ireland	Y	Liverpool	New York	05/01/1883	08/17/1886			Y	
Greeneberg, Frank	45	Germany	N	Bremen	New York	10/21/1866	?			Y	
Greener, John	34	Germany	Y	Havre	New York	07/18/1864	10/12/1880			Y	
Greenfield, Samuel	??	Russia	Y	?	?	08/??/1892	09/03/1894			Y	
Greenfinkel, Moses	??	Russia	Y	?	?	?	08/31/1895			Y	
Greenheim, George	38	Germany	N	Bremen	New York	09/21/1869	?			Y	
Greenwood, Bernard	32	Hanover	Y	Bremen	New York	08/23/1854	06/10/1859	17	457	N	
Greenwood, Henry	47	England	Y	Liverpool	New York	11/30/1852	03/30/1858	16	459	N	
Grefer, Barney	30	Hanover	Y	Bremen	Baltimore	06/13/1845	08/15/1848	22	121	N	
Gregoire, Laurent	23	Germany	Y	Havre	New York	09/19/1886	10/14/1890			Y	
Gregoire, Stephan	57	Germany	Y	Havre	New York	09/19/1886	01/30/1892			Y	
Gregoire, Stephen	22	Germany	Y	Havre	New York	09/19/1886	06/06/1892			Y	
Gregson, Thomas	??	Great Britain	Y	?	?	?	06/02/1890			Y	
Grehan, Patrick	26	Ireland	Y	Liverpool	New York	01/21/1850	04/15/1853	8	64	N	
Grehl, Charles	36	Germany	Y	Bremen	Baltimore	06/03/1883	09/14/1891			Y	
Grehl, Henry	27	Germany	Y	Bremen	New York	07/26/1882	08/26/1887			Y	
Greifenkamp, Bernard	25	Oldenburg	Y	Bremen	New York	11/05/1857	01/06/1860	27	35	N	
Greifenkamp, Joseph	23	Germany	Y	Bremen	New York	05/19/1872	04/15/1883			Y	
Greilich, Martin	50	Germany	N	Havre	New York	06/28/1857	?			Y	
Greiling, John	42	Prussia	Y	Bremen	New Orleans	12/20/1846	01/08/1850	23	482	N	

CITIZENSHIP RECORDS

APPLICANT	AGE	COUNTRY OF ORIGIN	DEC	DEPART PORT	ENTRY PORT	ARRIVE DATE	DEC DATE	VOL	PG.	FLD	NAT DATE
Greiling, William	26	Prussia	Y	Bremen	New York	10/06/1857	07/26/1858	16	524	N	
Greimann, William	26	Germany	Y	London	New York	01/06/1882	01/06/1886			Y	
Greimmann, Friedrich	32	Prussia	Y	Bremen	New York	02/27/1852	06/19/1852	25	296	N	
Greinberg, Henry	22	Russia	Y	?	New York	12/01/1891	01/05/1893			Y	
Greiner, Balthauser	48	Germany	Y	Hamburg	New York	04/30/1883	07/27/1894			Y	
Greiner, Charles	32	Germany	Y	Bremen	New York	08/03/1881	07/21/1892			Y	
Greiner, Charles J.	28	Germany	Y	Rotterdam	New York	03/28/1881	11/24/1890			Y	
Greiner, Ernst	56	Germany	N	Bremen	Baltimore	11/??/1857	?			Y	
Greiner, Frederick	24	Baden	Y	Havre	New Orleans	??/07/1846	12/05/1849	23	390	N	
Greiner, Gottlieb	26	Bavaria	Y	Bremen	New York	??/14/1849	02/12/1850	2	63	N	
Greiner, Henry	52	Germany	Y	Hamburg	New York	05/30/1886	10/28/1893			Y	
Greiner, Jacob	32	Baden	Y	Havre	New York	07/01/1847	09/14/1852	25	496	N	
Greiner, John	25	Bavaria	Y	Havre	New Orleans	05/09/1850	11/23/1855	13	245	N	
Greiner, John	30	Bavaria	Y	Havre	New York	05/04/1844	09/15/1848	22	352	N	
Greiner, Karl	??	Germany	N	?	?	03/15/1885				Y	10/19/1892
Greiner, Peter	31	Bavaria	Y	Havre	New York	08/27/1849	05/15/1852	25	22	N	
Greiner, Theodore	63	Germany	N	Freesland	New York	09/09/1847	??/??/1853	28	316	N	??/??/1853
Greiner, William	28	Baden	Y	Havre	New York	09/16/1849	01/12/1853	7	10	N	
Greinn, Theodore	18	Germany	N	Leer	New York	09/09/1847	00/00/1853			Y	00/00/1853
Greiser, Francis	26	Baden	Y	Havre	New Orleans	05/25/1847	02/06/1849	23	129	N	
Greissinger, John	39	Germany	Y	Rotterdam	New York	10/20/1881	02/28/1893			Y	
Greive, Hermann	23	Prussia	Y	Bremen	New York	06/25/1854	12/05/1857	16	194	N	
Greiwe, Christopher	58	Germany	N	?	Baltimore	07/??/1837	?	28	51	N	10/??/1851
Gremelspacher, Roman	25	Baden	Y	Havre	New York	02/09/1854	02/18/1856	26	97	N	
Gremmlsbacher, Frederick	31	Germany	Y	?	?	05/01/1887	10/24/1888			Y	
Grendelmeyer, John M.	25	Switzerland	Y	Havre	New York	09/25/1886	04/01/1889			Y	
Grenfield, Thomas	28	Germany	Y	Bremen	New York	06/08/1873	10/28/1887			Y	
Grenim, Frank	26	Baden	Y	Antwerp	New York	10/26/1847	10/09/1854	6	120	N	
Grennan, John	26	Ireland	Y	Queenstown	New York	04/30/1894	11/19/1897			Y	
Greppi, Gottlieb	36	Switzerland	Y	Havre	New York	05/25/1876	09/03/1887			Y	
Greskamp, Frank	32	Prussia	Y	Bremen	Baltimore	05/04/1854	12/04/1855	13	287	N	
Gress, Caspar	29	Germany	Y	Antwerp	New York	03/29/1882	12/30/1884			Y	
Gressler, Rudolph	24	Germany	Y	?	?	?	08/21/1896			Y	
Grethel, William	25	Germany	Y	Antwerp	Philadelphia	05/17/1897	03/17/1903			Y	
Grether, Gottlieb	24	Switzerland	Y	Havre	New York	09/09/1846	02/20/1849	23	233	N	
Grether, Herm	29	Germany	Y	Havre	New York	09/14/1880	10/05/1883			Y	
Greufe, Theodore	34	Germany	Y	Bremen	Baltimore	12/03/1878	01/06/1881			Y	
Greulich, Henry	28	Prussia	Y	Bremen	New York	09/04/1857	12/15/1859	17	504	N	
Greulich, John	42	Germany	Y	Bremen	Baltimore	12/20/1879	09/28/1885			Y	
Greve, Christian	23	Hanover	Y	Hamburg	New York	05/01/1849	01/??/1850	23	493	N	
Greve, Fred	30	Germany	Y	Bremen	New York	04/16/1873	07/06/1883			Y	
Greve, Hermann	30	Germany	Y	Bremen	New York	10/01/1889	11/28/1890			Y	
Greve, John	26	Hanover	Y	Bremen	New Orleans	12/??/1845	10/28/1850	2	319	N	
Greve, John	32	Prussia	Y	Bremen	New York	05/09/1848	11/01/1852	5	124	N	
Greve, John	32	Prussia	Y	Bremen	New York	05/09/1848	11/01/1852	6	250	N	
Grevers, Bernhard Henry	47	Holland	Y	London	New Orleans	12/25/1848	11/01/1852	5	155	N	
Greves, William	36	England	Y	Liverpool	New York	02/21/1848	05/22/1852	25	89	N	
Grewe, John H.W.	28	Hanover	Y	Bremen	Baltimore	08/18/1846	03/12/1851	3	256	N	
Grewe, William	37	Germany	Y	Bremen	New York	05/27/1883	01/03/1887			Y	
Grewer, William H.	21	Scotland	Y	?	Boston	04/14/1887	10/11/1889			Y	
Griahan, Michael	21	Ireland	Y	Liverpool	New York	08/06/1886	10/29/1888	19	199	N	
Gribbin, Thomas	40	Ireland	Y	Dublin	New York	04/21/1848	09/07/1852	25	404	N	
Gribi, Fritz	32	Germany	Y	Havre	New York	09/10/1878	10/09/1884			Y	
Grieb, Ferdinand	??	Germany	N	?	?	01/02/1887				Y	03/29/1892
Griemann, F.	36	Hanover	Y	Bremen	New Orleans	10/19/1854	11/02/1860	27	557	N	
Grieneisen, Christian	32	Germany	Y	Antwerp	New York	03/05/1891	01/11/1899			Y	
Gries, Frank	24	Baden	Y	Havre	New York	05/20/1850	04/12/1852	24	446	N	
Gries, John	22	Bavaria	Y	Havre	New York	05/12/1852	08/17/1855	11	446	N	
Griesbach, Christoph Ott	34	Germany	Y	Bremen	Baltimore	06/19/1871	10/13/1884			Y	

CITIZENSHIP RECORDS

APPLICANT	AGE	COUNTRY OF ORIGIN	DEC	DEPART PORT	ENTRY PORT	ARRIVE DATE	DEC DATE	VOL	PG.	FLD	NAT DATE
Griese, George H.	39	Hanover	Y	Bremen	Baltimore	04/16/1847	10/20/1851	4	340	N	
Griese, John	21	Hamburg	Y	Bremen	New Orleans	04/26/1854	02/17/1857	15	27	N	
Grieser, John M.	50	Germany	Y	?	New York	??/??/1884	01/20/1888			Y	
Grieseweld, Adam	45	Hanover	Y	Bremen	Baltimore	06/25/1850	04/08/1856	26	472	N	
Griesser, John	22	Germany	Y	Rotterdam	New York	03/01/1891	11/20/1893			Y	
Grieve, Chas H.	??	Germany	Y	Bremen	Baltimore	04/04/1891	08/08/1893			Y	
Griffig, Ernst	52	Prussia	Y	Bremen	New York	12/11/1853	10/29/1858	17	172	N	
Griffin, John	25	Ireland	Y	Waterford	Buffalo	09/20/1850	10/07/1854	10	535	N	
Griffin, John	25	Ireland	Y	Waterford	Buffalo	09/20/1850	10/07/1854	12	474	N	
Griffin, John	23	Ireland	Y	Liverpool	New York	04/01/1849	03/26/1856	26	351	N	
Griffin, Michael	24	Ireland	Y	London	New York	10/??/1848	10/??/1849	23	289	N	
Griffin, Patrick	30	Ireland	Y	Limerick	Burlington	05/25/1849	05/30/1854	9	460	N	
Griffin, Patrick	30	Ireland	Y	Limerick	Burlington	05/25/1849	05/31/1854	10	43	N	
Griffin, Patrick	37	Ireland	Y	Queenstown	New York	04/00/1866	03/28/1884			Y	
Griffin, Thomas	21	Ireland	Y	Galway	New York	09/20/1851	01/28/1856	13	513	N	
Griffith, James	46	Wales	Y	Liverpool	New York	08/12/1879	09/25/1878			Y	
Griffiths, John R.	35	Wales	Y	Liverpool	New York	10/??/1877	02/17/1888			Y	
Grigeois, Christoph	25	France	Y	Havre	New York	09/??/1852	09/21/1855	13	94	N	
Grigg, Jacob	29	England	Y	Plymouth	Buffalo	09/01/1849	10/06/1860	27	406	N	
Grill, Anton	31	Austria	Y	Bremen	Baltimore	06/21/1879	05/29/1882			Y	
Grim, Edward	22	Germany	Y	Antwerp	New York	07/12/1881	06/13/1884			Y	
Grimberg, Miki	??	Russia	Y	?	New York	12/??/1892	04/23/1894			Y	
Grimes, Michael	24	Ireland	Y	Queenstown	New York	05/25/1881	10/10/1885			Y	
Grimes, Thomas	35	Ireland	Y	Queenstown	New York	04/26/1882	10/26/1895			Y	
Grimm, Adolph	54	Reuss	Y	Liverpool	New York	05/26/1854	11/05/1860	18	21	N	
Grimm, Dominick	32	Wurttemberg	Y	Havre	New York	06/14/1852	10/01/1857	15	340	N	
Grimm, Frank	26	Baden	Y	Antwerp	New York	10/26/1847	10/09/1854	11	123	N	
Grimm, Henry	31	Hanover	Y	Bremen	New Orleans	10/25/1852	11/11/1857	16	9	N	
Grimm, Herman	31	Germany	Y	Antwerp	New York	07/02/1881	08/23/1884			Y	
Grimm, Jacob	30	Baden	Y	Havre	New Orleans	01/27/1847	11/01/1852	5	104	N	
Grimm, Jacob	36	Germany	Y	Bremen	New York	11/11/1869	01/13/1874			Y	
Grimm, Nicholaus	34	Bavaria	Y	Bremen	New York	05/16/1866	05/12/18??	17	542	N	
Grimm, Paul	31	Germany	Y	Bremen	New York	06/06/1880	10/08/1885			Y	
Grimm, Peter	40	Germany	Y	Antwerp	New York	?	12/22/1893	21	57	N	
Grimm, Peter	40	Germany	Y	Antwerp	New York	08/24/1889	12/22/1893			Y	
Grimme, John Joseph	58	Hanover	Y	Bremen	New Orleans	12/10/1848	01/26/1856	13	511	N	
Grimmelsmann, John F.	28	Germany	Y	Bremen	Baltimore	07/13/1887	04/01/1892			Y	
Grimsehl, Victor W.	35	Germany	Y	Hamburg	New York	04/10/1889	10/26/1893			Y	
Grin, Anton	31	Bavaria	Y	Antwerp	New York	07/16/1856	08/31/1857	15	207	N	
Grindrod, Kay	29	England	Y	Liverpool	New York	06/18/1849	10/07/1854	6	14	N	
Grindrod, Kay	29	England	Y	Liverpool	New York	06/18/1849	10/07/1854	11	15	N	
Gringel, Carl August	37	Germany	Y	Bremen	New York	02/24/1884	04/20/1888			Y	
Grippner, Adam	25	Bavaria	Y	Bremen	Baltimore	08/12/1852	10/09/1854	6	184	N	
Grischy, Heinrich	25	Bavaria	Y	Havre	New Orleans	03/14/1852	11/05/1852	6	352	N	
Grischy, Henry	25	Bavaria	Y	Havre	New Orleans	03/14/1852	11/05/1852	5	226	N	
Grischy, Michael	33	Germany	Y	Frankfurt	New York	08/31/1882	07/23/1886			Y	
Grisz, Caspar	29	Germany	Y	Antwerp	New York	03/29/1882	12/30/1884			Y	
Gritsch, Joseph	27	Austria	Y	Bremen	New York	05/10/1880	11/06/1886			Y	
Grivers, Bernard Henry	47	Holland	Y	London	New Orleans	12/25/1848	11/01/1852	6	281	N	
Groat, John	27	Scotland	Y	Aberdeen	New York	05/12/1856	02/06/1860	27	88	N	
Grob, Gottlieb	31	Germany	Y	Hamburg	New York	12/02/1880	12/01/1884			Y	
Grob, John G.	56	Germany	N	Havre	New York	03/??/1848	?			Y	
Grobbink, Henry	28	Holland	Y	Antwerp	New York	05/15/1890	04/24/1893			Y	
Grobbink, John	32	Holland	Y	Antwerp	New York	06/26/1885	03/28/1888			Y	
Grochawine, Joseph	25	Prussia	Y	Hamburg	New York	05/20/1853	09/29/1856	14	439	N	
Grodotzky, Wilhelm	32	Germany	Y	Bremen	Baltimore	05/14/1889	07/29/1895			Y	
Groebel, Henry	32	Prussia	Y	Rotterdam	Baltimore	05/04/1848	05/25/1854	8	542	N	
Groebel, Henry	32	Prussia	Y	Rotterdam	Baltimore	05/04/1848	05/25/1854	9	416	N	
Groeber, Heinrich Freder	28	Prussia	Y	Bremen	New Orleans	12/16/1850	11/05/1852	6	356	N	

CITIZENSHIP RECORDS

APPLICANT	AGE	COUNTRY OF ORIGIN	DEC	DEPART PORT	ENTRY PORT	ARRIVE DATE	DEC DATE	VOL	PG.	FLD	NAT DATE
Groedecke, Ludwig	54	Waldeck	Y	Bremen	New Orleans	08/??/1847	09/01/1857	15	213	N	
Groen, Louis	31	Germany	Y	Bremen	Baltimore	07/10/1881	10/17/1887			Y	
Groene, Eugene	??	Germany	Y	?	?	?	05/16/1893			Y	
Groene, Frederick	??	Hanover	Y	Bremen	Baltimore	09/27/1847	10/05/1848	22	429	N	
Groene, Heinrich	22	Germany	Y	Rotterdam	New York	06/05/1884	12/23/1887			Y	
Groenefeld, Herman	52	Holland	N	Rotterdam	New York	03/16/1871	?			Y	
Groener, Andreas	33	Germany	Y	Bremen	New York	05/25/1879	02/02/1888			Y	
Groeniger, Charles	30	Hesse Cassel	Y	Bremen	Baltimore	04/12/1849	01/??/1850	23	546	N	
Groeninger, Lewis	25	Kurhassen	Y	Bremen	Baltimore	09/18/1846	09/11/1848	22	329	N	
Groenland, Henry	33	Denmark	Y	Hamburg	New York	07/03/1852	10/02/1854	10	347	N	
Groenland, Henry	33	Denmark	Y	Hamburg	New York	07/08/1852	10/02/1854	12	286	N	
Grofer, Herman	25	Germany	Y	Amsterdam	New York	04/12/1884	12/08/1885			Y	
Groger, Theodore William	28	Hanover	Y	Liverpool	New York	07/19/1853	03/14/1856	26	198	N	
Groh, Peter	48	Prussia	Y	Antwerp	New Orleans	11/23/1848	08/18/1855	11	453	N	
Groh, Philip	27	Hesse Darmsta	Y	Bremen	Baltimore	12/22/1846	03/23/1853	7	374	N	
Grohs, Conrad	21	Wurttemberg	Y	Havre	New York	06/03/1854	08/17/1855	11	448	N	
Grohs, John	24	Germany	Y	Bremen	New York	05/24/1887	06/08/1888			Y	
Grohs, Nicholas	27	Prussia	Y	Havre	New York	05/01/1852	11/01/1852	5	113	N	
Groitie, Henry L.	38	Hanover	N	Bremen	Baltimore	11/11/1872	?			Y	
Groll, Franz	21	Kurhessen	Y	Bremen	New York	06/19/1859	05/17/1860	27	192	N	
Groll, Gerhard	23	Prussia	Y	Bremen	New York	06/16/1871	11/05/1860	18	17	N	
Groll, John	23	Bavaria	Y	Bremen	Baltimore	09/01/1850	04/04/1853	8	43	N	
Groll, Peter	21	Bavaria	Y	Bremen	New York	04/26/1853	10/07/1854	6	37	N	
Groll, Peter	21	Bavaria	Y	Bremen	New York	04/26/1853	10/07/1854	11	38	N	
Groll, William	??	Germany	N	?	?	12/01/1884				Y	10/28/1892
Grollig, Frederick	38	Germany	N	Rotterdam	New York	05/08/1870	?			Y	
Grolmes, Joseph	40	Germany	Y	Bremen	New York	04/02/1883	05/06/1887			Y	
Grom, Joseph	32	Germany	Y	Rotterdam	New York	10/28/1889	01/06/1893			Y	
Grone, Herman	30	Hanover	Y	Bremen	New Orleans	12/05/1842	10/14/1848	1	224	N	
Gronefelt, Girhard (Gran	31	Hanover	Y	Bremen	Baltimore	05/01/1843	08/15/1848	22	180	N	
Gronemann, George	9	Germany	N	?	Baltimore	00/00/1872				Y	10/22/1886
Groneweg, Frederick H.	23	Hanover	Y	Bremen	New York	06/27/1849	06/11/1852	25	239	N	
Groneweg, Philip	40	Hanover	Y	Bremen	New Orleans	12/16/1844	10/12/1848	1	172	N	
Gropp, Fritz	??	Germany	Y	?	?	?	10/25/1884			Y	
Groppenbacher, Jacob	21	Bavaria	Y	London	New York	03/03/1855	11/05/1855	13	163	N	
Groppenbacher, Maximilia	32	Bavaria	Y	Havre	New York	03/28/1852	05/31/1852	25	143	N	
Groppenbacher, William	28	Bavaria	Y	Havre	New York	07/23/1850	11/05/1855	13	160	N	
Groppenbecker, George	31	Bavaria	Y	Antwerp	New York	02/23/1852	11/05/1855	13	158	N	
Gros, Stene Selavo	26	Italy	Y	Naples	Philadelphia	08/21/1886	08/15/1894			Y	
Grosch, Balthasar	23	Germany	Y	Rotterdam	New York	02/04/1883	05/23/1884			Y	
Grosch, John	41	Germany	Y	Bremen	New York	03/22/1871	10/26/1889			Y	
Grosch, John J.	32	Germany	Y	Bremen	New York	09/20/1881	07/10/1884			Y	
Groschel, Anton	39	Germany	Y	Hamburg	New York	06/06/1880	03/01/1883			Y	
Grosdidier, Albert	25	Germany	Y	Antwerp	Philadelphia	11/??/1880	07/31/1884			Y	
Grosmann, Adam	23	Hesse Darmsta	Y	London	New York	04/30/1857	02/04/1861	18	86	N	
Gross, Albert	28	Germany	Y	Hamburg	New York	06/09/2874	03/29/1883			Y	
Gross, Ben	23	Russia	Y	Hamburg	New York	06/18/1882	04/06/1885			Y	
Gross, Charles	26	Germany	Y	?	New York	??/??/1877	12/24/1883			Y	
Gross, Christoph	28	Germany	Y	Antwerp	New York	07/07/1883	05/18/1883			Y	
Gross, Daniel	26	Germany	Y	Bremen	New York	09/10/1887	09/20/1889			Y	
Gross, George Michael	67	Germany	N	Havre	New York	06/??/1856	?			Y	
Gross, John Philip	26	Wurttemberg	Y	Antwerp	New York	05/15/1848	09/23/1854	10	183	N	
Gross, John Phillip	26	Wurttemberg	Y	Antwerp	New York	05/15/1848	09/23/1848	12	122	N	
Gross, Martin	24	Bavaria	Y	Havre	New Orleans	??/10/1847	10/09/1848	1	67	N	
Gross, Nicholas	35	France	Y	Havre	New Orleans	11/23/1851	02/09/1858	16	93	N	
Gross, Peter	48	Germany	N	Bremen	Baltimore	07/??/1862	?			Y	
Gross, Philip	31	Bavaria	Y	Havre	New York	08/28/1849	12/20/1852	5	434	N	
Gross, Theodor	27	Switzerland	Y	Antwerp	New York	07/21/1890	03/14/1893			Y	
Grosse, Christian	21	Germany	Y	Havre	New York	06/04/1881	09/17/1883			Y	

CITIZENSHIP RECORDS

APPLICANT	AGE	COUNTRY OF ORIGIN	DEC	DEPART PORT	ENTRY PORT	ARRIVE DATE	DEC DATE	VOL	PG.	FLD	NAT DATE
Grosse, Diederick	29	Oldenburg	Y	Bremen	New Orleans	11/04/1849	01/19/1851	24	25	N	
Grosse, Fred	37	Austria	Y	Bremen	New York	05/11/1883	04/11/1887			Y	
Grossenbacher, Samuel	23	Switzerland	Y	Havre	?	?	10/28/1893			Y	
Grosser, Charles	38	Germany	Y	Hamburg	New York	04/20/1881	10/14/1886			Y	
Grosser, Joseph	25	Bavaria	Y	Bremen	Baltimore	08/24/1853	10/09/1854	6	96	N	
Grosser, Joseph	25	Bavaria	Y	Bremen	Baltimore	08/30/1853	10/09/1854	11	99	N	
Grossheim, Hermann	18	Germany	Y	?	?	05/16/1888	05/06/1891			Y	
Grossheim, J. Henry	59	Germany	N	Hanover	New Orleans	11/10/1849	?	28	194	N	11/??/1856
Grosskopf, Conrad	30	Germany	Y	Hamburg	New York	06/26/1888	03/02/1889			Y	
Grossman, Herman	35	Germany	N	Bremen	New York	08/??/1875	?			Y	
Grossman, Max	33	Austria	Y	Hamburg	New York	06/29/1880	09/06/1888			Y	
Grossman, Pinkus	31	Russia	Y	Bremen	New York	10/28/1890	08/24/1896			Y	
Grossmann, Anton L.	25	Germany	Y	Bremen	Baltimore	10/19/1894	10/25/1899			Y	
Grossmann, Aron	36	Russia	N	Hamburg	New York	12/??/1869	?			Y	
Grossmann, Frank	24	Prussia	Y	Rotterdam	New York	07/03/1849	05/24/1852	25	97	N	
Grossmann, Gottlob	56	Hanover	Y	Bremen	New York	04/24/1857	04/09/1862	18	312	N	
Groszner, George	29	Saxe Meininge	Y	Bremen	Philadelphia	08/23/1851	05/10/1852	24	530	N	
Grote, Anton	31	Oldenburg	Y	Bremen	Baltimore	06/10/1848	03/11/1851	3	250	N	
Grote, B.	28	Germany	Y	Bremen	Baltimore	05/24/1879	11/01/1884			Y	
Grote, Clemens	34	Germany	Y	Bremen	Baltimore	05/29/1883	08/15/1887			Y	
Grote, Henry	32	Hanover	Y	Bremen	New Orleans	05/??/1847	10/28/1850	2	317	N	
Grote, Henry	??	Oldenburg	Y	?	Baltimore	07/12/18??	11/05/1856	14	495	N	
Grote, John Henry	23	Hanover	Y	Bremen	Baltimore	10/17/1848	11/03/1851	4	465	N	
Grothaus, Henry	25	Hanover	Y	Bremen	New York	10/06/1845	01/27/1849	1	523	N	
Grothe, Bernard	29	Oldenburg	Y	Bremen	Baltimore	10/13/1849	10/02/1856	14	159	N	
Grothe, Herman	53	Germany	N	Hamburg	New York	09/20/1866	?			Y	
Groti, Henry	32	Oldenburg	Y	Bremen	Baltimore	06/19/1848	08/16/1855	11	443	N	
Grotkafs, August	25	Hanover	Y	Hamburg	New York	08/30/1857	11/29/1858	17	364	N	
Grotschulte, Antoni	22	Germany	Y	Rotterdam	New York	11/01/1884	06/06/1888			Y	
Grotthaus, Henry	27	Prussia	Y	Bremen	Baltimore	06/27/1848	06/13/1851	3	371	N	
Grotz, Gustav	35	Germany	Y	Havre	New York	09/21/1880	03/11/1891			Y	
Groves, John T.	??	Canada	Y	?	?	?	09/19/1885			Y	
Grow, George	24	Hesse Cassel	Y	Bremen	New York	01/??/1850	11/06/1851	4	493	N	
Grub, Philip	32	Bavaria	Y	Havre	New York	08/02/1850	09/26/1856	14	393	N	
Grube, Fred	30	Germany	Y	Bremen	Baltimore	08/26/1881	05/25/1885			Y	
Grube, Henry	26	Prussia	Y	Bremen	New York	08/29/1849	08/06/1851	4	93	N	
Grubenhoff, Henry	52	Germany	Y	Bremen	Baltimore	11/12/1865	10/25/1890			Y	
Gruber, Freidoline	26	Switzerland	Y	Havre	New Orleans	12/04/1848	11/05/1852	6	354	N	
Gruber, Fridolin	36	Switzerland	Y	Havre	New Orleans	12/04/1848	11/05/1852	5	229	N	
Gruber, John Diomsimus	29	Bavaria	Y	Havre	New Orleans	??/22/1846	01/24/1850	23	543	N	
Gruber, Joseph	22	Germany	Y	Bremen	Baltimore	01/27/1884	12/28/1885			Y	
Gruber, Joseph	22	Bavaria	Y	Bremen	New York	05/01/1851	03/24/1856	26	279	N	
Gruber, Karl	27	Germany	Y	Bremen	New York	10/04/1885	09/07/1887			Y	
Gruenebach, Frederick	24	Prussia	Y	Rotterdam	Baltimore	06/16/1849	03/01/1852	24	205	N	
Gruenebaum, Leopold	37	Germany	Y	Bremen	New York	09/01/1882	05/24/1888			Y	
Gruener, John	54	Germany	Y	Bremen	New York	10/12/1888	12/29/1892			Y	
Gruenewald, John	27	Bavaria	Y	Bremen	New York	11/17/1853	06/09/1854	10	107	N	
Gruenewald, Valentine	42	Bavaria	Y	Antwerp	New York	09/27/1852	03/21/1856	26	241	N	
Gruenheim, Henry	44	Germany	Y	Bremen	Baltimore	07/20/1880	07/12/1890			Y	
Grueninger, Jacob	26	Switzerland	Y	Havre	New York	05/26/1881	03/19/1888			Y	
Grueninger, Louis	39	Germany	Y	Antwerp	Philadelphia	02/22/1883	04/26/1890			Y	
Gruenke, Hugo	37	Germany	Y	Bremen	New York	05/07/1885	10/06/1891			Y	
Gruenschlaeger, Johann P	39	Germany	Y	Bremen	Baltimore	08/29/1883	11/02/1889			Y	
Gruenthal, H.	59	Germany	N	Bremen	New Orleans	04/25/1849	?			Y	
Gruess, Henry	30	Germany	Y	Bremen	Baltimore	09/12/1886	08/26/1890			Y	
Grufe, Gottfried	48	Saxony	Y	Bremen	New Orleans	05/28/1849	10/13/1851	4	257	N	
Gruhler, Christian	23	Wurttemberg	Y	Havre	New York	06/17/1853	10/19/1857	15	458	N	
Gruhler, Elias	26	Wuerttemberg	Y	Havre	New York	05/11/1846	02/28/1852	24	181	N	
Grumanel, Johan	36	Germany	Y	Amsterdam	New York	04/17/1882	10/29/1892	19	401	N	

CITIZENSHIP RECORDS

APPLICANT	AGE	COUNTRY OF ORIGIN	DEC	DEPART PORT	ENTRY PORT	ARRIVE DATE	DEC DATE	VOL	PG.	FLD	NAT DATE
Grumbacher, Albert	27	Germany	Y	Havre	New York	06/28/1882	10/10/1889			Y	
Grunauer, Julius	40	Germany	Y	Hamburg	New York	07/??/1866	09/24/1884			Y	
Grunberg, Otto	28	Germany	Y	Bremen	Baltimore	05/01/1883	10/27/1890	19	304	N	
Grunder, Jacob	27	France	Y	Havre	New York	06/04/1844	01/22/1849	1	488	N	
Grundhoefer, Peter Willi	28	Bavaria	Y	Havre	New York	06/02/1853	07/29/1858	16	535	N	
Grundner, Andreas	78	Germany	N	Rotterdam	New York	07/03/1848	?			Y	
Grundorf, Peter	28	Bavaria	Y	Havre	New Orleans	09/29/1849	10/06/1854	10	477	N	
Grundorf, Peter	28	Bavaria	Y	Havre	New Orleans	09/29/1849	10/06/1854	12	416	N	
Grunefeld, John Wessel	34	Hanover	Y	Bremen	New Orleans	12/28/1853	11/05/1861	18	221	N	
Gruner, Emil	43	Germany	Y	Antwerp	Philadelphia	10/17/1873	10/23/1896			Y	
Gruner, Johann	25	Bavaria	Y	Hamburg	New York	10/10/1885	11/01/1886			Y	
Grunewald, Jacob	36	Prussia	Y	Antwerp	New York	04/21/1848	11/13/1848	1	255	N	
Grunewald, John	27	Bavaria	Y	Bremen	New Orleans	11/17/1853	06/09/1854	12	44	N	
Grunholz, Henry	23	Bavaria	Y	Havre	New York	10/12/1853	11/22/1858	17	346	N	
Gruninger, Fred	28	Germany	Y	Hamburg	New York	07/16/1880	01/24/1883			Y	
Gscheidle, Carl	27	Germany	Y	Antwerp	New York	04/17/1886	09/16/1887			Y	
Gsellmann, George	26	Hungary	Y	Antwerp	New York	06/02/1892	08/03/1896			Y	
Gshwendtner, George	??	Germany	Y	?	?	?	01/30/1879			Y	
Gtach, Andreas	27	Austria	Y	Havre	New York	04/14/1861	05/13/1861	18	166	N	
Guad, Mich.	66	Germany	Y	?	Baltimore	03/??/1889	11/01/1892			Y	
Gualano, Carmine	32	Italy	Y	Naples	New York	07/06/1887	08/30/1894			Y	
Guareo, Guissepa	34	Italy	Y	Naples	New York	04/01/1890	06/26/1894			Y	
Gucinotta, Guiseppe	39	Italy	Y	Missina	New York	09/28/1891	07/26/1899			Y	
Guckert, Conrad	42	Germany	Y	Hamburg	New York	07/02/1880	10/15/1888			Y	
Gude, August	26	Prussia	Y	Bremen	Baltimore	05/30/1851	02/03/1862	18	253	N	
Guellner, Frederick	27	Hanover	Y	Bremen	New York	08/10/1854	07/09/1855	11	353	N	
Guenen, Matthew	29	Ireland	Y	Limerick	Oswego	05/01/1848	04/04/1853	8	25	N	
Guenger, Louis	21	Germany	Y	Antwerp	New York	09/22/1881	05/07/1883			Y	
Guenthen, Conrad	57	Germany	N	Bremen	Baltimore	01/??/1838	?			Y	
Guenther, Andreas	25	Wuerttemberg	Y	Rotterdam	New York	06/21/1847	08/09/1848	22	82	N	
Guenther, Andrew	37	Bavaria	Y	Bremen	New York	11/15/1860	06/03/1861	18	182	N	
Guenther, John Conrad	35	Saxe Coburg	Y	Bremen	Baltimore	09/20/1853	05/06/1854	8	390	N	
Guenther, Nicholas	49	Bavaria	Y	Havre	New Orleans	12/23/1848	06/13/1851	3	370	N	
Guenther, Philipp	27	Bavaria	Y	Havre	New Orleans	02/20/1847	02/06/1851	3	103	N	
Guenther, Richard	??	Germany	Y	?	?	?	11/07/1882			Y	
Guenthlein, Martin	33	Germany	Y	Antwerp	New York	01/14/1883	10/24/1896			Y	
Guenthner, John	48	Germany	Y	Bremen	New York	05/20/1885	10/26/1903			Y	
Guenthner, Sebastian	43	Germany	Y	Bremen	Baltimore	02/28/1881	02/08/1886			Y	
Guenthner, Theodore	39	Baden	Y	Havre	New Orleans	03/28/1854	06/06/1854	10	97	N	
Guerges, Peter	29	Prussia	Y	Antwerp	New York	05/01/1852	10/09/1854	11	180	N	
Guerther, Peter	26	Switzerland	Y	Bremen	New York	02/02/1852	07/10/1855	11	375	N	
Guese, George	21	Germany	Y	Bremen	New York	01/07/1889	01/07/1893			Y	
Guethlein, Joseph	29	Germany	Y	Bremen	Baltimore	05/09/1882	03/05/1890			Y	
Guetting, Joseph	51	Bavaria	Y	Havre	New York	07/07/1847	04/05/1852	24	380	N	
Guggenheim, Daniel	16	Germany	N	?	New York	00/00/1881				Y	10/23/1886
Guggenheim, Max	34	Germany	N	Havre	New York	08/25/1873	?	28	312	N	04/02/1881
Guggenheim, Max	13	Germany	N	Havre	New York	08/25/1873				Y	04/02/1881
Gugger, Fred	30	Switzerland	Y	Havre	New York	02/07/1883	11/07/1888			Y	
Guhe, Peter Henry	23	Prussia	Y	Bremen	New York	11/04/1853	02/16/1857	15	22	N	
Guhmann, Jacob	29	Bavaria	Y	Antwerp	New Orleans	12/21/1849	03/01/1853	7	248	N	
Guhmann, John	32	Bavaria	Y	Havre	New Orleans	04/08/1854	11/06/1860	18	25	N	
Guhring, Emanuel Ludwig	26	Germany	Y	Antwerp	New York	09/17/1879	10/09/1882			Y	
Guien, Christopher	??	Ireland	Y	Liverpool	New York	05/03/1845	10/11/1848	1	135	N	
Guilfoxle, John	55	Ireland	N	Ireland	New Orleans	04/??/1849	?			Y	
Guillaume, Henry	36	Belgium	Y	Havre	New Orleans	12/10/1855	11/01/1858	17	212	N	
Guillerme, Charles	24	France	Y	Havre	New York	06/07/1848	05/30/1854	9	449	N	
Guillerme, Charles	24	France	Y	Havre	New York	06/07/1848	05/30/1854	10	32	N	
Guilmartin, Patrick	55	Ireland	Y	Liverpool	New Orleans	02/19/1851	10/22/1852	5	46	N	
Guinan, William	30	Ireland	Y	Liverpool	New Orleans	11/27/1850	11/01/1852	5	140	N	

CITIZENSHIP RECORDS

APPLICANT	AGE	COUNTRY OF ORIGIN	DEC	DEPART PORT	ENTRY PORT	ARRIVE DATE	DEC DATE	VOL	PG.	FLD	NAT DATE
Guisti, Edeliso	??	Italy	Y	?	New York	05/??/1892	10/26/1896			Y	
Gukenberger, George	24	Bavaria	Y	Bremen	Baltimore	06/18/1852	10/09/1854	11	124	N	
Gulde, John	40	Bavaria	Y	Havre	New York	10/10/1857	07/18/1860	27	226	N	
Guldi, Jacob	23	Wurttemberg	Y	Havre	New York	06/07/1853	01/24/1856	13	503	N	
Guleser, James T.	25	Turkey	Y	Smyrna	?	11/01/1890	05/27/1893			Y	
Gullemann, Peter H.	29	Germany	Y	Antwerp	New York	03/19/1887	10/25/1892			Y	
Gulon, John Henry	23	Hamburg	Y	Hamburg	New Orleans	11/08/1847	01/24/1853	7	61	N	
Gumbert, Karl F.	29	Germany	Y	Havre	New York	09/24/1884	03/20/1890			Y	
Gumbinger, George	32	Germany	Y	Rotterdam	New York	02/13/1884	07/03/1885			Y	
Gumley, Charles H.	26	Ireland	Y	Londonderry	New York	06/26/1892	04/11/1895			Y	
Gummersheimer, Geo.	28	Germany	Y	Bremen	New York	02/15/1884	04/14/1886			Y	
Gump, Joseph	27	Austria	Y	Bremen	Baltimore	01/25/1888	02/13/1891			Y	
Gump, Wenzel	24	Austria	Y	Bremen	Baltimore	10/17/1887	11/03/1890			Y	
Gundel, John George	30	Bavaria	Y	Bremen	Baltimore	06/26/1845	02/19/1849	23	189	N	
Gunning, Daniel	25	Scotland	Y	Glasgow	Boston	05/20/1849	11/01/1852	5	154	N	
Gunning, Daniel	25	Scotland	Y	Glasgow	Boston	05/20/1849	11/01/1852	6	280	N	
Gunther, Christian	28	Germany	Y	?	?	?	11/15/1898			Y	
Gunther, Frederick	25	Hanover	Y	Bremen	New York	08/02/1857	10/08/1860	27	423	N	
Gunther, John Conrad	35	Saxe Coburg	Y	Bremen	Baltimore	09/20/1853	05/06/1854	9	263	N	
Gunther, Julius	29	Saxe Weimar	Y	Hamburg	New York	06/19/1852	02/08/1853	7	131	N	
Gunther, Ludwig	29	Prussia	Y	Bremen	Baltimore	01/28/1859	08/08/1859	18	469	N	
Gunther, Oswald	15	Germany	N	?	New York	00/00/1881				Y	10/28/1886
Gunthner, Theodore	39	Baden	Y	Havre	New Orleans	03/28/1854	06/05/1854	12	34	N	
Gurcky, Philip	29	Germany	Y	Bremen	Baltimore	10/01/1886	10/27/1890	19	306	N	
Gurdding, Henry	23	Hanover	Y	Bremen	Baltimore	10/01/1858	09/07/1860	27	343	N	
Gureirtz, Israel	25	Russia	Y	Hamburg	New York	08/22/1891	06/23/1894			Y	
Gurges, Peter	29	Prussia	Y	Antwerp	New York	05/01/1852	10/09/1854	6	177	N	
Gurren, J.	5	Ireland	N	?	New York	00/00/1869				Y	04/05/1886
Gursch, Hamil	??	Germany	Y	?	?	?	02/17/1892			Y	
Gursky, Philip	29	Germany	Y	Bremen	Baltimore	10/01/1886	10/27/1890			Y	
Gusdorf, Jacob	30	Switzerland	Y	Liverpool	Boston	12/27/1857	10/06/1860	27	405	N	
Guse, Karl	41	Germany	N	Bremen	Baltimore	09/??/1876	?			Y	
Gushurst, Franz	46	Germany	Y	Havre	New York	03/29/1870	04/??/1875			Y	
Gushurst, Franz	46	Germany	N	Havre	New York	03/29/1870	?			Y	
Guss, Bernhard	40	Germany	Y	Havre	New York	10/06/1884	11/01/1886			Y	
Gustriech, Joseph	48	Prussia	Y	Bremen	Baltimore	08/02/1845	08/15/1848	22	150	N	
Gut, Rudolf	28	Austria	Y	Havre	New York	11/09/1882	06/15/1886			Y	
Gutbrodt, Joseph	23	Baden	Y	Rotterdam	New York	06/01/1850	09/08/1852	25	408	N	
Gutenberger, George	24	Bavaria	Y	Bremen	Baltimore	06/18/1852	10/09/1854	6	121	N	
Gutenberger, John	33	Wuerttemberg	Y	Havre	New York	07/09/1847	08/15/1849	23	114	N	
Gutfleisch, Philipp	35	Germany	Y	Bremen	New York	09/11/880	08/23/1888			Y	
Guth, George	21	Bavaria	Y	Havre	New York	11/11/1857	03/08/1858	16	380	N	
Gutheinz, Joseph Karl	25	Baden	Y	London	New York	09/20/1849	12/04/1852	5	375	N	
Guthlein, Albert	33	Germany	Y	Hamburg	New York	08/29/1867	05/25/1874			Y	
Gutjahn, Jacob	42	Germany	Y	Antwerp	New York	12/04/1887	11/02/1893			Y	
Gutjahr, Jacob	42	Germany	Y	Antwerp	New York	12/04/1887	11/02/1893	21	48		
Gutknecht, Heinrich	39	Germany	Y	Bremen	Baltimore	03/20/1875	11/01/1889			Y	
Gutknecht, William	37	Germany	N	Bremen	Baltimore	05/22/1871	?			Y	
Gutkowski, Joseph (Goodk	23	Poland	Y	?	New York	05/01/1887	10/04/1888			Y	
Gutmann, August	35	Hesse Darmsta	Y	Bremen	Baltimore	09/11/1857	09/18/1858	16	174	N	
Gutmann, Nicholas	31	Bavaria	Y	Havre	New Orleans	10/23/1846	08/16/1848	22	189	N	
Guttenberg, Gottlieb	29	Bavaria	Y	Bremen	Buffalo	08/25/1847	02/02/1850	2	32	N	
Guttermann, Anthony	28	Bavaria	Y	Havre	New Orleans	11/01/1845	02/19/1849	23	176	N	
Gutting, Peter	31	Germany	Y	Bremen	New York	07/24/1881	10/23/1884			Y	
Guttmann, Robert	42	Germany	N	Bremen	New York	09/??/1867	?			Y	
Guttmann, Simon	23	Bavaria	Y	Bremen	New York	09/28/1849	03/05/1853	7	284	N	
Gutzki, Frederick Willia	36	Germany	Y	?	Baltimore	??/??/1872	10/18/1880			Y	
Gutzweller, Fridolin	25	Switzerland	Y	Havre	New Orleans	05/??/1846	11/??/1849	23	374	N	
Gutzwiller, Anthony	39	Switzerland	Y	Havre	New York	07/28/1891	10/27/1896			Y	

CITIZENSHIP RECORDS

APPLICANT	AGE	COUNTRY OF ORIGIN	DEC	DEPART PORT	ENTRY PORT	ARRIVE DATE	DEC DATE	VOL	PG.	FLD	NAT DATE
Gutzwiller, Emil	29	Switzerland	Y	Havre	New York	06/22/1888	02/24/1892			Y	
Gutzwiller, Otto	28	Switzerland	Y	Havre	New York	08/10/1880	05/07/1883			Y	
Gutzwiller, Uers	33	Switzerland	Y	Havre	New Orleans	??/26/1846	11/28/1849	23	375	N	
Gutzwiller, Victor	30	Switzerland	Y	Havre	New York	07/15/1848	08/15/1851	4	133	N	
Guyman, Edward	24	Ireland	Y	Liverpool	New Orleans	??/04/1848	11/22/1849	23	363	N	
Guziotck, John	24	Germany	Y	Hamburg	Baltimore	04/28/1891	02/21/1894			Y	
Gysin, Louis	30	Germany	Y	Bremen	New York	11/08/1889	08/05/1895			Y	
Gyssels, Desire	60	Belgium	Y	Antwerp	Boston	10/29/1869	10/22/1896			Y	
Haab, Edward	34	Germany	Y	Antwerp	New York	05/05/1888	10/24/1888			Y	
Haag, Christian	26	Wurttemberg	Y	Havre	New York	04/09/1849	05/06/1850	3	46	N	
Haag, Clemens	27	Germany	Y	Antwerp	New York	04/03/1889	11/01/1889			Y	
Haag, Gottlieb	33	Wurttemberg	Y	Rotterdam	New York	05/28/18??	12/30/1852	5	476	N	
Haag, John	34	Germany	Y	London	New York	11/21/1882	01/30/1890			Y	
Haag, Karl Leonard	24	Germany	Y	?	Philadelphia	05/22/1896	07/30/1898			Y	
Haag, Leo	47	Austria	Y	Bremen	Baltimore	05/27/1882	09/24/1902			Y	
Haake, Anton	26	Prussia	Y	Bremen	New Orleans	12/15/1845	07/31/1848	22	20	N	
Haake, Gerhard Henry	23	Hanover	Y	Bremen	New Orleans	12/10/1848	06/08/1852	25	212	N	
Haake, Gustav	37	Germany	Y	Bremen	New York	11/19/1883	05/??/1883			Y	
Haake, Gustav	37	Germany	N	Bremen	New York	11/19/1882	?			Y	
Haake, Henry	26	Hanover	Y	Bremen	New Orleans	11/18/1850	02/25/1852	24	172	N	
Haap, Michael	17	Germany	N	?	New York	00/00/1873				Y	10/22/1886
Haarmann, W.F.	42	Germany	Y	Amsterdam	New York	03/12/1882	07/28/1885			Y	
Haarmeyer, Laurent	37	Germany	Y	Amsterdam	New York	03/01/1892	02/21/1894			Y	
Haas, Andreas	28	Baden	Y	Havre	New York	09/15/1853	04/18/1854	8	202	N	
Haas, Andreas	28	Baden	Y	Havre	New York	09/15/1853	04/18/1854	9	73	N	
Haas, Anton	21	Germany	Y	Antwerp	New York	06/18/1899	10/07/1892			Y	
Haas, Christian	21	Wurttemberg	Y	Bremen	New York	05/09/1854	08/17/1857	15	146	N	
Haas, Christian	21	Germany	Y	Havre	New York	09/15/1882	10/05/1883			Y	
Haas, Edward	34	Germany	Y	Antwerp	New York	05/05/1888	10/24/1888	19	174	N	
Haas, Frank A.	24	Germany	Y	Hamburg	New York	12/01/1872	04/16/1874			Y	
Haas, Franz	29	Bavaria	Y	Havre	New York	11/29/1856	11/22/1859	17	478	N	
Haas, George	36	Baden	Y	Havre	New Orleans	10/16/1847	09/13/1852	25	468	N	
Haas, Georges	35	Switzerland	Y	Havre	New York	04/14/1886	07/24/1895			Y	
Haas, Jacob	28	Bavaria	Y	Havre	New Orleans	03/01/1854	02/19/1857	15	36	N	
Haas, John	22	Germany	Y	Bremen	New York	08/28/1888	10/25/1889			Y	
Haas, John	30	Germany	Y	Antwerp	New York	06/06/1890	11/30/1895			Y	
Haas, Joseph	25	Baden	Y	Havre	New York	12/22/1854	08/24/1857	15	177	N	
Haas, Salomon	26	Baden	Y	Havre	New Orleans	06/??/1853	10/25/1858	17	104	N	
Haase, Fred	58	Germany	N	Germany	New Orleans	11/28/1865	07/29/1879	28	455	N	10/10/1881
Haase, Henry	27	Germany	Y	Hamburg	New York	09/21/1882	09/17/1883			Y	
Haasz, Charles	21	Baden	Y	Havre	New Orleans	03/01/1846	01/16/1849	1	435	N	
Haasz, Frederick	54	Baden	Y	Havre	New Orleans	03/01/1846	01/16/1849	1	434	N	
Habel, George Andrew	26	Wurttemberg	Y	Liverpool	New York	11/15/1853	04/08/1858	16	506	N	
Habel, Max	??	Germany	Y	?	?	?	01/09/1882			Y	
Haber, Henry	23	Hanover	Y	Bremen	Philadelphia	10/01/1845	11/22/1848	1	365	N	
Haberer, Louis	16	Germany	N	?	New York	00/00/1871				Y	10/23/1886
Haberkern, Anton	40	Wurttemberg	Y	London	New York	09/06/1849	11/01/1851	4	458	N	
Habermann, Friedrich	32	Germany	Y	Bremen	New York	08/29/1882	04/26/1890			Y	
Habermehl, John	36	Bavaria	Y	Havre	New York	02/18/1855	07/10/1862	18	372	N	
Habig, Michael	22	Luxembourg	Y	Antwerp	New York	09/29/1853	11/08/1858	17	297	N	
Habighorst, Henry W.	32	Prussia	Y	Bremen	Baltimore	10/10/1857	06/28/1860	27	15	N	
Hack, Michael	28	Baden	Y	Rotterdam	New York	09/08/1851	06/14/1852	25	255	N	
Hackenbruch, Ferdinand	26	Prussia	Y	Havre	New York	12/15/1855	02/10/1860	27	98	N	
Hackenburg, August	24	Germany	Y	Antwerp	New York	12/05/1870	04/28/1880			Y	
Hacker, Christian	61	Germany	Y	Bremen	Baltimore	06/15/1887	10/07/1893			Y	
Hacker, Conrad	30	Bavaria	Y	Bremen	New York	07/25/1854	10/17/1857	15	437	N	
Hacker, Conrad	30	Germany	Y	Bremen	New York	03/26/1883	03/13/1884			Y	
Hacker, Simon	39	Germany	Y	Bremen	New York	05/20/1885	09/26/1892			Y	
Hacket, John	49	Ireland	Y	Liverpool	Baltimore	06/01/1840	02/01/1850	2	24	N	

CITIZENSHIP RECORDS

APPLICANT	AGE	COUNTRY OF ORIGIN	DEC	DEPART PORT	ENTRY PORT	ARRIVE DATE	DEC DATE	VOL	PG.	FLD	NAT DATE
Hackett, John	25	Ireland	Y	Liverpool	New Orleans	04/04/1847	01/24/1861	18	68	N	
Hackl, Joseph	27	Austria	Y	Bremen	Baltimore	06/20/1895	12/31/1900			Y	
Hackmann, Fred	17	Germany	N	?	Baltimore	00/00/1881				Y	10/18/1886
Hackmann, Gerhard Freder	34	Hanover	Y	Bremen	Baltimore	10/20/1852	04/17/1862	18	317	N	
Hackmann, Henry	30	Germany	Y	Bremen	New York	10/15/1884	11/16/1895			Y	
Hackner, Franz	32	Germany	Y	Bremen	New York	04/25/1878	10/11/1881			Y	
Hackstedde, Herman Henry	24	Hanover	Y	Bremen	Baltimore	09/22/1854	09/23/1857	15	305	N	
Hadapp, Wendel	33	Baden	Y	Havre	New York	09/14/1848	09/22/1854	10	164	N	
Hadapp, Wendel	33	Baden	Y	Havre	New York	09/14/1848	09/22/1854	12	103	N	
Hadden, Joseph	21	Ireland	Y	Liverpool	New Orleans	10/20/1849	03/30/1852	24	341	N	
Haddock, Luke	70	Ireland	N	Liverpool	New York	06/25/1853	?			Y	
Hadler, Fred	27	Germany	Y	Bremen	Baltimore	07/30/1884	10/17/1890			Y	
Hadley, Charles	45	England	Y	Liverpool	New Orleans	03/17/1833	01/25/1850	23	547	N	
Haeberle, Mathias	46	Wuertemberg	Y	Havre	New York	04/18/1854	02/14/1856	26	83	N	
Haeckel, Casper	33	Bavaria	Y	Bremen	New York	06/21/1854	08/18/1857	15	158	N	
Haeckel, Edward	26	Saxe Weimar	Y	Bremen	New York	05/18/1854	04/02/1858	16	476	N	
Haeckl, Michael	35	Germany	Y	Bremen	Baltimore	06/15/1889	10/23/1891			Y	
Haefeley, Robert	35	Switzerland	Y	Havre	New York	02/24/1847	02/21/1849	23	237	N	
Haefeli, Charles	??	France	Y	?	New York	10/??/1885	04/29/1890			Y	
Haefker, H.	22	Germany	Y	Bremen	Baltimore	12/??/1880	07/15/1884			Y	
Haefler, Lorenz	47	France	Y	Havre	New Orleans	11/25/1845	08/02/1848	22	41	N	
Haefner, Charles	30	Germany	Y	Rotterdam	New York	01/15/1880	07/03/1884			Y	
Haefner, Conrad	25	Kurhessen	Y	Bremen	Baltimore	07/13/1850	09/29/1854	10	316	N	
Haefner, George	26	Germany	Y	Bremen	New York	06/02/1889	10/10/1892			Y	
Haefner, Heinrich	27	Germany	Y	Hamburg	New York	10/06/1880	05/02/1883			Y	
Haefner, John	31	Germany	Y	Bremen	New York	10/21/1880	04/06/1885			Y	
Haegel, Frank Xav.	28	Germany	Y	Havre	New York	01/24/1890	07/22/1893			Y	
Haegele, John George	46	Wuerttenberg	Y	London	New York	06/01/1847	09/27/1848	22	355	N	
Haegi, Jacob	21	Switzerland	Y	Havre	New York	06/13/1882	10/15/1884			Y	
Haehnel, Charles August	45	Saxony	Y	Bremen	New York	08/13/1849	10/16/1851	4	315	N	
Haeling, Albert	28	Germany	Y	?	Baltimore	??/??/1881	12/11/1884			Y	
Haelker, William	30	Hanover	Y	Bremen	New York	07/02/1842	09/02/1848	22	290	N	
Haelmig, Gerhard	29	Prussia	Y	Bremen	New Orleans	10/03/1845	08/04/1848	22	57	N	
Haelmreich, George	37	Bavaria	Y	Havre	New York	11/07/1849	12/04/1855	13	280	N	
Haenzler, Wm.	36	Germany	Y	Liverpool	New York	06/04/1894	01/07/1895			Y	
Haerdlein, William	44	Germany	Y	Bremen	New York	10/15/1873	09/29/1885			Y	
Haering, Fred	26	Germany	Y	Liverpool	New York	03/26/1882	03/03/1888			Y	
Haering, Joseph	22	Germany	Y	Bremen	New York	09/04/1880	09/28/1883			Y	
Haering, William	34	Germany	Y	Bremen	New York	04/06/1892	10/29/1898			Y	
Haeringer, Joseph	21	Baden	Y	Havre	New Orleans	04/??/1853	11/03/1856	14	454	N	
Haermmerlin, George	28	Germany	Y	Havre	New York	01/01/1894	06/30/1900			Y	
Haerth, George	30	Germany	Y	Hamburg	New York	05/??/1876	09/29/1885			Y	
Haese, Gustav	32	Germany	Y	Bremen	New York	08/05/1882	09/25/1885			Y	
Haesel, John	30	Germany	Y	Bremen	New York	09/26/1879	10/19/1883			Y	
Haeseler, Anton	36	Hanover	Y	Havre	New York	10/08/1851	04/04/1853	8	35	N	
Haeseler, Ernst	32	Hanover	Y	Havre	New Orleans	01/13/1850	04/02/1853	7	489	N	
Haessler, Conrad	49	Baden	Y	Havre	New Orleans	03/12/1852	11/02/1857	15	514	N	
Haeusel, Jacob	22	Bavaria	Y	Havre	New Orleans	12/01/1851	07/13/1855	11	384	N	
Haeusler, Anton	21	Germany	Y	Antwerp	Philadelphia	04/14/1892	03/25/1895			Y	
Haeusser, Sigismund	39	Kourhassen	Y	Havre	New Orleans	05/08/1849	04/08/1852	24	422	N	
Haey, Jacob	52	Bavaria	Y	Havre	New York	10/20/1849	09/13/1852	25	463	N	
Haey, Valentine	38	Bavaria	Y	Havre	New Orleans	12/04/1848	01/25/1849	1	512	N	
Haeyn, Frederick William	??	Germany	Y	?	?	?	07/01/1882			Y	
Hafen, Charles	30	Germany	Y	?	New Orleans	02/01/1884	09/21/1884			Y	
Hafenbraede, Joseph	28	Bavaria	Y	Bremen	New York	04/02/1855	09/27/1856	14	411	N	
Hafer, Friedrich Henry	25	Hanover	Y	Bremen	New Orleans	11/13/1847	02/02/1850	2	31	N	
Hafer, John Henry	33	Hanover	Y	Bremen	Baltimore	10/15/1854	10/28/1857	15	498	N	
Hafer, William	28	Germany	Y	Bremen	New York	07/10/1883	12/09/1889			Y	
Hafertepe, John Henry	34	Hanover	Y	Bremen	New Orleans	12/20/1856	11/01/1858	17	252	N	

CITIZENSHIP RECORDS

APPLICANT	AGE	COUNTRY OF ORIGIN	DEC	DEPART PORT	ENTRY PORT	ARRIVE DATE	DEC DATE	VOL	PG.	FLD	NAT DATE
Haffner, Wilhelm Ferdina	50	Wurttemberg	Y	Havre	New York	06/21/1854	09/30/1854	10	320	N	
Haffner, Wilhelm Ferdina	50	Wurttemberg	Y	Havre	New York	06/21/1854	09/30/1854	12	259	N	
Hafner, Conrad	25	Kurhessen	Y	Bremen	Baltimore	07/13/1850	09/29/1854	12	255	N	
Hafner, Stephan	31	Wurttemberg	Y	Havre	New York	07/04/1855	04/20/1858	16	480	N	
Hafner, Stephan	28	Germany	Y	Bremen	New York	08/26/1888	10/29/1892			Y	
Hafner, Stephen	28	Germany	Y	Bremen	New York	80/26/1888	10/29/1892	19	405	N	
Hafuer, William	38	Baden	Y	Havre	New York	06/17/1851	11/21/1855	13	241	N	
Hagagarty, John	23	Ireland	Y	Liverpool	New Orleans	02/20/1851	04/17/1854	9	31	N	
Hagarty, Anthony	36	Ireland	Y	Liverpool	New Orleans	01/01/1846	10/13/1851	4	226	N	
Hagedorn, Bernard	30	Prussia	Y	Bremen	New Orleans	12/07/1850	12/29/1855	13	385	N	
Hagedorn, Friedrich	58	Germany	Y	Bremen	New York	04/19/1885	07/05/1895			Y	
Hagedorn, Herman	21	Germany	Y	Amsterdam	New York	09/09/1890	08/15/1893			Y	
Hagedorn, John Diedrich	36	Prussia	Y	Bremen	New Orleans	11/26/1849	11/05/1852	5	238	N	
Hagedorn, John Diedrick	36	Prussia	Y	Bremen	New Orleans	11/26/1849	11/05/1852	6	362	N	
Hagedorn, Joseph	37	Germany	Y	Bremen	New York	08/05/1891	08/26/1893			Y	
Hagelstein, John	26	France	Y	Havre	New York	09/26/1853	10/28/1858	17	145	N	
Hageman, Bernard	35	Prussia	Y	Bremen	New Orleans	07/03/1847	01/27/1849	1	526	N	
Hageman, Conrad	30	Germany	Y	Bremen	New York	08/19/1877	04/08/1879			Y	
Hageman, Henry	40	Prussia	Y	Bremen	Baltimore	06/07/1844	01/27/1849	1	527	N	
Hageman, John William	26	Hanover	Y	Bremen	Baltimore	05/27/1845	10/07/1848	22	464	N	
Hagemann, Gerhard Freder	23	Hanover	Y	Bremen	Baltimore	06/20/1853	10/21/1857	15	467	N	
Hagemann, Henry	21	Germany	Y	Bremen	Baltimore	10/03/1887	08/14/1890			Y	
Hagemann, John	52	Germany	Y	Bremen	Baltimore	10/18/1866	09/24/1890			Y	
Hagemann, William	35	Prussia	Y	Bremen	New York	11/06/1869	07/16/1872	18	505	N	
Hagemeyer, John Christia	33	Bremen	Y	Bremen	Baltimore	05/14/1854	09/25/1854	10	192	N	
Hagemeyer, John Christia	33	Bremen	Y	Bremen	Baltimore	05/14/1854	09/25/1854	12	131	N	
Hagen, Charles W.L.	25	Germany	Y	Rotterdam	Boston	09/17/1888	11/15/1890			Y	
Hagen, George	28	Germany	Y	Bremen	Baltimore	05/24/1884	01/20/1888			Y	
Hagen, George	30	Germany	Y	Bremen	Baltimore	08/28/1892	10/19/1899			Y	
Hagen, John	37	Germany	Y	Bremen	New York	05/07/1888	03/27/1894			Y	
Hagen, John	30	Saxe Meininge	Y	Antwerp	New York	07/04/1849	06/03/1852	25	179	N	
Hagen, Karl	38	Germany	Y	Bremen	New York	04/18/1882	07/18/1888			Y	
Hagen, Max	55	Denmark	Y	?	New York	??/??/1878	10/19/1892			Y	
Hagen, William	27	Mecklenburg S	Y	Hamburg	New York	06/15/1855	10/30/1858	17	206	N	
Hagensieker, H.	39	Germany	Y	Bremen	Baltimore	07/26/1884	02/05/1887			Y	
Hager, George	27	Bavaria	Y	Bremen	New York	08/06/1849	12/08/1852	5	398	N	
Hagerty, Thomas	35	Ireland	Y	Liverpool	New York	02/??/1849	01/06/1853	5	523	N	
Haggarty, John	23	Ireland	Y	Liverpool	New Orleans	02/20/1851	04/17/1854	8	160	N	
Hagmeier, Jacob	30	Germany	Y	Havre	New York	05/17/1882	01/26/1889			Y	
Haguman, Joseph	33	Germany	Y	?	?	?	08/04/1873			Y	
Hahn, Charles Fred	31	Prussia	Y	Bremen	New York	05/01/1849	02/07/1852	24	72	N	
Hahn, George	50	Germany	Y	Rotterdam	New York	10/25/1892	08/09/1897			Y	
Hahn, George Adam	26	Wurttemberg	Y	Bremen	Baltimore	10/??/1853	09/21/1855	13	88	N	
Hahn, Gustave	34	Germany	Y	Bremen	Baltimore	10/11/1883	02/24/1885			Y	
Hahn, Henry	25	Hesse Darmsta	Y	Bremen	New York	10/10/1849	10/20/1851	4	339	N	
Hahn, Henry	27	Prussia	Y	Halifax	Boston	10/08/1856	03/19/1860	27	132	N	
Hahn, Jacob	28	Hanover	Y	Bremen	New York	06/17/1849	01/06/1853	5	525	N	
Hahn, Jacob	32	Baden	Y	Havre	New Orleans	11/11/1852	11/08/1858	17	287	N	
Hahn, John	25	Baden	Y	Antwerp	Galveston	02/25/1847	06/19/1851	3	407	N	
Hahn, John	28	Germany	Y	Hamburg	New York	03/03/1881	09/28/1885			Y	
Hahn, John	34	Germany	Y	Bremen	New York	08/18/1885	09/28/1896			Y	
Hahn, Philip	39	Germany	Y	?	New York	??/??/1880	11/03/1884			Y	
Hahn, William	33	Hesse Cassel	Y	Bremen	New York	06/06/1852	09/14/1857	15	270	N	
Hahne, Diedrich	25	Hanover	Y	Bremen	New Orleans	06/10/1848	01/27/1851	2	535	N	
Haider, John	27	Wurttemberg	Y	Havre	New York	12/??/1853	12/24/1855	13	355	N	
Haigis, John G.	21	Germany	Y	Hamburg	New York	09/14/1887	09/17/1890			Y	
Hail, Gabriel	21	Bavaria	Y	Bremen	New York	08/25/1851	06/19/1852	25	294	N	
Hailey, Martin	29	Ireland	Y	Liverpool	New York	03/02/1845	02/06/1849	23	118	N	
Haimerl, Michael	35	Germany	Y	Antwerp	New York	02/06/1881	02/09/1886			Y	

CITIZENSHIP RECORDS

APPLICANT	AGE	COUNTRY OF ORIGIN	DEC	DEPART PORT	ENTRY PORT	ARRIVE DATE	DEC DATE	VOL	PG.	FLD	NAT DATE
Hais, Sebastian	25	Heckingen	Y	Havre	New Orleans	12/20/1846	01/02/1851	2	443	N	
Haisch, Gottlieb	37	Wuerttenberg	Y	Havre	New Orleans	06/01/1849	05/31/1852	25	150	N	
Hake, Charles Friedrich	26	Hanover	Y	Bremen	Baltimore	11/06/1850	05/20/1852	25	59	N	
Hake, William	23	Hanover	Y	Bremen	New Orleans	06/12/1850	10/06/1854	10	476	N	
Hake, William	23	Hanover	Y	Bremen	New Orleans	06/12/1850	10/06/1854	12	415	N	
Hake, William	26	Germany	Y	Bremen	New York	04/31/1882	03/31/1883			Y	
Halblaut, John	36	Germany	Y	Antwerp	New York	04/16/1887	10/05/1896			Y	
Hale, Thomas	60	Ireland	Y	Liverpool	New Orleans	07/01/1851	10/12/1857	15	399	N	
Halenkamp, William	30	Oldenburg	Y	Bremen	New Orleans	12/08/1847	02/12/1851	3	126	N	
Haley, Edward	26	Ireland	Y	Liverpool	New York	10/21/1855	12/26/1857	16	265	N	
Haley, Humphrey	50	Ireland	Y	Cork	Boston	04/25/1846	10/22/1857	15	478	N	
Haley, James	50	Ireland	N	Liverpool	New York	05/??/1869	?			Y	
Haley, Michael	27	Ireland	Y	Liverpool	New Orleans	04/04/1848	12/27/1852	5	452	N	
Haley, Michael	35	Ireland	Y	Liverpool	New Orleans	12/24/1848	09/25/1856	14	371	N	
Haley, Michael	40	Ireland	Y	Dublin	New York	00/00/1869	10/05/1876			Y	
Hall, John	22	Ireland	Y	Liverpool	New York	11/15/1851	07/25/1855	11	428	N	
Hall, John	39	England	Y	?	New York	09/05/1868	12/10/1884			Y	
Hall, Patrick	40	Ireland	N	Queenstown	New York	08/11/1871	?			Y	
Hall, Peter W.	35	Ireland	Y	Liverpool	New York	06/22/1880	01/16/1886	19	29	N	
Hall, Peter W.	35	Ireland	Y	Liverpool	New York	06/22/1880	01/16/1886			Y	
Hall, Robert	29	Ireland	Y	Londonderry	Philadelphia	09/08/1844	02/01/1849	23	6	N	
Hall, William	??	?	Y	?	?	??/24/18??	10/25/1850	2	299	N	
Hall, William	42	Hesse Cassel	Y	Bremen	Baltimore	10/03/1846	06/16/1851	3	388	N	
Hall, William	32	England	Y	Liverpool	New Orleans	05/20/1849	10/07/1854	11	1	N	
Hall, William	32	England	Y	Liverpool	New Orleans	05/02/1849	10/07/1854	12	480	N	
Hallahan, Patrick O.	28	Ireland	Y	Liverpool	New York	11/30/1845	03/17/1851	3	286	N	
Hallandberger, Mathew	24	Germany	Y	?	?	?	05/13/1880			Y	
Hallasy, Daniel	25	Ireland	Y	Liverpool	New York	10/01/1851	10/06/1854	10	514	N	
Hallasy, Daniel	25	Ireland	Y	Liverpool	New York	10/01/1851	10/06/1854	12	453	N	
Halle, Max M.	??	Germany	Y	?	?	?	06/27/1888			Y	
Haller, Andreas	25	Germany	Y	Havre	New York	10/14/1888	05/19/1893			Y	
Haller, George	30	Germany	Y	Hamburg	New York	10/26/1889	10/29/1897			Y	
Haller, Henry	40	Bavaria	Y	Bremen	New York	08/19/1853	09/30/1854	10	330	N	
Haller, Henry	40	Bavaria	Y	Bremen	New York	08/19/1853	09/30/1854	12	269	N	
Haller, Jacob	28	Germany	Y	Bremen	New York	11/28/1885	09/29/1887			Y	
Haller, Jacob	37	Wuerttenberg	Y	Antwerp	New York	07/12/1847	05/20/1852	25	47	N	
Haller, John	24	Germany	Y	?	?	?	09/22/1887			Y	
Halleren, Frank	22	Ireland	Y	Liverpool	New York	11/30/1849	03/22/1853	7	372	N	
Hallermann, George	45	Germany	Y	Amsterdam	New York	05/18/1881	11/07/1892			Y	
Halliday, Philip	53	England	N	Liverpool	New York	06/??/1851	?			Y	
Halligan, John	21	Ireland	Y	Liverpool	New Orleans	12/25/1849	09/15/1852	25	534	N	
Halloran, Patrick J.	33	Ireland	N	Queenstown	New York	04/01/1872	?			Y	
Halpern, Israel	28	Russia	Y	Hamburg	Boston	01/??/1889	03/25/1890			Y	
Halpern, Samuel	21	Russia	Y	Bremen	Baltimore	09/30/1891	01/04/1894			Y	
Halpin, Anthony	34	Ireland	Y	Liverpool	New York	09/01/1852	03/17/1853	7	337	N	
Halpin, Cornelius	50	Ireland	Y	Ireland	New York	06/27/1880	05/06/1883	28	360	N	
Halpin, Cornelius	38	Ireland	Y	?	New York	06/27/1880	05/06/1883			Y	
Halpin, Cornelius	41	Ireland	Y	London	New York	06/27/1880	05/06/1883			Y	
Halpin, John	28	Ireland	Y	Eridge	New York	09/01/1883	03/20/1889			Y	
Halpin, John	32	Ireland	Y	London	New York	04/??/1849	12/??/1849	23	393	Y	
Halpin, Michael	??	Ireland	N	?	?	05/10/1875				Y	10/18/1892
Halpin, Patrick	26	Ireland	Y	Liverpool	New York	04/06/1849	06/21/1852	25	299	N	
Halton, John	??	England	Y	?	?	02/??/1885	03/07/1892			Y	
Halves, Fred	42	Germany	Y	Bremen	Baltimore	05/27/1882	04/01/1889			Y	
Hamann, Ernst	32	Prussia	Y	Bremen	Baltimore	10/15/1857	10/06/1860	27	410	N	
Hamann, Ernst A.	36	Germany	Y	Hamburg	Baltimore	10/02/1881	11/17/1883			Y	
Hamann, Gottlieb	28	Mecklenburg	Y	Hamburg	New York	08/17/1852	09/07/1852	25	396	N	
Hamann, Lewis	33	Hanover	Y	Bremen	New York	05/01/1857	09/13/1860			Y	
Hambacher, Jacob	36	Bavaria	Y	Antwerp	New Orleans	06/07/1850	07/28/1851	4	53	N	

143

CITIZENSHIP RECORDS

APPLICANT	AGE	COUNTRY OF ORIGIN	DEC	DEPART PORT	ENTRY PORT	ARRIVE DATE	DEC DATE	VOL	PG.	FLD	NAT DATE
Hamberg, Gerhard	30	Hanover	Y	Bremen	New Orleans	04/30/1848	01/10/1856	13	440	N	
Hamberger, Karl A.	33	Germany	Y	Antwerp	Philadelphia	11/04/1887	04/06/1903			Y	
Hambly, Thomas	49	England	Y	Fowey	Buffalo	03/10/1859	03/26/1883			Y	
Hambrock, Christian	31	Hanover	Y	Bremen	New York	05/25/1855	10/23/1857	15	483	N	
Hambrock, John Henry	27	Hanover	Y	Bremen	New Orleans	12/22/1846	03/14/1850	2	195	N	
Hamburger, Abraham	23	Kurhessen	Y	Bremen	Baltimore	07/04/1847	03/25/1850	2	246	N	
Hamburger, Andrew	25	Bavaria	Y	Havre	New York	06/09/1856	09/29/1856	14	24	N	
Hamburger, Jacob	25	Bavaria	Y	Havre	New York	09/14/1855	08/29/1862	18	421	N	
Hamerschmidt, Lenard	23	Kurhessen	Y	London	New York	06/25/1846	11/21/1848	1	353	N	
Hamester, Adolf Julius	34	Germany	Y	Hamburg	New York	02/07/1885	02/07/1888			Y	
Hamilton, James	54	Scotland	Y	Liverpool	New York	09/01/1845	10/09/1854	6	71	N	
Hamilton, James	54	Scotland	Y	Liverpool	New York	09/01/1845	10/09/1854	11	72	N	
Hamilton, Patrick	??	Ireland	N	?	?	09/14/1889				Y	10/24/1892
Hamilton, Robert	40	Ireland	Y	Liverpool	New York	10/27/1869	06/27/1885			Y	
Hamilton, William	54	Ireland	N	Liverpool	New York	07/??/1853	?			Y	
Hamlyn, John	54	England	Y	Liverpool	New York	06/09/1850	11/13/1855	13	222	N	
Hamma, Christ	29	Germany	Y	Hamburg	New York	03/??/1882	03/31/1887			Y	
Hammann, Mathias	31	Prussia	Y	Havre	New York	06/12/1853	03/03/1856	26	153	N	
Hammel, Adolph	??	Germany	Y	?	?	?	11/26/1883			Y	
Hammel, Charles	26	Bavaria	Y	Havre	New Orleans	05/30/1852	07/09/1855	11	363	N	
Hammel, Edward	26	Bavaria	Y	Havre	New York	07/02/1850	10/17/1857	15	443	N	
Hammel, Jacob	25	Bavaria	Y	London	New York	07/01/1849	05/08/1852	24	415	N	
Hammell, George William	33	Bavaria	Y	Havre	New Orleans	05/01/1855	06/28/1860	27	13	N	
Hammell, William	??	Bavaria	Y	?	?	03/08/1866	10/17/1870			Y	
Hammelstein, Henry	27	Russia	Y	Hamburg	New York	07/04/1882	10/08/1889			Y	
Hammer, Andreas	25	Germany	Y	Amsterdam	New York	09/29/1882	10/03/1885			Y	
Hammer, Casper	24	Bavaria	Y	Havre	New York	07/04/1853	05/02/1858	17	390	N	
Hammer, Joseph	22	Germany	Y	Bremen	New York	09/15/1891	03/27/1894			Y	
Hammers, Andrew	38	Germany	Y	?	?	?	10/08/1883			Y	
Hammerschmidt, Adalbert	30	Germany	Y	?	?	?	06/11/1881			Y	
Hammler, Philipp	31	Germany	Y	Bremen	Baltimore	08/17/1880	09/13/1886			Y	
Hammon, Jacob	28	Germany	Y	?	New York	?	10/25/1895			Y	
Hammond, John	35	England	Y	London	New York	06/30/1849	02/12/1853	7	147	N	
Hamp, Frank	??	Germany	Y	?	?	?	11/07/1887			Y	
Hampe, Joseph	30	Hanover	Y	Liverpool	New York	08/04/1849	06/19/1852	25	292	N	
Hanagan, Darbey	34	Ireland	Y	Liverpool	New York	04/06/1847	03/01/18??	7	254	N	
Hanahan, Daniel	29	Ireland	Y	Cork	New York	01/12/1853	09/01/1860	27	321	N	
Hanahan, Patrick	46	Ireland	Y	Limerick	Buffalo	05/??/1851	09/01/1860	27	322	N	
Hanaman, Lewis	10	Germany	N	Havre	New York	04/00/1836				Y	00/00/1847
Hanan, Bartholomew	42	Ireland	Y	Toronto	Buffalo	11/08/1846	10/13/1851	4	243	N	
Hanau, William	23	Germany	Y	Bremen	New York	10/08/1883	08/07/1884			Y	
Hanbrook, William	54	Germany	N	Bremen	New Orleans	12/??/1850	?			Y	
Hance, Robert Peter	??	England	Y	?	?	?	12/18/1882			Y	
Hancer, Emil	23	Baden	Y	Liverpool	New York	11/12/1852	03/28/1853	7	436	N	
Hanchen, Edward	48	Germany	Y	Bremen	New York	09/01/1882	10/26/1893	21	34		
Hanchen, Edward	48	Germany	Y	Bremen	New York	09/01/1882	10/26/1893			Y	
Hancock, Charles	24	England	Y	London	New York	02/06/1852	04/09/1856	26	476	N	
Hancox, Joseph	60	England	Y	Liverpool	New York	05/15/1883	11/05/1888			Y	
Hand, Michael	??	Ireland	Y	Liverpool	New Orleans	04/03/1849	03/25/1851	3	332	N	
Handel, Kasper	25	Germany	Y	Antwerp	New York	09/24/1883	01/31/1887			Y	
Handman, Lewis	66	Germany	N	Havre	New York	04/??/1836	?	28	328	Y	??/??/1847
Handrich, Daniel	25	Germany	Y	Antwerp	New York	06/30/1880	10/02/1882			Y	
Handrick, John	30	Germany	Y	Hamburg	New York	02/14/1885	06/05/1889			Y	
Handrick, Miles	35	Ireland	Y	Dublin	New York	05/04/1850	11/09/1852	5	263	N	
Handrick, Miles	35	Ireland	Y	Dublin	New York	05/04/1850	11/09/1852	6	387	N	
Handy, Michael	35	Ireland	Y	Limerick	Burlington	05/??/1843	05/06/1854	8	387	N	
Handy, Michael	35	Ireland	Y	Limerick	Burlington	05/??/1847	05/06/1854	9	260	N	
Handy, Patrick	41	Ireland	Y	Liverpool	New Orleans	04/19/1847	07/25/1851	4	38	N	
Hane, Henry	31	Hanover	Y	Bremen	New Orleans	05/19/1852	01/15/1853	7	29	N	

CITIZENSHIP RECORDS

APPLICANT	AGE	COUNTRY OF ORIGIN	DEC	DEPART PORT	ENTRY PORT	ARRIVE DATE	DEC DATE	VOL	PG.	FLD	NAT DATE
Haneberg, F. K.	30	Oldenburg	Y	Bremen	New Orleans	12/04/1849	01/06/1860	27	38	N	
Hanekamp, John	45	Germany	Y	Liverpool	New York	04/10/1872	08/24/1891			Y	
Hanewinkel, Herman	24	Germany	Y	Rotterdam	New York	03/??/1880	02/03/1883			Y	
Haney, James	23	Ireland	Y	Liverpool	New Orleans	06/01/1848	05/01/1854	8	303	N	
Haney, James	23	Ireland	Y	Liverpool	New Orleans	06/01/1848	05/01/1854	9	175	N	
Hanfalder, William	29	Hanover	Y	Bremen	New Orleans	11/01/1857	11/01/1860	27	513	N	
Hangartner, Anton	25	Switzerland	Y	Antwerp	New York	01/21/1886	11/20/1889			Y	
Hangbers, Bernard Wilhel	26	Germany	Y	Bremen	Baltimore	04/09/1880	01/12/1882			Y	
Hanisch, Edward	30	Germany	Y	Bremen	New York	04/15/1885	08/08/1887			Y	
Hankamp, Barney Frederick	41	Oldenburg	Y	Bremen	New Orleans	12/12/1848	09/17/1855	13	50	N	
Hanke, Ernst	29	Germany	Y	Havre	New York	07/27/1891	05/02/1894			Y	
Hanker, Gerhard Frederic	40	Hanover	Y	Bremen	New York	07/15/1851	11/06/1855	13	171	N	
Hankins, Isaac	42	England	Y	Liverpool	New York	05/06/1887	03/22/1896			Y	
Hanle, William Frederick	28	Wurttemberg	Y	Antwerp	New York	05/07/1849	02/25/1850	2	122	N	
Hanley, Daniel K.	36	Ireland	Y	Queenstown	Philadelphia	05/31/1887	10/23/1894			Y	
Hanley, James	23	Ireland	Y	Ross	Buffalo	05/08/1851	01/30/1857	14	518	N	
Hanley, Timothy	40	Ireland	N	Liverpool	?	?	?			Y	
Hanlin, Patrick	33	Ireland	Y	Canada	Burlington	08/??/1846	11/??/1849	23	364	N	
Hanlon, John	26	Ireland	Y	Dublin	Black Rock	07/04/1843	05/20/1852	25	55	N	
Hanlon, Peter	21	Ireland	Y	Liverpool	New York	05/06/1847	01/07/1850	23	470	N	
Hanlon, Roger	54	Ireland	Y	Liverpool	New Orleans	12/24/1848	12/23/1852	5	441	N	
Hanly, Jeremiah	30	Ireland	Y	Limerick	New York	05/18/1852	03/22/1858	16	433	N	
Hanly, Michael	24	Ireland	Y	Waterford	New York	05/10/1846	10/13/1851	4	239	N	
Hanly, Nicholas	27	Ireland	Y	Liverpool	New York	09/20/1848	10/13/1851	4	241	N	
Hanly, Patrick	23	Ireland	Y	Queenstown	New York	05/25/1888	11/09/1891			Y	
Hann, August	31	Bavaria	Y	Havre	New York	01/29/1860	11/01/1860	27	527	N	
Hannafan, John	28	Ireland	Y	Liverpool	New York	04/28/1851	12/26/1851	24	15	N	
Hannaghan, John	36	Ireland	Y	Liverpool	New York	08/24/1882	10/22/1888			Y	
Hannahan, John	36	Ireland	Y	Liverpool	New York	08/24/1887	10/22/1888	19	165	N	
Hannan, Daniel	30	Ireland	Y	Liverpool	New Orleans	12/24/1850	10/07/1857	15	367	N	
Hannan, John	34	Ireland	Y	Limerick	Buffalo	10/??/1842	09/11/1852	25	454	N	
Hannan, Michael	27	Ireland	Y	Liverpool	New York	11/13/1851	10/07/1857	15	368	N	
Hannan, Patrick	26	Ireland	Y	Liverpool	New York	11/10/1846	07/05/1851	3	491	N	
Hanneken, Louis	33	Germany	Y	Bremen	New York	10/02/1873	11/01/1881			Y	
Hannen, Martin	22	Ireland	Y	Liverpool	New York	03/05/1851	05/02/1854	9	224	N	
Hannibal, Adam	27	Germany	Y	Bremen	Philadelphia	06/14/1878	10/19/1882			Y	
Hannig, Geroge	30	Baden	Y	Havre	New York	05/17/1855	12/24/1859	17	515	N	
Hanning, Ferdinand	27	Germany	Y	Hamburg	Boston	01/15/1891	06/27/1894			Y	
Hanningan, Thomas (Hunni	32	France	Y	Havre	New Orleans	07/04/1846	08/15/1848	22	172	N	
Hannon, James	31	Ireland	Y	Liverpool	New Orleans	06/28/1847	10/14/1851	4	275	N	
Hannon, John	35	Ireland	Y	Queenstown	New York	05/26/1883	02/10/1890			Y	
Hannon, John P.	23	England	N	?	New York	00/00/1863				Y	10/23/1886
Hannon, Martin	22	Ireland	Y	Liverpool	New York	03/05/1851	05/02/1854	8	351	N	
Hannower, John Bernard	21	Oldenburg	Y	Bremen	Baltimore	10/23/1854	11/10/1855	13	203	N	
Hanny, Ferdinand	23	Baden	Y	Havre	New York	03/01/1851	06/19/1852	25	291	N	
Hanold, Mathias	26	Baden	Y	Havre	New York	04/02/1854	05/22/1856	26	531	N	
Hanrahan, Dennis	21	Ireland	Y	Liverpool	New York	10/15/1856	12/16/1859	17	506	N	
Hans, Franz Michael	37	Bavaria	Y	Havre	New Orleans	05/28/1852	11/21/1855	13	238	N	
Hans, Henry	24	Bavaria	Y	Havre	New York	08/16/1853	11/02/1857	15	522	N	
Hans, Jacob	22	Bavaria	Y	Havre	New York	12/15/1853	02/02/1856	26	9	N	
Hans, John	24	Bavaria	Y	Havre	New Orleans	04/12/1851	01/23/1856	13	499	N	
Hans, Peter	27	Germany	Y	Bremen	Baltimore	08/03/1887	09/15/1890			Y	
Hansan, Louis	22	Denmark	Y	Copenhagen	New York	05/22/1882	10/20/1886	19	56	N	
Hansberg, John	24	Ireland	Y	Liverpool	Philadelphia	05/??/1886	03/24/1890			Y	
Hanschmidt, Arnold	64	Germany	N	Bremen	New Orleans	12/??/1855	?			Y	
Hanselman, Franz	27	Bavaria	Y	Bremen	Baltimore	12/22/1852	11/05/1855	13	168	N	
Hanselman, John Louis	26	Wuerttemberg	Y	Bremen	Baltimore	07/18/1843	08/08/1848	22	81	N	
Hanselmann, George Micha	35	Wuerttemberg	Y	Bremen	Baltimore	07/17/1844	04/12/1852	24	437	N	
Hanselmann, Simon	24	France	Y	Havre	New York	11/01/1857	08/04/1860	27	248	N	

CITIZENSHIP RECORDS

APPLICANT	AGE	COUNTRY OF ORIGIN	DEC	DEPART PORT	ENTRY PORT	ARRIVE DATE	DEC DATE	VOL	PG.	FLD	NAT DATE
Hansen, Andrew	29	Denmark	Y	?	?	04/04/1883	01/28/1889			Y	
Hanser, Gustav	25	Baden	Y	Havre	New York	07/22/1848	09/14/1852	25	492	N	
Hanser, Heribut	??	Austria	Y	?	?		12/18/1882			Y	
Hanser, Simon	22	Germany	Y	Liverpool	Philadelphia	01/19/1893	01/15/1895			Y	
Hansfeld, Henry	28	Oldenburg	Y	Bremen	New Orleans	05/01/1849	10/09/1854	6	67	N	
Hansfeld, John Bernhard	22	Hanover	Y	Bremen	New York	10/13/1856	08/08/1860	27	257	N	
Hany, William	24	Ireland	Y	Liverpool	New York	12/16/1848	02/14/1853	7	151	N	
Hapelwander, Joseph	26	Bavaria	Y	Havre	New Orleans	04/02/8155	10/29/1858	17	177	N	
Hapip, Assed	45	Syria	Y	Beirut	New York	04/20/1894	07/06/1898			Y	
Happ, Jacob	36	Wurttemberg	Y	Antwerp	New York	10/24/1857	11/20/1861	18	227	N	
Happe, Henry B.	??	Prussia	Y	?	?	?	04/10/1885			Y	
Happersberger, C.	25	Germany	Y	Havre	New York	09/11/1879	10/22/1881			Y	
Haran, Michael	26	Ireland	Y	Liverpool	New Orleans	11/22/1852	02/11/1860	27	101	N	
Harbars, Johann Dietrich	29	Germany	Y	Bremen	New York	09/21/1887	08/27/1888			Y	
Harbers, Gerhard Henry	44	Prussia	Y	Bremen	New Orleans	11/13/1844	08/15/1848	22	141	N	
Harbron, George	59	England	Y	Liverpool	New York	??/??/1851	10/06/1884			Y	
Harburg, Jasse	25	England	Y	Liverpool	New York	11/01/1846	04/14/1852	24	503	N	
Harder, John	30	Switzerland	Y	Havre	New York	04/18/1847	03/29/1853	7	457	N	
Hardert, Fred	27	Germany	Y	Bremen	Baltimore	04/06/1881	01/30/1888			Y	
Hardick, Joseph	26	Hanover	Y	Bremen	New Orleans	11/22/1854	12/16/1857	16	226	N	
Hardway, Frederick	25	Ireland	Y	Liverpool	New York	10/27/1847	03/16/1852	24	315	N	
Hardy, Benjamin	67	England	Y	Liverpool	New York	09/20/1886	10/27/1893			Y	
Hare, James	??	Ireland	Y	Limerick	Massachusett	??/20/1847	03/25/1851	3	350	N	
Harenberg, Conrad	28	Hanover	Y	Bremen	New Orleans	11/30/1848	01/30/1849	1	545	N	
Harff, Paul	34	Germany	Y	Antwerp	New York	11/02/1893	10/03/1899			Y	
Harford, Michael	42	Ireland	Y	Londonderry	New York	08/10/1871	09/25/1889			Y	
Haring, Charles	32	Wurttemberg	Y	Bremen	Baltimore	10/28/1841	10/12/1857	15	295	N	
Haring, Theodore	30	Germany	Y	Bremen	New York	06/13/1884	01/02/1889			Y	
Harkas, Michael	28	Germany	Y	Amsterdam	Philadelphia	03/13/1878	03/16/1885			Y	
Harl, Cornelius	30	Ireland	Y	London	New York	07/17/1854	05/11/1859	17	409	N	
Harlein, William	35	Prussia	Y	Bremen	New Orleans	11/??/1846	12/02/1852	5	367	N	
Harley, James	22	Ireland	Y	Liverpool	New York	09/??/1848	12/26/1850	2	391	N	
Harlfinger, August	35	Baden	Y	Havre	New Orleans	05/26/1850	09/30/1856	14	55	N	
Harlow, John	23	Ireland	Y	Liverpool	New Orleans	02/20/1850	08/04/1851	4	82	N	
Harlow, Michael	23	Ireland	Y	Liverpool	New Orleans	02/01/1849	11/01/1852	5	99	N	
Harlow, Michael	23	Ireland	Y	Liverpool	New Orleans	02/01/1850	11/01/1852	6	242	N	
Harmann, George	40	Germany	Y	Rotterdam	New York	07/15/1872	01/03/1882			Y	
Harmann, Henry	55	Germany	Y	Bremen	New Orleans	12/29/1860	11/01/1888			Y	
Harmeier, Bernard	26	Prussia	Y	Bremen	New York	07/11/1866	11/06/1871	18	439	N	
Harmeling, Henry	35	Germany	Y	?	?	?	10/19/1896			Y	
Harmer, Peter	35	Ireland	Y	Liverpool	New Orleans	05/08/1848	05/11/1854	9	296	N	
Harmeyer, Casper Henry	26	Hanover	Y	Bremen	New Orleans	12/31/1845	11/04/1852	5	215	N	
Harmeyer, Casper Henry	26	Hanover	Y	Bremen	New Orleans	12/31/1845	11/04/1852	6	341	N	
Harmeyer, Louis	32	Hanover	Y	Bremen	Baltimore	07/01/1854	09/25/1856	14	370	N	
Harmis, William	??	Hanover	Y	?	New York	??/04/18??	11/05/1856	14	468	N	
Harms, William	33	Germany	Y	Bremen	New York	10/25/1885	10/31/1896			Y	
Harnberger, George	25	Germany	Y	Bremen	New York	03/17/1885	11/01/1889			Y	
Harne, John	32	Ireland	Y	St. Johns	Portland	06/14/1847	03/18/1852	24	330	N	
Harneck, John	21	Mecklenburg	Y	Hamburg	New York	04/16/1851	09/21/1854	10	144	N	
Harnett, Daniel	35	Ireland	Y	Liverpool	Boston	07/29/1842	02/13/1851	3	129	N	
Harnock, John	21	Mecklenburg	Y	Hamburg	New York	04/16/1851	09/21/1854	12	83	N	
Harper, Nehemiah	45	England	Y	Liverpool	New York	02/??/1880	09/16/1888			Y	
Harpman, Isaac	36	Holland	Y	London	New York	09/02/1854	07/01/1857	15	120	N	
Harpsky, Adam	35	Germany	Y	Hamburg	New York	07/08/1881	10/03/1891			Y	
Harran, Martin	33	Ireland	Y	Sligo	New York	06/??/1849	02/23/1856	26	117	N	
Harrard, William F.	??	?	N	?	?	?	?			Y	10/30/1844
Harrens, Richard	32	Germany	Y	Bremen	Baltimore	12/10/1880	11/02/1886			Y	
Harries, George H.	26	Hanover	Y	Bremen	New York	11/15/1858	02/27/1860	27	112	N	
Harrigan, John	25	Ireland	Y	Limerick	Philadelphia	07/29/1846	03/03/1851	3	194	N	

146

CITIZENSHIP RECORDS

APPLICANT	AGE	COUNTRY OF ORIGIN	DEC	DEPART PORT	ENTRY PORT	ARRIVE DATE	DEC DATE	VOL	PG.	FLD	NAT DATE
Harrigan, John	47	Ireland	N	Liverpool	New York	04/20/1863	?			Y	
Harrington, Daniel	??	Ireland	Y	Cork	New York	04/01/1849	03/24/1851	3	320	N	
Harrington, Herbert L.	35	Canada	Y	?	Brasher Fall	??/??/1878	11/03/1890			Y	
Harrington, Michael	??	Ireland	Y	?	?	?	02/18/1892			Y	
Harrington, T.	34	Ireland	Y	Queenstown	Boston	03/??/1874	10/10/1884			Y	
Harrington, Thomas	??	Ireland	Y	?	?	?	04/23/1883			Y	
Harris, Charles	??	England	Y	?	New York	08/??/1880	10/31/1894			Y	
Harris, Henry	38	Wales	Y	Liverpool	New York	02/??/1855	01/04/1872	18	546	N	
Harris, Henry	43	Germany	N	Germany	New York	05/15/1861	?			Y	
Harris, Jah.	23	England	Y	Liverpool	New York	10/??/1847	10/29/1850	2	331	N	
Harris, James	29	England	Y	Liverpool	Philadelphia	10/06/1846	03/01/1852	24	197	N	
Harris, Joseph	25	Prussia	Y	London	New York	07/02/1850	04/24/1854	8	254	N	
Harris, Joseph	25	Prussia	Y	London	New York	02/02/1850	04/24/1854	9	125	N	
Harris, Joseph	27	Poland	Y	Hamburg	New York	04/21/1883	09/22/1887			Y	
Harris, Joseph	42	Russia	Y	Liverpool	New York	06/29/1892	10/07/1892			Y	
Harris, Michael	25	Russia	Y	Hamburg	New York	05/10/1889	03/29/1894			Y	
Harris, Nathaniel R.	32	Ireland	Y	Liverpool	Philadelphia	10/07/1848	06/05/1852	25	211	N	
Harris, William	31	England	Y	Liverpool	New Orleans	06/04/1848	02/14/1851	3	132	N	
Harris, William	25	England	Y	Canada	Cleveland	03/17/1843	09/01/1848	22	286	N	
Harrison, William H.	30	Scotland	Y	Liverpool	New York	01/17/1848	02/19/1852	24	142	N	
Harrmann, Emil	23	Germany	Y	Amsterdam	New York	05/29/1882	07/05/1884			Y	
Harsch, Emanuel	24	Wertenburg	Y	Antwerp	New York	07/09/1847	07/28/1848	22	6	N	
Hart, Anthony	25	Ireland	Y	Liverpool	New Orleans	01/09/1846	04/24/1854	8	255	N	
Hart, Anthony	25	Ireland	Y	Liverpool	New Orleans	01/09/1846	04/24/1854	9	126	N	
Hart, Anthony	59	Ireland	N	Liverpool	New Orleans	01/??/1846	?			Y	
Hart, Isaac	40	Prussia	Y	Liverpool	New York	08/06/1851	08/18/1855	11	455	N	
Hart, James	36	Ireland	Y	Quebec	Troy	09/18/1847	02/01/1853	7	103	N	
Hart, James	38	Ireland	Y	Liverpool	New York	08/20/1871	10/13/1884			Y	
Hart, Patrick	22	Ireland	Y	Liverpool	New York	09/20/1849	12/08/1852	5	400	N	
Hart, Patrick	22	Ireland	Y	Liverpool	New Orleans	01/01/1848	01/20/1852	24	39	N	
Hart, Peter	36	Ireland	Y	Liverpool	New York	08/03/1849	06/07/1852	25	196	N	
Hart, Phillip	34	Hesse Cassel	Y	Bremen	Buffalo	08/09/1847	01/19/1849	1	472	N	
Hart, Thomas	28	Ireland	Y	Galway	New York	12/??/1850	03/15/1853	7	327	N	
Hartars, Johan Dietrich	29	Germany	Y	Bremen	New York	09/21/1887	08/27/1888	19	135	N	
Harte, August	28	Germany	Y	Bremen	New York	04/28/1881	11/10/1884			Y	
Harte, August F.	25	Hanover	Y	Bremen	Baltimore	10/23/1853	08/22/1855	11	479	N	
Harte, John Henry	27	Hanover	Y	Bremen	New Orleans	11/10/1849	08/12/1851	4	124	N	
Hartel, Frank	21	Germany	Y	?	New York	10/16/1885	10/16/1888			Y	
Harter, Benedict	26	Baden	Y	Havre	New Orleans	05/25/1846	01/22/1849	1	483	N	
Harter, Joseph	30	Baden	Y	Havre	New Orleans	05/20/1840	08/07/1848	22	62	N	
Harterer, Nicholas	22	Wurttemberg	Y	Havre	New York	09/18/1851	03/25/1853	7	399	N	
Hartgen, Frederick	24	Hanover	Y	Hamburg	New Orleans	11/04/1852	10/13/1857	15	417	N	
Harth, Jacob	35	Germany	Y	?	?	05/??/1886	09/08/1897			Y	
Hartig, Adam	31	Bavaria	Y	Bremen	Baltimore	09/25/1842	08/02/1848	22	43	N	
Hartig, Fritz	21	Germany	Y	Bremen	New York	09/18/1888	01/04/1892			Y	
Hartig, Hans	27	Germany	Y	Bremen	New York	03/21/1885	08/21/1886			Y	
Hartigan, Richard	21	Ireland	Y	Liverpool	New Orleans	03/28/1848	03/08/1850	2	168	N	
Hartigan, Richard	61	Ireland	N	Liverpool	New Orleans	05/??/1849	?			Y	
Harting, Herman	24	Hanover	Y	Bremen	New York	07/17/1845	08/14/1848	22	107	N	
Hartke, Henry	52	Germany	Y	Bremen	New York	08/21/1891	03/22/1898			Y	
Hartke, John G. H.	42	Oldenburg	Y	Bremen	Baltimore	05/15/1834	04/15/1852	24	505	N	
Hartkemeyer, Frank	36	Germany	Y	Bremen	New York	08/?//1863	03/25/1881			Y	
Hartken, Hermann Anton	32	Hanover	Y	Bremen	Baltimore	12/07/1858	10/10/1860	27	482	N	
Hartlage, Frank	27	Germany	Y	Hamburg	New York	11/15/1879	07/24/1885			Y	
Hartleib, Martin	27	Prussia	Y	Bremen	Baltimore	??/10/1848	01/07/1851	2	471	N	
Hartlein, George	33	Bavaria	Y	Hamburg	New York	12/22/1857	01/26/1860	27	73	N	
Hartley, Charles	37	England	Y	Liverpool	New York	10/10/1887	04/17/1894			Y	
Hartlieb, Frederick	28	Germany	Y	Antwerp	Philadelphia	10/23/1895	10/29/1898			Y	
Hartling, Franz	29	Germany	Y	Bremen	Baltimore	06/20/1873	10/09/1880			Y	

CITIZENSHIP RECORDS

APPLICANT	AGE	COUNTRY OF ORIGIN	DEC	DEPART PORT	ENTRY PORT	ARRIVE DATE	DEC DATE	VOL	PG.	FLD	NAT DATE
Hartly, Thomas	49	England	Y	Liverpool	New York	06/18/1849	05/29/1852	25	131	N	
Hartman, August	40	Germany	N	Bremen	Baltimore	06/01/1873	?			Y	
Hartman, Henry	21	Prussia	Y	Bremen	New Orleans	11/04/1854	12/15/1855	13	316	N	
Hartman, Johann	29	Germany	Y	Bremen	New York	06/14/1891	09/27/1893			Y	
Hartman, John	29	Germany	Y	Hamburg	New York	06/17/1888	10/19/1892			Y	
Hartman, Michael	64	Germany	N	Bremen	New York	05/09/1846	?			Y	
Hartmann, Anton	30	Germany	Y	Rotterdam	New York	06/04/1894	07/15/1897			Y	
Hartmann, Casper Ludwig	32	Germany	Y	Antwerp	New York	11/01/1881	03/25/1887			Y	
Hartmann, Christian Henr	24	Wurttemberg	Y	Havre	New York	05/02/1855	08/15/1857	15	140	N	
Hartmann, Daniel	40	Bavaria	Y	Havre	New Orleans	03/07/1845	03/18/1850	2	213	N	
Hartmann, Gottfried	24	Prussia	Y	Bremen	Baltimore	10/08/1854	03/24/1856	26	274	N	
Hartmann, Henry	29	Germany	Y	Bremen	New York	07/15/1878	01/03/1888			Y	
Hartmann, John	34	Russia	Y	Liverpool	Boston	10/05/1858	11/16/1858	17	336	N	
Hartmann, John	21	Germany	Y	Bremen	New York	05/07/1890	10/20/1892			Y	
Hartmann, John Joseph	25	Prussia	Y	Bremen	New Orleans	11/29/1851	02/21/1856	26	113	N	
Hartmann, Joseph	34	Bavaria	Y	Havre	New Orleans	07/29/1845	07/09/1851	3	515	N	
Hartmann, Oskar	??	Switzerland	Y	?	?	?	04/23/1892			Y	
Hartmann, Peter	30	Bavaria	Y	Harve	New Orleans	03/03/1847	03/18/1850	2	214	N	
Hartmann, Peter	39	Germany	Y	Bremen	New York	09/18/1880	03/22/1894			Y	
Hartmann, Peter Joseph	??	Bavaria	Y	Bremen	New York	08/09/1848	03/25/1851	3	348	N	
Hartmann, William	22	Germany	Y	?	Baltimore	??/??/1884	10/15/1889			Y	
Hartmann, William	40	Germany	N	Bremen	New York	05/01/1868	?	28	366	N	10/07/1878
Hartnagel, Jacob	31	Germany	Y	Rotterdam	New York	05/13/1881	09/24/1887			Y	
Hartoin, Nicholas	28	Germany	Y	Havre	New York	03/02/1889	07/08/1892			Y	
Hartstone, Frederick	33	England	Y	Liverpool	Philadelphia	04/22/1852	04/24/1854	8	245	N	
Hartstone, Frederick	33	England	Y	Liverpool	Philadelphia	04/22/1852	04/24/1853	9	116	N	
Hartt, Joseph	38	Canada	Y	?	Cincinnati	11/16/1879	10/29/1882			Y	
Hartung, Albert	29	Germany	Y	Bremen	New York	08/07/1880	07/26/1890			Y	
Hartung, Henry	38	Saxe Weimar	Y	Hamburg	Buffalo	09/05/1847	01/04/1853	5	508	N	
Hartung, Jacob	28	Germany	Y	Bremen	New York	04/28/1885	09/29/1887			Y	
Hartveld, Jacob	??	Holland	Y	?	?	?	03/30/1893			Y	
Hartweg, Jacob	30	France	Y	Havre	New York	05/??/1847	11/??/1849	23	372	N	
Hartwig, Frederick	26	Lippe Detmold	Y	Bremen	Baltimore	05/15/1846	03/01/1851	3	184	N	
Hartwig, John Baptist	34	Bavaria	Y	Hamburg	New York	07/21/1847	05/07/1859	17	401	N	
Hartwig, Otto	36	Germany	Y	Bremen	New York	10/24/1891	11/01/1897			Y	
Harty, Daniel	25	Ireland	Y	Liverpool	New York	01/01/1850	05/01/1854	8	341	N	
Harty, Daniel	25	Ireland	Y	Liverpool	New York	01/01/1850	05/01/1854	9	214	N	
Hartz, August	29	Saxony	Y	Bremen	New Orleans	09/28/1852	10/06/1856	14	211	N	
Harvey, George	30	England	Y	Liverpool	New York	03/02/1890	04/09/1897			Y	
Harz, George	36	Germany	Y	Bremen	New York	02/16/1881	06/06/1888			Y	
Hasch, Andrew	36	Hesse Darmsta	Y	Havre	New York	06/03/1837	07/31/1848	22	26	N	
Hase, William	29	Prussia	Y	Bremen	New York	12/??/1849	03/30/1853	7	465	N	
Hasebrock, Henry	35	Hanover	Y	Bremen	New Orleans	06/10/1851	11/07/1855	13	189	N	
Hasebrock, John	31	Hanover	Y	Bremen	New Orleans	05/19/1852	10/01/1856	14	96	N	
Hasekoster, Chrisopher	22	Germany	Y	Bremen	New York	10/29/1879	11/03/1884			Y	
Hasel, Frank Peter	30	Baden	Y	Havre	New Orleans	11/24/1847	01/31/1851	3	67	N	
Hasel, Fred	34	Germany	Y	Antwerp	New York	03/15/1882	08/28/1888			Y	
Haselbeck, Martin	23	Germany	Y	Bremen	New York	11/11/1893	10/10/1896			Y	
Hasemeier, John Diedrich	32	Germany	N	Bremen	Baltimore	08/19/1872	?			Y	
Hasenahr, Gustav	26	Saxony	Y	Bremerhafen	Baltimore	09/11/1857	01/28/1861	18	75	N	
Hasenohr, Albert	50	Germany	N	Bremen	Baltimore	09/??/1860	?			Y	
Hasenstab, George	56	Germany	Y	Antwerp	New York	10/21/1886	11/26/1894			Y	
Hasenzahl, Albrecht	45	Germany	Y	Bremen	Baltimore	07/09/1881	10/12/1887			Y	
Hasenzahl, Julius	39	Germany	Y	Bremen	Baltimore	10/22/1876	01/15/1894			Y	
Haskamp, Bernard	25	Oldenburg	Y	Bremen	New Orleans	11/15/1854	09/28/1858	16	113	N	
Haskamp, Herman Henry	30	Oldenburg	Y	Bremen	New Orleans	11/??/1847	09/10/1855	11	520	N	
Hasl, John	30	Germany	Y	Bremen	New York	09/26/1879	10/19/1883			Y	
Haslbeck, Franz	26	Germany	Y	Bremen	New York	12/28/1889	04/08/1893			Y	
Hasler, Frederick	44	Switzerland	Y	Havre	New York	10/01/1847	08/14/1848	22	100	N	

CITIZENSHIP RECORDS

APPLICANT	AGE	COUNTRY OF ORIGIN	DEC	DEPART PORT	ENTRY PORT	ARRIVE DATE	DEC DATE	VOL	PG.	FLD	NAT DATE
Haslvantal, Joseph	47	Germany	N	Bremen	New York	??/??/1872	??/??/1872	28	201	N	??/??/1877
Haslvantal, Joseph	33	Germany	N	Bremen	New York	00/00/1872	00/00/1872			Y	00/00/1877
Hass, Kafus	31	Baden	Y	Havre	New Orleans	12/24/1850	06/03/1859	17	452	N	
Hassan, Habeb	22	Syria	Y	Beruit	New York	06/10/1897	05/13/1899			Y	
Hasselbrock, Phillip H.J	24	Hanover	Y	Bremen	New Orleans	11/20/1851	11/01/1852	6	273	N	
Hassemeier, Henry	25	Hanover	Y	Bremen	Baltimore	06/01/1855	09/18/1858	16	179	N	
Hassenbusch, Lazarus	??	Kurhessen	Y	Bremen	New York	07/04/1853	04/20/1854	8	219	N	
Hassenbusch, Lazarus	59	Germany	N	Bremen	New York	06/??/1850	??/??/1850	28	68	N	08/??/1855
Hassenmeyer, Charles	28	Wurttemberg	Y	Havre	New York	07/23/1851	01/31/1856	13	524	N	
Hassenpflug, Daniel	29	Kurhassen	Y	Bremen	New York	07/09/1848	09/11/1848	22	324	N	
Hassett, James	23	Ireland	Y	?	?	?	08/11/1884			Y	
Hassler, Andrew	53	Switzerland	Y	Havre	New Orleans	06/02/1847	02/21/1853	7	198	N	
Hasslocher, Joseph	35	Hesse Darmsta	Y	Havre	New York	11/10/1852	08/28/1862	18	414	N	
Hassmann, Henry	63	Germany	N	Bremen	Baltimore	11/??/1866	?			Y	
Hastings, James	25	Ireland	Y	Liverpool	New York	05/01/1849	02/02/1856	26	3	N	
Hater, George B.	45	Germany	N	Hamburg	New York	09/??/1861	?			Y	
Hatke, Bernard	28	Prussia	Y	Bremen	Baltimore	05/29/1853	03/06/1860	27	119	N	
Hatke, Henry	32	Prussia	Y	Bremen	New York	10/20/1858	04/25/1862	18	329	N	
Hatke, John Gradus	23	Hanover	Y	Bremen	Baltimore	11/05/1848	01/22/1852	24	57	N	
Hatke, Joseph	26	Hanover	Y	Bremen	Baltimore	10/20/1846	10/20/1851	4	335	N	
Hatke, Joseph	32	Hanover	Y	Bremen	New Orleans	12/28/1855	03/25/1856	26	343	N	
Hatmaker, Henry	24	Prussia	Y	Antwerp	New York	06/04/1847	02/01/1849	23	3	N	
Hatten, Peter	22	Ireland	Y	Liverpool	New York	05/27/1855	10/26/1858	17	120	N	
Hatten, Thomas	60	Ireland	N	Liverpool	New York	07/??/1849	05/??/1850	28	109	N	10/??/1855
Hattendorf, August	42	Germany	Y	Bremen	New York	04/04/1883	10/22/1892			Y	
Hattermann, Albert	36	Prussia	Y	Bremen	New York	11/17/1845	10/14/1848	1	210	N	
Hattler, Mathaeus	31	Germany	Y	Hamburg	New York	08/05/1891	03/10/1896			Y	
Hatzky, Edward	47	Germany	Y	Bremen	New York	04/??/1864	01/04/1883			Y	
Haub, Henry	28	Nassau	Y	Liverpool	New York	09/01/1853	08/04/1856	14	317	N	
Hauber, John Geo.	32	Germany	Y	Havre	New York	07/15/1880	01/17/1889			Y	
Haubner, Andreas	49	Bavaria	Y	Hamburg	New York	09/03/1844	02/26/1853	7	235	N	
Haubner, Michael	39	Bavaria	Y	Hamburg	New York	08/29/1843	02/26/1853	7	234	N	
Hauck, Conrad	29	Bavaria	Y	Havre	New Orleans	11/17/1853	10/06/1856	14	194	N	
Hauck, Fred	36	Germany	N	Hamburg	New York	05/01/1867	?			Y	
Hauck, George Jacob	24	Bavaria	Y	Havre	New Orleans	11/26/1851	05/04/1854	8	362	N	
Hauck, George Jacob	24	Bavaria	Y	Havre	New Orleans	11/26/1851	05/04/1854	9	235	N	
Hauck, John	32	Germany	Y	Havre	New York	06/25/1881	02/11/1888			Y	
Hauck, John Frederick	27	Wurttemberg	Y	Havre	New York	04/01/1847	05/29/1854	9	443	N	
Hauck, John Frederick	27	Wurttemberg	Y	Havre	New York	04/01/1847	05/29/1854	10	26	N	
Hauck, Julius	21	Hesse Darmsta	Y	Antwerp	New Orleans	10/25/1849	09/06/1852	25	385	N	
Hauck, Michael	33	Bavaria	Y	Havre	New Orleans	05/23/1849	03/30/1857	15	107	N	
Hauck, Michael	36	Bavaria	Y	Havre	New Orleans	02/20/1846	11/27/1858	17	358	N	
Hauck, Peter Michael	51	Germany	Y	Hamburg	New York	03/13/1873	04/01/1889			Y	
Hauck, Theodore	24	Germany	Y	Bremen	Baltimore	08/24/1889	08/02/1894			Y	
Haucke, Ernst	??	Germany	Y	?	?	?	08/06/1881			Y	
Haucke, Ignatz Anton Hei	51	Prussia	Y	Hamburg	New York	08/02/1854	04/25/1861	18	147	N	
Hauenstein, Casper	29	Bavaria	Y	Bremen	New York	06/01/1858	12/03/1858	17	374	N	
Hauenstein, John	58	Bavaria	N	Germany	New York	06/18/1852	07/15/1852	28	280	N	06/18/1857
Hauenstein, Ludwig	30	Germany	Y	Rotterdam	New York	07/28/1881	10/27/1888			Y	
Hauenstein, William	30	Switzerland	Y	Havre	New York	06/14/1882	09/20/1887			Y	
Hauer, George	35	Austria	Y	Bremen	New York	03/29/1894	08/11/1897			Y	
Hauert, Henry	26	Switzerland	Y	Havre	New Orleans	02/07/1844	03/18/1850	2	207	N	
Haufe, Robert G.	40	Germany	Y	Bremen	Baltimore	09/30/1887	01/31/1898			Y	
Haufle, Joseph	42	Germany	Y	Bremen	New York	02/06/1881	12/09/1890			Y	
Hauflein, Jueuis	43	Prussia	N	Hamburg	New York	07/??/1865	?			Y	
Haufler, George G.	29	Germany	Y	Havre	New York	04/01/1888	10/23/1896			Y	
Haufler, Gottlief	26	Wurttemberg	Y	Havre	New York	12/04/1866	10/07/1872	18	525	N	
Haufner, John	36	Bavaria	Y	Bremen	Baltimore	09/20/1848	11/20/1848	1	331	N	
Haug, Charles	27	Wurttemberg	Y	Antwerp	New York	08/19/1847	12/12/1851	4	513	N	

149

CITIZENSHIP RECORDS

APPLICANT	AGE	COUNTRY OF ORIGIN	DEC	DEPART PORT	ENTRY PORT	ARRIVE DATE	DEC DATE	VOL	PG.	FLD	NAT DATE
Haug, Egide	35	Prussia	Y	Antwerp	New Orleans	11/14/1854	01/16/1862	18	244	N	
Haug, Fred	30	Germany	Y	Bremen	New York	04/21/1883	01/02/1886			Y	
Haug, Gottfried	38	Wurttemberg	Y	Havre	New York	11/27/1854	10/28/1858	17	151	N	
Haug, Martin	48	Germany	Y	Bremen	Baltimore	05/20/1880	05/09/1887			Y	
Hauger, Peter	36	Baden	Y	Havre	New York	02/23/1854	09/26/1854	10	246	N	
Hauger, Peter	36	Baden	Y	Havre	New York	02/23/1853	09/26/1854	12	185	N	
Hauk, Edward	21	Austria	Y	Hamburg	New York	07/08/1852	07/25/1855	11	426	N	
Haukish, Abdoo Abraham	??	Asia Turkey	Y	?	?	?	06/24/1895			Y	
Hauks, Henry	28	Ireland	Y	Cork	Boston	05/20/1844	05/28/1856	14	262	N	
Haulle, John	27	Baden	Y	Bremen	New York	06/20/1848	09/08/1852	25	420	N	
Haumeisser, Faustin	32	Germany	Y	Antwerp	New York	11/25/1882	09/22/1887			Y	
Haumesser, Michael	24	Germany	N	Bremen	New York	07/??/1877	?			Y	
Haun, Ewald	28	Germany	Y	Havre	New York	04/29/1890	06/30/1893			Y	
Haungs, Hermann	28	Germany	Y	Havre	New York	12/10/1891	01/11/1896			Y	
Haunss, George	25	Germany	Y	Bremen	New York	11/24/1883	08/03/1885			Y	
Haupern, Frederick	31	Schleswig	Y	Hamburg	New York	08/20/1855	12/28/1857	16	266	N	
Hausen, Bernard	??	Germany	Y	?	?	?	10/22/1884			Y	
Hausen, Johannes Alfred	30	Denmark	Y	Christeansan	Boston	03/01/1893	05/13/1901			Y	
Hausen, Mathias P.	34	Germany	Y	Hamburg	Philadelphia	05/27/1879	05/27/1882			Y	
Hauser, August	28	Germany	Y	Bremen	New York	07/23/1880	10/25/1888			Y	
Hauser, Christian	27	Wurttemberg	Y	Havre	New York	08/08/1854	07/30/1858	16	541	N	
Hauser, John	36	Austria	Y	Havre	New York	05/22/1853	10/22/1857	15	474	N	
Hauser, John	39	Switzerland	Y	Havre	New York	08/30/1891	10/23/1899			Y	
Hauser, John	52	Germany	Y	Bremen	New York	06/16/1882	11/08/1901			Y	
Hauser, John M.	31	Germany	Y	Antwerp	New York	05/18/1891	02/04/1892			Y	
Hauser, Markus	64	Switzerland	Y	Havre	New York	08/26/1880	08/14/1888			Y	
Hauser, Martin	26	Germany	Y	Havre	New York	06/08/1881	05/23/1887			Y	
Hauser, Paul	34	Switzerland	Y	Havre	New York	01/24/1870	02/02/1882			Y	
Hauser, Rudolph	22	Switzerland	Y	Antwerp	New York	05/31/1853	05/31/1856	14	274	N	
Hauserstein, Gothard	30	Baden	Y	Havre	New Orleans	03/28/1854	02/16/1857	15	20	N	
Hausfeld, Henry	28	Oldenburg	Y	Bremen	New Orleans	05/01/1849	10/09/1854	11	68	N	
Hausfield, Henry	28	Hanover	Y	Bremen	Baltimore	06/04/1845	01/15/1849	1	419	N	
Hausknecht, Charles Theo	29	Prussia	Y	Hamburg	New York	08/26/1854	11/09/1855	13	196	N	
Hausmann, Anton	22	Baden	Y	Havre	New Orleans	01/15/1855	12/15/1855	13	315	N	
Hausmann, E. O.	36	Germany	N	Hamburg	New York	12/15/1881	?			Y	
Hausmann, Ferdinand	29	Baden	Y	Havre	New York	10/03/1844	08/15/1848	22	161	N	
Hausmann, George	22	Prussia	Y	Bremen	Baltimore	06/05/1848	06/19/1851	3	414	N	
Hausmann, Joseph	29	Baden	Y	Havre	New Orleans	01/23/1855	12/29/1855	13	394	N	
Hausmann, Ludwig Frederi	24	Wurttemberg	Y	Antwerp	New York	02/13/1854	09/26/1857	15	321	N	
Hauss, Fred	29	Germany	Y	Havre	New York	09/12/1883	12/01/1887			Y	
Hauss, Frederick	27	Baden	Y	Liverpool	New York	07/10/1852	10/06/1856	14	224	N	
Hauss, Jacob	39	Germany	Y	Antwerp	Philadelphia	10/22/1886	09/13/1892			Y	
Hauss, Jacob	61	Germany	N	Havre	New York	05/07/1855	?			Y	
Haussmann, Emil	??	Germany	Y	?	?	?	02/06/1882			Y	
Haustater, John Bernhard	26	Lippe Detmold	Y	Bremen	New York	??/28/1849	12/20/1850	2	380	N	
Hauter, Nicolaus	24	Bavaria	Y	Havre	New York	10/04/1852	09/17/1755	13	56	N	
Hauth, Casper	37	Germany	Y	Antwerp	New York	04/27/1880	08/09/1892			Y	
Hautmann, Joseph	22	Bavaria	Y	Bremen	New York	06/04/1854	03/25/1856	26	319	N	
Hautz, John	49	Germany	Y	Bremen	New York	09/16/1892	10/28/1898			Y	
Hautz, John	31	Germany	N	Bremen	New York	07/14/1880	?			Y	
Hautz, Philip	31	Bavaria	Y	Havre	New York	06/20/1851	09/25/1854	10	207	N	
Havekamp, Henry	61	Germany	N	Bremen	New Orleans	07/??/1853	?			Y	
Havekorst, August	23	Hanover	Y	Bremen	New York	07/12/1854	03/02/1858	16	355	N	
Havekorst, Henry	30	Hanover	Y	Bremen	New York	09/04/1852	01/21/1856	13	487	N	
Haverkamp, August	52	Germany	N	Bremen	New York	05/??/1862	?			Y	
Haverkamp, Bernard	37	Germany	Y	Bremen	New York	11/01/1880	10/17/1887			Y	
Haverkamp, John Heinrich	26	Prussia	Y	Bremen	New Orleans	06/05/1852	09/20/1858	16	161	N	
Haverkamp, Joseph	32	Germany	Y	Bremen	Baltimore	03/30/1880	12/22/1887			Y	
Haverkamp, Mathias	33	Germany	Y	Bremen	New York	10/26/1881	10/??/1883			Y	

CITIZENSHIP RECORDS

APPLICANT	AGE	COUNTRY OF ORIGIN	DEC	DEPART PORT	ENTRY PORT	ARRIVE DATE	DEC DATE	VOL	PG.	FLD	NAT DATE
Haverkamp, Mathias	33	Germany	N	Bremen	New York	10/26/1881	?			Y	
Haverland, John Gerhard	41	Hanover	Y	Bremen	Baltimore	07/04/1845	11/18/1848	1	317	N	
Haverland, John H.	24	Germany	Y	Bremen	New York	06/19/1879	08/25/1885			Y	
Havermann, Theodore	32	Prussia	Y	Bremen	New Orleans	12/15/1847	10/27/1858	17	131	N	
Haverty, Thomas	30	Ireland	Y	Galway	New York	07/03/1850	05/22/1856	26	526	N	
Havey, John	40	Ireland	Y	Liverpool	New Orleans	12/??/1851	07/27/1857	15	135	N	
Hawells, Griffith	22	Wales	Y	Liverpool	New York	06/20/1850	03/22/1858	16	436	N	
Hawiekhorst, G.	32	Germany	Y	Oldenburg	New York	06/01/1879	10/06/1883			Y	
Hawken, W.F.	26	Canada	Y	London, Ont.	Detroit	08/02/1877	03/26/1884			Y	
Hawley, Michael	23	Ireland	Y	Derry	Ogdensburg	11/15/1848	10/05/1854	12	372	N	
Hawlik, Ernst	28	Germany	Y	Bremen	New York	05/08/1886	02/14/1893			Y	
Hawthorn, Charles E.	33	England	Y	Liverpool	New York	04/03/1844	12/01/1852	5	366	N	
Haxaire, John	31	Germany	Y	Bremen	New York	11/18/1882	10/29/1889			Y	
Hayen, Christian	25	Prussia	Y	Hamburg	New York	05/18/1850	04/12/1852	24	481	N	
Hayes, Edward M.	21	Ireland	Y	Queenstown	New York	03/03/1877	03/??/1881			Y	
Hayes, John	25	Ireland	Y	Queenstown	New York	08/01/1887	10/27/1893	21	40	N	
Hayes, John	25	Ireland	Y	Queenstown	New York	08/01/1887	10/23/1893			Y	
Hayes, John	43	Ireland	Y	Queenstwon	New York	04/20/1879	03/23/1885			Y	
Hayman, Garrett	27	Prussia	Y	Bremen	Baltimore	10/??/1845	10/16/1848	1	238	N	
Hayman, Louis	33	Hanover	Y	Bremen	New York	05/01/1857	09/13/1860			Y	
Haynes, C.T.	25	Ireland	Y	Liverpool	New York	08/27/1852	09/28/1858	16	109	N	
Hays, John	60	Ireland	Y	Liverpool	New York	05/12/1855	05/04/1861	18	156	N	
Hays, Patrick	28	Ireland	Y	Liverpool	Mobile	04/13/1850	05/12/1852	25	11	N	
Hays, Patrick	16	Ireland	N	?	Boston	00/00/1879				Y	10/23/1886
Hays, Samuel	26	England	Y	Liverpool	New York	09/30/1851	10/09/1854	6	100	N	
Hays, Samuel	26	England	Y	Liverpool	New York	09/30/1851	10/09/1854	11	103	N	
Hays, Thomas	33	England	Y	Liverpool	New York	08/07/1844	12/15/1852	5	418	N	
Head, John	26	England	Y	Liverpool	New Orleans	11/07/1849	11/03/1852	5	205	N	
Head, John	26	England	Y	Liverpool	New Orleans	11/07/1849	11/03/1852	6	331	N	
Headon, William	31	Ireland	Y	Liverpool	New York	04/23/1883	12/26/1888	19	222	N	
Heal, George	24	Germany	Y	Hamburg	New York	03/02/1881	03/19/1883			Y	
Healey, Charles	40	Ireland	Y	Cork	Portland	09/??/1841	03/07/1853	7	304	N	
Healey, John	35	Ireland	Y	Liverpool	New Orleans	03/??/1847	12/17/1850	2	373	N	
Healy, Daniel	27	Ireland	Y	Liverpool	New York	07/04/1846	03/23/1850	2	240	N	
Healy, James	22	Ireland	Y	St. Johns	Boston	09/15/1848	01/29/1852	24	30	N	
Healy, Jeremiah	22	Ireland	Y	Cork	Boston	05/05/1847	02/28/1852	24	180	N	
Healy, John	25	Ireland	Y	Limerick	New York	09/??/1851	09/17/1855	13	54	N	
Healy, John	21	Ireland	Y	Liverpool	New York	05/19/1857	10/20/1857	15	465	N	
Healy, John	24	Ireland	Y	Waterford	New York	09/29/1848	04/12/1852	24	478	N	
Healy, John	5	Ireland	N	?	New York	00/00/1862				Y	10/23/1886
Healy, Martin	31	Ireland	Y	Havre	New Orleans	11/??/1844	11/03/1851	4	473	N	
Healy, Matt	24	Ireland	Y	Queenstown	New York	05/06/1898	10/30/1901			Y	
Healy, Patrick	25	Ireland	Y	Liverpool	New Orleans	04/20/1849	05/10/1854	8	407	N	
Healy, Patrick	25	Ireland	Y	Liverpool	New Orleans	04/20/1849	05/10/1854	9	280	N	
Healy, Patrick John	29	Ireland	Y	Queenstown	New York	09/11/1891	02/18/1895			Y	
Healy, Thomas	25	Ireland	Y	Liverpool	New York	10/19/1848	12/26/1851	24	12	N	
Heamann, August	23	Bavaria	Y	Bremen	New Orleans	??/28/1848	02/18/1850	2	87	N	
Heard, John	31	England	Y	Portsmouth	New Algenack	12/27/1849	10/06/1856	14	201	N	
Hearly, Daniel	33	Ireland	Y	Cork	Burlington	05/13/1847	01/27/1851	2	530	N	
Hearn, Richard	30	Ireland	Y	Liverpool	New York	05/15/1844	11/06/1851	4	494	N	
Heath, John	33	England	Y	Liverpool	New York	02/??/1879	02/18/1884			Y	
Hebbeler, Adam	30	Hanover	Y	Bremen	Baltimore	10/01/18??	10/16/1848	1	243	N	
Hebel, August	28	Prussia	Y	Bremen	New Orleans	12/13/1851	09/13/1855	13	16	N	
Hebel, Conrad	30	Prussia	Y	Havre	New York	11/16/1854	02/15/1858	16	309	N	
Hebel, Engel	48	Prussia	Y	Bremen	New York	01/14/1853	11/07/1857	15	541	N	
Heber, Louis	27	Bavaria	Y	Hamburg	New York	08/24/1853	09/25/1858	16	129	N	
Heberle, Joseph	??	Bavaria	Y	?	?	?	07/03/1882			Y	
Heberlein, George	31	Bavaria	Y	Bremen	Philadelphia	06/25/1844	02/19/1849	23	201	N	
Heberstreit, Kasper	22	Germany	Y	Antwerp	New York	10/26/1888	03/27/1889			Y	

CITIZENSHIP RECORDS

APPLICANT	AGE	COUNTRY OF ORIGIN	DEC	DEPART PORT	ENTRY PORT	ARRIVE DATE	DEC DATE	VOL	PG.	FLD	NAT DATE
Hechinger, Adolph	29	Germany	Y	Antwerp	New York	10/12/1890	10/29/1892			Y	
Hechler, John	23	Germany	Y	Antwerp	New York	05/25/1888	10/14/1892			Y	
Hechler, Michael	29	Hesse Darmsta	Y	Havre	New York	06/20/1851	08/06/1851	4	89	N	
Hecht, Frances M.	24	Wurttemberg	Y	Amsterdam	New York	06/24/1845	10/12/1848	1	157	N	
Hecht, Fritz	29	Germany	Y	Bremen	New York	04/04/1887	09/19/1889			Y	
Heck, Alban	25	Germany	Y	Bremen	Baltimore	04/20/1884	04/04/1887			Y	
Heck, John	30	Prussia	Y	Antwerp	New York	09/10/1847	09/15/1852	25	510	N	
Heck, John Adam	35	Baden	Y	Havre	New York	07/08/1854	11/02/1857	15	518	N	
Heckel, William	23	Wurttemberg	Y	Havre	New York	04/??/1854	09/20/1855	13	80	N	
Heckendorn, Fred	27	Germany	Y	Havre	New York	10/14/1893	10/24/1898			Y	
Heckendorn, Johann Georg	26	Germany	Y	Antwerp	New York	04/13/1885	04/02/1888			Y	
Heckenmueller, John	34	Germany	Y	Antwerp	New York	05/29/1881	12/06/1886			Y	
Hecker, Christ	37	Germany	Y	Hamburg	New York	08/28/1867	08/28/1882			Y	
Hecker, Herman Bernard	28	Hanover	Y	Bremen	New York	05/29/1849	04/12/1852	24	476	N	
Heckinger, George	28	Germany	Y	Havre	New York	05/01/1891	10/29/1892			Y	
Heckle, Ferdinand	26	Baden	Y	Havre	New York	09/28/1849	12/13/1851	4	514	N	
Heckman, Francis Michael	26	Wuerttemberg	Y	Havre	New Orleans	05/26/1848	08/15/1848	22	164	N	
Heckman, Joseph Phillip	30	Wuerttemberg	Y	Antwerp	New York	07/29/1847	08/15/1848	22	166	N	
Heckmann, George	30	Hanover	Y	Bremen	New Orleans	11/15/1848	04/04/1853	7	524	N	
Heckmann, Heinrich	28	Prussia	Y	Bremen	Baltimore	11/10/1847	10/13/1851	4	262	N	
Heckmann, John	27	Prussia	Y	Bremen	New York	08/21/1854	02/02/1856	26	8	N	
Heckmann, Joseph	24	Germany	Y	Bremen	New York	11/09/1886	03/18/1889			Y	
Heckmann, Otto	29	Bremen	Y	Bremen	New Orleans	11/05/1846	02/20/1849	23	223	N	
Hector, Patrick	78	Ireland	Y	Liverpool	New York	12/04/1854	10/15/1860	27	500	N	
Heddergott, Florence	25	Germany	Y	Antwerp	New York	05/12/1883	08/22/1885			Y	
Heder, Louis	21	Hesse Cassel	Y	Bremen	New Orleans	11/20/1858	08/01/1861	18	213	N	
Hederman, William	??	England	Y	?	?	?	06/04/1879			Y	
Hedinger, William A.	40	Switzerland	Y	Havre	New York	09/11/1886	06/09/1896			Y	
Hedman, Charles	56	Sweden	Y	Goteborg	Boston	06/08/1872	07/17/1890			Y	
Heeg, Christian	23	Hesse Cassel	Y	London	New York	08/15/1854	10/03/1856	14	176	N	
Heeg, Henry	21	Hesse Cassel	Y	London	New York	09/17/1854	07/01/1857	15	121	N	
Heeker, Henry	31	Prussia	Y	Bremen	Baltimore	09/08/1837	10/05/184?			Y	10/10/1842
Heeman, Heinrich	50	Germany	Y	Bremen	Baltimore	08/29/1883	12/22/1887			Y	
Heemeyer, Christ	48	Germany	Y	Bremen	Baltimore	11/06/1881	09/08/1893			Y	
Heenan, Patrick	38	Ireland	N	Queenstown	New York	05/20/1877	10/??/1878	28	350	N	10/??/1882
Heenan, Patrick	23	Ireland	N	Queenstown	New York	05/20/1877	10/00/1878			Y	10/00/1882
Heenan, Roderick	48	England	Y	Liverpool	Detroit	03/18/1883	09/15/1886			Y	
Heeng, Henry	33	Prussia	Y	Bremen	New York	12/04/1854	09/24/1857	15	314	N	
Heerdink, John	23	Holland	Y	Rotterdam	New Orleans	01/06/1847	03/15/1852	24	308	N	
Heerlein, Michael	25	Germany	Y	Hamburg	New York	04/20/1883	06/01/1886			Y	
Heesselbrock, Henry	25	Hanover	Y	Bremen	New Orleans	11/04/1858	03/04/1862	18	267	N	
Hefat, Herman	34	Hanover	Y	Bremen	New Orleans	12/01/1848	04/12/1852	24	472	N	
Hefele, Chrisostomus	29	Germany	Y	Bremen	New York	04/04/1886	11/23/1888			Y	
Hefele, Xavier	27	Germany	Y	Bremen	Baltimore	04/29/1890	09/29/1893			Y	
Hefferan, William	33	Ireland	Y	Liverpool	New York	06/03/1867	04/12/1882			Y	
Hefke, Philip	??	Germany	N	?	?		11/00/1882			Y	10/17/1892
Hefkermahn, Barney Henry	35	Prussia	Y	Rotterdam	New Orleans	04/03/1847	11/03/1852	5	196	N	
Hefkermahn, Barney Henry	35	Prussia	Y	Rotterdam	New Orleans	04/03/1847	11/03/1852	6	322	N	
Hefner, C.M. Edward	21	Germany	Y	Rotterdam	New York	08/15/1891	10/30/1894				
Heft, Henry	29	Germany	Y	Hamburg	New York	11/01/1872	10/02/1880			Y	
Hefter, Theodore	55	Germany	N	Havre	New York	04/20/1865	?			Y	
Hegarty, Cornelius	22	Ireland	Y	Queenstown	New York	05/04/1894	12/31/1894			Y	
Hegarty, Daniel	24	Ireland	Y	Queenstown	New York	05/08/1892	12/31/1894			Y	
Hegarty, Jeremiah	28	Ireland	Y	Queenstown	New York	05/28/1890	12/31/1894			Y	
Hegberty, James	22	Ireland	Y	Liverpool	New York	08/31/1851	12/23/1851	4	550	N	
Hegener, Anton T. H.	28	Prussia	Y	Bremen	Baltimore	10/04/1845	08/19/1848	22	210	N	
Hegener, Ernst	33	Prussia	Y	Bremen	New Orleans	12/01/1852	02/25/1856	26	121	N	
Hegenhauker, Michael	23	France	Y	Havre	New Orleans	04/??/1852	04/16/1855	11	250	N	
Heger, Frank	??	?	Y	?	?	?	11/27/1883			Y	

CITIZENSHIP RECORDS

APPLICANT	AGE	COUNTRY OF ORIGIN	DEC	DEPART PORT	ENTRY PORT	ARRIVE DATE	DEC DATE	VOL	PG.	FLD	NAT DATE
Heger, George	25	Bavaria	Y	Hamburg	New York	07/20/1853	09/03/1857	15	227	N	
Heger, Michael	??	Bavaria	Y	Bremen	Baltimore	??/10/1845	12/??/1850	2	401	N	
Heger, Simon	24	Baden	Y	Antwerp	New York	05/10/1851	12/24/1859	17	514	N	
Hegertz, Patrick	48	Ireland	Y	Cuba	New Orleans	05/12/1847	10/13/1848	1	189	N	
Hegge, H. B.	55	Germany	N	Bremen	Baltimore	09/29/1858	?			Y	
Hegge, H.B.	29	Hanover	Y	Bremen	Baltimore	09/29/1858	02/25/1861	18	118	N	
Hegger, John Bernard	27	Hanover	Y	Bremen	New Orleans	01/17/1854	10/28/1858	17	141	N	
Hegner, Hugo	23	Prussia	Y	Havre	New York	06/14/1851	05/24/1854	8	510	N	
Hegner, Hugo	23	Prussia	Y	Havre	New York	06/11/1851	05/24/1854	9	384	N	
Hehe, Christian	38	Prussia	Y	Bremen	New York	04/20/1852	09/16/1858	16	164	N	
Hehe, Ernst	21	Germany	Y	Bremen	Baltimore	08/26/1880	02/03/1883			Y	
Hehe, Frederick	28	Hanover	Y	Bremen	Baltimore	11/08/1845	09/09/1848	22	314	N	
Heheman, Herman Henry	26	Hanover	Y	Bremen	Baltimore	07/16/1845	09/05/1848	22	304	N	
Hehl, Frank	22	Germany	Y	Bremen	New York	03/30/1872	05/06/1873			Y	
Hehmann, Henry	24	Germany	Y	Brmen	Baltimore	08/16/1886	04/01/1892			Y	
Hehms, John Kasper	24	Switzerland	Y	Havre	New York	05/23/1857	04/11/1860	27	145	N	
Hehn, Edward	29	Ireland	Y	Liverpool	New Orleans	02/01/1849	02/07/1850	2	52	N	
Hehn, John	49	Bavaria	Y	Rotterdam	New York	06/22/1845	03/20/1850	2	227	N	
Heho, James	28	Ireland	Y	Liverpool	New Orleans	05/06/1849	01/20/1853	7	47	N	
Hehre, Henry Adolph Herm	33	Germany	Y	Bremen	New York	05/??/1866	09/02/1880			Y	
Heiberger, Johan	28	Baden	Y	Havre	New York	06/29/1848	11/03/1851	4	475	N	
Heibertshausen, Eberhard	29	Prussia	Y	Havre	New York	07/11/1849	03/15/1852	24	313	N	
Heichelt, Joseph	40	Germany	Y	Rotterdam	New York	03/03/1882	05/11/1886			Y	
Heid, August	24	Germany	Y	?	New York	09/25/1880	12/03/1880			Y	
Heid, John B.	32	Germany	N	Bremen	Baltimore	06/28/1870	?			Y	
Heid, Philipp	28	Baden	Y	Havre	New York	06/01/1844	10/07/1851	4	218	N	
Heidelmann, Barney	21	Hanover	Y	Bremen	New Orleans	11/29/1850	09/26/1854	10	233	N	
Heidelmann, Barney	21	Hanover	Y	Bremen	New Orleans	11/29/1850	09/26/1854	12	172	N	
Heidemann, Henry	24	Germany	Y	Bremen	Baltimore	10/01/1888	05/02/1892			Y	
Heidemann, Paul	28	Germany	Y	Bremen	New York	06/16/1881	10/06/1884			Y	
Heidenreich, Charles	27	Hesse Cassel	Y	Liverpool	New York	04/23/1859	07/16/1861	18	208	N	
Heidenreich, Fred	49	Germany	N	Bremen	Baltimore	05/01/1857	?			Y	
Heider, Christoph	24	Bavaria	Y	Havre	New Orleans	03/15/1854	10/04/1858	17	48	N	
Heidgerker, John Gerhard	22	Oldenburg	Y	Bremen	New Orleans	11/10/1850	09/23/1854	10	181	N	
Heidgerker, John Gerhard	22	Oldenburg	Y	Bremen	New Orleans	11/10/1850	09/23/1854	12	120	N	
Heidle, Christ	21	Germany	Y	Rotterdam	New York	05/01/1879	04/03/1882			Y	
Heidler, John	23	Germany	Y	Bremen	Baltimore	08/09/1883	10/01/1886			Y	
Heidler, Joseph	21	Austria	Y	Bremen	Baltimore	07/21/1879	05/03/1882			Y	
Heidorn, August	33	Germany	Y	Bremen	New York	09/18/1880	11/21/1885			Y	
Heidorn, Frederick	33	Germany	Y	Bremen	New York	03/27/1880	05/16/1882			Y	
Heidorn, Herman	23	Germany	Y	Bremen	New York	06/27/1885	10/23/1889			Y	
Heidschuch, Charles	30	Germany	Y	Bremen	New York	03/03/1883	11/16/1892			Y	
Heidt, Michael	29	Bavaria	Y	Havre	New Orleans	12/04/1849	12/06/1852	5	386	N	
Heidtmann, Henry	43	Germany	Y	Hamburg	New York	08/??/1856	05/06/1878			Y	
Heiermann, Bernard	24	Germany	N	Bremen	New York	08/11/1887	12/27/1889			Y	
Heigis, Joseph	40	Germany	N	Bremen	New York	10/28/1871	?			Y	
Heil, George Phillip	40	Hesse Darmsta	Y	Bremen	New Orleans	12/25/1848	10/30/1852	5	70	N	
Heil, Hermann	37	Germany	Y	Rotterdam	New York	11/17/1887	10/18/1893	21	26	N	
Heil, Leonard	27	Bavaria	Y	Havre	New Orleans	02/10/1844	02/07/1850	2	166	N	
Heil, Valentine	23	Germany	Y	Rotterdam	New York	09/11/1883	10/27/1886			Y	
Heilbronner, Moses	23	Baden	Y	Havre	New York	03/01/1853	04/08/1856	26	470	N	
Heilbrunn, Alexander	27	Hanover	Y	Bremen	New York	11/11/1854	01/23/1860	27	70	N	
Heildebrandt, August	33	Germany	Y	?	New York	??/??/1879	01/16/1883			Y	
Heilemann, Herman Henry	28	Hanover	Y	Bremen	New York	06/14/1852	08/27/1855	11	493	N	
Heilemann, Jacob	21	Wurttemberg	Y	Antwerp	New York	05/16/1854	08/17/1855	11	449	N	
Heilholz, Johann	23	Germany	Y	Bremen	Baltimore	09/01/1886	01/28/1889			Y	
Heiligenthal, Frank A.	30	Germany	Y	Rotterdam	New York	12/02/1882	03/17/1892			Y	
Heilman, Andreus	29	Germany	Y	Hamburg	New York	01/17/1880	01/11/1884			Y	
Heilman, Gerhard John	24	Hanover	Y	Bremen	Baltimore	10/01/1853	04/03/1858	16	482	N	

CITIZENSHIP RECORDS

APPLICANT	AGE	COUNTRY OF ORIGIN	DEC	DEPART PORT	ENTRY PORT	ARRIVE DATE	DEC DATE	VOL	PG.	FLD	NAT DATE
Heilmann, Andrew	29	Germany	Y	Antwerp	New York	11/08/1883	10/05/1889			Y	
Heilmann, Heinrich	39	Germany	Y	Havre	New York	05/24/1877	09/29/1880			Y	
Heilmann, Henry	28	Germany	Y	Bremen	New York	08/08/1892	06/10/1897			Y	
Heilmann, Jacob	24	Germany	Y	Amsterdam	New York	09/20/1884	09/22/1887			Y	
Heilmann, Joseph	31	Bavaria	Y	Bremen	Baltimore	06/03/1844	02/19/1849	23	177	N	
Heilmann, Lorenz	27	Germany	Y	Hamburg	New York	10/26/1879	09/26/1884			Y	
Heilmann, Louis	29	Germany	Y	Bremen	New York	04/19/1881	08/15/1883			Y	
Heilos, Lorence	28	Bavaria	Y	Havre	New York	05/28/1851	10/21/1852	5	37	N	
Heim, Ignatius	31	Germany	Y	Bremen	New York	07/14/1888	10/14/1896			Y	
Heim, John	30	Wurttemberg	Y	Liverpool	New York	04/01/1853	04/21/1854	8	232	N	
Heim, John	30	Wurttemberg	Y	Liverpool	New York	04/01/1853	04/21/1854	9	103	N	
Heim, John	27	Germany	Y	Antwerp	New York	02/24/1880	02/13/1883			Y	
Heim, Max	31	Germany	Y	Antwerp	New York	12/02/1888	03/08/1895			Y	
Heim, Phillip	33	France	Y	Havre	New Orleans	10/20/1840	08/01/1848	22	29	N	
Heimberger, John Erhardt	41	Wuerttenberg	Y	London	New York	07/03/1849	06/18/1852	25	290	N	
Heimbold, Albert	24	Germany	Y	Hamburg	New York	11/17/1887	02/21/1888			Y	
Heimbrock, Frank	29	Germany	Y	Rotterdam	New York	08/18/1887	09/23/1896			Y	
Heimer, Cornelius	63	Germany	Y	Hamburg	New York	07/10/1866	04/25/1892			Y	
Heimerdinger, Friedrich	25	Germany	Y	Hamburg	New York	09/14/1880	12/21/1887			Y	
Heimkneiter, Frank	32	Bavaria	Y	Havre	New Orleans	09/25/1846	02/10/1851	3	117	N	
Heimler, George	34	Bavaria	Y	Bremen	New York	07/01/1854	06/13/1861	18	190	N	
Heimmel, Johan	??	Germany	Y	?	?	?	06/15/1887			Y	
Heimon, H.J.	35	Prussia	Y	Antwerp	New Orleans	12/06/1854	08/30/1862	18	426	N	
Heimrock, B. H.	47	Prussia	N	Bremen	Baltimore	08/??/1866	?			Y	
Heims, Christian Frederi	35	Prussia	Y	Hamburg	New York	05/18/1854	08/05/1856	14	341	N	
Heims, Henry	35	Germany	Y	Hamburg	New York	06/07/1881	03/30/1888			Y	
Heimsath, Casper Henry	25	Prussia	Y	Bremen	New Orleans	12/15/18??	10/11/1848	1	115	N	
Heimstock, Nicholas	35	Germany	Y	?	New York	??/??/1882	05/08/1884			Y	
Hein, August	27	Germany	Y	Stettin	New York	07/22/1891	12/19/1893			Y	
Hein, Fred	29	Germany	Y	Bremen	New York	04/28/1893	10/12/1897			Y	
Hein, Mathias	32	Bavaria	Y	Hamburg	New York	03/06/1851	01/15/1853	7	32	N	
Hein, Paul	28	Prussia	Y	?	?	01/15/1888	12/22/1888			Y	
Heinbach, John	28	Wurttemberg	Y	Rotterdam	New York	07/16/1845	10/16/1848	1	248	N	
Heine, Barney	26	Hanover	Y	Bremen	New Orleans	01/08/1847	01/??/1850	23	548	N	
Heine, Edward	48	Germany	N	Hamburg	New York	05/20/1858	?	28	274	N	08/??/1868
Heine, Frank	28	Germany	Y	Bremen	New York	12/19/1880	10/20/1885			Y	
Heine, William	28	Germany	Y	Bremen	New York	07/25/1880	12/20/1883			Y	
Heinebrodt, William	39	Germany	Y	Bremen	Baltimore	05/21/1882	07/09/1892			Y	
Heineccius, Henry	35	Brunswick	Y	Bremen	Baltimore	07/21/1846	01/04/1853	5	509	N	
Heinecke, Frederick	29	Prussia	Y	Hamburg	New York	08/28/1854	08/05/1856	14	345	N	
Heinecken, Bernard	22	Prussia	Y	Liverpool	Boston	11/10/1849	11/03/1851	4	482	N	
Heinekamp, Christ	30	Germany	Y	Bremen	New York	06/23/1880	04/08/1882			Y	
Heineke, August	25	Prussia	Y	Lehrte	Baltimore	09/16/1882	09/21/1885			Y	
Heineman, Timothy	22	Wurttemberg	Y	Liverpool	Boston	06/05/1853	08/15/1855	11	440	N	
Heinemann, Charles	31	Prussia	Y	Hamburg	New York	05/06/1857	12/26/1859	17	522	N	
Heinemann, Edward	22	Germany	Y	Amsterdam	New York	04/06/1889	08/22/1892			Y	
Heinemann, Felix	25	Germany	Y	Hamburg	New York	08/17/1888	03/05/1891			Y	
Heinemann, Frederick	29	Oldenburg	Y	Bremen	New York	06/25/1853	10/17/1857	15	439	N	
Heinemann, George	29	Kurhessen	Y	London	New York	08/07/1856	04/11/1860	27	148	N	
Heinemann, Marzell	25	Wurttemberg	Y	Liverpool	New York	??/05/1852	04/28/1855	11	318	N	
Heinen, Barney	31	Hanover	Y	Bremen	Baltimore	07/04/1846	08/15/1848	22	114	N	
Heinichen, Albert	43	Germany	Y	Amsterdam	New York	01/02/1886	03/27/1888			Y	
Heinichen, Frank Alwin	17	Germany	Y	Antwerp	Philadelphia	03/04/1891	03/13/1891			Y	
Heinichen, Frank Otto	22	Germany	Y	Antwerp	Philadelphia	03/04/1891	03/13/1891			Y	
Heinichen, Gustav	20	Germany	Y	Antwerp	New York	02/07/1891	04/07/1891			Y	
Heining, Bernard	24	Prussia	Y	Bremen	Baltimore	08/12/1846	03/30/1852	24	339	N	
Heinisch, Charles	29	Germany	N	Hamburg	New York	07/19/1881	?			Y	
Heinlein, George	31	Germany	Y	Bremen	New York	05/06/1883	09/11/1888			Y	
Heinlein, Henry	17	Germany	N	?	?	00/00/1866				Y	10/23/1886

CITIZENSHIP RECORDS

APPLICANT	AGE	COUNTRY OF ORIGIN	DEC	DEPART PORT	ENTRY PORT	ARRIVE DATE	DEC DATE	VOL	PG.	FLD	NAT DATE
Heinlein, J.J.	40	Germany	Y	?	?	07/01/1879	02/25/1889			Y	
Heinold, George	41	Wurttemberg	Y	Havre	New York	03/30/1852	09/14/1857	15	264	N	
Heinold, Valentine	55	Germany	Y	Bremen	Baltimore	03/28/1883	03/16/1886			Y	
Heinoss, Nicholas	58	Bavaria	Y	Havre	New Orleans	04/23/1851	09/27/1858	16	114	N	
Heinrich, Carle	27	Saxony	Y	Bremen	New Orleans	?	10/07/1854	6	1	N	
Heinrich, Charles	25	Wurttemberg	Y	Havre	New Orleans	05/01/1848	02/21/1853	7	207	N	
Heinrich, Charles	27	Saxony	Y	Bremen	New Orleans	05/09/1852	10/07/1854	11	2	N	
Heinrich, Christian	24	Germany	Y	Hamburg	New York	05/27/1880	06/01/1881			Y	
Heinrich, John Frdrick J	31	Saxony	Y	Bremen	New York	10/04/1848	04/29/1850	3	30	N	
Heinrich, Michael	28	Bavaria	Y	Bremen	Baltimore	06/16/1845	09/04/1848	22	293	N	
Heinrich, Peter Herman	26	Holstein	Y	Hamburg	New York	06/01/1853	04/17/1854	8	140	N	
Heinrich, Peter Herman	26	Holstein	Y	Hamburg	New York	06/01/1853	04/17/1854	9	11	N	
Heinrich, Phillip (Heinr	23	Prussia	Y	London	New York	07/25/1847	08/??/1848	22	99	N	
Heinrichs, John	26	Prussia	Y	Bremen	Philadelphia	06/22/1847	04/25/1854	8	257	N	
Heinrichs, Rudolph	32	Prussia	Y	Hamburg	New York	08/01/1854	11/09/1855	13	195	N	
Heins, John	43	Hanover	Y	Bremen	Baltimore	09/17/1854	03/24/1856	26	262	N	
Heinsius, Frederick	22	Holland	Y	Amsterdam	New York	09/15/1851	05/10/1854	8	420	N	
Heinsius, Frederick	22	Holland	Y	Amsterdam	New York	09/15/1851	05/10/1854	9	293	N	
Heintz, Adam	36	Bavaria	Y	Havre	New Orleans	04/??/1848	06/24/1860	27	4	N	
Heintz, Bartholomaeus	24	Bavaria	Y	Havre	New York	02/03/1853	02/05/1856	26	50	N	
Heintz, Jacob	28	Germany	Y	Antwerp	New York	09/02/1885	08/09/1890			Y	
Heintzelmann, Jacob	32	Germany	Y	Antwerp	New York	11/02/1884	04/11/1898			Y	
Heintzsch, George	26	Germany	Y	Hamburg	New York	07/22/1882	02/18/1884			Y	
Heinz, Adolph	17	Germany	N	?	New York	00/00/1880				Y	10/23/1886
Heinz, Albert L.	16	Germany	N	?	New York	00/00/1880				Y	10/23/1886
Heinz, Christian Ludwig	24	Wuerttemberg	Y	Antwerp	New York	05/04/1849	05/31/1852	25	155	N	
Heinz, Joseph	49	France	Y	Havre	New Orleans	04/25/1855	06/26/1862	18	362	N	
Heinze, Carl F. F.	31	Saxony	Y	Havre	New Orleans	06/25/1848	09/28/1848	22	359	N	
Heinzelmann, Matthias	21	Germany	Y	Antwerp	New York	11/23/1888	04/11/1889			Y	
Heire, Thomas	34	Ireland	Y	Limerick	Whitehall	09/13/1848	02/26/1853	7	237	N	
Heis, Michael	44	Bavaria	Y	Bremen	New York	01/??/1853	09/22/1855	13	117	N	
Heise, Charles	32	Prussia	Y	Bremen	New York	12/25/1855	01/14/1856	13	460	N	
Heise, Ernst Henry	28	Prussia	Y	Hamburg	New York	8/28/1854	09/12/1855	13	11	N	
Heise, Paul	38	Germany	Y	Bremen	New York	02/27/1882	09/09/1895			Y	
Heiser, Gerhard	32	Prussia	Y	Bremen	Philadelphia	06/23/1847	07/05/1851	3	498	N	
Heiser, Ludwig	44	Hesse Darmsta	Y	Rotterdam	New York	02/04/1850	05/20/1852	25	54	N	
Heiss, Allonnus	42	Bavaria	Y	Antwerp	New York	08/22/1850	01/03/1853	5	500	N	
Heiss, Otto	32	Germany	Y	Antwerp	Philadelphia	08/15/1883	03/27/1889			Y	
Heister, Henry	26	Germany	Y	Bremen	New York	02/04/1881	12/04/1883			Y	
Heister, Henry	61	Prussia	N	?	?	?	?			Y	
Heister, Wilhelm	24	Germany	Y	Bremen	Baltimore	10/18/1882	02/25/1884			Y	
Heisterkamp, Henry	32	Prussia	Y	Bremen	New Orleans	02/23/1845	02/09/1849	23	40	N	
Heitahrends, Henry	25	Hanover	Y	Bremen	New Orleans	12/11/1848	11/06/1855	13	178	N	
Heitel, Bernard	31	Germany	Y	Bremen	New York	04/25/1888	10/13/1896			Y	
Heitfeld, Herman	55	Germany	Y	Bremen	Baltimore	09/15/1885	11/01/1890			Y	
Heithaus, Bernard Henry	64	Germany	N	Bremen	New Orleans	04/??/1849	05/??/1851	28	33	N	05/??/1854
Heitkamp, Barney	24	Germany	Y	Rotterdam	New York	09/05/1876	11/01/1878			Y	
Heitkamp, Barney Herman	25	Hanover	Y	Bremen	New Orleans	12/18/1844	09/13/1848	22	342	N	
Heitkamp, Christian	30	Prussia	Y	Bremen	New Orleans	06/23/1853	03/17/1856	26	213	N	
Heitkamp, Frederick	30	Prussia	Y	Bremen	New Orleans	06/02/1854	09/30/1858	17	26	N	
Heitkamp, Frederick	24	Germany	Y	Rotterdam	New York	06/29/1883	10/26/1888			Y	
Heitker, Bernard	52	Germany	Y	Bremen	Baltimore	08/05/1874	04/28/1894			Y	
Heitker, Bernhard J.	30	Germany	Y	Bremen	New York	08/02/1883	10/19/1893			Y	
Heitling, Clemens	42	Germany	N	Amsterdam	New York	05/??/1869	?			Y	
Heitman, John Henry	30	Oldenburg	Y	Bremen	Baltimore	??/04/1844	12/13/1849	23	392	N	
Heitmann, Christian	25	Germany	Y	Bremen	New York	05/13/1881	10/31/1882			Y	
Heitmann, Heinrich Chris	20	Germany	Y	?	?	03/17/1880	03/29/1880			Y	
Heitmann, William	28	Germany	Y	Bremen	Baltimore	11/16/1883	11/04/1889	19	277	N	
Heitmann, William	26	Germany	Y	Bremen	Baltimore	05/21/1880	07/17/1882			Y	

155

CITIZENSHIP RECORDS

APPLICANT	AGE	COUNTRY OF ORIGIN	DEC	DEPART PORT	ENTRY PORT	ARRIVE DATE	DEC DATE	VOL	PG.	FLD	NAT DATE
Heitmann, William	28	Germany	Y	Bremen	Baltimore	11/16/1883	11/04/1889			Y	
Heitmann, William	34	Germany	N	Bremen	Baltimore	12/??/1864	?			Y	
Heitzler, George	34	Germany	Y	Havre	New York	06/26/1880	10/05/1885			Y	
Heitzmann, William	33	Germany	Y	Antwerp	New York	12/17/1882	10/24/1889	19	256	N	
Heitzmann, William	33	Germany	Y	Antwerp	New York	12/17/1882	10/24/1889			Y	
Helbig, Philip	34	Bavaria	Y	Antwerp	New York	02/08/1851	10/22/1858	17	92	N	
Helbing, Gustavus Adolph	29	Wurttemberg	Y	Antwerp	New York	05/30/1848	11/24/1857	16	50	N	
Helble, Geresimus	53	Germany	Y	Havre	New York	04/28/1847	07/10/1883			Y	
Helbling, F.H.	35	Germany	Y	Liverpool	New York	08/15/1871	07/27/1886			Y	
Helck, John	21	Bavaria	Y	Havre	New York	08/24/1853	10/03/1856	14	170	N	
Helck, John	33	Bavaria	Y	Havre	New York	05/27/1854	04/17/1860	27	162	N	
Held, John	23	Germany	Y	Hamburg	New York	05/30/1885	10/26/1889			Y	
Held, John	50	Germany	Y	Bremen	New York	09/??/1880	01/??/1883			Y	
Heldberg, Henry	53	Germany	Y	Hamburg	New York	09/12/1886	10/19/1896			Y	
Heldmeyer, Edward	39	Switzerland	Y	?	?	?	12/28/1892			Y	
Helen, John	30	Ireland	Y	Liverpool	New Orleans	01/01/1851	07/25/1857	15	132	N	
Helferich, Louis	33	Bavaria	Y	Havre	New York	08/30/1852	09/08/1860	27	347	N	
Helferich, Lucas	34	Germany	Y	Bremen	New York	03/06/1881	02/02/1888			Y	
Helfrich, Anton	55	Germany	Y	Antwerp	Philadelphia	08/19/1890	01/15/1894			Y	
Helfrich, John	21	Hesse Darmsta	Y	London	New York	10/10/1857	04/01/1861	18	124	N	
Helg, Adam	32	Germany	N	Bremen	Baltimore	03/27/1878	?			Y	
Helier, Christian	30	France	Y	Havre	New York	03/06/1854	05/24/1862	18	340	N	
Helken, Ignatz	25	Hanover	Y	Bremen	New Orleans	12/??/1853	07/18/1860	27	225	N	
Helkomp, John	28	Holland	Y	Rotterdam	New Orleans	??/02/1846	10/23/1851	4	379	N	
Hell, Adam	26	Germany	Y	Antwerp	New York	09/23/1891	10/26/1891	19	343	N	
Hell, Joseph	37	Bavaria	Y	Bremen	New York	05/22/1854	10/09/1854	6	188	N	
Hell, Joseph	31	Bavaria	Y	Bremen	New York	05/22/1854	10/09/1854	11	191	N	
Hell, Philip	50	Germany	N	Hamburg	New York	10/26/1865	?			Y	
Helle, Herman Henry	29	Hanover	Y	Bremen	New Orleans	12/07/1852	11/07/1855	13	187	N	
Helleberg, C. G.	35	Sweden	Y	Gottingberg	New York	08/19/1845	01/23/1850	23	541	N	
Heller, Elias	32	Germany	Y	Bremen	New York	03/14/1889	04/19/1892			Y	
Heller, Fritz	22	Switzerland	Y	Havre	New York	12/15/1884	09/21/1887			Y	
Heller, Geo	39	Germany	Y	Havre	New York	02/18/1897	07/28/1900			Y	
Heller, John Bernard	32	Hanover	Y	Bremen	New Orleans	10/24/1852	07/07/1855	11	344	N	
Heller, John Henry	40	Germany	N	Rotterdam	New York	09/14/1872	?			Y	
Heller, Lorenz	40	Germany	Y	Bremen	New York	06/22/1883	03/26/1890			Y	
Helligrath, Adam	35	Germany	Y	Rotterdam	Jersey City	09/04/1876	10/10/1881			Y	
Helling, Anton	27	Germany	Y	Antwerp	New York	07/07/1885	09/05/1889			Y	
Helling, Barney	27	Germany	Y	Bremen	New York	09/03/1872	09/02/1874			Y	
Helling, Carlos	54	Prussia	Y	Bremen	New York	07/12/1856	01/28/1857	14	515	N	
Hellinger, Leonhardt	56	Wurttemberg	Y	London	New York	10/19/1853	06/12/1854	10	116	N	
Hellkamp, Gerhard	29	Germany	Y	Bremen	Baltimore	12/26/1883	12/19/1888			Y	
Hellmann, George	25	Germany	Y	Bremen	New York	05/16/1884	01/26/1889			Y	
Hellmann, George Adam	37	Bavaria	Y	Havre	New York	12/17/1852	02/06/1856	26	59	N	
Hellmann, Henry	25	Hanover	Y	Bremen	New Orleans	01/01/1857	10/08/1860	27	426	N	
Hellmann, Hermann	34	Germany	Y	Bremen	Baltimore	08/30/1883	10/11/1888			Y	
Hellmann, J.P. Henry	30	Germany	Y	Bremen	Baltimore	11/03/1881	11/01/1882			Y	
Hellmann, Jacob	21	Bavaria	Y	Havre	New York	09/16/1847	01/22/1849	1	490	N	
Hellmann, Joseph	25	Germany	Y	Bremen	New York	04/30/1880	11/17/1882			Y	
Hellmann, Joseph	??	Germany	Y	?	?	?	08/29/1887			Y	
Hellmund, William	25	Prussia	Y	Rotterdam	New York	06/25/1852	04/17/1854	9	51	N	
Hellmuth, John	21	Baden	Y	Rotterdam	New York	04/21/1853	03/25/1856	26	338	N	
Hello, Vincent	35	Sicily	Y	Palermo	Boston	12/29/1835	07/15/1851	3	539	N	
Hellstein, Christian	49	Wurttemberg	Y	Havre	New Orleans	01/06/1848	10/07/1854	6	8	N	
Hellstein, Christian	49	Wurttemberg	Y	Havre	New Orleans	01/06/1848	10/07/1854	11	9	N	
Hellsten, Nels Herman	29	Sweden	Y	Goteborg	New York	06/11/1891	04/03/1893			Y	
Hellstern, Joachim	36	Sigmaringen	Y	Havre	New Orleans	01/06/1848	09/08/1852	25	414	N	
Hellwig, F.W.	49	Oldenburg	Y	Boake	New York	02/01/1857	11/02/1860	18	2	N	
Helman, Louis	??	Germany	Y	?	?	?	01/09/1891			Y	

CITIZENSHIP RECORDS

APPLICANT	AGE	COUNTRY OF ORIGIN	DEC	DEPART PORT	ENTRY PORT	ARRIVE DATE	DEC DATE	VOL	PG.	FLD	NAT DATE
Helmerich, Edward	26	Bavaria	Y	Havre	New York	06/21/1851	11/03/1851	4	483	N	
Helmers, Henry	22	Prussia	Y	Bremen	New York	07/25/1854	11/01/1858	17	229	N	
Helmes, Barney	44	Germany	N	Hanover	Baltimore	11/03/1864	?			Y	
Helmes, Henry J.	35	Germany	Y	Hamburg	New York	08/21/1882	11/02/1888	19	213	N	
Helmes, Herman	35	Oldenburg	Y	Bremen	New York	10/22/1847	01/30/1849	1	547	N	
Helmholz, William	24	Hanover	Y	Hamburg	New York	08/12/1859	08/06/1860	27	254	N	
Helmich, Bernard Henry	36	Hanover	Y	Bremen	Baltimore	07/18/1854	04/03/1858	16	483	N	
Helmich, Frederick	23	Prussia	Y	Carraccus	New York	05/25/1851	02/28/1852	24	182	N	
Helmick, Barney	30	Hanover	Y	Bremen	New Orleans	12/25/1856	06/28/1860	27	12	N	
Helmig, Gerhard	23	Hanover	Y	Bremen	Baltimore	05/01/1849	06/10/1852	25	311	N	
Helmig, Heinrich	26	Germany	Y	Bremen	Baltimore	08/25/1883	01/02/1886			Y	
Helmig, Henry	56	Hanover	Y	Bremen	New Orleans	12/05/1852	10/12/1858	17	66	N	
Helming, Geo. H.	34	Germany	Y	Rotterdam	New York	12/??/1870	03/03/1884			Y	
Helming, Herman	21	Hanover	Y	Bremen	Baltimore	09/10/1853	05/22/1856	26	530	N	
Helming, John	25	Hanover	Y	Bremen	Baltimore	10/06/1847	08/15/1851	4	149	N	
Helming, John	25	Hanover	Y	Bremen	New Orleans	05/25/1851	11/01/1852	5	90	N	
Helming, John	24	Hanover	Y	Bremen	Baltimore	05/02/1859	05/10/1862	18	332	N	
Helmingdircks, H.	22	Germany	Y	Rotterdam	New York	07/14/1880	05/24/1883			Y	
Helmkamp, August	25	Germany	Y	Bremen	Baltimore	10/08/1883	02/09/1888			Y	
Helmkamp, Henry	37	Germany	Y	Bremen	Baltimore	05/15/1883	11/22/1892			Y	
Helmke, John Gerhard	32	Bremen	Y	Bremen	Philadelphia	11/07/1852	03/31/1862	18	291	N	
Helmling, Louis	24	Germany	Y	Havre	New York	08/02/1893	04/25/1898			Y	
Helms, August	26	Bavaria	Y	Havre	New Orleans	11/14/1852	09/16/1857	15	274	N	
Helmsauer, Herman	??	Germany	Y	?	?	12/??/1889	05/04/1891			Y	
Helmsdorfer, Ludwig	32	Wuerttemberg	Y	Havre	New York	10/15/1854	10/08/1860	27	414	N	
Helmstetter, John	32	Bavaria	Y	Antwerp	New York	08/26/1845	10/05/1848	22	428	N	
Helmuth, Joseph	23	Baden	Y	London	New York	07/12/1847	08/30/1848	22	284	N	
Helpoltsteiner, Willabal	23	Bavaria	Y	Bremen	Baltimore	09/06/1849	10/07/1854	6	4	N	
Helpoltsteiner, Willibal	23	Bavaria	Y	Bremen	Baltimore	09/06/1849	10/07/1854	1	5	N	
Helscheo, John	26	Prussia	Y	Bremen	New Orleans	11/20/1847	04/27/1853	8	127	N	
Helwig, Philipp	30	Hesse Darmsta	Y	London	Whitehall	??/15/1847	09/09/1852	25	434	N	
Hemann, Edward	34	Prussia	Y	Bremen	Baltimore	??/04/1845	11/19/1849	23	349	N	
Hemann, Franz	34	Prussia	Y	Bremen	Baltimore	06/04/1849	09/17/1855	13	47	N	
Hemann, Henry	32	Prussia	Y	Bremen	Baltimore	05/04/1857	04/08/1862	18	308	N	
Hemann, Rudolph	47	Germany	Y	Bremen	New York	12/07/1872	11/13/1893			Y	
Hembrodt, Henry	27	Hanover	Y	Bremen	Baltimore	04/27/1846	12/20/1851	4	540	N	
Hemesacht, Friedrich	31	Hanover	Y	Bremen	New Orleans	10/05/1845	01/06/1851	2	452	N	
Hemesath, David	34	Germany	Y	Bremen	New York	11/27/1881	05/23/1890			Y	
Hemesath, John Henry	29	Hanover	Y	Hamburg	New York	09/29/1846	04/02/1852	24	350	N	
Heming, John	34	Germany	Y	Bremen	New York	05/19/1883	12/10/1889			Y	
Heminger, John Michael	32	Wurttemberg	Y	Havre	New York	09/03/1851	07/13/1855	11	383	N	
Hemings, William F.	40	England	Y	London	Detroit	01/??/1835	03/04/1856	26	163	N	
Heminn, Ernst	30	Germany	Y	Bremen	Baltimore	02/14/1868	01/02/1875			Y	
Hemler, Michael	54	Germany	N	Havre	New York	04/02/1847	?			Y	
Hemmelgarn, Henry	25	Hanover	Y	Bremen	New Orleans	11/02/1853	10/01/1856	14	100	N	
Hemmer, Henry	22	Bavaria	Y	Havre	New Orleans	12/29/1854	12/10/1857	16	212	N	
Hemmerle, John	34	Baden	Y	Havre	New York	05/12/1854	09/30/1856	14	73	N	
Hemmerle, Joseph	30	Baden	Y	Havre	New York	05/12/1854	09/30/1856	14	72	N	
Hemmersbach, Andrew	24	Germany	Y	Bremen	New York	08/12/1887	04/28/1892			Y	
Hemmet, Peter	40	Bavaria	Y	Havre	New York	07/30/1847	08/25/1848	22	254	N	
Hemmeter, Charles	??	Germany	Y	?	?	?	07/10/1888			Y	
Hemmings, George Edwin	38	England	Y	Liverpool	New York	09/29/1883	10/16/1896			Y	
Hempelmann, Bernard	72	Germany	N	Hamburg	New York	07/30/1848	09/??/1849	28	380	N	10/??/1855
Hempelmann, Frederick	31	Oldenburg	Y	Hamburg	New York	08/15/1848	10/29/1858	17	175	N	
Hemseth, Henry	23	Germany	Y	Bremen	Baltimore	12/24/1883	10/22/1886	19	71	N	
Henck, Frederick	25	Germany	Y	Amsterdam	New York	11/05/1888	12/04/1891			Y	
Hencke, Charles	49	Germany	N	Hamburg	New York	05/28/1860	?			Y	
Hencke, Christian	43	Germany	Y	Bremen	New York	08/26/1881	10/25/1886			Y	
Henderson, Jacob	36	Germany	Y	Hamburg	New York	08/01/1881	11/06/1882			Y	

CITIZENSHIP RECORDS

APPLICANT	AGE	COUNTRY OF ORIGIN	DEC	DEPART PORT	ENTRY PORT	ARRIVE DATE	DEC DATE	VOL	PG.	FLD	NAT DATE
Henderson, John	32	England	Y	Sunderland	Vermont	06/13/1839	12/22/1851	4	543	N	
Henegan, William	47	Ireland	Y	Liverpool	New Orleans	12/16/1849	03/05/1851	3	201	N	
Henemann, Otto	??	Hesse Cassel	N	?	?	?		18	561	N	10/11/1858
Henen, George	24	Hanover	Y	Bremen	New Orleans	12/12/1845	01/11/1849	1	400	N	
Henen, John	28	Hanover	Y	Bremen	New Orleans	11/30/1844	01/11/1849	1	394	N	
Henesy, Andrew	21	Ireland	Y	Liverpool	New Orleans	02/01/1850	12/07/1852	5	388	N	
Henesy, Peter	28	Ireland	Y	New Koss	Buffalo	06/10/1849	01/24/1853	7	55	N	
Henge, Andy	33	Germany	Y	Hamburg	New York	10/??/1879	10/05/1885			Y	
Hengehold, Frederick G.	39	Germany	N	Bremen	New York	09/12/1867	?			Y	
Henges, John	32	Bavaria	Y	Havre	New Orleans	09/??/1848	12/30/1852	5	473	N	
Henjes, George C.D.	41	Germany	Y	Hamburg	New York	05/10/1882	09/26/1891			Y	
Henke, B. Gerhard	28	Oldenburg	Y	Bremen	New Orleans	07/15/1846	07/27/1848	22	1	N	
Henke, Bernard	25	Germany	Y	Amsterdam	New York	10/23/1883	10/19/1886			Y	
Henke, Carl R.	26	Germany	Y	Bremen	New York	03/04/1881	03/28/1887			Y	
Henke, Charles	27	Germany	Y	Bremen	Baltimore	06/04/1884	10/01/1888			Y	
Henke, Henry	33	Oldenburg	Y	Bremen	New Orleans	11/??/1852	10/27/1857	15	493	N	
Henke, William	29	Germany	Y	Bremen	Baltimore	08/06/1886	07/05/1890			Y	
Henkel, Christian	28	Hesse Cassel	Y	Bremen	Baltimore	06/22/1851	07/09/1851	3	514	N	
Henkel, Christian	36	Germany	Y	Hamburg	New York	11/11/1875	02/04/1889			Y	
Henkel, Constantine	23	Saxe Weimar E	Y	Antwerp	New York	09/14/1857	10/08/1860	27	452	N	
Henkel, Leopold	52	Germany	Y	Bremen	New York	04/??/1854	10/23/1856	19	78	N	
Henkenberns, Anton	29	Germany	Y	Bremen	Baltimore	04/30/1881	11/14/1890			Y	
Henkenberns, B.H.	29	Germany	Y	Bremen	Baltimore	03/28/1879	03/25/1885			Y	
Henle, Moses	35	Germany	Y	Havre	New York	08/20/1880	08/27/1884			Y	
Henley, Patrick	27	Ireland	Y	Liverpool	New York	12/28/1846	10/03/1854	10	377	N	
Henley, Patrick	27	Ireland	Y	Liverpool	New York	12/28/1846	10/03/1854	12	316	N	
Henn, Carl J.	25	Germany	Y	Hamburg	New York	10/17/1884	10/26/1889			Y	
Henn, Daniel	53	Germany	Y	Antwerp	New York	04/27/1889	06/04/1894			Y	
Henn, Frank	28	Germany	Y	Bremen	New York	05/02/1882	10/26/1886	19	88	N	
Henn, John	49	Germany	Y	Havre	New York	12/05/1857	02/03/1883			Y	
Henne, Justus	48	Hanover	Y	Bremen	New Orleans	12/??/1844	03/04/1856	26	159	N	
Hennegan, Patrick	67	Ireland	N	Liverpool	New York	??/??/1842	?			Y	
Henneghan, James	53	Ireland	Y	Liverpool	New York	05/??/1872	04/01/1886			Y	
Henneker, J.G.	22	Hanover	Y	Antwerp	New York	06/01/1858	12/12/1859	17	503	N	
Hennekes, Anton	29	Holland	Y	Rotterdam	New York	07/28/1851	04/03/1852	24	361	N	
Hennekes, Henry	51	Germany	N	Bremen	New Orleans	10/10/1855	?			Y	
Hennenhofer, Peter	45	Prussia	Y	Bremen	New Orleans	??/28/1846	02/25/1850	2	126	N	
Hennessey, James	22	Ireland	Y	Liverpool	New Orleans	01/04/1852	03/05/1853	7	283	N	
Hennessy, John	25	Ireland	Y	Liverpool	New York	11/30/1853	11/02/1858	17	263	N	
Hennessy, John	40	Ireland	Y	Plymouth	New York	05/??/1835	02/21/1856	26	115	N	
Hennessy, Nicholas	28	Ireland	Y	Matanzas	New York	06/28/1847	01/02/1858	16	290	N	
Hennessy, Thomas	25	Ireland	Y	Liverpool	New Orleans	03/17/1851	03/01/1852	24	193	N	
Hennfrey, Thomas	22	England	Y	Liverpool	New York	11/01/1850	04/09/1856	26	479	N	
Hennig, Charles	34	Germany	Y	Hamburg	New York	03/18/1890	08/30/1894			Y	
Henninger, Herman	30	Germany	Y	Bremen	New York	07/04/1882	10/24/1890			Y	
Henninger, Karl	27	Germany	Y	Havre	New York	12/31/1881	07/14/1887			Y	
Hennis, Andrew	25	Hesse Darmsta	Y	Havre	New York	03/05/1854	01/02/1858	16	293	N	
Hennjes, Fred	27	Germany	Y	Bremen	Baltimore	11/15/1890	11/11/1892			Y	
Hennrich, Franz Karl	33	Germany	Y	Antwerp	New York	05/24/1890	11/02/1892			Y	
Henrich, Jacob	37	Germany	Y	Bremen	Baltimore	04/15/1888	03/03/1894			Y	
Henricks, John	26	Prussia	Y	Bremen	Philadelphia	06/22/1847	04/25/1854	9	128	N	
Henry, Anton (Heiny?)	55	Germany	Y	Antwerp	New York	06/01/1880	07/23/1883			Y	
Henry, Bernard	27	Germany	Y	Bremen	Baltimore	03/13/1883	09/30/1884			Y	
Henry, Francis	35	Baden	Y	Havre	New York	05/09/1846	04/30/1850	3	34	N	
Henry, Lawrence	26	Ireland	Y	Liverpool	New Orleans	11/??/1847	10/22/1851	4	370	N	
Henry, Martin	29	Baden	Y	Havre	New York	12/30/1854	10/06/1857	15	356	N	
Henry, Patrick	35	Ireland	Y	Liverpool	New York	11/??/1848	11/??/1849	23	325	N	
Henry, Pierre	32	France	Y	Havre	New Orleans	01/??/1852	04/23/1855	11	286	N	
Hens, Leonard	32	Bavaria	Y	London	New York	08/20/1847	05/31/1852	25	141	N	

CITIZENSHIP RECORDS

APPLICANT	AGE	COUNTRY OF ORIGIN	DEC	DEPART PORT	ENTRY PORT	ARRIVE DATE	DEC DATE	VOL	PG.	FLD	NAT DATE
Henschen, William	24	Prussia	Y	Bremen	New Orleans	12/22/1847	06/19/1851	3	440	N	
Hensel, M. Emil	26	Germany	Y	Amsterdam	New York	02/17/1882	04/02/1887			Y	
Hensel, William	??	Germany	Y	?	?	?	04/07/1882			Y	
Hensgen, Fred	23	Germany	Y	?	Philadelphia	08/07/1893	11/02/1905			Y	
Henshemeyer, Barney	38	Germany	N	Bremen	Baltimore	06/28/1880	?			Y	
Hensinger, Jacob	51	Germany	Y	Bremen	New York	02/10/1872	02/23/1889			Y	
Henson, Peter	28	Ireland	Y	Liverpool	New Orleans	04/18/1849	02/19/1853	7	187	N	
Henszler, John	28	Wurttemberg	Y	Bremen	New York	04/16/1852	04/17/1854	8	156	N	
Hentschel, Johann	22	Germany	Y	Bremen	Boston	12/24/1881	01/10/1883			Y	
Hentschel, Max	29	Germany	Y	Hamburg	New York	03/04/1880	07/27/1885			Y	
Henz, George	45	Germany	N	Havre	New York	01/25/1866	?			Y	
Henze, Julius	24	Hanover	Y	Bremen	New York	10/30/1857	08/26/1862	18	402	N	
Henzi, Fried	31	Switzerland	Y	Havre	New York	07/16/1900	07/05/1902			Y	
Heoffeld, Henry	37	Germany	N	Bremen	Baltimore	10/09/1868	?			Y	
Hepp, Markus	40	Switzerland	Y	Havre	New York	10/14/1880	10/14/1896			Y	
Heppes, Philipp	40	Germany	N	Antwerp	New York	06/24/1870	?			Y	
Hept, Louis	21	Germany	Y	Bremen	New York	12/08/1884	05/28/1887			Y	
Her, Christian	37	Wurttemberg	Y	London	New York	01/20/1853	09/01/1857	15	215	N	
Herault, Alexander	60	France	Y	Havre	New York	03/07/1863	12/23/1889			Y	
Herbener, Louis	24	Germany	Y	Hamburg	New York	03/22/1888	08/04/1893			Y	
Herber, Jacob	50	Prussia	Y	Antwerp	New Orleans	11/25/1848	02/07/1852	24	68	N	
Herberg, Xavier	27	Germany	Y	Bremen	New York	05/??/1874	05/??/1875			Y	
Herbers, Henry	??	Hanover	Y	Bremen	New Orleans	03/06/18??	10/11/1848	1	132	N	
Herbers, John Bernard	22	Hanover	Y	Bremen	Baltimore	05/27/1845	08/08/1848	22	76	N	
Herbert, Adam	68	Hesse Darmsta	Y	Bremen	New York	08/07/1854	03/24/1856	26	256	N	
Herbert, Anton	36	Prussia	Y	Bremen	New Orleans	01/23/1846	02/13/1849	23	85	N	
Herbert, August	36	Hesse Darmsta	Y	Bremen	New York	08/07/1854	03/24/1856	26	258	N	
Herbert, Frederick	28	England	Y	Liverpool	New York	02/21/1882	04/03/1885			Y	
Herbert, Henry	30	Germany	N	Bremen	Baltimore	03/??/1878	?			Y	
Herbert, John Ludwig	38	Hesse Darmsta	Y	Bremen	New York	08/07/1854	03/24/1856	26	257	N	
Herbert, Joseph	28	Germany	N	Bremen	Baltimore	06/14/1878	?			Y	
Herbert, Thomas	26	England	Y	Canada	Rochester	06/18/1848	03/24/1851	3	245	N	
Herbert, William	22	Hanover	Y	Bremen	New Orleans	11/??/1849	10/25/1851	4	402	N	
Herbig, Gustav	61	Germany	Y	Antwerp	New York	12/09/1881	12/24/1883			Y	
Herbig, Hugo	29	Germany	Y	Antwerp	New York	12/09/1881	12/24/1883			Y	
Herbolsheimer, John Geor	34	Bavaria	Y	Bremen	Buffalo	07/01/1846	02/19/1849	23	190	N	
Herbrecht, Jos	56	France	Y	Cherbourg	New York	08/19/1871	10/20/1894			Y	
Herbst, Herman	24	Brunswick	Y	Bremen	Philadelphia	12/04/1853	03/31/1856	26	380	N	
Herbst, Leman	??	Bavaria	Y	Bremen	Baltimore	??/??/1845	04/19/1855	11	276	N	
Herd, Andreas	31	Germany	Y	Hamburg	New York	06/??/1881	08/02/1884			Y	
Herd, Paul	32	Wurttemberg	Y	Havre	New Orleans	03/06/1854	02/10/1857	15	11	N	
Herdemann, Anton	23	Germany	Y	Rotterdam	Baltimore	09/16/1891	01/04/1894			Y	
Herdemann, Theodore	21	Germany	Y	?	?	?	01/16/1888			Y	
Herdy, Andreas	50	Bavaria	Y	Havre	New York	09/15/1852	02/26/1853	7	238	N	
Herfel, Franz	43	Bavaria	Y	Havre	New York	03/29/1852	11/26/1855	13	255	N	
Herfurt, Max Hugo	28	Germany	Y	Bremen	Baltimore	10/21/1883	09/30/1889			Y	
Herfurt, Robert L.	35	Germany	Y	Hamburg	New York	04/17/1883	10/15/1892			Y	
Hergeroeder, Phillip	26	Russia	Y	Hamburg	New York	04/12/1892	95/25/1894			Y	
Herget, Conrad F.	24	Germany	Y	Antwerp	New York	09/26/1893	01/31/1898			Y	
Herich, Casper	36	Prussia	Y	Bremen	New Orleans	11/24/1853	05/24/1854	9	376	N	
Herier, Jacob	23	Bavaria	Y	Havre	Boston	08/28/1846	05/20/1852	25	76	N	
Herig, Casper	36	Prussia	Y	Bremen	New Orleans	11/24/1853	05/24/1854	8	502	N	
Hering, Anton	31	Germany	Y	Havre	New York	05/29/1883	11/05/1886			Y	
Hering, August	25	Germany	Y	Bremen	Baltimore	11/15/1880	02/02/1882			Y	
Hering, Bruno	35	Germany	Y	Hamburg	New York	09/15/1882	05/21/1888			Y	
Hering, Ernst	25	Saxony	Y	Bremen	New York	05/29/1849	07/12/1851	3	523	N	
Hering, Ernst	60	Germany	N	Bremen	New York	06/03/1849	?			Y	
Hering, Moritz Oscar	26	Germany	Y	Hamburg	New York	05/14/1880	10/16/1882			Y	
Hering, Otto	??	Germany	Y	?	?	?	03/10/1888			Y	

CITIZENSHIP RECORDS

APPLICANT	AGE	COUNTRY OF ORIGIN	DEC	DEPART PORT	ENTRY PORT	ARRIVE DATE	DEC DATE	VOL	PG.	FLD	NAT DATE
Heringhaus, Bernhard	30	Germany	Y	Bremen	Baltimore	09/06/1888	07/08/1892			Y	
Heringhaus, Henry	24	Germany	Y	Rotterdam	New York	05/17/1882	12/08/1883			Y	
Herkert, August	24	Germany	Y	Bremen	New York	12/07/1884	04/27/1889			Y	
Herkert, Ludwig Joseph	29	Germany	Y	Bremen	New York	07/24/1894	12/08/1897			Y	
Herkes, Philip	30	Luxemburg	Y	Havre	New York	08/16/1853	03/19/1856	26	232	N	
Herl, Charles	30	Baden	Y	Havre	New York	10/20/1854	01/31/1857	14	521	N	
Herling, Emil	31	Germany	Y	Havre	New York	05/18/1894	03/04/1898			Y	
Herman, Albert O.	??	Germany	Y	?	?	?	10/21/1893			Y	
Herman, George	44	Germany	Y	Havre	New York	08/06/1864	10/08/1886			Y	
Herman, George	76	Germany	N	Bremen	New York	05/15/1872	01/??/1873	28	471	N	11/01/1876
Herman, John	30	Baden	Y	Havre	New York	04/13/1846	11/20/1848	1	335	N	
Herman, John	41	Wurttemberg	Y	Havre	New York	09/17/1854	09/22/1857	15	302	N	
Herman, Julius	21	Wurttemberg	Y	Havre	New York	06/15/1854	07/25/1857	15	134	N	
Hermann, Adam Henry	??	Germany	N	?	?	10/18/1881				Y	03/26/1892
Hermann, August	35	Germany	Y	Havre	New York	10/25/1882	04/06/1891			Y	
Hermann, Casper	57	Saxe Meininge	Y	Bremen	Baltimore	08/??/1845	11/21/1855	13	240	N	
Hermann, Conrad	26	Wurtemberg	Y	Havre	New York	03/30/1852	09/13/1852	25	470	N	
Hermann, Francis	28	Prussia	Y	Hamburg	New York	08/14/1854	03/24/1856	26	290	N	
Hermann, Jacob	23	Baden	Y	Rotterdam	New York	09/23/1851	12/29/1855	13	393	N	
Hermann, Jacob	45	Offenbach	Y	Rotterdam	New York	09/15/1854	09/09/1857	15	253	N	
Hermann, John	28	Bavaria	Y	Havre	New York	01/02/1859	08/30/1862	18	424	N	
Hermann, John Henry	26	Bremen	Y	Bremen	Baltimore	06/21/1852	11/12/1855	13	213	N	
Hermann, Samuel	43	Germany	N	Hamburg	New York	05/01/1866	?			Y	
Hermann, Valentine	22	Baden	Y	Havre	New Orleans	11/??/1852	12/26/1855	13	361	N	
Hermann, Xavier	39	Baden	Y	Havre	New Orleans	05/04/1853	10/31/1863			Y	
Hermerling, William	37	Germany	N	Bremen	Baltimore	07/02/1867	?			Y	
Hermersdoerfer, G.	36	Germany	Y	Antwerp	New York	07/05/1872	06/01/1886			Y	
Hermes, Bernhard	34	Germany	Y	Bremen	Baltimore	05/13/1882	02/13/1890			Y	
Hermes, Franz	24	Germany	Y	Antwerp	New York	07/25/1892	01/28/1893			Y	
Herninghausen, Ernst A.	28	Germany	Y	Hamburg	New York	12/16/1881	12/09/1889			Y	
Herold, John Charles	33	France	Y	Havre	New Orleans	11/10/1849	03/27/1856	26	353	N	
Herold, Morris	22	Bavaria	Y	Havre	New York	07/09/1850	03/14/1856	26	202	N	
Herper, Louis	22	Germany	Y	Hamburg	New York	07/27/1882	11/01/1882			Y	
Herr, Jacob	27	Bavaria	Y	Havre	New York	09/??/1847	11/??/1849	23	342	N	
Herr, Ruppert	48	Baden	Y	Havre	New York	09/02/1852	02/16/1858	16	312	N	
Herrberg, William	36	Germany	Y	Bremen	Baltimore	10/07/1881	07/21/1892			Y	
Herrel, John	21	Germany	Y	Havre	New York	08/29/1880	03/25/1881			Y	
Herren, Rudolf	22	Switzerland	Y	Havre	New York	03/15/1891	02/24/1892			Y	
Herrfurth, Heinrich Fran	30	Germany	Y	Hamburg	New York	10/01/1879	08/15/1881			Y	
Herrgult, Joseph	31	Germany	Y	Havre	New York	06/02/1896	11/05/1902			Y	
Herringhaus, Joseph	23	Germany	Y	Bremen	New York	09/06/1888	04/15/1892			Y	
Herrman, George	23	Baden	Y	Havre	New Orleans	01/22/1848	01/11/1849	1	389	N	
Herrmann, Andreas	54	Germany	Y	Bremen	New York	08/08/1881	04/08/1886			Y	
Herrmann, Bartholomew	27	Bavaria	Y	Bremen	Baltimore	08/08/1857	05/15/1860	27	191	N	
Herrmann, Christ	26	Germany	Y	Rotterdam	New York	09/10/1884	11/11/1886			Y	
Herrmann, Christian	40	Anhalt Dessau	Y	Bremen	New York	08/10/1858	08/15/1861	18	216	N	
Herrmann, George	27	Germany	Y	Havre	New York	10/23/1887	03/03/1894			Y	
Herrmann, George	27	Germany	Y	Havre	New York	10/23/1887	03/03/1894			Y	
Herrmann, George	35	Germany	Y	Hamburg	New York	07/20/1875	05/21/1888			Y	
Herrmann, George	45	Germany	Y	Havre	New York	06/01/1866	02/20/1883			Y	
Herrmann, Henry	35	Germany	Y	Havre	New York	10/26/1887	03/31/1897			Y	
Herrmann, J. Otto	22	Germany	Y	?	?	?	05/26/1886			Y	
Herrmann, Leopold	24	Germany	Y	Havre	New York	03/11/1881	12/13/1884			Y	
Herrmann, Otto C.	22	Germany	Y	Bremen	New York	05/02/1884	01/04/1887			Y	
Herrmann, Pius	32	Austria	Y	Hamburg	New York	10/31/1886	12/27/1887			Y	
Herrmanndoerfer, John	25	Germany	Y	Bremen	Baltimore	02/27/1889	03/25/1896			Y	
Herrschmann, William	29	Germany	Y	Bremen	New York	05/23/1883	01/24/1891			Y	
Hersberger, John	34	Baden	Y	London	New York	06/02/1846	06/14/1852	25	263	N	
Herschel, Hugo Edmund	28	Germany	Y	Amsterdam	New York	01/16/1882	12/29/1882			Y	

CITIZENSHIP RECORDS

APPLICANT	AGE	COUNTRY OF ORIGIN	DEC	DEPART PORT	ENTRY PORT	ARRIVE DATE	DEC DATE	VOL	PG.	FLD	NAT DATE
Herschler, John	29	Bavaria	Y	Havre	New York	06/20/1850	11/01/1852	5	100	N	
Herskamp, Herman	23	Hanover	Y	Bremen	New Orleans	05/02/1848	02/01/1851	3	80	N	
Hertel, John	31	Germany	Y	Bremen	Baltimore	04/10/1887	05/03/1894			Y	
Hertel, John	32	Bavaria	Y	Havre	New Orleans	03/04/1849	05/10/1852	24	532	N	
Hertenstein, Frederick	22	Baden	Y	Havre	New Orleans	11/06/1853	01/15/1856	13	470	N	
Herthel, Conrad	25	Germany	Y	Antwerp	New York	11/13/1881	03/03/1885			Y	
Hertlein, Martin	22	Wurttemberg	Y	Havre	New York	09/04/1854	02/23/1857	15	54	N	
Hertsenberg, Henry	58	Holland	Y	Amsterdam	New York	10/03/1882	10/23/1888	19	172	N	
Hertwig, John Christ.	27	Bavaria	Y	Havre	New York	??/10/1849	10/??/1849	23	276	N	
Hertzler, Christian	40	Bavaria	Y	Havre	New Orleans	05/27/1854	05/04/1861	18	158	N	
Hertzlin, Camille	32	Germany	Y	Havre	New York	05/10/1884	02/20/1888			Y	
Hertzoch, Nathan	27	Hesse Darmsta	Y	London	New York	11/02/1848	11/18/1848	1	325	N	
Herwegen, Henry	35	Prussia	Y	Liverpool	New York	08/??/1852	09/21/1855	13	90	N	
Herwig, Henry	34	Hanover	Y	Bremen	New York	09/15/1852	05/05/1854	8	381	N	
Herwig, Henry	34	Hanover	Y	Bremen	New York	09/15/1852	05/05/1854	9	254	N	
Herz, Isaac	26	Wurttemberg	Y	Liverpool	Philadelphia	05/20/1854	10/06/1856	14	227	N	
Herzdoerfer, Max	44	Germany	Y	Bremen	New York	07/02/1880	10/04/1883			Y	
Herzel, John	29	Germany	Y	Bremen	New York	10/01/1885	09/05/1887			Y	
Herzig, Peter A.	64	Germany	N	Havre	New York	05/08/1846	?			Y	
Herzner, John	50	Germany	N	Bremen	?	12/12/1865	?			Y	
Herzog, Bernard	38	Germany	Y	Amsterdam	New York	07/24/1881	11/01/1882			Y	
Herzog, Frederick	29	Oldenburg	Y	Bremen	New Orleans	12/10/1845	01/28/1850	2	12	N	
Herzog, Henry	60	Germany	Y	Hamburg	New York	04/25/1889	09/21/1894			Y	
Herzog, John Bernard	30	Oldenburg	Y	Bremen	New Orleans	09/24/1849	02/17/1852	24	128	N	
Herzog, Kark	76	Germany	N	Havre	New Orleans	??/??/1844	?			Y	
Herzog, Louis	24	Germany	Y	Hamburg	New York	06/12/1889	07/28/1893			Y	
Herzog, Maximilian	29	Germany	N	Antwerp	New York	01/15/1882	?			Y	
Heseding, Frank Ferdinan	30	Oldenburg	Y	Bremen	New York	07/??/1852	05/23/1856	26	545	N	
Heselbacher, Andreas	48	Bavaria	Y	Bremen	Baltimore	??/30/1848	12/04/1849	23	380	N	
Heselman, Herman	26	Prussia	Y	Bremen	New York	08/22/1848	10/16/1851	4	308	N	
Hesion, John	30	England	Y	Queenstown	New York	06/30/1881	10/11/1894			Y	
Heskamp, Herman	33	Hanover	Y	Bremen	New Orleans	05/10/1852	01/05/1856	13	424	N	
Heskamp, Herman	23	Hanover	Y	Bremen	Baltimore	10/02/1858	03/25/1862	18	278	N	
Heskamp, Johann H.	53	Germany	N	Bremen	New York	05/??/1864	?			Y	
Heskamp, John B. A.	27	Hanover	Y	Bremen	New Orleans	05/20/1848	06/08/1852	25	214	N	
Heslin, Peter	40	Ireland	Y	Liverpool	New Orleans	06/18/1843	03/01/1852	24	185	N	
Heslin, Thomas	38	Ireland	Y	Dublin	New York	05/20/1887	06/21/1894			Y	
Hesling, Herman	52	Germany	Y	Bremen	New York	09/19/1867	10/13/1892	19	361	N	
Hess, Adam	40	Hesse Cassel	Y	Bremen	New Orleans	11/25/1854	01/02/1858	16	294	N	
Hess, Adolphe	57	Germany	N	Hamburg	New York	03/??/1844	?			Y	
Hess, Anton	??	Germany	N	?	?	05/05/1879				Y	10/31/1892
Hess, Casper	52	Saxe Meininge	Y	Bremen	New York	05/18/1866	04/30/18??	17	461	N	
Hess, Christoph	24	Kurhessen	Y	Bremen	New York	06/16/1849	04/11/1853	8	56	N	
Hess, Ferdinand	57	Germany	Y	Hamburg	New York	05/08/1896	06/19/1899			Y	
Hess, Florian	35	Baden	Y	Havre	New Orleans	04/27/1849	05/12/1852	25	10	N	
Hess, Henry	21	Bavaria	Y	Liverpool	New York	07/28/1853	10/04/1854	10	412	N	
Hess, Henry	21	Bavaria	Y	Liverpool	New York	07/28/1853	10/04/1854	12	351	N	
Hess, John	32	Germany	Y	Antwerp	New York	06/22/1891	10/23/1895			Y	
Hess, John Liborius	22	Saxe Coburg G	Y	Bremen	New York	08/09/1852	05/26/1854	9	425	N	
Hess, John Liborius	22	Saxe Coburg G	Y	Bremen	New York	08/09/1852	05/26/1854	10	8	N	
Hess, Louis	35	Germany	Y	Bremen	New York	11/30/1884	10/11/1894			Y	
Hess, Sebastian	36	Germany	Y	Havre	New York	10/20/1872	10/22/1889			Y	
Hess, Valentine Charles	24	Saxe Weimar	Y	Bremen	Baltimore	07/04/1845	05/26/1852	25	116	N	
Hesse, Anton	29	Prussia	Y	Bremen	New York	09/20/1870	08/19/1872	18	512	N	
Hesse, Diederick Nichola	30	Hanover	Y	Bremen	New York	04/21/1850	03/21/1853	7	362	N	
Hesse, Gustav	28	Germany	Y	Hamburg	New York	10/21/1892	03/16/1900			Y	
Hesse, Justus	29	Germany	Y	Bremen	New York	10/06/1882	04/06/1887			Y	
Hesse, Lawrence	53	Hanover	Y	Bremen	New York	08/03/1854	08/15/1860	27	290	N	
Hesse, Theodore	21	Prussia	Y	Bremen	New York	??/??/1843	02/04/1862	18	254	N	

CITIZENSHIP RECORDS

APPLICANT	AGE	COUNTRY OF ORIGIN	DEC	DEPART PORT	ENTRY PORT	ARRIVE DATE	DEC DATE	VOL	PG.	FLD	NAT DATE
Hesse, William	22	Prussia	Y	Bremen	Baltimore	06/16/1856	05/04/1859	17	397	N	
Hessel, Gotfried	21	Germany	Y	Bremen	New York	10/20/1866	04/06/1868				Y
Hessel, Herman	24	Hanover	Y	Bremen	New Orleans	12/15/1853	10/05/1854	10	460	N	
Hessel, Hermann	24	Hanover	Y	Bremen	New Orleans	12/15/1853	10/05/1854	12	399	N	
Hesselbrock, Joseph	39	Germany	N	Bremen	Baltimore	10/28/1866	?				Y
Hesselbrock, Phillip H.J	24	Hanover	Y	Bremen	New Orleans	11/20/1851	11/01/1852	5	147	N	
Hesselbusch, Lazarus	21	Kurhessen	Y	Bremen	New York	07/04/1853	04/20/1854	9	90	N	
Hessing, Casper	23	Oldenburg	Y	Bremen	Baltimore	11/20/1847	05/06/1850	3	47	N	
Hessler, Joseph	34	Hanover	Y	Bremen	Baltimore	06/04/1846	05/25/1854	8	534	N	
Hessler, Joseph	34	Hanover	Y	Bremen	Baltimore	06/04/1846	05/25/1854	9	408	N	
Hessmann, Frank	31	Prussia	Y	Bremen	New York	12/10/1856	01/06/1860	27	31	N	
Hessmann, William	23	Prussia	Y	Bremen	New York	01/08/1853	08/15/1855	11	436	N	
Hester, James	27	Ireland	Y	Liverpool	New Orleans	07/25/1845	02/11/1851	3	122	N	
Hester, Nicholas	26	Ireland	Y	Liverpool	New Orleans	06/09/1848	02/16/1852	24	120	N	
Hester, Peter	29	Ireland	Y	Liverpool	New Orleans	04/04/1845	02/07/1852	24	73	N	
Hesz, George	43	Germany	Y	Havre	New York	10/05/1880	06/06/1881				Y
Heszler, John Heinrich	56	Kurhessen	Y	Bremen	Baltimore	07/26/1850	02/12/1853	7	148	N	
Hetsch, John	26	Bavaria	Y	Havre	New Orleans	06/16/1848	08/08/1851	4	99	N	
Hettemes, John	25	Prussia	Y	Antwerp	New York	06/23/1847	09/14/1848	22	343	N	
Hettersheimer, Wilhelm	33	Bavaria	Y	Havre	New Orleans	02/28/1852	09/29/1854	10	309	N	
Hettersheimer, William	33	Bavaria	Y	Havre	New Orleans	02/28/1852	09/39/1854	12	248	N	
Hettinger, Lorenz	22	Baden	Y	Havre	New York	08/08/1847	08/23/1848	22	236	N	
Hetz, George	37	Germany	N	Bremen	New York	04/02/1868	?				Y
Hetzelberger, Andreas	21	Wurttemberg	Y	Bremen	New York	01/07/1854	05/22/1854	8	489	N	
Hetzner, George	30	Bavaria	Y	Bremen	Baltimore	05/26/1850	09/08/1852	25	419	N	
Heubeck, John George	22	Germany	Y	Bremen	New York	11/15/1883	04/02/1889				Y
Heuberger, Xavier	32	Baden	Y	Havre	New York	08/01/1853	10/02/1856	14	143	N	
Heubner, Ernst	25	Germany	Y	Bremen	New York	09/23/1892	06/17/1896				Y
Heuck, Hermann	38	Germany	Y	Antwerp	New York	03/29/1888	03/17/1898				Y
Heuck, Hubert	21	Bavaria	Y	Havre	New York	05/02/1854	03/08/1856	26	173	N	
Heuckmann, Bernard	21	Holland	Y	Havre	New York	07/22/1854	08/20/1857	15	161	N	
Heuer, August	30	Germany	Y	Bremen	Baltimore	06/16/1882	10/06/1885				Y
Heuer, Ferdinand	25	Prussia	Y	Rotterdam	New York	10/19/1854	06/29/1857	15	114	N	
Heuer, Fritz	33	Germany	Y	Bremen	New York	06/28/1881	10/29/1888	19	196	N	
Heuer, Fritz	33	Germany	Y	Bremen	New York	06/28/1881	10/29/1888				Y
Heuer, Henry	28	Hanover	Y	Bremen	New Orleans	12/01/1848	01/21/1852	24	50	N	
Heuer, William	50	Germany	Y	Bremen	New York	11/15/1881	10/23/1888	19	168	N	
Heuke, Henry	25	Prussia	Y	Bremen	New Orleans	12/06/1851	04/01/1856	26	395	N	
Heule, John	27	Holland	Y	Rotterdam	New York	05/11/1854	02/04/1856	26	30	N	
Heulmann, Henry	??	Holland	Y	?	?	?	11/07/1892				Y
Heulse, Balz Henry	37	Hanover	Y	Bremen	New York	12/02/1853	02/23/1858	16	334	N	
Heumisch, Charles Freder	43	Baden	Y	Havre	New Orleans	12/20/1849	03/16/1850	2	199	N	
Heun, John	35	Nassau	Y	Antwerp	New York	12/18/1854	09/16/1857	15	272	N	
Heuning, Henry	27	Prussia	Y	Bremen	New Orleans	11/20/1844	10/11/1848	1	151	N	
Heunnecke, Ludwig	27	Oldenburg	Y	Bremen	New York	08/15/1857	02/23/1858	16	333	N	
Heuschling, Frank	29	Luxemburg	Y	Antwerp	New York	05/22/1882	01/04/1887				Y
Heuser, Charles	??	Germany	Y	?	?	?	11/01/1894				Y
Heusler, Sebastian	38	Bavaria	Y	Bremen	New York	11/30/1848	03/20/1853	7	260	N	
Heusmann, Joseph	25	Oldenburg	Y	Bremen	Baltimore	08/06/1856	07/27/1858	16	533	N	
Heuss, Gustav	29	Germany	Y	Antwerp	New York	02/10/1884	09/13/1887				Y
Heusser, Oscar W.	25	Germany	Y	?	?	10/30/1884	10/08/1892				Y
Heussing, Franz	??	Germany	Y	?	?	?	12/05/1891				Y
Heuszler, John	28	Wurttemberg	Y	Bremen	New York	04/16/1852	04/17/1854	9	27	N	
Heutel, Benedict	53	Germany	Y	Bremen	New York	03/09/1879	10/31/1884				Y
Heutle, George	48	Germany	Y	Antwerp	New York	02/02/1868	05/08/1882				Y
Heutschel, Robert	30	Germany	Y	Hamburg	New York	07/16/1883	10/24/1888				Y
Hevey, Denis	39	Ireland	Y	Liverpool	New Orleans	06/08/1852	11/27/1852	5	351	N	
Hewicker, Hermann	22	Prussia	Y	Bremen	New Orleans	11/02/1852	10/09/1854	6	49	N	
Hewiker, Herman	32	Prussia	Y	Bremen	New Orleans	11/15/1852	10/09/1854	11	50	N	

CITIZENSHIP RECORDS

APPLICANT	AGE	COUNTRY OF ORIGIN	DEC	DEPART PORT	ENTRY PORT	ARRIVE DATE	DEC DATE	VOL	PG.	FLD	NAT DATE
Hewitt, William	45	England	Y	Liverpool	Detroit	10/30/1872	05/29/1888			Y	
Hewson, James T.	??	England	Y	?	?	?	09/17/1864			Y	
Hexter, Max	35	Germany	Y	?	?	05/09/1881	10/19/1889			Y	
Hey, August	29	Germany	Y	Bremen	Baltimore	05/01/1888	02/21/1891			Y	
Hey, Christopher	48	Oldenburg	Y	Rotterdam	New Orleans	12/16/1844	10/06/1848	22	451	N	
Heydecker, Henry	44	Hanover	Y	Bremen	Baltimore	09/15/1844	10/02/1856	14	157	N	
Heyden, Patrick	28	Ireland	Y	Liverpool	Baltimore	03/07/1847	03/01/1851	3	182	N	
Heydrich, Theodore	40	Prussia	Y	Hamburg	New York	05/??/1853	11/06/1856	14	499	N	
Heyer, Bernard	49	Prussia	Y	Rotterdam	New Orleans	03/17/1846	02/13/1849	23	77	N	
Heyer, Franz	29	Bavaria	Y	Havre	New York	10/18/1849	04/18/1854	9	63	N	
Heyerhoff, Victor	29	Germany	Y	Hagen	New York	06/13/1890	06/09/1892			Y	
Heyl, Ben	43	Germany	Y	Bremen	Baltimore	10/06/1866	09/26/1885			Y	
Heyl, Henry	38	Prussia	Y	Bremen	Baltimore	07/07/1844	07/05/1851	3	499	N	
Heylen, Louis	27	Belgium	Y	Antwerp	New York	05/??/1848	02/07/1856	26	62	N	
Heymes, Victor	52	Germany	Y	Havre	New York	11/04/1894	01/11/1898			Y	
Heyn, John	35	Hesse Darmsta	Y	Bremen	New York	07/09/1852	07/09/1856	14	301	N	
Heyne, Richard	31	Germany	Y	Bremen	New York	06/28/1879	12/24/1888			Y	
Heynen, William	42	Germany	Y	Bremen	Hoboken	11/07/1879	05/22/1885			Y	
Heyroth, Hugh	26	Prussia	Y	Hamburg	New York	08/??/1849	12/??/1850	2	412	N	
Heyroth, Hugh	26	Prussia	Y	Hamburg	New York	08/21/1849	12/28/1850			Y	
Hezinger, Gottlieb	40	Germany	Y	Hamburg	New York	04/24/1870	09/24/1885			Y	
Hiabur, Carl	50	Wuerttemberg	Y	Havre	New York	06/24/1856	03/24/1860	27	135	N	
Hibbert, Alfred	27	England	Y	Liverpool	New York	10/09/1853	10/09/1854	6	138	N	
Hibbert, John	26	England	Y	Liverpool	New York	04/04/1848	07/07/1851	3	502	N	
Hickethier, Charles Egmo	35	Saxe Weimar	Y	Hamburg	New York	09/30/1852	07/10/1856	14	307	N	
Hickey, ?	??	?	Y	?	New Orleans	??/17/18??	10/30/1850	2	332	N	
Hickey, Andrew	30	Ireland	Y	Liverpool	New Orleans	12/25/1850	11/03/1852	5	202	N	
Hickey, Andrew	30	Ireland	Y	Liverpool	New Orleans	12/25/1850	11/03/1852	6	328	N	
Hickey, John	25	Ireland	Y	Liverpool	New Orleans	11/25/1850	04/04/1853	8	5	N	
Hickey, John	25	Ireland	Y	Liverpool	New York	10/28/1854	10/24/1857	15	487	N	
Hickey, Thomas	27	Ireland	Y	Liverpool	New York	04/22/1848	07/25/1851	4	35	N	
Hickey, William	35	Ireland	Y	Liverpool	New York	07/08/1848	10/18/1852	5	2	N	
Hickey, William	22	Ireland	Y	Liverpool	New Orleans	11/25/18??	09/26/1854	10	236	N	
Hickey, William	22	Ireland	Y	Liverpool	New Orleans	11/25/1851	90/26/1854	12	175	N	
Hickman, Issac	35	England	Y	Liverpool	New Orleans	12/26/1850	11/19/1852	5	309	N	
Hieber, Frank Anton	47	Wurttemberg	Y	London	New York	12/10/1852	10/09/1852	11	53	N	
Hieber, Franz Anton	47	Wurttemberg	Y	London	New York	10/10/1852	10/09/1854	6	52	N	
Hieman, Jacob	26	Bavaria	Y	Bremen	New York	??/20/1844	02/26/1850	2	129	N	
Hiestand, Henry	34	Switzerland	Y	Havre	New York	05/22/1854	06/12/1854	10	121	N	
Hiestand, Henry	34	Switzerland	Y	Havre	New York	05/22/1854	06/12/1854	12	58	N	
Higgins, John	51	Ireland	Y	Liverpool	New York	01/27/1865	09/25/1895			Y	
Higgins, Lawrence	21	Ireland	Y	Youghall	New York	08/07/1849	01/??/1850	23	454	N	
Higgins, Patrick	??	Ireland	Y	?	New York	??/23/18??	10/28/1850	2	322	N	
Higgins, Patrick J.	24	Ireland	Y	Liverpool	New Orleans	03/10/1854	12/28/1855	13	378	N	
Higgins, Thomas	25	Ireland	Y	Liverpool	New York	06/28/1857	11/01/1860	27	545	N	
Higgins, Thomas	45	Ireland	Y	Liverpool	New York	11/07/1859	02/09/1882			Y	
Highes, Thomas	30	Wales	Y	Liverpool	New York	??/08/1845	02/11/1850	2	57	N	
Highgate, John	27	Scotland	Y	Glasgow	New York	07/06/1848	01/02/1851	2	442	N	
Highland, Michael	28	Ireland	Y	Queenstown	New York	10/10/1880	03/17/1884			Y	
Highland, Michael	35	Ireland	Y	Queenstown	New York	07/26/1884	11/02/1889			Y	
Hiland, John C.	26	Ireland	Y	Dublin	New York	08/29/1847	03/11/1853	7	322	N	
Hilberg, John	33	Kurhessen	Y	Bremen	Baltimore	06/26/1853	12/01/1858	17	367	N	
Hilbert, Alfred	27	England	Y	Liverpool	New York	06/09/1853	10/09/1854	11	141	N	
Hilbert, Benjamin	25	Prussia	Y	Hamburg	New York	09/13/1856	10/09/1857	15	381	N	
Hilbert, John	21	Baden	Y	Havre	New York	09/07/1847	02/17/1849	23	161	N	
Hilbert, Michael	35	Baden	Y	Havre	New York	05/01/1851	02/06/1856	26	51	N	
Hilbert, Peter	29	Germany	Y	Antwerp	New York	07/16/1890	11/03/1892			Y	
Hilckmann, Paul	39	Germany	Y	Bremen	Baltimore	07/??/1868	05/29/1882			Y	
Hild, Michael	42	Austria	Y	Hamburg	New York	02/07/1883	08/02/1884			Y	

CITIZENSHIP RECORDS

APPLICANT	AGE	COUNTRY OF ORIGIN	DEC	DEPART PORT	ENTRY PORT	ARRIVE DATE	DEC DATE	VOL	PG.	FLD	NAT DATE
Hildebrand, Edward	28	Prussia	Y	Bremen	New York	07/04/1852	04/26/1853	8	226	N	
Hildebrandt, Henry	32	Prussia	Y	Hamburg	New York	08/01/1866	10/04/1872	18	524	N	
Hildebrandt, Ludwig F. E	52	Hesse Cassel	Y	Bremen	Baltimore	10/10/1848	02/12/1849	23	64	N	
Hildebrecht, Theodore	29	Brunswick	Y	Bremen	New York	08/18/1848	12/26/1851	24	5	N	
Hildemann, Frederick Cur	33	Germany	Y	Bremen	New York	05/13/1882	06/18/1885			Y	
Hildenbrand, Anton	26	Germany	Y	Antwerp	New York	06/10/1888	04/13/1891			Y	
Hilebrandt, Frintz	35	Prussia	Y	Bremen	New York	10/03/1852	10/10/1854	6	235	N	
Hilfinger, Joseph	??	Germany	Y	?	?	03/??/1897	05/05/1892			Y	
Hilgar, Henry	36	Prussia	Y	Bremen	New York	05/17/1846	04/14/1852	24	501	N	
Hilge, William	44	Prussia	Y	Bremen	New York	07/17/1846	04/17/1854	8	188	N	
Hilge, William	48	Germany	Y	Bremen	Balttimore	06/02/1883	10/19/1896			Y	
Hilgefort, Bernhard	32	Germany	Y	Bremen	New York	05/10/1884	05/01/1889			Y	
Hilgemaier, Herman	26	Prussia	Y	Bremen	New York	06/01/1857	09/28/1860	27	381	N	
Hilgemann, Henry	25	Germany	Y	Hamburg	New York	09/15/1884	03/12/1885			Y	
Hilgemann, Henry	49	Germany	N	Bremen	New York	08/13/1860	?			Y	
Hilgemann, William	28	Prussia	Y	Bremen	New Orleans	11/26/1849	10/16/1857	15	435	N	
Hilgenauer, Frederick	33	Prussia	Y	Bremen	Baltimore	11/09/1840	10/05/1848	22	430	N	
Hilger, Ernst	40	Prussia	Y	Bremen	New York	05/17/1846	04/14/1852	24	502	N	
Hilger, George	26	Germany	Y	Rotterdam	New York	12/10/1883	02/09/1886			Y	
Hilger, William	44	Prussia	Y	Bremen	New York	07/17/1746	04/17/1854	9	59	N	
Hilker, Rudolph H.	31	Hanover	Y	Bremen	New York	11/23/1847	03/10/1853	7	319	N	
Hilker,, Henry W.	24	Germany	Y	Glasgow	New York	09/01/1893	10/14/1895			Y	
Hilkert, Jacob	45	Wurttemberg	Y	Havre	New York	05/20/1852	06/29/1857	15	116	N	
Hill, John	22	Ireland	Y	Canada	Buffalo	??/20/1849	12/26/1850	2	390	N	
Hill, John	27	Kurhassen	Y	Bremen	New York	05/31/1848	04/09/1853	24	428	N	
Hill, Joseph	42	England	Y	Liverpool	New York	08/14/1880	08/27/1888			Y	
Hill, Richard	30	Ireland	Y	Liverpool	New York	09/08/1848	09/14/1852	25	497	N	
Hill, Richard C.	??	England	Y	?	?	?	06/25/1890			Y	
Hill, William G.	25	Wales	Y	Liverpool	Philadelphia	04/28/1888	06/23/1891			Y	
Hill, William	28	Ireland	Y	Liverpool	New York	06/23/1840	03/26/1853	7	413	N	
Hille, Albert	27	Germany	Y	Bremen	New York	11/06/1881	01/02/1884			Y	
Hillebrand, Fred	35	Prussia	Y	Bremen	New York	10/03/1852	10/10/1854	11	238	N	
Hillebrand, George Josep	??	Prussia	Y	Bremen	New Orleans	12/13/18??	10/09/1848	1	96	N	
Hillebrand, Leopold	29	Prussia	Y	Hamburg	New York	06/01/1849	12/07/1852	5	389	N	
Hillebrandt, August	37	Germany	Y	Bremen	New York	11/19/1884	09/27/1892			Y	
Hillebrandt, Henry	66	Germany	N	Bremen	New York	07/04/1852	?			Y	
Hillen, Henri	36	Germany	Y	Bremen	New York	09/22/1877	05/25/1882			Y	
Hillen, John	22	Ireland	Y	Liverpool	New York	??/26/18?3	04/16/1855	11	251	N	
Hillenhinrich, Joseph	23	Germany	Y	Amsterdam	New York	11/26/1884	09/29/1884			Y	
Hiller, Albert	33	Germany	Y	Bremen	New York	03/19/1884	03/10/1890			Y	
Hiller, Benedict Leonhar	36	Germany	Y	Hamburg	New York	10/04/1882	10/29/1887			Y	
Hiller, Christian	34	Germany	Y	Antwerp	Philadelphia	10/03/1880	10/03/1881			Y	
Hiller, Conrad	26	Germany	Y	Antwerp	New York	08/07/1880	08/23/1883			Y	
Hiller, Emil	33	Switzerland	Y	Havre	New York	05/23/1881	10/21/1895			Y	
Hiller, Gottlieb	21	Germany	Y	Havre	New York	05/27/1880	04/23/1883			Y	
Hiller, Gustav	28	Wuerttemberg	Y	Havre	New York	04/25/1854	07/31/1860	27	241	N	
Hillman, Henry S.	21	Russia	Y	Hamburg	New York	05/07/1892	10/22/1895			Y	
Hillmantel, Henry	26	Bavaria	Y	Rotterdam	New York	08/10/1850	04/10/1852	24	435	N	
Hilmer, Christ	40	Germany	Y	Bremen	Baltimore	05/15/1884	07/31/1890			Y	
Hilpoltsteiner, Frank	24	Bavaria	Y	Bremen	Baltimore	11/09/1849	10/09/1854	11	91	N	
Hilpoltsteiner, Franz	24	Bavaria	Y	Bremen	Baltimore	11/09/1849	10/09/1854	6	89	N	
Hilshorst, Henry	??	Prussia	Y	Bremen	Baltimore	09/04/18??	10/11/1848	1	130	N	
Hilsinger, Henry	40	Switzerland	Y	Havre	New York	03/??/1850	03/21/1853	7	356	N	
Hilsinger, Michael	54	Germany	N	Havre	New York	09/??/1857	?			Y	
Hilt, George	47	Germany	Y	Bremen	New York	08/25/1877	11/02/1894			Y	
Hiltenbrand, Leon	22	Germany	Y	Havre	New York	03/01/1883	10/30/1886			Y	
Hiltmann, Henry	49	Germany	Y	Coppenhagen	New York	04/09/1880	04/24/1882			Y	
Hilvert, Theodore	41	Germany	Y	Hamburg	New York	04/23/1870	02/11/1891			Y	
Hilwerth, Christian	23	Saxony	Y	Bremen	Baltimore	11/06/1848	03/15/1851	3	279	N	

CITIZENSHIP RECORDS

APPLICANT	AGE	COUNTRY OF ORIGIN	DEC	DEPART PORT	ENTRY PORT	ARRIVE DATE	DEC DATE	VOL	PG.	FLD	NAT DATE
Himmelfarb, N.	30	Russia	Y	Antwerp	New York	11/21/1881	06/14/1883			Y	
Himmelhan, Phillip Josep	34	Baden	Y	Havre	New York	05/01/1844	08/17/1848	22	202	N	
Himserth, Joseph	29	Hanover	Y	Bremen	New York	06/??/1851	10/29/1858	17	168	N	
Hinan, George	26	Hanover	Y	Bremen	New Orleans	12/01/1848	08/15/1851	4	144	N	
Hinan, Henry	42	Hanover	Y	Bremen	New Orleans	12/01/1848	08/15/1851	4	145	N	
Hinan, Julius	50	Germany	N	Bremen	Baltimore	11/11/1865	?			Y	
Hinchco, Benyan	27	England	Y	Liverpool	New York	05/19/1850	02/05/1856	26	42	N	
Hinchy, Thomas	42	Ireland	Y	Lewistown	Niagra	11/20/1850	09/20/1858	16	193	N	
Hinderberger, Martin	30	Germany	Y	?	New York	??/??/1882	04/14/1884			Y	
Hinderer, A.G.	23	Germany	Y	Bremen	New York	09/29/1882	12/26/1885	19	28	N	
Hinderer, A.G.	23	Germany	Y	Bremen	New York	08/29/1882	12/28/1885			Y	
Hine, Charles	29	Prussia	Y	Bremen	New York	08/31/1854	02/18/1857	15	33	N	
Hines, Edmund	64	Ireland	Y	Liverpool	New Orleans	04/28/1852	03/23/1853	7	382	N	
Hines, John	32	Ireland	Y	Waterford	New York	06/06/1851	09/24/1857	15	311	N	
Hines, Patrick	54	Ireland	Y	Liverpool	New Orleans	12/18/1849	03/23/1853	7	381	N	
Hines, Peter	30	Hanover	Y	Bremen	Baltimore	02/12/1845	05/06/1850	3	52	N	
Hines, Theodore	31	Oldenburg	Y	Bremen	New York	06/??/1847	05/24/1852	25	101	N	
Hinghaus, Bernhard Henry	31	Germany	Y	Bremen	New York	08/26/1879	06/15/1888			Y	
Hinghaus, Francis Henry	30	Hanover	Y	Bremen	New Orleans	11/15/1853	02/18/1857	15	30	N	
Hinkeler, John	28	France	Y	Havre	New Orleans	04/11/1850	08/23/1852	25	335	N	
Hinkelmann, Louis	23	Bavaria	Y	Havre	New York	05/26/1850	04/21/1853	8	91	N	
Hinken, Gert	41	Prussia	Y	Bremen	New Orleans	05/18/1849	10/10/1854	6	238	N	
Hinken, Gert	41	Prussia	Y	Bremen	New Orleans	05/18/1849	10/10/1854	11	241	N	
Hinking, Henry	22	Hanover	Y	Bremen	Baltimore	06/20/1849	08/15/1851	4	143	N	
Hinnah, W.	22	Germany	Y	Bremen	New York	10/02/1880	10/04/1883			Y	
Hinnan, Gerhard	21	Prussia	Y	Bremen	New York	12/24/1855	12/17/1857	16	231	N	
Hinnan, Gustav Adolph	23	Prussia	Y	Bremen	New Orleans	12/19/1855	12/17/1857	16	230	N	
Hinnekamp, August	33	Germany	Y	Bremen	Baltimore	11/18/1883	01/04/1888			Y	
Hinnekamp, George	57	Germany	N	Bremen	Baltimore	05/??/1853	?			Y	
Hinnen, Emanuel	28	Switzerland	Y	Antwerp	New Orleans	03/??/1850	03/21/1853	7	364	N	
Hinnenkamp, Gerhard Henr	26	Hanover	Y	Bremen	Baltimore	05/24/1854	09/03/1857	15	224	N	
Hinnenkamp, Joseph	26	Germany	Y	Amsterdam	New York	06/10/1882	06/05/1885			Y	
Hinnors, Henry	45	Hanover	Y	Bremen	New Orleans	10/18/1846	03/09/1850	2	176	N	
Hinrichs, Frederick	27	Germany	Y	?	New York	??/??/1872	09/25/1880			Y	
Hinrichs, Tobe	52	Germany	Y	Bremen	Baltimore	05/27/1880	11/01/1893	21	47	N	
Hinsel, Charles	36	Germany	Y	Hamburg	New York	06/29/1887	09/22/1892			Y	
Hinternesch, Frederick	??	Germany	Y	?	Baltimore	??/??/1880	03/20/1885			Y	
Hintz, John Charles	36	Denmark	Y	Hamburg	New Orleans	12/25/1846	10/04/1848	1	51	N	
Hinz, F.W.	33	Germany	Y	Bremen	New York	06/??/1872	10/23/1883			Y	
Hinz, Herrmann	29	Germany	Y	Hamburg	New York	02/07/1881	11/01/1887			Y	
Hippe, Henry	23	Germany	Y	Bremen	New York	06/03/1882	10/30/1888	19	205	N	
Hippe, Henry	23	Germany	Y	Bremen	New York	06/03/1882	10/30/1888			Y	
Hirlinger, Hermann	21	Germany	Y	Havre	New York	11/19/1886	01/16/1888			Y	
Hirlinger, Joseph	33	Germany	Y	Bremen	New York	04/14/1892	10/28/1895			Y	
Hirlinger, Matthias	35	Germany	Y	Havre	New York	03/30/1891	10/15/1896			Y	
Hirlinger, Silver	35	Hohenzollern	Y	Havre	New Orleans	04/28/1852	07/16/1855	11	389	N	
Hirn, Franz V.	28	Germany	Y	Bremen	New York	10/26/1881	03/23/1885			Y	
Hirn, John	23	Germany	Y	Bremen	New York	12/04/1882	05/23/1883			Y	
Hirsch, August	40	Germany	Y	Hamburg	New York	08/30/1883	10/17/1892	19	367	N	
Hirsch, August	40	Germany	Y	Hamburg	New York	08/30/1883	10/17/1892			Y	
Hirsch, Edmond	??	Germany	Y	?	?	?	08/38/1890			Y	
Hirsch, Felix	37	France	Y	Havre	New York	09/03/1840	02/25/1856	26	128	N	
Hirsch, George	23	Germany	Y	Bremen	New York	05/21/1886	09/13/1887			Y	
Hirsch, Henry	28	Wurttemberg	Y	Havre	New York	08/20/1840	03/02/1850	2	149	N	
Hirsch, Ike	31	Austria	Y	Hamburg	New York	11/22/1891	01/04/1896			Y	
Hirsch, Jacob	28	Wurttemberg	Y	Havre	New York	09/17/1848	07/11/1851	3	519	N	
Hirsch, Jacob	42	Bavaria	Y	Havre	New Orleans	02/??/1855	02/16/1861	18	102	N	
Hirsch, Nicholas	31	Bavaria	Y	Havre	New York	10/20/1846	10/21/1854	10	352	N	
Hirsch, Nicholaus	31	Bavaria	Y	Havre	New York	10/20/1846	10/02/1854	12	291	N	

CITIZENSHIP RECORDS

APPLICANT	AGE	COUNTRY OF ORIGIN	DEC	DEPART PORT	ENTRY PORT	ARRIVE DATE	DEC DATE	VOL	PG.	FLD	NAT DATE
Hirsch, Peter Jacob	63	Germany	N	Havre	New York	05/??/1844	?	28	306	N	03/25/1850
Hirsch, Phillip	25	Bavaria	Y	Havre	New York	07/28/1846	02/14/1849	23	100	N	
Hirsch, Samson	24	Wurttemberg	Y	London	New York	07/15/1849	09/30/1854	10	318	N	
Hirsch, Samson	24	Wurttemberg	Y	London	New York	07/15/1849	09/30/1854	12	257	N	
Hirsch, Simon	27	Germany	Y	Havre	New York	12/24/1888	08/26/1896			Y	
Hirschauer, Paul	66	Prussia	N	Havre	New York	04/02/1852	?			Y	
Hirschberg, Isador	61	Germany	N	Hamburg	New York	12/25/1866	?			Y	
Hirschberger, Christian	28	Germany	Y	Bremen	New York	11/30/1899	09/20/1897			Y	
Hirschfeld, Carl Theodor	48	Germany	Y	Bremen	New York	11/01/1882	10/28/1887			Y	
Hirschfeld, Isaac	36	Russia	Y	Hamburg	New York	04/17/1885	03/14/1890			Y	
Hirschle, Julius	29	Wuerttemberg	Y	Bremen	Baltimore	08/16/1858	09/28/1860	27	385	N	
Hirschmann, George	25	Wurttemberg	Y	Havre	New York	11/20/1853	05/18/1854	8	470	N	
Hirschmann, George	25	Wurttemberg	Y	Havre	New York	11/20/1853	05/18/1854	9	344	N	
Hirschmann, Joseph	50	Russia	Y	Rotterdam	New York	06/12/1889	06/02/1893			Y	
Hirst, James	28	England	Y	Liverpool	New York	03/26/1848	02/27/1852	24	178	N	
Hirt, Albert	41	Germany	Y	Rotterdam	New York	04/14/1884	10/29/1886			Y	
Hirt, Conrad	22	Germany	Y	Havre	New York	05/22/1885	10/17/1889			Y	
Hirt, Francis Xaver	22	Baden	Y	Havre	New York	09/12/1853	06/02/1856	14	276	N	
Hirt, John	28	Germany	Y	Rotterdam	New York	03/03/1881	08/15/1889			Y	
Hirtes, John	48	Bavaria	Y	Bremen	New York	05/01/1849	10/07/1854	6	3	N	
Hirtes, John	48	Bavaria	Y	Bremen	New York	05/01/1849	10/07/1854	11	4	N	
Hirth, Jacob	23	Bavaria	Y	Havre	New Orleans	12/25/1846	11/04/1851	4	485	N	
Hirth, Otto	31	Germany	Y	Bremen	New York	03/03/1883	12/02/1890			Y	
Hirttig, Charles W.	27	England	Y	Canada	Lockport	10/??/1849	11/04/1856	14	465	N	
Hirtzel, Mathias	24	Baden	Y	Antwerp	New York	08/16/1851	06/05/1854	12	20	N	
Hirtzel, Philipp	??	Germany	Y	?	?	?	10/21/1879			Y	
Hirzel, Mathias	24	Baden	Y	Amsterdam	New York	08/16/1851	06/05/1854	10	83	N	
Hirzel, Mathias	48	Baden	Y	Liverpool	New Orleans	11/29/1851	06/05/1854	10	84	N	
Hirzel, Mathias	48	Baden	Y	Liverpool	New Orleans	11/29/1851	06/05/1854	12	21	N	
Hiss, Charles Frederick	23	Baden	Y	Havre	New York	08/09/1854	10/27/1857	15	497	N	
Hitzelberger, Andreas	21	Wurttemberg	Y	Bremen	New York	01/07/1854	05/22/1854	9	363	N	
Hitzemann, Ernst Henry	50	Lippe Schauen	Y	Bremen	New Orleans	10/10/1852	04/26/1854	8	267	N	
Hitzemann, Ernst Henry	50	Lippe Schauen	Y	Bremen	New Orleans	10/10/1852	04/25/1854	9	138	N	
Hitzfeld, Joseph	24	Germany	Y	Havre	New York	07/01/1887	10/29/1887			Y	
Hitzman, Michael	29	Bavaria	Y	Havre	New Orleans	06/04/1846	11/14/1848	1	288	N	
Hjermstad, B.S.	25	Norway	Y	Christiania	New York	11/??/1890	08/19/1896			Y	
Hlubik, John	29	Hungaria	Y	Svedernik	Baltimore	01/??/1888	10/02/1889			Y	
Hoar, Bartholomew	30	Ireland	Y	Liverpool	New York	05/25/1849	12/21/1852	5	437	N	
Hoare, Patrick	30	Ireland	Y	Galway	New York	05/17/1857	04/03/1861	18	127	N	
Hoban, James	40	Ireland	Y	Liverpool	New Orleans	06/09/1849	?	25	321	N	
Hoban, John	70	Ireland	N	Dublin	New Orleans	05/??/1846	10/??/1847	28	334	N	10/??/1851
Hoban, John	24	Ireland	N	Dublin	New Orleans	05/00/1846	10/00/1847			Y	10/00/1851
Hoban, Martin L.	47	Ireland	Y	Dublin	?	05/26/1863	03/31/1887			Y	
Hobbin, Patrick	26	Ireland	Y	Liverpool	New York	10/17/1847	10/06/1856	14	223	N	
Hobell, Christian	30	Hanover	Y	Bremen	New York	11/02/1853	02/23/1856	26	116	N	
Hoberg, Ludwig	57	Germany	Y	Bremen	Baltimore	04/21/1891	07/22/1896			Y	
Hoborken, Joseph	??	Germany	Y	?	?	?	04/21/1887			Y	
Hobson, Matthew	32	England	Y	Liverpool	New York	03/17/1879	11/05/1888	19	219	N	
Hoch, Frank	33	Germany	Y	Hamburg	New York	05/18/1878	10/08/1884			Y	
Hochenlertner, Joseph	??	Bavaria	Y	?	?	??/??/18??	10/26/1850	2	313	N	
Hochscheid, Johann	60	Germany	Y	Havre	New York	04/13/1884	05/04/1889			Y	
Hochstetter, Alex	44	Germany	Y	Bremen	New York	06/25/1885	06/02/1896			Y	
Hochstetter, William	21	Wurttemberg	Y	Havre	New York	05/22/1854	12/11/1857	16	215	N	
Hock, Conrad	31	Germany	Y	Bremen	New York	04/01/1881	10/22/1889			Y	
Hock, George	32	Germany	N	Hamburg	New York	04/22/1868	?			Y	
Hock, George Adam	27	Bavaria	Y	Antwerp	New York	04/13/1857	08/27/1857	15	193	N	
Hock, Jacob	36	Bavaria	Y	Antwerp	New York	07/02/1848	11/01/1852	5	85	N	
Hock, John	45	Hesse Darmsta	Y	Havre	New Orleans	12/28/1846	08/28/1848	22	264	N	
Hock, Louis	33	Germany	Y	Antwerp	New York	04/18/1880	05/??/1880			Y	

CITIZENSHIP RECORDS

APPLICANT	AGE	COUNTRY OF ORIGIN	DEC	DEPART PORT	ENTRY PORT	ARRIVE DATE	DEC DATE	VOL	PG.	FLD	NAT DATE
Hock, Louis	33	Germany	N	Antwerp	New York	04/18/1881	?			Y	
Hocker, Dieck	30	Hanover	Y	Bremen	New Orleans	12/25/1850	11/02/1860	27	552	N	
Hockmann, Conrad Henry	25	Hanover	Y	Bremen	Baltimore	11/05/1853	10/10/1854	11	235	N	
Hockmann, Fritz	31	Hanover	Y	Bremen	New Orleans	11/04/1848	08/04/1851	4	86	N	
Hoctzel, Jopseh	45	Baiern	Y	Hamburg	New York	12/01/1867	11/27/1871			Y	
Hodapp, Henry	39	Germany	Y	Havre	New York	10/02/1865	12/05/1881			Y	
Hodeck, Oscar	??	Germany	Y	?	?	?	02/25/1889			Y	
Hodeke, Henry	23	Germany	Y	Antwerp	New York	09/12/1879	08/30/1882			Y	
Hodgkinson, George	43	Canada	Y	Canada	Lewiston	04/??/1850	06/05/1854	10	70	N	
Hodgkinson, George	43	Canada	Y	Canada	Lewiston	04/??/1850	06/05/1854	12	7	N	
Hodgson, William W.	40	England	Y	Liverpool	New York	11/09/1886	10/19/1891	19	337	N	
Hodgson, William W.	40	England	Y	Liverpool	New York	11/09/1886	10/19/1891			Y	
Hodler, John	37	Switzerland	Y	Havre	New York	05/13/1884	09/05/1887			Y	
Hoebbel, Frank	27	Germany	Y	Bremen	New York	01/16/1882	07/15/1889			Y	
Hoecker, Adolph	25	Germany	Y	Bremen	New York	08/13/1881	07/05/1883			Y	
Hoecker, John Henry	36	Hanover	Y	Bremen	Baltimore	01/30/1848	02/03/1851	3	81	N	
Hoedebecke, Frederick	21	Oldenburg	Y	Bremen	New Orleans	12/01/1853	10/06/1856	14	233	N	
Hoefenider, Wilhelm	43	Russia	Y	Hamburg	New York	04/08/1893	10/05/1900			Y	
Hoefer, Charles Jr.	??	Germany	N	?	?	05/00/1873				Y	10/28/1892
Hoefer, Herman	40	Germany	Y	Bremen	New York	05/12/1885	02/10/1887			Y	
Hoeffer, Herman	22	Germany	Y	Hamburg	New York	02/06/1882	02/16/1883			Y	
Hoefle, John	38	Germany	Y	Hamburg	New York	06/04/1881	05/08/1885			Y	
Hoegner, Ernst	28	Germany	Y	Antwerp	New York	06/26/1881	01/07/1886			Y	
Hoeh, Adam	58	Germany	Y	Amsterdam	New York	05/28/1882	08/11/1885			Y	
Hoehlein, Frank	37	Germany	N	Bremen	New York	10/11/1872	?			Y	
Hoehn, Jacob	29	Wuerttemberg	Y	Havre	New York	08/04/1860	08/11/1860	27	263	N	
Hoehnberger, William	??	Bavaria	Y	Havre	New York	??/04/1847	??/??/1851	3	225	N	
Hoekzema, Anton	33	Holland	Y	Bremen	New York	02/01/1848	03/01/1852	24	195	N	
Hoell, Philipp	35	Baden	Y	Havre	New York	05/30/1854	10/02/1856	14	150	N	
Hoeller, Christoph Gottl	28	Wuerttemberg	Y	Havre	New Orleans	08/15/1847	08/09/1848	22	84	N	
Hoelscher, Joseph	29	Prussia	Y	Bremen	New York	11/01/1854	04/07/1856	26	454	N	
Hoeltge, Henry Frederick	26	Hanover	Y	Bremen	New Orleans	12/19/1850	12/28/1855	13	382	N	
Hoeltge, John Henry Will	52	Hanover	Y	Bremen	Philadelphia	12/04/1853	12/28/1855	13	381	N	
Hoeltka, Ernst	25	Schoenburg Li	Y	Bremen	New Orleans	02/28/1844	06/12/1852	25	245	N	
Hoeltke, Frederick Chris	23	Lippe Schauen	Y	Bremen	New Orleans	10/10/1852	04/20/1854	8	268	N	
Hoelzen, Henry	22	Oldenburg	Y	Bremen	New Orleans	10/18/1850	10/04/1854	10	418	N	
Hoemmelmeier, Bernard	36	Hanover	Y	Bremen	Baltimore	07/03/1842	10/07/1854	11	42	N	
Hoene, Henry	21	Oldenburg	Y	Bremen	Baltimore	10/25/1854	11/12/1857	16	13	N	
Hoenig, Adolf	52	Austria	Y	Vienna	New York	12/03/1887	04/05/1892			Y	
Hoenig, Eduard	28	Baden	Y	Bremen	New York	01/27/1853	05/31/1854	10	46	N	
Hoening, Frank	36	Oldenburg	Y	Bremen	New Orleans	06/20/1845	11/01/1852	5	169	N	
Hoepfl, Philip	23	Hesse Darmsta	Y	Liverpool	New York	05/18/1854	01/23/1860	27	71	N	
Hoeppke, Ernst	51	Germany	Y	Bremen	New York	07/05/1882	12/21/1892			Y	
Hoermann, William	28	Germany	Y	Bremen	New York	04/10/1889	07/28/1893			Y	
Hoerner, Christoph	23	Bavaria	Y	Havre	New York	11/13/1851	07/18/1855	11	407	N	
Hoerner, Frank	29	Germany	Y	?	New York	08/??/1883	10/11/1884			Y	
Hoerner, George	43	Germany	Y	Bremen	New York	11/13/1874	11/19/1883			Y	
Hoerner, John	22	Bavaria	Y	Havre	New York	10/31/8151	09/26/1856	14	384	N	
Hoerner, Leopold	31	Germany	Y	Antwerp	New York	06/10/1883	06/12/1885			Y	
Hoernle, Frederick	30	Wurttemberg	Y	Havre	New Orleans	04/??/1850	10/27/1851	4	414	N	
Hoernstein, Peter	53	Wurttemberg	Y	Antwerp	New York	12/05/1849	09/08/1857	15	247	N	
Hoersken, William	28	Germany	Y	Antwerp	New York	04/26/1881	12/20/1883			Y	
Hoerstieg, Anton	29	Prussia	Y	Bremen	New Orleans	05/01/1849	04/02/1852	24	351	N	
Hoerth, Paskal	34	Germany	Y	Havre	New York	08/13/1879	10/25/1887			Y	
Hoerth, Thomas	37	Germany	Y	Havre	New York	08/13/1879	01/10/1888			Y	
Hoese, Ernst	25	Prussia	Y	Bremen	Philadelphia	05/01/1852	11/02/1852	5	188	N	
Hoese, Ernst	23	Prussia	Y	Bremen	Philadelphia	05/01/1852	11/02/1852	6	314	N	
Hoesmann, Wilhelm	21	Germany	Y	Bremen	Baltimore	11/01/1880	10/17/1882			Y	
Hoetker, Heinrich	34	Germany	N	Bremen	New York	09/09/1871	?			Y	

CITIZENSHIP RECORDS

APPLICANT	AGE	COUNTRY OF ORIGIN	DEC	DEPART PORT	ENTRY PORT	ARRIVE DATE	DEC DATE	VOL	PG.	FLD	NAT DATE
Hoeveler, Fred	??	Germany	N	?	?	08/25/1882				Y	11/07/1892
Hoeverman, Wm	27	Germany	Y	Antwerp	New York	11/01/1881	10/13/1885			Y	
Hoey, Robert	24	Ireland	Y	Belfast	New Orleans	01/29/1850	04/29/1850	3	28	N	
Hoey, Thomas	57	Ireland	N	Liverpool	New Orleans	12/23/1848	?			Y	
Hoey, Thomas P.	??	England	Y	?	?	?	05/14/1890			Y	
Hof, Otto	43	Switzerland	N	Havre	New Orleans	12/30/1859	?			Y	
Hofeekert, Melchoir	35	Bavaria	Y	Bremen	Baltimore	09/04/1843	02/25/1850	2	127	N	
Hofer, George	28	Germany	Y	Bremen	Baltimore	09/02/1884	04/16/1889			Y	
Hofer, Gotleib	27	Prussia	Y	Bremen	Baltimore	07/08/1848	10/02/1854	10	339	N	
Hofer, Gotleib	27	Prussia	Y	Bremen	Baltimore	07/08/1848	10/02/1854	12	278	N	
Hofer, Gustave	28	Germany	Y	Havre	New York	01/10/1892	03/26/1900			Y	
Hoferkamp, Otto	55	Germany	Y	Bremen	Baltimore	10/??/1864	10/11/1900			Y	
Hoff, Aloysius	37	France	Y	Havre	New York	04/07/1857	08/27/1862	18	409	N	
Hoff, Valentine	26	Bavaria	Y	Havre	New Orleans	03/05/1845	09/08/1848	22	309	N	
Hoffinger, Martin	51	Germany (Aust	Y	Bremen	New York	05/22/1892	12/21/1892			Y	
Hoffman, August	32	Germany	Y	Hamburg	New York	09/25/1890	10/13/1894			Y	
Hoffman, Fiet	71	Bavaria	Y	Bremen	Baltimore	11/27/1845	08/14/1848	22	106	N	
Hoffman, Fred Henry	50	Hesse Darmsta	Y	Bremen	New York	07/17/1852	12/18/1852	5	427	N	
Hoffman, Frederick	33	Bavaria	Y	Havre	New Orleans	10/11/1848	02/10/1853	7	138	N	
Hoffman, Frederick	31	Germany	Y	Rotterdam	?	01/03/1869	05/07/1872			Y	
Hoffman, Frederick	51	Germany	N	Bremen	New York	09/01/1853	?			Y	
Hoffman, Frederick Ludwi	38	Wurttemberg	Y	Havre	New Orleans	02/15/1848	05/07/1850	3	60	N	
Hoffman, George	??	Germany	Y	?	?	?	05/22/1883			Y	
Hoffman, George Peter	24	Bavaria	Y	Havre	New Orleans	03/??/1848	11/??/1849	23	321	N	
Hoffman, Henry	29	Hanover	Y	Bremen	New Orleans	12/24/1837	08/15/1848	22	174	N	
Hoffman, Jacob	37	Napan	Y	Havre	New Orleans	06/14/1848	07/28/1851	4	52	N	
Hoffman, John	28	Bavaria	Y	Havre	New York	12/29/1850	08/??/1851	4	160	N	
Hoffman, John	32	Bavaria	Y	Bremen	New York	09/01/1845	08/14/1848	22	101	N	
Hoffman, John	36	Bavaria	Y	Havre	New York	06/01/1848	08/18/1848	22	205	N	
Hoffman, Lewis	43	Baden	Y	Liverpool	New Orleans	11/25/1852	05/24/1854	9	383	N	
Hoffman, Louis	30	Baden	Y	Havre	New York	12/05/1849	01/20/1853	7	46	N	
Hoffman, Michael	31	Bavaria	Y	Havre	New Orleans	05/18/1848	??/??/1851	3	253	N	
Hoffman, Sebastian	52	Baden	Y	Havre	New Orleans	11/30/1843	07/09/1855	11	355	N	
Hoffmann, Adam	30	Prussia	Y	Antwerp	New York	09/27/1852	11/08/1855	13	193	N	
Hoffmann, Adam	37	Germany	Y	Antwerp	New York	06/19/1889	07/19/1897			Y	
Hoffmann, Anthony	28	Bavaria	Y	Havre	New York	09/16/1849	09/23/1858	16	150	N	
Hoffmann, Anton	40	Germany	Y	Antwerp	New York	06/29/1887	07/13/1892			Y	
Hoffmann, August	44	Germany	Y	Bremen	New York	09/13/1883	10/29/1889			Y	
Hoffmann, August	58	Germany	Y	Liverpool	New York	03/31/1888	07/06/1891			Y	
Hoffmann, Barney	28	Germany	Y	Bremen	Baltimore	07/30/1882	11/03/1888			Y	
Hoffmann, Ben	27	Germany	Y	Hamburg	New York	09/12/1881	10/22/1886			Y	
Hoffmann, Carl	26	Hanover	Y	Hamburg	New York	03/31/1859	12/19/1859	17	509	N	
Hoffmann, Carl O.	39	Germany	Y	Rotterdam	New York	09/17/1881	08/15/1883			Y	
Hoffmann, Charles	34	Germany	Y	Havre	New York	04/20/1880	03/23/1891			Y	
Hoffmann, Christian	25	Bavaria	Y	Havre	New York	05/10/1858	02/14/1860	27	110	N	
Hoffmann, Daniel	25	Bavaria	Y	Havre	New York	05/26/1854	11/15/1858	17	330	N	
Hoffmann, Emilius	22	Hesse Darmsta	Y	Bremen	New York	07/17/1852	03/05/1856	26	165	N	
Hoffmann, Frederick	24	Bavaria	Y	Havre	New York	03/03/1853	09/29/1857	15	332	N	
Hoffmann, Frederick	46	Bavaria	Y	Havre	New York	09/17/1857	08/23/1860	27	308	N	
Hoffmann, Frederick	26	Germany	Y	Havre	New York	05/01/1880	07/22/1884			Y	
Hoffmann, Frederick A.	??	Bavaria	Y	?	?	?	09/05/1866			Y	
Hoffmann, Frederick F.	30	Germany	N	Bremen	Baltimore	08/10/1872	?			Y	
Hoffmann, George	25	Germany	Y	Hamburg	New York	06/28/1879	09/29/1883			Y	
Hoffmann, George Philipp	28	Wurttemberg	Y	Havre	New York	04/07/1854	09/30/1856	14	53	N	
Hoffmann, Henry	59	Germany	N	Bremen	New Orleans	05/06/1849	?			Y	
Hoffmann, Jacob	36	France	Y	Havre	New York	06/24/1852	11/27/1855	13	260	N	
Hoffmann, Jacob	23	Germany	Y	Hamburg	Philadelphia	04/??/1881	10/09/1884			Y	
Hoffmann, Jacob	59	Germany	N	Havre	New York	08/??/1846	?			Y	
Hoffmann, Jacob	47	Germany	Y	Havre	New York	02/09/1865	10/15/1868	28	410	N	

CITIZENSHIP RECORDS

APPLICANT	AGE	COUNTRY OF ORIGIN	DEC	DEPART PORT	ENTRY PORT	ARRIVE DATE	DEC DATE	VOL	PG.	FLD	NAT DATE
Hoffmann, John	28	Hanover	Y	Bremen	New Orleans	12/10/1848	06/28/1851	3	466	N	
Hoffmann, John	27	Germany	Y	Bremen	New York	08/16/1889	10/28/1892			Y	
Hoffmann, John H.	28	Germany	Y	Bremen	New York	05/09/1891	10/09/1896			Y	
Hoffmann, John H. H.	29	Hanover	Y	Bremen	Baltimore	07/15/1845	09/30/1848	22	375	N	
Hoffmann, John Mike	23	Bavaria	Y	Bremen	Baltimore	09/16/1848	10/16/1848	1	237	N	
Hoffmann, Joseph	38	Germany	Y	Hamburg	New York	05/01/1881	02/18/1884			Y	
Hoffmann, Julius	26	Germany	Y	Hamburg	New York	08/??/1883	09/??/1883			Y	
Hoffmann, Julius	32	Germany	N	Hamburg	New York	08/??/1883	?			Y	
Hoffmann, Lewis	24	Russia	Y	Hamburg	New York	11/23/1886	09/11/1889			Y	
Hoffmann, Louis	43	Baden	Y	Liverpool	New Orleans	11/28/1852	05/24/1854	8	509	N	
Hoffmann, Martin	40	Bavaria	Y	Rotterdam	New York	05/01/1847	10/05/1848	22	441	N	
Hoffmann, Mathias	33	Bavaria	Y	Havre	New Orleans	12/28/1846	02/23/1850	2	121	N	
Hoffmann, Nicholas	28	Prussia	Y	Antwerp	New York	08/27/1854	11/01/1858	17	257	N	
Hoffmann, Peter	23	Bavaria	Y	Havre	New York	05/28/1851	02/16/1857	15	18	N	
Hoffmann, Philipp	35	Bavaria	Y	Havre	New Orleans	11/04/1849	09/06/1852	25	386	N	
Hoffmann, W. H.	48	Germany	N	Bremen	Baltimore	12/??/1854	?			Y	
Hoffmann, William	25	Germany	Y	Hamburg	New York	06/01/1882	03/02/1886			Y	
Hoffmeier, Adam	41	Germany	N	Bremen	Baltimore	09/??/1861	?			Y	
Hoffmeister, Ferdinand	59	Germany	N	Antwerp	New York	05/07/1848	?			Y	
Hoffmeister, Henry	26	Hanover	Y	Bremen	New Orleans	05/25/1849	10/09/1854	6	112	N	
Hoffmeister, Henry	26	Hanover	Y	Bremen	New Orleans	05/25/1849	10/09/1854	11	115	N	
Hoffmeister, Herman Henr	31	Hanover	Y	Bremen	Baltimore	09/21/1854	10/01/1856	14	129	N	
Hoffmeister, William	29	Germany	Y	Bremen	New York	04/17/1885	09/06/1892			Y	
Hoffmeyer, Jacob	35	Switzerland	Y	Havre	New Orleans	03/20/1848	03/29/1853	7	458	N	
Hoffmeyer, Otto	31	Germany	Y	Hamburg	New York	02/10/1881	02/21/1887			Y	
Hoffmockel, Francis Edwa	26	Prussia	Y	Bremen	New York	11/29/1845	10/09/1848	22	496	N	
Hoffrogge, Bernard Henry	24	Hanover	Y	Bremen	Baltimore	11/12/1854	10/01/1856	14	83	N	
Hoffrogge, John George	25	Hanover	Y	Bremen	New Orleans	12/25/1852	01/11/1856	13	452	N	
Hoffrogge, John Henry	27	Hanover	Y	Bremen	New Orleans	05/20/1851	06/02/1854	10	57	N	
Hoffstadt, Henry	26	Poland	Y	Hamburg	New York	08/03/1845	01/21/1852	24	48	N	
Hoffstedde, Henry	32	Germany	Y	Bremen	New York	06/14/1878	10/25/1883			Y	
Hoffstedde, Herman	30	Germany	Y	Bremen	Baltimore	05/03/1884	10/20/1886	19	55	N	
Hofken, John	40	Hanover	Y	Bremen	New Orleans	06/03/1847	08/29/1848	22	273	N	
Hofknecht, Frederick	32	Bavaria	Y	Hamburg	New York	08/27/1857	03/08/1858	16	377	N	
Hofman, Charles William	39	Saxony	Y	Hamburg	New York	05/01/1849	01/01/1853	5	494	N	
Hofman, John	26	Germany	Y	?	?	02/09/1890	11/21/1896			Y	
Hofmann, Andrew	27	Bavaria	Y	Hamburg	New York	02/04/1872	04/05/1872	18	488	N	
Hofmann, Anton	28	Bavaria	Y	Havre	New York	01/09/1857	02/19/1862	18	264	N	
Hofmann, Charles	39	Nassau	Y	Havre	New Orleans	03/06/1854	09/25/1858	16	127	N	
Hofmann, Frederick	25	Lippe Detmol	Y	Bremen	New Orleans	01/03/1853	02/16/1856	26	90	N	
Hofmann, J.B.	52	Germany	Y	Bremen	Baltimore	10/23/1873	04/03/1882			Y	
Hofmann, Jacob	28	Germany	Y	Antwerp	New York	04/18/1881	11/27/1883			Y	
Hofmann, Peter	??	Germany	Y	?	?	?	05/15/1882			Y	
Hofmann, Simon	23	Bavaria	Y	Bremen	New York	07/01/1852	08/04/1856	14	327	N	
Hofner, Philip	28	Germany	Y	Rotterdam	New York	04/09/1881	08/31/1888	19	137	N	
Hofrogge, John Henry	27	Hanover	Y	Bremen	New Orleans	05/20/1851	06/02/1854	9	474	N	
Hofstetter, John	??	Switzerland	Y	Havre	New York	02/21/1892	08/17/1896			Y	
Hogan James	30	Ireland	Y	Liverpool	New Orleans	01/01/1854	06/02/1856	14	280	N	
Hogan, Andrew	23	Ireland	Y	Liverpool	New York	02/14/1857	10/19/1857	15	460	N	
Hogan, James	??	Ireland	Y	Dublin	New York	06/10/1848	08/??/1851	4	187	N	
Hogan, James	22	England	Y	Liverpool	New York	09/03/1851	10/17/1851	4	322	N	
Hogan, James	??	Ireland	Y	Liverpool	New Orleans	12/??/18??	11/06/1856	14	493	N	
Hogan, Jeremiah	23	Ireland	Y	Liverpool	New York	07/22/1850	06/02/1856	14	279	N	
Hogan, John	28	Ireland	Y	Queenstown	New York	06/05/1885	09/08/1890			Y	
Hogan, Michael	40	Ireland	Y	Liverpool	New Orleans	01/24/1850	12/31/1852	5	487	N	
Hogan, Patrick	24	Ireland	Y	Liverpool	New York	07/22/1850	06/02/1856	14	281	N	
Hogan, Patrick	40	Ireland	Y	Liverpool	New Orleans	10/15/1852	09/28/1856	16	111	N	
Hogan, Thomas	33	Ireland	Y	Liverpool	New York	05/30/1853	10/22/1857	15	477	N	
Hogan, William	28	Ireland	Y	Limerick	Buffalo	12/16/1845	10/06/1851	4	201	N	

CITIZENSHIP RECORDS

APPLICANT	AGE	COUNTRY OF ORIGIN	DEC	DEPART PORT	ENTRY PORT	ARRIVE DATE	DEC DATE	VOL	PG.	FLD	NAT DATE
Hogarty, Michael	28	Ireland	Y	Liverpool	New York	08/22/1849	08/23/1852	25	324	N	
Hogbin, Thomas	37	England	Y	London	New York	01/01/1838	08/24/1848	22	251	N	
Hogenkamp, John	31	Hanover	Y	Bremen	New York	10/29/1859	11/28/1859	17	485	N	
Hogenkamp, Rudolph	21	Hanover	Y	Bremen	Baltimore	05/28/1854	01/14/1856	13	462	N	
Hogg, Robert	33	England	Y	Liverpool	New Orleans	11/08/1848	03/07/1853	7	302	N	
Hogg, Thomas	33	England	Y	Windsor	Detroit	09/??/1859	??/??/1860			Y	
Hogg, Thomas	66	England	N	Canada	?	09/??/1859	?			Y	
Hoglund, Charles E.	27	Sweden	Y	Christiana	New York	10/31/1880	09/08/1886			Y	
Hogrebe, Fred	57	Germany	Y	Bremen	New York	02/14/1868	11/11/1889			Y	
Hoh, Andreas	25	Germany	Y	Bremen	New York	12/01/1887	08/28/1888			Y	
Hoh, Carl	26	Germany	Y	Bremen	New York	07/02/1880	10/19/1885			Y	
Hohenbrink, Joseph	23	Hanover	Y	Bremen	New Orleans	05/20/1848	03/30/1852	24	337	N	
Hohl, Christian	21	Bavaria	Y	Havre	New York	05/03/1850	03/28/1850	7	420	N	
Hohman, Franz	50	Germany	Y	Bremen	Hoboken	11/30/1873	05/22/1885			Y	
Hohman, George	32	Germany	N	Bremen	Baltimore	07/??/1870	?			Y	
Hohmann, Bruno	35	Germany	Y	Havre	New York	08/03/1883	08/29/1888			Y	
Hohmann, Isaac	27	Bavaria	Y	Havre	New York	10/21/1847	03/18/1851	3	232	N	
Hohmann, John Henry	26	Prussia	Y	New Diep	Baltimore	10/16/1853	04/01/1856	26	401	N	
Hohmann, Moses	29	Bavaria	Y	Havre	New York	10/21/1847	03/18/1851	3	233	N	
Hohne, John	25	Oldenburg	Y	Bremen	Baltimore	09/14/1859	05/22/1861	18	176	N	
Hohneck, Emanuel	22	Austria	Y	Bremen	New Orleans	01/01/1855	10/05/1857	15	350	N	
Hohnhorst, Clemens	21	Germany	Y	Amsterdam	New York	11/10/1886	09/27/1887			Y	
Hohnstedt, Henry	28	Hanover	Y	Bremen	New Orleans	12/25/1846	03/12/1850	2	185	N	
Hohs, Abraham	23	Prussia	Y	Antwerp	New York	08/04/1847	12/20/1850	2	379	N	
Hohweiler, John George	23	Baden	Y	Liverpool	New York	08/13/1853	07/23/1855	11	425	N	
Hok, Jacob	29	Hesse Darmsta	Y	Antwerp	New York	??/??/1843	08/08/1848	22	79	N	
Holan, John	30	Ireland	Y	Liverpool	New Orleans	02/07/1849	10/13/1851	4	225	N	
Holbrock, John J.	41	Germany	Y	Bremen	New York	07/17/1866	06/22/1886			Y	
Holbrook, James J.	??	England	Y	?	?	?	11/20/1882			Y	
Holdan, John	32	Ireland	Y	Liverpool	New Orleans	11/30/1849	02/11/1860	27	99	N	
Holden, William	28	Ireland	Y	Liverpool	New York	01/20/1849	01/17/1853	7	35	N	
Holder, Gottlieb	30	Wuerttenberg	Y	London	New York	07/08/1849	04/09/1852	24	431	N	
Holderbach, Leo	31	Germany	Y	Antwerp	New York	04/21/1889	08/23/1894			Y	
Holdmeyer, Christian	33	Hanover	Y	Bremen	Baltimore	08/21/1848	03/15/1852	24	309	N	
Holdsworth, Benjamin	24	England	Y	Liverpool	New Orleans	05/18/1849	03/08/1852	24	256	N	
Holdt, Dr. G.	42	Russia	Y	Hamburg	New York	05/20/1871	01/18/1872	18	457	N	
Holehan, John	30	Ireland	Y	New Ross	Ogdensburg	07/12/1844	10/13/1851	4	224	N	
Hollaender, Anthony	45	France	Y	Havre	New York	04/20/1877	04/04/1892			Y	
Holland, Nicholas	30	Ireland	Y	Dublin	New Orleans	12/18/1848	11/03/1852	5	204	N	
Holland, Nicolas	30	Ireland	Y	Dublin	New Orleans	12/18/1848	11/03/1852	6	330	N	
Hollander, James	26	Holland	Y	Rotterdam	New Orleans	03/19/1853	08/05/1856	14	356	N	
Holldorf, Heinrich	39	Germany	Y	Bremen	Baltimore	09/05/1888	04/06/1896			Y	
Holle, Charles	28	Lippe Schauen	Y	Bremen	New York	04/29/1849	02/21/1856	26	111	N	
Holle, Christian Frederi	21	Prussia	Y	Bremen	New Orleans	05/28/1851	09/25/1854	10	217	N	
Holle, Christian Frederi	31	Prussia	Y	Bremen	New Orleans	05/28/1851	09/25/1854	12	156	N	
Holle, Frederick William	22	Prussia	Y	Bremen	New Orleans	06/08/1851	10/29/1852	5	63	N	
Holleker, Joseph	??	Prussia	Y	?	?	03/19/1880	10/31/1882			Y	
Hollenbach, Fritz	44	Germany	N	Hamburg	New York	12/24/1865	?			Y	
Hollenbeck, George	55	Germany	Y	Bremen	Baltimore	11/18/1866	09/23/1893			Y	
Hollenkamp, Joseph	25	Germany	Y	Bremen	Baltimore	09/09/1891	10/24/1893			Y	
Holler, John Michel	45	Germany	Y	?	New York	08/16/1881	10/13/1892			Y	
Hollerauer, Otto J.	32	Germany	Y	Antwerp	New York	05/14/1880	07/08/1887			Y	
Hollgrewe, Frederick	53	Germany	Y	Bremen	New York	06/14/1884	11/05/1886	19	127	N	
Hollinden, Barney	36	Germany	Y	Bremen	New York	10/15/1883	11/10/1892			Y	
Hollinger, Leonhardt	56	Wurttemberg	Y	London	New York	10/19/1853	06/12/1854	12	53	N	
Hollingsworth, Edward T.	28	Ireland	Y	Liverpool	New York	05/01/1849	05/01/1854	8	322	N	
Hollingsworth, Edward T.	28	Ireland	Y	Liverpool	New York	05/01/1849	05/01/1854	9	195	N	
Hollkamp, Joseph Henry	32	Prussia	Y	Rotterdam	New York	08/19/1846	10/02/1848	1	37	N	
Hollmann, Anton	21	Prussia	Y	Antwerp	New York	09/05/1852	01/24/1856	13	504	N	

CITIZENSHIP RECORDS

APPLICANT	AGE	COUNTRY OF ORIGIN	DEC	DEPART PORT	ENTRY PORT	ARRIVE DATE	DEC DATE	VOL	PG.	FLD	NAT DATE
Hollmann, Bernard	39	Germany	Y	Bremen	Baltimore	09/01/1883	11/21/1893			Y	
Hollmann, Bernard	27	Prussia	Y	Bremen	New Orleans	05/15/1848	02/21/1849	23	236	N	
Hollmann, Christian F. W	33	Prussia	Y	Bremen	Baltimore	12/15/18??	01/09/1850	23	490	N	
Hollmeyer, Eberhard	34	Germany	N	Bremen	New York	08/07/1869	?			Y	
Hollmeyer, Herman	34	Germany	Y	Bremen	New York	07/09/1869	09/27/1882			Y	
Holloran, Michael	22	Ireland	Y	Liverpool	New Orleans	01/10/1849	03/17/1856	26	210	N	
Hollstein, Christian	25	Bavaria	Y	Havre	New Orleans	03/01/1851	02/21/1853	7	200	N	
Holm, Arthur	35	Germany	Y	Bremen	New York	11/12/1888	03/20/1891			Y	
Holmes, James G.	29	England	Y	Liverpool	New York	09/15/1857	01/23/1861	18	111	N	
Holmes, Johannes	??	Germany	Y	?	?	?	12/09/1892			Y	
Holmes, Solomon	40	England	Y	Liverpool	New York	06/04/1880	03/24/1887			Y	
Holmes, William	33	England	Y	Liverpool	New York	07/06/1841	11/20/1848	1	344	N	
Holms, Robert	25	Ireland	Y	Liverpool	New York	07/16/1853	11/10/1858	17	318	N	
Holocher, William	26	Germany	Y	Antwerp	New York	02/17/1892	10/12/1896			Y	
Holohan, John	33	Ireland	Y	Waterford	Boston	02/22/1866	10/08/1880			Y	
Holohan, Michael	24	Ireland	Y	Dublin	New Orleans	01/01/1850	01/07/1856	13	428	N	
Holshu, Charles	28	Baden	Y	Havre	New Orleans	07/14/1846	09/04/1848	22	296	N	
Holstagge, Heinrich	28	Prussia	Y	Liverpool	New York	07/03/1868	03/29/1872	18	478	N	
Holste, William	21	Hanover	Y	Bremen	Baltimore	11/17/1854	09/25/1857	15	318	N	
Holstein, August	30	Prussia	Y	Hamburg	New York	10/04/1847	11/22/1848	1	376	N	
Holstein, Bernard	22	Germany	Y	Amsterdam	New York	06/31/1889	10/27/1893	21	38	N	
Holstein, Jacob	37	Bavaria	Y	Havre	New Orleans	03/01/1851	05/30/1854	9	459	N	
Holstein, Jacob	37	Bavaria	Y	Havre	New Orleans	03/01/1851	05/31/1854	10	42	N	
Holt, Joseph	38	England	Y	Liverpool	New York	07/04/1842	05/06/1850	3	55	N	
Holters, B. Gerhard	44	Oldenburg	Y	Bremen	New Orleans	12/05/1845	07/27/1848	22	2	N	
Holtgrefe, F. Heinrich	27	Germany	Y	Bremen	Baltimore	08/09/1883	05/11/1887			Y	
Holtgrefe, Fritz	20	Germany	Y	Rotterdam	New York	05/28/1888	08/13/1888			Y	
Holtgreiwe, Herman	27	Prussia	Y	Bremen	New Orleans	11/15/1855	08/21/1860	27	304	N	
Holtgrewe, Henry	25	Germany	Y	Amtserdam	New York	08/18/1885	11/05/1887	19	125	N	
Holtgrewe, Henry	25	Germany	Y	Amsterdam	New York	08/18/1886	11/05/1887			Y	
Holtgriewe, Henry	32	Germany	Y	Bremen	Baltimore	??/??/1865	12/16/1880			Y	
Holthaus, Bernard	50	Oldenburg	Y	Bremen	New Orleans	01/??/1846	10/03/1854	12	333	N	
Holthaus, Bernhard	50	Oldenburg	Y	Bremen	New Orleans	01/??/1846	10/03/1854	10	394	N	
Holthaus, G.	42	Germany	Y	Bremen	New York	03/22/1882	08/16/1884			Y	
Holthaus, Henry	28	Hanover	Y	Bremen	New York	06/01/1847	04/18/1854	8	201	N	
Holthaus, Henry	28	Hanover	Y	Bremen	New York	06/01/1847	04/18/1854	9	72	N	
Holthaus, Herman	26	Germany	Y	Bremen	Baltimore	10/07/1880	09/25/1884			Y	
Holthenrech, Henry	26	Germany	Y	Bremen	Baltimore	10/21/1883	10/09/1888	19	144	N	
Holthenrich, Henry	26	Germany	Y	Bremen	Baltimore	10/21/1883	10/09/1888			Y	
Holthinrichs, H.	32	Germany	Y	Amsterdam	New York	06/??/1880	11/05/1888	19	217	N	
Holthoff, August	45	Germany	Y	Bremen	Baltimore	06/??/1855	05/17/1884			Y	
Holtkamp, George	23	Germany	Y	Bremen	New York	08/09/1889	10/26/1895			Y	
Holtke, Frederick Christ	23	Lippe Schauen	Y	Bremen	New Orleans	10/10/1852	04/25/1854	9	139	N	
Holtke, Frederick Gottli	29	Lippe Schauen	Y	Bremen	Ne Orleans	03/01/1848	04/26/1854	8	266	N	
Holtke, Frederick Gottlo	29	Lippe Schauen	Y	Bremen	New Orleans	03/01/1849	04/25/1854	9	137	N	
Holtmeier, Francis	50	Hanover	Y	Bremen	New Orleans	01/05/1846	10/29/1858	17	174	N	
Holtmeier, Frank	28	Hanover	Y	Bremen	New Orleans	01/01/1847	10/05/1848	22	426	N	
Holtmeier, John	24	Hanover	Y	Bremen	Baltimore	09/29/1842	02/19/1849	23	215	N	
Holtvogt, Charles	45	Germany	Y	Bremen	Baltimore	09/22/1884	01/15/1889			Y	
Holweg, J.A.	36	Holland	Y	Rotterdam	New York	03/31/1881	04/03/1884			Y	
Holzbacher, Daniel	32	Holstein	Y	Liverpool	New York	08/03/1852	02/29/1856	26	141	N	
Holzbaur, Jacob	35	Wurttemberg	Y	Antwerp	New York	10/20/1848	12/15/1851	4	523	N	
Holzberg, David	22	Russia	Y	Hamburg	New York	07/05/1888	08/01/1890			Y	
Holzberg, Jacob	23	Russia	Y	Hamburg	New York	12/14/1886	07/26/1889			Y	
Holzberger, John	33	Bavaria	Y	Havre	New York	08/09/1846	01/02/1851	2	436	N	
Holze, Fritz	36	Germany	Y	Bremen	New York	03/12/1882	12/26/1885			Y	
Holzen, Henry	22	Oldenburg	Y	Bremen	New Orleans	10/18/1850	10/04/1854	12	357	N	
Holzer, Martin	47	Germany	N	Antwerp	New York	08/04/1865	?			Y	
Holzer, Philip	48	Baden	Y	Antwerp	New Orleans	10/20/1853	10/07/1854	10	522	N	

CITIZENSHIP RECORDS

APPLICANT	AGE	COUNTRY OF ORIGIN	DEC	DEPART PORT	ENTRY PORT	ARRIVE DATE	DEC DATE	VOL	PG.	FLD	NAT DATE
Holzer, Philip	48	Baden	Y	Antwerp	New Orleans	10/20/1853	10/07/1854	12	461	N	
Holzfarstar, Charles	30	Germany	Y	Bremen	Baltimore	04/29/1883	11/06/1893			Y	
Holzhausen, Wilhelm	39	Germany	Y	Bremen	New York	02/12/1891	11/13/1895			Y	
Holzhauser, Michael	39	Germany	Y	Bremen	New York	04/16/1881	10/26/1885			Y	
Holzinger, Michael	29	Germany	Y	Bremen	New York	05/01/1882	06/14/1886			Y	
Holzkaemper, August	25	Lippe Detmol	Y	Bremen	New Orleans	01/01/1853	02/28/1856	26	137	N	
Holzknecht, Louis	33	Austria	Y	Bremen	New York	07/18/1891	10/15/1896			Y	
Holzleiter, George	31	Bavaria	Y	Havre	New York	08/09/1849	03/15/1852	24	305	N	
Holzreuter, August	??	Germany	Y	?	?	?	09/28/1888			Y	
Holzschuh, Jacob	22	Germany	Y	Rotterdam	New York	03/29/1884	10/28/1887			Y	
Holzwarth, Charles	26	Germany	Y	Hamburg	New York	08/27/1883	08/18/1890			Y	
Holzwarth, Gottlieb	42	Germany	Y	Havre	New York	07/05/1880	04/16/1897			Y	
Holzwarth, Jacob	25	Germany	Y	Antwerp	New York	08/19/1881	05/22/1884			Y	
Holzwarth, Louis	29	Germany	Y	Hamburg	New York	12/09/1882	03/29/1886			Y	
Holzwarth, William	24	Wuertemberg	Y	Havre	New York	11/20/1852	05/21/1856	26	513	N	
Holzweiss, Hugo	22	Germany	Y	Bremen	Baltimore	07/15/1884	11/09/1886			Y	
Homan, Joseph	44	Prussia	Y	Bremen	New York	11/01/1857	02/10/1862	18	256	N	
Homann, Albert	35	Prussia	Y	Rotterdam	New Orleans	10/24/1846	10/30/1852	5	66	N	
Homann, Frederick	41	Hanover	Y	Bremen	Galveston	06/08/1846	10/11/1848	1	150	N	
Homann, Herman George	-1	Germany	N	?	Baltimore	00/00/1865				Y	10/18/1886
Homann, Johann A. H.	38	Belgium	Y	Liverpool	New York	09/12/1869	01/06/1872	18	452	N	
Homberg, Peter	56	Prussia	N	Bremen	New Orleans	12/21/1853	?			Y	
Homburgh, John	24	Hesse Cassel	Y	Bremen	New York	10/04/1851	02/15/1856	26	88	N	
Homehr, John	28	France	Y	Havre	New York	01/15/1848	03/12/1850	2	186	N	
Hommelmeier, Bernard	36	Hanover	Y	Bremen	Baltimore	07/03/1842	10/07/1854	6	41	N	
Homnig, Herman Heinrich	30	Prussia	Y	Bremen	New Orleans	11/05/1855	10/09/1860	27	462	N	
Homolle, B.	24	Germany	Y	Rotterdam	New York	11/03/1883	09/20/1886			Y	
Homung, Christian	25	Baden	Y	Havre	New York	08/02/1855	08/15/1860	27	289	N	
Homung, John Anton	27	Baden	Y	Havre	New York	08/02/1855	10/08/1860	27	454	N	
Honegger, Emil	28	Switzerland	Y	Havre	New York	04/03/1887	10/24/1892	19	381	N	
Honegger, Werner	31	Switzerland	Y	Havre	New York	10/06/1883	11/02/1886			Y	
Honemeier, Theodore	40	Germany	N	Bremen	Baltimore	05/18/1870	?			Y	
Honer, Frank Xaver	27	Wurttemberg	Y	Liverpool	New York	08/01/1852	10/09/1854	11	181	N	
Honer, Franz Xavier	27	Wurttemberg	Y	Liverpool	New York	08/01/1852	10/09/1854	6	178	N	
Honeyman, George	36	Ireland	N	Belfast	New York	10/??/1865	?			Y	
Honig, Eduard	28	Baden	Y	Bremen	New York	01/29/1853	05/30/1854	9	463	N	
Honig, John Henry	28	Hanover	Y	Bremen	New York	07/04/1846	01/06/1851	2	457	N	
Honigfort, Herman Bernar	31	Hanover	Y	Bremen	New Orleans	05/28/1847	03/15/1851	3	276	N	
Honkomp, F. F.	45	Germany	N	Liverpool	New York	12/??/1863	?			N	
Honning, Franz	36	Oldenburg	Y	Bremen	New Orleans	06/20/1845	11/01/1852	6	295	N	
Honning, John	24	Bavaria	Y	Bremen	New York	11/23/1848	07/29/1851	4	60	N	
Honold, Michael	27	Germany	Y	Bremen	New York	05/13/1889	10/07/1792			Y	
Honschopp, Albert	37	Germany	Y	Antwerp	New York	11/02/1881	09/23/1886			Y	
Hood, Hamilton	34	Ireland	Y	Glasgow	Philadelphia	06/17/1851	02/03/1858	16	74	N	
Hoogenberg, Jacob	??	?	Y	?	?	?	06/08/1895			Y	
Hook, Adolph	36	Germany	Y	Bremen	New York	05/09/1888	07/05/1900			Y	
Hook, Francis	38	Baden	Y	Havre	New York	10/13/1837	08/23/1852	25	337	N	
Hook, John M.	50	Germany	Y	Antwerp	New York	10/02/1890	09/30/1895			Y	
Hook, Joseph	??	Prussia	Y	?	?	?	03/18/1882			Y	
Hoot, John	24	Prussia	Y	Havre	New York	05/29/1856	09/22/1858	16	154	N	
Hopeia, Josef	??	Germany	Y	?	?	?	02/25/1892			Y	
Hopele, Vitus	25	Germany	Y	Bremen	New York	02/21/1885	09/16/1886			Y	
Hopf, Bernard	21	Prussia	Y	Bremen	New York	09/01/1854	07/10/1856	14	305	N	
Hopf, John	27	Germany	Y	Bremen	New York	02/24/1884	07/05/1888			Y	
Hopf, Matthias	31	Prussia	Y	Antwerp	New York	12/16/1856	12/28/1859	17	533	N	
Hopf, Peter	24	Bavaria	Y	Antwerp	New York	05/??/1848	12/??/1849	23	411	N	
Hopfeld, Frederick	25	Kurhessen	Y	Bremen	New York	??/03/1852	04/30/1855	11	329	N	
Hopkemeier, Rudolph H.	31	Hanover	Y	Bremen	Baltimore	08/03/1846	10/13/1848	1	183	N	
Hopkins, Owen	37	Ireland	Y	Liverpool	New Orleans	02/03/1849	09/06/1860	27	340	N	

CITIZENSHIP RECORDS

APPLICANT	AGE	COUNTRY OF ORIGIN	DEC	DEPART PORT	ENTRY PORT	ARRIVE DATE	DEC DATE	VOL	PG.	FLD	NAT DATE
Hopkins, Thomas	27	Ireland	Y	Liverpool	New Orleans	05/25/1848	11/16/1848	1	279	N	
Hopkins, Thomas	27	Ireland	Y	Liverpool	New York	05/28/1863	03/22/1872	18	474	N	
Hopkins, Thomas	22	Ireland	Y	Dublin	Burlington	08/15/1847	09/07/1852	25	400	N	
Hopkinson, John T.	32	England	Y	Hull	New York	04/24/1875	03/31/1886			Y	
Hopmann, John Herman	26	Holland	Y	Bremen	Baltimore	10/08/1854	01/11/1856	13	449	N	
Hopp, Heinrich	34	Prussia	Y	Bremen	New Orleans	05/06/1852	01/29/1853	7	87	N	
Hopp, Julius	30	Prussia	Y	Havre	New York	06/27/1853	09/25/1854	10	197	N	
Hopp, Julius	30	Prussia	Y	Havre	New York	06/27/1853	06/25/1854	12	136	N	
Hoppe, Charles	43	Germany	Y	Bremen	Baltimore	11/??/1865	08/12/1891			Y	
Hoppe, Fred	41	Prussia	Y	Bremen	Baltimore	09/17/1882	11/04/1893			Y	
Hoppe, Henry	33	Germany	Y	Bremen	Baltimore	07/05/1883	11/04/1892			Y	
Hoppe, John Paul	30	Germany	Y	Bremen	New York	10/05/1893	10/17/1900			Y	
Hor, Phillip (Hoer?)	61	France	N	Havre	New York	05/18/1847	??/??/1850	28	118	N	10/??/1852
Horan, Patrick	27	Ireland	Y	?	?	?	05/27/1896			Y	
Hore, James	32	Ireland	Y	New Ross	Ogdensburg	08/10/1850	10/04/1854	10	425	N	
Hore, James	32	Ireland	Y	New Ross	Ogdensburg	08/10/1850	10/04/1854	12	364	N	
Horlacher, Frederick	23	Wurttemberg	Y	Havre	New York	11/13/1853	01/27/1857	14	475	N	
Horlacher, John Conrad	26	Wurttemberg	Y	Havre	New York	04/??/1854	01/27/1857	14	508	N	
Horn, Bernard	23	Germany	Y	Bremen	Baltimore	05/27/1884	09/30/1887			Y	
Horn, George	33	Germany	Y	Bremen	New York	09/01/1883	10/17/1890			Y	
Horn, Henry	30	Bavaria	Y	Havre	New York	09/30/1854	10/30/1857	15	504	N	
Horn, Henry	34	Germany	Y	Bremen	New York	03/25/1881	09/26/1887			Y	
Horn, John	45	Baden	Y	Havre	New Orleans	11/26/1852	01/15/1853	7	27	N	
Horn, John	26	Hesse Darmsta	Y	Rotterdam	Baltimore	08/15/1844	08/23/1848	22	243	N	
Horn, John Jr.	24	Baden	Y	Havre	New Orleans	11/26/1852	02/07/1856	26	64	N	
Horn, Joseph	33	Bavaria	Y	Havre	New Orleans	05/25/1853	08/20/1855	11	463	N	
Horn, Joseph	26	Germany	Y	Bremen	New York	05/??/1879	11/03/1884			Y	
Hornbacher, John	24	Wurttemberg	Y	Havre	New Orleans	12/26/1847	01/11/1849	1	399	N	
Hornecker, Andreas	27	Baden	Y	Havre	New Orleans	04/28/1850	04/07/1852	24	413	N	
Horner, Robert	??	Ireland	Y	Liverpool	New York	??/09/18?4	04/14/1855	11	243	N	
Hornn, Richard	34	Germany	Y	Bremen	New York	07/??/1870	10/13/1884			Y	
Hornschemeier, Franz	21	Germany	Y	Bremen	Baltimore	05/26/1882	09/23/1885			Y	
Hornschemeier, L.	34	Germany	Y	Bremen	Baltimore	11/02/1880	09/29/1884			Y	
Hornschmeier, G.	24	Germany	Y	Bremen	Baltimore	09/13/1881	11/01/1884			Y	
Hornung, Henry	43	Germany	Y	Bremen	Baltimore	04/05/1883	04/06/1891			Y	
Horowitz, Lewis	27	Russia	Y	Hamburg	New York	08/10/1885	10/10/1891			Y	
Horr, Nicholas	32	Bavaria	Y	Havre	New York	05/16/1848	10/02/1848	22	390	N	
Horschfeld, Abraham	30	Prussia	Y	Hamburg	New Orleans	11/12/1848	01/20/1851	2	508	N	
Horselmann, Joseph	43	Germany	Y	Bremen	New York	05/??/1872	10/10/1882			Y	
Horsfall, Jonas	50	England	Y	Liverpool	New Orleans	11/01/1848	09/06/1852	25	376	N	
Horst, Bernard	31	Prussia	Y	Rotterdam	New Orleans	10/20/1846	01/11/1849	1	388	N	
Horst, Matt	35	Germany	Y	Antwerp	Philadelphia	06/13/1873	03/15/1888			Y	
Horstkamp, Hermann	24	Hanover	Y	Bremen	Baltimore	10/12/1858	04/27/1860	27	172	N	
Horstman, Gerhard Henry	24	Hanover	Y	Bremen	New York	01/25/1859	02/14/1862	18	260	N	
Horstman, Nicolaus	27	Prussia	Y	Bremen	New Orleans	06/19/1848	09/08/1852	25	409	N	
Horstmann, A.	25	Prussia	Y	Bremen	Baltimore	05/26/1859	02/14/1861	18	99	N	
Horstmann, Ernst	50	Germany	N	Bremen	New York	05/06/1857	?			Y	
Horstmann, John	36	Germany	Y	Bremen	Baltimore	05/19/1883	01/06/1887			Y	
Horstmann, John Frederic	28	Hanover	Y	Bremen	Baltimore	10/24/1853	04/01/1858	16	469	N	
Horstschneider, Joseph	25	Hanover	Y	Bremen	New Orleans	05/14/1848	01/20/1851	2	507	N	
Horwitz, Harry	24	Russia	Y	London	New York	07/04/1893	11/27/1897			Y	
Horwitz, Solomon J.	30	Russia	Y	Liverpool	New York	10/03/1880	04/15/1890			Y	
Horz, Joseph	??	Bavaria	Y	?	?	?	12/26/1885			Y	
Hosang, John M.	17	Switzerland	N	?	New York	00/00/1881				Y	10/23/1886
Hosp, Francis Philip	??	Germany	Y	?	?	?	09/25/1880			Y	
Hossfeld, Andrew	30	Saxony	Y	Bremen	Baltimore	10/25/1855	10/04/1858	17	38	N	
Hossli, John	22	Switzerland	Y	Bremen	Baltimore	05/22/1888	05/22/1890			Y	
Hossmann, William	26	Prussia	Y	Bremen	New Orleans	11/07/1851	10/03/1854	10	397	N	
Hossmann, William	26	Prussia	Y	Bremen	New Orleans	11/07/1851	09/03/1854	12	336	N	

CITIZENSHIP RECORDS

APPLICANT	AGE	COUNTRY OF ORIGIN	DEC	DEPART PORT	ENTRY PORT	ARRIVE DATE	DEC DATE	VOL	PG.	FLD	NAT DATE
Hostetter, Alexander	23	Switzerland	Y	?	?	?	11/07/1892			Y	
Hotel, John	48	Germany	Y	Antwerp	New York	01/17/1884	02/24/1887			Y	
Hotlhus, Frederick	44	Germany	Y	Bremen	Baltimore	07/20/1872	06/11/1889			Y	
Hottinger, Henry	25	Germany	Y	Havre	New York	05/27/1884	11/01/1887			Y	
Hottmann, Anton	32	Wurttemberg	Y	Havre	New York	05/01/1852	11/06/1857	15	536	N	
Hotz, Albert	24	Prussia	Y	Bremen	Baltimore	11/01/1857	06/02/1859	17	449	N	
Houden, Francis	22	Ireland	Y	Liverpool	New York	08/01/1853	10/30/1858	17	201	N	
Houlehan, Thomas	21	Ireland	Y	Liverpool	Baltimore	02/10/1846	02/19/1849	23	187	N	
Houlihan, Edmond	22	Ireland	Y	Liverpool	New York	06/03/1847	06/26/1851	3	455	N	
Housefield, Diedrich Hen	50	Hanover	Y	Bremen	Baltimore	06/03/1844	01/20/1849	1	481	N	
Housman, Henry	31	Waldeck	Y	Hamburg	New York	05/??/1850	12/23/1850	2	385	N	
Houz, Henry	31	Hanover	Y	Bremen	New Orleans	12/04/1849	03/28/1853	7	444	N	
Hovel, Lucas	21	Hanover	Y	Bremen	New Orleans	12/01/1853	12/06/1855	13	293	N	
Hover, John	24	Hanover	Y	Bremen	New Orleans	03/15/1854	01/18/1856	13	483	N	
Hoverborn, William	26	Prussia	Y	Bremen	Baltimore	08/01/1845	09/11/1848	22	330	N	
Howard, Charles	??	Ireland	Y	Liverpool	New York	??/15/18??	10/26/1850	2	308	N	
Howard, Daniel	??	England	Y	?	?	?	01/25/1888			Y	
Howard, Michael	33	Ireland	Y	Limerick	Whitehall	11/10/1847	04/04/1853	8	20	N	
Howard, William M.	28	Ireland	Y	Liverpool	New York	04/03/1844	04/30/1850	3	33	N	
Howden, Frank	51	Ireland	N	Liverpool	New York	06/??/1854	10/??/1858	28	107	N	10/??/1871
Howden, Richard	34	Ireland	Y	Liverpool	New York	02/14/1875	10/29/1892	19	402	N	
Howdley, John	29	England	Y	Southhampton	Oswego	09/18/1847	03/18/1851	3	298	N	
Howdon, William	26	England	Y	Liverpool	New York	08/21/1849	03/25/1856	26	328	N	
Howe, James S.	31	Scotland	Y	Glasgow	New York	04/20/1849	02/20/1850	2	109	N	
Howel, George	28	Germany	Y	Bremen	New York	07/14/1880	10/15/1886	19	50	N	
Howell, William H.	38	Canada	Y	Windsor	Detroit	03/28/1891	10/22/1896			Y	
Howells, Humphrey	29	Wales	Y	Liverpool	New York	06/21/1851	01/10/1856	13	442	N	
Howitz, Abraham Isaac	36	Russia	Y	Hamburg	New York	09/17/1888	10/24/1894			Y	
Howley, Michael	23	Ireland	Y	Derry	Ogdensburg	11/15/1848	10/05/1854	10	433	N	
Howroyd, Joseph	34	England	Y	Liverpool	New York	03/22/1883	09/22/1887			Y	
Howser, Ferdinand	30	Germany	Y	Bingen	New York	05/30/1882	03/07/1888			Y	
Howson, William	26	England	Y	London	New York	01/10/1856	05/07/1861	18	160	N	
Hoz, John	30	Prussia	Y	Havre	New York	04/26/1854	10/07/1856	14	260	N	
Hreze, Rudolph	48	Germany	Y	Bremen	New York	06/23/1881	10/23/1896			Y	
Huban, Thomas	28	Ireland	Y	Galway	New York	05/14/1848	03/13/1850	2	190	N	
Hubbert, Bernard Henry	31	Prussia	Y	Bremen	New Orleans	11/31/1844	06/11/1848	22	323	N	
Hubedenck, Frederick	50	Hanover	Y	Bremen	New Orleans	05/20/1849	02/11/1850	2	60	N	
Huber, Adam	38	Baden	Y	Hamburg	New York	08/28/1872	02/20/1888			Y	
Huber, Albert	24	Switzerland	Y	Antwerp	New York	07/04/1893	03/29/1899			Y	
Huber, Anton	23	Germany	Y	Havre	New York	10/19/1882	08/15/1887			Y	
Huber, Anton	32	Germany	Y	Havre	New York	06/11/1881	01/26/1888			Y	
Huber, Anton	33	Austria	Y	Antwerp	Jersey City	10/12/1882	01/27/1886			Y	
Huber, August	??	Germany	Y	?	?	?	04/30/1883			Y	
Huber, August	38	Germany	N	Antwerp	Philadelphia	09/22/1879	?			Y	
Huber, Babist	23	Baden	Y	London	New York	05/??/1852	09/22/1855	13	114	N	
Huber, Bernhard	21	Germany	Y	Havre	New York	09/29/1880	10/02/1882			Y	
Huber, Caspar	26	Austria	Y	Amsterdam	New York	09/16/1886	10/14/1887			Y	
Huber, Charles	24	Baden	Y	Havre	New York	07/11/1847	11/20/1848	1	334	N	
Huber, Conrad	52	Wuerttemberg	Y	Havre	New York	08/05/1846	09/29/1848	22	363	N	
Huber, George	24	Baden	Y	Havre	New York	11/05/1854	10/06/1860	27	413	N	
Huber, Hilar	26	Baden	Y	Havre	New York	12/01/1847	02/24/1852	24	163	N	
Huber, Ignaz	38	Germany	Y	Havre	New York	02/25/1885	01/24/1887			Y	
Huber, Jacob	40	Bavaria	Y	Havre	New York	08/01/1856	04/15/1861	18	105	N	
Huber, Jacob	30	Germany	Y	Antwerp	New York	03/02/1880	07/05/1890			Y	
Huber, Johann	37	Germany	Y	Bremen	New York	08/11/1882	08/19/1887			Y	
Huber, John	29	Germany	Y	Antwerp	New York	06/17/1882	11/12/1885			Y	
Huber, John James Edward	27	Bavaria	Y	Bremen	New York	10/27/1855	11/17/1857	16	31	N	
Huber, Joseph	24	Germany	Y	Bremen	New York	03/08/1880	02/02/1883			Y	
Huber, Joseph	24	Germany	Y	Havre	New York	11/19/1888	11/17/1891			Y	

CITIZENSHIP RECORDS

APPLICANT	AGE	COUNTRY OF ORIGIN	DEC	DEPART PORT	ENTRY PORT	ARRIVE DATE	DEC DATE	VOL	PG.	FLD	NAT DATE
Huber, Joseph	30	Germany	N	Antwerp	Philadelphia	09/22/1879	?			Y	
Huber, Leo	41	Germany	Y	Havre	New York	09/20/1873	04/04/1887			Y	
Huber, Leopold	25	Wuerttenberg	Y	Havre	New York	08/05/1846	09/30/1848	22	364	N	
Huber, Ludwig	39	Switzerland	Y	Havre	New York	02/23/1884	10/24/1888			Y	
Huber, Ludwig	40	Germany	Y	Bremen	New York	05/27/1873	10/23/1890			Y	
Huber, Michael	20	Germany	Y	Havre	New York	10/14/1885	07/24/1888			Y	
Huber, Robert	21	Germany	Y	Havre	New York	03/01/1896	08/05/1898			Y	
Huber, Thomas	31	Baden	Y	Havre	New Orleans	03/30/1852	10/29/1852	5	58	N	
Huber, Victor	27	Switzerland	Y	Havre	New York	03/26/1890	03/08/1894			Y	
Huber, Xaver	29	Germany	Y	Bremen	New York	03/08/1880	12/30/1882			Y	
Huber, Ziriack	25	Germany	Y	Bremen	Baltimore	10/05/1887	01/26/1888			Y	
Huberm Herman	22	Germany	Y	Hamburg	New York	04/29/1893	01/11/1896			Y	
Huberman, Conrad	??	Germany	Y	?	New York	??/??/1880	10/18/1884			Y	
Hubert, Heinrich	40	Switzerland	Y	Havre	New York	02/10/1887	01/03/1893			Y	
Hubert, Rudolf	??	Germany	Y	?	?	?	11/13/1882			Y	
Hubert, Wm.	53	Germany	Y	Bremen	New York	08/23/1881	08/07/1886			Y	
Hubzmiller, Louis	34	Prussia	Y	Bremen	New York	10/27/1847	04/02/1853	7	504	N	
Huck, Anton	26	Germany	Y	Antwerp	Philadelphia	10/19/1879	09/05/1887			Y	
Huck, Bernhard	34	Germany	Y	?	New York	??/??/1872	04/07/1884			Y	
Huck, Francis	28	Prussia	Y	Bremen	New Orleans	12/??/1849	03/30/1858	16	458	N	
Huck, Joseph	34	Baden	Y	Havre	New York	05/10/1850	05/03/1854	8	359	N	
Huck, Joseph	34	Baden	Y	Havre	New York	05/10/1850	05/03/1854	9	232	N	
Huck, Martin	37	Germany	Y	Havre	New York	08/31/1881	03/24/1886			Y	
Huck, Nicholas	39	Baden	Y	Havre	New Orleans	06/10/1850	03/03/1852	24	223	N	
Hucke, Caspar	34	Germany	Y	Bremen	Baltimore	11/16/1885	11/01/1890			Y	
Hucke, Charles	26	Germany	Y	Havre	New York	09/02/1886	06/15/1892			Y	
Huckmann, Conrad Henry	25	Hanover	Y	Bremen	Baltimore	11/05/1853	10/10/18??	6	232	N	
Huckriede, Herman Henry	30	Prussia	Y	Liverpool	New York	11/03/1853	11/03/1855	13	150	N	
Hudepohl, Henry	26	Hanover	Y	Bremen	New Orleans	02/12/1846	08/15/1851	4	129	N	
Huder, Nicholas	21	France	Y	Havre	New Orleans	03/07/1854	10/04/1858	17	36	N	
Hudson, William L.	36	Wales	Y	Liverpool	New York	06/16/1837	08/10/1848	22	88	N	
Hueber, Michael	31	Austria	Y	Brest	New York	05/22/1869	04/03/1872	18	487	N	
Hueber, Nicolas	35	Germany	Y	Havre	New York	03/02/1890	06/06/1894			Y	
Huebner, Gustav P. T.	23	Prussia	Y	Bremen	New York	08/15/1850	05/13/1852	25	13	N	
Huebner, John	34	Germany	Y	?	Philadelphia	??/??/1884	09/12/1884			Y	
Huebner, Joseph	42	Germany	Y	Bremen	New York	07/28/1882	08/17/1887			Y	
Huebner, Louis	27	Baden	Y	Havre	New York	08/05/1850	09/11/1852	25	455	N	
Huefe, Dietrich Herman	26	Hanover	Y	Bremen	New York	07/20/1845	10/02/1848	22	388	N	
Huefenberg, Frederick	28	Prussia	Y	Bremen	New York	10/12/1849	06/19/1851	3	412	N	
Huegel, Anton	31	Baden	Y	Havre	New Orleans	05/17/1846	10/06/1854	10	474	N	
Huegel, Daniel	33	Germany	Y	Havre	New York	10/04/1873	06/04/1883			Y	
Huehlefeld, Gerhard Henr	38	Hanover	Y	Bremen	New Orleans	12/29/1845	02/11/1851	3	118	N	
Hueil, John	28	Germany	Y	Amsterdam	New York	03/17/1883	04/24/1890			Y	
Huellemeier, B.	25	Germany	Y	Antwerp	New York	11/08/1882	11/16/1886			Y	
Huellermann, Bernard	22	Prussia	Y	Rotterdam	New York	06/26/1846	02/13/1849	23	75	N	
Huelsebusch, Herman H.	44	Germany	Y	Bremen	Baltimore	03/11/1884	02/01/1887			Y	
Huelsman, August	27	Germany	Y	Bremen	Baltimore	08/14/1884	05/19/1891			Y	
Huelsmann, Charles	26	Hanover	Y	Bremerhafen	Baltimore	07/02/1858	01/17/1861	18	65	N	
Huelsmann, Anton	48	Germany	Y	Bremen	Baltimore	09/23/1884	02/21/1888			Y	
Huelsmann, Anton	63	Germany	N	Bremen	Baltimore	?	?	28	442	N	08/30/1873
Huelsmann, Bernard	21	Hanover	Y	Bremen	New York	05/24/1855	03/24/1856	26	275	N	
Huelsmann, F. H.	51	Germany	N	Bremen	Baltimore	11/17/1872	?			Y	
Huelsmann, Ferdinand	22	Oldenburg	Y	Bremen	New Orleans	11/16/1853	10/10/1854	11	217	N	
Huelsmann, George	25	Germany	Y	Bremen	Baltimore	10/23/1884	04/05/1888			Y	
Huelsmann, Henry	35	Germany	Y	Bremen	Baltimore	03/28/1886	03/28/1894			Y	
Huenefeld, Henry	50	Germany	N	Bremen	New Orleans	01/??/1848	?	28	7	N	10/??/1856
Huenefeld, Henry	10	Germany	N	Bremen	New Orleans	01/00/1848				Y	10/00/1856
Hueneke, Charles	28	Germany	Y	Bremen	New York	02/16/1889	02/15/1897			Y	
Hueneke, Cord	54	Hanover	Y	Bremen	New York	06/10/1851	09/22/1854	10	156	N	

CITIZENSHIP RECORDS

APPLICANT	AGE	COUNTRY OF ORIGIN	DEC	DEPART PORT	ENTRY PORT	ARRIVE DATE	DEC DATE	VOL	PG.	FLD	NAT DATE
Hueneker, August	49	Germany	Y	Bremen	New York	05/10/1866	03/23/1889			Y	
Hueninghacke, Bernard	61	Germany	Y	Bremen	New York	09/15/1865	10/09/1896			Y	
Huerlemann, Henry	22	Switzerland	Y	Antwerp	New York	05/22/1854	06/12/1854	10	122	N	
Huermann, John	30	Germany	Y	Bremen	New York	08/20/1883	01/03/1895			Y	
Huerster, David	23	Baden	Y	Havre	New Orleans	10/20/1850	11/20/1855	13	236	N	
Huesing, John Theodore	32	Hanover	Y	Bremen	New Orleans	12/23/1852	08/22/1857	15	167	N	
Hueston, John	31	Ireland	Y	Liverpool	New York	05/28/1840	11/20/1848	1	343	N	
Hueston, John	31	Ireland	Y	Liverpool	New York	05/28/1840	11/20/1848	1	345	N	
Huether, Francis	49	Prussia	Y	Bremen	New York	07/16/1854	02/04/1856	26	33	N	
Huether, Henry	25	Germany	Y	Bremen	New York	05/19/1882	10/08/1883			Y	
Huether, Philip	57	Germany	Y	Antwerp	New York	01/03/1885	08/25/1896			Y	
Hueve, Clemens	55	Germany	N	Bremen	New York	09/??/1862	?			Y	
Huewe, Frederick	24	Prussia	Y	Bremen	New Orleans	12/18/1846	08/29/1848	22	271	N	
Hufer, Franz	28	Frankfort	Y	Bremen	New York	04/24/1852	02/28/1856	26	135	N	
Hufnagel, Henry	48	Bavaria	Y	Bremen	New York	07/29/1850	09/29/1858	16	102	N	
Hug, Leo	33	Switzerland	Y	Havre	New York	04/24/1880	05/15/1886			Y	
Hug, Max	??	Baden	Y	Bremen	Galveston	??/01/1848	12/07/1850	2	343	N	
Hug, Rudolph	32	Baden	Y	Havre	New York	08/01/1849	04/12/1852	24	444	N	
Hugel, Anton	31	Baden	Y	Havre	New Orleans	05/17/1846	10/06/1854	12	413	N	
Hugel, John	29	Bavaria	Y	Bremen	New York	08/04/1847	08/02/1848	22	34	N	
Hugenschmidt, John	26	Baden	Y	Havre	New York	05/04/1854	10/29/1857	15	501	N	
Hugentobler, Adolf	28	Switzerland	Y	Antwerp	Philadelphia	03/28/1873	11/13/1882			Y	
Hugentobler, Jacob	28	Switzerland	Y	Havre	New York	10/10/1871	08/29/1877			Y	
Hugentobler, Joseph	28	Switzerland	Y	Havre	New York	06/26/1848	10/06/1851	4	197	N	
Hugerschoff, Francis Gus	21	Saxony	Y	Hamburg	New York	07/06/1856	01/26/1857	14	507	N	
Hugger, Charles	22	Wurttemberg	Y	Havre	New York	04/??/1853	09/21/1855	13	105	N	
Hugger, Gothard	36	Germany	Y	Bremen	New York	07/04/1869	03/25/1885			Y	
Huggle, John Henry	32	Baden	Y	Havre	New York	08/04/1848	02/03/1853	7	112	N	
Hugher, Thomas	63	Ireland	Y	Queenstown	New York	07/05/1873	10/01/1885	19	8	N	
Hughes, Arthur	55	Ireland	N	Liverpool	New York	03/12/1871	?			Y	
Hughes, Charles T.	25	England	Y	Liverpool	New York	08/01/1884	07/16/1888			Y	
Hughes, David	22	England	Y	South Hampto	New York	10/01/1886	06/04/1888			Y	
Hughes, E.J.	21	England	Y	Liverpool	New York	03/01/1880	??/??/1881			Y	
Hughes, Enoch	33	Wales	Y	Liverpool	New York	05/15/1846	10/26/1858	17	114	N	
Hughes, John	28	Ireland	Y	Queenstown	New York	04/??/1880	10/25/1888			Y	
Hughes, John	42	Ireland	N	?	New York	11/07/1863	?			Y	
Hughes, Patrick	37	Ireland	Y	Havre	New York	08/17/1847	03/02/1853	7	255	N	
Hughes, Richard M.	28	Wales	Y	Liverpool	New York	06/11/1848	04/02/1853	7	493	N	
Hughes, Thomas	35	Ireland	Y	Canada	Boston	?	01/28/1850	2	3	N	
Hughes, Thomas	28	Ireland	Y	Liverpool	New Orleans	03/15/1850	04/04/1853	8	22	N	
Hughes, Thomas	25	Ireland	Y	Liverpool	New York	06/12/1883	12/19/1883			Y	
Hughes, Timothy	22	Ireland	Y	Liverpool	New York	04/23/1857	09/04/1860	27	335	N	
Hughes, William	36	Ireland	Y	Liverpool	New York	11/18/1854	10/04/1858	17	47	N	
Huging, Gerhard	21	Prussia	Y	Bremen	Baltimore	05/30/1861	02/03/1862	18	252	N	
Hugo, Charles	31	Prussia	Y	Bremen	Baltimore	08/20/1846	02/12/1849	23	56	N	
Hugon, John E.	26	Hesse Cassel	Y	Bremen	New York	10/05/1845	06/18/1851	3	391	N	
Huhn, Fred	36	Germany	Y	Havre	New York	08/13/1873	10/20/1885			Y	
Huie, John	70	Scotland	N	Scotland	New York	08/01/1839	?	28	254	N	10/??/1844
Huisman, William	48	Holland	Y	Amsterdam	New York	05/171889	03/22/1894			Y	
Huismann, Rudolf	34	Holland	Y	Rotterdam	New York	06/09/1882	05/29/1885			Y	
Hulefeld, Henry	34	Germany	Y	Hanover	New York	04/27/1885	01/15/1891	19	313	N	
Hulershom, Charles Augus	22	Prussia	Y	Bremen	New York	11/27/1855	02/22/1858	16	326	N	
Hull, Daniel	??	?	Y	Liverpool	New York	??/19/1848	??/??/1851	3	220	N	
Hull, Harry	28	Canada	Y	Windsor	Detroit	11/10/1888	10/16/1896			Y	
Hullebrand, Rudolph	22	Prussia	Y	Hamburg	New York	06/09/1849	01/21/1851	2	514	N	
Hullemeier, T.	25	Germany	Y	Amsterdam	New York	09/26/1882	11/01/1884			Y	
Hullmann, George	32	Hanover	Y	Bremen	New Orleans	11/28/1848	05/29/1852	25	129	N	
Hullmann, Henry	30	Oldenburg	Y	Bremen	New Orleans	02/20/1846	02/19/1851	3	145	N	
Hulsberger, Jacob	29	Baden	Y	Havre	New York	09/19/1848	06/16/1852	25	277	N	

CITIZENSHIP RECORDS

APPLICANT	AGE	COUNTRY OF ORIGIN	DEC	DEPART PORT	ENTRY PORT	ARRIVE DATE	DEC DATE	VOL	PG.	FLD	NAT DATE
Hulsemann, Gerhard	??	Germany	Y	?	?	?	09/11/1884			Y	
Hulsemann, Otto	38	Germany	Y	Bremen	Boston	11/12/1865	04/28/1879			Y	
Hulshaas, William	28	Prussia	Y	Bremen	Baltimore	09/04/1846	11/24/1848	1	386	N	
Hulshorst, Friedrich	25	Prussia	Y	Bremen	Baltimore	09/18/1846	06/21/1852	25	297	N	
Hulsing, John Gerard	25	Hanover	Y	Bremen	New Orleans	12/25/1845	10/03/1848	1	41	N	
Hulsmann, Ferdinand	22	Oldenburg	Y	Bremen	New Orleans	11/16/1853	10/10/1854	6	214	N	
Hulsmann, Frank	29	Oldenburg	Y	Bremen	New Orleans	06/08/1848	09/13/1852	25	476	N	
Hulsmann, George	22	Germany	Y	Bremen	New York	05/29/1885	01/26/1889			Y	
Humann, John	39	Prussia	Y	Bremen	New York	??/25/1848	02/04/1850	2	35	N	
Humbert, Bernard Henry	31	Hanover	Y	Bremen	Baltimore	05/30/1848	05/20/1852	25	79	N	
Humbert, William	20	Germany	N	Hanover	New York	09/04/1837	00/00/1838			Y	12/00/1843
Humbert, William (Humber	70	Germany	N	Hanover	New York	09/04/1837	??/??/1838	28	25	N	12/??/1843
Humbrecht, Victor	47	Germany	Y	Havre	New York	05/17/1863	03/26/1887			Y	
Humler, August	22	Baden	Y	Heping	Baltimore	07/15/1856	11/25/1858	17	353	N	
Humm, Michael	22	Germany	Y	Bremen	New York	10/03/1881	11/23/1885			Y	
Hummefeld, John	30	Hanover	Y	Bremen	Baltimore	10/01/1845	09/30/1856	14	68	N	
Hummel, August	21	Austria	Y	?	?	?	07/06/1889			Y	
Hummel, Benadict	22	Wurttemberg	Y	Bremen	New York	05/20/1848	02/22/1851	3	158	N	
Hummel, Christian	22	Germany	Y	Liverpool	New York	11/10/1873	03/04/1878			Y	
Hummel, David	25	Wuerttenberg	Y	Havre	New Orleans	05/12/1847	02/19/1849	23	206	N	
Hummel, Franz J.	49	Germany	Y	Rotterdam	New York	11/02/1881	11/17/1886			Y	
Hummel, Jacob	31	Wurttemberg	Y	Havre	New Orleans	05/20/1847	04/26/1854	8	272	N	
Hummel, Jacob	31	Wurttemberg	Y	Havre	New Orleans	05/20/1847	04/26/1854	9	143	N	
Hummel, Jacob	40	Austria	Y	Antwerp	New York	07/19/1890	07/28/1896			Y	
Hummel, Jacob Frederick	34	Wurttemberg	Y	Havre	New Orleans	12/29/1850	04/18/1853	8	70	N	
Hummel, John	28	Wurttemberg	Y	Bremen	Baltimore	06/10/1852	10/23/1855	13	146	N	
Hummel, John	32	Germany	Y	Bremen	New York	07/17/1881	04/12/1882			Y	
Hummel, John	26	Wuerttenberg	Y	Havre	New York	05/14/1846	10/05/1848	22	446	N	
Hummel, Joseph	34	Germany	Y	Bremen	New York	09/28/1883	02/09/1885			Y	
Hummel, Marcus	21	Wuertemberg	Y	Havre	New York	04/03/1854	02/13/1856	26	81	N	
Hummel, Michael	27	Wurttemberg	Y	London	New York	04/27/1853	05/22/1854	8	488	N	
Hummel, Michael	27	Wurttemberg	Y	London	New York	04/27/1853	05/22/1854	9	362	N	
Hummel, Pius	32	Germany	Y	Havre	New York	05/18/1882	10/27/1884			Y	
Hummpert, Joseph	39	Germany	Y	Havre	New York	10/26/1882	11/28/1887			Y	
Humpert, Joseph	31	Prussia	Y	Bremen	New York	06/01/1846	03/29/1850	2	281	N	
Humphreys, David	25	Wales	Y	Liverpool	New York	07/01/1841	10/14/1848	1	223	N	
Humphreys, Thomas	25	Wales	Y	Liverpool	Boston	04/16/1889	10/08/1891			Y	
Hund, Anselm	23	Germany	Y	Havre	New York	03/04/1880	11/21/1882			Y	
Hund, August	23	Hanover	Y	Bremen	Baltimore	07/01/1861	08/27/1862	18	405	N	
Hund, Sylvester	21	Baden	Y	Havre	New York	07/22/1845	03/11/1850	2	182	N	
Hund, Theodore	22	Germany	Y	Bremen	New York	06/17/1881	05/09/1882			Y	
Hundertmark, August	26	Prussia	Y	Bremen	New Orleans	06/18/1851	03/31/1856	26	392	N	
Hundertmark, Henry	36	Germany	Y	Bremen	Baltimore	08/28/1882	10/13/1892			Y	
Hundt, Frank	22	Baden	Y	Havre	New Orleans	04/??/1849	10/??/1849	23	279	N	
Huneke, Cord	54	Hanover	Y	Bremen	New York	06/10/1851	09/22/1854	12	95	N	
Hunemeier, Frederick	27	Hanover	Y	Bremen	Baltimore	10/27/1858	03/31/1862	18	286	N	
Hungeling, Herman	32	Hanover	Y	Bremen	Baltimore	07/02/1844	11/18/1848	1	320	N	
Hunger, Felix	28	Switzerland	Y	Havre	New York	06/??/1855	03/15/1858	16	407	N	
Hunker, John Martin	26	Germany	Y	?	?	?	10/08/1885			Y	
Hunn, Joseph	32	Germany	Y	Havre	New York	10/30/1875	03/30/1889			Y	
Hunnekuhl, Anton	34	Prussia	Y	Bremen	Baltimore	02/01/1854	04/22/1861	18	139	N	
Hunnemann, Henry	??	Hanover	Y	Bremen	Baltimore	??/09/1848	08/??/1851	4	179	N	
Hunningbacke, Bernhard	34	Germany	N	Bremen	Baltimore	05/??/1871	?			Y	
Hunsch, John Henry	29	Prussia	Y	Bremen	Baltimore	05/22/1866	09/19/1872	18	521	N	
Hunsche, Ernst	22	Prussia	Y	Bremen	Baltimore	09/30/1858	04/16/1860	27	159	N	
Hunsicker, Fred	41	Germany	Y	Rotterdam	New York	06/04/1881	10/15/1891			Y	
Hunsinger, Adam	??	Germany	N	?	?	05/26/1882				Y	10/24/1892
Hunt, Barney	24	Ireland	Y	?	New York	00/00/1884	04/03/1889			Y	
Hunt, Carl	28	Baden	Y	Havre	New York	07/22/1851	04/17/1854	9	5	N	

CITIZENSHIP RECORDS

APPLICANT	AGE	COUNTRY OF ORIGIN	DEC	DEPART PORT	ENTRY PORT	ARRIVE DATE	DEC DATE	VOL	PG.	FLD	NAT DATE
Hunt, Charles	28	Baden	Y	Havre	New York	07/22/1851	04/17/1854	8	134	N	
Hunt, Edward	24	Ireland	Y	Queenstown	New York	05/12/1883	10/16/1885			Y	
Hunt, George	26	Ireland	Y	Dublin	Buffalo	08/20/1845	08/??/1851	4	155	N	
Hunt, Martin	38	Ireland	Y	Liverpool	New Orleans	01/20/1853	08/13/1860	27	264	N	
Hunt, Theodore	22	Germany	Y	Bremen	New York	06/17/1881	05/09/1882			Y	
Huntebrincker, Henry	26	Hanover	Y	Bremen	Baltimore	06/01/1852	01/25/1860	27	72	N	
Hunziker, Charles	30	Switzerland	Y	Havre	New York	05/01/1884	08/20/1894			Y	
Hupong, Frederick	23	Baden	Y	Antwerp	New York	06/02/1851	06/19/1851	3	424	N	
Hupp, John	25	Bavaria	Y	Havre	New York	05/12/1853	03/25/1856	26	294	N	
Huppert, Adrian A.	38	Austria	Y	Hamburg	New York	11/08/1890	10/18/1898			Y	
Huppert, John David	33	Nassau	Y	Antwerp	New York	05/17/1850	05/29/1852	25	127	N	
Hurlemann, Henry	22	Switzerland	Y	Antwerp	New York	05/22/1854	06/12/1854	12	59	N	
Hurley, Michael	40	Ireland	Y	Cork	New York	09/01/1850	05/11/1859	17	410	N	
Hurley, Philip	17	Ireland	N	?	New York	00/00/1875				Y	10/28/1887
Hurlimann, Peter J.	32	Switzerland	Y	Antwerp	New York	06/25/1874	02/19/1884			Y	
Hurly, Dennis	49	Ireland	Y	Canada	New York	06/20/1825	03/18/1850	2	217	N	
Hurly, Dennis	32	Ireland	Y	Canada	Ogdensburg	09/26/1849	09/06/1852	25	360	N	
Hurly, Patrick	??	Ireland	Y	Dublin	New Orleans	??/01/1847	08/??/1851	4	189	N	
Hurner, Francis	48	Switzerland	Y	Havre	New Orleans	03/27/1854	04/19/1854	8	213	N	
Hurner, Francois	48	Switzerland	Y	Havre	New Orleans	03/27/1854	04/19/1854	9	84	N	
Hurrle, Thomas	33	Germany	Y	Antwerp	Philadelphia	01/16/1888	05/05/1894			Y	
Hurst, Emile	36	France	Y	Havre	New York	04/24/1872	04/05/1879			Y	
Hurst, Martin	30	Germany	Y	Bremen	New York	03/28/1880	02/01/1882			Y	
Hurst, Rochus	30	Baden	Y	Havre	New Orleans	01/17/1841	09/15/1852	25	513	N	
Hurst, Valentine	31	Baden	Y	Havre	New York	12/09/1858	04/17/1865			Y	
Hurstman, Gerhard	45	Hanover	Y	Bremen	Baltimore	11/??/1846	03/08/1853	3	312	N	
Hurter, Arnold	??	Switzerland	Y	?	?	?	03/14/1894			Y	
Hurter, Louis	48	Germany	Y	Rotterdam	New York	04/21/1868	10/28/1882			Y	
Hurzeler, Heinrich	44	Switzerland	Y	Havre	New Orleans	04/20/1857	05/07/1860	27	181	N	
Husck, Frank	60	Austria	Y	Bremen	Baltimore	07/02/1880	07/11/1892			Y	
Husecker, Henry	27	Hanover	Y	Bremen	New Orleans	01/08/1845	01/12/1849	1	401	N	
Huser, Andrew	53	France	Y	Rotterdam	New York	06/05/1848	10/11/1848	1	148	N	
Huser, George	34	Germany	Y	Bremen	New York	09/04/1888	07/13/1895			Y	
Huser, Henry	21	Germany	Y	Rotterdam	New York	10/03/1887	10/23/1888	19	170	N	
Huser, Henry	21	Germany	Y	Rotterdam	New York	10/03/1887	10/23/1888			Y	
Huser, Henry	41	Germany	Y	Bremen	New York	09/02/1888	10/15/1897			Y	
Huser, John Anton	38	Germany	Y	Bremen	New York	09/09/1881	01/24/1893			Y	
Husfar, Jacob	26	Baden	Y	Havre	New Orleans	02/02/1846	02/03/1849	23	21	N	
Husing, William	27	Hanover	Y	Bremen	New Orleans	11/25/1852	10/09/1854	6	153	N	
Husing, William	27	Hanover	Y	Bremen	New Orleans	11/25/1852	10/09/1854	11	156	N	
Husmann, Bernard	22	Oldenburg	Y	Bremen	New Orleans	12/04/1853	02/05/1857	14	540	N	
Husmann, Bernard	25	Germany	Y	Bremen	New York	08/22/1880	11/17/1882			Y	
Husmann, Frederick	21	Oldenburg	Y	Bremen	Baltimore	10/10/1857	07/27/1858	16	534	N	
Huss, John Adam	25	Wuertemberg	Y	Antwerp	New York	08/16/1854	02/07/1856	26	60	N	
Hussel, Adam	57	Bavaria	Y	Havre	New Orleans	12/15/1854	11/11/1857	16	8	N	
Hussey, Martin	43	Ireland	Y	Liverpool	New York	11/03/1854	09/28/1860	27	382	N	
Hussey, Michael	17	Ireland	Y	?	New York	00/00/1879				Y	10/20/1886
Hussey, Peter	38	Ireland	Y	Queenstown	New York	03/24/1884	10/12/1888			Y	
Hussmann, Henry	??	Hanover	N	?	?	?	06/19/1871			Y	06/21/1873
Hussner, Michael	35	Bavaria	Y	Havre	Boston	09/14/1837	05/31/1852	25	134	N	
Hust, Andrew	33	Bavaria	Y	Havre	New Orleans	03/03/1846	02/27/1850	2	137	N	
Hust, Jacob	25	Bavaria	Y	Havre	New Orleans	05/12/1852	09/27/1856	14	403	N	
Hust, Valentine	24	Germany	Y	Antwerp	Philadelphia	02/27/1881	12/08/1883			Y	
Husteden, Herman	29	Germany	Y	Rotterdam	New York	08/??/1879	03/31/1888			Y	
Husteden, Herman	27	Hanover	Y	Bremen	Baltimore	??/01/1845	12/04/1849	23	378	N	
Huster, Frederick	21	Hanover	Y	Bremen	Baltimore	10/27/1850	10/21/1854	10	354	N	
Huster, Frederick	21	Hanover	Y	Bremen	Baltimore	10/27/1850	10/02/1854	12	293	N	
Huster, William	24	Germany	Y	Rotterdam	New York	10/25/1887	01/15/1891			Y	
Huth, Heinrich	27	Germany	Y	Bremen	New York	04/07/1884	05/07/1886			Y	

CITIZENSHIP RECORDS

APPLICANT	AGE	COUNTRY OF ORIGIN	DEC	DEPART PORT	ENTRY PORT	ARRIVE DATE	DEC DATE	VOL	PG.	FLD	NAT DATE
Huth, Jacob	35	Nassau	Y	London	New York	08/02/1847	02/10/1849	23	42	N	
Huthmacker, Christian	32	Baden	Y	Havre	New Orleans	04/01/1846	10/02/1848	22	380	N	
Hutkin, Meier	26	Russia	Y	Hamburg	New York	06/17/1881	05/07/1883			Y	
Hutkin, Meier	31	Russia	Y	Hamburg	New York	06/17/1881	05/09/1883	28	182	N	
Hutlage, John Henry	26	Hanover	Y	Bremen	Baltimore	05/01/1848	06/10/1852	25	222	N	
Hutmann, Henry	29	Switzerland	Y	Havre	New York	06/16/1883	09/23/1887			Y	
Hutner, Harris	??	Russia	Y	?	?	?	03/02/1888			Y	
Hutner, Harris	??	Russian	Y	?	?	?	03/02/1888			Y	
Hutner, Saul	25	Russia	Y	Hamburg	New York	06/??/1880	09/29/1888			Y	
Hutte, John Henry	24	Hanover	Y	Bremen	New York	10/14/1854	11/06/1855	13	177	N	
Hutten, Henry	29	Germany	Y	Antwerp	New York	02/20/1882	02/23/1882			Y	
Huttenseiler, Frederick	41	Bavaria	Y	Havre	New York	09/15/1847	08/28/1848	22	266	N	
Hutterer, Philipp	43	Germany	Y	Rotterdam	New York	05/08/1884	12/19/1888			Y	
Huttl, Andrew	27	Austria	Y	Bremen	Baltimore	09/26/1883	11/02/1886	19	109	N	
Huttl, Andrew	27	Austria	Y	Bremen	Baltimore	09/26/1883	11/02/1886			Y	
Huttl, Karl	30	Germany	Y	Bremen	New York	05/20/1876	04/24/1882			Y	
Hutz, Philip	31	Bavaria	Y	Havre	New York	06/20/1851	09/25/1854	12	146	N	
Hutzelman, George Casper	26	Bavaria	Y	Bremen	Baltimore	07/04/1845	08/02/1848	22	39	N	
Huwel, Joseph	25	Prussia	Y	Bremen	New York	01/04/1854	11/26/1855	13	253	N	
Huxley, Henry	21	England	Y	Liverpool	New York	07/13/1850	03/18/1851	3	235	N	
Huy, Nicholas	28	Prussia	Y	Havre	New York	06/12/1847	02/27/1851	3	178	N	
Hyams, Nathan	72	England	N	Liverpool	New York	02/??/1834	??/??/1835	28	272	N	10/??/1840
Hyems, Isaac	36	England	Y	London	New York	10/22/1844	03/26/1853	7	409	N	
Hyland, John	27	Ireland	Y	Liverpool	New York	01/15/1858	08/15/1860	27	278	N	
Hyland, Thomas	24	Ireland	Y	Queenstown	New York	04/08/1884	10/26/1889	19	270	N	
Hyland, William	25	Ireland	Y	Liverpool	New Orleans	01/??/1854	09/10/1855	11	521	N	
Hyman, Charles	66	Germany	N	Bavaria	New York	06/28/1843	?			Y	
Hyman, Elias	23	Bavaria	Y	Havre	New York	04/01/1867	05/04/1867			Y	
Hyman, Jake	??	Russia	Y	?	?	?	06/07/1899			Y	
Hyman, Pincaus	36	Russia	Y	Hamburg	New York	06/29/1888	04/11/1890			Y	
Hynds, Thomas	28	Ireland	Y	Liverpool	New York	06/12/1852	08/27/1855	11	506	N	
Hynes, John	??	Ireland	Y	Liverpool	New York	06/21/1853	11/07/1856	14	488	N	
Ibach, Gildebent	25	Baden	Y	Havre	New York	05/29/1849	06/15/1852	25	270	N	
Ibold, Carl	30	Germany	Y	Bremen	New York	06/13/1892	08/06/1894			Y	
Ibold, Frank	43	Germany	N	Bremen	New York	08/??/1868	?			Y	
Ibold, Michael	21	Germany	Y	Bremen	New York	08/08/1880	04/10/1882			Y	
Idoux, John	25	France	Y	Antwerp	Galveston	02/01/1845	02/01/1850	2	25	N	
Ierstoefer, Conrad	44	Bavaria	Y	Bremen	Baltimore	07/01/1847	01/20/1852	24	38	N	
Iffland, Andrew	24	Germany	Y	Bremen	New York	06/10/1893	10/18/1899			Y	
Ifirmann, Frederick	22	Bavaria	Y	Havre	New York	05/30/1852	10/09/1854	6	169	N	
Igel, Frederick William	44	Prussia	Y	Liverpool	New York	04/06/1852	04/17/1854	9	16	N	
Igel, Henry	27	Germany	Y	Bremen	Baltimore	12/03/1882	10/13/1884			Y	
Igelbrink, John Christop	38	Hanover	Y	Bremen	Baltimore	01/01/1855	08/07/1860	27	255	N	
Igelmann, John G. H.	33	Oldenburg	Y	Bremen	Baltimore	10/09/1857	10/06/1860	27	411	N	
Igo, Martin	30	Ireland	Y	Liverpool	New York	04/26/1844	02/20/1857	15	39	N	
Ihle, Christian	28	Wurttemberg	Y	Havre	New York	04/15/1853	06/11/1859	17	453	N	
Ikkind, Gerhard	40	Holland	Y	Amsterdam	New York	12/03/1847	06/13/1861	18	191	N	
Ilg, Anton	30	Germany	Y	Havre	New York	10/14/1888	11/08/1893			Y	
Ilg, Jacob	25	Wuertemberg	Y	Havre	New York	06/01/1853	03/25/1856	26	309	N	
Ilges, Guido	21	Prussia	Y	Liverpool	New York	06/17/1855	05/16/1859			Y	
Ill, Charles	27	Baden	Y	London	New York	09/05/1848	02/05/1851	3	101	N	
Ilsen, Oscar	41	Germany	Y	Bremen	New York	10/??/1874	10/17/1890			Y	
Imbach, Aegidius	33	Switzerland	Y	Havre	New York	06/05/1879	10/29/1892			Y	
Imber, Napatali Herz.	37	Austria	Y	London	New York	09/15/1890	03/29/1894	21	67	N	
Imberg, Charles	26	Wurttemberg	Y	Havre	New Orleans	01/15/1850	01/14/1851	2	494	N	
Imbusch, Louis	28	Germany	Y	Bremen	New York	12/03/1888	12/18/1891			Y	
Imdieke, Joseph	27	Germany	Y	Hamburg	New York	03/17/1879	01/03/1885			Y	
Imenschuh, Philip	22	Baden	Y	Havre	New York	10/17/1848	01/16/1849	1	430	N	
Imhauser, Henry	25	Prussia	Y	Antwerp	New York	08/23/1848	10/06/1848	22	448	N	

CITIZENSHIP RECORDS

APPLICANT	AGE	COUNTRY OF ORIGIN	DEC	DEPART PORT	ENTRY PORT	ARRIVE DATE	DEC DATE	VOL	PG.	FLD	NAT DATE
Imhof, Herman	23	Prussia	Y	Bremen	Baltimore	10/30/1846	02/19/1849	23	196	N	
Imhof, Jacob	21	Bavaria	Y	Havre	New Orleans	09/28/1850	12/02/1852	5	373	N	
Imhof, John Jacob	28	Bavaria	Y	Liverpool	New York	06/02/1853	03/24/1856	26	289	N	
Imhof, Mathias	32	Baden	Y	Havre	New York	05/08/1854	04/05/1856	26	447	N	
Imhoft, Gerard	25	Prussia	Y	Bremen	Baltimore	08/31/1845	10/05/1848	22	438	N	
Imholt, Henry Anton	30	Hanover	Y	Bremen	Baltimore	07/22/1850	01/10/1856	13	477	N	
Immel, Henry	27	Germany	Y	Bremen	New York	12/29/1894	01/02/1895			Y	
Immig, Carl	34	Germany	Y	Havre	New York	11/02/1882	11/02/1886			Y	
Imphender, Fred	32	Germany	Y	Bremen	Baltimore	09/17/1874	05/29/1882			Y	
Imsande, August	29	Germany	Y	Hamburg	New York	07/01/1889	08/08/1892			Y	
Imsande, Fred	32	Germany	Y	Bremen	Baltimore	09/17/1874	05/29/1882			Y	
Imsonda, Deiderich	30	Hanover	Y	Bremen	Baltimore	12/15/1848	05/06/1854	8	385	N	
Imsonda, Diedrich	30	Hanover	Y	Bremen	Baltimore	12/15/1848	05/06/1854	9	258	N	
Imwalle, Henry	26	Hanover	Y	Bremen	New Orleans	11/08/1857	10/01/1860	27	396	N	
Imwalle, J. H. Joseph	48	Germany	N	Bremen	New York	09/13/1858	?			Y	
Imwalle, John	23	Hanover	Y	Bremen	New York	09/17/1858	12/18/1861	18	234	N	
Imwalle, Joseph	24	Germany	Y	Bremen	Baltimore	06/01/1882	11/05/1886			Y	
Imwalle, William	28	Germany	Y	Bremen	Baltimore	09/11/1891	10/28/1898			Y	
Inderrieden, Bernard	21	Germany	Y	Bremen	Baltimore	04/01/1880	04/13/1882			Y	
Ingram, Thomas	35	Ireland	Y	Liverpool	New York	10/03/1854	06/24/1860	27	5	N	
Ingwersen, John	23	Germany	Y	Hamburg	New York	06/05/1885	11/02/1889			Y	
Inkofer, Markas	43	Germany	Y	Bremen	New York	06/02/1885	07/09/1892			Y	
Inkofer, Martin	35	Germany	Y	Amsterdam	New York	07/18/1882	10/04/1886			Y	
Insprucher, Michael	26	Bavaria	Y	Bremen	Baltimore	10/15/1845	08/15/1848	22	134	N	
Inurez, Francisco Alvare	24	?	Y	?	?	?	08/13/1892			Y	
Inwalle, Herman	52	Germany	Y	Bremen	Baltimore	09/10/1891	11/01/1894			Y	
Irish, Andrew	36	Ireland	Y	Liverpool	New York	10/22/1850	11/12/1855	14	211	N	
Irvine, John	32	Scotland	Y	Glasgow	New York	09/19/1870	05/29/1883			Y	
Irving, Joseph Hoodles	24	England	Y	Liverpool	New York	09/23/1884	06/02/1887			Y	
Irwin, Henry	27	Ireland	Y	Liverpool	New Orleans	10/13/1851	04/17/1854	8	163	N	
Irwin, Henry	27	Ireland	Y	Liverpool	New Orleans	10/13/1851	04/17/1854	9	34	N	
Irwin, Thomas	24	Ireland	Y	Galway	Boston	10/08/1847	10/20/1852	5	23	N	
Irwin, William	33	Ireland	N	Dublin	New York	06/??/1869	?			Y	
Isaac, Isadore	36	Germany	Y	Hamburg	New York	08/18/1889	10/13/1896			Y	
Isaac, Samuel	25	Prussia	Y	Liverpool	New York	??/18/1850	04/23/1855	11	284	N	
Isele, Emil	28	Germany	Y	Havre	New York	09/12/1883	08/21/1888			Y	
Isenrich, Joseph Martin	31	Switzerland	Y	Antwerp	New York	03/20/1880	10/20/1887			Y	
Iseringhausen, August	31	Germany	Y	Bremen	Baltimore	08/31/1881	10/23/1889			Y	
Isherwood, John	33	England	Y	Liverpool	Boston	11/13/1848	04/12/1852	24	467	N	
Isphording, Anthony	30	Prussia	Y	Antwerp	New York	06/25/1845	03/04/1851	3	217	N	
Israel, Israel	53	Russia	Y	Hamburg	New York	04/30/1885	10/20/1891			Y	
Israel, Samuel L.	29	Russia	Y	Hamburg	New York	07/10/1886	10/20/1891			Y	
Issersohn, Nathan	37	Russia	Y	Hamburg	New York	11/11/1886	08/27/1892			Y	
Issler, Friedrich Wm	28	Germany	Y	Antwerp	Philadelphia	07/14/1892	08/13/1896			Y	
Ittig, William	46	Germany	N	Bremen	New Orleans	10/??/1854	?			Y	
Ivanovich, Stefano	??	?	Y	?	?	?	08/03/1903			Y	
Ivinson, John	25	England	Y	Liverpool	New Orleans	01/30/1850	02/22/1853	7	212	N	
Ivory, Patrick	35	Ireland	Y	Liverpool	Boston	12/20/1854	12/16/1861	18	233	N	
Jache, Otto	25	Germany	Y	Bremen	New York	04/12/1890	10/28/1892			Y	
Jacke, Fritz	36	Germany	Y	Bremen	New York	08/18/1887	05/04/1889			Y	
Jackman, Ike	27	Austria	Y	Hamburg	New York	09/27/1892	01/31/1893			Y	
Jackson, Allen	??	England	Y	?	?	?	12/27/1887			Y	
Jackson, Henry H.	??	Canada	Y	?	?	09/??/1862	10/15/1870			Y	
Jackson, John	32	Ireland	Y	Londonderry	Philadelphia	07/05/1839	06/26/1851	3	456	N	
Jackson, Joseph	??	Ireland	Y	?	?	?	12/16/1892			Y	
Jackson, Ralph	42	England	Y	Liverpool	New York	02/10/1849	04/02/1853	7	492	N	
Jackson, William	29	Ireland	Y	Liverpool	New York	04/18/1887	09/25/1896			Y	
Jacob, Christian	28	Bavaria	Y	Havre	New York	05/06/1845	10/09/1854	6	151	N	
Jacob, Christian	28	Bavaria	Y	Havre	New York	05/06/1845	10/09/1854	11	154	N	

CITIZENSHIP RECORDS

APPLICANT	AGE	COUNTRY OF ORIGIN	DEC	DEPART PORT	ENTRY PORT	ARRIVE DATE	DEC DATE	VOL	PG.	FLD	NAT DATE
Jacob, David	40	Austria	Y	Bremen	New York	12/18/1854	05/20/1856	26	500	N	
Jacob, George	26	Bavaria	Y	Liverpool	New York	09/28/1851	11/01/1852	4	278	N	
Jacob, George	30	Bavaria	Y	Bremen	New York	12/15/1854	08/24/1857	15	183	N	
Jacob, Gustav	34	Germany	Y	Antwerp	New York	06/16/1881	10/10/1881			Y	
Jacob, Henry Metzger	28	Baden	Y	Havre	New York	10/25/1859	08/15/1860	27	285	N	
Jacob, Leopold	25	Bavaria	Y	Bremen	Baltimore	10/20/1846	08/14/1849	23	112	N	
Jacob, Max	51	Canada	Y	Canada	Detroit	12/02/1889	07/01/1895			Y	
Jacob, Philip	38	Bavaria	Y	Bremen	Baltimore	05/15/1860	08/27/1860	27	317	N	
Jacob, Veis	43	Bavaria	Y	Havre	New Orleans	05/01/1849	06/12/1852	25	249	N	
Jacob, William	25	Hanover	Y	Bremen	New York	10/26/1852	10/10/1854	6	230	N	
Jacob, William	25	Hanover	Y	Bremen	New York	10/26/1852	10/01/1854	11	233	N	
Jacobi, Christ	29	Germany	Y	Havre	New York	05/01/1879	10/28/1887			Y	
Jacobi, Fredrich	41	Germany	Y	Bremen	New York	01/18/1883	05/01/1899			Y	
Jacobi, Peter	25	Prussia	Y	Liverpool	Boston	11/30/1853	09/25/1854	12	163	N	
Jacobi, Peter	33	Germany	N	Havre	New York	08/26/1871	?			Y	
Jacobs, Abraham	49	Germany	Y	Bremen	New York	10/07/1875	10/09/1882			Y	
Jacobs, Abraham	60	Poland	N	Liverpool	New York	09/??/1850	?			Y	
Jacobs, August	31	Germany	Y	Bremen	Baltimore	08/31/1879	10/22/1889	19	244	N	
Jacobs, August	31	Germany	Y	Bremen	Baltimore	08/31/1879	10/22/1889			Y	
Jacobs, George	31	Germany	Y	Bremen	Baltimore	08/24/1883	11/05/1890			Y	
Jacobs, Louis	28	Germany	Y	Bremen	New York	09/30/1887	12/19/1889			Y	
Jacobs, Max	39	Germany	Y	Liverpool	New York	10/10/1885	10/14/1897			Y	
Jacobs, Peter	41	France	Y	Liverpool	Philadelphia	11/30/1887	11/19/1894	21	76	N	
Jacobs, Simon	28	Canada	Y	Canada	Cincinnati	10/07/1889	10/27/1894			Y	
Jacobson, Joseph	??	Russia	N	?	?	09/10/1880				Y	10/29/1892
Jacobson, Simon	28	Poland	Y	Hamburg	New York	11/29/1882	10/14/1889			Y	
Jacoby, John	40	Germany	Y	Bremen	New York	07/??/1872	11/01/1886			Y	
Jacoby, Max	??	Russia	Y	?	?	05/05/1892	08/24/1897			Y	
Jacquemeier, John James	29	Belgium	Y	Antwerp	New York	07/12/1850	11/01/1852	5	87	N	
Jacques, John	35	France	Y	Havre	New Orleans	06/01/1846	11/05/1852	5	232	N	
Jacques, John	35	France	Y	Havre	New Orleans	06/01/1846	11/05/1852	6	358	N	
Jaeckin, Emil Albert	34	Germany	Y	Antwerp	New York	04/23/1889	10/22/1894			Y	
Jaeckle, Andreas George	34	Germany	Y	Havre	New York	11/30/1891	05/09/1892			Y	
Jaeger, Frank	28	Germany	Y	Bremen	Baltimore	03/05/1881	08/18/1888			Y	
Jaeger, George	30	Germany	Y	Antwerp	New York	07/07/1882	10/17/1885			Y	
Jaeger, Gottlieb	30	Wurttemberg	Y	Havre	New York	06/29/1854	09/30/1856	14	46	N	
Jaeger, Robert	48	Switzerland	N	Antwerp	Philadelphia	08/14/1882	?			Y	
Jaegers, Albert	30	Germany	Y	Amsterdam	New York	08/08/1881	03/25/1882			Y	
Jaenigen, Herman	22	Prussia	Y	Bremen	New York	06/02/1882	04/07/1890			Y	
Jaffe, Herman	23	Germany	Y	Bremen	New York	05/31/1888	03/28/1891			Y	
Jagen, Herman	25	Prussia	Y	Bremen	Baltimore	10/26/1858	04/16/1860	27	157	N	
Jahn, Charles	28	Hanover	Y	Bremen	New York	10/01/1853	10/02/1856	14	168	N	
Jahn, Charles	26	Hesse Cassel	Y	Bremen	Baltimore	01/15/1861	01/22/1862	18	250	N	
Jahn, Hilbert	32	Germany	Y	Bremen	New York	10/31/1880	10/28/1889			N	
Jahn, Max	26	Germany	Y	Hamburg	New York	03/22/1883	03/29/1884			Y	
Jahn, Michael	30	Bavaria	Y	Hamburg	New York	08/07/1844	09/04/1848	22	291	N	
Jahn, William	24	Braunschweig	Y	Bremen	New York	09/04/1854	10/12/1857	15	407	N	
Jahnle, Gottfried	42	Germany	Y	Bremen	New York	08/19/1883	12/27/1887			Y	
Jahnuseck, John	24	Austria	Y	Bremen	New York	01/10/1891	12/28/1892			Y	
Jakob, George	26	Bavaria	Y	Liverpool	New York	09/28/1851	11/01/1852	5	152	N	
Jakobi, Peter	25	Prussia	Y	Liverpool	Boston	11/30/1853	09/25/1854	10	224	N	
Jakobs, Heinrich	41	Germany	Y	Bremen	New York	10/01/1888	10/07/1892			Y	
Jakobs, Jacob	39	Germany	Y	Antwerp	?	05/24/1872	05/05/1874			Y	
Jakris, Leib	??	Austria	Y	?	?	?	06/02/1891			Y	
James, George	24	England	Y	Liverpool	New York	05/03/1886	04/22/1889			Y	
James, John	??	England	Y	Liverpool	New York	??/14/1847	12/13/1850	2	361	N	
Jamieson, Archibald W.H.	33	Ireland	Y	Londonderry	New York	07/06/1889	06/05/1897			Y	
Jamieson, Robert	??	Ireland	Y	?	?	?	06/16/1888			Y	
Jamison, Wilson	25	Ireland	Y	?	New York	??/??/1892	09/24/1896			Y	

CITIZENSHIP RECORDS

APPLICANT	AGE	COUNTRY OF ORIGIN	DEC	DEPART PORT	ENTRY PORT	ARRIVE DATE	DEC DATE	VOL	PG.	FLD	NAT DATE
Jana, John	30	Austria	Y	Bremen	Baltimore	05/28/1884	07/24/1889			Y	
Janisch, Henry	40	Germany	Y	Hamburg	New York	08/29/1884	12/29/1888			Y	
Janiszewski, Wladislaus	23	Germany	Y	Bremen	New York	07/04/1885	10/07/1887			Y	
Janning, John Herman	25	Hanover	Y	Bremen	New Orleans	12/25/1852	02/04/1856	26	34	N	
Janosik, John	38	Austria	Y	Bremen	New York	03/25/1897	03/24/1900			Y	
Jansen, John	37	Hanover	Y	Bremen	New Orleans	12/15/1845	09/30/1848	22	370	N	
Jansen, William	36	Oldenburg	Y	Bremen	New Orleans	11/14/1844	11/01/1852	5	95	N	
Jansen, William	36	Oldenburg	Y	Bremen	New Orleans	11/14/1844	11/01/1852	6	243	N	
Jansen, William	31	Hanover	Y	Bremen	Baltimore	10/13/1854	02/27/1858	16	346	N	
Jansh, Robert	48	Germany	Y	?	New Orleans	??/??/1882	09/30/1897			Y	
Jansing, Bernard H.	26	Germany	Y	Bremen	Baltimore	05/19/1873	11/10/1879			Y	
Jansing, G.H.	29	Germany	Y	Bremen	New York	05/21/1873	06/19/1883			Y	
Janssen, Fred	29	Germany	Y	Bremen	New York	10/13/1882	03/26/1888	19	131	N	
Janssen, Fred	29	Germany	Y	Bremen	New York	10/13/1882	03/26/1888			Y	
Janssen, Heinrich	45	Germany	N	Bremen	Baltimore	10/03/1881	?			Y	
Janssen, Henry	56	Germany	Y	Bremen	New York	10/14/1882	10/02/1903			Y	
Jantz, Frank Joseph	26	France	Y	Havre	New Orleans	05/19/1849	07/05/1851	3	500	N	
Janz, Charles F.	28	Baden	Y	Antwerp	New York	01/12/1850	02/27/1850	2	138	N	
Janz, George	31	Baden	Y	Antwerp	New York	08/27/1848	02/27/1850	2	141	N	
Janz, Samuel	25	Baden	Y	Havre	New York	??/04/1845	02/27/1850	2	140	N	
Jarehow, John H.	40	Germany	N	Hamburg	New York	04/15/1867	?			Y	
Jarrell, Patrick	28	Ireland	Y	Liverpool	New York	04/28/1888	11/06/1893			Y	
Jasper, Herman	31	Prussia	Y	Bremen	New Orleans	12/28/1851	09/12/1860	27	365	N	
Jaspers, Henry	21	Oldenburg	Y	Bremen	Baltimore	11/01/1850	05/25/1854	8	538	N	
Jaspers, Henry	21	Oldenburg	Y	Bremen	Baltimore	11/01/1850	05/25/1854	9	412	N	
Jaspers, Henry	65	Germany	N	Bremen	New Orleans	11/06/1856	?			Y	
Jaspers, Herman	39	Germany	Y	Bremen	Baltimore	01/03/1882	10/17/1892			Y	
Jasy, Jeremiah	25	Ireland	Y	Liverpool	New Orleans	05/??/1851	09/22/1857	15	303	N	
Jauch, George	32	Germany	Y	Hamburg	Baltimore	02/23/1880	07/17/1884			Y	
Jauch, Michael	48	Germany	Y	Bremen	New York	12/31/1887	10/27/1890			Y	
Jauch, Richard	36	Germany	Y	Bremen	New York	07/10/1880	10/26/1888	19	187	N	
Jauch, Richard	36	Germany	Y	Bremen	New York	07/10/1880	10/26/1888			Y	
Jeberien, H.F. Ludwig	46	Germany	Y	Hamburg	Philadelphia	11/27/1882	01/22/1889			Y	
Jeckel, Jacob	35	Bavaria	Y	Havre	New York	06/21/1853	12/05/1857	16	197	N	
Jecker, Joseph	26	Switzerland	Y	Liverpool	New York	05/05/1852	05/22/1856	26	538	N	
Jeffery, William	32	England	Y	Liverpool	New York	04/15/1851	03/21/1856	26	244	N	
Jeggi, Joseph	39	Baden	Y	Havre	New Orleans	07/14/1849	09/06/1852	25	382	N	
Jeggli, Francis Xavier	40	Switzerland	Y	Antwerp	New York	12/03/1853	03/04/1858	16	372	N	
Jeggli, Valentine	26	Switzerland	Y	Havre	New York	10/08/1857	04/02/1861	18	126	N	
Jendes, Adam	31	Germany	Y	Antwerp	New York	04/03/1887	10/22/1889	19	248	N	
Jenkins, Even L.	33	England	Y	Liverpool	New York	04/21/1881	03/28/1885			Y	
Jenkins, Thomas	63	England	N	Liverpool	New York	05/??/1846	?			Y	
Jenkner, Erich	49	Austria	Y	Bremen	New York	10/10/1883	11/04/1890			Y	
Jennewein, Peter	74	Germany	N	Germany	New York	06/03/1853	?			Y	
Jenni, Frederick	28	Germany (Swit	Y	?	?	04/??/1883	10/27/1884			Y	
Jennings, John	25	Ireland	Y	Queenstown	New York	06/22/1895	10/31/1896			Y	
Jepson, Hubert Edward	33	England	Y	?	Garret	01/27/1887	03/10/1892			Y	
Jermor, John	??	Prussia	Y	?	?	?	04/13/1868			Y	
Jernteman, John Frederic	31	Hanover	Y	Bremen	New Orleans	10/25/1846	09/05/1848	22	303	N	
Jeruk, Jacob	27	Bavaria	Y	Havre	New York	10/09/1845	09/30/1848	22	371	N	
Jervis, James M.	26	Wales	Y	Liverpool	New York	04/14/1882	03/17/1886			Y	
Jesse, Michael	29	Germany	Y	Bremen	Baltimore	06/22/1881	09/28/1883			Y	
Jessen, John	35	Denmark	Y	Copenhagen	Buffalo	10/05/1859	07/03/1860	27	204	N	
Jessop, Wm A.	??	England	Y	?	?	?	11/04/1882			Y	
Jetten, Jan William	??	Holland	Y	?	?	?	09/30/1890			Y	
Jetter, Balthas	33	Germany	Y	Bremen	New York	05/28/1880	08/26/1881			Y	
Jettinghoff, Henry	24	Germany	Y	Bremen	New York	07/08/1881	11/27/1882			Y	
Jifers, Thomas	34	Ireland	Y	Liverpool	New Orleans	12/??/1847	11/??/1849	23	318	N	
Jimpelmann, George	25	Bavaria	Y	Havre	New York	08/13/1849	10/13/1851	4	237	N	

CITIZENSHIP RECORDS

APPLICANT	AGE	COUNTRY OF ORIGIN	DEC	DEPART PORT	ENTRY PORT	ARRIVE DATE	DEC DATE	VOL	PG.	FLD	NAT DATE
Joachim, George	25	Germany	Y	Bremen	New York	10/10/1892	04/10/1893			Y	
Joachim, Joseph	33	Germany	Y	Bremen	New York	02/26/1880	07/15/1885			Y	
Jochem, Nick	34	Germany	Y	Antwerp	New York	08/07/1884	03/16/1887			Y	
Joehnk, August	24	Germany	Y	Hamburg	New York	02/10/1882	03/29/1884			Y	
Joehnk, Ben	26	Germany	Y	Hamburg	New York	02/10/1882	10/05/1885			Y	
Joerg, Gottlieb	34	Switzerland	Y	Havre	New York	09/14/1881	08/02/1882			Y	
Joerg, Simon	32	Germany	Y	Bremen	New York	10/01/1887	04/11/1895			Y	
Joerg, Theophile	34	Switzerland	Y	Havre	New York	09/14/1881	08/02/1882			Y	
Joergens, ?	28	Prussia	Y	Bremen	New Orleans	01/16/1847	10/07/1848	22	468	N	
Joergens, George Henry	28	Prussia	Y	Bremen	New York	05/08/1852	04/25/1854	8	258	N	
Joerger, Tobias	27	Germany	Y	Bremen	New York	04/04/1882	06/13/1887			Y	
Joering, Frederick	28	Hanover	Y	Bremen	Baltimore	06/15/1847	10/04/1854	10	417	N	
Joerling, Frank	27	Germany	Y	Bremen	New York	04/05/1889	09/05/1890			Y	
Joesting, Wm	28	Germany	Y	Bremen	New York	05/22/1881	08/23/1889			Y	
Joffee, Moses	48	Russia	Y	Bremen	Baltimore	06/07/1889	10/21/1903			Y	
Joge, J.B.	42	Germany	Y	?	Baltimore	??/??/1867	10/13/1884			Y	
Joggerst, Mathias	44	Germany	Y	Havre	New York	06/17/1883	03/05/1885			Y	
Johaentges, Reinhard	31	Germany	Y	Antwerp	New York	06/24/1884	02/13/1892			Y	
Johann, Frederick	25	Bavaria	Y	Havre	New Orleans	11/09/1843	11/13/1848	1	253	N	
Johann, Joseph	35	Bavaria	Y	Havre	New Orleans	11/09/1843	11/13/1848	1	273	N	
Johannes, George	25	Germany	Y	Antwerp	New York	09/20/1883	05/02/1887			Y	
Johannes, Herman	35	Saxe Meininge	Y	Bremen	New York	10/07/1848	03/13/1851	3	274	N	
Johannes, Peter	22	Baiern	Y	Havre	New York	10/19/1849	10/21/1852	5	43	N	
Johanning, Herman Heinri	30	Oldenburg	Y	Amsterdam	New York	06/14/1849	04/16/1852	24	517	N	
Johanning, William	23	Hanover	Y	Bremen	New Orleans	11/06/1857	08/20/1860	27	301	N	
Johansing, Charlie	??	Germany	N	?	?	05/15/1882				Y	10/28/1892
Johansing, William	31	Germany	Y	Bremen	New York	05/31/1882	03/12/1888			Y	
John, Henry	38	Germany	Y	Bremen	New York	07/06/1889	07/18/1894			Y	
John, Ott	34	Germany	Y	Hamburg	New York	09/24/1891	10/24/1899			Y	
Johnke, Herman	24	Germany	Y	Antwerp	New York	04/04/1882	10/06/1884			Y	
Johnke, Rudolph	27	Germany	Y	Hamburg	New York	02/17/1882	10/07/1884			Y	
Johnson, Andrew Peter	39	Sweden	Y	Goteborg	New York	07/??/1868	04/30/1883			Y	
Johnson, John	24	Sweden	Y	Goteborg	New York	11/19/1891	02/16/1891			Y	
Johnson, John W.	24	Sweden	Y	Goteborg	New York	02/24/1893	10/28/1899			Y	
Johnson, Leonard	48	Sweden	Y	Goteborg	Boston	06/14/1881	04/07/1886			Y	
Johnson, Louis	??	Sweden	Y	?	?	?	04/07/1885			Y	
Johnson, N. Ross	27	Canada	Y	Sarnia	Port Huron	12/24/1882	08/03/1891			Y	
Johnson, Sydney William	27	England	Y	Bristol	New York	06/10/1883	12/07/1888			Y	
Johnston, Francis	23	Ireland	Y	Liverpool	New York	08/17/1845	03/01/1852	24	196	N	
Johnston, James A.	35	Ireland	Y	Belfast	New York	05/30/1839	07/01/1851	3	474	N	
Johnston, John	23	England	Y	Liverpool	Philadelphia	08/15/1852	02/20/1856	26	110	N	
Johnston, Sam	??	Sweden/Norway	N	?	?	03/02/1882				Y	11/03/1892
Johnston, William	40	Ireland	Y	Canada	Buffalo	09/??/1849	12/15/1852	5	417	N	
Johnston, William	27	Ireland	Y	Liverpool	New York	12/22/1859	05/10/1862	18	333	N	
Johnston, William	30	Ireland	Y	Liverpool	New York	09/11/1885	06/21/1886			Y	
Jokers, Ludwig	26	Baden	Y	Havre	New York	09/22/1845	10/02/1848	22	387	N	
Jokers, Michael	24	Baden	Y	Havre	New York	08/26/1852	09/20/1855	13	87	N	
Jokisch, Thomas	44	Germany	Y	Hamburg	New York	09/14/1883	12/31/1886			Y	
Jonas, Henry W.	49	England	Y	Liverpool	New Orleans	02/??/1832	10/29/1857	15	500	N	
Jones, Abraham	30	Wales	Y	Liverpool	New York	07/10/1847	05/02/1850	3	43	N	
Jones, Benjamin	28	Wales	Y	Liverpool	New York	09/22/1890	10/16/1894			Y	
Jones, Charles Howell	46	England	Y	Liverpool	New York	07/19/1888	02/10/1890			Y	
Jones, David	37	Wales	Y	Liverpool	Philadelphia	03/23/1849	05/22/1854	9	369	N	
Jones, David	25	Wales	Y	Liverpool	New York	08/05/1851	11/26/1855	13	256	N	
Jones, David	36	Wales	Y	Liverpool	New York	07/07/1856	12/24/1861	18	237	N	
Jones, David H.	37	Wales	Y	Liverpool	New Orleans	??/??/1846	04/30/1855	11	333	N	
Jones, David L.	28	Wales	Y	Liverpool	New York	04/??/1880	01/29/1883			Y	
Jones, David T.	??	Wales	Y	?	?	?	10/07/1889			Y	
Jones, David W.	37	Wales	Y	Liverpool	Philadelphia	03/23/1849	05/22/1854	8	495	N	

CITIZENSHIP RECORDS

APPLICANT	AGE	COUNTRY OF ORIGIN	DEC	DEPART PORT	ENTRY PORT	ARRIVE DATE	DEC DATE	VOL	PG.	FLD	NAT DATE
Jones, Edward	25	England	Y	Liverpool	New York	04/05/1883	09/29/1886			Y	
Jones, George	34	England	Y	Liverpool	New York	05/28/1844	02/19/1851	3	144	N	
Jones, H.O.	23	Wales	Y	Liverpool	New York	05/29/1881	09/04/1884			Y	
Jones, James D.	40	Wales	Y	Liverpool	New York	06/03/1846	07/09/1855	11	354	N	
Jones, John	??	Ireland	Y	Liverpool	New Orleans	??/09/1849	12/??/1850	2	405	N	
Jones, John	26	England	Y	Liverpool	Boston	07/28/1883	04/13/1885			Y	
Jones, John H.	26	Wales	Y	Liverpool	New York	07/03/1849	02/05/1856	26	46	N	
Jones, John Henry Parry	??	Wales	Y	?	?	?	01/02/1883			Y	
Jones, John R.	54	England	Y	Liverpool	New York	03/27/1884	01/04/1889			Y	
Jones, Jonathon H.	37	England	Y	Liverpool	New Orleans	06/06/1848	06/16/1851	3	386	N	
Jones, Joseph	32	England	Y	Liverpool	New York	02/28/1885	09/03/1896			Y	
Jones, Joseph	21	England (Wale	Y	Liverpool	New York	04/11/1894	04/11/1895			Y	
Jones, Lodwick	24	Wales	Y	Nova Scotia	Boston	??/19/1845	12/03/1849	23	384	N	
Jones, Owen G.	25	Wales	Y	Liverpool	New York	05/18/1882	01/08/1885			Y	
Jones, Peter	26	Ireland	Y	Liverpool	New York	08/16/1849	10/13/1857	15	416	N	
Jones, Richard	27	Wales	Y	Liverpool	New York	05/01/1846	02/12/1851	3	127	N	
Jones, Richard	23	Wales	Y	Liverpool	New York	05/01/1851	04/04/1853	7	534	N	
Jones, Richard M.	??	Wales	Y	?	?	08/??/1880	04/25/1884			Y	
Jones, Robert	28	England	Y	Liverpool	New York	08/??/1849	03/25/1851	3	351	N	
Jones, Robert	47	England	Y	Liverpool	New York	05/18/1837	10/05/1860	27	399	N	
Jones, Rowland	32	North Wales	Y	Liverpool	New York	09/04/1849	01/07/1860	27	42	N	
Jones, Rupert M.	35	England	Y	?	?	?	09/28/1892			Y	
Jones, Samuel	40	England	N	Liverpool	New York	05/??/1861	?			Y	
Jones, Samuel William	34	Wales	Y	Liverpool	New York	06/11/1852	01/19/1856	13	485	N	
Jones, Thomas	22	Wales	Y	?	?	?	10/31/1888			Y	
Jones, Thomas S.	21	Wales	Y	?	?	08/01/1884	03/19/1885			Y	
Jones, William	31	England	Y	Liverpool	New Orleans	12/??/1848	10/31/1851	4	442	N	
Jones, William	27	Wales	Y	Liverpool	New York	08/15/1880	10/13/1884			Y	
Jonte, Peter	37	France	Y	Havre	New York	08/26/1852	12/30/1857	16	288	N	
Joos, Frederick	??	Baden	Y	?	New York	??/22/18??	11/03/1856	14	453	N	
Joos, Philipp Gottlob	24	Wurttemberg	Y	Havre	New York	01/02/1859	02/20/1861	18	115	N	
Jordan, John	29	Ireland	Y	Liverpool	New York	10/15/1857	05/21/1861	18	175	N	
Jordon, George Henry	37	Hanover	Y	Bremen	Baltimore	07/18/1846	02/10/1851	3	111	N	
Jordon, Hugo	??	Germany	Y	?	?	?	03/16/1892			Y	
Jorgens, George Henry	28	Prussia	Y	Bremen	New York	05/08/1852	04/25/1854	9	129	N	
Joring, Frederick	28	Hanover	Y	Bremen	Baltimore	06/15/1847	10/04/1854	12	356	N	
Jorling, Herman	59	Germany	Y	Bremen	New York	04/28/1864	03/20/1897			Y	
Jory, John	36	England	Y	Liverpool	New York	04/16/1854	06/02/1856	14	284	N	
Jory, Samuel	22	England	Y	Canada	Lewiston	06/10/1850	06/02/1852	25	173	N	
Josef, Henry	31	Germany	Y	Havre	New York	11/15/1890	03/14/1892			Y	
Joseph, ?	25	Germany	Y	Hamburg	New York	11/28/1873	04/??/1880			Y	
Joseph, Abraham	69	Germany	N	Hamburg	New York	08/25/1864	?			Y	
Joseph, Benzer F.	36	Austria	Y	Bremen	New York	05/28/1890	11/09/1893			Y	
Joseph, Christian D.	43	Russia	Y	Liverpool	New York	11/02/1885	03/29/1886			Y	
Joseph, Herman	30	Germany	Y	?	New York	??/??/1877	10/11/1884			Y	
Joseph, Joseph	48	Hassen Darmis	N	Hamburg	New York	11/10/1864	?			Y	
Joseph, Leopold	27	Germany	Y	Bremen	New York	04/30/1888	02/09/1891			Y	
Joseph, Leopold	16	Germany	N	?	New York	00/00/1880				Y	10/23/1886
Joseph, Samuel	25	Germany	Y	Hamburg	New York	11/18/1873	04/05/1880			Y	
Joseph, Simon	26	Turkey	Y	?	New York	??/??/1884	08/14/1890			Y	
Jost, Frederick	32	Switzerland	Y	Havre	New York	03/17/1880	06/06/1881			Y	
Jost, Henry William	28	Saxony	Y	Antwerp	New Orleans	11/25/1847	06/11/1852	25	236	N	
Josting, Herman	44	Germany	Y	Bremen	New York	07/27/1881	11/12/1890			Y	
Jourdern, George	32	Germany	Y	Havre	?	??/??/1884	10/30/1886			Y	
Jourkawitch, Nathan	33	Russia	Y	Hamburg	New York	06/10/1895	10/31/1899			Y	
Joyce, Edmund	65	Ireland	N	Queenstown	New Orleans	03/01/1851	08/??/1851	28	262	N	04/??/1856
Joyce, Edmund	29	Ireland	N	Queenstown	New Orleans	03/01/1851	08/00/1851			Y	04/00/1856
Joyce, Michael	32	Ireland	Y	Liverpool	New Orleans	01/04/1853	02/08/1853	7	126	N	
Joyce, Patrick	47	Ireland	Y	Liverpool	New Orleans	12/20/1850	08/27/1855	11	500	N	

CITIZENSHIP RECORDS

APPLICANT	AGE	COUNTRY OF ORIGIN	DEC	DEPART PORT	ENTRY PORT	ARRIVE DATE	DEC DATE	VOL	PG.	FLD	NAT DATE
Joyce, Thomas C.	31	Ireland	Y	Queenstown	New York	05/20/1868	03/31/1882			Y	
Joyce, Thomas C.	33	Ireland	N	Queenstown	New York	05/20/1868	?			Y	
Jucht, August F.	40	Bavaria	N	Hamburg	New York	08/??/1869	?			Y	
Judge, James	45	Ireland	Y	Canada	Sandusky	05/04/1848	12/06/1852	5	381	N	
Judge, William	35	Ireland	Y	Liverpool	New York	01/12/1852	11/03/1857	15	524	N	
Judlekofer, Edward	25	Baden	Y	Liverpool	New York	12/25/1853	02/20/1858	16	322	N	
Juehling, Hugo William	??	Germany	Y	?	?	?	05/02/1890			Y	
Jueilfs, Carl J.	39	Germany	Y	Bremen	New York	04/22/1882	02/01/1887			Y	
Juelch, Conrad	33	Bavaria	Y	Havre	New York	05/31/1841	11/06/1851	4	492	N	
Juelg, Michael	30	France	Y	Havre	New York	10/12/1848	06/19/1851	3	429	N	
Juergens, August	25	Germany	Y	Amsterdam	New York	09/09/1885	08/13/1888			Y	
Juergens, Bernard	32	Germany	Y	Bremen	New York	02/01/1890	05/20/1891			Y	
Juergens, John Frederick	33	Hanover	Y	Bremen	New York	09/??/1843	03/24/1856	26	277	N	
Juerger, Joseph	30	Baden	Y	Havre	New York	12/25/1856	11/11/1858	17	321	N	
Juerling, Herman	45	Germany	Y	Bremen	Baltimore	08/??/1868	10/04/1884			Y	
Juet, William	29	Nassau	Y	Rotterdam	New York	06/11/1851	04/05/1852	24	383	N	
Juettner, Alois Francis	30	Germany	Y	Havre	New York	08/27/1880	10/11/1882			Y	
Juhlmann, John	40	Germany	N	Hamburg	New York	04/??/1862	?			Y	
Juhmann, John	25	Bavaria	Y	Havre	New Orleans	01/21/1855	10/301/858	17	197	N	
Juister, George	53	Germany	Y	Bremen	Baltimore	05/??/1868	10/01/1885			Y	
Julian, William	35	England	Y	Liverpool	New Orleans	01/01/1848	03/22/1851	3	309	N	
Julier, John	29	Germany	Y	Hamburg	New York	05/17/1880	10/04/1887			Y	
Julio, Mike	28	Italy	Y	Roccodaspida	New York	04/02/1893	11/07/1898			Y	
Julte, John Henry	43	Germany	Y	Bremen	Baltimore	08/15/1879	11/02/1896			Y	
Junce, Dietrich	45	Germany	N	Bremen	Baltimore	04/17/1869	?			Y	
Juncker, Gustav Frank	??	France	Y	?	?	?	04/15/1889			Y	
Jund, George	24	Germany	Y	Antwerp	New York	05/10/1889	09/16/1891			Y	
Junemann, Henry	35	Hanover	Y	Bremen	Baltimore	08/08/1846	05/24/1852	25	92	N	
Jung, August	52	Germany	Y	Hamburg	Baltimore	07/25/1871	12/11/1890			Y	
Jung, Carl	56	Germany	N	Havre	New York	10/??/1847	?			Y	
Jung, Christian	34	Prussia	Y	Antwerp	New Orleans	05/19/1847	11/01/1851	4	459	N	
Jung, Christopher	50	Germany	N	Havre	New York	05/02/1853	?			Y	
Jung, Daniel	29	Germany	Y	Antwerp	New York	06/0/1881	08/29/1892			Y	
Jung, Herman	26	Germany	Y	?	New York	??/??/1881	08/31/1887			Y	
Jung, Jacob	26	Germany	Y	Bremen	New York	09/21/1888	01/20/1892			Y	
Jung, Jacob	49	Germany	N	Havre	New York	08/??/1853	?			Y	
Jung, Jacob M.	21	Germany	Y	Antwerp	New York	06/08/1888	11/02/1892			Y	
Jung, Jeangorg	33	France	Y	Havre	New York	05/19/1850	05/19/1852	25	44	N	
Jung, Johann	50	Germany	Y	Bremen	New York	05/07/1885	07/28/1887			Y	
Jung, John	40	Germany	Y	Bremen	New York	06/18/1880	10/23/1888			Y	
Jung, Louis C.	33	Germany	N	Bremen	Baltimore	03/03/1871	?			Y	
Jung, Maximiliam	22	Germany	Y	Antwerp	New York	09/29/1880	12/05/1881			Y	
Jung, Otto	??	Germany	Y	Bremen	New York	09/30/1891	08/17/1892			Y	
Jung, Peter	38	Bavaria	Y	Havre	New Orleans	05/06/1853	01/29/1856	13	517	N	
Jung, Peter	21	Germany	Y	Havre	New York	06/22/1882	05/25/1885			Y	
Jung, Theobald	25	Bavaria	Y	Havre	New York	08/26/1846	10/06/1851	4	191	N	
Jung, Theodore	34	Germany	Y	Hamburg	New York	08/15/1885	10/12/1893			Y	
Jung, Wilhelm	34	Germany	Y	Havre	New York	07/05/1883	12/17/1891			Y	
Jungakind, Christian	30	Baden	Y	Havre	New York	01/12/1854	10/01/1857	15	339	N	
Jungeblut, Henry	29	Hanover	Y	Bremen	New York	09/24/1868	05/22/1872	18	493	N	
Jungelas, Henry	53	Germany	Y	Bremen	New York	09/29/1863	10/22/1896			Y	
Junghoeni, George	41	Switzerland	Y	Havre	New York	08/12/1884	01/20/1890			Y	
Jungkunz, Michael	56	Germany	Y	Bremen	Baltimore	09/07/1887	10/16/1889			Y	
Jungmann, John Philip	40	Baden	Y	Havre	New Orleans	10/20/1851	09/26/1854	10	238	N	
Jungmann, John Philip	40	Baden	Y	Havre	New Orleans	10/20/1851	09/26/1854	12	177	N	
Junius, John	33	Germany	Y	Bremen	Baltimore	06/24/1886	11/13/1896			Y	
Junk, Creighton	30	Ireland	Y	Belfast	New York	04/??/1848	11/13/1855	13	218	N	
Junk, John	21	Kurhassen	Y	Bremen	Buffalo	06/20/1846	03/27/1849	23	259	N	
Junker, Fridel	28	Baden	Y	Rotterdam	New York	01/??/1847	12/05/1850	2	340	N	

CITIZENSHIP RECORDS

APPLICANT	AGE	COUNTRY OF ORIGIN	DEC	DEPART PORT	ENTRY PORT	ARRIVE DATE	DEC DATE	VOL	PG.	FLD	NAT DATE
Junker, George	33	Germany	Y	Bremen	New York	05/14/1886	10/09/1893			Y	
Junker, John	29	Germany	Y	Havre	New York	04/01/1889	01/12/1892			Y	
Junkermann, Otto	24	Prussia	Y	Antwerp	New York	07/29/1848	08/15/1851	4	130	N	
Jurg, Jacob	50	Germany	N	Bremen	New York	04/??/1862	08/??/1864			Y	
Jurgan, Andreas	??	Wuerttenberg	Y	Rotterdam	New York	07/02/1845	10/09/1848	22	509	N	
Jurgens, Franz	43	Germany	Y	Bremen	New York	11/07/1888	11/07/1892			Y	
Jurgens, John	53	Germany	Y	Bremen	Baltimore	??/??/1864	10/05/1880			Y	
Jurgensen, John Johannse	21	Germany	Y	Havre	New York	11/18/1880	01/16/1882				
Juskovski, Anton	28	Russia	Y	Hamburg	New York	04/05/1887	10/23/1895			Y	
Jutzi, Charles C.	23	Germany	Y	Rotterdam	New York	05/28/1887	06/24/1890			Y	
Jutzler, Henry	33	Baden	Y	Liverpool	New York	06/02/1853	05/29/1854	9	445	N	
Jutzler, Henry	33	Baden	Y	Liverpool	New York	06/02/1853	05/29/1854	10	28	N	
Jutzoamd, Henry	28	Hanover	Y	Bremen	New Orleans	12/20/1848	11/03/1851	4	469	N	
Juy, Michael	24	Ireland	Y	Liverpool	New York	10/07/1851	02/23/1853	7	225	N	
Kabus, Emil	39	Germany	Y	Havre	New York	05/23/1880	04/12/1899			Y	
Kade, Louis	35	Germany	Y	Hamburg	New York	02/15/1882	06/08/1883			Y	
Kaelen, Ambros	31	Switzerland	Y	Antwerp	New York	08/26/1886	04/18/1892			Y	
Kaelin, Herman	27	Switzerland	Y	Havre	New York	11/08/1882	04/20/1888			Y	
Kaelin, Jos Mar	32	Switzerland	Y	Havre	New York	03/17/1892	03/12/1896			Y	
Kaem, Maddis	30	Bavaria	Y	Havre	New Orleans	03/??/1851	01/10/1853	7	1	N	
Kaemerer, John	23	Baden	Y	Bremen	New York	10/07/1854	10/01/1856	14	136	N	
Kaemmerling, Gustav	33	Prussia	Y	Havre	New York	05/10/1850	01/03/1853	5	507	N	
Kaemper, Joseph	28	Prussia	Y	Bremen	New Orleans	12/29/1847	01/03/1850	23	461	N	
Kaeppner, Anton	39	Germany	Y	Bremen	New York	09/15/1883	11/12/1888			Y	
Kaeppner, Kaspar	37	Germany	Y	Bremen	New York	09/15/1883	12/12/1888			Y	
Kaerbel, David	28	Baden	Y	Havre	New York	07/20/1853	05/20/1854	8	481	N	
Kaercher, Alexander	34	Wurttemberg	Y	Havre	New York	??/23/1852	04/04/1855	11	279	N	
Kaertle, Karl	29	Germany	Y	Havre	New York	06/18/1896	06/04/1900			Y	
Kaeslin, Joseph	33	Switzerland	Y	Antwerp	New York	05/28/1887	05/19/1894			Y	
Kaestle, John	32	Germany	Y	Rotteredam	New York	09/11/1887	08/15/1893			Y	
Kaeufl, John	29	Germany	Y	Rotterdam	New York	08/30/1892	02/23/1894			Y	
Kahle, Christian	36	Hanover	Y	Bremen	Baltimore	10/21/1854	10/06/1856	14	191	N	
Kahle, Henry	27	Germany	Y	Bremen	?	09/23/1881	02/13/1884			Y	
Kahleis, Louis	43	Germany	Y	Bremen	New York	04/23/1882	12/26/1885			Y	
Kahling, Herman	26	Germany	Y	Bremen	Baltimore	05/19/1892	03/29/1900			Y	
Kahn, Alexander	53	Germany	Y	Antwerp	New York	11/13/1882	11/14/1884			Y	
Kahn, Arnold	25	Germany	Y	Havre	New York	12/26/1865	10/06/1868			Y	
Kahn, Henry	24	Bavaria	Y	Havre	New Orleans	12/29/1846	01/28/1950	2	9	N	
Kahn, Henry	62	Germany	N	Havre	New Orleans	12/??/1847	?			Y	
Kahn, Paul	??	Germany	Y	?	?	?	04/05/1894			Y	
Kahoe, Michael	60	Ireland	N	Queenstown	New York	03/25/1883	?			Y	
Kahtenbrink, Henry	32	Germany	Y	Bremen	New York	11/02/1881	07/03/1885			Y	
Kain, ?	??	?	Y	?	New York	??/19/18??	10/29/1850	2	329	N	
Kain, Edward (affidavit			N							N	
Kain, Martin	41	Ireland	N	Liverpool	New York	07/05/1864	?			Y	
Kain, Thomas	32	Ireland	Y	Dublin	Buffalo	06/04/1848	04/04/1853	7	514	N	
Kaise, Edward	25	Holland	Y	?	?	?	07/07/1884			Y	
Kaiser, Adolph	??	Germany	Y	?	?	?	07/02/1881			Y	
Kaiser, Anton	29	Baden	Y	Havre	New Orleans	01/11/1854	12/24/1855	13	356	N	
Kaiser, August	48	Germany	Y	Hamburg	New York	09/18/1887	10/16/1890			Y	
Kaiser, Benjamin	16	Germany	N	?	New York	00/00/1879				Y	10/22/1886
Kaiser, Bernard	23	Hanover	Y	Bremen	Baltimore	11/02/1857	10/17/1860	27	507	N	
Kaiser, Bernard	18	Germany	N	?	Baltimore	00/00/1883				Y	10/12/1888
Kaiser, Casper	26	Hanover	Y	Bremen	New Orleans	12/09/1848	05/25/1854	8	541	N	
Kaiser, Casper	26	Hanover	Y	Bremen	New Orleans	12/09/1848	05/25/1854	9	415	N	
Kaiser, Clemens	31	Germany	Y	Bremen	Baltimore	03/03/1882	11/12/1890			Y	
Kaiser, Diedrich	57	Hanover	Y	Bremen	Baltimore	11/02/1857	10/09/1860	27	465	N	
Kaiser, Fidel	38	Germany	Y	Havre	New York	04/28/1884	08/14/1888			Y	
Kaiser, Frank	40	Baden	Y	Havre	New Orleans	01/13/1852	10/09/1854	11	70	N	

CITIZENSHIP RECORDS

APPLICANT	AGE	COUNTRY OF ORIGIN	DEC	DEPART PORT	ENTRY PORT	ARRIVE DATE	DEC DATE	VOL	PG.	FLD	NAT DATE
Kaiser, Franz	??	Germany	Y	?	?	?	06/09/1887			Y	
Kaiser, George	39	Germany	N	Antwerp	New York	01/??/1854	?			Y	
Kaiser, Ignatz	22	Germany	Y	Amsterdam	New York	11/??/1881	04/07/1885			Y	
Kaiser, Jacob	36	Germany	N	Antwerp	New York	12/26/1880				Y	03/26/1892
Kaiser, John Henry (Kays	25	Hanover	Y	Bremen	Baltimore	11/25/1857	10/17/1860	27	506	N	
Kaiser, Joseph	??	Germany	Y	?	?	?	06/01/1887			Y	
Kaiser, Matheus	28	Hanover	Y	Bremen	New Orleans	11/16/1847	05/25/1854	9	414	N	
Kaiser, Matthias	28	Hanover	Y	Bremen	New Orleans	11/16/1847	05/25/1854	8	540	N	
Kaiser, Valentine	24	Hesse Cassel	Y	Bremen	New York	06/28/1847	02/11/1851	3	120	N	
Kaiser, Wilhelm	37	Germany	Y	Bremen	Baltimore	06/04/1880	03/07/1882			Y	
Kaiser, William	21	Prussia	Y	Havre	New York	04/24/1851	04/18/1854	8	204	N	
Kaiser, William	21	Prussia	Y	Havre	New York	04/24/1851	04/18/1854	9	75	N	
Kaiser, William	33	Germany	Y	Hamburg	New York	03/03/1881	01/09/1891			Y	
Kaizer, Valentine	37	Germany	N	Bremen	New York	06/05/1872	?			Y	
Kalaphatis, M. Apostolis	41	Greece	Y	?	New Orleans	00/00/1867	03/10/1881			Y	
Kalb, John Christian	22	Germany	Y	?	New York	12/01/1890	10/03/1894			Y	
Kalbel, Gottlieb	40	Saxony	Y	Bremen	New York	09/10/1858	04/12/1860	27	150	N	
Kaletzky, Julius	40	Russia	Y	Hamburg	New York	08/24/1880	10/26/1892			Y	
Kalin, Xaver	40	Switzerland	Y	Havre	New York	05/03/1853	11/12/1854	13	208	N	
Kalitzky, Pene	32	Russia	Y	Liverpool	New York	05/09/1890	04/07/1898			Y	
Kalkbrenner, Gregor	25	Baden	Y	Havre	New Orleans	03/18/1854	02/23/1858	16	339	N	
Kallendorf, Diedrich C.	23	Prussia	Y	Bremen	New Orleans	05/27/1850	08/23/1852	25	325	N	
Kallint, Casper	30	Bavaria	Y	Bremen	Baltimore	06/18/1845	08/15/1848	22	179	N	
Kallmeier, Henry	32	Baden	Y	Havre	New York	06/06/1852	10/07/1854	10	532	N	
Kallmeier, Henry	32	Baden	Y	Havre	New York	06/06/1852	10/07/1854	12	471	N	
Kallmeier, Henry	26	Oldenburg	Y	Bremen	New York	11/15/1851	09/28/1858	16	107	N	
Kallmeyer, William	42	Germany	Y	Bremen	New York	09/19/1881	04/29/1891			Y	
Kallomeck, Albert	35	Germany	Y	Bremen	Baltimore	04/08/1884	08/13/1886			Y	
Kallschmidt, Wilhelm	26	Germany	Y	Bremen	New York	04/15/1891	03/27/1894			Y	
Kalmbach, Daniel	27	Wurttemberg	Y	Antwerp	New York	06/01/1846	01/15/1849	1	427	N	
Kalmbacher, George	22	Germany	Y	Bremen	New York	09/00/1882	11/02/1888			Y	
Kalthoff, Frederick	47	Germany	N	Bremen	Baltimore	12/15/1863	?			Y	
Kalthoff, H. W.	58	Germany	N	Bremen	New York	11/??/1854	?			Y	
Kalthoff, Henry William	28	Hanover	Y	Bremen	New York	10/25/1854	10/28/1858	17	153	N	
Kaltwasser, Andreas	34	Germany	Y	Bremen	Baltimore	06/04/1892	02/20/1894			Y	
Kamfius, George	27	Prussia	Y	Bremen	Baltimore	10/01/1848	10/10/1854	6	215	N	
Kamleiter, William	35	Germany	Y	Antwerp	New York	10/20/1887	11/19/1898			Y	
Kamm, Daniel	35	Bavaria	Y	Antwerp	New York	11/29/1853	03/12/1856	26	190	N	
Kammann, Frederick	22	Hanover	Y	Bremen	New Orleans	12/11/1855	10/04/1858	17	29	N	
Kammann, Henry	27	Germany	Y	Bremen	New York	09/18/1881	08/15/1887			Y	
Kammer, Michael	??	Germany	Y	?	?	?	05/02/1883			Y	
Kammerer, Frederick	25	Baden	Y	Havre	New Orleans	06/02/1849	10/09/1854	6	149	N	
Kammerer, Frederick	25	Baden	Y	Havre	New Orleans	06/02/1849	10/09/1854	11	152	N	
Kammerer, Joseph	30	Baden	Y	Havre	New Orleans	05/16/1848	02/06/1852	24	66	N	
Kammerer, Nicholas	29	Bavaria	Y	Havre	New Orleans	01/08/1845	02/17/1849	23	155	N	
Kammerle, Frank	33	Germany	Y	Havre	New York	05/24/1883	04/30/1887			Y	
Kamp, F.	35	Holland	Y	Rotterdam	New Orleans	01/06/1847	10/12/1848	1	156	N	
Kamp, George	21	Germany	Y	Bremen	New York	09/04/1891	10/23/1896			Y	
Kamp, George	23	Germany	Y	Bremen	Baltimore	06/02/1886	01/09/1890			Y	
Kamp, Henry	35	Hanover	Y	Bremen	Baltimore	05/14/1847	03/12/1851	3	261	N	
Kamp, John	41	Germany	Y	Rotterdam	New York	09/01/1868	01/02/1886			Y	
Kamper, Ernst	35	Switzerland	Y	Havre	New York	01/12/1881	10/01/1886			Y	
Kamper, George	27	Hanover	Y	Bremen	New Orleans	11/15/1847	01/??/1850	23	462	N	
Kamper, Phillip (Kemper?	28	Hanover	Y	Bremen	New Orleans	01/27/1846	08/15/1848	22	177	N	
Kampf, John George	30	Wurttemberg	Y	London	New York	04/01/1853	11/30/1857	16	60	N	
Kampfmeyer, Henry	24	Hanover	Y	Bremen	Baltimore	11/01/1849	10/06/1854	10	504	N	
Kampfmeyer, Henry	24	Hanover	Y	Bremen	Baltimore	11/01/1849	10/06/1854	12	443	N	
Kamphaus, Herman	29	Prussia	Y	Bremen	New Orleans	11/11/1853	10/01/1857	15	341	N	
Kamphaus, John	34	Holland	Y	Bremen	New Orleans	05/28/1847	03/15/1851	3	277	N	

CITIZENSHIP RECORDS

APPLICANT	AGE	COUNTRY OF ORIGIN	DEC	DEPART PORT	ENTRY PORT	ARRIVE DATE	DEC DATE	VOL	PG.	FLD	NAT DATE
Kamphaus, John	68	Holland	Y	Amsterdam	New York	09/28/1865	10/26/1900			Y	
Kamphus, William	29	Prussia	Y	Bremen	New York	08/24/1847	10/02/1848	22	386	N	
Kampman, John	28	Prussia	Y	Bremen	New Orleans	05/30/1848	08/01/1848	22	33	N	
Kampmeyer, John Heinrich	30	Hanover	Y	Bremen	Baltimore	07/15/1845	08/15/1848	22	135	N	
Kamppmann, Barney L.	32	Prussia	Y	Bremen	New Orleans	06/30/1849	08/23/1852	25	328	N	
Kamps, Bernard	33	Prussia	Y	Rotterdam	New York	01/02/1852	09/27/1854	10	266	N	
Kamps, Bernard	33	Prussia	Y	Rotterdam	New York	01/21/1852	09/27/1854	12	205	N	
Kampsen, Bernard	26	Oldenberg, Ge	Y	?	?	06/27/1882	02/19/1883			Y	
Kampus, George	27	Prussia	Y	Bremen	Baltimore	10/01/1848	10/10/1854	11	218	N	
Kams, John	35	Saxony	Y	Bremen	Baltimore	05/09/1854	08/27/1857	15	195	N	
Kanamuller, H. Jurt	??	Germany	Y	?	?	?	12/12/1894			Y	
Kane, John	50	Ireland	Y	Limerick	New York	09/29/1849	09/09/1857	15	251	N	
Kane, John	77	Ireland	N	Liverpool	New Orleans	03/02/1848	??/??/1851	28	268	N	04/??/1854
Kane, Patrick	17	Ireland	N	?	New York	00/00/1880				Y	10/26/1888
Kangelmeyer, William	21	Hanover	Y	Bremen	New Orleans	07/01/1849	09/14/1852	25	500	N	
Kannally, Patrick	40	Ireland	Y	Liverpool	New Orleans	03/15/1852	03/26/1853	7	410	N	
Kanne, Friedrich	33	Lippe	Y	Bremen	Baltimore	09/06/1846	11/20/1848	1	350	N	
Kannemann, Carl	25	Hanover	Y	Hamburg	New York	06/27/1854	10/09/1854	6	161	N	
Kanner, David	??	Romania	Y	?	?	?	03/29/1888			Y	
Kanrup, Hugo	33	Germany	Y	?	New York	05/00/1883	08/02/1886			Y	
Kantor, Frederick	30	Russia	Y	Hamburg	Philadelphia	07/13/1882	09/26/1887			Y	
Kapelmann, Casper Henry	27	Hanover	Y	Bremen	New York	07/03/1857	08/15/1860	27	277	N	
Kapfer, Ulrach	37	Germany	Y	Bremen	New York	06/25/1882	02/15/1887			Y	
Kaplan, Jacob	21	Russia	Y	Kurschave	New York	08/12/1886	09/01/1888			Y	
Kaplan, John	??	Germany	Y	?	?	?	01/27/1892			Y	
Kaplan, Max	??	Russia	Y	?	?	?	07/19/1895			Y	
Kaplen, Joseph	22	Russia	Y	Bremen	New York	12/11/1896	04/28/1899			Y	
Kaplen, Nathan	40	Russia	Y	?	?	?	12/02/1891			Y	
Kapp, August	32	Wurttemberg	Y	Havre	New York	09/24/1854	06/26/1862	18	361	N	
Kappel, Henry	29	Prussia	Y	Bremen	New Orleans	05/22/1852	04/01/1856	26	396	N	
Kappel, Mike	32	Germany	Y	Antwerp	New York	06/08/1891	10/02/1896			Y	
Kappel, Roman	32	Germany	Y	Hamburg	New York	08/29/1885	04/04/1891			Y	
Kappler, Lorenz	25	Baden	Y	Liverpool	New York	06/01/1853	04/03/1856	26	423	N	
Kapsch, F. J.	??	Germany	Y	?	?	09/??/1864	07/21/1874			Y	
Karas, Hippolite	28	Germany	Y	Hamburg	New York	05/18/1888	04/11/1892			Y	
Karbel, David	28	Baden	Y	Havre	New York	07/20/1853	05/20/1854	9	355	N	
Karcher, Julius	22	Germany	Y	Amsterdam	New York	05/05/1883	05/23/1887			Y	
Karg, Nicholas	30	Germany	Y	Havre	New York	08/01/1876	09/13/1887			Y	
Karger, Moritz	23	Prussia	Y	Hamburg	New York	10/21/1856	03/01/1858	16	349	N	
Karl Kiefer	28	Germany	Y	Hamburg	New York	09/22/1891	07/02/1896			Y	
Karl, Francis	25	Bavaria	Y	Havre	New York	09/21/1856	12/10/1857	16	211	N	
Karl, Hans	??	Germany	Y	?	?	?	02/28/1887			Y	
Karl, Lorenz	37	Austria	Y	Bremen	Baltimore	08/23/1853	10/09/1854	6	124	N	
Karl, Lorenz	37	Austria	Y	Bremen	Baltimore	08/23/1853	10/09/1854	11	128	N	
Karle, Christian	22	Baden	Y	Liverpool	New York	07/30/1847	08/15/1848	22	167	N	
Karle, Conrad	26	Wurttemberg	Y	Havre	New York	04/20/1854	01/09/1856	13	438	N	
Karle, Noe	37	Germany	Y	Havre	New York	07/15/1880	03/19/1890			Y	
Karlin, Caspar	22	Switzerland	Y	Havre	New York	08/17/1889	10/27/1892	19	288	N	
Karlis, Caspar	22	Switzerland	Y	Havre	New York	08/17/1889	10/27/1892			Y	
Karlkamp, Herman	34	Germany	Y	Bremen	Baltimore	10/??/1858	10/05/1876			Y	
Karmann, Joseph	??	Germany	Y	?	?	?	11/10/1892			Y	
Karnagel, Alvin	29	Germany	Y	Bremen	Baltimore	11/28/1881	04/11/1887			Y	
Karp, George	30	Holland	Y	Antwerp	New York	06/28/1854	02/10/1858	16	98	N	
Karpales, Frank	37	Germany	N	Bremen	New York	07/??/1869	?			Y	
Karpf, Jacob	49	Germany	Y	Bremen	New York	03/13/1881	01/17/1898			Y	
Karrer, Martin	29	Germany	Y	Antwerp	New York	08/21/1888	06/29/1893			Y	
Karsch, Frederick Christ	35	Bavaria	Y	Havre	New York	04/13/1850	07/28/1851	4	48	N	
Karst, Herman Reinhold	34	Germany	Y	Hamburg	New York	11/19/1882	02/02/1883			Y	
Karst, Hermann Reinhold	34	Germany	N	Hamburg	New York	11/19/1882	?			Y	

188

CITIZENSHIP RECORDS

APPLICANT	AGE	COUNTRY OF ORIGIN	DEC	DEPART PORT	ENTRY PORT	ARRIVE DATE	DEC DATE	VOL	PG.	FLD	NAT DATE
Karstans, Henry	17	Germany	N	?	New York	00/00/1881				Y	10/19/1886
Kartemeyer, Clements	39	Prussia	N	Amsterdam	New York	07/15/1866	?			Y	
Kartenschlaeger, William	26	Bavaria	Y	Antwerp	New York	10/28/1849	11/01/1852	5	159	N	
Karthouse, Charles	24	Prussia	Y	Bremen	New York	01/22/1857	02/22/1858	16	328	N	
Karto, Philipp	41	Germany	Y	Bremen	New York	03/21/1884	08/28/1888			Y	
Karvisa, Charles	26	Poland	Y	Hamburg	New York	12/??/1872	05/00/1877			Y	
Kasel, Wolf	16	Russia	N	?	New York	00/00/1877				Y	10/12/1888
Kaser, Charles	43	Switzerland	Y	Havre	New York	05/18/1886	10/22/1895			Y	
Kasheimer, Herman	25	Germany	Y	Antwerp	New York	06/06/1890	04/26/1893			Y	
Kasper, August	29	Wurtemburg	Y	?	New York	??/??/1893	05/19/1896			Y	
Kasper, Ludwig	40	Baden	Y	Havre	New Orleans	04/27/1854	05/21/1856	26	515	N	
Kass, John B.	21	Hanover	Y	Bremen	Baltimore	10/24/1860	08/28/1862	18	418	N	
Kasselbaum, Frederick	39	Hanover	Y	Liverpool	New York	11/01/1846	01/15/1849	1	423	N	
Kasselmann, Bernard	30	Germany	Y	Bremen	New York	10/??/1880	12/08/1883			Y	
Kasselmann, F.	24	Germany	Y	Bremen	New York	07/15/1880	06/04/1883			Y	
Kasselmann, William	30	Germany	Y	Bremen	New York	05/28/1886	10/10/1888			Y	
Kassen, Charles	31	Prussia	Y	Bremen	Philadelphia	07/26/1857	08/24/1857	15	184	N	
Kassens, Fred	39	Germany	Y	Bremen	Baltimore	10/??/1882	01/10/1887			Y	
Kast, Jacob	24	Germany	Y	Hamburg	New York	09/28/1894	02/10/1897			Y	
Kastern, Frederick	28	Germany	Y	Bremen	New York	12/25/1866	10/08/1872	18	530	N	
Kasting, Henry	47	Germany	Y	Bremen	New York	09/21/1881	08/28/1884			Y	
Kastrup, Joseph	38	Germany	Y	Bremen	Baltimore	07/14/1873	09/16/1884			Y	
Kath, Andreas	30	Germany	Y	Bremen	New York	09/23/1878	01/29/1885			Y	
Kathanjanz, Mesach	30	Russia	Y	Havre	New York	05/30/1892	08/01/1892			Y	
Kathman, Herman H. W.	30	Prussia	Y	Bremen	New Orleans	12/20/1847	07/20/1849	23	225	N	
Kathmann, Clemens	27	Oldenburg	Y	Bremen	New Orleans	11/30/1845	03/31/1852	24	344	N	
Kathmann, Henry	38	Oldenburg	Y	Bremen	Baltimore	06/03/1848	08/15/1851	4	139	N	
Kathmann, John Clement	26	Oldenburg	Y	Bremen	New Orleans	11/23/1845	10/14/1848	1	232	N	
Kathmann, John Henry	28	Oldenburg	Y	Bremen	New Orleans	11/23/1845	02/19/1849	23	203	N	
Kathmann, William	24	Prussia	Y	Bremen	New Orleans	11/08/1851	08/27/1855	11	497	N	
Katoelge, Heinrich	20	Oldenburg	Y	Bremen	Baltimore	04/25/1846	01/15/1849	1	425	N	
Kattan, August	31	Germany	Y	Bremen	Baltimore	09/25/1887	02/17/1893			Y	
Kattan, Herman	35	Germany	Y	Bremen	?	04/08/1876	05/01/1882			Y	
Katte, John Frederick	25	Oldenburg	Y	Bremen	Baltimore	04/??/1854	01/26/1857	14	504	N	
Kattein, Conrad	34	Wurttemberg	Y	Havre	New York	09/24/1847	11/13/1848	1	261	N	
Kattelmann, Henry	38	Hanover	Y	Bremen	Baltimore	06/18/1848	12/16/1851	4	538	N	
Kattenhorn, A.	24	Hanover	Y	Bremen	New York	09/20/1853	10/03/1856	14	179	N	
Kattenhorn, Henry	28	Hanover	Y	Bremen	Philadelphia	??/01/1846	10/??/1849	23	282	N	
Katterjohann, Herman H.	22	Prussia	Y	Bremen	Baltimore	10/01/1844	10/02/1848	1	20	N	
Katterjohann, William	24	Germany	Y	Bremen	New York	05/01/1882	02/10/1888			Y	
Katterjohn, Ernst	25	Prussia	Y	Bremen	Baltimore	10/01/1844	10/02/1848	1	21	N	
Katting, Thomas	53	England	N	London	Buffalo	06/??/1868	?			Y	
Kattleman, William	40	Germany	Y	?	Baltimore	??/??/1872	10/04/1880			Y	
Kattman, Gerhard	30	Hanover	Y	Bremen	New Orleans	02/28/18??	10/13/1848	1	190	N	
Kattmann, Rudolf	53	Germany	N	Bremen	New York	11/??/1873	?			Y	
Katus, Valentine	24	Bavaria	Y	Havre	New Orleans	06/10/1852	11/24/1852	5	341	N	
Katz, Jonah	40	Russia	Y	Bremen	New York	09/15/1886	07/06/1893			Y	
Katzenberger, John	47	Germany	Y	Bremen	New York	06/02/1889	10/08/1897			Y	
Katzenstein, Aaron	23	Saxe Weiman	N	Bremen	New York	10/00/1852	03/27/1854			Y	10/02/1858
Katzenstein, Moses	21	Saxe Weimar	Y	Bremen	New York	12/28/1855	09/30/1858	17	27	N	
Katzenstein, Theodore	??	Hanover	Y	Bremen	New Orleans	12/26/1846	10/12/1848	1	170	N	
Katznelson, Lacer	34	Russia	Y	Hamburg	New York	07/01/1888	09/26/1889			Y	
Katzung, Louis	33	Kuhrhassen	Y	Bremen	New York	08/09/1846	10/03/1848	22	407	N	
Kaucher, Charles	21	Baden	Y	Havre	New York	03/07/1853	01/09/1856	13	476	N	
Kaucher, Louis	33	Germany	Y	Baden	Baltimore	06/22/1881	06/07/1884			Y	
Kaucher, Ludwig	27	Baden	Y	Havre	New York	10/25/1854	02/22/1858	16	330	N	
Kauet, Michael	40	Bavaria	Y	Havre	New Orleans	06/26/1847	07/31/1848	22	16	N	
Kaufel, Ferdinand	30	Hanover	Y	Bremen	New Orleans	11/18/1855	03/13/1858	16	399	N	
Kauffman, Caspar	21	France	Y	Havre	New York	07/03/1846	02/07/1850	2	48	N	

CITIZENSHIP RECORDS

APPLICANT	AGE	COUNTRY OF ORIGIN	DEC	DEPART PORT	ENTRY PORT	ARRIVE DATE	DEC DATE	VOL	PG.	FLD	NAT DATE
Kauffman, Lewis	24	Prussia	Y	Antwerp	New York	09/??/1852	09/27/1856	14	410	N	
Kauffmann, Louis	27	Hesse Cassel	Y	Bremen	New York	07/07/1852	07/09/1855	11	358	N	
Kauffung, Charles	29	Germany	Y	Bremen	Baltimore	03/22/1883	11/22/1886			Y	
Kaufman, Simon	27	Bavaria	Y	Havre	Baltimore	08/??/1846	01/??/1850	23	467	N	
Kaufmann, Emil	24	Saxe Coburg	Y	Hamburg	Buffalo	06/01/1850	12/09/1852	5	403	N	
Kaufmann, Ernest	30	France	Y	?	New York	??/??/1882	11/03/1887			Y	
Kaufmann, John	35	Germany	Y	Antwerp	New York	12/07/1880	06/14/1892			Y	
Kaufmann, John	60	Germany	Y	Bremen	Baltimore	10/28/1889	10/09/1896			Y	
Kaufmann, John Christian	24	Wuertemberg	Y	Havre	New York	05/15/1853	04/09/1856	26	481	N	
Kaufmann, Nicolas	24	France	Y	Havre	New Orleans	11/27/1850	10/06/1856	14	197	N	
Kaufmann, Valentine	??	Bavaria	Y	Havre	New York	07/20/1858	12/31/1860	18	36	N	
Kauper, John	25	Bavaria	Y	Bremen	Baltimore	08/11/1853	08/17/1857	15	145	N	
Kaurisch, Court	34	Germany	Y	Breman	New York	03/16/1870	08/17/1876			Y	
Kautz, Christian F.	27	Germany	Y	Bremen	New York	10/04/1892	01/26/1894			Y	
Kautz, John	24	Wuerttenberg	Y	Antwerp	New York	07/18/1846	09/04/1852	25	351	N	
Kautz, Karl	22	Germany	Y	Bremen	New York	10/24/1889	10/23/1890			Y	
Kavanagh, David	40	Ireland	Y	Liverpool	New York	03/12/1847	05/18/1852	25	38	N	
Kavanagh, Michael	22	Ireland	Y	Liverpool	New York	05/02/1851	12/31/1852	5	478	N	
Kawalerzik, Markus	34	Russia	Y	Bremen	Baltimore	01/02/1892	01/27/1893			Y	
Kawalske, John	30	Russia	Y	Bremen	Baltimore	04/02/1884	09/22/1896			Y	
Kay, Duncan	42	Canada	Y	Canada	Detroit	05/02/1872	11/06/1893			Y	
Kayata, Kaisr Antoon She	26	Syria	Y	Havre	New York	06/10/1891	01/02/1894			Y	
Kayata, Nackly Antoon Sh	32	Syria	Y	Beirut	New York	08/02/1889	01/03/1895			Y	
Kays, Kern	23	Ireland	Y	Liverpool	New Orleans	03/11/1853	10/26/1858	17	119	N	
Kayser, Conrad	36	Baden	Y	Havre	New York	05/22/1853	02/08/1858	16	86	N	
Kazenwadel, John	37	Germany	Y	Antwerp	New York	11/05/1882	11/23/1887			Y	
Keadian, Peter	23	Ireland	Y	Liverpool	New Orleans	04/26/1849	04/18/1853	8	76	N	
Kealey, Michael J.	42	Ireland	Y	Liverpool	New York	??/12/1847	02/20/1950	2	108	N	
Kean, Thomas	32	Ireland	Y	Liverpool	New York	10/12/1848	01/17/1849	1	444	N	
Kearney, Edward	34	Ireland	Y	Galway	Boston	06/05/1849	04/04/1853	8	48	N	
Kearns, John	30	Ireland	Y	Liverpool	New York	07/10/1851	03/09/1857	15	84	N	
Kearns, Martin	33	Ireland	Y	?	New York	??/??/1889	09/23/1897			Y	
Kearns, Walter	28	Ireland	Y	Queenstown	New York	11/25/1879	10/26/1889	19	265	N	
Keating, Edward	48	Ireland	N	Ireland	New York	07/??/1862	?			Y	
Keating, Michael	22	Ireland	Y	Liverpool	New Orleans	02/02/1852	12/04/1854	13	286	N	
Keating, Michael	22	Ireland	Y	Liverpool	New Orleans	12/22/1850	03/20/1856	26	234	N	
Keating, Michael A.	27	Ireland	Y	Dublin	New York	06/??/1845	12/31/1849	23	451	N	
Keating, Patrick	25	Ireland	Y	Liverpool	New Orleans	01/01/1851	10/07/1854	10	529	N	
Keating, Peter	25	Ireland	Y	Liverpool	New Orleans	01/01/1851	10/07/1854	12	468	N	
Keating, Thomas	31	Ireland	Y	Liverpool	New Orleans	04/10/1847	03/13/1851	3	264	N	
Keavery, Michael	25	Ireland	Y	Queenstown,	?	04/16/1895	11/07/1898			Y	
Keays, James	24	Ireland	Y	Liverpool	New Orleans	04/??/1849	12/09/1850	2	348	N	
Kech, Alexander	25	Germany	Y	Havre	New York	01/25/1887	10/19/1887			Y	
Kech, John George	33	Baden	Y	Bremen	Buffalo	07/??/1852	12/26/1855	13	367	N	
Kechel, John	31	Wurttemberg	Y	Liverpool	New York	09/20/1853	12/29/1855	13	391	N	
Keck, August	28	Nassau	Y	Antwerp	New York	07/20/1848	05/20/1852	25	77	N	
Keck, Christian	33	Germany	Y	Rotterdam	Boston	10/08/1882	04/16/1889			Y	
Keck, Edward	39	Germany	Y	Bremen	Baltimore	04/03/1889	05/07/1892			Y	
Keck, George	33	Germany	Y	Havre	New York	04/??/1880	10/29/1886			Y	
Keck, Jacob	21	Germany	Y	Bremen	New York	06/15/1884	10/23/1885			Y	
Keck, Michael	30	Germany	Y	Rotterdam	New York	10/04/1879	10/11/1884			Y	
Keck, William	28	Germany	Y	Hamburg	New York	08/22/1886	02/26/1889			Y	
Keefe, Timothy	26	Ireland	Y	Liverpool	Boston	12/21/1848	04/26/1854	8	270	N	
Keefe, Timothy	26	Ireland	Y	Liverpool	Boston	12/21/1848	04/26/1854	9	141	N	
Keefer, Francis	28	Baden	Y	Havre	New Orleans	05/26/1846	08/02/1848	22	48	N	
Keeffe, Cornelius	30	Ireland	Y	Cork	New York	09/29/1849	12/26/1857	16	257	N	
Keeffe, John	47	Ireland	Y	Canada	Oswego	05/16/1850	03/16/1852	24	321	N	
Keegan, Matthew	27	Ireland	Y	Liverpool	New York	??/26/1849	07/19/1851	4	6	N	
Keegan, Robert	29	Ireland	Y	Dublin	New York	06/01/1848	07/19/1851	4	5	N	

CITIZENSHIP RECORDS

APPLICANT	AGE	COUNTRY OF ORIGIN	DEC	DEPART PORT	ENTRY PORT	ARRIVE DATE	DEC DATE	VOL	PG.	FLD	NAT DATE
Keeghan, James	25	Ireland	Y	Liverpool	New Orleans	10/??/1849	10/22/1851	4	371	N	
Keegon, James	36	Ireland	Y	Liverpool	Boston	06/24/1849	01/23/1852	24	60	N	
Keeler, Philip	39	Germany	N	Rotterdam	New York	??/??/1855	?			Y	
Keelty, James	27	Ireland	Y	Liverpool	New York	05/05/1857	10/13/1860	27	492	N	
Keenan, Felix	19	Ireland	N	Queenstown	New York	09/00/1869				Y	10/20/1892
Keenan, Patrick	46	Ireland	Y	Liverpool	Whitehall	08/??/1847	03/25/1851	3	347	N	
Kees, Joseph	38	Bavaria	Y	Havre	New Orleans	12/20/1854	05/14/1861	18	169	N	
Keeti, Benedict	27	Russia	Y	Bremen	Baltimore	09/12/1890	09/26/1893			Y	
Kehald, John Henry	23	Hanover	Y	Bremen	New Orleans	12/01/1859	08/15/1860	27	283	N	
Keheler, John	36	Ireland	Y	Liverpool	Burlington	05/20/1845	03/04/1851	3	200	N	
Kehlenbeck, Henry	54	Germany	N	Bremen	New York	08/??/1854	?			Y	
Kehoe, Dennis	30	Ireland	Y	Liverpool	New York	07/16/1846	11/22/1848	1	372	N	
Kehoe, Dennis	27	Ireland	Y	Liverpool	New York	09/10/1852	08/04/1856	14	335	N	
Kehoe, Garrett	29	Ireland	Y	Liverpool	New York	02/??/1874	12/03/1883			Y	
Kehoe, Michael	24	Ireland	Y	Liverpool	New Orleans	03/03/1849	11/03/1851	4	470	N	
Kehoe, Patrick	25	Ireland	Y	Liverpool	New Orleans	11/05/1848	11/22/1848	1	373	N	
Kehoe, Thomas	25	Ireland	Y	Liverpool	New York	12/14/1851	10/07/1854	10	531	N	
Kehoe, Thomas	25	Ireland	Y	Liverpool	New York	12/14/1851	10/07/1854	12	470	N	
Kehoe, William	21	Ireland	Y	Liverpool	New Orleans	11/05/1848	11/22/1848	1	374	N	
Kehrer, Peter	34	Germany	Y	Bremen	New York	03/26/1882	07/07/1886			Y	
Keiber, Adam	30	Austria	Y	Havre	New York	06/01/1849	10/02/1854	12	298	N	
Keifel, Charles	22	Bavaria	Y	Havre	New York	08/02/1851	10/02/1854	10	356	N	
Keifel, Charles	22	Bavaria	Y	Havre	New York	08/02/1851	10/02/1854	12	295	N	
Keifel, Charles	31	Germany	Y	Hamburg	New York	05/20/1882	12/10/1888			Y	
Keifel, Frank	21	Germany	Y	Bremen	New York	01/09/1884	04/01/1886			Y	
Keifel, Frederick	34	Bavaria	Y	London	New York	08/28/1854	10/08/1860	27	442	N	
Keil, John	66	Germany	N	London	New York	06/07/1849	?			Y	
Keil, John	35	Hesse Darmsta	Y	London	New York	06/07/1849	04/07/1856	26	453	N	
Keil, Nicholas	23	Hesse Darmsta	Y	London	New York	10/01/1856	09/29/1858	17	17	N	
Keilson, Isaac	27	Russia	Y	Hamburg	New York	11/13/1884	03/29/1890			Y	
Keim, Mathias	22	Hesse Darmsta	Y	Bremen	New York	01/15/1851	03/05/1852	24	238	N	
Keimath, Mathew	28	Germany	Y	Havre	New York	04/12/1881	10/26/1886	19	89	N	
Keinath, Louis	20	Germany	Y	Havre	New York	04/24/1881	02/14/1882			Y	
Keinath, Mathew	28	Germany	Y	Havre	New York	04/12/1881	10/26/1886			Y	
Keinath, William	36	Germany	Y	Bremen	New York	10/30/1880	02/20/1883			Y	
Keirens, John	24	Ireland	Y	?	New York	??/??/1887	12/31/1891			Y	
Keiser, Conrad	43	Brunswick	Y	Bremen	New Orleans	10/26/1852	04/18/1854	8	199	N	
Keiser, Conrad	43	Brunswick	Y	Bremen	New Orleans	10/26/1852	04/18/1854	9	70	N	
Keiser, Fordmadusz	28	France	Y	Havre	New Orleans	04/08/1852	05/24/1852	25	99	N	
Keiser, Heinrich	43	Hanover	Y	Hamburg	New York	10/28/1867	02/09/1872	18	462	N	
Keiser, Jacob	??	Bavaria	Y	Bremen	New York	??/24/1843	03/27/1849	23	267	N	
Keisling, Jacob	25	Bavaria	Y	Bremen	New York	??/01/1847	12/31/1849	23	448	N	
Keister, Denis	26	Saxony	Y	Bremen	New York	04/30/1849	10/31/1851	4	443	N	
Keistermeier, John Ludwi	50	Oldenburg	Y	Bremen	New Orleans	11/08/1849	03/11/1852	24	285	N	
Keitel, August	32	Germany	Y	Bremen	New York	07/??/1863	04/05/1875			Y	
Kelihan, Michael	40	Ireland	Y	Liverpool	New Orleans	02/10/1851	04/02/1856	26	413	N	
Kelker, Herman B.	30	Hanover	Y	Bremen	Baltimore	07/06/1845	08/30/1848	22	279	N	
Keller, Andreas	37	Germany	Y	Rotterdam	New York	11/02/1881	12/31/1886			Y	
Keller, Benedict	28	Germany	Y	Constan	New York	10/05/1881	09/12/1885			Y	
Keller, Charles	43	Germany	Y	Antwerp	New York	07/02/1892	07/07/1898			Y	
Keller, Charles	48	Switzerland	Y	?	New York	?	10/29/1892			Y	
Keller, Ernst	33	Germany	Y	Bremen	Baltimore	01/29/1880	08/20/1889			Y	
Keller, Ferdinand J.	48	Hassecassel	N	Bremen	Baltimore	05/05/1861	?			Y	
Keller, Frank	34	Baden, German	Y	Havre	New York	02/??/1880	02/03/1890			Y	
Keller, Frederick	34	France	Y	Havre	New York	06/01/1851	04/20/1854	8	224	N	
Keller, Frederick	34	France	Y	Havre	New York	06/01/1851	04/20/1854	9	95	N	
Keller, Frederick	25	Prussia	Y	Hamburg	New York	10/08/1856	09/01/1857	15	212	N	
Keller, George	40	Hesse Darmsta	Y	Havre	New York	09/22/1856	06/20/1861	18	196	N	
Keller, George	28	Germany	Y	Hamburg	Boston	06/27/1882	10/03/1885			Y	

CITIZENSHIP RECORDS

APPLICANT	AGE	COUNTRY OF ORIGIN	DEC	DEPART PORT	ENTRY PORT	ARRIVE DATE	DEC DATE	VOL	PG.	FLD	NAT DATE
Keller, Henry	28	Hesse Darmsta	Y	Bremen	New York	06/01/1857	02/27/1862	18	266	N	
Keller, Jacob	37	France	Y	Havre	New York	06/02/1851	12/27/1852	5	454	N	
Keller, Jacob	38	Switzerland	Y	Havre	New Orleans	02/26/1846	01/12/1853	7	11	N	
Keller, Jacob	68	Germany	Y	Bremen	New York	08/30/1882	06/03/1889			Y	
Keller, Jacob	36	Switzerland	Y	Havre	New York	09/01/1882	04/19/1886			Y	
Keller, John	30	Bavaria	Y	Bremen	New York	09/05/1846	02/11/1850	2	56	N	
Keller, John	38	Bavaria	Y	Antwerp	New York	08/16/1852	10/01/1856	14	94	N	
Keller, John	24	Germany	Y	?	?	?	10/08/1885			Y	
Keller, John	52	Bavaria	Y	Havre	New Orleans	05/01/1843	08/17/1848	22	190	N	
Keller, John	23	Germany	Y	Baden	New York	04/14/1881	02/12/1885			Y	
Keller, John (Kaeler?)	27	Bavaria	Y	Havre	New Orleans	05/01/1843	08/16/1848	22	185	N	
Keller, John Christoph	26	Germany	Y	Bremen	Baltimore	06/08/1887	10/01/1890			Y	
Keller, John Frederick	25	Bavaria	Y	Antwerp	New York	05/20/1849	02/23/1852	24	155	N	
Keller, John George	36	Switzerland	Y	Bremen	New York	11/16/1851	04/12/1852	24	470	N	
Keller, Joseph	26	Prussia	Y	London	New York	07/09/1847	03/18/1851	3	234	N	
Keller, Joseph	31	Germany	Y	Rotterdam	New York	11/12/1880	10/29/1886			Y	
Keller, Joseph	49	Germany	N	?	New York	02/15/1852	?			Y	
Keller, Louis	26	Germany	Y	Antwerp	New York	04/04/1890	11/29/1893			Y	
Keller, Martin	38	Germany	Y	Bremen	New York	10/06/1882	11/12/1889			Y	
Keller, Nathan	37	Austria	Y	Bremen	New York	03/03/1886	04/07/1891			Y	
Keller, Nicholas	30	Bavaria	Y	Havre	New Orleans	12/31/1854	11/04/1857	15	528	N	
Keller, Othmer	61	Germany	N	Baden	New York	10/??/1874	?	28	462	N	11/??/1880
Keller, Peter Andrew	28	Prussia	Y	Bremen	New Orleans	12/25/1846	07/12/1851	3	530	N	
Keller, Rudolph	21	Germany	Y	Herclake	?	04/28/1883	11/01/1884			Y	
Keller, Timothy	33	Ireland	Y	Liverpool	New York	10/01/1851	10/09/1854	6	116	N	
Keller, Timothy	33	Ireland	Y	Liverpool	New York	10/01/1851	10/09/1854	11	119	N	
Kellerman, Charles A.	??	Holland	Y	?	?	?	09/29/1888			Y	
Kellerman, Conrad	35	Germany	Y	Liverpool	New York	05/21/1884	11/04/1893			Y	
Kellermann, Diederich	35	Germany	Y	Bremen	New York	06/14/1872	03/03/1883			Y	
Kellermann, Francis	35	Oldenburg	Y	Bremen	New Orleans	12/22/1846	11/21/1857	16	40	N	
Kellermann, George	31	Germany	Y	Hamburg	New York	04/01/1881	03/06/1888			Y	
Kellermann, Henry	35	Oldenburg	Y	Bremen	New York	10/??/1856	04/01/1861	18	122	N	
Kelley, Bernard	28	Ireland	Y	Liverpool	New York	03/12/1851	01/23/1860	27	69	N	
Kelley, Daniel	45	Ireland	Y	Liverpool	New York	11/09/1854	10/08/1860	27	450	N	
Kelley, Edmund	22	Ireland	Y	Liverpool	New York	06/28/1850	02/23/1853	7	223	N	
Kelley, John	25	Ireland	Y	Londonderry	New York	06/17/1885	02/18/1889			Y	
Kelley, John E.	24	Ireland	Y	Liverpool	New York	07/12/1881	12/24/1884			Y	
Kelley, Martin	25	Ireland	Y	Liverpool	New York	11/02/1857	10/04/1860	27	398	N	
Kelley, Stephen	60	Ireland	Y	Queenstown	New York	07/??/1882	03/24/1890	19	280	N	
Kelley, William H.	47	Ireland	N	London	New Orleans	12/23/1849	?			Y	
Kellner, Frederick	24	Brunswick	Y	Bremen	New York	11/??/1854	04/16/1854	11	249	N	
Kelly, Christopher	30	Ireland	Y	Drogeda	Boston	05/??/1846	03/25/1851	3	349	N	
Kelly, Daniel	45	Ireland	Y	Dublin	New York	05/29/1864	03/29/1889			Y	
Kelly, Dennis	24	Ireland	Y	Cork	New York	04/07/1849	02/13/1856	26	80	N	
Kelly, Edward	25	Ireland	Y	Liverpool	New York	02/23/1850	09/28/1854	10	295	N	
Kelly, Edward	25	Ireland	Y	Liverpool	New York	02/23/1850	09/28/1854	12	234	N	
Kelly, Edward	17	Ireland	N	?	New York	00/00/1880				Y	03/14/1887
Kelly, George	35	Ireland	Y	Drawhady	Philadelphia	09/24/1847	08/01/1851	4	68	N	
Kelly, George	32	Ireland	Y	Liverpool	New York	03/12/1853	08/04/1856	14	331	N	
Kelly, Henry	26	Ireland	Y	Liverpool	New York	10/01/1848	07/31/1851	4	65	N	
Kelly, James	29	Ireland	Y	Liverpool	New York	05/21/1840	12/12/1851	4	508	N	
Kelly, James	40	Ireland	Y	Liverpool	New Orleans	04/02/1848	10/18/1852	5	16	N	
Kelly, James	21	Ireland	Y	Liverpool	New Orleans	06/18/1849	02/04/1853	7	114	N	
Kelly, James	47	Ireland	Y	Liverpool	New Orleans	06/05/1847	10/07/1857	15	366	N	
Kelly, James	34	Italy	Y	Naples	New York	04/15/1887	05/17/1894			Y	
Kelly, James	26	Ireland	Y	Queenstown	New York	05/20/1883	10/18/1889			Y	
Kelly, Jas.	26	Ireland	Y	Queenstown	New York	05/20/1883	10/18/1889	19	241	N	
Kelly, John	25	Ireland	Y	Limerick	Troy	06/27/1847	09/07/1854	10	255	N	
Kelly, John	25	Ireland	Y	Limerick	Troy	06/27/1847	09/27/1854	12	194	N	

CITIZENSHIP RECORDS

APPLICANT	AGE	COUNTRY OF ORIGIN	DEC	DEPART PORT	ENTRY PORT	ARRIVE DATE	DEC DATE	VOL	PG.	FLD	NAT DATE
Kelly, John	50	Ireland	Y	Queenstown	New York	05/25/1881	02/19/1889			Y	
Kelly, John	??	Scotland	N	?	?	05/00/1878				Y	10/19/1892
Kelly, John	17	Ireland	N	?	New York	00/00/1883				Y	10/24/1888
Kelly, John G.	51	Ireland	N	Liverpool	New York	04/25/1849	09/??/1869	28	136	N	10/01/1869
Kelly, John G.	12	Ireland	N	Liverpool	New York	04/25/1849				Y	10/01/1869
Kelly, John J.	42	England	Y	London	New York	10/18/1880	05/03/1892	19	350	N	
Kelly, Lawrence	40	Ireland	Y	Liverpool	New Orleans	11/28/1849	09/12/1855	13	13	N	
Kelly, Malachy	21	Ireland	Y	Queenstown	New York	05/21/1892	10/24/1893			Y	
Kelly, Mathew	35	Ireland	Y	Liverpool	New Orleans	07/23/1844	10/03/1848	22	404	N	
Kelly, Michael	27	Ireland	Y	London	Boston	04/12/1845	11/14/1848	1	290	N	
Kelly, Michael	24	Ireland	Y	Cork	New York	06/15/1848	03/25/1851	3	327	N	
Kelly, Michael	30	Ireland	Y	Liverpool	New Orleans	02/03/1852	05/25/1854	8	528	N	
Kelly, Michael	30	Ireland	Y	Liverpool	New Orleans	02/03/1852	05/25/1854	9	402	N	
Kelly, Michael	28	Ireland	Y	Limerick	Oswego	08/30/1849	09/21/1854	10	150	N	
Kelly, Michael	28	Ireland	Y	Limerick	Oswego	08/30/1849	09/21/1854	12	89	N	
Kelly, Michael	29	Ireland	Y	Liverpool	Boston	05/02/1883	08/06/1883			Y	
Kelly, Michael	34	Ireland	Y	Liverpool	New York	05/22/1881	06/16/1892			Y	
Kelly, Morgon	50	Ireland	Y	Cork	New Orleans	01/23/1849	02/05/1851	3	99	N	
Kelly, Patrick	25	Ireland	Y	Liverpool	Boston	07/28/1846	02/28/1853	7	244	N	
Kelly, Patrick	21	Ireland	Y	Liverpool	New York	06/01/1879	08/15/1879			Y	
Kelly, Patrick	24	Ireland	Y	Queenstown	New York	05/16/1881	03/08/1884			Y	
Kelly, Patrick	22	Ireland	Y	Canada	Oswego	02/16/1848	02/13/1849	23	88	N	
Kelly, Patrick	23	Ireland	Y	Liverpool	New Orleans	06/20/1847	02/12/1852	24	100	N	
Kelly, Patrick	32	Ireland	Y	Kilkenny	New Orleans	02/18/1850	02/27/1852	25	122	N	
Kelly, Patrick	17	Ireland	N	?	New York	00/00/1883				Y	10/24/1888
Kelly, Thomas	38	Ireland	Y	Queenstown	New York	03/15/1884	11/06/1893	21	53	N	
Kelly, Thomas	38	Ireland	Y	Queenstown	New York	03/15/1884	11/06/1893			Y	
Kelly, Thomas	27	Ireland	Y	Queenstown	New York	05/26/1888	11/01/1893			Y	
Kelly, Thomas	44	Ireland	Y	Dublin	New Orleans	02/01/1850	12/26/1851	24	7	N	
Kelly, William	25	Ireland	Y	Liverpool	New Orleans	01/05/1854	09/29/1856	14	435	N	
Kelly, William	25	Ireland	Y	Liverpool	New Orleans	12/15/1848	02/12/1852	24	99	N	
Kelly, William F.	32	Ireland	Y	Liverpool	New York	09/30/1848	10/23/1851	4	385	N	
Kelm, August	45	Germany	Y	Bremen	Baltimore	04/12/1891	10/26/1895			Y	
Kelsch, John	44	Bavaria	Y	Havre	New Orleans	12/16/1850	04/07/1856	26	451	N	
Kemble, Arthur	29	England	Y	Liverpool	Boston	06/27/1883	05/10/1888			Y	
Kemken, H.	24	Germany	Y	Bremen	Baltimore	08/30/1881	06/07/1886			Y	
Kemme, August	25	Germany	Y	Bremen	Baltimore	11/03/1883	07/27/1887			Y	
Kemme, Theodore	53	Germany	Y	Bremen	Baltimore	??/??/1861	09/25/1884			Y	
Kemmell, Ferdinand	30	Hanover	Y	Bremen	Baltimore	05/01/1854	07/07/8159	17	460	N	
Kemmer, Francis	36	Mecklenburg	Y	Hamburg	Buffalo	06/19/1849	02/10/1851	3	115	N	
Kemmerer, Benedict	30	Bavaria	Y	Havre	New York	10/24/1850	11/06/1855	13	174	N	
Kemna, Barney	27	Prussia	Y	Bremen	New York	11/01/1846	01/14/1850	23	506	N	
Kemper, Bernard	24	Germany	Y	Bremen	New York	08/22/1885	11/02/1889			Y	
Kemper, Bernhard	28	Germany	Y	Amsterdam	New York	03/01/1883	12/08/1888			Y	
Kemper, Charles	31	Germany	Y	Bremen	Baltimore	06/09/1872	05/04/1881			Y	
Kemper, Evert	25	Hanover	Y	Bremen	New Orleans	11/07/1853	11/28/1855	13	263	N	
Kemper, Henry	37	Hanover	Y	Bremen	New Orleans	11/06/1853	09/27/1856	14	415	N	
Kemper, Henry	28	Germany	Y	Amsterdam	New York	10/24/1882	10/26/1888	19	178	N	
Kemper, Henry	31	Germany	Y	Bremen	New York	03/24/1883	10/22/1892	19	376	N	
Kemper, Henry	24	Germany	Y	Amsterdam	New York	10/25/1881	12/21/1881			Y	
Kemper, Henry	31	Germany	Y	Bremen	New York	03/24/1883	10/22/1892			Y	
Kemper, Henry	28	Prussia	Y	Bremen	Buffalo	07/??/1847	12/??/1849	23	409	N	
Kemper, Henry	22	Prussia	Y	Bremen	New Orleans	11/08/1849	06/03/1852	25	178	N	
Kemper, Henry	28	Germany	Y	Amsterdam	New York	10/24/1882	10/26/1888			Y	
Kemper, John	24	Prussia	Y	Bremen	Buffalo	??/13/1847	12/17/1849	23	406	N	
Kemper, John M.	44	Germany	N	Hanover	Baltimore	05/10/1870	?			Y	
Kempf, Jonathon	27	Wurttemberg	Y	Antwerp	New York	06/09/1851	09/14/1857	14	268	N	
Kempher, Herman	30	Hanover	Y	Bremen	New Orleans	11/01/1857	07/26/1858	16	526	N	
Kena, Frederick (Kichne?	??	Prussia	Y	?	?	?	09/24/1884			Y	

CITIZENSHIP RECORDS

APPLICANT	AGE	COUNTRY OF ORIGIN	DEC	DEPART PORT	ENTRY PORT	ARRIVE DATE	DEC DATE	VOL	PG.	FLD	NAT DATE
Kendall, Edward	17	England	N	?	New York	00/00/1881				Y	10/19/1886
Kenier, Henry	??	Prussia	Y	Bremen	New Orleans	??/07/1848	12/09/1850	2	347	N	
Kenkel, F. B.	23	Germany	Y	Bremen	Baltimore	06/05/1880	05/14/1885			Y	
Kenkel, Henry	22	Germany	Y	Bremen	Baltimore	10/28/1881	10/14/1885			Y	
Kennedy, Andrew	30	Ireland	Y	Belfast	Buffalo	10/??/1844	10/06/1856	14	206	N	
Kennedy, Edward	23	Ireland	Y	Liverpool	New York	04/18/1882	10/06/1885	19	15	N	
Kennedy, Hugh	38	Ireland	Y	Canada	Whitehall	06/??/1833	10/??/1849	23	268	N	
Kennedy, James	40	Ireland	Y	Canada	Oswego	08/07/1847	03/25/1850	2	264	N	
Kennedy, James	??	Ireland	Y	?	?	??/11/18??	10/24/1850	2	297	N	
Kennedy, James	26	Ireland	Y	Toronto	Buffalo	09/01/1848	01/21/1852	24	47	N	
Kennedy, James	28	Ireland	Y	Liverpool	New Orleans	08/??/1850	06/07/1852	25	198	N	
Kennedy, James	24	Ireland	Y	Liverpool	New Orleans	01/15/1850	09/07/1852	25	395	N	
Kennedy, John	27	Ireland	Y	Liverpool	New York	04/25/1844	10/29/1851	4	433	N	
Kennedy, John	29	Ireland	Y	Cork	Boston	11/04/1848	05/15/1854	8	446	N	
Kennedy, John	29	Ireland	Y	Cork	Boston	11/04/1848	05/15/1854	9	319	N	
Kennedy, Michael	28	Ireland	Y	Liverpool	Boston	11/01/1849	10/20/1852	5	24	N	
Kennedy, Michael	28	Ireland	Y	Liverpool	Detroit	01/31/1883	10/27/1890	19	305	N	
Kennedy, Michael	28	Ireland	Y	Liverpool	Detroit	01/31/1883	10/27/1890			Y	
Kennedy, Nicholas	??	Ireland	Y	Waterford	Boston	??/05/1846	12/13/1850	2	358	N	
Kennedy, Patrick	29	Ireland	Y	Liverpool	Philadelphia	12/08/1848	10/09/1854	6	142	N	
Kennedy, Patrick	29	Ireland	Y	Liverpool	Philadelphia	12/08/1848	10/09/1854	11	145	N	
Kennedy, Patrick	28	Ireland	Y	Liverpool	New Orleans	12/11/1851	10/30/1858	17	203	N	
Kennedy, Patrick	35	Ireland	Y	Liverpool	New Orleans	04/01/1852	02/18/1856	26	94	N	
Kennedy, Peter	26	Ireland	Y	Liverpool	New York	06/??/1846	01/28/1853	7	79	N	
Kennedy, Thomas	23	Ireland	Y	Liverpool	New York	05/20/1857	09/30/1858	17	28	N	
Kennedy, Thomas	30	Ireland	Y	South Hampto	New York	06/03/1894	01/08/1895	21	78	N	
Kennefrohn, Herman	24	Hanover	Y	Bremen	New Orleans	01/06/1848	01/03/1851	2	445	N	
Kennelly, John	26	England	Y	Liverpool	New York	06/15/1884	12/12/1887			Y	
Kennelly, Patrick	23	Ireland	Y	Quebec	Ohio	08/01/1847	11/09/1852	5	260	N	
Kennelly, Patrick	23	Ireland	Y	Quebec	Ohio	08/01/1847	11/09/1852	6	384	N	
Kenner, Charles	25	Germany	Y	Antwerp	New York	10/04/1879	10/15/1882			Y	
Kenneweg, Christian Henr	32	Bremen	Y	Bremen	New York	09/03/1854	12/05/1857	16	198	N	
Kenneweg, Frederick	21	Hanover	Y	Bremen	New Orleans	11/22/1848	07/14/1851	3	532	N	
Kenney, John	40	Ireland	Y	Liverpool	New Orleans	08/09/1847	09/24/1856	14	363	N	
Kenney, Patrick	33	Ireland	Y	Liverpool	New York	04/27/1849	05/08/1852	24	418	N	
Kenney, Patrick	17	Ireland	N	?	New York	00/00/1880				Y	10/22/1888
Kenning, Anton	45	Germany	Y	Bremen	Baltimore	09/24/1880	10/18/1883			Y	
Kenning, Anton	28	Germany	Y	Bremen	Baltimore	05/19/1890	11/07/1892			Y	
Kenny, Edward	28	Ireland	Y	Queenstown	New York	03/11/1883	02/02/1888			Y	
Kenny, Michael	22	Ireland	Y	Dublin	New York	??/03/1849	12/17/1849	23	408	N	
Kensella, Matthew	21	Ireland	Y	Waterford	New York	10/20/1853	03/15/1856	26	207	N	
Kent, William	43	England	Y	Liverpool	New York	10/07/1880	10/29/1889			Y	
Kentner, Christian	21	Wurttemberg	Y	Bremen	New York	08/15/1859	04/04/1861	18	133	N	
Kentrup, Henry	29	Prussia	Y	Bremen	Rochester	08/15/1847	02/19/1849	23	212	N	
Keogh, Edmund	30	Ireland	Y	Limerick	New York	07/09/1848	03/08/1850	2	170	N	
Keown, Bernard	33	Ireland	Y	Liverpool	New York	06/19/1843	04/05/1852	24	392	N	
Keparaitis, George	??	Russia	Y	Bremen	New York	03/05/1888	01/10/1896			Y	
Kepfer, Andrew	32	France	Y	Havre	New York	05/24/1855	04/08/1858	16	509	N	
Keppel, Ludwig	32	Germany	Y	Antwerp	New York	08/25/1885	04/06/1891			Y	
Keppler, John	52	Martemburg	N	Hamburg	New York	05/27/1848	?			Y	
Keppler, Louis	39	Wuertemberg	Y	Bremen	New York	05/14/1853	03/31/1856	26	390	N	
Keppner, Xaver	33	Baden	Y	Havre	New Orleans	12/03/1856	07/02/1862	18	369	N	
Kerans, Lyons	48	Ireland	Y	Liverpool	New York	10/13/1873	01/15/1885			Y	
Kercsmar, Adam	22	Austria	Y	Bremen	Baltimore	09/08/1892	05/03/1893			Y	
Kergel, John	22	Prussia	Y	Hamburg	New York	09/14/1854	10/14/1857	15	420	N	
Kerhert, Andreas	27	Baden	Y	Havre	New Orleans	11/??/1847	11/??/1849	23	295	N	
Kerigan, Geroge	30	Ireland	Y	Londonderry	New York	06/02/1848	08/04/1856	14	320	N	
Kerius, Patrick	??	Ireland	Y	?	?	?	09/29/1868			Y	
Kerkhoff, Anthony	??	Germany	N	?	?	?	?	28	446	N	03/16/1871

CITIZENSHIP RECORDS

APPLICANT	AGE	COUNTRY OF ORIGIN	DEC	DEPART PORT	ENTRY PORT	ARRIVE DATE	DEC DATE	VOL	PG.	FLD	NAT DATE
Kerley, Edwin J.	49	England	Y	London	New York	11/14/1884	11/01/1888	19	211	N	
Kerley, John A.	23	England	Y	Liverpool	Detroit	07/03/1885	11/01/1888	19	210	N	
Kern, Adolph	33	Germany	Y	Bremen	Baltimore	05/13/1884	12/31/1886			Y	
Kern, Adolph	30	Germany	Y	Antwerp	New York	07/30/1881	06/20/1888			Y	10/06/1890
Kern, Charles	24	Germany	Y	Bremen	Baltimore	08/11/1893	12/03/1894			Y	
Kern, Charles	41	Germany	N	Bremen	New York	09/03/1866	?			Y	
Kern, Dermian	26	Bavaria	Y	Liverpool	New York	12/17/1854	10/22/1858	17	94	N	
Kern, Frederick	27	Germany	Y	Havre	New York	05/05/1881	07/03/1884			Y	
Kern, George	50	Germany	Y	Havre	New Orleans	11/??/1867	10/27/1885			Y	
Kern, Isadore	56	Baden	Y	Havre	New York	01/01/1847	01/19/1852	24	27	N	
Kern, John	??	Napan	Y	London	New York	06/08/18??	10/11/1848	1	140	N	
Kern, John Leonard	36	Bavaria	Y	Bremen	New York	05/02/1851	09/29/1856	14	12	N	
Kern, Joseph	31	Switzerland	Y	Basil	Philadelphia	08/18/1890	03/11/1892			Y	
Kern, Louis	30	Germany	Y	Bremen	New York	03/28/1887	11/21/1890			Y	
Kern, Peter	27	Bavaria	Y	Havre	New York	08/14/1850	09/29/1856	14	29	N	
Kernan, Bernard	23	Ireland	Y	Londonderry	New York	03/10/1886	02/13/1890			Y	
Kerner, Mathias	28	Wuerttemberg	Y	Rotterdam	New York	07/25/1850	05/20/1852	25	71	N	
Kerner, William	23	Wurttemberg	Y	Havre	New York	12/01/1854	11/03/1858	17	268	N	
Kerr, David	22	Scotland	Y	Glasgow	New York	10/08/1884	06/04/1887			Y	
Kerrison, George Edward	50	England	Y	Liverpool	New York	10/03/1842	07/25/1851	4	41	N	
Kerschbaum, Frederick	27	Bavaria	Y	Amsterdam	New York	06/01/1849	03/02/1852	24	218	N	
Kerstens, John Hermann	24	Hanover	Y	Bremen	New Orleans	11/13/1854	11/01/1860	27	528	N	
Kersting, Bernard	36	Prussia	Y	Antwerp	New York	12/11/1857	11/01/1858	17	222	N	
Kersting, Heinrich	40	Germany	Y	Bremen	Baltimore	11/14/1881	11/04/1884			Y	
Kersting, Joseph	??	Germany	Y	?	?	11/??/1874	11/06/1882			Y	
Kerth, Charles	27	Bavaria	Y	Havre	New Orleans	12/27/1845	02/27/1850	2	134	N	
Kerwald, Valentine	30	Bavaria	Y	Havre	New Orleans	04/01/1851	12/03/1855	13	275	N	
Kesheimer, John	44	Baden	Y	Havre	New York	05/20/1840	08/21/1848	22	213	N	
Kesker, Herman H.	22	Hanover	Y	Bremen	Baltimore	10/17/1848	11/01/1852	6	271	N	
Kesker, Herman Henry	22	Hanover	Y	Bremen	Baltimore	10/17/1848	11/01/1852	5	145	N	
Kesse, Gerhard	35	Germany	Y	Amsterdam	Baltimore	08/22/1890	10/03/1892			Y	
Kessen, Bernard Henry	28	Hanover	Y	Bremen	New Orleans	12/11/1854	03/02/1851	16	354	N	
Kessen, Carl Anton	26	Germany	Y	Bremen	Baltimore	09/14/1881	08/24/1887			Y	
Kessen, Clemens	30	Germany	Y	Bremen	Baltimore	05/25/1887	10/25/1890			Y	
Kessens, Gerhard Heinric	24	Hanover	Y	Bremen	New Orleans	12/01/1851	09/25/1854	10	200	N	
Kessens, Gerhard Heinric	24	Hanover	Y	Bremen	New Orleans	12/01/1851	09/25/1854	12	139	N	
Kessheimer, Sebastian	25	Baden	Y	Havre	New York	02/24/1847	03/19/1850	2	220	N	
Kessler, Heinrich	48	Germany	Y	Rotterdam	New York	08/??/1880	07/00/1883			Y	
Kessler, Heinrich	48	Germany	N	Rotterdam	New York	08/??/1880	?			Y	
Kessler, John	32	Hessen	Y	Bremen	New York	11/20/1849	09/20/1858	16	187	N	
Kessler, Martin	??	Germany	Y	?	?	?	10/04/1890			Y	
Kessler, Michael	38	Germany	Y	Hamburg	New York	09/01/1880	07/25/1884			Y	
Kessler, P. Charles	16	Germany	N	?	New York	00/00/1882				Y	10/26/1888
Kessler, Peter	41	Switzerland	N	Havre	New York	10/03/1866	?			Y	
Kessler, Rudolph	34	Germany	Y	Bremen	New York	08/30/1881	08/06/1891			Y	
Kessling, Heinrich Josep	31	Hanover	Y	Bremen	New Orleans	12/08/1849	02/24/1853	7	226	N	
Keszler, Peter	31	Hesse Cassel	Y	Bremen	Baltimore	10/03/1846	07/17/1851	3	543	N	
Kett, Franz	36	Denmark	Y	Hamburg	New York	03/15/1878	11/27/1891			Y	
Ketterer, Kilian	21	Germany	Y	Havre	New York	09/08/1880	10/08/1880			Y	
Kettering, Valentine	27	Germany	Y	Antwerp	Boston	10/26/1881	11/02/1886			Y	
Ketterling, Henry	24	Germany	Y	Bremen	Baltimore	03/01/1883	03/02/1887			Y	
Kettertzech, August	22	Saxony	Y	Bremen	New Orleans	11/05/1848	08/??/1851	4	161	N	
Kettler, Gerard	30	Hanover	Y	Bremen	New Orleans	12/12/1845	03/18/1850	2	209	N	
Kettler, Herman	38	Germany	Y	Bremen	Baltimore	08/17/1871	12/18/1888			Y	
Kettler, Hermann	48	Germany	Y	Bremen	Baltimore	02/28/1892	02/29/1896			Y	
Kettman, Bernard	27	Hanover	Y	Bremen	New Orleans	11/??/1846	10/26/1850	2	312	N	
Keunneir, Robert	48	Scotland	Y	Glasgow	Philadelphia	09/15/1836	06/21/1851	3	437	N	
Keuse, Jean	43	France	Y	Havre	New Orleans	11/??/1853	11/08/1856	14	482	N	
Keuter, Herman	34	Germany	Y	Rotterdam	New York	09/24/1882	10/10/1894			Y	

CITIZENSHIP RECORDS

APPLICANT	AGE	COUNTRY OF ORIGIN	DEC	DEPART PORT	ENTRY PORT	ARRIVE DATE	DEC DATE	VOL	PG.	FLD	NAT DATE
Keutz, Barney Hermann	27	Hanover	Y	Bremen	New Orleans	11/20/1850	03/17/1853	7	342	N	
Key, George	25	England	Y	Liverpool	New York	10/25/1847	03/03/1853	7	263	N	
Keyser, Jacob	49	Germany	N	Havre	New York	10/??/1865	?			Y	
Keyser, John	30	Luxembourg	Y	Antwerp	New York	11/10/1882	05/19/1893			Y	
Keztermann, Hermann	29	Prussia	Y	Bremen	Baltimore	04/17/1869	03/29/1872	18	477	N	
Khol, Frank	45	Austria	Y	Bremen	Baltimore	06/16/1880	12/12/1883			Y	
Khough, Patrick	27	Ireland	Y	Liverpool	New Orleans	11/12/1850	11/23/1852	5	329	N	
Khriep, John	36	Bavaria	Y	Bremen	New Orleans	12/28/1844	03/09/1950	2	175	N	
Kiczkiwski, Joseph	25	Germany	Y	Antwerp	Philadelphia	12/17/1884	04/04/1889			Y	
Kidd, George	62	Ireland	Y	Liverpool	New York	04/14/1849	05/01/1854	8	324	N	
Kidd, George	62	Ireland	Y	Liverpool	New York	04/14/1849	05/01/1854	9	197	N	
Kidd, William H.	26	Ireland	Y	Liverpool	New York	05/10/1849	05/01/1854	8	323	N	
Kidd, William H.	26	Ireland	Y	Liverpool	New York	05/01/1849	05/01/1854	9	196	N	
Kidd, William H.	26	Ireland	Y	Belfast	New York	06/??/1879	10/13/1884			Y	
Kidney, James	40	Ireland	Y	Liverpool	New York	11/12/1842	08/30/1848	22	278	N	
Kieback, Charles	29	Prussia	Y	Bremen	New York	06/01/1857	02/15/1862	18	262	N	
Kieber, Adam	30	Austria	Y	Havre	New York	06/01/1849	10/02/1854	10	359	N	
Kiechle, Christian	53	Baden	Y	Rotterdam	New York	03/30/1846	02/18/1857	15	29	N	
Kieckbusch, Henry	52	Germany	Y	Hamburg	New York	04/15/1865	03/10/1887			Y	
Kief, Gerhard	49	Hanover	N	Bremen	New York	08/24/1866	?			Y	
Kiefer, Franz	30	Germany	Y	Bremen	Baltimore	07/01/1882	01/12/1889			Y	
Kiefer, Frederick	31	Germany	Y	Havre	New York	04/06/1882	07/01/1885			Y	
Kiefer, Fredrick	44	Germany	Y	Bremen	?	04/05/1884	10/12/1885			Y	
Kiefer, John	32	Germany	Y	Hamburg	New York	01/27/1882	03/17/1887			Y	
Kiefer, Joseph	30	Germany	Y	Havre	New York	02/05/1889	10/28/1896			Y	
Kiefer, Joseph	36	France	Y	Havre	New York	08/20/1852	03/01/1856	26	145	N	
Kiefer, Sebastian	28	Bavaria	Y	Havre	New Orleans	06/09/1847	07/17/1851	3	545	N	
Kieffer, Charles	42	Germany	Y	Havre	New York	04/04/1892	10/22/1897			Y	
Kieffer, Eugene Charles	??	France	Y	?	?	?	09/13/1890			Y	
Kieffer, Ferdinand	24	France	Y	Havre	New York	10/16/1871	05/05/1874			Y	
Kieffer, Joseph	30	Germany	Y	Antwerp	New York	12/21/1890	09/09/1896			Y	
Kieffer, Peter	26	Luxemburg	Y	Antwerp	New York	05/31/1885	12/27/1886			Y	
Kiehe, John Theodore	24	Bavaria	Y	Havre	New York	06/29/1849	02/16/1852	24	118	N	
Kiehl, Carl	??	Germany	Y	?	?	?	06/07/1882			Y	
Kielmann, John George	34	Wurttemberg	Y	Liverpool	Philadelphia	09/09/1852	09/21/1855	13	102	N	
Kiely, Edward	17	Ireland	N	?	New York	00/00/1879				Y	10/22/1886
Kiely, Jeremiah	24	Ireland	Y	Queenstown	New York	06/27/1885	03/31/1888			Y	
Kiely, John	41	Canada	Y	?	?	?	02/23/1893			Y	
Kiely, Patrick (Killy?)	??	Ireland	N	?	?	04/02/1886				Y	10/22/1892
Kiemle, Friedrich	30	Germany	Y	Bremen	New York	10/27/1891	10/29/1884			Y	
Kiene, John	26	Austria	Y	?	?	?	10/08/188?			Y	
Kienfl, Benedicht	32	Germany	Y	Bremen	New York	12/27/1872	11/09/1876			Y	
Kienker, Christ	26	Germany	Y	Bremen	Baltimore	04/17/1882	01/02/1885			Y	
Kienker, Fred	24	Germany	Y	Bremen	New York	11/12/1885	04/30/1887			Y	
Kienle, Henry	23	Germany	Y	Rotterdam	New York	09/09/1883	01/18/1887			Y	
Kienzle, John Martin	24	Baden	Y	Liverpool	New York	07/31/1852	10/02/1856	14	137	N	
Kienzli, Joseph	26	Switzerland	Y	Havre	New York	06/19/1850	09/27/1858	16	125	N	
Kiepling, Adam	21	Germany	Y	Bremen	New York	07/27/1892	10/24/1892			Y	
Kierns, Thomas	27	Ireland	Y	Liverpool	New York	06/25/1852	04/19/1853	8	86	N	
Kiesel, Charles	38	Germany	Y	Hamburg	New York	09/25/1861	10/07/1872			Y	
Kiesselbach, John	21	Kurhessen	Y	Liverpool	New York	05/05/1852	07/25/1855	11	427	N	
Kiessling, Friedrich	41	Germany	N	Bremen	New York	04/22/1873	?			Y	
Kiessling, John	32	Bavaria	Y	Bremen	New York	06/16/1852	08/23/1855	11	484	N	
Kiessling, Julius	45	Germany	Y	Havre	New York	12/06/1871	04/01/1886			Y	
Kietzmann, Rudolph	34	Germany	Y	Bremen	Baltimore	12/19/1889	10/28/1896			Y	
Kiezer, George	??	Hanover	Y	?	New Orleans	??/29/18??	10/28/1850	2	318	N	
Kiffe, August	26	Germany	Y	Bremen	New York	09/17/1881	10/15/1886	19	49	N	
Kilcoyne, Patrick	27	Ireland	Y	Liverpool	New York	10/28/1848	01/20/1852	24	42	N	
Kilfoil, John	28	Ireland	Y	Liverpool	New Orleans	05/15/1853	08/06/1860	27	253	N	

CITIZENSHIP RECORDS

APPLICANT	AGE	COUNTRY OF ORIGIN	DEC	DEPART PORT	ENTRY PORT	ARRIVE DATE	DEC DATE	VOL	PG.	FLD	NAT DATE
Kilgour, Peter Thomson	31	Canada	Y	Windsor	Detroit	03/15/1883	11/14/1891			Y	
Kilian, John	38	Baden	Y	Havre	New York	06/02/1852	10/06/1860	27	407	N	
Kilian, John George	??	Bavaria	Y	?	?	?	01/03/1888			Y	
Kilk, John Henry	29	Nassau	Y	London	New York	07/26/1854	09/20/1858	16	184	N	
Kilkenny, Bernard	??	Great Britain	Y	?	?	?	06/02/1886			Y	
Kilkeny, Anthony	26	Ireland	Y	Liverpool	New York	04/17/1848	10/25/1851	4	404	N	
Killan, Thomas	30	Ireland	Y	Liverpool	New Orleans	??/??/1852	02/23/1861	18	116	N	
Kille, Lorenz	55	Germany	Y	Bremen	New York	04/09/1882	01/21/1885			Y	
Killenn, Patrick	46	Ireland	N	Liverpool	New York	06/01/1870	?			Y	
Killian, August	41	Germany	Y	Hamburg	New York	07/28/1868	09/16/1882			Y	
Killinger, Henry	26	Germany	Y	Havre	New York	10/18/1880	04/05/1886	19	34	N	
Killinger, Henry	26	Germany	Y	Havre	New York	10/18/1880	04/05/1886			Y	
Killinger, John Michael	38	Wurttemberg	Y	London	New York	10/28/1847	02/03/1853	7	108	N	
Killoran, Michael	??	Ireland	Y	Sligo	Boston	11/01/1847	04/04/1853	7	530	N	
Killoran, Owen	36	Ireland	Y	?	?	07/17/1889	04/11/1894			Y	
Kimball, Hugo	35	Germany	Y	Antwerp	Philadelphia	11/30/1888	10/22/1896			Y	
Kimberley, Harry	??	England	Y	?	?	?	05/26/1883			Y	
Kimmerle, Herbert	26	Germany	Y	?	?	?	03/19/1889			Y	
Kimmerle, Theodore	37	Switzerland	Y	Havre	New York	05/03/1881	04/14/1892			Y	
Kimpel, Henry	25	Germany	Y	Hamburg	Baltimore	11/02/1891	08/16/1892			Y	
Kinan, Patrick	30	Ireland	Y	Liverpool	New Orleans	02/28/1847	02/09/1852	24	77	N	
Kindeley, Frederick	31	Germany	Y	Havre	New York	09/21/1882	02/21/1890			Y	
Kindt, Conrad	29	Germany	Y	Antwerp	New York	10/15/1882	04/07/1886			Y	
Kindt, Karl	25	Germany	Y	Antwerp	New York	07/31/1882	07/05/1887			Y	
Kine, Edward	30	Ireland	Y	Liverpool	New York	06/27/1840	10/02/1848	22	377	N	
King, George	26	Ireland	Y	Liverpool	New York	04/18/1853	04/02/1856	26	410	N	
King, John	35	Ireland	Y	Liverpool	New Orleans	06/05/1848	07/21/1851	4	22	N	
King, John	30	Ireland	Y	Liverpool	New York	04/??/1855	02/07/1861	18	93	N	
King, John C.	39	Ireland	N	Queenstown	New York	04/16/1865	?			Y	
King, Martin	39	Ireland	Y	Liverpool	New York	05/25/1879	10/22/1888	19	163	N	
King, Martin	27	Germany	Y	Havre	New York	05/02/1869	08/17/1875			Y	
King, Michael	40	Ireland	Y	Liverpool	Mobile	11/10/1849	03/07/1857	15	71	N	
King, Michael	28	Ireland	Y	Queenstown	New York	06/29/1880	08/07/1884			Y	
King, Patrick	29	Ireland	Y	Galway	Boston	11/01/1850	05/05/1859	17	400	N	
King, Patrick	32	Ireland	Y	Queenstown	New York	10/23/1864	11/04/1889	19	274	N	
King, Patrick	26	Ireland	Y	Queenstown	New York	06/12/1888	04/20/1893			Y	
King, Patrick	32	Ireland	Y	Queenstown	New York	10/23/1867	11/04/1889			Y	
King, Peter	68	France	N	Havre	New York	07/04/1840	10/??/1843	28	144	N	10/??/1848
King, Peter	20	France	N	Havre	New York	07/04/1840	10/00/1843			Y	10/00/1848
King, Thomas	25	Ireland	Y	Liverpool	New York	05/29/1846	07/15/1851	3	535	N	
Kinkal, Anton	28	Oldenburg	Y	Rotterdam	New York	07/18/1840	10/13/1851	4	258	N	
Kinker, William	34	Germany	Y	Bremen	Baltimore	07/04/1874	10/02/1878			Y	
Kinner, Gottlieb	40	Prussia	Y	Bremen	Baltimore	06/14/1860	06/11/1862	18	349	N	
Kinney, Bartholomew	45	Ireland	Y	Liverpool	New York	08/01/1848	12/03/1857	16	65	N	
Kinney, Christopher	27	Ireland	Y	Liverpool	New York	06/30/1855	10/11/1860	27	485	N	
Kinney, M. F.	45	Ireland	Y	Liverpool	New York	06/28/1864	10/06/1884			Y	
Kinney, Thomas	32	Ireland	Y	Liverpool	New Orleans	05/12/1846	11/20/1848	1	340	N	
Kinny, Martin	30	Ireland	Y	Dublin	New Orleans	03/??/1851	03/29/1853	7	455	N	
Kinny, Thomas	33	Ireland	Y	Liverpool	New Orleans	01/??/18??	10/??/1849	23	269	N	
Kinsela, Terrence	35	Ireland	Y	Queenstown	New York	06/??/1880	04/??/1883	28	310	N	?
Kinsella, James	38	Ireland	Y	Liverpool	New York	06/12/1848	03/20/1860	27	133	N	
Kinsella, John	20	Ireland	Y	?	?	06/15/1885	04/27/1893			Y	
Kintz, Ignatz	63	Baden	Y	Havre	New York	10/31/1850	04/20/1854	8	220	N	
Kinzler, Charles	??	Germany	Y	?	?	05/11/1890	12/03/1895			Y	
Kinzler, Franz Achaz	??	Baden	Y	Havre	New York	06/27/18??	10/11/1848	1	127	N	
Kipp, Ernst	29	Brunswick	Y	Hamburg	New York	01/13/1854	06/05/1854	10	66	N	
Kipp, Ernst	29	Brunswick	Y	Hamburg	New York	01/16/1854	06/05/1854	12	3	N	
Kippenberger, Jacob	39	Hesse Darmsta	Y	Havre	New York	04/25/1846	03/17/1851	3	288	N	
Kirbert, Casper Hermann	35	Hanover	Y	Bremen	New York	08/20/1857	08/15/1860	27	269	N	

CITIZENSHIP RECORDS

APPLICANT	AGE	COUNTRY OF ORIGIN	DEC	DEPART PORT	ENTRY PORT	ARRIVE DATE	DEC DATE	VOL	PG.	FLD	NAT DATE
Kirbey, John	22	Ireland	Y	Canada	Buffalo	07/01/1855	11/29/1858	17	365	N	
Kirby, Jeremiah	30	Ireland	Y	Queenstown	New York	05/02/1881	09/22/1885			Y	
Kirby, John	27	Ireland	Y	Liverpool	New York	09/25/1852	04/14/1853	8	61	N	
Kirby, Patrick	25	Ireland	Y	Canada	Oswego	10/04/1845	04/03/1852	24	359	N	
Kircher, Charles	27	Germany	Y	Antwerp	New York	03/19/1882	06/09/1886			Y	
Kircher, John	25	Wurttemberg	Y	Bremen	New York	08/??/1853	12/28/1855	13	377	N	
Kircher, John	28	Germany	Y	Antwerp	New York	03/04/1882	10/22/1889			Y	
Kirchgefsner, John Nepom	30	Baden	Y	London	New York	09/28/1856	03/28/1857	15	98	N	
Kirchheck, John Dietrich	25	Hanover	Y	Bremen	New Orleans	06/18/1845	10/03/1848	22	400	N	
Kirchhoeffer, George Wil	33	Saxony	Y	London	New York	02/26/1855	09/17/1858	16	167	N	
Kirchhofer, Henry	21	Switzerland	Y	Havre	New York	08/04/1856	09/19/1857	15	288	N	
Kirchhoff, Bernard	46	Germany	Y	Antwerp	Philadelphia	04/08/1881	02/19/1885			Y	
Kirchner, Charles	34	Germany	Y	Bremen	New York	10/10/1879	10/18/1890			Y	
Kirchner, Christian	23	Wuerttenberg	Y	London	New York	05/29/1849	04/05/1852	24	375	N	
Kirchner, Conrad	34	Germany	Y	Hamburg	New York	04/20/1857	10/08/1872	18	532	N	
Kirchner, Frederick	25	Baden	Y	Antwerp	New York	09/26/1849	04/18/1853	8	78	N	
Kirchner, Sebastian	33	Bavaria	Y	Antwerp	New York	09/29/1850	02/25/1852	24	168	N	
Kirk, James	27	Ireland	Y	Liverpool	New York	06/??/1849	12/??/1849	23	433	N	
Kirkhoefel, Ernst	40	Prussia	Y	Antwerp	New Orleans	01/17/1847	02/11/1850	2	55	N	
Kirks, Albert	29	Prussia	Y	Bremen	New York	06/05/1868	01/03/1872	18	448	N	
Kirlach, Joseph	25	Austria	Y	Bremen	Baltimore	05/11/1860	04/11/1861	18	107	N	
Kirsch, Andreas	??	Germany	Y	?	?	?	10/27/1882			Y	
Kirsch, Jacob	37	Germany	Y	Amsterdam	New York	06/24/1882	07/17/1890			Y	
Kirsch, Michael	33	Germany	Y	Bremen	Baltimore	05/05/1880	04/03/1886			Y	
Kirschdoerffer, Jules	29	Germany	Y	Havre	New York	05/10/1882	10/25/1886			Y	
Kirschner, Frederick	29	Hesse Darmsta	Y	London	New York	08/10/1850	06/05/1854	10	68	N	
Kirschner, Frederick	28	Saxony	Y	Hamburg	New York	05/05/1849	06/05/1854	10	88	N	
Kirschner, Frederick	29	Hesse Darmsta	Y	London	New York	08/10/1850	06/05/1854	12	5	N	
Kirschner, Frederick	28	Saxony	Y	Hamburg	New York	05/05/1849	06/05/1854	12	25	N	
Kirschner, Henry	16	Germany	N	?	Baltimore	00/00/1871				Y	10/26/1888
Kirschner, Herman	33	Switzerland	Y	Havre	New York	08/07/1881	10/24/1891			Y	
Kirschner, Herman	23	Germany	Y	Bremen	New York	02/03/1889	04/17/1893			Y	
Kirstein, Louis	33	Germany	Y	Bremen	Baltimore	03/10/1877	11/03/1882			Y	
Kirsten, Gustav Adolph	43	Germany	Y	Hamburg	New York	05/01/1881	04/08/1889			Y	
Kirstenhaker, Stephan	28	Bavaria	Y	Bremen	New York	07/07/1844	11/13/1848	1	269	N	
Kisif, Johannes Friedric	42	Germany	Y	Bremen	New York	11/04/1882	03/09/1901			Y	
Kiskar, Henry (Kisker?)	26	Hanover	Y	Bremen	Baltimore	10/20/1857	09/11/1860	27	357	N	
Kisker, Fred W.	24	Hanover	Y	Bremen	New Orleans	05/28/1848	03/??/1851	3	321	N	
Kisner, Gersten	45	Russia	Y	Hamburg	New York	03/00/1888	01/24/1891			Y	
Kison, Charles	32	Germany	Y	Antwerp	New York	07/06/1882	08/01/1889			Y	
Kissel, Edward	33	Germany	Y	Antwerp	New York	08/12/1882	02/17/1887			Y	
Kissel, Peter	29	Germany	Y	Rotterdam	New York	08/21/1881	06/10/1884			Y	
Kissten, Paul	15	Germany	N	?	New York	00/00/1879				Y	10/27/1888
Kist, Andreas	34	Germany	Y	Havre	New York	05/15/1888	07/21/1894			Y	
Kist, Charles	27	Germany	Y	Antwerp	New York	03/02/1884	11/01/1890			Y	
Kist, Joseph	30	Germany	Y	Havre	New York	09/02/1880	06/30/1884			Y	
Kistenberger, George	32	Germany	Y	Havre	New York	01/16/1868	10/04/1880			Y	
Kistner, John George	29	Wuerttenberg	Y	Bremen	Baltimore	07/??/1844	12/??/1849	23	383	N	
Kistner, Joseph	31	Wurzburg, Bav	Y	Germany	?	10/20/1883	09/16/1884			Y	
Kistner, Nicholas	28	Hesse Homberg	Y	Havre	New Orleans	05/19/1849	06/14/1852	25	264	N	
Kistner, Theodore	45	Baden	Y	Havre	New Orleans	11/17/1847	10/22/1858	17	95	N	
Kitt, Balthasar	78	Germany	N	Havre	New York	05/??/1850	?			Y	
Kitt, John	23	Hanover	Y	Bremen	Baltimore	09/30/1847	03/13/1850	2	189	N	
Kittelberger, Fred	15	Germany	Y	?	New York	00/00/1881				Y	04/02/1888
Kitten, Joseph	24	Prussia	Y	Bremen	Baltimore	05/01/1847	04/26/1850	3	11	N	
Kitzinger, Nicholas	31	Bavaria	Y	Bremen	New York	11/24/1854	03/19/1858	16	427	N	
Kizenberger, John Adam	38	Germany	Y	Rotterdam	New York	05/03/1887	01/04/1888			Y	
Klaasen, Herman H.	34	Hanover	Y	Bremen	New Orleans	04/11/1846	11/13/1848	1	276	N	
Klaer, George	44	Baden	Y	Rotterdam	New York	01/20/1847	10/20/1851	4	346	N	

CITIZENSHIP RECORDS

APPLICANT	AGE	COUNTRY OF ORIGIN	DEC	DEPART PORT	ENTRY PORT	ARRIVE DATE	DEC DATE	VOL	PG.	FLD	NAT DATE
Klages, August	26	Hanover	Y	Bremen	Baltimore	10/01/1854	09/02/1857	15	221	N	
Klahm, Frank	22	Germany	Y	Bremen	New York	09/22/1891	10/01/1894			Y	
Klaiber, John	35	Wurttemberg	Y	Havre	New York	12/30/1860	06/01/1861	18	181	N	
Klaiber, Michael	50	Germany	N	Bremen	New York	04/29/1869	?			Y	
Klang, John	40	Germany	Y	Havre	New York	10/23/1867	03/27/1888			Y	
Klanke, Christ.	28	Prussia	Y	Bremen	Baltimore	09/10/1848	10/13/1851	4	263	N	
Klanke, Frederick Henry	22	Hanover	Y	Bremen	New Orleans	10/27/1852	02/05/1856	26	41	N	
Klanker, Joseph (Klenke?)	27	Hanover	Y	Bremen	Baltimore	06/18/1845	08/15/1848	22	149	N	
Klann, Frederick	29	Germany	Y	?	Baltimore	??/??/1872	10/18/1880			Y	
Klapper, William	32	Prussia	Y	Bremen	New York	02/28/1854	02/04/1858	16	77	N	
Klar, August	40	Germany	Y	Hamburg	New York	03/21/1886	12/01/1890			Y	
Klar, Edward	25	Baden	Y	Havre	New York	02/22/1854	08/05/1856	14	357	N	
Klar, Edward	44	Prussia	Y	Hamburg	New York	04/15/1881	05/16/1882			Y	
Klara, Heinrich	30	Germany	Y	Bremen	Baltimore	05/13/1889	10/08/1896			Y	
Klare, Henry	33	Hanover	Y	Bremen	Baltimore	11/02/1857	12/26/1859	17	518	N	
Klare, Rudolph	45	Hanover	Y	Bremen	Baltimore	11/02/1857	12/26/1859	17	517	N	
Klas, Gustav	33	Germany	Y	Bremen	New York	10/??/1881	05/10/1887			Y	
Klasing, H.	26	Germany	Y	Bremen	Baltimore	06/10/1881	08/16/1884			Y	
Klatch, Abraham	40	Russia	Y	Antwerp	Philadelphia	08/10/1891	10/17/1896			Y	
Klatz, Engelhardt	28	Bavaria	Y	London	New Orleans	11/25/1852	07/09/1860	27	212	N	
Klauke, Henry	25	Germany	Y	Bremen	New York	09/06/1890	10/27/1892			Y	
Klaus, Albert	40	Prussia	Y	Bremen	Philadelphia	06/21/1847	08/22/1848	22	228	N	
Klaus, Emil	24	Germany	Y	Antwerp	Philadelphia	06/22/1882	09/12/1882			Y	
Klaus, Henry	43	Germany	Y	Hamburg	New York	07/14/1882	09/17/1894			Y	
Klaus, Joseph	35	Germany	Y	Antwerp	Philadelphia	07/15/1885	11/23/1885			Y	
Klause, Gottlieb	41	Germany	Y	Antwerp	New York	10/21/1885	12/27/1890			Y	
Klauseng, Alexander	58	Germany	Y	Bremen	Baltimore	00/00/1859	03/15/1886			Y	
Klausman, Karl	46	Germany	Y	Baden	New York	09/12/1881	10/18/1892	19	371	N	
Klawitter, Stanislaus	30	Germany	N	Bremen	Baltimore	06/17/1871	?			Y	
Klayer, Bernard	50	Germany	N	Bremen	Baltimore	11/01/1857	?	28	301	N	10/10/1863
Klebahn, Franz Ludwig	26	Bremen	Y	Bremen	Baltimore	12/19/1853	10/02/1856	14	149	N	
Kleber, Henry	42	Bavaria	Y	Havre	New York	01/20/1868	11/11/1872	18	542	N	
Kleeman, Philip	66	Germany	N	Havre	Baltimore	07/21/1852	?			Y	
Kleemann, Johann	24	Germany	Y	Bremen	New York	11/22/1885	09/15/1888			Y	
Kleemeier, John	64	Germany	N	Bremen	Baltimore	10/??/1845	?			Y	
Kleesattel, Fred.	28	Germany	Y	Amsterdam	New York	03/12/1882	01/28/1885			Y	
Klefens, Jacob	30	Germany	Y	Havre	New York	12/25/1878	04/01/1880			Y	
Kleiboecker, Anthony	27	Oldenburg	Y	Bremen	Baltimore	05/05/1849	09/26/1856	14	386	N	
Kleier, Bernard	52	Germany	Y	Bremen	New York	08/01/1866	10/27/1892			Y	
Kleimeier, Theodore	28	Hanover	Y	Bremerhafen	New York	01/03/1858	01/26/1861	18	71	N	
Kleimmann, Charles	21	Germany	Y	Havre	New York	03/20/1893	04/06/1896			Y	
Klein, Alois	44	Germany	Y	Bremen	New York	06/11/1883	06/06/1889			Y	
Klein, Andreas	35	Germany	Y	Hamburg	New York	04/01/1884	06/28/1889			Y	
Klein, August	43	Germany	Y	Hamburg	New York	03/25/1882	03/10/1885			Y	
Klein, Balthauser	28	Bavaria	Y	Havre	New Orleans	04/02/1855	11/24/1857	16	48	N	
Klein, Bernard	52	Germany	Y	Bremen	New York	08/01/1866	10/27/1892	19	385	N	
Klein, Casper	23	Hanover	Y	Bremen	New Orleans	01/01/1853	12/13/1855	13	308	N	
Klein, Charles	24	Nassau	Y	London	New York	04/18/1854	09/21/8155	13	106	N	
Klein, Charles	21	Austria	Y	Bremen	New York	02/03/1883	02/23/1886			Y	
Klein, Christ	26	Bavaria	Y	Havre	New York	07/17/1866	03/20/1869			Y	
Klein, Christ M.	5	Germany	N	?	New York	00/00/1872				Y	10/13/1888
Klein, Christ.	42	France	Y	Tealousi	New Orleans	12/02/1846	11/04/1852	5	219	N	
Klein, Christ.	42	France	Y	Tealouse	New Orleans	12/02/1847	11/04/1852	6	345	N	
Klein, Christian	27	Wurttemberg	Y	Bremen	New York	07/08/1854	08/27/1855	11	505	N	
Klein, Christophe	46	Germany	Y	Bremen	New York	10/18/1884	03/11/1889			Y	
Klein, Christopher	32	Germany	Y	Havre	New York	10/01/1881	11/05/1886			Y	
Klein, Edward	44	Germany	Y	Bremen	New York	07/27/1887	05/08/1894			Y	
Klein, Emanuel	30	Austria	Y	Hamburg	New York	06/26/1884	12/27/1887			Y	
Klein, Frank	21	Switzerland	Y	Havre	New York	04/12/1853	09/22/1855	13	108	N	

199

CITIZENSHIP RECORDS

APPLICANT	AGE	COUNTRY OF ORIGIN	DEC	DEPART PORT	ENTRY PORT	ARRIVE DATE	DEC DATE	VOL	PG.	FLD	NAT DATE
Klein, George	35	Wurttemberg	Y	Antwerp	New York	07/04/1848	07/22/1851	4	28	N	
Klein, George	24	Germany	Y	Havre	New York	11/07/1893	10/01/1896			Y	
Klein, George Peter	33	Bavaria	Y	Havre	New York	08/12/1849	06/19/1851	3	428	N	
Klein, Henry A.	16	Austria	N	?	New York	00/00/1883				Y	08/23/1888
Klein, Hermann	32	Germany	Y	Hamburg	New York	05/??/1891	04/20/1897			Y	
Klein, Jacob	24	Germany	Y	Antwerp	New York	07/25/1887	12/17/1890			Y	
Klein, John	44	Napan	Y	London	New York	07/08/1848	10/11/1848	1	139	N	
Klein, John	??	Germany	Y	?	?	?	06/10/1882			Y	
Klein, Joseph	47	Switzerland	Y	Havre	New York	02/18/1853	04/04/1853	7	537	N	
Klein, Joseph	46	Germany	Y	Havre	New York	10/10/1868	07/18/1888	19	134	N	
Klein, Joseph	26	Austria	Y	Breman	Baltimore	05/04/1882	09/25/1885			Y	
Klein, Joseph	46	Germany	Y	Havre	New York	10/10/1868	07/18/1888			Y	
Klein, Karl	30	Germany	Y	Antwerp	New York	08/01/1884	12/18/1890			Y	
Klein, L. M.	29	Germany	N	Havre	New York	01/??/1872	?			Y	
Klein, Leopold	38	Germany	N	Havre	New York	04/25/1875	?			Y	
Klein, Lorenz	27	Germany	Y	Havre	New York	09/09/1884	10/13/1885			Y	
Klein, Louis	23	Prussia	Y	Rotterdam	New York	07/04/1849	04/12/1852	24	440	N	
Klein, Martin August	40	Germany	Y	Bremen	New York	04/30/1882	09/23/1890			Y	
Klein, Max	52	Germany	N	Rotterdam	New York	08/??/1850	?			Y	
Klein, Michael	21	France	Y	Havre	New Orleans	11/25/1846	01/11/1849	1	390	N	
Klein, Michael	27	Prussia	Y	Havre	New York	05/10/1846	01/15/1849	1	417	N	
Klein, Moritz	41	Hungary	Y	Rotterdam	New York	04/29/1900	03/28/1903			Y	
Klein, Morris	60	Russia	Y	Hamburg	New York	07/11/1888	02/03/1897			Y	
Klein, Peter	42	Bavaria	Y	Antwerp	New York	09/04/1847	11/03/1852	5	192	N	
Klein, Peter	42	Bavaria	Y	Hautevergen	New York	09/04/1847	11/03/1852	6	318	N	
Klein, Peter	24	Bavaria	Y	Rotterdam	New York	07/03/1849	05/19/1854	8	473	N	
Klein, Peter	24	Bavaria	Y	Rotterdam	New York	07/03/1849	05/19/1854	9	347	N	
Klein, Peter	33	Prussia	Y	Antwerp	New Orleans	09/09/1852	10/26/1855	13	136	N	
Klein, Peter	21	Germany	Y	Havre	New York	09/27/1893	10/12/1895			Y	
Klein, Peter	41	Switzerland	Y	Havre	New York	03/02/1852	02/04/1856	26	38	N	
Klein, Philip	26	Prussia	Y	Liverpool	Boston	06/06/1853	08/28/1855	11	513	N	
Klein, Samuel	28	Hungary	Y	Hamburg	New York	03/??/1880	03/27/1888			Y	
Klein, Wilhelm	35	Germany	Y	Havre	New York	06/14/1872	06/27/1883			Y	
Kleinberger, Samuel S.	25	Austria	Y	Hamburg	New York	06/09/1880	10-24/1882			Y	
Kleine, Charles F.	25	Prussia	Y	Bremen	New Orleans	12/28/1848	01/21/1852	24	49	N	
Kleine, Frederick Gottli	23	Prussia	Y	Bremen	Baltimore	11/10/1847	10/13/1851	4	261	N	
Kleiner, Christian	30	Wuertemberg	Y	Bremen	New Orleans	05/04/1852	03/24/1856	26	268	N	
Kleiner, Munrad	29	Prussia	Y	Havre	New Orleans	11/25/1850	01/26/1853	7	72	N	
Kleinfelter, Adam	24	Hesse Cassel	Y	Bremen	Buffalo	08/03/1847	05/23/1851	3	441	N	
Kleinhauser, Moses	27	Germany	Y	Rotterdam	New York	08/??/1881	03/28/1887			Y	
Kleinke, Hermann	29	Germany	Y	Hamburg	New York	06/21/1890	05/05/1892			Y	
Kleinle, Jacob	59	Germany	Y	Amsterdam	New York	03/25/1882	03/30/1893			Y	
Kleinman, John Henry	30	Hanover	Y	Bremen	New York	11/12/1853	09/20/1858	16	191	N	
Kleinmann, Bernard	23	Germany	Y	Antwerp	New York	10/03/1880	02/12/1883			Y	
Kleintank, John	65	Holland	N	Rotterdam	New York	06/08/1846	??/??/1848	28	362	N	??/??/1852
Kleintank, John	23	Holland	N	Rotterdam	New York	06/08/1846	00/00/1848			Y	00/00/1852
Kleinwaechter, August	33	Germany	Y	Hamburg	New York	12/28/1881	06/15/1886			Y	
Kleisel, John	31	Hungary	Y	Bremen	New York	08/12/1901	09/17/1902			Y	
Klekamp, Frank	34	Germany	Y	Bremen	Baltimore	05/05/1869	10/06/1880			Y	
Klekamp, Matthias	38	Germany	Y	Bremen	New York	11/05/1868	01/05/1884			Y	
Klemann, Anthony	31	Prussia	Y	Bremen	Baltimore	10/18/1854	11/01/1858	17	255	N	
Klemann, Bernard/Benjami	23	Germany	Y	Bremen	Baltimore	09/15/1877	10/04/1880			Y	
Klemann, Henry	29	Germany	Y	Bremen	Baltimore	06/??/1881	05/01/1886			Y	
Klement, John A.	31	Germany	Y	Bremen	New York	05/21/1882	07/31/1885			Y	
Klement, Wolfgang	32	Germany	Y	Hamburg	New York	07/28/1881	10/14/1882			Y	
Klemme, Henry	31	Hanover	Y	Bremen	New York	05/18/1855	10/08/1860	27	420	N	
Klenck, Christian	52	Germany	Y	Amsterdam	New York	04/23/1882	10/14/1889			Y	
Klenger, August	??	Germany	Y	?	?	05/00/1882	10/27/1886			Y	
Klenk, Charles	34	Germany	Y	Bremen	New York	04/13/1881	10/03/1887			Y	

CITIZENSHIP RECORDS

APPLICANT	AGE	COUNTRY OF ORIGIN	DEC	DEPART PORT	ENTRY PORT	ARRIVE DATE	DEC DATE	VOL	PG.	FLD	NAT DATE
Klenk, George Michael	51	Germany	Y	Hamburg	New York	04/16/1882	09/23/1892			Y	
Klenk, John	20	Germany	Y	?	?	10/06/1881	07/27/1886			Y	
Klenk, William	27	Germany	Y	Antwerp	New York	09/12/1888	04/01/1890			Y	
Kleone, Casper	26	Prussia	Y	Rushendorf	Cincinnati	10/11/1873	10/01/1878			Y	
Klepper, Henry	16	Germany	N	?	New York	00/00/1882				Y	10/27/1888
Kless, Michael	43	Germany	Y	Bremen	Baltimore	08/16/1865	10/17/1881			Y	
Klett, Ernst	27	Germany	Y	Amsterdam	New York	07/21/1881	03/12/1884			Y	
Klettner, Charles	54	Germany	Y	Hamburg	New York	07/??/1866	10/15/1891			Y	
Kleuber, August	28	Hesse Cassel	Y	Bremen	New York	02/04/1857	09/08/1857	15	246	N	
Kleyer, Clemens	25	Oldenburg	Y	Bremen	New Orleans	02/06/1849	05/20/1852	25	80	N	
Klimkeiwicz, Theodore	38	Germany	Y	Hamburg	New York	12/??/1881	10/09/1888			Y	
Klimkiewicz, George	26	Germany	Y	Bremen	Baltimore	11/04/1882	09/17/1888			Y	
Klimper, Henry	52	Prussia	Y	Rotterdam	New York	07/03/1846	11/01/1852	5	107	N	
Klinckhamer, Henry	31	Hanover	Y	Bremen	New Orleans	09/01/1849	02/16/1857	15	17	N	
Kline, Adam	35	Bavaria	Y	Havre	New York	07/26/1845	07/29/1848	22	12	N	
Kline, Antone	25	Nassau	Y	Antwerp	New York	06/03/1848	10/05/1854	10	436	N	
Kline, Antone	25	Nassau	Y	Antwerp	New York	06/03/1848	10/05/1854	12	375	N	
Kline, Joe	21	Hungary	Y	?	?	07/??/1890	08/29/1892			Y	
Kline, John	25	Hesse Darmsta	Y	Rotterdam	New York	??/??/1845	11/??/1849	23	344	N	
Kling, Frederick	31	Hanover	Y	Bremen	New York	07/08/1849	06/08/1852	25	204	N	
Kling, Jacob	28	Bavaria	Y	Havre	New York	09/??/1848	01/04/1851	2	450	N	
Kling, Jacob	59	Germany	Y	Bremen	New York	10/15/1890	03/28/1891	19	320	N	
Kling, Lewis	27	France	Y	Havre	New Orleans	05/01/1840	10/12/1848	1	165	N	
Klinge, William	25	Prussia	Y	Bremen	New York	05/10/1856	02/24/1860	27	114	N	
Klingel, Jacob	28	Wuerttenberg	Y	Hamburg	New York	07/11/1847	01/18/1850	23	525	N	
Klingenberg, George	24	Prussia	Y	Bremen	Baltimore	10/??/1847	12/16/1850	2	369	N	
Klingenberg, John	32	Prussia	Y	Bremen	Baltimore	07/02/1846	08/28/1848	22	258	N	
Klingenmeier, John	??	Germany	N	?	?	06/24/1884				Y	10/05/1892
Klinger, Anton	32	Austria	Y	Havre	New York	06/04/1857	07/23/1860	27	235	N	
Klinger, Emil	24	Germany	Y	Havre	New York	10/05/1882	11/14/1885			Y	
Klinger, Max	27	Germany	Y	Antwerp	New York	07/03/1887	03/23/1891			Y	
Klinger, Otto	26	Germany	Y	?	?	?	07/22/1882			Y	
Klingler, Peter	34	Germany	Y	Bremen	New York	09/09/1882	10/27/1896			Y	
Klingner, Friedrich Augu	32	Saxony	Y	Hamburg	New York	10/25/1848	06/02/1852	25	176	N	
Klink, Gottleib	??	Germany	Y	?	?	?	09/06/1886			Y	
Klink, Gottlieb	25	Germany	Y	Bremen	New York	05/18/1890	04/15/1892			Y	
Klink, John	23	Holland	Y	Bremen	Boston	12/20/1856	09/06/1860	27	342	N	
Klinkicht, Adolph	26	Germany	Y	Hamburg	New York	06/17/1881	04/06/1885			Y	
Klinkosch, Edward	17	Germany	N	?	New York	00/00/1881				Y	10/27/1888
Klippel, Henry	52	Oldenburg	Y	Bremen	Baltimore	09/19/1851	01/11/1853	7	8	N	
Klitz, Henry	31	Prussia	Y	Bremen	New York	11/10/1847	11/01/1852	5	133	N	
Klitz, Henry	31	Prussia	Y	Bremen	New York	11/16/1847	11/01/1852	6	259	N	
Klitz, Henry	43	Germany	Y	Bremen	Baltimore	08/12/1881	10/06/1884			Y	
Kliwansky, Aaron J.	36	Russia	Y	?	?	?	06/13/1887			Y	
Klob, Joseph	23	Baden	Y	Havre	New York	06/23/1846	09/05/1848	22	299	N	
Klock, Henry	40	Bavaria	Y	Bremen	New York	06/14/1855	01/13/1860	27	52	N	
Klock, John P.	20	France	Y	Havre	New York	06/25/1849	03/23/1853	7	383	N	
Klockenkemper, H.	26	Prussia	Y	Bremerhafen	Baltimore	08/24/1858	02/12/1861	18	112	N	
Klody, Adam	25	Germany	Y	Bremen	Baltimore	10/02/1884	04/04/1887			Y	
Kloeb, Lorenz	27	France	Y	Havre	New York	07/02/1844	03/21/1849	23	256	N	
Kloeble, Charles	30	Wurttemberg	Y	Rotterdam	New York	10/02/1848	10/13/1851	4	228	N	
Kloeckler, Theodore	24	Germany	Y	Havre	New York	10/22/1881	12/27/1883			Y	
Kloekner, Henry	30	Prussia	Y	Antwerp	New York	09/19/1847	02/21/1849	23	241	N	
Kloenne, Heinrich Joseph	13	Germany	N	?	New York	00/00/1866				Y	10/18/1888
Kloepper, Henry	34	Prussia	Y	Bremen	Richmond	09/03/1846	11/01/1852	5	119	N	
Kloesner, Henry	30	Germany	Y	Rotterdam	New York	11/15/1881	01/28/1884			Y	
Kloetzle, Lorenz	34	Prussia	Y	Havre	New Orleans	05/07/1854	09/12/1857	15	260	N	
Kloha, Johann Leonhard	29	Germany	Y	Bremen	Baltimore	07/14/1890	06/11/1894			Y	
Klohe, Joseph Anton	33	Germany	Y	Antwerp	New York	05/14/1880	12/06/1881			Y	

CITIZENSHIP RECORDS

APPLICANT	AGE	COUNTRY OF ORIGIN	DEC	DEPART PORT	ENTRY PORT	ARRIVE DATE	DEC DATE	VOL	PG.	FLD	NAT DATE
Klohs, John	??	Germany	Y	?	?	10/20/1880	09/12/1881			Y	
Kloker, William	38	Germany	Y	Bremen	Baltimore	07/03/1884	06/13/1889			Y	
Kloppenberg, John Henry	35	Hanover	Y	Bremen	Baltimore	11/??/1850	04/27/1855	11	315	N	
Klopper, Heinrich	34	Prussia	Y	Bremen	Richmond	09/03/1841	11/01/1852	6	245	N	
Klosmann, Wilhelm	22	Hanover	Y	Bremen	New Orleans	12/03/1849	02/23/1853	7	218	N	
Klosterkemper, Alexander	23	Prussia	Y	Bremen	New York	10/01/1849	06/10/1852	25	322	N	
Klosterman, Bernard	25	Prussia	Y	Bremen	New York	11/17/1859	11/01/1860	27	540	N	
Klosterman, John Henry	48	Oldenburg	Y	Bremen	New Orleans	12/20/1845	10/02/1848	22	381	N	
Klostermann, Arnold	35	Oldenburg	Y	Bremen	Baltimore	05/24/1857	08/15/1860	27	288	N	
Klostermann, August	46	Germany	Y	Bremen	New York	08/28/1885	07/22/1889			Y	
Klostermann, Franz	17	Germany	N	?	Baltimore	00/00/1881				Y	06/28/1888
Klostermann, Herman	24	Germany	Y	Bremen	Baltimore	10/24/1882	06/16/1885			Y	
Klostermann, John	30	Prussia	Y	Antwerp	New York	09/15/1857	11/01/1860	27	537	N	
Klostermann, Joseph	30	Germany	Y	Bremen	Baltimore	10/21/1874	06/28/1886			Y	
Klotte, Henry	29	Germany	Y	Bremen	New York	09/06/1890	03/30/1894			Y	
Klotter, Jacob	52	Germany	Y	Havre	New York	10/12/1880	03/24/1888			Y	
Klotter, Michael	28	Baden	Y	Rotterdam	New York	06/01/1849	01/04/1851	2	449	N	
Klotz, Friedrich H.	??	Germany	Y	?	?	?	11/15/1893			Y	
Klotz, George	43	Germany	N	Rotterdam	New York	07/01/1871	?			Y	
Klotz, George	43	Germany	Y	Rotterdam	New York	07/01/1871	06/04/1883			Y	
Kluemper, Bernard	32	Hanover	Y	Bremen	New Orleans	05/09/1852	03/10/1856	26	180	N	
Kluemper, John Herman	40	Hanover	Y	Bremen	Baltimore	07/06/1845	08/15/1848	22	182	N	
Kluempke, Gerhard	48	Germany	Y	?	New York	08/28/1882	02/09/1886			Y	
Klug, Valtine	33	Bavaria	Y	Bremen	Baltimore	08/30/1844	09/06/1852	25	365	N	
Kluge, August	36	Germany	Y	Bremen	Baltimore	06/02/1881	09/06/1887			Y	
Kluger, Joseph	34	Germany	Y	Bremen	New York	08/31/1869	03/23/1883			Y	
Klugman, Nathan	30	Bavaria	Y	Antwerp	New York	07/08/1844	03/03/1852	24	224	N	
Klumper, William	24	Hanover	Y	Bremen	Baltimore	12/01/1848	08/15/1851	4	142	N	
Klumpp, David	23	Wurttemberg	Y	Havre	New York	10/23/1854	09/28/1858	16	105	N	
Klumpp, Moriz	66	Germany	Y	Havre	New York	03/08/1867	06/15/1882			Y	
Klumprink, E.	48	Holland	Y	Rotterdam	New York	06/07/1846	08/07/1848	22	69	N	
Klund, Philip Jacob	39	Bavaria	Y	Havre	New York	09/29/1849	07/28/1851	4	47	N	
Klundt, John	31	Germany	Y	Antwerp	New York	10/12/1879	10/10/1891			Y	
Klundt, Peter	73	Germany	N	Havre	New York	05/27/1857	?			Y	
Klus, Joseph	27	Hanover	Y	Bremen	Baltimore	10/06/1859	11/01/1860	27	549	N	
Klusman, Fred	26	Hanover	Y	Bremen	New Orleans	02/18/1845	02/19/1849	23	168	N	
Klusmann, Ludwig	22	Hanover	Y	Bremen	Baltimore	08/27/1846	11/22/1848	1	364	N	
Klussmann, George Henry	26	Hanover	Y	Bremen	New York	02/28/1844	08/09/1851	4	104	N	
Klyman, Julius	22	Prussia	Y	Liverpool	New York	12/14/1854	07/20/1858	16	516	N	
Kmell, John	32	Germany	Y	Hamburg	New York	09/18/1882	10/02/1884			Y	
Kmempelbeck, Charles	22	Germany	Y	Bremen	New York	05/21/1882	12/19/1884			Y	
Kmiekowski, John	28	Germany	Y	Bremen	Philadelphia	05/01/1887	11/03/1891			Y	
Knab, August	30	Germany	Y	Amsterdam	New York	07/09/1881	09/05/1884			Y	
Knabe, Louis	26	Schwarzburg S	Y	Bremen	Baltimore	09/15/1853	01/29/1856	13	516	N	
Knacht, George	58	Bavaria	Y	Havre	New Orleans	04/06/1849	01/02/1860	27	20	N	
Knackivefel, John Freder	28	Hanover	Y	Bremen	Baltimore	10/07/1846	01/17/1849	1	451	N	
Knaebel, George L.	35	Baden	Y	Havre	New York	07/16/1842	05/19/1852	25	42	N	
Knaebel, Michael	29	Germany	Y	Hamburg	New York	02/00/1881	10/28/1886			Y	
Knaeberd, John	47	Prussia	Y	Havre	New York	06/26/1846	02/17/1851	3	140	N	
Knaeuper, John	43	Germany	Y	Bremen	New York	05/26/1885	04/30/1894			Y	
Knaff, Alfons	25	Holland	Y	Antwerp	New York	11/13/1878	11/04/1881			Y	
Knaffl, Rudolph	45	Austria	Y	Hamburg	New York	09/29/1852	04/18/1853	8	83	N	
Knaggs, Robert	26	Ireland	Y	Dublin	New York	08/??/1849	?	23	316	N	
Knaggs, Thomas	25	Ireland	Y	Liverpool	New Orleans	??/07/1848	10/??/1849	23	290	N	
Knapke, Ignatz	35	Germany	N	Bremen	Baltimore	11/01/1883				Y	10/27/1888
Knapke, John Arend	27	Hanover	Y	Bremen	New Orleans	05/01/1849	03/20/1851	3	242	N	
Knapp, August	32	Germany	Y	Havre	New York	04/01/1881	03/21/1889			Y	
Knapp, Charles	25	Nassau	Y	Antwerp	New Orleans	12/07/1848	03/05/1851	3	203	N	
Knapp, Charles	29	Germany	Y	Antwerp	New York	05/21/1882	06/09/1886			Y	

CITIZENSHIP RECORDS

APPLICANT	AGE	COUNTRY OF ORIGIN	DEC	DEPART PORT	ENTRY PORT	ARRIVE DATE	DEC DATE	VOL	PG.	FLD	NAT DATE
Knapp, Frank	37	Wuerttemberg	Y	Havre	New York	05/18/1857	09/10/1860	27	356	N	
Knapp, Frederick	24	Germany	Y	Antwerp	Philadelphia	08/18/1887	11/03/1888			Y	
Knapp, Jacob	31	Oldenburg	Y	London	New York	07/09/1851	08/23/1855	11	483	N	
Knapp, John	25	Baden	Y	Havre	New York	07/24/1855	03/15/1858	16	403	N	
Knapp, Joseph	38	Baden	Y	Havre	New York	11/06/1854	10/06/1860	27	412	N	
Knaths, Friedrich	48	Germany	N	Bremen	New York	12/18/1865	?			Y	
Knauba, Francis	26	Bavaria	Y	Rotterdam	Philadelphia	12/10/1847	04/27/1850	3	12	N	
Knauber, Jacob	23	Bavaria	Y	Havre	New Orleans	12/01/1846	03/25/1850	2	257	N	
Knauber, John	24	Bavaria	Y	Havre	New Orleans	12/10/1849	01/13/1853	7	18	N	
Knauber, John	20	Bavaria	Y	Havre	New York	08/13/1849	09/13/1852	25	481	N	
Knauer, Christian	25	Wuerttemberg	Y	Havre	New York	??/30/1848	11/??/1849	23	305	N	
Knauf, Nick	36	Germany	Y	Antwerp	New York	04/??/1880	03/31/1885			Y	
Knauf, William	28	Germany	Y	Antwerp	New York	10/18/1883	10/27/1890			Y	
Knauper, John Henry	27	Hanover	Y	Bremen	Baltimore	11/10/1851	01/12/1856	13	454	N	
Knaus, Christ	50	Germany	N	Havre	New York	06/30/1867	?			Y	
Knaus, Frank	29	Prussia	Y	Antwerp	New York	01/16/1854	08/18/1857	15	157	N	
Knaus, George	30	Bavaria	Y	Bremen	New York	05/23/1848	05/15/1854	8	443	N	
Knaus, George	30	Bavaria	Y	Bremen	New York	05/23/1848	05/15/1854	9	316	N	
Knecht, Charles Leopold	26	Wurttemberg	Y	Bremen	New York	06/03/1854	03/03/1857	15	58	N	
Knecht, Gottlob	??	Germany	Y	?	?	?	04/03/1884			Y	
Knecht, Louis	40	France	Y	Havre	New Orleans	07/28/1849	06/01/1852	25	171	N	
Kneff, Balthasar	30	Germany	Y	Bremen	Baltimore	05/03/1886	03/07/1887			Y	
Kneiger, George	34	Hesse Cassel	Y	Hamburg	New York	07/09/1852	12/29/1857	16	278	N	
Kneip, John	28	Prussia	Y	Antwerp	New York	08/13/1846	07/31/1848	22	25	N	
Kneis, John Bernard	29	Oldenburg	Y	Bremen	New Orleans	05/25/1851	05/02/1854	8	344	N	
Kneis, John Bernard	29	Oldenburg	Y	Bremen	New Orleans	05/25/1851	05/02/1854	9	217	N	
Kneisle, Peter	??	Germany	Y	?	?	06/??/1877	03/26/1883			Y	
Kneitz, Andreas	30	Bavaria	Y	Bremen	New York	08/19/1846	03/14/1850	2	192	N	
Knell, Andrew	55	Germany	N	Germany	New York	10/02/1854	?			Y	
Knemeier, Henry	26	Prussia	Y	Bremen	New Orleans	11/12/1853	10/03/1854	10	380	N	
Knemeier, Henry	26	Prussia	Y	Bremen	New Orleans	11/12/1853	10/03/1854	12	319	N	
Kneuper, Henry	30	Germany	Y	Bremen	Baltimore	09/01/1881	10/12/1885	19	21	N	
Kneuper, Henry	30	Germany	Y	Bremen	Baltimore	09/01/1881	10/12/1885			Y	
Kneupper, Henry	21	Bavaria	Y	Bremen	Baltimore	10/28/1849	02/17/1851	3	138	N	
Knieling, George	42	Germany	Y	?	New York	04/13/1865	11/07/1876			Y	
Knieriehem, Louis	21	Hanover	Y	Bremen	New Orleans	05/??/1853	04/17/1855	11	261	N	
Knight, Arthur T.	25	England	Y	Liverpool	Baltimore	06/09/1885	03/30/1891			Y	
Knight, Edwin	39	England	Y	Liverpool	New York	06/08/1878	03/30/1891			Y	
Knight, Henry	49	England	Y	Liverpool	New York	08/04/1886	08/10/1889			Y	
Knight, Patrick	21	Ireland	Y	Liverpool	New York	04/04/1853	07/06/1855	11	342	N	
Knippenberg, Henry	22	Hanover	Y	Bremen	Baltimore	10/01/1852	10/06/1854	10	485	N	
Knippenberg, Henry	22	Hanover	Y	Bremen	Baltimore	10/01/1852	10/06/1854	12	424	N	
Knippenberg, Rudolph	22	Prussia	Y	Bremen	New York	09/26/1850	12/30/1852	5	474	N	
Knips, William	32	Germany	Y	Havre	New York	04/01/1881	06/29/1882			Y	
Knirr, Jacob	31	Bavaria	Y	Havre	New Orleans	09/??/1843	11/??/1849	23	350	N	
Knise, Christian	22	Prussia	Y	Bremen	Baltimore	10/28/1856	05/23/1859	17	427	N	
Knittal, Joseph	43	Wuerttemberg	Y	Bremen	New York	03/24/1852	03/12/1860	27	125	N	
Knittel, Henry	45	Germany	Y	Bremen	New York	10/28/1880	08/13/1885			Y	
Knobbe, Andrew	30	Hanover	Y	Bremerhafen	New Orleans	11/21/1854	01/19/1861	18	66	N	
Knobeloch, Nicolaus	26	Bavaria	Y	Havre	New Orleans	01/??/185	09/22/1855	13	107	N	
Knoble, Joseph	50	Austria	N	Bremen	Baltimore	05/??/1855	?			Y	
Knoch, Adolph	35	Germany	Y	Rotterdam	New York	11/10/1881	05/09/1893			Y	
Knoch, Arthur	25	Russia	Y	Bremen	New York	11/12/1888	11/13/1891			Y	
Knochenhauer, Charles	??	Germany	Y	?	?	10/15/1893	03/09/1896			Y	
Knock, Adolph	22	Germany	Y	Rotterdam	New York	06/03/1881	05/14/1885			Y	
Knockewiefel, Henry	24	Germany	Y	Bremen	New York	06/11/1892	11/09/1894			Y	
Knodel, Jacob	27	Wurttemberg	Y	Bremen	Galveston	11/04/1854	03/31/1857	15	109	N	
Knoebel, William	30	Germany	Y	?	?	?	10/27/1890			Y	
Knoechel, John George	46	Germany	Y	Bremen	New York	12/20/1890	10/25/1892			Y	

CITIZENSHIP RECORDS

APPLICANT	AGE	COUNTRY OF ORIGIN	DEC	DEPART PORT	ENTRY PORT	ARRIVE DATE	DEC DATE	VOL	PG.	FLD	NAT DATE
Knoeckel, Michael	23	Germany	Y	Hamburg	New York	12/10/1880	09/30/1882			Y	
Knoepfle, Engelbert	26	Bavaria	Y	Havre	New York	04/16/1854	10/07/1854	11	10	N	
Knoepfler, Michael	33	France	Y	Havre	New Orleans	03/01/1847	02/13/1849	23	81	N	
Knoerzer, Daniel	31	Germany	Y	Antwerp	Philadelphia	08/09/1893	12/30/1893			Y	
Knoll, Edward	31	Germany	Y	Havre	New York	07/04/1880	03/15/1890			Y	
Knoll, Hermann	??	Germany	Y	?	?	?	11/26/1890			Y	
Knoll, John	21	Wurttemberg	Y	Havre	New York	12/01/1853	01/28/1856	13	514	N	
Knollhoff, Christian Fre	26	Hanover	Y	Bremen	New Orleans	12/20/1848	10/21/1857	15	468	N	
Knollmann, Francis	25	Hanover	Y	Bremen	New Orleans	10/18/1853	11/08/1858	17	289	N	
Knollmann, Henry	30	Hanover	Y	Bremen	New Orleans	11/26/1854	11/08/1858	17	288	N	
Knollmann, Herman	25	Hanover	Y	Bremen	New Orleans	??/22/1852	04/20/1855	11	278	N	
Knoos, Ernst	25	Germany	Y	Bremen	New York	09/09/1882	03/04/1887			Y	
Knop, Frederick	38	Hanover	Y	Bremen	New Orleans	06/28/1848	01/17/1849	1	449	N	
Knopf, Leopold E. C.	51	Prussia	Y	Bremen	New York	08/24/1849	09/11/1852	25	451	N	
Knopfle, Engelbart	26	Bavaria	Y	Havre	New York	04/16/1854	10/07/1854	6	9	N	
Knopker, George	32	Prussia	Y	Bremen	New Orleans	06/02/1857	10/09/1860	27	476	N	
Knorr, Frederick	21	Wurttemberg	Y	Havre	New York	04/19/1854	08/04/1856	14	334	N	
Knorr, Peter	31	Germany	Y	Antwerp	Philadelphia	05/21/1887	02/20/1900			Y	
Knossel, John	46	Baden	Y	Havre	New Orleans	12/04/1846	10/20/1852	5	31	N	
Knost, John Henry	21	Prussia	Y	Bremen	Baltimore	??/19/1845	10/09/1848	1	101	N	
Knoth, Andrew	47	Bavaria	Y	Bremen	Baltimore	06/20/1847	08/02/1848	22	40	N	
Knox, John	27	London	Y	Liverpool	New York	10/19/1844	11/24/1852	5	339	N	
Knuepfer, Karl Herman	30	Germany	Y	Amsterdam	New York	05/21/1882	01/25/1889			Y	
Knuss, Emil	31	Switzerland	Y	Havre	New York	09/14/1881	08/02/1882			Y	
Knynin, Francis Frederic	33	Frankfurt	Y	Hamburg	New York	05/10/1855	10/30/1858	17	196	N	
Kobel, Joseph	37	Germany	Y	Hamburg	New York	03/04/1886	08/15/1887			Y	
Kober, Christoph	35	Wurttemberg	Y	Havre	New York	08/12/1849	05/31/1859	17	439	N	
Kober, Jacob	21	Germany	Y	?	?	10/20/1883	10/15/1884			Y	
Kober, John	??	Germany	Y	?	?	?	03/15/1871			Y	
Koberg, Hermann	43	Hanover	Y	Bremen	Baltimore	09/15/1852	10/07/1854	10	536	N	
Kobery, Hermann	43	Hanover	Y	Bremen	Baltimore	09/15/1852	10/07/1854	12	475	N	
Kobila, Anton	25	Schlesinger,	Y	?	Galveston	11/01/1884	04/03/1886			Y	
Kobmann, George	24	Germany	Y	Bremen	New York	11/26/1896	10/24/1897			Y	
Kobmann, John	26	Bavaria	Y	Bremen	New York	04/15/1859	04/21/1862	18	326	N	
Kobmann, John	22	Germany	Y	Bremen	Baltimore	06/21/1881	04/07/1883			Y	
Kobold, Charles H.	45	Germany	Y	?	New York	05/??/1881	10/28/1882			Y	
Kobs, William	45	Prussia	Y	Havre	New Orleans	04/01/1855	09/03/1860	27	327	N	
Koch, Adam	29	Austria	Y	Bremen	Baltimore	03/31/1893	07/13/1896			Y	
Koch, Bernard Herman	23	Hanover	Y	Bremen	New Orleans	02/??/1848	12/09/1850	2	350	N	
Koch, Ernst	40	Hesse Cassel	Y	Havre	New York	08/25/1854	11/16/1857	16	23	N	
Koch, Ernst	70	Germany	N	Havre	New York	10/16/1854	?			Y	
Koch, Ferdinand	29	Germany	Y	Hamburg	New York	06/20/1882	11/20/1886			Y	
Koch, Frank	45	Germany	N	Bremen	Baltimore	06/??/1881	?			Y	
Koch, Frederick	22	Prussia	Y	Bremen	Baltimore	09/15/1848	02/19/1849	23	178	N	
Koch, Frederick	42	Hanover	Y	Bremen	Baltimore	09/07/1857	10/13/1860	27	488	N	
Koch, Frederick Henry	21	Hanover	Y	Bremen	New Orleans	12/28/1851	10/03/1854	10	392	N	
Koch, Frederick Henry	21	Hanover	Y	Bremen	New Orleans	12/28/1851	10/03/1854	12	331	N	
Koch, Fritz	31	Germany	Y	Bremen	New York	08/28/1883	10/24/1887			Y	
Koch, George	22	Germany	Y	Antwerp	New York	03/23/1883	08/31/1885			Y	
Koch, George David	26	Bavaria	Y	Havre	New York	08/16/1854	09/27/1854	10	252	N	
Koch, George David	26	Bavaria	Y	Havre	New York	08/16/1854	09/26/1854	12	191	N	
Koch, George Henry	25	Hanover	Y	Bremen	New Orleans	11/22/1854	03/25/1856	26	335	N	
Koch, H. August	23	Germany	Y	Bremen	Baltimore	10/20/1892	02/15/1883			Y	
Koch, H. August	34	Germany	N	Bremen	Baltimore	04/20/1882	?			Y	
Koch, Henry	25	Prussia	Y	Bremen	Baltimore	09/15/1848	10/13/1848	1	197	N	
Koch, Henry	23	Saxony	Y	Bremen	New Orleans	05/30/1854	10/05/1854	10	457	N	
Koch, Henry	23	Saxony	Y	Bremen	New Orleans	05/30/1854	10/05/1854	12	396	N	
Koch, Henry	32	Germany	Y	Bremen	Baltimore	11/??/1871	05/18/1882			Y	
Koch, Henry	27	Switzerland	Y	Havre	New York	06/17/1881	03/23/1888			Y	

CITIZENSHIP RECORDS

APPLICANT	AGE	COUNTRY OF ORIGIN	DEC	DEPART PORT	ENTRY PORT	ARRIVE DATE	DEC DATE	VOL	PG.	FLD	NAT DATE
Koch, Henry	36	Hanover	Y	Bremen	New York	04/22/1857	09/07/1860	27	344	N	
Koch, Jacob	27	Germany	Y	Havre	?	06/14/1878	10/13/1882			Y	
Koch, John	35	Hesse Darmsta	Y	Havre	New York	03/09/1850	03/17/1858	16	418	N	
Koch, John	25	Wurttemberg	Y	Havre	New Orleans	11/06/1852	04/20/1858	16	472	N	
Koch, John	26	Bavaria	Y	Havre	New York	09/29/1853	09/29/1858	17	18	N	
Koch, John	35	Germany	Y	Antwerp	New York	12/13/1880	08/28/1882			Y	
Koch, John Baptist	33	Baden	Y	Havre	New Orleans	07/08/1845	02/16/1849	23	142	N	
Koch, John Bernard	27	Prussia	Y	Rotterdam	New Orleans	12/26/1846	10/03/1854	10	404	N	
Koch, John Bernard	27	Prussia	Y	Rotterdam	New Orleans	12/26/1846	10/03/1854	12	343	N	
Koch, John Frederich	40	Germany	Y	Antwerp	New York	07/??/1866	10/09/1882			Y	
Koch, Joseph	24	Prussia	Y	Bremen	New York	08/24/1849	05/20/1852	25	81	N	
Koch, Lorentz	34	Prussia	Y	Bremen	Buffalo	07/15/1851	07/28/1851	4	50	N	
Koch, Ludwig	37	Germany	N	Bremen	Baltimore	06/14/1867	?			Y	
Koch, Ludwig Heinrich	43	Germany	Y	Antwerp	New York	07/02/1881	10/03/1887			Y	
Koch, Melchior	27	Kurhessen	Y	Liverpool	New York	07/07/1851	10/02/1854	10	350	N	
Koch, Melchior	26	Kurhessen	Y	Liverpool	Liverpool (?	05/14/1851	10/02/1854	12	289	N	
Koch, Michael	34	Bavaria	Y	Bremen	Baltimore	06/19/1845	08/04/1848	22	56	N	
Koch, Nicholas	27	Baden	Y	London	New York	10/28/1846	04/19/1850	3	2	N	
Koch, Oscar	17	Germany	Y	?	New York	00/00/1878				Y	10/27/1888
Koch, Otto	22	Germany	Y	?	?	?	04/13/1885			Y	
Koch, Otto Johannes	29	Germany	Y	Bremen	New York	04/22/1892	09/13/1892			Y	
Koch, Paul	46	Germany	Y	Antwerp	New York	04/02/1882	10/28/1890			Y	
Koch, Peter	56	Bavaria	Y	Havre	New York	07/03/1849	10/01/1856	14	81	N	
Koch, Philipp	23	Bavaria	Y	Havre	New York	05/18/1858	06/12/1861	18	189	N	
Koch, Rev. Sigismund	28	Austria	Y	Havre	New York	05/25/1849	11/10/1852	5	266	N	
Koch, Robert	58	?	Y	?	New York	11/06/1883	11/01/1886			Y	
Koch, Rudolph	38	Russia	Y	Bremen	Baltimore	05/29/1888	10/29/1898			Y	
Koch, Simon	39	Germany	Y	Rotterdam	New York	11/18/1882	11/07/1893			Y	
Koch, Thomas	25	Wurttemberg	Y	Havre	New York	07/24/1852	05/22/1854	8	487	N	
Koch, Thomas	25	Wurttemberg	Y	Havre	New York	07/24/1852	05/22/1854	9	361	N	
Koch, Ursus	23	Switzerland	Y	Havre	New Orleans	01/26/1854	03/25/1856	26	306	N	
Koch, William	24	Germany	Y	Bremen	New York	01/13/1889	02/20/1895			Y	
Koch, William	36	Germany	Y	Bremen	Baltimore	07/19/1872	08/09/1884			Y	
Koch, William	76	Germany	N	Bremen	Baltimore	07/09/1842	01/31/1848	28	130	N	10/03/1850
Koch, William	30	Germany	N	Bremen	Baltimore	07/09/1842	01/31/1848			Y	10/07/1850
Koche, Martin	40	Ireland	Y	Liverpool	New Orleans	12/18/1849	07/07/1851	3	508	N	
Kocher, Andreas	41	Germany	N	Havre	New York	05/??/1869	?			Y	
Kochler, John	41	Bavaria	Y	Antwerp	New York	03/03/1851	07/31/1861	18	211	N	
Kock, F.	28	Germany	Y	Bremen	Baltimore	04/10/1881	03/25/1884			Y	
Kock, John Bernard	30	Hanover	Y	Bremen	New Orleans	11/29/1853	04/02/1856	26	411	N	
Kock, Klemens	36	Germany	Y	Bremen	Baltimore	05/27/1882	10/22/1892	19	377	N	
Kock, Rev. Sigismund	28	Austria	Y	Havre	New York	05/25/1849	11/10/1852	6	390	N	
Kocks, Bernard Henry	32	Prussia	Y	Bremen	New Orleans	12/16/1844	09/30/1848	22	367	N	
Koczorowski, John	39	Germany	Y	Hamburg	New York	03/02/1883	11/06/1893			Y	
Kodas, Harris	??	Russia	Y	?	?	?	10/26/1888			Y	
Koebele, John	28	Germany	Y	Havre	New York	03/06/1881	01/19/1885			Y	
Koefs, John Karl	30	Hanover	Y	Bremen	New Orleans	11/27/1849	11/10/1852	5	265	N	
Koegel, Caspar	59	Germany	N	Hamburg	?	01/??/1851	12/18/1855	28	260	N	03/18/1858
Koegel, Casper	26	Baden	Y	Liverpool	New York	09/07/1851	12/18/1855	13	330	N	
Koegel, Casper	23	Germany	N	Hamburg	?	01/00/1851	12/18/1855			Y	03/18/1858
Koegel, John B.	31	Germany	Y	Amsterdam	New York	02/22/1883	07/13/1888			Y	
Koehl, Frederick	31	Germany	Y	Hamburg	New York	03/10/1882	09/25/1886			Y	
Koehl, Henry	40	France	Y	Havre	New Orleans	12/06/1853	10/06/1856	14	189	N	
Koehl, Leo	46	France	N	Havre	New Orleans	01/??/1853	?			Y	
Koehle, Leonhardt	23	Bavaria	Y	Bremen	Baltimore	09/20/1851	11/18/1857	16	33	N	
Koehler, Andreas	43	Germany	Y	Bremen	New York	11/??/1867	02/19/1883			Y	
Koehler, Anton	21	Austria	Y	Hamburg	New York	08/30/1895	08/10/1900			Y	
Koehler, Conrad	24	Germany	Y	Bremen	New York	08/07/1871	07/01/1876			Y	
Koehler, Heinrich	29	Germany	Y	Bremen	New York	04/28/1883	10/27/1886			Y	

CITIZENSHIP RECORDS

APPLICANT	AGE	COUNTRY OF ORIGIN	DEC	DEPART PORT	ENTRY PORT	ARRIVE DATE	DEC DATE	VOL	PG.	FLD	NAT DATE
Koehler, John	34	Germany	Y	Bremen	New York	05/21/1885	01/15/1894			Y	
Koehler, John	35	Nassau	Y	Hamburg	New York	09/19/1850	09/08/1852	25	418	N	
Koehler, John Adam	28	Germany	Y	Antwerp	New York	04/17/1885	04/25/1892			Y	
Koehler, John H.	28	Bavaria	Y	Bremen	Baltimore	09/07/1845	08/02/1848	22	35	N	
Koehler, Joseph	26	Bavaria	Y	Havre	New York	10/01/1845	03/17/1851	3	293	N	
Koehler, Martin	24	Bavaria	Y	Havre	New Orleans	11/04/1852	03/17/1856	26	221	N	
Koehler, Max	??	Germany	Y	?	?	?	01/24/1881			Y	
Koehler, Max	36	Germany	Y	Hamburg	New York	04/15/1882	10/17/1889			Y	
Koehler, Paul	31	Germany	Y	Bremen	Baltimore	07/03/1879	08/03/1887			Y	
Koehler, Phillip	22	Bavaria	Y	Havre	New Orleans	06/24/1846	02/13/1849	23	86	N	
Koehler, Rudolph A.	50	Germany	Y	Hamburg	New York	11/04/1884	10/19/1900			Y	
Koehlhoeffer, George	23	France	Y	London	New York	??/28/1847	11/??/1849	23	299	N	
Koehm, Fred	31	Germany	Y	Bremen	New York	05/17/1883	11/01/1886			Y	
Koehn, Wilhelm	37	Germany	Y	Rotterdam	New York	09/11/1881	07/01/1886			Y	
Koehne, Joseph	28	Hanover	Y	Bremen	New Orleans	12/20/1848	10/06/1854	10	512	N	
Koehne, Joseph	28	Hanover	Y	Bremen	New Orleans	12/20/1848	10/06/1854	12	451	N	
Koehnig, Martin	34	Germany	Y	Rotterdam	New York	06/06/1878	10/22/1888			Y	
Koehnken, John H.	73	Germany	N	Bremen	Baltimore	07/??/1837	?	28	332	N	08/??/1842
Koehnken, John H.	18	Germany	N	Bremen	Baltimore	]07/00/183				Y	08/00/1842
Koeke, H.	24	Hanover	Y	Bremen	Baltimore	06/24/1858	11/01/1860	27	519	N	
Koel, Francis	42	France	Y	Havre	New Orleans	10/25/1849	11/26/1855	13	259	N	
Koelblin, Richard	37	Germany	Y	Bremen	New York	??/??/1870	06/05/1886			Y	
Koeller, John	28	Bavaria	Y	Hamburg	New York	11/28/1854	12/30/1857	16	287	N	
Koelpin, Gotfreid	38	Baden	Y	Havre	New York	09/??/1851	03/21/1853	7	358	N	
Koelsch, John	35	Prussia	Y	Antwerp	New York	06/27/1852	05/08/1854	8	394	N	
Koelsch, Peter	38	Bavaria	Y	Havre	New Orleans	05/15/1851	03/01/1856	26	143	N	
Koempel, Peter	28	Prussia	Y	Havre	New Orleans	09/08/1841	10/03/1848	22	403	N	
Koenig, Abraham	34	Germany	Y	Havre	New York	04/28/1881	01/28/1884			Y	
Koenig, Adam	20	Germany	Y	Bremen	New York	03/17/1883	02/08/1886			Y	
Koenig, Alois	49	Germany	Y	Hamburg	New York	07/18/1871	10/25/1889			Y	
Koenig, Arthur	28	Germany	Y	Bremen	New York	09/03/1889	10/26/1895			Y	
Koenig, August	29	Germany	Y	Rotterdam	New York	03/30/1888	10/16/1896			Y	
Koenig, Charles	28	Germany	Y	Bremen	Baltimore	08/29/1879	10/??/1881	28	166	N	
Koenig, Charles	21	Germany	Y	Bremen	Baltimore	08/29/1879	10/00/1881			Y	
Koenig, Charles A.	??	Germany	Y	?	?	?	08/24/1887			Y	
Koenig, Edward	25	Germany	Y	Amsterdam	New York	09/23/1881	07/11/1884			Y	
Koenig, Franz H.	30	Germany	Y	Bremen	Baltimore	05/01/1880	06/15/1892			Y	
Koenig, Henry	31	Germany	Y	Hamburg	New York	08/14/1885	04/03/1891			Y	
Koenig, Herman	33	Prussia	Y	Bremen	Baltimore	10/19/1854	03/25/1856	26	340	N	
Koenig, Herman Henry	??	Hanover	Y	Bremen	Baltimore	05/04/18??	10/09/1848	1	69	N	
Koenig, Jacob	25	Germany	Y	Rotterdam	New York	05/19/1881	03/03/1886			Y	
Koenig, John	32	Bavaria	Y	Havre	New Orleans	01/25/1847	03/17/1851	3	285	N	
Koenig, John	31	Germany	Y	Antwerp	New York	11/06/1882	03/22/1890			Y	
Koenig, John Andrew	28	Wurttemberg	Y	Rotterdam	New York	07/05/1846	01/23/1849	1	499	N	
Koenig, John B.	27	Germany	Y	Hamburg	New York	10/26/1895	08/25/1899			Y	
Koenig, John B.	38	Germany	Y	Bremen	Baltimore	10/27/1872	05/15/1891			Y	
Koenig, Paul	36	Germany	Y	Havre	New York	12/06/1890	11/06/1893			Y	
Koenig, Richard	31	Germany	Y	Liverpool	Philadelphia	05/07/1892	07/03/1897			Y	
Koenig, Theodore	48	Germany	Y	Havre	New York	03/25/1892	08/11/1892			Y	
Koenigsmann, Carl Franz	32	Germany	Y	Hamburg	Boston	07/02/1895	09/15/1898			Y	
Koenigsmann, Frank	28	Germany	Y	Bremen	New York	07/26/1891	04/19/1897			Y	
Koenigstein, Michael	22	Bavaria	Y	Havre	New York	10/22/1851	10/02/1854	10	336	N	
Koennen, Jacob	27	Holland	Y	Rotterdam	New York	05/27/1848	01/21/1851	2	515	N	
Koeper, Henry	31	Prussia	Y	Bremen	Baltimore	05/16/1850	02/18/1858	16	317	N	
Koepfle, Franz	27	Austria	Y	Havre	New York	05/01/1883	01/29/1889			Y	
Koepfle, Henry	22	Austria	Y	Havre	Neww York	11/04/1885	11/10/1888			Y	
Koeppel, Hermann	30	Germany	Y	Bremen	New York	03/17/1882	12/18/1886			Y	
Koeppens, Henry	33	Germany	N	Bremen	New York	07/10/1873	?			Y	
Koerbel, Otto	26	Germany	Y	Amsterdam	New York	04/24/1882	07/05/1884			Y	

CITIZENSHIP RECORDS

APPLICANT	AGE	COUNTRY OF ORIGIN	DEC	DEPART PORT	ENTRY PORT	ARRIVE DATE	DEC DATE	VOL	PG.	FLD	NAT DATE
Koering, Casper Henry	37	Hanover	Y	Bremen	New York	12/02/1846	02/22/1849	23	253	N	
Koerner, Charles	33	Prussia	Y	Hamburg	New York	05/01/1849	04/12/1852	24	451	N	
Koester, Charles	27	Prussia	Y	Bremen	Baltimore	08/24/1845	05/06/1850	3	54	N	
Koester, Johann	27	Germany	Y	?	Philadelphia	06/??/1881	10/31/1882			Y	
Koester, Louis	62	Germany	N	Hamburg	New York	08/??/1850	?			Y	
Koesters, Berard	28	Prussia	Y	Rotterdam	New Orleans	12/12/1848	07/05/1851	3	489	N	
Koesters, Dirck	??	Hanover	Y	Bremen	Baltimore	??/30/1847	12/??/1850	2	425	N	
Koesters, Gerhard	28	Hanover	Y	Bremen	New Orleans	12/11/1845	01/18/1849	1	460	N	
Koesters, Gerhard	29	Germany	Y	Bremen	New York	09/23/1881	10/11/1884			Y	
Koesters, William	47	Germany	N	Bremen	New York	11/28/1869	?			Y	
Koetitz, John	26	Saxony	Y	Bremen	New York	09/21/1853	05/30/1854	9	466	N	
Koetitz, John	26	Saxony	Y	Bremen	New York	09/21/1853	05/31/1854	10	49	N	
Koett, Gustav	29	Germany	Y	Bremen	New York	04/14/1891	09/04/1897			N	
Koettel, John	29	Bavaria	Y	Bremen	New York	10/28/1851	03/27/1856	26	360	N	
Koetter, August	29	Oldenburg	Y	Bremen	New York	10/01/1848	03/02/1852	24	208	N	
Koetter, John Herman	30	Oldenburg	Y	Bremen	New Orleans	12/18/1845	08/08/1848	22	80	N	
Koff, John	??	Switzerland	Y	?	?	?	06/04/1887			Y	
Koger, Charles	17	Germany	N	?	New York	00/00/1882				Y	10/26/1888
Kohan, Lewis	??	Russia	Y	?	?	?	09/27/1889			Y	
Koharske, John	39	Germany	Y	Hamburg	Philadelphia	05/09/1881	09/13/1888			Y	
Koher, Philipp	32	Bavaria	Y	Havre	New Orleans	04/03/1849	03/31/1852	25	146	N	
Kohl, Adam	24	Germany	Y	Bremen	Baltimore	06/25/1884	10/25/1889			Y	
Kohl, George	29	Wurttemberg	Y	Rotterdam	Baltimore	06/26/1846	01/15/1849	1	428	N	
Kohl, Heinrich	66	Germany	Y	Rotterdam	New York	07/02/1882	12/29/1890			Y	
Kohl, Henry	30	Germany	Y	Rotterdam	New York	01/07/1883	05/21/1890			Y	
Kohl, Herman Henry	24	Oldenburg	Y	Bremen	New York	06/04/1849	06/19/1851	3	416	N	
Kohl, Jacob	30	Oldenburg	Y	Liverpool	New York	05/02/1854	07/03/1857	15	125	N	
Kohl, John	32	Germany	N	Bremen	Baltimore	10/03/1871	?			Y	
Kohl, John S.	33	Bavaria	Y	Havre	New Orleans	06/09/1840	06/14/1852	25	260	N	
Kohl, Jos.	24	Germany	Y	Amsterdam	New York	06/24/1888	10/27/1893	21	37	N	
Kohl, Justus	32	Germany	Y	Rotterdam	New York	04/24/1881	10/27/1894			Y	
Kohlbrandt, F.	43	Germany	Y	Bremen	New York	12/24/1883	04/11/1887			Y	
Kohlem, Henry	28	Germany	Y	Rotterdam	New York	09/13/1892	10/26/1900			Y	
Kohler, Ernst W.	33	Germany	Y	Hamburg	New York	05/17/1895	10/16/1903			Y	
Kohler, George	29	Germany	Y	Hamburg	New York	06/11/1884	10/26/1889	19	269	N	
Kohler, Johann	30	Germany	Y	Havre	New York	12/03/1879	09/10/1886			Y	
Kohler, John	30	Wuertemberg	Y	Havre	New York	04/27/1853	03/21/1856	26	245	N	
Kohler, Joseph	27	France	Y	Havre	New York	12/05/1851	09/30/1856	14	48	N	
Kohler, Michael	36	Bavaria	Y	Bremen	Baltimore	08/09/1845	01/13/1849	1	414	N	
Kohler, Nicholas	39	Germany	Y	Bremen	New York	12/19/1872	09/11/1888			Y	
Kohlhagen, Max	23	Germany	Y	Antwerp	New York	08/20/1892	10/21/1896			Y	
Kohlhaupt, William	34	Germany	Y	Bremen	Baltimore	12/07/1880	12/28/1882			Y	
Kohlmann, John	45	Baden	Y	Rotterdam	Boston	06/17/1848	06/16/1852	25	276	N	
Kohlmeier, August	22	Germany	Y	Bremen	Baltimore	09/23/1882	10/03/1885			Y	
Kohlmeyer, William	39	Germany	Y	Bremen	Baltimore	05/27/1881	05/25/1895			Y	
Kohlsdorf, Francis	26	Prussia	Y	Bremen	New York	05/06/1855	03/25/1856	26	302	N	
Kohn, Franz	20	Austria	Y	Bremen	Baltimore	03/12/1887	08/29/1887			Y	
Kohn, Harries	36	Poland (Russi	Y	London	New York	03/07/1852	10/16/1852	5	1	N	
Kohn, Louis	22	Russia	Y	Hamburg	New York	12/27/1888	03/26/1892			Y	
Kohn, Max	29	Russia	Y	Hamburg	New York	07/15/1892	07/08/1898			Y	
Kohnen, Barney	28	Hanover	Y	Bremen	New Orleans	12/25/1844	09/15/1848	22	348	N	
Kohnen, Gerhard Henry	36	Hanover	Y	Bremen	New Orleans	01/01/1848	10/13/1860	27	490	N	
Kohner, Henry	31	Hanover	Y	Bremen	New Orleans	01/02/1847	02/01/1851	3	79	N	
Kohnert, Stephen	??	Prussia	Y	?	?	?	03/01/1891			Y	
Kohnky, Moses	47	Germany	N	Hamburg	New York	09/??/1860	?			Y	
Kohnle, Gottlieb	34	Germany	Y	Hamburg	New York	06/25/1890	04/15/1892			Y	
Kohorst, Barney	35	Germany	Y	Bremen	Baltimore	06/05/1881	10/28/1892	19	399	N	
Kohorst, Clem	30	Germany	Y	Bremen	New York	05/27/1885	10/27/1888	19	191	N	
Kohorst, Clem	30	Germany	Y	Bremen	New York	05/27/1885	10/27/1888			Y	

CITIZENSHIP RECORDS

APPLICANT	AGE	COUNTRY OF ORIGIN	DEC	DEPART PORT	ENTRY PORT	ARRIVE DATE	DEC DATE	VOL	PG.	FLD	NAT DATE
Kohos, Herman	27	Prussia	Y	Bremen	New Orleans	11/29/1852	06/05/1854	10	80	N	
Kohos, Herman	27	Prussia	Y	Bremen	New Orleans	11/29/1852	06/05/1854	12	17	N	
Kohrmann, Berhard	25	Hanover	Y	Bremen	New Orleans	12/25/1856	01/17/1860	27	57	N	
Kohrmann, Henry	23	Hanover	Y	Bremen	New York	04/04/1859	04/22/1862	18	327	N	
Kohrs, Henry	23	Germany	Y	Oldenberg	New York	05/??/1877	11/19/1880			Y	
Kohschulte, Anton	41	Germany	Y	Bremen	New York	05/04/1888	09/29/1894			Y	
Kohsiek, Frederick Willi	27	Hanover	Y	Bremen	Baltimore	??/30/1845	04/16/1855	11	258	N	
Kohur, Herman	27	Prussia	Y	Bremen	New Orleans	11/29/1852	06/05/1854	10	80	N	
Kok, John	42	Holland	Y	Rotterdam	New Orleans	03/20/1853	09/29/1858	17	20	N	
Kokans, Henry	24	Prussia	Y	Rotterdam	New York	07/30/1849	09/06/1852	25	383	N	
Kokenbrink, Bernard	32	Prussia	Y	Bremen	New York	06/18/1853	11/02/1857	15	516	N	
Kolb, Adam	31	Bavaria	Y	Havre	New York	07/10/1850	10/22/1852	5	44	N	
Kolb, Andy	27	Germany	Y	Bremen	New York	11/15/1893	02/04/1896			Y	
Kolb, Conrad	??	Hesse Cassel	Y	?	New York	??/28/18??	11/03/1856	14	448	N	
Kolb, Frederick	29	Bavaria	Y	Bremen	Baltimore	08/24/1844	02/14/1849	23	101	N	
Kolb, John	21	Bavaria	Y	Hamburg	New York	08/02/1854	10/17/1857	15	444	N	
Kolb, Michael	22	Bavaria	Y	Havre	New York	04/11/1850	06/04/1852	25	182	N	
Kolbe, Carl	45	Germany	Y	Hamburg	New York	03/05/1885	10/19/1889			Y	
Kolbe, Joseph	43	Germany	N	Bremen	New York	06/24/1864	?			Y	
Kolbe, Werner	52	Hesse Cassel	Y	Bremen	Buffalo	08/15/1847	05/26/1852	25	111	N	
Kolckmeier, Frederick	26	Hanover	Y	Bremen	New York	01/12/1847	01/18/1849	1	459	N	
Kolde, Fred	??	Prussia	Y	?	?	?	07/05/1892			Y	
Kolkmeier, Henry	22	Hanover	Y	Bremen	New Orleans	11/08/1853	09/16/1857	15	277	N	
Kolkmeyer, Henry	26	Hanover	Y	Bremen	New Orleans	12/05/1847	10/06/1854	10	497	N	
Kolkmeyer, Henry	26	Hanover	Y	Bremen	New Orleans	12/05/1847	10/06/1854	12	436	N	
Koll, Karl	31	Kurhessen	Y	Bremen	New York	04/27/1851	12/06/1859	17	494	N	
Kollar, Karl	30	Austria (Hung	Y	?	?	?	11/02/1896			Y	
Koller, John	??	Bavaria	Y	Bremen	New Orleans	10/01/18??	10/09/1848	1	82	N	
Koller, John	26	Bavaria	Y	Bremen	New York	11/01/1853	09/22/1854	10	170	N	
Koller, John	26	Bavaria	Y	Bremen	New York	11/01/1853	09/23/1854	12	109	N	
Koller, Joseph	31	Bavaria	Y	Bremen	Baltimore	08/10/1846	10/16/1851	4	307	N	
Kollmer, Jacob	36	Germany	Y	Hamburg	New York	08/14/1876	11/01/1893			Y	
Kolln, John Hermann	39	Holstein	Y	Hamburg	New York	07/12/1857	01/18/1860	27	61	N	
Kollner, Bernard	30	Prussia	Y	Antwerp	New York	07/21/1849	01/14/1853	7	25	N	
Kollner, Henry	32	Prussia	Y	Bremen	Baltimore	04/17/1847	01/14/1853	7	24	N	
Kollsh, Jacob	38	Bavaria	Y	Havre	New York	03/18/1859	11/03/1860	18	10	N	
Kolms, August	51	Germany	Y	Bremen	New York	05/12/1888	07/02/1891			Y	
Kolodzik, Adolph	21	Germany	Y	Rotterdam	New York	06/27/1891	11/21/1893			Y	
Kols, Charles B.	??	Germany	N	?	?	?	?	28	238	N	05/??/1875
Kols, Charles B.	??	Germany	N	?	?	?				Y	05/00/1875
Kols, Rudolph G. H.	??	Germany	N	?	?	09/15/1885				Y	08/05/1892
Kolsch, John	35	Prussia	Y	Antwerp	New York	06/29/1852	05/08/1854	9	267	N	
Kolte, John Gerhard	24	Hanover	Y	Bremen	New Orleans	12/15/1848	08/11/1851	4	109	N	
Kolz, Mathias	27	Prussia	Y	Havre	New Orleans	04/27/1854	05/27/1856	26	559	N	
Koman, Vaclar	??	Austria	Y	?	?	06/??/1900	02/09/1903			Y	
Kommaier, Julius	25	Baden	Y	Havre	New York	07/12/1853	09/25/1856	14	369	N	
Kommann, Jacob	25	Bavaria	Y	Havre	New York	80/10/1854	11/08/1858	17	293	N	
Kommer, Christian	25	Germany	Y	Bremen	New York	08/04/1881	09/20/1887			Y	
Kondasz, Michael	52	Austria	Y	Bremen	New York]	03/22/1884	09/20/1894			Y	
Kondretzer, Joseph	40	Russia	Y	Hamburg	New York	01/28/1892	04/21/1894			Y	
Kondring, John Anthony	36	Prussia	Y	Bremen	Baltimore	08/02/1855	07/20/1858	16	515	N	
Konen, Joseph	23	Germany	Y	Bremen	Baltimore	05/31/1882	09/21/1885			Y	
Konermann, Anton	25	Prussia	Y	Bremen	New York	10/09/1854	10/07/1856	14	243	N	
Konermann, Anton	21	Prussia	Y	Bremen	Baltimore	05/03/1849	06/10/1852	25	229	N	
Konermann, B.	24	Germany	Y	Rotterdam	New York	09/15/1883	10/10/1885			Y	
Konermann, Herman	23	Prussia	Y	Bremen	Baltimore	06/03/1848	06/10/1852	25	230	N	
Konersmann, George	24	Hanover	Y	Bremen	New York	08/24/1869	08/01/1872	18	501	N	
Konert, Bernard	34	Prussia	Y	Bremen	New Orleans	11/04/1850	04/02/1856	26	409	N	
Konigstein, Michael	22	Bavaria	Y	Havre	New York	10/22/1851	10/02/1854	12	275	N	

CITIZENSHIP RECORDS

APPLICANT	AGE	COUNTRY OF ORIGIN	DEC	DEPART PORT	ENTRY PORT	ARRIVE DATE	DEC DATE	VOL	PG.	FLD	NAT DATE
Konnan, Konrad	??	?	Y	?	?	?	07/14/1897			Y	
Konnerman, John E. F.	21	Hanover	Y	Bremen	New York	01/12/1846	10/07/1848	22	480	N	
Konrad, Frank	21	Germany	Y	Bremen	Baltimore	09/06/1892	10/25/1894			Y	
Konradi, Peter	30	Nassau	Y	London	New York	09/07/1854	10/03/1854	10	381	N	
Konradi, Peter	30	Nassau	Y	London	New York	09/07/1851	10/03/1854	12	320	N	
Konsheim, William	27	Hesse Cassel	Y	London	New York	11/02/1853	10/19/1857	15	456	N	
Koob, Ferdinand	22	Bavaria	Y	Bremen	Baltimore	09/20/1852	05/31/1856	14	271	N	
Koock, Charles	25	Hanover	Y	Bremen	New Orleans	11/02/1858	09/10/1860	27	355	N	
Koop, Clemens	34	Germany	Y	Bremen	Baltimore	06/14/1879	02/25/1893			Y	
Koop, Herman Stephan	18	Germany	Y	Bremen	New York	08/12/1881	10/16/1882			Y	
Koop, John B.	30	Germany	Y	Bremen	Baltimore	02/08/1882	10/01/1885			Y	
Koop, John Frederick	25	Hanover	Y	Bremen	New Orleans	11/10/1853	07/23/1855	11	419	N	
Koop, Wilhelm August	25	Hanover	Y	Bremen	New Orleans	10/01/1853	03/01/1858	16	350	N	
Koop, William	27	Hanover	Y	Bremen	New Orleans	11/15/1853	10/04/1858	17	41	N	
Koopmann, Joseph	31	Germany	Y	Bremen	Baltimore	03/21/1892	03/27/1901			Y	
Koops, Henry	50	France	Y	Havre	New Orleans	12/04/1848	10/30/1851	4	440	N	
Koors, Diedrich	40	Oldenburg	Y	Bremen	Baltimore	06/21/1841	11/01/1852	5	168	N	
Kopelent, Heribert	26	Germany	Y	Bremen	Baltimore	06/22/1881	02/03/1882			Y	
Koper, Fred	42	Germany	N	Bremen	Baltimore	10/02/1858	?			Y	
Kopf, Fortunas	30	Germany	Y	Hamburg	New York	10/20/1873	09/18/1879			Y	
Kopf, George	24	Baden	Y	Havre	New Orleans	04/19/1844	10/13/1848	1	188	N	
Kopferss, Jacob	23	Baden	Y	Havre	New Orleans	04/??/1849	01/06/1851	2	464	N	
Kopfman, Wilhelm	23	Germany	Y	Amsterdam	New York	08/10/1883	10/11/1887			Y	
Kopfmann, George	27	Germany	Y	Antwerp	New York	11/30/1882	06/06/1887			Y	
Kopka, Christian	30	Germany	Y	Hamburg	Baltimore	05/26/1891	11/08/1892			Y	
Kopke, John Henry	28	Germany	Y	Hamburg	New York	09/28/1873	05/08/1882			Y	
Kopke, William	??	Germany	Y	?	?	?	02/09/1886			Y	
Kopmann, John Bernard	26	Hanover	Y	Bremen	?	12/??/1850	11/30/1857	16	61	N	
Kopp, Constantine	30	Baden	Y	Havre	New York	07/22/1851	09/25/1854	10	211	N	
Kopp, Constantine	30	Baden	Y	Havre	New York	07/22/1851	09/25/1854	12	150	N	
Kopp, Felix	30	Baden	Y	Havre	New York	08/01/1854	03/24/1856	26	272	N	
Kopp, George	26	Bavaria	Y	Havre	New York	05/20/1848	10/09/1854	6	113	N	
Kopp, George	26	Bavaria	Y	havre	New York	05/30/1848	10/09/1854	10	116	N	
Kopp, John	34	Wurttemberg	Y	Havre	New York	05/12/1850	06/05/1854	10	94	N	
Kopp, John	34	Wurttemberg	Y	Havre	New York	05/12/1850	06/05/1854	12	31	N	
Kopp, Lois	39	Germany	Y	Bremen	Baltimore	05/30/1874	10/09/1883			Y	
Kopp, Louis (affidavit o	??		N							N	
Koppe, Hugo	29	Germany	Y	Bremen	New York	05/23/1883	12/08/1883			Y	
Koppel, Dominick	50	Baden	Y	Havre	New Orleans	02/29/1854	02/09/1860	27	96	N	
Koppen, John F.	??	Germany	Y	?	?	?	09/22/1896			Y	
Koppers, Henry	36	Germany	Y	Antwerp	New York	07/11/1881	10/05/1883			Y	
Kops, John Karl	30	Hanover	Y	Bremen	New Orleans	11/27/1849	11/10/1852	6	389	N	
Kopschinski, Hyman	39	Poland (Russi	Y	Hamburg	New York	06/20/1884	06/13/1890			Y	
Korb, David	30	Germany	Y	Bremen	New York	09/28/1888	05/22/1893			Y	
Korb, Franz	28	Austria	Y	Bremen	Baltimore	09/10/1855	10/06/1856	14	209	N	
Korbei, Joseph	37	Germany	Y	Havre	New York	09/22/1883	07/25/1887			Y	
Korbet, Martin	??	Germany	Y	?	?	?	02/08/1879			Y	
Kordes, J.	30	Prussia	Y	Bremen	New York	09/01/1856	01/06/1860	27	39	N	
Kordes, Valentine	26	Prussia	Y	Antwerp	New York	08/15/1853	03/31/1856	26	387	N	
Korell, Valentin	47	Germany	N	Bremen	Baltimore	07/07/1854	?			Y	
Korfhagen, George	17	Germany	N	?	Baltimore	00/00/1883				Y	10/26/1888
Korman, Robert	32	Germany	Y	Antwerp	Philadelphia	06/27/1881	01/04/1887			Y	
Kormann, Cornelius	23	Bavaria	Y	Havre	New York	05/03/1854	03/24/1856	26	270	N	
Kormann, Gerhard	32	Germany	Y	Bremen	Baltimore	01/27/1884	06/30/1888			Y	
Korn, Frank Joseph	17	Germany	N	?	New York	00/00/1880				Y	10/26/1888
Korn, Micke	24	Germany	Y	Bremen	Baltimore	11/24/1868	03/04/1872	18	468	N	
Kornfihrer, Jospeh	37	Germany	Y	Bremen	New York	05/15/1882	02/18/1884			Y	
Kornmeyer, August	31	Baden	Y	Liverpool	New York	06/08/1854	08/15/1855	11	433	N	
Korpien, Fred William	26	Germany	Y	Hamburg	New York	01/23/1890	09/25/1891			Y	

CITIZENSHIP RECORDS

APPLICANT	AGE	COUNTRY OF ORIGIN	DEC	DEPART PORT	ENTRY PORT	ARRIVE DATE	DEC DATE	VOL	PG.	FLD	NAT DATE
Korrhaus, George	28	Holland	Y	Bremerhafen	Baltimore	10/??/1857	01/30/1861	18	77	N	
Kors, Henry	32	Oldenburg	Y	Bremen	Baltimore	07/16/1845	08/15/1848	22	171	N	
Korsmann, Abraham	45	Russia	Y	Hamburg	New York	11/20/1891	10/28/1898			Y	
Korstow, Peter	??	?	N	?	?	?	?			Y	
Kortain, John	27	Holland	Y	Rotterdam	Philadelphia	07/20/1848	08/??/1851	4	153	N	
Korte, Herman	14	Germany	N	?	Baltimore	00/00/1882				Y	10/10/1888
Korte, Johann Heinrich	26	Germany	Y	Amsterdam	New York	05/25/1887	01/04/1889			Y	
Korte, Peter	43	Germany	Y	Rotterdam	New York	09/29/1870	04/05/1882			Y	
Korte, William	50	Germany	Y	Bremen	Baltimore	06/19/1881	07/05/1890			Y	
Kortekamp, George	29	Germany	Y	Bremen	Baltimore	04/26/1883	03/29/1890			Y	
Kortekamp, Henry	24	Germany	Y	Bremen	New York	10/13/1888	10/24/1894			Y	
Korthus, John	41	Germany	Y	Bremen	Baltimore	10/23/1881	08/02/1886			Y	
Kortkamp, John Henry	33	Prussia	Y	Bremen	Baltimore	11/08/1857	04/07/1862	18	306	N	
Korwan, Charles	16	Germany	N	?	New York	00/00/1883				Y	06/28/1888
Korzenborn, Frederick	23	Prussia	Y	Antwerp	New York	07/16/1845	10/03/1848	22	411	N	
Kosche, Kuno	55	Prussia	N	Hamburg	New York	04/17/1865	?			Y	
Koshover, Jacob	29	Austria	Y	Bremen	Baltimore	07/21/1897	09/22/1903			Y	
Kosky, Joseph	33	Germany	Y	?	New York	00/00/1871	10/18/1884			Y	
Koss, Nicholas	32	Germany	Y	Bremen	Baltimore	06/23/1872	07/21/1882			Y	
Kosse, Joseph	25	Germany	Y	Amsterdam	New York	09/10/1881	10/09/1884			Y	
Kost, Augustus Frederick	32	Wurttemberg	Y	Antwerp	New York	05/03/1848	03/05/1857	15	67	N	
Kostars, Frank	21	Oldenburg	Y	Bremen	Baltimore	11/15/1852	10/04/1858	17	32	N	
Kostermann, Herman	46	Hanover	N	Hanover	New Orleans	11/??/1852	?			Y	
Kosters, J.G.	31	Hanover	Y	Bremerhafen	Baltimore	05/??/1859	01/01/1861	18	41	N	
Koth, Michael	51	Germany	Y	?	New York	??/??/1874	11/03/1884			Y	
Kothe, Bernhardt	29	Germany	Y	Bremen	New York	08/06/1881	07/15/1885			Y	
Kothe, Frederick W.	36	Germany	Y	Bremen	New York	06/14/1880	06/07/1886			Y	
Kothe, Jacob W.	31	Germany	Y	Bremen	New York	06/12/1880	06/13/1883			Y	
Kotler, Johann	30	Germany	Y	Havre	New York	12/03/1879	09/10/1886	19	43	N	
Kotte, Herman	22	Hanover	Y	Bremen	New Orleans	12/24/1853	05/21/1856	26	517	N	
Kotte, J. Bernard	42	Germany	Y	Bremen	Baltimore	08/11/1879	06/20/1882			Y	
Kotte, Joseph	31	Germany	Y	Bremen	Baltimore	09/??/1875	10/10/1882			Y	
Kotter, Bernard	22	Prussia	Y	Bremen	New Orleans	01/01/1847	07/05/1851	3	488	N	
Kottig, George	22	Germany	Y	Amsterdam	New York	08/27/1882	05/10/1883			Y	
Kottmann, Anthony	32	Prussia	Y	Bremen	New Orleans	10/26/1851	10/29/1858	17	1	N	
Kottmeyer (Kottmann), F.	22	Germany	Y	Bremen	Baltimore	03/28/1880	12/26/1883			Y	
Kotz, Joseph	45	Germany	Y	Hamburg	Boston	06/16/1883	08/19/1892			Y	
Kotzorasilis, V.	28	Greece	Y	?	?	?	04/08/1898			Y	
Kouba, Frank	40	Austria	Y	Hamburg	New York	07/02/1893	12/08/1897			Y	
Koule, Sebastian	26	Bavaria	Y	?	?	10/07/1882	10/24/1888			Y	
Kouri, Assad	25	Arabia	Y	Beirut	New York	11/14/1888	08/30/1892			Y	
Kouschuetzky, L. R.	23	Germany	Y	Rotterdam	New York	02/27/1882	03/16/1886			Y	
Koutavzer, John	42	Germany	N	Bremen	New York	02/16/1869	?			Y	
Kouzak, John	36	Germany	Y	?	?	03/26/1889	02/07/1891			Y	
Kowalski, Bernard	29	Germany	Y	Antwerp	New York	10/18/1884	08/18/1887			Y	
Kowalski, Emil	37	Germany	Y	Antwerp	New York	06/02/1881	07/23/1894			Y	
Kowalski, Emil Leo	25	Germany	Y	Antwerp	New York	09/22/1885	10/26/1888			Y	
Kraatz, Carl	36	Germany	Y	Hamburg	New York	04/17/1896	01/30/1903			Y	
Krabacher, Edward	25	Germany	Y	Havre	New York	05/03/1883	08/03/1885			Y	
Krabacher, Joseph	25	Germany	Y	Antwerp	New York	07/17/1885	08/03/1885			Y	
Krabbe, Bernhard	36	Germany	Y	Bremen	New York	07/29/1883	10/21/1896			Y	
Krabbe, George	30	Germany	Y	Bremen	New York	10/14/1883	10/26/1895			Y	
Kracke, Hermann	37	Prussia	Y	Bremen	Baltimore	06/15/1848	10/06/1854	10	488	N	
Kracke, Hermann	37	Prussia	Y	Bremen	Baltimore	06/15/1848	10/06/1854	12	427	N	
Kracker, Michael	50	Bavaria	Y	Bremen	New York	02/24/1853	04/17/1854	8	190	N	
Kracker, Michael	50	Bavaria	Y	Bremen	New York	02/24/1853	04/17/1854	9	61	N	
Krackman, Charles	??	Germany	N	?	?	07/15/1885				Y	02/10/1892
Kraeckel, Charles	34	Bavaria	Y	Bremen	New York	10/12/1854	12/12/1855	13	304	N	
Kraehmer, Peter	42	Bavaria	Y	Havre	New Orleans	05/29/1846	06/18/1851	3	392	N	

CITIZENSHIP RECORDS

APPLICANT	AGE	COUNTRY OF ORIGIN	DEC	DEPART PORT	ENTRY PORT	ARRIVE DATE	DEC DATE	VOL	PG.	FLD	NAT DATE
Kraemer, Adam	50	Germany	Y	Bremen	Baltimore	09/30/1886	10/27/1890			Y	
Kraemer, Adolph	41	Germany	Y	Hamburg	New York	02/15/1884	06/27/1898			Y	
Kraemer, Cornel	41	Germany	Y	Antwerp	New York	02/20/1884	11/18/1889			Y	
Kraemer, Frank J.	22	Germany	Y	Antwerp	New York	10/13/1879	05/14/1883			Y	
Kraemer, Fritz	35	Germany	Y	Antwerp	New York	12/24/1881	09/18/1890			Y	
Kraemer, George	29	Germany	Y	Bremen	New York	05/03/1885	09/15/1890			Y	
Kraemer, Henry	29	Germany	Y	Amsterdam	New York	09/11/1881	09/11/1890			Y	
Kraemer, Jacob	25	Germany	Y	Bremen	New York	10/21/1891	09/13/1892			Y	
Kraemer, John	32	Germany	Y	Hamburg	New York	03/27/1881	10/31/1887			Y	
Kraemer, Peter	32	Germany	Y	Hamburg	New York	05/15/1882	10/07/1892			Y	
Kraemer, Theodore	22	Hanover	Y	Bremen	Baltimore	10/31/1847	10/27/1851	4	411	N	
Kraempelmann, B.	32	Germany	Y	Bremen	Baltimore	10/16/1878	04/06/1883			Y	
Kraengle, John	26	Bavaria	Y	Bremen	New York	06/25/1859	07/07/1859	17	459	N	
Krafft, Joseph	45	Germany	Y	Havre	Buffalo	05/08/1872	10/26/1892	19	383	N	
Krafft, William	25	Germany	Y	Bremen	New York	10/15/1880	01/02/1886			Y	
Kraft, Adam	40	Hesse Darmsta	Y	Havre	New York	09/10/1854	09/29/1858	17	19	N	
Kraft, Adam	33	Bavaria	Y	Bremen	Buffalo	07/28/1847	09/30/1848	22	373	N	
Kraft, Andreas	60	Germany	N	Bremen	Baltimore	06/20/1857	?			Y	
Kraft, August	32	Saxe Altenbur	Y	Bremen	New York	07/22/1858	11/01/1858	17	228	N	
Kraft, Carl	29	Germany	Y	Hamburg	New York	06/01/1880	10/08/1886			Y	
Kraft, Friedrich	25	Germany	Y	Rotterdam	Boston	09/17/1888	12/28/1888			Y	
Kraft, Henry	37	Germany	N	Bremen	New York	06/29/1867	?			Y	
Kraft, Karl	24	Germany	Y	Antwerp	New York	04/04/1885	12/05/1889			Y	
Kraft, Louis	22	Germany	Y	Antwerp	New York	03/22/1884	04/23/1886			Y	
Kraft, William	19	Germany	Y	Bremen	Baltimore	12/15/1882	06/15/1886			Y	
Kraheck, John	35	Germany	Y	Antwerp	New York	03/25/1884	04/15/1892			Y	
Krahenbuhl, John B.	38	Switzerland	Y	Havre	New York	02/19/1882	03/04/1886			Y	
Kraining, Gerhard Henry	25	Hanover	Y	Bremen	New York	10/04/1848	04/02/1853	7	502	N	
Krais, William	29	Wuerttenberg	Y	Havre	New York	??/05/1849	11/24/1849	23	369	N	
Krake, Dietrich	56	Germany	N	Bremen	New York	03/??/1849	?			Y	
Kralick, Wenzel	60	Austria	N	Bremen	New York	10/??/1854	?			Y	
Krambelbeck, Bernard Hen	25	Oldenburg	Y	Bremen	Baltimore	06/07/1850	10/12/1857	15	396	N	
Kramen, Herman	25	Germany	Y	?	Baltimore	??/??/1883	05/07/1888			Y	
Kramer, Adolph	72	Germany	N	Bremen	New Orleans	05/??/1842	??/??/1844	28	396	N	??/??/1848
Kramer, Andreas	39	Hungary	Y	Bremen	New York	03/14/1893	03/03/1904			Y	
Kramer, Anthony	29	Baden	Y	Havre	New Orleans	07/09/1849	12/18/1850	2	374	N	
Kramer, Anton	47	Germany	N	Hamburg	New York	09/??/1867	?			Y	
Kramer, August	26	Prussia	Y	Bremen	New Orleans	11/19/1852	02/09/1858	16	89	N	
Kramer, August	29	Germany	N	Bremen	New York	?//??/1865	?			Y	
Kramer, Charles	23	Germany	Y	Bremen	New York	07/28/1892	07/27/1895			Y	
Kramer, Christian	22	Prussia	Y	Rotterdam	Baltimore	06/14/1849	03/09/1852	24	274	N	
Kramer, Conrad	25	Bavaria	Y	Bremen	New York	07/11/1852	12/07/1857	16	202	N	
Kramer, Edward	33	Germany	Y	Havre	New York	06/10/1884	10/01/1889			Y	
Kramer, Emil	25	Germany	Y	Antwerp	New York	04/18/1884	05/05/1887			Y	
Kramer, F.	40	Germany	Y	Bremen	Baltimore	07/22/1881	09/22/1885			Y	
Kramer, Frank	28	Germany	Y	Bremen	New York	09/25/1880	12/15/1884			Y	
Kramer, Frank	14	Germany	N	?	Baltimore	00/00/1881				Y	08/23/1888
Kramer, Frederick	32	Hanover	Y	Bremen	New Orleans	11/07/1851	07/16/1855	11	393	N	
Kramer, Frederick	30	Bavaria	Y	Bremen	New York	08/20/1854	03/26/1857	15	90	N	
Kramer, Frederick	??	Germany	N	?	?	10/03/1884				Y	10/20/1892
Kramer, Friedarick	26	Germany	Y	Bremen	New York	01/18/1873	04/07/1879			Y	
Kramer, George	29	Prussia	Y	Havre	New York	07/20/1841	11/18/1848	1	321	N	
Kramer, Gerhard Heinrich	22	Germany	Y	Bremen	Baltimore	08/16/1883	10/05/1887			Y	
Kramer, Henry	18	Germany	Y	Hanover	?	09/01/1882	12/29/1886			Y	
Kramer, Henry	26	Germany	Y	Hamburg	Philadelphia	08/07/1882	11/03/1886			Y	
Kramer, Henry	72	Germany	N	Bremen	New Orleans	09/19/1844	?			Y	
Kramer, Henry	37	Oldenburg	Y	Bremen	New Orleans	12/25/1848	03/02/1852	24	209	N	
Kramer, Henry	30	Prussia	Y	Bremen	Baltimore	05/04/1854	03/25/1856	26	296	N	
Kramer, Henry	27	Germany	Y	Bremen	New York	09/25/1880				Y	08/30/1888

211

CITIZENSHIP RECORDS

APPLICANT	AGE	COUNTRY OF ORIGIN	DEC	DEPART PORT	ENTRY PORT	ARRIVE DATE	DEC DATE	VOL	PG.	FLD	NAT DATE
Kramer, Herman	28	Germany	Y	Bremen	Baltimore	05/27/1884	06/30/1888			Y	
Kramer, Herman	30	Germany	Y	Bremen	Baltimore	05/20/1888	11/01/1890			Y	
Kramer, J. Frank	23	Germany	Y	Bremen	Baltimore	05/18/1892	08/19/1897			Y	
Kramer, Jacob	24	Wuerttemberg	Y	Havre	New Orleans	09/10/1846	09/14/1848	22	346	N	
Kramer, Johann George	28	Germany	Y	Bremen	New York	05/26/1883	03/24/1886			Y	
Kramer, Johannes	37	Germany	Y	Bremen	New York	09/12/1893	10/27/1900			Y	
Kramer, John	29	Prussia	Y	Bremen	Baltimore	06/13/1846	10/13/1848	1	198	N	
Kramer, John	23	Germany	Y	Bremen	Baltimore	10/09/1884	08/18/1888			Y	
Kramer, John	23	Bavaria	Y	Antwerp	New York	07/08/1881	03/21/1884			Y	
Kramer, John Bernard	24	Hanover	Y	Bremen	New Orleans	06/04/1855	11/12/1857	16	14	N	
Kramer, John Jacob	50	Switzerland	Y	Havre	New York	07/24/1847	10/02/1848	1	34	N	
Kramer, Julius C.	40	Germany	Y	Bremen	New York	04/24/1871	11/10/1887			Y	
Kramer, Mike	??	Germamy	Y	?	New York	12/18/1891	10/13/1892			Y	
Kramer, Paul	28	Germany	Y	Hamburg	New York	10/10/1881	07/05/1884			Y	
Kramer, Peter	27	Germany	Y	Hamburg	New York	03/21/1886	04/02/1888			Y	
Kramer, Richard	32	Germany	Y	Bremen	Baltimore	05/24/1879	03/23/1885			Y	
Kramer, Sebastian	28	Wurttemberg	Y	Havre	New York	05/08/1848	11/01/1852	5	167	N	
Kramer, Sebastian	28	Wurttemberg	Y	Havre	New York	05/08/1848	11/01/1852	6	293	N	
Kramer, Simon	21	Prussia	Y	Antwerp	New York	08/01/1852	09/29/1856	14	440	N	
Kramer, Soloman	17	Russia	N	?	New York	00/00/1872				Y	10/15/1888
Kramer, Theodore	??	Germany	Y	?	?	?	03/12/1879			Y	
Kramer, William	40	Germany	Y	Bremen	New York	10/31/1865	10/28/1885			Y	
Kramer, William	35	Hanover	Y	Bremen	New Orleans	01/01/1843	06/10/1852	25	234	N	
Kraml, John	50	Bavaria	Y	Bremen	Baltimore	07/23/1848	02/18/1851	3	142	N	
Krampe, August	31	Germany	Y	Antwerp	New York	06/05/1881	10/12/1886			Y	
Krampe, Frederick	29	Germany	Y	Antwerp	New York	06/05/1881	10/12/1886			Y	
Krampner, Solomon	37	Austria	Y	Hamburg	New York	06/28/1879	10/19/1896			Y	
Kranning, Matthias	41	Hanover	Y	Bremen	New Orleans	12/??/1847	12/??/1849	23	417	N	
Krantz, Frank	24	Germany	Y	Antwerp	Philadelphia	06/??/1888	10/16/1890			Y	
Kranz, Henry	28	Germany	Y	Antwerp	New York	08/12/1882	07/05/1883			Y	
Kranz, John Frederick	40	Hanover	Y	Bremen	New Orleans	11/02/1853	11/05/1855	13	167	N	
Kranz, Zachary	26	Prussia	Y	Bremen	New York	11/19/1853	10/01/1854	14	78	N	
Kranzbuehler, Daniel	26	Bavaria	Y	Havre	New York	01/26/1850	10/15/1851	4	294	N	
Krapf, Gottlieb Edward	29	Germany	Y	Rotterdam	New York	07/07/1881	02/29/1888			Y	
Krass, Michael	26	Bavaria	Y	Bremen	Baltimore	08/??/1849	12/14/1852	5	412	N	
Kraszer, Gottlieb	39	Bavaria	Y	Bremen	Baltimore	07/12/1847	04/22/1850	3	7	N	
Kratt, Christian	38	Germany	Y	Bremen	New York	02/28/1869	02/02/1883			Y	
Kratzdorn, Rudolph	34	Baden	Y	Antwerp	New York	11/01/1848	02/08/1853	7	130	N	
Kraup, Frederick	50	Wuerttemberg	Y	Havre	New York	06/??/1849	11/??/1849	23	368	N	
Kraurer, Friedrich	27	Hanover	Y	Bremen	New Orleans	12/18/1851	09/09/1852	25	423	N	
Kraus, Abe	24	Germany	Y	Hamburg	New York	10/09/1889	10/26/1894			Y	
Kraus, Andreas	40	Bavaria	Y	Bremen	New York	07/05/1841	10/10/1854	6	211	N	
Kraus, Andreas	40	Bavaria	Y	Bremen	New York	07/05/1841	10/10/1854	11	214	N	
Kraus, Christian	32	Baden	Y	Antwerp	New York	08/08/1853	12/29/1855	13	397	N	
Kraus, Johann George	28	Bavaria	Y	Bremen	New York	08/03/1851	02/14/1853	7	154	N	
Kraus, John	27	Bavaria	Y	Bremen	Baltimore	09/04/1852	10/05/1854	10	448	N	
Kraus, John	27	Bavaria	Y	Bremen	Baltimore	09/04/1852	10/05/1854	12	387	N	
Kraus, John	27	Bavaria	Y	Bremen	New York	05/09/1870	04/01/1872	18	485	N	
Kraus, John	27	Bavaria	Y	Bremen	New York	05/09/1870	04/01/1872	18	485	N	
Kraus, John	59	Germany	Y	?	New York	00/00/1879	09/30/1884			Y	
Kraus, Michael	44	Bavaria	Y	Bremen	Baltimore	09/04/1852	10/05/1854	10	449	N	
Kraus, Michael	44	Bavaria	Y	Bremen	Baltimore	09/04/1852	10/05/1854	12	388	N	
Kraus, Sebastian	26	Germany	Y	?	?	02/14/1893	03/21/1896			Y	
Kraus, Walter	21	Prussia	Y	Bremen	New Orleans	12/23/1848	04/27/1850	3	14	N	
Krause, August	36	Germany	Y	Bremen	Baltimore	06/17/1883	03/30/1888			Y	
Krause, Emil	41	Germany	Y	Hamburg	New York	05/10/1869	10/06/1886			Y	
Krause, Ferdinand	49	Germany	Y	Bremen	New York	04/21/1881	10/24/1888			Y	
Krause, Hermann	24	Germany	Y	Bremen	New York	05/04/1880	09/28/1882			Y	
Krause, Karl	29	Germany	Y	Bremen	Baltimore	07/16/1896	07/30/1896			Y	

CITIZENSHIP RECORDS

APPLICANT	AGE	COUNTRY OF ORIGIN	DEC	DEPART PORT	ENTRY PORT	ARRIVE DATE	DEC DATE	VOL	PG.	FLD	NAT DATE
Krause, William	41	Germany	Y	Bremen	New York	10/04/1882	01/08/1886			Y	
Krauss, G. Eugen	27	Germany	Y	Bremen	New York	09/29/1884	12/06/1888			Y	
Krauss, John	26	Germany	Y	Antwerp	New York	03/24/1883	02/16/1885			Y	
Kraut, Hilar	36	Hesse Darmsta	Y	Antwerp	New York	08/25/1848	02/09/1849	23	38	N	
Kraut, John Casper	48	Wurttemberg	Y	Bremen	New York	06/10/1850	07/07/1851	3	505	N	
Krauter, Albert	46	Germany	N	Bremen	New York	04/??/1868	?			Y	
Krauter, Joseph	??	Germany	Y	?	?	?	10/20/1883			Y	
Krautz, Abraham	22	Bavaria	Y	Havre	New York	04/25/1850	03/15/1853	7	330	N	
Krauz, Alex	23	Russia	Y	Hamburg	New York	03/28/1890	12/19/1891			Y	
Krauz, Charles	29	Russia	Y	Hamburg	New York	07/04/1890	01/10/1896			Y	
Krebs, Casper	33	Prussia	Y	Rotterdam	New Orleans	04/02/1845	05/25/1854	8	530	N	
Krebs, Casper	33	Prussia	Y	Rotterdam	New Orleans	04/02/1846	05/25/1854	9	404	N	
Krebs, Charles	3	Germany	N	?	New York	00/00/1853				Y	10/22/1886
Krebs, Conrad Henry	25	Kurhessen	Y	Bremen	Baltimore	08/24/1853	07/25/1858	16	523	N	
Krebs, Daniel	16	Germany	N	?	New York	00/00/1881				Y	10/15/1886
Krebs, Ferdinand	53	Germany	Y	London	New York	09/20/1880	10/20/1903			Y	
Krebs, Frank	26	Germany	Y	Antwerp	New York	04/27/1883	03/29/1889			Y	
Krebs, Joseph	25	Bavaria	Y	Bremen	Baltimore	07/11/1844	08/22/1848	22	223	N	
Krebs, Laurent	21	Germany	Y	Havre	New York	10/19/1891	01/09/1894			Y	
Krebs, Louis	26	Baden	Y	Havre	New York	09/26/1846	02/20/1849	23	230	N	
Krebs, Martin	42	Germany	Y	Bremen	New York	01/01/1889	12/20/1897			Y	
Krebser, August Sr.	51	Switzerland	Y	Havre	New York	03/09/1882	03/12/1889			Y	
Krebsfanger, Henry	30	Germany	Y	Bremen	New York	08/22/1885	10/17/1890			Y	
Krechting, Frank	26	Germany	Y	Rotterdam	New York	08/06/1882	09/08/1888			Y	
Kreh, George	27	Hesse Darmsta	Y	Bremen	New York	06/18/1849	03/09/1852	24	275	N	
Krehe, August	32	Germany	Y	Amsterdam	New York	05/??/1872	10/24/1884			Y	
Krehe, George	36	Germany	Y	Bremen	New York	06/03/1881	10/13/1884			Y	
Krehe, George	55	Bavaria	Y	Havre	New York	06/29/1849	02/16/1852	24	119	N	
Krehe, Johann	31	Germany	Y	Bremen	New York	04/01/1881	09/01/1884			Y	
Kreich, Jacob	39	France	Y	Havre	New Orleans	05/??/1846	12/??/1849	23	419	N	
Kreideler, Bernard	47	Germany	Y	Bremen	Baltimore	05/01/1888	12/08/1891			Y	
Kreider, Frederick	26	Baden	Y	Havre	New York	06/21/1849	03/21/1853	7	355	N	
Kreidler, Mathias	24	Wuerttemberg	Y	Havre	New Orleans	03/08/1854	02/27/1860	27	111	N	
Kreienbuehl, Anton	28	Switzerland	Y	Havre	New York	07/08/1893	06/23/1896			Y	
Kreiger, Henry	21	Germany	Y	Bremen	?	06/??/1881	11/02/1886			Y	
Kreil, John Michael	25	Bavaria	Y	Bremen	New York	12/10/1844	10/03/1848	1	44	N	
Kreiler, Casper	30	Baden	Y	London	New York	07/09/1848	09/08/1852	25	410	N	
Kreiler, Dominick	37	Baden	Y	London	New York	07/09/1848	09/08/1852	25	411	N	
Kreimer, Charles	18	Germany	Y	Bremen	New York	09/19/1883	04/20/1886			Y	
Kreimer, Henry	24	Hanover	Y	Bremen	New York	07/11/1854	10/01/1856	14	88	N	
Kreimer, William	24	Hanover	Y	Bremen	New Orleans	12/??/1850	09/19/1855	13	74	N	
Kreiner, George	31	Germany	Y	Havre	New York	01/14/1885	10/20/1888			Y	
Kreiner, Jacob	25	Germany	Y	Havre	New York	05/06/1880	05/09/1882			Y	
Kreinest, Herman	34	Germany	Y	Bremen	Baltimore	06/04/1881	05/25/1885			Y	
Kreinhof, John	30	Hanover	Y	Bremen	New York	08/02/1846	11/08/1852	5	252	N	
Kreis, Adam	24	Baden	Y	Rotterdam	New York	06/06/1854	09/11/1855	13	1	N	
Kreis, Carl	27	Germany	Y	?	?	09/10/1894	03/04/1901			Y	
Kreis, Nicholas	23	Baden	Y	Bremen	New York	07/17/1852	04/17/1854	8	159	N	
Kreis, Nicolaus	23	Baden	Y	Bremen	New York	07/07/1852	04/17/1854	9	30	N	
Kreiss, Franz	37	Germany	Y	Bremen	New York	04/12/1879	12/05/1885			Y	
Kreiss, John	54	Saxe Weimar E	Y	Bremen	New York	07/02/1848	10/02/1854	10	362	N	
Kreiss, John	54	Saxe Weimar E	Y	Bremen	New York	07/02/1848	10/02/1854	12	301	N	
Kreitch, Fred.	32	Saxony	Y	Bremen	New York	08/19/1849	03/19/1853	7	351	N	
Kreitlein, John Andrew	27	Bavaria	Y	Bremen	Baltimore	09/??/1850	12/04/1850	2	336	N	
Krelans, Ferdinand	21	Prussia	Y	Bremen	New Orleans	05/07/1854	02/02/1856	13	539	N	
Krell, Frederick	25	Prussia	Y	Bremen	New Orleans	06/24/1853	12/10/1855	13	296	N	
Kremer, Arnold	22	Germany	Y	Bremen	Baltimore	05/22/1886	01/31/1890			Y	
Kremer, Frank	24	Germany	Y	Antwerp	New York	04/04/1881	10/01/1883			Y	
Kremer, Herman	32	Hanover	Y	Bremen	New Orleans	01/16/1848	02/21/1849	23	246	N	

CITIZENSHIP RECORDS

APPLICANT	AGE	COUNTRY OF ORIGIN	DEC	DEPART PORT	ENTRY PORT	ARRIVE DATE	DEC DATE	VOL	PG.	FLD	NAT DATE
Krempien, John	23	Germany	Y	?	New York	10/??/1884	12/09/1887			Y	
Kremsner, Charles	32	Germany	Y	Bremen	New York	06/02/1883	11/13/1884			Y	
Krenkel, Fred	30	Germany	Y	Havre	New York	04/20/1883	04/07/1886			Y	
Krenning, Frederick	49	Germany	Y	Bremen	New York	08/??/1865	10/21/1890	19	293	N	
Kreser, Michael	34	Bavaria	Y	Hamburg	New York	11/22/1857	01/14/1861	18	57	N	
Kresken, H. Anton	51	Germany	N	Hamburg	New York	05/??/1863	?			Y	
Kresse, Edward	41	Germany	Y	Havre	New York	06/01/1882	06/17/1884			Y	
Kressig, Ignatz	32	Germany	Y	Havre	New York	08/22/1881	10/26/1887			Y	
Kreter, August	60	Germany	Y	?	New York	??/??/1864	10/09/1880			Y	
Kreth, Henry	??	Germany	Y	?	?	06/??/1882	10/14/1885			Y	
Kretschmar, August	26	Saxe Altenbur	Y	Bremen	New York	01/04/1854	02/11/1856	26	70	N	
Kretzschmar, August	36	Germany	Y	Bremen	New York	05/17/1883	05/09/1890			Y	
Kreul, Adolf	31	Austria	Y	Hamburg	New York	04/11/1891	10/23/1894			Y	
Kreul, Ernst	21	Austria	Y	Havre	New York	08/01/1887	01/17/1890			Y	
Kreutzians, Christian	33	Hanover	Y	Bremen	New Orleans	06/13/1847	05/28/1852	25	126	N	
Kreuzkem, Frank	60	Germany	N	Hanover	?	??/??/1861	?			Y	
Kreuzmann, August Bruno	27	Germany	Y	Hamburg	New York	06/01/1882	04/11/1892			Y	
Krey, Julius	37	Germany	Y	Bremen	Baltimore	05/26/1883	03/24/1890			Y	
Kribb, Frank	26	Germany	Y	Antwerp	New York	04/27/1883	03/29/1888	19	224	N	
Krick, Daniel	34	Germany	Y	Rotterdam	New York	09/17/1878	11/02/1888	19	214	N	
Kriedler, Anton	30	Germany	Y	?	?	11/24/1887	04/02/1894			Y	
Krieg, Benedict	50	Baden	Y	Havre	New York	05/15/1846	03/25/1856	26	317	N	
Krieg, Charles	26	Germany	Y	Havre	New York	01/23/1881	02/02/1883			Y	
Krieg, G. W.	24	Germany	Y	Hamburg	New York	11/28/1880	10/22/1886			Y	
Krieg, Mathews	24	Wurttemberg	Y	Antwerp	New York	10/09/1848	10/06/1851	4	192	N	
Kriege, Heinrich	28	Germany	Y	Bremen	New York	09/11/1892	10/24/1893			Y	
Krieger, Bernard	30	Oldenburg	Y	Bremen	Baltimore	07/24/1854	09/29/1856	14	438	N	
Krieger, George	27	Baden	Y	Havre	New York	08/15/1850	03/25/1853	7	390	N	
Krieger, Herman	30	Germany	Y	Rotterdam	New York	05/30/1877	11/02/1887			Y	
Krieger, John	30	Baden	Y	Havre	New York	??/02/1848	10/??/1849	23	292	N	
Krieghoff, Ernst P.	43	Canada	Y	Toronto	Buffalo	07/01/1881	03/07/1894			Y	
Krieler, Frederick	36	Hanover	Y	Bremen	New Orleans	11/01/1848	10/30/1858	17	194	N	
Kriesmann, William	35	Germany	Y	Bremen	Baltimore	09/10/1872	10/27/1882			Y	
Krimme, Frank	52	Germany	Y	Bremen	Baltimore	05/04/1880	10/17/1887			Y	
Krimmel, William Ludwig	31	Wurttemberg	Y	Liverpool	Philadelphia	09/07/1853	02/23/1857	15	49	N	
Krimmer, Conrad	45	Bavaria	Y	Hamburg	New York	06/15/1852	03/11/1858	16	394	N	
Krincker, John	40	Argentina	Y	Buenas Aires	Philadelphia	12/12/1891	04/04/1900			Y	
Krinehop, John	30	Hanover	Y	Bremen	New York	08/02/1846	11/08/1852	6	376	N	
Krins, H.	30	Prussia	Y	Bremen	Baltimore	06/01/1860	06/26/1860	27	9	N	
Krippner, Adam	25	Bavaria	Y	Bremen	Baltimore	08/12/1852	11/09/1854	11	187	N	
Krisner, Francis Joseph	29	Wurttemberg	Y	Bremen	Philadelphia	05/01/1852	12/02/1852	5	374	N	
Krissmer, John	??	Germany	Y	?	New York	05/??/1873	11/03/1873			Y	
Krite, Henry	24	Prussia	Y	Bremerhafen	New Orleans	04/15/1859	01/10/1861	18	53	N	
Krobecki, Stanislaus	23	Poland	Y	Liverpool	New York	04/16/1852	03/26/1853	7	406	N	
Kroeger, Anton	51	Oldenburg	Y	Bremen	New York	04/01/1852	10/01/1856	14	118	N	
Kroeger, Frank W.	40	Germany	N	Bremen	Baltimore	08/03/1863	?			Y	
Kroeger, Gerard Henry	23	Hanover	Y	Bremen	New York	08/15/1854	09/30/1856	14	44	N	
Kroeger, Henry	40	Germany	Y	Bremen	New York	08/30/1872	12/02/1893			Y	
Kroeger, Joseph	33	Hanover	Y	Bremen	New Orleans	01/27/1851	02/11/1852	24	91	N	
Kroell, Francis	27	Prussia	Y	London	New York	09/04/1847	02/27/1851	3	172	N	
Kroemer, Henry	55	Germany	Y	Bremen	New York	05/12/1870	05/09/1898			Y	
Kroeper, Henry	27	Prussia	Y	Bremen	Baltimore	12/23/1846	10/03/1848	22	415	N	
Kroepsch, Julius	22	Prussia	Y	Bremen	Baltimore	10/20/1855	02/03/1857	14	535	N	
Krogall, Gottfried	28	Germany	Y	Bremen	Baltimore	11/05/1884	03/12/1888			Y	
Kroger, Fred	32	Germany	Y	Bremen	Baltimore	07/25/1875	11/16/1887			Y	
Kroger, J.H.	57	Holland	Y	New Diep	Baltimore	10/09/1853	10/06/1856	14	234	N	
Kroger, John Henry	31	Hanover	Y	Bremen	Baltimore	11/01/1845	01/17/1849	1	450	N	
Krohmer, Nicholas	30	Baden	Y	Havre	New York	12/20/1854	02/19/1857	15	28	N	
Krohn, John	31	Germany	Y	Hamburg	New York	05/00/1881	04/01/1886			Y	

CITIZENSHIP RECORDS

APPLICANT	AGE	COUNTRY OF ORIGIN	DEC	DEPART PORT	ENTRY PORT	ARRIVE DATE	DEC DATE	VOL	PG.	FLD	NAT DATE
Krohne, William	50	Prussia	N	Bremen	Baltimore	11/07/1867	?			Y	
Kroie, Fred	26	Germany	Y	?	?	06/27/1882	10/18/1884			Y	
Krolage, Henry	50	Germany	N	Bremen	New York	06/26/1866	?			Y	
Krome, Herman Henry	26	Hanover	Y	Bremen	Baltimore	10/21/1853	10/01/1856	14	126	N	
Kromer, Alphonso	24	Germany	Y	Havre	New York	06/06/1885	01/10/1890			Y	
Kromer, John	22	Wurttemberg	Y	Havre	New York	09/??/1852	03/26/1853	7	411	N	
Krommer, John	45	Baden	Y	Antwerp	New York	11/24/1853	10/06/1856	14	184	N	
Kronauer, Adam	29	Hesse Darmsta	Y	London	New Orleans	01/??/1853	11/24/1857	16	49	N	
Kronauer, John	73	Germany	N	Rotterdam	New York	06/10/1850	?			Y	
Kronberg, Gustave	??	Germany	Y	?	?	?	03/20/1893			Y	
Krone, Anton	36	Prussia	Y	Bremen	Baltimore	09/26/1852	09/27/1856	14	399	N	
Krone, Emil	38	Germany	Y	Montreal	Buffalo	05/13/1894	03/23/1896			Y	
Krones, John	35	Nassau	Y	Liverpool	New York	??/??/18?2	04/25/1855	11	305	N	
Kronmuller, John Michael	??	Baden	Y	London	New York	06/28/18??	10/11/1848	1	117	N	
Kronz, Carl	25	Prussia	Y	Liverpool	Boston	05/18/1853	05/04/1854	9	250	N	
Kronz, Charles	25	Prussia	Y	Liverpool	Boston	05/18/1853	05/05/1854	8	377	N	
Kroog, Frank Ludwig	33	Baden	Y	Havre	New York	10/20/1845	10/06/1848	22	449	N	
Kroos, John	32	Germany	Y	Bremen	New Orleans	03/13/1880	09/15/1886			Y	
Kropf, Christian	42	Switzerland	Y	Havre	New York	07/24/1883	08/25/1884			Y	
Kropf, John	24	Switzerland	Y	Havre	New York	03/27/1884	08/25/1884			Y	
Kropf, John Jacob	51	Baden	Y	Havre	New Orleans	09/10/1847	??/??/18??	3	236	N	
Krotz, John Friedrich	45	Germany	Y	Havre	New York	07/??/1864	03/15/1881			Y	
Krouse, Conrad	41	Bavaria	Y	Bremen	New York	09/04/1846	11/20/1848	1	332	N	
Krouse, Henry	24	Hanover	Y	Bremen	Baltimore	05/16/1856	11/25/1857	16	52	N	
Krouse, Herman Henry	26	Hanover	Y	Hamburg	New Orleans	05/22/1847	06/16/1852	25	278	N	
Krouse, Jacob	26	Bavaria	Y	Havre	New York	08/04/1846	03/25/1850	2	242	N	
Kruber, Robert	49	Germany	Y	Hamburg	New York	06/27/1882	10/15/1888			Y	
Krucker, John Frederick	29	Bavaria	Y	Havre	New Orleans	02/19/1848	03/13/1851	3	262	N	
Krueger, Albert	21	Germany	Y	Bremen	New York	12/31/1892	02/05/1894			Y	
Krueger, Carl	28	Germany	Y	Bremen	New York	12/18/1883	11/07/1887			Y	
Krueger, Franz	29	Germany	Y	?	?	?	07/13/1888			Y	
Krueger, John F.	52	Germany	Y	Hamburg	New York	01/28/1874	05/11/1898			Y	
Krueger, Wilhelm	32	Germany	Y	Antwerp	Philadelphia	06/16/1887	07/21/1890			Y	
Krueger, William	47	Germany	N	Hamburg	New York	??/??/1851	?			Y	
Kruegmann, Hans Christia	33	Denmark	Y	Hamburg	New York	05/11/1848	11/13/1848	1	251	N	
Kruellmann, Theodore H.	27	Germany	Y	?	New York	05/??/1872	11/02/1872			Y	
Kruemmel, Franz	54	Prussia	Y	Havre	New York	09/12/1850	05/29/1854	10	31	N	
Kruep, John Gerad	31	Hanover	Y	Bremen	New Orleans	11/12/1844	10/13/1851	4	244	N	
Kruesling, S. Bernard	27	Hanover	Y	Bremen	Baltimore	07/18/1844	08/29/1848	22	270	N	
Kruetz, Theobald	42	Germany	Y	Havre	New York	08/08/1866	04/04/1890	19	282	N	
Kruetz, Theobald	42	Germany	Y	Havre	New York	08/08/1866	04/04/1890			Y	
Krug, Alois	24	Wurttemberg	Y	Havre	New York	06/20/1854	10/25/1858	17	100	N	
Krug, Henry	46	Germany	N	Bremen	New York	03/18/1864	?			Y	
Krug, John	26	Germany	Y	Bremen	New York	10/19/1883	12/02/1885			Y	
Krug, Martin	29	Hesse Darmsta	Y	Antwerp	New York	06/26/1847	04/18/1853	8	72	N	
Krug, William	17	Germany	N	?	Baltimore	00/00/1868				Y	10/29/1886
Kruger, August	??	Germany	Y	?	?	?	11/01/1888			Y	
Kruger, John	27	Wurttemberg	Y	Liverpool	New York	05/01/1852	11/13/1855	13	223	N	
Kruger, Wilhelm	42	Germany	Y	Hamburg	New York	03/07/1880	01/08/1883			Y	
Krum, Cyriakus	45	Bavaria	Y	Havre	New York	04/15/1854	05/24/1854	8	507	N	
Krum, Cyriakus	45	Bavaria	Y	Havre	New York	04/15/1854	05/24/1854	9	381	N	
Krumdick, Henry	48	Germany	N	Bremen	New York	05/??/1858	?			Y	
Krumer, H.	25	Germany	Y	Rotterdam	New York	04/15/1880	04/19/1883			Y	
Krumm, William	38	Bavaria	Y	Bremen	New York	09/12/1852	10/07/1854	6	16	N	
Krumme, Herman	24	Hanover	Y	Bremen	New Orleans	12/17/1848	01/21/1852	24	46	N	
Krummel, Franz	54	Prussia	Y	Havre	New York	09/12/1850	05/29/1854	9	448	N	
Krummen, Clemens	??	Germany	Y	?	?	?	10/17/1890			Y	
Krummen, Henry	24	Germany	Y	Rotterdam	New York	10/23/1885	09/03/1888			Y	
Krumpe, Frederick	24	Schwartzburg	Y	Bremen	New York	07/02/1854	07/24/1860	27	236	N	

CITIZENSHIP RECORDS

APPLICANT	AGE	COUNTRY OF ORIGIN	DEC	DEPART PORT	ENTRY PORT	ARRIVE DATE	DEC DATE	VOL	PG.	FLD	NAT DATE
Krumphorn, Robert	37	Germany	Y	Hamburg	New York	05/04/1882	01/03/1887			Y	
Krun, John	27	Nassau	Y	Antwerp	New York	05/??/1850	12/29/1855	13	395	N	
Krun, William	38	Bavaria	Y	Bremen	New York	09/12/1852	10/07/1854	11	17	N	
Krunburger, Peter	23	Bavaria	Y	?	?	?	05/09/1892			Y	
Kruse, B.	27	Germany	Y	Bremen	Baltimore	03/28/1881	10/20/1884			Y	
Kruse, Billy	37	Prussia	Y	Bremen	Philadelphia	10/28/1843	04/29/1850	3	26	N	
Kruse, C. H.	72	Germany	N	Bremen	Baltimore	08/??/1848	?			Y	
Kruse, Ernst	34	Prussia	Y	Bremen	Baltimore	11/11/1854	07/30/1858	16	537	N	
Kruse, Frederick	32	Hanover	Y	Bremen	Philadelphia	06/11/1855	02/02/1860	27	86	N	
Kruse, Henry	30	Hanover	Y	Bremen	Baltimore	05/20/1848	11/01/1852	5	180	N	
Kruse, Henry	30	Hanover	Y	Bremen	Baltimore	05/20/1848	11/01/18??	6	305	N	
Kruse, Henry	33	Mecklenburg	Y	Hamburg	New York	09/21/1850	04/11/1853	8	58	N	
Kruse, Henry	30	Germany	Y	Bremen	New York	06/30/1881	10/22/1883			N	
Kruse, Herman	43	Prussia	Y	Bremen	New Orleans	01/10/1846	02/13/1849	23	76	N	
Kruse, John Bernard	24	Hanover	Y	Bremen	New York	06/18/1849	09/13/1852	25	475	N	
Kruse, John Gerhard	28	Hanover	Y	Bremen	New Orleans	12/12/1854	11/01/1858	17	225	N	
Kruse, Joseph	27	Germany	Y	Rotterdam	New York	10/27/1895	01/02/1903			Y	
Kruse, Joseph	28	Germany	Y	Bremen	New York	07/06/1874	04/06/1887			Y	
Kruse, Leonard	64	Hanover	Y	Bremen	New Orleans	01/18/1845	10/04/1858	17	55	N	
Kruse, William	21	Prussia	Y	Bremen	New York	04/??/1849	12/??/1849	23	389	N	
Kruse, William	48	Prussia	Y	Bremen	New York	06/21/1849	03/29/1856	26	375	N	
Kruse, William	21	Germany	Y	Bremen	New York	06/14/1880	11/01/1883			Y	
Krusemeier, Heinrich	33	Prussia	Y	Bremen	Baltimore	12/24/1854	05/31/1859	17	440	N	
Kruskal, Marcus	39	Russia	Y	Liverpool	New York	09/29/1886	01/27/1888			Y	
Krusmeier, John	38	Prussia	Y	Bremen	New York	05/01/1848	01/29/1853	7	86	N	
Kruss, Otto	30	Germany	Y	Hamburg	New York	05/22/1886	04/10/1890			Y	
Krussel, J. Hermann	22	Germany	Y	Bremen	Baltimore	03/21/1883	04/04/1886	19	36	N	
Krussel, J. Hermann	22	Germany	Y	Bremen	Baltimore	03/21/1883	04/06/1886			Y	
Krusze, Charles	28	Kurhessen	Y	Bremen	New York	06/15/1853	07/16/1855	11	398	N	
Krysling, George	22	Hanover	Y	Bremen	New Orleans	11/20/1854	02/23/1859	16	332	N	
Kubbler, Joseph	21	Germany	Y	Havre	New York	02/05/1887	02/13/1890			Y	
Kubel, Charles	31	Baden	Y	Havre	New Orleans	06/01/1848	09/09/1852	25	428	N	
Kubler, Henry	??	Germany	Y	?	?	?	11/21/1879			Y	
Kubler, Jacob	27	Germany	Y	Havre	New York	09/06/1889	07/05/1890			Y	
Kuchle, Joseph	??	Germany	Y	?	?	07/18/1893	12/20/1893			Y	
Kuckelmann, Henry	40	Germany	Y	Bremen	New York	01/14/1883	05/07/1890			Y	
Kuckelmann, Theodore	26	Germany	Y	Liverpool	New York	10/18/1883	05/07/1890			Y	
Kuckertz, Jacob Hubert	36	Germany	Y	Antwerp	New York	01/20/1883	10/30/1889			Y	
Kuckewith, C. H.	27	Prussia	Y	Bremen	New York	09/26/1859	01/03/1860	27	22	N	
Kudell, Ernst	23	Prussia	Y	Hamburg	Buffalo	09/??/1853	09/22/1855	13	119	N	
Kuderer, Ferdinand	21	Baden	Y	Havre	New Orleans	04/??/1846	01/??/1850	23	530	N	
Kuebler, Godlieb	24	Wurttemberg	Y	Havre	New York	07/20/1850	10/28/1858	17	144	N	
Kuebler, Stanislaus	28	Switzerland	Y	Havre	New York	01/14/1853	10/19/1857	15	461	N	
Kuebler, William	14	Germany	N	?	New York	00/00/1875				Y	10/28/1886
Kuechler, August	28	Prussia	Y	Bremen	New York	05/24/1859	04/03/1862	18	295	N	
Kueck, Henry	27	Hanover	Y	Bremen	New Orleans	11/26/1852	11/08/1858	17	303	N	
Kuefer, Frank	26	Germany	Y	Havre	New York	04/30/1891	07/30/1894			Y	
Kueffner, Frederick	35	Germany	Y	Bremen	New York	05/26/1883	03/13/1884			Y	
Kueffner, Konrad	39	Germany	Y	Bremen	Baltimore	08/11/1893	08/20/1896			Y	
Kuehhorn, Frederick	24	Bavaria	Y	Bremen	Baltimore	05/08/1848	02/12/1849	23	52	N	
Kuehhorn, John	22	Bavaria	Y	Bremen	Baltimore	07/06/1848	02/12/1849	23	51	N	
Kuehl, Herman	26	Hanover	Y	Bremen	New Orleans	??/01/1849	04/17/1855	11	263	N	
Kuehlenborg, John	25	Hanover	Y	Bremen	Baltimore	02/??/1848	02/20/1856	26	106	N	
Kuehn, Arthur	23	Germany	Y	Bremen	Baltimore	07/08/1893	09/14/1896			Y	
Kuehne, John	??	Germany	Y	?	?	?	09/30/1880			Y	
Kuehner, Max F.	23	Germany	Y	?	?	?	06/26/1897			Y	
Kuehnert, Robert	38	Prussia	N	Danzig	New York	01/16/1868	?			Y	
Kuehnle, John	43	Germany	Y	Hamburg	New York	03/16/1872	02/18/1892			Y	
Kuehnle, John Phillip	24	Baden	Y	Havre	New York	05/26/1847	01/17/1850	23	519	N	

216

CITIZENSHIP RECORDS

APPLICANT	AGE	COUNTRY OF ORIGIN	DEC	DEPART PORT	ENTRY PORT	ARRIVE DATE	DEC DATE	VOL	PG.	FLD	NAT DATE
Kuehnle, Joseph	32	Hohenzoller H	Y	Rotterdam	Richmond VA	07/04/1844	08/07/1848	22	60	N	
Kuehnle, Julius	29	Germany	Y	Havre	New York	04/05/1882	11/14/1887			Y	
Kuehnlein, John	32	Germany	Y	Hamburg	New York	02/26/1884	10/14/1891			Y	
Kuehter, Henry	32	Germany	N	Bremen	Baltimore	07/01/1875	?			Y	
Kuemmerle, Joseph Anton	38	Switzerland	Y	Havre	New York	05/12/1880	03/20/1889			Y	
Kuemmerle, Karl	24	Germany	Y	Bremen	Baltimore	08/23/1890	12/05/1892			Y	
Kuennemaier, William	46	Germany	Y	Bremen	New York	11/05/1862	10/30/1886			Y	
Kuennemann, Charles	25	Hanover	Y	Hamburg	New York	06/27/1854	10/09/1854	11	164	N	
Kuenneth, Charles	26	Bavaria	Y	Bremen	Baltimore	08/21/1849	03/29/1850	2	282	N	
Kuenning, Herman Henry W	27	Hanover	Y	Bremen	New Orleans	10/??/1852	10/16/1855	11	252	N	
Kueny, Joseph	28	Germany	Y	Havre	New York	09/02/1891	03/26/1897			Y	
Kuenz, Markus	17	Germany	Y	?	New York	03/00/1881	06/17/1872			Y	03/26/1884
Kuenzi, John	25	Switzerland	Y	Havre	New York	04/18/1854	05/13/1854	9	309	N	
Kuenzi, John	60	Switzerland	N	Havre	New York	04/??/1854	?			Y	
Kues, Frank	31	Germany	Y	Bremen	New York	11/27/1885	04/22/1895			Y	
Kues, Heinrich	24	Germany	Y	Bremen	New York	05/23/1883	12/08/1885			Y	
Kues, Herman	??	Germany	Y	?	?	?	02/06/1889			Y	
Kueth, John	17	Germany	N	?	New York	00/00/1881				Y	10/18/1886
Kueven, Theodore	36	Hanover	Y	Bremen	New Orleans	06/28/1847	08/15/1848	22	139	N	
Kuewen, Rudolf	29	Hanover	Y	Bremen	New York	06/24/1845	02/14/1849	23	107	N	
Kugel, Joseph	22	Hungary	Y	Hamburg	New York	05/30/1887	06/05/1889			Y	
Kugele, Jacob Frederick	24	Germany	Y	Havre	New York	04/28/1881	10/10/1887			Y	
Kugler, Karl	33	Germany	Y	Antwerp	Philadelphia	04/01/1890	10/29/1900			Y	
Kugler, Mathew	28	Prussia	Y	Havre	New York	01/13/1854	03/19/1858	16	423	N	
Kuhl, Charles	28	Germany	Y	Antwerp	New York	09/12/1885	07/21/1891			Y	
Kuhl, Conrad	28	Hesse Darmsta	Y	Havre	New Orleans	11/18/1852	01/03/1856	13	422	N	
Kuhl, John	38	Germany	Y	Hamburg	New York	04/??/1886	04/26/1894			Y	
Kuhl, Malte	35	Germany	Y	?	?	?	09/10/1888			Y	
Kuhle, Frederick	26	Prussia	Y	Bremen	New Orleans	05/07/1854	03/28/1856	26	367	N	
Kuhlenberg, Gerard Henry	40	Hanover	Y	Bremen	New York	06/16/1853	10/09/1854	6	171	N	
Kuhlenberg, Gerard Henry	40	Hanover	Y	Bremen	New York	06/16/1853	10/09/1854	11	174	N	
Kuhler, Constantine	28	Germany	Y	?	New York	05/??/1887	10/26/1892			Y	
Kuhlman, Frederick H.	??	Hanover	Y	Bremen	Baltimore	11/08/18??	10/11/1848	1	124	N	
Kuhlmann, Albert	27	Germany	Y	Bremen	Baltimore	05/22/1879	12/22/1881			Y	
Kuhlmann, Arnold	25	Germany	Y	Bremen	Baltimore	05/22/1879	12/22/1881			Y	
Kuhlmann, Bernhard	29	Germany	Y	Antwerp	New York	04/07/1883	12/10/1892			Y	
Kuhlmann, Christ	25	Germany	Y	Bremen	New York	05/04/1882	12/04/1884			Y	
Kuhlmann, Felix	??	Germany	Y	?	?	?	12/08/1890			Y	
Kuhlmann, Frank	34	Germany	Y	Bremen	Baltimore	05/07/1873	10/09/1880			Y	
Kuhlmann, Fred	28	Hanover	Y	Bremen	New York	10/04/1846	03/02/1852	24	210	N	
Kuhlmann, H.	25	Germany	Y	Rotterdam	New York	05/30/1880	04/25/1883			Y	
Kuhlmann, Heinrich	39	Germany	Y	Bremen	Baltimore	08/29/1882	02/19/1890			Y	
Kuhlmann, Heinrich	22	Germany	Y	Bremen	Baltimore	06/22/1879	01/07/1881			Y	
Kuhlmann, Henry	23	Oldenburg	Y	Bremen	Baltimore	11/08/1848	11/01/1851	4	461	N	
Kuhn, August	47	Mecklenburg S	Y	Hamburg	Galveston	08/28/1846	05/02/1854	8	345	N	
Kuhn, August	47	Mecklenburg S	Y	Hamburg	Galveston	08/28/1846	05/02/1854	9	218	N	
Kuhn, Carl Frederick	42	Wurttemberg	Y	Havre	New Orleans	01/08/1847	10/06/1854	10	473	N	
Kuhn, Carl Frederick	42	Wurttemberg	Y	Havre	New Orleans	01/08/1847	10/06/1854	12	412	N	
Kuhn, Charles	31	Germany	Y	Bremen	New York	09/26/1882	10/21/1889			Y	
Kuhn, Daniel	39	Germany	Y	Bremen	New York	07/26/1880	09/21/1883			Y	
Kuhn, Frank	23	Bavaria	Y	Antwerp	New York	11/25/1849	03/28/1853	7	437	N	
Kuhn, Franz	24	Germany	Y	Bremen	Baltimore	07/02/1891	10/28/1892			Y	
Kuhn, Fred	50	Germany	Y	Bremen	Baltimore	04/01/1874	10/27/1887			Y	
Kuhn, Fritz	28	Germany	Y	Bremen	New York	11/07/1887	04/14/1892			Y	
Kuhn, George	26	Bavaria	Y	Haarburg	New York	09/11/1854	10/02/1856	14	167	N	
Kuhn, George Jacob	23	Bavaria	Y	Havre	New Orleans	12/26/1852	05/12/1854	8	431	N	
Kuhn, George Jacob	23	Bavaria	Y	Havre	New Orleans	12/26/1852	05/12/1854	9	304	N	
Kuhn, John	30	Germany	Y	Bremen	Baltimore	10/13/1880	10/02/1888			Y	
Kuhn, John Adam	32	Bavaria	Y	Havre	New York	05/15/1852	02/28/1853	7	240	N	

CITIZENSHIP RECORDS

APPLICANT	AGE	COUNTRY OF ORIGIN	DEC	DEPART PORT	ENTRY PORT	ARRIVE DATE	DEC DATE	VOL	PG.	FLD	NAT DATE
Kuhn, Joseph	30	Bavaria	Y	Antwerp	New York	08/15/1853	05/09/1859	17	405	N	
Kuhn, Joseph	40	Germany	Y	Bremen	New York	04/12/1870	09/00/1881			Y	
Kuhn, Joseph	51	Germany	Y	Bremen	New York	04/12/1870	09/??/1881	28	326	N	
Kuhn, Joseph	29	Germany	Y	Bremen	New York	04/12/1870	09/00/1881			Y	
Kuhn, Peter	30	Bavaria	Y	Havre	New York	11/08/1849	11/12/1852	5	274	N	
Kuhn, Peter	30	Bavaria	Y	Havre	New York	11/08/1849	11/12/1852	6	398	N	
Kuhn, Peter	22	Bavaria	Y	Havre	New Orleans	04/16/1852	10/07/1854	10	524	N	
Kuhn, Peter	22	Bavaria	Y	Havre	New Orleans	04/16/1852	10/07/1854	12	463	N	
Kuhn, Philip	25	Prussia	Y	London	New York	04/23/1854	07/10/1856	14	303	N	
Kuhn, Valentine	22	Germany	Y	Bremen	New York	04/28/1885	08/01/1889			Y	
Kuhn, William	26	Baden	Y	London	New York	11/06/1854	05/15/1859	17	415	N	
Kuhn, William	24	Germany	Y	?	?	?	03/04/1884			Y	
Kuhne, Louis	??	Germany	Y	?	?	?	11/03/1884			Y	
Kuhner, Fredrick	26	Wurtemburg, G	Y	?	New York	03/22/1887	10/20/1892			Y	
Kuhnle, John	22	Baden	Y	Havre	New York	09/28/1856	09/01/1857	15	217	N	
Kuhr, Henry	22	Hanover	Y	Bremen	New Orleans	05/11/1852	09/21/1854	10	142	N	
Kuhr, Henry	22	Hanover	Y	Bremen	New Orleans	05/11/1852	09/21/1854	12	81	N	
Kuhr, Herman	22	Hanover	Y	Bremen	New Orleans	11/22/1849	04/04/1853	8	18	N	
Kuin, Anton	31	Holland	Y	Rotterdam	New York	04/27/1856	10/09/1860	27	466	N	
Kulenborg, Gerhard Herma	45	Germany	Y	Bremen	Baltimore	09/00/1858	10/28/1880			Y	
Kull, Frederick	24	Germany	Y	Amsterdam	New York	04/24/1881	10/14/1886			Y	
Kull, Jacob	31	Germany	Y	Antwerp	New York	04/23/1881	03/18/1885			Y	
Kullmann, W. P.	19	Germany	Y	Bremen	New York	06/21/1883	08/04/1885			Y	
Kulmann, John	30	Austria	Y	Bremen	New York	08/28/1849	04/16/1852	24	515	N	
Kulueke, August	40	Germany	Y	Bremen	Baltimore	08/27/1881	06/18/1888			Y	
Kumerle, Christian	26	Baden	Y	Havre	New Orleans	03/12/1854	12/05/1855	13	291	N	
Kumey, John	23	Ireland	Y	Liverpool	New Orleans	??/28/1848	10/24/1851	4	393	N	
Kummer, Andrew	32	Bavaria	Y	Havre	New Orleans	03/24/1854	03/08/1858	16	383	N	
Kummer, August	40	Germany	N	Bremen	New York	09/??/1867	?			Y	
Kummer, Ernest	19	Berne, Switze	Y	?	?	??/??/1880	06/30/1881			Y	
Kummerle, John Christian	30	Wurttemberg	Y	Havre	New York	09/16/1852	02/14/1853	7	149	N	
Kummerlen, Adolph	23	Wurttemberg	Y	Havre	New York	03/31/1852	09/22/1855	13	120	N	
Kummler, John	29	Germany	Y	Bremen	New York	10/11/1883	10/06/1892			Y	
Kumstat, Franz	31	Austria	Y	Bremen	Baltimore	05/20/1888	01/04/1890			Y	
Kunath, Frederick Alexan	28	Saxony	Y	Hamburg	New York	09/09/1853	02/12/1856	26	78	N	
Kunckel, Jacob	27	Bavaria	Y	Hamburg	Buffalo	10/09/1854	11/30/1857	16	58	N	
Kungler, Nicolaus	32	Prussia	Y	Havre	New Orleans	03/08/1852	04/22/1854	9	113	N	
Kunkel, John	41	Germany	Y	Hamburg	New York	05/12/1880	02/07/1884			Y	
Kunkelloveski, Herman	35	Germany	Y	Antwerp	New York	09/15/1881	10/23/1888			Y	
Kunkemoller, Frank	24	Germany	Y	Rotterdam	New York	10/18/1881	10/21/1886	19	62	N	
Kunkemoller, Frank	24	Germany	Y	Rotterdam	New York	10/18/1881	10/21/1886			Y	
Kunkemoller, George	42	Germany	N	Holland	New York	06/10/1873	?			Y	
Kunkemoller, Henry	30	Germany	Y	Rotterdam	New York	08/05/1881	10/21/1887	19	61	N	
Kunkemoller, Henry	30	Germany	Y	Rotterdam	New York	08/05/1881	10/21/1886			Y	
Kunkemoller, Herman	17	Germany	N	?	New York	00/00/1881				Y	10/21/1886
Kunkemoller, Johann	28	Germany	Y	Rotterdam	New York	08/05/1881	01/20/1888			Y	
Kunkemoller, Wilh.	14	Germany	N	?	New York	00/00/1881				Y	10/17/1888
Kunker, Henry	30	Hanover	Y	Bremen	New Orleans	11/24/1849	09/27/1854	10	271	N	
Kunker, Henry	30	Hanover	Y	Bremen	New Orleans	11/24/1849	09/27/1854	12	210	N	
Kunnen, A. S.	79	Prussia	N	Bremen	New York	09/??/1836	??/??/1838	28	138	N	09/??/1841
Kunnen, A. S.	27	Prussia	N	Bremen	New York	09/00/1836	09/00/1838			Y	09/00/1841
Kunnen, Henry	32	Germany	Y	Bremen	New York	05/29/1881	10/15/1890			Y	
Kunning, William	24	Hanover	Y	Bremen	New Orleans	11/02/1853	11/05/1855	13	166	N	
Kunsemueller, Christ	24	Germany	Y	Bremen	Baltimore	03/27/1887	02/15/1892			Y	
Kunsi, John	25	Switzerland	Y	Havre	New York	04/18/1854	05/13/1854	8	436	N	
Kuntz, Conrad	27	Bavaria	Y	Havre	New Orleans	03/24/1852	03/24/1856	26	291	N	
Kuntz, Ignatius	63	Baden	Y	Havre	New York	10/31/1850	04/20/1854	9	91	N	
Kuntz, John	46	Germany	N	Havre	New York	06/22/1871	?			Y	
Kuntz, Philip	24	Bavaria	Y	Havre	New York	07/01/1853	10/14/1857	15	418	N	

CITIZENSHIP RECORDS

APPLICANT	AGE	COUNTRY OF ORIGIN	DEC	DEPART PORT	ENTRY PORT	ARRIVE DATE	DEC DATE	VOL	PG.	FLD	NAT DATE
Kuntz, Phillip	21	Bavaria	Y	Havre	New York	10/07/1846	11/14/1848	1	292	N	
Kunz, Gottlieb	29	Baden	Y	Havre	New York	04/24/1852	08/22/1855	11	481	N	
Kunz, Henry	40	Germany	N	Bremen	New York	03/14/1871	?			Y	
Kunz, John	33	Switzerland	Y	Havre	New Orleans	12/28/1854	02/04/1861	18	88	N	
Kunz, Paul Jung	54	Germany	Y	Bremen	Baltimore	04/10/1881	01/29/1892			Y	
Kunz, Valentine	64	Germany	N	Havre	New Orleans	02/??/1847	?			Y	
Kunze, Hugo	33	Germany	Y	Hamburg	New York	08/28/1888	10/08/1894			Y	
Kunzel, George	30	Germany	Y	Havre	New York	06/21/1882	09/07/1885			Y	
Kunzer, Martin	31	Bavaria	Y	Bremen	New York	09/18/1868	03/30/1872	18	480	N	
Kunzer, Martin	27	Bavaria	Y	Bremen	New York	09/??/1868	05/00/1872			Y	
Kunzla, Franz	23	Baden	Y	Havre	New York	03/01/1856	02/09/1860	27	95	N	
Kunzler, John Jacob	??	Switzerland	Y	?	?	05/13/1892	08/27/1897			Y	
Kunzler, Nicholas	32	Prussia	Y	Havre	New Orleans	03/08/1852	04/22/1854	8	242	N	
Kunzler, Nicholas	26	Prussia	Y	Havre	New York	10/15/1854	01/02/1858	16	289	N	
Kunzmann, L.	58	Germany	N	Liverpool	New York	09/??/1855	?			Y	
Kuper, B.	50	Germany	Y	Bremen	Baltimore	08/29/1881	05/22/1884			Y	
Kuper, John Gerhard	32	Germany	Y	Bremen	Baltimore	04/27/1888	11/06/1889			Y	
Kuper, Wilhelm	27	Germany	Y	Antwerp	New York	05/19/1896	07/23/1896			Y	
Kuperman, Moses G.	49	Russia	Y	Hamburg	Philadelphia	05/20/1884	01/28/1890			Y	
Kupferschmid, Jacob	41	Germany	Y	?	New York	??/??/1881	12/12/1887			Y	
Kupferschmid, Leo	28	Wurttemberg	Y	Havre	New York	04/24/1854	10/09/1854	11	94	N	
Kupferschmidt, Leo	28	Wurttemberg	Y	Havre	New York	04/24/1854	10/09/1854	6	91	N	
Kupler, Xavier	21	Germany	N	Havre	New York	05/00/1867				Y	11/01/1888
Kuppens, Francis X.	??	Belgium	Y	?	?	?	10/11/1866			Y	
Kuren, John	29	Germany	Y	Havre	New York	08/09/1879	08/12/1884			Y	
Kurlander, Heinrich	24	Prussia	Y	Bremen	New Orleans	01/05/1856	09/20/1858	16	158	N	
Kurre, Gerhard	50	Oldenburg	Y	Bremen	Baltimore	09/04/1847	01/22/1849	1	489	N	
Kurrus, August	35	Germany	Y	?	?	?	05/27/1879			Y	
Kurs, George Henry	40	Germany	Y	Bremen	Baltimore	09/12/1882	12/31/1900			Y	
Kurtz, Albert	??	?	Y	?	?	?	11/00/1884			Y	
Kurtz, Antoinette Friedr	32	Prussia	Y	Liverpool	Portland	01/15/1870	01/22/1873	18	550	N	
Kurtz, Frederick William	24	Hanover	Y	Bremen	New Orleans	12/02/1855	06/17/1861	18	195	N	
Kurtz, Henry	34	Hanover	Y	Bremen	Baltimore	11/01/1846	10/02/1848	1	12	N	
Kurtz, William Albert	43	Prussia	Y	Liverpool	Portland	01/15/1870	01/22/1873	18	548	N	
Kurtze, H.	33	Germany	Y	Liverpool	New York	11/03/1883	10/27/1886			Y	
Kurz, Friedrich	26	Wurttemberg	Y	Liverpool	New York	06/10/1852	12/21/1852	5	436	N	
Kurz, George	29	Wurttemberg	Y	Havre	New York	05/09/1854	12/22/1857	16	240	N	
Kurz, John	33	Germany	Y	Havre	New York	06/04/1882	02/18/1885			Y	
Kurz, Leonhart	22	Bavaria	Y	Bremen	New York	07/27/1854	09/14/1857	15	265	N	
Kurz, W.	28	Germany	Y	Bremen	Baltimore	08/12/1880	09/22/1884			Y	
Kurzmieraitis, Anton	26	Russia	Y	Bremen	Baltimore	03/20/1889	12/29/1892			Y	
Kusel, Henry	35	Germany	Y	Bremen	New York	07/??/1870	08/30/1884			Y	
Kusgoerd, Alexander	??	Prussia	Y	?	?	?	12/09/1891			Y	
Kusgoerd, Henry A.	36	Prussia	Y	Rotterdam	Baltimore	09/17/1836	05/31/1852	25	159	N	
Kusiek, Thomas	26	Ireland	Y	Liverpool	New York	08/31/1850	04/23/1853	8	101	N	
Kusnierajtys, Frank	51	Poland	Y	Hamburg	New York	06/01/1884	09/15/1893			Y	
Kuster, Samuel	25	Switzerland	Y	Havre	New York	03/05/1860	06/02/1862	18	345	N	
Kusworm, Daniel	48	Germany	N	Hamburg	New York	08/??/1860	?			Y	
Kutzberger, Frederick	??	Germany	Y	?	?	05/??/1884	12/28/1895			Y	
Kutzberger, Konrad	27	Germany	Y	Bremen	Baltimore	04/25/1891	05/29/1894			Y	
Kutzmann, Phillip	24	Wurttemberg	Y	Antwerp	New York	10/01/1850	04/04/1853	7	531	N	
Kuyper, Cornelius	36	Holland	Y	Rotterdam	New York	04/24/1891	01/24/1894			Y	
Kuyper, Morinus	25	Holland	Y	Rotterdam	New York	04/14/1889	04/19/1892			Y	
Kylius, Ferdinand	21	Baden	Y	Havre	New Orleans	06/02/1849	06/18/1851	3	393	N	
Kyne, Martin	25	Ireland	Y	Galway	New Orleans	03/04/1849	03/13/1851	3	275	N	
LaForce, Albert E.	23	Canada	Y	Canada	Detroit	10/15/1894	10/04/1899			Y	
LaKamp, John Henry	23	Hanover	Y	Bremen	Baltimore	09/22/1854	11/05/1858	17	280	N	
Laagner, Joseph	40	Nassau	Y	Bremen	Baltimore	07/27/1857	07/05/1860	27	203	N	
Laakmann, Henry	24	Brunswick	Y	Bremen	New York	06/20/1857	10/09/1860	27	474	N	

CITIZENSHIP RECORDS

APPLICANT	AGE	COUNTRY OF ORIGIN	DEC	DEPART PORT	ENTRY PORT	ARRIVE DATE	DEC DATE	VOL	PG.	FLD	NAT DATE
Laarke, Gerhard Henry	30	Hanover	Y	Bremen	New Orleans	11/13/1842	08/15/1848	22	140	N	
Laarmann, Rudolph	29	Holland	Y	Bremen	New Orleans	10/28/1852	11/15/1852	5	289	N	
Laatsch, Carl	32	Prussia	Y	Hamburg	New York	05/31/1867	02/01/1872	18	461	N	
Laban, Martin	42	Holland	N	Liverpool	New York	09/18/1872	?			Y	
Labbert, Henry	21	Hanover	Y	Bremen	Baltimore	09/18/1856	05/21/1859	17	418	N	
Labbing, Henry	52	Germany		Bremen	Baltimore	05/28/1878	10/20/1892			Y	
Labermeier, Lorenz	28	Germany	Y	Antwerp	New York	06/14/1883	10/25/1886			Y	
Labinski, William	31	Prussia	Y	Hamburg	New York	09/10/1857	02/10/1858	16	101	N	
Laby, Thomas James	29	England	Y	London	New York	11/11/1847	03/09/1852	24	271	N	
Lace, William	29	England	Y	Liverpool	New York	05/28/1842	02/12/1849	23	61	N	
Lacherer, John	36	Austria	Y	Havre	New York	04/12/1884	10/15/1890	19	288	N	
Lacherer, John	36	Austria	Y	Havre	New York	04/12/1884	10/15/1890			Y	
Lachering, John Henry	24	Hanover	Y	Bremen	New York	06/26/1845	08/12/1848	22	97	N	
Lachman, Zeke	45	Russia	Y	Bremen	Baltimore	08/15/1888	08/22/1899			Y	
Lachmanski, Gustav	??	Germany	Y	?	?	?	01/21/1873			Y	
Lachora, Stamaty	35	Korfu	Y	Smyrna	Boston	10/??/1853	05/20/1854	9	354	N	
Lachore, Stamaty	35	Korfu	Y	Smyrna	Boston	10/??/1853	05/20/1854	8	480	N	
Lachtrupp, Henry	21	Germany	Y	Bremen	New York	05/09/1889	10/14/1891			Y	
Lack, Charles	26	Germany	Y	Havre	New York	01/24/1892	02/24/1893			Y	
Lacker, Casper Henry	22	Prussia	Y	Bremen	New Orleans	11/10/1854	03/28/1858	16	441	N	
Laderchi, Angelo	??	Italy	Y	?	?	?	09/16/1885			Y	
Laear, Christian	28	Saxony	Y	Bremen	New York	05/01/1849	07/02/1851	3	478	N	
Laeckamp, Conrad Henry	30	Hanover	Y	Bremen	Baltimore	10/18/1856	08/22/1860	27	307	N	
Laeger, Joseph A.	33	Switzerland	Y	?	?	?	05/07/1900			Y	
Laeneng, ?	??	Bavaria	Y	?	?	??/28/18??	10/24/1850	2	296	N	
Laesche, Clem	27	Germany	Y	Bremen	New York	04/02/1895	12/30/1897			Y	
Laesche, Frank	20	Germany	Y	Antwerp	New York	06/01/1887	08/15/1887			Y	
Laetsch, John	33	Switzerland	Y	Liverpool	New York	12/03/1857	02/15/1858	16	308	N	
Laeubly, Theobald	24	France	Y	Havre	New Orleans	04/25/1854	03/24/1856	26	273	N	
Laffey, James	28	Ireland	Y	Liverpool	New York	12/14/1878	10/12/1885	19	20	N	
Laffin, Mark	22	Ireland	Y	Liverpool	New York	12/16/1852	02/04/1856	26	17	N	
Lagai, Jacob (Laque)	33	Germany	Y	Amsterdam	New York	10/26/1884	09/03/1892			Y	
Lage, Clemens	23	Germany	Y	Hanover	Baltimore	10/??/1877	11/01/1880			Y	
Lageman, Henry	33	Hanover	Y	Bremen	New Orleans	11/30/1844	10/05/1848	22	439	N	
Lagemann, Fred	56	Germany	Y	Bremen	New York	07/14/1864	10/19/1894			Y	
Lagemann, John Bernard	33	Oldenburg	Y	Bremen	New Orleans	11/31/1849	09/25/1854	10	210	N	
Lagemann, John Bernard	33	Oldenburg	Y	Bremen	New Orleans	11/31/1849	09/25/1854	12	149	N	
Lagemann, Wilhelm	27	Germany	Y	Bremen	Baltimore	06/07/1881	09/16/1884			Y	
Lah, H.	22	Hanover	Y	Bremen	Baltimore	05/10/1858	04/04/1861	18	132	N	
Lahe, John Bernard	25	Hanover	Y	Bremen	New Orleans	12/??/1848	03/28/1851	3	365	N	
Lahmer, William	27	Germany	Y	Bremen	Baltimore	06/24/1889	10/14/1890			Y	
Lahnip, Conrad	34	Bavaria	Y	Bremen	Baltimore	07/04/1845	08/26/1848	22	255	N	
Lahrmann, Gerhard	25	Hanover	Y	Bremen	New York	05/04/1848	02/19/1849	23	210	N	
Laible, George	26	Germany	Y	Havre	New York	10/18/1882	06/06/1885			Y	
Laible, George	39	Germany	Y	Havre	New York	06/21/1870	12/28/1887			Y	
Laidlaw, Henry	23	Scotland	Y	?	New York	??/??/1880	10/08/1883			Y	
Laidlaw, Robert	46	Scotland	N	Glasgow	New York	04/17/1875	12/03/1879	28	423	N	03/08/1882
Laile, Charles	51	Germany	N	Havre	New York	05/??/1846	?			Y	
Lainck, John	36	Germany	Y	Amsterdam	New York	04/30/1881	08/25/1891			Y	
Laing, August	59	Germany	N	?	New York	06/??/1851	?			Y	
Lais, Jacob	24	Wuertemberg	Y	Havre	New York	03/07/1852	02/23/1856	26	118	N	
Laituf, Elais	32	Syria	Y	Marseilles	New York	12/08/1888	01/08/1894			Y	
Laiveling, Joseph	17	Germany	N	?	Baltimore	00/00/1881				Y	10/23/1888
Lakamp, David	45	Germany	N	Bremen	New York	08/??/1863	?			Y	
Lake, Francis Henry	38	Hanover	Y	Bremen	New Orleans	10/20/1852	08/18/1857	15	155	N	
Lake, Gerhard	51	Hanover	Y	Bremen	New Orleans	01/28/1846	01/04/1851	2	448	N	
Lake, Gerhard Hermann	42	Hanover	Y	Bremen	New Orleans	01/01/1847	02/05/1860	27	118	N	
Lake, John Henry	32	Hanover	Y	Bremen	New Orleans	12/20/1848	01/23/1852	24	62	N	
Lalbarre, Nicholas	65	Germany	Y	Bremen	New Orleans	11/17/1856	10/22/1896			Y	

CITIZENSHIP RECORDS

APPLICANT	AGE	COUNTRY OF ORIGIN	DEC	DEPART PORT	ENTRY PORT	ARRIVE DATE	DEC DATE	VOL	PG.	FLD	NAT DATE
Lamarche, Charles	48	France	Y	Havre	New York	07/28/1848	08/11/1851	4	110	N	
Lamarre, Henry	60	Germany	Y	Bremen	New York	04/07/1884	08/07/1900			Y	
Lamb, Jeremiah	57	England	Y	London	New York	07/03/1848	03/09/1857	15	82	N	
Lamb, John	21	Ireland	Y	Liverpool	New Orleans	04/21/1848	01/25/1849	1	518	N	
Lamb, John	25	Ireland	Y	Liverpool	New York	04/15/1857	01/04/1858	16	300	N	
Lamb, Michael	35	Ireland	N	Queenstown	New York	06/05/1869	?			Y	
Lambers, John Herman Ber	27	Hanover	Y	Bremen	New York	??/06/1853	04/28/1855	11	320	N	
Lambert, Charles	21	Baden	Y	Havre	New ?	03/??/1852	11/04/1856	14	459	N	
Lambert, Jacob	30	Baden	Y	Havre	New York	10/09/1845	08/11/1848	22	93	N	
Lambert, James	24	Ireland	Y	Liverpool	New Orleans	11/04/1848	12/29/1852	5	466	N	
Lambert, Nic	28	Germany	Y	Antwerp	New York	08/28/1890	01/26/1893			Y	
Lambion, Pitt	26	Holland	Y	Antwerp	New York	05/27/1848	10/13/1851	4	227	N	
Lamker, Conrad	30	Hanover	Y	Bremen	New York	06/??/1845	01/27/1853	7	74	N	
Lamles, Barney	24	Hanover	Y	Havre	New Orleans	05/01/1849	03/16/1851	3	382	N	
Lamm, Hermann	43	Germany	Y	Havre	New York	09/20/1882	04/06/1894			Y	
Lamm, Reinhard	44	Germany	Y	Antwerp	New York	10/18/1886	10/02/1891			Y	
Lammens, Henry	39	Germany	N	Bremen	Baltimore	09/??/1867	?			Y	
Lammerding, Frank Henry	45	Germany	Y	Bremen	New York	09/19/1878	09/21/1882			Y	
Lammerding, Joseph	22	Germany	Y	Hanover	Baltimore	10/28/1877	11/27/1880			Y	
Lammerding, Otto	22	Germany	Y	Bremen	Baltimore	11/19/1883	12/23/1886			Y	
Lammering, Bernard	34	Prussia	Y	Bremen	New Orleans	11/09/1844	10/02/1848	22	376	N	
Lammers, Charles	19	Germany	N	Bremen	New Orleans	12/00/1842	00/00/1843			Y	00/00/1847
Lammers, Charles (Carl)	64	Germany	N	Bremen	New Orleans	12/??/1842	??/??/1843	28	132	N	??/??/1878
Lammers, Herman Henry	24	Oldenburg	Y	Bremen	New Orleans	02/04/1849	01/19/1852	24	28	N	
Lammers, John	25	Hanover	Y	Bremen	New Orleans	06/23/1853	08/15/1855	11	437	N	
Lammers, John	37	Germany	Y	Bremen	Baltimore	10/16/1889	01/30/1893			Y	
Lammers, John Gerrard He	37	Prussia	Y	Bremen	New Orleans	06/02/1842	10/05/1848	1	57	N	
Lammers, Joseph	31	Oldenburg	Y	Bremen	New Orleans	12/30/1846	01/27/1849	1	525	N	
Lammers, William	29	Prussia	Y	Bremen	New Orleans	06/07/1850	10/22/1852	5	54	N	
Lammess, Carl	26	Germany	Y	Bremen	New York	04/15/1883	08/15/1883			Y	
Lammung, John Herman	??	Hanover	Y	Bremen	Buffalo	08/20/1847	03/24/1851	3	314	N	
Lampart, Karl	27	Prussia	Y	Bremen	New York	07/03/1857	07/09/1860	27	215	N	
Lampe, August	31	Germany	Y	Bremen	New York	11/04/1890	11/04/1897			Y	
Lampe, Bernard	25	Germany	Y	Rotterdam	New York	02/20/1893	08/02/1897			Y	
Lampe, Frank	30	Hanover	Y	Bremen	Baltimore	11/01/1846	04/25/1853	8	120	N	
Lampe, Franz	23	Germany	Y	Rotterdam	New York	09/24/1884	12/15/1886			Y	
Lampe, Fritz	31	Germany	Y	Bremen	Baltimore	08/08/1883	07/31/1886			Y	
Lampe, Gottlieb	21	Germany	Y	Bremen	Baltimore	03/28/1880	10/08/1883			Y	
Lampe, H.	34	Germany	Y	Bremen	New York	04/??/1866	10/14/1880			Y	
Lampe, Henry	21	Hanover	Y	Bremen	New Orleans	01/16/1853	02/04/1856	26	16	N	
Lamper, John	24	Hanover	Y	Bremen	New Orleans	12/??/1847	11/??/1849	23	310	N	
Lampert, Alois	27	Germany	Y	?	?	09/27/1883	04/05/1886			Y	
Lampert, Simon	21	Bavaria	Y	Bremen	New York	07/04/1845	01/??/1849	1	492	N	
Lamping, August	35	Germany	N	Rotterdam	New York	02/??/1872	?			Y	
Lamping, Bernard	30	Germany	Y	Bremen	Baltimore	11/28/1890	10/24/1896			Y	
Lamping, Bernard	29	Germany	Y	Bremen	Baltimore	05/19/1892	04/29/1895			Y	
Lamping, F.	21	Oldenburg	Y	Bremerhafen	Baltimore	09/01/1858	01/30/1861	18	80	N	
Lampp, Daniel	31	Germany	Y	Havre	New York	08/17/1893	10/28/1898			Y	
Lamppert, Anton	29	Baden	Y	Rotterdam	New York	12/02/1847	01/??/1850	23	485	N	
Lamprecht, Konrad	23	Germany	Y	?	Baltimore	??/??/1874	08/19/1878			Y	
Lanahan, Edward	50	Ireland	Y	Canada	Boston	10/27/1843	03/06/1850	2	163	N	
Lanbach, Christian	25	Nassau	Y	London	New York	05/05/1860	09/03/1860	27	324	N	
Landau, Louis	17	Russia	N	?	New York	00/00/1883				Y	10/20/1888
Landau, Thomas	33	Hesse Darmsta	Y	Havre	New York	09/15/1853	09/30/1856	14	52	N	
Lander, H.	44	Germany	N	?	New York	11/??/1890	?			Y	
Landers, John	25	Ireland	Y	Cork	Boston	05/29/1846	04/02/1852	24	358	N	
Landesco, Alexander	??	Rumania	Y	?	?	06/??/1900	01/05/1904			Y	
Landgraf, Ernst	37	Germany	Y	Bremen	New York	07/27/1887	07/11/1893			Y	
Landgraf, Friedrich W.	30	Germany	Y	Bremen	New York	06/27/1889	11/29/1889			Y	

CITIZENSHIP RECORDS

APPLICANT	AGE	COUNTRY OF ORIGIN	DEC	DEPART PORT	ENTRY PORT	ARRIVE DATE	DEC DATE	VOL	PG.	FLD	NAT DATE
Landgrof, August	26	Germany	Y	Bremen	New York	08/20/1893	10/16/1899			Y	
Landick, Ferdinand	32	Hanover	Y	Bremen	New York	07/03/1857	10/10/1860	27	477	N	
Landman, John	35	Holland	Y	?	?	?	03/08/1852	24	258	N	
Landman, Lewis	32	Russia	Y	Hamburg	New York	09/19/1887	10/21/1890			Y	
Landman, Solomon	39	Germany	Y	Hamburg	New York	09/01/1887	06/13/1893			Y	
Landower, Aron	40	Hesse Darmsta	Y	Bremen	Baltimore	10/22/1839	02/12/1849	23	54	N	
Landre, Henry Gottlieb	26	Prussia	Y	Bremen	Baltimore	07/06/1845	03/11/1850	2	183	N	
Landsberg, William	25	Prussia	Y	?	New York	??/04/1848	11/??/1849	23	309	N	
Landsee, Charles	26	Sigmaringen	Y	Havre	New Orleans	09/01/1846	10/03/1848	22	401	N	
Landwehr, Joseph	34	Germany	Y	Hamburg	New York	05/25/1882	04/15/1890			Y	
Landwehr, Louis	25	Hanover	Y	Bremen	New Orleans	11/02/1849	12/06/1852	5	384	N	
Landwer, Fred	??	Germany	N	?	?	09/14/1884				Y	10/29/1892
Landy, Phillip F.	22	Ireland	Y	Queenstown	New York	05/18/1891	06/05/1892			Y	
Lane, Emil C.	24	Germany	Y	Bremen	Baltimore	10/27/1881	10/27/1884			Y	
Lane, James H.	22	Ireland	Y	Canada	Buffalo	04/??/1849	03/28/1853	7	439	N	
Lang, Abraham	45	Germany	N	Bremen	New York	05/??/1866	?			Y	
Lang, Arbogast	31	Baden	Y	Havre	New Orleans	03/09/1854	03/09/1857	15	76	N	
Lang, Frank	31	Germany	Y	Havre	New York	12/12/1873	10/10/1881			Y	
Lang, George	26	Germany	Y	Antwerp	Baltimore	??/??/1853	10/05/1883			Y	
Lang, George J.	43	Germany	Y	Antwerp	New York	03/30/1889	04/03/1903			Y	
Lang, Gervus	30	Baden	Y	Havre	New York	07/08/1857	08/10/1859	17	473	N	
Lang, Henry Frederick	28	Prussia	Y	Hamburg	New York	??/31/1847	10/09/1848	1	85	N	
Lang, Jacob	34	Germany	Y	Bremen	New York	06/04/1889	12/20/1894			Y	
Lang, Jacob	50	Germany	N	Havre	New York	08/??/1854	?			Y	
Lang, John	??	Wurttemberg	Y	Havre	New York	??/03/1849	12/14/1850	2	362	N	
Lang, John	26	Bavaria	Y	Havre	New York	04/??/1845	12/14/1850	2	363	N	
Lang, John	40	Bavaria	Y	Havre	New York	12/15/1854	03/21/1856	26	239	N	
Lang, John Henry	24	Wurttemberg	Y	Havre	New York	06/30/1854	09/03/1857	15	226	N	
Lang, Martin	47	Ireland	Y	Liverpool	New Orleans	01/01/1848	04/18/1853	8	75	N	
Lang, Paul	22	Saxony	Y	Bremen	Baltimore	06/28/1853	04/21/1854	8	236	N	
Lang, Theodore	35	Germany	Y	Hamburg	New York	11/06/1883	10/27/1894			Y	
Lang, William	29	Germany	Y	Antwerp	New York	01/28/1882	05/06/1885			Y	
Langan, Thomas	34	Ireland	Y	Liverpool	New Orleans	02/04/1848	08/??/1851	4	171	N	
Langbein, Frederick	31	Meiningen Hil	Y	Bremen	New York	12/25/1853	04/17/1854	8	176	N	
Lange, Charles	25	Germany	Y	Hamburg	New York	10/01/1884	10/04/1889	19	234	N	
Lange, Charles	25	Germany	Y	Hamburg	New York	10/01/1884	10/04/1889			Y	
Lange, David	60	Germany	Y	Bremen	Baltimore	05/08/1869	03/07/1892			Y	
Lange, F.	29	Hanover	Y	Hamburg	New York	09/07/1855	01/31/1860	27	80	N	
Lange, George Fred	??	Germany	N	?	?	05/06/1887				Y	10/10/1892
Lange, Henry Christian	29	Hanover	Y	Bremen	New Orleans	11/12/1847	01/19/1849	1	466	N	
Lange, John Frederick	31	Hanover	Y	Bremen	Baltimore	10/02/1850	09/27/1854	10	279	N	
Lange, John Frederick	31	Hanover	Y	Bremen	Baltimore	10/02/1850	09/27/1854	12	218	N	
Lange, John Henry	24	Oldenburg	Y	Bremen	Baltimore	06/04/1848	12/22/1851	4	545	N	
Lange, John Henry	27	Oldenburg	Y	Bremen	New Orleans	02/06/1848	06/04/1852	25	189	N	
Lange, William	30	Germany	Y	?	New York	??/??/1881	02/19/1885			Y	
Lange, William	22	Germany	Y	Bremen	New York	04/23/1882	10/20/1885			Y	
Lange, William	23	Germany	Y	Bremen	New York	07/05/1864	10/10/1871			Y	
Lange, William	29	Prussia	Y	Bremen	Baltimore	04/17/1847	04/09/1852	24	424	N	
Langebracke, Herman Henr	38	Prussia	Y	Bremen	New Orleans	11/08/1851	08/23/1855	11	485	N	
Langebrake, William	31	Prussia	Y	Bremen	New Orleans	12/??/1847	10/27/1851	4	408	N	
Langefeld, Gustav	25	Germany	Y	Bremen	Baltimore	05/24/1887	08/20/1894			Y	
Langefels, John Henry	14	Prussia	Y	Bremen	New Orleans	11/21/1851	10/02/1854	10	368	N	
Langefels, John Henry	34	Prussia	Y	Bremen	New Orleans	11/21/1851	10/02/1854	12	307	N	
Langefels, Theodore	22	Prussia	Y	Bremen	New Orleans	12/09/1852	09/24/1855	13	126	N	
Langellier, Charles	31	Canada	Y	Montreal	Albany	07/07/1843	10/25/1858	17	107	N	
Langemann, John	38	Mecklenburg S	Y	Hamburg	New York	10/25/1854	09/08/1857	15	243	N	
Langenbeck, F.	24	Germany	Y	Bremen	New York	09/09/1857	08/06/1860	27	252	N	
Langendoerfer, Frederick	36	Germany	Y	Rotterdam	New York	03/16/1881	03/14/1892			N	
Langenstroeer, Bernard	22	Prussia	Y	Bremen	New York	06/20/1853	10/01/1856	14	86	N	

CITIZENSHIP RECORDS

APPLICANT	AGE	COUNTRY OF ORIGIN	DEC	DEPART PORT	ENTRY PORT	ARRIVE DATE	DEC DATE	VOL	PG.	FLD	NAT DATE
Langer, Franz	33	Austria	Y	Bremen	New York	06/24/1891	11/04/1895			Y	
Langer, Joseph	31	Germany	Y	Bremen	New York	03/17/1884	12/29/1890			Y	
Langfermann, Joseph	29	Oldenburg	Y	Bremen	New Orleans	12/23/1845	10/16/1848	1	247	N	
Langguth, August	26	Prussia	Y	Hamburg	New York	08/16/1850	03/01/1852	24	192	N	
Langhammer, Frederick	24	Austria	Y	Bremen	Baltimore	06/10/1882	09/19/1885			Y	
Langhans, Carl August	37	Germany	Y	Bremen	Baltimore	08/23/1885	05/02/1887			Y	
Langhauser, Simon	35	Bavaria	Y	Havre	New York	03/03/1851	11/12/1855	13	209	N	
Langhenry, Ernst	27	Bavaria	Y	Hamburg	New York	07/06/1847	09/11/1848	22	325	N	
Langhont, Hessel	24	Holland	Y	Antwerp	New York	06/19/1889	09/26/1892			Y	
Langhorst, August	29	Germany	Y	Bremen	New York	04/10/1884	03/25/1895			Y	
Langhorst, Daniel	40	Hanover	Y	Bremen	New Orleans	12/25/1846	11/13/1848	1	270	N	
Langhorst, Frederick	42	Germany	Y	Bremen	New York	08/19/1889	11/01/1892			Y	
Langhorst, John	43	Oldenburg	Y	Bremen	New Orleans	01/??/1838	07/30/1851	4	62	N	
Langhorst, William	28	Hanover	Y	Bremen	Baltimore	06/18/1845	07/28/1851	4	45	N	
Langhorst, William	50	Germany	Y	Bremen	Baltimore	04/01/1884	10/16/1893			Y	
Langmead, John	41	England	Y	Plymouth	Buffalo	06/02/1849	09/13/1852	25	484	N	
Langoine, Santo	30	Italy	Y	Naples	New York	11/28/1886	03/30/1891			Y	
Langold, John	22	Germany	Y	Hamburg	New York	04/??/1872	05/01/1875			Y	
Langstaff, Charles H.	40	England	Y	?	?	09/17/1882	07/19/1888			Y	
Langthim, William	22	Switzerland	Y	Havre	New York	11/04/1888	05/17/1890			Y	
Languth, John Julius	38	Germany	Y	Bremen	New York	09/12/1888	10/28/1893			Y	
Laninger, Joseph	32	Baden	Y	Havre	New Orleans	05/28/1849	11/01/1852	5	181	N	
Lankheet, Charles	39	Holland	Y	Amsterdam	New York	08/27/1882	10/13/1896			Y	
Lanmann, Joseph	28	Germany	Y	Bremen	Baltimore	05/10/1881	04/12/1894			Y	
Lannan, John	58	Ireland	Y	Liverpool	New Orleans	11/29/1849	03/30/1853	7	463	N	
Lanninger, Joseph	32	Baden	Y	Havre	New Orleans	05/28/1849	11/01/1852	6	307	N	
Lansing, Anton	26	Prussia	Y	Rotterdam	New York	06/14/1850	09/27/1854	10	267	N	
Lansing, Anton	26	Prussia	Y	Rotterdam	New York	06/14/1850	09/27/1854	12	206	N	
Lansing, Herman	31	Prussia	Y	Bremen	Baltimore	11/01/1854	10/08/1860	27	457	N	
Lantman, Louis	44	Holland	Y	Amsterdam	New York	12/30/1880	07/12/1888			N	
Lanzing, Christian	30	Wurttemberg	Y	Rotterdam	New York	07/15/1847	02/06/1850	2	42	N	
Laplace, Robert	43	Germany	Y	?	New York	??/??/1873	04/14/1884			Y	
Lapp, Otto	24	Germany	Y	Bremen	Baltimore	06/10/1893	12/30/1893			Y	
Lapthorn, George	26	England	Y	Bristol	New York	08/12/1849	10/21/1851	4	358	N	
Larberg, Heinrich	23	Germany	Y	Amsterdam	New York	08/08/1883	08/05/1887			Y	
Larbus, Henry	26	Germany	Y	Amsterdam	New York	10/24/1881	10/22/1888			Y	
Larenshaw, John O.	56	England	Y	Liverpool	New York	10/22/1881	10/27/1893			Y	
Larken, Thomas	25	Ireland	Y	Liverpool	New York	05/19/1845	10/18/1851	4	332	N	
Larkin, Coleman	14	Ireland	N	?	New York	00/00/1872				Y	10/15/1888
Larkin, Thomas	22	Ireland	Y	Liverpool	New York	05/06/1853	11/12/1855	13	206	N	
Larmann, Philipp	31	Germany	Y	Bremen	New York	05/26/1887	10/17/1888			Y	
Larsen, Edward	??	Denmark	Y	?	?	12/??/1882	09/09/1884			Y	
Lasance, August	26	Hanover	Y	Bremen	New Orleans	01/01/1848	02/21/1849	23	235	N	
Lasance, Herman	26	Hanover	Y	Bremen	New York	10/17/1856	01/30/1860	27	78	N	
Laschat, Samuel	26	Germany	Y	Bremen	New York	05/27/1881	10/07/1882			Y	
Laseta, Vincenzo	25	Italy	Y	Naples	New York	06/02/1894	10/18/1899			Y	
Lasito, Augustina	24	Italy	Y	Naples	New York	03/12/1898	05/14/1900			Y	
Lask, Nathan	28	Prussia	Y	Hamburg	New York	09/04/18??	01/02/1856	26	14	N	
Laster, Francis	30	Bavaria	Y	Havre	New York	07/26/1853	04/05/1858	16	493	N	
Latcher, Charles	30	France	Y	Havre	New Orleans	03/30/1854	10/28/1858	17	158	N	
Latker, Isaac	31	Russia	Y	Bremen	Baltimore	03/13/1897	06/12/1902			Y	
Latosinski, Joseph	27	Germany	Y	Hamburg	New York	10/21/1883	10/28/1887			Y	
Latoszynski, Simon	23	Prussia	Y	Stryelno	New York	03/20/1855	08/14/1860	27	268	N	
Latterner, John	35	Bavaria	Y	Havre	New York	??/13/1846	11/10/1849	23	331	N	
Latzarus, Frantz Anton	66	France	Y	Havre	New York	12/07/1853	11/08/1858	17	296	N	
Lau, John	38	Germany	Y	Amsterdam	New York	06/27/1885	03/30/1891			Y	
Laub, Gustav	27	Bavaria	Y	Havre	New York	05/??/1849	12/13/1852	5	406	N	
Laube, Rudolph	33	Switzerland	Y	Havre	New York	05/17/1850	02/07/1853	7	122	N	
Lauber, Carl	22	Germany	Y	Antwerp	New York	01/21/1885	09/24/1887			Y	

CITIZENSHIP RECORDS

APPLICANT	AGE	COUNTRY OF ORIGIN	DEC	DEPART PORT	ENTRY PORT	ARRIVE DATE	DEC DATE	VOL	PG.	FLD	NAT DATE
Lauchli, Samuel	28	Switzerland	Y	Antwerp	New York	12/11/1848	06/16/1851	3	380	N	
Laudenbach, Herman Henry	23	Hanover	Y	Bremen	Baltimore	11/01/1845	10/04/1848	22	417	N	
Laudenback, Henry	31	Hanover	Y	Bremen	New Orleans	12/08/1848	04/04/1853	7	512	N	
Laudes, Ernst (Lauders)	20	Germany	Y	Bremen	New York	05/29/1889	08/19/1891			Y	
Laudesvatten, Andreas	34	Wurtemburg, G	Y	Bremen	New York	06/??/1880	09/00/1882			Y	
Laue, Charles	32	Germany	N	Bremen	New York	01/??/1867	?			Y	
Lauer, Daniel	42	Germany	Y	Bremen	New York	08/18/1883	10/25/1886			Y	
Lauer, George	38	Wurttemberg	Y	Havre	New York	08/18/1851	02/21/1853	7	193	N	
Lauer, Jacob	30	Germany	Y	Hamburg	New York	10/23/1883	03/31/1893			Y	
Lauer, Levi	26	Saxony	Y	Bremen	New York	09/08/1853	12/04/1855	13	283	N	
Lauer, Meyer	22	Saxony	Y	Bremen	New York	09/08/1853	12/04/1855	13	284	N	
Laufer, Conrad	25	Germany	Y	Antwerp	New York	11/11/1882	03/09/1886			Y	
Lauffenberg, Philipp	29	France	Y	Havre	New York	05/23/1849	02/17/1851	3	137	N	
Laug, Frank	24	Germany	Y	Antwerp	New York	11/07/1884	09/29/1891			Y	
Laug, Paul	22	Saxony	Y	Bremen	Baltimore	06/28/1853	04/21/1854	9	107	N	
Laugbein, Frederick	31	Meiningen Hil	Y	Bremen	New York	12/23/1853	04/17/1854	9	47	N	
Laugel, John	31	France	Y	Havre	New York	08/27/1840	08/07/1848	22	495	N	
Laughlin, Michael	40	Ireland	Y	Liverpool	New York	05/20/1849	01/31/1853	7	94	N	
Laughman, John	54	Ireland	N	Dublin	Buffalo	04/01/1856	?			Y	
Laugkamp, J. H.	30	Germany	Y	?	?	02/27/1879	08/04/1886			Y	
Laugner, Henry	34	Saxony	Y	Hamburg	New York	01/05/1853	09/20/1858	16	192	N	
Lauk, Lucas	35	Germany	Y	Bremen	New York	07/19/1872	10/02/1884			Y	
Laukhuff, Christ	58	Germany	N	Bremen	New York	11/23/1870	?			Y	
Lauktrees, William James	28	Ireland	Y	Liverpool	New Orleans	04/22/1849	10/06/1856	14	221	N	
Laumann, Gus	36	Germany	Y	Bremen	New York	09/19/1888	09/30/1896			Y	
Laumeister, John Andrew	24	Bavaria	Y	Havre	New York	??/04/1846	10/09/1848	1	83	N	
Laurier, Fred	28	Germany	Y	Hamburg	New York	10/28/1880	06/14/1887			Y	
Lauringer, Lorenz	35	Germany	N	Hamburg	New York	08/14/1872	?			Y	
Lausberg, Frank	31	Germany	Y	Bremen	New York	06/27/1885	05/10/1888			Y	
Lausmann, Anselm	28	Baden	Y	Havre	New Orleans	05/31/1847	03/18/1853	7	345	N	
Laussmann, Franz Gunther	22	Germany	Y	Bremen	Baltimore	10/13/1886	11/01/1886			Y	
Lautenschlager, Wilhelm	40	Germany	Y	Havre	New York	12/18/1879	05/31/1880			Y	
Lauterbach, Dieterich	21	Bremen	Y	Bremen	Baltimore	06/15/1857	09/21/1857	15	297	N	
Lauterbach, Isaac	26	Austria	Y	Rotterdam	New York	02/16/1893	04/05/1897			Y	
Lauterbach, John	59	Germany	N	Bremen	Baltimore	05/??/1861	?			Y	
Lauterbach, John K.	40	Germany	Y	Bremen	Baltimore	11/18/1873	11/03/1886			Y	
Lauther, Adam	28	Hesse Darmsta	Y	Havre	New York	04/24/1848	04/03/1856	26	428	N	
Lauther, Jacob	27	Germany	Y	Antwerp	New York	10/07/1882	09/01/1884			Y	
Lauxtermann, John	26	Hanover	Y	Bremen	Baltimore	07/20/1850	09/07/1857	15	237	N	
Lavall, James	26	Ireland	Y	Liverpool	New York	09/18/1849	05/04/1854	8	375	N	
Lavall, James	26	Ireland	Y	Liverpool	New York	09/18/1849	05/04/1854	9	248	N	
Lavall, John (Lawall)	27	Germany	Y	?	New York	??/??/1881	08/31/1887			Y	
Lavan, Michael	35	Ireland	Y	Liverpool	New York	04/??/1848	10/28/1850	2	323	N	
Lavanier, Aloise	28	Germany	Y	Havre	New York	05/09/1884	04/03/1889			Y	
Lavell, Thomas	40	Ireland	Y	Liverpool	New Orleans	04/28/1846	04/02/1852	24	349	N	
Lavelle, Anthony	25	Ireland	Y	Liverpool	New York	04/15/1853	09/26/1856	14	392	N	
Lavelle, David	27	Ireland	Y	Liverpool	New York	10/01/1849	10/24/1855	13	145	N	
Lavelle, George	38	Canada	N	Canada	Toledo	??/??/1862	?			Y	
Lavender, Michael	25	Ireland	Y	Liverpool	Boston	04/20/1848	03/02/1852	24	217	N	
Lavender, Robert	28	Ireland	Y	Liverpool	New York	05/??/1852	04/24/1855	11	296	N	
Laverty, Dennis	30	Ireland	Y	Liverpool	Philadelphia	04/26/1885	10/30/1893	21	46	N	
Laverty, Dennis	30	Ireland	Y	Liverpool	Philadelphia	04/26/1885	10/03/1893			Y	
Lavin, John	27	Ireland	Y	Liverpool	New Orleans	05/20/1848	11/18/1852	5	305	N	
Lavin, John	27	Ireland	Y	Liverpool	New Orleans	03/27/1851	04/08/1856	26	475	N	
Lavin, Thomas	23	Ireland	Y	Liverpool	New York	10/08/1856	11/29/1859	17	486	N	
Lawall, Peter	26	Germany	Y	Hamburg	New York	11/16/1881	04/09/1886			Y	
Lawenstein, Henry	51	Hanover	Y	Bremen	New Orleans	01/01/1847	11/22/1848	1	371	N	
Lawler, David	25	Ireland	Y	Cork	New York	07/15/1846	01/01/1853	5	490	N	
Lawler, James	30	Ireland	Y	Liverpool	New Orleans	07/29/1851	10/14/1851	4	283	N	

CITIZENSHIP RECORDS

APPLICANT	AGE	COUNTRY OF ORIGIN	DEC	DEPART PORT	ENTRY PORT	ARRIVE DATE	DEC DATE	VOL	PG.	FLD	NAT DATE
Lawler, James	25	Ireland	Y	Limerick	New York	07/12/1849	03/17/1852	24	323	N	
Lawler, John	36	Ireland	Y	Liverpool	New York	04/03/1848	04/27/1850	3	13	N	
Lawler, Patrick	27	Ireland	Y	Queenstown	New York	04/??/1878	04/03/1886	19	32	N	
Lawler, Thomas	28	Ireland	Y	Liverpool	New York	11/04/1849	03/05/1852	7	274	N	
Lawless, Edmond	23	Ireland	Y	Dublin	New York	04/26/1852	03/18/1853	7	346	N	
Lawless, Patrick	29	Ireland	Y	Dublin	New Orleans	04/16/1852	08/24/1857	15	181	N	
Lawrence, Albert	38	England	Y	Liverpool	New York	09/02/1869	09/15/1884			Y	
Lawrence, William	55	England	Y	Liverpool	Port Huron	07/11/1868	10/28/1899			Y	
Lawson, Charles A.	??	Sweden	Y	?	?	06/15/1879	02/28/1883			Y	
Laxterkamp, Beatus	25	Germany	Y	Bremen	Baltimore	09/03/1887	10/28/1893			Y	
Lazarus, Joseph R.	25	Germany	Y	Havre	New York	02/08/1884	11/27/1888			Y	
Lazarus, Nathan	??	Germany	N	?	?	08/25/1887				Y	10/29/1892
Lazebnick, Frank	35	Germany	Y	Bremen	New York	10/10/1882	10/05/1885			Y	
LeDonn, Giovanni	34	Italy	Y	Naples	New York	05/21/1891	09/30/1896			Y	
LeDonne, Francesco	40	Italy	Y	Naples	New York	07/28/1887	03/10/1898			Y	
LeDonne, Peter	34	Italy	Y	Naples	New York	07/28/1887	03/10/1898			Y	
Leahy, John	21	Ireland	Y	Liverpool	New York	04/17/1853	10/22/1857	15	471	N	
Leahy, Michael	26	Ireland	Y	Cork	Boston	05/21/1846	04/15/1852	24	511	N	
Leahy, William	52	Ireland	Y	Liverpool	New Orleans	05/09/1852	09/28/1854	10	294	N	
Leahy, William	52	Ireland	Y	Liverpool	New Orleans	05/19/1852	09/28/1854	12	233	N	
Leaky, Thomas	45	Ireland	Y	Cork	New Orleans	07/08/1851	09/26/1854	10	244	N	
Leaky, Thomas	45	Ireland	Y	Cork	New Orleans	07/08/1857	09/26/1854	12	183	N	
Leaman, William	26	England	Y	Bristol	New York	08/??/1848	10/21/1851	4	357	N	
Learmann, Rulof	29	Holland	Y	Bremen	New Orleans	10/28/1852	11/15/1852	6	413	N	
Leary, Dennis	26	Ireland	Y	Canada	New York	05/29/1845	03/18/1850	2	212	N	
Leary, John	??	Ireland	Y	?	?	07/26/1855	08/01/1860			Y	
Leary, Michael	24	Ireland	Y	Liverpool	New York	04/16/1849	04/17/1854	8	136	N	
Leary, Michael	24	Ireland	Y	Liverpool	New York	04/16/1849	04/17/1854	9	7	N	
Leary, Patrick	50	Ireland	N	Liverpool	New York	01/??/1867	?			Y	
Leary, Timothy	??	Ireland	Y	Liverpool	New York	??/20/1849	04/24/1855	11	295	N	
Leber, Carl	34	Germany	Y	Antwerp	New York	05/02/1882	01/02/1886			Y	
Leber, Joseph	25	Germany	Y	Antwerp	New York	07/16/1881	08/15/1884			Y	
Leber, Matthaeus	30	Germany	Y	Bremen	New York	05/04/1891	03/08/1892			Y	
Lebowitz, Louis	35	Russia	Y	Hamburg	New York	03/17/1888	10/27/1894			Y	
Lebrecht, George	30	Bavaria	Y	Havre	New Orleans	12/31/1850	07/25/1855	11	429	N	
Lechleitner, Edward	25	Prussia	Y	Bremen	Baltimore	08/25/1848	07/11/1851	3	520	N	
Lechner, Frederick	31	Bavaria	Y	Havre	New Orleans	04/27/1849	04/12/1852	24	469	N	
Lechner, Henry	26	Germany	Y	Antwerp	New York	06/27/1894	01/27/1898			Y	
Lecht, Christopher	50	Germany	Y	Bremen	New York	11/06/1874	10/07/1876			Y	
Lecount, David	68	England	Y	Liverpool	New York	06/??/1833	12/24/1855	13	346	N	
Leddy, Michael	35	Ireland	Y	Liverpool	New Orleans	05/01/1850	12/07/1852	5	391	N	
Leddy, Michael	52	Ireland	Y	Liverpool	New Orleans	01/21/1849	04/05/1852	24	377	N	
Leder, Joseph	24	Switzerland	Y	Havre	New York	11/??/1849	12/18/1850	2	375	N	
Leder, Konrad	28	Switzerland	Y	Havre	New York	03/27/1881	12/16/1887			Y	
Leder, Otto	28	Germany	Y	Hamburg	New York	05/17/1881	07/17/1883			Y	
Lederberg, Max	??	Russia	Y	?	?	05/01/1888	04/22/1897			Y	
Lederer, Valentine	??	Germany	Y	?	?	?	04/07/1884			Y	
Lederhaus, Herman E. H.	??	Germany	Y	?	?	?	10/05/1881			Y	
Lederle, August	??	Baden	Y	Havre	New York	09/20/1849	08/??/1851	4	185	N	
Ledermair, Alois	45	Germany	Y	Antwerp	New York	05/27/1890	03/31/1902			Y	
Ledertlin, Charles	35	Baden	Y	Havre	New York	08/27/1849	02/07/1853	7	124	N	
Ledgor, Benjamin	45	England	Y	Liverpool	New Orleans	02/20/1851	04/04/1856	26	435	N	
Lee, Charlie	46	China	N	Hong Kong	Portland	10/??/1869	?			Y	
Lee, George	45	Ireland	Y	Liverpool	New Orleans	08/16/1847	02/28/1853	7	242	N	
Lee, Henry	22	Kurhessen	Y	Bremen	New York	10/18/1854	09/20/1858	16	155	N	
Lee, James	21	Ireland	Y	Liverpool	New York	09/18/1847	10/05/1848	22	432	N	
Lee, John	40	England	Y	Liverpool	Philadelphia	08/12/1885	10/22/1889			Y	
Lee, John	58	England	N	Liverpool	New York	07/??/1856	?			Y	
Lee, Martin	21	Ireland	Y	Liverpool	New Orleans	04/02/1849	10/30/1852	5	75	N	

CITIZENSHIP RECORDS

APPLICANT	AGE	COUNTRY OF ORIGIN	DEC	DEPART PORT	ENTRY PORT	ARRIVE DATE	DEC DATE	VOL	PG.	FLD	NAT DATE
Lee, William	46	Ireland	Y	?	New York	??/??/1873	08/31/1885			Y	
Lees, Israel	36	Austria	Y	Bremen	Baltimore	06/04/1890	04/24/1893			Y	
Leewe, Joseph	29	Germany	Y	Rotterdam	New York	07/01/1881	10/26/1885			Y	
Lefebvre, Henry Lewis	40	Holland	Y	Rotterdam	New York	06/19/1852	09/25/1854	10	216	N	
Lefebvre, Henry Lewis	80	Holland	Y	Rotterdam	New York	06/19/1852	09/25/1854	12	155	N	
Leffelad, John Gerard	32	Bavaria	Y	Bremen	New York	05/28/1849	04/05/1852	24	368	N	
Lefkowitsch, Max	27	Austria	Y	Bremen	New York	01/21/1887	09/02/1890			Y	
Legard, Peter	48	Denmark	Y	Hamburg	New York	??/??/1855	01/17/1883			Y	
Legendre, Ernest	39	Canada	Y	Montreal	Boston	00/00/1871	04/03/1886			Y	
Legenhausen, Ernest	24	Germany	Y	?	?	?	11/02/1894			Y	
Leggatt, Charles	34	England	Y	London	New York	07/16/1848	11/29/1852	5	357	N	
Lehman, Charles	??	Germany	Y	?	?	03/08/1889	04/16/1892			Y	
Lehman, John	23	Switzerland	Y	Havre	New York	08/17/1849	05/24/1852	25	103	N	
Lehman, John Joseph	46	Switzerland	Y	Havre	New York	07/20/1881	06/07/1886			Y	
Lehman, Kaspar	25	Germany	Y	Bremen	Baltimore	01/04/1891	04/06/1891			Y	
Lehman, Lippman	24	Baden	Y	Havre	New York	08/21/1850	01/12/1856	13	458	N	
Lehman, Nathan	22	Russia	Y	Antwerp	New York	11/22/1882	07/21/1884			Y	
Lehmann, Albert	28	Germany	Y	?	?	?	04/05/1892			Y	
Lehmann, Bernhard	54	Switzerland	Y	Havre	New York	10/15/1871	07/05/1884			Y	
Lehmann, Carl F.	56	Germany	Y	Bremen	New York	09/12/1884	01/17/1889			Y	
Lehmann, Frederick	34	Prussia	Y	Bremen	New York	07/07/1853	09/02/1857	15	219	N	
Lehmann, John	32	Switzerland	Y	Havre	New York	04/20/1886	09/12/1896			Y	
Lehmann, John	27	Germany	Y	Havre	New York	10/11/1881	01/02/1885			Y	
Lehmann, Joseph Michael	22	Bavaria	Y	Havre	New York	05/08/1854	03/31/1856	26	381	N	
Lehmbeck, John	??	Germany	Y	?	?	?	08/30/1884			Y	
Lehmhaus, Frederick Will	31	Hanover	Y	Bremen	Baltimore	05/19/1847	05/10/1854	9	284	N	
Lehmkuhl, Arnold	20	Germany	Y	Bremen	Baltimore	10/15/1885	10/21/1887			Y	
Lehmkuhl, George	34	Germany	Y	Bremen	Baltimore	06/04/1880	10/23/1894			Y	
Lehmkuhl, Henry	27	Germany	Y	Bremen	Baltimore	06/05/1880	09/07/1886			Y	
Lehmkuhler, Friedrich	22	Prussia	Y	Bremen	New Orleans	12/20/1846	03/18/1850	2	204	N	
Lehmluhl, Henry	27	Germany	Y	Bremen	Baltimore	06/05/1880	09/07/1885	19	42	N	
Lehmuth, Friedrich	71	Germany	N	Bremen	Baltimore	07/17/1845	?			Y	
Lehner, John	43	Bavaria	Y	Hamburg	New York	09/29/1848	10/14/1851	4	281	N	
Lehnkuhl, Bernard	44	Germany	Y	Bremen	New York	07/29/1881	08/10/1886			Y	
Lehr, Friedrich	26	Germany	Y	Bremen	New York	04/05/1893	10/14/1895			Y	
Lehr, Henry	25	Germany	Y	Antwerp	New York	07/08/1882	12/27/1887			Y	
Lehrer, John George	28	Wurttemberg	Y	Havre	New York	10/24/1854	12/31/1855	13	408	N	
Lehrmann, George Michael	32	Bavaria	Y	Havre	New York	12/20/1846	04/03/1856	26	427	N	
Lehssenich, Mathias	30	Prussia	Y	Antwerp	New York	03/04/1848	03/23/1850	2	239	N	
Lehwald, Carl	30	Germany	Y	Hamburg	New York	12/28/1881	04/12/1883			Y	
Lehy, Joseph	30	Ireland	Y	Liverpool	New Orleans	06/15/1845	10/06/1851	4	211	N	
Leib, Eberhard	40	Hesse Darmsta	Y	Havre	New York	11/10/1851	09/25/18??	10	195	N	
Leib, Eberhard	40	Hesse Darmsta	Y	Havre	New York	09/01/1851	09/25/1854	11	134	N	
Leibbrandt, Christian	39	Wuertemberg	Y	Antwerp	New York	05/07/1849	03/17/1856	26	218	N	
Leibeck, Sebastian	38	Bavaria	Y	Havre	New Orleans	05/??/1844	12/13/1850	2	359	N	
Leibel, Frank	34	Germany	Y	Bremen	Baltimore	06/26/1886	01/26/1891			Y	
Leiber, Rudolf	26	Hanover	Y	Bremen	New York	04/27/1851	11/27/1861	18	230	N	
Leibold, Charles	28	Prussia	Y	Havre	New York	10/28/1853	09/27/1856	14	417	N	
Leibold, John	24	Prussia	Y	Havre	New Orleans	01/15/1854	10/28/1858	17	143	N	
Leibolt, Joseph	27	Heckingen	Y	Antwerp	New York	06/??/1847	01/??/1850	23	542	N	
Leibovitz, Isac	28	Romania	Y	Hamburg	New York	07/11/1894	03/18/1901			Y	
Leibovitz, Philiph	24	Romania	Y	Bueuresty	New York	07/29/1899	10/28/1903			Y	
Leicht, Casper	53	Germany	Y	Bremen	New York	05/12/1883	03/08/1894			Y	
Leicht, Jacob	27	Germany	Y	Antwerp	Philadelphia	03/06/1889	09/11/1891			Y	
Leicht, Ludwig	24	Germany	Y	Antwerp	Philadelphia	08/08/1893	08/16/1893			Y	
Leicht, Matthew	15	Germany	N	?	New York	00/00/1882				Y	10/27/1888
Leidenfrost, Emil	24	Austria	Y	Bremen	New York	07/16/1887	07/16/1888			Y	
Leidheiser, Conrad	27	Germany	Y	Bremen	New York	08/04/1883	11/16/1889			Y	
Leidinger, Jacob	37	Prussia	Y	Havre	New York	07/29/1847	04/24/1850	3	9	N	

CITIZENSHIP RECORDS

APPLICANT	AGE	COUNTRY OF ORIGIN	DEC	DEPART PORT	ENTRY PORT	ARRIVE DATE	DEC DATE	VOL	PG.	FLD	NAT DATE
Leidlein, Frederick	47	Wurttemberg	Y	Liverpool	New York	06/28/1854	12/05/1869	17	489	N	
Leierer, Franz	29	Bavaria	Y	Havre	New York	11/02/1853	10/09/1854	6	76+	N	
Leifeling, George	21	Germany	N	Bremen	New York	09/29/1867	?			Y	
Leifeling, John X.	26	Hanover	Y	Bremen	New Orleans	05/20/1848	02/21/1849	23	250	N	
Leighton, George Johnson	30	England	Y	Glasgow	New York	03/10/1891	01/13/1894			Y	
Leimgruber, Martin	38	Germany	Y	Havre	New York	03/01/1892	04/22/1898			Y	
Leingang, John	22	Bavaria	Y	Havre	New Orleans	12/07/1848	03/29/1849	23	264	N	
Leingang, Joseph	36	Germany	Y	Havre	New York	04/25/1880	03/27/1885			Y	
Leinkuehler, William	25	Hanover	Y	Bremen	New York	11/16/1844	10/06/1856	14	226	N	
Leins, William Henry	??	Wurttemberg	Y	Havre	New York	05/03/1849	??/??/1851	3	223	N	
Leipelt, William	43	Germany	Y	?	New York	02/??/1882	04/04/1893			Y	
Leisch, J. Charles	36	Prussia	Y	Hamburg	New York	01/??/1855	01/10/1861	18	50	N	
Leischer, John	36	Germany	Y	Bremen	New York	02/01/1881	03/11/1885			Y	
Leischke, Edmund	??	Germany	Y	?	?	?	09/01/1894			Y	
Leiser, Martin M.	21	Prussia	Y	Hamburg	New York	03/18/1888	04/12/1892			Y	
Leising, Herman	??	Germany	Y	?	?	?	03/29/1902			Y	
Leisinger, Fritz	33	Germany	Y	Havre	New York	10/05/1884	12/31/1887			Y	
Leisinger, Jacob	35	Germany	Y	Havre	New York	06/25/1889	04/16/1894			Y	
Leisinger, Philipp	28	Germany	Y	Havre	New York	05/30/1887	12/08/1888			Y	
Leisle, Franz	40	Wuerttemberg	Y	Bremen	New York	12/28/1849	09/29/1860	27	389	N	
Leist, Andreas	34	Germany	Y	Rotterdam	New York	04/??/1882	05/25/1885			Y	
Leist, Peter	27	Baden	Y	Havre	New York	11/23/1854	01/08/1856	13	430	N	
Leist, Philipp	27	Germany	Y	Rotterdam	New York	10/28/1880	05/29/1882			Y	
Leist, William	25	Germany	Y	Rotterdam	New York	11/01/1880	10/13/1882			Y	
Leistikow, Charles	32	Prussia	Y	Hamburg	New York	08/07/1852	01/02/1858	16	292	N	
Leiter, Joseph	41	Germany	Y	Havre	New York	02/10/1866	06/02/1882			Y	
Leith, Jacob	31	Bavaria	Y	Bremen	Baltimore	08/06/1857	07/08/1859	17	465	N	
Leittel, Henry	29	Hanover	Y	Bremen	New Orleans	12/20/1849	03/08/1852	24	266	N	
Leitz, Matthaeus	57	Germany	Y	Bremen	New York	11/24/1876	04/16/1890			Y	
Leiva, John Henry (Leive	36	Germany	Y	Bremen	Baltimore	10/17/1839	10/05/1840			Y	10/30/1844
Leive, T. H.	23	Hanover	Y	Bremen	Baltimore	11/25/1845	08/01/1848	22	32	N	
Leiwenson, Ber Leib	??	Russia	Y	?	?	?	01/09/1893			Y	
Lejeune, Frederick	40	Prussia	Y	Hamburg	New York	08/20/1849	05/21/1856	26	512	N	
Lemacher, Charles A.	27	Austria	Y	Ku Rus	New York	07/26/1857	09/03/1857	15	225	N	
Lembike, Wilhelm	27	Mecklenburg	Y	Hamburg	New York	06/30/1851	09/21/1854	10	143	N	
Lembike, Wilhelm	27	Mecklenburg	Y	Hamburg	New York	06/30/1851	09/21/1854	12	82	N	
Lemken, Bernard Herman	30	Hanover	Y	Bremen	New Orleans	01/01/1846	11/04/1852	5	217	N	
Lemker, Bernard Hermann	30	Hanover	Y	Bremen	New Orleans	01/01/1846	11/04/1852	6	343	N	
Lemmel, John	30	Bavaria	Y	Havre	New York	04/09/1856	11/01/1860	27	542	N	
Lemmer, Carl	26	Germany	Y	?	?	?	04/16/1884			Y	
Lemming, H.	28	Hanover	Y	Bremen	Baltimore	10/09/1857	10/16/1860	27	503	N	
Lemon, Max	32	Russia	Y	Hamburg	New York	04/20/1884	10/09/1889			Y	
Lemonek, Simon	32	Russia	Y	Hamburg	New York	06/17/1881	05/??/1883	28	104	N	
Lemonek, Simon	27	Russia	Y	Hamburg	New York	06/17/1881	05/00/1883			Y	
Lemper, Joseph	27	Hanover	Y	Bremen	New York	09/30/1852	09/29/1854	10	306	N	
Lemper, Joseph	27	Hanover	Y	Bremen	New York	09/30/1852	09/28/1854	12	245	N	
Lenahan, Michael	46	Ireland	Y	Liverpool	Baltimore	06/08/1881	03/05/1885			Y	
Lenahan, Thomas	17	England	N	?	New York	00/00/1883				Y	10/31/1888
Lenamuth, Henry	28	Oldenburg	Y	Bremen	Baltimore	10/04/1846	02/21/1849	23	249	N	
Lender, George	28	Germany	Y	?	New York	??/??/1882	12/11/1884			Y	
Lenehan, John	41	Ireland	Y	Queenstown	New York	08/??/1870	03/28/1883			Y	
Leng, William Henry John	26	Germany	Y	Hamburg	New York	11/23/1887	09/22/1891			Y	
Lengan, James	29	Ireland	Y	Liverpool	New York	04/03/1845	06/13/1854	10	132	N	
Lengan, James	29	Ireland	Y	Liverpool	New York	04/03/1845	06/13/1854	12	69	N	
Lenger, Frank Frederick	34	Prussia	Y	Bremen	New Orleans	??/12/18??	02/12/1850	2	62	N	
Lenihan, James	24	England	Y	Liverpool	New York	11/27/1881	03/16/1887			Y	
Lennon, Christopher	28	Ireland	Y	Dublin	New York	05/05/1848	11/16/1848	1	282	N	
Lennon, James	28	Ireland	Y	?	?	03/25/1882	04/20/1891			Y	
Lennrich, Felix	27	Germany	Y	Amsterdam	New York	06/05/1887	08/15/1889			Y	

CITIZENSHIP RECORDS

APPLICANT	AGE	COUNTRY OF ORIGIN	DEC	DEPART PORT	ENTRY PORT	ARRIVE DATE	DEC DATE	VOL	PG.	FLD	NAT DATE
Lenny, James	42	England	Y	Liverpool	New York	08/07/1840	10/03/1848	1	46	N	
Lense, Albert	21	Germany	Y	Havre	New York	09/19/1884	12/16/1887			Y	
Lensink, R.	29	Holland	Y	Bremen	New York	08/23/1859	11/01/1860	27	514	N	
Lentsch, Pius	24	Germany	Y	Hamburg	New York	09/03/1883	10/06/1888			Y	
Lentz, John	26	Prussia	Y	Bremen	Galveston	03/01/1845	03/18/1850	2	210	N	
Lenz, August	29	Germany	Y	?	New York	??/??/1890	10/03/1894			Y	
Lenz, Herman	31	Germany	Y	Hamburg	New York	01/12/1867	10/04/1878			Y	
Lenz, John	36	Wurttemberg	Y	Bremen	New York	07/10/1854	12/29/1855	13	390	N	
Lenz, Joseph	33	Wuertemberg	Y	Bremen	New York	07/11/1854	03/24/1856	26	259	N	
Lenz, Mathias	41	Germany	Y	Bremen	New York	04/22/1889	10/22/1890			Y	
Lenz, Michael	49	Germany	Y	Hamburg	New York	03/28/1881	03/06/1885			Y	
Lenz, Nathan	21	Bavaria	Y	Havre	New York	09/06/1854	11/23/1857	16	45	N	
Lenze, Wilhelm	26	Germany	Y	Havre	New York	05/03/1896	01/19/1898			Y	
Leon, Joseph	31	Baden	Y	Havre	New York	11/18/1847	06/18/1851	3	396	N	
Leonard, John	28	Ireland	Y	Cork	New York	06/16/1849	01/14/1851	2	493	N	
Leonard, John	34	Ireland	Y	Liverpool	New Orleans	05/08/1848	09/29/1854	10	304	N	
Leonard, John	34	Ireland	Y	Liverpool	New Orleans	05/08/1848	09/29/1854	12	243	N	
Leonard, John	68	Ireland	N	Liverpool	New Orleans	05/15/1848	?			Y	
Leonard, Michael	35	Ireland	Y	Dublin	New York	05/20/1848	03/10/1853	7	318	N	
Leonard, Patrick	60	Ireland	N	Liverpool	New Orleans	02/??/1851	?			Y	
Leonard, Patrick	53	Ireland	N	Liverpool	New Orleans	06/??/1849	?			Y	
Leonard, Patrick	34	Ireland	Y	Liverpool	New York	02/24/1848	06/21/1852	25	303	N	
Leonard, Peter	29	Ireland	Y	Liverpool	New York	06/02/1851	12/16/1851	4	537	N	
Leonard, Robert	21	Ireland	Y	Liverpool	New York	03/30/1851	05/02/1854	8	347	N	
Leonard, Robert	21	Ireland	Y	Liverpool	New York	03/30/1851	05/02/1854	9	220	N	
Leonard, William	26	Ireland	Y	Liverpool	New York	04/18/1852	05/19/1856	26	499	N	
Leonardy, Charles	28	France	Y	Havre	New York	06/06/1849	08/23/1852	25	334	N	
Leonardy, Ernst	31	France	Y	Antwerp	New York	07/18/1850	08/23/1852	25	333	N	
Leonhard, Adam	??	Germany	N	?	?	05/15/1879				Y	10/29/1892
Leonhard, Karl (Leonard)	30	Germany	Y	Antwerp	New York	01/20/1884	11/09/1886			Y	
Leonhard, Michael	28	France	Y	Havre	New York	04/17/1854	01/04/1860	27	25	N	
Leonhardt, Bernhardt	54	Germany	Y	Hamburg	New York	05/20/1884	04/10/1888			Y	
Leonhardt, Philipp Walde	26	Germany	Y	Hamburg	New York	11/13/1887	03/08/1894			Y	
Leop, George	37	Russia	Y	Bremen	New York	??/??/1888	11/05/1894			Y	
Leopold, Paul	??	Germany	Y	?	?	?	04/07/1885			Y	
Lepnski, John	27	Germany	Y	Bremen	New York	08/14/1893	01/20/1896			Y	
Leppert, Erhard	52	Baden	Y	Liverpool	New Orleans	01/03/1852	06/08/1852	25	207	N	
Leppert, Leonhart	27	Baden	Y	Havre	New York	06/20/1849	09/08/1852	25	422	N	
Lerch, Carl	28	Germany	Y	Havre	New York	11/30/1882	03/29/1887			Y	
Lerch, Jacob	30	Germany	Y	Bremen	New York	12/07/1879	05/18/1888			Y	
Lerch, Michael	24	France	Y	Havre	New York	04/11/1853	03/03/1856	26	149	N	
Lergenmueller, Valentine	34	Germany	Y	Bremen	New York	05/16/1882	02/23/1886			Y	
Lerman, Joseph	17	Russia	N	?	Philadelphia	00/00/1883				Y	10/23/1888
Lerner, Nelson	??	Germany	Y	?	?	?	12/28/1895			Y	
Lerney, Owen	27	Ireland	Y	Liverpool	New York	03/04/1858	11/23/1858	17	349	N	
Lesage, Jules	44	France	Y	Havre	New York	04/??/1833	04/27/1854	8	275	N	
Lesage, Jules	44	France	Y	Havre	New York	04/??/1833	04/27/1854	9	146	N	
Lesch, John	28	Bavaria	Y	London	New York	09/26/1848	02/19/1849	23	172	N	
Leschke, Fritz	27	Germany	Y	?	Baltimore	??/??/1883	07/29/1886			Y	
Leschke, John	29	Prussia	Y	Hamburg	New York	07/30/1852	03/17/1856	26	222	N	
Leser, Andreas	30	Germany	Y	Bremen	Baltimore	12/01/1892	11/12/1896			Y	
Leslie, John	39	Scotland	Y	Liverpool	New York	07/04/1889	07/08/1895			Y	
Lessmann, Anton	30	Lippe Detmold	Y	Bremen	New Orleans	06/12/1853	04/02/1856	26	404	N	
Letang, Adolf	35	Germany	Y	Antwerp	New York	05/31/1880	04/02/1880			Y	
Letoger, Joseph	33	France	Y	Havre	New Orleans	11/29/1848	03/08/1852	24	264	N	
Letoile, Herman	31	Germany	Y	Bremen	New York	09/28/1881	01/25/1889			Y	
Lettermann, Henry	22	Prussia	Y	Bremen	New Orleans	11/04/1859	01/11/1860	27	49	N	
Letterst, Clemens	33	Germany	Y	Antwerp	New York	01/10/1881	04/25/1893	19	422	N	
Letterst, Clemens	33	Germany	Y	Antwerp	New York	01/10/1884	06/25/1893			Y	

CITIZENSHIP RECORDS

APPLICANT	AGE	COUNTRY OF ORIGIN	DEC	DEPART PORT	ENTRY PORT	ARRIVE DATE	DEC DATE	VOL	PG.	FLD	NAT DATE
Lettler, Siegfried	25	Germany	Y	Havre	New York	03/28/1882	08/04/1884			Y	
Letto, John	28	Mecklenburg S	Y	Hamburg	New York	08/15/1853	11/19/1855	13	230	N	
Letzer, Jacob	39	France	Y	Havre	New Orleans	03/27/1857	12/26/1859	17	528	N	
Letzler, Frederick	21	France	Y	Havre	New Orleans	05/03/1853	02/04/1856	26	21	N	
Leuaggi, Anthony	30	Italy	N	Geneva	New York	04/01/1880	?			Y	
Leuderalbert, Herman Hen	21	Prussia	Y	Bremen	New Orleans	11//13/184	02/01/1849	23	1	N	
Leukering, William	33	Hanover	Y	Bremen	New Orleans	12/12/1845	09/27/1848	22	354	N	
Leukhardt, John	25	Wurttemberg	Y	Havre	New York	02/24/1854	08/18/1857	15	159	N	
Leunig, Henry	26	Hanover	Y	Bremen	New Orleans	01/01/1847	09/05/1848	22	301	N	
Leuning, Carl	22	Hanover	Y	Bremen	New Orleans	12/18/1847	08/23/1848	22	247	N	
Leuser, Adam	35	Bavaria	Y	Havre	New York	05/04/1853	10/01/1856	14	101	N	
Levanier, Edward	37	Germany	Y	Havre	New York	07/04/1872	11/05/1888			Y	
Levenie, Hyman	31	Russia	Y	Hamburg	New York	04/21/1886	10/12/1896			Y	
Levenmann, B.	33	Germany	Y	Bremen	New York	07/??/1873	08/15/1883			Y	
Levi, Jacob	44	Germany	Y	Bremen	New York	06/??/1870	10/04/1880			Y	
Levi, Julius (Levy)	54	Germany	Y	?	New York	??/??/1884	10/13/1884			Y	
Levi, Lewis	55	Prussia	Y	Liverpool	New York	08/29/1848	01/13/1851	2	488	N	
Levi, Sampson	38	Germany	Y	Hamburg	New York	07/??/1872	10/11/1884			Y	
Levi, William	38	Russia	Y	Bremen	New York	01/22/1884	10/25/1894			Y	
Levin, Isodore M.	25	Russia	Y	?	New York	??/??/1881	07/27/1885			Y	
Levin, Sam	27	Russia	Y	Hamburg	New York	11/29/1886	04/05/1890	19	284	N	
Levin, Sam	27	Russia	Y	Hamburg	New York	11/29/1886	04/05/1890			Y	
Levine, Joseph	36	Russia	Y	Hamburg	New York	04/24/1891	10/27/1903			Y	
Levine, Leon W.	33	Russia	Y	Hamburg	New York	02/29/1892	06/11/1895	21	80	N	
Levine, Leon W.	33	Russia	Y	Hamburg	New York	07/29/1892	06/11/1895			Y	
Levine, Marcus	35	Russia	Y	Hamburg	Philadelphia	07/27/1882	07/16/1883			Y	
Levine, Moses	28	Russia	Y	Hamburg	New York	07/02/1900	10/27/1903			Y	
Levinger, Leopold	44	Germany	Y	Bremen	Philadelphia	??/??/1866	10/12/1886			Y	
Levinson, Peter	50	Russia	Y	Hamburg	New York	05/17/1891	06/30/1898			Y	
Levinson, Samuel	24	Russia	Y	Hamburg	New York	07/26/1886	04/07/1890			Y	
Levit, Mendel	32	Russia	Y	Glasgow	New York	11/19/1888	04/11/1890			Y	
Levitis, Isaac	26	Germany	Y	?	Boston	??/??/1885	10/06/1892			Y	
Levy, Henry	21	England	Y	London	New York	05/??/1847	12/31/1849	23	443	N	
Levy, Herman	43	Germany	N	Liverpool	New York	01/??/1868	10/??/1868	28	116	N	10/??/1873
Levy, Herman	23	Germany	N	Liverpool	New York	01/00/1868	10/00/1868			Y	10/00/1873
Levy, Isaac	33	Russia	Y	Hamburg	New York	08/15/1889	12/16/1892			Y	
Levy, Isaac	45	France	N	Harvar	New York	02/10/1866	?			Y	
Levy, Jonas	47	France	N	Havre	New York	10/08/1866	?	28	438	N	??/??/1871
Levy, Joseph	20	Russia	Y	Hamburg	New York	12/??/1886	09/06/1888			Y	
Levy, Lewis	90	Prussai	N	Liverpool	New York	08/20/1848	?			Y	
Levy, Max	36	Germany	Y	Hamburg	New York	03/04/1880	06/30/1883			Y	
Levy, Max	22	Germany	Y	Amsterdam	New York	08/26/1882	05/25/1883			Y	
Levy, Nathan	38	Prussia	Y	London	New York	08/14/1850	03/29/1856	26	372	N	
Levy, Philip	25	Russia	Y	Hamburg	New York	03/15/1896	06/11/1902			Y	
Levy, Raphard	44	Germany	N	Havre	New Orleans	12/??/1870	?			Y	
Levy, Samuel	53	Germany	Y	London	New York	05/30/1888	10/25/1894			Y	
Levy, Zadok	36	Napan	Y	Havre	New York	09/11/1847	03/18/1850	2	218	N	
Lewald, Oscar	29	Germany	Y	?	Boston	09/18/1882	01/30/1884			Y	
Lewe, Christian	29	Prussia	Y	Bremen	New York	05/01/1849	11/01/1852	5	10	N	
Lewe, Henry	31	Prussia	Y	Bremen	New Orleans	12/16/1844	10/05/1848	22	433	N	
Lewe, Joseph Otto	36	Austria	Y	Hamburg	New York	08/28/1856	08/15/1857	15	142	N	
Lewin, Benno	35	Germany	Y	Antwerp	New York	02/29/1883	02/03/1900			Y	
Lewin, Isaac	29	Poland	Y	Hamburg	New York	10/03/1887	10/14/1889			Y	
Lewin, Markus	37	Germany	Y	Bremen	Baltimore	07/19/1881	02/03/1900			Y	
Lewing, George	31	Germany	Y	Rotterdam	New York	06/14/1880	11/01/1889			Y	
Lewing, Louis	36	Germany	Y	Hamburg	New York	03/13/1881	02/26/1885			Y	
Lewis, Benjamin	50	Russia	Y	Hamburg	Baltimore	06/15/1886	10/28/1893			Y	
Lewis, John	31	Wales	Y	Liverpool	New Orleans	02/01/1849	10/06/1854	12	431	N	
Lewis, John C.	43	England	N	Liverpool	New York	11/09/1870	?			Y	

CITIZENSHIP RECORDS

APPLICANT	AGE	COUNTRY OF ORIGIN	DEC	DEPART PORT	ENTRY PORT	ARRIVE DATE	DEC DATE	VOL	PG.	FLD	NAT DATE
Lewis, Robert	21	Wales	Y	Liverpool	New York	06/02/1849	10/06/1854	10	491	N	
Lewis, Robert	21	Wales	Y	Liverpool	New York	06/02/1849	10/06/1854	12	430	N	
Lewis, W. W.	60	Wales	N	Liverpool	New York	??/??/1834	?	28	207	N	10/01/1848
Lewis, W. W.	6	Wales	N	Liverpool	New York	00/00/1834				Y	10/01/1848
Lewis, William	26	North Wales	Y	Liverpool	New York	08/19/1887	02/20/1888			Y	
Lewitz, John	33	Germany	Y	Bremen	Baltimore	03/02/1872	10/11/1879			Y	
Lewy, Sem	29	Poland	Y	Hamburg	New York	07/20/1854	09/30/1856	14	61	N	
Liar, John George	27	Bavaria	Y	Havre	New Orleans	11/27/1853	10/04/1854	10	427	N	
Liar, John George	27	Bavaria	Y	Havre	New Orleans	11/27/1853	10/04/1854	12	366	N	
Libers, Marzell	22	Germany	Y	Amsterdam	New York	08/09/1882	10/08/1885			Y	
Libes, Edward	39	Germany	N	Havre	New York	04/12/1880	?			Y	
Libis, Joseph	22	Germany	Y	Havre	New York	03/06/1887	10/20/1888			Y	
Librer, Fred	35	Italy	Y	Naples	New York	04/10/1884	05/09/1893			Y	
Licguire, Frederick	27	England	Y	London	New York	12/18/1850	01/09/1860	27	45	N	
Licht, Abraham	23	Russia	Y	Bremen	Baltimore	04/29/1888	09/26/1892			Y	
Lichtenberg, Friederich	59	Germany	Y	Bremen	Baltimore	06/??/1862	03/31/1888			Y	
Lichtenberg, Isaac	30	Prussia	Y	Bremen	Baltimore	10/11/1855	12/08/1858	17	387	N	
Lichtendahl, Bernard Her	23	Prussia	Y	Amsterdam	New Orleans	03/15/1847	11/17/1848	1	310	N	
Lichtenfeldt, Charles	??	Germany	Y	?	?	?	03/31/1886			Y	
Lichtenstein, Julius	23	Saxony	Y	Bremen	New York	08/??/1854	12/26/1855	13	369	N	
Lichtenstein, Ulrich	37	Germany	Y	Hamburg	New York	02/08/1882	04/08/1889			Y	
Lichtenwald, Adam	32	Bavaria	Y	Havre	New York	07/01/1850	04/25/1853	8	106	N	
Lickert, Frederick	21	Saxe Weimar	Y	Bremen	New York	09/01/1851	05/30/1854	9	455	N	
Lickert, Frederick	21	Saxe Weimar	Y	Bremen	New York	09/01/1851	05/30/1854	10	38	N	
Liddell, Andrew	32	Scotland	Y	London	New York	09/24/1848	07/07/1851	3	503	N	
Liddell, Andrew	25	Scotland	Y	Glasgow	New York	08/14/1850	09/06/1852	25	380	N	
Lieb, Andreas	38	Germany	Y	Bremen	Baltimore	06/12/1881	07/21/1886			Y	
Liebel, Henry	30	Germany	Y	Hamburg	New York	07/22/1888	10/23/1888			Y	
Liebel, Michael	28	Bavaria	Y	Havre	New Orleans	05/07/1852	05/13/1854	8	435	N	
Liebel, Michael	28	Bavaria	Y	Havre	New Orleans	05/07/1852	05/13/1854	9	308	N	
Liebelt, Adolf	31	Germany	Y	Bremen	Baltimore	09/17/1881	11/29/1884			Y	
Liebenberg, Carl A. F. B	28	Hanover	Y	Bremen	New York	08/29/1853	07/23/1860	27	233	N	
Lieber, William	43	Nassau	Y	London	New York	05/11/1854	09/29/1856	14	39	N	
Liebermann, Frank Xavier	32	Wuerttemberg	Y	Antwerp	New York	05/07/1849	02/??/1852	24	65	N	
Liebermann, Franz Joseph	29	Germany	Y	Bremen	New York	06/09/1892	01/06/1897			Y	
Liebermann, Jacob	52	Germany	Y	Antwerp	New York	04/25/1881	10/19/1892			Y	
Lieberth, Sebastian	28	Bavaria	Y	Bremen	Baltimore	07/13/1852	01/02/1858	16	291	N	
Liebig, Frank	24	Germany	Y	Rotterdam	New York	08/21/1881	02/27/1882			Y	
Liebler, Adam	38	Bavaria	Y	Liverpool	New York	04/??/1854	02/03/1857	14	534	N	
Liebschuetz, Myer	22	Germany	Y	Bremen	New York	05/15/1891	04/16/1894			Y	
Liebshevitz, Jacob	27	Russia	Y	Hamburg	New York	??/??/1881	04/14/1887			Y	
Liebshevitz, Joseph	60	Russia	Y	Hamburg	Philadelphia	07/20/1881	10/28/1892			Y	
Liedebrand, Henry	28	Kourhessen	Y	Bremen	New York	02/01/1848	06/15/1852	25	269	N	
Lieder, Alexander	29	Prussia	Y	Bremen	New York	10/14/1854	09/25/1856	14	378	N	
Lieder, John Charles Fre	33	Prussia	Y	Hamburg	New York	08/04/1850	01/25/1853	7	67	N	
Liehner, Adolph	37	Germany	Y	Havre	New York	01/27/1883	01/21/1889			Y	
Lielke, August	21	Germany	Y	Bremen	Baltimore	01/30/1890	07/31/1893			Y	
Liendhorst, Henry	39	Germany	Y	Bremen	New York	05/27/1881	10/22/1891			Y	
Lienert, Meinrad	28	Switzerland	Y	Havre	New York	04/08/1884	10/26/1889			Y	
Lienesch, Fred	22	Germany	Y	Bremen	Baltimore	08/20/1881	11/03/1884			Y	
Liesen, Henry	25	Germany	Y	Antwerp	New York	05/07/1882	09/22/1886			Y	
Lieve, Christ	54	Germany	Y	Bremen	Baltimore	08/20/1881	01/02/1885			Y	
Light, Thomas	22	England	Y	Liverpool	Philadelphia	12/31/1852	03/25/1853	7	393	N	
Lilie, August	32	Germany	Y	Bremen	Baltimore	06/23/1881	11/05/1888			Y	
Lilje, Adolf	31	Germany	Y	Hamburg	Detroit	07/01/1891	12/16/1891	19	345	N	
Lilje, Adolf	31	Germany	Y	Hamburg	Detroit	07/01/1891	12/16/1891			Y	
Liller, Michael	27	Bavaria	Y	Havre	New Orleans	11/19/1847	03/15/1852	24	312	N	
Lilley, Luke	38	England	Y	?	?	04/??/1868	03/06/1882			Y	
Lillis, Patrick	38	Ireland	Y	Liverpool	New Orleans	06/01/1843	03/22/1850	2	237	N	

CITIZENSHIP RECORDS

APPLICANT	AGE	COUNTRY OF ORIGIN	DEC	DEPART PORT	ENTRY PORT	ARRIVE DATE	DEC DATE	VOL	PG.	FLD	NAT DATE
Lillis, Thomas	27	Ireland	N	Queenstown	New York	05/12/1879	?			Y	
Limbeck, Henry	31	Germany	Y	Rotterdam	New York	06/15/1888	02/06/1894			Y	
Limbeck, Herman	25	Germany	Y	Rotterdam	New York	12/01/1892	12/31/1895			Y	
Limberger, Joseph	45	Germany	Y	Bremen	New York	10/10/1868	10/02/1891			Y	
Limke, Francis A.	35	Prussia	Y	Bremen	New York	05/02/1849	09/14/1852	25	507	N	
Limke, John Clemens	30	Prussia	Y	Bremen	New Orleans	06/30/1845	02/02/1853	7	107	N	
Limmer, Francis	30	Bavaria	Y	Bremen	New York	05/10/1852	06/04/1856	14	290	N	
Linch, Nathan	33	Germany	Y	Hamburg	New York	08/30/1880	10/15/1889			Y	
Lind, Benjamin	25	Germany	Y	Havre	New York	06/22/1880	09/02/1881			Y	
Lind, Christoph	36	Baden	Y	Liverpool	New York	11/28/1853	10/16/1860	27	504	N	
Lindauer, Joseph Meinrad	28	Switzerland	Y	Havre	New York	05/16/1854	10/03/1854	10	406	N	
Lindauer, Joseph Meinrad	28	Switzerland	Y	Havre	New York	05/16/1854	10/03/1854	12	345	N	
Lindeboom, B.	26	Germany	Y	Bremen	Baltimore	12/27/1881	08/12/1886			Y	
Lindeman, George	25	Prussia	Y	Rotterdam	New York	07/20/1850	08/11/1851	4	107	N	
Lindemann, Bernhard	49	Germany	Y	Bremen	Baltimore	08/13/1890	01/11/1894			Y	
Lindemann, Clemens	28	Hanover	Y	Bremen	Baltimore	12/10/1851	08/28/1855	11	511	N	
Lindemann, F.	57	Germany	N	Hamburg	New York	10/??/1854	?			Y	
Lindemann, F. W.	??	?	N	?	?	?	?			Y	
Lindemann, Fred	49	Germany	N	Havre	New Orleans	03/03/1858	?			Y	
Lindemann, Frederick	33	Prussia	Y	Bremen	Baltimore	12/02/1857	01/03/1860	27	23	N	
Lindemann, H. W.	59	Germany	N	Bremen	Baltimore	11/17/1845	?	28	215	N	10/??/1850
Lindemann, Henry	23	Prussia	Y	Bremen	New York	10/09/1852	09/27/1854	10	282	N	
Lindemann, Henry	23	Prussia	Y	Bremen	New York	10/09/1852	09/27/1854	12	221	N	
Lindemann, John	56	Germany	Y	Hamburg	New York	03/14/1880	10/19/1894			Y	
Lindemann, John Henry	36	Hanover	Y	Bremen	New York	07/10/1850	02/20/1858	16	324	N	
Lindemuth, Ludwig	24	Prussia	Y	Hamburg	New York	01/01/1857	02/23/1858	16	336	N	
Linden, N.	26	Germany	Y	Antwerp	New York	03/03/1887	09/05/1887			Y	
Lindenmaier, George	49	Bavaria	N	Hamburg	New York	08/15/1867	?			Y	
Lindenman, Charles	23	Baden	Y	Havre	New York	05/04/1848	11/06/1852	5	250	N	
Lindenmeyer, Charles	23	Baden	Y	Havre	New York	05/04/1848	11/06/1852	6	374	N	
Lindenmeyer, Moritz	24	Bavaria	Y	Bremen	New York	06/26/1854	04/05/1856	26	446	N	
Linder, Aaron	21	Finland	Y	Bremen	New York	09/12/1893	03/09/1894			Y	
Linder, Christoph Friedr	20	Germany	Y	Antwerp	New York	03/23/1879	11/07/1881			Y	
Linder, George	30	Wurttemberg	Y	Antwerp	New York	06/20/1846	10/13/1848	1	206	N	
Linder, Joseph	??	Germany	N	Havre	New Orleans	12/??/1839	?			Y	
Linder, Joseph	32	Wuerttemberg	Y	Rotterdam	New York	06/01/1848	02/14/1849	23	91	N	
Linder, Louis	33	Germany	Y	Havre	New York	06/29/1883	10/20/1884			Y	
Linder, Phillip	34	Bavaria	Y	Havre	New York	04/13/1851	05/01/1854	9	200	N	
Lindermann, Henry	17	Germany	N	?	New York	00/00/1882				Y	06/22/1887
Lindhorst, Frederick	34	Bremen	Y	Havre	New York	03/06/1849	01/31/1853	7	89	N	
Lindloff, William	32	Germany	Y	Hamburg	New York	10/18/1882	09/25/1885			Y	
Lindnar, Frederick	40	Bavaria	Y	Bremen	New York	10/09/1854	10/11/1860	27	484	N	
Lindner, August	??	Germany	Y	?	?	?	12/23/1885			Y	
Lindner, Ernst	29	Germany	Y	Bremen	Baltimore	06/27/1883	11/03/1886			Y	
Lindner, Hirronimus	??	Switzerland	Y	?	?	?	05/03/1886			Y	
Lindner, John	26	Germany	Y	Liverpool	Detroit	05/20/1892	10/02/1896			Y	
Lindner, Philip	34	Bavaria	Y	Havre	New York	04/13/1851	05/01/1854	8	327	N	
Lindower, Jacob	38	Hesse Darmsta	Y	Bremen	Baltimore	10/02/1840	02/26/1850	2	128	N	
Lines, Patrick	25	Ireland	Y	Liverpool	New Orleans	06/07/1847	10/06/1851	4	194	N	
Linfert, Henry	21	Prussia	Y	Rotterdam	New York	09/21/1851	09/28/1854	10	300	N	
Linfert, Henry	21	Prussia	Y	Rotterdam	New York	09/21/1851	09/28/1854	12	239	N	
Linfert, John	28	Prussia	Y	Rotterdam	New York	09/21/1851	09/28/1854	10	301	N	
Linfert, John	28	Prussia	Y	Rotterdam	New York	09/21/1851	09/28/8154	12	240	N	
Linfert, William	25	Prussia	Y	Rotterdam	New York	08/14/1852	09/28/1854	10	299	N	
Linfert, William	25	Prussia	Y	Rotterdam	New York	08/14/1852	09/28/1854	12	238	N	
Linfoot, Thomas	35	England	Y	Toronto	Lewistown	03/15/1837	12/24/1849	23	426	N	
Ling, Henry	33	Hesse Cassel	Y	Bremen	New York	08/20/1851	08/20/1857	15	162	N	
Lingart, George	28	Wuerttemberg	Y	Bremen	New York	09/26/1859	10/15/1860	27	499	N	
Lingemer, Louis	42	Germany	Y	Bremen	New York	10/09/1880	01/04/1887			Y	

CITIZENSHIP RECORDS

APPLICANT	AGE	COUNTRY OF ORIGIN	DEC	DEPART PORT	ENTRY PORT	ARRIVE DATE	DEC DATE	VOL	PG.	FLD	NAT DATE
Lingers, Henry	23	Hanover	Y	Bremen	New Orleans	12/07/1848	08/15/1851	4	141	N	
Lining, August Francis	32	Lombardy	Y	Havre	New York	07/30/1850	12/06/1852	5	383	N	
Linitzky, Abraham	17	Russia	N	?	New York	00/00/1881				Y	10/26/1888
Link, Ernst	32	Germany	Y	Bremen	Baltimore	03/26/1888	11/07/1893			Y	
Link, Ferdinand Frederic	29	Wurttemberg	Y	Liverpool	New York	11/11/1852	01/28/1856	13	512	N	
Link, Francis	33	Bavaria	Y	Bremen	New York	05/??/1852	12/24/1855	13	351	N	
Link, George	24	Bavaria	Y	Bremen	New York	05/11/1854	12/29/1855	13	389	N	
Link, Gotthief	22	Germany	Y	Bremen	New York	06/17/1891	08/17/1895			Y	
Link, John	28	Bavaria	Y	Havre	New York	05/16/1852	12/29/1855	13	388	N	
Link, John	32	Germany	Y	Bremen	New York	06/16/1877	04/10/1882			Y	
Link, Michael	42	Germany	Y	Bremen	New York	03/12/1888	03/25/1893			Y	
Link, Peter	40	Bavaria	Y	Havre	New York	05/16/1852	10/15/1860	27	498	N	
Linke, Edward	32	Germany	Y	Bremen	New York	05/01/1883	10/29/1892			Y	
Linkenbach, Carl	24	Nassau	Y	Havre	New York	05/21/1854	05/27/1854	9	432	N	
Linkenbach, Carl	24	Nassau	Y	Havre	New York	05/21/1854	05/27/1854	10	15	N	
Linkenbach, Phillip	33	Nassau	Y	Liverpool	New York	06/10/1854	10/05/1854	10	470	N	
Linkenbach, Phillip	23	Nassau	Y	Liverpool	New York	06/10/1854	10/05/1854	12	409	N	
Linkenbach, William	34	Nassau	Y	Havre	New York	10/13/1852	10/05/1854	10	469	N	
Linkenbach, William	34	Nassau	Y	Havre	New York	10/13/1852	10/05/1854	12	408	N	
Linley, Joseph	39	England	Y	Liverpool	New York	06/10/1847	11/06/1852	5	242	N	
Linley, Joseph	39	England	Y	Liverpool	New York	06/10/1847	11/06/1852	6	366	N	
Linne, Henry	28	Brunswick	Y	Bremen	New York	06/12/1852	04/18/1854	8	193	N	
Linne, Henry	28	Brunswick	Y	Bremen	New York	06/12/1852	04/18/1854	9	64	N	
Linnemann, Anton B.	34	Germany	Y	Rotterdam	New York	08/26/1880	11/01/1886			Y	
Linnemann, Henry	56	Hanover	Y	Bremen	New Orleans	11/29/1849	05/25/1854	9	419	N	
Linnemann, Henry	56	Hanover	Y	Bremen	New Orleans	11/29/1849	05/25/1854	10	2	N	
Linnemann, Herman	29	Germany	Y	Rotterdam	New York	03/25/1880	10/19/1886			Y	
Lins, Andrew	40	Austria	Y	Havre	New York	06/11/1873	03/25/1885			Y	
Linz, Anton	26	Germany	Y	Havre	New York	08/25/1880	02/13/1883			Y	
Linz, John	25	Bavaria	Y	Bremen	New York	07/03/1851	09/29/1856	14	17	N	
Linz, Lorenz	44	Baden	Y	Havre	New Orleans	06/26/1854	12/05/1855	13	289	N	
Linz, Pius	37	Baden	Y	Havre	New York	05/30/1854	10/02/1856	14	151	N	
Linz, Vinzens	32	Baden	Y	Havre	New York	12/01/1853	12/20/1855	13	336	N	
Lipman, Maier	36	Germany	N	Bremen	New York	03/16/1871	?			Y	
Lipp, Frederick	25	Germany	Y	?	New York	??/??/1881	05/05/1884			Y	
Lipp, John	27	Germany	Y	Hamburg	New York	05/31/1880	10/22/1888	19	161	N	
Lipp, John	24	Germany	Y	Hamburg	New York	05/31/1880	10/22/1888			N	
Lipp, Joseph	25	Germany	Y	Bremen	Baltimore	06/21/1882	10/13/1888	19	146	N	
Lipp, William	23	Germany	Y	Hamburg	New York	06/06/1880	07/30/1883			Y	
Lippe, William	31	Prussia	Y	Rotterdam	Baltimore	06/03/1849	03/24/1851	3	247	N	
Lippelman, Peter Henry	24	Prussia	Y	Bremen	New York	10/11/1852	10/02/1854	10	366	N	
Lippelmann, Peter Henry	24	Prussia	Y	Bremen	New York	10/11/1852	10/02/1854	12	305	N	
Lippert, Joseph	??	Germany	Y	?	?	10/22/1881	08/22/1885			Y	
Lippert, Lorenz	37	Germany	N	Bremen	Baltimore	04/10/1870	?			Y	
Lipps, Ferdinand	22	Baden	Y	Havre	New Orleans	01/26/1855	12/24/1855	13	341	N	
Lipps, Karl	42	Germany	Y	Havre	New York	03/23/1882	10/22/1888			Y	
Lippschuetz, Hosias (Jos	30	Turkey	Y	Hamburg	New York	10/15/1885	01/10/1891			Y	
Lippss, Christ.	36	Germany	Y	Antwerp	Philadelphia	06/10/1880	07/13/1892			Y	
Lippus, Sebastian	26	Wurttemberg	Y	Havre	New York	05/01/1849	01/02/1851	2	435	N	
Lipske, Ladislaus	33	Russia	Y	Hamburg	New York	04/24/1891	10/30/1894			Y	
Lisch, George	43	Austria	Y	Havre	New York	06/10/1873	03/25/1885			Y	
Lisker, Charles William	28	Saxe Weimar	Y	Bremen	New York	03/24/1857	07/30/1858	16	538	N	
Liss, Isaac	36	Russia	Y	Hamburg	New York	11/08/1885	02/18/1888			Y	
List, Joseph	26	Bavaria	Y	Liverpool	New York	05/24/1854	10/07/1854	6	5	N	
List, Joseph	26	Bavaria	Y	Liverpool	New York	05/24/1854	10/07/1854	11	6	N	
Listermann, Christopher	??	Prussia	Y	Bremen	Baltimore	06/14/18??	10/09/1848	1	102	N	
Listermann, William	??	Prussia	Y	Bremen	Baltimore	05/14/18??	10/09/1848	1	94	N	
Litmer, Herman H.C.	35	Prussia	Y	Bremen	New York	10/08/1864	10/09/1869			Y	
Litschgi, Frank	30	Germany	Y	Bremen	New York	10/06/1883	06/04/1891			Y	

CITIZENSHIP RECORDS

APPLICANT	AGE	COUNTRY OF ORIGIN	DEC	DEPART PORT	ENTRY PORT	ARRIVE DATE	DEC DATE	VOL	PG.	FLD	NAT DATE
Litshyi, Joe	27	Germany	Y	Antwerp	New York	10/06/1886	11/06/1893	21	52	N	
Litshyi, Joe	27	Germany	Y	Antwerp	New York	10/06/1886	11/06/1893			Y	
Littig, Christian	13	Germany	N	?	New York	00/00/1856				Y	10/17/1888
Little, John	40	Ireland	Y	Liverpool	New York	05/01/1838	01/20/1849	1	479	N	
Littlejohn, Thomas	36	Scotland	Y	Glasgow	Philadelphia	05/02/1888	10/18/1899			Y	
Littner, Charles F.	32	Germany	Y	Havre	New York	06/17/1886	07/19/1897			Y	
Litzinger, John	41	Bavaria	Y	Havre	New Orleans	06/01/1844	01/22/1853	7	52	N	
Litzler, Jacob	40	Germany	Y	Havre	New York	07/04/1889	07/21/1894			Y	
Litzowitz, Itzig	45	Russia	Y	Bremen	New York	06/24/1893	02/05/1895			Y	
Livingston, Meyer	21	Hesse Darmsta	Y	Bremen	New York	09/??/1852	09/21/1855	13	96	N	
Lizotte, L. Napoleon	42	Canada	Y	Windsor	Detroit	10/10/1868	11/17/1888			Y	
Lloyd, Thomas	24	Ireland	Y	Dublin	New York	04/17/1856	07/31/1860	27	240	N	
Lloyd, William	29	Wales	Y	Liverpool	New York	07/25/1887	08/15/1892			Y	
Lloyd, William P.	29	Ireland	Y	Liverpool	New York	08/26/1849	11/05/1852	5	234	N	
Lloyd, William P.	29	Ireland	Y	Liverpool	New York	08/26/1849	11/05/1852	6	358	N	
Lobker, H.	41	Germany	Y	Bremen	Baltimore	08/15/1864	08/13/1879			Y	
Lobnitz, Frank	54	Germany	Y	Hamburg	New York	05/13/1868	10/02/1884			Y	
Locherer, Apolinar	45	Baden	Y	Havre	New Orleans	04/23/1854	10/03/1854	12	322	N	
Locherer, Yrolinar	45	Baden	Y	Havre	New Orleans	04/23/1854	10/03/1854	10	383	N	
Lochschmidt, Frank	38	Austria	Y	Bremen	Baltimore	09/10/1881	06/21/1886			Y	
Lochte, Herman	32	Hanover	Y	Bremen	New Orleans	12/31/1853	09/29/1856	14	31	N	
Locker, John	25	Wurttemberg	Y	Havre	New York	05/05/1854	09/20/1855	13	79	N	
Loeb, Immanuel	40	Germany	N	Havre	New York	07/??/1865	?			Y	
Loeb, Isaac	40	Germany	N	Havre	New York	09/??/1869	?			Y	
Loeb, Jacob	21	Bavaria	Y	Hamburg	New York	12/20/1870	06/13/1872	18	500	N	
Loeb, Jacob	60	Germany	N	Havre	New York	01/10/1853	?			Y	
Loeb, Jacob	48	Germany	N	Havre	New York	07/10/1858	?			Y	
Loeb, Marcus	40	Hesse Darmsta	Y	Liverpool	New York	07/??/1853	02/21/1857	15	43	N	
Loeb, Simon	34	Germany	Y	Bremen	New York	05/20/1882	07/29/1886			Y	
Loeb, Solomon	28	Hesse Darmsta	Y	London	New York	05/04/1849	02/21/1857	15	42	N	
Loeber, Herman	58	Germany	Y	Bremen	New York	04/??/1850	08/27/1879			Y	
Loebker, Bernard	39	Hanover	Y	Bremen	Baltimore	05/26/1846	06/21/1851	3	439	N	
Loebker, Herman	59	Germany	N	Bremen	New York	05/01/1849	04/??/1851	28	17	N	08/??/1854
Loebker, Herman	21	Germany	N	Bremen	New York	05/07/1849	04/00/1851			Y	08/00/1854
Loebnitz, Charles Ferdin	36	Prussia	Y	Hamburg	New York	10/03/1854	03/27/1856	26	358	N	
Loeffelholz, Gottfried	30	Germany	Y	Bremen	Baltimore	09/10/1880	01/11/1889			Y	
Loeffler, Carl	65	Germany	N	Bremen	New York	02/05/1872	07/??/1872	28	72	N	10/??/1877
Loeffler, Carl	49	Germany	N	Bremen	New York	02/05/1872	07/00/1872			Y	10/00/1877
Loeffler, Theodore	34	Baden	Y	Havre	New Orleans	05/01/1854	12/10/1859	17	501	N	
Loehr, Jacob	32	Nassau	Y	London	New York	04/19/1852	04/17/1854	8	177	N	
Loehtefeld, Bernard	28	Prussia	Y	Bremen	New York	07/03/1855	10/10/1857	15	385	N	
Loelwer, Joseph	30	Germany	Y	Amsterdam	New York	10/21/1883	02/18/1887			Y	
Loepker, Gerhard Henry	31	Hanover	Y	Bremen	New Orleans	06/01/1854	09/24/1857	15	313	N	
Loer, Conrad	26	Hanover	Y	Bremen	New Orleans	12/10/1849	03/07/1853	7	306	N	
Loerke, Gustav	??	Germany	Y	?	New York	03/??/1884	10/21/1882			Y	
Loesche, Henry	36	Hanover	Y	Bremen	Philadelphia	10/01/1852	09/30/1856	14	67	N	
Loeser, Adam	52	Germany	Y	Bremen	New York	10/18/1869	10/06/1880			Y	
Loevs, Jacob	36	Bavaria	Y	Havre	New York	07/??/1850	12/05/1850	2	342	N	
Loew, Jacob	22	Wurttemberg	Y	Havre	New York	11/05/1853	03/26/1857	15	88	N	
Loewe, Christoph	33	Hesse Darmsta	Y	Liverpool	New York	09/29/1852	04/18/1854	8	196	N	
Loewe, Christoph	33	Hesse Darmsta	Y	Liverpool	New York	09/29/1852	04/18/1854	9	67	N	
Loewel, Johann	37	Germany	Y	Bremen	Baltimore	03/04/1885	01/23/1890			Y	10/26/1893
Loewensohn, Levi	??	Russia	Y	?	?	02/??/1873	08/12/1879			Y	
Loewinger, Charles	34	Saxe Meininge	Y	Bremen	New York	05/12/1856	05/06/1861	18	159	N	
Lohaus, Anton	24	Germany	Y	Amsterdam	New York	10/11/1880	10/25/1883			Y	
Lohaus, Bernard	24	Germany	Y	Bremen	New York	04/27/1884	06/03/1886			Y	
Lohbeck, George	27	Germany	Y	Bremen	Baltimore	10/20/1880	10/05/1892			Y	
Lohbeck, Henry	21	Germany	Y	Bremen	New York	04/09/1881	07/06/1882			Y	
Loheide, Frederick	23	Hanover	Y	Bremen	Baltimore	10/10/1857	04/09/1861	18	137	N	

CITIZENSHIP RECORDS

APPLICANT	AGE	COUNTRY OF ORIGIN	DEC	DEPART PORT	ENTRY PORT	ARRIVE DATE	DEC DATE	VOL	PG.	FLD	NAT DATE
Loheide, William	35	Germany	N	Bremen	Baltimore	06/24/1871	?			Y	
Lohekamp, Bernard	21	Hanover	Y	Bremen	New Orleans	12/15/1851	10/09/1854	11	106	N	
Lohle, Theo Bernard	32	Germany	Y	Bremen	New York	06/23/1888	12/24/1889			Y	
Lohmann, August	21	Germany	Y	Bremen	Baltimore	10/17/1885	04/03/1889			Y	
Lohmann, Barney	32	Germany	Y	Bremen	New York	09/23/1871	10/09/1882			Y	
Lohmann, Diedrich	25	Hanover	Y	Bremen	Baltimore	07/08/1848	10/21/1852	5	35	N	
Lohmann, Franz	34	Germany	Y	?	Baltimore	??/??/1884	10/24/1890			Y	
Lohmann, Fred	25	Germany	Y	Bremen	New York	05/02/1883	11/01/1889			Y	
Lohmann, Henry	27	Germany	Y	Bremen	Baltimore	06/01/1889	07/07/1891			Y	
Lohmann, Herman	22	Germany	Y	Antwerp	New York	03/31/1881	05/30/1883			Y	
Lohmann, Joseph	24	Germany	Y	Rotterdam	New York	10/22/1892	06/10/1897			Y	
Lohmann, Julius	43	Germany	Y	Bremen	New York	03/10/1870	03/26/1888			Y	
Lohmann, Theodor	22	Germany	Y	Bremen	Baltimore	05/10/1887	04/11/1891			Y	
Lohmasser, William	31	Bavaria	Y	Bremen	Baltimore	09/??/1850	03/12/1853	7	326	N	
Lohmeier, Christ	23	Prussia	Y	Bremen	Baltimore	06/24/1849	04/05/1852	24	371	N	
Lohmeier, Henry	25	Germany	Y	Bremen	New York	10/27/1881	09/24/1883			Y	
Lohmiller, John Bernard	32	Hanover	Y	Bremen	Baltimore	07/01/1845	08/07/1848	22	63	N	
Lohmuller, Carl	23	Germany	Y	Havre	New York	04/17/1884	02/24/1885			Y	
Lohr, John	65	Hanover	Y	Bremen	New Orleans	03/29/1847	04/01/1853	7	476	N	
Lohr, Michael	32	Bavaria	Y	Havre	New Orleans	12/15/1836	09/??/1848	22	360	N	
Lohrer, Charles	43	Switzerland	Y	Havre	New York	12/15/1854	03/08/1858	16	381	N	
Lohrer, Martin	25	Wurttemberg	Y	Havre	New York	06/01/1852	12/04/1855	13	282	N	
Lohrig, Peter	23	Prussia	Y	Liverpool	New York	05/12/1852	04/18/1854	8	200	N	
Lohrig, Peter	23	Prussia	Y	Liverpool	New York	05/12/1852	04/18/1854	9	71	N	
Lohse, Louis	29	Saxony	Y	Bremen	New York	08/??/1849	11/??/1849	23	323	N	
Loibl, Max	??	Germany	Y	?	?	?	09/24/1891			Y	
Loibl, Otto	??	Germany	Y	?	?	?	04/14/1893			Y	
Loichinger, Carl	29	Germany	Y	Bremen	New York	11/22/1881	03/21/1885			Y	
Lombard, Fred	30	Germany	Y	?	Baltimore	??/??/1890	08/22/1893			Y	
Lombardo, Battista	33	Italy	Y	Palermo	New York	05/08/1882	10/18/1893			Y	
Lombardo, Laverio	??	Italy	Y	?	?	?	10/29/1895			Y	
Lomler, Charles W.	21	Saxony	Y	Bremen	New York	06/23/1848	05/20/1852	25	62	N	
Lommer, Sylvester	42	Germany	Y	Bremen	New York	12/06/1880	06/09/1890			Y	
London, Arnold	25	Austria	Y	Bremen	Baltimore	11/01/1890	08/29/1891			Y	
Londy, Simon	32	Russia	Y	Hamburg	New York	07/17/1881	05/15/1883	28	97		
Londy, Simon	27	Russia	Y	Hamburg	New York	07/17/1881	05/15/1883			Y	
Lonergan, Patrick	28	Ireland	Y	Queenstown	New York	05/02/1883	10/31/1891			Y	
Lonergan, William J.	32	Ireland	Y	Queenstown	New York	05/02/1887	09/15/1893			Y	
Lonergau, James	35	Ireland	Y	Liverpool	New Orleans	12/20/1851	11/18/1858	17	340	N	
Long, Anthony	16	Germany	N	?	New York	00/00/1877				Y	10/26/1888
Long, Charles	33	Prussia	Y	Bremen	Baltimore	??/06/1945	10/09/1848	1	91	N	
Long, David	27	Ireland	Y	Liverpool	New Orleans	12/22/1849	07/24/1851	4	33	N	
Long, George	44	Bavaria	Y	Havre	New Orleans	12/28/1832	01/19/1850	23	529	N	
Long, James	21	Ireland	Y	Cork	New Orleans	06/13/1849	11/08/1851	4	504	N	
Long, Jerry	26	Ireland	Y	Queenstown	New York	05/16/1886	10/27/1893			Y	
Long, John	29	Ireland	Y	Liverpool	New Orleans	02/15/1849	02/27/1851	3	175	N	
Long, John	33	France	Y	Havre	New York	01/03/1854	10/01/1856	14	109	N	
Long, John	24	Ireland	Y	Liverpool	New Orleans	01/06/1852	08/05/1856	14	354	N	
Long, John	34	Bavaria	Y	Bremen	Richmond	07/10/1844	10/02/1848	22	394	N	
Long, Mathias	31	Bavaria	Y	Bremen	New York	12/??/1852	03/23/1853	7	376	N	
Long, Patrick	32	Ireland	Y	Canada	Buffalo	05/22/1848	06/18/1851	3	397	N	
Long, Patrick	26	Ireland	Y	Cork	New Orleans	??/17/1849	01/??/1850	23	453	N	
Long, Robert	26	Ireland	Y	Belfast	New York	06/??/1851	11/04/1856	14	461	N	
Long, Robert	62	Ireland	N	Belfast	New York	06/10/1851	?			Y	
Long, Robert	52	Ireland	N	Belfast	New York	06/10/1851	??/??/1853	28	87	N	10/??/1860
Long, Robert	15	Ireland	N	Belfast	New York	06/10/1851	00/00/1853			Y	10/00/1860
Long, Simon	42	Germany	N	Havre	New York	06/??/1862	?			Y	
Long, Thomas	40	Ireland	Y	Kilrush	Buffalo	07/??/1851	03/02/1858	16	358	N	
Longel, Anthony	63	France	N	Havre	New York	07/??/1848	??/??/1851	28	146	N	??/??/1855

CITIZENSHIP RECORDS

APPLICANT	AGE	COUNTRY OF ORIGIN	DEC	DEPART PORT	ENTRY PORT	ARRIVE DATE	DEC DATE	VOL	PG.	FLD	NAT DATE
Longel, Anthony	23	France	N	Havre	New York	07/00/1848	00/00/1851			Y	00/00/1855
Longinetti, Louis	29	Italy	Y	Havre	New York	12/15/1882	10/26/1892			Y	
Longini, Sol	23	Germany	Y	Havre	New York	01/06/1882	11/28/1885			Y	
Longinotti, John G.	??	Italy	Y	Havre	New York	08/10/1864	03/27/1897			Y	
Longo, Guiseppe	31	Italy	Y	Naples	New York	04/01/1890	06/26/1894			Y	
Longo, Joseph	47	Italy	Y	Palermo	New York	12/22/1883	10/11/1893	19	430	N	
Longo, Joseph	47	Italy	Y	Palermo	New York	12/22/1883	10/11/1893			Y	
Longo, Vincent	38	Italy	Y	Palermo	New York	12/15/1884	10/18/1893	21	22	N	
Longo, Vincent	38	Italy	Y	Palermo	New York	12/15/1884	10/18/1893			Y	
Lonney, Thomas	25	Ireland	Y	Dublin	New York	03/11/1881	03/30/1888			Y	
Loos, Christian	24	Bavaria	Y	Havre	New York	06/28/1853	09/14/1855	13	32	N	
Loos, Conrad	28	Bavaria	Y	Bremen	New York	05/22/1848	02/21/1852	24	147	N	
Loos, Henry	36	Kurhessen	Y	Bremen	Baltimore	11/19/1859	09/12/1860	27	359	N	
Loos, Joseph	??	Germany	Y	?	?	08/12/1890	10/22/1890			Y	
Loppacher, Jacob	29	Switzerland	Y	Havre	New York	08/07/1881	04/03/1891			Y	
Lopple, Henry	29	Wurttemberg	Y	Havre	New York	10/??/1853	01/27/1856	14	514	N	
Lorbeer, August	38	Germany	Y	Hamburg	New York	10/28/1877	09/30/1882			Y	
Lorch, William	21	Germany	Y	Bremen	New York	03/20/1881	08/17/1883			Y	
Lorentz, Michael	44	Bavaria	Y	Havre	New Orleans	05/27/1848	03/15/1852	24	303	N	
Lorenz, Alfons	37	Germany	Y	Antwerp	New York	??/??/1874	09/21/1886			Y	
Lorenz, Alois	20	Germany	Y	Havre	New York	03/19/1881	09/25/1882			Y	
Lorenz, Andreas	45	Germany	Y	Bremen	New York	02/14/1883	02/15/1892		1	Y	
Lorenz, Anton	28	Austria	Y	Bremen	Baltimore	03/10/1888	03/27/1891			Y	
Lorenz, Basilius	27	Baden	Y	Havre	New York	10/09/1845	04/29/1850	3	17	N	
Lorenz, Emanuel	36	Germany	Y	Antwerp	Philadelphia	06/25/1883	09/28/1896			Y	
Lorenz, Frank	27	Austria	Y	Bremen	Baltimore	05/15/1891	08/30/1892			Y	
Lorenz, Henry	24	Saxe Weimar	Y	Bremen	Baltimore	??/12/1850	10/31/1851	4	447	N	
Lorenz, Henry	??	Germany	Y	?	?	?	03/01/1884			Y	
Lorenz, Jacob	43	Germany	Y	Bremen	New York	03/04/1883	01/07/1890			Y	
Lorenz, Josph	34	France	Y	Havre	New York	09/17/1849	03/28/1853	7	418	N	
Lorenzino, John	48	Italy	Y	Havre	New York	08/25/1885	07/22/1896			Y	
Lorie, Henry	27	Prussia	Y	Liverpool	New York	05/15/1850	09/20/1856	14	360	N	
Lorke, A. Edwin	47	Prussia	Y	?	New York	05/06/1883	03/23/1887			Y	
Lorsbach, Adolph	22	Prussia	Y	Havre	New York	??/27/1849	10/??/1849	23	284	N	
Losche, Wilhelm	36	Germany	Y	Bremen	Baltimore	08/??/1866	10/11/1880			Y	
Loschiavo, John	42	Italy	Y	Palermo	New York	04/22/1884	10/19/1893			Y	
Loschinske, Carl	32	Germany	Y	Hamburg	New York	05/16/1882	12/27/1883			Y	
Losekamp, Bernard	21	Hanover	Y	Bremen	New Orleans	12/15/1851	10/09/1854	6	103	N	
Losekamp, Joseph	58	Germany	N	Bremen	New Orleans	05/??/1849	?			Y	
Losing, Joseph	25	Prussia	Y	Bremen	New York	09/17/1848	06/26/1851	3	457	N	
Losson, Gottlieb	24	Bavaria	Y	Havre	New York	04/??/1856	11/03/1856	14	458	N	
Loth, Michael	33	France	Y	Havre	New York	??/24/1846	08/??/1851	4	157	N	
Lothes, Eberhard	??	Bavaria	Y	Hamburg	Baltimore	05/29/1852	11/08/1856	14	502	N	
Lothes, Peter	19	Germany	Y	Bremen	New York	05/18/1890	11/16/1891			Y	
Lothian, Adam J.	??	England	Y	?	?	?	03/23/1888			Y	
Lotter, John	29	Bavaria	Y	Bremen	New York	08/15/1853	06/04/1856	14	289	N	
Lotterer, Albert	19	Germany	Y	Rotterdam	New York	09/03/1891	04/11/1892			Y	
Lotz, Henry	33	Hesse Darmsta	Y	London	New York	07/??/1848	10/23/1851	4	378	N	
Lotz, Ludwig	48	Nassau	Y	Bremen	New York	08/??/1840	04/25/1855	11	302	N	
Lotz, Ludwig	31	Hanover	Y	Bremen	New Orleans	12/20/1854	09/27/1856	14	414	N	
Loughlin, John	22	Ireland	Y	Liverpool	New Orleans	03/15/1851	02/27/1852	24	175	N	
Loughlin, Michael	25	Ireland	Y	Queenstown	New York	02/13/1867	??/??/1873			Y	
Loughlin, Michael	45	Ireland	N	Queenstown	New York	02/13/1867	?			Y	
Loughran, John	27	Ireland	Y	Liverpool	New Orleans	12/24/1848	03/09/1852	24	270	N	
Louis, John	33	Austria	Y	Bremen	Baltimore	04/01/1888	11/02/1895			Y	
Louis, Pierre	29	France	Y	Havre	New York	08/??/1845	02/04/1853	7	115	N	
Louis, Thomas	32	Poland (Pruss	Y	Liverpool	New Orleans	02/??/1847	12/15/1855	13	317	N	
Love, Robert	34	Ireland	N	Liverpool	Boston	09/??/1861	?			Y	
Lovett, Mathew R.	33	Ireland	N	Sligo	Buffalo	??/??/1870	?			Y	

CITIZENSHIP RECORDS

APPLICANT	AGE	COUNTRY OF ORIGIN	DEC	DEPART PORT	ENTRY PORT	ARRIVE DATE	DEC DATE	VOL	PG.	FLD	NAT DATE
Lovett, Thomas	30	Ireland	Y	London	New York	07/12/1852	04/25/1853	8	117	N	
Lowe, James	43	England	Y	London	New York	07/27/1839	01/26/1849	1	522	N	
Lowell, Richard	21	England	Y	Belfast	New York	12/15/1847	02/05/1853	7	117	N	
Lowenhirz, Solomon	34	Nassau	Y	London	New York	07/??/1848	11/??/1849	23	308	N	
Lowenthal, Berthold	21	Wurttemberg	Y	Havre	New York	08/15/1850	08/12/1851	4	116	N	
Lowry, John	42	Ireland	Y	Liverpool	New York	06/07/1849	04/05/1852	24	376	N	
Lowry, John	30	England	Y	Liverpool	New Orleans	05/12/1849	04/11/1856	26	491	N	
Luadefeld, Henry	22	Hesse Cassel	Y	Havre	New York	11/03/1854	10/01/1856	14	84	N	
Lubbe, Casper	40	Germany	Y	Bremen	Baltimore	06/07/1877	10/14/1894			Y	
Lubbe, John Jos	56	Germany	Y	Bremen	Baltimore	06/28/1861	10/23/1888	19	167	N	
Lubbers, Julius	26	Hamburg	Y	Southampton	New York	11/30/1857	11/26/1859	17	482	N	
Lubbert, Ernst Henry	23	Hanover	Y	Bremen	Baltimore	07/02/1859	12/23/1861	18	236	N	
Lubker, Lewis	22	Hanover	Y	Bremen	Baltimore	08/??/1847	10/26/1850	2	309	N	
Luc, John	42	Germany	Y	Antwerp	New York	12/12/1881	10/17/1892			Y	
Luchte, Anton	34	Prussia	Y	Bremen	New Orleans	11/14/1853	10/09/1854	6	193	N	
Luchte, Anton	34	Prussia	Y	Bremen	New Orleans	11/04/1853	10/09/1854	11	196	N	
Luckmann, Philip	??	Prussia	Y	Rotterdam	New Orleans	11/17/18??	10/11/1848	1	116	N	
Lucko, Otto	31	Germany	Y	Bremen	New York	10/02/1880	09/19/1885			Y	
Lucks, Herman	31	Germany	Y	Bremen	Baltimore	06/19/1891	05/23/1894			Y	
Lucks, Joseph	59	France	Y	Strassburg	New York	??/??/1852	11/01/1886	19	104	N	
Lucks, Joseph	59	France	Y	Strassburg	New York	00/00/1852	11/01/1886			Y	
Ludeke, Hermann	36	Hanover	Y	Bremen	New York	06/20/1853	05/13/1861	18	168	N	
Ludemann, Herman	27	Hanover	Y	Bremen	Baltimore	07/01/1854	12/02/1857	16	63	N	
Ludemeier, John	32	Austria	Y	Bremen	New York	04/18/1870	05/20/1871			Y	
Ludwig, Charles	29	Germany	Y	Antwerp	New York	09/11/1891	10/21/1896			Y	
Ludwig, Chrisitan	33	Baden	Y	Havre	New York	04/18/1854	10/02/1856	14	142	N	
Ludwig, Frank	22	Germany	Y	Havre	New York	10/19/1882	04/12/1884			Y	
Ludwig, Frederick Ferdin	31	Prussia	Y	Bremen	New York	12/08/1858	10/06/1860	27	408	N	
Ludwig, Heinz	24	Bavaria	Y	Havre	New York	04/23/1851	04/17/1854	8	187	N	
Ludwig, Heinz	24	Bavaria	Y	Havre	New York	04/23/1851	04/17/1854	9	58	N	
Ludwig, Herman	36	Germany	Y	Bremen	New York	04/07/1882	07/06/1885			Y	
Ludwig, Herman H.	28	Oldenburg	Y	Bremen	New Orleans	12/21/1845	11/01/1852	5	150	N	
Ludwig, Jacob	43	Germany	Y	Bremen	New York	06/17/1885	08/10/1887			Y	
Ludwig, John	23	Bavaria	Y	Havre	New York	??/12/1851	04/24/1855	11	301	N	
Ludwig, John	30	Hesse Darmsta	Y	Bremen	Baltimore	01/13/1854	06/03/1856	14	287	N	
Ludwig, Joseph	48	Bavaria	Y	Havre	New York	05/27/1846	09/14/1848	22	344	N	
Ludwig, Mathias	28	Prussia	Y	Liverpool	New York	06/24/1853	08/28/1855	11	515	N	
Ludwig, Mathias	44	Germany	Y	?	Cincinnati?	04/20/1864	04/06/1885			Y	
Ludwig, Peter	27	Kurhessen	Y	Bremen	Baltimore	05/08/1854	09/24/1856	14	361	N	
Ludwig, Peter	37	Germany	Y	Rotterdam	New York	09/07/1881	04/11/1887			Y	
Ludwig, Wendl	21	Germany	Y	Bremen	New York	07/23/1894	11/23/1896			Y	
Luebbehuesen, Henry	24	Oldenburg	Y	Bremen	New Orleans	12/20/1846	02/19/1849	23	202	N	
Luebben, J. H.	30	Germany	Y	Bremen	Baltimore	07/15/1880	07/16/1884			Y	
Luebbenjans, William	29	Germany	Y	Bremen	New York	05/25/1884	10/19/1888			Y	
Luebbermann, Heinrich	22	Germany	Y	Bremen	Baltimore	08/05/1882	10/14/1885			Y	
Luebbersmann, Anthony	22	Germany	Y	Bremen	Baltimore	06/06/1879	08/18/1881			Y	
Luebbersmann, Heinrich	22	Germany	Y	Bremen	Baltimore	08/05/1882	10/14/1885	19	25		
Luebbert, C.W.	53	Hanover	N	Bremen	Baltimore	07/01/1859	?			Y	
Luebbert, Henry	28	Germany	Y	Antwerp	New York	05/25/1881	06/17/1884			Y	
Luebbinjans, William	29	Germany	Y	Bremen	New York	05/25/1884	10/19/1888	19	157	N	
Lueben, Max	35	Germany	Y	Hamburg	New York	05/15/1882	10/30/1886	19	101	N	
Lueben, Max	35	Germany	Y	Hamburg	New York	05/15/1882	10/30/1886			Y	
Luebkert, Harry	36	Germany	Y	Hamburg	New Orleans	09/28/1889	10/14/1891			Y	
Luecher, Henry	38	Germany	Y	Bremen	Baltimore	??/??/1873	10/02/1883			Y	
Luechtefeld, Anton	34	Hanover	Y	Bremen	New Orleans	11/30/1849	03/25/1856	26	312	N	
Luecke, Henry	23	Germany	Y	Bremen	New York	08/20/1887	02/16/1892	19	348	N	
Luecke, Henry	23	Germany	Y	Bremen	New York	08/20/1884	02/16/1892			Y	
Luecke, William Edward	24	Germany	Y	Hamburg	New York	08/13/1890	10/22/1890			Y	
Lueckmann, Herman	16	Germany	N	?	New York	00/00/1882				Y	04/02/1888

CITIZENSHIP RECORDS

APPLICANT	AGE	COUNTRY OF ORIGIN	DEC	DEPART PORT	ENTRY PORT	ARRIVE DATE	DEC DATE	VOL	PG.	FLD	NAT DATE
Lueckner, Barney	32	Hanover	Y	Bremen	New Orleans	12/21/1845	02/19/1849	23	166	N	
Lueddecke, Charles	30	Brunswick	Y	Havre	New York	05/28/1852	03/19/1853	7	353	N	
Lueders, Karl	29	Germany	Y	Amsterdam	New York	05/07/1891	01/03/1899			Y	
Luedner, Michael	35	Bavaria	Y	Bremen	New York	09/25/1850	02/04/1851	3	93	N	
Luehner, Joseph	36	Hanover	Y	Bremen	New Orleans	12/20/1848	04/12/1852	24	448	N	
Luehrmann, H. W.	59	Germany	N	Bremen	Baltimore	11/17/1845	?	28	215	N	10/??/1850
Luehrmann, H. W.	16	Germany	N	Bremen	Baltimore	11/17/1845				Y	10/00/1850
Luehrs, Henry	26	Hanover	Y	Bremen	New York	07/10/1854	09/27/1856	14	412	N	
Lueken, John B. C.	36	Germany	Y	Amsterdam	New York	07/24/1881	02/26/1886			Y	
Luekens, Adolph	42	Germany	N	Bremen	Baltimore	11/??/1864	?			Y	
Luen, Gerhard	23	Hanover	Y	Bremen	Baltimore	10/04/1853	10/06/1856	14	188	N	
Luening, Anton F.	28	Oldenburg	Y	Bremen	Baltimore	05/06/1848	04/13/1852	24	488	N	
Luennemann, Henry	29	Hanover	Y	Bremen	Baltimore	05/16/1856	05/17/1860	27	193	N	
Luering, Adolf	42	Germany	N	Hamburg	New York	12/19/1881	?			Y	
Luerson, Henry	47	Oldenburg	Y	Bremen	New Orleans	10/12/1852	04/04/1853	8	55	N	
Luerss, Bernard	19	Germany	Y	Bremen	Baltimore	05/27/1882	08/15/1882			Y	
Luetgens, Fred	29	Germany	Y	Hamburg	New York	11/04/1881	02/15/1884			Y	
Luetticke, Henry	41	Prussia	Y	Bremen	Baltimore	08/19/1844	10/06/1848	22	452	N	
Luetzel, Christian	27	Bavaria	Y	Havre	New York	10/03/1854	09/30/1857	15	336	N	
Lugaur, Joseph	40	Germany	Y	Munich	Baltimore	05/04/1870	11/26/1880			Y	
Lugenbiehl, Peter	27	Germany	Y	?	New York	??/??/1879	10/10/1884			Y	
Lugtenburg, Peter	32	Holland	Y	Rotterdam	Boston	04/19/1854	04/09/1862	18	311	N	
Luhen, John Henry	41	Hanover	Y	Bremen	New Orleans	11/15/1851	08/27/1855	11	501	N	
Luhn, Gerhard	23	Hanover	Y	Bremen	Baltimore	10/08/1854	09/24/1858	16	140	N	
Luhn, John William	30	Hanover	Y	Bremen	New Orleans	10/28/1852	05/01/1854	8	311	N	
Luhn, John William	30	Hanover	Y	Bremen	New Orleans	10/28/1852	05/01/1854	9	184	N	
Luhn, Joseph	26	Germany	Y	Bremen	Baltimore	04/08/1880	03/25/1882			Y	
Luhr, Antone	43	Germany	Y	Baden	New York	01/14/1870	10/27/1895			Y	
Luhr, Jacob	32	Nassau	Y	London	New York	04/19/1852	04/17/1854	9	48	N	
Luhrmann, Henrich	29	Germany	Y	Bremen	New York	05/05/1886	01/11/1890			Y	
Luick, Emanuel	27	Wurttemberg	Y	Havre	New York	04/12/1854	06/29/1857	15	117	N	
Lukens, Charles	28	Hanover	Y	Bremen	Baltimore	05/05/1848	09/08/1852	25	415	N	
Lukovitz, John	29	Germany	Y	Hamburg	New York	03/07/1880	10/13/1885	19	24	N	
Lukowsky, Joseph	??	Russia	Y	?	?	??/??/1881	12/16/1881			Y	
Lumbert, August	31	Germany	Y	Hamburg	New York	09/20/1882	08/04/1885			Y	
Lumpp, Herman	25	Wurttemberg	Y	Havre	New York	05/05/1854	11/01/1858	17	216	N	
Lunas, William B.	??	Russia	Y	?	?		10/27/1890			Y	
Lund, Carl August	36	Sweden	Y	Antwerp	New York	10/05/1854	10/25/1858	17	101	N	
Lund, John	49	England	Y	Liverpool	Baltimore	01/26/1889	04/01/1896			Y	
Lund, William	54	Sweden	Y	?	?	05/29/1870	08/13/1884			Y	
Lundy, Michael	??	Ireland	Y	?	?	?	04/10/1882			Y	
Lung, Charles	40	Germany	Y	Antwerp	New York	03/01/1886	03/27/1888			Y	
Lungmus, Albert	42	Germany	Y	Bremen	New York	07/17/1867	03/28/1882			Y	
Lunne, Fred	33	Germany	N	?	Baltimore	11/12/1869	?			Y	
Lunne, Henry	31	Germany	Y	Bremen	Baltimore	08/18/1874	10/13/1884			Y	
Lunnemann, Bernhard	25	Hanover	Y	Bremen	New Orleans	11/29/1849	12/02/1852	5	370	N	
Lunsmann, B.	27	Germany	Y	Bremen	Baltimore	10/01/1882	04/08/1886			Y	
Luntz, John	34	Bavaria	Y	Bremen	New Orleans	12/01/1853	04/26/1854	8	271	N	
Luntz, John	34	Bavaria	Y	Bremen	New Orleans	12/01/1853	04/26/1854	9	142	N	
Lupkes, H.	22	Germany	Y	?	?	?	05/24/1892			Y	
Lupriore, Antonio	??	Italy	Y	?	?	?	08/31/1894			Y	
Lurie, Hirsch	36	Russia	Y	Liverpool	New York	09/21/1888	04/11/1890			Y	
Lurie, Joseph	29	Russia	Y	Hamburg	New York	10/07/1887	10/05/1888			Y	
Lurie, Thomas	??	Russia	Y	?	?	?	10/01/1885			Y	
Luring, Adolf	33	Germany	Y	Hamburg	New York	12/19/1881	03/00/1883			Y	
Lurz, August	61	Germany	Y	Bremen	New York	04/01/1888	10/31/1891			Y	
Lurz, John	23	Germany	Y	Bremen	New York	04/01/1888	05/06/1892			Y	
Lusch, J. George	51	Germany	Y	Bremen	New York	09/25/1880	02/20/1888			Y	
Luscher, Segmund	21	Switzerland	Y	Havre	New York	12/16/1852	10/05/1854	10	467	N	

CITIZENSHIP RECORDS

APPLICANT	AGE	COUNTRY OF ORIGIN	DEC	DEPART PORT	ENTRY PORT	ARRIVE DATE	DEC DATE	VOL	PG.	FLD	NAT DATE
Luscher, Segmund	21	Switzerland	Y	Havre	New York	12/16/1852	10/05/1854	12	406	N	
Lussy, Joseph	30	Germany	Y	Antwerp	New York	12/10/1889	05/14/1894			Y	
Lustenberger, Leon	34	Germany	Y	Havre	New York	09/09/1888	09/06/1894			Y	
Lustig, Nicholas	32	Bavaria	Y	Havre	New York	05/18/1849	09/15/1857	15	271	N	
Luter, Lorenzo	??	Italy	Y	?	?	?	11/10/1894			Y	
Luther, Charles	29	Prussia	Y	Bremen	New York	10/01/1860	06/25/1862	18	360	N	
Luther, Charles S.	58	Prussia	N	Bremen	New York	10/04/1861	?			Y	
Luthmann, Gerhard	25	Germany	Y	Amsterdam	New York	09/06/1891	06/29/1895			Y	
Luthringer, Phillip	25	Germany	Y	Havre	New York	09/05/1892	05/25/1896			Y	
Luthy, Edmund	51	Switzerland	N	Havre	New York	08/??/1854	?			Y	
Luthy, Samuel	30	Switzerland	Y	Havre	New York	05/01/1847	10/22/1852	5	50	N	
Lutja, George Henry	35	Hanover	Y	Bremen	Baltimore	07/14/1843	10/02/1848	1	11	N	
Lutker, David Henry (Joh	34	Hanover	Y	Bremen	Baltimore	10/21/1854	03/25/1856	26	337	N	
Lutman, H. (Luttmann)	40	Germany	Y	Bremen	New York	12/??/1866	03/19/1887			Y	
Lutterbeck, Friedrich	34	Germany	Y	Bremen	Baltimore	12/??/1865	10/13/1880			Y	
Lutterbein, William	30	Prussia	Y	Bremen	New Orleans	12/22/1847	02/13/1849	23	78	N	
Lutterbey, Rudolph	28	Prussia	Y	Bremen	New Orleans	11/25/1854	03/25/1858			Y	
Lutticke, Hubert	68	Germany	N	Antwerp	New York	06/??/1845	?			Y	
Luttigmann, William	28	Prussia	Y	Hamburg	New York	04/23/1860	11/05/1860	18	14	N	
Luttmann, Frederick	22	Germany	Y	Bremen	New York	11/08/1881	05/14/1885			Y	
Luttmann, Henry	21	Germany	Y	Bremen	New York	11/14/1881	08/15/1884			Y	
Lutz, Anton	22	Austria	Y	Bremen	New York	03/28/1881	04/02/1883			Y	
Lutz, Brunner	34	Germany	Y	Hamburg	New York	07/27/1886	10/25/1895			Y	
Lutz, Frank	24	Prussia	Y	Bremen	New Orleans	06/03/1854	10/09/1854	11	190	N	
Lutz, Frank	59	Germany	Y	Bremen	New York	03/16/1881	10/17/1896			Y	
Lutz, Franz	24	Prussia	Y	Bremen	New Orleans	06/03/1854	10/09/1854	6	187	N	
Lutz, Fred	34	Germany	Y	Hamburg	New York	07/04/1882	10/13/1893			Y	
Lutz, Frederick	29	Wurttemberg	Y	Havre	New York	11/06/1854	12/08/1858	17	386	N	
Lutz, George	26	Germany	Y	Bremen	New York	05/30/1893	08/21/1894			Y	
Lutz, Gustav Albert	43	Germany	Y	Hamburg	New York	10/20/1887	02/11/1891			Y	
Lutz, Joseph	33	Austria	Y	Antwerp	New York	10/21/1878	11/27/1886			Y	
Lux, Adalbert	21	Hungary	Y	Bremen	Baltimore	01/06/1889	01/27/1891			Y	
Lux, Gottfried	30	Germany	Y	Havre	New York	08/16/1872	09/09/1883			Y	
Lyden, Michael	26	Ireland	Y	Queenstown	New York	05/22/1885	06/16/1891			Y	
Lyer, John	34	Germany	Y	Bremen	New York	02/11/1888	02/05/1892			Y	
Lynam, William	25	Ireland	Y	Liverpool	New York	03/24/1848	09/03/1852	25	349	N	
Lynch, Dominic	17	England	N	?	New York	00/00/1882				Y	08/28/1888
Lynch, James	28	Ireland	Y	Liverpool	New York	07/12/1847	10/13/1848	1	196	N	
Lynch, James	29	Ireland	Y	Liverpool	New Orleans	02/10/1851	10/03/1854	10	378	N	
Lynch, James	29	Ireland	Y	Liverpool	New Orleans	02/10/1851	10/03/1854	12	317	N	
Lynch, James	40	Ireland	Y	Liverpool	New York	??/08/1844	11/12/1849	23	396	N	
Lynch, John	40	Ireland	Y	Cork	New Orleans	??/??/1851	04/25/1855	11	303	N	
Lynch, Michael	33	Ireland	Y	Liverpool	New Orleans	05/08/1847	10/29/1852	5	56	N	
Lynch, Michael	32	Ireland	Y	Queenstown	New York	05/01/1879	10/16/1885			Y	
Lynch, Michael	17	Ireland	N	?	New York	00/00/1883				Y	10/23/1888
Lynch, Morthey	29	Ireland	Y	Limmerick	New York	07/??/1846	10/??/1849	23	287	N	
Lynch, Patrick	25	Ireland	Y	Liverpool	New Orleans	05/09/1849	10/03/1854	10	379	N	
Lynch, Patrick	25	Ireland	Y	Liverpool	New Orleans	05/09/1849	10/03/1854	12	318	N	
Lynch, Stephen	24	Ireland	Y	Limerick	Buffalo	08/29/1850	09/30/1856	14	60	N	
Lynch, Thomas	??	Ireland	Y	?	?	?	11/20/1883			Y	
Lynch, Thomas	44	Ireland	N	?	New York	06/17/1865	?			Y	
Lynchiz, Dave	25	Russia	Y	Bremen	New York	03/18/1887	01/05/1893			Y	
Lynn, Patrick	24	Ireland	Y	Liverpool	New York	03/??/1847	10/20/1851	4	352	N	
Lyons, Bernard	23	Ireland	Y	?	?	?	03/19/1883			Y	
Lyons, Dennis	40	Ireland	Y	Cork	Buffalo	06/28/1847	02/15/1853	7	161	N	
Lyons, Denny	25	Ireland	Y	Cork	Baltimore	??/12/1849	07/18/1851	4	2	N	
Lyons, Francis	22	Ireland	Y	Liverpool	New Orleans	12/01/1848	03/08/1850	2	171	N	
Lyons, Frank	53	Ireland	N	Liverpool	New Orleans	05/??/1848	?			Y	
Lyons, James	26	Ireland	Y	Liverpool	New York	04/18/1854	03/22/1858	16	435	N	

CITIZENSHIP RECORDS

APPLICANT	AGE	COUNTRY OF ORIGIN	DEC	DEPART PORT	ENTRY PORT	ARRIVE DATE	DEC DATE	VOL	PG.	FLD	NAT DATE
Lyons, Jerry	??	Ireland	N	?	?	04/17/1886				Y	10/28/1892
Lyons, John	27	Ireland	Y	Queenstown	New York	04/03/1887	03/09/1894	21	63	N	
Lyons, John	??	Ireland	N	?	?	06/22/1885				Y	10/28/1892
Lyons, Michael R.	23	Ireland	Y	Liverpool	New Orleans	03/02/1850	02/19/1856	26	104	N	
Lyons, Patrick	30	Ireland	Y	Liverpool	New York	05/02/1851	11/12/1855	13	212	N	
Lyons, Peter	32	Ireland	N	Liverpool	New York	05/??/1870	?			Y	
Lyons, Timothy	25	Ireland	Y	Queenstown	New York	06/11/1883	10/10/1884			Y	
Lyons, William F.	28	Ireland	Y	Cork	Baltimore	04/12/1849	06/13/1851	3	374	N	
Lyttleton, John Joseph	24	Ireland	Y	Liverpool	New York	10/28/1848	02/17/1849	23	158	N	
Maag, Frederick	46	Oldenburg	Y	Bremen	New Orleans	11/28/1849	11/01/1852	5	132	N	
Maag, Frederick	46	Oldenburg	Y	Bremen	New Orleans	11/28/1849	11/01/1852	6	258	N	
Maag, Sebastian	31	Baden	Y	Liverpool	New York	12/22/1854	01/02/1858	16	296	N	
Maahan, James	32	Ireland	Y	Toronto	Buffalo	09/30/1849	01/20/1852	24	37	N	
Maas, Anton	30	Prussia	Y	Bremen	New York	05/28/1849	01/17/1853	7	34	N	
Maas, Carl	18	Mannheim, Ger	Y	?	?	11/12/1882	05/04/1885			Y	
Maas, Garrett William	25	Holland	Y	Rotterdam	New York	08/20/1850	11/15/1852	5	287	N	
Maas, Garrett William	25	Holland	Y	Rotterdam	New York	08/20/1850	11/15/1852	6	411	N	
Maas, Jacob	55	Germany	N	Rotterdam	New York	09/??/1852	?			Y	
Maas, John	55	Germany	N	Havre	New York	06/28/1870	?			Y	
Maas, John William	28	Holland	Y	Rotterdam	New Orleans	12/25/1845	09/27/1848	22	356	N	
Maas, Julius J.	48	Germany	N	Bremen	New York	07/??/1865	?			Y	
Maas, Leonardus Aloysius	37	Holland	Y	Rotterdam	New Orleans	12/29/1849	03/01/1852	24	206	N	
Maass, F.W.	45	Hanover	Y	Bremen	Baltimmore	10/24/1856	11/02/1860	18	3	N	
MacAvoy, Henry	48	England	Y	Liverpool	New York	05/02/1888	10/26/1891			Y	
MacDermott, Joseph	??	England	Y	?	?	02/??/1896	02/26/1900			Y	
MacLachlan, Alex	??	Great Britain	Y	?	?	?	09/25/1886			Y	
MacPhun, John	38	Scotland	Y	Quebec	Lewiston	09/05/1850	02/16/1853	7	170	N	
Macalusa, Michael	23	Italy	Y	Palermo	New York	12/25/1899	03/18/1903			Y	
Machenheimer, Christoph	29	Hesse Darmsta	Y	Havre	New York	??/28/1846	02/19/1850	2	100	N	
Machnovitz, Moses	50	Russia	Y	Bremen	Baltimore	05/15/1897	04/27/1900			Y	
Maciejensky, Martin	28	Prussia	Y	Hamburg	New York	06/04/1851	04/28/1854	8	280	N	
Maciejensky, Martin	28	Prussia	Y	Hamburg	New York	06/04/1851	04/28/1854	9	151	N	
Mack, Adam	23	Bavaria	Y	Antwerp	New Orleans	02/22/1849	01/14/1851	2	495	N	
Mack, Bernhard	44	Bavaria	Y	Havre	New Orleans	12/06/1852	09/26/1856	14	397	N	
Mack, Frank	23	Bavaria	Y	Antwerp	New Orleans	02/18/1848	01/22/1849	1	487	N	
Mack, Frank	47	Germany	Y	Antwerp	New York	10/26/1893	10/31/1902			Y	
Mack, Friedrich	27	Germany	Y	Bremen	New York	10/11/1880	08/30/1882			Y	
Mack, Henry	68	Bavaria	N	Hamburg	New York	09/??/1839	??/??/1841	28	276	N	11/01/1844
Mack, Joseph	35	Germany	Y	Bremen	New York	05/13/1881	03/13/1882			Y	
Mack, Martin	25	Bavaria	Y	Havre	New York	06/24/1846	10/14/1848	1	236	N	
Mack, Mathew	28	Ireland	Y	Limerick	New York	07/25/1844	04/15/1852	24	508	N	
Mackay, Patrick	22	Ireland	Y	Liverpool	New York	07/12/1848	02/20/1852	24	145	N	
Macke, Bernard	46	Germany	N	Bremen	Baltimore	08/16/1872	?			Y	
Macke, Bernard	28	Oldenburg	Y	Bremen	New Orleans	12/25/1845	04/05/1852	24	373	N	
Macke, Diedrick	22	Dinklaw	Y	Bremen	New Orleans	11/09/1849	06/28/1851	3	460	N	
Macke, Gerhard Heinrich	37	Germany	Y	Bremen	New York	07/05/1879	12/08/1880			Y	
Macke, Henry	23	Oldenburg	Y	Bremen	New Orleans	01/06/1844	01/16/1849	1	433	N	
Macke, Henry	26	Oldenburg	Y	Bremen	New York	05/03/1849	05/20/1852	25	66	N	
Macke, John H.	55	Germany	Y	Bremen	New Orleans	12/07/1853	03/26/1889			Y	
Macke, John Henry	25	Oldenburg	Y	Bremen	New Orleans	10/17/1852	10/05/1854	10	459	N	
Macke, John Henry	25	Oldenburg	Y	Bremen	New Orleans	10/17/1852	10/05/1854	12	398	N	
Mackey, Matthias	40	Ireland	Y	Waterford	New York	05/06/1850	08/13/1860	27	266	N	
Mackin, Patrick	22	Ireland	Y	Dublin	New Orleans	05/20/1850	03/18/1852	24	328	N	
Mackintosh, Alexander Ch	40	Scotland	Y	Liverpool	New York	09/07/1884	08/29/1889			Y	
Macnamara, Thomas	35	Canada	Y	Kingston	Cape Vincent	11/??/1866	04/22/1881			Y	
Madden, Edward	??	Ireland	Y	?	New Orleans	02/??/1849	11/03/1856	14	456	N	
Madden, James	39	Ireland	Y	Liverpool	New York	10/??/1832	05/01/1854	8	307	N	
Madden, James	39	Ireland	Y	Liverpool	New York	10/??/1832	05/01/1854	9	180	N	
Madden, Martin	50	Ireland	Y	Galway	New Orleans	02/26/1849	04/24/1854	8	256	N	

CITIZENSHIP RECORDS

APPLICANT	AGE	COUNTRY OF ORIGIN	DEC	DEPART PORT	ENTRY PORT	ARRIVE DATE	DEC DATE	VOL	PG.	FLD	NAT DATE
Madden, Martin	50	Ireland	Y	Galway	New Orleans	02/26/1849	04/24/1854	9	127	N	
Madden, Patrick	22	Ireland	Y	Queenstown	Philadelphia	06/12/1882	09/19/1885			Y	
Madden, Thomas	33	Ireland	N	Queenstown	New York	?	?			Y	
Maddis, Theobato	33	Bavaria	Y	Rotterdam	Baltimore	01/08/1849	11/17/1851			Y	
Maddis, Wolfgang	27	Bavaria	Y	Hamburg	New York	06/24/1845	11/20/1848	1	329	N	
Maddison, George	35	England	Y	Penzance	Albany	08/15/1847	05/09/1861	18	165	N	
Mader, Christian	30	Bavaria	Y	Bremen	New Orleans	06/20/1852	10/09/1854	6	77	N	
Mader, Christian	30	Bavaria	Y	Bremen	New Orleans	06/20/1852	10/09/1854	11	78	N	
Mader, Christian F.	24	Germany	Y	Hamburg	New York	10/15/1880	09/30/1884			Y	
Mader, Edmund	31	Saxony	Y	Bremen	Baltimore	09/14/1844	03/28/1853	7	433	N	
Mader, John Matthias	26	Bavaria	Y	Bremen	Baltimore	07/04/1853	07/02/1860	27	195	N	
Madigan, Thomas	23	Ireland	Y	Limerick	Burlington	08/24/1849	03/18/1851	3	301	N	
Madje, August	33	Germany	Y	Bremen	New York	11/16/1877	05/13/1882			Y	
Madlener, Adolph	37	Baden	Y	Havre	New York	06/14/1852	11/15/1852	5	290	N	
Madlener, Stefan	28	Austria	Y	Rotterdam	New York	02/08/1884	07/29/1889			Y	
Madlenner, Adolph	37	Baden	Y	Havre	New York	06/14/1852	11/15/1852	6	414	N	
Maecherle, Bernard	30	Bavaria	Y	Havre	New Orleans	09/29/1850	03/04/1852	24	234	N	
Maegly, Abraham	22	Bavaria	Y	Havre	New York	11/05/1853	09/20/1855	13	81	N	
Maehler, Henry	21	Hesse Cassel	Y	Hamburg	New York	05/28/1860	10/08/1860	27	435	N	
Maeir, Joseph	25	Baden	Y	Havre	New York	07/23/1849	12/27/1851	24	20	N	
Maertz, B.	48	Baden	Y	Havre	New York	01/??/1855	01/30/1861	18	81	N	
Maertz, Jacob	44	Germany	Y	Amsterdam	New York	06/01/1882	04/25/1895			Y	
Maertz, Peter	31	Germany	Y	Rotterdam	New York	05/03/1882	04/04/1887			Y	
Maerz, Frederick	30	Germany	Y	Bremen	New York	05/16/1883	10/22/1888			Y	
Maerz, John	23	Bavaria	Y	Havre	New Orleans	07/11/1855	11/08/1858	17	291	N	
Maerz, John	41	Germany	Y	Antwerp	New York	03/22/1886	04/23/1894			Y	
Maerz, Karl	27	Germany	Y	Rotterdam	New York	05/02/1882	04/02/1887			Y	
Maeski, Ernst	30	Switzerland	Y	Havre	New York	09/20/1884	09/20/1884			Y	
Maess, John Henry	66	Germany	N	Bremen	Baltimore	12/??/1846	?			Y	
Maestram, Joseph	38	Switzerland	Y	Marseilles	New York	04/02/1872	10/30/1888			Y	
Maeurer, M.	38	Germany	Y	Bremen	New York	10/30/1886	09/26/1896			Y	
Maeyer, George	48	Germany	Y	Antwerp	New York	10/21/1882	03/15/1886			Y	
Maeyrs, Michael	??	Russia	Y	?	?	?	09/24/1890			Y	
Maffey, Anthony	41	France	Y	Havre	Baltimore	06/??/1833	05/26/1856	26	556	N	
Magaletta Domenico	37	Italy	Y	Naples	New York	05/26/1890	03/17/1894			Y	
Magarill, Joseph	30	Germany	Y	Bremen	New York	06/14/1893	06/26/1893			Y	
Magee, Patrick	27	Ireland	Y	Belfast	Philadelphia	05/00/1880	10/20/1888			Y	
Maggio, Gaetano	33	Italy	Y	Naples	New York	04/25/1891	03/17/1894			Y	
Magher, Anthony	32	Ireland	Y	Liverpool	New York	05/10/1847	11/01/1852	5	91	N	
Magin, Jacob	42	Bavaria	Y	Havre	New Orleans	05/03/1853	02/21/1857	15	41	N	
Maginn, John	55	Ireland	Y	St Johns	Boston	09/03/1837	02/21/1851	3	150	N	
Maginnis, Peter M.	38	Greece	Y	Karristo	New York	05/??/1871	10/28/1886	19	94	N	
Maglin, Rudolph	23	Switzerland	Y	Havre	New York	09/03/1854	11/19/1855	13	229	N	
Magrish, Louis	??	Russia	Y	?	?	11/??/1890	12/21/1897			Y	
Maguff, Thomas	25	Ireland	Y	Liverpool	New Orleans	12/25/1848	03/12/1851	3	260	N	
Maguire, Francis	40	Ireland	Y	Canada	Albany	07/??/1831	11/??/1849	23	370	N	
Maguire, Ireland	43	Ireland	Y	Liverpool	Philadelphia	05/16/1847	02/23/1852	24	153	N	
Maguire, John	29	Ireland	Y	Liverpool	New Orleans	05/20/1847	12/??/1850	2	430	N	
Maguire, Joseph	29	Canada	Y	Sarnia	Port Huron	05/08/1883	08/20/1889			Y	
Maguire, Patrick	28	Ireland	Y	Liverpool	New Orleans	02/04/1850	05/14/1852	25	16	N	
Maguire, Philip	64	Ireland	N	Liverpool	New Orleans	05/14/1851	?			Y	
Maguire, Thomas	23	Ireland	Y	Sligo	New York	08/24/1849	12/24/1852	5	445	N	
Mahan, John	36	England	Y	Galway	New York	05/25/1847	06/12/1861	18	188	N	
Mahan, John M.	35	Ireland	Y	Toronto	Buffalo	09/15/1847	11/06/1852	5	244	N	
Mahan, John M.	35	Ireland	Y	Toronto	Buffalo	09/15/1847	11/06/1852	6	368	N	
Mahan, Michael	29	Ireland	Y	Limerick	Rochester	08/15/1850	10/20/1858	17	77	N	
Mahan, Michael	25	Ireland	Y	Liverpool	New Orleans	08/??/1851	03/13/1856	26	195	N	
Mahan, Patrick	40	Ireland	Y	Liverpool	New Orleans	02/03/1849	03/17/1853	7	338	N	
Mahan, Patrick	38	Ireland	Y	?	?	07/01/1874	11/07/1887			Y	

CITIZENSHIP RECORDS

APPLICANT	AGE	COUNTRY OF ORIGIN	DEC	DEPART PORT	ENTRY PORT	ARRIVE DATE	DEC DATE	VOL	PG.	FLD	NAT DATE
Mahan, William J.	39	Ireland	Y	Liverpool	New York	03/01/1891	03/28/1891	19	322	N	
Mahar, James	27	Ireland	Y	Liverpool	New Orleans	04/11/1851	09/21/1854	10	137	N	
Mahar, James	27	Ireland	Y	Liverpool	New Orleans	04/11/1851	09/21/1854	12	76	N	
Maharick, Simon	??	Drissa Witebs	Y	?	?	?	08/01/1893			Y	
Maher, Charles	24	Ireland	Y	Queenstown	Philadelphia	05/23/1887	10/17/1891			Y	
Maher, Daniel	29	Ireland	Y	Liverpool	New Orleans	05/10/1847	05/15/1854	8	441	N	
Maher, Daniel	29	Ireland	Y	Liverpool	New Orleans	04/10/1847	05/15/1854	9	314	N	
Maher, Edward	29	Ireland	Y	Queenstown	Philadelphia	05/28/1890	11/16/1897			Y	
Maher, Jeremiah	26	Ireland	Y	Canada	Albany	08/14/1847	02/17/1849	23	144	N	
Maher, John	20	Ireland	Y	Liverpool	New York	07/18/1852	09/27/1854	10	254	N	
Maher, John	20	Ireland	Y	Liverpool	New York	07/18/1852	09/27/1854	12	193	N	
Maher, Mathew	50	Ireland	Y	Queenstown	New York	08/05/1888	11/15/1897			Y	
Maher, Patrick	28	Ireland	Y	Quebec	Buffalo	08/10/1847	11/06/1852	5	240	N	
Maher, Patrick	28	Ireland	Y	Quebec	Buffalo	08/10/1847	11/06/1852	6	364	N	
Maher, Patrick	24	Ireland	Y	Liverpool	New York	05/01/1849	03/10/1852	24	279	N	
Maher, Philip	17	Ireland	N	?	New York	00/00/1880				Y	10/27/1888
Maher, William	27	Ireland	Y	Liverpool	New York	03/19/1845	10/13/1851	4	220	N	
Mahlecke, Rudolph	25	Germany	Y	Hamburg	New York	08/19/1880	08/15/1881			Y	
Mahler, Ludwig	35	Germany	Y	Antwerp	New York	03/20/1879	09/09/1884			Y	
Mahlke, August	30	Germany	Y	Hamburg	New York	03/16/1880	10/28/1892	19	398	N	
Mahlmeister, Adam	35	Germany	Y	Bremen	New York	11/28/1880	05/23/1888			Y	
Mahn, John	31	Germany	Y	Antwerp	New York	03/20/1882	01/17/1887			Y	
Mahne, Henry	46	Prussia	Y	?	New York	05/25/1864	10/20/1882			Y	
Mahnke, John Henry	33	Hanover	Y	Bremen	Philadelphia	??/14/1844	10/09/1848	1	62	N	
Mahon, Martin	25	Ireland	Y	Liverpool	New Orleans	12/25/1848	11/01/1852	5	157	N	
Mahon, Martin	25	Ireland	Y	Liverpool	New Orleans	12/25/1848	11/01/1852	6	283	N	
Mahon, Thomas	22	England	Y	Liverpool	New York	10/17/1896	10/17/1900			Y	
Mahon, William J.	39	Ireland	Y	Liverpool	New York	03/01/1891	03/28/1891			Y	
Mahoney, Barth	28	Ireland	Y	Queenstown	Philadelphia	05/29/1891	09/28/1895			Y	
Mahoney, Dennis	52	Ireland	N	Liverpool	New York	04/??/1850	??/??/1855	28	242	N	04/??/1857
Mahoney, James	35	Ireland	Y	Queenstown	New York	10/16/1880	02/18/1889			Y	
Mahoney, James	34	Ireland	Y	Queenstown	New York	04/26/1883	10/22/1896			Y	
Mahoney, Jeremiah	23	Ireland	Y	Canada	Boston	06/04/1845	03/06/1850	2	162	N	
Mahoney, Jerry	28	Ireland	Y	Queenstown	New York	03/11/1884	10/25/1889			Y	
Mahoney, John	27	Ireland	Y	Liverpool	New York	07/25/1849	05/01/1854	8	335	N	
Mahoney, John	27	Ireland	Y	Liverpool	New York	07/25/1849	05/01/1854	9	208	N	
Mahoney, John	34	Ireland	Y	London	New York	06/20/1879	04/01/1885	19	6	N	
Mahoney, John	37	England	Y	London	New York	06/20/1879	04/02/1885			Y	
Mahoney, Michael	53	Ireland	Y	Queenstown	Philadelphia	05/01/1892	10/22/1897			Y	
Mahoney, Timothy	21	Ireland	Y	Liverpool	New York	04/22/1853	02/04/1856	26	36	N	
Mahoney, William D.	23	Ireland	Y	Liverpool	New York	06/12/1849	03/06/1850	2	161	N	
Mahony, John	60	Ireland	N	Cork	Boston	06/??/1855	?			Y	
Mahony, William	40	Ireland	Y	Cork	New Orleans	12/24/1849	06/12/1852	25	243	N	
Mahrlein, Andreas	32	Bavaria	Y	Antwerp	New Orleans	12/28/1847	03/12/1850	2	188	N	
Mahy, Eugene	25	Belgium	Y	?	?	04/09/1895	07/24/1895			Y	
Mai, Frank	24	Germany	Y	Antwerp	New York	05/21/1881	01/20/1887			Y	
Maibach, Philipp Charles	42	Germany	Y	Bremen	New York	10/30/1880	05/31/1890			Y	
Maibohm, William	??	Germany	Y	?	?	?	04/27/1889			Y	
Maichle, Bernhard	30	Germany	Y	?	?	?	10/17/1888			Y	
Maichle, Herman Herkulan	24	Antwerp	Y	Antwerp	New York	12/15/1885	04/19/1888			Y	
Maichle, Stephan	34	Germany	Y	Liverpool	New York	08/13/1873	06/09/1882			Y	
Maier, Bonifaz	43	Germany	Y	Hamburg	New York	05/06/1884	12/27/1890			Y	
Maier, Christian	35	Germany	Y	Antwerp	New York	06/07/1881	11/27/1886			Y	
Maier, Constantine	30	Wurttemberg	Y	Havre	New York	02/28/1854	10/30/1858	17	16	N	
Maier, Fridolin	??	Germany	Y	?	New York	07/??/1891	10/17/1892			Y	
Maier, George	37	Austria	Y	Hamburg	Buffalo	05/15/1848	06/04/1852	25	186	N	
Maier, Gottlieb	27	Germany	Y	Bremen	New York	05/??/1884	12/27/1886			Y	
Maier, Ignatz	26	Germany	Y	Bremen	New York	09/02/1892	10/28/1897			Y	
Maier, Isiderer	35	Germany	Y	Hamburg	New York	07/??/1880	06/08/1888			Y	

CITIZENSHIP RECORDS

APPLICANT	AGE	COUNTRY OF ORIGIN	DEC	DEPART PORT	ENTRY PORT	ARRIVE DATE	DEC DATE	VOL	PG.	FLD	NAT DATE
Maier, Jacob	22	Hesse Darmsta	Y	Havre	New York	12/18/1851	11/22/1852	5	324	N	
Maier, Jacob	26	Germany	Y	Bremen	New York	03/02/1885	11/10/1888			Y	
Maier, Johann George	43	Germany	Y	Bremen	New York	08/27/1883	10/13/1885			Y	
Maier, John	24	Wurttemberg	Y	Bremen	New York	08/28/1848	01/24/1851	2	526	N	
Maier, John George Micha	29	Bavaria	Y	Bremen	Baltimore	11/02/1855	09/29/1856	14	9	N	
Maier, Joseph	29	Germany	Y	Bremen	New York	04/29/1892	01/19/1898			Y	
Maier, Ludwig	30	Germany	Y	Rotterdam	New York	07/23/1881	11/06/1886			Y	
Maier, Matz	36	Wuerttemberg	Y	Havre	New York	04/01/1854	10/08/1860	27	453	N	
Maier, Max	22	Baden	Y	Havre	New York	09/??/1849	10/23/1851	4	376	N	
Maier, Michael	27	Bavaria	Y	Havre	New Orleans	05/12/1854	11/05/1857	15	531	N	
Maier, Phillip	28	Wurttemberg	Y	Havre	New York	03/28/1854	10/29/1858	17	188	N	
Maier, William	??	Baden	Y	?	New York	??/28/18??	11/03/1865	14	449	N	
Mail, Hermann	34	Hesse Cassel	Y	Bremen	New York	12/??/1854	06/26/1860	27	6	N	
Maile, Leo	23	Germany	Y	Havre	New York	09/27/1883	09/06/1887			Y	
Mailes, Cuthbert S.	25	England	Y	Liverpool	New York	03/26/1852	11/27/1852	5	354	N	
Maisch, Andrew	36	Wurttemberg	Y	Havre	New York	12/30/1854	12/05/1857	16	69	N	
Maisch, John	25	Germany	Y	Antwerp	New York	05/24/1882	08/22/1882			Y	
Maisel, John E.	37	Germany	Y	Bremen	New York	05/03/1883	03/29/1884			Y	
Maitland, Samuel	25	Ireland	Y	Liverpool	New York	07/18/1853	11/17/1858	17	339	N	
Maiwurm, Peter	34	Germany	Y	Rotterdam	Jersey City	04/29/1887	05/26/1890			Y	
Majoewski, Henry	33	Germany	Y	Bremen	Baltimore	05/10/1880	10/09/1883			Y	
Majoewsky, Rudolph	27	Germany	Y	Bremen	Baltimore	03/22/1883	11/29/1886			Y	
Makenstorm, Cragor	32	Baden	Y	Havre	New Orleans	05/10/1853	07/18/1860	27	223	N	
Malespine, John	34	Italy (Sardin	Y	Genoa	New York	07/25/1845	02/18/1853	7	180	N	
Maley, Michael	45	Ireland	Y	Liverpool	New Orleans	05/01/1848	05/01/1854	8	313	N	
Maley, Michael	45	England	Y	Liverpool	New Orleans	05/01/1848	05/01/1854	9	186	N	
Maley, Pat	32	Ireland	Y	Liverpool	New York	08/18/1883	10/29/1888	19	200	N	
Maley, Pat	60	Ireland	Y	Dublin	New York	11/11/1856	03/22/1893			Y	
Maley, Patrick	32	Ireland	Y	Liverpool	New York	08/18/1883	10/29/1888			Y	
Mall, Fritz	28	Germany	Y	Bremen	New York	06/10/1886	01/23/1888			Y	
Mall, John Michael	27	Germany	Y	Hamburg	New York	11/10/1880	09/26/1882			Y	
Mall, Michael	23	Germany	Y	Bremen	New York	10/01/1883	09/06/1887			Y	
Mallen, Owen	33	Ireland	Y	Liverpool	Philadelphia	04/15/1891	07/22/1896			Y	
Mallet, Peter	33	Ireland	Y	Queenstown	New York	04/24/1886	05/14/1890			Y	
Malley, James	29	Ireland	Y	Liverpool	New York	05/08/1883	05/29/1886			Y	
Mallony, John	26	Ireland	Y	Liverpool	New York	01/20/1845	02/22/1850	2	115	N	
Malon, George	31	Germany	Y	Bremen	Baltimore	06/??/1884	10/19/1888			Y	
Malone, James J.	26	Ireland	Y	Queenstown	New York	05/15/1891	07/14/1891			Y	
Maloney, James	60	Ireland	Y	Liverpool	New York	03/29/1852	09/27/1853	12	208	N	
Maloney, John	52	Ireland	N	Liverpool	New York	04/??/1853	?			Y	
Maloney, Lawrence	??	Great Britain	Y	?	?	?	06/09/1893			Y	
Maloney, Martin	21	Ireland	Y	Liverpool	New York	05/30/1894	07/01/1895			Y	
Maloney, Michael	31	Ireland	Y	?	?	?	10/25/1884			Y	
Maloney, Michael	54	Ireland	N	Galway	New York	04/??/1856	?			Y	
Maloney, Patrick	22	Ireland	Y	Liverpool	New York	05/13/1882	10/20/1884			Y	
Maloney, William	25	Ireland	Y	?	?	?	10/24/1884			Y	
Maloschek, Joseph	35	Germany	Y	?	?	10/23/1883	04/19/1890			Y	
Malseed, John D.	30	Ireland	Y	Queenstown	New York	03/19/1873	09/06/1884			Y	
Maltry, John	17	Germany	N	?	New York	00/00/1872				Y	10/27/1888
Malzacher, Sebastian	29	Baden	Y	Havre	New Orleans	03/11/1852	07/09/1855	11	360	N	
Mancini, Giovanni	27	Italy	Y	Naples	New York	08/12/1890	08/08/1894			Y	
Mancino, Sebastiana	34	Italy	Y	Naples	New York	04/30/1890	09/29/1896			Y	
Mancuso, Fortunato	53	Italy	Y	Naples	New York	05/01/1883	05/22/1894			Y	
Mandeler, Charles	29	Bavaria	Y	Havre	New Orleans	06/??/1851	05/22/1854	9	366	N	
Manderi, Peter	29	Bavaria	Y	Havre	New York	05/28/1846	08/22/1848	22	230	N	
Mandler, Charles	29	Bavaria	Y	Havre	New Orleans	06/??/1851	05/22/1854	8	492	N	
Mandler, Herman	27	Bavaria	Y	Antwerp	New York	02/23/1851	05/22/1854	8	496	N	
Mandler, Herman	27	Bavaria	Y	Antwerp	New York	02/23/1850	05/22/1854	9	370	N	
Manegold, August	25	Brunswick	Y	Bremen	New York	07/09/1847	01/13/1849	1	408	N	

CITIZENSHIP RECORDS

APPLICANT	AGE	COUNTRY OF ORIGIN	DEC	DEPART PORT	ENTRY PORT	ARRIVE DATE	DEC DATE	VOL	PG.	FLD	NAT DATE
Manegold, Charles	22	Brunswick	Y	Bremen	New York	07/09/1847	01/13/1849	1	409	N	
Mang, August	38	Baden	Y	Bremen	New York	10/22/1851	04/17/1854	8	155	N	
Mang, August	38	Baden	Y	Bremen	New York	10/22/1851	04/17/1854	9	26	N	
Mangan, John	22	Ireland	Y	Liverpool	New York	06/29/1849	11/23/1852	5	328	N	
Manger, Jacob	42	Baden	Y	Rotterdam	New York	11/17/1848	08/26/1857	15	191	N	
Mangin, August	27	France	Y	Havre	New York	05/17/1847	07/18/1851	4	1	N	
Manginie, Antonio	30	Italy	Y	Naples	New York	02/26/1881	10/25/1890	19	303	N	
Mangionie, Antonio	30	Italy	Y	Naples	New York	02/26/1881	10/25/1881			Y	
Mangold, Jacob	29	Germany	Y	Antwerp	Philadelphia	01/28/1887	10/29/1892			Y	
Mangold, Urs	??	Switzerland	Y	?	?	?	11/07/1892			Y	
Manheimer, Abraham	30	Bavaria	Y	Bremen	New York	09/??/1847	10/06/1856	14	218	N	
Manischewitz, Behr	31	Russia	Y	Hamburg	New York	12/17/1885	10/11/1888			Y	
Mann, Anton	27	Wuertemberg	Y	Havre	New Orleans	03/27/1854	03/25/1856	26	298	N	
Mann, James	30	Canada	Y	Kingston	Cape Vincent	04/01/1892	10/19/1897			Y	
Mann, Jeannot	34	Russia	Y	Bremen	Baltimore	08/11/1887	02/04/1888			Y	
Mann, Joseph	22	Germany	Y	Antwerp	New York	04/14/1881	11/01/1881			Y	
Mann, Lazarus	60	Russia	Y	Bremen	Baltimore	09/05/1889	10/18/1892			Y	
Mann, Nicholas J.	29	Ireland	Y	Queenstown	New York	02/22/1889	09/10/1894			Y	
Mann, Robert F.	28	Canada	Y	St. John	Boston	09/15/1892	04/09/1891			Y	
Mannbeck, George	23	Germany	Y	Rotterdam	New York	11/10/1884	12/29/1886			Y	
Manne, Charles	28	France	Y	Havre	New Orleans	03/14/1854	07/16/1855	11	391	N	
Mannheimer, William	36	Austria	Y	Bremen	New York	09/21/1854	10/23/1857	15	485	N	
Manning, James	27	Ireland	Y	Liverpool	Whitehall	08/??/1847	12/08/1852	5	397	N	
Mannion, Andrew	22	Ireland	Y	Queenstown	New York	06/11/1883	12/15/1885			Y	
Mannix, Patrick	56	Ireland	Y	Queenstown	New York	09/??/1869	08/31/1886	19	40	N	
Mannix, Patrick	56	Ireland	Y	Queenstown	New York	09/??/1869	08/31/1886			Y	
Mannon, Dennis	24	Ireland	Y	Liverpool	Boston	05/05/1846	10/14/1851	4	276	N	
Mannshardt, John	24	Baden	Y	Havre	New York	07/02/1854	02/07/1856	26	63	N	
Manoosas, George	28	Greece	Y	?	?	?	06/05/1884			Y	
Manoque, Thomas	23	Ireland	Y	Liverpool	New Orleans	03/17/1849	01/06/1853	5	521	N	
Mansz, Ludwig	42	Hesse Darmsta	Y	London	New York	06/20/1848	01/16/1849	1	429	N	
Manthey, August	37	Germany	Y	Hamburg	New York	10/20/1885	04/06/1891			Y	
Manthey, William	35	Germany	Y	Bremen	Baltimore	02/18/1884	09/21/1887			Y	
Manuel, John	??	Wales	N	?	?	05/10/1881				Y	10/15/1892
Manz, Conrad	39	Wurttemberg	Y	London	New York	01/04/1854	04/25/1854	8	260	N	
Manz, Conrad	39	Wurttemberg	Y	London	New York	01/04/1854	04/25/1854	9	131	N	
Manz, Lorenz	31	Baden	Y	Havre	New York	08/09/1858	08/15/1860	27	275	N	
Manzey, Herman	29	Prussia	Y	Hamburg	New York	10/10/1851	01/13/1853	7	21	N	
Mappes, Henry	23	Bavaria	Y	Havre	New York	06/??/1849	10/24/1851	4	390	N	
Mara, James	55	Ireland	N	Liverpool	New York	06/??/1867	?			Y	
Mara, John	71	Ireland	N	Liverpool	New Orleans	04/20/1851	?	28	459	N	09/11/1856
Mara, Patrick	31	Ireland	Y	Dublin	New Orleans	02/27/1850	11/01/1852	5	114	N	
Marahrens, August	28	Germany	Y	Bremen	Baltimore	06/01/1882	10/13/1884			Y	
Marc, Blinveil Antoine	24	France	Y	Havre	New Orleans	??/10/1847	02/20/1850	2	110	N	
Marc, Mathias	33	Germany	Y	Havre	New York	10/30/1881	10/23/1886	19	83	N	
Marc, Mathias	35	Germany	Y	Havre	New York	10/30/1881	10/23/1886			Y	
Marchi, Edward	10	Italy	N	?	New York	00/00/1856				Y	10/20/1888
Marchmann, Theodore	24	Mecklenburg S	Y	Hamburg	New York	08/20/1854	10/30/1858	17	14	N	
Marcinkowski, John	28	Germany	Y	Bremen	Baltimore	09/01/1888	10/13/1888	19	147	N	
Marcinkowski, John	28	Germany	Y	Bremen	Baltimore	09/01/1880	10/13/1888			Y	
Marcomier, Alexander	34	France	Y	Havre	New Orleans	11/05/1843	09/13/1852	25	472	N	
Marcus, David	37	Russia	Y	Hamburg	New York	07/22/1888	11/15/1890			Y	
Marcus, John Herman	33	Hanover	Y	Bremen	New Orleans	06/05/1854	03/26/1856	26	350	N	
Marcus, Max	31	Russia	Y	Bremen	New York	09/15/1884	12/12/1896			Y	
Marcus, Nicholas John	28	Mecklenburg	Y	Hamburg	New York	09/25/1849	11/08/1852	5	258	N	
Marcus, Nicholas John	28	Mecklenburg	Y	Hamburg	New York	09/25/1849	11/08/1852	6	382	N	
Marcuse, John	??	Prussia	Y	?	?	?	10/27/1880			Y	
Mardon, William Campbell	??	England	Y	?	?	?	07/31/1896			Y	
Marenberg, John	38	Austria	Y	Liverpool	New York	04/19/1851	05/25/1854	8	512	N	

CITIZENSHIP RECORDS

APPLICANT	AGE	COUNTRY OF ORIGIN	DEC	DEPART PORT	ENTRY PORT	ARRIVE DATE	DEC DATE	VOL	PG.	FLD	NAT DATE
Mareno, James	37	Italy	Y	?	?	02/12/1882	04/16/1894			Y	
Marg, David	25	Bavaria	Y	Havre	New York	04/15/1853	09/25/1858	16	134	N	
Margreiter, Alois	29	Austria	Y	?	New York	11/??/1884	01/27/1888			Y	
Margua, Valentine	31	Bavaria	Y	Havre	New Orleans	02/03/1848	05/01/1854	9	193	N	
Marhmann, Frederick	21	Hanover	Y	Bremen	New Orleans	05/14/1853	05/29/1856	14	265	N	
Mariacher, Alois	42	Austria	Y	Antwerp	Philadelphia	05/15/1892	10/27/1894			Y	
Mariani, Domonico G. A.	47	Italy	Y	Genoa	New Orleans	01/11/1866	05/23/1888			Y	
Marien, Joseph	??	Belgium	Y	Antwerp	New York	10/29/1895	11/09/1895			Y	
Mark, Isaac Jacob	21	Russia	Y	Bremen	New York	07/05/1892	07/03/1893			Y	
Mark, Robert	24	Ireland	Y	Liverpool	New Orleans	04/28/1848	02/12/1852	24	104	N	
Mark, Theodore	53	Oldenburger	Y	Bremen	New Orleans	12/20/1844	02/01/1849	23	7	N	
Markart, Andreas	32	Bavaria	Y	Bremen	New York	06/18/1845	08/21/1848	22	214	N	
Markert, John C.F.G.	29	Saxe Weimar	Y	Bremen	New York	04/08/1852	05/29/1852	25	132	N	
Markert, Lorenz	30	Bavaria	Y	Havre	New York	05/09/1854	02/18/1856	26	98	N	
Markham, Joseph A.	29	Canada	Y	Port Elgin	Detroit	10/12/1882	06/20/1887			Y	
Markiewics, Sam	??	Russia	Y	?	?	?	06/08/1893			Y	
Markind, William	33	Hanover	Y	Bremen	Baltimore	12/??/1847	09/09/1852	25	436	N	
Markowski, Felix	32	Russia	Y	Hamburg	New York	06/01/1890	03/20/1894			Y	
Marks, Henry	49	Hanover	Y	Bremen	New Orleans	11/18/1848	10/06/1851	4	190	N	
Marks, Leopold	22	Saxe Weimar	Y	Bremen	New York	05/02/1851	04/18/1854	8	195	N	
Marks, Leopold	22	Saxe Weimar	Y	Bremen	New York	10/02/1851	04/18/1854	9	66	N	
Marks, Louis M.	??	Germany	Y	?	?	11/00/1870	10/07/1880			Y	
Markurth, Friedrich	39	Bremen	Y	Bremen	New York	04/10/1885	09/05/1887			Y	
Markus, John	36	Germany	N	Hamburg	New York	10/??/1873	?			Y	
Marlmann, Henry	30	Hanover	Y	Bremen	New York	08/21/1851	05/29/1856	14	266	N	
Marlmann, Lewis (Louis?)	26	Hanover	Y	Bremen	New York	08/20/1851	02/04/1856	26	18	N	
Marohn, Eugene	28	Germany	Y	Hamburg	New York	11/21/1883	03/25/1887			Y	
Marooden, Andes	27	Greece	Y	Sparta	New York	05/06/1888	11/08/1895			Y	
Maroodes, James	38	Greece	Y	?	?	05/10/1887	09/25/1893			Y	
Marorana, Vincenzo	22	Italy	Y	Naples	New York	12/03/1900	10/24/1903			Y	
Marqua, John	26	Germany	Y	Hamburg	New York	06/16/1889	08/23/1892			Y	
Marqua, John	26	Bavaria	Y	Havre	New Orleans	04/13/1852	03/11/1856	26	187	N	
Marqua, Valentine	31	Bavaria	Y	Havre	New Orleans	02/03/1848	05/01/1854	8	320	N	
Marquart, Paul	23	Wurttemberg	Y	Bremen	New York	11/23/1867	02/29/1872	18	466	N	
Marrenburg, John	38	Austria	Y	Liverpool	New York	04/19/1851	05/25/1854	9	386	N	
Marriott, Alfred	25	England	Y	Liverpool	Boston	07/13/1887	04/29/1892			Y	
Marron, Bartley	28	Ireland	Y	Liverpool	New Orleans	03/22/1847	10/18/1852	5	6	N	
Marron, Thomas	22	Ireland	Y	Liverpool	New Orleans	03/10/1851	10/18/1852	5	8	N	
Marsch, Andrew	24	Austria	Y	Hamburg	Boston	05/02/1869	06/14/1872	18	501	N	
Marschel, Gerard Herman	30	Hanover	Y	Havre	New Orleans	06/10/1849	12/08/1852	5	399	N	
Marschwert, Rudolph	39	Prussia	Y	Bremen	New Orleans	01/16/1847	10/07/1848	22	470	N	
Marsh, Alfred Richard	32	England	Y	London (Cana	Detroit	04/07/1890	12/31/1900			Y	
Marshall, Augustus	26	England	Y	Canada	New York	07/14/1878	10/13/1884			Y	
Marshall, David	38	Scotland	N	Glasgow	New York	12/28/1870	?			Y	
Marshall, George W.	23	England	Y	Liverpool	New York	09/20/1895	03/06/1899			Y	
Marshall, Hubert	17	England	N	?	Detroit	09/00/1883				Y	10/26/1888
Marshall, James G.	50	Scotland	Y	Glasgow	New York	04/16/1886	10/10/1900			Y	
Marshall, John	41	England	Y	?	Toledo, Ohio	??/??/1883	11/04/1884			Y	
Marst, Henry	31	Prussia	Y	Bremen	New Orleans	05/09/1849	03/28/1853	7	448	N	
Mart, Nicholas	25	Italy	Y	Naples	New York	04/13/1886	08/03/1892			Y	
Marte, Oswald	27	Austria	Y	Havre	New York	03/01/1887	03/01/1892			Y	
Marten, Heinrich	26	Germany	Y	Bremen	New York	02/15/1883	06/05/1883				
Martens, J. Bernard	45	Germany	Y	Bremen	Baltimore	11/01/1861	01/30/1882			Y	
Marter, John	28	Germany	Y	Havre	New York	11/09/1891	05/16/1895			Y	
Marthaler, Charles	36	Switzerland	Y	Havre	New York	07/23/1883	10/03/1887			Y	
Martin, Amand	31	Prussia	Y	Hamburg	New York	12/20/1854	08/31/1857	15	206	N	
Martin, Andreas	44	Hanover	Y	Bremen	New Orleans	10/28/1846	04/21/1854	8	234	N	
Martin, Andreas	44	Hanover	Y	Bremen	New Orleans	10/28/1846	04/21/1854	9	105	N	
Martin, Christoph	30	Germany	Y	Antwerp	Philadelphia	02/21/1887	11/19/1890			Y	

CITIZENSHIP RECORDS

APPLICANT	AGE	COUNTRY OF ORIGIN	DEC	DEPART PORT	ENTRY PORT	ARRIVE DATE	DEC DATE	VOL	PG.	FLD	NAT DATE
Martin, Daniel	28	Ireland	Y	?	New York	00/00/1857	10/27/1892			Y	
Martin, Edward	26	Ireland	Y	Liverpool	New York	04/18/1853	05/20/1856	26	511	N	
Martin, Emil	25	Germany	Y	Havre	New York	11/15/1891	04/16/1895			Y	
Martin, Ferdinand	28	Germany	Y	Bremen	Baltimore	05/26/1882	04/23/1886			Y	
Martin, Garret	22	Ireland	Y	Liverpool	New York	04/01/1847	03/01/1852	24	194	N	
Martin, George	25	Bavaria	Y	Antwerp	New York	05/09/1889	10/31/1890			Y	
Martin, Henry	37	Germany	Y	Bremen	Baltimore	03/15/1880	02/04/1888			Y	
Martin, Hugh	53	Ireland	Y	Glasgow	New York	03/26/1880	03/22/1894	21	64	N	
Martin, Hugh	53	Ireland	Y	Glasgow	New York	03/26/1880	03/22/1894			Y	
Martin, Joe	??	Italy	Y	?	New York	06/??/1891	11/22/1896			Y	
Martin, John	29	Ireland	Y	Liverpool	New Orleans	10/30/1850	05/22/1854	8	485	N	
Martin, John	29	Ireland	Y	Liverpool	New Orleans	10/30/1850	05/22/1854	9	359	N	
Martin, John	??	?	Y	?	New York	??/04/18??	11/03/1856	14	452	N	
Martin, John Henry	21	Germany	Y	Havre	New York	10/23/1891	01/05/1892			Y	
Martin, John M.	21	Scotland	Y	Glasgow	New York	??/01/1854	04/24/1855	11	292	N	
Martin, Joseph	38	Germany	N	Havre	Chicago	10/??/1873	?			Y	
Martin, Michael	28	Ireland	Y	Liverpool	New Orleans	03/26/1852	11/26/1858	17	356	N	
Martin, Nicholaus	58	Germany	N	Antwerp	New Orleans	12/17/1849	?			Y	
Martin, Philip	26	Wales	Y	Liverpool	New York	05/18/1857	08/24/1860	27	312	N	
Martin, William	32	England	Y	London	New Orleans	01/02/1852	12/08/1852	5	402	N	
Martin, William	27	Wales	Y	Liverpool	New York	08/25/1849	07/07/1855	11	347	N	
Marting, Herman	40	Germany	Y	Bremen	Baltimore	07/05/1891	03/22/1894			Y	
Marty, Lawrence	42	Switzerland	N	Havre	New York	04/24/1869	?			Y	
Martz, Stephan	25	Bavaria	Y	Havre	New York	08/10/18??	10/23/1851	4	381	N	
Maruca, Frank	28	Italy	Y	Naples	New York	12/24/1881	08/13/1888			Y	
Marx, Charles	27	Germany	Y	Bremen	New York	10/16/1891	07/23/1892			Y	
Marx, Frederick	27	Hanover	Y	Bremen	Baltimore	08/18/1851	08/31/1857	15	205	N	
Marx, John Joseph	24	Prussia	Y	Bremen	Charleston	06/03/1854	11/01/1858	17	254	N	
Marx, Nicolaus	32	Prussia	Y	Liverpool	New York	05/31/1853	09/10/1855	11	530	N	
Marx, Otto J.	27	Germany	Y	Bremen	New York	04/13/1894	04/20/1898			Y	
Marxan, Nicholas	26	Prussia	Y	Antwerp	New York	06/02/1857	01/10/1860	27	47	N	
Marz, Jenner	48	Germany	Y	Bremen	New York	02/13/1881	06/23/1886			Y	
Marz, John	33	Bavaria	Y	Hamburg	New York	08/13/1845	01/16/1849	1	440	N	
Marz, Leo	23	Baden	Y	Havre	New York	10/04/1852	10/09/1854	6	173	N	
Marz, Leo	23	Baden	Y	Havre	New York	10/04/1852	10/09/1854	11	176	N	
Marz, Paul	29	Germany	Y	Antwerp	New York	06/18/1881	04/30/1886			Y	
Marz, Philip	39	Bavaria	Y	Havre	New Orleans	01/28/1850	03/03/1853	7	262	N	
Marzer, Joseph	28	Bavaria	Y	Havre	New York	??/??/18??	10/07/1854	11	11	N	
Masa, John Gerhard	23	Oldenburg	Y	Bremen	Baltimore	09/20/1843	10/03/1848	1	45	N	
Mascari, Frank	38	Italy	Y	Palermo	New York	02/20/1884	10/23/1893			Y	
Mascari, Joseph	31	Italy	Y	Palermo	New York	10/26/1886	10/17/1893	21	20	N	
Mascari, Salvatore	40	Italy	Y	Palermo	New York	03/17/1887	10/16/1893	21	12	N	
Mascari, Salvatore	40	Italy	Y	Palermo	New York	03/17/1887	10/16/1893			Y	
Mascaro, Pietro	17	Italy	N	?	New York	00/00/1881				Y	10/20/1888
Maschman, Christian F.	45	Germany	Y	Hamburg	New York	01/12/1896	09/22/1902			Y	
Maschmeier, Henry D.	47	Germany	Y	?	Baltimore	??/??/1871	10/11/1880			Y	
Masconi, Joseph	31	Italy	Y	Palermo	New York	10/26/1886	10/17/1893			Y	
Maslanker, Valentine	29	Germany	Y	Hamburg	Baltimore	10/20/1881	11/01/1886			Y	
Masman, Henry	28	Hanover	Y	Bremen	Baltimore	10/??/1846	03/17/1851	3	295	N	
Mason, George A.	21	Bavaria	Y	Bremen	New Orleans	01/05/1845	02/12/1849	23	53	N	
Mason, John	32	England	Y	Liverpool	New York	04/??/1849	12/04/1850	2	338	N	
Mason, Robert	45	Ireland	Y	Liverpool	New York	09/28/1847	10/30/1852	5	84	N	
Mason, William B.	37	Canada	Y	Toronto	Niagara	04/??/1880	10/10/1880			Y	
Massa, Giacomo	45	Italy	Y	Genoa	New York	03/30/1892	10/10/1898			Y	
Masser, Nicolas	24	France	Y	Havre	New York	12/20/1850	10/05/1854	10	468	N	
Masser, Nicolas	24	France	Y	Havre	New York	12/20/1850	10/05/1854	12	407	N	
Massett, Bandlin	28	Bavaria	Y	Havre	New Orleans	12/03/1846	07/12/1851	3	528	N	
Massi, Antonio	29	Italy	Y	Havre	New York	01/21/1883	03/30/1891			Y	
Massman, Gerhard	21	Hanover	Y	Bremen	New Orleans	05/01/1849	03/20/1851	3	296	N	

CITIZENSHIP RECORDS

APPLICANT	AGE	COUNTRY OF ORIGIN	DEC	DEPART PORT	ENTRY PORT	ARRIVE DATE	DEC DATE	VOL	PG.	FLD	NAT DATE
Massmann, Paul	26	Germany	Y	Hamburg	New York	09/29/1886	10/03/1891			Y	
Massmann, Thomas	22	Hanover	Y	Bremen	New Orleans	11/21/1854	02/18/1858	16	315	N	
Massoni, Leopold	17	Italy	N	?	New York	00/00/1874				Y	10/27/1888
Mast, Sebastian	??	Germany	Y	?	?	04/??/1883	09/18/1884			Y	
Master, Louis	34	Russia	Y	Bremen	New York	03/11/1896	09/08/1904			Y	
Mastio, John	39	Germany	Y	Havre	New York	03/??/1865	10/31/1884			Y	
Masur, Anton	32	Germany	Y	Bremen	New York	08/02/1883	11/26/1889			Y	
Matacia, Ignazio	43	Italy	Y	Palermo	New York	12/24/1883	10/23/1893			Y	
Mateis, Mathew	31	Baden	Y	Havre	New York	05/??/1854	02/10/1857	15	9	N	
Matheisen, Souker	61	Denmark	N	Liverpool	New York	09/??/1859	?			Y	
Mather, Francis	40	Austria	Y	Rotterdam	New York	06/??/1848	11/19/1858	17	343	N	
Mather, John	22	England	Y	Liverpool	New York	05/16/1849	12/14/1852	5	415	N	
Matheson, Neil	28	Scotland	Y	Glasgow	New York	04/30/1850	09/26/1857	15	324	N	
Mathias, Charles	22	France	Y	Havre	New York	05/12/1859	08/27/1861	18	218	N	
Mathias, James D.	48	England	Y	Liverpool	New York	04/??/1880	10/24/1888			Y	
Mathie, James	53	Scotland	Y	Leith	Rochester, N	03/23/1860	04/11/1892			Y	
Mathies, Eagen	27	Austria	Y	Havre	New York	02/08/1884	03/30/1886	19	31	N	
Mathis, Daniel	34	France	Y	Havre	New York	12/23/1852	06/28/1862	18	364	N	
Matius, Abe	37	Russia	Y	Hamburg	New York	01/01/1892	08/23/1895			Y	
Matt, Francis	25	Bavaria	Y	Bremen	New York	08/01/1857	08/08/1859	17	468	N	
Matt, George	34	Germany	Y	Hamburg	New York	04/19/1883	10/18/1886			Y	
Mattei, Pasquale	37	Italy	Y	Naples	New York	09/03/1877	05/18/1894			Y	
Mattern, Charles	38	Germany	Y	Hamburg	New York	01/01/1893	10/13/1899			Y	
Mattert, Julius	44	Germany	Y	Bremen	Baltimore	05/28/1884	10/25/1889	19	262	N	
Mattert, Julius	44	Germany	Y	Bremen	Baltimore	05/28/1881	10/25/1889			Y	
Mattes, A.	??	France	Y	?	?	?	11/07/1882			Y	
Mattes, Anton	40	Germany	Y	Antwerp	New York	05/18/1882	10/23/1896			Y	
Mattes, Christian	22	Baden	Y	Havre	New Orleans	11/??/1852	12/24/1855	13	359	N	
Mattheis, Christian Mart	??	Saxe Weimar	Y	Hamburg	New York	06/24/18??	10/09/1848	1	88	N	
Matthes, Leo Michael	26	Bavaria	Y	Hamburg	New York	07/31/1847	11/20/1848	1	347	N	
Matthew, Frank	33	Germany	Y	Bremen	Baltimore	06/14/1888	04/07/1894			Y	
Matthews, John	27	Ireland	Y	Liverpool	Philadelphia	??/26/1849	12/17/1850	2	372	N	
Matthews, Thomas	28	Ireland	Y	Liverpool	New York	07/??/1841	05/04/1854	8	368	N	
Matthews, Thomas	28	Ireland	Y	Liverpool	New York	07/??/18??	05/04/1854	9	241	N	
Matthies, Ernst	25	Hanover	Y	Bremen	New York	11/25/1857	10/08/1860	27	439	N	
Matthiesen, Soenker	28	Denmark	Y	Flensburg	New York	09/01/1859	08/25/1860	27	313	N	
Matti, John	37	Switzerland	Y	Bremen	New York	04/00/1872	11/21/1885			Y	
Mattick, Henry	22	Bavaria	Y	Bremen	New Orleans	07/04/1848	02/23/1852	24	152	N	
Mattio, Matteo	31	Italy	Y	Naples	New York	04/23/1881	11/16/1891			Y	
Mattioli, Lina	37	Italy	Y	Havre	New York	10/23/1884	07/06/1891	19	330	N	
Mattioli, Lino	34	Italy	Y	Havre	New York	10/23/1884	07/06/1891			Y	
Mattler, John	26	France	Y	Havre	New Orleans	02/07/1849	01/29/1853	7	84	N	
Mattscheck, Gerhard	21	Hanover	Y	Bremen	New Orleans	12/09/1848	10/29/1851	4	437	N	
Mattscheck, John Phillip	26	Hanover	Y	Bremen	New Orleans	11/15/1844	09/12/1848	22	336	N	
Matz, Jacob	23	Bavaria	Y	Havre	New York	08/04/1852	09/20/1854	10	136	N	
Matz, Jacob	23	Bavaria	Y	Havre	New York	08/04/1852	09/20/1854	12	75	N	
Matz, Michael	30	Bavaria	Y	London	New York	09/29/1852	11/04/1852	6	346	N	
Matzke, Julius	34	Germany	Y	Hamburg	New York	03/24/1882	01/08/1883			Y	
Matzmor, August	27	Germany	Y	Bremen	New York	05/17/1892	09/29/1894			Y	
Matzner, Reinhold	27	Austria	Y	Bremen	New York	08/18/1883	12/03/1891			Y	
Mauch, Carl	25	Germany	Y	Havre	New York	02/05/1880	03/12/1883			Y	
Mauch, George	29	Wurttemberg	Y	Havre	New York	12/01/1851	04/04/1853	7	528	N	
Mauch, Paul	24	Germany	Y	Antwerp	New York	09/02/1880	01/02/1883			Y	
Maudel, Frederick	22	Hanover	Y	Bremen	New Orleans	06/25/1852	10/09/1854	6	98	N	
Maudel, Frederick	22	Hanover	Y	Bremen	New Orleans	06/25/1852	10/09/1854	11	101	N	
Maue, Frederick	25	Hanover	Y	Bremen	Philadelphia	10/03/1845	04/30/1850	3	32	N	
Maue, John	30	Germany	Y	Rotterdam	New York	09/15/1894	02/08/1898			Y	
Maune, Henry	59	Germany	Y	Bremen	New York	10/10/1884	10/22/1889			Y	
Mauntel, Frank	22	Hanover	Y	Bremen	Baltimore	07/15/1853	05/22/1856	26	533	N	

CITIZENSHIP RECORDS

APPLICANT	AGE	COUNTRY OF ORIGIN	DEC	DEPART PORT	ENTRY PORT	ARRIVE DATE	DEC DATE	VOL	PG.	FLD	NAT DATE
Mauntel, Louis	27	Hanover	Y	Bremen	New Orleans	06/03/1850	03/01/1853	7	246	N	
Maurath, Henry	21	Germany	Y	?	?	05/00/1884	10/11/1887			Y	
Maurer, Aloys	38	Austria	Y	Bremen	New York	04/07/1882	05/25/1889			Y	
Maurer, Emil	35	Germany	Y	Havre	New York	04/25/1891	10/14/1896			Y	
Maurer, Joseph	28	Germany	Y	Havre	New York	03/15/1888	10/18/1893			Y	
Mauritz, Joseph	22	Prussia	Y	Rotterdam	Baltimore	09/??/1853	07/10/1855	10	374	N	
Mause, Peter	35	Germany	Y	Bremen	New York	10/15/1885	09/12/1892			Y	
Maushart, John	27	Germany	Y	Havre	New York	01/28/1880	09/25/1882			Y	
Mautschka, Joseph	36	Austria	Y	Bremen	Baltimore	08/15/1853	05/23/1854	8	499	N	
Mautschka, Joseph	36	Austria	Y	Bremen	Baltimore	08/15/1853	05/23/1854	9	373	N	
May, Ambros	32	Germany	Y	Bremen	Baltimore	03/01/1897	10/24/1902			Y	
May, Benjamin	42	England	Y	Liverpool	Boston	04/18/1870	02/24/1893			Y	
May, Christian	38	Prussia	Y	Hamburg	New York	08/02/1871	01/27/1872	18	552	N	
May, Erwin	22	Prussia	Y	Bremen	New York	10/15/1854	11/23/1857	16	44	N	
May, Isaac	52	Germany	N	Liverpool	New York	09/27/1858	?			Y	
Mayer, Abraham	28	Hesse Darmsta	Y	Liverpool	New York	07/06/1853	11/02/1857	15	520	N	
Mayer, Benedict	25	Germany	Y	Antwerp	New York	11/22/1892	04/21/1898			Y	
Mayer, Carl	35	Wurttemberg	Y	Havre	New York	08/23/1853	10/09/1854	6	81	N	
Mayer, Charles	35	Wurttemberg	Y	Havre	New York	08/23/1853	10/09/1854	11	84	N	
Mayer, Charles	28	Austria	Y	Bremen	New York	08/13/1880	06/06/1883			Y	
Mayer, Charles	71	Germany	N	Havre	Philadelphia	06/??/1844	??/??/1855	28	256	N	04/??/1857
Mayer, Charles Jacob	??	?	N	?	?	?	?			Y	
Mayer, Christian	27	Wurttemberg	Y	Liverpool	New York	05/27/1854	07/01/1861	18	202	N	
Mayer, Daniel	21	Bavaria	Y	Havre	New Orleans	03/02/1854	02/11/1858	16	302	N	
Mayer, Fred	58	Germany	Y	Baden	New York	03/24/1866	07/26/1895			Y	
Mayer, Frederick	30	Wuerttemberg	Y	Havre	New Orleans	06/01/1849	05/31/1852	25	148	N	
Mayer, George	24	Bavaria	Y	Liverpool	Philadelphia	09/26/1854	03/15/1856	26	209	N	
Mayer, German	33	Baden	Y	Havre	New Orleans	03/11/1854	03/17/1856	26	216	N	
Mayer, Harry	??	Russia	N	?	?	04/20/1885				Y	10/24/1892
Mayer, Henry	54	Germany	Y	?	New York	??/??/1882	10/09/1885			Y	
Mayer, Isaac	45	Bavaria	Y	Havre	New York	06/01/1849	08/22/1855	11	478	N	
Mayer, John	25	Baden	Y	Havre	New Orleans	06/01/1853	02/05/1856	26	43	N	
Mayer, Joseph	??	Germany	Y	?	?	?	03/04/1887			Y	
Mayer, Julius	24	Germany	Y	Antwerp	New York	07/01/1880	10/21/1884			Y	
Mayer, Klemeus	21	Germany	Y	Bremen	New York	06/20/1880	12/26/1883			Y	
Mayer, Lorenz	28	Germany	Y	Havre	New York	03/26/1883	10/04/1887			Y	
Mayer, Philip	30	Bavaria	Y	Havre	New York	09/22/1858	04/27/1860	27	171	N	
Mayer, Simon	31	Hohenzollern	Y	Havre	New York	04/20/1854	10/20/1855	13	235	N	
Mayer, Valentine	40	Baden	Y	Havre	New Orleans	12/23/1853	09/23/1854	10	172	N	
Mayer, Valentine	40	Baden	Y	Havre	New Orleans	12/23/1853	09/23/1854	12	111	N	
Mayerratken, W.	35	Germany	Y	Bremen	New York	05/17/1881	10/27/1888	19	193	N	
Mayers, John F.W.	32	Hanover	Y	Bremen	Philadelphia	09/11/1842	03/23/1850	2	241	N	
Mayhaus, Henry	22	Germany	Y	Bremen	Baltimore	08/31/1888	05/26/1892			Y	
Mayne, Joseph	34	Ireland	Y	Liverpool	New York	05/17/1880	10/05/1885	19	13	N	
Mayos, Constantine	??	Germany	Y	?	?	?	04/26/1887			Y	
Mayr, Joseph	58	Germany	N	Bremen	New York	03/??/1867	?			Y	
Mazza, Basilio	50	Italy	Y	Genoa	New York	10/05/1877	09/29/1885			Y	
Mazzhauser, Charles	23	Prussia	Y	Antwerp	New York	05/01/1850	03/01/1852	24	201	N	
Mazzoni, John	39	Sardina	Y	Genoa	New Orleans	01/10/1848	11/03/1851	4	466	N	
McAdams, Patrick	31	Ireland	Y	Liverpool	Boston	07/01/1846	02/19/1850	2	102	N	
McAnally, Joseph	41	Ireland	Y	Liverpool	New York	05/28/1839	10/13/1848	1	186	N	
McAndrew, Patrick	61	Ireland	Y	Sligo	New York	03/17/1846	12/29/1859	17	534	N	
McAndrew, Peter	35	Ireland	Y	Liverpool	New Orleans	04/26/1847	05/01/1854	8	333	N	
McAndrew, Peter	35	Ireland	Y	Liverpool	New Orleans	04/26/1847	05/01/1854	9	206	N	
McAnespy, James	34	Ireland	Y	Liverpool	New York	04/18/1853	09/29/1856	14	14	N	
McArdle, Francis	24	Ireland	Y	?	Boston	08/10/1895	10/17/1896			Y	
McArdle, Hugh	30	Ireland	Y	Liverpool	New York	10/03/1848	08/06/1851	4	92	N	
McArdle, John	27	Ireland	Y	Liverpool	New York	06/02/1846	03/21/1853	7	359	N	
McArdle, Patrick	40	Ireland	Y	Liverpool	New Orleans	02/04/1849	01/20/1852	24	43	N	

CITIZENSHIP RECORDS

APPLICANT	AGE	COUNTRY OF ORIGIN	DEC	DEPART PORT	ENTRY PORT	ARRIVE DATE	DEC DATE	VOL	PG.	FLD	NAT DATE
McArthur, John	34	Canada	Y	Glencoe	Detroit	01/05/1891	12/30/1895			Y	
McArthur, John	37	Canada	Y	Windsor	Detroit	09/30/1892	11/05/1892			Y	
McAtees, John	??	Ireland	Y	Liverpool	New York	09/04/18??	11/08/1856	14	483	N	
McAuliff, Jerry	32	Ireland	Y	Liverpool	New York	05/07/1856	01/06/1860	27	34	N	
McAuliffe, Charles	32	Ireland	Y	Queenstown	New York	05/21/1887	02/07/1888			Y	
McAuliffe, Dennis L.	31	Ireland	Y	?	New York	??/??/1893	06/04/1896			Y	
McAuliffg, Simon	36	Ireland	N	Cork	New York	06/??/1866	?			Y	
McAvoy, Hugh	31	Ireland	Y	Liverpool	New Orleans	07/01/1845	10/11/1848	1	118	N	
McAvoy, John	31	Ireland	Y	Liverpool	New Orleans	04/26/1850	07/07/1855	11	350	N	
McAvoy, Timothy	21	Ireland	Y	Liverpool	New Orleans	04/26/1850	07/07/1855	11	351	N	
McBirney, Hugh	27	Ireland	Y	Belfast	New Orleans	01/27/1846	10/06/1851	4	200	N	
McBirney, Hugh	71	Ireland	N	Belfast	New Orleans	01/23/1846	12/01/1851	28	418	N	01/12/1854
McBriar, Robert	57	Ireland	N	Liverpool	New Orleans	??/??/1849	?			Y	
McBride, Patrick	26	Ireland	Y	Liverpool	Troy	07/04/1850	02/01/1853	7	102	N	
McBride, Thomas P.	7	Ireland	N	?	New York	00/00/1869				Y	10/20/1888
McCabe, James	23	Ireland	Y	Liverpool	New Orleans	12/??/1847	10/21/1851	4	363	N	
McCabe, John	40	Ireland	Y	Liverpool	Philadelphia	04/05/1886	08/18/1888			Y	
McCabe, Owen	35	Ireland	Y	Liverpool	New Orleans	10/22/1851	09/04/1860	27	331	N	
McCabe, Patrick	25	England	Y	Liverpool	New York	08/25/1893	06/22/1896			Y	
McCaffrey, Nicholas	27	Ireland	Y	Liverpool	New York	12/01/1848	02/28/1852	24	183	N	
McCallan, Francis	??	Ireland	Y	?	?	?	08/29/1889			Y	
McCamara, Martin	29	Ireland	Y	Liverpool	New Orleans	04/15/1853	10/03/1857	15	247	N	
McCann, James	21	Ireland	Y	Liverpool	New Orleans	12/23/1848	03/29/1853	7	454	N	
McCann, Michael	??	Ireland	N	?	?	07/12/1887				Y	10/26/1892
McCann, Patrick	40	Ireland	Y	Belfast	New York	08/??/1847	11/08/1856	14	484	N	
McCann, Patrick	26	Ireland	Y	Liverpool	New York	08/23/1882	10/10/1890			Y	
McCann, Peter	40	Ireland	Y	Liverpool	New York	06/01/1849	04/04/1853	8	42	N	
McCanna, Hugh	26	Ireland	Y	Liverpool	New York	10/06/1853	05/31/1859	17	442	N	
McCanna, Michael	25	Ireland	Y	Liverpool	New York	08/12/1845	01/22/1852	24	52	N	
McCarney, Terrence	23	Ireland	Y	Liverpool	New York	11/18/1845	12/30/1861	18	238	N	
McCarthy, Dan	30	Ireland	Y	Liverpool	New York	04/11/1851	04/18/1853	8	73	N	
McCarthy, Dennis	26	Ireland	Y	Queenstown	New York	05/09/1894	07/15/1898			Y	
McCarthy, Eugene	35	Ireland	Y	Queenstown	New York	05/??/1881	01/12/1887			Y	
McCarthy, Florence	26	Ireland	Y	Queenstown	New York	05/22/1891	05/22/1896			Y	
McCarthy, Jerry	27	Ireland	Y	Queenstown	New York	05/01/1881	05/04/1888			Y	
McCarthy, Michael	26	Ireland	Y	Queenstown	New York	04/30/1885	04/02/1892			Y	
McCarthy, Owen	29	Ireland	Y	Liverpool	New York	10/15/1849	10/26/1858	17	121	N	
McCarthy, Patrick	21	Ireland	Y	Queenstown	New York	05/13/1892	11/04/1893			Y	
McCarthy, Tim	44	Ireland	N	Ireland	New York	07/??/1865	?	28	209	N	12/17/1874
McCarthy, Tim	21	Ireland	N	?	New York	07/00/1865				Y	12/17/1874
McCarthy, William	51	Ireland	N	Liverpool	Philadelphia	09/??/1838	?			Y	
McCartney, Charles	35	Ireland	Y	Belfast	New York	10/08/1887	03/29/1894			Y	
McCartney, Charles	??	Ireland	Y	?	?	?	05/23/1891			Y	
McCartney, Hugh	30	Ireland	Y	Liverpool	New York	05/08/1883	03/29/1894			Y	
McCarty, Bernard	40	Ireland	Y	Liverpool	New Orleans	02/06/1849	03/17/1851	3	294	N	
McCarty, Dennis	23	Ireland	Y	Cork	New York	05/31/1851	06/07/1854	10	101	N	
McCarty, Dennis	23	Ireland	Y	Cork	New York	05/31/1851	06/07/1854	12	38	N	
McCarty, Eugene	30	Ireland	Y	London	New York	06/01/1852	09/29/1856	14	33	N	
McCarty, James	35	Ireland	Y	Bantry	Boston	09/01/1846	02/28/1853	7	243	N	
McCarty, James	27	Ireland	Y	Liverpool	New York	07/09/1853	03/27/1857	15	93	N	
McCarty, James	21	Ireland	Y	Liverpool	New Orleans	11/??/1841	03/17/1856	26	215	N	
McCarty, Jerry	23	Ireland	Y	Canada	Lewiston	07/22/1849	10/18/1851	4	327	N	
McCarty, John	23	Ireland	Y	Liverpool	New Orleans	12/29/1849	03/??/1851	3	317	N	
McCarty, John	25	Ireland	Y	Liverpool	New York	07/07/1848	09/29/1854	10	302	N	
McCarty, John	25	Ireland	Y	Liverpool	New York	07/07/1848	09/29/1854	12	241	N	
McCarty, Martin	36	Ireland	Y	Liverpool	New Orleans	04/08/1849	11/01/1852	5	170	N	
McCarty, Martin	36	Ireland	Y	Liverpool	New Orleans	04/08/1849	11/01/1852	6	296	N	
McCarty, Michael	23	Ireland	Y	Canada	Buffalo	05/03/1847	03/11/1850	2	180	N	
McCarty, Patrick	50	Ireland	Y	Westport	Philadelphia	08/09/1847	01/31/1850	2	21	N	

CITIZENSHIP RECORDS

APPLICANT	AGE	COUNTRY OF ORIGIN	DEC	DEPART PORT	ENTRY PORT	ARRIVE DATE	DEC DATE	VOL	PG.	FLD	NAT DATE
McCarty, Patrick	23	Ireland	Y	Liverpool	New Orleans	04/10/1849	03/25/1851	3	325	N	
McCarty, Peter	33	Ireland	Y	Galway	New York	04/20/1848	04/17/1852	24	526	N	
McCarty, Thomas	26	Ireland	Y	Liverpool	Boston	07/06/1847	03/07/1851	3	206	N	
McCasey, D. J.	41	Canada	Y	Wingham	Detroit	03/11/1889	10/09/1896			Y	
McCasey, John H.	26	Canada	Y	?	?	?	06/23/1887			Y	
McCassy, Edward George	??	Ireland	Y	?	?	?	01/02/1889			Y	
McCleary, Samuel	25	Ireland	Y	Liverpool	New York	??/21/1853	04/18/1855	11	270	N	
McColloch, George	55	Ireland	Y	Liverpool	New York	10/??/1845	09/11/1857	15	258	N	
McComb, William	7	Canada	N	?	Wyandott, MI	00/00/1850				Y	10/26/1888
McConnell, Peter	30	Ireland	Y	Liverpool	New York	04/23/1853	10/09/1854	11	146	N	
McCool, Hugh	51	Ireland	Y	Liverpool	New York	10/04/1873	10/25/1886	19	85	N	
McCool, Hugh	51	Ireland	Y	Liverpool	New York	10/04/1873	10/25/1886			Y	
McCormack, Patrick	28	Ireland	Y	Londonderry	Philadelphia	08/28/1848	05/02/1854	8	352	N	
McCormick, James	23	Ireland	Y	Liverpool	New Orleans	02/21/1851	05/25/1854	9	423	N	
McCormick, James	23	Ireland	Y	Liverpool	New Orleans	02/21/1851	05/25/1854	10	6	N	
McCormick, James	34	Scotland	Y	Greenwich	New York	07/19/1885	12/23/1895			Y	
McCormick, Luke	38	Ireland	Y	Liverpool	New Orleans	03/04/1828	10/14/1851	4	280	N	
McCormick, Mathew	21	Ireland	Y	Liverpool	New York	09/20/1851	09/09/1852	25	430	N	
McCormick, Patrick	28	Ireland	Y	Londonderry	Philadelphia	08/25/1848	05/02/1854	9	225	N	
McCormick, Patrick	28	Ireland	Y	Dublin	New York	06/21/1848	06/05/1854	10	76	N	
McCormick, Patrick	28	Ireland	Y	Dublin	New York	06/21/1848	06/05/1854	12	13	N	
McCourt, Henry	40	Ireland	Y	Belfast	New York	08/06/1850	08/05/1856	14	353	N	
McCoy, Barney	24	Ireland	Y	Londonderry	New York	05/22/1890	10/27/1892	19	387	N	
McCoy, Barney	24	Ireland	Y	Londonderry	New York	05/22/1890	10/27/1892			Y	
McCoy, John	32	Ireland	Y	Londonderry	New York	05/12/1870	08/15/1884			Y	
McCoy, Patrick	39	Ireland	Y	Canada	Burlington	06/29/1833	06/02/1852	25	209	N	
McCraith, William	22	Ireland	Y	Cork	New York	??/15/1851	04/23/1855	11	283	N	
McCready, G. W.	??	Great Britain	Y	?	?	?	11/09/1889			Y	
McCreary, Mathew	??	Ireland	Y	?	Philadelphia	04/22/1854	08/00/1856			Y	
McCurley, James	37	Liverpool	Y	Liverpool	New York	05/06/1868	02/19/1886			Y	
McDermott, Bryan	28	Ireland	Y	Halifax	Portland	08/28/1841	01/19/1852	24	31	N	
McDermott, Christopher	21	Ireland	Y	Liverpool	New York	05/19/1883	08/05/1886			Y	
McDermott, Dominick	28	Ireland	Y	Sligo	Boston	10/??/1843	09/14/1852	25	501	N	
McDermott, John	27	Ireland	Y	Liverpool	New Orleans	11/26/1847	11/21/1848	1	356	N	
McDermott, John	29	Ireland	Y	Dublin	New York	09/13/1881	12/01/1888			Y	
McDermott, Joseph	49	Ireland	N	Liverpool	Boston	06/24/1858	?			Y	
McDermott, Michael	34	Ireland	Y	Liverpool	New York	08/24/1849	11/03/1852	5	195	N	
McDermott, Michael	34	Ireland	Y	Liverpool	New York	08/24/1849	11/03/1852	6	321	N	
McDermott, Michael	21	Ireland	Y	Queenstown	Philadelphia	04/27/1895	07/27/1895			Y	
McDermott, Patrick	50	Ireland	Y	Liverpool	New York	05/??/1850	11/06/1851	4	491	N	
McDermott, Patrick	24	Ireland	Y	Queenstown	New York	05/22/1890	11/20/1890			Y	
McDermott, Phillip	23	Ireland	Y	Liverpool	Buffalo	07/??/1847	10/13/1848	1	201	N	
McDermott, Thomas	25	Ireland	Y	Canada	Cleveland	06/28/1845	10/13/1848	1	199	N	
McDermott, Thomas	22	Ireland	Y	Canada	Buffalo	06/12/1847	03/31/1852	24	342	N	
McDevitt, Charles	27	Ireland	Y	Londonderry	Philadelphia	07/01/1849	04/17/1854	8	158	N	
McDevitt, Charles	27	Ireland	Y	Londonderry	Philadelphia	07/01/1849	04/17/1854	9	29	N	
McDevitt, William	26	Ireland	Y	Londonderry	New York	06/01/1857	10/12/1857	15	409	N	
McDiarmid, Hugh	36	Canada	Y	?	Detroit	??/??/1864	02/03/1874			Y	
McDinnell, Anthony	25	Ireland	Y	Liverpool	New Orleans	04/25/1846	04/05/1852	24	378	N	
McDonagh, John	32	Ireland	Y	Liverpool	New Orleans	05/03/1846	10/18/1852	5	10	N	
McDonagh, John	16	Ireland	N	?	Boston	00/00/1881				Y	10/20/1888
McDonald, Charles	24	Ireland	Y	Liverpool	New York	06/29/1847	05/11/1852	25	3	N	
McDonald, Darby	40	England	Y	London	New York	06/04/1857	03/04/1858	16	361	N	
McDonald, David	??	Ireland	Y	Canada	Oswego	05/03/18??	10/11/1848	1	152	N	
McDonald, James	24	Ireland	Y	Liverpool	New York	12/02/1846	02/12/1849	23	62	N	
McDonald, James	36	Ireland	Y	Liverpool	New York	04/20/1848	06/14/1852	25	267	N	
McDonald, John	25	Ireland	Y	Liverpool	New York	04/18/1881	03/??/1882			Y	
McDonald, John	33	Ireland	Y	Liverpool	New York	04/18/1881	03/??/1882	28	270	N	?
McDonald, Martin	30	Ireland	Y	Liverpool	New York	04/14/1847	02/06/1850	2	44	N	

CITIZENSHIP RECORDS

APPLICANT	AGE	COUNTRY OF ORIGIN	DEC	DEPART PORT	ENTRY PORT	ARRIVE DATE	DEC DATE	VOL	PG.	FLD	NAT DATE
McDonald, Michael	48	Ireland	N	Liverpool	New York	06/??/1860	?			Y	
McDonald, Patrick	25	Ireland	Y	Liverpool	New York	11/04/1852	04/04/1853	8	9	N	
McDonald, Patrick	37	Ireland	Y	Liverpool	New York	09/01/1851	03/20/1858	16	429	N	
McDonald, William	29	Scotland	Y	Glasgow	New York	01/16/1882	04/04/1882			Y	
McDonnaugh, James	27	Ireland	Y	Liverpool	New York	05/06/1847	09/13/1852	25	486	N	
McDonnell, Patrick	33	Ireland	Y	Belfast	New Orleans	01/05/1852	02/11/1860	27	104	N	
McDonnell, Peter	30	Ireland	Y	Liverpool	New York	04/23/1853	10/09/1854	6	143	N	
McDonough, Andrew	25	Ireland	Y	Liverpool	New Orleans	12/??/1848	10/23/1851	4	382	N	
McDonough, Edward	34	Ireland	Y	Liverpool	New York	04/09/1847	03/15/1851	3	280	N	
McDonough, John	25	Ireland	Y	Liverpool	New Orleans	03/04/1849	04/05/1852	24	391	N	
McDonough, John Richard	23	Ireland	Y	Liverpool	New York	07/25/1847	02/17/1849	23	159	N	
McDonough, Patrick	30	Ireland	Y	Liverpool	New Orleans	03/22/1850	10/29/1858	17	187	N	
McDonough, Peter	37	Ireland	Y	Liverpool	New Orleans	05/05/1848	10/10/1854	6	217	N	
McDonough, Peter	37	Ireland	Y	Liverpool	New York	05/05/1848	10/10/1854	11	220	N	
McDonough, Richard	57	Ireland	N	Ireland	Philadelphia	05/??/1853	?			Y	
McDonough, Thomas	44	Ireland	N	Liverpool	New York	05/13/1864	?			Y	
McDougall, D. D.	26	Canada	Y	Windsor	Detroit	07/02/1879	10/12/1885			Y	
McDouglass, Thomas	50	Scotland	N	Liverpool	New York	08/26/1867	?			Y	
McDowell, Francis Edmund	35	Ireland	Y	Londonderry	New York	05/11/1881	10/07/1896			Y	
McElboy, Edward	53	Ireland	Y	Liverpool	New Orleans	04/27/1847	10/13/1851	4	222	N	
McElroy, Matthew	36	Ireland	Y	Glasgow	New York	11/19/1849	01/??/1853	7	96	N	
McElvoy, Frank	46	Ireland	Y	Liverpool	New York	04/14/1847	04/08/1852	24	419	N	
McEvilly, Thomas	28	Ireland	Y	Liverpool	New York	06/01/1854	12/28/1857	16	272	N	
McFadden, James	26	Ireland	Y	Liverpool	New York	09/01/1892	10/28/1897			Y	
McFarland, John	24	Ireland	Y	Liverpool	New Orleans	02/12/1847	01/23/1852	24	58	N	
McFarlane, John	33	Scotland	Y	Liverpool	New York	10/01/1852	10/30/1857	15	505	N	
McFeely, James	27	Ireland	Y	Canada	New York	04/01/1846	09/09/1852	25	424	N	
McFernan, John	28	Ireland	Y	Liverpool	Newport News	06/28/1888	03/30/1896			Y	
McGann, William J.	??	Canada	Y	?	?	?	09/20/1893			Y	
McGarahan, Thos.	30	Ireland	Y	Liverpool	New York	05/13/1844	03/24/1853	7	387	N	
McGarry, Michael	32	Ireland	Y	Queenstown	New York	03/01/1880	10/15/1890			Y	
McGearty, Barny	24	Ireland	Y	Liverpool	New Orleans	05/19/1849	10/14/1851	4	267	N	
McGeer, Patrick	24	Ireland	Y	Belfast	New York	04/26/1848	10/13/1851	4	256	N	
McGever, John	41	Ireland	Y	Sligo	Buffalo	12/25/1847	11/04/1852	5	218	N	
McGever, John	41	Ireland	Y	Sligo	Buffalo	12/25/1847	11/04/1852	6	344	N	
McGill, Patrick	22	Ireland	Y	Belfast	New York	03/02/1849	10/06/1854	10	495	N	
McGill, Patrick	22	Ireland	Y	Belfast	New York	03/02/1849	10/06/1854	12	434	N	
McGinn, Patrick	49	Ireland	N	Liverpool	New York	01/01/1850	?			Y	
McGinnis, John	25	Ireland	Y	Liverpool	New York	04/04/1850	07/11/1855	11	376	N	
McGinnis, Patrick	28	Ireland	Y	Liverpool	New York	06/19/1849	04/17/1852	24	525	N	
McGinny, Hugh	25	Ireland	Y	Liverpool	New York	06/01/1844	11/15/1848	1	301	N	
McGittrick, John	28	Ireland	Y	Liverpool	New Orleans	05/15/1850	06/29/1860	27	16	N	
McGiven, Michael	27	Ireland	Y	Liverpool	New York	04/21/1853	11/01/1858	17	236	N	
McGiven, Patrick	28	Ireland	Y	Liverpool	New York	06/04/1846	01/28/1851	2	537	N	
McGivern, David	37	Ireland	Y	Liverpool	New York	07/31/1834	05/24/1852	25	100	N	
McGlenn, Thomas	27	Ireland	Y	Liverpool	New York	04/10/1850	09/22/1854	12	104	N	
McGlinn, Thomas	27	Ireland	Y	Liverpool	New York	04/10/1850	09/22/18??	10	165	N	
McGlocklin, John	50	Ireland	Y	Liverpool	New York	07/11/1881	10/28/1899			Y	
McGoff, Daniel	31	Ireland	Y	Liverpool	New Orleans	12/30/1849	09/13/1852	25	488	N	
McGoldrick, Edward	??	?	Y	Canada	Buffalo	??/19/1847	03/28/1851	3	366	N	
McGoldrick, Thomas	28	Ireland	Y	Londonderry	Buffalo	08/15/1842	03/26/1850	2	271	N	
McGonnell, James	30	Ireland	Y	Liverpool	New Orleans	12/27/1848	11/10/1852	5	268	N	
McGonnell, James	30	Ireland	Y	Liverpool	New Orleans	12/27/1848	11/10/1852	6	392	N	
McGouran, James	56	Ireland	Y	Queenstown	Boston	07/19/1876	10/28/1899			Y	
McGovern, John	33	Ireland	Y	Liverpool	New York	04/10/1853	10/02/1856	14	165	N	
McGovern, Thomas	24	Ireland	Y	Liverpool	New York	05/13/1846	02/27/1852	24	179	N	
McGovern, Thomas	23	Ireland	Y	Liverpool	New York	04/14/1882	01/03/1884			Y	
McGowan, John	30	Ireland	Y	Liverpool	New York	04/14/1887	04/18/1894			Y	
McGowan, Laurence	23	Ireland	Y	Liverpool	New York	05/17/1882	04/03/1885			Y	

CITIZENSHIP RECORDS

APPLICANT	AGE	COUNTRY OF ORIGIN	DEC	DEPART PORT	ENTRY PORT	ARRIVE DATE	DEC DATE	VOL	PG.	FLD	NAT DATE
McGowan, Lawrence	27	Ireland	Y	Liverpool	New Orleans	05/10/1852	09/12/1860	27	361	N	
McGowan, Thomas	22	Ireland	Y	Queenstown	New York	04/28/1889	10/20/1892	19	373	N	
McGowan, Thomas	22	Ireland	Y	Queenstown	New York	04/28/1889	10/20/1892			Y	
McGowen, John	45	Ireland	Y	Liverpool	New York	03/??/1868	03/30/1891	19	314	N	
McGrain, Nicholas	22	Ireland	Y	Liverpool	New York	09/21/1851	01/25/1853	7	65	N	
McGrane, Bernard	24	Ireland	Y	Liverpool	New York	07/20/1853	04/11/1860	27	147	N	
McGrann, Thomas	30	Ireland	Y	Dublin	New Orleans	12/15/1851	09/15/1858	16	163	N	
McGrath, Dennis	50	Ireland	Y	Liverpool	New Orleans	01/03/1846	03/03/1856	26	157	N	
McGrath, James	30	Ireland	Y	Waterford	New York	07/29/1855	08/13/1860	27	267	N	
McGrath, John	35	Ireland	Y	Montreal	Whitehall	11/06/1848	02/17/1851	3	141	N	
McGrath, John	24	Ireland	Y	Waterford	New York	08/20/1859	07/20/1860	27	229	N	
McGrath, Michael	30	Ireland	Y	Liverpool	New Orleans	04/24/1849	08/15/1851	4	135	N	
McGrath, Michael	31	Ireland	Y	Canada	Troy	09/04/1846	04/25/1853	8	118	N	
McGrath, Morris	36	England	Y	Liverpool	New York	03/13/1886	10/21/1898			Y	
McGrath, Patrick	26	Ireland	Y	Liverpool	New York	03/12/1848	04/12/1852	24	438	N	
McGrath, Patrick Francis	21	Ireland	Y	Liverpool	New York	03/??/1852	03/28/1853	7	421	N	
McGrath, Thomas	24	Ireland	Y	Liverpool	New York	12/20/1848	09/07/1852	25	402	N	
McGrath, Timothy	32	Ireland	Y	London	New York	09/04/1853	04/20/1854	8	221	N	
McGrath, Timothy	32	Ireland	Y	London	New York	09/04/1853	04/20/1854	9	92	N	
McGrath, William	30	Ireland	Y	Canada	Whitehall	11/28/1844	08/16/1848	22	187	N	
McGraw, James	42	Ireland	Y	Liverpool	Philadelphia	12/29/1830	04/27/1861	18	150	N	
McGraw, Joseph Edward	22	England	Y	Liverpool	New York	06/26/1892	09/26/1892			Y	
McGreevy, John	22	England	Y	Liverpool	Philadelphia	09/03/1885	10/22/1888			Y	
McGrenn, John	30	Ireland	Y	Liverpool	Boston	05/10/1846	02/01/1850	2	27	N	
McGreth, John P.	29	Ireland	Y	Liverpool	New York	04/06/1849	03/01/1852	24	186	N	
McGrew, James	24	Ireland	Y	Queenstown	New York	05/30/1890	10/25/1893	21	31	N	
McGrew, James	24	Ireland	Y	Queenstown	New York	05/30/1890	10/25/1893			Y	
McGuckan, Michael	29	Ireland	Y	Belfast	Buffalo	??/07/1847	02/18/1850	2	94	N	
McGuff, Michael	28	Ireland	Y	Liverpool	Boston	04/15/1881	10/28/1886	19	95	N	
McGuff, Patrick	26	Ireland	Y	Liverpool	New Orleans	12/01/1848	11/01/1852	5	163	N	
McGuff, Patrick	22	Ireland	Y	Liverpool	New Orleans	12/01/1848	11/01/1852	6	289	N	
McGuiness, Thomas M.	36	Ireland	Y	Liverpool	New York	04/21/1894	10/27/1899			Y	
McGuinn, Michael	24	Ireland	Y	Liverpool	New York	05/02/1893	03/21/1896			Y	
McGuinn, Michael	30	Ireland	Y	Liverpool	New York	04/03/1883	06/18/1889			Y	
McGuinn, Patrick	23	Ireland	Y	Liverpool	New York	05/22/1887	11/03/1890			Y	
McGuinn, Patrick	75	Ireland	Y	Canada	Cleveland	05/??/1853	10/15/1889			Y	
McGuire, Austin	23	Ireland	Y	Liverpool	New Orleans	11/13/1851	10/06/1856	14	187	N	
McGuire, Christopher	21	Ireland	Y	Liverpool	New York	09/27/1851	10/22/1852	5	53	N	
McGuire, G. Alex	31	British West	Y	St. Croix	New York	11/14/1893	12/31/1896			Y	
McGuire, James	43	Ireland	N	Liverpool	New Orleans	05/??/1849	?				
McGuire, James	21	Ireland	Y	Liverpool	New Orleans	01/??/1848	11/??/1849	23	306	N	
McGuire, Matthew	4	Ireland	N	?	New York	00/00/1849				Y	11/02/1888
McGuire, Michael	24	Ireland	Y	Liverpool	New York	10/11/1883	12/13/1883			Y	
McGuire, Patrick	58	Ireland	Y	Liverpool	New Orleans	05/25/1851	10/06/1856	14	186	N	
McGuire, Richard J.	24	Ireland	Y	Liverpool	New York	08/04/1854	06/04/1856	14	292	N	
McGuire, William	26	Ireland	Y	Liverpool	New Orleans	04/21/1848	04/02/1853	6	485	N	
McGurrin, Patrick	75	Ireland	Y	Belleville	Cleveland	05/??/1853	10/15/1889	19	237	N	
McHale, James	10	Ireland	N	?	New York	00/00/1864				Y	10/26/1887
McHale, John	27	Ireland	Y	Liverpool	New York	05/13/1888	10/13/1892	19	360	N	
McHale, Patrick	28	Ireland	Y	Liverpool	New York	06/12/1881	10/23/1891			Y	
McHale, Patrick	43	Ireland	N	Liverpool	New York	05/20/1864	?			Y	
McHale, Patrick	16	Ireland	N	?	New Orleans	00/00/1852				Y	10/23/1888
McHugh, Daniel	26	England	Y	Liverpool	New York	02/14/1881	04/03/1886			Y	
McHugh, Dennis	23	Ireland	Y	Liverpool	New Orleans	04/24/1847	01/16/1849	1	442	N	
McHugh, Edward	??	Ireland	Y	?	New Orleans	03/15/1853	11/04/1856	14	460	N	
McHugh, James	24	Ireland	Y	Queenstown	New York	07/01/1885	10/19/1889			Y	
McHugh, James H.	21	Ireland	Y	Liverpool	New York	08/26/1851	04/04/1853	7	513	N	
McHugh, John	23	Ireland	Y	London	New York	07/20/1855	11/03/1858	17	271	N	
McHugh, John	22	Ireland	Y	Liverpool	New Orleans	12/22/1846	04/05/1852	24	379	N	

CITIZENSHIP RECORDS

APPLICANT	AGE	COUNTRY OF ORIGIN	DEC	DEPART PORT	ENTRY PORT	ARRIVE DATE	DEC DATE	VOL	PG.	FLD	NAT DATE
McHugh, Michael	32	Ireland	Y	Galway	Portland	05/??/1848	12/07/1852	5	394	N	
McHugh, Michael	28	Ireland	Y	Liverpool	New York	03/26/1852	05/29/1856	14	268	N	
McHugh, Michael	59	Ireland	Y	Liverpool	New York	08/16/1873	08/21/1890			Y	
McHugh, Michael	22	Ireland	Y	?	New York	??/??/1879	10/09/1882			Y	
McHugh, Patrick	23	Ireland	Y	Queenstown	New York	06/25/1885	03/14/1887	19	113	N	
McHugh, Patrick	23	Ireland	Y	Liverpool	New York	05/07/1853	05/20/1856	26	506	N	
McHugh, Peter	23	Ireland	Y	Queenstown	New York	07/02/1890	07/23/1893	19	424	N	
McHugh, Peter	23	Ireland	Y	Queenstown	New York	07/02/1890	06/23/1893			Y	
McHugh, Samuel	26	England	Y	Liverpool	New York	02/14/1881	04/03/1886	19	33	N	
McHugh, Thomas	35	Ireland	Y	Queenstown	New York	04/??/1869	06/14/1880			Y	
McHugh, Thomas	17	Ireland	N	?	Philadelphia	00/00/1879				Y	10/26/1888
McHugh, Timothy	30	Ireland	Y	Liverpool	New York	09/13/1849	03/25/1850	2	262	N	
McInany, James	??	Ireland	N	?	?	06/11/1886				Y	10/25/1892
McInerney, Michael J.	??	Great Britain	Y	?	?	?	06/27/1889			Y	
McInnes, James	21	Scotland	Y	Glasgow	New York	07/04/1856	10/20/1858	17	72	N	
McIntyre, Thomas	25	Ireland	Y	Queenstown	New York	05/05/1888	10/01/1894			Y	
McKale, Thomas	29	Ireland	Y	Queenstown	New York	07/21/1884	11/05/1892	19	411	N	
McKale, Thomas	29	Ireland	Y	Queenstown	New York	07/21/1884	11/05/1892			Y	
McKay, George	31	Scotland	Y	London	New York	04/03/1850	05/05/1854	8	380	N	
McKay, George	31	Scotland	Y	London	New York	04/03/1850	05/05/1854	9	253	N	
McKearny, John	27	Ireland	Y	Belfast	New York	05/01/1847	08/01/1851	4	69	N	
McKenne, Samuel	30	Scotland	Y	Glasgow	Buffalo	12/05/1841	11/03/1852	6	319	N	
McKenod, Hugh	27	Ireland	Y	Liverpool	New York	06/29/1849	04/04/1853	8	54	N	
McKeon, Lawrence	31	Ireland	Y	Liverpool	New York	11/07/1848	03/09/1852	24	273	N	
McKeown, Joseph	35	Ireland	Y	Liverpool	New York	06/26/1845	10/09/1854	11	118	N	
McKernan, John	29	Ireland	Y	Liverpool	New York	08/09/1843	10/04/1854	10	410	N	
McKernan, John	29	Ireland	Y	Liverpool	New York	08/09/1843	10/04/1854	12	349	N	
McKiernan, James	39	Ireland	Y	Liverpool	New Orleans	02/04/1852	04/25/1853	8	111	N	
McKinna, Samuel	30	Scotland	Y	Glasgow	Buffalo	12/05/1841	11/03/1852	5	193	N	
McKittrick, Michael S.	??	Great Britain	Y	?	?	?	10/14/1892			Y	
McKoen, Christopher	26	Ireland	Y	Liverpool	New York	10/01/1848	07/31/1851	4	66	N	
McKone, Michael	29	Ireland	Y	Liverpool	Boston	04/10/1850	07/21/1851	4	19	N	
McKown, Joseph	35	Ireland	Y	Liverpool	New York	06/26/1845	10/09/1854	6	115	N	
McLaughlin, James	40	Ireland	N	Liverpool	New York	05/??/1861	?			Y	
McLaughlin, James	61	Ireland	N	Liverpool	New York	01/02/1848	?	28	308	N	10/??/1855
McLaughlin, John	29	Ireland	Y	Dublin	New Orleans	03/09/1849	07/05/1851	3	481	N	
McLaughlin, John	20	Ireland	Y	Liverpool	New Orleans	12/23/1849	02/10/1853	7	137	N	
McLaughlin, John	40	Ireland	Y	Liverpool	New York	04/18/1848	01/23/1852	24	59	N	
McLaughlin, Martin	47	Ireland	N	Liverpool	New York	08/15/1866	04/16/1866	28	89	N	10/08/1872
McLaughlin, Martin	26	Ireland	N	Liverpool	New York	08/15/1865	04/16/1866			Y	10/08/1872
McLaughlin, Patrick	33	Ireland	Y	Liverpool	New Orleans	10/22/1848	05/19/1854	8	477	N	
McLaughlin, Patrick	33	Ireland	Y	Liverpool	New Orleans	10/22/1848	05/19/1854	9	351	N	
McLaughlin, Patrick	37	Ireland	Y	Londonderry	New York	06/??/1871	06/13/1888			Y	
McLaughlin, Paul	21	Ireland	Y	Liverpool	New Orleans	04/16/1847	11/21/1848	1	359	N	
McLaughlin, Richard	54	Ireland	N	Liverpool	New York	10/07/1857	?			Y	
McLaughlin, William	25	Ireland	Y	London	Philadelphia	04/23/1848	07/26/1851	4	42	N	
McLaughlin, William	28	Ireland	Y	Liverpool	New York	04/22/1889	11/03/1893			Y	
McLauglin, James	23	Ireland	Y	Londonderry	New York	12/01/1848	05/17/1854	9	334	N	
McLean, Archibald	44	Canada	N	Summersie	Boston	06/20/1868	?			Y	
McLean, Daniel	30	Ireland	Y	London	Philadelphia	??/12/1846	02/15/1850	2	83	N	
McLellan, David	23	Canada	Y	Ontario	Port Huron,	08/25/1881	08/04/1884			Y	
McLeod, A. H.	49	Canada	Y	?	Boston	00/00/1854	10/10/1884			Y	
McLeod, Murdock	54	Scotland	Y	Glasgow	New York	10/02/1889	06/09/1894			Y	
McLeon, Samuel	28	Ireland	Y	Liverpool	Buffalo	03/??/1880	10/30/1888	19	202	N	
McMahan, Bernard	25	Ireland	Y	Liverpool	New Orleans	12/01/1852	09/30/1854	10	334	N	
McMahan, Bernard	25	Ireland	Y	Liverpool	New Orleans	12/01/1852	09/30/1854	12	273	N	
McMahan, John	35	Ireland	Y	Liverpool	New Orleans	03/??/1850	12/27/1852	5	449	N	
McMahan, John	25	Ireland	Y	Limerick	Burlington	07/??/1847	09/25/1854	12	152	N	
McMahan, Philip	30	Ireland	Y	Liverpool	New Orleans	03/01/1850	09/30/1854	10	333	N	

CITIZENSHIP RECORDS

APPLICANT	AGE	COUNTRY OF ORIGIN	DEC	DEPART PORT	ENTRY PORT	ARRIVE DATE	DEC DATE	VOL	PG.	FLD	NAT DATE
McMahan, Philip	30	Ireland	Y	Liverpool	New Orleans	03/01/1850	09/30/1854	12	272	N	
McMahen, David	32	Ireland	Y	Queenstown	New York	06/00/1881	01/16/1885			Y	
McMahon, Christopher	40	Ireland	Y	Liverpool	New York	02/21/1851	12/29/1852	5	463	N	
McMahon, John	25	Ireland	Y	Limerick	Burlington	07/??/1847	09/25/1854	10	213	N	
McMahon, John	32	Ireland	Y	?	?	?	06/02/1879			Y	
McMahon, Joseph	??	Ireland	Y	Liverpool	New York	06/17/18??	10/09/1848	1	70	N	
McManimin, Michael	24	Ireland	Y	Liverpool	New York	04/20/1884	09/22/1888	19	140	N	
McMannus, Dominic	35	Ireland	N	Liverpool	New York	05/10/1869	?			Y	
McManny, James	29	Ireland	Y	Liverpool	New York	04/16/1881	06/15/1889			Y	
McManus, James	21	Ireland	Y	Liverpool	New Orleans	01/06/1853	03/03/1856	26	156	N	
McManus, John	25	Ireland	Y	Sligo	New York	04/04/1845	11/01/1852	5	117	N	
McManus, John	31	Ireland	Y	Dublin	Baltimore	01/18/1889	04/10/1893			Y	
McManus, Michael	27	Ireland	Y	Liverpool	New York	06/11/1850	06/04/1856	14	293	N	
McMeara, John	28	Ireland	Y	Liverpool	New Orleans	03/27/1850	10/13/1851	4	253	N	
McMillan, D. G.	??	Great Britain	Y	?	?	?	04/05/1886			Y	
McMillan, James	29	Canada	Y	Canada	Cincinnati	11/17/1888	10/12/1894			Y	
McMillin, James T.	26	Ireland	Y	Galway	New York	10/13/1858	01/11/1862	18	242	N	
McMillons, Alexander	24	Scotland	Y	Glasgow	New York	07/09/1843	10/07/1848	22	488	N	
McMoran, Charles	40	Ireland	Y	Londonderry	Philadelphia	07/10/1830	11/01/1851	4	449	N	
McMullen, John	29	Ireland	Y	Liverpool	Baltimore	03/22/1886	10/26/1895			Y	
McMullen, Patrick	??	Great Britain	Y	?	?	?	10/27/1890			Y	
McMullen, Thomas	27	Ireland	Y	Liverpool	New York	05/03/1845	02/17/1853	7	172	N	
McNair, Archibald	21	Scotland	Y	Glasgow	New York	07/23/1850	10/06/1854	10	517	N	
McNair, Archibald	21	Scotland	Y	Glasgow	New York	07/23/1850	10/06/1854	12	456	N	
McNally, Thomas	22	Ireland	Y	Canada	Buffalo	06/08/1847	11/13/1848	1	278	N	
McNamara, James P.	48	Ireland	N	Liverpool	New York	03/03/1861	?			Y	
McNamara, Jeremiah	23	Ireland	Y	Liverpool	New York	06/12/1847	11/17/1848	1	305	N	
McNamara, John	39	Ireland	N	Liverpool	New York	07/??/1850	?			Y	
McNamara, Michael	22	Ireland	Y	Queenstown	New York	04/27/1882	04/09/1885			Y	
McNamara, Patrick	27	Ireland	Y	Liverpool	New York	09/??/1847	09/22/1855	13	110	N	
McNamara, Patrick	26	Ireland	Y	Liverpool	New York	05/26/1847	02/12/1849	23	73	N	
McNamara, Philipp	37	Ireland	Y	Liverpool	Boston	05/22/1849	10/02/1856	14	152	N	
McNamee, Charles	65	Ireland	Y	Canada	Rochester	09/??/1846	12/28/1857	16	269	N	
McNamee, James	42	Ireland	N	Queenstown	New York	04/21/1871	?			Y	
McNamee, Laughlin	27	Ireland	Y	Canada	Buffalo	05/05/1849	05/20/1852	25	56	N	
McNearney, Rody	28	Ireland	Y	Liverpool	New Orleans	06/27/1849	10/01/1856	14	103	N	
McNeff, Patrick	23	Ireland	Y	Liverpool	New York	05/06/1889	10/23/1891			Y	
McNeill, George	23	Ireland	Y	Liverpool	New York	04/19/1851	11/13/1855	13	219	N	
McNeill, Thomas	21	Ireland	Y	Liverpool	New York	04/29/1853	10/06/1856	14	236	N	
McNichols, Patrick	27	Ireland	Y	Liverpool	New Orleans	01/16/1851	05/24/1852	25	93	N	
McNoulty, John	38	Ireland	Y	London	New York	11/01/1848	02/11/1851	3	123	N	
McNulty, Edward	25	Ireland	Y	Liverpool	New York	06/20/1849	08/08/1851	4	98	N	
McNulty, John	35	Ireland	Y	Dublin	New York	11/14/1886	03/23/1891			Y	
McNulty, Thomas	28	Ireland	Y	Londonderry	New Orleans	02/04/1850	10/03/1854	10	372	N	
McNulty, Thomas	28	Ireland	Y	Londonderry	New Orleans	02/04/1850	10/03/1854	12	311	N	
McNutt, William	23	Ireland	Y	Londonderry	Philadelphia	06/27/1852	08/29/1857	15	201	N	
McPartlin, Patrick	21	Ireland	Y	Liverpool	New York	05/23/1880	05/29/1882			Y	
McPherson, Robert	38	Scotland	Y	Liverpool	New York	04/01/1849	08/12/1851	4	121	N	
McPhillips, Henry	34	Ireland	N	London	New York	05/10/1873	?			Y	
McQuaid, William S.	30	Ireland	Y	Liverpool	New York	06/??/1844	05/22/1854	8	493	N	
McQuaid, William S.	30	Ireland	Y	Liverpool	New York	06/??/1844	05/22/1854	9	367	N	
McQue, John	29	Ireland	Y	Liverpool	New Orleans	06/05/1846	07/21/1851	4	20	N	
McQueen, George	??	Scotland	Y	Belfast	New York	04/14/18??	10/11/1848	1	145	N	
McQueen, Samuel	29	Ireland	Y	Liverpool	New York	05/16/1880	08/06/1885			Y	
McQueety, John	22	Ireland	Y	Liverpool	New York	07/03/1844	10/07/1848	22	483	N	
McQuillan, William	30	Ireland	Y	Liverpool	New York	03/16/1851	11/10/1852	5	267	N	
McQuillan, William	30	Ireland	Y	Liverpool	New York	03/15/1851	11/10/1852	6	391	N	
McRoberts, Gavanius	21	Ireland	Y	Liverpool	New York	04/30/1850	05/06/1854	9	255	N	
McRoberts, Gavinus	21	Ireland	Y	Liverpool	New York	04/30/1850	05/06/1854	8	382	N	

CITIZENSHIP RECORDS

APPLICANT	AGE	COUNTRY OF ORIGIN	DEC	DEPART PORT	ENTRY PORT	ARRIVE DATE	DEC DATE	VOL	PG.	FLD	NAT DATE
McShane, Frank	49	Ireland	Y	Derry	Fairburg	07/09/1885	01/06/1890			Y	
McShane, Hugh	36	Ireland	N	Belfast	Canada	08/??/1867	?			Y	
McShane, Hugh M.	36	Ireland	Y	Londonderry	New York	06/01/1882	06/02/1893			Y	
McShene, Condy	28	Ireland	Y	Liverpool	New York	04/23/1848	08/23/1852	25	338	N	
McSweeney, Roderick	22	Ireland	Y	Liverpool	New York	10/10/1855	04/03/1858	16	486	N	
McSweeny, Morgan	34	Ireland	Y	Liverpool	New Orleans	01/27/1848	03/10/1852	24	280	N	
McTaggert, Robert	30	Ireland	Y	Canada	Vermont	06/??/1846	03/11/1853	7	323	N	
McTiermy, Patrick	32	Ireland	Y	Liverpool	New Haven	06/28/1843	03/01/1851	3	185	N	
McTigue, William	47	Ireland	Y	Liverpool	New Orleans	11/23/1847	01/??/1850	23	540	N	
McVey, James	26	Ireland	Y	Liverpool	New Orleans	04/25/1848	04/12/1852	24	484	N	
McVitie, Robert	36	Scotland	Y	Liverpool	New York	05/30/1842	07/29/1848	22	10	N	
McWilliams, John	22	Ireland	Y	Liverpool	Philadelphia	07/16/1889	03/12/1894			Y	
Mead, Patrick	54	Ireland	N	Cove of Cork	Quebec	??/??/1842	?			Y	
Meagher, William J.	22	Ireland	Y	Queenstown	New York	11/06/1877	10/30/1880			Y	
Meakin, Joseph	37	England	Y	Liverpool	New York	05/19/1851	03/29/1853	7	454	N	
Meale, Henry	24	Italy	Y	Naples	New York	02/22/1892	10/04/1896			Y	
Meany, Michael	26	Ireland	Y	Limerick	Whitehall	10/15/1847	04/25/1852	8	109	N	
Meany, Patk. B.	25	Ireland	Y	Limerick	Brooklyn	06/21/1855	05/19/1862	18	338	N	
Meara, John	30	Ireland	Y	Liverpool	New York	04/08/1847	07/25/1851	4	37	N	
Meara, Patrick	30	Ireland	Y	Queenstown	New York	04/20/1882	11/03/1890			Y	
Meara, William	23	Ireland	Y	Liverpool	New Orleans	12/24/1851	02/21/1853	7	203	N	
Meara, William	27	Ireland	Y	Liverpool	New York	12/15/1851	09/25/1854	10	209	N	
Meara, William	27	Ireland	Y	Liverpool	New York	12/15/1851	09/15/1854	12	148	N	
Mearzer, Joseph	23	Bavaria	Y	Havre	New York	??/20/18??	10/07/1854	6	10	N	
Meath, Thomas	27	Ireland	Y	Liverpool	New Orleans	11/19/1852	04/17/1854	8	151	N	
Meath, Thomas	27	Ireland	Y	Liverpool	New Orleans	11/19/1852	04/17/1854	9	22	N	
Mechel, Franz	32	Bavaria	Y	Havre	New Orleans	12/23/1846	11/04/1852	6	342	N	
Mechlenburg, Louis	18	Germany	Y	Hamburg	New York	09/12/1881	10/27/1882			Y	
Mecke, William	27	Hanover	Y	Bremen	New York	06/27/1858	07/08/1859	17	462	N	
Mecke, William	26	Germany	Y	Hamburg	New York	04/06/1886	01/16/1891			Y	
Meckel, Christian	40	Germany	Y	Bremen	New York	04/10/1867	10/10/1883			Y	
Meckor, Orr	24	Scotland	Y	Liverpool	New York	12/??/1852	03/25/1853	7	395	N	
Meder, Adam	33	Germany	Y	Hamburg	New York	04/20/1890	10/08/1903			Y	
Meder, Dominicus	24	Bavaria	Y	Havre	New Orleans	12/22/1854	02/02/1857	14	524	N	
Meder, Joseph	29	Germany	Y	Bremen	New York	10/17/1887	12/22/1891			Y	
Medeweller, Frank	25	Germany	Y	Amsterdam	New York	03/14/1887	12/15/1892			Y	
Meehan, John	43	Ireland	Y	St. John, N.	Boston	10/18/1832	01/08/1850	23	480	N	
Meehan, John	59	Ireland	N	Liverpool	New Orleans	05/02/1850	??/??/1853	28	58	N	03/??/1856
Meehan, John	21	Ireland	N	Liverpool	New Orleans	05/02/1850	00/00/1853			Y	03/00/1856
Meehan, Morris	25	Ireland	Y	Liverpool	New Orleans	05/??/1848	03/28/1853	7	432	N	
Meehan, Peter	??	Ireland	Y	?	?	?	03/28/1876			Y	
Meek, Arthur	32	England	Y	London	New York	09/13/1891	04/07/1898			Y	
Meerhoff, Herman Henry	23	Hanover	Y	Bremen	New York	11/24/1848	12/23/1851	4	547	N	
Meerse, Adrian	52	Holland	Y	Rotterdam	New York	07/25/1881	01/26/1884			Y	
Meese, John	49	Germany	Y	Bremen	Baltimore	07/02/1868	09/20/1888			Y	
Megel, Jakob	??	Germany	Y	?	?	?	11/39/1887			Y	
Meglitsch, Martin	40	Austria	Y	Antwerp	Philadelphia	12/20/1883	01/02/1892			Y	
Mehan, James	28	Ireland	Y	Liverpool	New Orleans	02/??/1848	08/27/1855	11	495	N	
Mehegan, David	29	Ireland	Y	St. Johns	Boston	08/21/1847	03/16/1852	24	317	N	
Mehers, Nicholas	27	Ireland	Y	Liverpool	New York	08/12/1842	02/12/1849	23	63	N	
Mehnert, Gottfried	52	Germany	Y	Bremen	Baltimore	12/01/1869	09/22/1879			Y	
Mehrer, John	29	Wuerttenberg	Y	Rotterdam	New York	06/04/1848	03/13/1852	24	296	N	
Mehringer, Joseph	26	Bavaria	Y	Bremen	New York	09/05/1854	09/29/1856	14	38	N	
Mehrwald, August	44	Germany	Y	Bremen	Baltimore	05/07/1892	04/19/1894			Y	
Meichel, Martin	35	Germany	Y	Antwerp	New York	05/??/1881	12/13/1884			Y	
Meidel, Dennis	31	Germany	Y	Bremen	New York	09/07/1886	09/28/1891			Y	
Meidel, Roman	33	Bavaria	Y	Bremen	New York	08/19/1859	04/11/1860	27	142	N	
Meier, Anton	27	Prussia	Y	Bremen	New Orleans	12/08/1855	11/01/1860	27	538	N	
Meier, August	31	Germany	Y	Bremen	New York	02/20/1881	04/10/1889			Y	

254

CITIZENSHIP RECORDS

APPLICANT	AGE	COUNTRY OF ORIGIN	DEC	DEPART PORT	ENTRY PORT	ARRIVE DATE	DEC DATE	VOL	PG.	FLD	NAT DATE
Meier, Augustus	31	Baden	Y	Havre	New York	12/20/1846	03/25/1850	2	248	N	
Meier, Balthasar	25	Germany	Y	Bremen	New York	02/28/1887	04/03/1888			Y	
Meier, Bernard	24	Oldenburg	Y	Bremen	New Orleans	11/17/1854	11/01/1858	17	218	N	
Meier, Bernard	24	Germany	Y	Rotterdam	New York	11/13/1891	04/18/1895			Y	
Meier, Charles	33	Austria	Y	Bremen	New York	09/14/1849	07/22/1851	4	24	N	
Meier, Charles	48	Germany	Y	Bremen	Baltimore	07/28/1883	10/26/1888			Y	
Meier, Edward	28	Prussia	Y	Bremen	New Orleans	??/26/1845	11/23/1849	23	367	N	
Meier, Erich	31	Germany	Y	Hamburg	New York	02/20/1901	02/24/1902			Y	
Meier, Frank Henry	26	Oldenburg	Y	Bremen	New Orleans	12/04/1847	07/07/1851	3	510	N	
Meier, Frederick	32	Hanover	Y	Bremerhafen	New York	01/08/1858	02/02/1861	18	84	N	
Meier, Frederick	29	Prussia	Y	Bremen	Baltimore	??/29/1846	12/03/1849	23	376	N	
Meier, Gebhard	25	Wuerttemberg	Y	Hamburg	New York	09/07/1857	09/04/1860	27	332	N	
Meier, George	??	Baden	Y	?	New Orleans	04/24/18??	11/06/1856	14	492	N	
Meier, George	33	Germany	Y	Bremen	New York	04/25/1887	10/23/1895			Y	
Meier, Heinrich	29	Germany	Y	Bremen	Baltimore	05/04/1886	09/02/1889			Y	
Meier, Heinrich	38	Germany	Y	Bremen	Baltimore	10/28/1881	01/02/1895			Y	
Meier, Henry	25	Hanover	Y	Bremen	New York	06/24/1849	05/06/1854	8	386	N	
Meier, Henry	25	Hanover	Y	Bremen	New York	06/24/1849	05/06/1854	9	259	N	
Meier, Henry	25	Hanover	Y	Bremen	New Orleans	06/15/1856	10/08/1857	15	378	N	
Meier, Henry	63	Germany	Y	Bremen	New Orleans	??/??/1854	10/06/1882			Y	
Meier, Henry	25	Switzerland	Y	Havre	New York	12/26/1880	01/28/1885			Y	
Meier, Henry	38	Germany	N	Bremen	Baltimore	11/18/1865	?			Y	
Meier, Henry	27	Oldenburg	Y	Bremen	New Orleans	11/20/1849	04/02/1856	26	419	N	
Meier, Herman	24	Prussia	Y	Bremen	New Orleans	11/15/1851	10/03/1854	10	391	N	
Meier, Herman	22	Prussia	Y	Bremen	New Orleans	11/15/1851	10/03/1854	12	330	N	
Meier, Herman	27	Germany	Y	Havre	New York	04/07/1881	10/11/1884			Y	
Meier, Jacob	24	Bavaria	Y	Havre	New Orleans	12/14/1851	12/10/1855	13	300	N	
Meier, John	22	Prussia	Y	Havre	New York	04/06/1849	03/15/1853	7	329	N	
Meier, John	23	Germany	Y	Antwerp	New York	07/08/1881	08/15/1883			Y	
Meier, John	27	Switzerland	Y	Antwerp	New York	10/21/1886	06/19/1894			Y	
Meier, John	37	Germany	Y	Hamburg	Baltimore	08/30/1878	05/03/1890			Y	
Meier, John Bernard	26	Hanover	Y	Bremen	New Orleans	11/09/1856	12/06/1858	17	377	N	
Meier, John Clemens	27	Oldenburg	Y	Bremen	New York	06/04/1854	08/05/1856	14	352	N	
Meier, John Diedrich	23	Hanover	Y	Bremen	New York	10/06/1848	10/29/1852	5	57	N	
Meier, John M. (Mayer?)	50	Wuerttemberg	Y	Antwerp	New York	05/10/1847	02/12/1852	24	98	N	
Meier, Joseph	25	Oldenburg	Y	Bremen	New Orleans	12/20/1849	10/09/1854	6	146	N	
Meier, Joseph	25	Oldenburg	Y	Bremen	New Orleans	12/20/1849	10/09/1854	11	149	N	
Meier, Louis	55	Prussia	Y	Bremen	Baltimore	11/??/1842	10/06/1860	27	404	N	
Meier, Robert William	37	Germany	Y	Bremen	New York	04/22/1866	05/11/1882			Y	
Meier, Simon	25	Lippe Detmol	Y	Bremen	New York	05/01/1848	05/17/1852	25	33	N	
Meier, Theobald	31	Germany	Y	Bremen	New York	11/27/1888	08/17/1896			Y	
Meier, Theodore	64	Germany	Y	Bremen	Baltimore	10/11/1881	10/01/1885			Y	
Meierhoff, Henry	33	Hanover	Y	Bremen	New Orleans	11/12/1855	09/29/1856	14	3	N	
Meierl, Anton	29	Germany	Y	Bremen	Baltimore	04/21/1893	10/26/1895			Y	
Meierose, Fritz	34	Germany	Y	Bremen	Baltimore	06/10/1882	10/26/1889	19	266	N	
Meierose, Fritz	34	Germany	Y	Bremen	New York	06/10/1882	10/26/1889			Y	
Meierrenke, Bernard	25	Germany	Y	Amsteerdam	New York	10/22/1882	10/13/1886			Y	
Meiers, Henry	25	Oldenburg	Y	Bremen	New Orleans	12/30/1844	03/25/1850	2	261	N	
Meighan, John	24	Ireland	Y	Liverpool	New Orleans	05/12/1850	01/03/1853	5	505	N	
Meighan, John	51	Ireland	Y	Liverpool	New York	05/08/1838	09/28/1854	10	298	N	
Meighan, John	51	Ireland	Y	Liverpool	New York	05/08/1838	09/28/1854	12	237	N	
Meighan, John	22	Ireland	Y	Liverpool	New York	09/24/1853	06/04/1856	14	291	N	
Meighan, Thomas	22	Ireland	Y	Liverpool	New Orleans	12/18/1852	01/29/1856	13	519	N	
Meihaus, George	27	Germany	Y	Bremen	Baltimore	03/05/1881	10/01/1887			Y	
Meihaus, Herman	46	Germany	N	Bremen	New York	01/21/1861	?			Y	
Meinders, Henry	32	Hanover	Y	Bremen	New Orleans	03/19/1852	11/07/1855	13	188	N	
Meinecke, Adolph	43	Hanover	Y	Havre	New York	06/03/1847	02/19/1856	26	102	N	
Meineke, Charles	32	Germany	N	Bremen	Baltimore	06/??/1864	?			Y	
Meiner, John	22	Germany	Y	Antwerp	Philadelphia	02/20/1887	02/19/1890			Y	

CITIZENSHIP RECORDS

APPLICANT	AGE	COUNTRY OF ORIGIN	DEC	DEPART PORT	ENTRY PORT	ARRIVE DATE	DEC DATE	VOL	PG.	FLD	NAT DATE
Meiners, Fredrick J.	35	Germany	Y	Amsterdam	New York	09/??/1880	03/29/1886			Y	
Meiners, Joseph	23	Germany	Y	Bremen	Baltimore	03/28/1880	12/08/1883			Y	
Meininger, Joseph	30	Baden	Y	Liverpool	New York	?	05/01/1855	11	337	N	
Meinken, Diedrick	29	Germany	N	Bremen	New York	10/??/1871	?			Y	
Meinlschmidt, Charles	49	Austria	Y	Antwerp	Philadelphia	10/24/1891	10/23/1893			Y	
Meinlschmidt, Julius	21	Austria	Y	Antwerp	Philadelphia	10/22/1891	12/31/1894			Y	
Meins, John	30	Ireland	Y	Liverpool	New York	07/13/1845	03/04/1856	26	160	N	
Meinsen, Henry	31	Prussia	Y	Bremen	New Orleans	12/10/1849	10/04/1860	27	397	N	
Meinshausen, August	??	Saxony	Y	Liverpool	New York	??/18/1852	04/17/1855	11	266	N	
Meirose, Herman	21	Germany	Y	Bremen	Baltimore	06/12/1881	11/01/1883			Y	
Meisel, Henry	25	Germany	Y	Bremen	New York	06/20/1882	10/05/1883			Y	
Meisner, Max	??	Germany	Y	?	?	?	12/31/1883			Y	
Meisner, Michael	22	Hesse Cassel	Y	Bremen	New York	06/06/1855	09/29/1856	14	23	N	
Meissner, Dietrich	42	Germany	Y	Bremen	New York	07/27/1885	06/19/1895			Y	
Meissner, George	24	Wurttemberg	Y	Havre	New York	05/28/1848	02/23/1850	2	119	N	
Meissner, Henry	50	Kurhessen	Y	Bremen	New York	06/06/1855	09/30/1856	14	59	N	
Meissner, William	23	Anhalt Dessau	Y	Bremen	New York	08/28/1852	04/25/1854	9	134	N	
Meister, George	??	Switzerland	Y	?	?	?	08/06/1896			Y	
Meister, Mathias	24	Bavaria	Y	Bremen	Baltimore	07/06/1848	11/22/1852	5	321	N	
Meister, Michael	27	Germany	Y	Bremen	Baltimore	06/05/1890	10/21/1893			Y	
Meisz, Fistel	29	France	Y	Havre	New Orleans	05/17/1848	03/16/1850	2	202	N	
Meiszber, William	23	Anhalt Dessau	Y	Bremen	New York	08/28/1852	04/25/1854	8	263	N	
Meitus, Joseph	28	Russia	Y	Hamburg	New York	08/24/1884	12/02/1893			Y	
Meitzger, Joseph	33	Austria	Y	Antwerp	New York	06/12/1883	04/06/1886			Y	
Meixner, Adolph	32	Germany	Y	Amsterdam	New York	10/04/1891	09/21/1891			Y	
Meixner, Valentin	32	Baden	Y	Antwerp	Baltimore	01/10/1846	02/11/1853	7	143	N	
Meizner, George	39	Bavaria	Y	Bremen	New York	02/??/1848	10/27/1851	4	412	N	
Melcher, Carl	25	Prussia	Y	Bremen	New York	05/??/1853	09/19/1855	13	70	N	
Melcher, Joseph	??	Germany	Y	?	?	?	06/26/1884			Y	
Melcher, Louis	22	Prussia	Y	Bremen	New York	08/05/1858	08/21/1860	27	305	N	
Melchers, Franz	21	Prussia	Y	Bremen	New York	11/11/1854	03/25/1856	26	327	N	
Melchionno, Pietro	??	Italy	Y	?	?	?	09/26/1896			Y	
Meley, John	27	Ireland	Y	Queenstown	New York	05/05/1894	07/16/1897			Y	
Melican, Michael	24	Ireland	Y	Kilbrush	New York	10/26/1847	11/03/1852	5	200	N	
Melican, Thomas	28	Ireland	Y	Liverpool	New York	08/01/1844	11/03/1852	5	201	N	
Melican, Thomas	28	Ireland	Y	Liverpool	New York	08/01/1844	10/03/1852	6	327	N	
Melitz, Otto	46	Germany	Y	Hamburg	New York	01/24/1884	04/06/1884			Y	
Melleish, Thomas	28	England	Y	?	New York	??/??/1880	07/13/1885			Y	
Meller, August	32	France	Y	Havre	New York	01/15/1888	11/29/1892			Y	
Meller, Jacob (Miller)	22	Germany	Y	Liverpool	New York	06/04/1872	03/12/1874			Y	
Meller, Joseph Gerhard	24	Prussia	Y	Bremen	New York	05/05/1849	05/17/1852	25	28	N	
Mellert, George	25	Germany	Y	?	?	05/00/1885	03/11/1890			Y	
Melly, Charles	21	Ireland	Y	Liverpool	New York	05/25/1853	07/18/1855	11	409	N	
Melville, Robert B.	36	Scotland	Y	Liverpool	Boston	03/15/1848	09/09/1852	25	425	N	
Melzer, Frederick Willia	24	Saxony	Y	Bremen	New York	08/11/1854	08/04/1856	14	339	N	
Melzian, Christ	52	Germany	Y	Hamburg	New York	07/03/1882	06/28/1886			Y	
Memory, William	45	England	Y	Liverpool	New York	09/23/1888	10/26/1895			Y	
Menadier, Louis	51	Wurttemberg	Y	Antwerp	New York	07/26/1847	07/16/1855	11	392	N	
Menchen, Matthias	41	France	Y	Havre	New Orleans	02/28/1847	02/02/1853	7	106	N	
Mendel, Martin	46	Germany	Y	Bremen	Baltimore	05/16/1881	09/02/1890			Y	
Mendel, Samuel A.	36	Prussia	Y	Liverpool	New York	09/19/1847	04/25/1854	8	261	N	
Mendel, Samuel A.	36	Prussia	Y	Liverpool	New York	09/19/1847	04/25/1854	9	132	N	
Mendelsohn, Emil	24	Russia	Y	Bremen	Baltimore	12/23/1892	05/19/1894			Y	
Mendelsohn, Iki	23	Russia	Y	Hamburg	New York	11/20/1887	04/05/1890	19	283	N	
Mendelsohn, Iki	23	Russia	Y	Hamburg	New York	11/20/1887	04/05/1890			Y	
Mendelsohn, Samuel C.	??	Poland	Y	?	?	?	09/18/1888			Y	
Mendes, Nathan	29	Russia	Y	Hamburg	Philadelphia	07/12/1882	10/22/1888			Y	
Mengdehl, Christoph S. T	27	Prussia	Y	Bremen	New Orleans	11/01/1849	09/11/1852	25	452	N	
Mengden, Friedrich Carl	35	Germany	Y	Bremen	New York	08/08/1882	04/03/1891	19	327	N	

256

CITIZENSHIP RECORDS

APPLICANT	AGE	COUNTRY OF ORIGIN	DEC	DEPART PORT	ENTRY PORT	ARRIVE DATE	DEC DATE	VOL	PG.	FLD	NAT DATE
Menge, L. F.	25	Hanover	Y	Hamburg	New York	09/18/1859	10/16/1860	27	505	N	
Menier, Charles	24	Germany	Y	Bremen	New York	07/29/1889	01/04/1894			Y	
Menke, Arnold	31	Prussia	Y	Bremen	Philadelphia	01/07/1847	11/01/1851	4	457	N	
Menke, Ben	26	Germany	Y	Hamburg	New York	11/10/1895	09/07/1899			Y	
Menke, Ben	14	Russia	N	?	New York	00/00/1881				Y	10/17/1888
Menke, Bernard	24	Germany	Y	Rotterdam	New York	10/25/1889	10/23/1896			Y	
Menke, Herman A.	31	Germany	Y	Bremen	New York	04/08/1882	09/09/1885			Y	
Menke, Herman Henry	26	Hanover	Y	Bremen	Baltimore	09/30/1850	09/18/1858	16	181	N	
Menke, John	25	Hanover	Y	Bremen	New Orleans	??/22/1845	12/31/1849	23	444	N	
Menke, John	62	Prussia	Y	Bremen	Baltimore	04/15/1847	04/05/1852	24	396	N	
Menke, John Bernhard	75	Germany	N	Germany	Cincinnati	09/18/1839	10/20/1841	28	62	N	01/03/1845
Menke, John Bernhard	26	Germany	N	?	Cincinnati	09/18/1839	10/20/1841			Y	01/03/1845
Menke, Joseph	37	Germany	Y	Antwerp	Philadelphia	09/28/1881	10/29/1895			Y	
Menke, Joseph	31	Prussia	Y	Bremen	Philadelphia	01/07/1847	02/19/1849	23	214	N	
Menke, Mathias	32	Germany	Y	Bremen	Baltimore	07/26/1886	11/13/1888			Y	
Menkedick, Henry	28	Oldenburg	Y	Rotterdam	Baltimore	06/15/1849	05/20/1852	25	69	N	
Menkhaus, Franz	32	Germany	Y	Bremen	New York	10/??/1871	04/15/1881			Y	
Menkhaus, William	53	Germany	Y	Bremen	New York	07/06/1864	10/14/1889			Y	
Menner, Edward	27	Germany	Y	Havre	New York	03/20/1874	08/11/1880			Y	
Menner, John	30	Baden	Y	Havre	New York	05/08/1848	03/01/1851	3	188	N	
Menner, John	37	Germany	Y	Havre	New York	04/27/1889	04/21/1896			Y	
Menphy, Michael	43	Ireland	Y	Liverpool	New York	03/12/1849	04/04/1853	8	37	N	
Menrath, Charles	24	Germany	Y	Bremen	New York	08/13/1887	03/07/1890			Y	
Mensing, Charles	21	Bremen	Y	Bremen	Baltimore	06/22/1857	05/07/1860	27	183	N	
Mensing, P.F.H.	49	Hanover	Y	Bremen	Baltimore	10/021856	12/30/1859	17	536	N	
Mentel, Henry	42	Hesse Cassel	Y	Bremen	New Orleans	06/01/1854	09/29/1854	10	308	N	
Mentel, Henry	42	Hesse Cassel	Y	Bremen	New Orleans	06/01/1854	09/29/1854	12	247	N	
Mentges, Jacob	31	Prussia	Y	Antwerp	New York	05/16/1854	09/07/1857	15	231	N	
Mentges, Martin	24	Prussia	Y	Antwerp	New York	05/16/1854	09/07/8157	15	230	N	
Mentink, Richard	40	Holland	Y	Rotterdam	New York	06/23/1878	04/17/1882			Y	
Mentrup, Heinrich	30	Germany	Y	Bremen	New York	11/13/1881	06/08/1887			Y	
Mentzel, Charles	??	Germany	N	?	?	08/17/1881				Y	10/19/1892
Menz, Conrad	48	Nassau	Y	Havre	New York	06/28/1854	07/06/1857	15	128	N	
Menz, Eugene	23	Germany	Y	Antwerp	New York	11/29/1889	09/18/1890			Y	
Menz, William	33	Germany	Y	Antwerp	New York	04/03/1886	05/10/1893			Y	
Menzel, Conrad	31	Hesse Darmsta	Y	London	New York	11/20/1851	09/07/1852	25	398	N	
Merckel, William	33	Germany	Y	Stettin	New York	07/06/1888	06/26/1893			Y	
Mercurio, Guissepe	36	Italy	Y	Palermo	New York	04/26/1890	10/26/1900			Y	
Mercurio, Mariano	42	Italy	Y	Palermo	New York	06/02/1890	03/26/1901			Y	
Mercurio, Vincent	34	Italy	Y	Palermo	New York	02/06/1887	10/16/1893	21	10	N	
Mercurio, Vincent	34	Italy	Y	Palermo	New York	02/06/1887	10/16/1893			Y	
Meredith, Ephraim	30	Wales	Y	Canada	Michigan	05/16/1845	01/20/1849	1	480	N	
Mergel, Adam	56	Baden	Y	Havre	New Orleans	03/??/1854	08/15/1857	15	137	N	
Mergel, George	30	Germany	Y	Bremen	New York	05/15/1881	07/03/1890			Y	
Mergy, Sebastian	45	France	Y	Bordeaux	New York	04/??/1868	11/11/1884			Y	
Merk, George	41	Germany	Y	Bremen	Baltimore	06/14/1888	05/15/1900			Y	
Merk, John	38	Baden	Y	Antwerp	New York	10/18/1853	10/07/1856	14	259	N	
Merkel, George	27	Turkey	Y	?	New York	??/??/1884	08/14/1890			Y	
Merkel, Henry	30	Germany	Y	Beruak	New York	11/01/1868	03/19/1879			Y	
Merkel, Louis	??	Germany	Y	?	?	?	10/29/1881			Y	
Merkert, Sebastian	36	Germany	Y	Hamburg	New York	03/28/1881	11/02/1887			Y	
Merkisch, Eugen	24	Prussia	Y	Hamburg	New York	06/25/1853	05/13/1854	9	306	N	
Merkisotz, Eugene	24	Prussia	Y	Hamburg	New York	06/25/1853	05/13/1854	8	433	N	
Merkl, George	26	Bavaria	Y	Bremen	New York	08/26/1850	05/10/1854	8	415	N	
Merkl, George	26	Bavaria	Y	Bremen	New York	08/26/1850	05/10/1854	9	288	N	
Merland, H.	27	Germany	Y	Antwerp	New York	06/19/1879	03/19/1887			Y	
Merland, Theodor	37	Germany	N	Liverpool	New York	08/06/1872	?			Y	
Merling, Casper	26	France	Y	Havre	New Orleans	05/26/1847	02/19/1849	23	169	N	
Merna, Joseph	23	Ireland	Y	Liverpool	New Orleans	12/21/1850	06/16/1852	26	280	N	

CITIZENSHIP RECORDS

APPLICANT	AGE	COUNTRY OF ORIGIN	DEC	DEPART PORT	ENTRY PORT	ARRIVE DATE	DEC DATE	VOL	PG.	FLD	NAT DATE
Merren, William	73	England	N	London	Baltimore	??/??/1854	10/15/1856	28	457	N	03/15/1859
Merrick, Frederick	25	Wurttemberg	Y	Bremen	New York	04/26/1849	08/07/1851	4	96	N	
Merriman, John P.	81	England	Y	Liverpool	New York	11/10/1836	08/12/1899			Y	
Merritt, Patrick	34	Ireland	Y	Liverpool	New Orleans	02/10/1850	04/27/1854	8	273	N	
Merritt, Patrick	34	Ireland	Y	Liverpool	New Orleans	02/10/1850	04/27/1854	9	144	N	
Mersch, Charles H.	26	Germany	Y	Bremen	New York	04/03/1885	09/06/1888			Y	
Mersch, Gerhard	23	Prussia	Y	Bremen	New Orleans	05/03/1849	05/10/1852	25	1	N	
Mersmann, Anton	37	Prussia	Y	Antwerp	New York	08/12/1848	05/01/1854	8	302	N	
Mersmann, Anton	37	Prussia	Y	Antwerp	New York	08/12/1848	05/01/1854	9	174	N	
Mersmann, T. B.	24	Germany	Y	Bremen	New York	10/30/1880	11/01/1883			Y	
Merten, Henry	37	Prussia	Y	Bremen	New Orleans	01/01/1846	12/30/1852	5	471	N	
Merten, John	27	Waldecker	Y	Bremen	New York	09/13/1851	05/31/1852	25	160	N	
Merten, Rudolph	35	Prussia	Y	Bremen	New Orleans	11/02/1850	01/03/1853	5	502	N	
Mertens, Charles	30	Bremen	Y	Bremen	New York	04/15/1846	08/28/1848	22	260	N	
Mertes, John	31	Bavaria	Y	London	New York	06/21/1854	08/18/1857	15	153	N	
Mertes, Peter	34	Prussia	Y	London	New York	06/27/1854	11/10/1857	16	4	N	
Mertz, Adolph	9	Germany	N	?	New York	00/00/1873				Y	10/26/1888
Mertz, Anton	6	Germany	N	?	New York	00/00/1873				Y	10/26/1888
Mertz, John W.	21	Bavaria	Y	Havre	New York	09/16/1856	12/12/1859	17	502	N	
Merz, Adam	28	Bavaria	Y	Havre	New York	09/20/1845	12/13/1851	4	515	N	
Merz, Gustav	50	Germany	Y	Hamburg	New York	05/10/1880	10/18/1888			Y	
Merz, John George M.	34	Wuertemberg	Y	Havre	New Orleans	04/07/1854	02/20/1856	26	107	N	
Merz, Wilhelm	41	Germany	Y	Antwerp	New York	05/09/1874	07/31/1882			Y	
Mesch, Herman	22	Hanover	Y	Bremen	New Orleans	12/26/1854	11/01/1858	17	239	N	
Meschar, Fredrick	32	Wuerttenberg	Y	Havre	New Orleans	11/21/1846	08/23/1848	22	246	N	
Mescher, Bernard	25	Germany	Y	Bremen	Baltimore	11/00/1880	01/07/1886			Y	
Meskil, Cornelius	30	Ireland	Y	Liverpool	New York	09/15/1852	09/09/1857	15	252	N	
Mesmer, Frank	49	Germany	Y	Havre	New York	12/17/1878	05/06/1889			Y	
Mess, Simon	21	Hesse Darmsta	Y	Antwerp	New York	09/22/1850	02/15/1853	7	164	N	
Messer, George	42	Nassau	Y	London	New York	10/26/1852	09/29/1856	14	42	N	
Messer, Joseph	21	Germany	Y	Antwerp	New York	11/01/1888	07/15/1889			Y	
Messinger, Louis	29	Austria	Y	Bremen	New York	11/02/1884	04/07/1891			Y	
Messink, Frederick John	29	Holland	Y	Rotterdam	New Orleans	03/15/1845	??/??/1852	25	317	N	
Messink, Henry	31	Hanover	Y	Bremen	New Orleans	09/04/1853	10/12/1857	15	401	N	
Messmann, Franz	34	Germany	Y	Amsterdam	New York	07/10/1882	12/04/1888			Y	
Messmann, John	24	Oldenburg	Y	Bremen	Baltimore	06/24/1859	05/31/1861	18	180	N	
Messmer, Andrew	31	Germany	Y	Hamburg	New York	07/23/1874	12/11/1882			Y	
Messner, Casper	30	Prussia	Y	London	New York	10/??/1857	02/14/1857	15	16	N	
Messner, Christ	32	Germany	Y	Bremen	New York	05/19/1883	10/04/1890			Y	
Messner, Emil	30	Germany	Y	Bremen	New York	08/08/1887	08/06/1895			Y	
Mestebrock, William	22	Oldenburg	Y	Bremen	New Orleans	11/01/1851	06/13/1854	10	126	N	
Mestebrock, William	22	Oldenburg	Y	Bremen	New York	11/01/1851	06/13/1854	12	63	N	
Mestel, Florrian	59	Germany	N	Bremen	New York	05/??/1870	?			Y	
Mestel, Fred	5	Germany	N	?	New York	00/00/1870				Y	10/27/1888
Mestemacher, Ernst	30	Germany	Y	Bremen	New York	05/26/1878	10/31/1882			Y	
Mester, George	22	Prussia	Y	Bremen	Baltimore	12/15/1853	11/28/1857	16	54	N	
Metan, Ans	26	Greece	Y	Athens	New York	05/05/1885	02/04/1891			Y	
Meter, Dominick	58	Germany	N	Havre	New Orleans	01/??/1853	?			Y	
Metres, Peter	??	Greece	Y	?	?	?	11/27/1888			Y	
Mette, Conrad	35	Hanover	Y	Bremen	New Orleans	11/11/1853	02/18/1856	26	100	N	
Mette, William	27	Waldeck	Y	Amsterdam	New York	09/18/1849	09/06/1852	25	381	N	
Mettey, Henry	17	France	N	France	New York	09/19/1863	?			Y	
Metz, Adam	33	Bavaria	Y	Havre	New York	10/06/1852	01/30/1856	13	520	N	
Metz, Charles Joseph	30	Bavaria	Y	Havre	New Orleans	06/30/1847	03/25/1856	26	333	N	
Metz, Edward	48	France	Y	Havre	New York	08/02/1891	11/05/1895			Y	
Metz, George	27	Bavaria	Y	Havre	New Orleans	05/15/1847	02/27/1850	2	139	N	
Metz, John	35	France	Y	Havre	New York	08/01/1849	10/06/1860	27	400	N	
Metz, John Henry	23	Prussia	Y	Antwerp	New York	10/29/1854	11/06/1855	13	170	N	
Metz, Joseph	26	Bavaria	Y	Havre	New York	06/??/1854	12/28/1855	13	379	N	

CITIZENSHIP RECORDS

APPLICANT	AGE	COUNTRY OF ORIGIN	DEC	DEPART PORT	ENTRY PORT	ARRIVE DATE	DEC DATE	VOL	PG.	FLD	NAT DATE
Metz, Joseph	26	Germany	Y	?	?	?	09/09/1885			Y	
Metz, Joseph	37	Germany	N	Havre	New York	09/19/1873	?			Y	
Metz, Michael	30	Bavaria	Y	London	New York	09/29/1852	11/04/1852	5	220	N	
Metz, Philip	34	Germany	Y	Bremen	New York	05/01/1880	09/??/1881	28	354	N	
Metz, Philip	23	Germany	Y	Bremen	New York	05/01/1880	09/00/1881			Y	
Metzch, George M.	??	Germany	Y	?	?	?	08/21/1879			Y	
Metzdorf, John	23	Germany	Y	Hamburg	New York	09/07/1895	12/22/1898			Y	
Metze, Adam	36	Prussia	Y	Bremen	New York	06/28/1849	01/31/1851	3	68	N	
Metze, George Joseph	24	Germany	Y	Rotterdam	Jersey City	06/12/1887	05/26/1890			Y	
Metze, John	36	Prussia	Y	Bremen	New York	05/20/1854	02/02/1856	26	11	N	
Metzer, Ferdinand	58	Austria	N	Hamburg	New York	06/??/1859	?			Y	
Metzger, Alexander	24	Prussia	Y	Antwerp	New York	??/03/1847	02/11/1850	2	59	N	
Metzger, Alphonse	35	Germany	Y	Havre	New York	03/10/1884	09/27/1894			Y	
Metzger, Andreas	28	Bavaria	Y	Bremen	New York	??/28/1847	11/26/1849	23	373	N	
Metzger, Anton	44	Bavaria	Y	?	New York	??/??/1865	03/01/1882			Y	
Metzger, George Michael	43	Wurttemberg	Y	Havre	New York	05/24/1854	07/14/1855	11	387	N	
Metzger, Gottfried	27	Germany	Y	Antwerp	New York	06/14/1882	12/02/1885			Y	
Metzger, Henry Jacob ?	28	Baden	Y	Havre	New York	10/25/1859	08/15/1860	27	285	N	
Metzger, Jacob	31	Baden	Y	Havre	New York	05/12/1850	05/09/1854	8	406	N	
Metzger, John	21	Wurttemberg	Y	London	New York	07/10/1859	08/28/1862	18	417	N	
Metzger, John	29	Bavaria	Y	Havre	New York	04/02/8165	10;08/1872	18	527	N	
Metzger, Martin	41	Wurttemberg	Y	Havre	New York	09/20/1854	11/06/1857	15	535	N	
Metzger, Michael	25	Baden	Y	Havre	New York	04/17/1853	10/29/1858	17	173	N	
Metzler, August	32	Germany	Y	Bremen	Baltimore	06/16/1891	06/03/1892			Y	
Metzler, George	29	Wurttemberg	Y	Antwerp	New York	06/20/1847	01/28/1850	2	2	N	
Metzler, Jacob	26	Baden	Y	Rotterdam	New York	05/??/1848	10/27/1851	4	422	N	
Metzler, Paul	26	Wurttemberg	Y	Havre	New York	05/28/1849	03/10/1851	3	269	N	
Metzler, Theodor	24	Germany	Y	Bremen	New York	03/18/1883	03/31/1887			Y	
Metzner, Charles	25	Germany	Y	Bremen	Baltimore	05/01/1888	05/11/1892			Y	
Metzner, Henry	29	Bavaria	Y	Havre	New York	04/23/1853	05/09/1854	8	405	N	
Metzner, Henry	29	Bavaria	Y	Havre	New York	04/23/1853	05/09/1854	9	278	N	
Metzner, Jacob	31	Baden	Y	Havre	New York	05/12/1850	05/09/1854	9	279	N	
Metzner, Louis	21	Bavaria	Y	Havre	New York	03/24/1858	01/23/1862	18	248	N	
Metzroth, John	27	Prussia	Y	Antwerp	New York	04/25/1849	05/10/1854	8	417	N	
Metzroth, John	27	Prussia	Y	Antwerp	New York	04/25/1849	05/10/1854	9	290	N	
Meuerer, George Friedric	54	Germany	Y	Havre	New York	05/26/1863	01/05/1880			Y	
Meuleman, Mourist	23	Holland	Y	New Diepe	Baltimore	10/09/1853	09/29/1856	14	6	N	
Meure, John	25	Switzerland	Y	Havre	New Orleans	05/10/1848	06/10/1852	25	224	N	
Meurer, John Nicholas	27	Prussia	Y	Havre	New Orleans	08/17/1852	12/31/1855	13	405	N	
Meurer, Peter	29	Prussia	Y	Antwerp	New York	10/28/1852	03/06/1856	26	168	N	
Meuri, Franz Martin	29	Switzerland	Y	Havre	New Orleans	01/13/1850	09/27/1854	10	265	N	
Meuri, Franz Martin	29	Switzerland	Y	Havre	New Orleans	01/13/1849	09/27/1854	12	204	N	
Meusch, Frank	38	Germany	Y	Amsterdam	New York	12/30/1881	10/11/1890			Y	
Meuse, Hubert	23	Germany	Y	Rotterdam	New York	07/02/1881	07/09/1884			Y	
Meustoeckel, William	37	France	Y	Havre	New Orleans	05/??/1849	12/26/1850	2	393	N	
Meuttmann, Jacob	24	Hanover	Y	Bremen	New York	04/15/1851	03/19/1856	26	226	N	
Mey, Thomas	40	Ireland	Y	Liverpool	New York	06/08/1875	04/12/1890			Y	
Meyer, Adolph	24	Baden	Y	Havre	New Orleans	05/18/1848	12/20/1851	4	533	N	
Meyer, Ahrend Henry	33	Hanover	Y	Bremen	New Orleans	11/05/1852	07/16/1855	11	390	N	
Meyer, Ahrend Henry	30	Hanover	Y	Bremen	Baltimore	06/??/1846	11/??/1849	23	358	N	
Meyer, Albert	39	Hanover	Y	Bremen	New Orleans	06/14/1845	10/09/1854	6	128	N	
Meyer, Albert	39	Hanover	Y	Bremen	New Orleans	06/14/1845	10/09/1854	11	131	N	
Meyer, Albert	23	Bremen	Y	Bremen	New York	07/01/1853	10/07/1854	12	466	N	
Meyer, Albert N.	23	Bremen	Y	Bremen	New York	07/01/1853	10/07/1854	10	527	N	
Meyer, Anton	28	Switzerland	Y	Rotterdam	New York	11/11/1886	02/17/1890			Y	
Meyer, August	25	Germany	Y	Amsterdam	New York	08/27/1882	03/29/1886			Y	
Meyer, August	34	Germany	Y	Bremen	New York	06/20/1884	05/31/1890			Y	
Meyer, August	42	Prussia	Y	Havre	New York	09/30/1842	07/31/1848	22	24	N	
Meyer, Barney	28	Prussia	Y	Havre	New Orleans	05/03/1849	03/28/1853	7	433	N	

CITIZENSHIP RECORDS

APPLICANT	AGE	COUNTRY OF ORIGIN	DEC	DEPART PORT	ENTRY PORT	ARRIVE DATE	DEC DATE	VOL	PG.	FLD	NAT DATE
Meyer, Benjamin	23	Germany	Y	Bremen	Baltimore	08/08/1883	07/25/1887			Y	
Meyer, Bernard	32	Germany	Y	Bremen	Baltimore	10/08/1881	10/06/1884			Y	
Meyer, Bernard	28	Oldenburg	Y	?	Baltimore	??/01/1844	10/??/1849	23	288	N	
Meyer, Bernard August	23	Oldenburg	Y	Bremen	Baltimore	05/20/18??	10/12/1848	1	176	N	
Meyer, Bernard H.	26	Germany	Y	Rotterdam	New York	10/01/1882	11/05/1886			Y	
Meyer, Bernard Henry	36	Prussia	Y	Bremen	Baltimore	07/30/1847	03/02/1852	24	219	N	
Meyer, Bernd Henry	36	Hanover	Y	Bremen	New Orleans	02/10/1845	08/07/1848	22	64	N	
Meyer, Bernhard	31	Germany	Y	Bremen	Baltimore	10/14/1889	01/27/1891			Y	
Meyer, Bonaventur	34	Switzerland	Y	Havre	New York	06/30/1881	08/04/1888			Y	
Meyer, Carl	30	Germany	Y	Hamburg	New York	07/29/1885	01/15/1891	19	312	N	
Meyer, Carl	30	Germany	Y	Hamburg	New York	07/29/1885	01/15/1891			Y	
Meyer, Carl	49	Germany	Y	Hamburg	New York	05/26/1884	11/01/1887			Y	
Meyer, Caspar	28	Germany	Y	Bremen	New York	06/19/1885	10/19/1888			Y	
Meyer, Charles	26	Hanover	Y	Bremen	New Orleans	11/11/1846	11/15/1848	1	299	N	
Meyer, Charles	38	Switzerland	Y	Havre	New York	08/01/1879	12/24/1890			Y	
Meyer, Christ	27	Germany	Y	Amsterdam	New York	07/16/1880	07/07/1887			Y	
Meyer, Christian	26	Hanover	Y	Bremen	New Orleans	11/16/1850	04/22/1854	8	241	N	
Meyer, Christian	26	Hanover	Y	Bremen	New Orleans	11/16/1850	04/22/1854	9	112	N	
Meyer, Christian	??	Prussia	Y	?	New York	??/29/18??	11/05/1856	14	470	N	
Meyer, Christoph	41	Germany	Y	Hamburg	New York	06/19/1882	10/18/1893			Y	
Meyer, Conrad	25	Bavaria	Y	Bremen	New York	06/18/1852	04/08/1856	26	465	N	
Meyer, Daniel	33	Switzerland	Y	Antwerp	New York	09/28/1851	06/14/1852	25	252	N	
Meyer, Dietrido	38	Germany	Y	?	New York	??/??/1867	10/13/1884			Y	
Meyer, Edward	37	Germany	Y	Hamburg	New York	06/12/1872	07/07/1882			Y	
Meyer, Felix	23	Wurttemberg	Y	Liverpool	New York	05/06/1852	03/15/1853	7	332	N	
Meyer, Florien	28	Germany	Y	Austria?	New York	07/??/1879	11/01/1880			Y	
Meyer, Frank	32	Bavaria	Y	Bremen	Baltimore	10/01/1845	10/13/1851	4	249	N	
Meyer, Frank	29	Bavaria	Y	Havre	New York	10/18/1849	04/18/1854	8	192	N	
Meyer, Frank	33	Germany	Y	Hamburg	New York	05/12/1890	10/03/1893			Y	
Meyer, Frank	33	Germany	Y	Bremen	Baltimore	05/16/1884	01/30/1888			Y	
Meyer, Frank	49	Germany	Y	Bremen	Baltimore	09/03/1867	12/31/1891			Y	
Meyer, Fred	22	Prussia	Y	?	Baltimore	08/20/1880	11/06/1882			Y	
Meyer, Fred	32	Germany	Y	Bremen	Baltimore	03/??/1882	10/05/1885			Y	
Meyer, Fred	26	Germany	Y	London	New York	08/15/1883	01/28/1889			Y	
Meyer, Fred	34	Germany	Y	Bremen	Baltimore	10/14/1880	10/28/1889			Y	
Meyer, Fred	26	Germany	Y	London	New York	08/15/1883	01/28/1889			Y	
Meyer, Frederick	32	Oldenburg	Y	Bremen	Baltimore	05/20/1844	02/10/1849	23	45	N	
Meyer, Frederick August	30	Germany	Y	Bremen	New York	05/17/1882	10/21/1891			Y	
Meyer, Frederick K.	28	Lippe Detmold	Y	Bremen	Philadelphia	05/??/1848	12/23/1850	2	387	N	
Meyer, George	26	Oldenburg	Y	Bremen	New York	08/28/1860	08/08/1862	18	389	N	
Meyer, George	41	Germany	Y	Bremen	Baltimore	03/09/1883	12/15/1896			Y	
Meyer, George	30	Germany	Y	Amsterdam	New York	11/03/1888	10/26/1895			Y	
Meyer, George	40	Switzerland	Y	?	New York	08/04/1872	11/01/1880			Y	
Meyer, George	62	Germany	N	Bremen	New York	07/??/1854	?			Y	
Meyer, George	40	Germany	N	Bremen	Baltimore	09/??/1869	?			Y	
Meyer, Geroge	16	Germany	N	?	New York	00/00/1873				Y	10/26/1888
Meyer, Gustav Adolph	41	Saxony	Y	Bremen	Baltimore	09/13/1853	03/22/1858	16	434	N	
Meyer, Heinrich Wilhelm	21	Hanover	Y	Bremen	New Orleans	11/15/1857	01/06/1860	27	40	N	
Meyer, Henry	26	Hanover	Y	Bremen	New Orleans	12/02/1846	02/27/1851	3	179	N	
Meyer, Henry	25	Oldenburg	Y	Bremen	New Orleans	05/??/1849	12/01/1852	5	365	N	
Meyer, Henry	46	Hanover	Y	Bremen	New Orleans	11/04/1853	11/06/1855	13	173	N	
Meyer, Henry	48	Prussia	Y	Bremen	New Orleans	01/01/1847	02/23/1857	15	51	N	
Meyer, Henry	23	Hanover	Y	Bremen	New York	08/03/1854	03/05/1857	15	65	N	
Meyer, Henry	37	Hanover	Y	Bremen	Baltimore	05/01/1849	09/07/1857	15	232	N	
Meyer, Henry	27	Oldenburg	Y	Bremen	Baltimore	05/17/1859	11/07/1861	18	222	N	
Meyer, Henry	39	Germany	Y	Bremen	Baltimore	??/??/1870	03/19/1886			Y	
Meyer, Henry	30	Germany	Y	Bremen	New York	04/28/1884	10/15/1888			Y	
Meyer, Henry	29	Germany	Y	Bremen	Baltimore	07/28/1883	03/29/1886			Y	
Meyer, Henry	41	Germany	Y	Bremen	Baltimore	06/24/1890	07/12/1893			Y	

CITIZENSHIP RECORDS

APPLICANT	AGE	COUNTRY OF ORIGIN	DEC	DEPART PORT	ENTRY PORT	ARRIVE DATE	DEC DATE	VOL	PG.	FLD	NAT DATE
Meyer, Henry	59	Germany	Y	Bremen	New York	12/17/1880	03/28/1897			Y	
Meyer, Henry	29	Germany	Y	Bremen	New York	04/23/1895	04/27/1898			Y	
Meyer, Henry	24	Germany	Y	Bremen	New York	11/??/1881	08/04/1884			Y	
Meyer, Henry	27	Germany	Y	Rotterdam	New York	10/13/1885	08/18/1892			Y	
Meyer, Henry	31	Germany	Y	Bremen	Baltimore	04/21/1884	10/24/1891			Y	
Meyer, Henry	22	Oldenburg	Y	Bremen	New Orleans	01/04/1850	03/01/1852	24	199	N	
Meyer, Henry	54	Bavaria	Y	Havre	New Orleans	04/10/1849	03/08/1852	24	254	N	
Meyer, Henry	26	Denmark	Y	Martinique	Salem	07/04/1848	06/14/1852	25	262	N	
Meyer, Henry	15	Germany	N	?	New York	00/00/1881				Y	08/23/1888
Meyer, Henry (Maer)	45	Germany	Y	Bremen	New York	08/28/1892	10/23/1896			Y	
Meyer, Henry Christ	23	Hanover	Y	Bremen	Baltimore	12/01/1849	04/20/1853	8	88	N	
Meyer, Herman	21	Oldenburg	Y	Bremen	New Orleans	05/20/1851	05/05/1854	8	378	N	
Meyer, Herman	21	Oldenburg	Y	Bremen	New Orleans	05/20/1851	05/05/1854	9	251	N	
Meyer, Herman	59	Germany	N	Bremen	New York	06/27/1844	?			Y	
Meyer, Herman	23	Hanover	Y	Bremen	New Orleans	07/01/1849	09/14/1852	25	499	N	
Meyer, Herman Henry	29	Oldenburg	Y	Bremen	Baltimore	04/29/1848	12/20/1851	4	541	N	
Meyer, Herman Henry	23	Oldenburg	Y	Bremen	New Orleans	11/28/1845	02/21/1849	23	248	N	
Meyer, Hermann	25	Germany	Y	Antwerp	New York	07/10/1883	11/27/1886			Y	
Meyer, Hermanus	27	Hanover	Y	Bremen	Baltimore	06/24/1868	07/13/1872	18	504	N	
Meyer, Ignatz	24	Baden	Y	Havre	New York	07/28/1853	04/17/1854	8	175	N	
Meyer, Ignatz	24	Baden	Y	Havre	New York	??/28/18??	04/17/1854	9	46	N	
Meyer, Ike	??	Germany	N	?	?	09/05/1880				Y	10/14/1892
Meyer, Jacob	28	Baden	Y	Manheim	New York	01/25/1854	11/08/1858	17	299	N	
Meyer, Jacob	61	France	Y	Havre	New York	07/28/1888	10/14/1895			Y	
Meyer, Jacob	30	Germany	Y	Hamburg	New York	07/23/1873	05/24/1881			Y	
Meyer, Jacob Frederick	23	Baden	Y	Havre	New York	??/28/1852	04/24/1855	11	293	N	
Meyer, Johann H.	42	Germany	Y	Bremen	Baltimore	07/04/1867	10/22/1888	19	159	N	
Meyer, John	30	Hesse Cassel	Y	Bremen	New York	05/07/1846	02/14/1850	2	72	N	
Meyer, John	28	Bavaria	Y	Bremen	Baltimore	08/??/1849	12/21/1852	5	433	N	
Meyer, John	29	Bavaria	Y	Bremen	New Orleans	06/14/1853	10/30/1858	17	193	N	
Meyer, John	34	Germany	Y	Antwerp	New York	09/01/1881	07/05/1883			Y	
Meyer, John	30	Germany	Y	Rotterdam	New York	11/05/1891	11/21/1893			Y	
Meyer, John	31	Germany	Y	Bremen	New York	06/13/1885	11/14/1893			Y	
Meyer, John	36	Switzerland	Y	Havre	New York	04/10/1881	10/16/1896			Y	
Meyer, John Barney	38	Germany	Y	Bremen	Baltimore	08/16/1882	10/25/1888			Y	
Meyer, John Bernard	26	Hanover	Y	Bremen	Baltimore	11/06/1850	09/23/1854	10	185	N	
Meyer, John Bernard	26	Hanover	Y	Bremen	Baltimore	11/06/1850	09/23/1854	12	124	N	
Meyer, John Conrad	45	Hanover	Y	Bremen	New York	10/??/1838	09/07/1852	25	391	N	
Meyer, John Diedrich	28	Hanover	Y	Bremen	New York	01/21/1851	09/29/1856	14	16	N	
Meyer, John Frederick	22	Hanover	Y	Bremen	Baltimore	06/04/1854	10/08/1857	15	373	N	
Meyer, John George	26	Hanover	Y	Bremen	New Orleans	10/??/1847	12/15/1852	5	413	N	
Meyer, John H.	40	Hanover	Y	Bremen	Baltimore	11/02/1856	11/02/1860	18	1	N	
Meyer, John H.	41	Holland	Y	Rotterdam	New York	03/01/1889	10/29/1892			Y	
Meyer, John H.	48	Germany	N	Bremen	New York	??/??/1867	?			Y	
Meyer, John Harm	28	Hanover	Y	Rotterdam	New York	07/27/1849	08/15/1851	4	150	N	
Meyer, John Henry	??	Hanover	Y	Bremen	Baltimore	10/21/1845	10/11/1848	1	137	N	
Meyer, John Henry	??	Oldenburg	Y	Bremen	New Orleans	01/06/1849	03/25/1851	3	328	N	
Meyer, John Henry	26	Oldenburg	Y	Bremen	Baltimore	06/28/1857	08/15/1860	27	280	N	
Meyer, John Hermann	23	Hanover	Y	Bremen	Baltimore	07/07/1850	03/31/1853	7	467	N	
Meyer, John J.	25	Switzerland	Y	Havre	New York	07/05/1882	10/28/1884			Y	
Meyer, Joseph	37	Germany	Y	Bremen	New York	08/27/1881	12/30/1886			Y	
Meyer, Joseph	34	Germany	Y	Amsterdam	New York	10/26/1881	05/03/1890			Y	
Meyer, Joseph	27	Germany	Y	Bremen	New York	11/01/1884	10/24/1887			Y	
Meyer, Joseph	31	Germany	Y	Bremen	New York	10/27/1873	12/05/1881			Y	
Meyer, Joseph	25	Germany	Y	Bremen	Baltimore	04/30/1881	12/31/1883			Y	
Meyer, Joseph	24	Baden	Y	Havre	New York	06/04/1846	01/??/1850	23	475	N	
Meyer, Joseph	26	Oldenburg	Y	Bremen	Baltimore	04/20/1846	05/14/1852	25	17	N	
Meyer, Joseph	27	France	Y	Havre	New York	04/25/1854	04/16/1860	27	160	N	
Meyer, Joseph	42	Hanover	Y	Bremen	Baltimore	11/02/1856	07/16/1860	27	221	N	

CITIZENSHIP RECORDS

APPLICANT	AGE	COUNTRY OF ORIGIN	DEC	DEPART PORT	ENTRY PORT	ARRIVE DATE	DEC DATE	VOL	PG.	FLD	NAT DATE
Meyer, Levi	24	Bavaria	Y	Havre	New York	08/20/1848	10/07/1851	4	212	N	
Meyer, Lewis	21	Hamburg	Y	Bremen	Baltimore	05/16/1856	08/17/1857	15	144	N	
Meyer, Lewis	50	Germany	N	Havre	New York	04/??/1852	?			Y	
Meyer, Louis	25	Germany	Y	Bremen	Philadelphia	01/31/1899	09/10/1904			Y	
Meyer, Louis	17	Germany	N	?	New York	00/00/1873				Y	10/12/1888
Meyer, Martin	36	Prussia	Y	Bremen	Galveston	12/26/1846	02/16/1850	2	86	N	
Meyer, Martin	29	Prussia	Y	Bremen	New Orleans	01/01/1850	10/09/1854	5	141	N	
Meyer, Martin	29	Prussia	Y	Bremen	New Orleans	01/01/1850	10/09/1854	11	144	N	
Meyer, Martin	56	Germany	Y	Bremen	New York	12/23/1889	12/02/1893			Y	
Meyer, Nickolaus	31	Germany	Y	Bremen	Baltimore	03/05/1886	03/02/1889			Y	
Meyer, Peter	32	Hanover	Y	Bremen	Baltimore	06/01/1839	02/16/1849	23	143	N	
Meyer, Philip	24	Hanover	Y	Bremen	New Orleans	11/05/1854	10/08/1857	15	376	N	
Meyer, Richard	27	Baden	Y	Havre	New York	09/06/1853	04/22/1854	8	243	N	
Meyer, Richard	27	Baden	Y	Havre	New York	09/06/1853	04/22/1854	9	114	N	
Meyer, Robert	24	Germany	Y	Bremen	New York	08/01/1884	10/24/1890			Y	
Meyer, Rudolf	26	Germany	Y	Amsterdam	New York	08/05/1883	11/12/1889			Y	
Meyer, Rudolph	37	Germany	Y	Hamburg	New York	11/09/1883	10/28/1893			Y	
Meyer, Theodore	25	Hanover	Y	Bremen	Baltimore	10/14/1849	04/20/1853	8	90	N	
Meyer, Theodore	24	Germany	Y	Bremen	Baltimore	10/28/1886	11/05/1888			Y	
Meyer, Tony	35	Germany	N	Hanover	New York	04/27/1871	?			Y	
Meyer, Wilhelm	22	Germany	Y	Bremen	New York	11/04/1882	11/19/1885			Y	
Meyer, William	22	Brunswick	Y	Bremen	New Orleans	06/07/1857	12/05/1859	17	488	N	
Meyer, William	25	Germany	Y	Hamburg	New York	11/21/1883	12/27/1886	19	111	N	
Meyer, William	30	Germany	Y	Bremen	New York	09/20/1887	11/04/1891			Y	
Meyer, William	25	Germany	Y	Hamburg	New York	11/21/1883	12/27/1886			Y	
Meyer, William	43	Germany	N	Antwerp	New York	06/??/1867	?			Y	
Meyer, William John	59	Hanover	Y	Bremen	New Orleans	12/20/1844	01/08/1851	2	477	N	
Meyerose, Henry	24	Germany	Y	Bremen	New York	10/27/1880	11/03/1884			Y	
Meyerratken, William	35	Germany	Y	Bremen	New York	05/04/1881	10/24/1888			Y	
Meyers, Frank	26	Germany	Y	Antwerp	New York	09/17/1882	10/23/1888	19	169	N	
Meyers, Frank	26	Germany	Y	Antwerp	New York	09/17/1882	10/23/1888				
Meyers, Frederick	27	Hanover	Y	Bremen	New Orleans	01/04/1848	01/29/1849	1	538	N	
Meyers, Henry	23	Germany	Y	Bremen	New York	06/??/1880	03/03/1883			Y	
Meyers, Henry	24	Hanover	Y	Bremen	Baltimore	05/24/1845	02/17/1849	23	153	N	
Meyers, John	55	Switzerland	Y	Havre	New Orleans	06/04/1846	08/15/1848	22	111	N	
Meyersberg, Carl R.	31	Germany	Y	Hamburg	New York	07/09/1873	10/09/1876			Y	
Meyhers, Mathias	22	Hanover	Y	Bremen	New Orleans	12/25/1852	03/12/1856	26	191	N	
Meynng, Joseph	24	Germany	Y	Havre	New York	11/14/1892	02/05/1895			Y	
Mezetti, Agostino	52	Italy	Y	?	New York	??/??/1872	01/04/1893			Y	
Michael, Andrew	34	Saxe Coburg	Y	Bremen	New York	12/03/1848	01/15/1849	1	422	N	
Michael, Bernhard	21	Hesse Darmsta	Y	Havre	New York	10/26/1854	03/14/1856	26	201	N	
Michael, Charles	22	Hesse Cassel	Y	Bremen	New York	10/16/1854	10/20/1858	17	78	N	
Michael, Franics Henry W	21	Hanover	Y	Bremen	New Orleans	12/01/1854	09/25/1856	14	279	N	
Michael, Henry	28	Germany	Y	Amsterdam	New York	08/15/1887	10/29/1898			Y	
Michael, Herman Henry	23	Hanover	Y	Bremen	New Orleans	06/01/1849	03/08/1852	24	265	N	
Michael, John	26	Bavaria	Y	Havre	New Orleans	12/28/1847	01/13/1853	7	17	N	
Michael, Karl	??	Germany	Y	?	?	?	01/02/1883			Y	
Michael, Michael	25	France	Y	Havre	New York	03/13/1852	05/03/1854	8	356	N	
Michael, Michael	25	France	Y	Havre	New York	03/13/1852	05/03/1854	9	229	N	
Michaelis, William	25	Germany	Y	Bremen	Baltimore	01/28/1880	12/24/1883			Y	
Michaels, Cord	35	Hanover	Y	Bremen	New York	08/??/1854	09/20/1855	13	78	N	
Michaels, Peter (Mayil)	31	Germany	Y	Bremen	?	05/12/1881	09/10/1881			Y	
Michel, Frank	32	Bavaria	Y	Havre	New Orleans	12/23/1846	11/04/1852	5	216	N	
Michel, Frederick	42	Germany	Y	Bremen	New York	11/14/1868	10/17/1882			Y	
Michel, Jacob	28	Bavaria	Y	Havre	New Orleans	11/15/1846	01/28/1850	2	7	N	
Michel, John B.	29	Germany	Y	Antwerp	New York	05/01/1880	01/03/1885			Y	
Michelsen, Johan	50	Germany	Y	Hamburg	New York	10/22/1882	10/19/1888			Y	
Michelson, M.	26	Prussia	Y	?	New York	07/15/1878	11/04/1884			Y	
Michoff, George	27	Germany	Y	Rotterdam	New York	08/14/1893	10/27/1899			Y	

CITIZENSHIP RECORDS

APPLICANT	AGE	COUNTRY OF ORIGIN	DEC	DEPART PORT	ENTRY PORT	ARRIVE DATE	DEC DATE	VOL	PG.	FLD	NAT DATE
Middelbeck, Pieter	44	Holland	Y	Amsterdam	New York	07/15/1887	02/21/1889	19	223	N	
Middelbeek, Pieter	44	Holland	Y	Amsterdam	New York	07/15/1884	02/21/1889			Y	
Middeler, Frank	34	Germany	Y	Bremen	New York	06/??/1881	11/01/1886	19	108	N	
Middeler, Frank	34	Germany	Y	Bremen	New York	06/00/1881	11/01/1886			Y	
Middendorf, Ben	26	Germany	Y	Amsterdam	New York	09/20/1891	10/25/1897			Y	
Middendorf, Fred	36	Germany	Y	Amsterdam	New York	08/19/1888	05/07/1894			Y	
Middendorf, George	27	Oldenburg	Y	Bremen	New Orleans	12/09/1845	10/06/1851	4	209	N	
Middendorf, Gerhard Henr	27	Hanover	Y	Bremen	Baltimore	10/25/1855	04/10/1858	16	470	N	
Middendorf, Henry	33	Hanover	Y	Bremen	New Orleans	11/16/1847	05/25/1854	8	539	N	
Middendorf, Henry	33	Hanover	Y	Bremen	New Orleans	11/16/1847	05/25/1854	9	413	N	
Middendorf, Henry	34	Germany	Y	Bremen	Baltimore	09/18/1885	04/23/1894			Y	
Middendorf, John	25	Germany	Y	Amsterdam	New York	12/29/1881	11/24/1884			Y	
Middendorf, John H.	45	Germany	Y	Amsterdam	New York	09/02/1889	09/11/1894			Y	
Middendorf, Joseph	30	Germany	Y	Bremen	Baltimore	04/01/1881	11/12/1888			Y	
Middendorf, Klemens	16	Germany	N	?	Baltimore	00/00/1883				Y	11/01/1888
Middendorff, Franz	25	Hanover	Y	Bremen	New York	08/20/1855	11/01/1860	27	525	N	
Middlecamp, Henry	32	Germany	Y	Rotterdam	New York	11/06/1886	03/24/1894			Y	
Middleman, Sam	32	Russia	Y	Bremen	Baltimore	05/19/1891	01/10/1900			Y	
Miedeling, Henry	23	Hanover	Y	Bremen	Baltimore	10/02/1852	05/21/1856	26	519	N	
Miefert, George	17	Germany	N	?	Baltimore	00/00/1882				Y	10/24/1887
Miefert, Henry	21	Germany	Y	Bremen	Baltimore	08/01/1883	10/26/1885			Y	
Miefert, Henry	27	Germany	Y	Bremen	New York	09/01/1881	01/03/1885			Y	
Miefert, William	24	Germany	Y	Amsterdam	New York	12/29/1881	01/03/1885			Y	
Miehle, Adolphus	28	Hesse Cassel	Y	Bremen	Philadelphia	12/13/1844	07/12/1851	3	526	N	
Miele, Frank	33	Italy	Y	Naples	New York	11/13/1885	03/28/1891			Y	
Miemeyer, Theodore	37	Germany	N	?	New York	08/??/1873	?			Y	
Miensen, Henry	24	Prussia	Y	Bremen	Baltimore	12/24/1846	05/06/1850	3	53	N	
Mierenfeld, John Andrew	31	Prussia	Y	Havre	New York	05/02/1849	11/03/1852	5	197	N	
Mierenfeld, John Andrew	31	Prussia	Y	Havre	New York	05/02/1849	11/03/1852	6	324	N	
Mieth, John	28	Prussia	Y	Bremen	New Orleans	11/26/1853	08/05/1856	14	355	N	
Mihalovitch, Ignatz	68	Austria (Hung	Y	Bremen	New York	11/01/1863	10/16/1889			Y	
Mihalowitz, Ignatz	29	Romania	Y	Hamburg	New York	06/20/1899	05/03/1904			Y	
Mihas, Peter	24	Greece	Y	Athens	New York	06/02/1886	02/04/1891			Y	
Mike, Joseph	43	Syria	Y	Havre	New York	03/29/1890	11/02/1896			Y	
Milady, John	25	England	Y	Liverpool	New York	08/??/1881	07/00/1883			Y	
Milch, Philipp	29	Hesse Darmsta	Y	Havre	New York	10/02/1850	09/15/1852	25	522	N	
Mildner, Karl Wilhelm	54	Germany	Y	Bremen	Baltimore	06/04/1883	11/22/1887			Y	
Mildner, Otto	55	Germany	N	Bremen	New York	09/08/1863	?			Y	
Milenbach, Barnet	??	Russia	Y	?	?	?	10/30/1890			Y	
Miles, Albert	36	England	Y	Liverpool	New York	10/20/1891	11/18/1895			Y	
Militz, Otto	46	Germany	Y	Hamburg	New York	01/24/1884	04/06/1886	19	120	N	
Millanay, Charles Anthon	26	Bavaria	Y	Havre	New York	12/24/1845	11/13/1848	1	250	N	
Millbach, Henry	25	Nassau	Y	Antwerp	New York	08/17/1854	02/17/1857	15	24	N	
Miller, Abraham	38	Russia	Y	Hamburg	New York	07/04/1891	10/16/1896			Y	
Miller, Adam	23	Kurhessen	Y	Bremen	Baltimore	10/??/1847	03/25/1853	7	397	N	
Miller, Adam	23	Germany	Y	Havre	New York	11/20/1880	05/01/1882			Y	
Miller, Adolph	27	Hanover	Y	Bremen	New Orleans	11/01/1849	01/21/1851	2	518	N	
Miller, Ansolam	22	Baden	Y	Havre	New Orleans	05/20/1846	08/02/1848	22	36	N	
Miller, August	??	Germany	Y	?	?	?	12/14/1882			Y	
Miller, August	51	Germany	N	Bremen	Baltimore	10/??/1860	?			Y	
Miller, Christian	24	Bavaria	Y	Havre	New York	01/01/1854	02/01/1856	13	532	N	
Miller, David	26	Wurttemberg	Y	Rotterdam	New York	05/17/1854	10/05/1854	10	440	N	
Miller, David	36	Wurttemberg	Y	Rotterdam	New York	05/17/1854	10/05/1854	12	379	N	
Miller, David	34	Russia	Y	Hamburg	New York	05/01/1886	10/11/1892	19	357	N	
Miller, Edward	30	Germany	Y	?	?	?	10/17/1880			Y	
Miller, Ernest	27	England	Y	Liverpool	New York	08/??/1886	09/10/1889			Y	
Miller, Ernst	29	Lippe Detmold	Y	Bremen	Philadelphia	05/15/1846	02/22/1851	3	153	N	
Miller, Ferdinand	28	Hesse Cassel	Y	Bremen	Philadelphia	??/10/1848	12/23/1850	2	386	N	
Miller, Francis Anton	24	France	Y	Havre	New Orleans	09/30/1854	11/16/1857	16	18	N	

CITIZENSHIP RECORDS

APPLICANT	AGE	COUNTRY OF ORIGIN	DEC	DEPART PORT	ENTRY PORT	ARRIVE DATE	DEC DATE	VOL	PG.	FLD	NAT DATE
Miller, Frank	43	Switzerland	Y	Bremen	New York	05/22/1854	03/09/1857	15	80	N	
Miller, Frank	41	Germany	Y	Havre	New York	06/17/1866	10/18/1886			Y	
Miller, Frederick	55	Prussia	Y	Bremen	New Orleans	12/25/1846	08/12/1848	22	98	N	
Miller, George	33	Bavaria	Y	Bremen	Baltimore	??/27/1844	02/27/1850	2	142	N	
Miller, Henry	21	Hanover	Y	Hamburg	New Orleans	01/01/1848	11/13/1848	1	275	N	
Miller, Henry	29	Prussia	Y	Hamburg	New York	06/10/1854	09/14/1857	15	267	N	
Miller, Henry	24	Germany	Y	Antwerp	New York	04/16/1882	12/16/1887			Y	
Miller, Herman	??	Prussia	Y	Bremen	New Orleans	06/20/18??	10/11/1848	1	105	N	
Miller, Herman	50	Germany	N	Bremen	Baltimore	10/09/1855	?			Y	
Miller, Jacob	31	France	Y	Havre	New Orleans	11/18/1848	10/09/1854	6	133	N	
Miller, Jacob	37	France	Y	Havre	New Orleans	01/28/1847	10/04/1854	10	414	N	
Miller, Jacob	31	France	Y	Havre	New Orleans	11/18/1848	10/09/1854	11	136	N	
Miller, Jacob	37	France	Y	Havre	New Orleans	01/28/1847	10/04/1854	12	353	N	
Miller, Jacob	37	Germany	Y	?	New York	??/??/1867	10/06/1880			Y	
Miller, John	25	Saxony	Y	Bremen	Baltimore	06/11/1849	04/30/1850	3	36	N	
Miller, John	40	Baden	Y	Liverpool	New Orleans	01/20/1852	10/10/1854	6	207	N	
Miller, John	22	Ireland	Y	Dublin	New Orleans	04/01/1852	10/03/1854	10	388	N	
Miller, John	22	Ireland	Y	Dublin	New Orleans	04/01/1852	09/03/1854	12	327	N	
Miller, John	25	Wurttemberg	Y	Havre	New York	10/23/1850	09/29/1856	14	434	N	
Miller, John	27	France	Y	Havre	San Francisc	12/??/1883	09/21/1886			Y	
Miller, John	38	Poland	N	Hamburg		08/??/1878	?			Y	
Miller, John F.	33	Ireland	Y	Queenstown	New York	05/01/1882	10/22/1886	19	64	N	
Miller, John George	25	Bavaria	Y	Havre	New York	08/13/1846	10/02/1848	1	6	N	
Miller, John N.	59	Germany	Y	Bremen	New York	10/15/1869	10/25/1900			Y	
Miller, Joseph	30	Prussia	Y	Bremen	New Orleans	11/11/1845	08/15/1848	22	117	N	
Miller, Joseph	35	Baden	Y	Liverpool	New York	07/08/1852	02/16/1856	26	92	N	
Miller, Louis	27	Saxony	Y	Havre	New York	08/10/1849	11/16/1852	5	298	N	
Miller, Louis	27	Saxony	Y	Havre	New York	08/10/1849	11/16/1852	6	421	N	
Miller, Louis	??	Germany	Y	?	?	?	03/15/1886			Y	
Miller, Ludwig	28	Germany	Y	Bremen	New York	09/??/1879	10/03/1884			Y	
Miller, Martin	45	Hesse Darmsta	Y	Havre	New Orleans	12/25/1852	07/20/1858	16	512	N	
Miller, Martin	59	Germany	Y	Amsterdam	New York	04/12/1882	10/25/1889			Y	
Miller, Martin	30	Russia	Y	?	?	?	11/04/1892			Y	
Miller, Michael	21	Bavaria	Y	Havre	New York	09/29/1853	09/29/1856	14	18	N	
Miller, Morris	20	Russia	Y	?	New York	07/??/1893	02/23/1895			Y	
Miller, Moses	30	Poland	Y	Hamburg	New York	05/01/1880	08/15/1888			Y	
Miller, Robert Carr	26	Scotland	Y	Glasgow	New York	05/20/1894	08/06/1894			Y	
Miller, Rudolph	28	Germany	Y	Bremen	New York	04/06/1889	08/15/1896			Y	
Miller, Samuel	30	Russia	Y	Hamburg	New York	06/30/1888	11/02/1897			Y	
Miller, Soeren W.	40	Denmark	Y	Hamburg	?	?	05/??/1882	28	382	N	
Miller, Soeren W.	28	Germany	Y	Hamburg	New York	02/19/1880	05/00/1882			Y	
Miller, Victor	24	Germany	Y	Rotterdam	New York	07/01/1892	11/23/1897			Y	
Miller, Walter	29	Scotland	Y	Liverpool	New York	05/16/1857	04/04/1861	18	131	N	
Miller, William	23	Canada	Y	Napanee	Cincinnati?	09/07/1888	10/20/1892			Y	
Miller, William	45	Germany	Y	Bremen	Baltimore	05/15/1870	01/04/1883			Y	
Milligan, Michael	24	Ireland	Y	Kilrush	New York	10/26/1847	11/03/1852	6	326	N	
Milligan, Patrick	24	Ireland	Y	Liverpool	New York	04/13/1844	07/07/1851	3	507	N	
Mills, William	22	Ireland	Y	Liverpool	New York	11/??/1852	03/19/1856	26	227	N	
Milmo, John	28	Ireland	Y	Dublin	New York	05/16/1886	10/16/1890			Y	
Miltz, George	??	Germany	Y	?	?	09/11/1889	12/28/1897			Y	
Minahan, Daniel	22	Ireland	Y	Canada	Troy	08/01/1847	03/25/1850	2	258	N	
Minahan, John	21	Ireland	Y	Liverpool	New Orleans	03/29/1851	04/02/1853	7	486	N	
Minardo, Samuel (Minarco	30	Italy	Y	Palermo	New York	09/28/1882	10/20/1893			Y	
Minckwitz, Benno	27	Prussia	Y	Bremen	New York	11/03/1848	11/20/1848	1	348	N	
Mindermann, Albert	31	Hanover	Y	Delphsial(?)	New York	08/20/1849	06/18/1851	3	402	N	
Mindermann, C.	25	Germany	Y	Bremen	New York	01/09/1883	10/25/1886			Y	
Mine, Oscar	36	France	Y	Paris	New York	07/20/1891	10/31/1892			Y	
Minges, Daniel	48	Bavaria	Y	Havre	New Orleans	03/08/1854	03/08/1856	26	174	N	
Minich, Richard	21	Germany	Y	?	?	05/??/1883	08/04/1896			Y	

CITIZENSHIP RECORDS

APPLICANT	AGE	COUNTRY OF ORIGIN	DEC	DEPART PORT	ENTRY PORT	ARRIVE DATE	DEC DATE	VOL	PG.	FLD	NAT DATE
Mink, Histus	27	Wurttemberg	Y	Havre	New Orleans	12/29/1847	01/16/1849	1	436	N	
Mink, Joseph	33	Germany	Y	Bremen	New York	07/07/1880	09/29/1885			Y	
Minninghoff, John	30	Germany	Y	Bremen	New York	04/30/1881	05/03/1883			Y	
Minsch, Alphonse	22	France	Y	Havre	New York	02/10/1881	06/22/1883			Y	
Minten, Henry J.	57	Germany	N	Antwerp	New York	08/15/1857				Y	08/25/1888
Mintz, Charles	55	Germany	N	Germany	Baltimore	08/02/1857	?			Y	
Mirabello, Carmeco	38	Italy	Y	Palermo	New York	04/05/1888	11/06/1893			Y	
Mirabello, Cormelo	38	Italy	Y	Palermo	New York	04/05/1888	11/06/1893	21	51	N	
Misch, Carl	43	Germany	Y	Hamburg	New York	09/28/1891	10/25/1894			Y	
Mischler, Louis	21	Bavaria	Y	Havre	New York	04/03/1852	10/02/1854	10	348	N	
Mischler, Louis	21	Bavaria	Y	Havre	New York	04/03/1852	10/02/1854	12	287	N	
Mistler, Henry	26	Germany	Y	Antwerp	New York	05/15/1882	10/06/1882			Y	
Mitchel, James	25	Ireland	Y	Liverpool	New Orleans	12/25/1852	05/01/1854	8	295	N	
Mitchel, James	22	Ireland	Y	Liverpool	New Orleans	12/25/1852	05/01/1854	9	167	N	
Mitchel, Michael	25	Ireland	Y	Liverpool	New Orleans	02/17/1849	05/01/1854	8	294	N	
Mitchel, Michael	25	Ireland	Y	Liverpool	New Orleans	02/17/1849	05/01/1854	9	166	N	
Mitchel, Patrick	23	Ireland	Y	Liverpool	New Orleans	02/09/1850	06/13/1854	10	128	N	
Mitchel, Patrick	23	Ireland	Y	Liverpool	New Orleans	02/09/1850	06/13/1854	12	65	N	
Mitchel, William	??	?	Y	?	New Orleans	04/18/18??	11/05/1856	14	464	N	
Mitchell, Daniel	23	England	Y	Liverpool	New York	09/09/1848	06/04/1852	25	188	N	
Mitchell, Henry	31	England	Y	Liverpool	New York	05/03/1887	10/26/1891			Y	
Mitchell, James	27	Ireland	Y	Liverpool	New Orleans	03/25/1853	09/27/1854	10	277	N	
Mitchell, James	27	Ireland	Y	Liverpool	New Orleans	03/25/1853	09/27/1854	12	216	N	
Mitchell, John	56	Scotland	N	Glasgow	New York	07/06/1858	?			Y	
Mitchler, Frederick	??	Germany	Y	?	?	?	09/14/1880			Y	
Mittenberger, T.	??	Germany	Y	?	?	?	03/07/1887			Y	
Mittendarp, Eberhardt	22	Hanover	Y	Bremen	New York	10/31/1855	11/04/1858	17	275	N	
Mittenderp, Herman Henry	24	Hanover	Y	Bremen	New Orleans	12/15/1853	03/09/1857	15	78	N	
Mittenderp, John	28	Hanover	Y	Bremen	New Orleans	12/15/1853	03/09/1857	15	79	N	
Mittendorf, Frederick	25	Hanover	Y	Bremen	New Orleans	12/15/1847	01/??/1850	23	528	N	
Mittendorf, Joseph	37	Prussia	Y	Bremen	New Orleans	12/26/1846	10/10/1854	6	227	N	
Mittendorf, Joseph	37	Prussia	Y	Bremen	New Orleans	12/26/1846	10/10/1854	11	230	N	
Mittenzwei, William	29	Germany	Y	Hamburg	New York	06/13/1885	08/06/1887			Y	
Mitter, Lorenz	30	Germany	Y	Bremen	New York	04/04/1883	08/21/1885			Y	
Mittonberger, Charles	36	Baden	Y	London	New York	10/03/1856	10/12/1858	17	57	N	
Mizgayski, Alexander	32	Prussia	Y	Hamburg	New York	05/26/1853	10/21/1857	15	470	N	
Mobius, Fredrick Otto	22	Germany	Y	Bremen	?	03/03/1881	11/01/1884			Y	
Moch, Adolph	22	Germany	Y	Havre	Philadelphia	09/05/1892	09/19/1895			Y	
Mock, Nicholas	??	Prussia	Y	Hamburg	Buffalo	??/23/1847	12/11/1850	2	356	N	
Mockridge, George	32	England	Y	Bristol	New York	05/02/1848	10/19/1852	5	18	N	
Moder, Joseph	30	Bavaria	Y	Havre	New Orleans	03/17/1845	10/16/1851	4	306	N	
Moder, Karl	28	Austria	Y	Amsterdam	New York	12/04/1884	06/13/1889			Y	
Moebus, Charles	30	Germany	Y	Hamburg	New York	01/25/1883	01/03/1890			Y	
Moebus, Elbert	25	Germany	Y	Bremen	New York	05/27/1887	01/04/1888			Y	
Moecker, Herman	40	Prussia	Y	Bremen	New Orleans	04/04/1846	01/25/1849	1	516	N	
Moedinger, Friedrich	16	Germany	N	?	New York	00/00/1883				Y	10/19/1888
Moegling, Carl	63	Germany	N	Havre	New Orleans	05/19/1849	?			Y	
Moegling, Charles	27	Wuerttemberg	Y	Havre	New Orleans	05/19/1849	05/31/1852	25	161	N	
Moehl, Herman	??	Germany	Y	?	?	?	10/15/1886			Y	
Moehlman, Fred	27	Germany	Y	Bremen	New York	09/21/1881	10/28/1887			Y	
Moehlmann, Fritz	37	Germany	Y	Bremen	New York	10/09/1881	01/18/1895			Y	
Moelenkamp, William	21	Hanover	Y	Bremen	New York	01/05/1854	02/06/1856	26	57	N	
Moellenhoff, Joseph	35	Germany	Y	Rotterdam	New York	10/14/1882	04/21/1898			Y	
Moellenkamp, Frederick	33	Hanover	Y	Bremen	New York	12/16/1847	03/11/1851	3	251	N	
Moeller, Anthony	24	Germany	Y	Rotterdam	New York	06/22/1892	08/30/1895			Y	
Moeller, Bernard	33	Prussia	Y	Bremen	New Orleans	07/20/1845	10/11/1848	1	106	N	
Moeller, Bernard	25	Germany	Y	Bremen	New York	11/15/1874	10/11/1879			Y	
Moeller, David	24	Germany	Y	Bremen	Baltimore	05/15/1882	10/06/1885			Y	
Moeller, George	17	Germany	N	?	New York	00/00/1883				Y	10/13/1888

CITIZENSHIP RECORDS

APPLICANT	AGE	COUNTRY OF ORIGIN	DEC	DEPART PORT	ENTRY PORT	ARRIVE DATE	DEC DATE	VOL	PG.	FLD	NAT DATE
Moeller, Gottlieb (Muell	58	Germany	Y	Wittemburg	New York	06/07/1886	01/26/1891			Y	
Moeller, Henry	28	Germany	Y	Bremen	Baltimore	10/26/1881	01/31/1884			Y	
Moeller, John Frederick	22	Hanover	Y	Bremen	Baltimore	01/04/1845	01/17/1849	1	452	N	
Moeller, John G.	33	Germany	Y	Saxon	New York	04/24/1882	06/07/1884			Y	
Moeller, Philipp	31	Hanover	Y	Bremen	Baltimore	06/04/1845	03/25/1850	2	252	N	
Moeller, Theodore	33	Germany	Y	Bremen	New York	03/26/1884	12/07/1889			Y	
Moellers, Hermann	27	Germany	Y	Amsterdam	New York	05/14/1882	08/15/1887			Y	
Moellmann, Joseph	17	Germany	N	?	Baltimore	05/00/1883				Y	10/27/1888
Moellner, Joseph	26	Austria	Y	Havre	New York	04/12/1890	05/11/1892			Y	
Moerlein, Andrew	31	Germany	Y	Rotterdam	New York	09/27/1883	01/16/1894			Y	
Moerlein, George	27	Germany	Y	Antwerp	New York	09/29/1882	05/13/1886			Y	
Moerlein, John	26	Germany	Y	Bremen	New York	08/21/1882	06/07/1886			Y	
Moersch, Daniel	45	Germany	Y	Antwerp	Philadelphia	06/11/1880	09/16/1889			Y	
Moersell, Meyer	58	Austria	N	Hamburg	Philadelphia	11/??/1873	??/??/1874	28	330	N	??/??/1878
Moersell, Meyer	39	Austria	N	Hamburg	Philadelphia	11/00/1873	00/00/1874			Y	08/00/1878
Moeschlich, Anton	42	Bavaria	Y	Rotterdam	New York	10/??/1845	12/??/1849	23	427	N	
Moeskops, Christian P.	24	Holland	Y	Rotterdam	New York	03/28/1886	10/28/1889			Y	
Moeskops, John M.	26	Holland	Y	Antwerp	New York	03/28/1885	10/28/1889			Y	
Moesser, Julius	28	Hesse Darmsta	Y	Bremen	New York	10/24/1854	03/29/1858	16	457	N	
Moewes, Adolph	44	Germany	Y	Hamburg	New York	05/14/1867	07/16/1888			Y	
Mog, Max	26	Germany	Y	Bremen	New York	02/27/1880	05/25/1886			Y	
Mogen, Patrick	36	Ireland	Y	Liverpool	New Orleans	12/27/1848	05/01/1854	8	299	N	
Mogin, Patrick	36	Ireland	Y	Liverpool	New Orleans	12/27/1848	05/01/1854	9	171	N	
Mohan, John	33	Ireland	Y	Sligo	New York	03/28/1849	03/05/1853	7	275	N	
Moher, Michael	25	Ireland	Y	Cork	New York	11/10/1849	03/10/1852	24	278	N	
Mohlen, Mathias	40	Hanover	Y	Bremen	New Orleans	11/18/1841	11/13/1848	1	274	N	
Mohlenkamp, Gerhard	39	Germany	Y	Bremen	New York	03/28/1889	02/27/1892			Y	
Mohlenkamp, Henry	33	Germany	Y	Bremen	New York	05/11/1886	03/05/1894			Y	
Mohlenkamp, Theodore Ant	23	Germany	Y	Bremen	New York	06/15/1887	10/26/1891			Y	
Mohlmann, August (Moehlm	22	Germany	Y	Bremen	Baltimore	10/29/1883	06/09/1885			Y	
Mohlmann, Frank	31	Germany	Y	Bremen	New York	04/14/1894	10/28/1896			Y	
Mohlmann, Theodore	26	Germany	Y	Bremen	New York	08/29/1883	10/22/1887			Y	
Mohnlein, Casper	35	Bavaria	Y	Bremen	New Orleans	05/18/1848	08/30/1848	22	282	N	
Mohr, George	31	Hesse Darmsta	Y	Havre	New Orleans	01/28/1852	11/08/1858	17	292	N	
Mohr, Jacob	23	Germany	Y	Liverpool	New York	12/18/1874	10/31/1876			Y	
Mohr, Jacob E.	??	Germany	Y	?	?	?	07/15/1884			Y	
Mohr, Joseph	30	Germany	Y	Bremen	Baltimore	10/29/1883	05/07/1890			Y	
Mohr, Kilian Balthasar	49	Germany	Y	Antwerp	New York	05/24/1882	07/13/1893			Y	
Mohr, Valentin	24	Germany	Y	Bremen	New York	05/01/1883	07/06/1885			Y	
Mohren, Carl	??	Germany	Y	?	?	09/??/1895	02/15/1897			Y	
Mohrhoff, August	26	Germany	Y	Hanover	New York	02/01/1882	04/08/1882			Y	
Mohring, Heinrich	24	Prussia	Y	Bremen	New York	11/02/1857	06/26/1860	27	10	N	
Mohrmann, Henry	25	Germany	Y	Bremen	New York	06/15/1886	04/20/1891			Y	
Mohrmann, Henry Herman	34	Hanover	Y	Bremen	New Orleans	06/10/1851	01/16/1856	13	473	N	
Mohrmann, William	34	Germany	Y	Bremen	New York	08/29/1882	12/15/1884			Y	
Mok, Henry	35	Wurttemberg	Y	Havre	New York	05/??/1853	04/28/1855	11	321	N	
Moldenhauer, Robert C. A	??	Germany	Y	?	?	06/16/1892	07/11/1898			Y	
Molen, Barney	38	Hanover	Y	Bremen	Baltimore	05/20/1843	03/25/1850	2	251	N	
Molenda, Vincent	28	Germany	Y	Bremen	Baltimore	03/15/1887	12/18/1890			Y	
Molers, Henry	25	Prussia	Y	Bremen	Baltimore	10/05/1854	08/02/1856	14	315	N	
Molin, Timothy	24	Ireland	Y	Liverpool	New York	05/04/1847	08/21/1848	22	215	N	
Moll, Jacob	30	Germany	Y	Havre	New York	06/17/1881	05/07/1889			Y	
Mollath, Philipp	29	Germany	Y	Bremen	Baltimore	10/05/1883	07/01/1889			Y	
Mollenkamp, Henry Rudolp	31	Prussia	Y	Bremen	New Orleans	11/15/1853	11/05/1855	13	156	N	
Mollenkramer, George	40	Germany	Y	Bremen	New York	05/14/1880	10/26/1888	19	182	N	
Moller, Charles	32	Hanover	Y	Bremen	New York	07/24/1858	03/24/1862	18	277	N	
Moller, Conrad	39	Kurhessen	Y	Bremen	New Orleans	01/15/1859	04/01/1861	18	121	N	
Moller, Edward	28	Germany	Y	Bremen	New York	03/15/1881	03/24/1884			Y	
Moller, Franz	19	Germany	Y	Hamburg	New York	03/30/1881	10/11/1882			Y	

CITIZENSHIP RECORDS

APPLICANT	AGE	COUNTRY OF ORIGIN	DEC	DEPART PORT	ENTRY PORT	ARRIVE DATE	DEC DATE	VOL	PG.	FLD	NAT DATE
Moller, Henry	32	Germany	Y	Bremen	Baltimore	07/09/1880	06/14/1886			Y	
Moller, Joseph	23	Oldenburg	Y	Bremen	New Orleans	10/03/1852	11/27/1855	13	261	N	
Mollmann, Henry	46	Germany	Y	Bremen	Baltimore	09/01/1888	11/07/1898			Y	
Mollmann, Theodore	29	Germany	Y	Bremen	Baltimore	08/03/1888	11/01/1893			Y	
Molloy, Francis	21	Ireland	Y	Liverpool	New York	11/01/1854	10/02/1857	15	515	N	
Molloy, Henry	28	Ireland	Y	Liverpool	New York	06/04/1853	06/02/1856	14	283	N	
Molloy, John	27	Ireland	Y	Canada	Buffalo	08/01/1847	12/26/1851	24	18	N	
Molloy, Lawrence	67	Ireland	Y	Liverpool	New Orleans	02/03/1848	09/07/1857	15	241	N	
Molloy, Morris	26	Ireland	Y	Dublin	New York	05/01/1849	10/09/1860	27	473	N	
Molloy, William	30	Ireland	Y	Galway	Boston	05/09/1884	06/15/1889			Y	
Molnar, Stephen	33	Austria	Y	Hamburg	New York	07/13/1889	02/20/1894			Y	
Moloney, Edward	??	Ireland	Y	Liverpool	New York	11/20/1848	11/04/1856	14	466	N	
Moloney, Frank	25	Ireland	Y	Liverpool	New Orleans	12/25/1849	11/25/1852	5	345	N	
Moloney, James	60	Ireland	Y	Liverpool	New York	03/29/1852	09/27/1854	10	269	N	
Moloney, Patrick	24	Ireland	Y	Liverpool	New York	11/10/1848	02/07/1849	23	132	N	
Moloney, Richard	40	Ireland	Y	Liverpool	New Orleans	02/10/1851	03/25/1856	26	318	N	
Moloney, Thomas	26	Ireland	Y	Queenstown	New York	05/00/1879	11/13/1884			Y	
Moloney, Tim	40	Ireland	Y	Queenstown	New York	05/10/1890	04/01/1903			Y	
Molony, Dennis	31	Ireland	Y	Limerick	Burlington	09/15/1846	08/11/1851	4	112	N	
Molony, James	26	Ireland	Y	Liverpool	New York	09/??/1851	04/30/1855	11	334	N	
Molony, Martin	38	Ireland	Y	Liverpool	New Orleans	10/06/1852	11/06/1857	15	534	N	
Moloy, Peter	26	Ireland	Y	Canada	New York	03/??/1854	08/17/1857	15	149	N	
Momback, Samuel	24	Germany	Y	Hamburg	?	04/18/1864	05/07/1869			Y	
Momke, John	21	Oldenburg	Y	Bremen	New Orleans	11/??/1851	09/21/18??	10	149	N	
Momke, John	21	Oldenburg	Y	Bremen	New Orleans	11/20/1851	09/21/1854	12	88	N	
Momonto, Giuseppo	41	Italy	Y	Naples	New York	06/02/1898	03/30/1903			Y	
Monahan, John	45	Ireland	Y	Liverpool	Baltimore	05/??/1850	06/22/1852	25	304	N	
Monahan, Patrick	50	Ireland	Y	Liverpool	New Orleans	02/02/1850	12/29/1852	5	465	N	
Monahan, William	25	Ireland	Y	Liverpool	New York	06/22/1848	01/11/1851	2	479	N	
Monarty, Jeremiah	21	Ireland	Y	Kilbrush	New York	04/26/1851	09/26/1854	10	232	N	
Monasch, Leo	30	Hungary	Y	Bremen	New York	04/01/1886	07/15/1889			Y	
Moncke, Heinrich	23	Prussia	Y	Bremen	New York	09/28/1852	02/03/1853	7	110	N	
Monderscheld, Fred	36	Germany	N	Bremen	New York	10/??/1871	?			Y	
Mondshein, Isaac	17	Germany	N	?	New York	00/00/1872				Y	10/27/1888
Mongan, Terrence	33	Ireland	Y	Liverpool	New York	07/10/1855	11/05/1858	17	281	N	
Monikhoff, Henry (Monokk	30	Prussia	Y	Bremen	Baltimore	05/06/1846	08/15/1848	22	127	N	
Monks, Daniel	26	Ireland	Y	Dublin	New York	01/05/1850	09/26/1854	10	249	N	
Monks, Daniel	26	Ireland	Y	Dublin	New York	01/05/1850	09/26/1854	12	188	N	
Monnig, Ferdinand	28	Prussia	Y	Bremen	New York	09/20/1845	01/??/1850	23	479	N	
Monnig, Frank	24	Germany	Y	Amsterdam	New York	03/07/1885	11/01/1888	19	209	N	
Monnig, Frank Joseph	24	Germany	Y	Amsterdam	New York	03/07/1885	11/01/1888			Y	
Monninger, Christoph	35	Germany	Y	Hamburg	New York	05/06/1883	03/23/1891			Y	
Monstens, Bernard	59	Germany	N	Bremen	Baltimore	05/01/1856	?			Y	
Montag, Charles	32	Prussia	Y	Bremen	Baltimore	06/20/1845	03/25/1851	3	331	N	
Montag, Jacob	28	Baden	Y	Havre	New York	11/13/1847	06/09/1852	25	213	N	
Montague, Bernard	27	Ireland	Y	Londonderry	New York	09/20/1881	12/26/1885			Y	
Montague, Frank H. Grand	32	France?	Y	Antwerp	New York	02/20/1881	07/20/1886			Y	
Montague, Michael	34	Ireland	N	Liverpool	New York	05/??/1872	?			Y	
Monte, Max	40	Germany	Y	Amsterdam	New York	10/14/1881	11/05/1901			Y	
Montgomery, Campbell	27	Ireland	Y	Belfast	New Orleans	03/21/1848	01/24/1851	2	524	N	
Montgomery, Harry J.	24	Ireland	Y	Liverpool	New Orleans	03/11/1845	09/29/1848	22	361	N	
Montgomery, William A.	50	Ireland	Y	Glasgow	New York	08/??/1854	03/28/1885			Y	
Monypeny, William	23	Ireland	Y	Liverpool	New York	09/29/1848	12/07/1852	5	395	N	
Mook, Solomon	28	Bavaria	Y	Havre	New Orleans	01/31/1851	09/27/1856	14	407	N	
Mooney, Patrick	??	Ireland	Y	Westport	New York	07/02/1847	04/03/1852	24	360	N	
Mooney, Thomas	24	Ireland	Y	Liverpool	New York	12/31/1846	09/29/1756	14	428	N	
Mooney, William	24	Ireland	Y	Liverpool	New York	10/14/1847	01/15/1853	7	28	N	
Moorbrink, August	26	Germany	Y	Bremen	Baltimore	08/31/1888	01/02/1891			Y	
Moore, Alexander	38	Ireland	Y	Liverpool	New York	05/16/1851	11/01/1852	5	134	N	

CITIZENSHIP RECORDS

APPLICANT	AGE	COUNTRY OF ORIGIN	DEC	DEPART PORT	ENTRY PORT	ARRIVE DATE	DEC DATE	VOL	PG.	FLD	NAT DATE
Moore, Alexander	38	Ireland	Y	Liverpool	New York	05/16/1851	11/01/1852	6	260	N	
Moore, Frank	37	England	Y	Manchester	New York	05/29/1879	09/01/1886			Y	
Moore, George	40	Ireland	Y	Liverpool	New Orleans	11/10/1848	03/06/1852	24	243	N	
Moore, James	70	Ireland	N	Liverpool	New Orleans	04/??/1849	?			Y	
Moore, John	27	Ireland	Y	Liverpool	New Orleans	01/11/1849	01/20/1852	24	44	N	
Moore, Michael	24	Ireland	Y	Liverpool	New York	03/07/1848	06/10/1852	25	310	N	
Moore, Peter	??	?	Y	Dublin	New York	06/16/1849	03/26/1851	3	356	N	
Moore, Robert	59	Ireland	Y	Liverpool	New York	05/28/1856	05/26/1859	17	432	N	
Moorhouse, Thomas	32	Ireland	Y	Liverpool	Buffalo	11/16/1847	10/02/1854	10	346	N	
Moorhouse, Thomas	28	Ireland	Y	Liverpool	Buffalo	11/16/1847	10/02/1854	12	285	N	
Moorman, John Henry	29	Oldenburg	Y	Bremen	Baltimore	05/18/1844	08/15/1848	22	110	N	
Moormann, Anton	33	Germany	Y	Rotterdam	New York	07/25/1887	01/14/1895			Y	
Moormann, Clemens	37	Germany	N	Bremen	New York	06/??/1871	?			Y	
Moormann, Eugen	27	Germany	Y	Rotterdam	New York	07/25/1887	06/01/1893			Y	
Moormann, Eugene	37	Germany	Y	Rotterdam	New York	07/25/1887	04/01/1893	19	418	N	
Moormann, Ferdinand H.	23	Germany	Y	Bremen	Baltimore	08/26/1880	09/29/1885			Y	
Moormann, Friedrich	26	Hanover	Y	Bremen	Baltimore	07/04/1847	06/21/1852	25	302	N	
Moormann, Ignatz	26	Germany	Y	Rotterdam	New York	07/25/1887	01/14/1895			Y	
Moormann, Joseph	22	Oldenburg	Y	Bremen	Baltimore	10/25/1856	01/19/1860	27	63	N	
Moormann, Joseph	??	Germany	N	?	?	09/02/1886				Y	10/24/1892
Moormann, Theodore	28	Oldenburg	Y	Bremen	New York	02/15/1849	01/13/1851	2	490	N	
Moormann, William	35	Hanover	Y	Bremen	New Orleans	01/03/1849	11/03/1855	13	154	N	
Moorwessel, John Bernard	30	Prussia	Y	Bremen	New York	09/09/1871	01/20/1873	18	547	N	
Moorwessel, John G.	30	Germany	Y	Bremen	Baltimore	09/19/1888	10/23/1896			Y	
Moorwood, John	58	England	N	Liverpool	New York	01/??/1841	?	28	150	N	09/??/1853
Moorwood, John	11	England	N	Liverpool	New York	01/00/1841				Y	09/00/1853
Moosbrugger, Joseph	25	Switzerland	Y	Havre	New York	07/15/1893	10/23/1899			Y	
Moran, Daniel	23	Ireland	Y	Galway	Whitehall	11/21/1846	10/30/1852	5	73	N	
Moran, Edward	25	Ireland	Y	Liverpool	New York	07/14/1850	10/07/1854	6	34	N	
Moran, Edward	25	Ireland	Y	Liverpool	New York	07/14/1850	10/07/1854	11	35	N	
Moran, Edward	30	Ireland	Y	Liverpool	New Orleans	02/04/1848	07/16/1855	11	396	N	
Moran, James	23	Ireland	Y	Liverpool	New Orleans	02/23/1849	01/08/1851	2	475	N	
Moran, James	27	Ireland	Y	Queenstown	New York	06/21/1886	03/23/1894	21	66	N	
Moran, James	24	Ireland	Y	Queenstown	New York	05/22/1892	01/04/1896			Y	
Moran, John	24	Ireland	Y	Liverpool	New Orleans	??/20/1848	12/??/1850	2	421	N	
Moran, John	22	Ireland	Y	Liverpool	New Orleans	11/24/1847	12/29/1852	5	467	N	
Moran, John	24	Ireland	Y	Liverpool	New Orleans	04/01/1851	04/20/1854	8	229	N	
Moran, John	40	Ireland	Y	Liverpool	New York	03/19/1850	05/01/1854	8	334	N	
Moran, John	24	Ireland	Y	Liverpool	New Orleans	04/01/1851	04/20/1854	9	100	N	
Moran, John	40	Ireland	Y	Liverpool	New York	03/19/1850	05/01/1854	9	207	N	
Moran, Martin	17	Ireland	N	?	New York	00/00/1879				Y	10/13/1888
Moran, Michael	30	Ireland	Y	Liverpool	New York	09/13/1848	11/16/1852	5	295	N	
Moran, Michael	30	Ireland	Y	Liverpool	New York	09/13/1848	11/16/1852	6	419	N	
Moran, Michael	23	Ireland	Y	Liverpool	New Orleans	09/20/1848	03/29/1853	7	456	N	
Moran, Michael	33	Ireland	Y	Queenstown	New York	04/10/1881	10/24/1891	19	342	N	
Moran, Michael	36	Ireland	N	Liverpool	New York	07/31/1868	?			Y	
Moran, Michael	28	Ireland	Y	Liverpool	Whitehall	06/28/1847	04/05/1852	24	385	N	
Moran, Michael	??	Ireland	Y	?	?	?	08/27/1874			Y	
Moran, Nicholas	36	England	Y	London	New York	02/13/1888	10/16/1891			Y	
Moran, Owen	44	Ireland	Y	Liverpool	New Orleans	02/15/1848	05/03/1854	8	357	N	
Moran, Owen	44	Ireland	Y	Liverpool	New Orleans	02/15/1849	05/03/1854	9	230	N	
Moran, Patrick	30	Ireland	Y	Liverpool	New York	11/25/1848	11/20/1848	1	341	N	
Moran, Patrick	26	Ireland	Y	Liverpool	New Orleans	04/21/1850	05/20/1856	26	505	N	
Moran, Patrick	23	Ireland	Y	Queenstown	New York	04/14/1875	10/07/1876			Y	
Moran, Peter	17	Ireland	N	?	New York	00/00/1883				Y	10/23/1888
Moran, Thomas	30	Ireland	Y	Liverpool	New Orleans	04/14/1847	01/31/1850	2	20	N	
Moran, Thomas	25	Ireland	Y	Liverpool	New York	02/22/1853	02/19/1857	15	35	N	
Moran, Thomas, W.	39	Ireland	N	Dublin	New York	03/??/1864	?			Y	
Moran, William	31	Ireland	Y	Liverpool	New York	05/04/1849	07/08/1851	3	511	N	

CITIZENSHIP RECORDS

APPLICANT	AGE	COUNTRY OF ORIGIN	DEC	DEPART PORT	ENTRY PORT	ARRIVE DATE	DEC DATE	VOL	PG.	FLD	NAT DATE
Moran, William	30	Ireland	Y	Liverpool	New Orleans	02/15/1851	04/20/1854	8	228	N	
Moran, William	30	Ireland	Y	Liverpool	New Orleans	02/15/1851	04/20/1854	9	99	N	
Morebach, Anton	62	Baden	Y	Havre	New Orleans	05/09/1847	10/07/1851	4	216	N	
Moreley, James	21	Ireland	Y	Liverpool	New York	04/08/1850	04/02/1852	24	356	N	
Morelli, John	75	Italy	N	Liverpool	New Orleans	11/01/1843	??/??/1845	28	15	N	10/??/1850
Morelli, John	31	Italy	N	Liverpool	New Orleans	11/01/1843	00/00/1845			Y	10/00/1850
Morgan, George Edward	31	Wales	Y	Liverpool	New York	07/04/1849	12/13/1851	4	511	N	
Morgan, Henry	55	Ireland	Y	Queenstown	New York	05/??/1865	10/05/1883			Y	
Morgan, John	37	Wales	Y	?	?	?	05/03/1886			Y	
Morgan, John D.	35	Wales	Y	Liverpool	New York	11/30/1884	02/21/1894			Y	
Morgan, Patrick	28	Ireland	Y	Liverpool	New York	03/01/1849	03/03/1852	24	229	N	
Morgan, Thomas	24	England	Y	Liverpool	New York	05/05/1882	04/13/1885			Y	
Morganroth, Edward	25	Germany	Y	?	Baltimore	09/02/1891	08/01/1893			Y	
Morganstern, Daniel	23	Bavaria	Y	Bingen	New York	04/08/1851	09/22/1855	13	124	N	
Morganthan, Lippmann	21	Bavaria	Y	Bremen	New York	07/27/1848	03/??/1850	2	158	N	
Morgener, Fred	34	Germany	Y	Hamburg	New York	08/18/1892	10/28/1895			Y	
Morgenrote, Henry	33	Oldenburg	Y	Bremen	Baltimore	05/30/1845	10/11/1848	1	110	N	
Morgenthal, Anton	52	Germany	Y	Bremen	New York	07/04/1882	11/03/1890	19	310	N	
Morgenthal, Anton	52	Germany	Y	Bremen	New York	07/04/1882	11/03/1890			Y	
Morgenthaler, Max	45	Germany	Y	Havre	New York	04/06/1883	10/02/1890			Y	
Morgenthau, Lippman	??	Germany	N	Germany	New York	??/??/1848	03/05/1850	28	478	N	09/04/1854
Morgenthau, Lippman	??	Germany	N	?	New York	00/00/1848	03/05/1850			Y	09/04/1854
Morhardt, Adam	26	Germany	Y	Bremen	New York	04/13/1883	03/31/1885			Y	
Moriarity, Timothy	57	Ireland	N	Paris	Buffalo	10/??/1857	09/??/1860	28	99	N	04/??/1863
Moriarty, Timothy	26	Ireland	N	Paris Canada	Buffalo, NY	10/00/1857	09/00/1860			Y	04/00/1863
Morio, Andrew	57	Bavaria	Y	Havre	New Orleans	02/04/1852	03/25/1856	26	307	N	
Moritz, Mayer	22	Hesse Darmsta	Y	Havre	New Orleans	04/24/1849	09/15/1852	25	520	N	
Morkowsky, John	33	Russia	Y	Hamburg	Buffalo	08/23/1890	10/28/1893			Y	
Morley, George	26	England	Y	Nottinghamsh	?	09/05/1880	05/16/1881			Y	
Morlock, Adolph	??	Germany	Y	?	?	?	02/25/1884			Y	
Mormann, John	23	Oldenburg	Y	Bremen	New Orleans	12/22/1856	11/01/1858	17	219	N	
Morrell, August	24	Wurttemberg	Y	Havre	New York	04/08/1854	07/16/1855	11	401	N	
Morrin, Michael	40	Ireland	Y	Westport	Philadelphia	12/??/1848	11/06/1857	15	539	N	
Morris, Abraham	54	Russia	Y	Hamburg	New York	11/17/1886	02/28/1890			Y	
Morris, Edward	30	Ireland	Y	Liverpool	New York	07/18/1846	10/27/1851	4	409	N	
Morris, Jacob	26	Russia	Y	Hamburg	New York	11/17/1886	09/16/1890			Y	
Morris, James	28	Ireland	Y	Liverpool	New York	06/10/1847	06/30/1851	3	469	N	
Morris, John	30	Ireland	Y	Queenstown	New York	06/19/1887	03/22/1893			Y	
Morris, Lewis F.	20	Wales	Y	Liverpool	New York	04/15/1882	01/10/1884			Y	
Morrisey, Jeremiah	??	Ireland	N	?	?	02/21/1884				Y	10/24/1892
Morrisey, Richard	27	Ireland	Y	Queenstown	New York	04/29/1880	10/28/1887	19	122	N	
Morrison, George	27	Ireland	Y	Liverpool	New York	10/01/1849	06/10/1852	25	223	N	
Morrison, Irad H.	31	Scotland	Y	Glasgow	Portland	08/15/1873	10/08/1878			Y	
Morrison, John E.	33	Ireland	Y	Wexford	New York	05/??/1831	03/15/1856	26	206	N	
Morrison, Robert	34	Canada	Y	?	Detroit	??/??/1885	10/22/1892			Y	
Morrissey, James	48	Ireland	N	Queenstown	New York	06/21/1869	?			Y	
Morrissey, John	8	Ireland	N	?	New York	00/00/1872				Y	10/27/1888
Morrissey, William	35	Ireland	Y	Liverpool	New York	12/20/1875	08/31/1891			Y	
Mors, Siskind	37	Hesse Darmsta	Y	Bremen	Baltimore	10/??/1851	03/28/1853	7	429	N	
Morshaeuser, Martin	51	Germany	Y	Antwerp	Boston	06/14/1880	10/28/1886			Y	
Morstadt, Frederick Will	42	Baden	Y	Havre	New York	01/12/1849	12/24/1857	16	244	N	
Mortiz, Hyman	??	Russia	Y	?	?	?	07/24/1897			Y	
Mortiz, Solomon	65	Hessen Darmst	N	Havre	New York	10/??/1852	10/12/1857	28	453	N	10/12/1857
Morvinkel, Heinrich	61	Germany	N	Hamburg	New York	05/06/1858	?			Y	
Mory, Wilhelm	35	Germany	Y	Bremen	Baltimore	07/04/1881	11/06/1882			Y	
Mosbacher, Anton	??	Germany	Y	?	New York	05/??/1883	10/06/1884			Y	
Moschal, Peter	33	Germany	Y	Hamburg	New York	09/12/1895	10/27/1900			Y	
Moscisker, Abraham	28	Austria	Y	Hamburg	New York	08/27/1886	11/01/1892			Y	
Moser, Adam	30	Baden	Y	Antwerp	New Orleans	12/24/1947	10/??/1848	1	25	N	

CITIZENSHIP RECORDS

APPLICANT	AGE	COUNTRY OF ORIGIN	DEC	DEPART PORT	ENTRY PORT	ARRIVE DATE	DEC DATE	VOL	PG.	FLD	NAT DATE
Moser, August	30	Germany	Y	Havre	New York	05/27/1889	07/01/1896			Y	
Moser, Frederick Conrad	33	France	Y	Havre	New York	11/17/1854	03/15/1858	16	404	N	
Moser, Joseph F.	27	Germany	Y	Hamburg	New York	10/30/1873	03/27/1883			Y	
Moser, Otto	32	Germany	Y	Bremen	New York	12/16/1885	09/08/1892			Y	
Moser, Robert	46	Austria	Y	Bremen	Baltimore	05/25/1878	10/19/1881			Y	
Moser, William	21	Baden	Y	Bremen	New York	07/16/1852	12/17/1855	13	319	N	
Moses, Jerusalem	24	Russia	Y	Bremen	New York	12/18/1888	09/04/1890			Y	
Mosey, Chiku (Monsi)	25	Arabia	Y	Beirut	New York	11/14/1888	08/30/1892			Y	
Moskowitz, Julius	26	Hungaria-Aust	Y	Hamburg	New York	06/02/1888	10/25/1894	21	73	N	
Moss, Frank	40	Italy	Y	Naples	New York	05/27/1882	07/25/1893			Y	
Moss, Johann	31	Hanover	Y	Havre	New York	07/15/1848	10/09/1854	6	110	N	
Moss, John	23	Hanover	Y	Bremen	New Orleans	??/08/1848	11/01/1851	4	455	N	
Moss, John	31	Hanover	Y	Havre	New York	07/15/1848	10/09/1854	11	113	N	
Moss, William	45	England	Y	Liverpool	Detroit	06/27/1884	11/26/1884			Y	
Mossler, Aaron	21	Prussia	Y	Hamburg	New York	07/13/1853	09/10/1855	11	526	N	
Mossler, Liebermann	21	Poland (Pruss	Y	Hamburg	New York	09/20/1852	11/03/1855	13	153	N	
Mossop, Stephan	34	?	Y	Canada	Buffalo	08/20/1849	03/05/1851	3	215	N	
Moszbacher, John	31	Bavaria	Y	Havre	New York	03/28/1852	05/31/1852	25	167	N	
Moticka, Frank	??	Austria	Y	?	?	?	10/14/1889			Y	
Motschmann, Adam	31	Bavaria	Y	Bremen	New York	04/30/1848	02/05/1850	2	40	N	
Mott, Carl	??	Prussia	Y	Havre	New York	02/09/1848	12/20/1850	2	378	N	
Motz, Frank	39	Germany	N	Bremen	New York	11/??/1868	?			Y	
Motz, Herman	24	Germany	Y	Antwerp	New York	09/05/1890	04/04/1893			Y	
Motz, Jacob	28	Germany	Y	Hamburg	New York	02/28/1882	05/25/1885			Y	
Motzer, Charles	34	Wurttemberg	Y	Havre	New York	08/01/1852	08/24/1857	15	172	N	
Mouarty, Jeremiah	21	Ireland	Y	Kilriss	New York	04/26/1851	09/26/1854	12	171	N	
Mouse, Philip	??	Germany	Y	?	?	?	03/28/1872			Y	
Moussi, Calil	2?	Turkey	Y	Beirut	New Orleans	12/20/1887	10/17/1892			Y	
Mriesek, Ignatz	29	Germany	Y	Hamburg	New York	07/11/1882	09/01/1886	19	41	N	
Mrusek, Ignatz	29	Germany	Y	Hamburg	New York	07/11/1882	09/01/1886			Y	
Muche, Rudolph	30	Germany	Y	?	?	?	10/03/1892			Y	
Mucherheide, Arnold	45	Oldenburg	Y	Bremen	Baltimore	11/01/1848	03/01/1852	24	203	N	
Muck, John	29	Germany	Y	Bremen	New York	05/27/1882	03/31/1887			Y	
Mucker, Henry	29	Germany	Y	Bremen	Baltimore	09/13/1881	10/17/1891	19	335	N	
Muckerheide, August	??	Germany	N	?	?	05/01/1887				Y	10/04/1892
Mudersbach, Henry	30	Prussia	Y	Bremen	New York	10/06/1857	09/12/1860	27	360	N	
Mueckisch, Herman	38	Germany	Y	Hamburg	New York	06/26/1881	03/21/1893			Y	
Muegel, Peter	40	Germany	Y	Havre	New York	08/21/1885	10/28/1889			Y	
Mueggenborg, August	24	Germany	Y	Bremen	Baltimore	08/10/1883	11/10/1888			Y	
Mueggenborg, Bernard	25	Germany	Y	Bremen	Baltimore	10/30/1884	12/29/1892			Y	
Muehe, Frederick William	28	Brunswick	Y	Bremen	New Orleans	11/18/1854	07/14/1855	11	385	N	
Muehe, Jacob	38	Germany	Y	Antwerp	New York	03/01/1882	10/13/1894			Y	
Muehe, Joseph	33	Germany	Y	?	?	07/03/1880	11/04/1892			Y	
Muehlbeyer, Jacob Fred	28	Germany	Y	Hamburg	New York	07/30/1882	10/13/1885			Y	
Muehler, Gustav	26	Germany	Y	Hamburg	New York	03/22/1884	03/08/1886			Y	
Muehlhaeuser, Andreas	31	Germany	Y	Bremen	New York	05/21/1886	05/24/1892			Y	
Muehlhausen, John M.	56	Germany	N	Havre	New York	05/01/1851	?			Y	
Muehlheuser, Michael	24	Wurttemberg	Y	Havre	New York	05/02/1851	09/10/1855	11	525	N	
Muehrlein, Conrad	28	Bavaria	Y	Havre	New York	03/04/1851	05/29/1854	10	22	N	
Mueller, Adam	25	Bavaria	Y	Havre	New Orleans	04/28/1845	02/24/1853	7	227	N	
Mueller, Adam	31	Hesse Darmsta	Y	Havre	New Orleans	04/22/1850	04/13/1852	24	497	N	
Mueller, Andreas	42	Bavaria	Y	Havre	New Orleans	11/05/1852	03/02/1853	7	257	N	
Mueller, Andreas	31	Germany	Y	Bremen	New York	04/??/1881	10/14/1886			Y	
Mueller, Anton	26	Germany	Y	Bremen	New York	09/11/1878	10/05/1885			Y	
Mueller, Anton	26	Hesse Darmsta	Y	Antwerp	New Orleans	12/08/1848	04/12/1852	24	441	N	
Mueller, August	22	Germany	Y	Havre	New York	09/25/1887	01/07/1889			Y	
Mueller, August	39	Germany	Y	Hamburg	New York	05/17/1880	11/07/1887			Y	
Mueller, Augustus	21	Saxe Altenbur	Y	Bremen	New York	11/15/1854	11/14/1857	16	16	N	
Mueller, Balthaser	31	Switzerland	Y	Havre	New York	09/04/1847	02/11/1852	24	94	N	

CITIZENSHIP RECORDS

APPLICANT	AGE	COUNTRY OF ORIGIN	DEC	DEPART PORT	ENTRY PORT	ARRIVE DATE	DEC DATE	VOL	PG.	FLD	NAT DATE
Mueller, Balthaser	34	Hesse Darmsta	Y	Havre	New Orleans	04/22/1850	09/15/1852	25	508	N	
Mueller, Batte	34	Germany	Y	Hamburg	New York	05/20/1882	07/11/1891			Y	
Mueller, Bernard	35	Hanover	Y	Bremen	New York	06/05/1853	04/17/1854	8	172	N	
Mueller, Charles	39	Germany	Y	Rotterdam	New York	10/20/1880	10/22/1896			Y	
Mueller, Charles	23	Austria	Y	Bremen	Baltimore	08/27/1881	11/06/1882			Y	
Mueller, Charles	48	Prussia	N	Hamburg	New York	03/17/1869	?			Y	
Mueller, Charles	26	Prussia	Y	Havre	New York	06/04/1845	09/11/1848	22	321	N	
Mueller, Charles W. F.	32	Hanover	Y	Bremen	New Orleans	??/20/1848	10/09/1848	22	498	N	
Mueller, Christ.	29	Prussia	Y	Bremen	Philadelphia	07/09/1845	01/20/1851	2	509	N	
Mueller, Christian	28	Germany	Y	South Hampto	New York	12/12/1894	06/01/1898			Y	
Mueller, Conrad	21	Baden	Y	Havre	New Orleans	11/12/1854	11/09/1857	15	547	N	
Mueller, Conrad	45	Germany	Y	?	?	08/20/1890	04/30/1892			Y	
Mueller, Conrad	33	Germany	Y	?	New York	??/??/1887	10/29/1887			Y	
Mueller, Conrad	52	Germany	N	Havre	New Orleans	11/12/1854	?			Y	
Mueller, Danrenz (Franz)	44	Bavaria	Y	Havre	New York	03/01/1846	08/11/1848	22	95	N	
Mueller, Edward	29	Germany	Y	Bremen	Baltimore	06/16/1882	02/02/1884			Y	
Mueller, Edward	34	Germany	N	Bremen	Baltimore	10/17/1871	?			Y	
Mueller, Edward	35	Germany	N	Havre	New York	04/09/1881	?			Y	
Mueller, Ferdinand	28	Prussia	Y	Bremen	Galveston	12/23/1843	08/28/1848	22	262	N	
Mueller, Florente	27	France	Y	Havre	New York	12/20/1854	04/05/1858	16	498	N	
Mueller, Frank	25	Germany	Y	Havre	New York	02/13/1887	09/13/1890			Y	
Mueller, Frank Anton	34	Wurttemberg	Y	Antwerp	New York	05/01/1852	10/12/1857	15	402	N	
Mueller, Franz	23	Prussia	Y	Bremen	New York	09/17/1852	03/31/1856	26	394	N	
Mueller, Frederick	24	Bavaria	Y	Havre	New York	08/17/1846	02/10/1851	3	114	N	
Mueller, Frederick	37	Germany	Y	Bremen	Baltimore	06/01/1883	09/04/1884			Y	
Mueller, Frederick Anton	28	Saxony	Y	Hamburg	New York	10/25/1856	03/04/1857	15	63	N	
Mueller, Fritz	40	Germany	Y	Bremen	New York	12/06/1885	11/26/1890			Y	
Mueller, Georg	??	Hesse Cassel	Y	?	Baltimore	06/28/18??	11/07/1856	14	487	N	
Mueller, George	38	Hesse Darmsta	Y	Antwerp	New York	09/18/1852	02/09/1858	16	90	N	
Mueller, George	35	Germany	Y	Bremen	Hoboken	09/21/1879	10/17/1887			Y	
Mueller, George	45	Germany	Y	Antwerp	New York	06/02/1881	10/28/1886			Y	
Mueller, George	42	Germany	N	Bremen	New York	03/09/1869	?			Y	
Mueller, George	35	Baden	Y	Havre	New York	10/20/1845	08/22/1848	22	226	N	
Mueller, George	21	Bavaria	Y	Havre	New Orleans	10/20/1853	04/07/1856	26	463	N	
Mueller, George Henry	46	Bavaria	Y	Havre	New York	06/12/1852	03/27/1857	15	91	N	
Mueller, Gust	25	Germany	Y	Bremen	Baltimore	09/21/1891	10/27/1898			Y	
Mueller, Gustav R.	27	Germany	Y	Bremen	New York	09/01/1882	10/13/1886			Y	
Mueller, Henry	34	Prussia	Y	Antwerp	New Orleans	12/22/1848	06/16/1851	3	390	N	
Mueller, Henry	36	Hanover	Y	Bremen	New Orleans	12/31/1850	04/17/1854	8	174	N	
Mueller, Henry	33	Bavaria	Y	Havre	New York	09/19/1854	10/09/1857	15	382	N	
Mueller, Henry	28	Hanover	Y	Hamburg	New York	08/29/1855	03/15/1858	16	406	N	
Mueller, Henry	34	Germany	Y	Antwerp	New York	02/08/1884	02/01/1894			Y	
Mueller, Henry	24	Prussia	Y	Antwerp	New Orleans	05/26/1847	09/13/1852	25	477	N	
Mueller, Henry	26	Hanover	Y	Bremen	New Orleans	05/23/1849	04/07/1856	26	462	N	
Mueller, Henry	31	Germany	Y	Bremen	Baltimore	11/14/1880	03/02/1886			Y	
Mueller, Henry F.	34	Prussia	Y	Hamburg	New York	10/06/1863	05/30/1870			Y	
Mueller, Herman	53	Germany	Y	Hamburg	Baltimore	05/13/1881	10/09/1886			Y	
Mueller, Herman	21	Germany	Y	Hamburg	New York	08/28/1880	12/18/1882			Y	
Mueller, Herman Edward	45	Germany	Y	Bremen	New York	09/17/1884	10/10/1887			Y	
Mueller, Hermann	42	Germany	Y	Antwerp	New York	04/11/1887	03/27/1889			Y	
Mueller, Hermann Henry	39	Germany	Y	Bremen	New York	08/09/1869	11/09/1881			Y	
Mueller, Ignatz	57	Baden	Y	Havre	New Orleans	04/25/1846	08/26/1848	22	261	N	
Mueller, J.	49	Germany	Y	Bremen	New York	08/01/1865	10/10/1884			Y	
Mueller, Jacob	30	Hesse Cassel	Y	Bremen	New York	05/05/1849	06/13/1854	10	125	N	
Mueller, Jacob	25	Germany	Y	Antwerp	New York	06/11/1890	10/19/1891			Y	
Mueller, Jacob	30	Switzerland	Y	Havre	New Orleans	05/03/1849	03/17/1856	26	223	N	
Mueller, Jacob Charles	??	Germany	Y	?	?	?	10/20/1897			N	
Mueller, John	40	Baden	Y	Liverpool	New Orleans	01/20/1852	10/10/1854	10	210	N	
Mueller, John	28	Germany	Y	Antwerp	New York	06/06/1883	08/03/1886			Y	

CITIZENSHIP RECORDS

APPLICANT	AGE	COUNTRY OF ORIGIN	DEC	DEPART PORT	ENTRY PORT	ARRIVE DATE	DEC DATE	VOL	PG.	FLD	NAT DATE
Mueller, John	32	Germany	Y	Bremen	New York	11/26/1890	08/03/1892			Y	
Mueller, John H.	28	Germany	Y	Bremen	New York	01/27/1883	09/06/1887			Y	
Mueller, John Rudolph	30	Hanover	Y	Bremen	Baltimore	01/10/1846	08/28/1848	22	267	N	
Mueller, Jonas	22	Kurhessen	Y	Bremen	Baltimore	06/07/1851	08/27/1855	11	504	N	
Mueller, Joseph	34	Bavaria	Y	?	New Orleans	06/05/1847	09/29/1858	16	103	N	
Mueller, Joseph	??	Germany	Y	Havre	New York	05/06/1879	10/26/1888			Y	
Mueller, Joseph	31	Germany	Y	Antwerp	New York	12/18/1876	04/14/1892			Y	
Mueller, Joseph	43	Germany	N	Hamburg	New York	03/28/1875	?			Y	
Mueller, Joseph	28	Germany	Y	Antwerp	New York	05/12/1887	04/09/1888			Y	
Mueller, Joseph Gustave	??	Prussia	Y	?	?	?	05/07/1883			Y	
Mueller, Karl Caesar Edm	28	Germany	Y	?	?	?	11/17/1884			Y	
Mueller, Lorenz	30	Bavaria	Y	Havre	New York	06/11/1851	03/08/1852	24	269	N	
Mueller, Ludwig	40	Prussia	Y	London	New York	09/25/1853	05/01/1854	8	329	N	
Mueller, Ludwig	36	Germany	Y	Havre	New York	01/08/1880	10/12/1892			Y	
Mueller, Mathew	23	Baden	Y	Havre	New York	06/20/1847	12/16/1851	4	524	N	
Mueller, Matthias	42	Bavaria	Y	Bremen	New York	04/??/1849	03/25/1851	3	355	N	
Mueller, Matthias	28	Bavaria	Y	Havre	New York	04/27/1846	02/12/1849	23	65	N	
Mueller, Michael	33	Switzerland	Y	Havre	New York	09/21/1847	10/10/1854	6	212	N	
Mueller, Michael	33	Switzerland	Y	Havre	New York	09/21/1847	10/10/1854	11	215	N	
Mueller, Michael	23	Baden	Y	Havre	New Orleans	01/17/1852	08/21/1855	11	472	N	
Mueller, Peter	28	Prussia	Y	Antwerp	New York	07/04/1849	03/03/1851	3	191	N	
Mueller, Peter	41	Germany	Y	Bremen	New York	10/03/1871	08/19/1893			Y	
Mueller, Peter	26	Germany	Y	Bremen	New York	11/04/1881	05/25/1888			Y	
Mueller, Philip	44	Germany	Y	Hamburg	New York	12/23/1868	12/06/1887			Y	
Mueller, Philip	60	Germany	N	Havre	New York	08/??/1850	?			Y	
Mueller, Philipp	26	Bavaria	Y	Havre	New York	09/??/1850	01/06/1853	5	527	N	
Mueller, Phillip	56	Austria	Y	Hamburg	New York	08/13/1880	05/28/1895			Y	
Mueller, Reinhard	50	Germany	N	Bremen	Baltimore	09/29/1869	?			Y	
Mueller, Rudolf	52	Switzerland	N	Havre	New York	05/??/1857	?			Y	
Mueller, Rudolph B.	31	Germany	Y	Hamburg	Philadelphia	10/28/1882	11/01/1886			Y	
Mueller, Sebastian	28	Baden	Y	Havre	New York	08/19/1847	01/23/1849	1	503	N	
Mueller, Sebastian	39	Germany	N	Bremen	New York	06/18/1876	?			Y	
Mueller, Theodore	25	Germany	Y	Bremen	New York	07/13/1889	05/26/1890			Y	
Mueller, Tobias	32	Wurttemberg	Y	Antwerp	New York	09/21/1852	10/19/1857	15	459	N	
Mueller, Victor	17	France	Y	?	?	?	??/??/1869			Y	
Mueller, William	21	Hanover	Y	Bremen	New York	04/30/1851	04/24/1854	8	244	N	
Mueller, William	24	Germany	Y	Liverpool	New York	07/30/1895	11/10/1897			Y	
Muench, Conrad	16	Germany	N	?	Baltimore	00/00/1880				Y	10/27/1888
Muench, Gus W.	22	Germany	Y	Bremen	New York	04/18/1884	10/19/1888			Y	
Muennich, George	33	Germany	Y	Antwerp	New York	11/13/1881	05/10/1888			Y	
Muermann, Ernst	25	Prussia	Y	Bremen	New Orleans	01/06/1846	09/09/1848	22	316	N	
Muess, John Henry	27	Hanover	Y	Bremen	Baltimore	11/01/1848	03/24/1851	3	318	N	
Muff, Henry	26	Germany	Y	Antwerp	Philadelphia	09/11/1880	12/31/1885			Y	
Muffy, Daniel	28	Ireland	Y	Waxford	Buffalo	06/28/1854	04/03/1858	16	489	N	
Mugel, George	37	Germany	Y	Havre	New York	05/18/1886	10/03/1891			Y	
Muggenberg, John Henry	29	Oldenburg	Y	Bremen	New Orleans	01/08/1855	02/08/1858	16	87	N	
Muglach, Joseph	43	Austria	Y	Boulogna	New Orleans	06/03/1890	10/09/1895	21	81	N	
Muhlebach, John	??	Switzerland	Y	?	New York	02/??/1882	10/30/1884			Y	
Muhlemann, John	28	Switzerland	Y	Havre	New York	05/24/1885	06/15/1888			Y	
Muhlenpah, Henry	24	Germany	Y	Bremen	New York	11/15/1880	05/25/1886			Y	
Muhlhauser, Johannes	??	Germany	Y	?	?	?	12/23/1889			Y	
Muhling, Joachim	23	Baden	Y	Havre	New Orleans	05/16/1852	12/24/1855	13	340	N	
Muhr, Julius	22	Prussia	Y	Bremen	Boston	04/28/1857	07/25/1860	27	237	N	
Muhrlein, Conrad	28	Bavaria	Y	Havre	New York	03/04/1851	05/29/1854	9	439	N	
Muhrmann, Peter	34	Prussia	Y	Rotterdam	New Orleans	01/29/1847	01/28/1850	2	11	N	
Muir, Archibald	32	Scotland	Y	Glasgow	New York	04/01/1887	01/04/1888			Y	
Muirden, James	26	Scotland	Y	Glasgow	New York	06/28/1886	12/11/1889			Y	
Mulcahy, Dennis	46	Ireland	N	Liverpool	New York	??/??/1860	?			Y	
Mulcahy, Thomas	46	Ireland	Y	Queenstown	New York	10/01/1867	10/15/1890			Y	

CITIZENSHIP RECORDS

APPLICANT	AGE	COUNTRY OF ORIGIN	DEC	DEPART PORT	ENTRY PORT	ARRIVE DATE	DEC DATE	VOL	PG.	FLD	NAT DATE
Mulcahy, William	76	Ireland	N	Queenstown	Eastport ME	??/??/1832	??/??/1835	28	148	N	??/??/1837
Mulcahy, William	20	Ireland	N	Queenstown	East Port Ma	00/00/1832	00/00/1835			Y	00/00/1837
Mulder, Nicholas B.	30	Germany	Y	Hamburg	New York	09/17/1880	10/18/1888	19	155	N	
Mulder, Nicholas B.	30	Germany	Y	Hamburg	New York	09/17/1880	10/19/1888			Y	
Muldoon, Edmond	28	Ireland	Y	Liverpool	New York	11/13/1884	11/01/1889	19	273	N	
Mulfinger, August	33	Germany	Y	Hamburg	New York	06/24/1870	07/03/1880			Y	
Mulhall, James	37	Ireland	Y	Queenstown	New York	05/??/1871	03/26/1884			Y	
Mulheran, Michael	22	Ireland	Y	Liverpool	New Orleans	03/07/1851	12/28/1852	5	459	N	
Mulholland, Robert	46	Ireland	Y	Londonderry	Boston	08/07/1848	04/17/1852	24	520	N	
Mulholland, William	27	Ireland	Y	Liverpool	New York	05/20/1873	03/23/1881			Y	
Mulholland, William	45	Ireland	Y	Liverpool	New Orleans	11/26/1852	03/04/1856	26	162	N	
Mulkehy, Thomas	25	Ireland	Y	Liverpool	New York	??/15/1847	10/23/1851	4	383	N	
Mullagan, Patrick	27	Ireland	Y	Coburg	Buffalo	05/03/1849	02/01/1853	7	99	N	
Mullally, Roger	26	Ireland	Y	Liverpool	New York	05/25/1848	09/08/1852	25	417	N	
Mullana, James	30	Ireland	Y	Liverpool	Quebeck	07/08/1849	10/04/1858	17	56	N	
Mullany, James	24	Ireland	Y	Dublin	New York	04/28/1879	10/06/1884			Y	
Mullarkey, John I.	30	England	Y	Liverpool	New York	04/23/1880	04/16/1886			Y	
Mullen, Bartley	17	Ireland	N	Liverpool	New York	05/09/1858				Y	10/01/1875
Mullen, James	23	Ireland	Y	Liverpool	Portland	07/??/1844	10/24/1851	4	392	N	
Mullen, Luke	44	Ireland	N	Queenstown	New York	07/05/1872	?			Y	
Mullen, Thomas	27	Ireland	Y	Liverpool	Boston	04/03/1846	11/06/1852	5	227	N	
Mullen, Thomas	27	Ireland	Y	Liverpool	Boston	04/03/1846	11/05/1852	6	353	N	
Mullen, Thomas	36	Ireland	Y	Queenstown	New York	06/04/1886	11/23/1889			Y	
Mullenger, George	44	England	N	London	New York	04/??/1856	?			Y	
Muller, Adam	33	Baden	Y	Havre	New York	08/08/8154	12/26/1859	17	516	N	
Muller, Adam	72	Germany	N	Bremen	New Orleans	06/??/1842	?			Y	
Muller, Andrew	25	Bavaria	Y	Wurms	New York	05/01/1860	01/25/1861	18	69	N	
Muller, Antoine	38	Germany	Y	Havre	New York	08/27/1892	07/12/1895			Y	
Muller, Anton	29	Germany	Y	Bremen	New York	09/17/1881	10/17/1889			Y	
Muller, August	34	Germany	Y	Glascow	New York	05/09/1900	09/10/1904			Y	
Muller, Benjamin	??	Germany	N	?	?	08/23/1884				Y	10/28/1892
Muller, Bernard	35	Hanover	Y	Bremen	New York	06/05/1853	04/17/1854	9	43	N	
Muller, Casper	30	Bavaria	Y	London	New York	09/01/1853	09/29/1856	14	20	N	
Muller, Charles	28	Germany	Y	Antwerp	New York	11/16/1872	04/09/1877			Y	
Muller, Charles	29	Mecklenburg S	Y	Hamburg	New York	06/27/1852	09/13/1852	25	487	N	
Muller, Christ.	30	Germany	Y	Bremen	Baltimore	03/28/1883	05/22/1889			Y	
Muller, Constantine	38	Nassau	Y	Bremen	New York	09/09/1848	10/09/1860	27	468	N	
Muller, Edward	34	Prussia	Y	Liverpool	New York	06/01/1850	06/06/1854	10	99	N	
Muller, Edward	30	Prussia	Y	Liverpool	New York	07/12/1850	06/06/1854	12	36	N	
Muller, Ernst	27	Germany	Y	Rotterdam	New York	10/01/1882	11/16/1885			Y	
Muller, Franz	27	Prussia	Y	Bremen	New York	04/27/1854	01/18/1856	13	481	N	
Muller, Fred	28	Germany	Y	Bremen	Baltimore	04/08/1876	05/19/1881			Y	
Muller, Fritz	25	Germany	Y	Rotterdam	New York	03/10/1882	01/09/1883			Y	
Muller, Gerhard Henry	57	Germany	Y	Bremen	New York	11/01/1870	05/08/1878			Y	
Muller, Gottfried	41	Bavaria	Y	Havre	New Orleans	11/04/1853	06/05/1861	18	185	N	
Muller, Henry	36	Hanover	Y	Bremen	New Orleans	12/31/1850	04/17/1854	9	45	N	
Muller, Henry	27	Wurttemberg	Y	Havre	New Orleans	05/01/1854	06/05/1854	10	92	N	
Muller, Henry	27	Wurttemberg	Y	Havre	New Orleans	05/01/1854	06/05/1854	12	29	N	
Muller, Henry	25	Hesse Darmsta	Y	Havre	New York	06/02/1853	09/30/1856	14	71	N	
Muller, Henry (Mueller)	??	Germany	Y	?	?	?	04/04/1892			Y	
Muller, Henry Conrad	24	Furstindon Lu	Y	Bremen	Philadelphia	05/10/1847	10/02/1848	1	19	N	
Muller, Jacob	30	Hesse Cassel	Y	Bremen	New York	05/05/1849	06/13/1854	12	62	N	
Muller, Johann	45	Germany	Y	Bremen	New York	05/23/1873	10/25/1889			Y	
Muller, John	30	Baden	Y	Rotterdam	New York	06/10/1851	11/13/1855	13	220	N	
Muller, John	28	Switzerland	Y	Havre	New York	12/02/1854	11/05/1860	18	18	N	
Muller, John	29	Germany	Y	Bremen	Baltimore	04/29/1881	08/21/1888			Y	
Muller, John George	35	Baden	Y	Havre	New York	09/01/1852	12/04/1855	13	288	N	
Muller, John H.	??	Prussia	Y	Havre	New York	09/14/1853	06/27/1860	27	11	N	
Muller, Joseph	34	France	Y	Havre	New York	06/03/1849	11/01/1852	5	93	N	

CITIZENSHIP RECORDS

APPLICANT	AGE	COUNTRY OF ORIGIN	DEC	DEPART PORT	ENTRY PORT	ARRIVE DATE	DEC DATE	VOL	PG.	FLD	NAT DATE
Muller, Joseph	36	Germany	Y	Hamburg	New York	05/28/1881	06/13/1881			Y	
Muller, Karl	22	Germany	Y	Bremen	New York	05/19/1876	03/18/1881			Y	
Muller, Leopold	33	Germany	Y	Havre	New York	10/23/1882	05/20/1883			Y	
Muller, Lewis	40	Prussia	Y	London	New York	09/25/1853	05/01/1854	9	202	N	
Muller, Louis Phillip	37	Holland	Y	Amsterdam	New York	08/10/1849	07/03/1851	3	471	N	
Muller, Michael	17	Austria	N	?	New York	00/00/1876				Y	08/14/1888
Muller, Nickolaus	27	Bavaria	Y	Havre	New York	08/28/1855	09/28/1860	27	383	N	
Muller, Peter	34	Ireland	Y	Liverpool	New York	06/15/1868	10/06/1882			Y	
Muller, Reinhart	34	Saxe Meininge	Y	Bremen	Baltimore	09/29/1868	09/20/1872	18	522	N	
Muller, Sebastian	29	Baden	Y	London	New York	06/17/1853	12/06/1855	13	292	N	
Muller, Simon	26	Germany	Y	Rotterdam	New York	03/25/1881	05/02/1883			Y	
Muller, Theodore	53	Germany	Y	Bremen	New York	06/04/1880	12/22/1881			Y	
Muller, Thomas	30	Ireland	Y	Queenstown	New York	06/04/1886	11/23/1889	19	279	N	
Muller, Thomas	21	Ireland	Y	Liverpool	New York	05/01/1882	10/08/1883			Y	
Muller, William	21	Hanover	Y	Bremen	New York	04/30/1851	04/24/1854	9	115	N	
Muller, Willie	16	Germany	N	?	New York	00/00/1883				Y	10/27/1888
Mulligan, James A.	??	Ireland	Y	?	?	?	10/31/1899			Y	
Mulligan, Mathias	29	Ireland	Y	Dublin	New Orleans	03/10/1849	03/15/1852	24	300	N	
Mulligan, Michael	35	Ireland	Y	Dublin	New York	05/03/1841	10/21/1851	4	361	N	
Mulligan, Patrick		Pages missing	N				9/21/1854?	10	139	N	
Mulligan, Patrick	36	Ireland	Y	Liverpool	New Orleans	05/11/1847	09/21/1854	12	78	N	
Mulligan, Thomas	30	Ireland	Y	Liverpool	New York	03/23/1847	03/08/1853	7	313	N	
Mulligan, Timothy	29	Ireland	N	Liverpool	New York	03/28/1867	?			Y	
Mullin, James	23	Ireland	Y	Liverpool	New York	09/15/1850	10/09/1854	6	125	N	
Mullin, James	23	Ireland	Y	Liverpool	New York	09/15/1850	10/09/1854	11	127	N	
Mullins, Con	23	Ireland	Y	Coforth	Boston	05/18/1851	10/09/1854	6	123	N	
Mullins, Con	23	Ireland	Y	Coforth	Boston	05/18/1851	10/09/1854	11	126	N	
Mullins, John	28	Ireland	Y	Limerick	?	05/16/1850	09/28/1858	16	110	N	
Mullowney, Michael	35	Ireland	Y	Liverpool	New Orleans	01/01/1851	01/22/1856	13	493	N	
Mulloy, Patrick	30	Ireland	Y	Sligo	New York	06/09/1849	01/20/1852	24	41	N	
Mullur, John	21	Baden	Y	Havre	New York	05/05/1858	08/06/1860	27	250	N	
Muloany, Edward	28	Ireland	Y	Liverpool	New Orleans	04/12/1846	10/16/1851	4	302	N	
Mulryan, Thomas	26	Ireland	Y	Liverpool	Baltimore	05/30/1881	10/23/1886	19	73	N	
Mulryan, Thomas	26	Ireland	Y	Liverpool	Baltimore	05/03/1881	10/23/1886			Y	
Mulvaney, James	28	Ireland	Y	Liverpool	Philadelphia	06/29/1890	08/06/1895			Y	
Mulvey, Thomas	23	Ireland	Y	Sligo	New York	04/01/1847	09/28/1854	10	292	N	
Mulvey, Thomas	23	Ireland	Y	Sligo	New York	04/01/1847	09/28/1854	12	231	N	
Mulvihill, John	25	Ireland	Y	Liverpool	New York	06/23/1848	01/19/1849	1	468	N	
Mulvihill, Roger	17	Ireland	N	?	New York	00/00/1881				Y	10/20/1887
Mulvihill, William	25	Ireland	Y	Liverpool	New York	06/23/1848	01/19/1849	1	469	N	
Mulville, Alexander	26	Ireland	Y	Limerick	Whitehall	07/04/1845	08/02/1851	4	74	N	
Mulvy, Charles	40	Ireland	Y	Liverpool	New York	06/11/1883	09/15/1884			Y	
Mumm, Michael	23	Hesse Darmsta	Y	Liverpool	New York	03/29/1852	04/03/1856	26	422	N	
Muncey, William	28	England	Y	London	New York	04/25/1851	04/18/1854	8	205	N	
Muncey, William	28	England	Y	London	New York	04/25/1851	04/18/1854	9	76	N	
Munchhausen, Marks	23	Prussia	Y	Bremen	Baltimore	10/12/1845	03/25/1850	2	259	N	
Munck, Jacob	29	Prussia	Y	Bremen	New York	06/26/1846	01/12/1849	1	402	N	
Mund, Conrad	28	Hanover	Y	Bremen	New Orleans	06/28/1844	01/13/1851	2	486	N	
Mund, Herman	43	Hanover	Y	Bremen	New Orleans	05/18/1850	03/23/1858	16	439	N	
Mund, Ludwig	33	Hamburg	Y	Hamburg	New York	01/10/1854	05/01/1854	9	211	N	
Munder, Henry	32	Brunswick	Y	Hamburg	New York	06/28/1853	10/09/1854	6	90	N	
Munder, Henry	32	Brunswick	Y	Hamburg	New York	06/28/1853	10/09/1854	11	92	N	
Mundi, Gustav	31	Germany	Y	Bremen	New York	06/03/1887	03/06/1893			Y	
Mundrug, Henry	21	Prussia	Y	Bremen	Baltimore	09/15/1856	07/31/1858	16	544	N	
Mundt, Bernard	25	Germany	Y	Bremen	New York	04/30/1881	03/05/1883			Y	
Mundt, Ludwig	33	Hamburg	Y	Hamburg	New York	01/10/1854	05/01/1854	8	338	N	
Mungovin, John	46	Ireland	Y	Liverpool	New Orleans	12/25/1848	03/07/1853	7	286	N	
Mungovin, Peter	24	Ireland	Y	Liverpool	New York	08/09/1849	03/05/1853	7	277	N	
Munich, Frank	32	Baden	Y	Havre	New York	08/01/1846	01/13/1849	1	412	N	

CITIZENSHIP RECORDS

APPLICANT	AGE	COUNTRY OF ORIGIN	DEC	DEPART PORT	ENTRY PORT	ARRIVE DATE	DEC DATE	VOL	PG.	FLD	NAT DATE
Munro, Alexander	25	Scotland	Y	Glasgow	New York	10/01/1851	10/04/1854	12	348	N	
Munro, Alexander K.	25	Scotland	Y	Glasgow	New York	10/01/1851	10/04/1854	10	409	N	
Munro, Willis C.	32	Canada	Y	Sarnia	Port Huron	07/??/1870	10/04/1882			Y	
Munsch, Victor	25	Germany	Y	Antwerp	New York	06/28/1884	08/15/1890			Y	
Munsh, George	23	France	Y	Havre	New Orleans	05/08/1850	11/03/1852	5	207	N	
Munsh, George	23	France	Y	Havre	New Orleans	05/08/1850	11/03/1852	6	333	N	
Munsinger, Adam	42	Bavaria	N	Havre	New York	??/??/1865	?			Y	
Munt, Thomas Herbert	35	England	Y	London	New York	08/22/1880	11/12/1895			Y	
Muntel, Gerhard Herman	29	Hanover	Y	Rotterdam	New Orleans	06/01/1849	01/23/1856	13	498	N	
Muntel, Gerhard John	30	Hanover	Y	Rotterdam	New Orleans	06/01/1859	01/26/1856	13	509	N	
Munter, Carl Friedrich	24	Prussia	Y	Bremen	New York	11/??/1849	11/01/1851	4	448	N	
Munz, George	32	Germany	Y	Rotterdam	New York	06/04/1881	11/13/1886			Y	
Murdia, Edward	35	Ireland	Y	?	New York	??/??/1872	03/05/1885			Y	
Mure, John	27	France	Y	Havre	New York	04/10/1854	02/28/1856	26	138	N	
Murley, James	24	Ireland	Y	Liverpool	New York	10/05/1851	11/19/1852	5	312	N	
Murphy, Charles	50	Ireland	Y	Liverpool	New Orleans	03/03/1850	02/21/1853	7	210	N	
Murphy, Daniel	28	Ireland	Y	Liverpool	New York	04/01/1847	04/04/1853	8	17	N	
Murphy, Daniel	25	Ireland	Y	Liverpool	New Orleans	04/06/1849	12/26/1851	24	9	N	
Murphy, Daniel	22	Ireland	Y	Liverpool	New York	03/08/1849	06/17/1852	25	282	N	
Murphy, Daniel	17	Ireland	N	?	New York	00/00/1881				Y	10/02/1888
Murphy, Dennis	24	Ireland	Y	Liverpool	New York	08/24/1849	07/21/1851	4	16	N	
Murphy, Dennis	26	Ireland	Y	Cork	New York	02/??/1850	12/24/1855	13	345	N	
Murphy, Dennis	25	Ireland	Y	Queenstown	New York	04/18/1870	10/04/1875			Y	
Murphy, Dennis	66	Ireland	Y	Liverpool	New Orleans	03/00/1851	10/00/1856			Y	
Murphy, Edmund	??	?	Y	Liverpool	New Orleans	??/27/1847	12/??/1850	2	415	N	
Murphy, Edward	25	Ireland	Y	Waterford	New York	06/01/1849	10/21/1851	4	367	N	
Murphy, Edward	33	Ireland	Y	Queenstown	New York	06/11/1880	10/28/1880			Y	
Murphy, Edward	67	Ireland	N	Liverpool	New York	09/??/1849	?			Y	
Murphy, Eugene	40	Ireland	Y	Liverpool	New Orleans	02/08/1851	07/31/1851	4	63	N	
Murphy, Henry	58	Ireland	Y	Belfast	New York	04/09/1878	10/18/1888	19	153	N	
Murphy, James	28	England	Y	Liverpool	New York	07/30/1891	08/28/1894			Y	
Murphy, James	58	Ireland	N	Liverpool	New York	07/13/1853	?			Y	
Murphy, James	30	Ireland	Y	Liverpool	New York	10/01/1848	01/09/1850	23	488	N	
Murphy, James	45	Ireland	Y	Liverpool	Philadelphia	07/04/1849	09/07/1852	25	403	N	
Murphy, James	24	Ireland	Y	Liverpool	Philadelphia	07/04/1850	02/19/1856	26	103	N	
Murphy, Jeremiah	26	Ireland	Y	Liverpool	New York	12/10/1848	08/12/1851	4	123	N	
Murphy, Jeremiah	36	Ireland	Y	Limerick	Detroit	12/23/1859	02/08/1860	27	94	N	
Murphy, Jerry	25	Ireland	Y	Liverpool	New York	11/20/1849	10/14/1851	4	282	N	
Murphy, John	28	Ireland	Y	Liverpool	New York	07/08/1852	11/19/1852	5	314	N	
Murphy, John	28	Ireland	Y	Waterford	New York	07/01/1848	05/04/1854	8	369	N	
Murphy, John	28	Ireland	Y	Waterford	New York	07/01/1848	05/04/1854	9	243	N	
Murphy, Martin	32	England	Y	Liverpool	Boston	05/22/1875	09/07/1885			Y	
Murphy, Matthew	27	Ireland	Y	Glasgow	New York	12/08/1848	05/10/1854	8	413	N	
Murphy, Matthew	27	Ireland	Y	Glasgow	New York	12/08/1848	05/10/1854	9	286	N	
Murphy, Michael	23	Ireland	Y	Liverpool	Buffalo	07/29/1844	02/28/1851	3	181	N	
Murphy, Michael	27	Ireland	Y	Liverpool	New Orleans	02/14/1851	02/10/1852	24	82	N	
Murphy, Miles	23	Ireland	Y	Dublin	New York	04/18/1887	03/16/1892			Y	
Murphy, Patrick	22	Ireland	Y	Youghal	Rutland	06/28/1852	04/17/1854	8	154	N	
Murphy, Patrick	22	Ireland	Y	Youghal	Rutland	06/28/1852	04/17/1854	9	25	N	
Murphy, Patrick	33	Ireland	Y	Liverpool	New York	06/04/1881	05/08/1888			Y	
Murphy, Patrick	40	Ireland	Y	Queenstown	New York	??/??/1872	09/04/1882			Y	
Murphy, Patrick	17	Ireland	N	?	Detroit	00/00/1881				Y	08/11/1888
Murphy, Thomas	26	Ireland	Y	Liverpool	New Orleans	12/17/1849	08/04/1851	4	78	N	
Murphy, Thomas	31	Ireland	Y	Liverpool	New York	05/28/1842	11/15/1852	5	281	N	
Murphy, Thomas	31	Ireland	Y	Liverpool	New York	05/28/1842	11/15/1852	6	405	N	
Murphy, Thomas	28	Ireland	Y	London	New York	05/??/1851	06/03/1854	9	475	N	
Murphy, Thomas	28	Ireland	Y	London	New York	05/??/1851	06/03/1854	10	58	N	
Murphy, Thomas	27	Ireland	Y	Liverpool	New York	12/25/1849	08/04/1856	14	340	N	
Murphy, Thomas	29	Ireland	Y	Queenstown	Boston	95/22/1877	05/12/1882			Y	

CITIZENSHIP RECORDS

APPLICANT	AGE	COUNTRY OF ORIGIN	DEC	DEPART PORT	ENTRY PORT	ARRIVE DATE	DEC DATE	VOL	PG.	FLD	NAT DATE
Murphy, Thomas	44	Ireland	N	Queenstown	New York	05/??/1867	?			Y	
Murphy, Thomas	35	Ireland	Y	Liverpool	New York	06/15/1846	06/04/1852	25	190	N	
Murphy, Thomas	21	Ireland	Y	Queenstown	New York	06/29/1883	07/08/1886			Y	
Murphy, Timothy	22	Ireland	Y	?	Boston	04/02/1869	07/05/1867			Y	
Murphy, William	38	Ireland	Y	Liverpool	New York	05/05/1846	10/22/1851	4	375	N	
Murphy, William	31	Ireland	Y	Dublin	New York	12/05/1847	01/01/1853	5	488	N	
Murphy, William	24	Ireland	Y	Liverpool	New Orleans	02/??/1852	03/28/1853	7	451	N	
Murphy, William	21	Ireland	Y	Liverpool	New York	07/26/1855	01/27/1857	14	509	N	
Murphy, William	27	Ireland	Y	Canada	Portland	05/16/1848	02/16/1852	24	123	N	
Murr, August K. H.	21	Germany	Y	?	?	10/01/1885	10/03/1888			Y	
Murray, Annie	40	Scotland	Y	Glasgow	New York	11/03/1886	06/23/1892			Y	
Murray, Bartholomew	33	Ireland	Y	Liverpool	New Orleans	07/26/1847	11/02/1852	5	185	N	
Murray, Bartholomew	33	Ireland	Y	Liverpool	New Orleans	07/26/1847	11/01/1852	6	311	N	
Murray, Daniel	39	Ireland	Y	Liverpool	New York	04/??/1848	01/01/1861	18	39	N	
Murray, David	??	Ireland	Y	?	?	?	09/29/1885			Y	
Murray, Edward	30	Ireland	Y	Liverpool	New York	06/26/1846	11/17/1848	1	314	N	
Murray, Eugene	59	Ireland	N	Liverpool	New Orleans	07/06/1851	?			Y	
Murray, Hugh W.	29	Ireland	Y	Liverpool	New York	05/30/1845	10/30/1852	5	79	N	
Murray, James	26	Ireland	Y	Liverpool	Philadelphia	07/07/1846	09/08/1852	25	416	N	
Murray, James	??	Ireland	N	?	?	10/16/1887				Y	11/04/1892
Murray, John	38	Scotland	Y	London	New York	04/07/1849	10/07/1854	5	23	N	
Murray, John	28	Ireland	Y	Liverpool	New York	05/17/1851	06/08/1854	10	103	N	
Murray, John	26	Ireland	Y	Liverpool	New Orleans	12/10/1853	10/06/1854	10	506	N	
Murray, John	38	Scotland	Y	London	New York	04/07/1849	10/07/1854	11	24	N	
Murray, John	28	Ireland	Y	Liverpool	New York	05/17/1851	06/08/1854	12	40	N	
Murray, John	26	Ireland	Y	Liverpool	New Orleans	12/10/1853	10/06/1854	12	445	N	
Murray, John	44	Ireland	Y	Liverpool	New York	11/21/1882	03/07/1892			Y	
Murray, John	24	Ireland	Y	Westport	Buffalo	11/15/1850	03/27/1856	26	362	N	
Murray, John	39	Ireland	Y	Liverpool	New York	08/27/1857	08/23/1860	27	311	N	
Murray, John	56	Ireland	N	Liverpool	New Orleans	07/??/1848	07/18/1849	28	74	N	08/??/1861
Murray, John	16	Ireland	N	Liverpool	New Orleans	07/00/1848	07/18/1849			Y	08/00/1861
Murray, John W.	66	Ireland	N	Ireland	New York	08/??/1857	?			Y	
Murray, Martin	70	Ireland	N	Galway	St. John's	??/??/1850	?			Y	
Murray, Michael	34	Ireland	Y	Liverpool	New Orleans	06/27/1848	07/03/1851	3	479	N	
Murray, Michael	??	England	Y	?	?	?	07/14/1884			Y	
Murray, Patrick	26	Ireland	Y	Liverpool	New York	04/05/1848	08/11/1851	4	113	N	
Murray, Patrick	32	Ireland	Y	Liverpool	New York	04/11/1846	12/27/1852	5	446	N	
Murray, Patrick	25	Ireland	Y	Dublin	New Orleans	12/24/1848	01/01/1853	5	489	N	
Murray, Richard	45	Ireland	Y	Liverpool	New York	06/13/1870	12/31/1892			Y	
Murray, Thomas	??	Ireland	N	?	?	10/16/1887				Y	11/04/1892
Murren, Thomas	21	Ireland	Y	Liverpool	New York	08/12/1854	06/29/1857	15	115	N	
Murrin, Maurice	40	Ireland	Y	Liverpool	New York	04/11/1852	11/24/1857	16	47	N	
Murry, Joseph	30	Ireland	Y	Liverpool	New York	06/10/1853	10/08/1857	15	379	N	
Murry, Martin	40	Ireland	Y	Galway	Burlington	08/16/1847	09/29/1858	17	23	N	
Muschal, Nicolaus	39	Hohenzollern	Y	Havre	New Orleans	01/17/1854	10/25/1855	13	139	N	
Muschler, Peter	21	Bavaria	Y	Havre	New Orleans	11/15/1852	01/02/1856	13	415	N	
Muschmann, Joseph Philli	48	Prussia	Y	Bremen	New Orleans	06/02/1847	09/07/1848	22	307	N	
Musen, Philip	36	Austria	Y	Bremen	New York	07/15/1888	03/28/1891			Y	
Muth, Henry	26	Germany	Y	Bremen	New York	07/12/1880	04/22/1886			Y	
Muth, Jacob	25	Baden	Y	Antwerp	New York	09/29/1850	02/25/1852	24	169	N	
Muth, Joseph	36	Germany	Y	Bremen	New York	10/17/1880	10/22/1886	19	67	N	
Mutschler, Adolf	14	Germany	N	?	New York	00/00/1880				Y	03/21/1887
Mutschler, Joseph	39	Baden	Y	Bremen	New Orleans	01/20/1846	11/07/1855	13	181	N	
Mutter, Pierra	37	Prussia	Y	Havre	New York	08/15/1852	11/23/1852	5	330	N	
Mutz, John	44	Hungary	Y	Bremen	Baltimore	04/08/1893	07/15/1896			Y	
Mutzbauer, Thomas	57	Germany	Y	Bremen	New York	08/24/1872	08/24/1873			Y	
Myer, Casper	35	Germany	Y	Antwerp	New York	12/29/1891	10/18/1899			Y	
Myer, George	53	Germany	N	Bremen	Baltimore	05/??/1846	?			Y	
Myers, Joseph	34	Bavaria	Y	Havre	New Orleans	02/04/1846	01/11/1849	1	396	N	

CITIZENSHIP RECORDS

APPLICANT	AGE	COUNTRY OF ORIGIN	DEC	DEPART PORT	ENTRY PORT	ARRIVE DATE	DEC DATE	VOL	PG.	FLD	NAT DATE
Naas, Alfred	23	Germany	Y	Bremen	New York	06/03/1893	04/14/1897			Y	
Naber, Aloysius	23	Germany	Y	Amsterdam	New York	05/01/1881	10/24/1882			Y	
Naber, Andrew	23	Oldenburg	Y	Bremen	New Orleans	10/01/1852	07/13/1855	11	380	N	
Naber, B.	40	Germany	Y	Bremen	Baltimore	05/16/1873	10/15/1883			Y	
Naber, Bernhard	28	Oldenburg	Y	Bremen	Baltimore	08/13/1845	10/05/1854	10	432	N	
Naber, Bernhard	28	Oldenburg	Y	Bremen	Baltimore	08/13/1845	10/05/1854	12	371	N	
Naber, Henry	38	Germany	Y	Hamburg	Baltimore	12/01/1895	03/24/1900			Y	
Naber, John	37	Germany	Y	Bremen	Baltimore	04/19/1890	10/16/1900			Y	
Naber, William	28	Oldenburg	Y	Bremen	New York	11/10/1848	01/17/1853	7	36	N	
Naberhaus, Henry	23	Germany	Y	Bremen	New York	09/29/1889	04/26/1893			Y	
Naberhaus, Joseph	28	Germany	Y	Bremen	Baltimore	03/12/1879	09/01/1887			Y	
Nachtmann, Anton	33	Austria	Y	Hamburg	New York	05/12/1882	01/08/1885			Y	
Nack, John	??	Germany	Y	?	?	?	01/26/1885			Y	
Nacke, Henry	29	Germany	Y	Bremen	Baltimore	03/05/1881	01/06/1885			Y	
Nadelman, Sam	40	Russia	Y	Bremen	Baltimore	07/29/1892	12/08/1899			Y	
Naden, Henry	??	Ireland	Y	Liverpool	New Orleans	??/15/1849	03/25/1851	3	352	N	
Nadermann, Albert	34	Hanover	Y	Bremen	New Orleans	11/12/1854	09/27/1858	16	120	N	
Nadermann, Casper (Cehra	32	Hanover	Y	Bremen	Baltimore	05/21/1848	06/19/1851	3	406	N	
Nadermann, Henry	55	Hanover	Y	Bremen	Baltimore	11/03/1849	11/02/1858	17	264	N	
Nadler, Ferdinand	37	Austria	Y	Hamburg	New York	06/27/1854	10/09/1854	6	180	N	
Nadler, Ferdinand	37	Austria	Y	Hamburg	New York	06/27/1854	10/09/1854	11	183	N	
Nadler, Franz	29	Austria	Y	Hamburg	New York	06/29/1854	07/23/1855	11	423	N	
Nadler, Kosmos	??	Germany	Y	Havre	New York	03/16/1878	09/29/1885			Y	
Naegele, Herman	21	Germany	Y	Havre	New York	05/27/1880	08/07/1883			Y	
Naegeler, Herbert	37	Luxemburg	Y	Antwerp	New York	11/08/1854	05/22/1856	26	535	N	
Naegle, Frederick	25	Bavaria	Y	Havre	New York	08/31/1846	05/20/1852	25	50	N	
Naetebus, William	27	Prussia	Y	Havre	New York	10/08/1854	10/23/1857	15	482	N	
Naf, Andrew	33	Switzerland	Y	Havre	New York	11/13/1852	12/24/1855	13	352	N	
Naftalen, Mendel	52	Russia	Y	Stettiner	New York	08/??/1885	10/21/1890	19	292	N	
Nagel, Bernard	26	Germany	N	Antwerp	New York	06/24/1881	?			Y	
Nagel, Bernhard	51	Germany	Y	Antwerp	New York	06/23/1881	06/05/1884			Y	
Nagel, Frank	57	Germany	N	Bremen	Baltimore	10/17/1849	?			Y	
Nagel, Frederick Jacob	30	Bavaria	Y	Havre	New York	06/20/1854	02/11/1856	26	71	N	
Nagel, George	15	Germany	N	?	New York	00/00/1882				Y	10/26/1888
Nagel, Henry	33	Wurttemberg	Y	Bremen	New York	01/17/1852	10/09/1854	6	87	N	
Nagel, Henry	33	Wurttemberg	Y	Bremen	New York	01/17/1852	10/09/1854	11	90	N	
Nagel, Konrad	30	Germany	Y	Rotterdam	New York	07/05/1893	01/29/1896			Y	
Nagel, Nicholas	37	Germany	Y	Antwerp	New York	05/25/1887	10/30/1893			Y	
Nagel, Thomas	27	Germany	Y	Bremen	New York	11/30/1887	11/12/1890			Y	
Nagel, Thomas	28	Bavaria	Y	Bremen	Baltimore	06/10/1845	08/24/1848	22	249	N	
Nagel, Tobias	27	Bavaria	Y	Havre	New York	05/27/1857	09/24/1857	15	310	N	
Nagele, Anton	26	Switzerland	Y	?	New York	??/??/1880	03/04/1882			Y	
Nagele, Frank	8	Austria	N	?	New York	00/00/1872				Y	10/26/1888
Nageleisen, Karl	28	Germany	Y	Havre	New York	02/28/1892	10/08/1894			Y	
Nageleisen, Lorenz	39	Baden	Y	Havre	New Orleans	07/05/1847	10/20/1852	5	25	N	
Nagengast, Michael	37	Bavaria	Y	Bremen	New Orleans	06/12/1845	08/16/1848	22	184	N	
Nagg, John William	28	Austria	Y	Vliessengen	New York	05/08/1878	09/22/1882			Y	
Nagle, John	30	Ireland	Y	Galway	Boston	09/12/1848	09/06/1852	25	362	N	
Naglo, Arnold	28	Prussia	Y	Bremen	New York	09/05/1872	02/10/1873	18	554	N	
Nahlbach, Francis Joseph	23	Prussia	Y	Antwerp	New York	04/28/1852	04/08/1856	26	466	N	
Nahm, George	28	Baden	Y	Antwerp	New York	08/??/1849	10/23/1851	4	384	N	
Nahn, William	25	Prussia	Y	Bremen	New Orleans	05/06/1854	03/25/1856	26	346	N	
Nahrup, John	31	Prussia	Y	Bremen	New York	04/07/1859	11/01/1860	27	524	N	
Nahrwold, Diesderich	24	Prussia	Y	Bremen	New York	07/01/1854	09/03/1857	15	223	N	
Nalein, Thomas	43	Ireland	Y	Canada	Buffalo	10/04/1846	02/07/1849	23	131	N	
Namur, Emile	40	France	Y	?	?	01/10/1894	02/04/1896			Y	
Nangle, James	25	Ireland	Y	Liverpool	New Orleans	01/12/1851	05/02/1854	8	348	N	
Nanjoks, Herman	40	Germany	Y	Bremen	New York	03/25/1881	08/13/1888			Y	
Napier, Robert	??	Scotland	Y	Glasgow	New York	03/27/1887	10/20/1898			Y	

CITIZENSHIP RECORDS

APPLICANT	AGE	COUNTRY OF ORIGIN	DEC	DEPART PORT	ENTRY PORT	ARRIVE DATE	DEC DATE	VOL	PG.	FLD	NAT DATE
Napolitano, Giacomo	41	Italy	Y	Naples	New York	07/28/1885	11/06/1893	21	50	N	
Napolitano, Giacomo	41	Italy	Y	Naples	New York	07/28/1885	11/06/1893			Y	
Napp, Frederick C.	27	Germany	Y	Bremen	Baltimore	09/22/1881	12/02/1884			Y	
Narbach, Joseph	29	Baden	Y	Havre	New Orleans	05/09/1847	10/02/1856	14	139	N	
Narup, Barnie (Nahrup?)	35	Prussia	Y	Hamburg	New York	05/01/1860	11/01/1860	27	523	N	
Nasemann, August	30	Hanover	Y	Bremen	New York	01/05/1854	08/04/1856	14	323	N	
Nash, Alfred T.	44	England	Y	London	New York	04/05/1874	06/19/1900			Y	
Nassano, Pietro	25	Italy	Y	Havre	New York	08/28/1888	10/28/1893	21	41	N	
Nassano, Pietro A.	25	Italy	Y	Havre	New York	08/28/1888	10/28/1893			Y	
Nast, Jacob	36	Germany	Y	Bremen	Baltimore	04/28/1886	05/28/1886			Y	
Nastold, Eugene	30	Germany	Y	Bremen	New York	06/25/1882	10/07/1887			Y	
Nater, Frederick	32	Prussia	Y	Bremen	New Orleans	10/20/1845	07/05/1851	3	496	N	
Nater, Gottlieb	22	Prussia	Y	Bremen	New Orleans	05/15/1852	09/23/1854	10	186	N	
Nater, Gottlieb	22	Prussia	Y	Bremen	New Orleans	05/15/1852	09/23/1854	12	125	N	
Nathan, ?	??	Bavaria	Y	?	New York	??/30/18??	10/24/1850	2	289	N	
Nathan, Abraham	27	Bavaria	Y	Havre	New Orleans	04/12/1849	02/10/1852	24	90	N	
Nathan, H.	35	Poland	N	Hamburg	New York	03/??/1867	?			Y	
Nathan, Jacob	21	Bavaria	Y	Havre	New Orleans	02/01/1852	10/07/1854	6	44	N	
Nathan, Jacob	21	Bavaria	Y	Havre	New Orleans	02/01/1852	10/07/1854	11	45	N	
Nathan, Marx	32	Baden	Y	Havre	New York	09/22/1853	12/01/1855	13	269	N	
Nation, Frederick W.	52	Canada	Y	Toronto	Buffalo	06/??/1863	09/??/1873	28	352	N	?
Nation, Frederick W.	33	Canada	Y	Toronto	Buffalo, NY	06/00/1863	09/00/1873				
Natter, Milad	40	Arabia	Y	?	?	?	11/02/1896			Y	
Nau, Henry	32	Germany	Y	Bremen	New York	04/01/1881	04/08/1887			Y	
Nau, Michael	28	Germany	Y	Bremen	New York	10/07/1881	04/18/1890			Y	
Nau, Phillip	35	Kurhassen	Y	Bremen	New York	12/17/1846	01/14/1850	23	496	N	
Nau, Valentine	30	Kurhassen	Y	Bremen	Baltimore	11/18/1848	01/??/1850	23	495	N	
Naughtin, Mark	27	Ireland	Y	Galway	New York	10/15/1849	09/30/1854	10	326	N	
Naughtin, Mark	27	Ireland	Y	Galway	New York	10/15/1849	09/30/1854	12	265	N	
Naugle, James	25	Ireland	Y	Liverpool	New Orleans	01/12/1851	05/02/1854	9	221	N	
Naukam, John	27	Baden	Y	Bremen	Baltimore	06/13/1849	11/04/1852	6	347	N	
Nausieda, Anthony	36	Russia	Y	Hamburg	New York	05/01/1885	09/26/1889			Y	
Naylan, Anthony	36	Ireland	Y	Liverpool	New York	09/29/1847	05/20/1852	25	68	N	
Naylor, John Edwin	17	England	N	?	Detroit	00/00/1877				Y	10/24/1887
Naylor, William	??	England	N	?	?	05/00/1874				Y	10/29/1892
Neabauer, George	37	Bavaria	Y	Bremen	Baltimore	07/??/1844	11/??/1849	23	362	N	
Neal, William	50	England	Y	Liverpool	Baltimore	09/01/1886	09/26/1889			Y	
Nealis, Michael	48	Ireland	N	Liverpool	New York	05/18/1857	?			Y	
Nealis, Patrick	58	Ireland	N	Liverpool	New York	12/27/1859	?			Y	
Nealy, Thomas P.	26	Ireland	Y	Queenstown	New York	05/07/1899	04/30/1903			Y	
Near, Dave	??	Russia	N	?	?	05/00/1884				Y	10/22/1892
Nebel, Andy	44	Germany	Y	Havre	New York	09/18/1866	07/31/1891			Y	
Nee, Owen	55	Ireland	Y	Queenstown	New York	06/01/1863	10/30/1897			Y	
Needham, John	45	Ireland	Y	Dublin	New York	09/16/1865	04/07/1890			Y	
Neels, J.F.M.	27	Mecklenburg S	Y	Hamburg	New York	11/15/1854	11/02/1858	17	259	N	
Neely, Abednego Benjamin	36	West India	Y	Nassau	Baltimore	06/22/1872	10/26/1886			Y	
Neely, William	27	Ireland	Y	Liverpool	New York	05/29/1845	02/18/1852	24	137	N	
Neff, Charles	24	Wuerttenberg	Y	London	New York	05/14/1848	03/06/1852	24	251	N	
Neff, Heinrich	24	Bavaria	Y	Bremen	Baltimore	08/06/1851	02/21/1853	7	191	N	
Neff, William	33	Germany	Y	Antwerp	New York	07/01/1882	09/25/1886			Y	
Nehlig, Andrew	??	France	Y	Havre	New Orleans	12/10/1840	10/14/1848	1	233	N	
Nehls, Fredrick	??	Germany	Y	?	New York	10/24/1883	11/03/1884			Y	
Nehr, Kilean	28	Bavaria	Y	Havre	New York	??/10/1846	12/26/1849	23	432	N	
Nehring, John Christian	33	Prussia	Y	Hamburg	New York	10/04/1847	11/22/1848	1	378	N	
Nehrkamp, Bernard Lucas	24	Hanover	Y	Bremen	New Orlean	05/??/1852	04/27/1855	11	325	N	
Neiber, Paul	45	Baden	Y	Bremen	New York	03/03/1857	10/08/1860	27	444	N	
Neidhard, John	33	Germany	Y	Havre	New York	07/13/1889	05/03/1894			Y	
Neightman, Matthew	22	England	Y	Liverpool	New York	07/09/1853	05/02/1854	9	223	N	
Neilan, Patrick	30	Ireland	Y	Liverpool	Boston	08/10/1846	03/11/1850	2	184	N	

CITIZENSHIP RECORDS

APPLICANT	AGE	COUNTRY OF ORIGIN	DEC	DEPART PORT	ENTRY PORT	ARRIVE DATE	DEC DATE	VOL	PG.	FLD	NAT DATE
Neill, John	74	Ireland	Y	Liverpool	New York	08/??/1868	10/30/1884			Y	
Neinert, Charles	26	Germany	Y	Rotterdam	New York	10/17/1884	08/15/1887			Y	
Neis, Nicholas	25	Prussia	Y	Havre	New York	04/05/1850	09/27/1854	10	268	N	
Neis, Nicolaus	25	Prussia	Y	Havre	New York	04/05/1850	09/27/1854	12	207	N	
Neitfeld, Anthony	34	Oldenburg	Y	Bremen	New Orleans	10/27/1846	10/14/1848	1	218	N	
Nelinson, Joseph	27	Russia	Y	Hamburg	Philadelphia	07/02/1888	11/03/1893			Y	
Nelle, Henry	29	Germany	Y	Bremen	New York	06/23/1882	10/26/1886			Y	
Nelling, J. B.	51	Germany	Y	Bremen	New York	03/24/1864	12/18/1883			Y	
Nelsen, William	27	Sweden	Y	Eustadt	New York	09/16/1854	08/26/1857	15	189	N	
Nelson, Andrew	29	Hamburg	Y	Hamburg	Boston	01/16/1850	03/02/1852	24	207	N	
Nelson, Basil	37	Baden	Y	Rotterdam	New York	07/20/1844	11/21/1848	1	363	N	
Nelson, Christian M.	??	Sweden	Y	?	?	?	10/23/1886			Y	
Nelson, Henry	50	Germany	N	Havre	New Orleans	12/12/1860	?			Y	
Nelson, S. P.	44	Denmark	Y	Copenhagen	New York	09/??/1871	11/29/1886			Y	
Nemenger, Joseph	26	Baden	Y	Antwerp	New York	08/27/1848	02/04/1851	3	92	N	
Nenninger, John	34	Baden	Y	Rotterdam	New York	06/16/1846	03/31/1856	26	389	N	
Nepper, Herman	34	Oldenburg	Y	Bremen	New Orleans	05/19/1851	11/01/1852	5	184	N	
Nepper, Herman	34	Oldenburg	Y	Bremen	New Orleans	05/19/1851	11/01/1852	6	310	N	
Nerenberg, Julius	46	Russia	Y	Hamburg	New York	10/05/1890	10/26/1895			Y	
Nerhein, Frederick	25	Mecklenburg S	Y	Hamburg	New York	??/??/1854	04/18/1855	11	268	N	
Nerl, Franz	23	Germany	Y	Bremen	Baltimore	10/06/1883	09/06/1887			Y	
Nerl, Joseph	26	Germany	Y	Hamburg	Boston	06/05/1882	09/01/1887			Y	
Nerpel, Karl	24	Germany	Y	Bremen	New York	06/02/1883	12/26/1885			Y	
Nerreter, John	26	Bavaria	Y	Hamburg	New York	01/02/1855	01/02/1858	16	297	N	
Nerva, Isaac	30	Finland	Y	Liverpool	New York	03/02/1889	10/30/1894			Y	
Nesen, John	25	Hanover	Y	Bremen	Baltimore	05/12/1847	11/13/1848	1	266	N	
Nesselhuf, Alois	35	Germany	Y	Havre	New York	01/10/1881	10/02/1890			Y	
Nester, Martin	21	Ireland	Y	Liverpool	New Orleans	01/20/1847	10/20/1851	4	351	N	
Nestler, Adolph	25	Saxony	Y	Bremen	New Orleans	12/09/1847	03/10/1851	3	268	N	
Nestler, Bernhardt Oswal	32	Germany	Y	Bremen	Baltimore	09/18/1880	02/08/1889			Y	
Nett, Jacob	36	Germany	Y	Antwerp	New York	07/26/1883	09/26/1891			Y	
Neu, Adolph	32	Bavaria	Y	Havre	New York	03/30/1852	09/08/1857	15	245	N	
Neu, Michael	40	Germany	Y	Bremen	New York	11/18/1870	10/15/1890			Y	
Neu, William	??	Germany	Y	?	New York	03/??/1881	11/01/1884			Y	
Neubacher, F.	43	Austria	N	Bremen	New York	12/??/1849	?			Y	
Neubauer, Adolf	27	Austria	Y	?	?	?	10/11/1879			Y	
Neubauer, William	40	Germany	Y	Bremen	New York	11/19/1882	06/18/1883			Y	
Neubert, Robert	29	Germany	Y	Amsterdam	New York	02/24/1882	04/01/1886			Y	
Neuenkirchen, George	27	Germany	Y	Bremen	Baltimore	09/07/1883	09/17/1888			Y	
Neuer, Imen	28	Russia	Y	Bremen	Baltimore	03/30/1887	08/22/1891			Y	
Neuer, Valentine	26	Hesse Darmsta	Y	Antwerp	New York	10/21/1848	02/25/1852	24	167	N	
Neugebauer, Charles	37	Germany	Y	Bremen	New York	02/16/1868	10/11/1880			Y	
Neuhaus, William	37	Germany	Y	Antwerp	New York	09/07/1883	10/15/1888			Y	
Neukam, Anton	23	Wurttemberg	Y	Havre	New York	10/27/1854	07/24/1857	15	129	N	
Neukam, George	21	Bavaria	Y	Bremen	New Orleans	06/12/1853	07/10/1856	14	304	N	
Neukam, John	27	Baden	Y	Bremen	Baltimore	06/13/1849	11/04/1852	5	221	N	
Neukam, John	32	Bavaria	Y	Bremen	Philadelphia	12/27/1844	09/15/1852	25	516	N	
Neukom, Conrad	52	Switzerland	Y	Havre	New York	12/01/1873	02/13/1892			Y	
Neulander, David	??	?	Y	?	?	?	01/03/1887			Y	
Neuls, Adam	22	Prussia	Y	Antwerp	New York	08/03/1855	09/22/1858	16	151	N	
Neumaier, Joseph	31	Germany	Y	Havre	New York	10/13/1881	10/20/1887			Y	
Neumaier, Sigmund	32	Germany	Y	Bremen	New York	11/14/1884	10/30/1895			Y	
Neuman, David	26	Wurttemberg	Y	Antwerp	New York	12/02/1849	11/03/1852	5	206	N	
Neumann, Carl	33	Prussia	Y	Bremen	Philadelphia	06/08/1857	08/10/1859	17	472	N	
Neumann, Fred	30	Mecklenburg	Y	Hamburg	New York	09/19/1850	08/23/1852	25	331	N	
Neumann, Louis	30	Germany	Y	Bremen	Baltimore	12/07/1883	10/25/1888			Y	
Neumann, Rudolph	36	Germany	Y	Bremen	Baltimore	05/03/1883	04/08/1886			Y	
Neumann, S.	26	Germany	Y	Bremen	New York	10/01/1885	02/26/1887			Y	
Neumann, Theodore	21	Germany	Y	Bremen	Baltimore	04/27/1883	09/02/1885			Y	

CITIZENSHIP RECORDS

APPLICANT	AGE	COUNTRY OF ORIGIN	DEC	DEPART PORT	ENTRY PORT	ARRIVE DATE	DEC DATE	VOL	PG.	FLD	NAT DATE
Neumann, William	28	Germany	Y	Bremen	New York	03/20/1883	03/12/1888			Y	
Neumeyer, Bernard	33	Oldenburg	Y	Havre	New Orleans	05/20/1849	02/06/1852	24	64	N	
Neumeyer, Conrad Frederi	??	Germany	Y	?	?	?	11/05/1883			Y	
Neumeyer, John Ludwig	30	Hesse Cassel	Y	Bremen	New York	07/04/1852	09/26/1856	14	390	N	
Neun, Christian	33	Germany	Y	Bremen	New York	06/05/1880	07/30/1883			Y	
Neuner, Johann Peter	??	Germany	Y	?	?	?	12/31/1883			Y	
Neusch, John	27	Switzerland	Y	Havre	New York	04/30/1857	10/05/1857	15	352	N	
Neustetter, Abraham	45	Austria	Y	Bremen	New York	05/30/1883	06/04/1892			Y	
Neuwirth, Ludwig	28	Wurttemberg	Y	Havre	New York	04/18/1852	03/16/1858	16	415	N	
Neven, William	31	England	Y	Liverpool	New York	06/13/1857	12/26/1857	16	256	N	
Nevill, James	30	Ireland	Y	Queenstown	New York	05/15/1891	10/19/1898			Y	
Neville, Joseph	23	Ireland	Y	Queenstown	New York	05/18/1889	10/27/1892	19	389	N	
Neville, Joseph	23	Ireland	Y	Queenstown	New York	05/18/1889	10/27/1892			Y	
Neville, Tim	24	Ireland	Y	Queenstown	New York	05/01/1886	06/21/1886			Y	
Newberg, John	28	Sweden	Y	Guttenberg	New York	06/29/1888	04/03/1893			Y	
Newbiggin, Thomas	48	Scotland	Y	Toronto	Buffalo	04/15/1878	05/23/1898			Y	
Newburger, Leopold	58	Germany	Y	Havre	New York	12/20/1857	10/23/1900			Y	
Newey, Albert	??	England	Y	?	?	?	10/26/1893			Y	
Newfield Samuel	21	Hungary	Y	?	?	?	09/10/1888			Y	
Newhaus, Jacob	27	Bavaria	Y	Havre	New York	06/??/1841	10/??/1849	23	277	N	
Newland, Andrew	32	Prussia	Y	Bremen	Baltimore	04/28/1846	09/05/1848	22	306	N	
Newley, Samuel	65	England	Y	Liverpool	Portland	03/21/1867	11/05/1883			Y	
Newmaier, Alexander	32	Germany	Y	Rotterdam	New York	11/01/1881	08/03/1885			Y	
Newman, David	26	Wurttemberg	Y	Antwerp	New York	12/02/1849	11/03/1852	6	332	N	
Newman, Henry	50	England	Y	Liverpool	Philadelphia	03/00/1879	10/20/1886			Y	
Newman, Solomon	??	Germany	N	Prussia	New York	06/??/1852	04/24/1855	28	290	N	09/26/1859
Newmann, Augustus	30	Mecklenburg	Y	Bremen	New York	09/??/1848	01/??/1850	2	18	N	
Newmann, Henry	??	Bavaria	Y	Bremen	Baltimore	07/06/1846	10/14/1848	1	215	N	
Newmann, Henry	50	England	Y	Liverpool	Philadelphia	03/??/1879	10/20/1886	19	57	N	
Newmann, Henry	28	Germany	Y	Antwerp	New York	03/18/1883	01/26/1889			Y	
Newmann, John Brunner	22	Oldenburg	Y	Bremen	New Orleans	11/17/1854	07/31/1858	16	545	N	
Newmann, Robert	??	Germany	Y	?	?	?	10/19/1893			Y	
Newmann, Solomon	45	Prussia	Y	Liverpool	New York	??/??/1851	04/24/1855	11	297	N	
Newmark, Solomon	??	Russia	Y	?	?	?	04/03/1883			Y	
Newsberger, Joseph	24	Baden	Y	Havre	New Orleans	04/20/1848	08/13/1851	4	126	N	
Newstab, Jacob	35	Germany	Y	Hamburg	New York	07/03/1897	05/17/1902			Y	
Ney, John Adam	41	Hesse Cassel	Y	Bremen	Baltimore	06/12/1859	01/22/1862	18	249	N	
Neyer, Joseph	22	Germany	Y	Amsterdam	New York	11/13/1882	08/08/1884			Y	
Nezhiba, Thomas	44	Austria	Y	Bremen	Baltimore	06/01/1888	08/21/1893			Y	
Nhuee, John	39	Bavaria	Y	Havre	New York	08/13/1852	05/26/1856	26	546	N	
Niaswander, Godfrey	23	Switzerland	Y	?	?	06/02/1879	10/11/1880			Y	
Nicholas, Marks	27	Prussia	Y	Havre	New York	08/15/1852	11/23/1852	5	331	N	
Nichols, George	32	Bavaria	Y	Havre	New York	10/23/1853	12/27/1855	13	372	N	
Nichols, Levi	21	England	Y	Liverpool	New York	10/12/1851	01/31/1853	7	91	N	
Nichols, Thomas	30	Scotland	Y	Liverpool	New Orleans	09/01/1850	05/02/1854	8	346	N	
Nichols, William	53	England	N	London	New York	12/??/1849	?			Y	
Nichting, Anton	22	Germany	Y	Bremen	New York	04/22/1889	07/23/1890			Y	
Nickard, Jacob	23	Baden	Y	Havre	New York	07/08/1849	10/09/1854	6	179	N	
Nickart, Jacob	23	Baden	Y	Havre	New York	07/08/1849	10/09/1854	11	182	N	
Nickel, Adolf	25	Wurttemberg	Y	London	New York	09/07/1853	06/01/1854	10	54	N	
Nickel, John G.	50	Germany	Y	Hamburg	New York	06/26/1881	05/25/1885			Y	
Nickels, Herman	30	Germany	Y	Hamburg	New York	09/11/1883	01/20/1888			Y	
Nicklaus, Jacob	30	Bavaria	Y	Havre	New York	11/22/1849	05/19/1852	25	45	N	
Nickle, Adolf	25	Wurttemberg	Y	London	New York	09/07/1853	06/01/1854	9	471	N	
Nickles, Carl	47	Germany	N	Antwerp	New York	05/??/1877	?			Y	
Nickols, Thomas	30	Scotland	Y	Liverpool	New Orleans	09/01/1850	05/02/1854	9	219	N	
Nickum, George	21	Germany	Y	Antwerp	New York	04/04/1884	09/17/1887			Y	
Nickum, Jacob	70	Germany	Y	Bremen	Baltimore	05/04/1888	09/14/1888			Y	
Nickum, Nicholas	34	Germany	Y	Bremen	Baltimore	05/04/1888	02/23/1899			Y	

CITIZENSHIP RECORDS

APPLICANT	AGE	COUNTRY OF ORIGIN	DEC	DEPART PORT	ENTRY PORT	ARRIVE DATE	DEC DATE	VOL	PG.	FLD	NAT DATE
Nickum, William	30	Germany	Y	Bremen	New York	04/26/1882	07/05/1884			Y	
Nicol, John	25	Germany	Y	Bremen	New York	09/13/1880	03/04/1885			Y	
Nicol, John D.	??	Great Britain	Y	?	?	?	12/07/1892			Y	
Nicol, William	22	Ireland	Y	London	New Orleans	02/26/1849	02/01/1850	2	23	N	
Nicola, Benedict	34	Germany	Y	Antwerp	New York	10/27/1880	02/03/1880			Y	
Nicolai, Charles	17	Germany	N	?	New York	00/00/1872				Y	10/26/1888
Nicolai, Michael	41	Germany	Y	Bremen	New York	09/26/1867	09/30/1882			Y	
Nicolassen, Fred A.	70	Germany	N	Amsterdam	New York	06/27/1844	03/03/1849	28	303	N	12/08/1852
Nicolassen, Fred H.	67	Germany	N	Hamburg	New York	06/??/1844	03/03/1849	28	9	N	12/08/1852
Nicolassen, Fred. A.	24	Germany	N	Hamburg	New York	06/00/1844	03/03/1849			Y	12/08/1852
Nicolay, Adam	33	Prussia	Y	Havre	Baltimore	07/19/1836	07/22/1851	4	29	N	
Nicolette, Michael	33	Italy	Y	Naples	New York	05/28/1887	05/21/1894			Y	
Nieberding, Clemens	28	Oldenburg, Ge	Y	Bremen	Baltimore	05/29/1875	10/??/1877			Y	
Nieberg, Frank	25	Germany	Y	Bremen	New York	04/08/1881	10/30/1888			Y	
Niebrugge, John Henry	21	Hanover	Y	Bremen	New York	10/20/1845	02/09/1849	23	39	N	
Niebur, Joseph	29	Germany	Y	Bremen	Baltimore	03/07/1883	04/02/1888			Y	
Nieburger, Jacob	40	Bavaria	Y	Bremen	Baltimore	09/06/1842	10/06/1848	22	460	N	
Niedergang, Charles	24	Germany	Y	Havre	New York	07/04/1892	06/18/1896			Y	
Niederhellmann, William	23	Germany	Y	Bremen	New York	09/26/1885	04/15/1889			Y	
Niederhelman, Ernst	47	Germany	N	Bremen	Baltimore	11/17/1859	?			Y	
Niederloehner, Leonhard	25	Bavaria	Y	London	New York	06/22/1854	09/29/1857	15	333	N	
Niedfeld, Clemens	38	Germany	Y	Bremen	Baltimore	08/26/1882	03/18/1889			Y	
Niedfeld, Henry William	28	Hanover	Y	Bremen	New York	05/02/1853	11/04/1858	17	272	N	
Nienborg, John Henry	30	Prussia	Y	Bremen	New Orleans	06/??/1847	11/01/1851	4	450	N	
Niehaus, Adolph	39	Germany	Y	Bremen	New York	08/20/1882	01/19/1889			Y	
Niehaus, August	22	Germany	Y	Amsterdam	New York	09/08/1888	08/06/1889			Y	
Niehaus, Bernard	30	Holland	Y	Bremen	Baltimore	05/24/1859	10/01/1860	27	395	N	
Niehaus, Clemens	22	Germany	Y	Bremen	Baltimore	09/16/1891	04/03/1893			Y	
Niehaus, Conrad	24	Germany	Y	Bremen	Baltimore	05/15/1882	10/06/1885			Y	
Niehaus, Frank	29	Germany	Y	Bremen	Portland, Ma	05/??/1871	04/19/1881			Y	
Niehaus, Fred	60	Germany	Y	Bremen	Baltimore	09/12/18??	10/25/1900			Y	
Niehaus, George	31	Germany	Y	Amsterdam	New York	05/19/1873	01/14/1884			Y	
Niehaus, Gerhard Henry	28	Hanover	Y	Bremen	Baltimore	07/06/1846	03/18/1852	24	326	N	
Niehaus, Henry	41	Hanover	Y	Bremen	Baltimore	05/??/1845	12/07/1850	2	346	N	
Niehaus, Henry	25	Hanover	Y	Bremen	Baltimore	06/24/1848	06/19/1851	3	422	N	
Niehaus, Henry	25	Hanover	Y	Bremen	New York	08/10/1854	11/18/1857	16	34	N	
Niehaus, Henry	26	Hanover	Y	Bremen	New York	12/21/1866	01/11/1872	18	454	N	
Niehaus, Herman	30	Holland	Y	Bremen	New Orleans	11/11/1852	08/05/1856	14	350	N	
Niehaus, Herman	25	Germany	Y	Amsterdam	New York	12/31/1883	12/15/1888			Y	
Niehaus, John	33	Holland	Y	New Diep	Baltimore	12/??/1853	09/15/1855	13	37	N	
Niehaus, John	42	Germany	N	Bremen	Baltimore	06/06/1870	?			Y	
Niehaus, John Frederick	21	Oldenburg	Y	Bremen	New Orleans	12/01/1849	09/13/1852	25	462	N	
Niehaus, John Gerhard	32	Hanover	Y	Bremen	Baltimore	05/02/1849	05/20/1852	25	67	N	
Niehaus, John H.	24	Germany	Y	Bremen	Baltimore	03/03/1882	03/10/1882			Y	
Niehaus, John Henry	34	Oldenburg	Y	Bremen	New Orleans	05/01/1849	04/24/1854	8	252	N	
Niehaus, John Henry	34	Oldenburg	Y	Bremen	New Orleans	05/01/1849	04/24/1854	9	123	N	
Niehaus, John Henry	24	Oldenburg	Y	Bremen	Baltimore	08/02/1845	08/17/1848	22	196	N	
Niehaus, John Joseph	60	Oldenburg	Y	Bremen	Baltimore	05/20/1844	04/20/1854	8	226	N	
Niehaus, John Joseph	60	Oldenburg	Y	Bremen	Baltimore	05/20/1848	04/20/1854	9	97	N	
Niehoff, B.	24	Germany	Y	Rotterdam	New York	05/23/1882	09/10/1884			Y	
Niehoff, George	32	Germany	Y	Amsterdam	New York	11/04/1891	02/05/1894			Y	
Niehoff, Joseph	32	Germany	Y	Bremen	Baltimore	06/03/1876	02/01/1887			Y	
Niehoff, Theodore Edward	29	Prussia	Y	Bremen	Baltimore	08/28/1869	05/20/1872	18	494	N	
Niehring, Bernard Valent	27	Bavaria	Y	Bremen	Baltimore	06/18/1854	03/19/1858	16	426	N	
Niehuser, Ignatz	24	Germany	Y	Rotterdam	New York	01/17/1881	01/06/1885			Y	
Nieland, Hermann	29	Germany	Y	Amsterdam	New York	09/05/1885	09/05/1888			Y	
Nieland, John	26	Hanover	Y	Bremen	New Orleans	02/14/1846	02/14/1849	23	102	N	
Nielsen, Christian M.	??	Denmark	Y	?	?	?	10/01/1894			Y	
Nieman, Charles	25	Hanover	Y	Bremen	New Orleans	12/01/1849	04/24/1854	8	253	N	

CITIZENSHIP RECORDS

APPLICANT	AGE	COUNTRY OF ORIGIN	DEC	DEPART PORT	ENTRY PORT	ARRIVE DATE	DEC DATE	VOL	PG.	FLD	NAT DATE
Nieman, Frederick	25	Hanover	Y	Bremen	New Orleans	07/10/1849	07/19/1851	4	11	N	
Nieman, George	53	Germany	N	Bremen	New Orleans	11/??/1850	?			Y	
Nieman, Henry	36	Hanover	Y	Bremen	New Orleans	11/15/1847	02/05/1849	23	31	N	
Nieman, Joseph	30	Oldenburg	Y	Bremen	New Orleans	11/05/1847	03/22/1850	2	238	N	
Niemann, Bernard	28	Germany	Y	Antwerp	Philadlephia	05/22/1885	10/27/1888	19	190	N	
Niemann, Bernard	28	Germany	Y	Antwerp	Philadelphia	05/22/1885	10/27/1888			Y	
Niemann, Bernard Henry	55	Hanover	Y	Bremen	New Orleans	12/24/1850	09/04/1860	27	330	N	
Niemann, Charles	25	Hanover	Y	Bremen	New Orleans	12/01/1849	04/24/1854	9	134	N	
Niemann, Clemens	41	Germany	Y	Bremen	New York	10/??/1868	02/08/1889			Y	
Niemann, Frank	32	Germany	Y	Bremen	New York	05/19/1875	10/16/1886			Y	
Niemann, Fritz	19	Hanover	Y	Bremen	New Orleans	11/22/1854	10/04/1858	17	40	N	
Niemann, Henry	21	Hanover	Y	Bremen	New Orleans	11/04/1857	11/01/1858	17	241	N	
Niemann, Henry	41	Germany	Y	Bremen	Baltimore	10/17/1882	07/22/1884			Y	
Niemann, Henry	53	Hanover	N	Bremen	New Orleans	12/??/1854	?			Y	
Niemann, Henry	23	Hanover	Y	Bremen	New Orleans	12/04/1848	09/09/1852	25	427	N	
Niemann, Herman	28	Prussia	Y	Bremen	New Orleans	05/04/1849	06/19/1851	3	410	N	
Niemann, John Frederick	27	Hanover	Y	Bremen	Baltimore	10/10/1857	04/07/1862	18	303	N	
Niemann, Joseph	23	Prussia	Y	Bremen	New Orleans	10/31/1849	10/30/1852	5	77	N	
Niemann, Theodore Clemen	33	Oldenburg	Y	Bremen	New Orleans	10/30/1852	08/27/1855	11	503	N	
Niemann, William	23	Hanover	Y	Bremen	New Orleans	11/22/1849	03/28/1853	7	416	N	
Niemann, William	43	Hanover	Y	Bremen	New Orleans	12/22/1850	10/20/1858	17	67	N	
Niemeier, Andrew	33	Prussia	Y	Bremen	Baltimore	08/26/1846	08/15/1848	22	120	N	
Niemeier, Henry	31	Prussia	Y	Bremen	New Orleans	11/18/1845	06/05/1854	12	12	N	
Niemeier, Henry	25	Prussia	Y	Bremen	New York	12/17/1854	04/02/1858	16	474	N	
Niemeier, Henry	30	Hanover	Y	Bremen	New Orleans	12/15/1846	05/20/1852	25	78	N	
Niemeier, Hermann	34	Germany	Y	Bremen	Baltimore	05/04/1866	02/08/1881			Y	
Niemeier, John	33	Hanover	Y	Bremen	Philadelphia	10/14/1842	09/01/1848	22	287	N	
Niemeier, John	33	Hanover	Y	Bremen	New Orleans	11/29/1844	02/19/1849	23	199	N	
Niemes, Henry	48	Bavaria	N	Bavaria	New York	03/??/1858	?			Y	
Niemeyer, Arnold	28	Prussia	Y	Bremen	Baltimore	05/19/1849	06/19/1851	3	405	N	
Niemeyer, Bernhard	28	Germany	Y	Rotterdam	New York	05/27/1882	11/05/1888	19	216	N	
Niemeyer, Bernhard	28	Germany	Y	Rotterdam	New York	05/27/1882	11/05/1888			Y	
Niemeyer, Charles	28	Brunswick	Y	Liverpool	Philadelphia	04/10/1850	05/01/1854	8	310	N	
Niemeyer, Charles	28	Brunswick	Y	Liverpool	Philadelphia	04/10/1854	05/01/1854	9	183	N	
Niemeyer, Clemens	34	Prussia	Y	Bremen	Baltimore	08/31/1845	10/05/1848	22	440	N	
Niemeyer, Gehard	22	Germany	Y	Bremen	Baltimore	09/22/1890	05/18/1891			Y	
Niemeyer, Henry	31	Prussia	Y	Bremen	New Orleans	11/18/1845	06/05/1854	10	75	N	
Niemeyer, Henry	30	Germany	Y	Bremen	Baltimore	04/14/1882	04/20/1883			Y	
Niemeyer, Herman Henry	44	Germany	Y	Bremen	Baltimore	11/02/1883	10/11/1893			Y	
Niemeyer, John	40	Germany	Y	Bremen	Baltimore	07/28/1880	10/13/1884			Y	
Niemeyer, Joseph	28	Prussia	Y	Bremen	New Orleans	12/25/1846	02/07/1850	2	51	N	
Niemeyer, Theodore	24	Germany	Y	Rotterdam	New York	04/08/1887	02/03/1890			Y	
Niemeyer, William	27	Germany	Y	Bremen	Baltimore	05/20/1881	12/21/1881			Y	
Niemeyer, William	28	Germany	Y	Bremen	Baltimore	11/04/1883	04/29/1889			Y	
Niemoeller, H.	26	Germany	Y	Bremen	Baltimore	07/01/1880	04/17/1883			Y	
Niemoeller, John Henry	23	Oldenburg	Y	Bremen	New Orleans	11/25/1854	01/27/1857	14	513	N	
Niemoller, Ferdinand	39	Prussia	Y	Leer	New York	08/21/1849	10/03/1854	10	370	N	
Niemoller, Ferdinand	39	Prussia	Y	Leer	New York	08/21/1849	10/03/1854	12	309	N	
Nienaber, Frederick	40	Germany	N	Bremen	Baltimore	10/??/1871	?			Y	
Nienaber, Herman	32	Oldenburg	Y	Bremen	Baltimore	09/??/1844	12/17/1855	13	321	N	
Nienauber, Henry	25	Oldenburg	Y	Bremen	Baltimore	05/??/1849	10/27/1851	4	416	N	
Nienhaus, Gerhard	24	Germany	Y	Amsterdam	New York	05/18/1887	03/26/1888			Y	
Nieparte, Diederick	24	Hanover	Y	Bremen	New Orleans	??/26/1851	10/06/1854	10	482	N	
Nieparte, Diederick	24	Hanover	Y	Bremen	New Orleans	01/26/1851	10/06/1854	12	421	N	
Nieporte, Anthony Diedri	26	Hanover	Y	Bremen	New York	10/16/1856	11/01/1858	17	250	N	
Nieporte, Diedrich	59	Germany	N	Bremen	New Orleans	02/??/1851	?			Y	
Niermann, Gerard	29	Hanover	Y	Bremen	New Orleans	06/01/1848	10/09/1854	6	84	N	
Niermann, Gerhard	29	Hanover	Y	Bremen	New Orleans	06/01/1848	10/09/1854	11	87	N	
Niermann, John	34	Germany	Y	Antwerp	New York	08/12/1888	11/04/1889			Y	

CITIZENSHIP RECORDS

APPLICANT	AGE	COUNTRY OF ORIGIN	DEC	DEPART PORT	ENTRY PORT	ARRIVE DATE	DEC DATE	VOL	PG.	FLD	NAT DATE
Niestz, Henry	27	Kuer Hessen	Y	Havre	New York	08/27/1849	09/11/1852	25	456	N	
Nietert, Wilhelmus J. H.	30	Holland	Y	Rotterdam	New York	08/26/1853	04/10/1856	26	484	N	
Niewers, Johann H. C.	29	Germany	Y	Hamburg	New York	08/16/1881	07/03/1882			Y	
Niewoehner, Gerhard H.	32	Prussia	Y	Bremen	Baltimore	05/10/1850	01/22/1851	2	519	N	
Niewon, Henry	48	Germany	Y	Bremen	Baltimore	09/07/1875	??/??/1879	28	425	N	
Niggemann, Frederick	27	Prussia	Y	Bremen	New York	11/12/1853	04/01/1856	26	398	N	
Nimmo, Henry F.	16	Canada	N	?	Detroit	00/00/1881				Y	10/23/1888
Nimmo, Robert	51	Scotland	Y	Glasgow	Detroit	09/??/1881	10/23/1888	19	173	N	
Nimmo, Robert	51	Scotland	Y	Glasgow	Detroit	09/??/1881	10/23/1888			Y	
Nipkow, Julius	48	Germany	Y	Hamburg	Baltimore	12/00/1880	02/07/1887			Y	
Nipper, John	30	Oldenburg	Y	Bremen	Baltimore	11/01/1858	11/02/1860	27	560	N	
Nippert, Lewis/Louis See	??	France	N	France	?	?	?	28	485	N	04/??/1850
Nippert, Louis** See Pg	??	Gosdorf	N	France	?	?	?	28	469	N	01/??/1850
Nippert, Louis/Lewis	4	France	N	?	?	?				Y	04/09/1850
Nippgen, Michael	??	Bavaria	Y	Rotterdam	New Orleans	04/13/18??	10/11/1848	1	121	N	
Nissen, Julius	32	Germany	Y	Hamburg	New York	08/04/1885	05/23/1892			Y	
Nissen, Theodor	??	Germany	Y	?	?	?	10/15/1888			Y	
Nistler, Martin	23	Austria	Y	Bremen	Baltimore	07/13/1893	03/09/1896			Y	
Nitsche, Gotthard	??	Austria	Y	?	?	?	09/01/1885			Y	
Nitzschman, Ernst	30	Germany	Y	Havre	New York	11/12/1872	12/12/1883			Y	
Nixdorf, Oswald	31	Germany	Y	Hamburg	New York	09/25/1882	10/13/1888			Y	
Nixon, Stennet	51	England	Y	London	New York	08/08/1849	04/29/1850	3	29	N	
Noe, George	37	Germany	Y	Antwerp	New York	03/22/1880	09/02/1891			Y	
Noe, Gustav	27	Germany	Y	Hamburg	Philadelphia	01/16/1881	10/16/1889			Y	
Noe, Louis Joseph	31	Scicily	Y	London	New York	09/20/1855	03/28/1856	26	370	N	
Noel, Eugene	21	Germany	Y	Havre	New York	07/25/1891	10/29/1892			Y	
Noelker, H.	30	Germany	Y	Bremen	Baltimore	??/??/1875	04/12/1886			Y	
Noeltzly, Henry	32	Switzerland	Y	Havre	New York	07/15/1848	10/06/1854	12	426	N	
Noeth, Adam	34	Bavaria	Y	Hamburg	New York	05/30/1853	04/02/1858	16	477	N	
Noetker, Anton	??	Hanover	Y	Bremen	New Orleans	01/06/1850	03/25/1851	3	335	N	
Noetker, Gerhard	40	Hanover	Y	Bremen	New Orleans	12/13/1848	09/12/1857	15	263	N	
Noetzly, Henry	32	Switzerland	Y	Havre	New York	07/15/1848	10/06/1854	10	487	N	
Noga, Michael	35	Austria	Y	Bremen	New York	03/03/1885	11/02/1894			Y	
Nogaller, Sigismund S.	22	Russia	Y	Liverpool	New York	09/08/1854	09/22/18??	10	163	N	
Nogaller, Sigismund S.	22	Russia	Y	Liverpool	New York	09/08/1854	09/22/1854	12	102	N	
Noggler, John	32	Austria	Y	Antwerp	New York	05/06/1848	02/14/1852	24	108	N	
Nogt, Rudolph	28	Germany	Y	Hamburg	New York	02/18/1888	04/03/1893			Y	
Nolan, James	28	Ireland	Y	Liverpool	New Orleans	02/04/1851	11/01/1852	5	98	N	
Nolan, James	28	Ireland	Y	Liverpool	New Orleans	02/04/1851	11/01/1852	6	241	N	
Nolan, James	42	Ireland	Y	Liverpool	New York	09/26/1852	03/31/1862	18	288	N	
Nolan, John	45	Ireland	Y	Liverpool	New York	07/08/1848	04/08/1862	18	307	N	
Nolan, John	26	Ireland	Y	?	New York	?	04/11/1883			Y	
Nolan, Michael	30	Ireland	Y	Canada	Buffalo	09/??/1848	10/25/1850	2	300	N	
Nolan, Patrick	71	Ireland	Y	Canada	Buffalo	11/03/1848	10/20/1851	4	341	N	
Nolan, Patrick	33	Ireland	Y	Liverpool	New York	05/13/1846	05/20/1852	25	53	N	
Nolan, Thomas	27	Ireland	Y	Liverpool	New York	05/12/1885	10/21/1889	19	243	N	
Nolan, Thomas	27	Ireland	Y	Liverpool	New York	05/12/1885	10/21/1889			Y	
Nolan, William	28	Ireland	Y	Galway	Boston	07/05/1882	03/02/1888			Y	
Nolan, William	27	Ireland	Y	Liverpool	New York	04/08/1849	03/25/1856	26	300	N	
Nold, Frederick	28	Baden	Y	Havre	New Orleans	10/10/1847	11/13/1852	5	276	N	
Nold, Frederick	28	Baden	Y	Havre	New Orleans	10/10/1847	11/13/1852	6	400	N	
Nold, John	40	Bavaria	Y	Havre	New York	06/19/1837	10/13/1848	1	193	N	
Nold, Valentine	27	Baden	Y	Havre	New York	05/25/1852	10/03/1856	14	171	N	
Nolkamper, Frederick W.	28	Prussia	Y	Bremen	Baltimore	06/08/1859	07/12/1860	27	219	N	
Noll, Adam	39	Germany	Y	Bremen	New York	08/09/1881	11/01/1886			Y	
Noll, Anton	25	Germany	Y	Liverpool	Philadelphia	03/05/1883	03/03/1885			Y	
Noll, Carl	22	Germany	Y	Amsterdam	New York	02/16/1883	12/26/1884			Y	
Noll, Christian	33	Baden	Y	Havre	New Orleans	03/22/1852	09/25/1856	14	383	N	
Noll, George	41	Germany	Y	Bremen	New York	12/??/1865	09/27/1884			Y	

CITIZENSHIP RECORDS

APPLICANT	AGE	COUNTRY OF ORIGIN	DEC	DEPART PORT	ENTRY PORT	ARRIVE DATE	DEC DATE	VOL	PG.	FLD	NAT DATE
Noll, John	44	Germany	Y	Bremen	New York	05/20/1888	09/14/1893			Y	
Noll, Peter	45	Bavaria	Y	Havre	New Orleans	07/10/1857	08/26/1862	18	400	N	
Nollan, Robert	48	Germany	Y	Amsterdam	New York	12/31/1879	09/20/1892			Y	
Nollenberger, Albert	25	Germany	Y	Liverpool	New York	03/03/1884	02/28/1887			Y	
Nolte, Anthony	28	Prussia	Y	Bremen	New Orleans	10/29/1854	10/28/1858	17	140	N	
Nolte, Henry	27	Bavaria	Y	Havre	New Orleans	04/29/1846	01/30/1850	2	14	N	
Nolte, Henry	24	Hanover	Y	Bremen	New York	01/03/1847	01/27/1851	2	532	N	
Nolte, Henry	33	Germany	Y	Bremen	New York	08/24/1888	10/09/1896			Y	
Nolte, Henry	31	Germany	Y	Hamburg	New York	09/08/1880	12/29/1883			Y	
Nolte, Henry	26	Hanover	Y	Canada	Buffalo	05/21/1847	08/21/1848	22	216	N	
Nolte, James	28	Germany	Y	Rotterdam	New York	06/17/1881	06/21/1883			Y	
Nolte, John Henry	28	Hanover	Y	Bremen	New Orleans	12/28/1843	10/05/1848	1	59	N	
Nonner, Frank	32	Germany	Y	Hamburg	New York	05/01/1890	02/20/1894			Y	
Nonweiler, Gustav	36	Bavaria	Y	Antwerp	New York	06/28/1847	10/30/1858	17	202	N	
Noohaus, Ludwig	22	Prussia	Y	Bremen	New Orleans	01/01/1847	02/22/1849	23	252	N	
Noonan, John	31	Ireland	Y	Liverpool	New Orleans	12/24/1849	06/10/1852	25	309	N	
Noonan, Michael	50	Ireland	Y	Liverpool	New York	05/03/1849	01/30/1850	2	15	N	
Noonan, William	25	Ireland	Y	Liverpool	New Orleans	02/01/1849	10/14/1851	4	288	N	
Noone, John A.	23	Ireland	Y	?	Philadelphia	??/??/1886	05/17/1890			Y	
Noony, Timothy	31	Ireland	Y	Cork	Boston	10/31/1840	10/14/1851	4	277	N	
Noortwyck, Gustav	53	Germany	Y	Antwerp	New York	06/12/1878	07/05/1890			Y	
Noppert, Herman	37	Germany	Y	Havre	New York	06/20/1880	09/10/1896			Y	
Norback, Gustav	??	Sweden	Y	?	?	?	05/04/1891			Y	
Nordhorn, Herman	26	Hanover	Y	Bremen	New Orleans	11/24/1848	12/15/1851	4	519	N	
Nordloh, John H.	37	Oldenburg	Y	Bremerhafen	Baltimore	10/??/1842	01/26/1861	18	72	N	
Nordlohne, Johan Heinric	40	Germany	Y	Bremen	New York	04/08/1882	10/25/1889			Y	
Nordman, Casper	24	Hanover	Y	Bremen	New Orleans	12/??/1847	12/09/1850	2	351	N	
Nordmann, Henry	47	Germany	N	Bremen	New York	09/??/1859	?			Y	
Nordmann, John Gerd	52	Hanover	Y	Bremen	Baltimore	10/08/1854	10/12/1857	15	390	N	
Noreman, F. L.	??	Germany	Y	?	?	?	11/01/1878			Y	
Norman, Thomas	43	Ireland	Y	Liverpool	New Orleans	04/21/1849	04/22/1854	8	238	N	
Norman, Thomas	43	Ireland	Y	Liverpool	New Orleans	04/21/1849	04/22/1854	9	109	N	
Normann, Erdmann	26	Germany	Y	Bremen	New York	10/21/1888	10/26/1896			Y	
Normann, John	45	Ireland	N	Queenstown	New York	07/??/1865	?			Y	
Normann, William	34	Germany	Y	Bremen	Baltimore	08/02/1882	12/??/1883			Y	
Normann, William	43	Germany	N	Bremen	Baltimore	08/02/1882	?			Y	
Normez-Lopes, Alfred	40	France	Y	Antwerp	New York	08/20/1895	02/24/1898			Y	
Norris, John	30	Ireland	Y	Liverpool	New York	09/01/1855	01/03/1856	13	420	N	
North, James	45	Ireland	Y	Liverpool	New York	03/25/1848	11/08/1858	17	301	N	
Northcott, Peter W.	30	England	Y	Liverpool	New York	11/12/1882	06/10/1890			Y	
Northeim, John	32	Germany	Y	Bremen	New York	03/24/1885	03/23/1891			Y	
Nortmann, George	32	Hanover	Y	Bremen	New York	08/01/1847	01/06/1853	5	524	N	
Norton, Edward	23	Ireland	Y	Liverpool	New York	05/30/1851	02/02/1856	26	4	N	
Norton, James	48	England	Y	Liverpool	New York	10/31/1851	05/02/1854	8	349	N	
Norton, John	48	England	Y	Liverpool	New York	10/31/1851	05/02/1854	9	222	N	
Noschang, Franz	43	Bavaria	Y	Rotterdam	New York	09/05/1850	11/01/1852	5	105	N	
Nothelfer, Francis Josep	30	France	Y	Havre	New York	11/05/1883	04/12/1889			Y	
Nothelfer, Mathias	??	France	Y	?	?	?	06/28/1889			Y	
Nottage, John G.	12	England	N	?	Key West, FL	00/00/1873				Y	04/04/1887
Notter, Gottlieb	29	Germany	Y	Bremen	New York	02/06/1888	12/30/1891			Y	
Notton, James	25	Ireland	Y	Liverpool	Philadelphia	05/25/1855	05/14/1860	27	189	N	
Nougaret, Andre	??	France	Y	Bordeaux	New York	05/30/1887	03/27/1894			Y	
Noumann, John	35	Prussia	Y	Havre	New York	06/15/1853	08/11/1860	27	261	N	
Nowack, Charles A. Ch.	52	Germany	Y	Havre	New York	10/19/1882	01/28/1884			Y	
Nowak, Frank	46	Germany	Y	Hamburg	New York	06/03/1871	10/11/1892	19	356	N	
Nowak, Frank	46	Germany	Y	Hamburg	New York	06/03/1871	10/11/1892			Y	
Nower, John Gerhard	21	Oldenburg	Y	Bremen	Baltimore	11/02/1855	11/10/1855	13	204	N	
Nowick, Christian	35	Saxeweimer	Y	Bremen	New Orleans	01/01/1841	08/09/1848	22	83	N	
Nowlan, Francis	32	Ireland	Y	Liverpool	New Orleans	05/28/1848	02/19/1850	2	105	N	

CITIZENSHIP RECORDS

APPLICANT	AGE	COUNTRY OF ORIGIN	DEC	DEPART PORT	ENTRY PORT	ARRIVE DATE	DEC DATE	VOL	PG.	FLD	NAT DATE
Nowlan, Thomas	28	Ireland	Y	Liverpool	New York	06/09/1854	02/04/1858	16	76	N	
Nowlen, John	25	Ireland	Y	Liverpool	New York	04/26/1847	05/14/1852	25	18	N	
Nubling, George	25	Baden	Y	Havre	New Orleans	03/14/1847	10/05/1848	1	58	N	
Nuding, Michael	27	Wurttemberg	Y	Havre	New York	04/20/1854	10/07/1854	12	478	N	
Nuebling, Frank	27	Bavaria	Y	Havre	New York	08/28/1851	08/15/1855	11	438	N	
Nueding, Michael	27	Wurttemberg	Y	Havre	New York	04/20/1854	10/07/1854	10	539	N	
Nuegele, Joseph	34	Baden	Y	Havre	New York	09/18/1857	12/27/1859	17	530	N	
Nuehring, William	27	Hanover	Y	Bremen	Baltimore	05/01/1854	08/28/1857	15	196	N	
Nuenning, Bernard	30	Prussia	Y	Amsterdam	New York	11/10/1848	02/14/1849	23	99	N	
Nuenning, Joseph	25	Germany	Y	Bremen	Baltimore	04/10/1882	06/12/1884			Y	
Nuessle, Frederick	31	Germany	Y	Amsterdam	New York	10/23/1883	07/28/1891			Y	
Nuetzel, Konrad	25	Germany	Y	Antwerp	Philadelphia	02/18/1887	12/10/1889			Y	
Nugent, Christopher	36	Ireland	Y	Liverpool	New Orleans	07/??/1849	12/13/1852	5	407	N	
Nugent, Edward B.	27	Ireland	Y	Liverpool	New York	09/29/1849	03/20/1850	2	226	N	
Nugent, George	38	Ireland	Y	?	Portland, ME	00/00/1867	09/03/1875			Y	
Nugent, Michael	63	Ireland	N	Liverpool	New York	04/??/1848	?			Y	
Nuhring, Conrad	67	Germany	Y	Bremen	New York	05/??/1860	02/18/1884			Y	
Nuhs, George	25	Bavaria	Y	Havre	New York	08/22/1851	11/18/1852	5	307	N	
Nuld, Nicolaus	27	Baden	Y	Havre	New York	04/10/1850	05/27/1854	9	429	N	
Nuld, Nicolaus	27	Baden	Y	Havre	New York	04/10/1850	05/27/1854	10	12	N	
Nulello, Nicola	??	Italy	Y	?	?	?	07/06/1897			Y	
Nunn, George	21	Ireland	Y	Liverpool	New Orleans	11/04/1849	03/29/1853	7	461	N	
Nunn, Nathaniel	49	Ireland	Y	Liverpool	New Orleans	11/04/1849	03/29/1853	7	462	N	
Nunsgern, Peter	28	France	Y	Havre	New Orleans	10/09/1846	01/20/1851	2	511	N	
Nuss, Franz	31	Germany	Y	Antwerp	New York	04/10/1887	08/05/1891			Y	
Nuss, Gabriel	21	Germany	Y	Bremen	New York	08/22/1887	08/14/1890			Y	
Nuss, George	44	Hesse Darmsta	Y	Havre	New Orleans	05/14/1852	10/30/1858	17	192	N	
Nusse, William	17	Germany	N	?	Baltimore	00/00/1879				Y	10/23/1888
Nuszberger, Anton	37	Bavaria	Y	Havre	New Orleans	01/27/1852	03/03/1853	7	267	N	
Nuszdorfer, Jacob	42	Germany	Y	Havre	New York	11/14/1865	04/17/1880			Y	
Nuttle, Patrick	23	Ireland	Y	Liverpool	New Orleans	01/01/1852	04/17/1854	8	191	N	
Nuttle, Patrick	23	Ireland	Y	Liverpool	New Orleans	01/01/1852	04/17/1854	9	62	N	
Nutzel, George	29	Germany	Y	Bremen	New York	03/25/1888	10/14/1892			Y	
Nuxoll, Clemens	38	Oldenburg	Y	Bremen	New Orleans	11/15/1845	11/20/1848	1	342	N	
Nuxoll, Henry	49	Oldenburg	Y	Bremen	Baltimore	09/17/1833	06/14/1852	25	259	N	
Nuxoll, Herman Henry	22	Oldenburg	Y	Bremen	Baltimore	06/12/1848	03/25/1851	3	322	N	
Nye, Conrad	41	Bavaria	Y	Havre	New York	08/18/1847	10/02/1848	1	38	N	
O'Beirne, Peter J.	40	Ireland	Y	Queenstown	New York	05/11/1889	07/30/1894			Y	
O'Boertin, Alphonse	11	France	N	?	New Orleans	00/00/1875				Y	10/29/1887
O'Brian, Dermott	22	Ireland	Y	Liverpool	New York	06/02/1857	11/08/1858	17	306	N	
O'Brian, Henry	40	Ireland	Y	St. Johns	Whitehall	08/10/1849	05/30/1854	10	37	N	
O'Brian, James	28	Ireland	Y	Liverpool	New York	10/15/1848	07/26/1858	16	531	N	
O'Brian, John	22	Ireland	Y	Liverpool	New York	10/22/1847	11/16/1848	1	285	N	
O'Brien, Bartholmew	39	Ireland	Y	Liverpool	New Orleans	06/14/1851	05/17/1854	9	339	N	
O'Brien, Bartholomew	39	Ireland	Y	Liverpool	New Orleans	06/14/1851	05/17/1854	8	465	N	
O'Brien, Dennis P.	25	Ireland	Y	Limerick	Burlington	06/17/1849	09/19/1857	15	289	N	
O'Brien, Edward	29	Ireland	Y	Liverpool	New York	11/12/1853	02/04/1857	14	537	N	
O'Brien, Henry	40	Ireland	Y	St. Johns	Whitehall	08/10/1849	05/30/1854	9	454	N	
O'Brien, James	35	Ireland	Y	Liverpool	New York	04/11/1873	04/25/1888			Y	
O'Brien, James Sweeny	35	Ireland	Y	Liverpool	New York	08/25/1845	10/06/1848	22	456	N	
O'Brien, John	30	Ireland	Y	Dublin	New York	06/16/1849	03/25/1851	3	324	N	
O'Brien, John	22	Ireland	Y	Liverpool	New Orleans	12/01/1850	02/17/1853	7	176	N	
O'Brien, John	59	Ireland	Y	Liverpool	New York	01/16/1848	05/10/1854	8	409	N	
O'Brien, John	59	Ireland	Y	Liverpool	New York	01/16/1848	05/10/1854	9	382	N	
O'Brien, John	34	Ireland	N	Queenstown	Boston	11/??/1875	?			Y	
O'Brien, Mathias	26	Ireland	Y	Cork	New York	02/12/1851	03/16/1852	24	319	N	
O'Brien, Michael	30	Ireland	Y	Liverpool	New York	06/12/1839	02/14/1851	3	130	N	
O'Brien, Michael	34	Ireland	Y	Cork	New Orleans	02/10/1852	07/01/1861	18	200	N	
O'Brien, Michael	54	Ireland	N	Liverpool	New York	05/01/1866	?			Y	

CITIZENSHIP RECORDS

APPLICANT	AGE	COUNTRY OF ORIGIN	DEC	DEPART PORT	ENTRY PORT	ARRIVE DATE	DEC DATE	VOL	PG.	FLD	NAT DATE
O'Brien, Michael	27	Ireland	Y	Cork	Boston	05/01/1847	04/10/1852	24	434	N	
O'Brien, Michael	35	Ireland	Y	Liverpool	New Orleans	12/25/1847	11/02/1860	27	554	N	
O'Brien, Patrick	28	Ireland	Y	Canada	Buffalo	08/17/1848	08/11/1851	4	111	N	
O'Brien, Patrick	30	Ireland	Y	Quebec	Lewistown	??/24/18??	02/21/1853	7	195	N	
O'Brien, Patrick	38	Ireland	N	Queenstown	New York	09/??/1870	?			Y	
O'Brien, Terrence	23	Ireland	Y	Liverpool	New York	09/17/1851	09/27/1854	10	256	N	
O'Brien, Terrence	23	Ireland	Y	Liverpool	New York	09/17/1851	09/27/1854	12	195	N	
O'Brien, Thomas	31	Ireland	Y	Queenstown	New York	05/??/1870	03/09/1882			Y	
O'Brine, Dennis	40	Ireland	N	Liverpool	Philadelphia	??/??/1848	?			Y	
O'Bryan, Patrick	24	Ireland	Y	Liverpool	New Orleans	12/24/1852	02/16/1858	16	311	N	
O'Bryan, Thomas	32	Ireland	Y	Liverpool	New York	01/??/1850	10/27/1851	4	418	N	
O'Bryne, James	34	Ireland	N	London	New York	11/29/1879	?			Y	
O'Byrne, James	29	Ireland	Y	Londonderry	New York	11/29/1879	03/??/1883			Y	
O'Byrne, Michael	35	Ireland	Y	Liverpool	New York	05/11/1854	10/06/1857	15	358	N	
O'Callaghan, Daniel	30	Ireland	Y	Canada	Boston	09/??/1844	03/07/1853	7	296	N	
O'Callaghan, John	26	Ireland	Y	Waterford	Boston	05/??/1848	11/06/1851	4	495	N	
O'Callahan, Cornelius	50	Ireland	N	Queenstown	New York	08/01/1854	?			Y	
O'Connel, Daniel	30	Ireland	Y	Liverpool	New Orleans	04/17/1847	03/28/1849	23	262	N	
O'Connell, Daniel A.S.	22	Ireland	Y	Liverpool	Boston	12/09/1848	10/18/1851	4	326	N	
O'Connell, James	21	Ireland	Y	Liverpool	New Orleans	04/28/1849	03/01/1852	24	190	N	
O'Connell, John	??	Ireland	N	?	?	03/08/1887				Y	10/17/1892
O'Connell, Michael	36	Ireland	Y	Liverpool	New Orleans	06/28/1848	01/04/1853	5	512	N	
O'Connell, Pat	37	Ireland	N	Queenstown	New York	07/25/1863	?			Y	
O'Connell, Patrick	32	Ireland	Y	Waterford	Robinson	01/??/1848	05/19/1854	8	476	N	
O'Connell, Patrick	32	Ireland	Y	Waterford	Robinson	01/??/1848	05/19/1854	9	350	N	
O'Connell, Patrick	36	Ireland	Y	Liverpool	New York	04/16/1892	05/11/1892			Y	
O'Connell, Thomas	28	Ireland	Y	Cork	Boston	08/??/1845	01/24/1856	13	506	N	
O'Connell, Thomas W.	28	Ireland	Y	Liverpool	New Orleans	04/??/1846	12/??/1850	2	428	N	
O'Conner, Cornelius	21	Ireland	Y	Cork	New York	10/12/1851	09/04/1852	25	355	N	
O'Conner, Michael	21	Ireland	Y	Liverpool	New Orleans	05/24/1851	04/06/1852	24	399	N	
O'Conner, Thomas C.	??	Ireland	Y	Montreal	Buffalo	??/06/1848	12/16/1850	2	366	N	
O'Connor, Bernard	63	Ireland	Y	Londonderry	New York	06/11/1893	10/23/1896			Y	
O'Connor, Hugh	31	Ireland	Y	Londonderry	New York	02/06/1888	09/22/1893			Y	
O'Connor, James Hugh	30	Ireland	Y	Liverpool	New York	09/26/1852	03/09/1853	7	317	N	
O'Connor, Jeremiah	26	Ireland	Y	Tralee	New York	05/01/1852	09/29/1856	14	30	N	
O'Connor, John	30	Ireland	Y	Newport	Cape Cod	09/03/1850	03/05/1853	7	276	N	
O'Connor, John	44	Ireland	N	Queenstown	New York	06/??/1867	?			Y	
O'Connor, Joseph	22	Ireland	Y	Londonderry	New York	03/17/1893	10/05/1894			Y	
O'Connor, Michael	29	Ireland	Y	Limerick	Buffalo	05/10/1849	04/04/1853	8	19	N	
O'Connor, Michael	24	Ireland	Y	Queenstown	New York	05/07/1889	06/04/1890			Y	
O'Connor, Patrick	23	Ireland	Y	Queenstown	New York	09/28/1881	04/02/1883			Y	
O'Connor, Patrick	26	Ireland	Y	Londonderry	New York	06/24/1891	10/07/1893			Y	
O'Connor, Patrick	40	Ireland	Y	Liverpool	New Orleans	08/07/1848	04/12/1852	24	464	N	
O'Connor, Richard	28	Ireland	Y	Liverpool	New York	05/22/1847	10/12/1857	15	408	N	
O'Day, Patrick	30	Ireland	Y	Canada	Buffalo	10/04/1850	06/08/1852	25	203	N	
O'Day, Patrick	33	Ireland	Y	Liverpool	New York	05/04/1849	03/20/1856	26	233	N	
O'Day, Thomas	27	Ireland	Y	Liverpool	New York	05/09/1847	06/08/1852	25	202	N	
O'Donald, Cornelius	22	Ireland	Y	Limerick	Burlington	07/07/1850	10/22/1852	5	52	N	
O'Donnall, James	35	Ireland	Y	Quebeck	New Hampshir	08/22/1847	11/03/1852	6	325	N	
O'Donnell, Bartholomew	32	Ireland	Y	Waterford	New York	06/01/1848	11/01/1852	5	174	N	
O'Donnell, Bartholomew	32	Ireland	Y	Waterford	New York	06/01/1848	11/01/1852	6	300	N	
O'Donnell, Bryon	51	Ireland	Y	Liverpool	New York	08/15/1844	09/04/1852	25	352	N	
O'Donnell, Con	30	Ireland	Y	Liverpool	New York	02/25/1847	04/26/1853	8	123	N	
O'Donnell, Frank	53	Ireland	N	Ireland	New York	11/05/1850	?	28	226	N	10/??/1858
O'Donnell, Frank	15	Ireland	N	?	New York	11/05/1850				Y	10/00/1858
O'Donnell, Isaac	29	Ireland	Y	Belfast	New York	10/31/1850	03/12/1852	24	294	N	
O'Donnell, James	25	Ireland	Y	Quebec	New Hampshir	08/22/1847	11/03/1852	5	198	N	
O'Donnell, Jeremiah	24	Ireland	Y	Liverpool	New York	03/29/1849	02/03/1851	3	83	N	
O'Donnell, John	24	Ireland	Y	Liverpool	New York	03/17/1848	11/29/1852	5	259	N	

CITIZENSHIP RECORDS

APPLICANT	AGE	COUNTRY OF ORIGIN	DEC	DEPART PORT	ENTRY PORT	ARRIVE DATE	DEC DATE	VOL	PG.	FLD	NAT DATE
O'Donnell, John	30	Ireland	Y	Limerick	New York	10/25/1847	03/26/1853	7	408	N	
O'Donnell, John	24	Ireland	Y	?	Boston	05/04/1851	11/03/1868			Y	
O'Donnell, Joseph	62	Ireland	N	Liverpool	New York	09/??/1864	?			Y	
O'Donnell, Owen	35	Ireland	Y	Liverpool	New York	03/28/1852	10/07/1854	6	30	N	
O'Donnell, Owen	34	Ireland	Y	Liverpool	New York	03/28/1852	10/07/1854	11	31	N	
O'Donnell, Patrick	35	Ireland	Y	Waterford	New York	11/04/1846	06/19/1851	3	418	N	
O'Donnell, Peter	25	Ireland	Y	Glasgow	New York	02/20/1848	04/12/1852	24	480	N	
O'Donnell, Richard	25	Ireland	Y	Queenstown	New York	10/13/1894	10/18/1894			Y	
O'Donnell, William	35	Ireland	Y	Londonderry	Enfield	09/01/1836	02/01/1850	2	28	N	
O'Donnell, William	37	Ireland	Y	Queenstown	New York	04/27/1882	10/25/1889			Y	
O'Donnovan, Timothy	31	Ireland	Y	Liverpool	New Orleans	04/02/1849	01/21/1853	7	50	N	
O'Dowd, James	38	Ireland	Y	Liverpool	New York	02/12/1843	11/01/1858	17	256	N	
O'Dowd, Michael	35	Ireland	N	Queenstown	New York	??/??/1869	?			Y	
O'Dowd, Owen	37	Ireland	Y	Sliga	New York	06/??/1874	10/09/1882			Y	
O'Farrell, Frank	??	Ireland	Y	?	?	05/23/1887	02/06/1889			Y	
O'Ferrell, Bernard	45	Ireland	Y	Canada	New York	11/01/1831	01/18/1851	2	505	N	
O'Flaherty, Patrick	19	Ireland	Y	Queenstown	?	07/12/1865	11/11/1865			Y	
O'Gara, James	34	England	Y	Toronto	Buffalo	12/07/1883	04/02/1889			Y	
O'Gara, Michael	24	Ireland	Y	Dublin	New York	05/02/1884	04/02/1889			Y	
O'Gara, Patrick	27	Ireland	Y	Liverpool	New York	08/31/1888	11/17/1894			Y	
O'Garra, John	40	Ireland	Y	Liverpool	New York	06/20/1859	09/29/1860	27	386	N	
O'Hara, Michael	23	Ireland	Y	Liverpool	New Orleans	11/28/1852	08/23/1855	11	488	N	
O'Hara, Michael	22	Ireland	Y	Queenstown	New York	04/18/1887	02/28/1890			Y	
O'Hara, Patrick	30	Ireland	Y	Liverpool	New Orleans	12/01/1849	09/30/1858	17	22	N	
O'Hara, Thomas	26	Ireland	Y	Liverpool	New York	09/??/1889	11/03/1893	21	49	N	
O'Hara, Thomas	26	Ireland	Y	Liverpool	New York	09/??/1889	11/03/1893			Y	
O'Hara, Thomas	56	Ireland	Y	Queenstown	New York	04/20/1887	03/16/1892			Y	
O'Hare, John	35	Ireland	Y	Liverpool	New York	05/??/1846	09/25/1858	16	146	N	
O'Hearn, Lawrence	25	Ireland	Y	Liverpool	New Orleans	10/22/1851	03/25/1856	26	316	N	
O'Hearn, Michael	24	Ireland	Y	Liverpool	New Orleans	10/22/1851	03/27/1856	26	356	N	
O'Hearn, Patrick	22	Ireland	Y	Liverpool	New Orleans	03/25/1853	03/27/1856	26	357	N	
O'Keefe, Michael	43	Ireland	Y	Queenstown	Cleveland	09/??/1857	04/??/1877			Y	
O'Keefe, Michael	58	Ireland	N	Queenstown	Cleveland	09/??/1857	?			Y	
O'Keefe, Thomas	37	Ireland	N	Queenstown	New York	05/??/1869	?			Y	
O'Keeffe, Arthur	24	Ireland	Y	Liverpool	New York	08/15/1848	05/22/1852	25	88	N	
O'Keeffe, Patrick	31	Ireland	Y	Liverpool	New York	07/08/1886	10/26/1892			Y	
O'Ker, Joseph	66	Germany	N	Antwerp	New York	05/05/1849	?			Y	
O'Ker, Joseph	68	Germany	N	Antwerp	New York	05/??/1849	?			Y	
O'Larty, Francis	34	France	Y	Havre	New York	03/06/1849	10/02/1857	15	342	N	
O'Laughlan, John	28	Ireland	Y	Limerick	Burlington	05/10/1845	09/25/1854	10	214	N	
O'Laughlan, John	28	Ireland	Y	Limerick	Burlington	05/10/1845	09/25/1954	12	153	N	
O'Laughlin, Thomas	28	Ireland	Y	Liverpool	Mobile	12/25/1851	02/??/1853	7	179	N	
O'Leary, James	24	Ireland	Y	Liverpool	New Orleans	12/26/1847	04/21/1850	3	8	N	
O'Leary, James	38	Ireland	Y	Liverpool	New Orleans	08/01/1850	11/16/1852	5	297	N	
O'Leary, James	38	Ireland	Y	Liverpool	New Orleans	08/01/1850	11/16/1852	6	422	N	
O'Leary, James	28	Ireland	Y	Tralee	Sandusky	07/04/1853	02/04/1860	27	87	N	
O'Leary, James J.	26	Ireland	Y	Liverpool	New York	11/??/1876	12/03/1883			Y	
O'Leary, John J.	24	Ireland	Y	Liverpool	New York	02/00/1874	12/03/1883			Y	
O'Mailley, Cornelius	36	Ireland	Y	Liverpool	New Orleans	04/23/1849	06/03/1852	25	177	N	
O'Maley, Patrick	45	Ireland	Y	Liverpool	New York	06/02/1847	09/04/1860	27	333	N	
O'Maley, Thomas	21	Ireland	Y	Galway	New York	02/29/1860	09/04/1860	27	334	N	
O'Malley, John	26	Ireland	Y	Queenstown	New York	08/24/1884	10/29/1892	19	404	N	
O'Malley, John	26	Ireland	Y	Queenstown	New York	08/14/1887	10/29/1892			Y	
O'Mara, John	26	Ireland	Y	Liverpool	Brooklyn	05/22/1847	05/17/1854	8	457	N	
O'Mara, John	26	Ireland	Y	Liverpool	Brooklyn	05/22/1847	05/17/1854	9	330	N	
O'Meara, James	24	Ireland	Y	Liverpool	New Orleans	05/09/1851	12/17/1852	5	420	N	
O'Meara, Thomas	17	Ireland	N	?	New York	07/00/1879				Y	10/27/1888
O'Mera, John	23	Ireland	Y	Liverpool	New York	06/06/1845	11/16/1848	1	280	N	
O'Molloy, John C.	34	Ireland	Y	Limrick	Buffalo	11/00/1882	05/19/1884			Y	

CITIZENSHIP RECORDS

APPLICANT	AGE	COUNTRY OF ORIGIN	DEC	DEPART PORT	ENTRY PORT	ARRIVE DATE	DEC DATE	VOL	PG.	FLD	NAT DATE
O'More, John	21	Ireland	Y	Liverpool	New York	07/16/1848	07/07/1851	3	504	N	
O'Neaill, Michael	24	Ireland	Y	Liverpool	New York	05/03/1846	06/08/1852	25	215	N	
O'Neal, James	22	Ireland	Y	Limerick	Buffalo	11/10/1849	02/18/1850	2	93	N	
O'Neal, Owen	23	Ireland	Y	Liverpool	New Orleans	05/03/1849	11/19/1852	5	311	N	
O'Neil, Daniel	25	Ireland	Y	Liverpool	New York	04/27/18??	08/27/1855	11	502	N	
O'Neil, John	21	Ireland	Y	Liverpool	New Orleans	12/23/1848	11/07/1851	4	499	N	
O'Neil, John	22	Ireland	Y	Liverpool	New York	10/02/1851	03/01/1853	7	253	N	
O'Neil, John	40	Ireland	Y	Queenstown	New York	07/23/1881	04/09/1891			Y	
O'Neil, Michael	35	Ireland	N	Liverpool	New York	05/??/1874	?			Y	
O'Neil, Patrick	25	Ireland	Y	Queenstown	Baltimore	06/02/1887	05/03/1892			Y	
O'Neil, Timothy	28	Ireland	Y	Canada	Boston	07/25/1839	02/02/1849	23	15	N	
O'Neil, William	30	Ireland	Y	Liverpool	New York	05/21/1848	04/14/1852	24	504	N	
O'Neill, Felix	9	Ireland	N	?	New York	00/00/1860				Y	10/23/1888
O'Neill, James W.	66	Ireland	N	Liverpool	New York	03/??/1858	?			Y	
O'Neill, John McKown	54	Ireland	Y	Dublin	New York	09/18/1847	02/19/1853	7	188	N	
O'Neill, Michael	27	Ireland	Y	Liverpool	New York	07/??/1845	11/03/1856	14	451	N	
O'Neill, Thomas	34	Ireland	Y	Queenstown	New York	05/03/1885	11/21/1893			Y	
O'Neill, Thomas	25	Ireland	Y	Liverpool	New York	10/08/1857	05/04/1860	27	179	N	
O'Reilly, John	??	Ireland	Y	Liverpool	New York	??/02/18??	04/19/1855	11	274	N	
O'Reilly, Philip	??	Ireland	Y	?	?	?	10/01/1886				
O'Rouke, John	23	Newfoundland	Y	St. John	Baltimore	10/??/1888	10/28/1893	21	44	N	
O'Rourke, Michael	24	Ireland	Y	Liverpool	New Orleans	11/??/1848	10/26/1850	2	311	N	
O'Shaughnessy, William	51	Ireland	N	Queenstown	Boston	09/12/1870	10/??/1874	28	53	N	10/??/1876
O'Shaughnessy, William	33	Ireland	N	Queenstown	Boston	09/12/1870	10/00/1874			Y	10/00/1876
O'Shea, Michael	28	Ireland	Y	Liverpool	New Orleans	04/20/1850	02/21/1857	15	40	N	
O'Sullivan, Michael	30	Ireland	Y	Limerick	Burlington	05/06/1850	05/06/1854	8	388	N	
O'Sullivan, Michael	30	Ireland	Y	Limerick	Burlington	05/06/1850	05/06/1854	9	261	N	
O'Sullivan, Michael	36	Ireland	Y	Liverpool	New Orleans	01/04/1850	06/04/1852	25	185	N	
O'Toole, Albert	26	Ireland	Y	Dublin	New York	06/22/1847	03/24/1853	7	378	N	
O'Toole, James	25	Ireland	Y	?	Port Huron	??/??/1891	07/27/1893			Y	
O'Toole, John	??	Ireland	N	?	?	04/22/1886				Y	10/14/1892
O'Toole, Michael	29	Ireland	Y	Queenstown	New York	09/01/1883	12/06/1886			Y	
Oakley, John	7	Ireland	N	?	New York	00/00/1852				Y	10/12/1888
Obendoerfer, George	24	Russia	Y	Hamburg	New York	04/12/1892	05/25/1894			Y	
Oberacher, Ludwig/Louis	17	Germany	N	?	New York	00/00/1878				Y	10/27/1888
Oberfell, Henry	42	Germany	N	Bremen	Baltimore	02/22/1871	09/30/1878	28	412	N	09/30/1895
Obergfell, Christian	29	Wurttemberg	Y	Liverpool	New York	03/30/1858	11/15/1861	18	225	N	
Oberhage, Henry	??	Germany	Y	Bremen	Baltimore	10/20/1883	10/26/1888			Y	
Oberhen, Ferdinand	63	Hanover	Y	Bremen	New York	06/18/1848	01/16/1849	1	438	N	
Oberhuber, Jacob	40	Austria	Y	Havre	New York	03/17/1882	02/06/1888			Y	
Oberhuber, William	29	Germany	Y	Hamburg	Philadelphia	09/29/1880	07/29/1884			Y	
Oberlaender, George	28	Germany	Y	Bremen	New York	10/12/1888	10/20/1888			Y	
Oberle, Edmond	27	Bavaria	Y	Havre	New York	06/09/1852	07/18/1855	11	408	N	
Oberlin, Christian	32	Mecklenburg S	Y	Hamburg	New York	12/??/1852	03/20/1856	26	236	N	
Obermann, Charles Freder	26	Hesse Darmsta	Y	Liverpool	New York	01/24/1850	02/16/1852	24	114	N	
Obermann, Henry	28	Germany	Y	Bremen	Baltimore	09/01/1891	04/10/1894			Y	
Obermann, John	33	Hesse Darmsta	Y	Bremen	New York	09/10/1850	06/04/1852	24	117	N	
Obermeier, Andrew	35	Bavaria	Y	Bremen	New York	08/15/1845	11/08/1858	17	302	N	
Obermeyer, Simon	76	Germany	N	Hamburg	New York	08/??/1837	10/??/1838	28	21	N	10/??/1842
Obermeyer, Simon	26	Germany	N	Hamburg	New York	08/00/1837	10/00/1838			Y	10/00/1842
Obermeyer, Tony	26	Germany	Y	Bremen	Baltimore	05/02/1883	12/19/1884			Y	
Oberreuther, Augustus	33	Saxony	Y	Bremen	New York	08/02/1848	10/21/1852	5	39	N	
Oberst, Lorenz	34	Bavaria	Y	Havre	New York	10/24/1854	03/07/1856	26	170	N	
Obertscheider, John	28	Austria	Y	Havre	New York	12/19/1889	10/15/1892			Y	
Oberwegner, Adolf	29	Germany	Y	Hamburg	New York	03/04/1881	03/30/1886			Y	
Oberwitte, Henry	26	Germany	Y	Bremen	New York	10/20/1882	07/25/1888			Y	
Obser, John	39	Germany	Y	Antwerp	New York	09/04/1890	12/05/1892			Y	
Obst, William	30	Prussia	Y	Hamburg	New York	08/??/1854	12/24/1855	13	357	N	
Ochner, Vital	32	Switzerland	Y	?	?	08/11/1877	04/02/1888			Y	

CITIZENSHIP RECORDS

APPLICANT	AGE	COUNTRY OF ORIGIN	DEC	DEPART PORT	ENTRY PORT	ARRIVE DATE	DEC DATE	VOL	PG.	FLD	NAT DATE
Ochs, John	33	Germany	Y	Bremen	New York	06/14/1890	10/20/1899			Y	
Ochs, John S.	65	Germany	N	Bremen	New York	09/14/1848	?			Y	
Ochs, Michael	24	Hesse Darmsta	Y	London	New York	04/??/1850	08/18/1855	11	451	N	
Ochsner, Meinrad	36	Switzerland	Y	Havre	New York	05/13/1854	10/29/1858	17	181	N	
Ocke, Heinrich	50	Germany	Y	Bremen	New York	07/??/1866	10/24/1888			Y	
Ocker, H. W.	22	Hanover	Y	Bremen	New York	05/25/1857	10/08/1860	27	429	N	
Ockermann, William	34	Germany	Y	Havre	New York	10/08/1877	10/02/1882			Y	
Ockert, Matthew	22	Germany	Y	Havre	New York	03/26/1890	05/02/1893			Y	
Ockrant, Abraham	27	Russia	Y	Hamburg	New York	09/13/1888	04/21/1894			Y	
Oeder, George	56	Germany	N	Bremen	New York	09/10/1853	?			Y	
Oeder, John Conrad	24	Bavaria	Y	Bremen	New York	12/13/1855	02/27/1856	26	133	N	
Oefinger, Mattheus	25	Germany	Y	Havre	New York	04/09/1884	11/04/1887			Y	
Oeftiger, Albert	27	Prussia	Y	Bremen	New York	05/??/1848	11/??/1849	23	296	N	
Oeh, Conrad	31	Bavaria	Y	Bremen	New York	08/19/1848	09/13/1852	25	483	N	
Oehlering, Henry	21	Prussia	Y	Bremen	New Orleans	11/15/1853	10/10/1854	6	224	N	
Oehmann, Franz	27	Baden	Y	Havre	New York	07/01/1857	02/06/1860	27	90	N	
Oehne, William	26	Hanover	Y	Bremen	New York	07/04/1853	03/15/1856	26	204	N	
Oehr, George	26	Bavaria	Y	Bremen	Baltimore	12/13/1853	04/11/1856	26	487	N	
Oehrling, Henry	21	Prussia	Y	Bremen	New York	11/15/1853	10/10/1854	11	227	N	
Oeleker, Joseph	46	Prussia	Y	?	New Orleans	04/17/1854	09/22/18??	10	169	N	
Oeler, Karl Ulrich	??	Switzerland	Y	?	?	?	12/31/1892			Y	
Oelgemueller, George	38	Prussia	Y	Bremen	Baltimore	10/16/1849	11/01/1852	5	123	N	
Oelgeschlaeger, Wilhelm	23	Germany	Y	Hamburg	New York	04/27/1884	04/13/1888			Y	
Oelker, Joseph	46	Prussia	Y	Bremen	New Orleans	04/17/1854	09/22/1854	12	018	N	
Oelkers, John Christophe	23	Hanover	Y	Hamburg	New York	09/21/1859	05/25/1861	18	178	N	
Oelschlaegel, Fredrick	36	Germany	N	Bremen	New York	10/??/1876	?			Y	
Oelschlaeger, George Dav	31	Germany	Y	Havre	New York	12/31/1880	03/23/1891			Y	
Oenbrink, Clemens	26	Germany	Y	Bremen	Baltimore	06/02/1881	02/08/1884			Y	
Oerthle, Louis	35	Germany	Y	Rotterdam	New York	06/15/1882	09/26/1887			Y	
Oertker, Herman	37	Prussia	Y	Bremen	New York	12/20/1846	12/15/1851	4	520	N	
Oertlly, John	26	Switzerland	Y	Havre	New York	09/24/1885	04/10/1893	19	421	N	
Oertly, John	26	Switzerland	Y	Havre	New York	09/24/1885	04/10/1893			Y	
Oeser, John	26	Mecklenburg S	Y	Bremen	New Orleans	03/26/1853	03/27/1856	26	363	N	
Oesper, George	38	Bavaria	Y	Bremen	Buffalo	08/06/1847	04/04/1853	8	36	N	
Oesten, John	52	Germany	N	Bremen	New York	05/08/1860	?			Y	
Oesteneicher, Samuel	??	Austria	Y	?	?	?	10/15/1895			Y	
Oestenling, Joachim	27	Hesse Darmsta	Y	Havre	New York	??/05/18??	10/09/1848	1	97	N	
Oesterle, Henry	25	Baden	Y	Havre	New York	10/26/1853	08/15/1857	15	138	N	
Oesterle, Jacob	23	Hohenzoller	Y	Havre	New York	??/08/1845	11/06/1849	23	322	N	
Oesterle, John George	??	Wurttemberg	Y	Havre	New York	06/22/1847	04/20/1850	3	4	N	
Oesting, Henry	27	Germany	Y	Bremen	New York	07/19/1893	12/06/1895			Y	
Oestreicher, Valentin Al	52	Bavaria	Y	Hamburg	New York	07/29/1852	02/28/1853	7	241	N	
Oetting, Fredrich	60	Germany	N	Bremen	New Orleans	??/??/1856	?			Y	
Offenbacher, Frederick	29	Bavaria	Y	Havre	New York	11/07/1852	10/06/1854	12	438	N	
Offenbaecher, Frederick	29	Bavaria	Y	Havre	New York	11/07/1752	10/06/1854	10	499	N	
Offergeld, Wilhelm Heinr	37	Germany	Y	Rotterdam	Jersey City	06/25/1889	09/15/1892			Y	
Ogden, Samuel	31	England	Y	Liverpool	New Orleans	02/07/1849	05/21/1852	25	85	N	
Ogdon, Thomas	37	England	Y	Liverpool	New York	06/20/1841	01/23/1849	1	501	N	
Ogul, Solomon	21	Russia	Y	Hamburg	Boston	01/20/1897	10/29/1897			Y	
Ogulin, Johann	45	Austria	Y	Bremen	Baltimore	05/02/1857	04/25/1861	18	146	N	
Ohl, William	15	Canada	N	?	Detroit	00/00/1876				Y	10/24/1888
Ohlemacher, Phillip	58	Germany	N	Germany	New York	11/01/1851	?			Y	
Ohlendorf, Louis	19	Germany	Y	Bremen	New York	01/04/1891	04/18/1892			Y	
Ohler, Nick	48	Germany	Y	Bremen	New York	07/24/1863	07/05/1890			Y	
Ohlesen, Hans	25	Delstem	Y	Hamburg	New York	11/30/1859	12/26/1859	17	527	N	
Ohleyer, George	23	Bavaria	Y	Havre	New York	11/15/1853	03/24/1856	26	267	N	
Ohlhant, Martin	51	Germany	Y	Bremen	New York	04/13/1892	10/26/1900			Y	
Ohliger, Lewis	22	Germany	Y	Zwerboncken	New York	04/07/1877	09/13/1878			Y	
Ohlmeier, John H.	22	Hanover	Y	Bremen	Baltimore	05/16/1854	02/04/1856	26	27	N	

CITIZENSHIP RECORDS

APPLICANT	AGE	COUNTRY OF ORIGIN	DEC	DEPART PORT	ENTRY PORT	ARRIVE DATE	DEC DATE	VOL	PG.	FLD	NAT DATE
Ohmer, Frank Peter	32	Bavaria	Y	Havre	New York	04/12/1852	02/09/1856	26	67	N	
Ohmor, Nik	44	Germany	Y	Antwerp	New York	04/10/1885	03/30/1891	19	325	N	
Ohnesorgen, H. W. C.	38	Germany	Y	Bremen	Baltimore	09/09/1881	04/06/1885			Y	
Ohnesorgen, Henry	27	Germany	Y	Bremen	New York	05/02/1888	10/12/1892			Y	
Ohnstein, George	25	Germany	Y	?	New York	04/02/1893	10/04/1893			Y	
Ohr, Henry	26	Oldenburg	Y	Bremen	Baltimore	11/14/1859	11/01/1860	27	543	N	
Okrant, Joseph	32	Russia	Y	Bremen	Baltimore	08/01/1889	10/08/1896			Y	
Olberding, Anton	25	Oldenburg	Y	Bremen	Baltimore	06/??/1845	12/31/1849	23	445	N	
Olberding, Henry Ferdina	24	Oldenburg	Y	Bremen	New Orleans	11/11/1849	01/19/1852	24	24	N	
Olbert, Bernard	22	Germany	Y	Antwerp	New York	05/07/1888	08/05/1892			N	
Oldegering, Henry	27	Hanover	Y	Bremen	New Orleans	11/27/1849	11/01/1852	5	115	N	
Olderding, Joseph	42	Oldenburg	Y	Oldenburg	Baltimore	05/02/1849	08/04/1851	4	83	N	
Oldewage, August	31	Germany	Y	Hanover	New York	11/??/1877	10/26/1889	19	268	N	
Oldewage, August	31	Germany	Y	Hanover	New York	11/??/1877	10/26/1889			Y	
Oldewage, Lewis	24	Germany	Y	Bremen	New York	10/15/1879	09/26/1884			Y	
Olding, Henry	27	Germany	Y	Bremen	Baltimore	07/04/1892	02/21/1893			Y	
Olgee, Barney	23	Hanover	Y	Bremen	New Orleans	12/29/1847	01/06/1851	2	467	N	
Olgemuller, George	38	Prussia	Y	Bremen	Baltimore	10/16/1849	11/01/1852	6	249	N	
Olges, Herman	25	Hanover	Y	Bremen	New Orleans	11/01/1852	10/09/1854	11	80	N	
Olges, Hermann	25	Hanover	Y	Bremen	New Orleans	11/01/1852	10/09/1854	6	77+	N	
Oliver, Alexander H.	56	Scotland	Y	Canada	Detroit	11/15/1856	10/23/1896			Y	
Olliger, Herman	27	Germany	Y	Amsterdam	New York	10/29/1891	10/25/1898			Y	
Olliges, Christian	24	Germany	Y	Bremen	Baltimore	05/04/1899	10/29/1900			Y	
Olliges, Heinrich	34	Germany	Y	Bremen	Baltimore	05/14/1889	09/05/1891			Y	
Olschinsky, Fred	23	Austria	Y	Bremen	New York	07/16/1887	06/02/1888			Y	
Olshewitz, Nathan	30	Russia	Y	Hamburg	New York	05/13/1880	10/00/1883			Y	
Olswang, Raphael	42	Russia	Y	Hamburg	New York	12/26/1887	09/06/1889			Y	
Olthaus, Barney	50	Bremen	N	Bremen	Baltimore	10/??/1864	??/??/1876	28	134	N	??/??/1878
Oltheus, Bernard	39	Holland	Y	Rotterdam	New Orleans	12/12/1848	02/19/1849	23	200	N	
Oltheus, Herman	35	Holland	Y	Rotterdam	New York	05/28/1847	02/19/1849	23	164	N	
Olthous, Barney	26	Germany	N	Bremen	Baltimore	10/00/1864	00/00/1876			Y	00/00/1878
Omnitz, Charles	59	Germany	Y	Bremen	Baltimore	10/15/1891	08/31/1896			Y	
Omnitz, John	30	Germany	Y	Bremen	New York	04/17/1892	10/08/1896			Y	
Onnen, Michael Ferdinand	42	Oldenburg	Y	London	New York	07/11/18??	02/28/1853	7	245	N	
Onoroto, Pasqualino	24	Italy	Y	Naples	New York	04/27/1890	03/22/1894			Y	
Ons, John	27	Hanover	Y	Bremen	New Orleans	11/15/1845	01/23/1849	1	493	N	
Ontrup, Henry	??	Germany	Y	?	?	?	02/10/1887			Y	
Oonk, John D.	40	Holland	Y	Rotterdam	New York	06/18/1848	09/15/1855	13	36	N	
Oostendorp, Hubert	37	Germany	Y	Rotterdam	New York	04/11/1880	01/29/1883			Y	
Opel, William	??	Germany	Y	?	?	10/00/1881	11/01/1886			Y	
Oppel, George	40	Germany	Y	Bremen	Baltimore	10/06/1874	10/01/1885			Y	
Oppenheimer, Asser Moses	27	Holland	Y	Rotterdam	New York	01/15/1857	03/31/1862	18	292	N	
Oppenheimer, Charles	25	Bavaria	Y	Havre	New York	10/12/1852	10/07/1854	6	45	N	
Oppenheimer, Charles	25	Bavaria	Y	Havre	New York	10/12/1852	10/07/1852	11	46	N	
Oppenheimer, Lee	25	Bavaria	Y	Bremen	New York	05/13/1868	02/22/1872	18	557	N	
Oppermann, John Balthase	40	France	Y	Havre	New York	11/12/1852	02/10/1853	7	139	N	
Ording, Herman	38	Oldenburg	Y	Bremen	New Orleans	01/??/1846	10/03/1854	10	393	N	
Ording, Herman	38	Oldenburg	Y	Bremen	New Orleans	01/??/1846	10/03/1854	12	332	N	
Ording, Joseph	30	Germany	Y	Bremen	New York	09/11/1888	03/19/1894			Y	
Orlik, Louis	35	Austria	Y	Bremen	Baltimore	08/11/1887	04/06/1891			Y	
Orlin, Noah	42	Russia	Y	Hamburg	New York	08/16/1886	10/23/1896			Y	
Ornstein, Anshel	40	Russia	Y	Bremen	New York	11/28/1886	11/26/1887			Y	
Orr, John	32	Ireland	Y	Sligo	Buffalo	07/01/1847	06/10/1861	18	187	N	
Orsi, Raffale	33	Italy	Y	Naples	New York	03/19/1887	12/03/1897			Y	
Orstmann, Henrich	55	Germany	Y	Bremen	New York	10/11/1883	10/30/1896			Y	
Orszmann, John Casper	25	Hanover	Y	Bremen	Baltimore	10/03/1850	06/10/1852	25	314	N	
Ortell, Joseph	36	Germany	Y	Bremen	Baltimore	06/03/1883	07/30/1886			Y	
Orth, Lorentz	20	Bavaria	Y	Havre	New Orleans	12/03/1850	09/27/1858	16	119	N	
Orthig, Charles	32	Prussia	Y	Hamburg	New York	06/20/1848	06/18/1851	3	395	N	

CITIZENSHIP RECORDS

APPLICANT	AGE	COUNTRY OF ORIGIN	DEC	DEPART PORT	ENTRY PORT	ARRIVE DATE	DEC DATE	VOL	PG.	FLD	NAT DATE
Orthmann, Fred	27	Wuerttenberg	Y	London	New York	06/15/1849	05/31/1852	25	139	N	
Orthwein, John	29	Germany	Y	Hamburg	Philadelphia	07/04/1881	02/28/1889			Y	
Ortlepp, Fred	??	Germany	Y	?	?	04/01/1882	10/26/1886			Y	
Ortman, Charles	49	Hanover	Y	Bremen	New Orleans	01/08/1847	03/19/1850	2	222	N	
Ortman, Herman	33	Oldenburg	Y	Bremen	Baltimore	10/19/1844	07/29/1848	22	9	N	
Ortmann, August	23	Germany	Y	Bremen	New York	07/13/1880	05/06/1882			Y	
Ortmann, Barney	22	Oldenburg	Y	Bremen	Baltimore	08/01/1858	11/01/1860	27	534	N	
Ortmann, Emanuel Adolph	42	Prussia	Y	Bremen	New Orleans	11/20/1853	11/06/1860	18	26	N	
Ortmann, Friederich	48	Germany	Y	Bremen	Baltimore	10/05/1883	12/26/1885			Y	
Ortmann, Henry Frederick	26	Hanover	Y	Bremen	New York	09/15/1856	10/20/1858	17	68	N	
Ortner, Max	17	Austria	N	?	New York	00/00/1879				Y	10/15/1888
Ortwerth, Henry	28	Hanover	Y	Bremen	New Orleans	11/20/1853	03/26/1857	15	89	N	
Osborne, Jabez	22	England	Y	Liverpool	New York	09/10/1889	07/07/1892			Y	
Osborne, James	28	England	Y	Liverpool	New York	05/03/1887	10/26/1891			Y	
Osburg, Joseph	29	Prussia	Y	Bremen	New York	07/15/1859	10/08/1860	27	432	N	
Oscherowitz, Louis	22	Russia	Y	Hamburg	New York	05/29/1897	04/29/1902			Y	
Oscherwitz, Isaac	32	Russia	Y	Hamburg	New York	12/17/1885	10/11/1888			Y	
Oscherwitz, Samuel	23	Russia	Y	Hamburg	New York	12/17/1885	10/11/1888			Y	
Oser, Ernst	31	Baden	Y	Havre	New York	06/26/1855	12/16/1859	17	505	N	
Oser, Leopold	43	Germany	N	Bremen	New York	03/14/1868	?			Y	
Oser, Matheus	22	Baden	Y	Havre	New Orleans	01/15/1853	12/26/1855	13	363	N	
Oshrovitz, George	24	Russia	Y	Hamburg	Philadelphia	08/16/1891	03/20/1894			Y	
Osiander, Charles Theodo	24	Wurttemberg	Y	Havre	New York	08/16/1851	07/17/1855	11	402	N	
Osseforth, John Herman	24	Hanover	Y	Bremen	New Orleans	11/29/1855	03/17/1858	16	419	N	
Osseforth, John Joseph	55	Germany	N	Bremen	New Orleans	10/28/1851	?			Y	
Ossege, H.	34	Hanover	Y	Bremen	Baltimore	11/03/1857	11/01/1860	27	520	N	
Osselski, Jacob	42	Russia	Y	Hamburg	New York	07/25/1890	06/11/1894			Y	
Ossenbeck, John Frederic	23	Altenburgh	Y	Bremen	New Orleans	??/12/1847	02/12/1850	2	61	N	
Ossenschmidt, Charles	22	Germany	Y	Bremen	New York	09/12/1891	09/25/1894			Y	
Ossenschmidt, Christ.	23	Germany	Y	Bremen	Baltimore	10/07/1880	01/12/1883			Y	
Osswald, Emanuel	21	Wurttemberg	Y	Hamburg	New York	04/23/1860	01/07/1861	18	45	N	
Osten, Charles	26	Mecklenburg S	Y	Hamburg	New York	11/09/1851	11/01/1852	5	139	N	
Osten, Charles	26	Mecklenburg S	Y	Hamburg	New York	11/09/1851	11/01/1852	6	265	N	
Ostendorf, Bernard Henry	30	Hanover	Y	Bremen	New Orleans	12/04/1849	09/25/1854	10	222	N	
Ostendorf, Bernard Henry	30	Hanover	Y	Bremen	New Orleans	12/04/1849	09/25/1854	12	161	N	
Ostendorf, Casper Henry	??	Oldenburg	Y	Bremen	New Orleans	01/14/1845	10/09/1848	22	503	N	
Ostendorf, Edward	17	Germany	N	?	New York	00/00/1879				Y	11/05/1888
Ostendorf, George	38	Hanover	Y	Bremen	Baltimore	08/18/1847	02/21/1850	2	113	N	
Ostendorf, Henry	??	Oldenburg	Y	Bremen	Baltimore	05/26/18??	10/11/1848	1	113	N	
Ostendorf, John Henry	51	Prussia	Y	Bremen	New Orleans	01/26/1854	08/05/1856	14	344	N	
Ostendorf, Joseph	45	Prussia	Y	Bremen	Baltimore	08/06/1846	10/17/1851	4	316	N	
Ostendorf, Mathias	23	Hanover	Y	Bremen	Baltimore	05/22/1847	01/15/1853	7	26	N	
Osterfeld, George	25	Germany	Y	?	?	?	01/27/1881			Y	
Osterhoff, Anton H.	22	Germany	Y	Bremen	Baltimore	11/19/1882	08/04/1886			Y	
Osterholt, Anton	22	Holland	Y	Rotterdam	New York	09/25/1849	11/01/1852	5	179	N	
Osterholt, Anton	22	Holland	Y	Rotterdam	New York	09/25/1849	11/01/1852	6	306	N	
Osterhus, Friederich	25	Germany	Y	Bremen	New York	08/02/1893	12/26/1894			Y	
Osterkamp, Joseph	35	Oldenburg	Y	Bremen	New Orleans	10/28/1852	10/02/1856	14	154	N	
Osterlitz, Frank	39	Germany	Y	Bremen	Baltimore	07/26/1885	01/11/1892			Y	
Osterlitz, Theodor	34	Germany	Y	Bremen	New York	04/21/1884	01/14/1892			Y	
Ostermaier, Peter	32	Germany	Y	Antwerp	New York	03/27/1887	10/28/1892			Y	
Ostermann, Conrad	38	Bavaria	Y	Havre	New York	06/09/1852	07/09/1855	11	362	N	
Ostermann, Eugene	34	Germany	Y	Havre	New York	10/01/1893	11/11/1898			Y	
Ostermeier, Lorenz	36	Germany	Y	Bremen	New York	02/18/1882	05/29/1885			Y	
Osterroth, Aug	29	Brunswick	Y	Bremen	New York	06/02/1857	02/14/1860	27	107	N	
Osterwisch, Frederick	52	Prussia	Y	Bremen	New Orleans	11/15/1857	11/23/1861	18	228	N	
Osterwisch, L. W.	24	Germany	Y	Bremen	New York	07/28/1883	03/11/1886			Y	
Ostheimer, August	49	Germany	Y	Havre	New York	06/09/1879	10/27/1888			Y	
Ostheimn, August	49	Germany	Y	Havre	New York	06/09/1879	10/27/1888	19	189	N	

291

CITIZENSHIP RECORDS

APPLICANT	AGE	COUNTRY OF ORIGIN	DEC	DEPART PORT	ENTRY PORT	ARRIVE DATE	DEC DATE	VOL	PG.	FLD	NAT DATE
Ostholthoff, Barney	56	Germany	N	Antwerp	New York	09/22/1867	?			Y	
Ostkotte, John H.	33	Germany	Y	Antwerp	New York	08/10/1885	04/15/1892			Y	
Ostler, John	35	England	Y	London	New York	05/02/1848	11/19/1855	13	231	N	
Ostler, William	31	England	Y	Liverpool	Boston	07/26/1846	11/19/1855	13	232	N	
Ostmeyer, Henry	31	Germany	Y	Amsterdam	New York	05/28/1881	06/08/1886			Y	
Ostrop, John	29	Germany	Y	Bremen	New York	10/19/1886	08/21/1893			Y	
Ostrovsky, Max	28	Russia	Y	Hamburg	Philadelphia	08/15/1891	02/02/1897			Y	
Ostrovsky, Morris	25	Russia	Y	Hamburg	Philadelphia	09/29/1891	01/05/1894			Y	
Oswald, Edward	30	Germany	Y	Havre	New York	11/07/1891	03/26/1894			Y	
Oswald, Franz	19	Germany	Y	Bremen	New York	04/08/1880	07/21/1882			Y	
Oswald, Gottlieb	??	Germany	N	?	?	07/27/1886					10/14/1892
Oswald, John	27	Hesse Cassel	Y	Havre	New York	12/01/1847	01/16/1849	1	431	N	
Oswald, John	28	Hohenzollern	Y	Bremen	New York	05/12/1853	06/05/1854	10	95	N	
Oswald, John	28	Hohenzollen S	Y	Bremen	New York	05/12/1853	06/05/1854	12	32	N	
Oswald, Joseph	32	Germany	N	Antwerp	Philadelphia	11/03/1874	?			Y	
Oswaldt, August	29	Prussia	Y	Bremen	New Orleans	02/15/1849	05/20/1852	25	73	N	
Oszwein, George	??	Germany	N	?	?	?	04/07/1879	28	404	N	10/11/1881
Othling, Herman	50	Germany	N	Bremen	New York	09/16/1864	?			Y	
Otke, Peter	23	Hanover	Y	Bremen	Baltimore	11/12/1848	03/15/1852	24	314	N	
Otleib, Jacob	29	Wuerttemberg	Y	Bremen	New York	04/20/1857	01/09/1860	27	46	N	
Otner, Harris	??	Russia	Y	?	?	?	03/02/1888			Y	
Ott, Adam	64	Germany	N	Havre	New York	05/10/1845	?			Y	
Ott, Anton	45	Germany	Y	Bremen	New York	09/28/1882	10/02/1897			Y	
Ott, August	16	Germany	N	?	Baltimore	00/00/1883				Y	10/25/1888
Ott, Bernard	26	Wuerttemberg	Y	Antwerp	New York	10/26/1848	01/15/1850	23	514	N	
Ott, Christoph	28	Germany	Y	Bremen	New York	04/23/1880	09/23/1887			Y	
Ott, Edward	19	Germany	Y	Antwerp	New York	02/25/1890	06/30/1890			Y	
Ott, Edward	41	Germany	Y	Hamburg	New York	09/27/1882	01/29/1889			Y	
Ott, Eugene	26	Germany	Y	Rotterdam	New York	11/01/1889	11/03/1892			Y	
Ott, Fred	34	Germany	Y	Bremen	New York	02/24/1873	06/09/1887			Y	
Ott, George Valentine	43	Germany	Y	Antwerp	New York	06/29/1887	11/01/1890			Y	
Ott, Henry	27	Bavaria	Y	Hamburg	New York	07/19/1845	03/11/1851	3	249	N	
Ott, John	30	Hohenzollern	Y	Havre	New Orleans	07/04/1846	01/07/1851	2	472	N	
Ott, John	45	Wuerttemberg	Y	Antwerp	New York	10/26/1848	01/??/1850	23	513	N	
Ott, John George	22	Bavaria	Y	Havre	New York	07/28/1845	10/02/1848	1	30	N	
Ott, John Meier	30	Bavaria	Y	Bremen	New Orleans	01/??/1855	01/01/1861	18	37	N	
Ott, Martin	27	Germany	Y	Bremen	New York	07/21/1882	10/29/1887			Y	
Ott, Philip	23	Germany	Y	?	New York	??/??/1881	07/21/1884			Y	
Ott, William	22	Baden	Y	Havre	New York	04/03/1854	08/04/1856	14	329	N	
Otte, August	29	Germany	Y	Bremen	Baltimore	07/24/1881	02/11/1885			Y	
Otte, Bernard	32	Prussia	Y	Bremen	New Orleans	05/05/1849	11/05/1855	13	159	N	
Otte, Charles	??	Germany	Y	?	?	?	01/17/1890			Y	
Otte, H.	24	Germany	Y	Bremen	New York	03/12/1882	10/06/1884			Y	
Otte, Henry	24	Prussia	Y	Bremen	New York	11/12/1845	08/12/1851	4	120	N	
Otte, Henry	28	Germany	Y	Bremen	Baltimore	09/01/1881	10/10/1884			Y	
Otte, Henry	23	Hanover	Y	Bremen	Baltimore	08/28/1858	09/03/1860	27	326	N	
Otte, Hermann	??	Germany	Y	?	?	?	08/12/1868			Y	
Ottens, George	42	Germany	Y	Amsterdam	New York	01/??/1884	01/??/1884			Y	
Otting, Barney	28	Hanover	Y	Bremen	New Orleans	11/02/1848	11/22/1852	5	326	N	
Otting, John H.	30	Germany	Y	Rotterdam	Boston	09/30/1877	09/07/1880			Y	
Otting, William	32	Hanover	Y	Bremen	Baltimore	11/04/1848	11/01/1851	4	463	N	
Ottke, John Herman	17	Germany	N	Bremen	New Orleans	02/01/1842				Y	10/00/1848
Ottke, John Hermann	64	Germany	N	Bremen	New Orleans	02/01/1842	?	28	31	N	10/??/1848
Ottmann, Michael	32	Germany	Y	Rotterdam	New York	08/10/1880	09/25/1885			Y	
Ottnad, Frederick	46	Germany	Y	Hamburg	New York	06/15/1880	03/27/1891	19	319	N	
Otto, Augustus	38	Schwarzburg R	Y	Bremen	New York	08/??/1848	03/08/1858	16	385	N	
Otto, Ferdinand	30	Germany	Y	Bremen	New York	05/04/1893	03/25/1898			Y	
Otto, Frederick	26	Hanover	Y	Bremen	New York	09/??/1844	12/??/1849	23	421	N	
Otto, G.	52	Germany	Y	Bremen	Baltimore	07/06/1870	02/19/1883			Y	

CITIZENSHIP RECORDS

APPLICANT	AGE	COUNTRY OF ORIGIN	DEC	DEPART PORT	ENTRY PORT	ARRIVE DATE	DEC DATE	VOL	PG.	FLD	NAT DATE
Otto, William	23	Hesse Cassel	Y	Bremen	Baltimore	07/18/1855	05/23/1856	26	542	N	
Otto, William H.	29	Germany	Y	Hamburg	New York	03/04/1878	03/05/1883			Y	
Overbeck, Henry	30	Oldenburg	Y	Bremen	New Orleans	07/??/1849	11/26/1852	5	346	N	
Overbeck, Henry William	21	Hanover	Y	Bremen	New Orleans	05/03/1849	06/14/1852	25	266	N	
Overbeck, Henry William	86	Germany	N	Bremen	New Orleans	05/03/1849	06/14/1852	28	567	N	09/27/1854
Overbecke, Henry	35	Hanover	Y	Bremen	New Orleans	12/??/1851	12/11/1851	4	507	N	
Overbecks, Gerhard Henri	29	Hanover	Y	Bremen	New Orleans	01/12/1848	10/18/1851	4	333	N	
Overberg, Henry	40	Hanover	Y	Bremen	New Orleans	02/01/1857	09/03/1860	27	323	N	
Overberg, Joseph	21	Hanover	Y	Bremen	New Orleans	11/03/1849	02/??/1853	7	185	N	
Overdick, John Henry	27	Prussia	Y	Bremen	Baltimore	05/02/1851	09/21/1854	12	91	N	
Overdieck, John Henry	27	Prussia	Y	Bremen	Baltimore	05/21/1851	09/21/1854	10	152	N	
Overheu, Frederick Augus	42	Hanover	Y	Bremen	Baltimore	11/04/1840	03/25/1850	2	249	N	
Overman, Henry	53	Germany	Y	Bremen	Baltimore	09/??/1865	10/04/1880			Y	
Overmann, Henry	32	Germany	Y	Bremen	New York	05/08/1888	12/09/1890			Y	
Overmann, Ph.	31	Prussia	Y	Bremerhafen	Baltimore	05/??/1859	01/16/1861	18	62	N	
Overmeyer, B.	32	Germany	Y	Bremen	New York	07/11/1880	07/30/1883			Y	
Owen, Richard	24	Wales	Y	Liverpool	New York	09/23/1881	01/08/1885			Y	
Owens, Michael	??	Ireland	N	?	?	02/14/1884				Y	10/13/1892
Owens, Patrick	30	Ireland	Y	Liverpool	New Orleans	04/02/1849	02/10/1852	24	87	N	
Owens, Terence	26	England	Y	Liverpool	Philadelphia	10/23/1891	10/26/1897			Y	
Owens, William	??	Wales	N	?	?	01/02/1884				Y	11/04/1892
Pabst, Konrad	41	Germany	Y	Bremen	New York	04/14/1883	02/21/1882			Y	
Pace, Agostina	26	Italy	Y	Naples	New York	07/07/1892	10/18/1899			Y	
Pace, Biaggio	56	Italy	Y	Naples	New York	04/15/1879	10/22/1900			Y	
Pace, Giacomo	32	Italy	Y	Palermo	New York	08/01/1888	10/17/1893	21	16	N	
Pace, Giacomo	32	Italy	Y	Palermo	New York	08/01/1888	10/17/1893			Y	
Pachet, Francis	17	France	N	?	New York	00/00/1864				Y	10/22/1888
Pade, William	27	Switzerland	Y	Havre	New York	06/23/1885	10/31/1893			Y	
Padley, Herbert	42	England	Y	Liverpool	Cincinnati?	10/26/1878	02/20/1886			Y	
Padmore, Albert Edward	19	England	Y	?	?	?	07/20/1886			Y	
Paetow, Otto	34	Germany	Y	Hamburg	New York	08/11/1881	11/25/1889			Y	
Paffryman, James	33	England	Y	Liverpool	New York	09/17/1853	09/08/1857	15	244	N	
Pagani, Gaetano	46	Italy	Y	Genova	New York	05/22/1885	10/25/1900			Y	
Page, Noah	42	England	Y	Liverpool	New York	09/12/1868	11/04/1889			Y	
Pagel, Otto	21	Germany	Y	Bremen	New York	04/29/1893	06/15/1896			Y	
Pagenhardt, Julius	??	Germany	Y	?	?	?	12/24/1888			Y	
Pahl, Anthony	29	Germany	Y	Winterberg	New York	02/07/1870	11/05/1880			Y	
Pahls, Heinrich	33	Oldenburg	Y	Bremen	Baltimore	07/29/1860	11/01/1860	27	544	N	
Pahls, Henry	23	Germany	Y	Rotterdam	New York	10/11/1884	03/14/1884			Y	
Pahls, Wilhelm	23	Germany	Y	Bremen	Baltimore	06/27/1883	11/01/1887			Y	
Pallat, Charles	51	Germany	N	Germany	New York	09/22/1871	09/27/1876	28	219	N	10/03/1878
Palmer, Charles Edward	67	England	Y	?	?	08/18/1870	09/01/1882			Y	
Palmisano, Francesco	30	Italy	Y	Palermo	New York	01/05/1888	02/28/1888			Y	
Palmisano, Frank	27	Italy	Y	Palermo	New York	09/27/1882	11/17/1887			Y	
Palmisano, John	34	Italy	Y	Palermo	New York	12/10/1882	10/20/1893			Y	
Palmisano, Rosana	54	Italy	Y	Palermo	New York	04/21/1883	01/24/1890			Y	
Palmisano, Vincenzo	38	Italy	Y	Palermo	New York	03/26/1891	10/19/1893			Y	
Paluska, Joseph	39	Hungary	Y	Hamburg	New York	10/??/1853	10/09/1860	27	471	N	
Pandorf, Charles	28	Saxony	Y	Hamburg	New York	05/17/1854	03/13/1856	26	194	N	
Pandorf, Ernst C.	??	Germany	Y	?	?	?	04/26/1886			Y	
Pann, Carl	30	Mecklenburg S	Y	Hamburg	New York	11/20/1853	09/27/1854	12	196	N	
Panner, John	40	Baden	Y	Havre	New York	06/29/1848	01/02/1851	2	441	N	
Pantel, Joseph	26	Germany	Y	Rotterdam	Jersey City	04/29/1887	05/26/1890			Y	
Panter, Ignatz	42	Germany	N	Hamburg	New York	02/??/1872	?			Y	
Panzer, Jacob	31	Germany	Y	Hamburg	New York	06/06/1881	10/06/1885			Y	
Paono, Marco	42	Italy	Y	Naples	New York	04/22/1891	10/11/1894			Y	
Pape, Conrad	33	Brunswick	Y	Bremen	New Orleans	11/04/1853	03/15/1858	16	405	N	
Pape, Franz	40	Hanover	Y	Bremen	New Orleans	12/13/1856	06/13/1859	17	456	N	
Pape, Fred	24	Germany	Y	Antwerp	New York	08/17/1882	04/10/1886			Y	

CITIZENSHIP RECORDS

APPLICANT	AGE	COUNTRY OF ORIGIN	DEC	DEPART PORT	ENTRY PORT	ARRIVE DATE	DEC DATE	VOL	PG.	FLD	NAT DATE
Pape, Gerhard	21	Germany	Y	Bremen	New York	05/30/1885	01/14/1888			Y	
Pape, Paul	17	Germany	N	?	Philadelphia	00/00/1877				Y	10/24/1888
Papenberg, George	29	Hanover	Y	Bremen	New York	12/07/1857	03/31/1862	18	287	N	
Papke, Hermann	??	Germany	Y	?	?	?	02/12/1884			Y	
Papke, John	37	Germany	Y	Bremen	New York	04/04/1882	03/01/1887			Y	
Papke, William	30	Germany	Y	Berlin	Baltimore	07/15/1881	07/06/1883			Y	
Paquet, Frank	39	Holland	N	Antwerp	New York	08/14/1870	?			Y	
Paradise, John	48	England	Y	Liverpool	Philadelphia	05/08/1834	11/14/1848	1	294	N	
Pardi, Augusto	29	Italy	Y	Havre	New York	08/25/1881	04/02/1890			Y	
Pardi, Walter	32	Italy	Y	Antwerp	New York	11/04/1888	11/27/1896			Y	
Parino, Vincenzo	47	Italy	Y	Naples	New York	03/21/1882	03/21/1898			Y	
Park, Richard	27	Ireland	Y	Londonderry	Philadelphia	05/04/1851	04/02/1853	7	494	N	
Parker, William T.	??	Ireland	Y	?	?	?	07/08/1892			Y	
Parkin, Edwin E.	??	Ireland	Y	?	?	?	02/26/1890			Y	
Parkin, Samuel	26	Russia	Y	Antwerp	New York	07/12/1900	06/12/1903			Y	
Parlan, Patrick	35	Ireland	Y	Liverpool	New York	05/01/1848	04/01/1861	18	123	N	
Parmisano, James	41	Italy	Y	Palermo	New York	10/02/1888	11/13/1893	21	56	N	
Parmisano, James	41	Italy	Y	Palermo	New York	10/02/1888	11/13/1893			Y	
Parnell, Charles	46	England	Y	London	New York	04/15/1853	10/17/1857	15	438	N	
Parrell, Nicholaus	26	Ireland	Y	Liverpool	New York	11/18/1854	11/09/1857	15	548	N	
Parrott, John	??	Ireland	Y	Liverpool	New Orleans	11/16/18??	10/11/1848	1	125	N	
Parrott, Joseph	58	England	Y	Liverpool	New Orleans	10/20/1845	02/07/1849	23	133	N	
Parsons, Charles H.	30	England	Y	Liverpool	Su. St. Mary	??/??/1877	08/04/1886			Y	
Partel, Frank	44	Austria	Y	Bremen	New York	06/??/1866	10/28/1892	19	396	N	
Parthey, Gustav Friedric	54	Germany	Y	Bremen	Baltimore	04/16/1892	09/19/1894			Y	
Partheymuller, Casper	46	Germany	Y	Bremen	New York	08/05/1879	09/25/1885			Y	
Partmann, John W.	28	Germany	Y	Hamburg	New York	10/29/1881	09/17/1884			Y	
Partusch, Frank	25	Germany	Y	Bremen	Baltimore	06/10/1882	07/07/1883			Y	
Pascarelli, Pasquale	39	Italy	Y	Naples	New York	02/24/1881	10/24/1890	19	298	N	
Paschen, William	49	Prussia	Y	Bremen	Baltimore	08/18/1845	09/13/1852	25	465	N	
Pasker, Henry	25	Prussia	Y	Bremen	Baltimore	11/04/1847	11/25/1852	5	344	N	
Paskin, Bennie	21	Russia	Y	Hamburg	New York	07/01/1891	08/28/1893			Y	
Pasmark, Otto	33	Germany	Y	Bremen	New York	06/01/1893	01/10/1898			Y	
Pasquale, Velli Carprini	39	Italy	Y	Naples	New York	11/15/1891	12/12/1899			Y	
Passarge, Franz	26	Prussia	Y	Bremen	New York	06/13/1853	09/27/1854	10	259	N	
Passarge, Franz	26	Prussia	Y	Bremen	New York	06/13/1853	09/27/1854	12	198	N	
Passauer, Christian	25	Bavaria	Y	Havre	New Orleans	01/02/1852	10/12/1857	15	389	N	
Pastoff, George	36	Prussia	Y	Hamburg	New York	05/20/1850	05/16/1854	8	447	N	
Pastoff, George	36	Prussia	Y	Hamburg	New York	05/20/1850	05/16/1854	9	320	N	
Pastor, Isaac	30	Austria	Y	Hamburg	New York	06/17/1889	06/17/1891			Y	
Patrick, John	27	Ireland	Y	Liverpool	New York	08/20/1848	09/02/1853	7	490	N	
Patridge, Daniel	31	Ireland	Y	Montreal	Whitehall	10/06/1843	10/07/1848	22	486	N	
Pattem, John	33	Prussia	Y	Antwerp	New Orleans	06/11/1845	11/09/1855	13	199	N	
Patterson, Abraham	24	Ireland	Y	Liverpool	New York	07/10/1851	02/14/1857	15	15	N	
Patterson, James	30	Ireland	Y	Londonderry	New York	08/13/1900	03/26/1903			Y	
Patterson, James	25	England	Y	Liverpool	Boston	07/12/1850	05/27/1852	25	121	N	
Patterson, Meroyn	28	Ireland	Y	Larne	New York	06/26/1886	02/17/1888			Y	
Pattison, James E.	33	England	Y	London	New York	02/02/1849	04/25/1850	3	10	N	
Patton, Dominick	50	Ireland	N	Liverpool	New York	05/14/1856	??/??/1864	28	19	N	10/??/1868
Patton, Dominick	19	Ireland	N	Liverpool	New York	05/14/1856	00/00/1864			Y	10/00/1868
Patton, Owen	26	Ireland	Y	Liverpool	New Orleans	02/15/1849	11/01/1852	5	146	N	
Patton, Owen	26	Ireland	Y	Liverpool	New Orleans	02/15/1849	11/01/1852	6	272	N	
Patton, Patrick	40	Ireland	Y	Queenstown	New York	08/02/1883	11/08/1886			Y	
Patzold, Joseph	43	Germany	Y	Hamburg	Philadelphia	05/07/1883	10/25/1886			Y	
Pauckner, John Adam	25	Bavaria	Y	Bremen	New York	07/25/1852	04/23/1853	8	96	N	
Paudert, Frederick Augus	42	Saxe Weimar	Y	Bremen	New York	06/10/1853	08/17/1857	15	152	N	
Paul, Gerhard Henry	25	Hanover	Y	Bremen	New York	05/18/1850	04/25/1853	8	107	N	
Paul, Henry	22	Hanover	Y	Bremen	New Orleans	04/28/1849	02/07/1853	7	120	N	
Paul, Julius	56	Germany	N	Bremen	New York	10/01/1856	?			Y	

CITIZENSHIP RECORDS

APPLICANT	AGE	COUNTRY OF ORIGIN	DEC	DEPART PORT	ENTRY PORT	ARRIVE DATE	DEC DATE	VOL	PG.	FLD	NAT DATE
Paul, Peter	33	Bavaria	Y	Havre	New York	05/29/1854	03/16/1858	16	412	N	
Paulmann, Albert	39	Germany	Y	Bremen	New York	07/23/1888	11/28/1888			Y	
Paulowski, John	29	Poland (Russi	Y	Havre	New York	08/17/1850	05/20/1856	26	503	N	
Pauls, John D.A.	28	Germany	Y	Hamburg	New York	12/10/1890	11/09/1893			Y	
Paulus, Herman Joseph	30	Hesse Darmsta	Y	Hanover	New York	01/09/1854	08/04/1856	14	325	N	
Paulus, Michael	49	Germany	N	Antwerp	New York	05/31/1867	?			Y	
Pauly, Anton	26	Germany	Y	Bremen	New York	10/13/1884	03/21/1887			Y	
Pauly, Frederick	22	Germany	Y	Havre	New York	04/20/1880	08/10/1883			Y	
Pauly, Henry	21	Prussia	Y	Bremen	New York	05/27/1853	02/23/1857	15	53	N	
Pauly, William	27	Germany	Y	Havre	New York	04/20/1880	08/10/1883			Y	
Paustian, Johann Jurgen	37	Denmark	Y	Bremen	New York	06/23/1856	08/09/1859	17	470	N	
Paveglio, Luigi	??	Italy	Y	?	?	?	04/23/1894			Y	
Pavely, Fred J.	25	England	Y	London	New York	04/30/1888	09/29/1893			Y	
Pavlos, Nicholas	28	Greece	Y	Athens	New York	09/??/1884	09/24/1889			Y	
Pawlak, Mathias	42	Germany	Y	Bremen	Baltimore	08/17/1884	11/08/1893			Y	
Payne, William	30	England	Y	Liverpool	New York	09/06/1853	09/07/1857	15	240	N	
Payne, William James	31	Ireland	Y	Liverpool	New York	08/26/1837	07/31/1848	22	18	N	
Payson, Herbert	??	Great Britain	Y	?	?	?	10/28/1898			Y	
Pearce, Samuel	39	England	Y	Windsor, Can	Detroit	09/17/1891	09/01/1887			Y	
Pearson, Thomas	31	Scotland	Y	Greenock	New York	10/20/1852	04/02/1856	26	417	N	
Pearson, William	25	Canada	Y	Port Pearry	Rochester, N	09/21/1890	04/07/1894			Y	
Pearsson, Peter	??	Sweden	Y	?	?	?	05/28/1894			Y	
Peddenpohl, August	49	Germany	Y	Bremen	New York	08/15/1880	11/01/1888	19	207	N	
Pedercini, James	41	Italy	Y	Havre	New York	05/29/1882	01/07/1888			Y	
Pedretti, Peter	53	Italy	Y	Havre	New York	12/19/1856	10/19/1889			Y	
Peek, Adolph	28	Hanover	Y	Bremen	New York	09/08/1852	12/14/1852	5	413	N	
Peep, George	38	Germany	Y	Havre	New York	07/05/1850	10/09/1866			Y	
Peetz, John George	44	Germany	Y	Bremen	New York	05/23/1882	02/27/1894			Y	
Pegee, Max	22	Germany	N	Hamburg	New York	09/02/1871	?			Y	
Peichohourki, Maciae Ale	31	Prussia	Y	Hamburg	New York	06/23/1854	10/10/1854	11	203	N	
Peiker, Jon	24	Hesse Cassel	Y	Bremen	New Orleans	12/18/1854	01/04/1860	27	27	N	
Peiker, Wigand	28	Hesse Cassel	Y	Bremen	Baltimore	12/26/1855	01/04/1860	27	28	N	
Peikert, Albert	37	Germany	Y	Bremen	New York	05/17/1873	04/06/1887	19	119	N	
Peikert, Albert	37	Germany	Y	Bremen	New York	05/17/1873	04/06/1887			Y	
Peitz, Arnold	34	Prussia	Y	Bremen	New York	10/23/1865	08/26/1872	18	514	N	
Pele, Henri	??	France	Y	?	?	05/14/1894	01/18/1900			Y	
Pelecky, Joseph (Pelechi	25	Russia	Y	Bremen	Baltimore	05/25/1892	03/10/1894			Y	
Pelger, Nicholas	38	Prussia	Y	Canada	Troy, NY	08/09/1846	02/02/1849	23	18	N	
Pelizaeus, Edward	26	Germany	Y	Bremen	New York	11/13/1889	08/11/1893			Y	
Pell, Arnold (Pelle)	??	Prussia	Y	Bremen	New Orleans	11/03/18??	10/12/1848	1	155	N	
Pelle, August	??	Prussia	Y	Bremen	Baltimore	10/22/18??	10/12/1848	1	159	N	
Pelle, Florence	24	Prussia	Y	Bremen	New Orleans	11/03/1846	10/12/1848	1	160	N	
Pellens, George William	45	Hanover	Y	Bremen	New York	??/11/1832	11/20/1849	23	357	N	
Peller, John	32	Bavaria	Y	Hamburg	New York	08/12/1852	04/02/1856	26	405	N	
Pellerin, George	39	Germany	Y	Havre	New York	05/12/1893	01/30/1894			Y	
Pellerin, Joseph	22	Germany	Y	Havre	New York	03/19/1887	07/24/1890			Y	
Pelljohan, Henry	32	Prussia	Y	Bremen	New York	04/22/1847	10/30/1852	5	72	N	
Pellmann, August	32	Germany	Y	Hamburg	New York	05/15/1884	03/31/1886			Y	
Pellmann, Henry	23	Prussia	Y	Bremen	New Orleans	10/26/1857	01/31/1860	27	83	N	
Pelster, F.	25	Hanover	Y	Bremen	Baltimore	10/12/1856	01/19/1860	27	62	N	
Peltz, Hermann	24	Germany	Y	Antwerp	New York	01/28/1882	10/23/1888			Y	
Pelzel, Vincenz	33	Germany	Y	Bremen	New York	05/09/1882	08/08/1893			Y	
Pelzer, Bernard	26	Prussia	Y	London	New Orleans	05/14/1848	06/18/1851	3	400	N	
Pelzer, Henry	41	Germany	N	Bremen	New York	11/10/1863	?			Y	
Pemberton, Charles	42	England	Y	Liverpool	New York	09/21/1882	06/27/1892			Y	
Pendergast, Andrew	26	Ireland	Y	New Ross	Boston	08/20/1847	02/18/1850	2	91	N	
Pendergast, Terrence	22	Ireland	Y	Waterford	New York	08/01/1844	02/18/1850	2	92	N	
Pendergast, Thomas	25	Ireland	Y	Queenstown	New York	05/10/1891	10/30/1894			Y	
Pengelly, Richard H.I.P.	31	England	Y	Liverpool	New York	01/21/1879	09/30/1889			Y	

CITIZENSHIP RECORDS

APPLICANT	AGE	COUNTRY OF ORIGIN	DEC	DEPART PORT	ENTRY PORT	ARRIVE DATE	DEC DATE	VOL	PG.	FLD	NAT DATE
Pening, Richard	16	Germany	N	?	New York	00/00/1871				Y	10/27/1888
Penker, Max	38	Germany	Y	Bremen	New York	07/02/1880	03/28/1890			Y	
Penn, Albert E.	26	England	Y	Liverpool	Baltimore	08/28/1872	03/17/1881			Y	
Penn, Carl	30	Mecklenburg S	Y	Hamburg	New York	11/20/1853	09/27/1854	10	257	N	
Pennekamp, William	65	Germany	N	Rotterdam	New York	09/??/1851	?			Y	
Pepinsky, Robert	21	Russia	Y	Hamburg	Philadelphia	07/01/1886	10/06/1888			Y	
Pepper, Frank	37	Germany	Y	Bremen	New York	12/26/1880	06/20/1887			Y	
Pepping, John	58	Holland	N	Rotterdam	New York	10/31/1854	?			Y	
Peraldo, Ilario	??	Italy	Y	?	?	?	06/23/1896			Y	
Perazza, Aurelio	46	Italy	Y	Genoa	New York	07/02/1879	10/28/1899			Y	
Perk, Henry	35	Germany	Y	Amsterdam	New York	09/16/1883	04/26/1898			Y	
Perkuhn, Albert	36	Germany	Y	Hamburg	New York	10/03/1877	02/18/1881			Y	
Permentier, John Adam	36	France	Y	Havre	New York	12/28/1852	11/06/1858	17	284	N	
Perra, Vincent	53	Italy	Y	Sagorn	New York	09/24/1856	10/02/1888	19	142	N	
Perrano, Felice	45	Italy	Y	London	New York	01/05/1884	11/21/1888			Y	
Perraut, Frederick	28	Germany	Y	Havre	New York	02/19/1886	10/28/1889			Y	
Perrly, Charles	47	England	Y	London	New York	09/15/1849	03/18/1850	2	206	N	
Perry, Richard	38	Wales	Y	Liverpool	New York	06/01/1838	04/04/18??	8	52	N	
Persching, Heinrich	33	Germany	Y	Hamburg	New York	06/18/1881	10/13/1885			Y	
Person, Olaf	??	Sweden	Y	?	?	?	03/25/1893			Y	
Perugini, Nicolo	47	Italy	Y	Naples	New York	05/05/1887	06/07/1897			Y	
Peruzzo, J.	??	Italy	Y	?	New York	02/??/1875	04/27/1892			Y	
Perwig, Alias	36	Austria	Y	Bremen	Baltimore	03/28/1880	11/05/1892			Y	
Perzel, John	32	Austria	Y	Bremen	New York	05/??/1888	04/27/1894			Y	
Pesa, Florindo	29	Italy	Y	Naples	New York	11/12/1891	10/11/1900			Y	
Pessler, John M.	47	Germany	Y	Bremen	Baltimore	10/??/1866	01/31/1884			Y	
Peter, Antoine	38	Germany	Y	Havre	New York	10/20/1884	01/12/1889			Y	
Peter, Bernard	47	Wurttemberg	Y	Havre	New York	05/03/1855	02/08/1858	16	88	N	
Peter, Bernard	27	Germany	Y	Rotterdam	New York	08/28/1889	10/31/1894			Y	
Peter, Charles	20	Wurttemberg	Y	Bremen	Nwe York	04/01/1872	06/10/1872	18	498	N	
Peter, Conrad	29	Germany	Y	Bremen	New York	08/08/1886	07/29/1889			Y	
Peter, Dominique	32	Germany	Y	Havre	New York	07/13/1890	06/23/1891			Y	
Peter, Eckhart	24	Prussia	Y	Bremen	New York	10/??/1853	09/21/18??	10	147	N	
Peter, Eckhart	24	Prussia	Y	Bremen	New York	10/15/1853	09/21/1854	12	86	N	
Peter, Erhard	27	Baden	Y	Antwerp	New York	08/10/1854	11/01/1860	27	518	N	
Peter, Francois Joseph	37	Germany	Y	Havre	New York	05/21/1884	01/12/1889			Y	
Peter, Frank	25	Germany	Y	Rotterdam	New York	12/07/1889	12/26/1894			Y	
Peter, Henry	28	Kurhessen	Y	London	New York	04/20/1850	04/24/1854	8	250	N	
Peter, Henry	28	Kurhessen	Y	London	New York	04/20/1850	04/24/1854	9	121	N	
Peter, Henry	26	Germany	Y	Bremen	Baltimore	05/06/1876	10/03/1876			Y	
Peter, Jacob	23	Bavaria	Y	Havre	New York	12/23/1855	03/05/1858	16	373	N	
Peter, John	25	Germany	Y	Antwerp	New York	07/04/1893	10/15/1896			Y	
Peter, John	26	Germany	Y	Antwerp	New York	05/18/1880	04/10/1882			Y	
Peter, Paul	??	Turkey	Y	?	?	08/30/1892	05/05/1897			Y	
Peter, Sebold	27	Baden	Y	Havre	New Orleans	12/01/1846	08/??/1851	4	167	N	
Peter, Wilbrand	33	Hanover	Y	Bremen	Baltimore	10/30/1853	10/09/1854	6	165	N	
Peter, Wilbrand	33	Hanover	Y	Bremen	Baltimore	10/30/1853	10/09/1854	11	168	N	
Petering, Henry	25	Germany	Y	Bremen	Baltimore	09/19/1883	07/18/1885			Y	
Peterman, John	26	Bavaria	Y	Havre	New York	08/29/1849	08/23/1852	25	330	N	
Peterman, Theodore	33	Germany	Y	Bremen	New York	06/19/1884	09/22/1888	19	138	N	
Peters, August	35	Germany	Y	?	Baltimore	??/??/1881	01/02/1885			Y	
Peters, Charles	21	Germany	Y	Bremen	New York	04/13/1870	??/??/1870			Y	
Peters, Charles	41	Germany	N	Bremen	New York	04/13/1870	?			Y	
Peters, Fred	34	Germany	Y	Antwerp	New York	04/28/1880	03/29/1890			Y	
Peters, Gerard	30	Hanover	Y	Bremen	New York	06/01/1845	10/12/1848	1	166	N	
Peters, Henry	34	Prussia	Y	Bremen	Baltimore	06/12/1849	04/12/1852	24	483	N	
Peters, Herman	30	Prussia	Y	Bremen	Baltimore	06/12/1849	05/20/1852	25	61	N	
Peters, Herman C.	23	Germany	Y	?	?	12/02/1893	10/05/1898			Y	
Peters, John	32	Mecklenburg S	Y	Hamburg	New York	07/04/1852	10/06/1856	14	193	N	

CITIZENSHIP RECORDS

APPLICANT	AGE	COUNTRY OF ORIGIN	DEC	DEPART PORT	ENTRY PORT	ARRIVE DATE	DEC DATE	VOL	PG.	FLD	NAT DATE
Peters, John Henry	28	Scotland	Y	Glasgow	Boston	05/06/1884	11/30/1888			Y	
Peters, Rudolph William	28	Prussia	Y	Bremen	Baltimore	05/01/1854	02/12/1856	26	76	N	
Peters, Theodore	??	Germany	N	?	?	11/20/1880				Y	10/27/1892
Peters, William	31	Germany	Y	Rotterdam	New York	09/29/1882	10/12/1893			Y	
Petersen, August	22	Bremen	Y	Bremen	Baltimore	05/04/1854	09/25/1854	10	194	N	
Petersen, August	22	Bremen	Y	Bremen	Baltimore	05/04/1854	09/25/1854	12	133	N	
Petersen, Jurgen Christi	54	Bremen	Y	Bremen	New York	07/01/1853	09/25/1854	10	193	N	
Petersen, Jurgen Christi	54	Bremen	Y	Bremen	New York	07/01/1853	09/25/1854	12	132	N	
Petersmann, Franz	21	Germany	Y	Bremen	Baltimore	11/21/1883	11/18/1884			Y	
Petersmann, Joseph	31	Hanover	Y	Bremen	Baltimore	10/14/1842	10/14/1848	1	229	N	
Peterson, Albin	24	Sweden	Y	Guttenberg	Boston	05/23/1890	09/28/1895			Y	
Peterson, Charles	27	Oldenburg	Y	Bremen	New York	09/??/1853	03/06/1858	16	376	N	
Peterson, Christ	60	Denmark	N	Hamburg	New York	05/??/1852	?			Y	
Peterson, Hans C.	??	Germany	Y	?	?	?	05/22/1893			Y	
Peterson, John	22	Denmark	Y	Flanceburg	New York	03/?/1849	02/09/1857	15	6	N	
Peterson, John	??	Sweden	Y	?	?	?	08/05/1882			Y	
Peterson, Julius	29	Denmark	Y	?	Philadelphia	00/00/1879	10/15/1884			Y	
Peterson, Peter	22	Denmark	Y	Hamburg	New York	07/26/1854	10/06/1857	15	363	N	
Peterson, Peter	33	Denmark	Y	Amsterdam	Boston	??/??/1836	12/03/1849	23	386	N	
Petit, Anton	27	Germany	Y	Havre	New York	05/02/1895	07/18/1898			Y	
Petit, Edward	??	Ireland	N	?	?	09/15/1887				Y	10/22/1892
Petit, Gust	30	Germany	Y	Havre	New York	03/07/1887	04/14/1897			Y	
Petkus, Clem	31	Russia	Y	Bremen	Baltimore	04/09/1899	10/27/1903			Y	
Petraffke, Herman	34	Germany	Y	Bremen	Baltimore	11/09/1890	09/13/1897			Y	
Petri, Daniel	35	Baden	Y	Baden	New York	10/29/1881	03/??/1892	28	386	N	
Petrosch, Franz	55	Germany	Y	Rotterdam	New York	07/28/1879	10/04/1886			Y	
Petry, Daniel	31	Germany	Y	Bremen	New York	10/26/1887	12/26/1891			Y	
Petry, Michael	??	Germany	N	?	?	09/08/1884				Y	10/07/1892
Petsch, Adolph	37	Germany	Y	?	New York	09/25/1882	04/02/1900			Y	
Petti, Peitro	??	Italy	Y	?	?	?	01/02/1898			Y	
Pezold, Henry	32	Germany	Y	Antwerp	New York	06/25/1879	12/20/1881			Y	
Pfab, John	27	Germany	Y	Bremen	New York	05/12/1882	09/28/1887			Y	
Pfad, Michael	32	Baden	Y	Havre	New York	01/07/1853	01/28/1857	14	516	N	
Pfaefflin, Francis	31	Wurttemberg	Y	Havre	New York	06/22/1849	02/25/1853	7	232	N	
Pfaender, John Michael	30	Wurttemberg	Y	London	New York	12/03/1854	09/22/1857	15	301	N	
Pfaff, Frank	27	Germany	Y	Havre	New York	06/02/1880	10/11/1883			Y	
Pfaff, John	40	Wuerttemberg	Y	Havre	New York	05/20/1849	04/06/1852	24	403	N	
Pfaffenberger, George	29	Germany	Y	Bremen	New York	07/28/1888	08/02/1892			Y	
Pfahler, Adolph	27	Germany	Y	Bremen	New York	04/02/1872	10/25/1880			Y	
Pfahler, George	44	Germany	Y	Antwerp	Philadelphia	03/14/1881	03/25/1885			Y	
Pfaller, Andreas	33	Germany	Y	Bremen	New York	04/09/1888	05/20/1892			Y	
Pfaller, George	43	Bavaria	Y	Bremen	Baltimore	02/28/1884	02/09/1885			Y	
Pfaller, John	23	Germany	Y	Hamburg	New York	05/08/1896	05/12/1896			Y	
Pfalzgraf, Peter	30	Germany	Y	Havre	New York	10/09/1881	01/24/1887			Y	
Pfanner, Philipp	22	Bavaria	Y	Havre	New Orleans	12/06/1857	01/16/1861	18	63	N	
Pfannkuchen, Christian	35	Hanover	Y	Bremen	New York	07/25/1854	08/02/1862	18	383	N	
Pfanz, Johann	25	Germany	Y	Havre	New York	06/30/1881	09/04/1885			Y	
Pfarr, John Adam	38	Bavaria	Y	Bremen	New York	08/12/1854	09/10/1855	11	518	N	
Pfau, Gustav	30	Germany	Y	?	?	?	03/18/1884			Y	
Pfau, John	32	Wurttemberg	Y	London	New Orleans	11/28/1852	10/01/1856	14	79	N	
Pfau, John Gottlieb	31	Baden	Y	Havre	New York	05/25/1852	11/28/1857	16	55	N	
Pfeffer, Pius	??	Germany	Y	?	?	?	05/10/1889			Y	
Pfefferkorn, Joseph	23	Germany	Y	Havre	New York	05/??/1884	05/01/1888			Y	
Pfeifer, Frederick	28	Prussia	Y	Rotterdam	Baltimore	??/21/1846	11/20/1849	23	355	N	
Pfeifer, George	37	Germany	Y	Antwerp	New York	04/01/1881	04/16/1889			Y	
Pfeifer, George	28	Bavaria	Y	Bremen	New Orleans	01/05/1845	02/12/1849	23	50	N	
Pfeifer, Henry	24	Bavaria	Y	Bremen	Baltimore	08/08/1844	01/??/1850	23	456	N	
Pfeifer, Markus	28	Wurttemberg	Y	London	New York	04/25/1847	08/04/1851	4	80	N	
Pfeifer, Otto	46	Germany	N	Havre	New York	12/06/1860	?			Y	

297

CITIZENSHIP RECORDS

APPLICANT	AGE	COUNTRY OF ORIGIN	DEC	DEPART PORT	ENTRY PORT	ARRIVE DATE	DEC DATE	VOL	PG.	FLD	NAT DATE
Pfeifer, Philip	28	Germany	N	Antwerp	New York	12/??/1881	?			Y	
Pfeifer, William	30	Hesse Darmsta	Y	Havre	New York	01/??/1847	??/??/1851	3	219	N	
Pfeiff, Henry	51	Hesse Darmsta	Y	Liverpool	New York	10/02/1849	10/06/1851	4	206	N	
Pfeiffer, Adam	30	France	Y	Havre	New York	07/15/1852	02/11/1860	27	100	N	
Pfeiffer, Anton	35	Germany	Y	Bremen	New York	03/26/1888	03/27/1895			Y	
Pfeiffer, Chrisitan Fred	23	Wurttemberg	Y	Havre	New York	04/15/1852	10/25/1858	17	99	N	
Pfeiffer, Christian	26	Saxe Gotha	Y	Hamburg	New York	06/24/1853	04/28/1854	8	281	N	
Pfeiffer, Christian	26	Saxe Gothe	Y	Hamburg	New York	06/24/1853	04/28/1853	9	153	N	
Pfeiffer, Daniel	23	Germany	Y	Bremen	New York	05/18/1883	05/31/1884			Y	
Pfeiffer, Edward	24	Austria	Y	Bremen	Baltimore	02/06/1886	09/28/1891			Y	
Pfeiffer, Emil	43	Switzerland	Y	Havre	New York	01/28/1881	01/30/1889			Y	
Pfeiffer, George	38	Germany	Y	Havre	New York	05/27/1891	10/11/1897			Y	
Pfeiffer, Henry	31	Prussia	Y	Bremen	New York	11/15/1867	11/19/1868			Y	
Pfeiffer, Henry	55	Germany	Y	Antwerp	Philadelphia	08/17/1876	07/31/1894			Y	
Pfeiffer, Isaac	81	Germany	N	Hamburg	New York	07/07/1872	07/13/1874	28	473	N	08/27/1874
Pfeiffer, Isaac	35	Germany	N	Hamburg	New York	07/07/1872	07/13/1874			Y	08/27/1874
Pfeiffer, Jacob	32	Bavaria	Y	Havre	New York	07/01/1854	10/02/1856	14	140	N	
Pfeiffer, Jacob	36	Germany	Y	Havre	New York	02/25/1880	10/11/1889	19	235	N	
Pfeiffer, Philipp	28	Germany	Y	Antwerp	New York	12/??/1881	01/??/1882			Y	
Pfeiffer, Stephan	31	Germany	Y	Hamburg	New York	12/22/1881	06/13/1887			Y	
Pfeil, Philip	32	Bavaria	Y	Havre	New York	01/15/1849	04/04/1853	8	47	N	
Pfeimer, Jacob	27	Baden	Y	Havre	New York	04/10/1854	09/19/1855	13	73	N	
Pfennig, George	48	Germany	Y	Havre	New York	09/24/1882	10/31/1884			Y	
Pfennig, George	21	Germany	Y	Havre	New York	03/19/1882	05/25/1885			Y	
Pfenninger, John Jacob	24	Switzerland	Y	Havre	New York	03/25/1849	10/06/1851	4	196	N	
Pfiester, George Peter	45	Bavaria	Y	Havre	New York	06/12/1847	08/23/1848	22	239	N	
Pfirmann, August	37	Germany	Y	Antwerp	New York	05/19/1880	04/22/1889			Y	
Pfirmann, Frederick	22	Bavaria	Y	Havre	New York	05/30/1852	10/09/1854	11	172	N	
Pfister, Bartholomew	30	Prussia	Y	Havre	New Orleans	11/19/1852	10/06/1857	15	360	N	
Pfister, Henry	68	Switzerland	N	Havre	New York	05/16/1847	??/??/1848	28	374	N	??/??/1852
Pfister, Herman	25	Switzerland	Y	Liverpool	New York	12/01/1867	11/09/1872	18	540	N	
Pfister, Kasper	23	Germany	Y	Havre	New York	09/02/1884	03/27/1885			Y	
Pfister, Michael	65	Bavaria	N	Havre	New York	07/04/1849	?			Y	
Pfister, Theodre	29	Germany	Y	Hamburg	New York	11/24/1877	09/26/1885			Y	
Pfisterer, Friederich	23	Germany	Y	Amsterdam	New York	11/15/1881	09/20/1886			Y	
Pfisterer, George	31	Germany	Y	Hamburg	New York	05/24/1883	09/05/1887			Y	
Pfisterer, Philip Fred	24	Wurttemberg	Y	Antwerp	New Orleans	05/04/1849	12/31/1852	5	482	N	
Pfitzner, Albert	??	Germany	Y	?	?	?	06/29/1887			Y	
Pfitzner, Christian Gust	30	Holstein	Y	Hamburg	New York	08/21/1853	02/25/1856	26	124	N	
Pflueger, Frederick Jaco	34	Bremen	Y	Bremen	Baltimore	06/28/1854	09/25/1854	10	191	N	
Pflueger, Frederick Jaco	34	Bremen	Y	Bremen	Baltimore	06/28/1854	09/25/1854	12	130	N	
Pflumm, Adolph	29	Germany	Y	?	New York	04/19/1885	05/19/1885			Y	
Pflumm, Anton	29	Germany	Y	Rotterdam	New York	04/26/1886	09/18/1889			Y	
Pflumm, Simon	24	Germany	Y	Bremen	New York	09/01/1882	10/26/1888	19	188	N	
Pfohl, George	45	Germany	N	France	New York	06/15/1868	?			Y	
Pfursick, Johannes	37	Wuerttemberg	Y	Havre	New Orleans	03/28/1854	11/01/1860	27	516	N	
Phair, Robert James	26	England	Y	Glasgow	New York	02/29/1894	11/30/1900			Y	
Phelan, Albert	35	Ireland	Y	Queenstown	New York	06/02/1880	09/25/1896			Y	
Phelan, John	39	Ireland	Y	New Ross	New York	10/15/1850	10/29/1858	17	185	N	
Phelan, Joseph	34	Canada	Y	Blyth	Detroit	07/02/1889	03/10/1903			Y	
Phelan, Michael D.	28	Ireland	Y	Liverpool	New York	07/01/1848	12/10/1852	5	405	N	
Phelan, Patrick	55	Ireland	Y	Liverpool	New York	04/14/1850	12/26/1851	24	10	N	
Phelan, William	31	Ireland	Y	Dublin	New Orleans	03/09/1849	08/??/1851	4	178	N	
Phelan, William	21	Ireland	N	Queenstown	Philadelphia	09/01/1879	?			Y	
Philipp, Boell	29	Germany	Y	Havre	New York	09/16/1885	10/27/1892			Y	
Philipp, Ernst	31	Germany	Y	Hamburg	New York	08/17/1883	09/05/1887			Y	
Philippe, Eugene	34	France	N	Havre	New York	05/16/1872	?			Y	
Philippi, Charles Philip	30	Hesse Darmsta	Y	London	New York	02/18/1853	11/05/1855	13	162	N	
Philips, Fred	35	Germany	Y	Bremen	New York	08/??/1869	04/27/1888			Y	

CITIZENSHIP RECORDS

APPLICANT	AGE	COUNTRY OF ORIGIN	DEC	DEPART PORT	ENTRY PORT	ARRIVE DATE	DEC DATE	VOL	PG.	FLD	NAT DATE
Philips, Henry	47	Germany	Y	Bremen	New York	10/00/1870	10/07/1885			Y	
Phillip, Abraham	32	Nassau	Y	London	Baltimore	06/24/1847	08/07/1851	4	97	N	
Phillips, Francis	55	Wales	Y	Glamorganshi	New York	05/00/1882	04/05/1886			Y	
Phillips, Franics	55	Wales	Y	Gamorganshir	New York	05/??/1882	04/05/1886	19	35	N	
Phillips, Henry	21	Brunswick	Y	Bremen	Buffalo	07/09/1856	05/30/1859	17	436	N	
Phillips, Henry	47	Germany	Y	Bremen	New York	10/??/1870	10/07/1885	19	17	N	
Phillips, Robert	46	Germany	Y	Bremen	New York	??/??/1869	10/18/1888			Y	
Phillips, William F.	28	Wales	Y	Liverpool	New York	05/12/1882	06/09/1886			Y	
Phillips, William J.	23	Wales	Y	Liverpool	New York	04/27/1884	09/02/1886			Y	
Phipp, Hanz	32	Bavaria	Y	Havre	New Orleans	10/18/1846	02/01/1849	23	10	N	
Phippard, William	40	England	Y	Havre	Philadelphia	04/14/1876	03/20/1891			Y	
Piarkowski, George	42	Russia	Y	Bremen	Baltimore	05/05/1893	10/23/1897			Y	
Piatez, Harris	32	Russia	Y	Hamburg	New York	07/23/1881	05/10/1883	28	42	N	
Piatez, Harris	27	Russia	Y	Hamburg	New York	07/23/1881	05/10/1883			Y	10/12/1888
Piatez, Harris	25	Russia	Y	Hamburg	New York	07/23/1881	05/10/1883			Y	
Piazzi, John	32	Wurttemberg	Y	Havre	New York	04/07/1854	10/12/1857	15	410	N	
Piccioni, Mariano	45	Italy	Y	Havre	New York	02/21/1881	05/08/1894			Y	
Pich, Phillip	22	France	Y	Havre	New York	08/10/1849	07/16/1851	3	547	N	
Pichard, John	47	England	Y	Hull	New York	06/16/1845	11/22/1848	1	366	N	
Pichlik, Mathias	22	Austria	Y	Hamburg	New York	09/21/1894	01/29/1897			Y	
Pick, Emil	??	Germany	Y	?	?	?	10/20/1884			Y	
Pick, Joseph	57	France	Y	Havre	New Orleans	05/17/1852	02/17/1858	16	313	N	
Pickartz, Peter Joseph	44	Germany	Y	Bremen	New York	01/26/1878	03/16/1889			Y	
Pickel, Max	28	Bavaria	Y	Havre	New York	11/18/1846	04/04/1853	8	34	N	
Picker, Frederick	??	Prussia	Y	Bremen	Baltimore	07/07/1844	10/09/1848	22	497	N	
Picket, Anton	49	Hanover	Y	Rotterdam	New York	09/24/1855	02/10/1858	16	96	N	
Picket, Ignatz Bernard A	21	Holland	Y	Rotterdam	New York	09/27/1855	02/10/1858	16	95	N	
Picone, Luigi	38	Italy	Y	Naples	New York	04/09/1877	04/07/1894			Y	
Piechohourkei, Maciae Ale	31	Prussia	Y	Hamburg	New York	06/25/1854	10/10/1854	6	200	N	
Piechota, Jacob	32	Prussia	Y	Hamburg	New York	10/08/1853	10/10/1854	6	202	N	
Piechota, Jacob	32	Prussia	Y	Hamburg	New York	10/08/1853	10/10/1854	11	205	N	
Pieck, Edmond	30	Prussia	Y	Hamburg	New York	09/04/1851	01/31/1853	7	93	N	
Pieczonka, Alexander	27	Germany	Y	Hamburg	New York	09/11/1889	04/01/1897			Y	
Pielage, Joseph	22	Hanover	Y	Bremen	New Orleans	12/25/1852	12/28/1855	13	380	N	
Piemann, Frank	17	Germany	N	?	Baltimore	00/00/1876				Y	10/16/1888
Piening, John Henry	24	Oldenburg	Y	Bremen	New Orleans	06/01/1847	10/22/1851	4	369	N	
Piennig, August	24	Germany	Y	Rotterdam	New York	03/12/1891	10/09/1893			Y	
Piennig, Bernard	47	Germany	Y	Bremen	New York	03/13/1866	12/28/1888			Y	
Piennig, Frank	24	Germany	Y	Bremen	Baltimore	03/31/1881	03/03/1884			Y	
Piennig, John Bernard	22	Germany	Y	Bremen	Baltimore	09/13/1888	10/28/1891			Y	
Pieper, August	24	Germany	Y	Bremen	New York	05/14/1884	09/09/1890			Y	
Pieper, Bernhard	52	Germany	Y	Bremen	Baltimore	09/15/1883	02/28/1898			Y	
Pieper, Herman	25	Germany	Y	Bremen	New York	01/12/1889	10/23/1896			Y	
Pieper, John	27	Germany	Y	Bremen	Baltimore	10/06/1892	04/13/1897			Y	
Pieper, John Bernard	27	Hanover	Y	Bremen	New Orleans	11/06/1853	11/02/1858	17	262	N	
Pieper, William	61	Hanover	Y	Bremen	New Orleans	09/15/1841	08/04/1856	14	322	N	
Piepmeier, Henry	??	Hanover	Y	Bremen	Baltimore	??/17/1854	04/25/1855	11	307	N	
Pieran, August	??	Germany	Y	?	?	?	04/03/1886			Y	
Pierre, Yaegere	35	France	Y	Havre	New York	08/25/1846	03/25/1850	2	250	N	
Pierrot, Theodore	26	Germany	Y	Antwerp	Philadelphia	05/30/1877	10/11/1882			Y	
Pieters, Henry	42	Prussia	Y	Bremen	Baltimore	04/20/1848	11/02/1852	5	189	N	
Pieters, Henry	42	Prussia	Y	Bremen	Baltimore	04/20/1848	11/02/1852	6	315	N	
Pieters, J. B.	30	Belgium	Y	Antwerp	New York	07/12/1895	12/07/1896			Y	
Pietsch, Franz	44	Austria	Y	Hamburg	New York	06/25/1887	06/23/1893			Y	
Piker, Isaac	23	Russia	Y	Hamburg	New York	07/21/1881	05/07/1883	28	228	N	
Piker, Isaac	23	Russia	Y	Hamburg	New York	07/27/1881	05/07/1883			Y	
Piker, Isaac	21	Russia	Y	Hamburg	New York	07/27/1881	05/07/1883			Y	
Piker, Sam	30	Russia	Y	Hamburg	New York	01/10/1887	12/05/1892			Y	
Piket, Isaac	28	Russia	Y	Hamburg	New York	07/27/1881	05/07/1883	28	160	N	?

CITIZENSHIP RECORDS

APPLICANT	AGE	COUNTRY OF ORIGIN	DEC	DEPART PORT	ENTRY PORT	ARRIVE DATE	DEC DATE	VOL	PG.	FLD	NAT DATE
Pilderwasser, Aaron	26	Russia	Y	?	?	04/15/1889	04/02/1892			Y	
Pilderwasser, Hirsch	55	Russia	Y	Hamburg	New York	08/20/1891	07/13/1897			Y	
Pilkington, John	72	Ireland	N	Liverpool	New York	07/18/1839	07/??/1840	28	23	N	07/??/1845
Pilkington, John	24	Ireland	N	Liverpool	New York	07/18/1839	07/00/1840			Y	07/00/1845
Pill, Israel	45	Russia	Y	Hamburg	Baltimore	09/19/1891	10/16/1900			Y	
Pille, Bernard	44	Germany	Y	Bremen	Baltimore	06/01/1888	10/08/1896			Y	
Pille, Henry	27	Germany	Y	Bremen	New York	03/24/1883	06/04/1885			Y	
Pille, Herman	23	Oldenburg	Y	Bremen	New Orleans	09/10/1846	02/14/1849	23	95	N	
Pille, Hermann	39	Germany	Y	Bremen	Baltimore	10/09/1884	05/21/1888			Y	
Piller, Andrew	24	Germany	Y	Bremen	New York	11/13/1882	02/13/1883			Y	
Piller, Joseph	23	Switzerland	Y	Hamburg	New York	07/04/1892	04/20/1893			Y	
Pilni, Charles	32	Saxony	Y	Hamburg	New York	05/04/1849	03/25/1850	2	260	N	
Pilon, Joseph	39	Canada	Y	Windsor	Detroit	09/02/1879	04/05/1901			Y	
Pinkus, Charles	44	Germany	N	Hamburg	New York	04/30/1865	?			Y	
Pinkvoss, Heinrich Louis	43	Hanover	Y	Bremen	New Orleans	01/10/1858	08/28/1862	18	413	N	
Pinne, Ernst	38	Germany	Y	Bremen	New York	10/03/1885	10/04/1887			Y	
Pinnel, Peter	30	Germany	Y	Antwerp	New York	09/02/1881	08/26/1884			Y	
Pinoki, Morris	32	Prussia	Y	Glasgow	New York	07/16/1880	03/10/1888	19	130	N	
Pipe, James	61	England	Y	Liverpool	New York	05/??/1857	03/20/1884			Y	
Piper, Gerhard	43	Germany	Y	Amsterdam	New York	05/15/1890	05/22/1893			Y	
Pipir, Barney Henry	24	Oldenburg	Y	Bremen	New Orleans	12/??/1844	11/??/1849	23	303	N	
Pipp, Phillip	24	Hesse Darmsta	Y	Antwerp	New York	07/14/1849	01/22/1852	24	53	N	
Pirkin, Herman	29	Hanover	Y	Bremen	Baltimore	05/01/1857	10/08/1860	27	449	N	
Pirmann, Henry	22	Bavaria	Y	Havre	New Orleans	05/30/1852	11/06/1855	13	176	N	
Pischopink, Ludwig	32	Prussia	Y	Bremen	New Orleans	11/20/1852	03/25/1856	26	329	N	
Pistner, Christoph	25	Bavaria	Y	Bremen	Buffalo	10/28/1847	01/16/1851	2	501	N	
Pistor, Ludwig	37	Germany	Y	Bremen	New York	11/25/1887	06/09/1890			Y	
Pitrosky, Henry	21	Germany	Y	Havre	New York	08/10/1893	01/16/1894			Y	
Pitt, Thomas D.	28	England	Y	Liverpool	New York	05/18/1846	05/22/1856	26	541	N	
Plaatenkamp, George	17	Germany	N	?	New York	00/00/1870				Y	10/23/1888
Plachecki, Michael	29	Germany	Y	Bremen	Baltimore	11/01/1887	04/23/1890			Y	
Placke, Frank	26	Germany	Y	Liverpool	Boston	09/15/1884	10/30/1889			Y	
Placke, Fred	26	Germany	Y	Rotterdam	New York	09/09/1881	12/28/1887			Y	
Placke, Frederick August	30	Hanover	Y	Bremen	New York	12/01/1845	01/31/1851	3	73	N	
Placke, Herman	47	Germany	N	Bremen	Baltimore	11/??/1866	?			Y	
Placke, Herman	22	Germany	Y	Bremen	New York	05/22/1882	10/11/1886			Y	
Plagemann, Anton	27	Germany	Y	Rotterdam	New York	06/26/1886	10/15/1892	19	364	N	
Plagemann, F.	21	Germany	Y	Rotterdam	New York	08/07/1886	10/24/1889			Y	
Plagemann, Joseph	31	Germany	Y	Rotterdam	New York	06/26/1886	10/15/1892	19	365	N	
Plagemann, Joseph	31	Germany	Y	Rotterdam	New York	06/26/1886	10/15/1892				
Plagennum, F.	21	Germany	Y	Rotterdam	New York	08/07/1886	10/24/1889	19	255	N	
Plagge, Henry	30	Germany	Y	Amsterdam	New York	05/15/1884	10/28/1889			Y	
Plagge, Hermann	16	Germany	N	?	New York	00/00/1881				Y	10/26/1888
Plank, Joseph	30	Bavaria	Y	Havre	New Orleans	11/28/1851	05/24/1854	8	504	N	
Plank, Joseph	30	Bavaria	Y	Havre	New Orleans	11/28/1851	05/24/1854	9	378	N	
Plantholt, Fred	31	Germany	Y	Bremen	Baltimore	06/24/1884	11/09/1889			Y	
Plapp, Gottlieb	28	Germany	Y	Bremen	New York	03/05/1887	03/09/1888			Y	
Plas, G.	21	Germany	Y	Amsterdam	New York	10/27/1881	02/11/1884			Y	
Platen, Martin	32	Germany	Y	Bremen	Baltimore	08/21/1882	09/27/1886			Y	
Plath, Ferdinand	63	Germany	Y	?	?	?	09/26/1884			Y	
Plattner, Martin	30	Austria	Y	Antwerp	New York	04/21/1890	10/18/1897			Y	
Platvoet, Gerrit	27	Holland	Y	Amsterdam	New York	12/17/1847	01/06/1853	5	529	N	
Platwet, Theodore	41	Holland	Y	Amsterdam	New York	12/17/1847	10/12/1848	1	153	N	
Plaul, Michael	50	Saxe Weimar	Y	Hamburg	New York	09/15/1854	04/09/1858	16	510	N	
Pledderman, Herman	26	Hanover	Y	Bremen	New Orleans	12/14/1852	08/20/1855	11	465	N	
Pleisenberger, Friedrich	30	Germany	Y	Bremen	New York	03/28/1882	11/27/1883			Y	
Pleisenberger, Friedrich	30	Germany	N	Bremen	New York	03/28/1882	?			Y	
Pleiter, Bernhard	36	Germany	Y	Amsterdam	New York	10/29/1882	10/24/1896			Y	
Plesk, John	40	Austria	Y	Hamburg	Baltimore	07/23/1893	11/03/1900			Y	

CITIZENSHIP RECORDS

APPLICANT	AGE	COUNTRY OF ORIGIN	DEC	DEPART PORT	ENTRY PORT	ARRIVE DATE	DEC DATE	VOL	PG.	FLD	NAT DATE
Plessner, Abraham	21	Austria	Y	Hamburg	New York	03/31/1853	05/28/1856	14	263	N	
Plessner, Anton	21	Austria	Y	Hamburg	New York	03/31/1854	05/28/1856	26	560	N	
Pletscher, John	24	Switzerland	Y	Havre	New York	03/26/1856	02/02/1857	14	529	N	
Pletz, Carl	??	Germany	Y	?	?	?	09/07/1887			Y	
Pletzer, Henry	38	Germany	Y	Bremen	New York	08/04/1892	07/13/1898			Y	
Pletzer, Joseph	45	Germany	Y	Bremen	New York	03/26/1873	09/17/1885			Y	
Plitman, Alex	23	Russia	Y	Hamburg	New York	10/00/1881	07/01/1883			Y	
Plitman, Alex (Aleck?)	30	Russia	N	Hamburg	New York	10/??/1881	07/??/1883	28	158	N	?
Plitsch, Jacob	37	Germany	Y	Hamburg	New York	06/06/1881	01/02/1886			Y	
Plochg, Anton	31	Oldenburg	Y	Bremen	New York	08/22/1852	08/21/1855	11	466	N	
Ploebst, Gabriel	23	Germany	Y	Havre	New York	11/01/1883	03/29/1887			Y	
Ploeger, Bernard	26	Germany	Y	Bremen	New York	05/01/1883	01/22/1884			Y	
Plogmann, Fred	21	Germany	Y	Bremen	Baltimore	08/18/1886	07/10/1889			Y	
Plogsted, Henry	37	Germany	Y	Bremen	New York	10/05/1865	05/17/1880			Y	
Plogsterd, John Frederic	30	Hanover	Y	Bremen	Baltimore	10/08/1854	10/12/1857	15	391	N	
Plogsterth, Henry	30	Hanover	Y	Bremen	Baltimore	09/20/1854	08/27/1857	15	194	N	
Plueckebaum, Charles Ant	42	Prussia	Y	Bremen	New York	08/12/1855	03/31/1858	16	455	N	
Pluemer, Henry	22	Germany	Y	Bremen	Baltimore	04/13/1882	06/12/1884			Y	
Pluennecke, Adolf	28	Germany	Y	Bremen	Baltimore	04/20/1887	02/23/1888			Y	
Plume, Dominick	31	Germany	Y	Havre	New York	02/27/1891	10/12/1896			Y	
Plume, Eugene	??	Germany	Y	?	?	?	06/09/1891			Y	
Plummer, Cecil H.	??	England?	Y	?	?	?	07/10/1888			Y	
Plump, Gerhard	35	Oldenburg	Y	Bremen	New Orleans	11/12/1851	10/06/1856	14	232	N	
Plump, John H.	80	Germany	N	Bremen	New Orleans	10/??/1852	?			Y	
Plunger, Gerard	27	Hanover	Y	Bremen	New Orleans	12/10/1844	01/13/1849	1	416	N	
Plunkett, Thomas	24	Ireland	Y	Liverpool	New York	04/01/1851	04/17/1854	8	149	N	
Plunkett, Thomas	24	Ireland	Y	Liverpool	New York	04/01/1851	04/17/1854	9	20	N	
Plust, Carl	33	Germany	Y	Hamburg	New York	09/06/1882	11/01/1886			Y	
Pochat, Louis	25	Prussia	Y	Hamburg	New Orleans	11/09/1852	12/10/1855	13	297	N	
Pocock, Oliver	39	England	Y	Bristol	New York	07/13/1880	10/11/1890			Y	
Podesta, James	37	Sardina	Y	Liverpool	New York	11/12/1844	02/18/1852	24	136	N	
Podesta, John	30	Sardina	Y	Genoa	New York	11/07/1846	03/29/1850	2	279	N	
Podesta, John	23	Sardinia	Y	Genoa	New York	05/02/1845	03/28/1849	23	263	N	
Podesta, John	28	Sardinia	Y	Havre	New York	07/??/1847	12/??/1849	23	379	N	
Podesta, Louis	27	Italy	Y	Liverpool	New Orleans	11/18/1847	09/23/1858	16	147	N	
Podurgiel, Kasamer	??	Russia	Y	?	?	?	06/11/1894			Y	
Poehl, Henry W.	45	Germany	N	Bremen	New Orleans	10/??/1859	?			Y	
Poeling, Henry	42	Germany	Y	Rotterdam	New York	04/20/1886	03/11/1892			Y	
Poerschke, Edward	24	Germany	Y	Hamburg	New York	07/18/1889	03/21/1892			Y	
Poerschke, Frederick	27	Germany	Y	Bremen	Baltimore	05/21/1891	11/02/1896			Y	
Poeschel, Franz	39	Germany	Y	Bremen	New York	12/28/1884	10/20/1888			Y	
Poetz, George Adam	35	Kurhassen	Y	Antweerp	New York	07/06/1848	04/12/1852	24	471	N	
Poetzlberger, John	33	Austria	Y	Havre	New Orleans	09/29/1842	03/02/1850	2	147	N	
Pogue, Thomas	22	Ireland	Y	Dublin	New Orleans	12/23/1849	10/10/1854	6	222	N	
Pogue, Thomas	22	Ireland	Y	Dublin	New Orleans	12/23/1849	10/10/1854	11	225	N	
Pogue, William	54	Ireland	N	Dublin	New Orleans	12/24/1849	?	28	70	N	03/??/1856
Pogue, William	15	Ireland	N	Dublin	New Orleans	12/24/1849				Y	03/00/1856
Pohl, B. William	30	Hanover	Y	Bremerhafen	Baltimore	10/??/1859	01/30/1861	18	79	N	
Pohl, Carl	36	Germany	Y	Bremen	Baltimore	07/01/1888	02/05/1894			Y	
Pohl, Henry	46	Germany	Y	Bremen	Baltimore	08/20/1875	12/04/1889			Y	
Pohl, Hermann	29	Germany	Y	Rotterdam	New York	02/22/1884	04/04/1887			Y	
Pohl, Johann	50	Germany	Y	Bremen	New York	06/27/1885	05/11/1889			Y	
Pohl, Joseph	38	Prussia	Y	Bremen	Indianolo TX	12/17/1852	04/08/1856	26	473	N	
Pohl, Oscar	30	Germany	Y	Hamburg	Philadelphia	03/03/1885	01/21/1888			Y	
Pohl, William	23	Germany	Y	Rotterdam	New York	10/28/1881	10/25/1882			Y	
Pohl, William	50	Prussia	Y	Bremen	New Orleans	11/13/1851	09/15/1852	25	519	N	
Pohler, Heinrich	35	Austria	Y	Bremen	New York	05/31/1891	11/04/1895			Y	
Pohlkamp, John B.	33	Germany	Y	Amsterdam	New York	10/06/1883	12/24/1888			Y	
Pohlmann, Anton	30	Germany	Y	?	?	?	05/11/1878			Y	

CITIZENSHIP RECORDS

APPLICANT	AGE	COUNTRY OF ORIGIN	DEC	DEPART PORT	ENTRY PORT	ARRIVE DATE	DEC DATE	VOL	PG.	FLD	NAT DATE
Pohlmann, Diedrich	36	Hanover	Y	Bremen	Baltimore	05/18/1846	01/15/1849	1	426	N	
Pohlmann, Henry	27	Oldenburg	Y	Bremen	Baltimore	05/24/1844	01/02/1851	2	439	N	
Pohlmann, Henry	29	Germany	Y	Bremen	Baltimore	10/10/1890	06/18/1895			Y	
Pohlmann, Herman H. H.	47	Prussia	Y	Bremen	Baltimore	08/01/1846	02/19/1849	23	181	N	
Pohlmeyer, Henry Carl	32	Prussia	Y	Bremen	Baltimore	11/27/1847	03/30/1852	24	334	N	
Poitinger, Lambert	5	Germany	N	?	New York	00/00/1872				Y	10/10/1888
Polaski, Henry	34	Russia	Y	Hamburg	New York	10/??/1882	12/03/1887			Y	
Polekoff, Morris	30	Russia	Y	London	New York	07/02/1889	11/27/1897			Y	
Pollack, Leopold	44	Germany	Y	Havre	New York	09/21/1881	08/15/1885			Y	
Pollak, David	58	Russia	Y	Bremen	Baltimore	03/22/1890	07/25/1899			Y	
Pollak, Lewis	27	Austria	Y	Hamburg	New York	01/02/1889	06/20/1892			Y	
Pollak, Otto	??	Austria	N	?	?	04/19/1886				Y	10/13/1892
Pollatschek, Hugo	??	Hungary	Y	?	?	?	10/04/1892			Y	
Polman, Gerhard	58	Holland	Y	Rotterdam	New York	05/09/1892	11/07/1898			Y	
Polman, Tony	26	Holland	Y	Rotterdam	New York	05/09/1892	11/07/1898			Y	
Polster, August	34	Saxe Weimar	Y	Hamburg	New York	10/15/1854	09/18/1858	16	169	N	
Polster, Charles Clemens	27	Hanover	Y	Bremen	New Orleans	11/12/1847	09/27/1856	14	400	N	
Polster, John G.	24	Germany	Y	Bremen	New York	12/09/1888	07/12/1893			Y	
Polster, Konrad	32	Germany	Y	Bremen	New York	07/08/1882	07/14/1882			Y	
Polster, Robert	36	Saxony	Y	Hamburg	New York	10/04/1854	09/28/1858	16	112	N	
Pomeranetz, Jacob	37	Russia	Y	Bremen	Baltimore	04/06/1889	10/06/1896			Y	
Ponsch, Louis W.	40	Germany	Y	Bremen	New York	07/18/1883	03/16/1892			Y	
Poole, Henry	26	England	Y	London	New York	02/28/1890	08/28/1890			Y	
Pope, William Coleman	57	England	Y	Liverpool	New York	10/??/1847	10/25/1855	13	143	N	
Popp, Andrew	43	Bavaria	Y	Bremen	New York	08/15/1853	09/27/1856	14	404	N	
Popp, Christian	34	Saxe Coburg G	Y	Bremen	New York	07/01/1852	07/14/1855	11	388	N	
Popp, Henry	??	Russia	Y	?	?	?	09/16/1893			Y	
Popp, Johann L.	??	Germany	Y	?	?	?	02/28/1889			Y	
Popp, John David	35	Saxony	Y	Bremen	Baltimore	08/06/1852	03/03/1858	16	366	N	
Popp, Michael	30	Bavaria	Y	Bremen	Buffalo	08/04/1847	02/21/1851	3	149	N	
Popp, Michael	32	Bavaria	Y	London	New York	04/20/1852	12/12/1855	13	306	N	
Poppe, Frederick	44	Hanover	Y	Bremen	Baltimore	10/23/1854	09/29/1856	14	21	N	
Poppe, George Edward	48	Hanover	Y	Bremen	New York	09/21/1856	09/27/1858	16	118	N	
Poppe, John A. K.	22	Germany	Y	Bremen	New York	11/28/1888	04/08/1890			Y	
Poppel, George	??	Germany	Y	?	?	06/??/1883	10/22/1888			Y	
Poppel, Johann	45	Germany	Y	Hamberg	New York	04/22/1887	09/10/1896			Y	
Poradjinski, Ludwik	34	Germany	Y	Bremen	Baltimore	05/21/1885	10/15/1896			Y	
Poradricki, Wlady	29	Germany	Y	Bremen	New York	03/07/1884	10/15/1888			Y	
Poradriski, Wlady	29	Germany	Y	Bremen	New York	03/07/1884	10/13/1888	19	148	N	
Porman, Henry	22	Hanover	Y	Bremen	Baltimore	05/12/1847	08/21/1848	22	217	N	
Porter, Michael	27	Ireland	Y	Queenstown	New York	04/30/1896	03/17/1903			Y	
Porter, William	24	Ireland	Y	Liverpool	New York	09/18/1853	08/21/1857	15	163	N	
Portier, Charles	31	Wurttemberg	Y	Antwerp	New York	08/??/1848	02/14/1850	2	70	N	
Portier, William	26	Wurttemberg	Y	Bremen	New York	07/12/1854	10/05/1857	15	348	N	
Poske, Frank Henry	22	Germany	Y	Bremen	Baltimore	08/19/1890	01/18/1894			Y	
Poske, Heinrich	59	Germany	Y	Bremen	Baltimore	08/19/1890	08/29/1896			Y	
Poske, Henry	22	Germany	Y	Amsterdam	New York	12/08/1882	05/25/1885			Y	
Poske, Herman	26	Germany	Y	Amsterdam	New York	08/09/1881	11/14/1883			Y	
Posner, Frank	26	Russia	Y	Antwerp	Philadelphia	07/09/1899	07/09/1903			Y	
Posner, Leopold	28	Poland (Russi	Y	?	New Orleans	06/04/1887	10/02/1891			Y	
Posquale, Lorenzo D.	38	Italy	Y	Naples	New York	04/15/1883	08/04/1892			Y	
Post, Henry	40	Prussia	Y	Bremen	Baltimore	05/??/1848	04/18/1855	11	265	N	
Postel, George	24	Germany	Y	Bremen	Baltimore	09/20/1881	04/04/1885			Y	
Postel, Jacob	25	Germany	Y	Antwerp	New York	11/28/1882	12/28/1888			Y	
Potenberg, Charles	29	Prussia	Y	Hamburg	New York	05/03/1849	02/19/1850	2	97	N	
Pothast, William	30	Hanover	Y	Bremen	New Orleans	11/29/1854	12/03/1857	16	67	N	
Potrafke, Herman	28	Germany	Y	Bremen	New York	06/18/1892	12/28/1895			Y	
Pottebaum, Frederick	34	Prussia	Y	Havre	Baltimore	10/30/1846	10/10/1854	6	221	N	
Pottebaum, Frederick (Jo	34	Prussia	Y	Havre	Baltimore	10/30/1846	10/10/1854	11	222	N	

CITIZENSHIP RECORDS

APPLICANT	AGE	COUNTRY OF ORIGIN	DEC	DEPART PORT	ENTRY PORT	ARRIVE DATE	DEC DATE	VOL	PG.	FLD	NAT DATE
Pottebaum, Frederick W.	62	Germany	N	Bremen	New York	07/19/1854	?			Y	
Potthoff, Fritz	27	Germany	Y	Bremen	New York	03/25/1893	07/14/1897			Y	
Potthoff, Henry	40	Hanover	Y	Bremen	New Orleans	12/08/1845	10/02/1848	1	16	N	
Potthoff, Joseph	34	Hanover	Y	Bremen	New York	09/11/1846	10/02/1848	1	17	N	
Pottker, William	24	Germany	Y	Bremen	Baltimore	09/07/1884	10/24/1890	10	206	N	
Pottker, William	24	Germany	Y	Bremen	Baltimore	09/07/1884	10/24/1890			Y	
Pottman, Fred	24	Germany	Y	Bremen	New York	05/18/1885	10/26/1891			Y	
Pottmeier, Anton	33	Prussia	Y	Bremen	Baltimore	05/??/1849	09/24/1855	13	129	N	
Potts, Fred	30	Germany	Y	Bremen	New York	05/16/1882	04/19/1887			Y	
Potts, John	30	England	Y	Liverpool	New York	03/24/1884	03/09/1894			Y	
Pottschmidt, Louis	27	Germany	Y	Bremen	Baltimore	10/20/1891	10/18/1899			Y	
Potuznik, Waclav	36	Germany	Y	Bremen	New York	04/17/1889	11/22/1897			Y	
Pouer, Richard	23	Ireland	Y	Waterford	New York	04/15/1847	10/13/1851	4	254	N	
Poulsen, N.F.L.	??	Denmark	Y	?	?	?	05/03/1881			Y	
Powell, Edward W.	21	Ireland	Y	Liverpool	New York	09/02/1856	06/02/1859	17	448	N	
Powell, Jesse D.	22	Wales	Y	Liverpool	Newport News	08/20/1887	11/21/1889			Y	
Powell, John	30	Ireland	Y	Liverpool	New Orleans	01/23/1850	10/13/1851	4	240	N	
Powell, John	49	England	Y	Liverpool	New York	07/10/1855	01/28/1860	27	74	N	
Power, John	25	Ireland	Y	Liverpool	New Orleans	06/15/1852	04/02/1858	16	475	N	
Power, Michael	40	Ireland	Y	Queenstwon	New York	02/26/1879	10/23/1886	19	80	N	
Power, Michael	40	Ireland	Y	Queenstown	New York	02/26/1879	10/23/1886			Y	
Power, Robert	26	Ireland	Y	Liverpool	New Orleans	01/01/1854	04/03/1856	26	430	N	
Power, Thomas	23	Ireland	Y	Waterford	Boston	08/29/1854	03/17/1860	27	129	N	
Powers, Edward	28	Ireland	Y	Waterford	Boston	08/04/1855	02/11/1860	27	102	N	
Pownall, Thomas	34	England	Y	Liverpool	New York	10/08/1847	04/04/1853	8	40	N	
Poyn, Henry	??	China	Y	?	?	?	10/12/1885			Y	
Prabsting, August	49	Germany	Y	Bremen	Baltimore	11/25/1866	10/21/1895			Y	
Pracht, Albert	32	Germany	Y	Havre	New York	02/21/1890	09/23/1896			Y	
Pracht, J.G.	32	Baden	Y	Antwerp	New York	07/04/1850	08/29/1862	18	422	N	
Pradel, Charles	25	Prussia	Y	Bremen	New York	10/06/1856	07/26/1858	16	527	N	
Praechter, Peter	24	Germany	Y	Antwerp	New York	03/19/1882	03/03/1887			Y	
Pranger, Lambert	38	Hanover	Y	Bremen	New Orleans	05/26/1857	07/23/1862	18	379	N	
Pratt, Isaac	40	Ireland	Y	Queenstown	Newport News	04/20/1888	10/16/1893			Y	
Pratt, Thomas	44	Ireland	Y	Queenstown	Newport News	04/20/1888	10/16/1893			Y	
Prees, Griffith W.	??	Wales	Y	?	?	?	03/20/1879			Y	
Prehn, Christian	31	Mecklenburg S	Y	Hamburg	New York	08/01/1859	12/26/1859	17	526	N	
Preifer, Thomas	??	Germany	Y	?	?	?	10/18/1886			Y	
Preiner, August	25	Germany	Y	Hamburg	New York	09/23/1876	11/03/1884			Y	
Preiser, John	35	Germany	Y	Antwerp	New York	09/06/1884	01/23/1888			Y	
Preising, Adam Friedrich	25	Germany	Y	Hamburg	New York	09/17/1879	12/18/1882			Y	
Prell, Ludwig	26	Hanover	Y	Bremen	Baltimore	06/23/1855	11/01/1858	17	234	N	
Prelle, Ernst	17	Germany	N	?	New York	00/00/1880				Y	03/30/1888
Prelle, George F.	29	Germany	Y	Amsterdam	New York	12/11/1882	08/23/1889			Y	
Prendergast, Mathew	42	Ireland	Y	Queenstown	New York	05/23/1880	10/29/1894			Y	
Prendirgrass, James	24	Ireland	Y	Liverpool	New Orleans	04/22/1849	01/??/1850	23	491	N	
Prest, John George	32	Hesse Cassel	Y	Bremen	Baltimore	05/04/1848	06/19/1851	3	433	N	
Prestenbach, William	25	Baden	Y	Havre	New York	??/02/1845	11/12/1849	23	337	N	
Preun, John Theodore	26	Hanover	Y	Bremen	New York	09/20/1853	08/05/1856	14	347	N	
Preus, Benjamin	35	Russia	Y	Bremen	Baltimore	09/30/1894	10/28/1898			Y	
Preuss, Caesar	31	Germany	Y	Bremen	New York	12/18/1892	11/25/1896			Y	
Preuth, Barney	29	Germany	Y	Bremen	Baltimore	07/27/1881	10/13/1885			Y	
Prevot, Hellwig	61	Germany	Y	Hamburg	New York	02/19/1866	10/25/1886			Y	
Price, George	34	Scotland	Y	Glasgow	Cleveland	02/10/1872	10/05/1885			Y	
Price, George	29	England	Y	Liverpool	New York	07/01/1849	02/07/1852	24	69	N	
Price, James	??	Ireland	Y	?	?	06/??/1880	09/17/1886			Y	
Price, John	29	Wales	Y	Liverpool	Philadelphia	07/08/1849	08/04/1856	14	326	N	
Price, Simon	??	Austria	Y	?	?	?	10/25/1883			Y	
Price, William	23	England	Y	Liverpool	New Orleans	12/??/1847	12/??/1850	2	406	N	
Price, William	54	England	Y	Liverpool	New York	08/31/1888	11/05/1889			Y	

CITIZENSHIP RECORDS

APPLICANT	AGE	COUNTRY OF ORIGIN	DEC	DEPART PORT	ENTRY PORT	ARRIVE DATE	DEC DATE	VOL	PG.	FLD	NAT DATE
Price, William	31	England	Y	London	New Orleans	09/06/1886	10/31/1895			Y	
Priebs, William	??	Russia	Y	?	?	?	10/26/1893			Y	
Prieshoff, Bernard	23	Oldenburg	Y	Bremen	Baltimore	11/04/1857	03/25/1862	18	283	N	
Prieshoff, Gerhard Henry	29	Hanover	Y	Bremen	Baltimore	09/03/1857	12/04/1858	17	375	N	
Priessmann, John	23	Germany	Y	Antwerp	New York	10/25/1889	11/02/1889			Y	
Priesthoff, John Henry	22	Oldenburg	Y	Bremen	New Orleans	03/??/1851	09/18/1855	13	69	N	
Priga, Ernst	53	Germany	Y	Bremen	Baltimore	??/??/1861	11/03/1886			Y	
Prigge, Herman	31	Prussia	Y	Bremen	New York	09/28/1848	07/28/1851	4	43	N	
Prince, Henry	28	England	Y	Liverpool	New Orleans	10/15/1848	02/12/1853	7	146	N	
Prindergast, James	27	Ireland	Y	Liverpool	New York	05/08/1882	03/30/1888			Y	
Prinsen, Barney A.	26	Holland	Y	Bremen	Baltimore	06/15/1848	10/12/1848	1	163	N	
Prinz, Gustav	29	Germany	Y	Hamburg	New York	09/06/1880	01/06/1885			Y	
Prinz, Valentine	??	Germany	N	Havre	New York	07/04/1856	12/10/1856	28	250	N	03/08/1862
Prinzbach, F. Xavier	21	Baden	Y	Havre	New York	10/07/1869	04/01/1872	18	484	N	
Pristler, Matthias	27	Wurttemberg	Y	Havre	New York	05/11/1854	11/28/1859	17	483	N	
Pritchard, John	28	Wales	Y	Liverpool	New York	06/26/1847	01/31/1851	3	71	N	
Pritchard, John	28	Wales	Y	Liverpool	New York	07/04/1849	01/04/1853	5	516	N	
Pritki, Valentine	36	Germany	Y	Dunkirk	New York	07/16/1885	10/08/1896			N	
Pritsch, George	31	Hesse Darmsta	Y	Antwerp	New York	06/01/1850	04/24/1854	8	246	N	
Pritsch, George	31	Hesse Darmsta	Y	Antwerp	New York	06/01/1850	04/24/1854	9	117	N	
Probert, Thomas Woodward	??	England	Y	?	?	?	10/18/1888			Y	
Probst, Bernard	38	Germany	Y	Bremen	New York	05/26/1882	02/04/1887			Y	
Probst, Fred	29	Oldenburg	Y	Bremen	Baltimore	09/27/1858	11/01/1860	27	533	N	
Probst, John	21	Germany	Y	Antwerp	New York	07/23/1891	07/24/1893			Y	
Probst, Peter	37	Germany	N	London	New York	03/01/1880	04/??/1883	28	232	N	?
Probst, Vinzenz	31	Switzerland	Y	Antwerp	New York	09/09/1887	03/12/1889			Y	
Prochaska, John	35	Austria	Y	Hamburg	New York	09/28/1880	07/18/1882			Y	
Procher, John	30	Germany	Y	Bremen	New York	08/12/1881	03/25/1885			Y	
Procher, John Baptist	54	Austria	Y	Bremen	New York	08/08/1881	08/13/1881			Y	
Proeger, George	56	Germany	Y	Havre	New York	07/08/1862	10/27/1888			Y	
Proehl, Charles	29	Germany	Y	Antwerp	New York	11/04/1878	10/06/1884			Y	
Proes, Peter	35	Bavaria	Y	Hamburg	New York	07/20/1843	03/01/1851	3	187	N	
Proeschel, Christoph	23	Bavaria	Y	Rotterdam	New York	08/16/1854	02/16/1856	26	91	N	
Pronizius, Franz	46	Baden	Y	Havre	New Orleans	12/12/1852	09/29/1856	14	430	N	
Prophet, Johann August An	26	Prussia	Y	Bremen	Baltimore	09/29/1869	01/05/1872	18	450	N	
Propheter, Adam	51	Germany	N	Rotterdam	New Orleans	01/??/1851	?			Y	
Propheter, Michael	50	Bavaria	Y	Havre	New Orleans	11/30/1850	05/20/1854	8	479	N	
Propheter, Michael	50	Bavaria	Y	Havre	New Orleans	11/30/1850	05/20/1854	9	353	N	
Prospero, Ulricko	45	Italy	N	Naples	New York	11/??/1871	?			Y	
Prosstring, Bernard	27	Prussia	Y	Bremen	New York	10/12/1846	01/06/1853	5	522	N	
Prowd, Henry D.	44	Jamaica West	Y	Kingston	New Orleans	09/??/1891	07/16/1898			Y	
Prudent, Francis	58	France	Y	Havre	New Orleans	01/20/1853	04/23/1861	18	143	N	
Pruehl, Charles	29	Germany	Y	Antwerp	New York	11/04/1878	10/06/1884			Y	
Prues, Herman	17	Germany	N	?	Baltimore	00/00/1882				Y	10/29/1888
Prueser, Herman	28	Hanover	Y	Bremen	New York	05/05/1853	10/06/1854	10	518	N	
Prullage, Arnold	37	Oldenburg	Y	Bremen	New York	09/01/1846	11/20/1848	1	346	N	
Prune, Bernd Henry	31	Oldenburg	Y	Bremen	New Orleans	10/??/1852	12/26/1855	13	365	N	
Prunello, Louis	31	Italy	Y	Genova	New York	11/15/1899	04/27/1903			Y	
Prus, Bernard	25	Germany	Y	Bremen	Baltimore	12/30/1880	06/25/1885			Y	
Prus, H.	22	Germany	Y	Amsterdam	New York	03/17/1880	10/10/1885			Y	
Prus, John Frederick	21	Hanover	Y	Bremen	New Orleans	11/20/1854	10/02/1857	15	344	N	
Pruschansky, Solomon	34	Russia	Y	Hamburg	Philadelphia	05/17/1885	04/25/1894			Y	
Pruser, Herman	28	Hanover	Y	Bremen	New York	05/05/1853	10/06/1854	12	457	N	
Pryce, John L.	38	England	Y	Liverpool	New York	01/??/1876	11/29/1887			Y	
Pryor, Frederick	46	England	Y	London	New York	10/20/1856	01/15/1861	18	61	N	
Puchner, Joseph	36	Austria	Y	Bremen	Baltimore	08/15/1853	05/23/1854	9	372	N	
Puchta, Lorenz	23	Bavaria	Y	Bremen	New York	04/16/1852	10/22/1857	15	475	N	
Puechner, Joseph	36	Austria	Y	Bremen	Baltimore	08/15/1853	04/23/1854	8	498	N	
Puening, Ferdinand	26	Hanover	Y	Bremen	New York	05/17/1849	04/18/1853	8	69	N	

CITIZENSHIP RECORDS

APPLICANT	AGE	COUNTRY OF ORIGIN	DEC	DEPART PORT	ENTRY PORT	ARRIVE DATE	DEC DATE	VOL	PG.	FLD	NAT DATE
Pues, Ferdinand	26	Hanover	Y	Bremen	New Orleans	12/18/1850	02/21/1853	7	190	N	
Puetz, John Joseph	35	Prussia	Y	Antwerp	New York	05/27/1848	02/21/1849	23	240	N	
Puff, Martin	17	Germany	N	?	New York	00/00/1882				Y	10/26/1888
Pugh, Daniel	??	Wales	Y	?	?	?	11/01/1887			Y	
Pugh, Richard	48	England	Y	Liverpool	New Orleans	12/04/1849	11/08/1852	5	257	N	
Pugh, Richard	48	England	Y	Liverpool	New Orleans	12/04/1849	11/08/1852	6	380	N	
Puhl, Herman	39	Germany	Y	Hamburg	New York	02/11/1891	01/07/1896			Y	
Puhlmann, Carl	46	Germany	Y	Hamburg	New York	12/12/1880	04/04/1885			Y	
Pullinger, William S.	28	England	Y	London	New York	03/30/1884	10/25/1890			Y	
Pullman, Thomas	31	England	Y	Bristol	New York	06/12/1883	10/20/1890	19	290	N	
Pund, Henry	48	Germany	N	Bremen	Baltimore	12/??/1858	?			Y	
Pund, John H.C.	24	Germany	Y	Bremen	New York	02/16/1882	11/03/1884			Y	
Pund, John Henry	22	Oldenburg	Y	Bremen	Baltimore	11/20/1857	04/16/1860	27	155	N	
Pundsack, Frank	44	Germany	Y	Bremen	Baltimore	07/17/1877	11/03/1879			Y	
Puntt, August	17	Germany	N	?	New York	00/00/1883				Y	11/01/1888
Purcell, Bartholomew	30	Ireland	Y	Canada	Ogdensburg	03/01/1848	10/17/1851	4	317	N	
Purcell, Frank L.	??	Canada	N	?	?		11/00/1869			Y	10/17/1892
Purcell, John	36	Ireland	Y	Liverpool	New York	04/03/1863	07/26/1881				
Purcell, Joseph	5	Canada	N	?	Buffalo	00/00/1869				Y	10/13/1888
Purcell, Michael Carey	47	Ireland	Y	Liverpool	New Orleans	05/05/1848	10/06/1851	4	199	N	
Purcell, Patrick James	35	Ireland	Y	London	New York	08/31/1856	05/01/1860	27	175	N	
Purchase, Thomas	28	England	Y	Liverpool	Philadelphia	08/05/1854	05/25/1859	17	431	N	
Purfield, James	34	Ireland	Y	Liverpool	New York	12/12/1849	03/07/1857	15	72	N	
Purtell, John	??	Ireland	Y	?	?	?	10/25/1884			Y	
Purvan, Wolf	39	Poland	Y	?	?	05/??/1881	02/24/1891			Y	
Pushin, Simon	36	Russia	Y	Hamburg	New York	11/27/1885	05/22/1890			Y	
Puthoff, Henry	60	Germany	N	Bremen	New York	09/01/1853	??/??/1855	28	348	N	09/15/1860
Puthoff, Henry	21	Germany	N	Bremen	New York	09/01/1853	00/00/1855			Y	09/15/1860
Puthoff, John	29	Oldenburg	Y	Bremen	New York	05/10/1852	03/12/1860	27	123	N	
Putthoff, Barney	26	Prussia	Y	Havre	New York	11/01/1846	01/15/1850	23	508	N	
Putthoff, Christopher	40	Oldenburg	Y	Bremen	New Orleans	02/20/1845	08/07/1848	22	65	N	
Putting, Ferdinand	31	Germany	Y	Bremen	?	05/??/1860	10/09/1876			Y	
Putzel, George	29	Germany	Y	Bremen	New York	03/25/1888	10/14/1892	19	362	N	
Pye, John	26	Ireland	Y	Liverpool	New Orleans	??/25/1850	04/27/1855	11	314	N	
Quanta, John Frederick	53	Hanover	Y	Bremen	New Orleans	??/25/1847	02/12/1850	2	65	N	
Quartman, August	38	Germany	Y	Bremen	Baltimore	07/08/1882	04/05/1898			Y	
Quarto, Nicola	??	Italy	Y	?	?	01/04/1880	04/14/1891			Y	
Quast, Jacob	54	Baden	Y	Havre	?	?	09/22/1854	10	168	N	
Quast, Jacob	54	Baden	Y	Havre	New York	03/02/1850	09/22/1854	12	107	N	
Quattlander, Reinhold	25	Germany	Y	?	?	?	01/15/1887			Y	
Quayle, Robert James	21	England	Y	?	?	?	09/05/1889			Y	
Quealy, Martin	55	Ireland	Y	Queenstown	New York	06/07/1886	12/30/1893			Y	
Quebbermann, Joseph	48	Germany	N	Bremen	Baltimore	11/??/1860	?			Y	
Quekenstedt, Herman	27	Germany	Y	Bremen	Baltimore	06/22/1883	08/02/1886			Y	
Quenzer, Charles	26	Germany	Y	Antwerp	Philadelphia	05/26/1884	05/02/1888			Y	
Querner, Gottlieb Benjam	38	Prussia	Y	Hamburg	New York	06/??/1852	03/21/1853	7	360	N	
Quettner, Bernhard	55	Austria	Y	Bremen	New York	05/19/1890	01/16/1893			Y	
Quibell, James	43	England	Y	Liverpool	New York	05/28/1884	11/03/1887			Y	
Quigley, Michael	21	Ireland	Y	Liverpool	New Orleans	05/16/1853	05/20/1856	26	507	N	
Quigley, William	43	Ireland	Y	Londonderry	Philadelphia	10/04/1848	07/11/1851	3	518	N	
Quimke, Bernard	22	Prussia	Y	Bremen	New Orleans	10/03/1857	03/25/1858	16	446	N	
Quimke, Henry	31	Prussia	Y	Bremen	Galveston	11/03/1854	03/25/1858	16	445	N	
Quin, John	38	Ireland	Y	Quebec	Rochester	08/11/1848	11/06/1851	4	497	N	
Quinker, Francis	33	Prussia	Y	Bremen	Baltimore	06/01/1856	10/04/1858	17	30	N	
Quinlan, Daniel	31	Ireland	Y	Waterford	Rochester	08/15/1847	03/23/1853	7	375	N	
Quinlan, Edward	21	Ireland	Y	?	?	07/10/189?	03/21/1894			Y	
Quinlan, Jeremiah	24	Ireland	Y	Liverpool	New York	06/29/1849	03/16/1852	24	318	N	
Quinlan, John	26	Ireland	Y	Liverpool	New York	12/16/1847	09/10/1852	25	447	N	
Quinlan, Patrick	25	Ireland	Y	Queenstown	New York	05/18/1886	10/27/1893	21	39	N	

CITIZENSHIP RECORDS

APPLICANT	AGE	COUNTRY OF ORIGIN	DEC	DEPART PORT	ENTRY PORT	ARRIVE DATE	DEC DATE	VOL	PG.	FLD	NAT DATE
Quinlan, Patrick	25	Ireland	Y	Queenstown	New York	05/18/1886	10/27/1893			Y	
Quinlisk, Patrick	22	Ireland	Y	Liverpool	New York	05/??/1852	07/07/1855	11	348	N	
Quinn, Edward	37	Ireland	Y	Liverpool	New Orleans	01/??/1849	05/23/1854	8	500	N	
Quinn, Edward	37	Ireland	Y	Liverpool	New Orleans	01/??/1849	05/23/1854	9	374	N	
Quinn, James	38	Ireland	N	Ireland	New York	06/01/1873	?			Y	
Quinn, John	32	Ireland	Y	Liverpool	Boston	06/26/1852	09/17/1858	16	168	N	
Quinn, John	25	Ireland	Y	Canada	Lewiston	05/??/1847	06/21/1852	25	300	N	
Quinn, John	17	Ireland	N	?	New York	00/00/1882				Y	10/19/1888
Quinn, Patrick	24	Ireland	Y	Liverpool	New Orleans	01/20/1850	02/10/1853	7	136	N	
Quinn, Robert Orr	36	Ireland	Y	Cork	New York	10/05/1836	02/12/1850	2	64	N	
Quint, David	44	Russia	Y	Hamburg	New York	04/30/1889	11/01/1900			Y	
Quint, Henry	27	Hanover	Y	Bremen	Baltimore	10/03/1846	11/17/1848	1	307	N	
Quirk, Michael	29	Ireland	Y	Cork	New York	01/14/1851	05/11/1852	25	7	N	
Quirke, Patrick	??	Ireland	Y	Liverpool	Philadelphia	10/15/18??	11/05/1856	14	473	N	
Quirke, Patrick	23	Ireland	Y	Galway	New Orleans	12/25/1848	02/18/1852	24	139	N	
Quist, Lars	33	Sweden	Y	Hamburg	Baltimore	05/27/1881	11/05/1886			Y	
Quista, John	40	Sardinia	Y	Liverpool	Black Rock,	12/04/1831	03/28/1849	23	260	N	
Quittschreiber, Michael	31	Saxony	Y	Hamburg	New York	05/28/1858	12/31/1858			Y	
Raap, William	26	Germany	Y	Bremen	New York	01/14/1897	10/25/1898			Y	
Raas, Casper	26	Switzerland	Y	Havre	New York	03/??/1852	03/21/1853	7	365	N	
Rabanus, Henry	30	Kurhessen	Y	Bremen	New York	11/01/1851	10/09/1854	6	148	N	
Rabanus, Henry	30	Kurhessen	Y	Bremen	New York	11/18/1851	10/09/1854	11	151	N	
Rabbe, Henry	34	Germany	Y	?	New York	??/??/1883	10/06/1892			Y	
Rabbe, William	30	Brunswick	Y	Bremen	New York	08/15/1848	01/21/1851	2	517	N	
Rabe, Clemens	45	Germany	Y	Bremen	New York	08/01/1866	10/10/1884			Y	
Rabe, Henry	56	Oldenburg	Y	Bremen	Baltimore	04/29/1849	10/06/1854	10	471	N	
Rabe, Henry	56	Oldenburg	Y	Bremen	Baltimore	04/29/1849	10/06/1854	12	410	N	
Rabe, John Frederick	66	Prussia	Y	Hamburg	New York	07/29/1852	01/28/1853	7	77	N	
Rabe, Joseph	28	Oldenburg	Y	Bremen	New Orleans	01/01/1850	10/09/1854	6	140	N	
Rabe, Joseph	28	Oldenburg	Y	Bremen	New Orleans	01/01/1850	10/09/1854	11	143	N	
Rabe, Theodore	21	Germany	Y	?	New York	00/00/1883	10/19/1887			Y	
Raber, Balthaser	25	Bavaria	Y	Havre	New York	05/11/1849	10/09/1854	11	74	N	
Raber, Balthiser	25	Bavaria	Y	Havre	New York	05/11/1849	10/09/1854	6	73	N	
Raber, Henry	22	Hanover	Y	Bremen	Baltimore	10/15/1850	11/03/1852	5	203	N	
Raber, Henry	22	Hanover	Y	Bremen	Baltimore	09/18/1850	11/03/1852	6	329	N	
Rabinowitsch, Elias	44	Russia	Y	Hamburg	New York	08/31/1886	05/10/1889			Y	
Rabinowitz, Sam	24	Russia	Y	Hamburg	New York	02/20/1887	08/21/1888			Y	
Rackebrandt, Henry Willi	29	Hanover	Y	Bremen	New York	11/03/1851	06/01/1852	25	172	N	
Radar, Henry	39	Germany	Y	Bremen	Baltimore	05/??/1872	10/22/1886	19	69	N	
Radatz, Friedrick	26	Russia	Y	Bremen	New York	01/27/1891	07/23/1896			Y	
Radcliff, Smyth	28	Ireland	Y	Belfast	Oswego	06/??/1843	05/04/1854	8	367	N	
Radcliff, Smyth	28	Ireland	Y	Belfast	Oswego	06/??/1847	05/04/1854	9	240	N	
Radefeld, B.	32	Germany	N	Rotterdam	New York	10/02/1878	??/??/1880	28	85	N	10/??/1883
Radefeld, B.	22	Germany	N	Rotterdam	New York	10/02/1878	00/00/1880			Y	10/00/1883
Radeloff, Frederick	38	Prussia	Y	Bremen	Baltimore	08/02/1857	11/02/1857	15	509	N	
Radeloff, Gustav	21	Prussia	Y	Bremen	Galveston	12/12/1856	11/02/1857	15	510	N	
Rademacher, Anton	31	Germany	Y	Bremen	New York	08/21/1888	11/14/1893			Y	
Rademacher, Diederich	36	Hanover	Y	Bremen	New Orleans	05/04/1850	01/23/1856	13	500	N	
Rademacher, Franz	46	Germany	Y	Havre	New York	07/30/1866	10/11/1884			Y	
Rademakers, William	31	Hanover	Y	Bremen	Baltimore	06/04/1845	11/14/1848	1	296	N	
Rader, Gustav	21	Prussia	Y	Bremen	New York	08/18/1854	10/30/1857	15	503	N	
Rader, Henry	39	Germany	Y	Bremen	Baltimore	05/00/1872	10/22/1886			Y	
Radina, Alois	41	Germany	Y	Hamburg	New York	03/17/1891	11/29/1899			Y	
Radloff, Ludwig	31	Mecklenburg S	Y	Hamburg	New York	09/02/1852	04/12/1856	26	494	N	
Radtke, Friedrich	34	Germany	Y	?	New York	??/??/1881	07/28/1884			Y	
Radunsky, Max	26	Russia	Y	Hamburg	New York	09/18/1887	06/12/1891			Y	
Rae, John	36	Scotland	Y	Liverpool	New York	08/??/1846	12/26/1857	16	255	N	
Raebel, John	27	Germany	Y	Bremen	New York	12/21/1889	02/28/1894			Y	
Raechard, George Adam	38	Wuerttemberg	Y	Bremen	Galveston	??/16/1846	11/??/1849	23	341	N	

CITIZENSHIP RECORDS

APPLICANT	AGE	COUNTRY OF ORIGIN	DEC	DEPART PORT	ENTRY PORT	ARRIVE DATE	DEC DATE	VOL	PG.	FLD	NAT DATE
Raechard, Joseph Frederi	33	Wuerttenberg	Y	Bremen	Galveston	07/??/1846	11/??/1848	23	340	N	
Raeckmann, Henry	26	Prussia	Y	Bremen	New York	05/29/1847	04/29/1850	3	23	N	
Raeder, Max	29	Germany	Y	Hamburg	New York	10/29/1885	10/05/1896			Y	
Rafalo, Isaac	28	Turkey	Y	Hamburg	Philadelphia	07/23/1881	05/07/1883	28	170	N	
Rafalo, Isaac	23	Turkey	Y	Hamburg	Philadelphia	07/23/1881	05/07/1883			Y	
Rafferty, James	48	Ireland	Y	Liverpool	New York	05/12/1847	06/23/1851	3	444	N	
Rafferty, John	28	Ireland	Y	Liverpool	New Orleans	12/16/1849	09/22/1858	16	152	N	
Raffl, Louis	30	Austria	Y	Havre	New York	06/11/1858	01/06/1862	18	241	N	
Raffra, George Michael	26	Bavaria	Y	Havre	New Orleans	12/01/1853	03/24/1856	26	292	N	
Rager, George	30	Germany	Y	Antwerp	New York	12/04/1880	12/05/1884			Y	
Raggen, Eugene	47	Switzerland	Y	Havre	New York	05/12/1892	10/29/1898			Y	
Raggio, August	22	Sardina	Y	Giona	New York	05/09/1847	04/05/1852	24	395	N	
Ragie, Christian	25	Bavaria	Y	Havre	New Orleans	01/10/1852	11/05/1855	13	157	N	
Rahe, Frederick	30	Germany	Y	Rotterdam	Boston	04/??/1872	07/03/1882			Y	
Rahe, Herman	50	Germany	N	Bremen	Charleston	12/15/1868	?			Y	
Rahe, John Rudolph	25	Hanover	Y	Bremen	Baltimore	11/10/1845	08/28/1848	22	268	N	
Rahe, Wilhelm	24	Germany	Y	Amsterdam	New York	07/06/1892	03/03/1896			Y	
Rahenkamp, John Henry	22	Hanover	Y	Bremen	Baltimore	09/??/1852	09/22/1855	13	109	N	
Rahill, Patrick	33	Ireland	Y	Liverpool	New York	03/17/1892	10/22/1892			Y	
Rahn, Gustav	38	Germany	Y	Stettin	New York	05/20/1885	03/13/1893			Y	
Rahn, Gustav	??	Germany	N	?	?	12/23/1886				Y	10/11/1892
Rahn, Jacob	30	Bavaria	Y	Havre	New York	04/14/1853	08/19/1857	15	160	N	
Rahn, John	31	Germany	Y	Bremen	Baltimore	09/01/1883	03/29/1895			Y	
Rahner, Bernard	30	Wuerttenberg	Y	Havre	New York	07/03/1849	02/16/1852	24	113	N	
Raible, Stephan	27	Hohenzollern	Y	Havre	New York	01/12/1855	04/03/1856	26	426	N	
Railly, Owen	59	Ireland	N	Liverpool	New York	06/??/1856	?			Y	
Rainfroth, Job	33	England	Y	Liverpool	New Orleans	05/23/1846	04/04/1853	8	41	N	
Rairden, Daniel	21	Ireland	Y	Liverpool	New York	01/12/1850	02/03/1851	3	91	N	
Rairden, Jeremiah	30	Ireland	Y	Liverpool	New Orleans	07/02/1848	10/31/1857	15	508	N	
Rairden, Timothy	26	Ireland	Y	Liverpool	New York	10/14/1847	04/28/1854	8	282	N	
Rairden, Timothy	26	Ireland	Y	Liverpool	New York	10/14/1847	04/28/1854	9	153	N	
Rairdon, Daniel	45	Ireland	Y	Dundas	Buffalo	10/??/1863	06/07/1888	19	132	N	
Rairdon, Daniel	45	Ireland	Y	Dundas	Buffalo	10/00/1863	06/07/1888			Y	
Raisbeck, John E.	??	England	Y	?	?	?	06/06/1881			Y	
Raisch, Matheus	44	Wurttemberg	Y	Havre	New York	04/11/1851	05/29/1854	9	437	N	
Raisch, Matheus	44	Wurttemberg	Y	Havre	New York	04/11/1851	05/29/1854	10	20	N	
Raisch, Matthias	21	Wurttemberg	Y	Havre	New York	04/18/1851	02/14/1853	7	158	N	
Raiser, Franz	40	Baden	Y	Havre	New Orleans	01/13/1852	10/09/1854	6	69	N	
Rakavag, John	34	Hanover	Y	Bremen	Baltimore	08/06/1840	10/06/1848	22	458	N	
Rake, Heinrich	59	Germany	N	Bremen	Baltimore	10/??/1846	?			Y	
Rake, John	22	Germany	Y	Rotterdam	New York	06/19/1885	09/22/1887			Y	
Rakel, Gerd Luke	27	Hanover	Y	Bremen	New Orleans	11/07/1856	12/20/1859	17	511	N	
Rakel, John Henry	24	Hanover	Y	Bremen	Baltimore	01/27/1848	06/10/1852	25	316	N	
Rakel, John Herman	31	Hanover	Y	Bremen	New Orleans	11/27/1845	10/03/1848	1	42	N	
Raker, Diedrich	43	Germany	Y	Bremen	Baltimore	12/??/1878	10/11/1882			Y	
Rakmann, Henry (Reckman	23	Germany	Y	Bremen	Baltimore	10/06/1880	11/08/1884			Y	
Ralff, Anthony	28	Germany	Y	Bremen	Baltmire	06/03/1881	10/05/1885	19	12	N	
Rallo, Joseph M.	24	Italy	Y	Palermo	New York	06/29/1892	11/21/1895			Y	
Ramazzotto, Benedetto	47	Sardinia	Y	Genoa	New York	08/01/1852	09/11/1855	11	532	N	
Rambach, Anthony	39	France	Y	Havre	New York	02/12/1873	04/25/1892	19	349	N	
Rambach, Anthony	39	France	Y	Havre	New York	02/12/1873	04/25/1892			Y	
Rameier, William	24	Prussia	Y	Bremen	New Orleans	06/04/1850	11/22/1852	5	322	N	
Ramelt, Henry	??	Saxony	Y	Havre	New York	08/24/1847	10/07/1848	22	473	N	
Ramien, Carl Ludwig	57	Prussia	Y	Hamburg	New Orleans	11/13/1847	10/02/1848	1	35	N	
Rammler, Henry	34	Saxony	Y	Hamburg	New York	09/04/1851	08/23/1852	25	341	N	
Ramp, Bernard	31	Oldenburg	Y	Bremen	New Orleans	02/05/1849	??/??/1852	25	320	N	
Rampe, Bernard	27	Hanover	Y	Bremen	New York	12/??/1846	10/21/1851	4	362	N	
Rampendahl, F. H.	25	Prussia	Y	Bremen	New Orleans	01/16/1854	01/21/1860	27	65	N	
Ramsdale, Joseph	25	England	Y	London	New York	06/02/1849	12/18/1852	5	426	N	

307

CITIZENSHIP RECORDS

APPLICANT	AGE	COUNTRY OF ORIGIN	DEC	DEPART PORT	ENTRY PORT	ARRIVE DATE	DEC DATE	VOL	PG.	FLD	NAT DATE
Ranchini, Raffaele	30	Italy	Y	?	New York	??/??/1890	05/21/1894			Y	
Raney, Peter	45	Canada	Y	Canada	Albany	07/01/1825	02/18/1852	24	138	N	
Ranf, George	27	Germany	Y	Bremen	New York	02/19/1880	11/08/1887			Y	
Ranke, Charles	30	Germany	Y	Bremen	New York	10/20/1883	10/08/1888			Y	
Ranke, William	29	Germany	Y	Bremen	New York	06/06/1881	10/27/1884			Y	
Rankle, Joseph R.	14	Germany	N	?	New York	00/00/1880				Y	10/27/1888
Ranninger, George	30	Bavaria	Y	Havre	New York	09/18/1846	11/13/1848	1	265	N	
Rape, Adolph (Anton?)	61	Germany	Y	Bremen	Baltimore	09/28/1881	09/29/1886			Y	
Rapien, Bernard H.	23	Germany	Y	Rotterdam	New York	07/11/1886	10/21/1890	19	294	N	
Rapien, Bernard H.	23	Germany	Y	Rotterdam	New York	07/11/1886	10/21/1890			Y	
Rapien, Johan Bernard	45	Germany	Y	Bremen	Baltimore	03/27/1884	12/08/1890			Y	
Rapking, Frederick	27	Germany	Y	Bremen	Baltimore	04/10/1881	10/17/1884			Y	
Rapp, Andrew	28	Germany	Y	Bremen	Baltimore	06/23/1880	11/??/1887	19	126	N	
Rapp, Charles	25	Baden	Y	Havre	New York	06/20/1852	08/21/1855	11	468	N	
Rapp, Christ.	51	Germany	Y	Antwerp	New York	10/30/1865	08/19/1889			Y	
Rapp, Christian	31	Wuerttenberg	Y	Antwerp	New York	05/04/1849	05/31/1852	25	154	N	
Rapp, Frederick	22	Wurttemberg	Y	Havre	New York	09/03/1852	10/09/1854	6	64	N	
Rapp, Frederick	22	Wurttemberg	Y	Havre	New York	09/03/1852	10/09/1854	11	65	N	
Rapp, Frederick	23	Bavaria	Y	Havre	New York	11/06/1853	10/26/1857	15	489	N	
Rapp, Freed	32	Germany	Y	Antwerp	New York	09/20/1884	04/21/1890			Y	
Rapp, George	30	Wurttemberg	Y	London	Baltimore	06/24/1847	10/09/1854	6	63	N	
Rapp, George	30	Wurttemberg	Y	London	Baltimore	06/24/1847	10/09/1854	11	64	N	
Rapp, Jacob Frederick	32	Wurttemberg	Y	Havre	New York	08/08/1854	12/24/1855	13	354	N	
Rapp, John	??	Wurttemberg	Y	?	New York	06/04/18??	11/07/1856	14	489	N	
Rapp, John Gottlieb	28	Wurttemberg	Y	Havre	New York	08/??/1854	12/24/1855	13	353	N	
Rapp, Joseph	67	Germany	Y	Bremen	Baltimore	12/08/1880	04/21/1891			Y	
Rapp, Karl	39	Germany	Y	Bremen	New York	11/04/1882	07/27/1888			Y	
Rapp, Mathias	23	Baden	Y	Havre	New York	12/16/1848	01/23/1849	1	495	N	
Rapp, Philipp	23	Bavaria	Y	Havre	New York	12/25/1859	11/08/1861	18	223	N	
Rapply, Adam	32	Baden	Y	Havre	New York	09/14/1848	12/20/1851	4	534	N	
Raquet, Andreas	52	Germany	Y	Germany	New York	06/03/1880	05/01/1882	28	321	N	
Raquet, Andreas	40	Germany	Y	Germany	New York	06/03/1880	05/01/1882			Y	
Rarvir, John Casper	29	Hanover	Y	Bremen	Baltimore	08/02/1845	11/01/1852	5	94	N	
Rasch, Theodore	24	Prussia	Y	Hamburg	New York	05/05/1849	02/08/1850	2	54	N	
Rasche, Charles	28	Oldenburg	Y	Bremen	New York	05/04/1858	01/30/1860	27	76	N	
Rasche, Frederick	21	Hanover	Y	Bremen	New Orleans	??/03/1849	10/25/1851	4	399	N	
Rasfeld, Gustav	22	Germany	Y	Bremen	Baltimore	09/17/1881	07/12/1889			Y	
Rasfeld, Henry	21	Germany	Y	Bremen	New York	09/01/1882	01/08/1885			Y	
Rashbach, Peter Laurenti	25	Germany	Y	Antwerp	New York	10/04/1888	07/09/1889			Y	
Rasmussen, Charles	38	Norway	Y	Throndhjem	Baltimore	04/28/1887	10/28/1893	21	43	N	
Rasmussen, Nels Peter	??	Denmark	Y	?	New York	09/??/1881	02/06/1885			Y	
Rassenfoss, Frank	34	Germany	Y	Bremen	New York	10/28/1882	01/22/1892			Y	
Rasser, Jacob	25	Germany	Y	Antwerp	New York	03/25/1884	11/05/1888			Y	
Ratcliffe, Thomas	30	England	Y	Liverpool	New York	06/01/1879	09/30/1880			Y	
Raterman, George	26	Hanover	Y	Bremen	New Orleans	12/10/1846	04/04/1853	7	521	N	
Ratermann, Bernard	26	Hanover	Y	Liverpool	Portland	12/23/1866	05/03/1872	18	492	N	
Raters, William	36	Germany	Y	Bremen	Baltimore	09/21/1881	04/12/1888			Y	
Ratgers, Henry	42	Germany	Y	Bremen	New York	06/25/1886	10/29/1892			Y	
Rath, Adam	39	Germany	Y	Bremen	Baltimore	03/28/1875	09/29/1882			Y	
Rath, Jacob	27	Germany	Y	Bremen	New York	09/28/1880	10/27/1881			Y	
Rath, Johfinn	32	Germany	N	Hamburg	New York	07/16/1881	?			Y	
Rathert, Frederick	27	Prussia	Y	Bremen	New York	07/01/1845	09/08/1848	22	310	N	
Rathjen, Fred	32	Germany	Y	Bremen	Baltimore	10/08/1880	04/22/1889			Y	
Rathjen, Herman	??	Germany	Y	?	?	?	01/30/1888			Y	
Rathkamp, Herman Fred	22	Hanover	Y	Bremen	Baltimore	06/25/1859	04/05/1862	18	300	N	
Ratje, John	28	Hanover	Y	Hamburg	New York	10/06/1867	01/03/1872	18	446	N	
Ratner, Ben	33	Russia	Y	Hamburg	New York	05/01/1889	01/05/1893			Y	
Ratte, Frank	70	Germany	Y	Bremen	New York	06/16/1868	10/11/1894			Y	
Rattelmueller, Michael	35	Germany	Y	Bremen	New York	09/20/1890	01/26/1893			Y	

CITIZENSHIP RECORDS

APPLICANT	AGE	COUNTRY OF ORIGIN	DEC	DEPART PORT	ENTRY PORT	ARRIVE DATE	DEC DATE	VOL	PG.	FLD	NAT DATE
Ratz, Frank	23	Bavaria	Y	Graves End	Boston	01/23/1857	10/19/1857	15	455	N	
Ratz, Mathias	27	Wurttemberg	Y	Antwerp	New York	08/07/1846	06/24/1851	3	447	N	
Rau, Charles	52	Wurtenberg	N	Hamburg	New York	09/24/1867	?			Y	
Rau, Ferdinand	34	Saxony	Y	Bremen	New York	08/18/1852	12/06/1855	13	273	N	
Rau, George	45	Germany	Y	Havre	New York	09/21/1864	10/30/1882			Y	
Rau, George	50	Germany	N	Bremen	New York	09/??/1851	?			Y	
Rau, John	25	Wurttemberg	Y	Havre	New York	05/??/1854	10/02/1854	10	355	N	
Rau, John	25	Wurttemberg	Y	Havre	New York	05/11/1854	10/02/1854	12	294	N	
Rau, Max	25	Bavaria	Y	Amsterdam	New York	09/29/1847	03/31/1853	7	475	N	
Rau, William	57	Germany	Y	Havre	New York	09/19/1882	06/10/1890			Y	
Raub, Nikolaus	22	Germany	Y	Bremen	Baltimore	07/02/1881	10/11/1883			Y	
Rauber, Arnold	42	Switzerland	Y	Antwerp	Boston	06/24/1871	04/15/1880			Y	
Rauber, Jacob	42	Switzerland	Y	Havre	New York	07/18/1882	07/20/1888			Y	
Rauber, William	47	Baden	Y	Havre	New York	11/14/1856	01/27/1860	27	75	N	
Rauch, Martin	32	Germany	Y	Hamburg	New York	05/11/1890	03/27/1895			Y	
Rauchenberger, Frank	28	Germany	Y	Hamburg	New York	12/14/1880	10/11/1886			Y	
Rauh, Ludwig	48	Germany	Y	Hamburg	New York	11/22/1890	06/09/1894			Y	
Rauh, Otto	??	Switzerland	Y	?	?	10/21/1891	06/06/1895			Y	
Raulf, Theodore	22	Germany	Y	Antwerp	New York	09/28/1881	05/03/1883			Y	
Rauly, Charles?	44	Germany	Y	Bremen	Baltimore	01/16/1884	10/24/1896			Y	
Rauner, Joseph	39	Germany	Y	Havre	New York	??/??/1866	03/22/1883			Y	
Raurers, George Linhart	31	Bavaria	Y	Bremen	New York	06/24/1844	08/25/1848	22	253	N	
Rausch, John P.	26	Germany	Y	Antwerp	New York	09/05/1883	03/21/1887			Y	
Rausch, William	36	Germany	Y	Antwerp	New York	04/07/1883	01/09/1888			Y	
Rauscher, John	28	Bavaria	Y	Havre	New Orleans	??/25/1846	12/31/1849	23	450	N	
Rauscher, John Christoph	27	Wurttemberg	Y	Antwerp	New York	05/10/1853	12/01/1855	13	271	N	
Rauscher, Louis	??	Germany	Y	?	?	?	03/05/1894			Y	
Raushenberger, Frederick	21	Germany	Y	?	?	03/23/1884	10/11/1886			Y	
Rauther, John	25	Bavaria	Y	Havre	New York	07/01/1854	09/29/1860	27	391	N	
Ravaux, Joseph	26	Mecklenburg	Y	Hamburg	Buffalo	08/15/1851	03/25/1853	7	401	N	
Rave, Ernst	36	Germany	Y	Bremen	Baltimore	08/27/1872	06/23/1883			Y	
Ravin, Jacob	29	Romania	Y	Galitz	Philadelphia	08/01/1880	05/28/1885			Y	
Rawe, James	28	England	Y	Canada	New York	07/02/1848	04/25/1853	8	119	N	
Rawe, Joseph	24	Oldenburg	Y	Bremen	Baltimore	03/01/1848	03/03/1852	24	230	N	
Ray, Henry	33	Hanover	Y	Bremen	Baltimore	07/01/1859	08/20/1860	27	300	N	
Ray, Samuel	39	Germany	Y	Havre	New York	05/01/1869	10/15/1886			Y	
Rayel, Patrick	26	Ireland	Y	Queenstown	New York	04/29/1891	11/30/1896			Y	
Razas, Simon	39	Russia	Y	Hamburg	New York	02/20/1889	12/02/1895			Y	
Re, Vincenzo	33	Italy	Y	Palermo	New York	01/05/1888	02/28/1888			Y	
Reada, Charles	25	Kurhassen	Y	Bremen	New York	07/02/1847	01/14/1850	23	494	N	
Reagan, Michael	43	Ireland	Y	Canada	Boston	08/21/1844	03/11/1850	2	179	N	
Reagan, Michael	26	Ireland	Y	Liverpool	Neww Orleans	02/05/1848	05/11/1852	25	6	N	
Reagan, Thomas	22	Ireland	Y	Liverpool	New Orleans	07/10/1846	10/11/1848	1	123	N	
Reany, James	40	Ireland	Y	Liverpool	New Orleans	03/21/1849	11/01/1852	5	128	N	
Reany, Martin	38	Ireland	Y	Liverpool	New Orleans	12/31/1846	01/28/1851	2	536	N	
Reapahoff, Joseph	25	Hanover	Y	Bremen	New Orleans	10/20/1847	02/14/1852	24	110	N	
Rearden, Owen	25	Ireland	Y	Cork	New York	08/05/1852	09/14/1855	13	30	N	
Reardon, Daniel	40	Ireland	Y	Varlee	Philadelphia	09/??/1829	?	23	266	N	
Reardon, Jeremiah	27	Ireland	Y	Liverpool	Boston	10/04/1847	08/15/1851	4	146	N	
Reardon, William N.	??	Ireland	Y	?	?	?	08/02/1898			Y	
Reber, Nicolaus	23	Bavaria	Y	Havre	New York	08/20/1851	04/08/1856	26	469	N	
Rebermack, George	26	Germany	Y	Antwerp	New York	03/24/1884	03/09/1891			Y	
Rebhorn, John	29	Germany	Y	Bremen	Baltimore	04/15/1886	10/23/1893			Y	
Rebing, Henry	26	Prussia	Y	Bremen	New York	06/01/1847	01/30/1849	1	548	N	
Rebman, Henry	22	Germany	Y	?	?	?	10/03/1892			Y	
Rebmann, Conrad	23	Germany	Y	Hamburg	New York	02/11/1881	03/11/1884			Y	
Rebmann, John	29	Germany	Y	Antwerp	Philadelphia	11/21/1884	12/08/1888			Y	
Rebstok, Ottmar	??	Germany	Y	?	?	?	03/12/1892			Y	
Rech, Christian	28	Bavaria	Y	Havre	New York	06/??/1848	03/24/1851	3	313	N	

CITIZENSHIP RECORDS

APPLICANT	AGE	COUNTRY OF ORIGIN	DEC	DEPART PORT	ENTRY PORT	ARRIVE DATE	DEC DATE	VOL	PG.	FLD	NAT DATE
Reche, Ernst	35	Prussia	Y	Bremen	New York	11/24/1854	10/19/1857	15	446	N	
Rechelhoff, Henry	40	Hanover	Y	Bremen	New Orleans	11/??/1848	10/03/1854	12	329	N	
Rechsteiner, Ulrich	24	Switzerland	Y	Havre	New York	08/27/1889	10/13/1890			Y	
Rechterman, Henry	34	Hanover	Y	Bremen	New York	06/03/1858	06/11/1859	17	455	N	
Rechtiene, Barney	32	Hanover	Y	Bremen	New York	06/01/1845	06/19/1851	3	427	N	
Rechtin, Bernard H.	57	Germany	N	Bremen	New Orleans	11/??/1849	?			Y	
Rechtsteiner, Kasper	29	Germany	Y	Bremen	New York	09/31/1891	05/13/1892			Y	
Reckelman, Herman	33	Hanover	Y	Bremen	New York	12/30/1848	03/28/1853	7	445	N	
Recker, Conrad	30	Hanover	Y	Bremen	New Orleans	11/08/1854	03/03/1858	16	362	N	
Recker, Franz	38	Germany	Y	Antwerp	New York	10/01/1881	02/27/1882			Y	
Recker, John Casper	32	Hanover	Y	Bremen	New Orleans	05/27/1851	03/04/1856	26	161	N	
Reckers, Herman	22	Hanover	Y	Bremen	New Orleans	12/26/1853	09/27/1856	14	419	N	
Reckers, John Christian	22	Hanover	Y	Bremen	New Orleans	12/24/1853	10/28/1858	17	146	N	
Reckert, August	33	Germany	Y	Amsterdam	New York	04/18/1893	09/12/1898			Y	
Recklingloh, Bernard	29	Germany	Y	Bremen	Baltimore	06/25/1886	09/24/1887			Y	
Reddan, Thomas	42	Ireland	Y	Liverpool	New York	07/14/1879	10/13/1879			Y	
Reddehase, Friedrich	32	Germany	Y	Bremen	Baltimore	09/01/1881	04/17/1882			Y	
Reddington, James	29	Ireland	Y	Queenstown	New York	05/23/1882	10/22/1888	19	162	N	
Reddington, Martin	24	Ireland	Y	Queenstown	New York	04/29/1890	04/26/1893			Y	
Reddy, James	40	Ireland	Y	Queenstown	New York	04/06/1867	10/13/1885	19	23	N	
Reddy, John	31	Ireland	Y	Queenstown	New York	??/??/1874	10/26/1898	19	186	N	
Reddy, John	31	Ireland	Y	Queenstown	New York	??/??/1874	10/26/1888			Y	
Reddy, John	??	?	Y	?	?	?	??/??/1851	28	284	N	10/??/1856
Redeker, Christ	46	Germany	N	Bremen	New York	10/03/1867	?			Y	
Redeker, John Frederick	21	Hanover	Y	Bremen	Baltimore	10/23/1853	10/01/1856	14	125	N	
Redel, Michael	35	Bavaria	Y	Havre	New Orleans	05/17/1847	10/06/1854	10	481	N	
Redel, Michael	35	Bavaria	Y	Havre	New Orleans	05/17/1847	10/06/1854	12	420	N	
Redelsheimer, Louis	61	Germany	N	Germany	New York	04/18/1850	07/01/1854	28	295	N	09/19/1857
Redmond, William	32	Ireland	Y	New Ross	Ross Point	09/07/8150	01/25/1856	13	508	N	
Redolatti, Charles	25	Italy	Y	Havre	New York	02/27/1890	03/20/1893			Y	
Reece, Samuel	25	England	Y	Liverpool	New York	07/07/1885	02/07/1891			Y	
Reed, George	41	England	Y	Amsterdam	New York	10/18/1890	03/22/1893			Y	
Reed, Thomas	22	Canada	Y	?	?	05/24/1883	03/04/1890			Y	
Reef, George	26	Holland	Y	Rotterdam	New Orleans	10/10/1846	03/03/1851	3	198	N	
Reeg, Anton	27	Germany	Y	Bremen	Baltimore	09/01/1892	06/11/1894			Y	
Reehard, George Frederic	52	France	Y	Havre	New Orleans	??/06/1847	02/03/1851	3	89	N	
Reenar, James	40	Ireland	Y	Liverpool	New Orleans	11/01/1847	03/31/1852	24	346	N	
Rees, Abel	25	Wales	Y	Liverpool	Philadelphia	06/18/1856	05/07/1860	27	184	N	
Rees, Howell	26	England	Y	Liverpool	New York	01/23/1893	10/12/1893			Y	
Rees, Jacob	36	Germany	Y	Hamburg	New York	11/30/1880	03/28/1891			Y	
Rees, Theobald	27	Germany	Y	?	?	?	?			Y	
Reese, Robert D.	30	Wales	Y	Liverpool	New York	07/01/1837	02/13/1849	23	89	N	
Refi, Michele	32	Italy	Y	Naples	New York	04/12/1889	11/03/1892			Y	
Rega, Adam	34	Prussia	Y	Havre	New Orleans	06/26/1846	02/17/1851	3	139	N	
Regan, Cornelius	56	Ireland	Y	Queenstown	New York	05/01/1887	10/27/1892	19	390	N	
Regan, Cornelius	56	Ireland	Y	Queenstown	New York	05/01/1887	10/27/1892			Y	
Regan, James	30	Ireland	Y	Queenstown	New York	05/??/1886	10/26/1895			Y	
Regan, James	25	Ireland	Y	Liverpool	New York	04/06/1850	04/01/1856	26	399	N	
Regan, John	39	Ireland	N	Queenstown	New York	06/14/1866	?			Y	
Regan, Michael	26	Ireland	Y	Liverpool	New York	04/10/1879	10/08/1883			Y	
Regan, Michael	64	Ireland	N	Cork	Portland	11/??/1847	??/??/1849	28	266	N	??/??/1856
Regan, Michael	23	Ireland	N	Cork	Portland, ME	11/00/1847	00/00/1849			Y	00/00/1856
Regan, Pat	40	Ireland	N	Queenstown	New York	05/03/1867	?			Y	
Regan, Patrick	30	Ireland	Y	Liverpool	New York	01/20/1849	04/07/1852	24	411	N	
Regan, William	28	Ireland	Y	Queenstown	Philadelphia	11/10/1886	10/29/1894			Y	
Regan, William	28	Ireland	Y	Kinsale	New York	08/12/1845	02/25/1852	24	170	N	
Regener, Richard F.	??	Germany	Y	?	?	?	12/29/1882			Y	
Regensburger, Alois	31	Austria	Y	Bremen	Baltimore	06/17/1888	11/25/1891			Y	
Regensburger, Ludwig	50	Austria	Y	Hamburg	New York	06/05/1865	08/02/1880			Y	

CITIZENSHIP RECORDS

APPLICANT	AGE	COUNTRY OF ORIGIN	DEC	DEPART PORT	ENTRY PORT	ARRIVE DATE	DEC DATE	VOL	PG.	FLD	NAT DATE
Reger, Michael	49	Bavaira	Y	Bremen	New York	08/14/1853	10/04/1858	17	52	N	
Reggen, Henry	40	Germany	Y	Bremen	Baltimore	12/24/1868	10/05/1880			Y	
Regitz, Christian	33	Prussia	Y	Havre	New York	04/07/1849	08/18/1855	11	454	N	
Regmann, August	30	Hanover	Y	Bremen	New York	05/25/1855	01/23/1860	27	68	N	
Regnath, Kaspar	29	Germany	Y	Bremen	New York	11/02/1873	09/15/1881			Y	
Regus, Conrad	24	Bavaria	Y	Bremen	New York	02/01/1848	04/09/1852	24	429	N	
Regus, John Ulrich	30	Bavaria	Y	Bremen	New York	08/07/1854	08/22/1855	11	482	N	
Reh, Martin	38	Bavaria	Y	Hamburg	New York	11/05/1854	02/04/1858	16	79	N	
Rehage, Theodor	46	Germany	Y	Bremen	New York	05/20/1884	05/12/1896			Y	
Rehbach, Friedrich	26	Germany	Y	Bremen	New York	10/19/1883	03/06/1886			Y	
Rehbach, William	24	Germany	Y	Antwerp	New York	09/25/1882	04/06/1886			Y	
Rehm, Arnold	31	Bavaria	Y	Havre	New York	05/10/1850	05/31/1852	25	152	N	
Rehm, Edward	25	Germany	Y	Antwerp	New York	07/28/1880	11/03/1884			Y	
Rehme, Henry	41	Germany	N	Bremen	Baltimore	10/??/1864	?			Y	
Rehme, Mathias	63	Germany	Y	Bremen	New York	09/22/1870	10/??/1879			Y	
Rehme, Mathias	63	Germany	N	Bremen	New York	09/22/1870	?			Y	
Rehmert, F. William	30	Prussia	Y	Bremen	New Orleans	12/28/1847	10/02/1856	14	148	N	
Rehmet, August	39	Germany	Y	Bremen	New York	06/15/1883	02/09/1886			Y	
Rehn, Frederick	24	Hesse Darmsta	Y	Bremen	New York	09/18/1851	01/22/1856	13	494	N	
Rehn, William G.	33	Germany	Y	Hamburg	New York	05/16/1882	03/25/1890			Y	
Rehring, George	27	Germany	Y	Rotterdam	New York	10/28/1883	11/03/1888			Y	
Rehse, Fritz	29	Hanover	Y	Bremen	New York	06/02/1857	02/14/1860	27	108	N	
Rehse, Theodore	31	Schwarzburg S	Y	Bremen	New York	07/??/1854	09/27/1858	16	121	N	
Reibel, Aliois	51	France	Y	Havre	New Orleans	04/15/1851	03/29/1856	26	371	N	
Reibel, John	37	Bavaria	Y	Bremen	Baltimore	09/??/1845	11/??/1849	23	332	N	
Reibel, Peter	38	France	Y	Havre	New Orleans	12/24/1854	11/09/1857	16	1	N	
Reich, Emil	30	Germany	Y	Hamburg	New York	11/07/1887	03/31/1894			Y	
Reichard, Herman	42	Germany	Y	Hamburg	New York	09/04/1883	11/01/1895			Y	
Reiche, Gottleib	40	Saxony Prussi	Y	Bremen	Galveston	04/25/1846	10/02/1848	1	7	N	
Reichel, Fred	27	Germany	Y	Antwerp	Philadelphia	08/20/1885	08/23/1890			Y	
Reichel, Philip	34	Austria	Y	Hamburg	New York	02/19/1883	01/25/1887			Y	
Reichenbacher, John	30	Bavaria	Y	Havre	New York	07/10/1851	03/05/1853	7	285	N	
Reichenstein	32	Russia	Y	Stettin	New York	01/11/1892	02/09/1893			Y	
Reichers, John	27	Brunswick	Y	Bremen	New York	11/29/1851	03/05/1856	26	166	N	
Reichert, Adolph	54	Baden	N	Havre	New York	12/??/1857	?	28	436	N	10/09/1855
Reichert, Adolph	??	Baden	N	?	?	?				Y	10/09/1866
Reichert, Adolph	12	Baden	N	Havre	New York	12/00/1857				Y	10/09/1866
Reichert, Herman	??	?	Y	?	?	?	??/??/1882			Y	
Reichert, Joseph	43	Germany	Y	Hamburg	New York	07/11/1882	11/25/1889			Y	
Reiching, Mathias	33	Wurttemberg	Y	Havre	New York	05/12/1849	12/27/1855	13	374	N	
Reichle, John C.	23	Wurttemberg	Y	Havre	New York	09/02/1849	12/02/1852	5	372	N	
Reichle, Matthaus	30	Germany	Y	Antwerp	New York	04/18/1884	09/23/1887			Y	
Reichle, Michael	33	Germany	Y	Liverpool	Philadelphia	11/05/1880	09/25/1885			Y	
Reichler, Markus	??	Austria	Y	?	?	03/21/1897	04/26/1897			Y	
Reichmann, Henry	35	Russia	Y	Bremen	Baltimore	04/05/1891	02/27/1897			Y	
Reichow, Herman	29	Prussia	Y	Bremen	New York	06/07/1855	11/24/1858	17	351	N	
Reichs, Anton	25	Austria	Y	Antwerp	Philadelphia	10/24/1891	10/23/1897			Y	
Reichwein, Christ.	47	Germany	Y	Bremen	New York	03/20/1866	10/15/1888			Y	
Reid, Andrew	26	Ireland	Y	Belfast	Cincinnati?	12/29/1887	08/03/1889			Y	
Reid, John	45	Ireland	Y	Liverpool	New York	01/26/1890	03/24/1892			Y	
Reid, Thomas	38	Ireland	Y	Belfast	Detroit	10/02/1887	05/09/1893			Y	
Reid, William	33	Scotland	Y	Glasgow	New York	10/16/1857	08/08/1860	27	258	N	
Reidy, Michael	27	Ireland	Y	Queenstown	New York	11/14/1863	10/05/1868			Y	
Reiering, Joseph	26	Germany	Y	Bremen	New York	10/11/1880	11/19/1885			Y	
Reif, David	28	Germany	Y	Havre	New York	08/25/1880	01/31/1884			Y	
Reif, Jacob	38	Baden	Y	Havre	New York	11/04/1848	01/13/1851	2	492	N	
Reif, Jacob	27	France	Y	Havre	New Orleans	02/27/1848	03/03/1856	26	151	N	
Reif, Karl	35	Germany	Y	Antwerp	New York	10/26/1886	03/28/1889			Y	
Reif, Louis	40	Austria	N	Bremen	New York	??/??/1864	?			Y	

CITIZENSHIP RECORDS

APPLICANT	AGE	COUNTRY OF ORIGIN	DEC	DEPART PORT	ENTRY PORT	ARRIVE DATE	DEC DATE	VOL	PG.	FLD	NAT DATE
Reifenberger, John	54	Germany	Y	Bremen	New York	06/13/1880	09/25/1894			Y	
Reiff, George	61	Wurttemberg	Y	London	New York	06/15/1846	11/10/1858	17	314	N	
Reihs, Wendelin	46	Austria	Y	Antwerp	Philadelphia	10/21/1891	04/03/1893			Y	
Reikmann, Frederick Henr	26	Hanover	Y	Bremen	New York	08/04/1846	10/05/1848	22	423	N	
Reil, Sebastian	30	Bavaria	Y	Rotterdam	New York	09/29/1845	02/20/1849	23	221	N	
Reiley, Daniel	35	Ireland	Y	Queenstown	New York	06/09/1892	03/29/1899			Y	
Reilhammer, Tony	14	Germany	N	?	New York	00/00/1880				Y	10/27/1888
Reilhofer, Franz	??	Bavaria	Y	?	?	12/??/1884	09/21/1885			Y	
Reiling, Frederick	29	Fuerst of Wal	Y	Bremen	Baltimore	05/07/1843	08/01/1848	22	28	N	
Reilley, Michael	43	Ireland	Y	Liverpool	New Orleans	05/10/1852	05/01/1854	8	318	N	
Reilly, Anthony	25	Ireland	Y	Liverpool	New York	01/31/1848	10/20/1852	5	30	N	
Reilly, Bernard	21	Ireland	Y	Liverpool	New Orleans	02/10/1853	10/07/1854	10	537	N	
Reilly, Bernard	21	Ireland	Y	Liverpool	New Orleans	02/10/1853	10/07/1854	12	476	N	
Reilly, John	24	Ireland	Y	Londonderry	New York	05/09/1893	12/28/1896			Y	
Reilly, Patrick	28	Ireland	Y	Liverpool	New York	12/??/1848	03/25/1851	3	341	N	
Reilly, Patrick	??	Ireland	N	?	?	09/00/1884				Y	10/26/1892
Reilly, Peter	33	Ireland	Y	?	?	?	04/11/1892			Y	
Reilly, Thomas	??	Ireland	Y	Liverpool	New York	04/01/1844	03/25/1851	3	344	N	
Reilly, Thomas	32	Ireland	Y	Liverpool	New Orleans	06/29/1848	01/25/1856	13	507	N	
Reilly, Thomas	51	Ireland	N	Liverpool	Boston	05/??/1855	?			Y	
Reilly, Thomas	42	Ireland	N	?	?	??/??/1856	?			Y	
Reilmann, George	24	Germany	Y	Bremen	Baltimore	01/01/1883	01/01/1883			Y	
Reilmann, Theodore	36	Germany	Y	Bremen	New York	03/06/1890	05/05/1892			Y	
Reily, Peter	31	Ireland	Y	Glasgow	New York	03/01/1849	08/02/1856	14	313	N	
Reily, Philip	36	Ireland	Y	Liverpool	New York	05/28/1855	10/04/1858	17	37	N	
Reimbolt, Francis	21	Baden	Y	Havre	New York	05/17/1860	11/18/1860	27	508	N	
Reimer, Adolph	45	Germany	Y	Bremen	New York	05/01/1866	04/07/1890			Y	
Reimer, August	??	Germany	Y	?	?	?	11/28/1882			Y	
Reimer, Franz	24	Germany	Y	Hamburg	New York	10/04/1881	01/28/1884			Y	
Reimer, Johann	30	Germany	Y	Hamburg	New York	04/12/1883	02/11/1888			Y	
Reimers, Otto	24	Germany	Y	?	New York	05/00/1871	11/05/1872			Y	
Reimler, Christian	44	Germany	N	Bremen	Baltimore	06/15/1866	?			Y	
Reinberg, Mendel	55	Russia	Y	Hamburg	New York	04/??/1864	10/27/1880			Y	
Reinbold, Gregor	26	Baden	Y	Havre	New Orleans	04/23/1854	10/06/1856	14	216	N	
Reinbold, John M.	43	Austria	N	Antwerp	New York	09/05/1866	?			Y	
Reinbold, Peter	26	?	Y	?	New York	11/??/1878	04/26/1880			Y	
Reinders, John B.	30	Holland	Y	Amsterdam	New York	09/29/1883	11/01/1887			Y	
Reineke, Conrad	33	Prussia	Y	Bremen	New York	07/04/1845	02/20/1849	23	222	N	
Reinekenn, Herman	29	Hanover	Y	Bremen	New Orleans	05/19/1851	04/11/1856	26	486	N	
Reiner, Albert	54	Austria	Y	Hamburg	New York	01/15/1882	03/28/1891			Y	
Reiner, Billy	23	Russia	Y	Bremen	Baltimore	12/14/1890	01/02/1895			Y	
Reiner, Joseph	39	France	Y	Havre	New York	05/13/1850	03/18/1858	16	421	N	
Reiner, Ludwig	24	Wuerttemberg	Y	Havre	New York	07/09/1847	02/15/1849	23	117	N	
Reinermann, Adolph Anton	32	Germany	Y	Rotterdam	New York	05/23/1885	06/28/1887			Y	
Reinermann, Henry	23	Holland	Y	Bremen	New York	07/24/1884	07/03/1888			Y	
Reinert, Florien	42	Germany	Y	Antwerp	New York	04/25/1880	10/18/1884			Y	
Reinhard, August	22	Prussia	Y	Bremen	New York	09/26/1850	04/11/1853	8	59	N	
Reinhard, Charles	34	Hanover	Y	Bremen	New Orleans	11/27/1855	08/24/1857	15	178	N	
Reinhard, Ferdinand	42	Luxembourg	Y	Liverpool	New York	03/27/1873	04/25/1894	21	70	N	
Reinhard, Ferdinand	42	Luxemburg	Y	Liverpool	New York	03/27/1873	04/25/1894			Y	
Reinhard, Frank	30	Baden	Y	Antwerp	New York	05/17/1854	02/11/1856	26	69	N	
Reinhardt, August	23	Germany	Y	Bremen	New York	10/27/1883	10/17/1884			Y	
Reinhardt, Jost Henry	26	Hesse Darmsta	Y	London	New York	10/16/1854	10/08/1857	15	374	N	
Reinhardt, Michael	28	Bavaria	Y	Havre	New Orleans	12/10/1853	09/29/1856	14	433	N	
Reinhart, Alexander	28	Bavaria	Y	Bremen	New York	12/05/1847	10/03/1854	10	374	N	
Reinhart, Alexander	28	Bavaria	Y	Bremen	New York	12/05/1847	10/03/1854	12	313	N	
Reinhart, Christian	34	Hanover	Y	Bremen	New Orleans	11/19/1846	02/11/1852	24	92	N	
Reinhart, George	27	Germany	Y	?	New York	07/25/1881	10/04/1883			Y	
Reinhold, Jodocus Henric	22	Hanover	Y	Bremen	New York	12/19/1854	05/19/1856	26	497	N	

CITIZENSHIP RECORDS

APPLICANT	AGE	COUNTRY OF ORIGIN	DEC	DEPART PORT	ENTRY PORT	ARRIVE DATE	DEC DATE	VOL	PG.	FLD	NAT DATE
Reining, John	30	Hanover	Y	Bremen	Baltimore	05/08/1845	09/15/1848	22	349	N	
Reinke, Clemens August	28	Oldenburg	Y	Bremen	New Orleans	12/01/1849	06/04/1852	25	187	N	
Reinke, Joseph	38	Oldenburg	Y	Bremen	New Orleans	11/15/1848	11/03/1858	17	269	N	
Reinking, Christian	26	Prussia	Y	?	New York	10/29/1880	11/06/1883			Y	
Reinmuth, Henry	30	Germany	Y	Bremen	New York	07/22/1887	09/14/1888			Y	
Reinold, Josef	34	Austria	Y	Amsterdam	New York	09/01/1881	12/28/1887			Y	
Reinschmid, Celestin	40	Baden	Y	Havre	New York	06/26/1854	12/05/1855	13	290	N	
Reinschmidt, Zelestin	73	Germany	N	Havre	New Orleans	07/07/1855	?			Y	
Reiring, Anton	46	Germany	Y	Bremen	Baltimore	10/20/1883	10/26/1886			Y	
Reis, Lambert	??	Germany	N	?	?	?	10/08/1875	28	448	N	10/07/1878
Reis, Max (Reihs)	49	Germany	Y	Havre	New York	08/13/1885	11/07/1898			Y	
Reisbach, Robert	27	Germany	Y	Hamburg	New York	10/12/1880	08/31/1887			Y	
Reisch, John	33	Germany	Y	Antwerp	New York	05/17/1883	10/04/1890			Y	
Reischel, Frederick	30	Prussia	Y	Bremen	New York	06/04/1853	06/05/1854	10	73	N	
Reischel, Frederick	30	Prussia	Y	Bremen	New York	06/04/1853	06/05/1854	12	10	N	
Reiser, Andrew	21	Baden	Y	Havre	New Orleans	03/29/1854	11/19/1855	13	233	N	
Reiser, Anton	??	Wurttemberg	Y	Havre	New Orleans	12/28/18??	10/09/1848	1	86	N	
Reiser, Franz	19	Germany	Y	Havre	New York	10/19/1891	10/26/1891			Y	
Reiser, George	30	Germany	Y	?	?	?	03/12/1894			Y	
Reiser, George Michael	25	Wurttemberg	Y	Antwerp	New York	08/07/1851	10/21/1852	5	36	N	
Reiser, Jacob	30	Baden	Y	London	New York	06/20/1853	11/13/1855	13	221	N	
Reiser, John George	31	Germany	Y	Rotterdam	New York	06/23/1883	07/26/1890			Y	
Reisiger, George	38	Germany	Y	Bremen	Baltimore	06/09/1881	08/15/1887			Y	
Reising, George	53	Bavaria	Y	Antwerp	New York	??/13/18??	?	18	144	N	
Reising, Leonard	32	Bavaria	Y	Antwerp	New York	05/04/1848	10/05/1848	22	427	N	
Reisingen, Joseph	29	Hanover	Y	Bremen	New Orleans	12/20/1845	02/15/1849	23	137	N	
Reisner, Gustav	??	Germany	Y	?	?	?	12/15/1892			Y	
Reiss, Peter (Reihs)	20	Germany	Y	Bremen	Baltimore	12/02/1888	03/19/1891			Y	
Reiss, William	27	Germany	Y	Hamburg	New York	03/10/1881	06/21/1884			Y	
Reisz, Michael	34	Austria	Y	Bremen	New York	05/??/1854	11/03/1856	14	447	N	
Reitemeyer, Fred	22	Hanover	Y	Bremen	Baltimore	10/04/1847	02/21/1849	23	244	N	
Reith, Bernhard	45	Germany	N	Bremen	New York	06/08/1866	?			Y	
Reith, Frank	17	Germany	N	?	New York	00/00/1880				Y	10/26/1888
Reith, Herman	33	Germany	Y	Bremen	Baltimore	04/11/1861	06/11/1864			Y	
Reith, Herman	61	Germany	N	Bremen	Baltimore	04/11/1861	?			Y	
Reitkamp, Theodore	45	Prussia	Y	Bremen	New York	05/28/1854	12/29/1857	16	275	N	
Reitmann, John	56	Bavaria	Y	Havre	New Orleans	06/29/1852	11/10/1858	17	317	N	
Reitz, Conrad	45	Kurhessen	Y	Bremen	Baltimore	07/??/1841	01/03/1853	5	506	N	
Reitz, Conrad	28	Germany	Y	Frankfort	New York	07/28/1880	08/12/1887			Y	
Reitz, John	23	Germany	Y	Antwerp	Philadelphia	11/26/1883	01/06/1886			Y	
Reitz, John	40	Germany	Y	Bremen	Baltimore	11/18/1881	07/30/1888			Y	
Reitz, Martin J.	33	Prussia	Y	Havre	New York	07/03/1857	05/12/1862	18	334	N	
Reitz, Peter	30	England	Y	Liverpool	Boston	??/27/1848	04/27/1855	11	316	N	
Reivever, John Frederick	33	Hanover	Y	Bremen	New York	10/15/1857	12/23/1859	17	513	N	
Rekate, Gustave	24	Germany	Y	Bremen	New York	11/14/1880	03/08/1883			Y	
Rekow, Carl	36	Germany	Y	Bremen	Baltimore	04/12/1881	11/01/1892			Y	
Reling, Joseph	36	France	Y	Havre	New York	02/20/1854	11/08/1858	17	298	N	
Relker, Henry	23	Hanover	Y	Bremen	New Orleans	??/??/1845	11/??/1849	23	338	N	
Relph, Richard	??	England	Y	?	?	?	10/22/1890			Y	
Remke, John	46	Hanover	Y	Bremen	New York	12/13/1854	08/04/1862	18	385	N	
Remme, George	40	Hanover	Y	Bremen	New York	05/22/1848	09/13/1852	25	474	N	
Remmer, Franz	25	Germany	Y	Rotterdam	New York	02/22/1882	03/04/1887			Y	
Remmers, John H.	??	Germany	Y	?	?	?	11/03/1884			Y	
Remmler, Edward	33	Saxony	Y	Havre	New Orleans	07/09/1849	04/29/1850	3	27	N	
Rempe, Theodore	30	Hanover	Y	Bremen	Baltimore	05/29/1849	05/25/1854	8	532	N	
Rempe, Theodore	30	Hanover	Y	Bremen	Baltimore	05/29/1849	05/25/1854	9	406	N	
Remper, Frank	37	Hanover	Y	Bremen	New York	10/??/1846	10/27/1851	4	406	N	
Rempoldi, Louis	31	Italy	Y	Geneva	New York	12/??/1873	09/29/1885			Y	
Rendler, Frederick	34	Baden	Y	Havre	New Orleans	01/24/1855	02/20/1858	16	321	N	

CITIZENSHIP RECORDS

APPLICANT	AGE	COUNTRY OF ORIGIN	DEC	DEPART PORT	ENTRY PORT	ARRIVE DATE	DEC DATE	VOL	PG.	FLD	NAT DATE
Rene, Gerhard H.	29	Oldenburg	Y	Bremen	New Orleans	12/??/1845	08/??/1851	4	18-	N	
Reneer, Anthony	33	Baden	Y	Havre	New York	10/10/1850	09/24/1858	16	145	N	
Rengel, John	29	Prussia	Y	Bremen	New York	05/25/1857	08/20/1860	27	302	N	
Renken, August	24	Germany	Y	Amsterdam	New York	09/11/1890	04/14/1894			Y	
Renken, Ignatz	26	Germany	Y	Bremen	Baltimore	10/07/1889	11/14/1892			Y	
Renn, John	24	Germany	Y	Rotterdam	New York	09/24/1891	10/22/1892			Y	
Rennard, Adam	32	Bavaria	Y	Havre	New York	08/06/1851	03/28/1853	7	440	N	
Rennebarth, Paul	31	Germany	Y	Hamburg	New York	08/19/1881	07/15/1884			Y	
Renneberg, Henry	54	Germany	N	Bremen	New York	11/16/1866	?			Y	
Renneker, John H.	28	Oldenburg	Y	Bremen	New Orleans	03/16/18??	10/12/1848	1	182	N	
Rennenger, Frederick	27	Hanover	Y	Bremen	New York	12/01/1848	10/25/1851	4	403	N	
Renneo, Albert	??	Germany	Y	?	?	?	11/25/1890			Y	
Renner, Daniel	36	Bavaria	Y	Antwerp	New Orleans	02/08/1847	02/23/1850	2	118	N	
Renner, Daniel	75	Germany	N	Havre	New Orleans	??/??/1847	?			Y	
Renner, Jacob	58	Bavaria	Y	Havre	New York	06/20/1847	08/18/1848	22	204	N	
Renner, Johann	23	Germany	Y	Bremen	New York	05/09/1893	08/02/1894			Y	
Renner, John Adam	31	Bavaria	Y	Havre	New York	05/16/1848	10/02/1848	22	389	N	
Renner, Michael	60	Germany	N	Bremen	New York	11/20/1854	?			Y	
Renner, Peter	36	Prussia	Y	London	New York	06/19/1854	10/06/1856	14	230	N	
Rennert, Charles	28	Saxony	Y	Bremen	New York	09/20/1848	07/05/1851	3	493	N	
Rennick, Henry	28	Prussia	Y	Bremen	Baltimore	12/06/1845	05/25/1854	8	527	N	
Rennick, Henry	28	Prussia	Y	Bremen	Baltimore	12/06/1845	05/25/1854	9	401	N	
Renold, John Martin	??	Switzerland	Y	?	New York	10/??/1892	02/18/1901			Y	
Renschen, Henry	41	Germany	Y	Rotterdam	New York	11/01/1881	07/22/1887			Y	
Rensen, Gerhard Andreas	28	Germany	Y	Rotterdam	New York	06/10/1885	08/02/1890			Y	
Rensing, Bernard A.	49	Germany	Y	Bremen	Baltimore	11/03/1864	04/04/1887			Y	
Renter, Henry	34	Hesse Cassel	Y	Bremen	New York	11/29/1856	10/15/1860	27	502	N	
Rentner, Herman	28	Mecklenburg S	Y	Hamburg	New York	05/05/1852	04/19/1854	8	214	N	
Renz, Joseph	36	Germany	Y	Antwerp	Philadelphia	05/09/1889	09/14/1897			Y	
Renz, Theodore	40	Wurttemberg	Y	Havre	New York	05/??/1849	10/24/1851	4	398	N	
Reony, James	40	Ireland	Y	Liverpool	New Orleans	03/21/1849	11/01/1852	6	254	N	
Reottmann, John E.	21	Saxony	Y	Hamburg	New York	05/18/1858	08/13/1860	27	265	N	
Repetto, Alexander	29	Sardini	Y	Genoa	New York	03/07/1848	11/03/1851	4	480	N	
Repke, Paul	25	Germany	Y	Bremen	New York	09/01/1887	01/08/1891			Y	
Repker, William	39	Hanover	Y	Bremen	New Orleans	11/07/1845	01/23/1849	1	506	N	
Repking, Anton	22	Oldenburg	Y	Bremen	Baltimore	08/06/1846	09/12/1848	22	331	N	
Rervier, Casper	29	Hanover	Y	Bremen	Baltimore	08/21/1845	11/01/1852	6	244	N	
Resch, Joseph	24	Germany	Y	Havre	New York	10/??/1882	01/28/1886			Y	
Resplandin, Charles Fred	23	Bavaria	Y	Havre	New Orleans	01/25/1850	10/19/1852	5	17	N	
Ress, Valentine	24	Hesse Darmsta	Y	Liverpool	New York	04/10/1854	09/12/1857	15	259	N	
Restorff, George Henry	24	Holstein	Y	Sidney	Boston	06/20/1852	12/14/1852	5	408	N	
Reszka, Adam	39	Germany	Y	Hamburg	New York	08/28/1883	02/21/1887			Y	
Reter, Herman	30	Hanover	Y	Bremen	Baltimore	06/11/1846	01/??/1850	23	473	N	
Rethemeyer, Christ.	28	Germany	Y	?	?	?	12/24/1887			Y	
Rethey, August	??	Austria	Y	?	?	?	08/29/1889			Y	
Rettich, Matthew	25	Prussia	Y	Havre	New Orleans	03/15/1853	07/16/1855	11	399	N	
Rettich, Paul	33	Wurttemberg	Y	Bremen	New York	11/05/1851	02/14/1853	7	153	N	
Rettich, Stephan	24	Germany	Y	Rotterdam	New York	01/15/1886	02/04/1889			Y	
Rettig, Fidel	22	Prussia	Y	Havre	New York	06/50/1854	12/03/1855	13	277	N	
Rettig, Frank Anton	24	Hesse Darmsta	Y	Havre	New York	11/01/1848	12/16/1851	4	525	N	
Rettig, John	23	Hesse Darmsta	Y	Havre	New Orleans	05/19/1852	07/10/1855	11	373	N	
Retze, John	28	Hesse Cassel	Y	Bremen	Baltimore	08/28/1838	10/07/1848	22	489	N	
Reuber, Henry	52	Hanover	Y	Bremen	New Orleans	12/14/1845	11/17/1848	1	312	N	
Reucher, Anton	43	Bavaria	Y	Antwerp	New York	04/11/1853	03/28/1856	26	368	N	
Reugan, Timothy	21	Ireland	Y	Liverpool	New York	01/23/1849	10/21/1851	4	366	N	
Reum, Herman F.	22	Hamburg	Y	Bremen	New York	08/28/1856	12/10/1859	17	499	N	
Reumuth, John Adam	47	Baden	Y	Havre	New Orleans	05/14/1852	09/23/1858	16	148	N	
Reus, Robert	29	Wales	Y	Liverpool	New York	05/20/1842	02/17/1849	23	146	N	
Reusch, John	15	Germany	N	?	New York	00/00/1881				Y	10/23/1888

CITIZENSHIP RECORDS

APPLICANT	AGE	COUNTRY OF ORIGIN	DEC	DEPART PORT	ENTRY PORT	ARRIVE DATE	DEC DATE	VOL	PG.	FLD	NAT DATE
Reusch, Kilian	28	Germany	Y	Bremen	New York	09/18/1882	08/07/1888			Y	
Reusing, Adam	33	Germany	Y	Hamburg	New York	03/02/1880	08/14/1883			Y	
Reuss, Adam	25	Germany	Y	Antwerp	New York	09/30/1882	12/20/1886			Y	
Reuss, William	25	Germany	Y	Bremen	Baltimore	02/27/1880	12/16/1884			Y	
Reusser, Gottfried	43	Switzerland	Y	Havre	New York	02/09/1884	01/09/1889			Y	
Reuter, Bror. O.J.	21	Sweden	Y	Goteborg	New Orleans	01/06/1846	10/13/1851	4	242	N	
Reuter, Christoph John	26	Hanover	Y	Bremen	New Orleans	05/17/1849	02/27/1851	3	177	N	
Reuter, Frederick	67	Germany	N	Hanover	New York	06/24/1853	?			Y	
Reuter, Frederick Willia	26	Hanover	Y	Bremen	New York	11/01/1852	03/25/1856	26	303	N	
Reuter, John Rudolph Wil	30	Hanover	Y	Bremen	New Orleans	06/16/1850	07/07/1851	3	512	N	
Reuter, Julius	29	Germany	Y	Bremen	Baltimore	08/13/1884	11/05/1889			Y	
Reutermann, Henry	28	Oldenburg	Y	Bremen	New Orleans	12/22/1844	04/08/1852	24	421	N	
Reuthe, Carl	30	Bavaria	Y	Havre	New York	06/23/1847	10/06/1854	10	507	N	
Reuthe, Carl	30	Bavaria	Y	Havre	New York	06/23/1847	10/06/1854	12	446	N	
Reuther, Herman	32	Wurttemberg	Y	London	New York	03/30/1851	04/17/1854	8	185	N	
Reuther, Herman	32	Wurttemberg	Y	London	New York	03/30/1851	04/17/1854	9	56	N	
Reutner, Herman	28	Mecklenburg S	Y	Hamburg	New York	05/05/1852	04/19/1854	9	85	N	
Reuwer, Henry	25	Hanover	Y	Bremen	Baltimore	12/01/1848	03/08/1852	24	268	N	
Reuwer, William	22	Hanover	Y	Bremen	New Orleans	12/24/1845	10/13/1848	1	184	N	
Reuwer, William	30	Germany	Y	Bremen	New York	12/20/1882	03/29/1894			Y	
Revogli, Augustus	30	Italy	Y	Rome	New York	01/01/1881	12/27/1881			Y	
Rewald, Henry	32	Mecklenburg S	Y	Bremen	New Orleans	03/07/1845	10/09/1854	6	145	N	
Rewald, Henry	32	Mecklenburg S	Y	Bremen	New Orleans	03/07/1842	10/09/1854	11	148	N	
Rewwer, Frederick Willia	32	Hanover	Y	Bremen	Baltimore	10/27/1851	12/01/1855	13	267	N	
Reynold, Michael	43	Ireland	Y	Liverpool	New York	04/??/1850	10/24/1850	2	290	N	
Reynolds, ?	??	?	Y	?	Philadelphia	??/05/18??	10/26/1850	2	305	N	
Reynolds, Andrew	38	Ireland	Y	Wexford	New Orleans	12/27/1851	04/30/1860	27	174	N	
Reynolds, Francis	19	Ireland	Y	Queenstown	New York	05/20/1889	05/25/1889			Y	
Reynolds, George	40	Ireland	Y	Cork	New Orleans	08/12/1847	05/19/1852	25	41	N	
Reynolds, James	35	Ireland	Y	Liverpool	New Orleans	05/29/1848	06/02/1859	17	447	N	
Reynolds, Patrick	30	Ireland	Y	Liverpool	New Orleans	11/15/1849	05/17/1854	8	456	N	
Reynolds, Patrick	30	Ireland	Y	Liverpool	New Orleans	11/15/1849	05/17/1854	9	329	N	
Reynolds, Patrick Willia	26	Ireland	Y	Liverpool	New York	06/27/1848	01/28/1850	23	549	N	
Reynolds, Stephen	50	Ireland	Y	Wexford?	New Orleans	12/27/1851	04/30/1860	27	173	N	
Reynolds, William	26	Ireland	Y	Liverpool	New York	04/04/1843	03/26/1850	2	268	N	
Reynolds, William	40	England	Y	Liverpool	New York	06/30/1840	09/30/1858	17	24	N	
Rhedius, Euslachius	37	Wurttemberg	Y	Havre	New Orleans	12/02/1849	03/16/1850	2	200	N	
Rhegard, Ante	37	Bavaria	Y	Havre	New Orleans	10/20/1844	07/05/1851	3	483	N	
Rhein, George	24	Germany	Y	Antwerp	Philadelphia	03/24/1888	12/01/1891			Y	
Rheinecker, George Fred	43	Germany	N	Hamburg	New York	09/??/1871	?			Y	
Rheinheimer, Nathan	24	Bavaria	Y	Havre	New York	04/06/1853	11/23/1857	16	43	N	
Rheinstrom, Jacob	29	Germany	Y	Bremen	New York	09/07/1884	03/09/1888			Y	
Rhoda, John	36	Kurhessen	Y	Bremen	New York	09/08/1857	09/13/1860	27	371	N	
Rhyn, Fritz	44	Switzerland	Y	Antwerp	New York	08/20/1881	02/06/1896			Y	
Rhys, David	25	South Wales	Y	Liverpool	New York	08/19/1887	12/19/1887			Y	
Riaes, Paul	39	Bavaria	Y	Havre	New Orleans	12/24/1847	02/21/1849	23	234	N	
Rian, Joseph	47	Germany	Y	Havre	New York	05/26/1882	10/06/1886			Y	
Riardon, Jeramiah	23	Ireland	Y	Liverpool	New York	04/20/1852	10/05/1854	12	391	N	
Ribbers, John	26	Germany	Y	Antwerp	New York	10/09/1889	06/15/1894			Y	
Ribeaud, Xavier	28	Switzerland	Y	Havre	New York	07/16/1883	10/24/1892	19	380	N	
Ricci, Gioachino	29	Italy	Y	Naples	New York	03/19/1884	09/12/1894			Y	
Rice, Issac	41	Germany	N	Antwerp	New York	05/??/1867	?			Y	
Rice, James	23	Ireland	Y	Portsmouth	Port Huron	11/03/1852	12/19/1855	13	333	N	
Rice, John	43	Ireland	Y	Liverpool	New York	07/07/1870	05/21/1883			Y	
Rice, William (Reisz)	28	Bavaria	Y	Bremen	New York	08/06/1845	08/15/1848	22	118	N	
Rich, Henry	30	Bavaria	Y	Havre	New York	10/19/1846	08/21/1848	22	220	N	
Rich, Leo	27	Germany	Y	Havre	New York	06/04/1889	03/26/1894			Y	
Richacht, Carl	24	Prussia	Y	Bremen	New York	06/30/1853	04/17/1854	9	33	N	
Richacht, Charles	24	Prussia	Y	Bremen	New York	06/30/1853	04/17/1854	8	162	N	

CITIZENSHIP RECORDS

APPLICANT	AGE	COUNTRY OF ORIGIN	DEC	DEPART PORT	ENTRY PORT	ARRIVE DATE	DEC DATE	VOL	PG.	FLD	NAT DATE
Richard, Herman Gottfrie	26	Hanover	Y	Bremen	New York	09/29/1852	08/22/1855	11	475	N	
Richard, John Henry	31	Prussia	Y	Bremen	New York	10/22/1854	11/09/1857	15	546	N	
Richards, James	21	England	Y	Liverpool	New York	06/02/1853	05/01/1854	8	306	N	
Richards, James	21	England	Y	Liverpool	New York	06/02/1853	05/01/1854	9	179	N	
Richards, John M.	??	Wales	Y	?	New York	05/03/1883	01/26/1889			Y	
Richards, Stephen	37	Wales	Y	Liverpool	New York	07/07/1855	09/15/1860	27	376	N	
Richards, Thomas	25	England	Y	Liverpool	New York	08/02/1853	04/29/1854	8	286	N	
Richards, Thomas	25	England	Y	Liverpool	New York	08/02/1853	04/29/1854	9	158	N	
Richards, W. H.	18	Wales	Y	?	New York	05/03/1883	01/26/1889			Y	
Richards, William	35	England	Y	?	New York	06/00/1879	09/28/1888			Y	
Richardson, ?	??	Ireland	Y	Liverpool	New Orleans	11/09/1847	10/07/1848	22	477	N	
Richardson, Edward	21	Ireland	Y	Liverpool	New Orleans	11/09/1847	10/07/1848	22	478	N	
Richardson, George	28	Ireland	Y	Belfast	New York	06/28/1841	03/14/1850	2	193	N	
Richardson, John	22	Ireland	Y	Liverpool	New York	09/25/1851	02/04/1856	26	35	N	
Richel, Daniel	23	Hesse Darmsta	Y	Rotterdam	New York	06/10/1850	04/04/1853	7	536	N	
Richerd, Aloys	??	Germany	Y	?	?	?	07/17/1880			Y	
Richert, John	27	Canada	Y	Victoria	Buffalo	04/02/1888	12/10/1892			Y	
Richey, Joseph	38	Ireland	Y	Liverpool	New York	09/??/1846	04/28/1855	11	323	N	
Richmann, Anton	60	Bohemia	Y	Bremen	New York	07/25/1857	09/05/1860	27	336	N	
Richmann, Bernard Henry	37	Hanover	Y	Bremen	Baltimore	10/08/1848	04/20/1854	9	101	N	
Richt, Christian	49	Germany	N	Bremen	New York	06/15/1868	?			Y	
Richter, Alois	26	Austria	Y	Bremen	New York	05/27/1884	02/01/1888			Y	
Richter, August	35	Prussia	Y	Bremen	New Orleans	10/21/1854	01/25/1860	27	64	N	
Richter, Diedrich	33	Hanover	Y	Bremen	New Orleans	07/06/1842	01/11/1851	2	480	N	
Richter, Frank	26	Austria	Y	Bremen	Baltimore	03/04/1883	01/30/1886			Y	
Richter, Frederick	26	Germany	Y	Bremen	New York	11/01/1889	07/17/1893			Y	
Richter, Harry	28	Russia	Y	Hamburg	New York	07/06/1892	09/17/1896			Y	
Richter, Heinrich	??	Germany	Y	?	?	?	04/06/1896			Y	
Richter, Henry	??	Hanover	Y	Bremen	New Orleans	??/16/1845	12/10/1850	2	354	N	
Richter, Henry	21	Prussia	Y	Bremen	New Orleans	11/24/1850	04/28/1854	8	284	N	
Richter, Henry	21	Prussia	Y	Bremen	New Orleans	11/24/1850	04/28/1854	9	155	N	
Richter, Henry	35	Germany	Y	Bremen	Baltimore	03/27/1886	03/20/1894			Y	
Richter, Herman Albert	37	Germany	Y	Rotterdam	New York	06/13/1890	06/02/1899			Y	
Richter, Louis	49	Wurttemberg	Y	Bremen	New York	09/??/1837	10/25/1851	4	400	N	
Richter, Norbert	47	Austria	Y	Bremen	New York	09/14/1849	07/22/1851	4	25	N	
Richter, Oscar	36	Germany	Y	Hamburg	New York	06/26/1882	09/14/1896			Y	
Richter, Robert	23	Germany	Y	Bremen	Philadelphia	04/05/1880	10/23/1884			Y	
Richter, Theodore	50	Germany	Y	Hamburg	New York	11/??/1866	11/05/1888	19	218	N	
Richter, William	36	Hanover	Y	Bremerhafen	Baltimore	07/01/1857	02/06/1861	18	92	N	
Richters, Anton	33	Prussia	Y	Bremen	New Orleans	11/10/1849	05/20/1852	25	52	N	
Richthammer, Anton	27	Bavaria	Y	Bremen	New York	06/29/1854	03/24/1858	16	431	N	
Rickel, William	22	Hesse Cassel	Y	Bremen	New Orleans	01/11/1850	03/11/1852	24	284	N	
Rickers, George	24	Germany	Y	Rotterdam	New York	10/17/1884	06/04/1888			Y	
Rickert, Emil	22	Prussia	Y	Antwerp	New York	07/02/1848	11/29/1852	5	363	N	
Ridder, Ernst	36	Germany	Y	Bremen	Baltimore	06/03/1883	03/02/1892			Y	
Ridel, Leonard	34	Bavaria	Y	?	Baltimore	06/20/1869	10/10/1874			Y	
Rider, George	34	England	Y	Liverpool	Philadelphia	09/14/1882	02/06/1891			Y	
Ridgley, Thomas	29	England	Y	Liverpool	New York	10/16/1849	10/06/1856	14	222	N	
Riebel, George	28	Baden	Y	Havre	New York	06/22/1848	03/24/1856	26	271	N	
Riebel, Michael	29	Germany	Y	Bremen	New York	10/20/1878	03/29/1883			Y	
Riebrecht, Andreas	33	Wurttemberg	Y	Havre	New York	09/12/1849	01/27/1851	2	534	N	
Riebs, Ludwig Michael	39	Germany	Y	Havre	New York	11/25/1887	12/01/1887			Y	
Riechers, Heinrich	38	Germany	Y	Bremen	Baltimore	03/02/1882	05/26/1890			Y	
Rieck, Charles J.	17	Germany	N	?	New York	00/00/1869				Y	11/03/1888
Rieckhoff, Carl	30	Mecklenburg S	Y	Hamburg	New York	09/02/1851	10/04/1854	10	415	N	
Rieckhoff, Carl	30	Mecklenburg S	Y	Hamburg	New York	09/02/1851	10/04/1854	12	354	N	
Riede, Charles Frederick	21	Wuertemberg	Y	Havre	New York	09/05/1854	03/01/1856	26	144	N	
Riede, Demeter	30	Germany	Y	Havre	New York	05/26/1883	08/30/1886			Y	
Riedel, Carl	41	Germany	Y	Bremen	Baltimore	06/22/1892	09/13/1892			Y	

CITIZENSHIP RECORDS

APPLICANT	AGE	COUNTRY OF ORIGIN	DEC	DEPART PORT	ENTRY PORT	ARRIVE DATE	DEC DATE	VOL	PG.	FLD	NAT DATE
Riedel, Marcus	26	Germany	Y	Antwerp	Philadelphia	06/01/1882	09/25/1889			Y	
Riedel, Moritz	22	Saxony	Y	Bremen	Baltimore	01/03/1848	01/15/1849	1	418	N	
Riedel, Paul	42	Germany	Y	Hamburg	New York	09/22/1882	12/15/1890			Y	
Riedel, Paul C.O.	25	Germany	Y	Rotterdam	New York	11/03/1883	10/28/1886			Y	
Riedeman, Henry	25	Hanover	Y	Bremen	Baltimore	05/14/1848	07/19/1851	4	10	N	
Riedemann, Henry	23	Germany	Y	?	Cincinnati?	09/09/1881	04/06/1885			Y	
Riedenbeck, Bernard	23	Prussia	Y	Bremen	Baltimore	06/23/1855	10/28/1858	17	159	N	
Rieder, August	25	Hesse Cassel	Y	Bremen	New York	06/09/1847	01/29/1849	1	532	N	
Riederner, Andrew	35	Switzerland	Y	?	New York	05/18/1881	05/31/1886			Y	
Riedinger, Ferdinand	37	Baden	Y	Bremen	New York	06/01/1853	11/07/1855	13	185	N	
Riedinger, Joseph	27	Germany	Y	Havre	New York	02/11/1882	07/21/1885			Y	
Riedinger, Louis	26	Germany	Y	Hamburg	New York	06/27/1884	12/04/1885			Y	
Riedinger, Philipp	32	Hesse Darmsta	Y	London	New York	10/28/1857	06/06/1862	18	348	N	
Riedmatter, Charles	29	Germany	Y	Havre	New York	10/05/1882	01/19/1887			Y	
Riedmatter, Joseph	56	Germany	Y	Antwerp	New York	10/07/1882	01/19/1887			Y	
Riedy, James	22	Ireland	Y	Liverpool	New York	??/02/1852	04/26/1855	11	208	N	
Riedy, John	25	Ireland	Y	Queenstown	New York	04/03/1891	01/06/1893			Y	
Riedy, Thomas	25	Ireland	Y	Limerick	New York	07/??/1851	04/26/1855	11	306	N	
Riedy, William	27	Ireland	Y	Liverpool	New York	08/08/1849	03/06/1856	26	169	N	
Riefenstahl, Christ	52	Germany	N	Bremen	New York	11/??/1853	?			Y	
Riefenstahl, Christopher	26	Brunswick	Y	Bremen	New York	11/18/1853	08/02/1856	14	309	N	
Rieffer, Joseph	26	Germany	Y	Havre	New York	03/08/1888	07/08/1893			Y	
Riefstahl, Julius	34	Germany	Y	Bremen	New York	07/03/1880	07/31/1880			Y	
Rieg, G. Fred	43	Germany	Y	Bremen	New York	05/08/1885	06/09/1890			Y	
Riegar, John	38	Wurttemberg	Y	London	New York	01/18/1848	04/04/1853	7	519	N	
Riege, John Henry	28	Prussia	Y	Bremen	New Orleans	01/01/1848	02/15/1851	3	135	N	
Riegel, Gustav Joseph	40	Germany	Y	Bremen	New York	08/28/1875	04/04/1887			Y	
Riegel, Henry	43	Wuertemberg	Y	Bremen	Baltimore	06/28/1850	03/08/1856	26	171	N	
Riegel, Jacob	52	Germany	Y	Rotterdam	New York	07/01/1883	12/26/1885			Y	
Rieger, Bernard	33	Bavaria	Y	Havre	New York	06/18/1850	09/23/1857	15	307	N	
Rieger, Julius	25	Germany	Y	Bremen	Baltimore	12/01/1892	12/08/1893			Y	
Rieger, Michael	28	Germany	Y	Bremen	New York	05/03/1877	10/23/1882			Y	
Rieger, William	32	Germany	Y	Bremen	Baltimore	02/10/1878	02/27/1888			Y	
Riegger, Emil	??	Germany	N	?	?	05/03/1882				Y	10/29/1892
Riegler, Michael	26	Germany	Y	Amsterdam	New York	08/07/1881	03/12/1884			Y	
Riehemann, Bernard Henry	37	Hanover	Y	Bremen	Baltimore	10/08/1848	04/20/1854	8	230	N	
Riehl, George	19	Germany	Y	Havre	New York	05/06/1879	10/27/1880			Y	
Rieke, Henry	44	Germany	Y	Bremen	New York	11/??/1865	03/23/1881			Y	
Rieke, William	31	Hanover	Y	Liverpool	Baltimore	08/29/1839	10/02/1848	22	378	N	
Rieksen, Lambert	??	Holland	Y	?	?	?	09/22/1888			Y	
Rielage, Christopher	42	Germany	Y	Bremen	Baltimore	10/11/1865	10/22/1885			Y	
Riele, William	44	Germany	Y	Bremen	New York	07/06/1881	03/21/1894			Y	
Riely, John	25	Ireland	Y	Queenstown	New York	04/03/1891	01/06/1892	19	415	N	
Riely, Martin	25	Ireland	Y	Queenstown	New York	06/01/1882	?	19	74	N	
Riely, Martin	25	Ireland	Y	Queenstown	New York	06/01/1882	10/23/1886			N	
Riely, Michael	40	Ireland	Y	Liverpool	New Orleans	01/13/1851	11/19/1852	5	313	N	
Riely, Patrick	36	Ireland	Y	Queenstown	New York	03/12/1874	10/22/1888	19	164	N	
Riemann, H. H.	27	Germany	Y	Bremen	Baltimore	05/04/1883	04/06/1886			Y	
Riemann, Henry	49	Germany	Y	Antwerp	New York	10/06/1873	10/15/1888			Y	
Riemeke, Herman	43	Prussia	Y	Hamburg	New York	05/04/1849	01/07/1850	23	468	N	
Riemenschneider, Conrad	50	Germany	Y	Liverpool	New York	03/14/1872	12/03/1888			Y	
Riemenschneider, George	54	Germany	Y	Rotterdam	New York	03/16/1872	11/21/1888			Y	
Riemenschneider, George	46	Germany	N	Bremen	Baltimore	10/??/1866	?			Y	
Riemenschnieder, Henry	??	Germany	Y	?	?	?	09/20/1877			Y	
Rienjes, Leonardus	35	Holland	Y	Amsterdam	New York	09/22/1883	10/23/1888	19	171	N	
Riepe, Herman	25	Hesse Cassel	Y	Bremen	New Orleans	05/01/1849	01/13/1851	2	489	N	
Ries, Anthony	40	Wurttemberg	Y	Havre	New York	06/11/1852	03/23/1858	16	442	N	
Ries, Daniel	53	Germany	Y	?	Baltimore	??/??/1881	06/29/1885			Y	
Ries, Edward	41	England	Y	Liverpool	New Orleans	04/??/1849	11/08/1849	23	328	N	

CITIZENSHIP RECORDS

APPLICANT	AGE	COUNTRY OF ORIGIN	DEC	DEPART PORT	ENTRY PORT	ARRIVE DATE	DEC DATE	VOL	PG.	FLD	NAT DATE
Ries, Frederick	21	Germany	Y	Antwerp	New York	04/14/1884	10/12/1885			Y	
Ries, John	29	Bavaria	Y	London	New York	06/03/1854	09/25/1856	14	372	N	
Ries, John	30	Germany	Y	Antwerp	New York	07/23/1887	11/03/1894			Y	
Ries, John Gottlieb	57	Germany	Y	London	New York	12/??/1867	10/08/1883			Y	
Ries, Michael	31	Bavaria	Y	Bremen	Buffalo	08/20/1847	10/13/1851	4	245	N	
Ries, Michael	26	Germany	Y	Bremen	New York	09/20/1880	05/07/1887			Y	
Ries, Peter	46	Germany	Y	Bremen	New York	02/18/1882	01/02/1892			Y	
Riesch, Hermann	31	Germany	Y	Bremen	New York	10/08/1887	11/01/1888			Y	
Riese, Friedrich	??	Germany	Y	?	?	?	03/10/1891			Y	
Riese, George	26	Prussia	Y	Bremen	New York	11/17/1853	02/02/1856	26	12	N	
Rieselman, Henry	25	Oldenburg	Y	Bremen	New Orleans	??/28/1851	04/30/1855	11	335	N	
Riesenbeck, Ben	27	Germany	Y	Bremen	Baltimore	11/06/1891	10/27/1894			Y	
Riesner, Anton	28	Austria	Y	Bremen	New Orleans	12/03/1849	09/04/1852	25	356	N	
Riess, George	23	Germany	Y	Antwerp	New York	12/03/1887	11/02/1889			Y	
Riess, Hermann	??	Germany	Y	?	?	?	06/22/1894			Y	
Riess, John	35	Germany	Y	Bremen	Baltimore	03/31/1887	05/31/1888			Y	
Riess, Martin	25	Baden	Y	Havre	New York	04/23/1856	05/21/1856	26	514	N	
Riesterer, Cellestin	23	Baden	Y	Havre	New Orleans	10/19/1848	04/07/1852	24	407	N	
Riestoven, Phillip	??	Baden	Y	Havre	New Orleans	??/29/1847	12/07/1850	2	345	N	
Rieth, Valentine	29	Germany	Y	Bremen	Baltimore	05/19/1888	09/03/1889			Y	
Riethmann, Christian Hen	27	Hanover	Y	Bremen	New Orleans	12/04/1846	08/25/1848	22	252	N	
Riethmann, John	44	Switzerland	Y	Havre	New York	08/24/1848	02/04/1851	3	96	N	
Rietner, Jacob	30	Wuerttenberg	Y	Havre	New York	05/01/1849	05/17/1852	25	27	N	
Riffelamcher, George	32	Bavaria	Y	Bremen	Baltimore	06/04/1854	03/16/1858	16	411	N	
Rifkin, Bar	36	Russia	Y	Hamburg	New York	11/15/1881	09/20/1887			Y	
Rigby, Arthur	15	England	N	?	Philadelphia	00/00/1879				Y	08/24/1888
Rigert, Thomas	34	Switzerland	Y	Havre	New York	09/16/1879	10/04/1888			Y	
Riggs, Arthur James	23	England	Y	London	New York	05/09/1891	11/20/1895			Y	
Rigney, Joseph	30	Ireland	Y	Queenstown	New York	04/20/1888	07/29/1892			Y	
Rigney, Michael	46	Ireland	N	Queenstown	New York	05/30/1860	?			Y	
Rigney, William	26	Ireland	Y	Liverpool	New Orleans	12/??/1851	04/25/1855	11	300	N	
Riley, James	25	Ireland	Y	Liverpool	New Orleans	07/15/1847	05/04/1854	8	364	N	
Riley, James	25	Ireland	Y	Liverpool	New Orleans	07/15/1847	05/04/1854	9	237	N	
Riley, James	35	Ireland	Y	Queenstown	New York	05/05/1870	09/26/1883			Y	
Riley, James	30	Ireland	Y	Liverpool	New York	05/15/1847	03/09/1852	24	272	N	
Riley, John	30	Ireland	Y	Liverpool	New Orleans	02/01/1849	02/05/1853	7	118	N	
Riley, Martin	25	Ireland	Y	Liverpool	New York	01/15/1856	04/27/1861	18	149	N	
Riley, Michael	43	Ireland	Y	Liverpool	New Orleans	05/10/1852	05/01/1854	9	191	N	
Riley, Patrick	28	Ireland	Y	Liverpool	New Orleans	02/25/1852	10/02/1854	10	351	N	
Riley, Patrick	28	Ireland	Y	Liverpool	New Orleans	02/25/1852	10/02/1854	12	290	N	
Riley, Peter	50	Ireland	Y	Liverpool	New Orleans	06/10/1848	04/15/1853	8	67	N	
Riley, Thomas	25	Ireland	Y	Liverpool	New Orleans	03/25/1851	04/04/1853	8	16	N	
Riley, Thomas	22	Ireland	Y	Liverpool	New Orleans	02/02/1852	10/01/1856	14	90	N	
Riley, Thomas	21	Ireland	Y	Liverpool	New Orleans	02/02/1852	10/01/1856	14	93	N	
Riley, William	36	Ireland	Y	Liverpool	Boston	05/??/1849	03/16/1853	7	335	N	
Rimele, Rupert	31	Germany	Y	Antwerp	New York	10/27/1880	12/08/1886			Y	
Rimkus, John	??	Russia	Y	?	?	?	04/06/1897			Y	
Rimmele, Karl	30	Germany	Y	Rotterdam	New York	02/08/1880	09/28/1882			Y	
Rimmler, Christ.	39	Germany	Y	Rotterdam	New York	09/24/1880	10/14/1889			Y	
Rinaldo, Antonio	48	Italy	Y	Naples	New York	05/13/1889	06/26/1894			Y	
Rinaldo, Frangecco	38	Italy	Y	Naples	New York	05/19/1889	02/28/1894			Y	
Rinchausen, Louis	30	Hanover	Y	Bremen	Baltimore	??/22/1849	12/22/1849	23	416	N	
Rinck, John	29	Germany	Y	Bremen	Baltimore	03/26/1882	05/14/1886			Y	
Rinckenberger, Albert	26	Germany	Y	Havre	New York	10/28/1885	01/14/1890			Y	
Rind, Edward	??	Austria	Y	?	?	?	06/23/1891			Y	
Rindinger, Constantine	27	Baden	Y	Havre	New York	05/21/1854	09/29/1856	14	27	N	
Rindlinger, Charles	32	Wuerttenberg	Y	Havre	New York	11/29/1851	06/17/1852	25	287	N	
Rindsfoos, Samuel	54	Bavaria	N	Bavaria	New Orleans	??/??/1851	?			Y	
Ring, Daniel	31	Ireland	Y	Cork	New York	08/01/1849	03/17/1858	16	417	N	

CITIZENSHIP RECORDS

APPLICANT	AGE	COUNTRY OF ORIGIN	DEC	DEPART PORT	ENTRY PORT	ARRIVE DATE	DEC DATE	VOL	PG.	FLD	NAT DATE
Ringel, Albert	22	Germany	Y	Hamburg	New York	03/18/1882	11/17/1885			Y	
Ringhand, Gustav (Rinkul	??	Germany	Y	?	New York	04/??/1885	10/28/1886			Y	
Ringwald, Gottfried	25	Germany	Y	Havre	New York	09/18/1889	03/31/1894			Y	
Rininger, Casper	68	Switzerland	Y	Amsterdam	Baltimore	09/??/1816	11/25/1852	5	343	N	
Rink, Frederick Victor	26	Nassau	Y	London	New York	04/18/1852	04/07/1856	26	450	N	
Rink, George	26	Germany	Y	Hamburg	New York	11/18/1881	12/29/1883			Y	
Rink, Joseph	40	Germany	Y	Havre	Baltimore	01/23/1874	10/25/1888			Y	
Rink, Peter	29	Wuerttemberg	Y	Liverpool	New York	07/10/1853	08/15/1860	27	274	N	
Rinker, Friedrich	38	Wurttemberg	Y	Rotterdam	New York	11/04/1848	10/24/1851	4	387	N	
Rinklin, Matthias	42	Germany	Y	Havre	New York	11/23/1886	10/16/1889			Y	
Rinz, Fidal	48	Heckingen	Y	Havre	New Orleans	11/30/1847	02/05/1849	23	30	N	
Rinzelmann, Henry	30	Hanover	Y	Bremen	New Orleans	01/13/1848	02/25/1858	16	341	N	
Riordan, Mathew	26	Ireland	Y	Liverpool	New Orleans	11/21/1850	02/21/1856	26	112	N	
Riorden, Jeremiah	23	Ireland	Y	Liverpool	New York	04/20/1853	10/05/1854	10	452	N	
Riordon, Con.	21	Ireland	Y	Cork	New York	07/16/1848	10/13/1851	4	236	N	
Ripking, Bernard Fred.	52	Hanover	Y	Bremen	New Orleans	10/29/1852	11/19/1852	5	210	N	
Rippe, Frank	34	Germany	Y	Bremen	Baltimore	06/20/1882	08/15/1889	19	229	N	
Rippe, Frank	34	Germany	Y	Bremen	Baltimore	06/20/1882	08/15/1889			Y	
Rippe, Henry	29	Hanover, Germ	Y	Bremen	New York	12/05/1880	11/28/1884			Y	
Rippel, Vinzenz	42	Austria	Y	Bremen	Baltimore	03/07/1883	10/30/1886	19	100	N	
Rippel, Vinzenz	42	Austria	Y	Bremen	Baltimore	03/07/1883	10/30/1886				
Ripploh, William	30	Prussia	Y	Bremen	New Orleans	11/20/1848	03/17/1852	24	322	N	
Rippmann, David	28	Baden	Y	Havre	New York	07/06/1855	08/18/1860	27	297	N	
Ripsch, John	49	Bavaria	Y	Havre	New York	09/15/1852	10/05/1854	10	442	N	
Ripsch, John	49	Bavaria	Y	Havre	New York	09/15/1852	10/05/1854	12	381	N	
Rirdon, Owen	32	Ireland	Y	Cork	New Orleans	01/12/1848	03/26/1850	2	270	N	
Risch, Hermann Gotthilf	26	Germany	Y	Bremen	Baltimore	05/09/1888	07/11/1891			Y	
Risch, Jacob	34	Germany	N	Bremen	New York	10/??/1855	?			Y	
Risch, William	36	Bavaria	Y	Havre	New York	02/??/1854	04/24/1855	11	298	N	
Rischmann, Ignatz	36	Antwerp	Y	Antwerp	New York	05/28/1892	01/02/1895			Y	
Rischmueller, Henry F. W	20	Prussia	Y	Bremen	New York	08/04/1853	10/09/1854	11	57	N	
Rischmueller, Henry Frede	29	Prussia	Y	Bremen	New York	08/04/1853	10/09/1854	6	56	N	
Riskowsky, Louis	32	Russia	Y	Hamburg	New York	05/21/1893	01/03/1895			Y	
Rissert, John Michael	33	Germany	Y	Havre	New York	04/01/1890	12/19/1892			Y	
Rist, Leonard	35	Bavaria	Y	Rotterdam	New York	07/23/1844	04/27/1850	3	16	N	
Rist, Simon	28	Wurttemberg	Y	Havre	New York	07/05/1851	12/02/1852	5	369	N	
Ritchie, Andrew	24	Scotland	Y	Glasgow	New York	07/06/1848	10/07/1851	4	214	N	
Ritchie, George	??	England	Y	Glasgow	New York	08/01/1845	10/09/1848	22	501	N	
Ritchie, John	33	Scotland	Y	Grunock	Boston	07/18/1849	06/21/1852	25	301	N	
Riter, Alexander	24	Bavaria	Y	Bremen	New York	07/08/1848	10/13/1851	4	255	N	
Riter, Robert	22	Prussia	Y	Hamburg	New York	08/14/1858	07/19/1860	27	228	N	
Ritter, Albert	31	Germany	Y	Havre	New York	03/01/1883	02/21/1889			Y	
Ritter, Charles	44	Germany	N	Antwerp	New York	04/30/1867	03/??/1868	28	297	N	10/??/1874
Ritter, Charles	??	Germany	N	?	?	12/20/1886				Y	03/26/1892
Ritter, Charles G.	25	Germany	Y	Havre	New York	05/07/1880	12/29/1885			Y	
Ritter, Christ	25	Germany	Y	Havre	New York	05/11/1880	08/06/1883			Y	
Ritter, Christian	26	Germany	Y	Antwerp	New York	05/29/1881	03/22/1886			Y	
Ritter, Edward A.	49	Germany	Y	Hamburg	New York	11/23/1869	10/26/1900			Y	
Ritter, Eugene	35	France	Y	Havre	New York	09/27/1872	12/30/1882			Y	
Ritter, F.L.	31	France	Y	Havre	New York	10/07/1852	05/05/1859	17	398	N	
Ritter, Ferdinand	26	Austria	Y	Havre	New York	02/24/1882	10/10/1888			Y	
Ritter, Francis	24	Bavaria	Y	Bremen	New York	06/01/1854	05/22/1856	26	522	N	
Ritter, Henry	22	France	Y	?	New York	??/??/1882	05/12/1884			Y	
Ritter, John	26	Bavaria	Y	Bremen	Baltimore	02/07/1854	03/24/1856	26	286	N	
Ritter, John Casper	21	Wurttemberg	Y	Bremen	New Orleans	11/27/1855	09/25/1856	14	377	N	
Ritter, Joseph	36	Germany	Y	Havre	New York	06/26/1884	10/05/1887			Y	
Ritter, Lorenz	48	France	Y	Havre	New York	11/01/1854	12/10/1857	16	214	N	
Ritter, Peter	52	Hungary	Y	Hamburg	New York	09/12/1900	09/30/1902			Y	
Ritter, Rochus	26	Austria	Y	Havre	New York	03/01/1887	02/20/1890			Y	

CITIZENSHIP RECORDS

APPLICANT	AGE	COUNTRY OF ORIGIN	DEC	DEPART PORT	ENTRY PORT	ARRIVE DATE	DEC DATE	VOL	PG.	FLD	NAT DATE
Ritter, Rupert	31	Bavaria	Y	Hamburg	New York	07/01/1845	01/23/1849	1	510	N	
Ritterhoff, John	34	Hanover	Y	Bremen	Baltimore	09/15/1842	02/20/1849	23	227	N	
Rittimann, Peter	23	Germany	Y	Havre	New York	09/25/1887	11/02/1891			Y	
Ritting, Theodore	29	Hanover	Y	Bremen	New Orleans	11/27/1846	09/29/1856	14	423	N	
Rittlinger, George	29	Bavaria	Y	Havre	New York	04/12/1852	09/25/1856	14	367	N	
Rittweger, George C.	37	Wurttemberg	Y	Bremen	New York	10/27/1835	01/31/1849	1	552	N	
Ritz, Leopold	24	Baden	Y	Havre	New York	06/22/1852	11/03/1855	13	152	N	
Ritz, Otto	??	?	N	?	?	?	?			Y	
Ritze, Charles	27	Baden	Y	Havre	New York	04/17/1857	10/08/1860	27	425	N	
Ritzel, George	37	Germany	Y	Liverpool	New York	07/18/1886	10/22/1888	19	160	N	
Ritzer, Joseph	28	Bavaria	Y	Bremen	Baltimore	06/11/1852	05/17/1854	8	462	N	
Ritzer, Joseph	28	Bavaria	Y	Bremen	Baltimore	06/11/1852	05/17/1854	9	336	N	
Ritzi, Gebhard	??	Baden	Y	?	?	?	09/14/1866			Y	
Ritzi, Michael	32	Germany	Y	Havre	New York	05/11/1883	02/11/1888			Y	
Rivers, Dennis	29	Ireland	Y	Queenstown	New York	08/29/1888	10/22/1895	21	83	N	
Rivers, Dennis	29	Ireland	Y	Queenstown	New York	08/29/1888	10/22/1895			Y	
Rix, John	32	England	Y	Liverpool	New York	04/01/1845	02/25/1856	26	130	N	
Rizer, Israel	28	Russia	Y	Liverpool	Philadelphia	04/19/1881	10/12/1883			Y	
Rizolli, John	45	Austria	Y	Bremen	Baltimore	04/19/1874	04/26/1880			Y	
Rizzo, Agostino	35	Italy	Y	Palermo	New York	03/20/1883	10/23/1893	21	28	N	
Rizzo, Augustino	35	Italy	Y	Palermo	New York	03/20/1883	10/23/1893			Y	
Rizzo, Gaetano	31	Italy	Y	Palermo	New York	01/26/1884	10/17/1893	21	19	N	
Rizzo, Gartano	31	Italy	Y	Palermo	New York	01/26/1884	10/17/1893			Y	
Rizzo, Ignazio	43	Italy	Y	Palermo	New York	10/12/1882	11/13/1893	21	55	N	
Rizzo, Ignazio	43	Italy	Y	Palermo	New York	10/12/1882	11/13/1893			Y	
Rizzo, Salvatore	33	Italy	Y	Palermo	New York	01/02/1884	10/16/1893	21	5	N	
Rizzo, Salvatore	27	Italy	Y	Palermo	New York	12/16/1889	10/17/1893	21	15	N	
Rizzo, Salvatore	32	Italy	Y	Palermo	New York	02/01/1886	10/18/1893	21	21	N	
Rizzo, Salvatore	27	Italy	Y	Palermo	New York	12/15/1889	10/17/1893			Y	
Rizzo, Salvatore	33	Italy	Y	Palermo	New York	02/01/1884	10/16/1893			Y	
Rizzo, Salvatore	32	Italy	Y	Palermo	New York	02/01/1886	10/18/1893			Y	
Roa, Frederick William	28	Prussia	Y	Liverpool	New York	06/24/1853	08/28/1855	11	512	N	
Roa, Nicholas	33	Prussia	Y	Havre	New York	05/12/1854	09/25/1857	15	319	N	
Roach, Joseph	35	Ireland	Y	Westford	New York	05/25/1851	11/27/1852	5	350	N	
Roach, Michael	27	Ireland	Y	Liverpool	New York	04/26/1889	07/27/1891			Y	
Roach, Patrick	30	Ireland	N	Queenstown	New York	05/15/1883	?			Y	
Roark, Joseph	24	Ireland	Y	Liverpool	New Orleans	11/25/1850	??/05/1853	7	116	N	
Roarke, William	27	Ireland	Y	Waterford	New York	04/04/1852	02/20/1856	26	108	N	
Rob, August	??	Wuerttenberg	Y	Rotterdam	New York	06/02/1845	10/09/1848	22	500	N	
Robbeloth, Sebastian	33	Germany	Y	Liverpool	New York	07/13/1874	06/05/1882			Y	
Robben, Tony	30	Germany	Y	Bremen	New York	06/02/1886	01/27/1890			Y	
Robbes, George	50	Germany	N	Bremen	Baltimore	09/??/1866	?			Y	
Rober, Mathias	48	Bavaria	Y	Havre	New York	12/22/1854	11/09/1858	17	309	N	
Roberts, Alexander	27	Canada	Y	Canada	Buffalo	05/??/1848	09/14/1852	25	506	N	
Roberts, Charles John	36	England	Y	Bristol	New York	03/07/1840	11/24/1852	5	336	N	
Roberts, David	29	Wales	Y	Liverpool	New York	05/02/1846	11/03/1852	5	194	N	
Roberts, David	29	Wales	Y	Liverpool	New York	05/02/1846	11/03/1852	6	320	N	
Roberts, David	47	Wales	Y	Liverpool	New York	09/18/1852	01/14/1856	13	468	N	
Roberts, David	29	Wales	Y	Liverpool	Philadelphia	08/23/1854	03/09/1857	15	85	N	
Roberts, John	31	Wales	Y	Liverpool	?	?	09/10/1888			Y	
Roberts, John C.	27	Wales	Y	?	New York	??/??/1893	05/08/1896			Y	
Roberts, Richard	42	Wales	Y	Liverpool	New Orleans	11/20/1850	09/28/1854	10	290	N	
Roberts, Richard	42	Wales	Y	Liverpool	New Orleans	11/20/1850	09/28/1854	12	229	N	
Roberts, William H.	36	Wales	Y	Liverpool	Philadelphia	09/??/1850	09/20/1854	12	70	N	
Roberts, William John	27	England	Y	Liverpool	New York	06/04/1857	12/07/1857	16	201	N	
Robertson, Alexander	25	England	Y	Liverpool	Philadelphia	11/16/1892	05/15/1894			Y	
Robertson, Frank	33	Scotland	Y	Glasgow	New York	08/28/1885	11/07/1894			Y	
Robertson, Robert	17	Norway	N	?	New York	00/00/1880				Y	10/15/1888
Robertson, Thomas	38	Scotland	Y	Glasgow	New York	04/16/1876	04/04/1882			Y	

CITIZENSHIP RECORDS

APPLICANT	AGE	COUNTRY OF ORIGIN	DEC	DEPART PORT	ENTRY PORT	ARRIVE DATE	DEC DATE	VOL	PG.	FLD	NAT DATE
Robertson, William Clark	31	England	Y	Liverpool	New York	09/28/1848	10/30/1851	4	439	N	
Robertson, William D.	24	Scotland	Y	Glasgow	New York	03/04/1891	10/24/1894			Y	
Roberz, Anton	37	Germany	Y	Havre	New York	10/01/1883	10/25/1886			Y	
Roberz, John	30	Germany	Y	Havre	New York	10/01/1883	10/25/1886			Y	
Robin, Morris	40	Russia	Y	Hamburg	New York	03/01/1892	09/06/1899			Y	
Robinson, Arthur	29	Ireland	Y	Liverpool	New York	05/20/1852	04/11/1862	18	315	N	
Robinson, George	17	England	N	?	New York	00/00/1876				Y	10/22/1888
Robinson, Henry	??	Ireland	Y	Liverpool	New Orleans	04/25/1847	10/11/1848	1	147	N	
Robinson, John	34	England	Y	Liverpool	Liverpool	01/05/1846	02/22/1853	7	214	N	
Robinson, Noble	22	Ireland	Y	Londonderry	New Orleans	11/24/1849	01/??/1850	23	544	N	
Robinson, Thomas	51	England	N	Liverpool	New Orleans	01/??/1854	?			Y	
Robinson, Thomas C.	46	Canada	N	Toronto	Cincinnati?	10/??/1846	?			Y	
Robinson, W. L.	48	Canada	N	Toronto	Cincinnati?	10/??/1846	?			Y	
Robmann, Frederick	23	Bavaria	Y	Bremen	New York	07/02/1853	08/04/1856	14	333	N	
Rocelus, Antonio	26	Italy	Y	Naples	New York	06/16/1899	03/28/1903			Y	
Roche, David	38	Ireland	Y	Liverpool	New York	05/01/1851	08/04/1856	14	332	N	
Roche, Stephen	50	Ireland	N	Liverpool	New York	07/??/1866	?			Y	
Rochmann, John	45	Austria	Y	Rotterdam	New York	08/22/1886	11/22/1886			Y	
Rockelhoff, Henry	40	Hanover	Y	Bremen	New Orleans	11/??/1848	10/03/1854	10	390	N	
Rocker, Hermann	26	Germany	Y	Antwerp	New York	11/18/1891	08/04/1893			Y	
Rocker, Jacob	31	Germany	Y	?	New York	??/??/1884	04/16/1890			Y	
Rocker, Michael	36	Germany	Y	Antwerp	New York	10/13/1881	10/07/1891	19	332	N	
Rocker, Michael	36	Germany	Y	Antwerp	New York	10/13/1881	10/07/1891			Y	
Rockford, John	29	Ireland	Y	Liverpool	New York	07/20/1847	06/10/1852	25	225	N	
Rockford, Pierce	36	Ireland	Y	Waterford	New York	07/26/1847	06/10/1852	25	226	N	
Rodamer, Andrew	28	Hesse Darmsta	Y	Bremen	New Orleans	08/22/1849	01/24/1853	7	60	N	
Rodde, Edward Philip Fra	25	Bavaria	Y	Bremen	New York	11/26/1854	11/17/1857	16	30	N	
Rode, Henry	22	Germany	Y	Bremen	New York	11/28/1889	09/14/1891			Y	
Roden, Edward	24	Hanover	Y	Bremen	New York	11/02/1854	09/28/1857	15	329	N	
Roden, Vincence	27	Prussia	Y	Antwerp	New York	07/16/1857	09/15/1860	27	375	N	
Rodenberg, Carl	25	Germany	Y	Bremen	New York	05/29/1880	04/20/1885			Y	
Roder, Lawrence	22	Bavaria	Y	Bremen	Baltimore	05/11/1849	05/01/1854	9	162	N	
Rodger, James	30	Scotland	Y	Liverpool	New York	07/15/1842	05/06/1850	3	57	N	
Rodgers, John	26	Ireland	Y	Liverpool	New York	04/13/1853	04/01/1856	26	400	N	
Rodler, Frederick	27	Bavaria	Y	Bremen	Baltimore	11/11/1854	09/30/1856	14	57	N	
Rodler, Frederick	58	Germany	N	Bremen	Baltimore	11/10/1854	?			Y	
Roecke, Charles	32	Prussia	Y	Havre	New York	06/06/1855	10/27/1858	17	132	N	
Roeckert, Charles Freder	24	Hesse Darmsta	Y	Havre	New York	02/09/1853	08/24/1857	15	173	N	
Roedemeister, Frank	34	Prussia	Y	Central Amer	New Orleans	04/01/1855	10/20/1857	15	463	N	
Roeder, Lawrence	22	Bavaria	Y	Bremen	Baltimore	05/11/1849	05/01/1854	8	290	N	
Roedig, Robert	22	Austria	Y	Bremen	Baltimore	07/28/1893	10/28/1896			Y	
Roedig, Wenzl	21	Germany	Y	Bremen	Baltimore	06/17/1881	03/13/1883			Y	
Roefer, Theodore	15	Germany	N	?	New York	00/00/1881				Y	10/23/1888
Roehm, Caspar	23	Bavaria	Y	Bremen	Baltimore	11/13/1857	12/16/1857	16	224	N	
Roehm, Fred	29	Germany	Y	Havre	New York	06/08/1888	03/13/1893			Y	
Roehm, Jacob	22	Wurttemberg	Y	Antwerp	New York	04/04/1850	08/27/1855	11	496	N	
Roehm, John	31	Wuertemberg	Y	Havre	New York	11/17/1853	05/26/1856	26	554	N	
Roehm, Simon	37	Wuerttemberg	Y	London	New York	05/19/1848	02/08/1849	23	122	N	
Roehne, John Simon	32	Wurttemberg	Y	Antwerp	New York	04/18/1850	09/22/1854	10	166	N	
Roehnn, George	41	Germany	N	Bremen	New Orleans	12/18/1870	?			Y	
Roehr, F.	40	Germany	Y	Bremen	New York	06/27/1881	10/05/1885			Y	
Roelkenberg, Heinrich	24	Hanover	Y	Bremerhafen	Baltimore	06/??/1859	02/13/1861	18	97	N	
Roelker, Benjamin	30	Germany	Y	Bremen	Baltimore	10/20/1883	10/17/1893			Y	
Roell, Christoph	24	Bavaria	Y	Havre	New York	08/08/1849	03/11/1850	2	181	N	
Roell, Simon	36	Germany	Y	Antwerp	New York	06/22/1883	10/24/1889			Y	
Roeller, Christoph	48	Bavaria	Y	Havre	New Orleans	08/08/1850	10/09/1854	11	199	N	
Roeller, Ludwig	39	Germany	Y	Bremen	New York	05/25/1894	03/27/1900			Y	
Roeller, Peter	33	Germany	Y	Antwerp	New York	09/13/1881	02/18/1890			Y	
Roellig, John G.	38	Germany	Y	Bremen	New York	05/13/1882	11/03/1886			Y	

CITIZENSHIP RECORDS

APPLICANT	AGE	COUNTRY OF ORIGIN	DEC	DEPART PORT	ENTRY PORT	ARRIVE DATE	DEC DATE	VOL	PG.	FLD	NAT DATE
Roelver, William	40	Prussia	Y	Bremen	New Orleans	06/20/1851	05/25/1854	8	536	N	
Roemer, Charles	??	Germany	N	?	?	06/01/1883				Y	10/28/1892
Roemer, Henry	62	Germany	N	Hamburg	New York	09/22/1854	?			Y	
Roemer, Valentine	26	Bavaria	Y	Havre	New York	07/11/1850	05/25/1854	8	516	N	
Roemer, Valentine	36	Bavaria	Y	Havre	New York	07/10/1850	05/25/1854	9	390	N	
Roemheld, Ferdinand	36	Saxe Coburg	Y	Bremen	New Orleans	11/24/1850	04/18/1854	8	207	N	
Roepking, Dietrich	30	Oldenburg	Y	Bremen	Baltimore	11/??/1847	11/??/1849	23	348	N	
Roepking, John Henry	34	Oldenburg	Y	Bremen	Baltimore	05/28/1850	04/17/1854	8	161	N	
Roerwater, Gerd Henry	62	Oldenburg	Y	Bremen	New Orleans	11/04/1851	10/06/1856	14	237	N	
Roesch, Jacob	24	Germany	Y	Bremen	New York	05/15/1875	09/30/1880			Y	
Roesche, G. W. A.	50	Germany	N	Bremen	New Orleans	05/??/1852	?			Y	
Roescher, Leopold	22	Wurttemberg	Y	Liverpool	Philadelphia	10/16/1854	10/17/1857	15	445	N	
Roeschke, Alexander	37	Germany	Y	Stettin	New York	09/28/1871	12/03/1881			Y	
Roese, E.G. Hermann	??	Germany	Y	?	?	?	03/27/1875			Y	
Roeser, Gottlieb	45	Germany	Y	Bremen	New York	05/18/1880	07/06/1883			Y	
Roesh, Henry	33	Germany	Y	Bremen	New York	11/09/1881	02/10/1893			Y	
Roesler, John Nepomuck	33	Baden	Y	Havre	New York	11/11/1856	06/10/1861	18	186	N	
Roesler, Julius	34	Germany	Y	Bremen	New York	05/07/1884	10/06/1892			Y	
Roessel, Albrecht (Alber	32	Germany	Y	Hamburg	New York	05/27/1882	09/03/1889			Y	
Roester, Fred.	31	Germany	Y	Bremen	Baltimore	11/01/1869	04/05/1880			Y	
Roetker, Franz	34	Prussia	Y	Bremen	Baltimore	05/28/1845	05/16/1854	8	453	N	
Roettele, August	38	Germany	Y	Havre	Boston	05/??/1869	05/??/1872			Y	
Roettele, August	38	Germany	N	Havre	Boston	05/??/1869	?			Y	
Roettele, Blasius	35	Baden	Y	Havre	New Orleans	03/16/1846	10/06/1848	22	453	N	
Roetter, Max	19	Germany	Y	Bremen	New York	02/05/1890	02/29/1892			Y	
Roettger, Fred	45	Germany	Y	Bremen	New York	09/28/1881	12/14/1889			Y	
Roetting, Bernard Herman	46	Germany	Y	Liverpool	New York	05/20/1872	10/31/1896			Y	
Roetting, Herman	31	Germany	Y	Bremen	New York	03/18/1882	12/28/1894			Y	
Roevekamp, Herrick	46	Germany	Y	?	Baltimore	11/10/1864	10/11/1880			Y	
Roewekamp, Herman	30	Hanover	Y	Bremen	Baltimore	10/24/1855	10/22/1858	17	93	N	
Roewekamp, Louis	48	Germany	Y	Bremen	New York	10/18/1865	10/25/1886			Y	
Roewer, Herman Rudolph	31	Prussia	Y	Bremen	New Orleans	05/28/1852	03/01/1858	16	351	N	
Rofalsky, Joseph	36	Germany	Y	Hamburg	New York	07/27/1890	06/30/1892			Y	
Rofs, Clements	28	Prussia	Y	Bremen	New Orleans	12/26/1847	06/20/1851	3	467	N	
Rofskoesky, Louis	27	Russia	Y	Hamburg	New York	07/15/1888	07/01/1893			Y	
Rogers, Harry K.	22	Nova Scotia	Y	Yarmouth	Boston	04/20/1887	05/29/1890			Y	
Rogers, Patrick	55	Ireland	Y	Liverpool	New York	11/15/1852	02/26/1872	18	465	N	
Rogers, Phelim	24	Ireland	Y	Liverpool	New York	05/??/1846	10/05/1848	22	445	N	
Rogers, Samuel J.	28	Wales	Y	Liverpool	New York	07/03/1849	01/04/1853	5	515	N	
Rogers, Thomas	30	Ireland	Y	Liverpool	South Amborg	08/20/1836	11/13/1848	1	277	N	
Rogers, Thomas	24	Ireland	Y	Liverpool	New York	05/14/1850	01/11/1851	2	481	N	
Rogge, Franz	29	Hanover	Y	Bremen	New York	10/03/1854	09/17/1855	13	52	N	
Rogge, William	35	Germany	Y	Bremen	Baltimore	11/00/1868	09/13/1881			Y	
Rohde, Casper (Rode?)	38	Oldenburg	Y	Bremen	Baltimore	06/28/1845	08/15/1848	22	116	N	
Rohde, Martin	27	Germany	Y	Bremen	Baltimore	04/09/1887	11/08/1889			Y	
Rohe, Anton	59	Germany	N	Bremen	New Orleans	11/??/1853	?			Y	
Rohe, Christ	17	Germany	N	?	Baltimore	00/00/1878				Y	10/18/1888
Rohe, Clemens	17	Germany	N	?	New York	00/00/1867				Y	10/17/1888
Rohe, Henry	21	Oldenburg	Y	Bremen	New Orleans	11/04/1853	05/25/1854	8	533	N	
Rohe, Henry	21	Oldenburg	Y	Bremen	New Orleans	11/04/1853	05/25/1854	9	407	N	
Rohensteder, Andre	40	Germany	Y	Harvard	New York	06/20/1864	10/05/1871			Y	
Roherberger, Simon	40	Austria	Y	Hamburg	New York	07/08/1887	12/16/1892			Y	
Rohing, Joseph	52	Prussia	Y	Bremen	New Orleans	01/20/1848	03/03/1851	3	199	N	
Rohler, Joseph	35	Prussia	Y	Havre	New York	06/10/1852	11/20/1852	5	319	N	
Rohlf, August	39	Germany	Y	Hamburg	New York	07/04/1882	06/22/1891			Y	
Rohlfs, Hermann	29	Germany	Y	Bremen	New York	10/28/1880	10/23/1888			Y	
Rohling, Barney	27	Hanover	Y	Havre	New York	05/28/1847	10/07/1854	6	20	N	
Rohling, Leonard	27	Hanover	Y	Havre	New York	05/28/1847	10/07/1854	11	21	N	
Rohm, John George	35	Wurttemberg	Y	Havre	New York	04/27/1857	04/25/1862	18	330	N	

CITIZENSHIP RECORDS

APPLICANT	AGE	COUNTRY OF ORIGIN	DEC	DEPART PORT	ENTRY PORT	ARRIVE DATE	DEC DATE	VOL	PG.	FLD	NAT DATE
Rohm, John Simon	32	Wurttemberg	Y	Antwerp	New York	04/18/1850	09/22/1854	12	105	N	
Rohm, Philip	32	Prussia	Y	Antwerp	New York	04/22/1848	01/23/1849	1	502	N	
Rohmann, Charles	22	Brunswick	Y	Bremen	New York	11/24/1854	10/27/1858	17	130	N	
Rohmann, Frank Joseph	25	Bavaria	Y	Havre	New Orleans	08/04/1848	12/15/1851	4	517	N	
Rohmann, John	23	Hanover	Y	Bremen	New Orleans	06/??/1849	08/??/1851	4	164	N	
Rohmann, Peter	26	Hesse Darmsta	Y	Liverpool	Baltimore	05/28/1852	08/20/1855	11	459	N	
Rohr, Conrad	28	Prussia	Y	Antwerp	New Orleans	11/11/1852	11/24/1855	13	246	N	
Rohrer, Anton	65	Germany	N	London	Boston	10/??/1848	?				Y
Rohrer, Samuel	??	Switzerland	N	Bremen	New York	??/??/1861	?				Y
Rohrkaste, Frederick Chr	34	Prussia	Y	Bremen	Philadelphia	06/18/1845	01/13/1849	1	410	N	
Rohsmeihsl, Carl	31	Austria	Y	Bremen	Baltimore	05/21/1875	08/01/1885				Y
Roiderer, Joseph	44	Germany	Y	Hamburg	New York	01/26/1881	07/05/1890				Y
Roidl, Anton	25	Germany	Y	Antwerp	New York	03/12/1893	10/06/1896				Y
Roidol, Christian	31	Bavaria	Y	Hamburg	New York	07/??/1846	12/??/1849	23	407	N	
Roland, William	27	Germany	Y	Antwerp	New York	02/27/1883	03/25/1887				Y
Rolfer, John Henry	43	Hanover	Y	Bremen	New Orleans	12/??/1848	05/10/1854	8	412	N	
Rolfer, John Henry	43	Hanover	Y	Bremen	New Orleans	12/??/1848	05/10/1854	9	285	N	
Rolfes, A.	40	Germany	Y	Bremen	New York	10/??/1881	10/29/1884				Y
Rolfes, Barney	32	Germany	Y	Rotterdam	New York	10/??/1870	10/13/1884				Y
Rolfes, Frank	43	Germany	Y	Bremen	New York	05/15/1869	12/03/1889				Y
Rolfes, George H.	47	Germany	Y	Bremen	Baltimore	10/??/1865	10/02/1882				Y
Rolfes, Henry	35	Germany	Y	Bremen	Bremen	06/18/1881	10/07/1882				Y
Rolfes, Henry	26	Germany	Y	Amsterdam	New York	12/26/1891	10/22/1897				Y
Rolfes, Henry	27	Germany	Y	Bremen	New York	08/06/1890	06/29/1894				Y
Rolfes, Herman	22	Germany	Y	Bremen	Baltimore	11/29/1881	07/10/1884				Y
Rolfes, Herman Christian	25	Hanover	Y	Bremen	New Orleans	12/23/1853	10/29/1858	17	178	N	
Rolfes, Ignatz	24	Germany	Y	Rotterdam	New York	05/04/1892	01/11/1897				Y
Rolfes, Johann H.	43	Germany	N	Bremen	New York	02/20/1867	?				Y
Rolfes, John William	29	Oldenburg	Y	Bremen	New Orleans	11/12/1852	02/04/1856	26	19	N	
Rolff, Anthony	28	Germany	Y	Bremen	Baltimore	06/03/1881	10/05/1885				Y
Rolfsen, Bernard	28	Oldenburg	Y	Bremen	Baltimore	04/15/1849	11/12/1855	13	207	N	
Roling, Bernard	27	Prussia	Y	Bremen	New Orleans	12/26/1846	10/04/1848	1	49	N	
Roling, Charles	26	Germany	Y	Rotterdam	New York	02/21/1887	04/09/1892				Y
Roling, Frank	30	Germany	Y	Rotterdam	New York	04/18/1874	03/19/1884				Y
Roling, Herman	28	Germany	Y	Bremen	New York	05/06/1885	12/08/1887				Y
Rolke, Albert	31	Germany	Y	Amsterdam	New York	05/20/1882	05/03/1883				Y
Rolker, Ferdinand	26	Germany	Y	Hanover	Baltimore	07/20/1879	12/10/1880				Y
Roll, David	37	Wurtemberg	Y	Bremen	New York	10/01/1864	09/27/1869				Y
Roll, John Frederick	27	Bavaria	Y	Liverpool	New York	05/18/1854	10/03/1856	14	177	N	
Roller, Cristoph	48	Bavaria	Y	Havre	New Orleans	08/08/1850	10/09/1854	6	196	N	
Roller, Ulrich	43	Bavaria	Y	Havre	New Orleans	11/24/1847	02/14/1849	23	98	N	
Rollins, Joseph	33	Switzerland	Y	Havre	New York	03/27/1882	08/04/1884				Y
Rollwagen, Louis Heinric	27	Hanover	Y	Bremen	New York	11/14/1851	03/07/1853	7	290	N	
Rols, Bernard	52	Germany	Y	Bremen	Baltimore	04/10/1870	04/06/1885				Y
Rolzler, Jacob Frederick	32	Baden	Y	Havre	New York	05/25/1857	11/20/1861	18	226	N	
Roma, Antonio	27	Italy	Y	Naples	New York	08/18/1896	10/17/1900				Y
Roman, Fergus	37	Ireland	Y	Liverpool	New Orleans	11/29/1849	01/08/1853	5	535	N	
Roman, Mathias	51	Baden	Y	Havre	New York	11/26/1854	10/30/1858	17	4	N	
Romane, Friederich Wilhe	30	Prussia	Y	Hamburg	New York	07/12/1857	02/26/1861	18	120	N	
Romanowisz, Lukas	25	Prussia	Y	Bremen	New York	09/25/1856	10/06/1856	14	192	N	
Romath, Joseph	55	Germany	Y	Bremen	Baltimore	05/26/1867	01/29/1890				Y
Romer, Fred	??	Germany	N	?	?	?	?				Y
Romer, Joseph	42	Baden	Y	Havre	New Orleans	02/28/1852	09/30/1856	14	58	N	
Romheld, Ferdinand	36	Saxe Coburg	Y	Bremen	New Orleans	11/24/1850	04/18/1854	9	78	N	
Romich, Michael	36	Bavaria	Y	Antwerp	New York	08/28/1848	11/20/1848	1	328	N	
Rominger, Jacob	38	Baden	Y	Havre	New Orleans	05/27/1849	09/30/1854	10	317	N	
Rominger, Jacob	38	Baden	Y	Havre	New Orleans	05/27/1849	09/30/1854	12	256	N	
Ronan, John	23	Ireland	Y	Cork	New Orleans	04/12/1850	10/27/1851	4	417	N	
Rondi, Karl Paul	29	Germany	Y	Bremen	Baltimore	11/15/1884	09/14/1891				Y

CITIZENSHIP RECORDS

APPLICANT	AGE	COUNTRY OF ORIGIN	DEC	DEPART PORT	ENTRY PORT	ARRIVE DATE	DEC DATE	VOL	PG.	FLD	NAT DATE
Roney, Martin	32	Ireland	Y	Liverpool	New Orleans	??/??/1849	04/27/1855	11	312	N	
Roolmann, Gerhard	38	Prussia	Y	Bremen	New Orleans	12/30/1856	03/04/1862	18	268	N	
Rooney, George	23	Ireland	Y	Liverpool	New Orleans	??/10/1848	12/19/1849	23	412	N	
Rooney, George	62	Ireland	N	Liverpool	New Orleans	05/??/1853	??/??/1854	28	406	N	10/??/1859
Rooney, John	22	Ireland	Y	Liverpool	New York	12/17/1852	01/31/1856	13	527	N	
Rooney, John	44	Ireland	Y	Liverpool	New Orleans	11/20/1853	08/27/1860	27	316	N	
Rooney, Michael	25	Ireland	Y	Liverpool	New Orleans	11/24/1848	10/14/1851	4	272	N	
Rooney, Philip	27	Ireland	Y	Liverpool	New York	06/??/1851	08/25/1857	15	186	N	
Roos, Charles	30	Saxony	Y	Bremen	New York	10/06/1854	01/11/1856	13	448	N	
Roos, Henry	29	Germany	Y	Hamburg	New York	06/06/1881	10/11/1883			Y	
Roose, John	28	France	Y	Havre	New Orleans	05/28/1846	01/15/1849	1	421	N	
Ropking, John Henry	34	Oldenburg	Y	Bremen	Baltimore	05/28/1850	04/17/1854	9	32	N	
Roppelt, John	30	Germany	Y	Bremen	Baltimore	03/10/1882	03/10/1885			Y	
Rosazza, Bernard G.	??	Italy	Y	?	?	?	05/31/1895			Y	
Rosche, Anton	49	Germany	N	Hanover	Quebec	05/??/1863	?			Y	
Rose, Bernard	30	Prussia	Y	Nubedeb	Baltimore	10/18/1852	10/09/1854	6	95	N	
Rose, Bernard	30	Prussia	Y	Nubedeb	Baltimore	10/18/1852	10/09/1854	11	98	N	
Rose, Carl	??	Germany	Y	?	?	?	05/29/1882			Y	
Rose, Gustav	34	Germany	Y	Hamburg	New York	11/28/1883	10/31/1891			Y	
Rose, Henry	26	Germany	Y	Bremen	Baltimore	10/23/1881	08/10/1882			Y	
Rose, Nicholas (Roos?)	25	Prussia	Y	Antwerp	New Orleans	05/12/1848	01/??/1850	23	538	N	
Rose, Oscar	28	Germany	Y	Bremen	New York	03/27/1880	05/22/1882			Y	
Rose, Richard	27	Germany	Y	Bremen	New York	05/22/1885	04/02/1888			Y	
Rosembaum, Moses	68	Russia	N	Russia	New York	08/??/1866	?	28	465	N	10/14/1878
Rosemeier, Henry	27	Hanover	Y	Bremen	New York	10/15/1854	10/01/1856	14	82	N	
Rosemeyer, Gerhard Henry	23	Hanover	Y	Bremen	Baltimore	10/04/1846	03/25/1850	2	247	N	
Rosen, Ernst	21	Saxe Aldenbur	Y	Bremen	Baltimore	12/12/1850	11/01/1852	5	151	N	
Rosen, Ernst	21	Saxe Aldenbur	Y	Bremen	Baltimore	12/12/1850	11/01/1852	6	277	N	
Rosen, Henry	27	Hanover	Y	Havre	New York	05/04/1849	06/16/1851	3	381	N	
Rosenbaum, David	22	Germany	Y	Hamburg	New York	04/10/1893	03/23/1896			Y	
Rosenbaum, Fritz	25	Germany	Y	Bremen	New York	12/30/1893	04/28/1894			Y	
Rosenbaum, Isaac	??	Egypt	Y	?	?	12/??/1877	04/09/1886			Y	
Rosenbaum, Lazarus	30	Russia	Y	Hamburg	New York	11/15/1881	11/02/1891			Y	
Rosenbaum, Sam	??	Russia	Y	?	?	?	09/23/1891			Y	
Rosenberg, Samuel	29	Russia	Y	Hamburg	New York	06/19/1887	10/23/1891			Y	
Rosenberg, Wolf	17	Russia	N	?	New York	00/00/1883				Y	10/17/1888
Rosenberger, Casper	37	Switzerland	Y	Antwerp	New York	05/25/1854	02/25/1856	26	128	N	
Rosenbloom, David	50	Poland	Y	Liverpool	New York	05/05/1881	05/26/1888			Y	
Rosenblum, Henry	22	Russia	Y	Hamburg	Philadelphia	06/01/1882	06/11/1883			Y	
Rosendahl, Peter	27	Prussia	Y	Antwerp	New York	06/25/1852	10/10/1854	11	219	N	
Rosendahle, Peter	27	Prussia	Y	Antwerp	New York	06/25/1852	10/10/1854	6	216	N	
Rosener, Herman	40	Oldenburg	Y	Bremen	Baltimore	09/01/1845	10/01/1848	1	169	N	
Rosenfeld, Adolph	42	Hungary	Y	Hamburg	New York	06/02/1885	10/24/1896			Y	
Rosenfeld, Adolph	36	Austria	Y	Bremen	New York	10/13/1886	09/03/1891			Y	
Rosenfeld, Max	40	Hungary	Y	Hamburg	Philadelphia	06/26/1891	10/24/1896			Y	
Rosenfelder, Franz Josep	30	Baden	Y	Havre	New Orleans	01/16/1854	09/26/1854	10	247	N	
Rosenfelder, Franz Josep	30	Baden	Y	Havre	New Orleans	01/16/1854	09/26/1854	12	186	N	
Rosenfelder, Theodore	29	Germany	Y	Antwerp	New York	09/24/1890	11/07/1893			Y	
Rosenfeldt, Julius	58	Germany	N	Hamburg	New York	07/??/1850	?			Y	
Rosenhamer, Simon	41	Germany	Y	Hamburg	New York	07/15/1881	06/15/1886			Y	
Rosenkranz, Joseph	??	Prussia	Y	?	?	10/??/1881	10/17/1882			Y	
Rosenkranz, Joseph	29	Austria	Y	Havre	New York	02/02/1883	07/25/1885			Y	
Rosenmond, Samuel	23	Austria	N	Galicia	New York	06/00/1879	00/00/1880			Y	00/00/1883
Rosenstein, Max	??	Hungary	Y	Hamburg	New York	01/02/1891	03/26/1897			Y	
Rosental, Bennett	23	Romania	Y	Liverpool	New York	09/00/1881	05/27/1883			Y	
Rosenthal, Abraham	49	Russia	Y	Liverpool	New York	08/??/1858	06/04/1888			Y	
Rosenthal, Christoph	28	Prussia	Y	Bremen	New Orleans	11/07/1847	02/19/1849	23	220	N	
Rosenthal, Hyman	36	Russia	Y	Hamburg	New York	01/29/1887	11/05/1895			Y	
Rosenthal, Isaac	47	Germany	Y	Bremen	New York	07/05/1877	10/24/1888			Y	

CITIZENSHIP RECORDS

APPLICANT	AGE	COUNTRY OF ORIGIN	DEC	DEPART PORT	ENTRY PORT	ARRIVE DATE	DEC DATE	VOL	PG.	FLD	NAT DATE
Rosenthal, Jacob	22	Russia	Y	Bremen	Baltimore	12/18/1888	08/20/1892			Y	
Rosenthal, Joseph	30	Russia	Y	Hamburg	New York	06/09/1886	05/17/1893			Y	
Rosenzweig, David	46	Russia	Y	Hamburg	Detroit	08/20/1891	11/06/1891			Y	
Rosenzweig, John	31	Germany	Y	Bremen	Baltimore	05/26/1890	05/11/1893			Y	
Rosenzweig, Louis	34	Russia	Y	Liverpool	New York	07/15/1882	10/14/1896			Y	
Roser, Matheus	29	Baden	Y	Havre	New Orleans	02/17/1853	05/30/1854	9	467	N	
Roser, Matheus	29	Baden	Y	Havre	New Orleans	02/17/1851	05/31/1854	10	50	N	
Rosewarne, William Henry	36	England	Y	Liverpool	New York	06/22/1876	08/09/1882			Y	
Rosewich, Mathias	47	Germany	Y	Hamburg	New York	09/??/1868	10/??/1875			Y	
Rosewich, Mathias	47	Germany	N	Hamburg	New York	09/??/1868	?			Y	
Rosinthal, Bennett	28	Romania	Y	Liverpool	New York	09/??/1881	05/27/1883	28	164	N	
Rosler, Alexander	34	Hesse Darmsta	Y	Havre	New Orleans	04/25/1859	03/21/1862	18	276	N	
Rosmann, Gerhard Bernard	60	Hanover	Y	Bremen	Baltimore	01/09/1849	10/28/1858	17	161	N	
Ross, Donald	29	Scotland	Y	Glasgow	New York	06/23/1882	03/30/1891	19	324	N	
Ross, Donald	29	Scotland	Y	Glasgow	New York	06/23/1882	03/30/1891			Y	
Ross, George (Rohsz?)	35	Baden	Y	Havre	New Orleans	02/01/1840	08/22/1848	22	227	N	
Ross, Herman Henry	33	Hanover	Y	Bremen	New Orleans	12/24/1852	12/26/1857	16	252	N	
Ross, John Gerhard	27	Prussia	Y	Bremen	New Orleans	05/02/1851	10/02/1854	10	367	N	
Ross, John Gerhard	27	Prussia	Y	Bremen	New Orleans	05/02/1851	10/02/1854	12	306	N	
Ross, Wilhelm	43	Germany	Y	Hamburg	Buffalo	11/23/1868	02/09/1892			Y	
Ross, William	29	England	Y	London	New York	08/??/1848	02/01/1853	7	100	N	
Rossel, Jacob	57	France	Y	Havre	New York	10/07/1869	04/29/1879			Y	
Rossi, Tobias	37	Rome	Y	Liverpool	New York	12/25/1855	04/19/1860	27	166	N	
Rost, August	33	Germany	Y	Antwerp	New York	04/19/1881	01/11/1886			Y	
Rost, George	22	Germany	Y	Bremen	Baltimore	08/04/1882	09/29/1885			Y	
Rost, John Henry	32	Hanover	Y	Bremen	New Orleans	10/??/1851	07/12/1855	11	379	N	
Rost, Ludwig	??	Wurttemberg	Y	Antwerp	New York	08/27/1848	12/??/1850	2	423	N	
Rost, Tobias	55	Germany	N	Bremen	Baltimore	07/26/1850	?			Y	
Rostentscher, Lothar T.C	41	Germany	Y	Hamburg	New York	09/14/1882	11/03/1886			Y	
Rostert, Lud	38	Wuerttemberg	Y	Havre	New York	08/16/1848	07/10/1860	27	217	N	
Rotermann, George	50	Germany	Y	?	?	09/15/1866	10/25/1893			Y	
Roth, Alois	26	Baden	Y	Liverpool	New York	08/05/1852	10/06/1854	10	478	N	
Roth, Alois	26	Baden	Y	Liverpool	New York	08/05/1852	10/06/1854	12	417	N	
Roth, Andrew	??	Germany	Y	?	?	?	12/13/1886			Y	
Roth, Anton	31	Prussia	Y	Havre	New York	06/18/1856	08/02/1860	27	243	N	
Roth, Conrad	28	Baden	Y	Havre	New York	05/09/1854	06/02/1856	14	277	N	
Roth, Conrad	36	Switzerland	Y	Havre	New York	07/24/1887	10/30/1889	19	272	N	
Roth, Diedrich	35	Hanover	Y	Bremen	Baltimore	05/14/1847	03/12/1851	3	255	N	
Roth, Fred	38	Germany	Y	Bremen	New York	04/07/1885	10/13/1892			Y	
Roth, Frederick	27	Germany	Y	Bremen	New York	06/14/1891	07/13/1898			Y	
Roth, George	38	Kurhessen	Y	Bremen	Baltimore	05/12/1846	01/28/1850	2	8	N	
Roth, George	54	Germany	Y	Havre	New York	11/10/1867	10/26/1894			Y	
Roth, Geroge	25	Germany	Y	Antwerp	New York	04/15/1882	03/31/1887	19	116	N	
Roth, Gustav	32	Germany	Y	Bremen	Baltimore	01/04/1883	10/29/1887			Y	
Roth, Henry	34	Hesse Darmsta	Y	Bremen	New York	05/20/1848	08/??/1851	4	163	N	
Roth, Henry	17	Germany	N	?	New York	00/00/1879				Y	10/26/1888
Roth, Herman	??	Germany	Y	?	?	?	08/01/1888			Y	
Roth, Jacob	19	Austria	Y	Hamburg	New York	08/15/1890	04/07/1891			Y	
Roth, Jacob	30	Germany	Y	Hamburg	New York	09/20/1882	10/20/1887			Y	
Roth, John	24	Hohenzollern	Y	Havre	New York	10/08/152	12/04/1855	14	279	N	
Roth, John	33	Wurttemberg	Y	Havre	New York	02/19/1853	10/01/1857	15	338	N	
Roth, John	45	Germany	Y	Havre	New York	05/28/1892	09/22/1893			Y	
Roth, Leon	42	Austria	Y	Rotterdam	New York	08/01/1891	01/27/1893			Y	
Roth, Lorenz	26	Baden	Y	Havre	New York	05/01/1854	06/02/1856	14	278	N	
Roth, Louis	26	Austria	Y	Bremen	Baltimore	07/13/1891	04/24/1893			Y	
Roth, Louis	26	Austria	Y	Bremen	Baltimore	07/13/1891	04/24/1893			Y	
Roth, Osias	27	Austria	Y	Hamburg	New York	05/04/1887	04/07/1891			Y	
Roth, Peter	35	Germany	Y	Antwerp	New York	06/??/1874	10/30/1884			Y	
Roth, Samuel	23	Austria	Y	Hamburg	New York	06/20/1892	04/24/1893			Y	

CITIZENSHIP RECORDS

APPLICANT	AGE	COUNTRY OF ORIGIN	DEC	DEPART PORT	ENTRY PORT	ARRIVE DATE	DEC DATE	VOL	PG.	FLD	NAT DATE
Roth, Xavier	41	France	Y	Havre	New Orleans	03/21/1848	05/31/1852	25	162	N	
Rothacker, Gottfried	26	Switzerland	Y	Antwerp	New York	05/02/1884	06/05/1888			Y	
Rothaus, Frederick	58	Germany	N	Havre	New York	08/20/1859	?			Y	
Rothe, Charles	34	Germany	Y	Liverpool	New York	10/27/1884	11/05/1888			Y	
Rothe, Traugott	27	Saxony	Y	Havre	New Orleans	06/??/1849	12/24/1850	2	389	N	
Rothenbach, John	24	Germany	Y	Bremen	Baltimore	03/14/1891	02/16/1893			Y	
Rothenbach, Lorenz	32	Germany	Y	Bremen	New York	08/08/1879	09/30/1884			Y	
Rothenberg, Herman	30	Germany	N	Bremen	Baltimore	08/??/1879	?			Y	
Rothenbuecher, Henry Sev	22	Germany	Y	Bremen	New York	09/20/1880	12/18/1880				
Rother, Oscar	30	Germany	Y	Hamburg	Baltimore	09/28/1889	03/07/1898			Y	
Rother, Richard	36	Germany	Y	Bremen	Baltimore	07/14/1881	02/07/1887			Y	
Rothermel, Valentine	22	Hesse Darmsta	Y	Rotterdam	New York	08/22/1846	02/06/1849	23	35	N	
Rothert, August	21	Hanover	Y	Bremen	Baltimore	05/24/1854	10/10/1854	6	218	N	
Rothert, August	21	Hanover	Y	Bremen	Baltimore	05/24/1854	10/10/1854	11	221	N	
Rothert, Heddo	21	Hanover	Y	Bremen	New Orleans	12/04/1849	01/31/1851	3	65	N	
Rothert, Henry	??	Hanover	Y	Bremen	Philadelphia	??/02/1845	12/04/1850	2	337	N	
Rothfuss, George	32	Wurttemberg	Y	Antwerp	New York	11/12/1853	02/21/1857	15	47	N	
Rothfuss, Lewis	25	Wurttemberg	Y	Antwerp	New York	11/05/1853	11/09/1858	17	310	N	
Rothhaas, George	45	Germany	Y	Havre	New York	08/??/1859	06/03/1879			Y	
Rothlauf, Christoph	24	Bavaria	Y	Bremen	Buffalo	06/??/1852	05/26/1856	26	549	N	
Rothmann, Christ F.	42	Germany	Y	Bremen	New York	08/15/1872	09/15/1883			Y	
Rothmann, Henry	36	Prussia	Y	Bremen	Richmond	09/03/1846	11/01/1852	5	88	N	
Rothschild, Emanuel	??	Germany	Y	?	?	?	03/17/1890			Y	
Rothschild, Max	40	Germany	N	Hamburg	New York	09/??/1865	?			Y	
Rothstein, Isaac	38	Russia	Y	Hamburg	New York	11/22/1885	10/24/1892			Y	
Rothus, Francis	22	Prussia	Y	Rotterdam	New York	09/02/1871	02/24/1873	18	559	N	
Rotker, Franz	34	Prussia	Y	Bremen	Baltimore	05/28/1845	05/16/1854	9	326	N	
Rotring, Henry	22	Prussia	Y	Havre	New Orleans	09/??/1846	02/17/1849	23	154	N	
Rotring, William	23	Prussia	Y	Bremen	New Orleans	09/20/1846	02/17/1849	23	151	N	
Rotter, Frank	54	Germany	N	Bremen	Baltimore	05/10/1860	06/??/1861	28	336	N	10/??/1866
Rotter, Frank	22	Germany	N	Bremen	Baltimore	05/10/1860	06/00/1861			Y	10/00/1866
Rotting, Theodore	??	Germany	Y	Liverpool	New York	03/14/1876	10/25/1890			Y	
Rottinghaus, Francis Jos	21	Oldenburg	Y	Bremen	New Orleans	12/29/1852	02/05/1856	26	40	N	
Rottinghaus, Henry	26	Oldenburg	Y	Bremen	New Orleans	06/13/1853	06/02/1856	14	275	N	
Rottinghaus, Henry	27	Germany	Y	Bremen	Baltimore	07/01/1880	06/13/1888			Y	
Rottinghaus, John Freder	23	Oldenburg	Y	Bremen	New Orleans	08/29/1851	09/05/1854			Y	
Rottker, Bernard	26	Germany	Y	Bremen	Baltimore	04/10/1882	04/11/1885			Y	
Rottler, Simon	36	Wuerttenberg	Y	Havre	New York	11/18/1851	06/17/1852	25	288	N	
Rottmann, Casper Henry	22	Prussia	Y	Bremen	New Orleans	01/17/1854	05/23/1856	26	543	N	
Rottmann, Frank	42	Germany	Y	Bremen	Baltimore	11/21/1869	10/05/1880			Y	
Rottmann, Peter	24	Prussia	Y	Bremen	New Orleans	05/??/1852	12/23/1852	5	443	N	
Rottmann, Sigmund	24	Saxony	Y	Bremen	Baltimore	06/04/1849	01/13/1851	2	491	N	
Rottmann, William	25	Germany	Y	Bremen	New York	12/24/1883	09/28/1889			Y	
Rottmueller, Frank	26	Germany	Y	Bremen	New York	07/10/1880	09/29/1883			Y	
Rottstein, Isaac	38	Russia	Y	Hamburg	New York	11/29/1885	10/24/1892	19	379	N	
Rottweiler, Andreas	27	Germany	Y	Bremen	New York	06/23/1888	10/30/1894			Y	
Rotzler, Gustav	30	Germany	Y	Havre	New York	05/26/1882	10/16/1888	19	150	N	
Rotzler, Gustav	30	Germany	Y	Havre	New York	05/26/1882	10/16/1888			Y	
Roughton, Gervase	??	Great Britain	Y	?	?	?	12/08/1887			Y	
Rourke, James	28	Ireland	Y	Dublin	New Orleans	11/??/1852	03/16/1858	16	409	N	
Rourke, Michael	30	Ireland	Y	Liverpool	New York	10/22/1847	11/14/1848	1	289	N	
Rourke, Patrick	23	Ireland	Y	Dublin	New York	06/??/1848	08/??/1851	4	186	N	
Rouse, John	28	Bavaria	Y	Bremen	New York	10/01/1845	10/02/1848	1	27	N	
Roust, Henry William	24	Hanover	Y	Bremen	Baltimore	06/08/1855	02/27/1858	16	345	N	
Routman, Louis	35	Russia	Y	Hamburg	New York	01/29/1891	12/19/1893			Y	
Rover, Henry	43	Germany	N	Bremen	New York	09/??/1865	?			Y	
Rover, Wilhelm	??	Germany	Y	?	?	?	09/14/1883			Y	
Rovler, William	40	Prussia	Y	Bremen	New Orleans	06/20/1851	05/25/1854	9	410	N	
Rowe, Edward	34	Ireland	Y	Liverpool	New York	12/10/1854	10/09/1860	27	472	N	

CITIZENSHIP RECORDS

APPLICANT	AGE	COUNTRY OF ORIGIN	DEC	DEPART PORT	ENTRY PORT	ARRIVE DATE	DEC DATE	VOL	PG.	FLD	NAT DATE
Rowe, James	43	England	Y	Liverpool	New York	07/05/1843	08/26/1862	18	401	N	
Rowe, Robert	34	England	Y	?	?	?	07/30/1896			Y	
Rower, Frederick	28	Prussia	Y	Bremen	New Orleans	05/22/1850	09/15/1852	25	528	N	
Rowin, Patrick	29	Ireland	Y	Liverpool	New Orleans	06/04/1843	02/08/1849	23	121	N	
Rowley, Joseph William	28	England	Y	London	New York	09/16/1849	03/18/1850	2	205	N	
Roy, Cornelius	53	Netherlands	N	Netherlands	New York	05/26/1866	?			Y	
Royan, Wilhelm	47	Germany	Y	Bremen	Baltimore	10/02/1883	08/02/1886			Y	
Ruane, Michael	24	Ireland	Y	Liverpool	New Orleans	12/15/1848	09/25/1856	14	374	N	
Rubel, John	23	Bavaria	Y	Havre	New York	02/28/1853	01/14/1856	13	461	N	
Ruben, Ben	17	Germany	N	?	Philadelphia	00/00/1883				Y	10/13/1888
Ruben, Jacob	25	Prussia	Y	London	Boston	07/30/1848	06/25/1851	3	443	N	
Ruberg, Gerhard Henry	55	Hanover	Y	Bremen	New Orleans	12/25/1844	01/12/1853	7	16	N	
Rubin, Davis	??	Russia	Y	?	?	?	09/06/1886			Y	
Rubin, Mendel	31	Russia	Y	Bremen	New York	05/20/1886	09/15/1891			Y	
Rubin, Moses	37	Russia	Y	Hamburg	New York	08/08/1885	07/18/1888			Y	
Rubinow, Isaac	26	Russia	Y	Hamburg	New York	02/28/1885	09/25/1891			Y	
Rubrecht, Louis	32	Wuerttemberg	Y	Havre	New York	11/02/1851	05/31/1852	25	153	N	
Ruckart, Alexander	30	Mecklenburg S	Y	Hamburg	New York	06/28/1852	05/01/1854	9	173	N	
Ruckdeschel, John Lorenz	22	Bavaria	Y	Bremen	New York	05/04/1852	11/03/1852	5	209	N	
Ruckdeschel, John Lorenz	22	Bavaria	Y	Bremen	New York	05/04/1852	11/03/1852	6	335	N	
Ruckhaber, Carl	30	Baden	Y	Antwerp	New Orleans	12/27/1854	01/02/1857	16	298	N	
Ruckriegel, John	29	Bavaria	Y	Bremerhafen	New York	10/20/1858	02/05/1861	18	90	N	
Ruckriegel, Stephen	33	Germany	Y	Hamburg	New York	04/23/1881	10/30/1884			Y	
Rucktaschel, Otto	25	Germany	Y	Bremen	New York	01/18/1880	04/04/1881			Y	
Rudd, Richard	36	England	Y	Liverpool	New Orleans	04/02/1848	03/19/1856	26	228	N	
Ruddy, Nicholas	26	Ireland	Y	Canada	Buffalo	12/25/1845	02/12/1849	23	74	N	
Rude, George	24	Prussia	Y	London	New Orleans	12/22/1849	03/14/1850	2	194	N	
Ruder, Charles	28	Wuertemberg	Y	Havre	New York	08/28/1853	04/07/1856	26	461	N	
Ruderer, Joseph	30	France	Y	Havre	New Orleans	05/20/1849	10/30/1851	4	441	N	
Rudler, Theophile	40	France	Y	?	New York	??/??/1871	09/27/1884			Y	
Rudloff, August	27	Germany	Y	?	New York	07/24/1877	12/22/1883			Y	
Rudolf, Matthias	30	Germany	Y	Bremen	Baltimore	09/02/1886	05/01/1893			Y	
Rudolf, Max	23	Germany	Y	Havre	New York	11/01/1879	09/19/1881			Y	
Rudolph, Aloys	33	Germany	Y	Antwerp	New York	07/09/1881	02/23/1882			Y	
Rudolph, George	33	Bavaria	Y	Bremen	New York	09/01/1854	03/19/1856	26	229	N	
Rudolph, Henry	23	Germany	Y	Rotterdam	New York	05/14/1888	10/12/1891			Y	
Rudolph, Max	??	Germany	Y	?	?	?	10/23/1890			Y	
Rudolphi, John	46	Germany	N	Rotterdam	New York	09/17/1881	?			Y	
Rudolphsen, John Frederi	44	Germany	Y	?	New York	11/06/1848	04/11/1871			Y	
Ruebelmann, Conrad	21	Baden	Y	Havre	New Orleans	03/04/1853	03/03/1856	26	152	N	
Ruebusch, John	61	Germany	Y	Bremen	Baltimore	11/12/1866	04/06/1885			Y	
Rueckert, Alexander	30	Mecklenburg S	Y	Hamburg	New York	06/28/1852	05/01/1854	8	301	N	
Rueckert, Philip	29	Germany	Y	Hamburg	New York	02/15/1877	03/09/1887			Y	
Ruecking, William	32	Germany	Y	Bremen	New York	05/27/1883	11/08/1889			Y	
Ruedi, John	28	Switzerland	Y	Havre	New York	02/25/1854	09/07/8157	15	235	N	
Ruediger, Carl	29	Germany	Y	Bremen	Baltimore	06/27/1883	11/26/1883			Y	
Ruehlmann, Adam	24	Germany	Y	Antwerp	New York	11/25/1888	03/30/1892			Y	
Ruelisch, Henry	24	Oldenburg	Y	Bremen	New York	10/20/1847	06/19/1851	3	431	N	
Ruelle, Bernard	28	Prussia	Y	Bremen	New York	03/01/1853	02/22/1858	16	329	N	
Ruemmel, Karl	33	Germany	Y	Bremen	Baltimore	07/06/1882	04/02/1888			Y	
Ruennebaum, H.	26	Germany	Y	Bremen	New York	01/28/1879	10/27/1884			Y	
Ruesch, Robert	26	Switzerland	Y	Havre	New York	04/01/1885	11/14/1887			Y	
Ruese, Conrad	25	Hanover	Y	Bremen	Baltimore	10/30/1853	09/25/1858	16	135	N	
Ruesse, Diederich	24	Hanover	Y	Bremen	New Orleans	05/25/1852	10/12/1857	15	392	N	
Ruesse, Henry	23	Hanover	Y	Bremen	Baltimore	10/31/1855	11/04/1858	17	274	N	
Ruesz, John Martin	48	Wurttemberg	Y	Havre	New York	07/04/1848	07/05/1851	3	482	N	
Rueter, Mathias	24	Germany	Y	Bremen	New York	06/19/1885	10/31/1890			Y	
Ruether, Joseph	36	Germany	Y	Bremen	Baltimore	08/25/1883	10/22/1884			Y	
Ruettinger, Emil	35	Coburg	Y	Hamburg	New York	??/07/1848	12/??/1850	2	413	N	

CITIZENSHIP RECORDS

APPLICANT	AGE	COUNTRY OF ORIGIN	DEC	DEPART PORT	ENTRY PORT	ARRIVE DATE	DEC DATE	VOL	PG.	FLD	NAT DATE
Ruewe, John Henry	23	Oldenburg	Y	Bremen	New Orleans	05/28/1849	10/13/1851	4	260	N	
Ruf, Albert	38	Germany	Y	Havre	New York	04/08/1882	10/23/1896			Y	
Ruf, Alexander	38	Wurttemberg	Y	Havre	New York	02/08/1847	01/18/1849	1	454	N	
Ruf, Charles (Karl?)	28	Baden	Y	Havre	New York	07/22/1858	10/08/1860	27	427	N	
Ruf, Isadore	30	Wuerttemberg	Y	London	New York	05/12/1848	02/10/1849	23	47	N	
Rufinbergen, John	54	Germany	Y	Bremen	New York	06/13/1880	09/25/1894	21	72	N	
Rufli, Mathias	26	Switzerland	Y	Havre	New York	??/12/1851	04/18/1855	11	273	N	
Rufli, Michael	41	Switzerland	Y	Havre	New York	12/12/1851	04/04/1853	7	529	N	
Ruge, Anton	33	Germany	Y	Bremen	Baltimore	11/05/1891	03/04/1897			Y	
Ruh, Henry	48	Hanover	Y	Bremen	New Orleans	01/02/1843	02/08/1849	23	120	N	
Ruh, Peter	41	Germany	Y	Havre	New York	03/15/1892	03/17/1897			Y	
Ruhe, Herman	24	Oldenburg	Y	Bremen	New York	06/02/1850	09/23/1854	10	180	N	
Ruhe, Herman	24	Oldenburg	Y	Bremen	New York	06/02/1850	09/23/1854	12	119	N	
Ruhl, Clemens	26	Hesse Darmsta	Y	Bremen	Baltimore	07/07/1857	10/08/1860	27	424	N	
Ruhl, Engelbert	28	Hesse Darmsta	Y	Rotterdam	New York	07/04/1855	11/01/1858	17	244	N	
Ruhl, Henry	35	Germany	Y	Bremen	New York	11/01/1880	02/08/1890			Y	
Ruhl, Konrad	21	Germany	Y	Rotterdam	New York	12/27/1885	12/29/1885			Y	
Ruhl, Louis	23	Germany	Y	Antwerp	New York	08/31/1885	12/28/1889			Y	
Ruhle, Christ	32	Wurttemberg	Y	Havre	New York	07/26/1853	11/11/1861	18	224	N	
Ruhling, Herman	??	Germany	Y	?	?	02/08/1882	10/30/1884			Y	
Ruhsmeyer, Henry	34	Germany	N	Bremen	New York	11/02/1871	?			Y	
Rukin, Meier	38	Russia	Y	Hamburg	New York	09/25/1887	09/06/1889			Y	
Rukin, Meyer	24	Russia	Y	?	New York	11/00/1889	09/09/1892			Y	
Ruls, Marks	??	Prussia	Y	Antwerp	New York	??/27/1846	12/05/1850	2	339	N	
Rume, August (Ruwe?)	34	Germany	Y	Havre	New York	12/16/1881	09/21/1883			Y	
Ruminski, Joseph	38	Germany	Y	Havre	New York	08/01/1873	10/11/1884			Y	
Rumker, Johan Gerhard	35	Germany	Y	Bremen	New York	05/02/1888	05/29/1895			Y	
Rumker, John Hermann	33	Germany	Y	Bremen	New York	05/02/1888	10/19/1895			Y	
Rummel, John	43	Germany	Y	Rotterdam	New York	11/24/1881	11/27/1885			Y	
Rump, Arthur R.	??	England	Y	?	?	?	06/27/1890			Y	
Rump, Henry	33	Germany	Y	Bremen	New York	05/15/1883	09/26/1891			Y	
Rumpel, John	44	Germany	N	Rotterdam	New York	06/20/1869	?			Y	
Rumpf, Andreas	33	Germany	Y	Antwerp	New York	08/10/1885	02/27/1889			Y	
Rumpke, Frederick	36	Germany	Y	Bremen	New York	10/01/1884	11/30/1887			Y	
Rumpke, Herman	26	Germany	Y	?	New York	??/??/1882	05/08/1884			Y	
Rumpke, Theodore	22	Germany	Y	?	New York	05/04/1882	07/13/1885			Y	
Rumpke, August	38	Germany	Y	Bremen	New York	05/21/1872	03/18/1892			Y	
Rund, Frederick	38	Baden	Y	Havre	New York	06/??/1846	10/06/1856	14	213	N	
Rund, Jacob	46	Bavaria	Y	Havre	New Orleans	??/04/1846	11/20/1849	23	353	N	
Runde, John Herman	24	Hanover	Y	Bremen	New York	06/18/1849	01/06/1851	2	465	N	
Runge, H. William	63	Germany	N	Hanover	New York	05/02/1849	?			Y	
Runge, Herman	34	Germany	Y	Bremen	Baltimore	06/16/1882	11/04/1886	19	110	N	
Runge, Herman	34	Germany	Y	Bremen	Baltimore	06/16/1882	03/04/1890			Y	
Runge, Joseph	25	Germany	Y	Amsterdam	New York	11/29/1887	01/11/1888			Y	
Runge, Philip	40	Prussia	Y	Bremen	New York	05/25/1854	04/17/1862	18	319	N	
Runge, William Victor	??	Hanover	Y	Bremen	Baltimore	05/25/1844	10/09/1848	22	499	N	
Runk, Peter	47	Hesse Darmsta	Y	Antwerp	New York	07/14/1849	01/22/1852	24	54	N	
Runtz, Marx	66	Germany	N	Havre	New Orleans	05/19/1841	06/??/1846	28	5	N	06/??/1848
Runtz, Marx	20	Germany	N	Havre	New Orleans	05/19/1841	06/00/1846			Y	06/00/1848
Ruoff, Gottfried	26	Wurttemberg	Y	Havre	New York	04/28/1854	03/31/1857	15	112	N	
Rupell, Patrick	23	Ireland	Y	Liverpool	New York	10/14/1852	10/01/1856	14	132	N	
Rupertus, Gottfried	26	Prussia	Y	Hamburg	New York	08/25/1853	09/22/1854	10	160	N	
Rupertus, Gottfried	26	Prussia	Y	Hamburg	New York	08/25/1853	09/22/18??	12	99	N	
Rupertus, Gottleib	23	Hanover	Y	Hamburg	New York	08/30/1854	09/22/1854	10	161	N	
Rupertus, Gottlieb	23	Prussia	Y	Hamburg	New York	08/30/1854	09/22/1854	12	100	N	
Rupp, Adolf	30	Switzerland	Y	South Hampto	New York	07/29/1894	10/15/1900			Y	
Rupp, Frederick	24	Bavaria	Y	Rotterdam	New York	07/01/1846	02/19/1849	23	174	N	
Rupp, Paul	44	Bavaria	Y	Havre	New York	04/11/1852	10/27/1858	17	122	N	
Rupp, Valentine	23	Bavaria	Y	Havre	New Orleans	10/01/1847	02/23/1852	24	150	N	

CITIZENSHIP RECORDS

APPLICANT	AGE	COUNTRY OF ORIGIN	DEC	DEPART PORT	ENTRY PORT	ARRIVE DATE	DEC DATE	VOL	PG.	FLD	NAT DATE
Ruppel, Simon	30	Hesse Homberg	Y	London	New York	07/15/1848	01/22/1852	24	55	N	
Ruppersberg, John	22	Hesse Cassel	Y	Bremen	Baltimore	10/10/1858	10/08/1860	27	401	N	
Ruppert, Gottfried	22	Bavaria	Y	Havre	New York	10/01/1852	03/25/1856	26	295	N	
Ruppiler, Theodore	34	Prussia	Y	Bremen	New Orleans	?	03/18/1851	3	304	N	
Rupprecht, Anton	29	Austria	Y	Havre	New York	05/04/1882	05/22/1884			Y	
Rusche, Fred	17	Germany	N	?	New York	00/00/1877				Y	10/23/1888
Ruschenbeck, Frank	66	Germany	N	Bremen	New York	06/??/1849	?			Y	
Ruscher, F.H.H.	26	Germany	Y	Bremen	Baltimore	03/29/1883	10/28/1886			Y	
Ruscher, Henry	52	Germany	Y	Bremen	New York	11/20/1892	01/27/1904			Y	
Ruscher, Wilhelm	30	Germany	Y	Bremen	New York	09/02/1887	11/11/1891			Y	
Ruschke, August	48	Germany	Y	Stettin	New York	08/31/1880	10/23/1884			Y	
Ruschulte, George	28	Hanover	Y	Bremen	Baltimore	06/01/1857	09/13/1860	27	372	N	
Russell, Benjamin E.	27	England	Y	?	?	11/05/1885	07/15/1893			Y	
Russell, Forster	??	Ireland	Y	?	?	04/??/1886	05/08/1895			Y	
Russell, Henry	32	England	Y	Liverpool	Buffalo	??/??/1872	02/13/1882			Y	
Russell, James	32	Ireland	Y	Liverpool	New Orleans	12/??/1849	03/28/1853	7	430	N	
Russell, John	34	Scotland	Y	Liverpool	New York	06/07/1849	03/31/1853	7	468	N	
Russell, Michael	25	Ireland	Y	Liverpool	New Orleans	09/13/1848	09/11/1852	25	449	N	
Russell, Patrick	39	Ireland	Y	Liverpool	New York	05/06/1854	12/04/1868			Y	
Russo, Antonio	50	Italy	Y	Naples	New York	06/14/1884	03/30/1902			Y	
Russo, Michele	26	Italy	Y	Naples	New York	06/07/1891	05/15/1894			Y	
Rust, Herman	33	Bremen	Y	Bremen	New York	07/01/1841	09/06/1852	25	387	N	
Rusthe, J. Hermann	??	Germany	Y	?	?	?	07/30/1896			Y	
Rutemeyer, Fred	32	Germany	Y	Bremen	New York	07/04/1872	10/09/1884			Y	
Ruter, Henry	25	Hanover	Y	Bremen	New Orleans	11/13/1847	02/05/1849	23	34	N	
Ruth, Robert	29	Baden	Y	London	New York	08/17/1853	12/31/1855	13	410	N	
Ruthe, Gustav H.A.	33	Germany	Y	Bremen	New York	09/11/1869	09/05/1879			Y	
Ruthmann, Henry	24	Hanover	Y	Bremen	New Orleans	11/12/1854	02/02/1856	13	536	N	
Rutter, Heinrich	27	Germany	Y	Bremen	New York	10/02/1892	10/27/1899			Y	
Ruttinger, Joseph	22	Baden	Y	Havre	New York	04/16/1857	09/06/1860	27	341	N	
Ruttolph, Nicolaus	21	Bavaria	Y	London	New York	04/20/1852	12/12/1855	13	305	N	
Rutz, John	23	Germany	Y	Antwerp	New York	09/09/1886	04/11/1887			Y	
Ruwe, George Herman	27	Hanover	Y	Bremen	New Orleans	10/12/1852	10/09/1854	11	54	N	
Ruwe, George Hermann	27	Hanover	Y	Bremen	New Orleans	10/12/1852	10/09/1854	6	53	N	
Ruwe, Henry	45	Germany	N	Bremen	New York	09/05/1860	?			Y	
Ruwe, Theodor A.	22	Germany	Y	Bremen	Baltimore	08/31/1881	06/05/1885			Y	
Ruzirka, John	26	Switzerland	Y	Havre	New York	06/22/1887	10/27/1892	19	392	N	
Ryan, Cornelius	46	Ireland	Y	Liverpool	New York	09/20/1848	06/23/1851	3	442	N	
Ryan, Denis	40	Ireland	Y	Liverpool	New Orleans	02/12/1852	10/21/1852	5	38	N	
Ryan, Dennis	26	Ireland	Y	Liverpool	New Orleans	04/12/1852	08/04/1856	14	338	N	
Ryan, Edward	29	Ireland	Y	Queenstown	New York	08/29/1889	01/22/1891			Y	
Ryan, Francis	25	Ireland	Y	Liverpool	Boston	04/01/1848	03/22/1850	2	234	N	
Ryan, James	28	Ireland	Y	Liverpool	New Orleans	12/20/1850	12/15/1851	4	521	N	
Ryan, James	28	Ireland	Y	Liverpool	New York	04/08/1846	02/14/1853	7	155	N	
Ryan, James	41	Ireland	Y	Liverpool	New York	09/??/1880	10/30/1883			Y	
Ryan, James	37	Ireland	Y	Dublin	Philadelphia	05/30/1849	05/20/1852	25	57	N	
Ryan, James	26	Ireland	Y	Dublin	New York	09/13/1849	09/10/1852	25	440	N	
Ryan, John	25	Ireland	Y	Liverpool	New Orleans	10/22/1845	11/20/1848	1	338	N	
Ryan, John	35	Ireland	Y	Liverpool	Messina	06/15/1837	02/18/1850	2	88	N	
Ryan, John	27	Ireland	Y	Liverpool	New Orleans	11/19/1849	01/29/1853	7	82	N	
Ryan, John	32	Ireland	Y	Liverpool	New York	09/28/1881	10/15/1889	19	239	N	
Ryan, John	32	Ireland	Y	Liverpool	New York	09/28/1881	10/15/1889			Y	
Ryan, John	28	Ireland	N	Queenstown	New York	07/??/1879	?			Y	
Ryan, John	25	Ireland	Y	Liverpool	New York	04/04/1847	04/14/1852	24	500	N	
Ryan, John	47	Ireland	Y	Liverpool	New Orleans	03/19/1849	08/23/1852	25	340	N	
Ryan, John	20	Ireland	Y	Queenstown	New York	05/20/1882	10/12/1882			Y	
Ryan, John J. Jr.	??	Ireland	N	?	?	09/25/1879				Y	10/20/1892
Ryan, John Joseph	37	Ireland	N	Ireland	New York	06/15/1867	?			Y	
Ryan, Michael	22	Ireland	Y	Canada	Buffalo	10/29/1848	02/12/1851	3	124	N	

CITIZENSHIP RECORDS

APPLICANT	AGE	COUNTRY OF ORIGIN	DEC	DEPART PORT	ENTRY PORT	ARRIVE DATE	DEC DATE	VOL	PG.	FLD	NAT DATE
Ryan, Michael	25	Ireland	Y	Liverpool	New Orleans	01/10/1849	10/16/1851	4	312	N	
Ryan, Michael	34	Ireland	Y	Liverpool	New York	12/08/1851	11/15/1852	5	279	N	
Ryan, Michael	34	Ireland	Y	Liverpool	New York	12/08/1851	11/15/1852	6	403	N	
Ryan, Michael	25	Ireland	Y	Liverpool	New York	05/12/1847	02/17/1853	7	173	N	
Ryan, Michael	24	Ireland	Y	Limerick	New York	04/01/1849	09/25/1854	10	188	N	
Ryan, Michael	24	Ireland	Y	Liverpool	New York	04/01/1849	09/25/1854	12	127	N	
Ryan, Michael	22	Ireland	Y	Liverpool	New York	03/28/1859	06/19/1862	18	357	N	
Ryan, Michael	40	Ireland	Y	Liverpool	New York	09/11/1887	10/17/1892	19	366	N	
Ryan, Michael	26	Ireland	Y	Liverpool	New York	10/31/1882	01/07/1888			Y	
Ryan, Michael	40	Ireland	Y	Liverpool	New York	09/11/1887	10/17/1892			Y	
Ryan, Michael	50	Ireland	N	Liverpool	New Orleans	12/??/1852	?			Y	
Ryan, Michael	25	Ireland	Y	Liverpool	New York	09/??/1854	02/04/1856	26	39	N	
Ryan, Patrick	24	Ireland	Y	Queenstown	Boston	05/28/1888	10/18/1892	19	370	N	
Ryan, Patrick	19	Ireland	Y	Queenstown	New York	10/13/1888	03/25/1890			Y	
Ryan, Patrick Joseph	??	Ireland	N	?	?	03/21/1868				Y	10/20/1892
Ryan, Peter	25	Ireland	Y	Liverpool	New Orleans	04/15/1848	10/30/1852	5	76	N	
Ryan, Thomas	28	Ireland	Y	Liverpool	New York	09/28/1853	09/27/1854	10	278	N	
Ryan, Thomas	28	Ireland	Y	Liverpool	New York	09/28/1853	09/27/1854	12	217	N	
Ryan, Timothy F.	49	Ireland	N	Queenstown	New York	03/23/1866	?			Y	
Ryan, William	49	Ireland	N	Liverpool	New York	05/03/1859	?			Y	
Ryan, William	22	Ireland	Y	Liverpool	New York	05/01/1859	10/09/1860	27	470	N	
Ryan, William	58	Ireland	N	Waterford	Ellensburg N	07/12/1849	09/??/1859	28	230	N	10/??/1871
Ryan, William	21	Ireland	N	Waterford	Ellensburg,	07/12/1849	09/00/1849			Y	10/00/1871
Ryder, Gideon W.	49	Canada	Y	Delhi, Canad	Drayton, Dak	03/10/1893	10/20/1899			Y	
Ryder, Patrick B.	28	Canada	Y	Sarnia	Port Huron	10/14/1892	07/31/1896			Y	
Saal, Gerhard	31	Bavaria	Y	Antwerp	New York	11/24/1847	03/22/1853	7	367	N	
Saaln, August Christian	27	Hanover	Y	Bremen	Baltimore	08/18/1846	02/05/1849	23	26	N	
Saalwachter, Heinrich	45	Germany	Y	Hamburg	New York	11/07/1880	02/12/1883			Y	
Saalwachter, William	24	Germany	Y	Rotterdam	New York	08/16/1884	05/11/1886			Y	
Saalwaechter, Casper	61	Germany	Y	Rotterdam	New York	08/10/1884	11/01/1886			Y	
Sabath, Jacob	31	Germany	Y	Hamburg	New York	11/17/1881	02/19/1889			Y	
Sabirowsky, Wilhelm	29	Germany	Y	Bremen	Baltimore	06/02/1881	10/27/1884			Y	
Sachs, Alexander J.	40	Austria	Y	Bremen	New York	07/20/1890	01/08/1897			Y	
Sachs, Christian	30	Germany	Y	Hamburg	New York	08/11/1891	07/01/1903			Y	
Sachs, Elias	39	Russia	Y	Hamburg	New York	09/30/1881	06/20/1893			Y	
Sachs, Harry	46	Russia	Y	Hamburg	New York	01/16/1890	11/16/1894			Y	
Sachs, Kolman	22	Germany	Y	Hamburg	Philadelphia	10/03/1887	04/07/1890			Y	
Sack, Jacob	40	Prussia	Y	Bremen	Baltimore	11/28/1853	11/08/1855	13	194	N	
Sack, John H.	23	Oldenburg	Y	Bremen	Baltimore	10/25/1857	10/06/1860	27	403	N	
Sackmann, Charles	22	Germany	Y	Havre	New York	04/20/1881	10/15/1883			Y	
Sadelfeld, Frederick	32	Oldenburg	Y	Bremen	Baltimore	10/14/1845	06/01/1852	25	169	N	
Sadelfeld, Herman	38	Germany	Y	Hamburg	New York	09/15/1874	12/08/1893			Y	
Sadiet, Whoby Joseph	??	Syria	Y	?	?	?	08/16/1888			Y	
Sadler, Anton	49	Baden	Y	Havre	New York	05/??/1846	10/28/1850	2	315	N	
Sadler, F.	43	Germany	Y	Bremen	Baltimore	12/03/1882	01/04/1886			Y	
Sadouski, Julius	??	Germany	Y	?	?	?	03/29/1887			Y	
Saeger, Michael	31	Germany	N	Liverpool	New York	01/23/1872	?			Y	
Saehr, George P.	29	Germany	Y	Bremen	Baltimore	03/10/1892	02/10/1897			Y	
Saehr, Gustav	39	Germany	Y	Bremen	Baltimore	03/12/1892	08/14/1895			Y	
Saelinger, Andrew	42	Baden	Y	Havre	New Orleans	01/20/1854	02/08/1855	13	294	N	
Saenger, Fred	53	Germany	Y	Havre	New York	03/01/1881	10/18/1886			Y	
Saffran, Max	??	Russia	Y	?	?	?	10/06/1893			Y	
Saga, Albert	42	Germany	Y	Havre	New York	07/11/1873	10/09/1884			Y	
Sage, John Charles	27	France	Y	Havre	New Orleans	11/13/1847	10/13/1848	1	194	N	
Sagel, Henry	40	Germany	Y	Bremen	New York	09/06/1875	10/09/1880			Y	
Sagmeister, Joseph	30	Germany	Y	Antwerp	New York	05/04/1872	04/01/1882			Y	
Sahner, Wendell	57	Prussia	Y	Havre	New York	07/01/1852	10/25/1858	17	105	N	
Sahrbeck, Gerhard	26	Prussia	Y	Bremen	New Orleans	11/29/1852	06/05/1854	10	79	N	
Sahrbeck, Gerhard	26	Prussia	Y	Bremen	New Orleans	11/29/1852	06/05/1854	12	16	N	

CITIZENSHIP RECORDS

APPLICANT	AGE	COUNTRY OF ORIGIN	DEC	DEPART PORT	ENTRY PORT	ARRIVE DATE	DEC DATE	VOL	PG.	FLD	NAT DATE
Sahrbeck, Joseph	30	Prussia	Y	Bremen	New Orleans	12/14/1854	06/05/1854	10	78	N	
Sahrbeck, Joseph	30	Prussia	Y	Bremen	New Orleans	12/14/1851	06/05/1854	12	15	N	
Saile, George	26	Wurttemberg	Y	Havre	New York	02/12/1853	11/05/1860	18	19	N	
Sailer, Frederick	21	Wuerttemberg	Y	Antwerp	New York	??/10/1849	11/24/1849	23	371	N	
Sailer, John	41	Baden	Y	Havre	New York	12/26/1854	04/21/1862	18	325	N	
Sailer, Joseph	25	Germany	Y	?	?	?	10/20/1884			Y	
Saisall, Thomas	??	Great Britain	Y	?	?	?	10/26/1887			Y	
Sajovitz, Mendel	30	Russia	Y	Bremen	New York	01/09/1888	05/19/1890			Y	
Sakenhen, John Jovokus	??	Germany	Y	?	?	?	10/04/1883			Y	
Salamone, Antonino	34	Italy	Y	Palermo	New York	08/30/1889	10/18/1893			Y	
Salamone, Antonio	34	Italy	Y	Palermo	New York	08/30/1889	10/18/1893	21	25	N	
Salathin, Henry	32	Switzerland	Y	Havre	New Orleans	05/16/1848	07/03/1851	3	480	N	
Salheb, John	38	Syria	Y	Tripolis	New Orleans	12/25/1888	02/02/1892			Y	
Salimano, Bengdeto	??	Italy	N	Genoa	New York	05/10/1850	?			Y	
Sallaz, Charles Rudolf	23	Switzerland	Y	?	?	00/00/1883	11/02/1886			Y	
Salm, Andrew	29	Baden	Y	Antwerp	New York	08/20/1847	08/23/1848	22	237	N	
Salm, Jacob	40	Germany	Y	Bremen	New York	09/17/1883	03/07/1901			Y	
Salmon, Joseph	38	Russia	Y	Rotterdam	New York	07/05/1891	12/14/1895			Y	
Salpius, August	42	Prussia	Y	Bremen	New York	12/24/1851	02/18/1858	16	316	N	
Salvatorelli, Guisseppe	??	Italy	Y	?	?	?	09/19/1894			Y	
Salwasser, Conrad	40	Russia	Y	Bremen	Baltimore	03/26/1892	06/01/1903			Y	
Salway, Harry	24	England	Y	London	New York	11/10/1890	11/28/1892			Y	
Salzer, John	27	Wuertemberg	Y	Havre	New York	09/11/1854	03/24/1856	26	263	N	
Salziger, George	48	Nassau	Y	London	New York	08/24/1852	11/06/1855	13	180	N	
Salziger, Henry George	44	Nassau	Y	London	New York	08/24/1852	11/06/1855	13	179	N	
Salzmann, George	35	Prussia	Y	Bremen	New York	08/23/1849	07/15/1851	3	542	N	
Salzmann, Henry	??	Prussia	Y	Bremen	New Orleans	??/02/1847	12/??/1850	2	427	N	
Samkovy, Mayer	29	Russia	Y	Liverpool	New York	04/15/1887	07/20/1891			Y	
Samm, Charles	28	Mecklenburg S	Y	Hamburg	New York	05/28/1855	07/09/1855	11	367	N	
Sammet, Heinrich	30	Hesse Darmsta	Y	Bremen	New York	08/06/1854	11/09/1855	13	202	N	
Sammet, Wilhelm	24	Germany	Y	Bremen	Baltimore	05/27/1888	07/18/1889			Y	
Sampson, James B.	23	Ireland	Y	Liverpool	Philadelphia	11/08/1848	10/10/1854	6	220	N	
Sampson, James B.	23	Ireland	Y	Liverpool	Philadelphia	11/08/1848	10/10/1854	11	224	N	
Sampson, Joseph	60	Ireland	Y	Liverpool	Philadelphia	11/07/1848	04/04/1853	7	518	N	
Samson, Charles	26	Germany	Y	Havre	New York	04/20/1889	09/22/1890			Y	
Samuels, Aaron	??	Russia	Y	?	?	?	12/21/1889			Y	
Samuels, Benjamin	39	Russia	Y	Hamburg	New York	03/20/1891	01/17/1896			Y	
Samuels, Moses	35	Poland	Y	Southhampton	New York	03/12/1857	09/16/1857	15	276	N	
Samuels, Saul	39	Russia	Y	London	New York	01/15/1855	04/10/1858	16	465	N	
Sand, Gerd Christian	40	Hanover	Y	Bremen	New Orleans	06/14/1854	02/27/1860	27	113	N	
Sand, Henry	27	Hanover	Y	Bremen	New York	04/30/1849	03/20/1851	3	241	N	
Sand, Herman	25	Hanover	Y	Bremen	Baltimore	10/17/1848	03/20/1851	3	240	N	
Sand, J. H. Clements	41	Germany	Y	Bremen	New York	08/28/1887	07/05/1893			Y	
Sand, Jacob	27	Germany	Y	Havre	New York	08/01/1883	09/10/1883			Y	
Sand, Joseph	34	Hanover	Y	Bremen	Havre	03/15/1847	02/10/1862	18	257	N	
Sand, William	31	Hanover	Y	Bremen	New Orleans	02/27/1846	03/20/1851	3	239	N	
Sandbeck, Hugo Conrad	35	Germany	Y	Hamburg	New York	01/20/1884	10/21/1889			Y	
Sandbrink, Diedrich	40	Germany	Y	Bremen	New York	05/01/1878	03/31/1899			Y	
Sandemann, Ferdinand	31	Germany	Y	Bremen	Baltimore	09/17/1871	10/07/1878			Y	
Sandemann, Heinrich	47	Germany	Y	Bremen	Baltimore	05/26/1882	03/30/1888			Y	
Sander, Bernard Henry	22	Hanover	Y	Bremen	New Orleans	05/30/1852	10/06/1854	10	500	N	
Sander, Bernard Henry	22	Hanover	Y	Bremen	New Orleans	05/30/1852	10/06/1854	12	439	N	
Sander, Clements	??	Oldenburg	Y	Bremen	Baltimore	10/06/1847	10/07/1848	22	475	N	
Sander, Franz Henry	28	Hanover	Y	Bremen	New Orleans	01/01/1853	10/06/1854	10	502	N	
Sander, Franz Henry	28	Hanover	Y	Bremen	New Orleans	01/01/1853	10/06/1854	12	441	N	
Sander, Frederick	21	Prussia	Y	Bremen	New York	09/??/1854	09/14/1857	15	269	N	
Sander, Frederick	62	Germany	Y	Bremen	Baltimore	05/25/1866	10/20/1886	19	60	N	
Sander, Frederick	62	Germany	Y	Bremen	Baltimore	05/25/1866	10/21/1886			Y	
Sander, George	39	Germany	Y	Bremen	Baltimore	04/28/1873	08/15/1884			Y	

CITIZENSHIP RECORDS

APPLICANT	AGE	COUNTRY OF ORIGIN	DEC	DEPART PORT	ENTRY PORT	ARRIVE DATE	DEC DATE	VOL	PG.	FLD	NAT DATE
Sander, Gerhard	55	Germany	Y	Bremen	Baltimore	07/11/1882	05/08/1886			Y	
Sander, Gottlieb	25	Brunswick	Y	Hamburg	New Orleans	01/02/1846	11/17/1848	1	311	N	
Sander, Heinrich	23	Germany	Y	Rotterdam	New York	08/10/1892	12/30/1893			Y	
Sander, Henry	54	Mecklenburg S	Y	Hamburg	New York	12/20/1851	05/30/1856	14	270	N	
Sander, Henry	22	Hanover	Y	Bremen	New York	09/13/1868	01/10/1872	18	453	N	
Sander, Henry	31	Germany	Y	Bremen	Baltimore	07/30/1884	04/08/1889			Y	
Sander, Henry	35	Germany	N	Bremen	Baltimore	06/??/1866	?			Y	
Sander, John	21	Germany	Y	Rotterdam	New York	08/13/1892	11/17/1894			Y	
Sander, Theodor	24	Germany	Y	Antwerp	Boston	03/24/1887	12/28/1891			Y	
Sanderberger, Peter	24	Sweden	Y	Liverpool	New York	07/17/1854	12/17/1855	13	324	N	
Sandermann, Heinrich	22	Oldenburg	Y	Bremen	New York	09/12/1857	11/01/1860	27	532	N	
Sandermann, Henry	??	Oldenburg	Y	Bremen	Baltimore	??/15/1848	03/28/1851	3	364	N	
Sanders, Fred	35	Germany	Y	Amsterdam	New York	08/22/1885	12/27/1894			Y	
Sanders, William	40	Germany	N	Bremen	Baltimore	09/??/1864	?			Y	
Sanderson, James	36	Scotland	Y	Lieth	New York	05/16/1882	01/17/1888			Y	
Sanderson, Morris W.	16	England	N	?	New York	00/00/1867				Y	10/23/1888
Sandheger, H.	23	Germany	Y	Bremen	New York	06/??/1881	07/11/1884			Y	
Sandherr, Joseph	44	Germany	Y	Bremen	Baltimore	05/19/1887	11/02/1891			Y	
Sandker, William	26	Germany	Y	Bremen	?	?	10/29/1888	19	201	N	
Sandker, William	29	Germany	Y	Bremen	New York	09/04/1882	10/30/1888			Y	
Sandman, John F.	30	Oldenburg	Y	Bremen	New Orleans	11/15/1850	06/10/1852	25	312	N	
Sandmann, Frederick	26	Hanover	Y	Bremen	Baltimore	07/??/1845	01/??/1850	23	452	N	
Sandmann, Henry Herman	22	Hanover	Y	Bremen	New Orleans	12/14/1852	02/06/1856	26	53	N	
Sandmann, Joseph	23	Oldenburg	Y	Bremen	New Orleans	05/04/1849	05/24/1852	25	98	N	
Sandmeier, Jacob William	32	Prussia	Y	Bremen	Galveston	??/25/1846	11/??/1849	23	313	N	
Sandowitz, Jacob	60	Russia	Y	Hamburg	New York	07/29/1886	10/24/1903			Y	
Sandoz, Wilhelm	28	Germany	Y	Amsterdam	New York	08/27/1881	11/30/1888			Y	
Sands, Edward	22	Ireland	Y	Liverpool	New York	02/04/1849	02/27/1850	2	135	N	
Sandstrom, John	34	Sweden	Y	Stockholm	New York	10/12/1883	02/05/1894			Y	
Sanftleben, Heinrich	30	Prussia	Y	Bremen	Baltimore	11/18/1859	01/04/1860	27	29	N	
Sange, Otto	36	Germany	Y	Antwerp	New York	03/29/1883	07/15/1886			Y	
Sanger, Joseph	39	Germany	N	Hamburg	New York	07/01/1854	?			Y	
Sanguinete, Dominic	44	Sardinia	Y	Montovidel	New York	05/18/1847	10/20/1858	17	76	N	
Sannemann, Herman	27	Germany	Y	Bremen	New York	09/24/1894	12/20/1897			Y	
Sanning, Theodore	25	Hanover	Y	Bremen	New Orleans	06/15/1849	11/04/1852	5	222	N	
Sanning, Theodore	25	Hanover	Y	Bremen	New Orleans	06/15/1849	11/04/1852	6	348	N	
Sans, Lucius	22	Germany	Y	Bremen	New York	06/07/1889	11/02/1893			Y	
Sansone, Vincenzo	26	Italy	Y	Palermo	New York	10/14/1883	02/06/1889			Y	
Santas, Julius	23	Baden	Y	Havre	New York	05/29/1854	09/29/1856	14	26	N	
Santel, Henry	23	Hanover	Y	Liverpool	New York	05/03/1868	12/08/1871	18	442	N	
Santen, William	27	Germany	Y	Amsterdam	New York	11/02/1890	10/28/1895			Y	
Santo, Edward	31	Germany	Y	Havre	New York	11/12/1887	02/10/1896			Y	
Santoro, Michael	37	Italy	Y	Naples	New York	04/10/1882	09/21/1891			Y	
Sanz, John	23	Bavaria	Y	Liverpool	New York	06/03/1851	04/17/1854	8	132	N	
Sanz, John	23	Bavaria	Y	Liverpool	New York	06/03/1851	04/17/1854	9	4	N	
Sapinski, Frank	22	Russia	Y	Hamburg	New York	05/04/1892	01/17/1894			Y	
Sarnbitz, Lorenz	26	Baden	Y	Havre	New Orleans	10/01/1847	07/??/1848	22	4	N	
Sarsfield, James	24	Ireland	Y	Liverpool	New Orleans	05/20/1852	04/25/1853	8	115	N	
Sarsfield, Michael	30	Ireland	Y	Canada	Boston	08/??/1844	03/28/1853	7	428	N	
Sarson, Emil	??	Italy	Y	?	?	?	06/05/1901			Y	
Sarteri, Martin	21	Baden	Y	Havre	New Orleans	05/27/1850	12/24/1851	24	1	N	
Sas, Frederick	26	Mecklenburg S	Y	Hamburg	New York	07/01/1852	04/27/1854	9	147	N	
Saslavsky, Samuel	36	Russia	Y	Hamburg	Philadelphia	05/15/1882	10/30/1886			Y	
Sass, Harris	32	Russia	Y	Glasgow	New York	01/??/1887	10/06/1892	19	355	N	
Sass, Max	40	Russia	Y	Bremen	Baltimore	06/20/1889	07/02/1898			Y	
Sasse, Carl	42	Germany	Y	Bremen	Baltimore	02/28/1884	12/04/1889			Y	
Sasse, Mathias	29	Germany	Y	Amsterdam	New York	11/21/1883	03/25/1889			Y	
Sasslasky, Nathan	25	Russia	Y	Bremen	New York	12/13/1892	01/19/1897			Y	
Satter, Edward	32	Baden	Y	Havre	New York	05/20/1854	12/12/1857	16	218	N	

CITIZENSHIP RECORDS

APPLICANT	AGE	COUNTRY OF ORIGIN	DEC	DEPART PORT	ENTRY PORT	ARRIVE DATE	DEC DATE	VOL	PG.	FLD	NAT DATE
Sattler, George	38	Brunswick	Y	Bremen	Baltimore	07/08/1846	09/07/1852	25	389	N	
Sattler, Martin	21	Wurttemberg	Y	Havre	New York	05/08/1852	09/07/1857	15	234	N	
Satz, John	33	Bavaria	Y	Bremen	Philadelphia	09/06/1848	04/02/1853	7	491	N	
Sauer, Adam	35	Bavaria	Y	Havre	New York	10/05/1854	10/03/1856	14	175	N	
Sauer, Anton	??	Germany	Y	?	?	?	10/13/1888			Y	
Sauer, Carl	30	Germany	Y	Bremen	Baltimore	06/21/1881	08/30/1882			Y	
Sauer, Charles Fred	46	Hesse Cassel	Y	Bremen	New York	09/04/1847	09/07/1852	25	392	N	
Sauer, Christoph	24	Germany	Y	Rotterdam	New York	10/15/1882	08/30/1884			Y	
Sauer, Conrad	45	Germany	N	Bremen	New York	08/28/1866	?			Y	
Sauer, Frank	30	Kurhassen	Y	Bremen	New York	05/28/1848	04/06/1852	24	400	N	
Sauer, Frank	17	Germany	N	?	New York	00/00/1880				Y	10/27/1888
Sauer, Joseph	30	Germany	Y	Antwerp	New York	03/17/1877	11/03/1884			Y	
Sauer, Joseph	35	Germany	N	Bremen	New York	02/23/1872	?			Y	
Sauer, Michael	40	Germany	Y	Antwerp	New York	07/01/1874	03/15/1883			Y	
Sauer, Sebastian	48	Germany	N	Bavaria	New York	11/??/1866	?			Y	
Sauer, Thomas Joseph	29	Baden	Y	Bremen	New Orleans	02/12/1848	09/15/1852	25	526	N	
Sauer, Wendelein	29	Baden	Y	London	New York	04/01/1852	12/12/1855	13	303	N	
Sauerbeck, George	60	Germany	N	Havre	New York	10/??/1847	?			Y	
Sauerland, William	24	Prussia	Y	Bremen	New York	06/30/1854	12/11/1861	18	232	N	
Sauermann, George Edward	33	Hesse Darmsta	Y	London	New York	10/14/1849	02/01/1853	7	98	N	
Sauerwein, Conrad	60	Germany	N	Havre	New Orleans	03/??/1855	?			Y	
Saul, Moritz Charles	??	Germany	Y	?	?	?	03/31/1884			Y	
Sauler, Bernard	35	Bavaria	Y	Bremen	New York	11/12/1853	03/17/1856	26	220	N	
Sauler, Fred	??	Germany	Y	?	?	?	09/08/1885			Y	
Saurbeck, George	35	Baden	Y	Havre	New Orleans	02/15/1849	05/31/1856	14	272	N	
Sauro, Saverio	??	Italy	Y	?	New York	12/??/1882	04/23/1888			Y	
Sauten, Barney	26	Hanover	Y	Bremen	New Orleans	11/15/1858	11/04/1861	18	220	N	
Sauter, Anton	28	Germany	Y	Bremen	New York	12/03/1880	10/28/1885			Y	
Sauter, John	21	Wuertemberg	Y	Havre	New York	04/02/1854	02/04/1856	26	31	N	
Sautmann, John	38	Prussia	Y	Amsterdam	New York	11/29/1850	04/10/1854	8	408	N	
Sautmann, John	38	Prussia	Y	Amsterdam	New York	11/29/1850	05/10/1854	9	281	N	
Sautmann, Joseph	27	Prussia	Y	Bremen	New York	11/04/1854	09/14/1855	13	27	N	
Sautter, Fred	29	Germany	Y	Bremen	New York	05/16/1884	05/14/1885			Y	
Savage, John	25	Ireland	Y	Liverpool	?	?	?	7	2	N	
Savage, John	25	Ireland	Y	Liverpool	New York	08/29/1848	05/01/1854	8	340	N	
Savage, John	25	Ireland	Y	Liverpool	New York	08/29/1848	05/01/1854	9	213	N	
Save, Felix	32	Italy	Y	Naples	New York	12/29/1889	09/10/1896			Y	
Saven, Max	35	Russia	Y	Hamburg	New York	09/02/1887	10/08/1896			Y	
Saven, Morris	16	Russia	N	?	New York	00/00/1882				Y	10/26/1888
Savers, Anton	??	Germany	N	?	?	02/02/1883				Y	10/26/1892
Savin, Barnett	55	Russia	Y	Hamburg	New York	06/26/1888	10/28/1893			Y	
Savin, Harry	25	Russia	Y	Hamburg	New York	03/15/1887	10/21/1893			Y	
Sawyer, Charles Spencer	52	Scotland	Y	Liverpool	New York	11/??/1851	10/23/1883			Y	
Sax, Alois	22	Germany	Y	Bremen	New York	10/04/1889	11/06/1889			Y	
Sax, Louis	17	Germany	N	?	Boston	00/00/1882				Y	11/03/1888
Saxby, Howard	36	England	Y	Liverpool	New York	06/25/1874	04/03/1891	19	328	N	
Saxby, William L.	50	England	Y	Liverpool	Philadelphia	07/16/1897	05/02/1898			Y	
Scahill, Thomas	29	Ireland	Y	Liverpool	New York	10/10/1851	02/11/1853	7	140	N	
Scal, James	50	Ireland	Y	Liverpool	New York	08/12/1847	01/??/1850	23	509	N	
Scalea, Antonio	39	Italy	Y	Palermo	New York	09/25/1887	01/18/1894	21	58	N	
Scallia, Salvatore	50	Italy	Y	Palermo	New York	05/30/1879	10/26/1900			Y	
Scally, John	30	Ireland	Y	Havre	New Orleans	03/02/1850	08/26/1857	15	192	N	
Scally, Thomas	30	Ireland	Y	Belfast	Philadelphia	10/10/1846	11/01/1852	5	130	N	
Scally, Thomas	30	Ireland	Y	Belfast	Philadelphia	10/10/1846	11/01/1852	6	256	N	
Scally, Thomas	33	Ireland	Y	Liverpool	New Orleans	11/18/1852	11/02/1860	27	553	N	
Scanlan, James	43	Ireland	N	Queenstown	New York	01/??/1862	?			Y	
Scanlan, James	32	Ireland	Y	Liverpool	Buffalo	09/04/1847	09/15/1852	25	525	N	
Scanlan, James J.	29	Ireland	N	Liverpool	New York	03/??/1876	?			Y	
Scanlan, John	2	Ireland	N	?	New York	00/00/1867				Y	10/27/1888

CITIZENSHIP RECORDS

APPLICANT	AGE	COUNTRY OF ORIGIN	DEC	DEPART PORT	ENTRY PORT	ARRIVE DATE	DEC DATE	VOL	PG.	FLD	NAT DATE
Scanlin, John	24	Ireland	Y	Limerick	Burlington	06/01/1848	10/22/1852	5	51	N	
Scanlin, Martin	27	Ireland	Y	Liverpool	New Orleans	12/18/1849	04/17/1854	8	148	N	
Scanlin, Martin	27	Ireland	Y	Liverpool	New Orleans	12/18/1849	04/17/1854	9	19	N	
Scanlon, Michael	28	Ireland	Y	Queenstown	New York	05/02/1890	04/10/1893			Y	
Scanlon, Thomas	26	Ireland	Y	?	Philadelphia	??/??/1892	08/31/1897			Y	
Scannel, James	24	Ireland	Y	Canada	Boston	06/??/1845	10/22/1851	4	368	N	
Scanton, John	53	Ireland	Y	Liverpool	New Orleans	04/03/1849	07/21/1851	4	21	N	
Scardino, Virgilio	30	Italy	Y	Palermo	New York	06/16/1890	10/19/1893			Y	
Scarlett, Edward	33	Ireland	N	Glasgow	New York	03/22/1871	?			Y	
Scarlett, John	39	Ireland	N	Liverpool	New York	10/??/1866	?			Y	
Scarvunes, George	??	Greece	Y	?	?	?	11/27/1888			Y	
Scary, Patrick	28	Ireland	Y	Liverpool	Boston	05/29/1848	02/16/1852	24	122	N	
Scaunter, William	36	Wurttemberg	Y	Havre	New York	07/29/1849	03/11/1851	3	252	N	
Schaaf, Adam	16	Germany	N	?	New York	00/00/1870				Y	10/26/1888
Schaaf, Gottlob Frederic	23	Wurttemberg	Y	Rotterdam	New York	05/16/1850	06/06/1865	10	96	N	
Schaaf, Gottlob Frederic	23	Wurttemberg	Y	Rotterdam	New York	05/16/1850	06/05/1854	12	33	N	
Schaaf, Oswald	31	Prussia	Y	Antwerp	New York	06/30/1852	10/04/1854	10	428	N	
Schaaf, Oswald	31	Prussia	Y	Antwerp	New York	06/30/1852	10/04/1854	12	367	N	
Schaapvelt, Gerhardus	28	Holland	Y	New Diep	Baltimore	10/04/1853	05/25/1854	8	519	N	
Schaar, George Caspar	29	Bavaria	Y	Hamburg	Detroit	06/17/1862	06/28/1862	18	362	N	
Schabel, August	30	Germany	Y	Bremen	New York	09/05/1890	03/31/1898			Y	
Schabel, John	32	France	Y	Havre	New York	05/30/1850	11/05/1860	18	11	N	
Schach, Jacob	32	Bavaria	Y	Rotterdam	New York	06/03/1849	03/01/1852	24	189	N	
Schachet, Eli	30	Russia	Y	Bremen	New York	04/10/1885	08/29/1895			Y	
Schachet, Max	50	Russia	Y	Hamburg	New York	01/01/1894	10/26/1901			Y	
Schachter, John (Schoghu	28	Bavaria	Y	Bremen	Baltimore	10/14/1846	08/15/1848	22	168	N	
Schack, Henry	44	Saxe Gotha	Y	Bremen	New York	05/30/1850	10/29/1858	17	2	N	
Schad, Stephan A.	52	Germany	Y	Bremen	New York	05/25/1883	10/15/1886			Y	
Schadle, August	41	Germany	Y	Hamburg	New York	11/25/1881	12/27/1886			Y	
Schadler, Joseph	31	Germany	Y	Bremen	New York	01/15/1885	05/13/1896			Y	
Schaefer, Bernhard	40	Germany	Y	Hamburg	New York	02/16/1890	08/18/1902			Y	
Schaefer, Charles	25	Hanover	Y	Bremen	Baltimore	10/??/1854	10/14/1857	15	428	N	
Schaefer, Charles	24	Germany	Y	Amsterdam	New York	06/22/1881	05/14/1883			Y	
Schaefer, Charles	??	Germany	N	?	?	02/00/1881				Y	10/31/1892
Schaefer, Conrad	53	Hesse Cassel	Y	Bremen	New York	06/16/1846	06/16/1851	3	387	N	
Schaefer, Daniel	31	Germany	Y	Bremen	New York	06/??/1879	11/17/1886			Y	
Schaefer, Emil	21	Germany	Y	Bremen	New York	03/22/1885	04/10/1888			Y	
Schaefer, Emil Theodor	36	Germany	Y	Hamburg	New York	01/04/1882	07/31/1882			Y	
Schaefer, F. William	37	Germany	Y	Bremen	Baltimore	10/17/1888	08/21/1893			Y	
Schaefer, Fred	24	Germany	Y	Antwerp	New York	04/16/1891	09/29/1896			Y	
Schaefer, Frederick	32	Germany	Y	Bremen	New York	10/17/1880	10/13/1884			Y	
Schaefer, George	32	Wurttemberg	Y	London	New York	07/20/1848	12/20/1851	4	539	N	
Schaefer, George Ferdina	26	Hesse	Y	Bremen	New York	11/27/1853	09/29/1856	14	15	N	
Schaefer, George H.	49	Germany	N	Hamburg	New York	10/27/1859	?			Y	
Schaefer, George Heinric	49	Germany	Y	Hamburg	New York	10/27/1859	08/??/1868			Y	
Schaefer, Gottlieb	73	Germany	Y	Bremen	Baltimore	09/11/1890	04/21/1894			Y	
Schaefer, Gottlob Freder	22	Wurttemberg	Y	Havre	New York	09/14/1854	01/10/1856	13	446	N	
Schaefer, Gustav Adolph	28	Wuertemberg	Y	Havre	New York	09/01/1852	05/22/1856	26	536	N	
Schaefer, Heinrich	26	Germany	Y	Hanover	New York	05/16/1882	10/03/1885	19	10	N	
Schaefer, Henry	22	Bavaria	Y	Havre	New York	05/07/1848	11/03/1852	5	210	N	
Schaefer, Henry	22	Bavaria	Y	Havre	New York	05/07/1848	11/03/1852	6	336	N	
Schaefer, Henry	34	Bavaria	Y	Rotterdam	New York	08/04/1854	11/12/1858	17	323	N	
Schaefer, Henry	34	Germany	Y	?	New York	??/??/1882	04/04/1890			Y	
Schaefer, Henry	33	Germany	N	Bremen	New York	11/20/1881	?			Y	
Schaefer, Jacob	35	Germany	Y	Antwerp	New York	11/27/1885	06/05/1890			Y	
Schaefer, Jacob	23	Germany	Y	Antwerp	New York	04/21/1881	04/23/1883			Y	
Schaefer, Jacob	46	Baden	N	South Hampto	New Orleans	??/??/1855	?			Y	
Schaefer, Jacob	66	Germany	N	Bremen	New York	03/02/1851	?			Y	
Schaefer, Jakob	??	?	Y	?	?	?	10/07/1889			Y	

CITIZENSHIP RECORDS

APPLICANT	AGE	COUNTRY OF ORIGIN	DEC	DEPART PORT	ENTRY PORT	ARRIVE DATE	DEC DATE	VOL	PG.	FLD	NAT DATE
Schaefer, Johann	25	Austria	Y	Hamburg	New York	12/14/1899	12/31/1901			Y	
Schaefer, John	36	Germany	Y	Bremen	New York	01/01/1882	10/28/1893			Y	
Schaefer, Justus	38	Hanover	Y	Bremen	Baltimore	06/27/1855	05/20/1861	18	172	N	
Schaefer, Karl	26	Germany	Y	Hamburg	New York	02/19/1881	07/11/1882			Y	
Schaefer, Lazarus	52	Germany	Y	Bremen	New York	12/??/1869	10/09/1882			Y	
Schaefer, Ludwig	??	Hesse Darmsta	N	?	?	07/04/1852	?			Y	09/28/1858
Schaefer, Nicolaus	32	Bavaria	Y	Havre	New Orleans	04/12/1847	09/25/1854	10	212	N	
Schaefer, Reinhardt	28	Germany	Y	Bremen	New York	08/01/1882	01/03/1884			Y	
Schaefer, Reinhold	29	Germany	Y	Bremen	Baltimore	09/24/1890	01/22/1894			Y	
Schaefers, Frank	32	Germany	Y	Bremen	New York	08/09/1884	10/18/1887			Y	
Schaeffer, Charles	22	France	Y	Havre	New Orleans	01/22/1850	10/06/1851	4	208	N	
Schaeffer, Emil	25	Germany	Y	Sherbouth	New York	10/09/1891	09/22/1896			Y	
Schaeffer, Leon	32	Germany	Y	Havre	New York	07/24/1892	08/06/1895			Y	
Schaeffer, William	40	Germany	Y	Hamburg	New York	03/05/1882	03/05/1884			Y	
Schaeffer, William	30	Hanover	Y	Bremen	Baltimore	07/24/1857	08/18/1860	27	294	N	
Schaeffler, Gottlieb	42	Germany	Y	Antwerp	New York	03/11/1881	08/29/1883			Y	
Schaenfele, Frederick	30	Wuerttemberg	Y	Liverpool	New York	08/22/1852	04/30/1856			Y	09/28/1858
Schaerpf, John	33	Bavaria	Y	Bremerhafen	Baltimore	12/??/1860	01/14/1861	18	58	N	
Schaetzle, Joseph	43	Baden	Y	Havre	New York	04/03/1853	04/05/1856	26	448	N	
Schaeven, Joseph	34	Prussia	Y	Bremen	New York	05/01/1849	09/05/1857	15	229	N	
Schafeld, Gerhard	28	Holland	Y	New Diep	Baltimore	10/04/1853	05/25/1854	9	393	N	
Schafer, Adam	38	Hesse Cassel	Y	Bremen	Philadelphia	07/09/1847	10/14/1857	15	426	N	
Schafer, Alexander	26	Baden	Y	London	New York	06/30/1857	07/06/1860	27	208	N	
Schafer, Anton	23	Baden	Y	Havre	New York	05/10/1850	01/19/1852	24	34	N	
Schafer, Christian Gottl	24	Hanover	Y	Bremen	Baltimore	11/05/1853	01/05/1856	13	425	N	
Schafer, Clemens	24	Hanover	Y	Bremen	New Orleans	12/21/1847	01/27/1853	7	73	N	
Schafer, Frank Joseph	25	Oldenburg	Y	Bremen	Baltimore	06/28/1846	01/19/1849	1	464	N	
Schafer, Frederick Willi	27	Prussia	Y	Bremen	Baltimore	10/06/1850	11/15/1855	13	226	N	
Schafer, George	33	Germany	N	Bremen	New York	07/17/1878	?			Y	
Schafer, George Frederic	31	Hesse Cassel	Y	Havre	New York	09/22/1847	11/15/1852	6	404	N	
Schafer, George Fredk.	31	Hesse Cassel	Y	Havre	New York	09/22/1847	11/15/1852	5	280	N	
Schafer, George H.	29	Hanover	Y	Bremen	New Orleans	11/27/1857	10/08/1860	27	418	N	
Schafer, H.	39	Germany	N	Bremen	New York	09/??/1866	?			Y	
Schafer, Henry	31	Bavaria	Y	Havre	New York	05/07/1848	05/11/1854	9	294	N	
Schafer, Henry	33	Germany	Y	Bremen	New York	11/20/1881	07/15/1883			Y	
Schafer, John	30	Baden	Y	Havre	New York	02/26/1854	10/09/1854	11	158	N	
Schafer, Joseph	30	Bavaria	Y	Havre	New York	12/??/1854	11/05/1856	14	472	N	
Schafer, Julius	24	Bavaria	Y	Havre	New York	01/02/1848	02/23/1852	24	157	N	
Schafer, Karl	24	Germany	Y	Bremen	New York	04/24/1880	05/02/1882			Y	
Schafer, Leonhard	24	Bavaria	Y	Havre	New York	11/24/1856	03/07/1860	27	120	N	
Schafer, Nicolaus	32	Bavaria	Y	Havre	New Orleans	04/12/1847	09/25/1854	12	151	N	
Schafer, Theodor	53	Germany	Y	Bremen	Baltimore	07/05/1882	12/26/1885			Y	
Schaffele, Barney	38	Holland	Y	Rotterdam	New York	05/29/1846	02/03/1851	3	88	N	
Schaffer, Math	27	Austria	Y	Hamburg	Baltimore	06/09/1889	09/24/1894			Y	
Schaffhauser, Charles	42	Germany	Y	Havre	New York	06/22/1885	10/01/1898			Y	
Schaffner, Sebastian	29	Baden	Y	Havre	New Orleans	01/22/1848	10/02/1848	22	392	N	
Schafhentle, Frank	26	Germany	Y	Havre	New York	06/14/1889	02/20/1894			Y	
Schaible, Frederick	32	Wurttemberg	Y	Antwerp	New York	09/30/1847	09/21/1855	13	97	N	
Schaible, John	24	Wurttemberg	Y	Havre	New Orleans	11/11/1852	10/06/1854	10	516	N	
Schaible, John	24	Wurttemberg	Y	Havre	New Orleans	11/11/1852	10/06/1852	12	455	N	
Schaible, Michael	35	Wurttemberg	Y	Havre	New Orleans	11/11/1852	04/05/1858	16	499	N	
Schaich, Carl	30	Germany	Y	Bremen	New York	05/30/1889	02/19/1894			Y	
Schaich, Joseph	35	Germany	Y	?	New York	08/19/1880	11/01/1884			Y	
Schalcher, John G.	51	Switzerland	Y	Rotterdam	New York	05/15/1868	09/16/1889			Y	
Schaleman, J. Martin	49	Germany	N	Rotterdam	New York	11/02/1866	?			Y	
Schall, Joseph	48	Germany	Y	Bremen	Baltimore	03/19/1882	11/05/1900			Y	
Schallenmueller, Fred	33	Germany	N	Bremen	New York	11/05/1877	?			Y	
Schaller, Ferdinand	30	Germany	Y	Hamburg	New York	06/20/1881	10/03/1882			Y	
Schaller, George	28	Hesse Darmsta	Y	Havre	New York	07/18/1847	02/19/1850	2	99	N	

CITIZENSHIP RECORDS

APPLICANT	AGE	COUNTRY OF ORIGIN	DEC	DEPART PORT	ENTRY PORT	ARRIVE DATE	DEC DATE	VOL	PG.	FLD	NAT DATE
Schaller, Michael	33	Germany	Y	Havre	New York	07/04/1885	09/21/1891			Y	
Schaller, Paul	38	Baden	Y	Havre	New York	11/13/1855	10/21/1858	17	89	N	
Schamber, William	43	Germany	Y	Antwerp	New York	09/29/1881	10/09/1888			Y	
Schan, Victor	27	Nassau	Y	London	New York	04/18/1852	08/18/1855	11	452	N	
Schander, Alfred	21	Prussia	Y	Bremen	New York	11/12/1847	02/22/1851	3	159	N	
Schandig, George	30	Bavaria	Y	Bremen	New York	08/01/1845	01/15/1849	1	424	N	
Schanhorst, Henry	31	Prussia	Y	Bremen	Baltimore	10/01/1849	09/28/1854	10	285	N	
Schanhorst, Henry	31	Prussia	Y	Bremen	Baltimore	10/01/1849	09/28/1854	12	224	N	
Schantz, Michael	28	Bavaria	Y	Havre	New York	07/??/1846	12/26/1849	23	431	N	
Schapere, Nathan	52	Russia	Y	Hamburg	New York	06/15/1889	11/06/1896			Y	
Schapker, Engelbert	26	Prussia	Y	Bremen	New York	11/??/1843	02/17/1847	23	152	N	
Schapmann, Bernard	28	Hanover	Y	Bremen	New Orleans	12/31/1850	04/17/1854	9	44	N	
Schappach, Joseph	30	Baden	Y	Havre	New York	09/29/1848	06/13/1851	3	373	N	
Schappacher, William	22	Baden	Y	Liverpool	New York	01/01/1857	12/14/1857	16	219	N	
Schardt, Jacob	25	Bavaria	Y	Havre	New York	10/24/1851	10/30/1858	17	10	N	
Schardt, Jacob	55	Germany	Y	Bremen	New York	08/22/1885	03/18/1890			Y	
Scharenberg, G. Jan	22	Holland	Y	Rotterdam	New York	09/11/1846	08/15/1848	22	125	N	
Scharer, John	40	Switzerland	Y	Havre	New Orleans	12/12/1854	08/25/1859	17	474	N	
Scharf, Anton	35	Germany	Y	Hamberg	New York	12/28/1881	05/28/1887			Y	
Scharfheide, William	38	Germany	Y	Bremen	Baltimore	06/25/1873	?			Y	
Scharfscheer, Heinrich C	30	Hanover	Y	Bremen	Baltimore	10/18/1842	11/05/1852	6	359	N	
Scharfscheer, Henry Chri	30	Hanover	Y	Bremen	Baltimore	10/18/1842	11/05/1852	5	233	N	
Scharholtz, Frederick	31	Hanover	Y	Bremen	New Orleans	05/25/1852	10/09/1854	6	175	N	
Scharmann, Frederick	??	Prussia	Y	Bremen	New Orleans	05/29/1852	04/13/1855	13	134	N	
Scharphoff, Barni	29	Germany	Y	Rotterdam	New York	06/21/1890	06/26/1893			Y	
Scharre, Ferdinand Henry	33	Saxony	Y	Bremen	New York	04/26/1849	02/23/1852	24	156	N	
Schartz, John	69	Germany	N	Hamburg	New York	07/??/1855	?			Y	
Scharzinger, Max	32	Germany	Y	Havre	New York	01/22/1890	09/23/1896			Y	
Schatt, Martin	29	Hesse Darmsta	Y	Havre	New York	06/??/1847	11/02/1857	15	517	N	
Schatz, David	39	Hungary	Y	Hamburg	New York	01/28/1865	??/30/18??	17	540	N	
Schatz, Nicholas	28	Bavaria	Y	Havre	New Orleans	05/26/1847	02/09/1852	24	81	N	
Schatzle, Raimund	??	Germany	N	?	?	09/12/1885				Y	10/27/1892
Schaub, Isador	33	Germany	Y	Havre	New York	07/01/1892	09/17/1895			Y	
Schaub, Martin	29	Germany	Y	Rotterdam	New York	07/30/1880	06/01/1889			Y	
Schaub, Robert	33	Switzerland	Y	Havre	New York	02/15/1882	04/18/1892			Y	
Schaudig, Carl	27	Germany	Y	Antwerp	Detroit	01/26/1893	06/27/1893			Y	
Schauefele, John	28	Wurttemberg	Y	Bremen	New York	06/02/1852	08/27/1855	11	507	N	
Schaufler, Albert	25	Germany	Y	Hamburg	New York	05/25/1893	07/29/1899			Y	
Schaufler, Frank	22	Germany	Y	Bremen	Baltimore	07/29/1880	11/01/1884			Y	
Schaum, Rudolph	??	Germany	Y	?	?	?	11/05/1883			Y	
Schaumann, Louis	34	Wurttemberg	Y	Antwerp	New York	11/18/1849	01/03/1853	5	503	N	
Schaurer, John Jacob	32	Baden	Y	Havre	New York	06/20/1843	02/19/1849	23	180	N	
Schaurer, Nicolaus	58	Germany	Y	Havre	New York	06/16/1864	10/??/1868			Y	
Schaurer, Peter	42	Bavaria	Y	Havre	New Orleans	11/23/1853	09/14/1855	13	34	N	
Schave, Mathias	22	Germany	Y	Bremen	Baltimore	07/17/1883	07/18/1887			Y	
Schavin, Henry	30	Switzerland	Y	Havre	New York	05/29/1848	02/19/1849	23	192	N	
Schawe, A.	35	Germany	Y	Bremen	Baltimore	04/10/1870	03/18/1872	18	472	N	
Schear, Jacob	??	Russia	N	?	?	07/05/1885				Y	10/20/1892
Schearrer, Peter	??	Prussia	Y	?	?	?	02/01/1872			Y	
Scheben, Bernard	24	France	Y	Havre	New York	03/20/1851	02/04/1856	26	22	N	
Scheben, Ferdinand	41	France	Y	Havre	New York	10/15/1850	10/09/1854	6	102	N	
Scheben, Ferdinand	41	France	Y	Havre	New York	10/15/1850	10/09/1854	11	105	N	
Scheben, Lorenz	31	France	Y	Havre	New York	04/02/1847	05/08/1854	8	397	N	
Scheben, Lorenz	31	France	Y	Havre	New York	04/02/1847	05/08/1854	9	270	N	
Schechter, Moses	45	Roumania	Y	Hamburg	Philadelphia	03/31/1899	02/18/1903			Y	
Scheck, John Jacob	22	Wurttemberg	Y	Liverpool	New York	07/18/1852	10/10/1854	11	237	N	
Scheele, Ludwig	22	Hanover	Y	Bremen	New York	10/18/1855	10/14/1857	15	427	N	
Scheer, Charles	22	Germany	Y	Bremen	New York	09/22/1881	10/27/1884			Y	
Scheer, G. A.	21	Germany	Y	Bremen	New York	09/24/1881	10/18/1884			Y	

CITIZENSHIP RECORDS

APPLICANT	AGE	COUNTRY OF ORIGIN	DEC	DEPART PORT	ENTRY PORT	ARRIVE DATE	DEC DATE	VOL	PG.	FLD	NAT DATE
Scheer, John	23	Bavaria	Y	Havre	New York	12/11/1854	10/04/1858	17	50	N	
Scheerer, Alois	25	Baden	Y	Havre	New York	07/10/1852	04/17/1854	9	55	N	
Scheerer, John Casper	30	Hesse Darmsta	Y	Bremen	Baltimore	11/??/1848	10/27/1857	15	494	N	
Scheeve, John David	31	Mecklenburg	Y	Hamburg	New Orleans	11/13/1847	03/27/1849	23	550	N	
Scheffer, Adam	28	Germany	Y	Antwerp	Philadelphia	07/31/1890	05/24/1894			Y	
Scheffer, Conrad (Schaef	27	Bavaria	Y	Bremen	Baltimore	05/01/1847	08/15/1848	22	138	N	
Scheffer, Heinrich	40	Germany	Y	Bremen	New York	04/01/1884	03/27/1900			Y	
Scheffer, Johann Gerhard	24	Germany	Y	Amsterdam	New York	08/21/1885	09/27/1889	19	233	N	
Scheffer, Johann Gerhard	24	Germany	Y	Amsterdam	New York	08/24/1885	09/27/1889			Y	
Scheffer, Johann Herman	35	Germany	Y	Bremen	Baltimore	04/30/1884	09/27/1889	19	232	N	
Scheffer, Johann Herman	35	Germany	Y	Bremen	Baltimore	04/30/1884	09/27/1889			Y	
Scheffer, Joseph	29	Germany	Y	Bremen	New York	09/03/1882	05/??/1883			Y	
Scheffer, Joseph	28	Germany	N	Bremen	New York	09/03/1882	?			Y	
Scheffler, Michael	65	Germany	Y	Bremen	Baltimore	12/24/1872	06/13/1892			Y	
Schehr, Michael	45	Germany	Y	Havre	New York	08/17/1872	04/07/1879			Y	
Schehr, Peter Paul	26	France	Y	Havre	New Orleans	01/28/1852	05/11/1854	8	425	N	
Schehr, Peter Paul	26	France	Y	Havre	New Orleans	01/08/1852	05/11/1854	9	298	N	
Scheib, Theobald	44	Bavaria	Y	Havre	New York	06/24/1846	10/01/1856	14	111	N	
Scheibe, Robert	29	Germany	Y	Rotterdam	New York	11/03/1883	12/15/1890			Y	
Scheiber, William	27	Saxony	Y	Bremen	Baltimore	09/11/1849	01/27/1851	2	533	N	
Scheibert, Emil	22	Kurhessen	Y	Bremen	Baltimore	10/01/1847	11/21/1848	1	354	N	
Scheible, Gottlieb	49	Wuertemberg	Y	Havre	New York	07/16/1854	03/17/1856	26	212	N	
Scheick, George	43	Bavaria	Y	Amsterdam	New York	08/10/1849	07/05/1851	3	485	N	
Scheid, Friedrich	30	France	Y	Havre	New Orleans	??/14/1848	02/23/1850	2	120	N	
Scheid, John	31	Bavaria	Y	Havre	New York	06/02/1848	02/03/1853	7	109	N	
Scheid, Joseph	24	France	Y	Havre	New York	03/23/1851	03/24/1856	26	293	N	
Scheid, Nicholaus	32	France	Y	Havre	New Orleans	12/26/1839	09/10/1852	25	448	N	
Scheidegger, Alfred	22	Switzerland	Y	Havre	New York	05/10/1884	03/30/1887			Y	
Scheidel, Carl	30	Germany	Y	Antwerp	New York	04/04/1882	10/05/1883			Y	
Scheidemann, John	29	Hanover	Y	Bremen	New Orleans	07/06/1850	04/13/1852	24	491	N	
Scheidemendel, Justin	55	Germany	Y	Havre	New Orleans	07/01/1860	10/27/1893			Y	
Scheidle, Max	29	Austria	Y	Antwerp	New York	04/12/1880	06/14/1889			Y	
Scheidler, Frederick	28	Germany	Y	Hamburg	New York	06/03/1882	05/07/1883			Y	
Scheidt, Balthaser	32	France	Y	Havre	New York	05/02/1849	06/24/1851	3	448	N	
Scheidt, Charles	26	Germany	Y	Antwerp	New York	08/08/1884	03/12/1891			Y	
Scheidt, John	61	Germany	Y	Antwerp	New York	08/02/1884	08/16/1895			Y	
Scheier, Nicholas	26	Bavaria	Y	Havre	New York	06/24/1848	12/27/1851	24	19	N	
Scheifers, Augustus	29	Prussia	Y	Hamburg	New York	06/08/1858	07/07/1860	27	211	N	
Scheifers, Rudolph Franc	22	Prussia	Y	Bremen	Baltimore	06/18/1856	05/03/1859	17	396	N	
Scheir, Joseph (Scheer)	??	Russia	Y	?	New York	??/??/1883	10/20/1894			Y	
Scheisl, William	28	Germany	Y	Bremen	New York	07/03/1880	08/22/1888			Y	
Scheland, Theodore	32	Germany	Y	?	Baltimore	??/??/1872	09/20/1880			Y	
Schelies, Frank	31	Germany	Y	Hamburg	New York	05/07/1885	02/28/1888			Y	
Schell, George	27	Bavaria	Y	Bremen	Baltimore	??/14/1847	01/09/1850	23	484	N	
Schell, Michael Alois	21	Baden	Y	London	New York	04/01/1852	04/04/1853	8	21	N	
Schelle, Bernard	40	Prussia	Y	Bremen	Baltimore	07/01/1857	11/20/1858	17	344	N	
Schellenberg, Jacob	30	Prussia	Y	Antwerp	New York	12/12/1848	02/05/1848	23	33	N	
Scheller, Caspar	63	Switzerland	Y	Hamburg	New York	01/10/1873	07/13/1889			Y	
Scheller, Jacob	36	Switzerland	Y	Havre	New York	12/10/1854	03/11/1856	26	182	N	
Schellheimer, John	62	Germany	N	Havre	New York	04/??/1857	?			Y	
Schelling, John Jacob	36	Switzerland	Y	Havre	New York	06/29/1886	09/10/1887			Y	
Schellmueller, Joseph	30	Germany	Y	Bremen	New York	12/30/1892	12/09/1897			Y	
Schenck, Felix	50	Germany	Y	Antwerp	Philadelphia	10/19/1882	10/17/1896			Y	
Schenck, Hyacinth	33	Prussia	Y	Havre	New York	09/26/1852	10/07/1854	6	18	N	
Schenck, John	36	Germany	Y	Bremen	New York	04/15/1883	05/24/1889			Y	
Schenerle, Paul	48	Germany	Y	Bremen	Baltimore	03/28/1884	04/11/1887			Y	
Schengber, Henry	24	Germany	Y	Rotterdam	New York	10/26/1888	07/30/1892			Y	
Schenk, Frederick	24	Wurttemberg	Y	Havre	New York	12/14/1853	09/21/1857	15	293	N	
Schenk, Hyamth	33	Prussia	Y	Havre	New York	09/26/1852	10/07/1854	11	20	N	

CITIZENSHIP RECORDS

APPLICANT	AGE	COUNTRY OF ORIGIN	DEC	DEPART PORT	ENTRY PORT	ARRIVE DATE	DEC DATE	VOL	PG.	FLD	NAT DATE
Schenk, Michael	28	Germany	Y	Hamburg	New York	08/07/1882	05/03/1889			Y	
Schenke, B.	23	Oldenburg	Y	Bremen	New Orleans	12/17/1857	01/06/1860	27	33	N	
Schenkel, Jacob	21	Bavaria	Y	Havre	New York	12/29/1850	04/12/1852	24	482	N	
Schenplein, Andrew	26	Germany	Y	Bremen	Baltimore	03/26/1894	06/22/1896			Y	
Schepe, Wilhelm	31	Germany	Y	Hamburg	New York	11/03/1880	06/21/1886			Y	
Schepen, August	30	Germany	Y	Bremen	New York	05/19/1884	08/15/1887			Y	
Scheper, Clemens	22	Germany	Y	Bremen	New York	09/09/1881	08/03/1883			Y	
Scheper, John	35	Oldenburg	Y	Bremen	Baltimore	06/20/1845	11/17/1848	1	316	N	
Schepers, Bernhard	28	Germany	Y	Rotterdam	New York	06/19/1888	10/15/1896			Y	
Scher, Jacob	25	Bavaria	Y	Havre	New York	05/20/1860	04/28/1862	18	331	N	
Scherer, Alois	24	Baden	Y	Havre	New York	07/10/1852	04/17/1854	8	184	N	
Scherer, Christian	52	Germany	Y	Antwerp	New York	12/07/1890	07/11/1892			Y	
Scherer, Emil	33	Hesse Darmsta	Y	Rotterdam	New York	08/14/1847	08/22/1848	22	229	N	
Scherer, Ferdinand	26	Germany	Y	Antwerp	New York	06/28/1882	08/30/1884			Y	
Scherer, Fred	26	Germany	Y	Bremen	New York	12/23/1890	10/24/1896			Y	
Scherer, George	27	Baden	Y	Havre	New Orleans	01/27/1852	11/26/1858	17	357	N	
Scherer, John	36	Bavaria	Y	Havre	New York	06/20/1854	10/07/1856	14	246	N	
Scherger, Michael	47	Bavaria	Y	Havre	New Orleans	??/30/1845	10/09/1848	22	502	N	
Scherl, Charles	26	Austria	Y	Bremen	New York	12/29/1892	09/13/1893			Y	
Scherland, Joachim	39	Prussia	Y	Bremen	New York	01/14/1850	10/21/1858	17	85	N	
Scherm, Anton	39	Germany	Y	Antwerp	New York	09/02/1882	10/27/1892	19	391	N	
Scherpf, Peter	35	Bavaria	Y	Havre	New York	09/28/1851	10/30/1858	17	7	N	
Scherr, Louis	38	Germany	Y	?	?	06/11/1861	11/01/1888			Y	
Scherrer, John	26	Germany	Y	Antwerp	New York	12/02/1886	01/10/1890			Y	
Scherrer, Joseph	24	Germany	Y	Antwerp	New York	12/04/1885	04/09/1888			Y	
Scherrer, Peter	23	Germany	Y	?	New York	04/18/1879	10/09/1882			Y	
Scherzer, John	40	Germany	Y	Antwerp	Philadelphia	11/13/1890	11/18/1893			Y	
Scherzinger, Friedrich	??	Germany	Y	?	?	?	11/13/1879			Y	
Schettwitz, Charles	33	Saxony	Y	Havre	New Orleans	07/09/1849	03/02/1850	2	150	N	
Scheuer, Louis	30	Bavaria	Y	Liverpool	New York	02/01/1857	09/29/1860	27	388	N	
Scheuer, William	42	Bavaria	Y	Havre	New York	05/06/1854	10/08/1857	15	370	N	
Scheuerer, August	64	Germany	Y	Havre	New York	03/12/1865	11/15/1883			Y	
Scheuerman, Adam	45	Germany	Y	Rotterdam	New York	08/26/1880	08/04/1884			Y	
Scheuermann, Henry	27	Germany	Y	Hamburg	New York	06/27/1882	11/19/1883			Y	
Scheuermann, Martin	34	Baden	Y	Bremen	New York	10/24/1854	07/30/1858	16	540	N	
Scheuermann, William	22	Germany	Y	Antwerp	New York	08/27/1881	09/05/1882			Y	
Scheumann, Wolfgang Schn	30	Germany	Y	Bremen	New York	02/26/1880	12/19/1882			Y	
Scheuplein, Paul	25	Germany	Y	Hamburg	New York	06/29/1882	03/17/1886			Y	
Scheurer, Friedrich	21	Germany	Y	Antwerp	New York	07/01/1887	07/29/1890			Y	
Scheurer, John	24	Wuertemberg	Y	Liverpool	Philadelphia	05/26/1854	03/22/1856	26	248	N	
Scheurer, Joseph	32	Germany	Y	Antwerp	New York	05/03/1881	06/23/1891			Y	
Scheve, Joseph	32	Oldenburg	Y	Bremen	New Orleans	01/09/1847	11/01/1852	5	136	N	
Scheve, Joseph	32	Oldenburg	Y	Bremen	New Orleans	01/09/1847	11/01/1852	6	262	N	
Schewe, Charles	23	Oldenburg	Y	Bremen	New Orleans	11/01/1852	10/07/1854	6	42	N	
Schewe, Charles	23	Oldenburg	Y	Bremen	New Orleans	09/01/1852	10/07/1854	11	43	N	
Schiber, Seraphin	23	France	Y	Havre	New York	03/04/1847	11/22/1848	1	367	N	
Schibi, Michael	24	France	Y	Havre	New Orleans	05/25/1854	08/21/1855	11	469	N	
Schick, Henry	26	Germany	Y	Antwerp	New York	03/23/1883	03/16/1885			Y	
Schick, John	29	Germany	Y	Hamburg	New York	09/02/1882	05/21/1887			Y	
Schick, John	30	Germany	Y	Bremen	Baltimore	05/20/1872	11/20/1883			Y	
Schick, Joseph	33	Hesse Cassel	Y	Bremen	New York	07/31/1844	08/15/1848	22	158	N	
Schickling, John	53	Germany	N	Havre	New York	05/01/1852	?			Y	
Schiebel, Gottfried	32	Saxony	Y	Bremen	Baltimore	06/01/1854	09/20/1858	16	160	N	
Schieber, Albert	55	Germany	Y	Bremen	Baltimore	04/17/1889	07/25/1898			Y	
Schieber, Charles	38	Germany	Y	Antwerp	New York	08/10/1886	02/27/1891			Y	
Schiedler, John	??	Bavaria	Y	Hamburg	New York	??/05/1847	12/??/1850	2	403	N	
Schiedrich, Charles	??	Germany	N	?	?	08/18/1884				Y	10/27/1892
Schieferdecker, Julius	49	Prussia	Y	Bremen	New York	08/22/1851	11/16/1855	13	228	N	
Schieferle, Ulrich	47	Germany	Y	Rotterdam	New York	10/18/1881	11/10/1890			Y	

CITIZENSHIP RECORDS

APPLICANT	AGE	COUNTRY OF ORIGIN	DEC	DEPART PORT	ENTRY PORT	ARRIVE DATE	DEC DATE	VOL	PG.	FLD	NAT DATE
Schiefner, Louis	22	Schwartzburg	Y	Liverpool	New York	05/21/1854	02/17/1857	15	23	N	
Schiele, Fred	25	Germany	Y	Antwerp	Boston	04/29/1883	10/09/1883			Y	
Schiele, Heinrich	48	Germany	Y	Bremen	New York	08/08/1892	05/13/1898			Y	
Schierberg, Joseph	39	Oldenburg	N	Bremen	Baltimore	03/??/1866	?			Y	
Schierholtz, Frederick	31	Hanover	Y	Bremen	New Orleans	05/25/1852	10/09/1854	11	178	N	
Schierstein, Charles	27	Bremen	Y	Bremen	Baltimore	04/22/1852	05/12/1862	18	335	N	
Schievelbein, Frank	41	Germany	Y	Bremen	New York	12/17/1892	12/07/1897			Y	
Schiff, Charles	46	Austria	Y	Trieste	New York	10/27/1884	02/16/1885	19	3	N	
Schiff, Charles	46	Austria	Y	Frieste	New York	10/27/1884	02/16/1895			Y	
Schiff, Isaac	51	Russia	Y	Hamburg	New York	12/30/1891	10/22/1897			Y	
Schiffers, Joseph H. L.	25	Germany	Y	Antwerp	New York	10/16/1877	10/29/1883			Y	
Schiffman, Gabriel	44	Austria	Y	Bremen	New York	10/06/1872	09/19/1890			Y	
Schiffmann, Fred	??	Germany	Y	?	New York	11/29/1889	12/31/1892			Y	
Schiffmeyer, Joseph	27	Bavaria	Y	London	New York	07/21/1852	07/23/1855	11	421	N	
Schilder, Frederick	30	Bavaria	Y	Bremen	New York	12/07/1857	05/30/1859	17	438	N	
Schilffarth, Fritz	35	Germany	Y	Antwerp	Philadelphia	09/20/1882	06/06/1894			Y	
Schilhorst, William	25	Prussia	Y	Bremen	New Orleans	12/25/1852	10/08/1860	27	459	N	
Schill, Cosmas	49	Germany	N	Antwerp	Philadelphia	06/15/1881	?			Y	
Schill, George	37	Germany	Y	Bremen	New York	04/02/1873	10/11/1884			Y	
Schill, Wendelin	30	Germany	Y	Hamburg	New York	09/24/1887	01/21/1893			Y	
Schille, Leonhard	30	Germany	Y	Havre	New York	08/24/1881	10/01/1885			Y	
Schiller, Ferdinand	25	Saxony	Y	Bremen	New Orleans	10/20/1856	10/14/1857	15	424	N	
Schiller, Gustav	28	Saxony	Y	Hamburg	New York	10/13/1848	01/08/1850	23	476	N	
Schiller, Jacob	26	Germany	Y	Bremen	New York	03/05/1887	10/26/1888			Y	
Schilling, Alexander Gus	28	Prussia	Y	Hamburg	New York	09/18/1851	03/28/1853	7	424	N	
Schilling, Anton	31	Germany	Y	Rotterdam	New York	01/04/1881	02/05/1887			Y	
Schilling, Constantine	32	Germany	Y	Bremen	New York	05/17/1867	04/18/1881			Y	
Schilling, Gottlieb	37	Germany	Y	Bremen	New York	05/09/1883	11/10/1887			Y	
Schilling, Hans Carl Nic	31	Holstein	Y	Hamburg	New York	06/01/1853	04/17/1854	9	12	N	
Schilling, Hans Charles	31	Holstein	Y	Hamburg	New York	06/01/1853	04/17/1854	8	141	N	
Schilling, Michael	31	Kurhassen	Y	Bremen	New York	08/17/1844	08/03/1848	22	49	N	
Schillinger, John	69	Prussia	N	Havre	New Orleans	12/13/1854	?			Y	
Schimanski, John	32	Germany	Y	Bremen	Baltimore	05/02/1883	04/28/1886			Y	
Schimer, Frank	48	Austria	Y	Bremen	New York	09/14/1849	07/21/1851	4	23	N	
Schimke, Herman	35	Germany	Y	Bremen	New York	08/28/1881	09/07/1885			Y	
Schimmel, Emil Cornelius	25	Germany	Y	Hamburg	New York	05/28/1888	11/19/1890			Y	
Schimmelmann, Morris	43	Germany	Y	Hamburg	New York	03/15/1880	10/23/1886	19	81	N	
Schimmelmann, Morris	43	Germany	Y	Hamburg	New York	03/15/1880	10/23/1886			Y	
Schimmelpfeng, Valentine	40	Kuerfuerst Ha	Y	Bremen	Baltimore	07/16/1845	08/01/1848	22	30	N	
Schimmelpfening, John Ge	31	Hesse Cassel	Y	Hamburg	New York	06/??/1853	12/24/1855	13	347	N	
Schimmrock, Carl	28	Germany	Y	Hamburg	New York	04/24/1884	07/08/1887			Y	
Schimweg, Conrad	21	Germany	Y	Bremen	Baltimore	05/20/1887	09/17/1890			Y	
Schindeldecker, Henry	46	Germany	N	Havre	New York	05/??/1857	?			Y	
Schindeldecker, Reinhard	23	Bavaria	Y	Havre	New Orleans	02/11/1853	01/09/1856	13	436	N	
Schindelin, Gottfried	21	Germany	Y	Antwerp	New York	05/20/1885	06/11/1888			Y	
Schindler, August	29	Prussia	Y	Hamburg	New York	06/17/1852	05/06/1854	10	67	N	
Schindler, August	29	Prussia	Y	Hamburg	New York	06/17/1852	06/05/1854	12	4	N	
Schindler, Leonhard	25	Switzerland	Y	Havre	New York	10/05/1853	01/02/1856	13	413	N	
Schindlin, Jacob	24	Switzerland	Y	Havre	New Orleans	04/13/1848	11/20/1848	1	351	N	
Schinesohn, A.	40	Russia	Y	Bremen	New York	07/03/1888	06/19/1896			Y	
Schinkel, Andreas	26	Prussia	Y	Bremen	New Orleans	11/13/1847	02/10/1851	3	110	N	
Schinkel, Philip	23	Baden	Y	London	New York	06/02/1846	10/14/1848	1	228	N	
Schinner, John B.	59	Germany	N	Bremen	Baltimore	09/10/1853	?			Y	
Schipfer, Michael	28	Germany	Y	Bremen	New York	02/06/1884	10/07/1886			Y	
Schirmann, Charles	32	Germany	Y	Hamburg	New York	11/04/1885	11/01/1892			Y	
Schirmann, Mike	24	Germany	Y	Havre	New York	05/02/1887	01/13/1893			Y	
Schirrey, Carl	34	Germany	Y	Bremen	New York	07/13/1867	11/01/1871	18	434	N	
Schitz, Anton (Schilz?)	50	Germany	Y	Amsterdam	New York	05/21/1882	01/21/1885			Y	
Schlachter, Anton	27	Germany	Y	Bremen	New York	09/12/1887	02/11/1888			Y	

CITIZENSHIP RECORDS

APPLICANT	AGE	COUNTRY OF ORIGIN	DEC	DEPART PORT	ENTRY PORT	ARRIVE DATE	DEC DATE	VOL	PG.	FLD	NAT DATE
Schlachter, Henry	23	Germany	Y	Havre	New York	12/27/1882	09/08/1885			Y	
Schlachter, Jacob	53	Germany	N	Havre	New York	06/??/1851	?			Y	
Schlachter, Joseph	17	Germany	N	?	New York	00/00/1874				Y	10/28/1887
Schlachter, Martin	35	Germany	Y	Bremen	New York	02/23/1885	10/18/1893			Y	
Schlademann, August	21	Oldenburg	Y	Bremen	Baltimore	10/12/1846	10/16/1848	1	242	N	
Schlademann, John A.	53	Oldenburg	Y	Bremen	Baltimore	10/12/1846	10/16/1848	1	241	N	
Schlaechter, Adam	48	Germany	Y	Antwerp	New York	05/18/1881	04/30/1887			Y	
Schlaechter, Lorenz	37	Germany	Y	Bremen	New York	08/23/1876	10/14/1893			Y	
Schlaepfer, Conrad	33	Switzerland	Y	Havre	New York	08/28/1884	05/10/1894			Y	
Schlafer, Christoph	47	Wuerttemberg	Y	Rotterdam	New Orleans	11/13/1845	08/17/1848	22	198	N	
Schlafer, Ehrhardt	40	Wuerttemberg	Y	Havre	New York	05/29/1844	02/16/1852	24	111	N	
Schlagbaum, George	29	Prussia	Y	Bremen	Baltimore	06/12/1846	10/05/1848	1	55	N	
Schlagengei, John	26	Germany	Y	Antwerp	New York	02/08/1893	03/18/1893			Y	
Schlagengeil, Marcus	22	Germany	Y	Rotterdam	New York	08/20/1892	12/29/1892			Y	
Schlagheck, Bernard	24	Germany	Y	Bremen	New York	10/06/1888	04/29/1891			Y	
Schlake, Frank	22	Hanover	Y	Bremen	Baltimore	08/03/1845	11/21/1848	1	362	N	
Schlanski, Benjamin	36	Russia	Y	Bremen	Baltimore	08/18/1892	02/21/1894			Y	
Schlarb, Andreas	21	Prussia	Y	Liverpool	New York	05/07/1852	06/05/1854	10	89	N	
Schlarb, Andreas	21	Prussia	Y	Liverpool	New York	05/07/1852	06/05/1854	12	26	N	
Schlarmann, Bernard	34	Oldenburg	Y	Bremen	New Orleans	??/16/1844	10/09/1848	1	68	N	
Schlarmann, George	32	Germany	Y	Bremen	Baltimore	09/30/1888	09/27/1897			Y	
Schlatter, John	32	Switzerland	Y	Havre	New York	03/28/1881	01/22/1887			Y	
Schlatter, Ulrich	46	Switzerland	N	Havre	New York	05/15/1871	?			Y	
Schlecht, Gottlieb	23	Wurttemberg	Y	Liverpool	New York	09/12/1850	10/09/1854	11	195	N	
Schleck, Gottleib	23	Wurttemberg	Y	Liverpool	New York	09/12/1850	10/09/1854	6	192	N	
Schlegel, August	43	Germany	Y	London	New York	09/20/1894	06/16/1897			Y	
Schlegel, Frederick Augu	41	Germany	Y	Hamburg	Baltimore	11/??/1881	08/??/1882			Y	
Schlegel, Friedrich Augu	41	Germany	N	Hamburg	Baltimore	11/??/1881	?			Y	
Schlegel, Henry	30	Germany	Y	Rotterdam	New York	06/01/1888	04/02/1894			Y	
Schleibaum, George Henry	23	Hanover	Y	Bremen	New Orleans	01/04/1846	10/05/1848	22	424	N	
Schleich, Anton	63	France	N	Havre	New Orleans	03/08/1846	?			Y	
Schleicher, Frank	23	Germany	Y	Amsterdam	New York	04/12/1884	10/26/1885			Y	
Schleicher, John	48	Germany	Y	Hamburg	New York	04/06/1881	02/14/1889			Y	
Schleicher, Karl	22	Germany	Y	Havre	New York	05/03/1883	10/26/1885			Y	
Schleicher, Leopold	45	Germany	Y	Havre	New York	07/04/1868	10/26/1888			Y	
Schleitzer, Charles	37	Germany	Y	Bremen	Baltimore	10/07/1880	10/30/1897			Y	
Schleman, Louis	21	Russia	Y	Hamburg	New York	07/04/1889	10/12/1892			Y	
Schlemm, Louis	21	Russia	Y	Hamburg	New York	07/04/1889	10/12/1892	19	358	N	
Schlemmer, Emil	26	Bavaria	Y	Havre	New York	04/27/1853	10/30/1858	17	189	N	
Schlemmer, Henry	40	Wuerttemberg	Y	Havre	New York	10/29/1849	06/14/1852	25	258	N	
Schlenker, John	27	Germany	Y	Havre	New York	07/14/1881	11/01/1888			Y	
Schlenker, Martin	2	Germany	N	?	New York	00/00/1867				Y	04/04/1887
Schlensker, Heinrich C.F	32	Germany	Y	Bremen	Baltimore	08/16/1880	03/09/1888			Y	
Schlereth, Burkard	27	Germany	Y	Antwerp	New York	10/30/1880	11/10/1886			Y	
Schlereth, Conrad	45	Germany	N	Bremen	New York	05/??/1869	?			Y	
Schlesinger, William	37	Germany	Y	Hamburg	New York	02/27/1882	04/28/1887			Y	
Schlesselmann, Christ	55	Germany	Y	Bremen	New York	05/08/1881	02/12/1889			Y	
Schlesselmann, H. H.	34	Germany	N	Bremen	New York	06/09/1874	?			Y	
Schlesselmann, John	28	Germany	Y	Bremen	New York	05/07/1881	08/30/1889			Y	
Schlestmann, John Benj	26	Germany	Y	Bremen	New York	03/10/1885	10/28/1892	19	395	N	
Schletker, Eberhardt	39	Germany	Y	Bremen	New York	05/03/1881	03/01/1889			Y	
Schlett, Henry	21	Hesse Cassel	Y	Bremen	New York	09/15/1854	11/02/1860	27	559	N	
Schleunig, Theodore	27	Russia	Y	Hamburg	New York	06/08/1851	09/11/1857	15	257	N	
Schlewinsky, Ferdinand	58	Poland	N	Hamburg	New York	04/08/1864	?			Y	
Schlicht, Andrew	54	Bavaria	Y	Bremen	Baltimore	10/03/1844	08/15/1848	22	144	N	
Schlicht, John	27	Bavaria	Y	Bremen	Baltimore	10/03/1846	08/15/1848	22	142	N	
Schlicht, Joseph	24	Bavaria	Y	Bremen	Baltimore	10/01/1846	07/31/1848	22	23	N	
Schlichter, Christoph	32	Hesse Darmsta	Y	Hull	New York	08/12/1847	03/24/1853	7	385	N	
Schlick, John	38	Germany	Y	Antwerp	New York	05/27/1883	01/06/1886			Y	

CITIZENSHIP RECORDS

APPLICANT	AGE	COUNTRY OF ORIGIN	DEC	DEPART PORT	ENTRY PORT	ARRIVE DATE	DEC DATE	VOL	PG.	FLD	NAT DATE
Schlick, John	40	Germany	Y	Antwerp	New York	12/02/1865	11/03/1884			Y	
Schlickmann, Henry Rudol	32	Prussia	Y	Bremen	New Orleans	11/12/1843	01/25/1849	1	514	N	
Schlie, Henry	25	Germany	Y	Amsterdam	New York	08/25/1882	11/26/1883			Y	
Schlieckmann, Frank	26	Germany	Y	Bremen	Baltimore	08/28/1881	04/11/1887			Y	
Schlief, Bernard	29	Germany	Y	Hamburg	New York	06/18/1882	05/02/1885			Y	
Schliemann, Joseph	23	Mecklenburg S	Y	Hamburg	New York	05/15/1854	09/02/1857	15	220	N	
Schlieper, Friedrich	40	Germany	Y	Bremen	New York	10/??/1862	10/16/1880			Y	
Schlierf, John	49	Germany	Y	Bremen	New York	11/??/1864	05/20/1889			Y	
Schliewen, Richard	35	Germany	Y	Hamburg	New York	04/10/1885	11/04/1890			Y	
Schlimmer, John	27	Prussia	Y	Bremen	Baltimore	10/12/1846	10/07/1854	6	29	N	
Schlmeyer, Frederick	23	Hanover	Y	Bremen	New Orleans	10/25/1853	03/08/1858	16	384	N	
Schloemer, John	27	Prussia	Y	Bremen	Baltimore	10/12/1846	10/07/1854	11	30	N	
Schlohsnagel, Andreas	27	Germany	Y	Bremen	New York	08/09/1887	03/25/1889			Y	
Schlolein, Charles	21	Germany	Y	Antwerp	New York	05/15/1885	11/01/1886			Y	
Schlomann, Anton	40	Austria	Y	Bremen	New York	01/17/1867	04/20/1870			Y	
Schloss, Joseph Jr.	53	Germany	N	Hamburg	New York	07/22/1866	?			Y	
Schloss, Louis	30	Germany	Y	Antwerp	New York	11/??/1879	10/??/1881			Y	
Schlosser, Felix	23	Baden	Y	Havre	New York	05/02/1849	10/05/1854	10	463	N	
Schlosser, Felix	23	Baden	Y	Havre	New York	05/02/1849	10/05/1854	12	402	N	
Schlossstein, Charles	29	Bavaria	Y	Havre	New York	06/30/1849	08/12/1851	4	122	N	
Schlosstein, Frederick	22	Bavaria	Y	Hamburg	Buffalo	10/17/1853	02/12/1858	16	305	N	
Schloth, Gottfried	33	Hesse Darmsta	Y	Bremen	New York	07/14/1851	05/27/1854	10	17	N	
Schlothans, George	40	Germany	N	Amsterdam	New York	11/01/1867	?			Y	
Schlotmann, John Benjami	26	Germany	Y	Bremen	New York	03/10/1885	10/28/1892			Y	
Schlotterbeck, Christian	22	Wurttemberg	Y	Havre	New Orleans	10/??/1847	11/03/1851	4	478	N	
Schlotterbeck, John	29	Wurttemberg	Y	Havre	New York	08/16/1849	11/03/1851	4	479	N	
Schlottmann, Joseph	31	Oldenburg	Y	Bremen	New Orleans	12/25/1845	01/18/1849	1	457	N	
Schloz, Otto	27	Germany	Y	?	?	10/31/1887	10/31/1896			Y	
Schlueter, Franz	29	Germany	Y	Bremen	Baltimore	09/12/1880	02/12/1883			Y	
Schlueter, Fred	42	Germany	Y	Bremen	Baltimore	09/11/1882	01/08/1892			Y	
Schlupp, Philipp	27	Germany	Y	Antwerp	New York	05/22/1885	02/11/1892			Y	
Schluter, Gerhard	29	Prussia	Y	Bremen	New Orleans	11/20/1854	09/11/1860	27	358	N	
Schmackers, Henry	27	Hanover	Y	Bremen	New Orleans	05/16/1853	10/01/1856	14	135	N	
Schmaelzle, Jacob	40	Wuertemberg	Y	Bremen	Baltimore	04/10/1853	03/17/1856	26	211	N	
Schmalenberger, Peter	25	Germany	Y	Antwerp	New York	03/25/1887	07/21/1892			Y	
Schmalholz, George	33	Bavaria	Y	Bremen	New York	05/31/1853	06/02/1856	14	282	N	
Schmaltz, Gottlieb	34	Germany	Y	Bremen	Baltimore	09/15/1890	10/10/1892			Y	
Schmaltz, John Frederick	26	Bremen	Y	Bremen	New York	09/16/1854	09/21/1857	15	298	N	
Schmalz, Bernhard	26	Baden	Y	Havre	New Orleans	01/19/1848	09/21/1855	13	100	N	
Schmalz, Frank	32	Germany	Y	Havre	New York	09/14/1881	09/19/1885			Y	
Schmalz, Gustave	27	Germany	Y	Amsterdam	New York	04/09/1882	02/24/1885			Y	
Schmalz, Michael	55	Baden	Y	Havre	New Orleans	01/19/1848	09/21/1855	13	99	N	
Schmarr, Melchior	29	Germany	Y	Hamburg	New York	06/24/1882	06/02/1884			Y	
Schmas, Bernard	25	Germany	Y	Rotterdam	New York	06/27/1880	10/09/1883			Y	
Schmeder, William	30	Baden	Y	Dover	Buffalo	02/26/1857	08/15/1860	27	282	N	
Schmedinghoff, Joseph	25	Prussia	Y	Bremen	New York	09/21/1848	01/06/1851	2	454	N	
Schmeh, Anton	39	Germany	Y	Bremen	New York	05/??/1864	09/28/1882			Y	
Schmeing, Henry	34	Prussia	Y	Antwerp	New York	09/15/1857	11/01/1860	27	536	N	
Schmelsly, John	31	Wurttemberg	Y	Havre	New York	09/??/1847	12/17/1850	2	371	N	
Schmelter, Albert	33	Germany	Y	Hamburg	New York	11/30/1884	04/02/1894			Y	
Schmelzle, Fred	34	Germany	N	Rotterdam	New York	09/15/1872	?			Y	
Schmelzle, Michael	34	Germany	Y	Bremen	New York	10/11/1882	10/25/1888			Y	
Schmenger, Friederick	52	Germany	Y	Rotterdam	New York	06/10/1883	04/23/1886			Y	
Schmer, John	29	Germany	Y	Bremen	New York	06/29/1873	07/07/1879			Y	
Schmerge, John Bernard	31	Prussia	Y	Bremen	New Orleans	03/??/1846	11/??/1849	23	302	N	
Schmeussen, John Frederi	29	Germany	Y	Bremen	Baltimore	12/02/1882	10/16/1886			Y	
Schmey, Salo	41	Prussia	N	Prussia	New York	05/30/1867	?			Y	
Schmich, George	42	Germany	Y	Hamburg	New York	07/04/1878	10/22/1896			Y	
Schmid, Adam	32	Wurttemberg	Y	Havre	New York	10/01/1854	09/29/1856	14	2	N	

CITIZENSHIP RECORDS

APPLICANT	AGE	COUNTRY OF ORIGIN	DEC	DEPART PORT	ENTRY PORT	ARRIVE DATE	DEC DATE	VOL	PG.	FLD	NAT DATE
Schmid, Andrew	22	Wurttemberg	Y	Havre	New York	06/18/1854	02/19/1858	16	320	N	
Schmid, Casper	22	Wurttemberg	Y	London	New York	09/21/1853	09/25/1856	14	376	N	
Schmid, Christian	28	Wurttemberg	Y	Havre	New York	09/29/1854	10/20/1858	17	69	N	
Schmid, Christoph Freder	52	Wurttemberg	Y	Havre	New York	??/06/1854	04/30/1855	11	332	N	
Schmid, Edward	30	Germany	Y	Rotterdam	New York	08/28/1881	08/23/1890			Y	
Schmid, Emil	35	Switzerland	Y	Havre	New York	05/16/1881	05/28/1889			Y	
Schmid, Eugene	18	Germany	Y	?	?	?	04/01/1903			Y	
Schmid, Frank	34	Austria	Y	Hamburg	New York	04/10/1892	10/18/1900			Y	
Schmid, Franz Xavier	26	Germany	Y	Bremen	New York	07/15/1881	07/15/1882			Y	
Schmid, Frederick	55	Germany	N	Havre	New York	05/08/1854	?			Y	
Schmid, George	41	Germany	Y	Bremen	Baltimore	05/01/1888	02/03/1891			Y	
Schmid, John	32	Germany	Y	?	?	??/??/1881	05/02/1884			Y	
Schmid, John George	31	Wuerttenberg	Y	Havre	New York	11/08/1844	10/07/1848	22	482	N	
Schmid, John M.	41	Germany	N	Rotterdam	New York	11/??/1865	?			Y	
Schmid, Joseph	31	Germany	Y	Havre	New York	06/19/1882	06/22/1887			Y	
Schmid, Joseph	31	Germany	Y	Hamburg	New York	05/12/1893	10/22/1900			Y	
Schmid, Kasper	31	Germany	Y	Antwerp	New York	11/11/1881	09/15/1886			Y	
Schmid, Lambert	23	Germany	Y	Hamburg	New York	12/31/1881	01/30/1882			Y	
Schmid, Louis	33	Wuerttenberg	Y	London	New York	05/12/1848	02/10/1849	23	46	N	
Schmid, Mathias Adam	54	Germany	Y	Antwerp	New York	01/29/1883	09/19/1890			Y	
Schmid, Matthaus	23	Germany	Y	Hamburg	New York	12/31/1881	01/30/1882			Y	
Schmid, Matthew	35	Prussia	Y	Havre	New York	11/04/1854	03/31/1857	15	111	N	
Schmid, William	31	Germany	Y	Antwerp	Philadelphia	11/15/1889	06/16/1892			Y	
Schmidek, Theodore	26	Germany	Y	Bremen	New York	05/30/1884	12/15/1884			Y	
Schmidgall, Fred	36	Germany	Y	Bremen	New York	08/07/1893	06/09/1903			Y	
Schmidle, Joseph	40	Germany	N	Bremen	New York	07/07/1868	?			Y	
Schmidlin, Ambrose	29	Switzerland	Y	Havre	New York	05/03/1850	10/19/1852	5	20	N	
Schmidt, August	25	Germany	Y	Amsterdam	New York	08/24/1881	08/15/1884			Y	
Schmidt, August	30	Germany	Y	Bremen	New York	05/01/1880	06/04/1885			Y	
Schmidt, Benjamin	25	Germany	Y	Bremen	Baltimore	10/18/1887	11/01/1893			Y	
Schmidt, Benne	30	Prussia	Y	Bremen	Baltimore	??/06/1845	02/22/1850	2	116	N	
Schmidt, Bernard Henry	33	Hanover	Y	Bremen	New Orleans	11/06/1846	10/09/1854	6	57	N	
Schmidt, Bernard Henry	33	Hanover	Y	Bremen	New Orleans	11/06/1846	10/09/1854	11	58	N	
Schmidt, Carl	28	Germany	Y	Bremen	New York	09/21/1883	10/20/1887			Y	
Schmidt, Carl	38	Prussia	N	Hamburg	New York	07/??/1870	?			Y	
Schmidt, Casper H.	32	Prussia	Y	Bremen	New Orleans	07/04/1848	01/31/1851	3	66	N	
Schmidt, Charles	31	Hanover	Y	Bremen	Philadelphia	06/23/1846	02/15/1853	7	163	N	
Schmidt, Charles	28	Germany	Y	Bremen	New York	02/17/1887	03/21/1892			Y	
Schmidt, Charles	29	Germany	Y	Bremen	New York	04/??/1881	01/24/1887			Y	
Schmidt, Charles	26	Germany	Y	Bremen	New York	04/27/1884	05/05/1888			Y	
Schmidt, Charles	60	Germany	N	Bremen	New York	05/??/1851	?			Y	
Schmidt, Charles	25	Kurhassen	Y	Bremen	Baltimore	07/28/1847	01/21/1850	23	533	N	
Schmidt, Christ	21	Germany	Y	Bremen	New York	10/29/1888	12/09/1890			Y	
Schmidt, David	21	Germany	Y	Havre	New York	03/06/1882	03/21/1884			Y	
Schmidt, Diederich	27	Germany	Y	Bremen	New York	05/29/1886	07/18/1889			Y	
Schmidt, F. W.	40	Germany	Y	Bremen	New York	04/15/1881	12/26/1885			Y	
Schmidt, Ferdinand	29	Germany	Y	Amsterdam	New York	05/14/1883	04/04/1887			Y	
Schmidt, Francis	30	Prussia	Y	Antwerp	New Orleans	12/24/1853	11/02/1857	15	521	N	
Schmidt, Fred K.	39	Germany	N	Germany	New York	10/09/1856	?			Y	
Schmidt, Frederick	21	Bavaria	Y	Havre	New York	11/13/1853	01/12/1856	13	456	N	
Schmidt, Frederick	42	Prussia	Y	Bremen	New Orleans	11/10/1852	08/02/1856	14	308	N	
Schmidt, Frederick	37	Germany	Y	Bremen	New York	06/14/1880	02/07/1884			Y	
Schmidt, Frederick	34	Baden	Y	Antwerp	Galveston	08/15/1845	08/16/1848	22	188	N	
Schmidt, Frederick	51	Germany	N	Havre	New York	11/??/1853	01/??/1856	28	29	N	10/??/1860
Schmidt, Frederick	17	Germany	N	Havre	New York	11/00/1853	01/00/1856			Y	10/00/1860
Schmidt, Frederick Willi	35	Hanover	Y	Hamburg	Quebec	06/10/1849	10/05/1854	10	462	N	
Schmidt, Frederick Willi	35	Hanover	Y	Hamburg	Quebec	06/09/1849	10/05/1854	12	401	N	
Schmidt, Friedrich	23	Germany	Y	Bremen	Baltimore	05/28/1889	10/22/1889			Y	
Schmidt, George	37	Germany	Y	Liverpool	New York	04/19/1882	01/02/1886			Y	

CITIZENSHIP RECORDS

APPLICANT	AGE	COUNTRY OF ORIGIN	DEC	DEPART PORT	ENTRY PORT	ARRIVE DATE	DEC DATE	VOL	PG.	FLD	NAT DATE
Schmidt, George	39	Germany	Y	Bremen	New York	09/20/1890	10/08/1895			Y	
Schmidt, George	25	Germany	Y	Bremen	New York	??/??/1879	??/??/1881			Y	
Schmidt, George	35	Germany	Y	?	Baltimore	??/??/1869	10/11/1880			Y	
Schmidt, George	36	Germany	N	Bremen	New York	11/??/1879	?			Y	
Schmidt, George	27	Kurhessen	Y	Bremen	New York	09/08/1857	09/13/1860	27	370	N	
Schmidt, George M.	29	Bavaria	Y	Havre	New York	05/26/1849	05/26/1852	25	115	N	
Schmidt, Gottlieb F.	44	Germany	Y	Rotterdam	New York	05/29/1882	02/16/1888			Y	
Schmidt, Gustav	32	Germany	Y	Bremen	New York	10/01/1883	10/30/1888	19	204	N	
Schmidt, Gustav	32	Germany	Y	Bremen	New York	10/01/1883	10/30/1888			Y	
Schmidt, Gustav	31	Germany	Y	Bremen	Baltimore	06/08/1886	11/16/1886			Y	
Schmidt, Gustav	42	Germany	Y	Bremen	New York	05/24/1893	05/18/1895			Y	
Schmidt, Gustav Adolph	29	Baden	Y	Havre	New York	03/28/18??	06/05/1854	10	85	N	
Schmidt, Gustav Adolph	29	Baden	Y	Havre	New York	03/28/1852	06/05/1854	12	22	N	
Schmidt, H.	24	Germany	Y	Bremen	New York	04/07/1880	01/08/1885			Y	
Schmidt, H.	35	Germany	Y	Bremen	Baltimore	05/07/1875	11/01/1884			Y	
Schmidt, Henry	26	Hanover	Y	Bremen	New Orleans	12/10/1844	01/13/1849	1	415	N	
Schmidt, Henry	32	Prussia	Y	Antwerp	New York	06/30/1847	02/14/1850	2	76	N	
Schmidt, Henry	48	Bavaria	Y	Havre	New Orleans	05/25/1849	03/20/1850	2	228	N	
Schmidt, Henry	??	Prussia	Y	Bremen	New Orleans	??/16/1854	04/18/1855	11	269	N	
Schmidt, Henry	62	Hanover	Y	Brake	Baltimore	09/12/1860	09/05/1872	18	517	N	
Schmidt, Henry	25	Germany	Y	Hamburg	New York	08/19/1881	04/24/1882			Y	
Schmidt, Henry	30	Germany	Y	Bremen	New York	05/27/1883	01/07/1889			Y	
Schmidt, Henry	27	Germany	Y	Bremen	Baltimore	05/28/1884	04/18/1885			Y	
Schmidt, Henry	23	Hanover	Y	Bremen	Baltimore	06/10/1845	02/14/1849	23	92	N	
Schmidt, Henry	39	Germany	Y	Bremen	Baltimore	02/23/1887	07/05/1890			Y	
Schmidt, Herman	21	Hanover	Y	Bremen	Baltimore	10/18/1854	10/07/1857	15	365	N	
Schmidt, Herman	31	Switzerland	Y	Havre	New York	05/18/1881	10/15/1891			Y	
Schmidt, Herman	43	Germany	Y	Bremen	New York	01/24/1890	11/07/1892			Y	
Schmidt, Hermann	27	Germany	Y	Antwerp	New York	04/14/1881	09/16/1886			Y	
Schmidt, Jacob	30	Germany	Y	Bremen	New York	08/13/1880	01/19/1882			Y	
Schmidt, Jacob	24	Germany	Y	Rotterdam	New York	07/27/1884	10/01/1885			Y	
Schmidt, Johan J. F.	28	Germany	Y	Hamburg	New York	04/01/1880	05/21/1883			Y	
Schmidt, Johann	29	Hesse Darmsta	Y	Havre	New York	08/08/1853	12/20/1854	13	337	N	
Schmidt, John	34	Schwarzburg S	Y	Bremen	New York	08/01/1854	08/21/1855	11	473	N	
Schmidt, John	47	Holland	Y	Antwerp	New York	11/15/1854	04/03/1858	16	487	N	
Schmidt, John	24	Germany	Y	Havre	New York	06/02/1870	09/24/1872			Y	
Schmidt, John	36	Germany	Y	Bremen	Baltimore	05/31/1883	06/25/1889			Y	
Schmidt, John	36	Prussia	Y	Rotterdam	Baltimore	09/??/1846	11/??/1849	23	354	N	
Schmidt, John	40	Germany	Y	?	New York	06/01/1873	04/20/1888			Y	
Schmidt, John B.	43	Germany	Y	Bremen	New York	05/11/1887	01/23/1894			Y	
Schmidt, John Bernard	27	Hanover	Y	Bremen	New Orleans	12/31/1843	08/18/1848	22	206	N	
Schmidt, John F.	??	Germany	Y	?	?	?	05/13/1889			Y	
Schmidt, John Henry	25	France	Y	Havre	New York	05/04/1847	01/06/1851	2	458	N	
Schmidt, John Henry	27	Germany	Y	Bremen	Baltimore	04/31/1891	10/31/1895			Y	
Schmidt, John Martin	42	Wuerttemberg	Y	Havre	New Orleans	04/03/1851	04/10/1852	24	432	N	
Schmidt, Joseph	34	Bavaria	Y	Havre	New York	05/26/1849	03/19/1853	7	349	N	
Schmidt, Joseph	32	Germany	Y	Amsterdam	New York	08/25/1881	01/26/1892			Y	
Schmidt, Joseph	23	Germany	Y	Hamburg	New York	04/04/1884	12/04/1891			Y	
Schmidt, Joseph	30	Germany	Y	Hamburg	New York	06/07/1882	11/05/1888			Y	
Schmidt, Joseph	53	Austria	N	Hamburg	New York	06/06/1865	?			Y	
Schmidt, Joseph	23	Nassau	Y	Antwerp	New Orleans	11/25/1849	05/20/1852	25	51	N	
Schmidt, Louis	27	Germany	Y	Liverpool	New York	01/25/1866	02/01/1891			Y	
Schmidt, Louis	16	Germany	N	?	New York	00/00/1882				Y	10/26/1888
Schmidt, Martin	27	Germany	Y	Rotterdam	New York	11/27/1884	10/20/1891			Y	
Schmidt, Mathew	51	Germany	N	Havre	New York	08/14/1845	?			Y	
Schmidt, Max	31	Germany	Y	?	?	?	07/15/1892			Y	
Schmidt, Peter	25	Bavaria	Y	Havre	New Orleans	12/01/1858	04/09/1862	18	313	N	
Schmidt, Peter	49	Germany	N	Hamburg	New York	11/??/1863	?			Y	
Schmidt, Peter Henry	27	Prussia	Y	Bremen	Baltimore	05/17/1847	10/02/1848	22	384	N	

CITIZENSHIP RECORDS

APPLICANT	AGE	COUNTRY OF ORIGIN	DEC	DEPART PORT	ENTRY PORT	ARRIVE DATE	DEC DATE	VOL	PG.	FLD	NAT DATE
Schmidt, Peter Henry	28	Prussia	Y	Bremen	Baltimore	06/02/1847	02/14/1849	23	103	N	
Schmidt, Philip Charles	30	Prussia	Y	Antwerp	New York	06/02/1851	09/14/1855	13	33	N	
Schmidt, Philipp	32	Germany	Y	Antwerp	Philadelphia	06/22/1882	12/26/1883			Y	
Schmidt, Phillip	24	Hanover	Y	Bremen	Baltimore	07/04/1846	08/23/1848	22	238	N	
Schmidt, Sigmund	36	Baden	Y	Havre	New Orleans	11/30/1846	09/29/1856	14	422	N	
Schmidt, Theodore	33	Germany	N	Amsterdam	New York	07/23/1881	?			Y	
Schmidt, Theodore	26	Germany	Y	Bremen	Baltimore	06/30/1886	08/12/1890			Y	
Schmidt, Valentine	32	Germany	Y	Bremen	New York	06/01/1867	10/11/1872	18	534	N	
Schmidt, Wilhelm	44	Germany	Y	Hamburg	New York	06/03/1882	01/05/1886			Y	
Schmidt, Wilhelm	47	Germany	N	Bremen	New York	10/27/1862	?			Y	
Schmidt, William	32	Nassau	Y	Bremen	New York	01/15/1851	01/24/1853	7	54	N	
Schmidt, William	28	Hanover	Y	Bremen	Baltimore	07/22/1858	12/04/1858	17	376	N	
Schmidt, William	23	Germany	Y	Bremen	New York	10/01/1891	11/12/1896			Y	
Schmidtgall, Frederick	29	Wurtemberg	Y	Havre	New York	04/06/1849	09/13/1852	25	461	N	
Schmiedeke, William	44	Germany	Y	Stettin	New York	11/11/1874	09/27/1894			Y	
Schmiedeknecht, Friedric	21	Schwarzburg R	Y	Hamburg	New York	??/11/1846	10/09/1848	1	87	N	
Schmiemann, Henry	32	Germany	Y	Bremen	New York	09/20/1892	08/28/1894			Y	
Schmier, Herman	36	Germany	Y	Amsterdam	New York	09/23/1881	12/28/1883			Y	
Schmieth, Konrad	23	Germany	Y	Bremen	Baltimore	09/09/1881	12/19/1883			Y	
Schmiltekop, Herman	36	Hanover	Y	Bremen	Baltimore	10/01/1845	01/19/1849	1	474	N	
Schmit, John	23	Bavaria	Y	Bremen	Baltimore	08/14/1854	09/27/1854	10	272	N	
Schmit, John	23	Bavaria	Y	Bremen	Baltimore	08/14/1854	09/27/1854	12	211	N	
Schmit, John F.	58	Germany	Y	Havre	New Orleans	12/??/1872	10/07/1880			Y	
Schmit, Mathew	46	Baden	Y	Havre	New Orleans	12/24/1852	10/30/1858	17	209	N	
Schmit, Nicholas	??	Holland	Y	?	?	05/??/1883	06/03/1886			Y	
Schmithorst, Frederick	23	Prussia	Y	Bremen	New York	04/22/1857	05/13/1861	18	110	N	
Schmitker, Fritz	31	Germany	Y	Bremen	Baltimore	08/11/1881	04/29/1885			Y	
Schmitker, Henry	53	Prussia	N	Bremen	Baltimore	??/??/1861	?			Y	
Schmits, George	28	Germany	Y	Bremen	New York	06/22/1889	10/20/1892	19	274	N	
Schmits, George	28	Germany	Y	Bremen	New York	06/22/1889	10/20/1892			Y	
Schmitt, Adam	35	Baden	Y	Rotterdam	New Orleans	04/15/1848	01/28/1853	7	80	N	
Schmitt, Adam	30	Bavaria	Y	Rotterdam	New York	06/29/1849	05/01/1854	8	309	N	
Schmitt, Adam	24	Germany	Y	Bremen	New York	02/21/1885	09/02/1887			Y	
Schmitt, Adam	29	Germany	Y	Hamburg	New York	05/12/1880	03/13/1884			Y	
Schmitt, Alois	30	Germany	Y	Havre	New York	12/04/1892	11/16/1893			Y	
Schmitt, Andrew	21	Hesse Cassel	Y	Bremen	Philadelphia	05/27/1854	03/27/1856	26	361	N	
Schmitt, Berhard	28	Bavaria	Y	Bremen	Baltimore	10/24/1860	05/03/1861	18	155	N	
Schmitt, Charles	28	Germany	Y	Liverpool	New York	10/25/1884	03/30/1891			Y	
Schmitt, Charles	??	Prussia	Y	?	?	?	11/07/1882			Y	
Schmitt, Claude	27	Germany	Y	Havre	New York	03/01/1884	01/27/1891			Y	
Schmitt, Conrad P.	33	Germany	Y	?	New York	00/00/1871	10/17/1887			Y	
Schmitt, Franz	40	Germany	Y	Bremen	Baltimore	05/08/1882	10/19/1885			Y	
Schmitt, Frederick	26	Germany	Y	Bremen	New York	06/02/1880	12/26/1883			Y	
Schmitt, George	??	Bavaria	Y	Bremen	New York	05/28/18??	10/12/1848	1	161	N	
Schmitt, George	34	France	Y	Havre	New York	05/??/1852	04/16/1855	11	257	N	
Schmitt, George	33	Germany	Y	Anwterp	New York	01/01/1889	10/20/1891	19	338	N	
Schmitt, George	33	Germany	Y	Antwerp	New York	01/01/1889	10/20/1891			Y	
Schmitt, Henry	25	Hesse Cassel	Y	Antwerp	New York	07/19/1849	04/13/1852	24	495	N	
Schmitt, Herman	35	Germany	Y	Rotterdam	New York	08/24/1876	01/14/1889			Y	
Schmitt, Jean Pierre	33	France	Y	Havre	New York	09/26/1846	05/28/1852	25	124	N	
Schmitt, John	26	France	Y	Havre	New Orleans	12/09/1854	12/08/1857	16	208	N	
Schmitt, John	22	Germany	Y	Bremen	New York	06/03/1889	05/14/1891			Y	
Schmitt, John Frederick	30	Bavaria	Y	London	New York	05/15/1854	05/26/1856	26	553	N	
Schmitt, John Henry	38	Hanover	Y	Bremen	New Orleans	??/25/1843	10/09/1848	22	505	N	
Schmitt, Joseph	28	Bavaria	Y	London	New Orleans	03/13/1851	03/03/1856	26	150	N	
Schmitt, Laurent	32	France	Y	Havre	New Orleans	??/16/1852	04/16/1855	11	256	N	
Schmitt, Leopold	37	Germany	Y	Antwerp	New York	10/20/1883	08/16/1898			Y	
Schmitt, Louis	59	Germany	N	Bremen	New Orleans	04/??/1857	?			Y	
Schmitt, Michael	32	Germany	Y	Amsterdam	New York	03/18/1882	05/26/1890			Y	

CITIZENSHIP RECORDS

APPLICANT	AGE	COUNTRY OF ORIGIN	DEC	DEPART PORT	ENTRY PORT	ARRIVE DATE	DEC DATE	VOL	PG.	FLD	NAT DATE
Schmitt, Peter	30	Bavaria	Y	Havre	New York	09/27/1846	02/20/1849	23	226	N	
Schmitt, Valentine	29	Baden	Y	Havre	New Orleans	12/03/1846	02/12/1852	24	102	N	
Schmitt, Wilhelm	29	Germany	Y	Havre	New York	06/14/1883	08/20/1889			Y	
Schmitt, Zuirin	35	Baden	N	Havre	New York	03/08/1883	?			Y	
Schmitz, Arnold	31	Germany	Y	Bremen	New York	10/23/1887	01/03/1891			Y	
Schmitz, G. A.	49	Germany	Y	Bremen	New York	10/15/1863	09/25/1885			Y	
Schmitz, Gerhard Herman	36	Hanover	Y	Bremen	Baltimore	11/15/1853	11/01/1858	17	249	N	
Schmitz, H. B.	27	Germany	Y	Amsterdam	New York	09/22/1881	09/30/1885			Y	
Schmitz, Heinrich	49	Germany	Y	Amsterdam	New York	05/28/1882	08/15/1889			Y	
Schmitz, Heinrich Eugeni	36	Prussia	Y	Bremen	New York	05/09/1848	02/07/1853	7	121	N	
Schmitz, Henry	22	Prussia	Y	Bremen	Antwerp	08/20/1851	03/11/1852	24	291	N	
Schmitz, John	24	Germany	Y	Antwerp	New York	06/01/1897	11/05/1900			Y	
Schmitz, John Jost	49	Prussia	Y	Liverpool	Boston	05/28/1852	11/07/1855	13	184	N	
Schmoeller, Bernard	28	Prussia	Y	Bremen	Philadelphia	10/30/1858	02/14/1861	18	101	N	
Schmolke, Joseph	36	Germany	Y	Hamburg	New York	11/05/1872	09/29/1885			Y	
Schmoll, Jackob	29	Germany	Y	Hamburg	New York	07/13/1884	09/30/1884			Y	
Schmoll, Joseph	44	Germany	Y	Bremen	New York	05/17/1892	10/10/1893			Y	
Schmuck, Michael	35	Germany	Y	Rotterdam	New York	06/03/1881	12/18/1886			Y	
Schmuck, Peter	??	Germany	Y	?	?	?	07/28/1888			Y	
Schmucker, Martin	30	Bavaria	Y	Hamburg	New York	09/14/1855	03/25/1856	26	308	N	
Schmuelling, Frank	40	Germany	Y	Hamburg	New York	08/??/1875	04/26/1889			Y	
Schmuhl, William	23	Mecklenburg S	Y	Hamburg	New York	06/20/1852	09/13/1852	25	489	N	
Schmurtz, Frank	26	Hanover	Y	Bremen	New Orleans	03/07/1846	01/16/1849	1	441	N	
Schmutte, Ben	13	Germany	N	?	Baltimore	00/00/1880				Y	10/26/1888
Schmutte, Fred	19	Germany	N	Bremen	New York	11/01/1866	?			Y	
Schnabel, Henry	37	Saxe Gotha	Y	Bremen	Baltimore	12/16/1852	06/02/1854	9	476	N	
Schnabel, Henry	37	Saxe Gotha	Y	Bremen	Baltimore	12/16/1852	06/02/1854	10	59	N	
Schnabel, Richard T.	42	Germany	Y	Hamburg	New York	04/13/1881	07/12/1886			Y	
Schnaberger, Fred.	35	Switzerland	Y	Berne	New York	11/25/1893	05/04/1896			Y	
Schnake, Christian W. F.	21	Hanover	Y	Bremen	New York	05/31/1853	02/06/1856	26	54	N	
Schnarre, Casper	34	Prussia	Y	Bremen	Baltimore	09/01/1845	09/08/1852	25	421	N	
Schnebeck, Hermann	39	Germany	Y	Bremen	Baltimore	09/01/1881	03/27/1889			Y	
Schnebecke, John Henry	36	Prussia	Y	Bremen	Baltimore	05/03/1849	09/11/1855	13	3	N	
Schnebelt, Charles	17	Germany	N	?	New York	00/00/1880				Y	10/17/1888
Schneck, William	40	Germany	Y	Amsterdam	New York	05/28/1882	10/27/1893			Y	
Schnederbernd, H.	22	Germany	Y	Bremen	Baltimore	09/22/1881	11/01/1883			Y	
Schneebeli, Adolf	25	Switzerland	Y	Havre	New York	03/24/1885	05/10/1890			Y	
Schneeberger, Godfrey	??	Switzerland	Y	?	?	?	10/06/1884			Y	
Schneehain, John H.	28	Hesse Cassel	Y	Bremen	New York	07/??/1848	09/06/1852	25	384	N	
Schneemann, William	26	Prussia	Y	Bremen	New Orleans	01/01/1849	01/21/1851	2	513	N	
Schneider, Abraham	29	Russia	Y	Bremen	Baltimore	08/17/1891	03/20/1893			Y	
Schneider, Anton	47	Austria	Y	Hamburg	New York	10/09/1878	08/22/1884			Y	
Schneider, August	24	Germany	Y	Havre	New York	06/01/1882	09/10/1887			Y	
Schneider, August	24	Saxony	Y	Bremen	New York	10/01/1858	03/17/1860	27	128	N	
Schneider, Baptist	33	Holland	Y	Antwerp	New York	06/16/1854	02/10/1858	16	99	N	
Schneider, Benedict	35	Switzerland	Y	Havre	New York	10/26/1882	02/09/1886			Y	
Schneider, Bernard	28	Prussia	Y	Antwerp	New York	08/12/1849	03/12/1851	3	258	N	
Schneider, Bonaventur	25	Wurtemburg	Y	Havre	New York	05/13/1852	09/06/1852	25	379	N	
Schneider, Carl Gustav	38	Wurttemberg	Y	Havre	New Orleans	05/18/1849	10/07/1854	6	43	N	
Schneider, Charles Gusta	38	Wurttemberg	Y	Havre	New Orleans	05/18/1849	10/07/1854	11	44	N	
Schneider, Christian	46	Germany	Y	Hamburg	New York	12/03/1879	09/26/1885			Y	
Schneider, Conrad	46	Germany	N	?	Philadelphia	05/??/1854	??/??/1857	28	285	N	09/20/1860
Schneider, Daniel	23	Baden	Y	Havre	New Orleans	03/10/1846	08/07/1848	22	74	N	
Schneider, Edward	34	Germany	Y	Havre	New Orleans	11/28/1884	01/31/1894			Y	
Schneider, Felix	30	Germany	Y	Bremen	New York	07/17/1880	10/30/1889			Y	
Schneider, Francis	37	France	Y	Havre	New Orleans	05/19/1846	08/18/1848	22	203	N	
Schneider, Frank M.	42	Germany	Y	Bremen	New York	11/06/1885	10/31/1903			Y	
Schneider, Franz	30	Prussia	Y	Antwerp	New York	09/20/1850	09/24/1854	10	203	N	
Schneider, Franz	30	Prussia	Y	Antwerp	New York	09/20/1850	09/25/1854	12	142	N	

CITIZENSHIP RECORDS

APPLICANT	AGE	COUNTRY OF ORIGIN	DEC	DEPART PORT	ENTRY PORT	ARRIVE DATE	DEC DATE	VOL	PG.	FLD	NAT DATE
Schneider, Frederick	30	Germany	Y	Bremen	New York	06/02/1870	04/03/1882			Y	
Schneider, George	24	Bavaria	Y	Bremen	New York	05/19/1854	02/19/1858	16	319	N	
Schneider, George	35	Germany	Y	Bremen	New York	08/16/1883	10/10/1889			Y	
Schneider, Heinrich	36	Bavaria	Y	Havre	New York	06/03/1849	11/15/1852	6	418	N	
Schneider, Heinrich	29	Switzerland	Y	Havre	New York	03/23/1881	11/03/1885			Y	
Schneider, Henry	34	Switzerland	Y	Havre	New Orleans	04/27/1849	03/04/1850	2	155	N	
Schneider, Henry	26	Bavaria	Y	Havre	New York	06/03/1849	11/15/1852	5	293	N	
Schneider, Henry	34	Hesse Darmsta	Y	Antwerp	New York	05/18/1853	12/18/1855	13	332	N	
Schneider, Henry	47	Hesse Darmsta	Y	London	New York	06/10/1849	11/01/1858	17	258	N	
Schneider, Henry	17	Russia	N	?	New York	00/00/1878				Y	10/23/1888
Schneider, Henry F.	24	Germany	Y	Rotterdam	?	11/21/1880	11/04/1882			Y	
Schneider, Herman	17	Germany	N	?	New York	00/00/1874				Y	10/24/1888
Schneider, Jacob	41	Bavaria	Y	Havre	New York	08/26/1848	11/01/1852	5	153	N	
Schneider, Jacob	41	Bavaria	Y	Havre	New York	08/26/1848	11/01/1852	6	279	N	
Schneider, Jacob	24	Bavaria	Y	Havre	New York	10/??/1851	03/25/1853	7	400	N	
Schneider, Jacob	40	Germany	Y	Bremen	New York	05/17/1884	11/01/1892			Y	
Schneider, Jacob	52	Germany	Y	Bremen	New York	03/17/1882	02/24/1885			Y	
Schneider, Jean	29	Wurttemberg	Y	Antwerp	New York	08/17/1847	11/13/1848	1	262	N	
Schneider, John	23	Prussia	Y	London	Baltimore	06/29/1847	11/01/1852	5	126	N	
Schneider, John	23	Prussia	Y	London	Baltimore	06/27/1847	11/01/1852	6	252	N	
Schneider, John	38	Switzerland	Y	Havre	New York	01/16/1852	04/17/1854	8	142	N	
Schneider, John	27	Switzerland	Y	Havre	New York	11/20/1853	04/17/1854	8	144	N	
Schneider, John	38	Switzerland	Y	Havre	New York	01/16/1852	04/17/1854	9	13	N	
Schneider, John	27	Switzerland	Y	Havre	New York	11/20/1853	04/17/1854	9	15	N	
Schneider, John	30	Hesse Cassel	Y	Bremen	New York	08/15/1848	10/04/1854	10	430	N	
Schneider, John	30	Hesse Cassel	Y	Bremen	New York	08/15/1848	10/04/1854	12	369	N	
Schneider, John	21	Bavaria	Y	London	New York	09/12/1852	12/17/1855	13	320	N	
Schneider, John	22	Bavaria	Y	Bremen	Baltimore	08/14/1855	01/30/1856	13	521	N	
Schneider, John	50	Hesse Darmsta	Y	Antwerp	New York	11/28/1848	11/23/1857	16	41	N	
Schneider, John	35	Bavaria	Y	London	New York	09/01/1854	04/04/1862	18	298	N	
Schneider, John	29	Germany	Y	Bremen	New York	07/26/1881	08/20/1883			Y	
Schneider, John	22	Germany	Y	Amsterdam	New York	03/03/1890	10/28/1892			Y	
Schneider, John	33	Russia	Y	Bremen	New York	03/14/1887	03/06/1895			Y	
Schneider, John Baptist	29	Bavaria	Y	Bremen	New York	09/04/1854	05/20/1856	26	502	N	
Schneider, John George	52	Bavaria	Y	Havre	New Orleans	03/02/1852	11/13/1855	13	215	N	
Schneider, John George	31	Austria	Y	Bremen	Baltimore	02/02/1873	05/02/1879			Y	
Schneider, John Henry	29	Hanover	Y	Bremen	Baltimore	06/15/1845	06/10/1852	25	318	N	
Schneider, John Jacob	27	Bavaria	Y	Bremen	New York	04/29/1848	04/02/1853	7	503	N	
Schneider, John Mathias	22	Prussia	Y	Liverpool	New York	05/29/1853	04/04/1856	26	437	N	
Schneider, Joseph	40	Germany	Y	Bremen	New York	05/28/1881	10/20/1890	19	291	N	
Schneider, Joseph	40	Germany	Y	Bremen	New York	05/28/1881	10/20/1890			Y	
Schneider, Karl	??	Germany	Y	?	?	?	02/27/1899			Y	
Schneider, Karl	61	Germany	N	Havre	New York	04/??/1851	?			Y	
Schneider, Louis	28	Hesse Darmsta	Y	Antwerp	New York	09/14/1851	01/13/1853	7	22	N	
Schneider, Louis	22	Wurttemberg	Y	Havre	New York	01/03/1854	12/17/1857	16	227	N	
Schneider, Louis	34	Germany	Y	Hamburg	New York	06/01/1881	11/03/1887			Y	
Schneider, Louis	24	Baden	Y	Havre	New York	??/18/1846	11/??/1849	23	311	N	
Schneider, Louis Phillip	33	Baden	Y	Havre	New York	05/??/1842	07/07/1855	11	345	N	
Schneider, Ludwig	27	Germany	Y	Bremen	New York	05/15/1882	04/06/1885			Y	
Schneider, Martin	29	Wuerttemberg	Y	Havre	New York	08/19/1846	03/15/1852	24	306	N	
Schneider, Michael	31	Prussia	Y	Bremen	Baltimore	05/15/1857	02/08/1860	27	93	N	
Schneider, Nicholas	24	Hesse Darmsta	Y	Bremen	Baltimore	05/03/1850	03/08/1852	24	255	N	
Schneider, Nicholas	22	Prussia	Y	Liverpool	New York	05/29/1853	04/04/1856	26	438	N	
Schneider, Peter	31	Bavaria	Y	Bremen	New York	01/19/1858	09/03/1860	27	329	N	
Schneider, Philip	32	Bavaria	Y	Havre	New Orleans	05/28/1852	12/05/1857	16	195	N	
Schneider, Philip	??	Germany	Y	?	?	05/05/1885	11/05/1889			Y	
Schneider, Rudolph	25	Germany	Y	Rotterdam	New York	05/??/1883	10/23/1886	19	79	N	
Schneider, Sebastian	28	Bavaria	Y	London	New York	06/27/1854	12/13/1855	13	307	N	
Schneider, Thomas	58	Darmstadt	N	Liverpool	Baltimore	04/??/1852	?			Y	

346

CITIZENSHIP RECORDS

APPLICANT	AGE	COUNTRY OF ORIGIN	DEC	DEPART PORT	ENTRY PORT	ARRIVE DATE	DEC DATE	VOL	PG.	FLD	NAT DATE
Schneider, Valentine	31	Bavaria	Y	Havre	New Orleans	10/27/1854	10/16/1857	16	436	N	
Schneider, Victor	27	Germany	Y	Havre	New York	04/02/1892	03/14/1894			Y	
Schneider, Walter	28	Germany	Y	Antwerp	New York	06/17/1882	06/10/1889			Y	
Schneider, William	27	Bavaria	Y	Rotterdam	New York	12/??/1847	11/24/1852	5	340	N	
Schneiderlochner, Freder	30	France	Y	Havre	New Orleans	05/29/1849	05/17/1852	25	31	N	
Schneiderlochner, Martin	32	France	Y	Havre	New Orleans	05/29/1849	05/17/1852	25	29	N	
Schneiderloechner, John B	24	France	Y	Havre	New York	11/24/1856	12/29/1859	17	535	N	
Schneiter, Michael	28	Germany	Y	Bremen	Baltimore	04/02/1887	06/09/1890			Y	
Schnell, Christian	51	Bavaria	Y	Havre	New York	09/19/1854	10/04/1854	10	424	N	
Schnell, Christian	51	Bavaria	Y	Havre	New York	09/19/1854	10/04/1854	12	363	N	
Schnell, Heinrich	60	Germany	Y	Bremen	New York	05/30/1880	07/21/1890			Y	
Schnell, Herman	26	Germany	Y	Antwerp	New York	07/07/1882	03/23/1891			Y	
Schnell, Jacob	52	Bavaria	Y	Havre	New York	09/19/1854	10/04/1854	10	423	N	
Schnell, Jacob	52	Bavaria	Y	Havre	New York	09/19/1854	10/04/1854	12	362	N	
Schnell, John Henry Ludw	25	Brunswick	Y	Bremen	New York	10/08/1853	09/27/1854	12	203	N	
Schnell, Wilhelm	31	Germany	Y	Bremen	Baltimore	10/30/1889	10/26/1893			Y	
Schnellbacher, Carl	24	Germany	Y	Antwerp	New York	11/28/1894	06/24/1895			Y	
Schnelle, Carl	22	Germany	Y	Bremen	Baltimore	10/18/1882	01/13/1883			Y	
Schnelle, John Henry Lud	25	Brunswick	Y	Bremen	New York	10/08/1853	09/27/1854	10	264	N	
Schnelle, William	37	Brunswick	Y	Bremen	New Orleans	11/24/1845	11/13/1848	1	268	N	
Schneller, Bernard	30	Baden	Y	Havre	New Orleans	04/22/1851	03/28/1854	14	94	N	
Schneller, Laurenz	44	Hesse Darmsta	Y	Havre	New Orleans	04/24/1850	10/03/1854	10	387	N	
Schneller, Laurenz	44	Hesse Darmsta	Y	Havre	New Orleans	04/24/1850	10/03/1854	12	326	N	
Schnellke, Adolph	46	Germany	Y	Antwerp	New York	11/05/1882	12/12/1888			Y	
Schnepf, Andreas	53	Germany	Y	Bremen	New York	04/07/1890	10/14/1895			Y	
Schnepferling, George	23	Germany	Y	Bremen	Baltimore	10/02/1895	01/14/1897			Y	
Schnetschenan,	33	Germany	Y	Bremen	Baltimore	07/24/1890	11/02/1895			Y	
Schnetzer, Joseph	23	Germany (Aust	Y	Bremen	New York	06/01/1883	03/19/1885			Y	
Schnibling, Charles	25	Prussia	Y	Bremen	New Orleans	05/28/1848	08/02/1848	22	46	N	
Schnicke, Ernst William	54	Saxony	Y	Bremen	New York	08/16/1854	09/22/1857	15	299	N	
Schnieders, Bernard	29	Germany	Y	Rotterdam	New York	08/10/1884	10/24/1888	19	175	N	
Schnieders, Bernard	29	Germany	Y	Rotterdam	New York	08/10/1884	10/24/1888			N	
Schnieders, Frederick	37	Germany	Y	Rotterdam	New York	11/??/1871	07/31/1886			Y	
Schnier, Louis	25	Prussia	Y	Bremen	New York	10/??/1846	11/03/1851	4	474	N	
Schnitgocke, Joseph	25	Prussia	Y	Bremen	New York	06/12/1849	04/18/1854	9	79	N	
Schnitgoeke, Joseph	25	Prussia	Y	Bremen	New York	06/12/1849	04/18/1854	8	208	N	
Schnitker, John	52	Hanover	Y	Bremen	New York	10/12/1846	06/19/1851	3	426	N	
Schnitker, William	29	Hanover	Y	Bremen	Baltimore	08/08/1849	10/09/1854	6	109	N	
Schnitt, Adam	30	Bavaria	Y	Rotterdam	New York	06/29/1849	05/01/1854	9	182	N	
Schnitzler, Oscar	??	Germany	N	?	?	?	09/04/1901			Y	
Schnokelborg, Herman	40	Germany	N	Bremen	New York	12/03/1871	?			Y	
Schnorbus, Adam	29	Prussia	Y	Bremen	New Orleans	01/28/1852	04/01/1856	26	397	N	
Schnuck, Herman	21	Hanover	Y	Bremen	Baltimore	01/27/1860	02/17/1862	18	263	N	
Schnuerer, Jonas Marcus	22	Austria	Y	Hamburg	New York	08/15/1852	04/22/1854	8	240	N	
Schnull, Augustus	21	Prussia	Y	Bremen	Baltimore	05/17/1849	02/07/1852	24	71	N	
Schnuman, Charles	61	Germany	N	Bremen	New Orleans	01/01/1848	?			Y	
Schnurbusch, Anton	29	Prussia	Y	Bremen	New York	09/24/1854	10/07/1856	14	257	N	
Schnurer, Jonas Marcus	22	Austria	Y	Hamburg	New York	08/15/1852	04/22/1854	9	111	N	
Schnurr, Erman	54	Germany	Y	Hamburg	New York	06/10/1867	10/11/1884			Y	
Schober, John	34	Prussia	Y	Hamburg	New Orleans	11/08/1847	02/20/1849	23	228	N	
Schoberg, George	32	Hanover	Y	Bremen	Baltimore	06/05/1845	09/13/1852	25	458	N	
Schoberg, Joseph	41	Hanover	Y	Bremen	New Orleans	07/04/1849	11/26/1852	5	347	N	
Schobert, John	64	Germany	Y	Bremen	New York	11/09/1868	10/12/1900			Y	
Schoberth, George	23	Germany	Y	Bremen	Baltimore	03/26/1891	11/28/1891			Y	
Schoch, Louis	??	Germany	N	?	?	12/27/1871				Y	10/29/1892
Schoch, Rudolf	39	Switzerland	Y	Bremen	New Orleans	11/14/1870	02/28/1888			Y	
Schockenbaumer, Fred Wm.	31	Prussia	Y	Bremen	New Orleans	06/02/1847	04/26/1853	8	125	N	
Schockmann, John Gerhard	23	Hanover	Y	Bremen	Baltimore	05/24/1857	08/15/1860	27	284	N	
Schodel, Theodore	37	Prussia	Y	Bremen	Baltimore	10/04/1845	02/19/1849	23	184	N	

CITIZENSHIP RECORDS

APPLICANT	AGE	COUNTRY OF ORIGIN	DEC	DEPART PORT	ENTRY PORT	ARRIVE DATE	DEC DATE	VOL	PG.	FLD	NAT DATE
Schoeberl, Erhart	23	Wurttemberg	Y	Havre	New York	01/19/1870	11/11/1872	18	541	N	
Schoeffer, Henry	31	Bavaria	Y	Havre	New York	05/07/1848	05/11/1854	8	421	N	
Schoefler, Jacob	??	Germany	Y	?	?	?	07/20/1885			Y	
Schoellhammer, Albert	38	Germany	Y	Hamburg	New York	02/20/1881	01/14/1883			Y	
Schoellhammer, William	38	Germany	Y	Antwerp	New York	06/12/1884	05/10/1888			Y	
Schoemer, John	28	Prussia	Y	Havre	New York	04/24/1851	04/04/1853	8	30	N	
Schoemer, Nicholas	30	Prussia	Y	Antwerp	New York	09/10/1846	03/06/1850	2	164	N	
Schoen, Ferdinand	30	Prussia	Y	Bremen	Baltimore	08/??/1853	11/10/1856	14	479	N	
Schoen, Henry	27	Saxe Weimar E	Y	Bremen	New York	09/25/1855	10/03/1856	14	174	N	
Schoen, Henry	21	Germany	Y	Antwerp	Philadelphia	07/18/1883	08/09/1883			Y	
Schoen, Isaac	24	Saxe Weimar E	Y	Bremen	New York	07/01/1854	10/03/1856	14	173	N	
Schoen, John	23	Bavaria	Y	Bremen	Baltimore	08/15/1854	02/08/1858	16	84	N	
Schoene, Ernest	25	Germany	Y	Rotterdam	New York	11/13/1881	05/27/1884			Y	
Schoeneberger, Theodor E	23	Germany	Y	Antwerp	New York	02/20/1888	05/15/1893			Y	
Schoenecker, Frank	22	Austria	Y	Bremen	Baltimore	08/07/1883	05/25/1885			Y	
Schoenfeld, Abraam	39	Russia	Y	Bremen	Baltimore	04/??/1887	10/14/1892			Y	
Schoenfeld, Adaam	39	Russia	Y	Bremen	Baltimore	04/??/1887	10/14/1892	19	363	N	
Schoenfeld, Henry	38	Germany	Y	Bremen	Baltimore	12/05/1872	01/17/1887			Y	
Schoenhart, Simon	28	Germany	Y	Rotterdam	New York	05/10/1893	10/26/1896			Y	
Schoenhoft, Bernard	35	Germany	Y	Rotterdam	New York	05/08/1873	08/15/1882			Y	
Schoenig, J. William	37	Germany	N	Hamburg	New York	03/29/1870	?			Y	
Schoepf, Joseph	41	Austria	Y	Rotterdam	New York	02/17/1881	11/05/1892			Y	
Schoeppe, George	30	Germany	Y	Hamburg	New York	08/18/1881	08/16/1892			Y	
Schoeppel, Friedrich	17	Germany	N	?	New York	00/00/1882				Y	08/22/1888
Schoermaker, Charles	35	Baden	Y	Liverpool	New York	09/26/1852	10/01/1856	14	106	N	
Schoerzinger, Joseph	34	Baden	Y	Havre	New York	03/01/1851	04/17/1854	8	135	N	
Schoetker, Wilhelm	??	Germany	Y	?	Baltimore	08/??/1882	10/27/1886			Y	
Schoetmer, Jacob	22	Hanover	Y	Bremen	New Orleans	05/09/1851	12/03/1855	13	274	N	
Schoettelkott, John	63	Prussia	Y	Bremen	New York	??/04/1842	10/09/1848	1	95	N	
Schoettinger, Conrad	35	Bavaria	Y	Havre	New York	03/31/1845	09/30/1848	22	369	N	
Schoettinger, Martin	48	Germany	N	Havre	New Orleans	11/??/1853	?			Y	
Schoettinger, Peter	34	Bavaria	Y	Havre	New York	10/12/1847	02/19/1852	24	140	N	
Schoettle, Eugene	26	Germany	Y	Bremen	New York	05/02/1887	10/29/1890			Y	
Schoettlin, John	27	Switzerland	Y	Havre	New Orleans	03/27/1852	12/21/1855	13	338	N	
Schoettmer, John Bernard	26	Hanover	Y	Bremen	New York	11/30/1845	01/07/1850	23	474	N	
Schoettner, Henry	33	Hanover	Y	Bremen	New Orleans	11/??/1845	01/??/1850	23	471	N	
Schoh, John Henry	24	Prussia	Y	Bremen	Baltimore	11/??/1847	01/06/1851	2	462	N	
Schohl, Wolf	39	Bavaria	Y	Havre	New York	06/18/1847	06/12/1852	25	247	N	
Scholl, Christian	44	Wurttemberg	Y	Bremen	Baltimore	09/04/1843	05/02/1859	17	393	N	
Scholl, Daniel	28	Bavaria	Y	Havre	New Orleans	12/20/1848	09/13/1852	25	464	N	
Scholl, Mathias	38	Baden	Y	Havre	New York	10/10/1845	11/14/1848	1	293	N	
Scholl, Mike	40	Baden	Y	London	New York	01/18/1848	01/22/1849	1	485	N	
Scholl, Philipp	??	Germany	Y	?	?	?	03/13/1893			Y	
Scholl, Wolfgang	25	Germany	Y	Antwerp	Philadelphia	03/05/1889	03/18/1892			Y	
Scholle, Ernst Frederick	28	Germany	Y	Bremen	Baltimore	07/28/1891	07/22/1893			Y	
Scholle, Ferdinand	32	Germany	Y	Bremen	New York	01/08/1893	01/13/1898			Y	
Scholle, Frank	37	Hanover	Y	Bremen	Baltimore	10/15/1857	10/15/1860	27	495	N	
Scholle, Heinrich	44	Germany	Y	Bremen	New York	05/21/1881	10/01/1885			Y	
Scholle, Wilhelm	17	Germany	N	?	New York	00/00/1882				Y	11/03/1888
Scholz, J. T. J.	27	Germany	Y	Hamburg	Philadelphia	02/21/1879	12/28/1883			Y	
Scholz, William	39	Prussia	Y	Bremen	New York	10/22/1853	08/18/1860	27	293	N	
Schomaker, B. H.	24	Germany	Y	Rotterdam	New York	09/07/1878	03/01/1882			Y	
Schomaker, Gerhard H.	54	Germany	Y	Rotterdam	New York	09/07/1878	01/27/1881			Y	
Schomberg, Ernst	39	Germany	N	Bremen	New York	06/25/1868	?			Y	
Schomberg, William	28	Prussia	Y	Bremen	New Orleans	11/06/1849	11/06/1851	4	496	N	
Schomecker, Henry	50	Germany	Y	Bremen	New York	06/??/1863	10/25/1893	21	33	N	
Schomecker, Henry	50	Germany	Y	Bremen	New York	06/??/1863	10/25/1893			Y	
Schone, Ernst	30	Prussia	Y	Bremen	New York	07/18/1846	01/25/1849	1	513	N	
Schone, George Frank	25	Germany	Y	Bremen	New York	09/04/1888	11/01/1893			Y	

CITIZENSHIP RECORDS

APPLICANT	AGE	COUNTRY OF ORIGIN	DEC	DEPART PORT	ENTRY PORT	ARRIVE DATE	DEC DATE	VOL	PG.	FLD	NAT DATE
Schone, Theodore	23	Germany	Y	Bremen	New York	09/04/1888	10/26/1893	21	35	N	
Schone, Theodore	23	Germany	Y	Bremen	New York	09/04/1888	10/26/1893			Y	
Schoneberg, Fred	27	Germany	Y	Bremen	New York	06/08/1883	02/08/1884			Y	
Schoop, Adolph	28	Germany	Y	Hamburg	New York	05/23/1881	06/02/1884			Y	
Schopp, John George	25	Wuertemberg	Y	Havre	New York	09/23/1854	03/25/1856	26	299	N	
Schoppenhorst, Herman He	29	Prusia	Y	Bremen	Baltimore	09/12/1846	10/03/1848	22	409	N	
Schopper, Henry	36	Prussia	Y	Bremen	Baltimore	04/25/1847	09/24/1855	13	128	N	
Schorfheide, Henry W.	28	Hanover	Y	Bremen	Baltimore	09/24/1850	09/10/1852	25	441	N	
Schorl, Nicolaus	21	Baden	Y	Havre	New Orleans	01/01/1854	05/25/1854	9	392	N	
Schorle, Nicolaus	21	Baden	Y	Havre	New Orleans	01/01/1854	05/25/1854	8	518	N	
Schorli, Martin	33	Germany	Y	Antwerp	New York	05/02/1882	03/30/1888			Y	
Schorr, George	??	Bavaria	Y	?	New York	07/02/1852	11/03/1856	14	462	N	
Schorr, John A.	42	Germany	Y	Bremen	New York	10/21/1882	11/13/1883			Y	
Schorr, Saul	??	Turkey	Y	?	?	?	08/31/1893			Y	
Schott, Alois	24	Germany	Y	?	New York	??/??/1879	02/24/1886			Y	
Schott, Emil	30	Germany	Y	Bremen	New York	09/11/1888	12/17/1892	19	414	N	
Schott, Emil	30	Germany	Y	Bremen	New York	09/11/1888	12/17/1892			Y	
Schott, Ferdinand	32	Germany	Y	Havre	New York	11/12/1884	06/29/1891	19	329	N	
Schott, Ferdinand	32	Germany	Y	Havre	New York	11/12/1884	06/29/1891			Y	
Schott, Fred W.	32	Germany	Y	Bremen	New York	09/24/1880	08/19/1890			Y	
Schott, Gustav	33	Germany	Y	Havre	New York	06/05/1880	07/08/1887			Y	
Schott, John	44	Baden	Y	Havre	New Orleans	02/02/1851	10/02/1857	15	345	N	
Schott, John	28	Hesse Darmsta	Y	Bremen	New York	01/13/1853	02/12/1856	26	74	N	
Schott, Lorenz	29	France	Y	Havre	New Orleans	05/03/1853	06/09/1854	10	108	N	
Schott, Lorenz	29	France	Y	Havre	New Orleans	05/03/1853	06/09/1854	12	45	N	
Schottenfels, Jacob	35	Germany	Y	Hamburg	New York	11/??/1873	07/19/1890			Y	
Schrader, Ferdinand	35	Saxony	Y	Havre	New York	05/08/1846	10/05/1848	22	444	N	
Schrader, Justis	23	Kurhassen	Y	Bremen	New York	09/06/1847	08/01/1848	22	31	N	
Schraebski, Michael	38	Prussia	Y	Liverpool	New York	09/14/1849	01/15/1853	7	33	N	
Schraeck, Franz	39	Germany	Y	Bremen	Baltimore	07/17/1881	10/28/1886			Y	
Schraenkler, Henry	25	Baden	Y	Havre	New York	04/15/1847	11/03/1851	4	477	N	
Schraffenberger, Fred	16	Germany	N	?	New York	00/00/1883				Y	10/15/1888
Schrage, George Anton	26	Germany	Y	Bremen	New York	05/24/1884	04/17/1888			Y	
Schrameyer, Joseph	28	Prussia	Y	Bremen	Baltimore	06/03/1848	06/10/1852	25	228	N	
Schramm, Ernst Julius	??	Germany	Y	?	?	?	09/13/1881			Y	
Schramm, Henry	25	Germany	Y	Bremen	Baltimore	05/13/1881	03/22/1887			Y	
Schramm, John	45	Germany	Y	Bremen	Baltimore	03/02/1888	12/06/1897			Y	
Schramm, John	21	Germany	Y	Bremen	New York	04/07/1887	03/31/1887			Y	
Schramm, Karl	33	Germany	Y	Antwerp	New York	11/17/1882	04/02/1894			Y	
Schrand, Theodore	44	Germany	Y	Bremen	New York	06/03/1884	01/14/1895			Y	
Schrauder, John	29	Bavaria	Y	Bremen	New York	09/10/1852	06/01/1854	9	469	N	
Schrauder, John	29	Bavaria	Y	Bremen	New York	09/10/1852	06/01/1854	10	52	N	
Schrauder, Ulrich	21	Bavaria	Y	Bremen	Baltimore	05/01/1853	10/02/1856	14	160	N	
Schray, Gottlieb	36	Wuerttemberg	Y	Antwerp	New York	07/02/1853	08/20/1860	27	299	N	
Schray, Jacob	24	Germany	Y	?	?	?	01/23/1891			Y	
Schreck, John	32	Bavaria	Y	Havre	New Orleans	06/01/1855	11/24/1855	13	248	N	
Schreck, John	46	Bavaria	Y	Bremen	New York	05/28/1876	01/21/1891			Y	
Schreck, William	48	Bavaria	Y	Havre	New York	03/28/1852	05/31/1852	25	166	N	
Schreibeis, Valentine	36	Baden	Y	Liverpool	New York	05/19/1854	10/28/1858	17	138	N	
Schreiber, Emil	21	Germany	Y	Bremen	Baltimore	04/31/1892	09/13/1892			Y	
Schreiber, Gus Adolf	45	Switzerland	Y	Hamburg	New York	01/31/1872	04/04/1887			Y	
Schreiber, Joseph	26	Germany	Y	Havre	New York	06/03/1880	10/19/1887			Y	
Schreiber, Leonhard	66	Germany	N	Bremen	New York	10/07/1849	10/??/1849	28	414	N	10/??/1854
Schreiber, Peter	34	Germany	Y	Bremen	New York	06/19/1882	12/02/1885			Y	
Schreiber, Peter	41	Germany	N	Hamburg	New York	08/02/1871	?			Y	
Schreibers, Michael	28	Germany	Y	Havre	New York	04/01/1882	11/02/1889			Y	
Schreider, Henry	26	Denmark	Y	Hamburg	New York	09/07/1859	12/08/1859	17	497	N	
Schreieck, John	5	Germany	N	?	Baltimore	00/00/1872				Y	08/28/1888
Schreiner, Anton	24	Baden	Y	Havre	New Orleans	12/25/1856	10/15/1859			Y	

CITIZENSHIP RECORDS

APPLICANT	AGE	COUNTRY OF ORIGIN	DEC	DEPART PORT	ENTRY PORT	ARRIVE DATE	DEC DATE	VOL	PG.	FLD	NAT DATE
Schreiner, Christian	27	Wurttemberg	Y	London	New York	09/04/1853	10/19/1857	15	457	N	
Schreiner, Conrad	24	Hasse Cassel	Y	Bremen	New York	07/02/1845	08/15/1848	22	153	N	
Schreiner, George	42	Bavaria	Y	Bremen	Buffalo	10/24/1847	03/15/1852	24	304	N	
Schreiner, Jacob	29	Bavaria	Y	Havre	New Orleans	03/20/1843	07/29/1848	22	13	N	
Schreiner, Jacob	38	Hesse Cassel	Y	Bremen	New Orleans	05/03/1847	09/08/1852	25	407	N	
Schreiner, Johann	29	Germany	Y	Antwerp	New York	10/01/1883	10/29/1888			Y	
Schreiner, John	39	Nassau	Y	Havre	New York	12/20/1855	10/28/1858	17	139	N	
Schreiner, John	??	Germany	Y	Rotterdam	New York	11/30/1892	03/25/1897			Y	
Schreiner, Peter	28	Germany	Y	?	?	?	11/01/1894			Y	
Schreivogel, Bernhardt	40	Germany	Y	Bremen	New York	03/27/1880	05/21/1880			Y	
Schremker, Adam	32	Bavaria	Y	Bremen	Buffalo	08/20/1847	05/03/1854	8	360	N	
Schrencker, Adam	32	Bavaria	Y	Bremen	Buffalo	08/20/1847	05/03/1854	9	233	N	
Schrenker, John	32	Bavaria	Y	Bremen	Baltimore	07/10/1846	10/04/1848	1	53	N	
Schrenker, Pankroz	31	Germany	Y	Bremen	Baltimore	03/08/1882	10/26/1892			Y	
Schreyer, William	34	Germany	Y	?	?	?	10/23/1888			Y	
Schrichten, Gerhard	23	Holland	Y	Bremen	Baltimore	06/13/1845	06/12/1851	3	367	N	
Schriefer, Jacob	31	Germany	Y	Bremen	Baltimore	06/10/1882	07/12/1886			Y	
Schriekell, Frederick	30	Saxe Weimar	Y	Bremen	New York	12/25/1854	08/10/1860	27	260	N	
Schrigten, John Herman	33	Hanover	Y	Bremen	New Orleans	05/??/1851	09/22/1855	13	112	N	
Schriver, Peter	31	Germany	Y	?	?	?	10/20/1888			Y	
Schrock, Henry	39	Germany	Y	Bremen	Baltimore	04/27/1882	09/05/1887			Y	
Schroder, Bernard	65	Germany	Y	Bremen	Baltimore	05/18/1883	10/23/1889	19	252	N	
Schroder, Frederick	50	Hanover	Y	Bremen	New Orleans	10/??/1848	09/20/1855	13	84	N	
Schroder, Friedrich	76	Germany	Y	Bremen	New Orleans	11/27/1859	04/01/1880			Y	
Schroder, George	22	Germany	Y	Rotterdam	New York	10/22/1885	02/26/1889			Y	
Schroder, H.	22	Germany	Y	Hamburg	New York	04/15/1884	08/15/1887			Y	
Schroder, Heinrich	28	Germany	Y	Rotterdam	New York	04/16/1882	10/23/1889	19	253	N	
Schroder, Heinrich	28	Germany	Y	Rotterdam	New York	04/16/1882	10/23/1889			Y	
Schroder, Henry	24	Germany	Y	Amsterdam	New York	08/05/1883	11/04/1889			Y	
Schroder, John Cord	35	Hanover	Y	New Diep	Baltimore	10/25/1849	09/22/1854	12	98	N	
Schroder, Martin	23	Hesse Darmsta	Y	Liverpool	New York	07/04/1853	05/20/1854	9	552	N	
Schroder, Peter	30	Hanover	Y	Bremen	New York	06/25/1845	11/13/1848	1	256	N	
Schroeder, C. A.	27	Germany	Y	Rotterdam	New York	05/02/1881	01/06/1884			Y	
Schroeder, Charles	37	Prussia	Y	Bremen	New Orleans	11/30/1854	02/11/1858	16	303	N	
Schroeder, Charles	28	Saxe Coburg	Y	Hamburg	New York	12/01/1854	10/26/1858	17	113	N	
Schroeder, Charles Augus	36	Saxony	Y	Antwerp	New York	07/05/1849	07/17/1851	3	544	N	
Schroeder, Ferdinand	50	Germany	N	Bremen	Baltimore	05/19/1860	?			Y	
Schroeder, Frank	27	Hanover	Y	Bremen	New Orleans	11/18/1850	02/25/1852	24	171	N	
Schroeder, Fred	39	Germany	Y	Havre	New York	05/09/1883	12/28/1889			Y	
Schroeder, Frederick	32	Germany	Y	Bremen	New York	08/15/1885	10/16/1893			Y	
Schroeder, Frederick Hen	25	Hanover	Y	Bremen	Baltimore	09/14/1846	10/02/1848	22	383	N	
Schroeder, Frederick W.	58	Germany	N	Bremen	New York	10/??/1843	?	28	222	N	03/31/1851
Schroeder, Frederick W.	13	Germany	N	Bremen	New York	10/00/1843				Y	03/31/1851
Schroeder, H.	41	Germany	Y	Bremen	Baltimore	08/09/1883	11/23/1885			Y	
Schroeder, Henry	38	Oldenburg	Y	Bremen	New Orleans	11/16/1845	08/15/1851	4	134	N	
Schroeder, Henry	39	Hanover	Y	Bremen	Baltimore	08/22/1848	01/02/1856	13	417	N	
Schroeder, Henry	22	Prussia	Y	Bremen	Baltimore	11/02/1857	11/01/1858	17	238	N	
Schroeder, Henry	26	Germany	Y	Bremen	Baltimore	03/30/1882	10/10/1889			Y	
Schroeder, Henry	31	Oldenburg	Y	Bremen	Baltimore	06/14/1848	02/19/1849	23	186	N	
Schroeder, Henry F. D.	32	Hanover	Y	Bremen	New Orleans	06/09/1850	06/07/1852	25	197	N	
Schroeder, Hubert	30	Germany	Y	Antwerp	New York	06/27/1881	08/12/1884			Y	
Schroeder, John	26	Bavaria	Y	Bremen	New York	08/12/1853	10/10/1854	11	229	N	
Schroeder, John Albert	21	Hanover	Y	Bremen	New Orleans	11/20/1848	10/18/1851	4	325	N	
Schroeder, John Cord	35	Hanover	Y	New Diep	Baltimore	10/25/1849	09/22/1854	10	159	N	
Schroeder, John Gerhard	27	Hanover	Y	Bremen	New Orleans	11/20/1848	10/18/1851	4	324	N	
Schroeder, John Henry	36	Oldenburg	Y	Bremen	New Orleans	11/26/1846	02/19/1849	23	182	N	
Schroeder, John Henry	31	Hanover	Y	Bremen	New York	11/15/1845	04/03/1852	24	363	N	
Schroeder, John Henry	24	Oldenburg	Y	Bremen	Baltimore	05/04/1854	03/25/1856	26	332	N	
Schroeder, Martin	23	Hesse Darmsta	Y	Liverpool	New York	07/04/1853	05/30/1854	10	35	N	

CITIZENSHIP RECORDS

APPLICANT	AGE	COUNTRY OF ORIGIN	DEC	DEPART PORT	ENTRY PORT	ARRIVE DATE	DEC DATE	VOL	PG.	FLD	NAT DATE
Schroeder, Peter	44	Germany	Y	Hamburg	New York	05/01/1880	12/06/1880			Y	
Schroeder, R.	28	Germany	Y	Amsterdam	New York	07/27/1881	11/30/1886			Y	
Schroeder, W.	23	Germany	Y	Amsterdam	New York	11/20/1881	11/29/1884			Y	
Schroeder, William	28	Germany	Y	Bremen	New York	05/13/1882	10/01/1884			Y	
Schroeder, William	22	Germany	Y	Bremen	New York	09/11/1882	10/12/1885			Y	
Schroeker, John	25	Wurttemberg	Y	Havre	New York	08/18/1853	10/06/1854	10	508	N	
Schroeker, John	25	Wurttemberg	Y	Havre	New York	08/18/1853	10/06/1854	12	447	N	
Schroell, Frank	27	Prussia	Y	Antwerp	New York	10/20/1851	12/04/1852	5	377	N	
Schroer, Barney	23	Prussia	Y	Bremen	Baltimore	04/28/1847	02/03/1849	23	23	N	
Schroer, Bernhard	40	Germany	Y	Bremen	Baltimore	08/20/1890	10/06/1897			Y	
Schroer, George	24	Prussia	Y	Bremen	Baltimore	06/10/1858	03/11/1862	18	271	N	
Schroer, George Henry	29	Prussia	Y	Bremen	Baltimore	??/02/1845	08/13/1851	4	127	N	
Schroer, Herman Henry	26	Hanover	Y	Bremen	New Orleans	12/09/1848	12/10/1855	13	298	N	
Schroer, J. Bernard	22	Oldenburg	Y	Bremen	Baltimore	07/02/1859	05/13/1862	18	336	N	
Schroermeyer, Bernard	28	Prussia	Y	Bremen	New Orleans	10/21/1846	02/09/1852	24	80	N	
Schroff, Frank	45	Germany	Y	Bremen	New York	09/11/1878	10/09/1884			Y	
Schroff, Louis	23	Germany	Y	Bremen	New York	08/13/1881	11/27/1883			Y	
Schrohenlohr, John	53	Germany	Y	Antwerp	New York	10/29/1887	01/30/1893			Y	
Schrorrer, Walter	22	Switzerland	Y	Havre	New York	09/27/1880	10/03/1881			Y	
Schroth, Frederick	30	Wurttemberg	Y	Havre	New York	06/10/1853	02/18/1857	15	31	N	
Schroth, Gottfried	33	Hesse Darmsta	Y	Bremen	New York	07/14/1851	05/27/1854	9	434	N	
Schroth, Peter	40	Germany	Y	Bremen	New York	04/10/1884	11/14/1891			Y	
Schrotke, Christian Herm	37	Bavaria	Y	Bremen	New York	09/21/1854	10/12/1857	15	394	N	
Schuabel, Leonard Heinri	29	Germany	Y	?	?	04/29/1882	01/10/1887			Y	
Schub, Frederick	??	Germany	Y	?	?	?	06/15/1895			Y	
Schubach, Philip	36	Baden	Y	Havre	New Orleans	05/17/1854	08/26/1857	15	187	N	
Schuback, Charles G.	27	Germany	Y	?	New York	00/00/1882	04/17/1887			Y	
Schuber, John	36	Bavaria	Y	Havre	New York	01/16/1858	06/10/1859	17	458	N	
Schubert, August	31	Germany	Y	Rotterdam	New York	02/02/1883	03/30/1885			Y	
Schubert, Ernst	28	Germany	Y	?	?	12/18/1880	10/02/1888			Y	
Schubert, George	27	Bavaria	Y	Hamburg	New York	07/12/1846	06/16/1851	3	379	N	
Schubert, John	23	Bavaria	Y	Bremen	New York	10/05/1851	01/20/1852	24	36	N	
Schubert, John	25	Hamburg	Y	Hamburg	New Orleans	06/27/1851	05/25/1852	25	108	N	
Schuberth, William	41	Prussia	Y	Hamburg	New York	11/15/1851	10/06/1856	14	212	N	
Schuch, Henry	45	Germany	Y	Antwerp	New York	02/17/1888	10/26/1895			Y	
Schuch, Valentine	33	Germany	Y	Hamburg	New York	06/22/1882	12/26/1883			Y	
Schuchert, Philipp	27	Saxe Weimar E	Y	Hamburg	Buffalo	07/01/1855	10/08/1860	27	451	N	
Schuck, Jacob	27	Germany	Y	Amsterdam	New York	04/17/1882	05/25/1885			Y	
Schuck, Jacob	35	Germany	N	Antwerp	New York	05/25/1872	?			Y	
Schuck, John Eberhard	24	Hesse Cassel	Y	Bremen	New York	04/05/1845	08/15/1848	22	154	N	
Schuck, Robert	34	Germany	N	Bremen	?	??/??/1855	?			Y	
Schuckmann, G. H.	23	Germany	Y	Rotterdam	New York	08/30/1881	07/05/1884			Y	
Schuckmann, Henry	38	Germany	Y	Bremen	New York	08/07/1885	03/04/1887			Y	
Schudel, John	25	Switzerland	Y	Havre	New York	06/17/1888	10/01/1894			Y	
Schuderer, George	29	Bavaria	Y	Bremen	Baltimore	??/15/1847	12/15/1849	23	402	N	
Schudonia, Gustav	??	Germany	Y	?	?	?	10/29/1892			Y	
Schuele, George Frederic	49	Wurttemberg	Y	Bremen	New York	06/??/1853	04/01/1858	16	452	N	
Schuele, Jacob	26	Baden	Y	Havre	New York	07/01/1849	07/16/1855	11	394	N	
Schueler, Erich	38	Germany	Y	Bremen	New York	05/10/1864	06/27/1881			Y	
Schueler, Gregory	30	Germany	Y	Bremen	New York	10/08/1881	10/20/1886			Y	
Schueler, Valentine	25	Bavaria	Y	Havre	New York	09/??/1848	05/29/1854	10	18	N	
Schueler, William	26	Germany	Y	Hamburg	New York	08/18/1883	08/11/1887			Y	
Schuelkens, Henry	25	Hanover	Y	Bremen	New Orleans	05/24/1852	09/30/1856	14	45	N	
Schuelle, Joseph	28	Baden	Y	Havre	New Orleans	12/14/1854	09/14/1857	15	266	N	
Schueller, John	35	Baden	Y	Havre	New Orleans	03/14/1854	02/03/1857	14	533	N	
Schuelting, Gerhard	32	Germany	Y	Bremen	Baltimore	08/21/1884	10/22/1892	19	378	N	
Schuer, George	37	Germany	Y	Bremen	Baltimore	08/29/1877	12/03/1886			Y	
Schuer, John	33	Mecklenburg	Y	Hamburg	New Orleans	11/17/1847	02/19/1849	23	183	N	
Schuerer, Wenzel	26	Austria	Y	Bremen	Baltimore	08/22/1852	10/03/1854	10	405	N	

CITIZENSHIP RECORDS

APPLICANT	AGE	COUNTRY OF ORIGIN	DEC	DEPART PORT	ENTRY PORT	ARRIVE DATE	DEC DATE	VOL	PG.	FLD	NAT DATE
Schuering, Friedrich	25	Prussia	Y	Havre	New Orleans	12/17/1844	01/23/1849	1	494	N	
Schuering, Herman	26	Hanover	Y	Bremen	Baltimore	08/05/1846	10/03/1854	10	376	N	
Schuering, John Gerhard	32	Hanover	Y	Bremen	New Orleans	??/09/1852	04/28/1855	11	328	N	
Schuermann, Herman	29	Prussia	Y	Bremen	Baltimore	12/28/1849	11/20/1852	5	315	N	
Schuermann, Rudolph	38	Germany	Y	Bremen	Baltimore	08/29/1869	10/01/1883			Y	
Schuernstuhl, George	24	Germany	Y	Bremen	Baltimore	10/17/1888	12/08/1891			Y	
Schueschner, Richard	28	Germany	Y	Antwerp	New York	12/15/1892	10/05/1893			Y	
Schuester, Karl	25	Bavaria	Y	London	New York	04/26/1851	09/24/1854	10	202	N	
Schuett, Charles	33	Germany	Y	Bremen	New York	05/21/1881	11/19/1883			Y	
Schuettemeier, George	28	Germany	Y	Bremen	Baltimore	02/10/1882	02/25/1886			Y	
Schuetterle, Andreas	32	Germany	Y	Havre	New York	09/02/1880	08/09/1884			Y	
Schuetz, Lorenz	22	Baden	Y	Havre	New York	05/01/1854	03/25/1856	26	341	N	
Schuetze, John D.	23	Germany	Y	Bremen	New York	05/04/1869	12/16/1897			Y	
Schueve, Hanz Henry	33	Mecklenburg	Y	Hamburg	New Orleans	11/13/1847	03/27/1849	23	551	N	
Schug, Joseph	27	Germany	Y	Bremen	Baltimore	07/21/1879	05/08/1882			Y	
Schughardt, Herman Willi	26	Hesse Darmsta	Y	Bremen	Baltimore	09/04/1845	09/07/1848	22	308	N	
Schuh, Christian	35	Wurttemberg	Y	Bremen	New York	07/01/1845	01/26/1849	1	528	N	
Schuh, Daniel	29	Baden	Y	Havre	New York	09/29/1845	09/04/1848	22	292	N	
Schuh, John	22	Germany	Y	Bremen	New York	09/22/1883	09/25/1886			Y	
Schuhmacher, Paul	25	Wurttemberg	Y	Rotterdam	New York	06/29/1851	12/31/1855	13	399	N	
Schuhnacker, William	35	Germany	N	Bremen	New York	06/??/1869	?			Y	
Schukraft, Christian	22	Wuertemberg	Y	Havre	New York	08/15/1854	03/24/1856	26	254	N	
Schuldhois, John	32	Baden	Y	Havre	New Orleans	11/28/1851	05/24/1854	9	377	N	
Schulenberg, Gerhard	24	Prussia	Y	Bremen	New Orleans	12/07/1848	10/07/1851	4	213	N	
Schuler, Anthony	52	Bavaria	Y	Havre	New York	09/21/1854	10/04/1854	10	411	N	
Schuler, Anthony	52	Bavaria	Y	Havre	New York	09/21/1854	10/04/1854	12	350	N	
Schuler, Anton	28	Germany	Y	Bremen	Baltimore	09/23/1880	01/28/1886			Y	
Schuler, Edward	22	Germany	Y	Bremen	New York	03/05/1881	03/06/1883			Y	
Schuler, Frederick	22	Bavaria	Y	Ilbersheim	New York	05/07/1855	09/20/1858	16	159	N	
Schuler, George	30	Wurttemberg	Y	Liverpool	New York	12/06/1852	12/05/1855	13	272	N	
Schuler, John	31	Wurttemberg	Y	Rotterdam	New York	07/04/1845	02/25/1850	2	123	N	
Schuler, Joseph	29	Germany	Y	Bremen	New York	03/23/1884	10/14/1887			Y	
Schuler, Joseph	30	Germany	Y	Bremen	New York	05/28/1890	05/28/1895			Y	
Schuler, Mathias	28	Wurttemberg	Y	Havre	New York	04/26/1854	02/12/1858	16	306	N	
Schuler, Robert	24	Germany	Y	Bremen	New York	10/22/1880	02/03/1885			Y	
Schuler, Valentine	25	Bavaria	Y	Havre	New York	09/??/1848	05/27/1854	9	435	N	
Schuler, William C.	26	Germany	Y	Bremen	New York	02/15/1875	10/10/1881			Y	
Schulle, Joseph	??	Germany	Y	?	New York	04/21/1881	09/06/1883			Y	
Schuller, Hermann	32	Germany	Y	Hamburg	New York	11/04/1875	03/07/1883			Y	
Schuller, Mathias	23	Holland	Y	Havre	New York	06/12/1859	06/16/1862	18	351	N	
Schullman, P.	33	Russia	Y	Hamburg	New York	06/28/1881	05/15/1883			Y	
Schullman, Peter	40	Russia	Y	Hamburg	New York	06/28/1881	05/15/1883	28	92	N	?
Schullman, Peter	35	Russia	Y	Hamburg	New York	06/28/1881	05/15/1883			Y	
Schulman, A. S.	24	Austria	Y	Hamburg	New York	02/05/1883	02/15/1883			Y	
Schulman, A. S.	24	Austria	N	Hamburg	New York	02/05/1883	?			Y	
Schulman, Joe	16	Russia	N	?	New York	00/00/1882				Y	10/09/1888
Schulte, Albert	54	Germany	Y	Bremen	Baltimore	06/23/1882	10/18/1888			Y	
Schulte, August	22	Germany	Y	Amsterdam	New York	05/15/1882	02/27/1885			Y	
Schulte, B.	35	Germany	Y	Amsterdam	New York	03/09/1884	10/26/1895			Y	
Schulte, B. Clemens	36	Germany	Y	Bremen	Baltimore	08/00/1866	03/31/1883			Y	
Schulte, Bernard	24	Germany	Y	Rotterdam	New York	10/25/1887	11/01/1890			Y	
Schulte, Bernard Henry	45	Hanover	Y	Bremen	New Orleans	11/30/1857	04/25/1861	18	148	N	
Schulte, Edward	48	Prussia	Y	Antwerp	New York	10/08/1879	10/13/1884			Y	
Schulte, George	26	Germany	Y	Bremen	Baltimore	11/19/1873	10/14/1879			Y	
Schulte, Gerhard	32	Germany	Y	Bremen	New York	11/24/1892	01/27/1899			Y	
Schulte, Heinrich	26	Hanover	Y	Bremen	Baltimore	10/26/1857	11/18/1860	27	530	N	
Schulte, Henry	25	Hanover	Y	Bremen	Baltimore	11/25/1852	04/18/1862	18	320	N	
Schulte, Henry	22	Germany	Y	Bremen	Baltimore	06/22/1882	12/03/1885			Y	
Schulte, Herman	33	Germany	Y	Bremen	New York	05/??/1875	05/03/1883			Y	

CITIZENSHIP RECORDS

APPLICANT	AGE	COUNTRY OF ORIGIN	DEC	DEPART PORT	ENTRY PORT	ARRIVE DATE	DEC DATE	VOL	PG.	FLD	NAT DATE
Schulte, John B.	24	Oldenburg	Y	Bremen	New York	12/14/1858	02/16/1861	18	103	N	
Schulte, John Barney	25	Hanover	Y	Bremen	New Orleans	06/12/1845	09/30/1848	22	372	N	
Schulte, John Bernard	25	Hanover	Y	Bremen	New Orleans	12/20/1845	12/13/1852	5	410	N	
Schulte, John George	29	Hanover	Y	Bremen	New Orleans	06/01/1845	09/12/1848	22	335	N	
Schulte, Joseph	33	Prussia	Y	Bremen	Baltimore	11/05/1846	06/19/1851	3	423	N	
Schulte, Joseph	33	Prussia	Y	Bremen	Baltimore	09/??/1848	10/23/1851	4	380	N	
Schulte, Rudolph V.	29	Germany	Y	Antwerp	Philadelphia	06/11/1881	11/06/1889			Y	
Schulte, Theodore	24	Hanover	Y	Bremen	New Orleans	12/09/18??	10/28/1851	4	423	N	
Schulte, William	??	Prussia	Y	Bremen	New York	05/27/18??	10/09/1848	1	100	N	
Schulte, William	27	Prussia	Y	Bremen	Galveston	05/??/1851	04/16/1855	11	259	N	
Schulte, William	28	Prussia	Y	Bremen	New Orleans	05/08/1857	11/01/1860	27	546	N	
Schulten, Bernard Herman	29	Hanover	Y	Havre	New Orleans	04/07/1849	11/09/1855	14	198	N	
Schulten, Gerhard	25	Germany	Y	Bremen	Baltimore	04/08/1880	04/06/1883			Y	
Schulten, Herman	27	Germany	Y	Bremen	Baltimore	04/30/1882	03/24/1885			Y	
Schulten, John Bernard	22	Hanover	Y	Bremen	Baltimore	08/10/1859	06/19/1862	18	356	N	
Schultes, Anton	27	Germany	Y	Hamburg	New York	07/26/1882	02/15/1884			Y	
Schultheis, Johann	21	Germany	Y	Antwerp	Philadelphia	07/21/1897	08/06/1900			Y	
Schultheis, John G.	21	Wurttemberg	Y	Havre	New York	06/05/1852	03/09/1857	15	77	N	
Schultheis, Joseph	40	Wurttemberg	Y	Havre	New York	09/25/1848	04/21/1853	8	93	N	
Schultheiss, August	25	Wurttemberg	Y	Havre	New York	11/21/1853	09/21/18??	10	145	N	
Schultheiss, August	25	Wurttemberg	Y	Havre	New York	11/21/1853	09/21/18??	12	84	N	
Schultheiss, Peter	36	Germany	Y	Havre	New York	02/27/1880	10/27/1888			Y	
Schultheisz, John	32	Baden	Y	Havre	New Orleans	11/28/1851	05/24/1854	8	503	N	
Schultz, Aloys	37	Germany	Y	Bremen	New York	11/01/1894	02/18/1896			Y	
Schultz, Carl Hermann	23	Switzerland	Y	Hamburg	New York	08/02/1884	05/05/1888			Y	
Schultz, Charles	28	Germany	Y	Bremen	Baltimore	09/27/1883	09/17/1888			Y	
Schultz, Charles	??	Germany	Y	Antwerp	New York	06/09/1882	02/18/1886			Y	
Schultz, Christian Louis	45	Hanover	Y	Bremen	New York	07/01/1846	10/26/1858	17	118	N	
Schultz, Edward	26	Germany	Y	Antwerp	New York	11/20/1892	04/14/1893			Y	
Schultz, Frank	38	Austria	Y	Hamburg	New York	10/02/1885	10/21/1893			Y	
Schultz, Fred	34	Germany	Y	Antwerp	Philadelphia	05/14/1881	10/12/1896			Y	
Schultz, George	32	Mecklenburg S	Y	Hamburg	New York	06/01/1853	04/19/1854	8	215	N	
Schultz, George	32	Mecklenburg S	Y	Hamburg	New York	06/01/1853	04/19/1854	9	86	N	
Schultz, Hermann	30	Germany	Y	Bremen	New York	06/28/1880	07/06/1885			Y	
Schultz, John	27	Germany	Y	Hamburg	New York	08/28/1883	04/28/1891			Y	
Schultz, John	32	Prussia	Y	Bremen	Baltimore	08/01/1845	08/15/1848	22	148	N	
Schultz, John	21	Bavaria	Y	Havre	New York	05/07/1857	04/19/1860	27	167	N	
Schultz, Joseph	31	Germany	Y	Antwerp	New York	06/04/1885	04/22/1891			Y	
Schultz, Ludwig	25	Bavaria	Y	Liverpool	New York	??/06/1846	02/15/1850	2	79	N	
Schultz, Mathaus	25	Germany	Y	Antwerp	New York	11/01/1888	08/25/1890			Y	
Schultz, Peter	44	Bavaria	Y	Havre	New Orleans	11/18/1851	10/02/1854	10	335	N	
Schultz, Peter	44	Bavaria	Y	Havre	New Orleans	11/18/1851	10/02/1854	12	274	N	
Schultz, Philipp	31	Germany	Y	Amsterdam	New York	08/27/1883	10/08/1889			Y	
Schultz, Robert	23	Prussia	Y	Bremen	New York	07/10/1848	07/05/1851	3	497	N	
Schultz, Theodore	41	Germany	N	Hamburg	New York	04/02/1872	?			Y	
Schultz, Theophile	32	Germany	Y	Havre	New York	03/02/1891	09/24/1892			Y	
Schultz, Valentine	29	Germany	Y	Havre	New York	04/11/1880	01/13/1883			Y	
Schultz, William	34	Hamburg	Y	Liverpool	New Orleans	02/05/1851	05/01/1854	8	336	N	
Schultz, William	34	Hamburg	Y	Liverpool	New Orleans	02/05/1851	05/01/1854	9	209	N	
Schultz, William	25	Hanover	Y	Bremen	Baltimore	05/??/1854	02/07/1857	14	544	N	
Schultze, Adolph Frederi	36	Hesse Cassel	Y	Bremen	New York	04/21/1857	05/23/1859	17	424	N	
Schultze, Bernard	26	Oldenburg	Y	Bremen	New Orleans	06/25/1849	05/02/1854	8	342	N	
Schultze, Bernard	26	Oldenburg	Y	Bremen	New Orleans	06/25/1849	05/02/1854	9	215	N	
Schultze, Frederick	29	Prussia	Y	Bremen	New York	07/08/1853	09/20/1855	13	83	N	
Schultze, George	23	Bremen	Y	Bremen	New York	07/23/1853	10/03/1854	10	373	N	
Schultze, George	23	Bremen	Y	Bremen	New York	07/23/1853	10/03/1854	12	312	N	
Schultze, Herman	33	Germany	Y	Liverpool	New York	07/19/1887	10/23/1896			Y	
Schulz, Albert	??	Germany	Y	?	?	?	10/26/1891			Y	
Schulz, Charles	32	Saxony	Y	Bremen	New York	09/13/1850	12/27/1852	5	453	N	

CITIZENSHIP RECORDS

APPLICANT	AGE	COUNTRY OF ORIGIN	DEC	DEPART PORT	ENTRY PORT	ARRIVE DATE	DEC DATE	VOL	PG.	FLD	NAT DATE
Schulz, Charles	32	Prussia	Y	Bremen	New York	02/28/1854	02/04/1858	16	75	N	
Schulz, Herman	??	Germany	Y	?	?	06/15/1885	03/30/1886			Y	
Schulz, John	35	Prussia	Y	Hamburg	New Orleans	11/??/1853	01/27/1857	14	512	N	
Schulz, John	41	Wuerttenberg	Y	Rotterdam	Baltimore	06/23/1846	08/23/1848	22	233	N	
Schulz, John	43	Wuerttemberg	Y	Havre	New York	07/17/1857	10/08/1860	27	421	N	
Schulz, Joseph	27	Germany	Y	Liverpool	New York	05/??/1881	02/25/1888			Y	
Schulz, Markus	30	Germany	Y	Havre	New York	05/26/1882	06/08/1888			Y	
Schulz, Reinhold	35	Germany	Y	Bremen	New York	05/10/1885	11/06/1893			Y	
Schulz, Stephan	66	Wuerttemberg	Y	Antwerp	New York	05/??/1854	02/07/1865	28	356	N	?
Schulz, Stephen	48	Wurtemberg	Y	Antwerp	New York	05/00/1854	02/07/1865				
Schulz, William	44	Prussia	Y	Bremen	New York	11/02/1848	10/14/1851	4	284	N	
Schulz, William	22	Hanover	Y	Hamburg	New York	01/24/1868	11/04/1871	18	438	N	
Schulze, Bernard Henry	31	Oldenburg	Y	Bremen	New Orleans	11/21/1852	03/14/1856	26	197	N	
Schulze, Carl	26	Germany	Y	Hamburg	New York	08/15/1883	08/21/1886			Y	
Schulze, F. William	20	Prussia	Y	Bremen	Baltimore	05/01/1848	12/31/1852	5	481	N	
Schulze, Oscar	??	Germany	Y	?	?	?	01/14/1895			Y	
Schum, Adam	31	Hesse Darmsta	Y	Havre	New York	10/28/1855	04/05/1856	26	442	N	
Schumacher, Alexander	45	Germany	Y	Rotterdam	New York	05/24/1882	07/06/1895			Y	
Schumacher, Charles H.	45	Germany	Y	Antwerp	Philadelphia	09/20/1884	11/14/1890			Y	
Schumacher, Ernst	26	Germany	Y	Hamburg	New York	06/04/1878	02/21/1881			Y	
Schumacher, Frederick	28	Wurttemberg	Y	Havre	New York	08/20/1852	12/27/1859	17	529	N	
Schumacher, H.	24	Germany	Y	Bremen	New York	09/13/1880	02/09/1884			Y	
Schumacher, Henry	29	Germany	Y	Hamburg	New York	05/22/1883	10/01/1883			Y	
Schumacher, John	27	Germany	Y	Bremen	Hoboken	11/07/1879	05/22/1885			Y	
Schumacher, Rudolph	27	Germany	Y	Bremen	Baltimore	05/24/1874	11/05/1892			Y	
Schumacker, Anton	28	Prussia	Y	Bremen	New Orleans	01/12/1847	02/19/1849	23	213	N	
Schumacker, Charles	22	Mecklenburg S	Y	Hamburg	New York	10/24/1851	03/28/1853	7	423	N	
Schumacker, John Christ.	33	Mecklenburg S	Y	Hamburg	New York	10/24/1851	03/28/1853	7	422	N	
Schumaker, George	28	Germany	Y	Bremen	Baltimore	12/00/1881	10/27/1890			Y	
Schumaker, John Henry	47	Oldenburg	Y	Bremen	Baltimore	08/30/1846	03/17/1851	3	282	N	
Schuman, Jacob	38	Russia	Y	Bremen	Baltimore	07/15/1890	12/21/1895			Y	
Schumann, Fred William	23	Saxony	Y	Hamburg	New Orleans	08/08/1847	02/20/1849	23	231	N	
Schumann, Frederick Erns	23	Saxony	Y	Hamburg	New York	10/20/1850	03/07/1853	7	292	N	
Schumann, Fridolin	27	Saxony	Y	Bremen	New York	09/01/1854	12/10/1857	16	213	N	
Schumann, John F. A.	24	Prussia	Y	Bremen	New Orleans	07/06/1850	05/14/1852	25	20	N	
Schumann, Nathan	32	Russia	Y	Havre	New York	10/22/1888	10/25/1900			Y	
Schumer, George	41	Bavaria	Y	Havre	New Orleans	04/17/1848	03/26/1853	7	405	N	
Schumm, John	24	Germany	Y	Hamburg	New York	04/12/1881	12/17/1885			Y	
Schunder, John	39	Baden	Y	Havre	New York	10/27/1853	10/23/1857	15	481	N	
Schunemann, Theodor	35	Germany	Y	Hamburg	New York	03/28/1881	03/29/1887			Y	
Schungel, Martin	40	Germany	Y	Havre	New York	01/01/1881	09/13/1881			Y	
Schunk, Andrew	48	Germany	N	Bremen	Baltimore	05/??/1857	?			Y	
Schunk, John	28	Germany	Y	Bremen	New York	09/27/1882	03/13/1884			Y	
Schupert, August	27	Saxony	Y	Bremen	New York	08/19/1850	12/23/1851	4	552	N	
Schupp, Conrad	22	France	Y	Havre	New York	10/18/1848	02/27/1851	3	176	N	
Schur, Max	34	Russia	Y	Liverpool	New York	01/08/1885	10/17/1891			Y	
Schurer, Wenzel	26	Austria	Y	Bremen	Baltimore	08/23/1852	10/03/1854	12	344	N	
Schuring, Herman	26	Hanover	Y	Bremen	Baltimore	08/05/1846	10/03/1854	12	315	N	
Schurkamp, Philip	26	Prussia	Y	Bremen	Baltimore	08/08/1845	10/02/1848	1	22	N	
Schurz, William	45	Germany	Y	Hamburg	New York	03/01/1878	10/12/1893	21	1	N	
Schurzinger, Joseph	34	Baden	Y	Havre	New York	03/01/1851	04/17/1854	9	6	N	
Schuster, George	40	Bavaria	Y	Bremen	Baltimore	02/14/1849	11/05/1858	17	278	N	
Schuster, George	40	Germany	Y	Bremen	New York	05/29/1873	01/29/1884			Y	
Schuster, Gottlieb	34	Prussia	Y	Bremen	New York	03/09/1857	03/11/1860	27	122	N	
Schuster, Henry	28	Germany	Y	Bremen	Baltimore	05/28/1881	03/23/1885			Y	
Schuster, John	23	Bavaria	Y	Bremen	New York	07/08/1852	10/07/1854	10	523	N	
Schuster, John	23	Bavaria	Y	Bremen	New York	07/08/1852	10/07/1854	12	462	N	
Schuster, John G.	49	Germany	Y	Bremen	Baltimore	11/??/1882	03/06/1886			Y	
Schuster, Joseph	25	Prussia	Y	Antwerp	New York	06/20/1854	08/25/1855	11	490	N	

CITIZENSHIP RECORDS

APPLICANT	AGE	COUNTRY OF ORIGIN	DEC	DEPART PORT	ENTRY PORT	ARRIVE DATE	DEC DATE	VOL	PG.	FLD	NAT DATE
Schuster, Karl	25	Bavaria	Y	London	New York	04/26/1851	09/25/1854	12	141	N	
Schuster, Nicolaus	35	Bavaria	Y	Havre	New York	08/29/1852	03/15/1856	26	208	N	
Schuster, Paul	28	Germany	Y	Bremen	Baltimore	10/02/1892	12/26/1893			Y	
Schuster, Samuel	54	Germany	N	Bremen	New York	07/25/1860	?			Y	
Schuster, Sebastian	22	Baden	Y	Antwerp	New York	09/11/1848	03/12/1851	3	257	N	
Schuster, Theodore	27	Wurtemberg	Y	London	New York	10/11/1848	09/07/1852	25	405	N	
Schuster, Thomas	34	Bavaria	Y	Bremen	New York	09/??/1846	10/28/1858	17	166	N	
Schuster, William	25	Nassau	Y	Antwerp	New York	09/01/1849	02/25/1852	24	165	N	
Schuster, William August	26	Wurttemberg	Y	London	New York	10/04/1847	04/18/1853	8	79	N	
Schutte, Anthony	56	Germany	Y	Bremen	Baltimore	09/??/1872	10/13/1884			Y	
Schutte, Anton	29	Hanover	Y	Bremen	Baltimore	06/03/1845	08/24/1848	22	248	N	
Schutte, Herman	38	Oldenburg	Y	Bremen	New Orleans	11/04/1846	11/08/1851	4	501	N	
Schutte, W.	30	Germany	Y	Bremen	Baltimore	09/12/1874	10/08/1880			Y	
Schutte, William	27	Prussia	Y	Bremen	Baltimore	05/12/1848	06/19/1851	3	420	N	
Schutter, Geory	40	Germany	Y	Antwerp	New York	10/20/1885	03/26/1900			Y	
Schutterle, Michael	27	Baden	Y	Havre	New Orleans	12/31/1846	08/14/1848	22	108	N	
Schvener, Michael	37	Prussia	Y	Hamburg	Buffalo	01/01/1856	02/06/1858	16	82	N	
Schwaab, John	29	Bavaria	Y	Hamburg	New York	09/21/1880	04/28/1881			Y	
Schwab, ?	??	Baden	Y	?	New York	??/21/18??	10/28/1850	2	325	N	
Schwab, Abraham	46	Switzerland	Y	Havre	New York	02/09/1883	08/06/1898			Y	
Schwab, Christian	24	Bavaria	Y	Havre	New Orleans	01/29/1853	08/15/1857	15	141	N	
Schwab, Fred	28	Bavaria	Y	Havre	New York	05/25/1848	04/15/1853	8	65	N	
Schwab, George	27	Bavaria	Y	Rottterdam	New York	06/17/1844	11/05/1852	5	224	N	
Schwab, George	27	Bavaria	Y	Rotterdam	New York	06/17/1844	11/05/1852	6	350	N	
Schwab, Leo	44	Germany	Y	Bremen	New York	10/??/1875	09/28/1889			Y	
Schwab, Louis	24	Germany	Y	Antwerp	New York	10/11/1882	10/30/1884			Y	
Schwab, Martin	??	Germany	Y	?	?	04/17/1884				Y	10/11/1892
Schwab, Nicholas	36	Baden	Y	Havre	New Orleans	06/04/1840	08/15/1848	22	131	N	
Schwab, Wilhelm	47	Germany	Y	Hamburg	Baltimore	04/13/1883	01/20/1887			Y	
Schwaegerle, Jacob	23	Bavaria	Y	Havre	New York	07/06/1854	02/16/1857	15	19	N	
Schwaighart, August	25	Germany	Y	Bremen	New York	12/16/1890	07/01/1893			Y	
Schwali, Andreas	62	Baden	Y	Havre	New York	07/04/1850	06/20/1862	18	358	N	
Schwanecke, John George	32	Hanover	Y	Bremen	Galveston	12/22/1846	09/28/1848	22	358	N	
Schwanghaus, G. Hermann	38	Hanover	Y	Bremen	Baltimore	10/25/1867	11/10/1871	18	440	N	
Schwank, Conrad	30	Bavaria	Y	Hamburg	Buffalo	09/04/1851	12/16/1851	4	526	N	
Schwanke, C. F.	17	Germany	N	?	Baltimore	00/00/1868				Y	10/29/1888
Schwanzen, Salva	50	Norway	Y	London	New York	10/15/1831	09/12/1848	22	337	N	
Schwarberg, Henry	24	Germany	Y	Amsterdam	New York	08/26/1882	07/03/1885			Y	
Schwarberg, Herman	22	Germany	Y	Rotterdam	New York	09/10/1883	11/02/1886			Y	
Schwarle, Herman	33	Hanover	Y	Bremen	New Orleans	??/29/1847	10/09/1848	22	508	N	
Schwarmann, Frank Joseph	28	Prussia	Y	Bremen	New Orleans	01/03/1847	10/06/1848	22	459	N	
Schwarte, William A.	35	Germany	Y	?	New York	07/15/1889	03/26/1891			Y	
Schwarting, George	36	Germany	Y	Bremen	Baltimore	08/31/1888	01/02/1891			Y	
Schwartz, Adolph	52	Austria	Y	Hamburg	New York	04/12/1869	10/26/1895			Y	
Schwartz, Adolph	35	Austria	N	Bremen	New York	07/??/1870	?			Y	
Schwartz, Anton	??	Germany	Y	?	?	?	06/02/1890			Y	
Schwartz, Felix	32	Germany	Y	Havre	New York	09/14/1881	05/05/1883			Y	
Schwartz, Gustav	31	Saxe Weimar	Y	Bremen	New York	11/24/1849	03/05/1851	3	202	N	
Schwartz, Isaac	48	Russia	Y	Hamburg	New York	09/16/1891	06/21/1895			Y	
Schwartz, Jacob	29	Germany	Y	Hamburg	New York	06/??/1882	10/??/1883			Y	
Schwartz, Jacob	29	Russia	N	Hamburg	New York	06/??/1882	?			Y	
Schwartz, John A.	??	Germany	Y	?	?	04/10/1893	08/17/1899			Y	
Schwartz, John P.	48	Germany	Y	Hamburg	New York	03/05/1880	01/22/1884			Y	
Schwartz, Joseph	44	Oldenburg	Y	Bremen	Baltimore	??/06/1845	01/06/1851	2	459	N	
Schwartz, Lorenz	46	Prussia	Y	Havre	New York	05/14/1853	11/07/1855	13	183	N	
Schwartz, Louis	30	Russia	Y	Hamburg	New York	09/12/1887	10/26/1895			Y	
Schwartz, Louis	40	Germany	Y	Bremen	New York	06/02/1881	05/31/1895			Y	
Schwartz, Michael	34	Bavaria	Y	Rotterdam	Baltimore	??/03/1847	10/??/1849	23	280	N	
Schwartz, Nicholas	42	Bavaria	Y	Havre	New York	07/15/1842	08/15/1848	22	159	N	

CITIZENSHIP RECORDS

APPLICANT	AGE	COUNTRY OF ORIGIN	DEC	DEPART PORT	ENTRY PORT	ARRIVE DATE	DEC DATE	VOL	PG.	FLD	NAT DATE
Schwartz, Philip	63	Germany	Y	Havre	New York	11/10/1880	10/28/1899			Y	
Schwartz, Samuel	43	Austria	Y	Hamburg	New York	11/21/1885	04/05/1892			Y	
Schwarz, Anton	35	Bavaria	Y	Havre	New York	05/20/1851	05/01/1854	8	330	N	
Schwarz, Anton	35	Bavaria	Y	Havre	New York	05/20/1851	05/01/1854	9	203	N	
Schwarz, August	27	Germany	Y	Havre	New York	06/29/1889	10/10/1896			Y	
Schwarz, Ernst G.	21	Germany	Y	Bremen	Baltimore	05/03/1883	04/29/1886			Y	
Schwarz, Frederich	32	Germany	Y	Bremen	Baltimore	10/21/1883	03/29/1887			Y	
Schwarz, Frederick	24	Wurttemberg	Y	London	New York	10/12/1853	09/25/1856	14	380	N	
Schwarz, George	27	Bavaria	Y	Havre	New York	06/13/1849	01/13/1851	2	485	N	
Schwarz, Henry	35	Germany	Y	Bremen	Baltimore	06/01/1891	10/02/1893			Y	
Schwarz, Jacob	53	Switzerland	N	Bremen	New York	09/??/1863	?			Y	
Schwarz, John	26	Germany	Y	Bremen	New York	08/21/1881	05/31/1883			Y	
Schwarz, Joseph	27	Germany	Y	Bremen	New York	07/17/1880	02/14/1884			Y	
Schwarz, Julius	??	Austria	Y	?	?	02/05/1900	02/11/1904			Y	
Schwarz, Ludwig	24	Wurttemberg	Y	Rotterdam	New York	05/29/1848	10/20/1851	4	354	N	
Schwarz, Michael	32	Bavaria	Y	Havre	New York	09/01/1852	11/20/1860			Y	
Schwarz, Nicholas	27	Germany	Y	Havre	New York	05/03/1887	08/19/1891			Y	
Schwarz, Rudolf	25	Switzerland	Y	Havre	New York	08/10/1875	10/07/1880			Y	
Schwarz, Valentine	28	Bavaria	Y	Bremen	Baltimore	12/17/1847	01/26/1849	1	521	N	
Schwarze, Heinrich	26	Germany	Y	Bremen	New York	05/22/1893	10/21/1895			Y	
Schwarzenhoebzer, Christ	30	Wurttemberg	Y	Havre	New Orleans	02/06/1851	11/05/1852	6	355	N	
Schwarzenhoelzer, Christ	30	Wurttemberg	Y	Havre	New Orleans	02/06/1851	11/05/1852	5	228	N	
Schwarzer, Karl	42	Germany	Y	Bremen	Baltimore	01/27/1879	09/05/1882			Y	
Schwarzkopf, Joseph	28	Bavaria	Y	Hamburg	Boston	08/22/1859	03/12/1860	27	124	N	
Schwarztrauber, Wendel	27	Bavaria	Y	Havre	New York	08/??/1849	12/26/1850	2	395	N	
Schwatz, Gustav	31	Rumania	Y	Rotterdam	New York	08/21/1900	09/11/1903			Y	
Schwcizer, Emile	??	Switzerland	Y	?	?	?	09/22/1890			Y	
Schweer, Henry	31	Germany	Y	Bremen	Baltimore	06/20/1887	10/21/1896			Y	
Schweere, Ludecus	33	Hanover	Y	Bremen	New York	09/10/1845	11/15/1848	1	300	N	
Schwegler, Victor	23	Wurttemberg	Y	Havre	New York	06/29/1854	09/24/1857	15	309	N	
Schwegman, Herman Henry	??	Hanover	Y	Bremen	Baltimore	09/01/1845	10/07/1848	22	479	N	
Schwegmann, A.	25	Germany	Y	Bremen	Baltimore	05/22/1880	03/25/1885			Y	
Schwegmann, Heinrich	30	Hanover	Y	Bremen	New York	10/11/1858	08/05/1862	18	387	N	
Schweibold, William	31	Germany	Y	Havre	New York	04/07/1880	05/02/1881			Y	
Schweigel, George	41	Bavaria	Y	Bremen	Baltimore	09/20/1845	01/18/1851	2	506	N	
Schweiger, John	29	Germany	Y	Bremen	Baltimore	05/13/1892	01/09/1893			Y	
Schweigert, Michael	24	Baden	Y	Havre	New York	09/28/1856	11/11/1857	16	7	N	
Schweigmann, T. Anton	35	Prussia	Y	Bremen	Baltimore	10/28/1856	06/19/1862	18	355	N	
Schweikert, Raimund	40	Germany	Y	Bremen	New York	05/25/1874	09/15/1896			Y	
Schweinefuss, Herman	25	Germany	Y	Bremen	New York	10/19/1883	09/02/1889			Y	
Schweinfest, George	23	Bavaria	Y	Bremen	New York	08/26/1854	04/10/1858	16	466	N	
Schweinheer, Henry	40	Prussia	Y	Bremen	Baltimore	07/04/1833	09/23/1854	12	113	N	
Schweinlin, Jacob F.	26	Germany	Y	Havre	New York	08/28/1893	10/19/1894			Y	
Schweitzer (Switzer), He	29	Prussia	Y	Bremen	Baltimore	12/22/1846	04/29/1850	3	24	N	
Schweitzer, Albert	28	Germany	Y	Havre	New York	11/02/1890	03/26/1894			Y	
Schweitzer, Aloise	28	Germany	Y	Havre	New York	04/15/1888	09/24/1892			Y	
Schweitzer, Anton	47	Germany	Y	Antwerp	New York	10/06/1882	10/26/1888			Y	
Schweitzer, August	24	Germany	Y	Havre	New York	07/15/1892	01/06/1896			Y	
Schweitzer, Casper	28	Hesse Darmsta	Y	Havre	New York	05/18/1857	11/25/1857	16	51	N	
Schweitzer, Henry	43	Germany	Y	Amsterdam	New York	08/26/1882	01/07/1892			Y	
Schweitzer, John	36	Wurttemberg	Y	Antwerp	New York	05/04/1848	01/16/1851	3	389	N	
Schweitzer, Joseph	32	Baden	Y	Havre	New Orleans	12/??/1854	11/04/1856	14	463	N	
Schweitzer, Philip	40	Germany	Y	Antwerp	New York	09/07/1875	03/25/1897			Y	
Schweitzer, Wendelin	23	Germany	Y	Havre	New York	06/04/1884	10/26/1888	19	181	N	
Schweitzer, Wendelin	23	Germany	Y	Havre	New York	06/04/1884	10/26/1888			Y	
Schweizer, George	26	Wurttemberg	Y	Liverpool	New York	04/01/1851	11/24/1855	13	250	N	
Schweizer, Jacob	22	Wurttemberg	Y	Havre	New York	07/03/1854	11/13/1858	17	325	N	
Schweizer, Jacob	??	Germany	Y	?	?	04/25/1886	09/15/1888			Y	
Schweizer, Karl	22	Switzerland	Y	Antwerp	New York	04/21/1889	08/01/1890			Y	

CITIZENSHIP RECORDS

APPLICANT	AGE	COUNTRY OF ORIGIN	DEC	DEPART PORT	ENTRY PORT	ARRIVE DATE	DEC DATE	VOL	PG.	FLD	NAT DATE
Schweizerhof, Frederick	26	Wurttemberg	Y	Havre	New York	04/12/1850	04/17/1854	8	170	N	
Schweizerhoff, Frederick	26	Wurttemberg	Y	Havre	New York	04/12/1850	04/17/1854	9	41	N	
Schweizerhoff, Simon	22	Wurttemberg	Y	Havre	New York	11/09/1856	10/21/1858	17	86	N	
Schwemmlein, John	37	Bavaria	Y	Bremen	New Orleans	05/12/1852	05/25/1854	8	511	N	
Schwemmlein, John	37	Bavaria	Y	Bremen	New Orleans	05/12/1852	05/25/1854	9	385	N	
Schwenberger, Charles	36	Baden	Y	Havre	New Orleans	01/13/1852	05/13/1854	8	437	N	
Schwenberger, Charles	36	Baden	Y	Havre	New Orleans	01/13/1852	05/13/1854	9	310	N	
Schwendke, Julius	33	Prussia	Y	Hamburg	New York	06/03/1857	08/28/1860	27	319	N	
Schwengmeyer, Frederick	??	Prussia	Y	Bremen	Baltimore	??/06/1848	08/??/1851	4	177	N	
Schwenifus, John	25	Oldenburg	Y	Bremen	New York	05/16/1853	11/16/1857	16	20	N	
Schwennesen, Erich Johan	35	Germany	Y	Hamburg	New York	08/08/1868	04/03/1882			Y	
Schweppe, Frederick	32	Prussia	Y	Bremen	New Orleans	11/25/1851	02/23/1857	15	52	N	
Schwer, Barney	26	Hanover	Y	Bremen	New Orleans	05/26/1851	01/31/1853	7	90	N	
Schwer, H.	31	Germany	Y	Bremen	Baltimore	05/23/1881	12/08/1884			Y	
Schwerdtfeger, Charles	54	Prussia	Y	Hamburg	New York	09/15/1850	03/25/1856	26	311	N	
Schwerin, Carl	29	Germany	Y	Havre	New York	04/15/1888	01/02/1889			Y	
Schwering, Heinrich	30	Germany	Y	Bremen	New York	09/22/1883	08/15/1889			Y	
Schwert, Charles	23	Germany	Y	Antwerp	New York	01/08/1891	04/03/1893	19	420	N	
Schwetmann, Christoff	33	Germany	Y	Bremen	New York	01/01/1889	12/29/1903			Y	
Schwettmann, Francis Hen	40	Hanover	Y	Bremen	New York	12/06/1856	03/09/1858	16	387	N	
Schwettmann, Friedrich	29	Germany	Y	Bremen	New York	01/28/1886	11/09/1889			Y	
Schwettmann, Louis H.	28	Germany	Y	Bremen	New York	06/08/1887	10/23/1890			Y	
Schwey, George	49	France	Y	Havre	New Orleans	02/02/1852	10/01/1856	14	107	N	
Schweyer, Christian	23	Germany	Y	Havre	New York	03/29/1886	09/09/1887			Y	
Schwiekhard, Franz J.	27	Germany	Y	Rotterdam	New York	04/17/1882	12/26/1885			Y	
Schwienheer, Henry	40	Prussia	Y	Bremen	Baltimore	07/04/1833	09/23/1854	10	174	N	
Schwier, Christ	22	Germany	Y	Bremen	New York	06/22/1881	06/02/1884			Y	
Schwier, Henry	24	Germany	Y	Bremen	New York	09/29/1883	06/02/1884			Y	
Schwierling, Joseph	21	Hanover	Y	Bremen	Baltimore	11/20/1854	12/05/1857	16	68	N	
Schwietering, Herman	??	Germany	N	?	?	10/17/1884				Y	10/29/1892
Schwietert, John H.	23	Germany	Y	Rotterdam	New York	11/03/1883	12/03/1883			Y	
Schwind, Adam	40	Bavaria	Y	Bremen	New York	08/09/1853	07/19/1860	27	227	N	
Schwind, Bada	42	Switzerland	Y	Antwerp	Baltimore	06/14/1901	08/15/1904			Y	
Schwind, Leopold	40	Germany	Y	Bremen	Baltimore	08/22/1883	12/11/1889			Y	
Schwindt, Ludwig	31	Hesse Darmsta	Y	Bremen	New ?	05/??/1854	11/05/1856	14	496	N	
Schwindt, Peter	37	Germany	Y	Bremen	New York	07/28/1881	12/15/1886			Y	
Schwing, Valentine	32	Baden	Y	Havre	New York	11/11/1845	01/13/1849	1	405	N	
Schwinn, John S.	35	Germany	Y	Rotterdam	New York	01/09/1891	05/02/1894			Y	
Schwitzerhof, Gottlob	50	Wurttemberg	Y	Havre	New York	05/??/1843	10/28/1850	2	321	N	
Schwitzgebele, William	21	Wurttemberg	Y	Havre	New York	??/24/1854	04/28/1855	11	326	N	
Schwoeppe, William	27	Germany	Y	Bremen	Baltimore	09/30/1886	11/14/1888			Y	
Schwoerer, Edward	31	Baden	Y	Havre	New York	06/30/1849	05/24/1852	25	102	N	
Schwoerer, Louis	21	Germany	Y	Havre	New York	12/01/1890	12/07/1893			Y	
Schwoerer, Sylvester	31	Germany	Y	Havre	New York	08/09/1893	10/11/1900			Y	
Schwokowsky, Carl	35	Germany	Y	Stettin	New York	05/20/1872	08/05/1884			Y	
Schwope, Carl	30	Germany	Y	?	?	?	09/11/1891			Y	
Schwy, Henry	30	Switzerland	Y	Havre	New Orleans	12/02/1847	03/26/1850	2	267	N	
Sciarra, Antonio	25	Italy	Y	Naples	New York	03/24/1890	10/09/1893	19	427	N	
Sciarra, Antonio	25	Italy	Y	Naples	New York	03/14/1890	10/09/1893			Y	
Scollan, Michael	41	Ireland	Y	Dublin	New York	06/11/1869	08/27/1888			Y	
Scotece, Pasquale	??	Italy	Y	?	?	04/15/1900	06/09/1902			Y	
Scott, Francis	42	Ireland	Y	Liverpool	New York	08/05/1849	01/11/1856	13	451	N	
Scott, George	31	Scotland	Y	Glasgow	New York	03/27/1888	10/17/1894			Y	
Scott, James	25	Canada	Y	Hamilton	Lewiston	01/06/1847	11/16/1848	1	287	N	
Scott, James M.	28	Canada	Y	Hamilton	Lewiston	01/06/1847	03/15/1851	3	278	N	
Scott, John	??	Canada	Y	Hamilton W.C	Louisville K	10/01/1845	08/08/1848	22	78	N	
Scott, Michael	24	Ireland	Y	Queenstown	New York	04/17/1880	10/09/1882			Y	
Scott, Thomas	26	Ireland	Y	Liverpool	Savannah	??/02/1839	10/09/1848	1	71	N	
Scott, William Robert	39	Canada	Y	Montreal	Buffalo	08/??/1852	11/01/1858	17	223	N	

CITIZENSHIP RECORDS

APPLICANT	AGE	COUNTRY OF ORIGIN	DEC	DEPART PORT	ENTRY PORT	ARRIVE DATE	DEC DATE	VOL	PG.	FLD	NAT DATE
Scruny, Patrick	28	Ireland	Y	Liverpool	New York	06/??/1846	02/21/1849	23	251	N	
Scully, John	26	Ireland	Y	Liverpool	New York	06/29/1845	11/24/1848	1	383	N	
Scully, Lawrence	25	Ireland	Y	Liverpool	New Orleans	03/01/1852	04/25/1853	8	103	N	
Scully, Michael	34	Ireland	Y	Liverpool	New Orleans	03/02/1849	11/01/1852	5	144	N	
Scully, Michael	34	Ireland	Y	Liverpool	New Orleans	03/02/1849	11/01/1852	6	270	N	
Scully, William	32	Ireland	Y	Liverpool	New York	10/01/1847	02/18/1850	2	89	N	
Seamer, Clemens	51	Germany	N	Bremen	Baltimore	08/??/1845	?				Y
Seasongood, Alfred	50	Bavaria	N	Liverpool	New York	08/17/1860	?				Y
Seasongood, Siegfried	22	Germany	Y	South Hampto	New York	06/24/1893	06/27/1896				Y
Seaway, John	23	Ireland	Y	Liverpool	New York	08/04/1848	10/15/1851	4	292	N	
Sebald, John	32	Germany	Y	Bremen	Baltimore	05/26/1882	02/20/1889				Y
Sebastian, Kieny	35	Germany	Y	Havre	New York	01/20/1891	05/18/1898				Y
Sebastian, Martin	48	Germany	N	Liverpool	New York	08/06/1865	?				Y
Sebel, Adolph	26	Hungary	Y	Hamburg	New York	11/28/1882	01/30/1889				Y
Sebel, Joseph	38	Hungary	Y	Hamburg	New York	03/15/1879	01/17/1898				Y
Sechtelebend, Frederick	23	Hanover	Y	Bremen	Baltimore	05/22/1854	02/04/1857	14	536	N	
Seckmayer, John	26	Bavaria	Y	Bremen	New York	07/12/1853	10/02/1854	12	280	N	
Sedat, Christian	37	Germany	Y	Antwerp	New York	09/16/1882	08/12/1886				Y
Sedelke, August	29	Germany	Y	Bremen	New York	06/18/1889	07/06/1891				Y
Sedlmeyer, John	26	Bavaria	Y	Bremen	New York	07/12/1853	10/02/1854	10	341	N	
Seebach, Jacob	29	Bavaria	Y	Havre	New York	03/29/1853	09/21/1857	15	292	N	
Seeber, Andrew	44	Saxony	Y	Bremen	New Orleans	11/04/1849	12/??/1850	2	429	N	
Seebode, Henry	29	Germany	Y	Bremen	New York	10/01/1886	12/16/1889				Y
Seeger, Anton	30	Germany	Y	Bremen	Baltimore	04/28/1897	02/19/1902				Y
Seeger, Diderick Henry	38	Hanover	Y	Bremen	New York	11/??/1835	06/02/1854	10	60	N	
Seeger, Ludwig	27	Baden	Y	Havre	New York	07/01/1846	10/14/1848	1	231	N	
Seegers, George	27	Hanover	Y	Bremen	Baltimore	07/12/1850	04/05/1852	24	374	N	
Seegmiller, Ludwig	??	Germany	Y	?	?	?	03/11/1889				Y
Seelig, Paul	26	Wurttemberg	Y	Liverpool	New York	02/28/1854	03/24/1858	16	444	N	
Seelinger, Frederick	30	Germany	Y	Bremen	New York	05/19/1883	11/20/1889				Y
Seelmeyer, Frederick	26	Hanover	Y	Bremen	New York	06/03/1855	03/24/1856	26	265	N	
Seep, Herman Heinrich	24	Oldenburg	Y	Bremen	Baltimore	10/01/1859	01/30/1860	27	79	N	
Seeran, Neell	63	Ireland	Y	Liverpool	New Orleans	12/18/1848	10/07/1854	11	18	N	
Seerin, Neil	63	Ireland	Y	Liverpool	New Orleans	12/18/1848	10/07/1854	6	17	N	
Seery, James	35	Ireland	Y	Dublin	New York	05/26/1850	12/26/1857	16	258	N	
Seeser, Andreas Ludwig	33	Germany	Y	Hamburg	New York	08/20/1880	01/31/1881				Y
Seeser, George	31	Bavaria	Y	Bremen	New Orleans	05/18/1848	11/18/1848	1	306	N	
Seetiger, Herman	22	Prussia	Y	Hamburg	New York	12/24/1851	10/09/1854	11	140	N	
Seetiger, Hermann	22	Prussia	Y	Hamburg	New York	12/24/1851	10/09/1854	6	137	N	
Segal, Moses	32	Germany	Y	Hamburg	New York	08/23/1883	01/03/1888				Y
Segal, Simon	31	Germany	Y	Hamburg	Philadelphia	11/10/1886	10/16/1889				Y
Segar, Francis	40	Sardinia	Y	Genoa	New Orleans	03/05/1854	10/20/1858	17	75	N	
Segel, Ludwig	29	Hesse Darmsta	Y	Havre	New York	06/20/1851	03/30/1857	15	108	N	
Segel, Samuel	46	Russia	Y	Hamburg	New York	03/20/1888	04/07/1890				Y
Segen, Henry	25	Oldenburg	Y	Bremen	New Orleans	05/26/1852	08/05/1856	14	349	N	
Seger, Diedrich Herman	38	Hanover	Y	Bremen	New York	11/??/1834	06/02/1854	9	477	N	
Seger, Nicholas	26	Germany	Y	Antwerp	New York	09/02/1885	02/23/1888				Y
Segmiller, Daniel	22	Germany	Y	Antwerp	New York	11/12/1888	10/07/1892				Y
Segmiller, Joseph	42	France	Y	Havre	New Orleans	01/14/1851	01/22/1856	13	488	N	
Segtmeier, Frederick	32	Prussia	Y	Bremen	New Orleans	06/27/1851	10/03/1854	10	398	N	
Sehlken, John Henry	27	Mecklenburg	Y	Hamburg	New Orleans	11/13/1847	03/27/1849	23	257	N	
Sehmhausen, Frederick Wi	31	Hanover	Y	Bremen	Baltimore	05/19/1847	05/10/1854	8	411	N	
Sehn, Adam	31	Germany	Y	Bremen	New York	09/07/1887	10/27/1892	19	393	N	
Sehn, Adam	31	Germany	Y	Bremen	New York	09/07/1887	10/27/1892				Y
Sehner, John	43	Bavaria	Y	Bremen	Baltimore	??/04/1845	11/12/1849	23	335	N	
Sehrer, Stephan	32	Germany	Y	Antwerp	New York	06/02/1881	07/09/1888				Y
Seiber, Peter	42	Germany	Y	Hamburg	New York	06/??/1866	10/02/1882				Y
Seibert, Christian	36	Hesse Darmsta	Y	Rotterdam	New York	11/10/1847	08/06/1851	4	90	N	
Seibert, Ferd.	21	Germany	Y	Hamburg	New York	06/17/1882	06/02/1884				Y

CITIZENSHIP RECORDS

APPLICANT	AGE	COUNTRY OF ORIGIN	DEC	DEPART PORT	ENTRY PORT	ARRIVE DATE	DEC DATE	VOL	PG.	FLD	NAT DATE
Seibert, Jacob	61	Germany	N	Bremen	Baltimore	07/25/1843	?			Y	
Seibert, John	44	Baden	Y	Bremen	Baltimore	09/18/1830	07/12/1851	3	522	N	
Seibert, Valentine	34	Germany	Y	Bremen	New York	03/28/1884	10/20/1893			Y	
Seibertz, Jacob	36	Germany	Y	Bremen	New York	10/20/1891	10/27/1896			Y	
Seibl, John	33	Austria	Y	Havre	New York	05/26/1888	10/30/1888			Y	
Seidel, Wilhelm	36	Germany	Y	Bremen	Baltimore	03/27/1883	11/01/1888			Y	
Seidenspinner, Gottlieb	29	Wuertemberg	Y	Liverpool	New York	07/23/1852	04/02/1856	26	407	N	
Seidenspinner, John	??	Germany	Y	?	?	?	03/21/1887			Y	
Seidenspinner, Joseph (J	71	Germany	Y	Bremen	New York	03/??/1866	09/28/1885			Y	
Seidenspinner, Konrad	35	Germany	Y	Antwerp	New York	12/31/1880	01/07/1891			Y	
Seidenspinner, Thomas	50	Germany	Y	Bremen	New York	01/27/1866	09/25/1885			Y	
Seidenstuecker, Frederic	52	Schwazburg So	Y	Bremen	New York	05/25/1854	12/04/1858	17	373	N	
Seidl, Joseph	25	Bavaria	Y	Bremen	New Orleans	11/01/1846	03/29/1850	2	287	N	
Seiferheld, Andrew	35	Wuerttenberg	Y	Rotterdam	New York	??/??/1847	10/??/1849	23	281	N	
Seifert, Andreas	47	Germany	Y	Havre	New York	10/21/1853	10/17/1882			Y	
Seifert, Carl	23	Germany	Y	Bremen	Baltimore	10/05/1889	04/04/1893			Y	
Seifert, Charles Herman	30	Kurhessen	Y	Bremen	New York	09/24/1848	01/24/1853	7	62	N	
Seifert, John	35	Baden	Y	Havre	New Orleans	04/15/1846	01/19/1852	24	26	N	
Seifert, Michael	63	Germany	N	Havre	New York	01/??/1857	?			Y	
Seifest, Henry	23	Hanover	Y	Bremen	Baltimore	09/02/1845	07/31/1848	22	21	N	
Seiffert, Zacharias	25	Bavaria	Y	London	Buffalo	07/10/1847	03/18/1852	24	329	N	
Seifke, Joseph H.	24	Germany	Y	Amsterdam	New York	09/22/1881	12/01/1884			Y	
Seifried, Stephen	27	Baden	Y	Havre	New York	11/25/1853	10/01/1856	14	102	N	
Seigel, George	48	Germany	N	Havre	New York	03/24/1866	?			Y	
Seigel, Max	25	Russia	Y	Bremen	New York	01/26/1889	12/07/1892			Y	
Seigel, Wendelin	36	Baden	Y	Havre	New York	01/15/1848	02/01/1849	23	9	N	
Seiger, John Joseph	24	Bavaria	Y	Havre	New Orleans	05/16/1845	10/03/1848	22	410	N	
Seigers, Franz	34	Prussia	Y	Bremen	Galveston	10/29/1846	09/11/1848	22	319	N	
Seigwolf, John	41	Baden	Y	Rotterdam	New Orleans	12/16/1844	10/06/1848	22	450	N	
Seilacher, Henry	26	Wurtemburg	Y	Havre	New York	09/01/1852	09/10/1852	25	442	N	
Seiler, Joseph	26	Germany	Y	Havre	New York	07/02/1883	11/13/1886			Y	
Seim, Conrad	28	Germany	Y	?	New York	03/11/1881	01/09/1885			Y	
Seip, Emil	35	Prussia	Y	Hamburg	New York	10/13/1849	10/08/1860	27	416	N	
Seip, William	35	Austria	Y	Hamburg	New York	05/??/1882	04/02/1887			Y	
Seirer, Frank	29	Bavaria	Y	Havre	New York	11/02/1853	10/09/1854	11	79	N	
Seiser, Gottfried	28	Prussia	Y	Bremen	Baltimore	05/25/1856	05/07/1860	27	182	N	
Seiter, August	25	Wuerttemberg	Y	Rotterdam	New York	06/02/1848	01/21/1852	24	45	N	
Seiter, Joseph	27	Baden	Y	Havre	New York	09/26/1851	03/04/1853	7	272	N	
Seiter, Mike	30	Baden	Y	Havre	New Orleans	04/20/1849	03/20/1850	2	223	N	
Seitz, Amor	22	Bavaria	Y	Havre	New York	12/31/1852	01/12/1856	13	459	N	
Seitz, George Andreas	45	Germany	Y	Hamburg	New York	11/27/1885	01/20/1888			Y	
Seitz, John Michael	35	Germany	Y	Bremen	New York	04/12/1892	10/08/1897			Y	
Seitz, Louis	26	Bavaria	Y	Liverpool	New York	07/28/1853	05/05/1854	8	379	N	
Seitz, Louis	26	Bavaria	Y	Liverpool	New York	05/20/1851	05/05/1854	9	252	N	
Seitz, Paul	46	Austria	Y	Bremen	Baltimore	02/10/1887	08/30/1894			Y	
Seitz, R. W. Hans	32	Germany	Y	Liverpool	New York	12/21/1895	05/02/1898			Y	
Seiwert, Peter	27	Germany	Y	Antwerp	New York	08/24/1884	08/25/1887			Y	
Sekundi, Paul	33	Prussia	Y	Bremen	New York	07/09/1853	04/17/1854	8	138	N	
Sekundi, Paul	33	Prussia	Y	Bremen	New York	07/09/1853	04/17/1854	9	9	N	
Selb, Joseph	52	Baden	Y	Havre	New Orleans	11/22/1847	06/17/1852	25	285	N	
Selhorst, Anton	22	Prussia	Y	Bremen	New Orleans	12/26/1854	10/06/1856	14	231	N	
Selig, Conrad	??	Kenzoller Hec	Y	Rotterdam	Richmond	07/04/1844	05/07/1848	22	476	N	
Selig, John	29	Prussia	Y	Rotterdam	New York	07/03/1844	03/15/1852	24	297	N	
Seligsohn, Wolf	35	Russia	Y	Hamburg	New York	09/05/1891	01/06/1893			Y	
Selinger, Alois	40	Baden	Y	Havre	New Orleans	07/01/1854	02/02/1858	16	72	N	
Selker, William	29	Hanover	Y	Bremen	New Orleans	??/17/1843	10/09/1848	1	65	N	
Selkmann, William	34	Germany	Y	Hamburg	New York	04/14/1880	11/29/1882			Y	
Sell, Charles	26	Germany	Y	Hamburg	New York	08/30/1886	09/18/1888			Y	
Selle, Moritz	42	Germany	Y	?	Baltimore	??/??/1869	10/07/1889			Y	

359

CITIZENSHIP RECORDS

APPLICANT	AGE	COUNTRY OF ORIGIN	DEC	DEPART PORT	ENTRY PORT	ARRIVE DATE	DEC DATE	VOL	PG.	FLD	NAT DATE
Sellen, Mary E. (Sellers	33	England	Y	?	?	?	10/02/1888			Y	
Sellenings, Fred.	29	Germany	Y	Hamburg	Philadelphia	01/05/1877	12/11/1884			Y	
Seller, John Michael	24	France	Y	Havre	New Orleans	04/23/1850	10/27/1851	4	413	N	
Sellet, Joseph C.	30	Germany	Y	Havre	New York	10/05/1890	01/08/1895			Y	
Sellin, Gustav	38	Prussia	Y	Bremen	Baltimore	05/28/1848	02/10/1851	3	109	N	
Sellman, Anton	30	Prussia	Y	Bremen	Baltimore	08/02/1845	09/05/1848	22	302	N	
Selscher, Casper Louis A	26	Hanover	Y	Bremen	New Orleans	11/14/1845	09/28/1854	10	286	N	
Selscher, Casper Louis A	26	Hanover	Y	Bremen	New Orleans	11/14/1845	09/28/1854	12	225	N	
Selter, John Henry	38	Prussia	Y	Antwerp	New York	05/01/1856	12/29/1857	16	282	N	
Seltzer, Jacob	56	Russia	Y	Hamburg	New York	11/24/1884	03/22/1894			Y	
Selz, Andreas	33	Baden	Y	Havre	New York	06/14/1847	10/13/1851	4	265	N	
Selz, Xaver	29	Baden	Y	Havre	New York	07/11/1856	07/06/1857	15	126	N	
Selzerman, Adam	14	Russia	N	?	New York	00/00/1881				Y	10/18/1888
Seminara, Salvatore	34	Italy	Y	Palermo	New York	09/20/1890	10/24/1893			Y	
Seminara, Salvatore C.	34	Italy	Y	Palermo	New York	09/20/1890	10/24/1893	21	30	N	
Semper, Christian	58	Germany	N	Bremen	New York	10/??/1864	?			Y	
Sena, Antonio	37	Italy	Y	Naples	New York	04/20/1888	05/21/1894			Y	
Sendelbach, Adam	30	Germany	Y	Hamburg	New York	02/16/1882	01/02/1883			Y	
Sendelback, Andreas	53	Bavaria	Y	Havre	New Orleans	11/01/1852	09/21/18??	10	151	N	
Sendelback, Andreas	53	Bavaria	Y	Havre	New Orleans	11/13/1852	09/21/1854	12	90	N	
Sendelbeck, George	38	Germany	Y	Antwerp	Philadelphia	02/19/1887	10/26/1900			Y	
Sendfeld, Herman	28	Prussia	Y	Bremen	Buffalo	08/12/1845	10/09/1854	6	176	N	
Sendfeld, Herman	28	Prussia	Y	Bremen	Buffalo	08/12/1845	10/09/1854	11	179	N	
Sene, Pasquale	25	Italy	Y	?	New York	??/??/1880	08/18/1888			Y	
Seng, Henry	24	Germany	Y	Havre	New York	08/26/1884	07/09/1887			Y	
Seng, Konrad	20	Germany	Y	Bremen	Baltimore	04/12/1889	12/06/1890			Y	
Senge, Liborius	37	Germany	Y	Bremen	New York	01/18/1892	01/23/1895			Y	
Senger, Adam	27	Germany	Y	Antwerp	New York	05/31/1883	02/04/1889			Y	
Senger, Tobias	30	Baden	Y	Havre	New Orleans	12/08/1846	02/19/1849	23	207	N	
Senia, Costontino	41	Italy	Y	Naples	New York	05/07/1882	03/21/1900			Y	
Senkpeil, Charles	32	Prussia	Y	Hamburg	New York	11/16/1853	03/15/1858	16	400	N	
Senn, Frederick	??	Switzerland	Y	?	?	?	02/26/1884			Y	
Sentelbeck, Conrad	29	Germany	Y	Amsterdam	New York	07/21/1883	05/01/1886			Y	
Sepen, Peter Jopeph	40	Prussia	Y	Antwerp	New York	07/12/1852	08/05/1856	14	346	N	
Septant, William	??	France	Y	?	?	?	11/11/1878			Y	
Septenfeld, Frantz	34	Prussia	Y	Bremen	New Orleans	12/26/1851	11/17/1852	6	426	N	
Seradino, Herman	30	Prussia	Y	Darmstadt	Boston	??/09/1849	11/??/1849	23	297	N	
Sermersheim, Frank J.	33	Germany	Y	Havre	New York	08/19/1882	06/13/1887			Y	
Serodina, Joseph	30	Prussia	Y	Bremen	Norfold	10/23/1847	04/02/1852	24	353	N	
Serpossian, Hinter H.	??	Turkey	Y	?	?	?	02/14/1893			Y	
Serrieskoetter, Theodore	29	Prussia	Y	Bremen	Baltimore	05/??/1849	12/??/1849	23	399	N	
Sessler, John	31	Wuerttemberg	Y	Havre	New York	05/15/1850	09/15/1860	27	377	N	
Setter, Joseph	36	Germany	Y	Hamburg	New York	08/12/1880	10/06/1882			Y	
Settler, Michael	35	Bavaria	Y	Havre	New York	07/11/1852	08/28/1855	11	514	N	
Settler, Michael	70	Bavaria	N	Bavaria	New York	07/16/1852	?			Y	
Setzinger, F.	28	Germany	Y	Hamburg	New York	10/04/1881	03/15/1887			Y	
Setzler, Nicholas	24	France	Y	Havre	New Orleans	07/10/1847	03/07/1851	3	207	N	
Seubert, Christ	39	Germany	Y	Bremen	New York	04/21/1882	09/26/1887			Y	
Seubert, John	27	Germany	Y	Antwerp	New York	07/02/1893	09/10/1897			Y	
Seubert, Joseph	25	Bavaria	Y	Havre	New Orleans	??/15/1848	02/06/1851	3	104	N	
Seurig, Adolph	44	Germany	Y	Hamburg	New York	02/20/1882	02/03/1885			Y	
Sevy, Abraham	40	Russia	Y	Rotterdam	New York	03/02/1895	03/05/1897			Y	
Sewlon, Franz	36	Mecklenburg S	Y	Bremen	Baltimore	08/08/1855	02/10/1860	27	97	N	
Sexton, Edward	17	Ireland	N	?	New York	00/00/1881				Y	10/12/1888
Sexton, John	44	Ireland	Y	Liverpool	New Orleans	12/13/1851	10/27/1857	15	495	N	
Sexton, Patrick	29	Ireland	Y	Queenstown	New York	04/08/1891	06/02/1898			Y	
Sexton, Thomas	28	England	Y	London	New York	?	06/07/1852	25	199	N	
Sexton, William	45	Ireland	Y	Liverpool	Philadelphia	05/00/1881	09/29/1885			Y	
Seybold, Charles	26	Germany	Y	Hamburg	New York	08/11/1878	01/14/1884			Y	

CITIZENSHIP RECORDS

APPLICANT	AGE	COUNTRY OF ORIGIN	DEC	DEPART PORT	ENTRY PORT	ARRIVE DATE	DEC DATE	VOL	PG.	FLD	NAT DATE
Seybold, Frederick	38	Wurttemberg	Y	London	New York	10/22/1857	12/09/1858	17	389	N	
Seyfert, Gottlieb	24	Germany	Y	Rotterdam	New York	06/07/1881	05/05/1882			Y	
Seyffer, John Gottlieb	29	Wurttemberg	Y	Antwerp	New York	06/12/1854	11/03/1858	17	270	N	
Seyfferle, John	41	Germany	Y	Rotterdam	New York	08/07/1881	02/09/1886			Y	
Seyfried, Conrad	25	Germany	Y	Hamburg	New York	01/27/1883	11/06/1885			Y	
Seyler, Adam	24	Bavaria	Y	Havre	New York	03/03/1851	11/12/1855	13	210	N	
Seyler, Adolph	23	Prussia	Y	Bremen	Galveston	11/18/1852	05/03/1854	8	355	N	
Seyler, Adolph	23	Prussia	Y	Bremen	Galveston	11/18/1852	05/03/1854	9	228	N	
Seyppel, Ferdinand	37	Prussia	Y	Rotterdam	New York	07/20/1850	08/11/1851	4	106	N	
Shafer, Charles	??	Germany	Y	Bremen	New York	05/16/1884	10/24/1889			Y	
Shafer, John	22	Oldenburg	Y	Bremen	New Orleans	11/20/1845	10/11/1848	1	135	N	
Shafer, John	30	Baden	Y	Havre	New York	02/26/1854	10/09/1854	6	155	N	
Shafer, Louis	26	Germany	Y	Bremen	New York	08/21/1878	01/19/1883			Y	
Shaffer, Franz H.	??	Germany	Y	?	?	10/??/1875	03/25/1878			Y	
Shaffer, John F.	23	Hanover	Y	Bremen	Baltimore	06/??/1845	11/??/1849	23	336	N	
Shales, Frederick	24	England	Y	?	New York	03/21/1883	10/12/1883			Y	
Shandly, Daniel	25	Ireland	Y	Liverpool	New York	04/25/1839	02/15/1850	2	84	N	
Shanker, Harry	34	Russia	Y	Liverpool	Baltimore	08/29/1891	11/03/1894			Y	
Shannon, J. H.	??	England	Y	?	?	?	11/04/1882			Y	
Shannon, James	21	Ireland	Y	Liverpool	New York	05/12/1857	04/23/1861	18	142	N	
Shannon, James	45	Ireland	N	Sligo	New York	05/??/1857	?			Y	
Shannon, John	45	Ireland	N	Liverpool	New York	07/??/1861	?			Y	
Shannon, Patrick	25	Ireland	Y	Liverpool	New York	05/09/1853	12/30/1857	16	284	N	
Shannon, Patrick	24	Scotland	Y	Liverpool	New York	11/29/1879	04/12/1883			Y	
Shannon, Patrick	??	Ireland	N	?	?	05/07/1887				Y	10/18/1892
Shannon, Patrick J.	41	Ireland	N	Queenstown	New York	09/02/1861	?			Y	
Shannon, Peter	26	Ireland	Y	hLiverpool	New York	06/02/1846	02/15/1849	23	115	N	
Shannon, Timothy	40	Ireland	Y	Liverpool	New Orleans	02/??/1849	02/02/1856	26	6	N	
Shanvelen, Pat	59	Ireland	Y	Londenderry	New York	06/02/1852	01/16/1882			Y	
Shapera, William	33	Russia	Y	Hamburg	New York	04/05/1886	11/13/1894			Y	
Shappi, John	36	Switzerland	Y	Havre	New Orleans	03/06/1847	09/11/1848	22	326	N	
Sharkey, Bryan	22	Ireland	Y	Liverpool	New Orleans	12/18/1848	06/14/1852	25	261	N	
Sharland, Edward	25	England	Y	Liverpool	New York	08/01/1880	05/08/1885			Y	
Sharpe, Enoch	30	England	Y	Liverpool	New York	09/20/1880	11/04/1892	19	409	N	
Sharpe, Enoch	30	England	Y	Liverpool	New York	09/30/1880	11/04/1892			Y	
Sharples, John	35	England	Y	Liverpool	Philadelphia	08/30/1886	05/22/1894			Y	
Shaurer, John Nicholas	25	Bavaria	Y	Havre	New York	05/11/1854	03/16/1858	16	413	N	
Shaw, Morris	??	?	Y	St. Johns N.	Bangor	??/24/1844	12/??/1850	2	419	N	
Shay, James	46	England	Y	Antwerp	New York	05/29/1882	10/20/1892	19	372	N	
Shay, John	45	Ireland	Y	Liverpool	Boston	04/20/1845	03/04/1850	2	154	N	
Shay, Martin	26	Ireland	Y	Liverpool	New York	08/??/1845	12/??/1850	2	414	N	
Shay, Martin	30	Ireland	Y	Liverpool	New Orleans	02/28/1849	10/14/1851	4	269	N	
Shay, Michael	53	Ireland	Y	Liverpool	New York	04/??/1872	10/09/1882			Y	
Shay, Richard	24	Ireland	Y	Liverpool	New York	??/24/1847	02/16/1850	2	85	N	
Shay, Thomas	25	?	Y	Liverpool	New York	??/11/1848	12/??/1850	2	411	N	
Shay, Timothy	28	Ireland	Y	Cork	Boston	06/04/1842	03/04/1850	2	153	N	
Shayesohn, Mendel	??	Germany	Y	?	?	?	01/07/1892			Y	
Shea, Dennis	34	Ireland	Y	?	?	05/29/1879	10/10/1893			Y	
Shea, Dennis	36	Ireland	Y	Queenstown	New York	05/25/1880	07/20/1892			Y	
Shea, Jeremiah	24	Ireland	Y	Liverpool	New Orleans	12/??/1848	12/??/1850	2	418	N	
Shea, John	25	Ireland	Y	Liverpool	New Orleans	11/??/1846	10/13/1848	1	203	N	
Shea, John	35	Ireland	Y	Liverpool	New Orleans	01/??/1848	12/??/1850	2	416	N	
Shea, John	39	Ireland	Y	Cork	New York	12/20/1847	01/24/1852	24	63	N	
Shea, Matthew	25	Ireland	Y	Waterford	New York	05/15/1847	05/25/1854	8	259	N	
Shea, Matthew	25	Ireland	Y	Waterford	New York	05/15/1847	04/25/1854	9	130	N	
Shea, Michael	28	Ireland	Y	Liverpool	Boston	04/20/1849	12/26/1851	24	13	N	
Shea, Patrick	53	Ireland	Y	Liverpool	New Orleans	12/23/1849	05/18/1852	25	34	N	
Shea, William	26	Ireland	Y	Liverpool	New Orleans	11/04/1850	10/30/1852	5	67	N	
Sheay, John	50	Ireland	Y	Liverpool	New Orleans	11/15/1848	08/02/1862	18	384	N	

CITIZENSHIP RECORDS

APPLICANT	AGE	COUNTRY OF ORIGIN	DEC	DEPART PORT	ENTRY PORT	ARRIVE DATE	DEC DATE	VOL	PG.	FLD	NAT DATE
Sheehan, Jeremiah	37	Ireland	Y	Queenstown	New York	05/29/1884	10/27/1898			Y	
Sheehan, Patrick	33	Ireland	Y	Liverpool	New Orleans	03/28/1852	10/01/1856	14	131	N	
Sheehey, James	29	Ireland	Y	Liverpool	Boston	02/02/1848	06/10/1852	25	235	N	
Sheehy, James	36	Ireland	Y	Queenstown	New York	06/24/1874	02/03/1887			Y	
Sheehy, Pat	34	Ireland	Y	Queenstown	New York	05/15/1881	04/20/1887			Y	
Sheehy, Timothy	26	Ireland	Y	Queenstown	New York	09/11/1885	07/17/1888			Y	
Sheehy, William	23	Ireland	Y	Limerick	New York	07/20/1849	11/01/1852	5	143	N	
Sheehy, William	23	Ireland	Y	Limerick	New York	07/20/1849	11/01/1852	6	269	N	
Sheen, Frederick	27	England	Y	Liverpool	New Orleans	04/19/1849	04/29/1850	3	18	N	
Sheeran, Patrick J.	33	Ireland	Y	Liverpool	New Orleans	02/05/1850	02/27/1858	16	247	N	
Sheeran, Thomas	28	Ireland	Y	Dublin	New Orleans	01/21/1851	08/01/1851	4	70	N	
Sheeran, William	31	Ireland	Y	Liverpool	New York	03/12/1853	10/06/1856	14	190	N	
Sheeren, Michael	23	Ireland	Y	Liverpool	New York	07/29/1851	02/21/1853	7	206	N	
Sheerle, John	28	Germany	Y	Bremen	New York	10/02/1887	01/23/1893			Y	
Sheil, Michael	29	Ireland	Y	Liverpool	New York	09/31/1845	11/18/1848	1	322	N	
Sheil, Michael	36	Ireland	Y	London	Long Island	06/28/1851	10/20/1852	5	29	N	
Sheol, James	29	Ireland	Y	Dublin	New York	04/??/1847	03/25/1851	3	353	N	
Shepherd, James	39	Scotland	Y	Greenock	New York	06/12/1840	04/04/1853	8	53	N	
Shepherd, William Luther	35	Canada	Y	London, Ont.	Detroit	10/17/1896	11/25/1903			Y	
Sheridan, Lawrence	22	Ireland	Y	Liverpool	New York	03/17/1852	09/14/1855	13	31	N	
Sheridan, Martin	28	Ireland	Y	Liverpool	Boston	08/02/1846	03/02/1853	7	259	N	
Sheridan, Michael	24	Ireland	Y	Liverpool	Boston	06/21/1846	01/??/1850	23	469	N	
Sherlock, John	26	Ireland	Y	Liverpool	New York	06/11/1848	07/06/1855	11	341	N	
Sherman, Isaac	22	Russia	Y	Hamburg	New York	06/01/1885	06/15/1888			Y	
Sherridan, John	25	Ireland	Y	Liverpool	New York	04/18/1862	06/02/1870			Y	
Shevnin, John	23	Ireland	Y	Liverpool	New Orleans	11/04/1849	10/20/1851	4	349	N	
Shields, Edward	22	Ireland	Y	Liverpool	New York	01/01/1849	06/10/1852	25	308	N	
Shields, Patrick	26	Ireland	Y	Liverpool	New York	05/02/1881	08/19/1886			Y	
Shielen, Daniel	??	Germany	Y	?	?	?	06/23/1882			Y	
Shilly, Hugh	26	Ireland	Y	Liverpool	New Orleans	12/09/1848	01/06/1851	2	455	N	
Shimkowiak, Joseph	54	Germany	Y	Bremen	Baltimore	05/27/1873	11/26/1887			Y	
Shine, James	24	Ireland	Y	Queenstown	New York	06/15/1893	04/19/1898			Y	
Shipton, T.B.	49	England	Y	Rotterdam	New York	07/24/1884	10/25/1889	19	261	N	
Shlenker, Jacob	21	Baden	Y	Liverpool	New York	04/27/1858	10/09/1860	27	475	N	
Shmid, John	37	Germany	Y	Bremen	New York	06/14/1872	10/13/1884			Y	
Shmid, Michael	29	Baden	Y	Havre	New Orleans	05/24/1854	12/24/1855	13	348	N	
Shnoebelen, Antoine	41	Germany	Y	Havre	New York	06/16/1882	11/29/1887			Y	
Shobe, Rudolph	37	Switzerland	Y	Havre	New Orleans	05/25/1844	09/20/1858	16	178	N	
Shoch, Franz	33	Germany	Y	Antwerp	New York	06/04/1881	10/18/1884			Y	
Shochet, Solomon	??	Russia	Y	?	?	?	09/04/1890			Y	
Shoghtman, Henry	24	Bavaria	Y	Bremen	Baltimore	10/14/1846	08/15/1848	22	173	N	
Shoh, John Bernard	22	Prussia	Y	Bremen	Baltimore	10/02/1848	10/14/1851	4	291	N	
Sholomov, R.	30	Russia	Y	Hamburg	New York	06/12/1880	02/12/1883	28	180	N	
Sholomov, Rubin	25	Russia	Y	Hamburg	New York	06/12/1880	02/10/1883			Y	
Shopea, Benjamin	40	Russia	Y	Hamburg	New York	08/14/1888	05/22/1893			Y	
Shorten, Edward	41	Ireland	Y	Kilkenny	New Orleans	01/22/1850	09/26/1854	10	248	N	
Shorten, Edward	41	Ireland	Y	Kilkenny	New Orleans	01/22/1850	09/26/1854	12	187	N	
Shorten, James	21	Ireland	Y	Cork	New York	05/15/1851	11/09/1858	17	312	N	
Shorten, Richard	45	Ireland	Y	Liverpool	New Orleans	11/13/1848	03/29/1853	7	460	N	
Shorten, William	50	Ireland	Y	Liverpool	New York	12/??/1840	03/29/1853	7	459	N	
Shroder, Samuel	27	Bavaria	Y	Bremen	New York	07/28/1842	11/13/1848	1	264	N	
Shroder, Wolf	25	Bavaria	Y	Havre	New York	07/25/1845	11/13/1848	1	263	N	
Shroeder, John	26	Bavaria	Y	Bremen	New York	08/12/1853	10/10/1854	6	226	N	
Shuck, Henry	38	Switzerland	Y	Havre	New Orleans	12/??/1848	03/21/1853	7	357	N	
Shuhan, John	39	Ireland	Y	Canada	Eastport	??/10/1837	12/24/1849	23	424	N	
Shuk, Alois	50	Hesse Darmsta	Y	Hamburg	New York	02/20/1851	03/25/1853	7	392	N	
Shulkers, Herman	21	Hanover	Y	Bremen	Baltimore	10/28/1850	01/10/1853	7	3	N	
Shumacher, John Alexande	26	Wurttemberg	Y	Havre	New York	10/15/1854	07/26/1858	16	530	N	
Shumacher, Mathias	51	Prussia	Y	Antwerp	New York	07/02/1853	09/29/1856	14	41	N	

CITIZENSHIP RECORDS

APPLICANT	AGE	COUNTRY OF ORIGIN	DEC	DEPART PORT	ENTRY PORT	ARRIVE DATE	DEC DATE	VOL	PG.	FLD	NAT DATE
Shurbesmann, Engelbert	30	Prussia	Y	Bremen	New York	10/17/1860	11/05/1869	18	13	N	
Shurmann, George	26	Hanover	Y	Bremen	New Orleans	12/23/1845	02/06/1849	23	119	N	
Shuster, John	39	Germany	Y	Hamburg	New York	11/17/1874	11/03/1884			Y	
Shutz, Joseph	25	Germany	Y	Amsterdam	New York	07/23/1883	06/21/1889			Y	
Shwenk, Peter	27	Prussia	Y	Havre	New York	06/05/1857	12/09/1858	17	388	N	
Siano, Pasula	32	Italy	Y	Naples	New York	??/??/1877	11/25/1884			Y	
Sicker, Adam	??	Germany	Y	?	?	?	11/08/1883			Y	
Sicker, Anton	30	Prussia	Y	Bremen	New York	05/03/1847	03/30/1852	24	336	N	
Sickermeier, Henry	24	Hanover	Y	Bremen	New Orleans	12/18/1856	12/26/1859	17	519	N	
Sicking, Henry	22	Germany	Y	Rotterdam	New York	10/31/1881	10/02/1884			Y	
Sicking, John	30	Prussia	Y	Rotterdam	New York	09/10/1851	01/29/1856	13	518	N	
Sicking, John Bernard	23	Prussia	Y	Rotterdam	New York	09/02/1871	02/24/1872	18	560	N	
Sickinger, Adam	28	Germany	Y	Antwerp	New York	05/23/1880	04/11/1887			Y	
Sickinger, Charles Willi	31	Germany	Y	Bremen	New York	09/13/1887	10/21/1893			Y	
Sickinger, Florian	28	Germany	Y	Havre	New York	04/18/1888	02/08/1898			Y	
Sickinger, William	36	Germany	Y	Antwerp	New York	05/26/1880	07/07/1886			Y	
Sickinger, William	30	Germany	Y	Rotterdam	New York	10/14/1880	11/03/1886			Y	
Sickler, John	30	Wurttemberg	Y	Havre	New York	01/15/1854	11/15/1858	17	332	N	
Sickman, John	30	Germany	Y	Bremen	New York	09/13/1883	10/24/1884			Y	
Sickmann, Frank	30	Oldenburg	Y	Bremen	New Orleans	11/08/1847	10/13/1851	4	221	N	
Sickmann, Henry	50	Germany	Y	Bremen	Baltimore	10/??/1864	10/08/1884			Y	
Siddel, Jonathan	34	England	Y	Liverpool	New York	10/25/1848	02/16/1852	24	115	N	
Sidovski, Simon	35	Germany	Y	Bremen	New York	03/18/1881	04/06/1886			Y	
Siebel, Frederick Willia	45	Hanover	Y	Bremen	New York	08/12/1854	08/22/1856	15	169	N	
Siebenburgen, Joseph	32	Germany	Y	Bremen	Baltimore	05/29/1881	12/03/1887			Y	
Sieber, Franz	32	Austria	Y	Bremen	Baltimore	05/15/1889	01/23/1890			Y	
Sieber, Jacob	29	Bavaria	Y	Havre	New Orleans	08/08/1854	11/04/1857	15	529	N	
Sieber, Josef	31	Germany	Y	Bremen	New York	05/14/1887	12/24/1888			Y	
Sieber, Karl	24	Germany	Y	Bremen	Baltimore	10/26/1881	11/07/1882			Y	
Siebermann, Frank	34	Germany	Y	Bremen	Baltimore	03/08/1885	09/28/1887			Y	
Siebert, Herman	37	Germany	Y	Bremen	New York	10/08/1882	09/27/1888			Y	
Siebshevitz, David	17	Russia	N	?	New York	00/00/1881				Y	10/26/1888
Sieck, William	36	Hanover	Y	Bremen	New Orleans	12/15/1842	11/15/1852	5	278	N	
Sieck, William	36	Hanover	Y	Bremen	New Orleans	12/15/1842	11/15/1852	6	402	N	
Sieckmeier, Christian	26	Hanover	Y	Bremen	Baltimore	09/22/1857	09/29/1860	27	390	N	
Siedel, Edward	42	Bohemia, Aust	Y	Liverpool	New York	07/08/1852	01/07/1853	5	533	N	
Siedler, Pius	34	Germany	Y	Bremen	New York	12/12/1879	11/23/1887			Y	
Siedling, Christian	53	Germany	Y	Bremen	Baltimore	09/22/1882	07/09/1888			Y	
Siefert, Joseph	33	France	Y	?	New York	??/??/1873	09/30/1880			Y	
Siefert, Sefrim	35	Baden	Y	Havre	New Orleans	04/02/1854	09/12/1855	13	7	N	
Siefried, Jacob	22	Switzerland	Y	Havre	New York	03/09/1887	04/07/1890			Y	
Siefried, Joseph	33	Germany	Y	Rotterdam	New York	10/16/1873	10/08/1884			Y	
Siegenbaum, Ernst	33	Prussia	Y	Bremen	New Orleans	11/10/1843	11/13/1848	1	257	N	
Siegle, George	39	Wuerttemberg	Y	Havre	New York	07/09/1847	02/15/1849	23	116	N	
Siegle, John George	27	Wurttemberg	Y	Havre	New York	08/26/1853	04/29/1854	8	289	N	
Siegle, John Gerhard	27	Wurttemberg	Y	Havre	New York	08/26/1853	04/29/1854	9	161	N	
Sieglitz, Francis (Franz	50	Hesse Darmsta	Y	Havre	New York	09/04/1846	08/28/1848	22	263	N	
Siegmund, August	32	Germany	Y	Hamburg	New York	09/13/1890	01/17/1898			Y	
Siegrist, Albert	26	Switzerland	Y	Havre	New York	08/25/1896	09/09/1897			Y	
Siehl, Fred	72	Germany	Y	Havre	New York	04/20/1867	07/21/1884			Y	
Siek, John	25	Germany	Y	Bremen	New York	05/01/1882	08/12/1884			Y	
Siekman, Diedrick	35	Oldenburg	Y	Bremen	New Orleans	10/01/1844	08/03/1848	22	52	N	
Sielfleisch, Wilhelm	27	Germany	Y	Hamburg	New York	09/18/1880	04/10/1882			Y	
Sielschott, Barney	74	Germany	N	Bremen	Baltimore	11/01/1841	08/01/1842	28	1	N	11/01/1847
Sielschott, Barney	28	Germany	N	Bremen	Baltimore	11/01/1841	08/01/1842			Y	11/01/1847
Sieman, Henry	28	Hanover	Y	Bremen	Baltimore	05/01/1849	04/30/1850	3	37	N	
Siemer, Bernd.	23	Oldenburg	Y	Bremen	New Orleans	06/12/1850	10/30/1852	5	74	N	
Siemer, Carsten	65	Germany	Y	Bremen	Baltimore	05/09/1882	08/29/1888			Y	
Siemer, John Henry	27	Hanover	Y	Bremen	New York	11/25/1854	12/26/1857	16	249	N	

CITIZENSHIP RECORDS

APPLICANT	AGE	COUNTRY OF ORIGIN	DEC	DEPART PORT	ENTRY PORT	ARRIVE DATE	DEC DATE	VOL	PG.	FLD	NAT DATE
Siemer, Joseph	32	Oldenburg	Y	Bremen	Baltimore	06/25/1846	10/12/1848	1	174	N	
Siermann, Andreas	33	Prussia	Y	Bremen	New Orleans	11/17/1847	02/17/1849	23	147	N	
Sieve, Henry	53	Germany	Y	Bremen	New York	07/17/1866	10/30/1893			Y	
Sieve, L. G.	??	Germany	Y	?	?	?	11/01/1892			Y	
Siever, John Frederick	26	Hanover	Y	Bremen	Baltimore	11/08/1845	10/14/1848	1	213	N	
Sieverglade, Joseph	47	Russia	Y	Antwerp	New York	05/05/1887	10/08/1896			Y	
Sievermann, Anton	26	Hanover	Y	Bremen	New York	05/27/1857	08/27/1860	27	315	N	
Sievers, Heinrich	24	Germany	Y	Bremen	New York	04/04/1885	09/16/1886	19	44	N	
Sieveveld, Peter	46	Holland	Y	Rotterdam	New York	10/08/1883	10/29/1886			Y	
Sieving, John Henry	23	Hanover	Y	Bremen	Baltimore	07/28/1858	04/07/1862	18	304	N	
Siewe, Anthony	31	Switzerland	Y	Bremen	New York	10/05/1857	10/23/1858	17	98	N	
Sigel, Anton	31	Germany	Y	Bremen	New York	07/09/1871	10/31/1884			Y	
Sigel, Nathan	41	Russia	Y	Hamburg	New York	11/28/1886	10/08/1889			Y	
Sigg, Philipp	34	Germany	Y	Havre	New York	01/04/1891	08/27/1894			Y	
Sighe, Dominick	33	Ireland	Y	Queenstown	New York	09/??/1869	10/23/1872	18	536	N	
Sigling, Michael	26	Bavaria	Y	Bremen	Baltimore	06/25/1854	11/03/1855	13	151	N	
Sigloch, George David	27	Wurttemberg	Y	Havre	New York	08/18/1847	01/31/1849	1	551	N	
Sigloch, Gottlieb	52	Germany	Y	Bremen	New York	07/25/1880	03/17/1884			Y	
Sigloch, Gottlieb	??	Germany	N	?	?	07/00/1880				Y	10/25/1892
Sigmund, Wilhelm	41	Austria	Y	Bremen	New York	03/01/1887	07/07/1894			Y	
Sika, Josef	25	Austria	Y	Bremen	New York	08/11/1849	03/08/1850	2	174	N	
Silber, Charles	28	Germany	Y	Bremen	New York	05/21/1882	10/01/1885			Y	
Silber, H.	26	Austria	Y	Hamburg	Baltimore	05/18/1880	05/11/1887			Y	
Silber, Jacob	28	Roumania	Y	Bremen	Baltimore	09/29/1888	03/24/1894			Y	
Silber, Louis	27	Germany	Y	Rotterdam	New York	09/15/1882	09/19/1887			Y	
Silberberg, William	32	Germany	Y	Hamburg	Boston	08/21/1880	01/06/1883			Y	
Silberman, S.	25	Poland	Y	Antwerp	New York	10/04/1881	02/16/1883			Y	
Silbernagel, Fred	29	Sweden	Y	Gottenburg	New York	06/27/1881	11/09/1888			Y	
Silbersack, Casper	53	Germany	Y	Bremen	Baltimore	07/13/1887	03/21/1892			Y	
Silberstein, A. Philip	22	Russia	Y	Hamburg	New York	05/??/1882	10/23/1886			Y	
Silberstein, Abraham	49	Poland (Russi	Y	Stettin	New York	08/28/1885	06/13/1890			Y	
Silk, August	??	Ireland	N	?	?	05/00/1871				Y	10/24/1892
Silking, William	54	Prussia	Y	Bremen	New York	07/20/1845	02/10/1849	23	43	N	
Sillies, John	33	Germany	Y	Bremen	New York	06/26/1888	11/03/1892			Y	
Sillies, John Theodore	29	Hanover	Y	Bremen	Baltimore	10/13/1853	10/20/1858	17	195	N	
Sils, Theodore	30	Hanover	Y	Bremen	Baltimore	06/20/1848	07/23/1851	4	31	N	
Silver, James	38	Ireland	Y	Galway	Boston	10/20/1847	06/03/1856	14	288	N	
Silverglad, Meyer	30	Russia	Y	Hamburg	Philadelphia	07/15/1882	10/25/1887	19	121	N	
Silverman, Israel	22	Russia	Y	Bremen	Baltimore	02/06/1891	07/27/1895			Y	
Silverman, Michael Henry	22	Poland	Y	Liverpool	New Orleans	08/28/1851	05/15/1854	8	442	N	
Silverman, Michael Henry	22	Poland	Y	Liverpool	New Orleans	08/28/1851	05/15/1854	9	315	N	
Silvermann, Benjamin	53	Russia	Y	Hamburg	Boston	05/28/1885	10/29/1892			Y	
Silvers, Frank D.	20	Isle of Mader	N	?	Charleston,	03/00/1835	07/00/1837			Y	06/00/1840
Silvers, Frank D. (DeSil	73	Portuguese Ma	N	?	Charleston	03/??/1835	07/??/1837	28	40	N	06/??/1840
Silversmith, Oscar	24	Germany	Y	Bremen	New York	04/21/1893	10/22/1895			Y	
Silverson, Gottfried	23	Bavaria	Y	Bremen	New Orleans	02/06/1848	10/14/1851	4	287	N	
Silverstein, Herman	33	Russia	Y	Bode	New York	09/18/1882	03/21/1891			Y	
Simbeck, Bernhard	21	Germany	Y	Rotterdam	New York	12/01/1892	10/31/1894			Y	
Simendinger, Christ	15	Germany	N	?	New York	00/00/1882				Y	10/17/1888
Simeone, John	38	Italy	Y	Naples	New York	06/22/1882	10/16/1893	21	9	N	
Simeone, John	38	Italy	Y	Naples	New York	06/22/1882	10/16/1893			Y	
Simes, Mathew	26	Ireland	Y	Liverpool	New York	05/04/1852	09/27/1854	12	217	N	
Simister, William	46	England	Y	Liverpool	New Orleans	05/26/1849	03/20/1851	3	243	N	
Simmes, Matthew	26	Ireland	Y	Liverpool	New York	05/04/1852	09/27/1854	10	280	N	
Simmons, James	24	Ireland	Y	Limerick	New York	11/01/1848	06/18/1851	3	394	N	
Simms, Henry	36	England	Y	Liverpool	New York	06/10/1871	10/29/1884			Y	
Simon, Adolph	32	Prussia	Y	Hamburg	New York	08/26/1854	10/06/1856	14	225	N	
Simon, Adolph	17	Austria	N	?	New York	00/00/1878				Y	10/22/1888
Simon, Barney	28	Hanover	Y	Bremen	Baltimore	09/27/1853	09/25/1854	10	189	N	

CITIZENSHIP RECORDS

APPLICANT	AGE	COUNTRY OF ORIGIN	DEC	DEPART PORT	ENTRY PORT	ARRIVE DATE	DEC DATE	VOL	PG.	FLD	NAT DATE
Simon, Barney	28	Hanover	Y	Bremen	Baltimore	09/27/1853	09/25/1854	12	128	N	
Simon, Charles	21	Hesse Cassel	Y	Bremen	New York	08/01/1854	11/20/1855	13	234	N	
Simon, David	25	Meiningen Hil	Y	Bremen	New York	07/08/1854	07/25/1857	15	131	N	
Simon, Frank	29	Germany	Y	Rotterdam	New York	05/22/1883	04/04/1893			Y	
Simon, Frederich	25	Germany	Y	Hamburg	New York	11/26/1881	02/19/1883			Y	
Simon, Gabriel	47	Bavaria	Y	Havre	New York	06/24/1845	02/01/1849	23	4	N	
Simon, Henry	38	Germany	Y	Hamburg	New York	06/26/1875	12/08/1886			Y	
Simon, Isaac	14	Russia	N	?	New York	00/00/1881				Y	10/18/1888
Simon, Jacob	21	Germany	Y	Liverpool	?	04/02/1875	02/04/1878			Y	
Simon, Leopold	31	Kurhessen	Y	Liverpool	New York	06/??/1853	04/30/1855	11	327	N	
Simon, Max	40	Russia	Y	Lasja	New York	06/??/1881	05/15/1886			Y	
Simon, Mike	26	Bavaria	Y	Bremen	Baltimore	07/10/1845	01/25/1849	1	515	N	
Simon, Richard	23	Germany	Y	Havre	New York	06/10/1882	09/03/1884			Y	
Simon, Robert P.	26	Germany	Y	Hamburg	New York	06/03/1882	05/07/1883			Y	
Simon, Robert P.	37	Germany	N	Hamburg	New York	06/03/1882	?			Y	
Simon, Simeon	26	France	Y	Havre	New York	05/04/1885	09/30/1890			Y	
Simon, Theodore	??	Germany	Y	?	?	?	10/01/1886			Y	
Simon,Francis Anthony Ev	28	Hanover	Y	Hamburg	New York	05/01/1858	05/22/1862	18	339	N	
Simonwitz, Samuel	32	Russia	Y	Hamburg	Philadelphia	07/07/1881	08/20/1892			Y	
Simowitz, Henry	38	Hungary	Y	Hamburg	Boston	08/27/1894	06/15/1897			Y	
Simpson, James	28	Scotland	Y	Glasgow	New York	09/13/1848	10/22/1852	5	48	N	
Simpson, William	36	England	Y	London	Rochester NY	07/25/1833	05/21/1852	25	84	N	
Sinclair, Daniel	??	Scotland	Y	?	?	?	02/20/1902			Y	
Singelton, John	32	Ireland	Y	Queenstown	New York	06/27/1883	10/25/1889	19	259	N	
Singer, John	24	Bavaria	Y	Hamburg	New York	05/27/1854	01/07/1856	13	426	N	
Singer, Joseph	36	Baden	Y	London	New York	04/26/1849	11/29/1852	5	362	N	
Singer, Michael	60	Bavaria	Y	Havre	New Orleans	03/01/1853	04/04/1856	26	433	N	
Singleton, John	32	Ireland	Y	Queenstown	New York	06/27/1883	10/25/1889			Y	
Singleton, Thomas	22	England	Y	Liverpool	Baltimore	09/01/1886	01/30/1888			Y	
Singleton, Thomas	27	Ireland	Y	Liverpool	New Orleans	12/06/1848	01/??/1850	23	507	N	
Singleton, William	32	Ireland	Y	London	New Orleans	11/15/1852	07/09/1865	14	298	N	
Singman, John (Landman?)	31	Holland	Y	Rotterdam	New Orleans	01/14/1847	08/15/1848	22	130	N	
Sink, Charles	30	Germany	Y	Bremen	Baltimore	05/28/1889	03/25/1896			Y	
Sinn, Ludwig	21	Germany	Y	Genoa	New York	02/22/1898	02/14/1900			Y	
Sinn, Peter	34	Bavaria	Y	Havre	New York	08/10/1852	11/02/1852	5	186	N	
Sinn, Peter	34	Bavaria	Y	Havre	New York	08/10/1852	11/02/1852	6	312	N	
Sinnige, Henry C.	32	Holland	Y	Rotterdam	New York	06/09/1882	05/29/1885			Y	
Sinz, Martin	35	Germany	Y	Havre	New York	08/28/1882	01/21/1892			Y	
Sisto, Vincenzo	40	Italy	Y	Naples	New York	04/01/1887	11/07/1892			Y	
Sites, Christian	21	Wurttemberg	Y	Havre	New York	08/01/1852	03/26/1853	7	412	N	
Sittaker, Charles	30	Brunswick	Y	Havre	New York	05/28/1852	03/19/1853	7	352	N	
Sittel, Theodore	26	Prussia	Y	Havre	New York	05/30/1855	12/13/1855	13	309	N	
Sittenfeld, Hyman	49	Germany	Y	Hamburg	New York	09/??/1865	01/14/1884			Y	
Sitterle, Joseph	30	Baden	Y	Havre	New York	05/04/1860	07/11/1861	18	206	N	
Sive, Harry	16	Russia	N	?	New York	00/00/1879				Y	10/20/1888
Sive, Rophol	16	Russia	N	?	New York	00/00/1880				Y	10/25/1888
Skelley, Robert	26	Ireland	Y	Liverpool	New York	07/14/1856	01/09/1860	27	44	N	
Skelly, Peter	21	Ireland	Y	Liverpool	New York	07/22/1853	01/26/1857	14	505	N	
Skuse, Samjel	??	Great Britain	Y	?	?	?	06/04/1887			Y	
Slack, Peter	33	England	Y	Liverpool	New York	11/14/1851	06/01/1854	9	470	N	
Slack, Peter	33	England	Y	Liverpool	New York	11/14/1851	06/01/1854	10	53	N	
Slagter, H.	??	Netherlands	Y	?	?	?	11/07/1898			Y	
Slake, Diedrick	36	Hanover	Y	Bremen	Baltimore	05/15/1848	03/25/1853	7	398	N	
Slamon, Thomas	32	Ireland	Y	Liverpool	New Orleans	04/12/1851	11/22/1852	5	327	N	
Slane, Alexander	25	Ireland	Y	Liverpool	New York	06/??/1844	11/??/1849	23	314	N	
Slane, Dominick	35	Ireland	Y	Sligo	Eastport	07/04/1842	01/02/1856	13	412	N	
Slater, Simeon	42	England	Y	London	New York	11/04/1886	07/16/1888			Y	
Slatter, William	46	England	Y	London	New Orleans	03/12/1849	12/31/1852	5	479	N	
Slattery, John	23	Ireland	Y	Liverpool	New York	11/10/1847	03/08/1850	2	169	N	

CITIZENSHIP RECORDS

APPLICANT	AGE	COUNTRY OF ORIGIN	DEC	DEPART PORT	ENTRY PORT	ARRIVE DATE	DEC DATE	VOL	PG.	FLD	NAT DATE
Slattery, William	27	Ireland	Y	Liverpool	New Orleans	11/20/1844	01/17/1851	2	503	N	
Slayer, Henry	48	France	Y	Havre	New Orleans	07/01/1847	02/03/1849	23	22	N	
Sleper, George Henry	??	Hanover	Y	Bremen	New Orleans	02/28/18??	10/09/1848	1	74	N	
Sliney, John	26	Ireland	Y	Liverpool	New York	10/??/1852	03/30/1857	15	101	N	
Slittker, William	30	Prussia	Y	Bremen	New Orleans	11/??/1846	11/??/1849	23	327	N	
Slone, James	35	Ireland	Y	Londonderry	New York	06/24/1834	10/13/1848	1	205	N	
Sluter, Frank	30	Prussia	Y	?	?	?	10/19/1861			Y	
Small, Patrick	25	Ireland	Y	Liverpool	New York	08/??/1852	12/26/1855	13	370	N	
Small, Richard	50	Ireland	Y	Liverpool	New Orleans	07/??/1852	09/10/1855	11	524	N	
Small, Thomas	31	England	Y	Liverpool	New York	06/30/1888	06/08/1894			Y	
Smart, Henry Amos	31	England	Y	Bristol	New York	08/28/1848	02/25/1853	7	231	N	
Smecker, Frederick	25	Prussia	Y	Bremen	New Orleans	12/03/1852	08/28/1855	11	510	N	
Smickler, Ike	26	Russia	Y	Hamburg	New York	08/15/1891	01/19/1894	21	59	N	
Smickler, Isaac	26	Russia	Y	Hamburg	New York	08/15/1891	01/19/1894			Y	
Smickler, Solomon	24	Russia	Y	Hamburg	Philadelphia	07/08/1882	10/22/1887			Y	
Smidt, Charles	??	Germany	Y	?	?	01/00/1882	03/25/1884			Y	
Smidt, Heinrich	27	Prussia	Y	Bremen	New Orleans	05/23/1852	10/06/1854	10	511	N	
Smidt, Henry	27	Prussia	Y	Bremen	New Orleans	05/23/1852	10/06/1854	12	450	N	
Smith, Alexander	49	Scotland	Y	Glasgow	New York	08/10/1875	09/27/1892			Y	
Smith, Andrew	??	Bavaria?	Y	?	?	?	04/05/1870			Y	
Smith, Charles F.	28	Prussia	Y	Bremen	New York	09/24/1856	08/01/1857	15	211	N	
Smith, David	30	Ireland	Y	London	Philadelphia	05/23/1845	07/08/1856	14	299	N	
Smith, David	67	Ireland	N	London	Philadelphia	06/??/1840	?			Y	
Smith, Frederick	22	Meiningen	Y	Bremen	New York	06/21/1849	12/09/1852	5	401	N	
Smith, Henry	31	Bavaria	Y	Havre	New York	05/08/1849	04/04/1853	7	510	N	
Smith, Henry	22	Hanover	Y	Bremen	Baltimore	10/15/1857	08/15/1860	27	287	N	
Smith, Herman	28	Prussia	Y	Hamburg	New York	06/25/1856	08/06/1860	27	251	N	
Smith, James	35	Ireland	Y	Liverpool	New Orleans	01/14/1851	11/01/1852	5	175	N	
Smith, James	24	Ireland	Y	Liverpool	New York	02/??/1850	12/07/1852	5	392	N	
Smith, James	35	Ireland	Y	Liverpool	New Orleans	01/14/1851	11/01/1852	6	301	N	
Smith, John	33	Ireland	Y	Belfast	Robbinstown	07/06/1842	02/21/1853	7	211	N	
Smith, John	26	Scotland	Y	Greenock	New York	04/15/1887	09/02/1889			Y	
Smith, John	22	Ireland	Y	Queenstown	New York	06/04/1881	03/30/1882			Y	
Smith, John	30	England	Y	Liverpool	New York	??/06/1849	11/??/1849	23	307	N	
Smith, Joseph	24	Scotland	Y	Liverpool	New York	09/01/1853	08/17/1857	15	148	N	
Smith, Martin	40	Prussia	Y	Antwerp	New York	01/03/1847	01/30/1851	3	63	N	
Smith, Patrick	30	Ireland	Y	Liverpool	New York	12/24/1846	05/31/1859	17	441	N	
Smith, Patrick	??	Ireland	N	?	?	??/??/1834	10/10/1836	28	188	N	08/12/1844
Smith, Patrick Francis	26	Ireland	Y	Liverpool	New Orleans	05/09/1855	03/13/1858	16	396	N	
Smith, Peter	26	Ireland	Y	Liverpool	New Orleans	??/01/1850	02/13/1850	2	69	N	
Smith, Peter	26	Scotland	Y	Glasgow	New York	01/03/1851	09/26/1856	14	389	N	
Smith, Richard	25	Ireland	Y	Liverpool	New York	??/01/1841	11/08/1849	23	329	N	
Smith, Sam	17	Russia	N	?	New York	00/00/1880				Y	10/16/1888
Smith, Terrence Joseph	24	Ireland	Y	Liverpool	New Orleans	05/01/1852	01/09/1856	13	439	N	
Smith, Thomas	34	Ireland	Y	Liverpool	New York	05/08/1891	03/25/1903			Y	
Smith, Thomas	62	Ireland	N	Liverpool	New York	05/??/1852	?			Y	
Smith, Thomas J.	24	Ireland	Y	Queenstown	New York	03/23/1881	02/07/1883			Y	
Smith, William	40	England	Y	Liverpool	Philadelphia	08/09/1840	08/16/1848	22	183	N	
Smith, William	38	Ireland	Y	Liverpool	Philadelphia	07/04/1847	02/09/1849	23	41	N	
Smith, William James	44	England	Y	Liverpool	New York	10/15/1882	10/01/1892			Y	
Smits, Henry B.	28	Germany	Y	Amsterdam	New York	12/23/1891	11/02/1899			Y	
Smolky, Charles	23	Austria	Y	Hamburg	New York	12/30/1882	03/15/1886			Y	
Smolt, Charles	22	Oldenburg	Y	Bremen	New Orleans	05/19/1851	03/21/1853	7	354	N	
Smyrl, Gabriel	28	Ireland	Y	Belfast	New York	11/14/1879	12/16/1885			Y	
Smyth, Andrew	23	Ireland	Y	Liverpool	New York	07/03/1849	02/25/1852	24	166	N	
Smyth, Henry	23	Ireland	Y	Cork	New York	11/13/1855	04/03/1856	26	429	N	
Smyth, Patrick	31	Ireland	Y	Liverpool	New York	02/01/1849	03/15/1852	24	301	N	
Smyth, William	28	Ireland	Y	Liverpool	New York	05/01/1847	03/25/1850	2	245	N	
Smyth, William P.	26	Ireland	Y	Liverpool	New Orleans	10/??/1847	11/08/1852	5	256	N	

CITIZENSHIP RECORDS

APPLICANT	AGE	COUNTRY OF ORIGIN	DEC	DEPART PORT	ENTRY PORT	ARRIVE DATE	DEC DATE	VOL	PG.	FLD	NAT DATE
Smyth, William P.	26	Ireland	Y	Liverpool	New Orleans	10/??/1847	11/08/1852	6	381	N	
Sneath, John	70	England	N	Liverpool	New York	??/??/1850	?				Y
Sneebeli, Frederick	26	Switzerland	Y	Havre	New York	04/13/1850	04/12/1852	24	463	N	
Sneyra, Henry	27	Hesse Cassel	Y	Bremen	New York	06/22/1846	07/01/1851	3	473	N	
Snider, George F.	33	Canada	Y	Hamilton	Manchester	02/25/1886	07/11/1892				Y
Snider, Martin	29	Germany	Y	Greuth	New York	08/17/1882	05/04/1886				Y
Snider, T.A.	31	Canada	Y	Toronto	Chicago	04/19/1865	04/24/1874				Y
Snitker, William	29	Hanover	Y	Bremen	Baltimore	08/08/1849	10/09/1854	11	112	N	
Snow, Norbert (Affidavit	??	?	Y	?	?	??/??/1852	?				Y
Snyder, John	22	Bavaria	Y	Havre	New York	09/19/1846	01/??/1850	23	458	N	
Soal, Louis	35	Germany	Y	Hamburg	New York	08/15/1883	10/12/1898				Y
Sobatka, Gustave	51	Austria	Y	Hamburg	New York	05/??/1880	03/??/1881				Y
Sobel, Nathan	23	Austria	Y	London	New York	01/10/1881	10/10/1885				Y
Sodnig, Franz	26	Oldenburg	Y	Bremen	New Orleans	05/01/1849	??/??/18??	9	52	N	
Soehngen, George	24	Germany	Y	Hamburg	New York	10/21/1887	08/28/1888				Y
Soehnlein, George	43	Bavaria	Y	Hamburg	New York	07/02/1845	01/29/1849	1	530	N	
Soerker, Philip	21	Bavaria	Y	Havre	New York	05/01/1852	09/27/1856	14	405	N	
Soeter, William	30	Prussia	Y	Bremen	New Orleans	05/31/1849	10/27/1851	4	407	N	
Soetje, John	25	Germany	Y	Hamburg	New Orleans	09/13/1879	04/04/1883				Y
Sohler, Joseph	25	Baden	Y	Havre	New York	10/17/1848	10/15/1851	4	298	N	
Sohler, Karl	27	Baden	Y	Havre	New York	04/01/1854	10/02/1854	10	369	N	
Sohler, Karl	27	Baden	Y	Havre	New York	04/01/1854	10/02/1854	12	308	N	
Sohlmann, Ernest	24	Hanover	Y	Bremen	Baltimore	11/14/1858	02/15/1862	18	261	N	
Sohloeffel, John	30	Prussia	Y	Bremen	New Orleans	12/06/1845	09/28/1848	22	357	N	
Sohmann, Diederick	39	Hanover	Y	Bremen	New Orleans	06/23/1845	09/17/1855	13	45	N	
Sohmine, Tony	21	Italy	Y	Naples	New York	01/22/1900	10/29/1904				Y
Sohn, George	25	France	Y	Havre	New Orleans	01/10/1847	04/09/1852	24	430	N	
Sohnerzinger, Charles	53	Germany	Y	Hamburg	New York	08/??/1864	09/19/1883				Y
Sohngen, William	23	Nassau	Y	Antwerp	New York	01/24/1848	03/01/1852	24	198	N	
Soholowski, August	33	Germany	Y	Bremen	New York	08/28/1888	02/11/1891				Y
Sohrey, George	34	Hesse Cassel	Y	Bremen	New York	06/02/1848	10/02/1854	10	360	N	
Sohrey, George	34	Hesse Cassel	Y	Bremen	New York	06/02/1848	10/02/1854	12	299	N	
Solara, Augustino	64	Italy	N	Genoa	New York	12/22/1840	?				Y
Solasky, Joe	27	Russia	Y	Liverpool	New York	09/30/1890	09/20/1893				Y
Solbrig, Charles	25	Bavaria	Y	Havre	New York	03/10/1848	08/29/1848	22	276	N	
Solewski, Valentine	33	Germany	Y	Bremen	Baltimore	03/03/1890	07/05/1895				Y
Solger, Roman	38	Germany	Y	Rotterdam	New York	08/15/1887	06/11/1892				Y
Solimine, Francesco	??	Italy	Y	?	New York	03/15/1892	07/13/1897				Y
Solimon, Abraham	35	Russia	Y	Hamburg	New York	12/??/1883	02/01/1887				Y
Solko, Abraham	36	Russia	Y	Bremen	New York	11/05/1900	11/03/1902				Y
Sollmann, William	28	Germany	Y	Bremen	New York	10/10/1881	05/23/1888				Y
Sollner, John	33	Germany	Y	Antwerp	New York	03/01/1882	03/26/1885				Y
Solms, Heinrich	23	Prussia	Y	Bremen	Baltimore	07/22/1856	10/02/1856	14	162	N	
Soloman, Raphael	27	Syria (Turkey	Y	Beirut	Philadelphia	04/??/1889	03/08/1897				Y
Solomon, Benjamin	31	Russia	Y	Hamburg	New York	07/02/1888	09/14/1892				Y
Solomon, Henry	29	Russia	Y	Hamburg	New York	10/19/1886	10/13/1888				Y
Solomon, Michael Gabriel	26	Poland (Russi	Y	Hamburg	New York	11/12/1886	10/24/1890				Y
Solosky, Nathan	31	Russia	Y	Liverpool	New York	09/30/1890	09/20/1893				Y
Somers, Henry	24	Germany	Y	Bremen	New York	05/17/1881	10/18/1882				Y
Somers, John Henry	25	Hanover	Y	Bremen	New Orleans	06/01/1846	05/25/1852	25	105	N	
Somers, Patrick	??	Ireland	Y	?	?	?	12/31/1891				Y
Sommer, Daniel Reinhold	21	Prussia	Y	Hamburg	Buffalo	06/01/1854	03/27/1856	26	359	N	
Sommer, Feis	70	Germany	Y	Liverpool	New York	07/07/1883	10/29/1888				Y
Sommer, Gottlob	29	Germany	Y	Bremen	New York	06/19/1880	04/12/1883				Y
Sommer, Heinrich	40	Germany	Y	Bremen	New York	09/28/1866	10/28/1888	19	197	N	
Sommer, Heinrich	40	Germany	Y	Bremen	New York	09/28/1866	10/29/1888				Y
Sommer, Henry	29	Hesse Cassel	Y	Bremen	Baltimore	06/15/1861	03/31/1862	18	289	N	
Sommer, Henry	28	Germany	Y	Bremen	New York	05/04/1885	10/23/1886	19	82	N	
Sommer, Henry	28	Germany	Y	Bremen	New York	05/04/1885	10/23/1886				Y

CITIZENSHIP RECORDS

APPLICANT	AGE	COUNTRY OF ORIGIN	DEC	DEPART PORT	ENTRY PORT	ARRIVE DATE	DEC DATE	VOL	PG.	FLD	NAT DATE
Sommer, Henry Gerhard	35	Hanover	Y	Bremen	Baltimore	08/07/1846	09/03/1852	25	344	N	
Sommer, J. Henry F.	43	Germany	Y	Hamburg	New York	06/17/1873	07/12/1882				Y
Sommer, John	25	Germany	Y	Hamburg	New York	03/17/1879	03/29/1880				Y
Sommer, Julius	31	Germany	Y	Copenhagen	New York	10/22/1883	10/19/1894				Y
Sommer, Rudolf	39	Austria	Y	Bremen	Baltimore	04/09/1882	09/01/1886				Y
Sommerfield, Abraham	40	Germany	Y	Hamburg	New York	03/09/1872	10/18/1890				Y
Sommerfield, W.	52	Prussia	Y	Hamburg	New York	07/??/1856	04/01/1885	19	4	N	
Sommerkamp, Peter	26	Prussia	Y	Bremen	New Orleans	12/31/1846	10/14/1848	1	216	N	
Sommerlatte, Fred	35	Germany	Y	Hamburg	New York	08/17/1890	07/27/1896				Y
Sommerman, Christ	38	Germany	Y	?	Baltimore	12/01/1881	10/25/1894				Y
Sommers, Fred H.	39	Germany	Y	Ontario	Detroit	07/01/1886	03/31/1894				Y
Sommers, John	34	Germany	N	Bremen	New York	11/03/1878	?				Y
Sommers, Sigmund	22	Hesse Darmsta	Y	London	New York	08/22/1851	04/19/1854	8	210	N	
Sommers, Sigmund	22	Hesse Darmsta	Y	London	New York	08/22/1851	04/19/1854	9	81	N	
Sonantag, Aloysius	32	Germany	N	Bremen	New York	??/??/1865	?				Y
Sonders, Abraham	39	Turkey	Y	Hamburg	New York	02/08/1891	09/23/1896				Y
Sondiren, John Gradus	32	Holland	Y	Rotterdam	New York	09/11/1846	08/07/1848	22	71	N	
Sonmann, Joseph	30	Hanover	Y	Bremen	Baltimore	10/15/1865	03/13/1872	18	470	N	
Sonne, William	38	Prussia	Y	Antwerp	New York	10/28/1852	01/14/1856	13	464	N	
Sonnentag, Augustin	32	Wurttemberg	Y	Liverpool	New York	05/25/1852	11/04/1857	15	527	N	
Sonnentag, Conrad	30	Wurttemberg	Y	Havre	New Orleans	07/04/1846	01/31/1849	1	549	N	
Sonnleithner, John	34	Austria	Y	Havre	New York	05/01/1882	10/29/1886				Y
Sonntag, John	24	Germany	Y	Bremen	New York	06/05/1892	09/28/1894				Y
Sontag, Herman	29	Germany	Y	Bremen	New York	04/01/1881	11/30/1886				Y
Sontag, John	30	Prussia	Y	Liverpool	New York	12/15/1853	12/29/1855	13	396	N	
Sontag, Julius	28	Germany	Y	Hamburg	Philadelphia	06/06/1880	07/05/1888				Y
Sontheimer, Karl	24	Germany	Y	Antwerp	New York	05/30/1882	03/12/1884				Y
Sorenten, Joseph M.	29	Switzerland	Y	Havre	New York	02/25/1891	10/16/1897				Y
Sorg, Henry	31	Germany	Y	Bremen	New York	05/28/1885	09/09/1887				Y
Sorn, John	32	Germany	Y	Antwerp	New York	07/26/1890	12/22/1896				Y
Sosinsky, Anton	29	Germany	Y	?	?	?	01/03/1891				Y
Soverreign, Daniel L.	33	Canada	Y	Canada	Detroit	05/10/1847	03/28/1853	7	425	N	
Sowers, Harvey	26	Canada	Y	Sarnia	Port Huron	03/22/1886	10/26/1892				Y
Soyez, Daniel	49	Germany	Y	Rotterdam	New York	07/24/1880	10/22/1889				Y
Spaeth, Charles	24	Germany	Y	Antwerp	New York	04/12/1892	10/09/1893				Y
Spaeth, Frank	31	Germany	Y	Bremen	New York	06/18/1891	01/18/1898				Y
Spaeth, George	21	Wurttemberg	Y	Havre	New York	08/??/1859	02/04/1861	18	85	N	
Spaeth, John	49	Baden	Y	Rotterdam	New York	12/24/1846	02/10/1849	23	44	N	
Spaeth, Ziriack	22	Baden	Y	Havre	New York	08/05/1854	08/22/1857	15	170	N	
Spaeth, Ziriack	24	Baden	Y	Havre	New York	08/05/1854	08/22/1857	15	171	N	
Spagnola, Marino	43	Italy	Y	Palermo	New York	11/06/1889	10/16/1893				Y
Spagnolo, Marino	43	Italy	Y	Palermo	New York	11/06/1889	10/16/1893	21	11	N	
Spahn, Joseph	??	Germany	Y	?	?	?	12/01/1881				Y
Spahr, Michael	21	Baden	Y	Havre	New York	05/03/1854	04/02/1856	26	414	N	
Spaith, George	34	Germany	N	Antwerp	New York	07/12/1857	?				Y
Spamer, Hugo	34	Hesse Darmsta	Y	Havre	New York	09/09/1853	01/23/1856	13	497	N	
Spang, Nikolaus	25	Germany	Y	Antwerp	New York	11/23/1884	02/10/1887				Y
Spangenberg, William	33	Prussia	Y	Bremen	New York	07/24/1868	09/03/1872	18	516	N	
Sparenberg, Adolph	30	Germany	Y	Bremen	Baltimore	09/09/1880	09/26/1883				Y
Sparow, Batt	30	Ireland	Y	Liverpool	New Orleans	02/04/1850	09/25/1854	10	220	N	
Sparow, Batt	30	Ireland	Y	Liverpool	New Orleans	02/04/1850	09/25/1854	12	159	N	
Spataro, Francesco	37	Italy	Y	Massini	Boston	09/04/1889	10/25/1900				Y
Spath, George	45	Bavaria	Y	Bremen	Baltimore	10/01/1844	09/14/1848	22	347	N	
Spathe, Charles Frederic	??	Saxony	Y	Hamburg	New York	02/07/1845	10/06/1848	22	455	N	
Specht, Kaspar	35	Germany	Y	Antwerp	New York	11/25/1881	01/02/1890				Y
Speck, Conrad	32	Germany	Y	Bremen	Baltimore	06/12/1892	10/26/1893				Y
Speckman, Herman H.	30	Germany	Y	?	?	07/21/1876	01/13/1887				Y
Specks, Anton	27	Germany	Y	Bremen	New York	04/11/1892	08/21/1893				Y
Spector, Sam	40	Russia	Y	Hamburg	New York	07/29/1889	11/07/1895				Y

CITIZENSHIP RECORDS

APPLICANT	AGE	COUNTRY OF ORIGIN	DEC	DEPART PORT	ENTRY PORT	ARRIVE DATE	DEC DATE	VOL	PG.	FLD	NAT DATE
Speelman, Lion	46	Holland	Y	London	New York	09/02/1854	07/03/1857	15	124	N	
Speidel, August	24	Germany	Y	?	New York	02/27/1885	10/29/1886			Y	
Speidel, Henry	27	Germany	Y	Havre	New York	04/03/1882	10/15/1888			Y	
Speigel, John Mathias	34	Bavaria	Y	Havre	New Orleans	12/24/1851	01/24/1856	13	501	N	
Speiker, Henri	26	Germany	Y	Hamburg	New York	05/25/1880	10/29/1886	19	96	N	
Speiser, Arnold	50	Oldenberg	N	Bremen	New York	06/24/1866	?			Y	
Speith, Jacob	30	Wurttemberg	Y	Bremen	New York	11/??/1848	04/28/1855	11	219	N	
Spekemeyer, Henry	57	Germany	N	Bremen	New York	06/??/1846	?	28	211	N	??/??/1852
Spekemeyer, Henry	15	Germany	N	Bremen	New York	06/00/1846				Y	00/00/1852
Spelbrink, John	48	Germany	Y	Bremen	Baltimore	05/??/1864	02/18/1884			Y	
Spellbring, Herman	40	Hanover	Y	Bremen	Baltimore	07/01/1863	10/08/1872	18	531	N	
Speller, Clemens	32	Germany	Y	Bremen	New York	05/20/1882	07/31/1890			Y	
Speller, John	29	Germany	Y	Amsterdam	New York	08/10/1882	10/01/1883			Y	
Spellman, John	40	Ireland	Y	Liverpool	New Orleans	02/??/1849	12/07/1852	5	393	N	
Spellman, John	45	Ireland	Y	Cork	New Orleans	05/08/1852	09/26/1854	10	245	N	
Spellman, John	40	Ireland	Y	Cork	New Orleans	05/08/1852	09/26/1854	12	184	N	
Spellman, Thomas	35	Ireland	Y	Liverpool	New York	07/06/1853	09/30/1856	14	74	N	
Spelman, Daniel	40	Ireland	Y	Cork	New Orleans	05/08/1852	09/24/1857	15	315	N	
Spencer, John	22	Ireland	Y	Cork	New Orleans	04/15/1849	03/06/1852	24	247	N	
Spengel, Carl	23	Germany	Y	?	?	11/??/1880	12/10/1880			Y	
Spengemann, William	21	Prussia	Y	Bremen	New York	09/29/1856	11/01/1858	17	226	N	
Spengler, Gottfried	46	Switzerland	Y	Havre	New York	07/14/1872	03/22/1882			Y	
Spenneberg, Melchoir	31	Prussia	Y	Bremen	New York	08/20/1853	12/29/1857	16	283	N	
Spenner, John	35	Germany	Y	Hamburg	New York	08/25/1880	03/02/1881			Y	
Sperber, Andrew	47	Bavaria	Y	Havre	Baltimore	07/04/1852	12/17/1855	13	323	N	
Sperber, Nicholas	32	Germany	Y	?	New York	??/??/1872	10/13/1884			Y	
Sperl, Michael	66	Bavaria	Y	Havre	New York	05/31/1848	09/24/1855	13	130	N	
Sperlich, Frank	??	Germany	N	?	?	06/00/1872				Y	10/14/1892
Sperry, Nicholas	41	Bavaria	N	Havre	New York	05/??/1866	?			Y	
Speyer, Noah	21	Saxe Weimar E	Y	Bremen	New York	12/22/1855	01/12/1856	13	457	N	
Spichtig, Peter	40	Switzerland	Y	Havre	New York	05/07/1871	10/19/1888			Y	
Spicker, John Gottlieb	21	Prussia	Y	Bremen	New York	10/03/1855	02/01/1856	13	533	N	
Spiegel, Jonas	47	Austria	N	Hamburg	New York	12/09/1865	?			Y	
Spieks, Adam	26	Germany	Y	Antwerp	New York	05/09/1891	11/07/1892			Y	
Spielmann, Barni	34	Germany	Y	Rotterdam	New York	06/01/1883	11/12/1890			Y	
Spielmann, Henry	26	Kurhessen	Y	Bremen	Baltimore	08/26/1852	07/17/1855	11	403	N	
Spiering, Henry	40	Germany	Y	Bremen	New York	11/05/1871	10/26/1889	19	271	N	
Spies, Jacob	23	Hesse Darmsta	Y	Havre	New York	08/24/1848	10/16/1851	4	305	N	
Spies, Stephan	32	Germany	Y	Bremen	Baltimore	03/28/1884	01/24/1889			Y	
Spieser, Joseph	33	Germany	Y	Havre	New York	12/07/1889	11/11/1891			Y	
Spiess, Barthold Henry	??	Germany	Y	?	?	?	10/04/1892			Y	
Spiess, Fred	27	Germany	Y	Bremen	New York	05/10/1890	08/24/1895			Y	
Spiess, Phillip	24	Germany	Y	Antwerp	New York	05/13/1889	01/19/1894			Y	
Spiesz, George Charles	31	Hesse Darmsta	Y	Havre	New York	06/11/1846	04/12/1852	24	460	N	
Spilker, Fred	21	Germany	Y	Bremen	New York	04/26/1885	06/16/1887			Y	
Spillmann, Casper	40	Switzerland	Y	Havre	New York	03/09/1849	10/01/1852	5	171	N	
Spillmann, Casper	40	Switzerland	Y	Havre	New York	03/09/1849	11/01/1852	6	297	N	
Spina, Carmino	??	Italy	Y	?	?	?	06/02/1893			Y	
Spindler, Philipp	29	Germany	Y	Bremen	New York	08/07/1889	10/10/1894			Y	
Spinner, John	34	Baden	Y	Havre	New Orleans	04/16/1846	08/17/1848	22	194	N	
Spissman, George	28	Wurttemberg	Y	Havre	New York	07/09/1852	09/23/1854	12	123	N	
Spissmann, George	28	Wurttemberg	Y	Havre	New York	07/09/1852	09/23/1854	10	184	N	
Spitz, Ferdinand	44	France	Y	Havre	New York	01/19/1873	10/25/1887			Y	
Spitz, Louis	23	Russia	Y	Hamburg	New York	09/14/1892	05/23/1892			Y	
Spitz, Nicolaus	30	Baden	Y	Havre	New York	08/04/1854	04/04/1856	26	432	N	
Spitz, Sebastian	22	Baden	Y	Havre	New York	10/15/1853	10/12/1857	15	400	N	
Spitzle, Charles H.	29	Switzerland	Y	Havre	New York	08/14/1871	10/12/1880			Y	
Spitzmueller, Richard	31	Germany	Y	Havre	New York	03/01/1878	02/06/1886			Y	
Spitznagel, Julius	??	Germany	Y	Hamburg	New York	10/16/1880	09/24/1885			Y	

CITIZENSHIP RECORDS

APPLICANT	AGE	COUNTRY OF ORIGIN	DEC	DEPART PORT	ENTRY PORT	ARRIVE DATE	DEC DATE	VOL	PG.	FLD	NAT DATE
Splatt, William	41	England	Y	Liverpool	New York	05/25/1869	08/19/1886			Y	
Splinter, John	36	Hanover	Y	Bremen	New Orleans	12/20/1845	06/16/1851	3	383	N	
Spoltman, John	38	Holland	Y	Rotterdam	New York	09/11/1846	08/15/1848	22	123	N	
Sponagel, Valentine	25	Germany	Y	Amsterdam	New York	11/10/1882	09/04/1885			Y	
Sponsel, Christoph	38	Germany	Y	Bremen	New York	06/02/1878	03/24/1891			Y	
Sponsel, Henry	32	Germany	Y	Bremen	New York	01/09/1880	09/25/1885			Y	
Sponsel, John	32	Germany	Y	Hamburg	New York	06/11/1872	04/15/1882			Y	
Spormann, August	??	Germany	Y	?	Baltimore	01/??/1882	04/01/1884			Y	
Spranz, John Christopher	36	Hanover	Y	Bremen	Baltimore	09/08/1854	04/10/1858	16	451	N	
Spraul, Karl	25	Germany	Y	Antwerp	New York	08/18/1892	03/30/1896			Y	
Spreadburg, George J.	42	England	Y	Liverpool	New York	07/??/1865	03/27/1883			Y	
Spreen, Charles	23	Prussia	Y	Bremen	Baltimore	05/25/1858	02/18/1861	18	104	N	
Spreen, Christian	24	Prussia	Y	Bremen	Baltimore	05/20/1848	04/15/1852	24	512	N	
Spreen, William	22	Germany	Y	Bremen	New York	04/25/1881	10/27/1882			Y	
Sprekelmeier, Henry	28	Germany	Y	Antwerp	New York	04/23/1880	07/12/1888			Y	
Sprekels, John	44	Hanover	Y	Bremen	New Orleans	11/02/1851	08/10/1872	18	511	N	
Sprengelmeier, Henry	26	Hanover	Y	Bremen	New York	06/01/1867	02/15/1872	18	464	N	
Sprenger, Christian	28	Hanover	Y	Bremen	New York	08/06/1852	11/08/1852	5	254	N	
Sprenger, Franz	40	Germany	Y	Antwerp	New York	04/20/1881	01/12/1888			Y	
Spresser, Christoph	40	Wurtemberg	Y	Antwerp	New York	05/01/1845	09/15/1852	25	523	N	
Spriegel, Charles	34	Wurttemberg	Y	Antwerp	New York	09/01/1848	08/27/1855	11	492	N	
Springer, Adolph	31	Germany	Y	Bremen	Baltimore	08/25/1883	03/14/1887			Y	
Springer, Albert	27	Baden	Y	Havre	New York	08/28/1857	05/30/1859	17	435	N	
Springer, Charles	22	Wurttemberg	Y	Bremen	New York	06/28/1953	01/10/1856	13	445	N	
Springer, Christian	28	Hanover	Y	Bremen	New York	08/06/1852	11/08/1852	6	378	N	
Springer, Emil	41	Germany	Y	Hamburg	New York	09/05/1883	02/25/1884			Y	
Springman, Joseph	22	Baden	Y	Havre	New York	05/20/1854	02/02/1856	13	534	N	
Springmann, August	34	Germany	Y	Havre	New York	05/19/1882	10/28/1892			Y	
Springmeier, Henry	50	Germany	Y	Bremen	New York	11/??/1870	10/08/1884			Y	
Springmeier, Herman	24	Hanover	Y	Bremen	New York	01/15/1850	09/15/1852	25	512	N	
Sprokelkamp, Henry	36	Holland	Y	Rotterdam	New York	09/11/1846	08/15/1848	22	122	N	
Spruck, Konrad	29	Germany	Y	Antwerp	Philadelphia	04/11/1896	09/15/1899			Y	
Spruessky, Henry	62	Prussia	N	Bremen	New York	11/26/1853	?			Y	
Spruetzky, Henry	25	Prussia	Y	Bremen	New York	11/21/1853	04/17/1854	8	137	N	
Sprung, John Henry	30	Oldenburg	Y	Bremen	New Orleans	10/21/1848	03/05/1852	24	240	N	
Sprutzky, Henry	25	Prussia	Y	Bremen	New York	11/21/1853	04/17/1854	9	8	N	
Spuhler, Frederick	23	Germany	Y	Antwerp	New York	10/13/1881	10/08/1883			Y	
Spurgin, Joseph Miles	35	England	Y	Liverpool	New Orleans	11/08/1848	05/15/1854	8	440	N	
Spurgin, Joseph Miles	35	England	Y	Liverpool	New Orleans	11/08/1848	05/15/1854	9	313	N	
Spurk, Johann	39	Germany	Y	Antwerp	Philadelphia	10/24/1888	02/04/1889			Y	
Sputh, Oscar	23	Germany	Y	Bremen	New York	06/28/1878	10/20/1882			Y	
Spydraj, Walenty	??	Germany	Y	?	?	?	11/29/1887			Y	
Squires, John H.	40	England	Y	?	?	?	12/19/1891			Y	
Sreuser, Bernard	28	Germany	Y	Rotterdam	New York	04/16/1888	11/09/1896			Y	
St. Claire, Daniel	27	Scotland	Y	Glasgow	Philadelphia	05/15/1886	03/25/1893			Y	10/22/1895
Staab, Adam	??	Bavaria	Y	?	New York	11/07/1854	11/07/1856	14	486	N	
Staab, Adam J.	57	Germany	Y	Antwerp	New York	12/15/1869	10/13/1880			Y	
Staab, Conrad	48	Germany	Y	Bremen	New York	07/02/1883	07/10/1891			Y	
Staab, G.	49	Germany	Y	Hamburg	New York	??/??/1868	10/11/1884			Y	
Staab, Leo	45	Germany	Y	Bremen	New York	06/17/1870	02/18/1888			Y	
Staab, Lorenz	27	Bavaria	Y	Rotterdam	New York	06/29/1849	05/31/1852	25	149	N	
Staab, William	30	Germany	Y	Bremen	New York	05/01/1883	09/05/1887			Y	
Staak, Emil	27	Germany	Y	Bremen	New York	06/06/1887	11/01/1890	19	309	N	
Staak, Ernie	27	Germany	Y	Bremen	New York	06/06/1887	11/01/1890			Y	
Stack, Michael	23	Ireland	Y	Dublin	New York	05/06/1848	10/09/1854	6	190	N	
Stack, Michael	23	Ireland	Y	Dublin	New York	05/06/1848	10/09/1854	11	193	N	
Stack, Richard	28	Ireland	Y	Liverpool	New Orleans	11/28/1849	03/22/1853	7	370	N	
Stack, Thomas Cooke	31	Ireland	Y	Liverpool	Philadelphia	03/20/1849	05/01/1854	9	187	N	
Stadelbauer, Joseph	45	Bavaria	Y	Bremen	New York	05/??/1853	04/28/1855	11	317	N	

CITIZENSHIP RECORDS

APPLICANT	AGE	COUNTRY OF ORIGIN	DEC	DEPART PORT	ENTRY PORT	ARRIVE DATE	DEC DATE	VOL	PG.	FLD	NAT DATE
Stadelmann, Fritz	27	Germany	Y	Bremen	New York	05/02/1880	06/25/1883			Y	
Stader, John	44	Baden	Y	Bremen	New Orleans	01/??/1854	09/21/1855	13	98	N	
Stadermann, Gustav	30	Germany	Y	Bremen	New York	10/19/1880	04/11/1892			Y	
Stadler, Gabriel	21	Bavaria	Y	Havre	New York	05/??/1860	01/10/1861	18	48	N	
Stadler, George	34	Germany	Y	Rotterdam	New York	05/19/1883	10/03/1887			Y	
Stadler, Leonhard	37	Switzerland	Y	Antwerp	New York	07/01/1852	10/06/1856	14	199	N	
Stadt, Thomas Cooke	31	Ireland	Y	Liverpool	Philadelphia	03/20/1849	05/01/1854	8	314	N	
Stadtlaender, Henry	27	Hanover	Y	Baltimore?	New Orleans	12/18/1844	09/15/1848	22	351	N	
Stadtlaender, William	22	Hanover	Y	Bremen	New Orleans	12/25/1846	09/15/1848	22	350	N	
Staender, Philip	29	Prussia	Y	Bremen	New York	07/16/1854	02/04/1856	26	32	N	
Staffan, Nicholas	34	Prussia	Y	Rotterdam	New York	07/29/1849	10/07/8154	12	469	N	
Stafford, Thomas	40	England	Y	Liverpool	New York	??/28/1841	08/13/1851	4	135	N	
Stafke, Ignatius George	37	Germany	Y	Bremen	Baltimore	09/30/1888	09/24/1894			Y	
Stagge, Fritz	43	Germany	N	Bremen	New York	08/??/1868	?			Y	
Stagge, Herman	34	Germany	Y	Rotterdam	New York	06/01/1874	03/20/1885			Y	
Stagge, Johann Friedrick	55	Germany	Y	Bremen	Baltimore	09/09/1881	05/31/1887			Y	
Stagge, William	21	Hanover	Y	Bremen	Baltimore	10/11/1857	10/08/1860	27	417	N	
Staggenborg, Barney	??	Oldenburg	Y	?	New Orleans	11/04/18??	11/10/1856	14	480	N	
Stagmann, Adam	??	Germany	N	?	?	10/14/1884				Y	10/19/1892
Stahl, Bernard	32	Germany	Y	Bremen	Baltimore	03/24/1883	02/05/1889			Y	
Stahl, George	28	Germany	Y	Bremen	Baltimore	11/06/1890	11/06/1894			Y	
Stahl, John	36	Bavaria	Y	Bremen	New York	12/15/1846	10/20/1852	5	27	N	
Stahl, John	30	Bavaria	Y	Havre	New York	10/06/1848	02/19/1849	23	173	N	
Stahl, Louis	29	Kurhessen	Y	Bremen	New York	07/10/1840	10/11/1848	1	146	N	
Stahl, Peter	30	Germany	Y	Antwerp	New York	12/24/1885	03/26/1888			Y	
Stahl, Peter	27	Germany	Y	Bremen	New York	05/02/1882	04/07/1885			Y	
Stahl, Phillip Peter	24	Bavaria	Y	Havre	New York	08/17/1852	03/10/1853	7	320	N	
Stahlmann, Fred	24	Germany	Y	Bremen	New York	08/27/1880	02/02/1882			Y	
Staib, Robert	25	Baden	Y	Liverpool	New York	12/25/1852	09/26/1854	10	230	N	
Staib, Robert	25	Baden	Y	Liverpool	New York	12/25/1852	09/26/1854	12	169	N	
Stalf, Carl	45	Germany	Y	Bremen	New York	03/09/1883	11/16/1885			Y	
Stalf, Peter	53	Germany	Y	Bremen	New York	08/08/1864	06/15/1889			Y	
Stall, B. George	25	Oldenburg	Y	Amsterdam	New York	12/26/1848	04/04/1853	8	44	N	
Stallfort, Herbert (Stah	33	Germany	Y	Bremen	New York	06/11/1885	05/07/1891			Y	
Stallo, Fritz	32	Germany	Y	Amsterdam	New York	09/25/1887	03/18/1889			Y	
Stallo, Henry (Staller?)	26	Germany	Y	Bremen	Baltimore	10/04/1884	10/26/1891			Y	
Stallo, Joseph	23	Germany	Y	Bremen	Baltimore	09/24/1881	09/25/1885			Y	
Stammeier, Christian	39	Germany	Y	Bremen	Baltimore	03/29/1880	03/04/1895			Y	
Stammeier, Gottlieb	28	Germany	Y	Bremen	Baltimore	03/29/1880	10/25/1890			Y	
Stammeier, Joseph	28	Prussia	Y	Bremen	Baltimore	11/07/1853	12/29/1855	13	383	N	
Stammel, Gerhard	23	Kurhessen	Y	Bremen	New York	01/05/1854	09/30/1856	14	63	N	
Stammler, John	26	Germany	Y	Bremen	New York	06/02/1892	07/14/1892			Y	
Standan, Rudolph	35	Prussia	N	Bremen	Baltimore	07/08/1877	?			Y	
Stander, John	31	Prussia	Y	Bremen	New York	10/05/1852	10/04/1858	17	35	N	
Standt, Henry	35	Germany	Y	Havre	New York	09/01/1890	10/11/1893			Y	
Stanger, Adam	55	Wurttemberg	Y	Antwerp	New York	06/20/1846	10/13/1848	1	207	N	
Stanger, William	26	Wurttemberg	Y	Bremen	New York	05/24/1854	05/21/1859	17	422	N	
Stanley, John	23	Ireland	Y	Queenstown	New York	05/22/1881	10/03/1885			Y	
Stanley, Martin	47	Ireland	N	Liverpool	New York	05/??/1857	?			Y	
Stanley, William H.	27	England	Y	Liverpool	Buffalo	09/15/1849	09/07/1857	15	238	N	
Stanten, Edward	38	England	Y	Liverpool	Detroit	05/??/1877	11/01/1884			Y	
Stanter, Henry	35	Bavaria	Y	Havre	New York	03/28/1856	11/28/1859	17	484	N	
Stanton, Mathew	27	Ireland	Y	Liverpool	New York	04/02/1852	04/17/1854	9	35	N	
Stapel, Frederick	46	Germany	Y	Bremen	Baltimore	06/01/1866	10/28/1884			Y	
Stapelton, James	34	Ireland	Y	Waterford	Buffalo	06/02/1847	04/04/1853	8	38	N	
Stapf, William	24	Saxony	Y	Bremen	New York	12/??/1848	12/11/1850	2	357	N	
Stapleton, Edmond	24	Ireland	Y	Liverpool	New Orleans	02/07/1852	04/04/1853	7	515	N	
Stapleton, James	38	Ireland	Y	Liverpool	New Orleans	11/20/1845	06/23/1851	3	445	N	
Stapleton, James	33	Ireland	Y	Liverpool	New Orleans	04/11/1849	04/04/1853	8	15	N	

CITIZENSHIP RECORDS

APPLICANT	AGE	COUNTRY OF ORIGIN	DEC	DEPART PORT	ENTRY PORT	ARRIVE DATE	DEC DATE	VOL	PG.	FLD	NAT DATE
Stapleton, John	27	Ireland	Y	Liverpool	New Orleans	04/05/1851	10/21/1852	5	41	N	
Stapleton, Michael	40	Ireland	Y	Liverpool	New York	04/01/1850	04/25/1853	8	104	N	
Stapleton, Richard	27	Ireland	Y	Liverpool	New York	11/03/1848	03/22/1850	2	233	N	
Stapleton, William	25	England	Y	Liverpool	New Orleans	11/08/1848	03/07/1848	7	303	N	
Stargardt, Julius	33	Germany	Y	Bremen	New York	07/08/1891	10/06/1896			Y	
Stargardt, Morris	28	Germany	Y	Bremen	New York	07/18/1891	10/06/1896			Y	
Stark, Franz	45	Germany	Y	Havre	New York	06/16/1881	09/20/1887			Y	
Stark, William	23	Wurttemberg	Y	Bremen	New York	10/10/1854	11/09/1857	16	2	N	
Starke, Adolph	34	Prussia	Y	?	?	09/20/1868	01/02/1875			Y	
Starke, August	29	Hanover	Y	Bremen	Baltimore	08/23/1860	08/04/1862	18	386	N	
Starke, Rudolph	28	Germany	Y	Hamburg	New York	11/04/1883	10/27/1890			Y	
Starman, Joseph	25	Germany	Y	Bremen	New York	03/28/1888	11/15/1894			Y	
Starmann, Bernhard	21	Germany	Y	Amsterdam	New York	09/01/1895	12/10/1896			Y	
Starmon, Joseph	25	Germany	Y	Bremen	New York	03/28/1888	11/15/1894	21	75	N	
Starzmann, Jacob	27	Germany	Y	Bremen	New York	05/29/1881	05/08/1886			Y	
Statfeldt, H.	39	Germany	Y	Bremen	Baltimore	08/03/1883	09/22/1885			Y	
Stattman, Benjamin H.	31	Germany	N	Bremen	New Orleans	??/??/1859	?			Y	
Stau, Theo	45	Germany	Y	Hamburg	New York	07/27/1891	03/17/1893			Y	
Staub, Benedict	29	Germany	Y	Antwerp	New York	10/21/1886	08/21/1889			Y	
Staub, John	25	Bavaria	Y	Havre	New York	04/19/1851	04/17/1854	8	169	N	
Staub, John	25	Bavaria	Y	Havre	New York	04/19/1851	04/17/1854	9	40	N	
Staub, John	25	Germany	Y	Havre	New York	07/03/1887	12/10/1889			Y	
Staub, Theobald	25	Germany	Y	Havre	New York	05/24/1881	06/16/1881			Y	
Stauber, George	54	Bavaria	Y	Bremen	New York	11/15/1854	10/07/1856	14	251	N	
Staubitz, Johannes	59	Germany	Y	Antwerp	New York	08/12/1882	03/24/1890			Y	
Staubitz, Peter	20	Germany	Y	Antwerp	New York	09/29/1881	11/29/1881			Y	
Stauch, Louis	60	Germany	N	Havre	New York	06/02/1857	?			Y	
Staud, Peter Paul	39	Germany	Y	Bremen	Baltimore	05/21/1882	08/15/1889			Y	
Staudenmaier, Martin	21	Germany	Y	Rotterdam	New York	05/03/1881	11/28/1884			Y	
Staunton, Mathew	27	Ireland	Y	Liverpool	New York	04/02/1852	04/17/1854	8	164	N	
Staus, Baltus	23	Heckingen	Y	Havre	New Orleans	06/23/1846	02/02/1849	23	19	N	
Stauss, Joseph	21	Germany	Y	Havre	New York	06/27/1892	08/14/1893			Y	
Stautner, George	30	France	Y	Havre	New York	06/18/1854	09/17/1857	15	283	N	
Stautner, Jacob	33	France	Y	Havre	New York	06/18/1854	09/17/1857	15	282	N	
Stauvermann, Bernard	26	Prussia	Y	Bremen	New Orleans	12/06/1848	07/28/1851	4	55	N	
Stauvermann, William	23	Hanover	Y	Bremen	New Orleans	12/24/1852	03/25/1856	26	342	N	
Stavanevege, Jovan Ivan	??	Austria	Y	?	?	?	07/13/1896			Y	
Stecher, Peter	28	Wurttemberg	Y	Antwerp	New York	04/20/1847	01/29/1849	1	537	N	
Stecher, Stefan	27	Germany	Y	Hamburg	New York	09/07/1883	06/02/1886			Y	
Stecher, William	27	Germany	Y	Bremen	New York	04/25/1891	11/10/1899			Y	
Steck, Louis	33	Germany	Y	Antwerp	New York	05/01/1883	08/05/1891			Y	
Steck, William	35	Germany	Y	Bremen	Baltimore	09/25/1883	12/09/1892			Y	
Steding, Christian	48	Kurhessen	Y	Bremen	New York	05/29/1848	11/15/1852	5	294	N	
Steding, Christian	48	Kurhessen	Y	Bremen	New York	05/29/1848	11/15/1852	6	416	N	
Stedtefeld, Henry	23	Germany	Y	Amsterdam	New York	10/13/1884	12/26/1885			Y	
Stedtefeld, Hermann	22	Germany	Y	Amsterdam	New York	05/19/1887	12/24/1888			Y	
Stedtefeld, John	22	Germany	Y	Amsterdam	New York	10/11/1884	09/08/1886			Y	
Stedtefeldt, William	23	Germany	Y	Amsterdam	New York	09/13/1884	12/26/1885			Y	
Steegmueller, Julius	24	Wurttemberg	Y	Antwerp	New York	08/16/1849	10/09/1854	11	109	N	
Steegmuller, Julius	24	Wurttemberg	Y	Antwerp	New York	08/16/1849	10/09/1854	6	106	N	
Steel, David	30	Ireland	Y	Liverpool	New York	05/02/1843	01/28/1851	2	539	N	
Steele, Thomas	23	Ireland	Y	Liverpool	New York	09/01/1847	07/15/1851	3	537	N	
Steer, George H.	??	Canada	Y	?	?	?	09/29/1892			Y	
Steerlin, Conrad	28	Switzerland	Y	Havre	New Orleans	12/02/1848	03/26/1850	2	266	N	
Steers, James	29	Ireland	Y	Liverpool	Boston	11/29/1848	12/29/1849	23	436	N	
Stefener, Henry	26	Germany	Y	Bremen	Baltimore	12/01/1892	06/06/1895			Y	
Steffan, Nicolas	34	Prussia	Y	Rotterdam	New York	07/29/1849	10/07/1854	10	530	N	
Steffe, George	31	Baden	Y	Havre	New York	08/16/1854	09/12/1855	13	8	N	
Steffen, John	48	Prussia	Y	Hamburg	New York	09/07/1849	04/13/1860	27	152	N	

CITIZENSHIP RECORDS

APPLICANT	AGE	COUNTRY OF ORIGIN	DEC	DEPART PORT	ENTRY PORT	ARRIVE DATE	DEC DATE	VOL	PG.	FLD	NAT DATE
Steffen, John Mathias	30	Hanover	Y	Bremen	New Orleans	11/22/1854	03/25/1856	26	336	N	
Steffen, Peter	30	Germany	Y	Havre	New York	09/16/1894	05/14/1900			Y	
Steffens, Charles	39	Prussia	Y	Liverpool	New York	07/15/1852	07/09/1855	11	366	N	
Steffens, H.C.	27	Germany	Y	Bremen	Baltimore	04/18/1883	02/07/1885			Y	
Steffes, William	34	Luxembourg	Y	Antwerp	New York	11/10/1854	12/09/1857	16	210	N	
Steffins, Henry	11	Holland	N	?	New York	00/00/1866				Y	10/23/1888
Stefft, Harris	27	Russia	Y	Liverpool	New Orleans	12/24/1849	03/24/1851	3	246	N	
Stefke, Frank	30	Austria	Y	Hamburg	New York	11/06/1881	11/02/1886			Y	
Stegemann, A. J.	21	Germany	Y	Bremen	Baltimore	10/04/1881	12/11/1884			Y	
Stegemann, Gerhard	25	Hanover	Y	Bremen	New Orleans	06/05/1855	01/01/1856	14	120	N	
Stegemann, Henri	24	Germany	Y	Rotterdam	New York	10/30/1885	08/15/1889			Y	
Stegemann, Henry	34	Prussia	Y	Bremen	Baltimore	10/12/1859	05/08/1861	18	163	N	
Stegemeier, Henry	30	Hanover	Y	Bremen	Baltimore	05/01/1849	10/28/1851	4	427	N	
Stegemen, Adam	35	Prussia	Y	Rotterdam	New York	11/11/1847	02/17/1849	23	150	N	
Stegemoeller, Louis	46	Prussia	Y	Bremen	Baltimore	09/20/1847	02/08/1851	3	107	N	
Steger, George	36	Germany	Y	Bremen	New York	06/20/1883	03/11/1897			Y	
Stegle, Michael	28	Germany	Y	Antwerp	New York	10/??/1882	02/18/1889			Y	
Stegmaier, Charles	32	Germany	Y	Antwerp	New York	03/01/1881	02/01/1884			Y	
Stegman, John A.	36	Bavaria	Y	Havre	New York	05/15/1853	08/23/1862	18	396	N	
Stegmann, Bonefacius	24	Germany	Y	Bremen	Baltimore	06/29/1880	02/06/1882			Y	
Stegmann, David	63	Hanover	Y	Bremen	Baltimore	11/14/1854	10/25/1858	17	110	N	
Stegmann, Frank	25	Hanover	Y	Havre	Baltimore	12/29/1854	11/01/1860	27	515	N	
Stegmann, Franz	34	Bavaria	Y	Amsterdam	New York	05/02/1849	01/29/1853	7	83	N	
Stegmann, Frederick	22	Hanover	Y	Bremen	Baltimore	11/14/1854	10/25/1858	17	109	N	
Stegmann, Joseph	65	Germany	N	Liverpool	New York	04/23/1857	?			Y	
Stegmann, William	29	Germany	Y	Bremen	New York	08/13/1880	02/02/1884			Y	
Stegmess, Paul	32	Germany	Y	Hamburg	New York	12/02/1887	03/07/1898			Y	
Stegner, Daniel	30	Bavaria	Y	Havre	New Orleans	12/15/1846	08/27/1855	11	498	N	
Stehle, August	22	Wurttemberg	Y	Havre	New Orleans	??/15/1848	02/14/1850	2	75	N	
Stehman, Joseph	31	Hanover	Y	Bremen	Baltimore	02/04/1848	02/23/1852	24	158	N	
Stehr, Herman H.	24	Germany	Y	Bremen	Baltimore	01/05/1882	06/02/1886			Y	
Steidel, Ernst	23	Germany	Y	Antwerp	New York	09/07/1887	11/05/1890			Y	
Steidel, Mathias	32	Wurttemberg	Y	Bremen	New York	08/10/1853	06/05/1854	10	74	N	
Steidel, Mathias	32	Wurttemberg	Y	Bremen	New York	08/10/1853	06/05/1854	12	11	N	
Steidle, Ignatius	23	Germany	Y	?	?	08/15/1879	09/12/1882			Y	
Steier, Alois	26	Germany	Y	Havre	New York	07/12/1882	10/24/1888			Y	
Steiger, Casper	32	Wurttemberg	Y	Havre	New York	04/15/1853	09/17/1857	15	281	N	
Steiger, Robert	??	Austria	Y	?	?	?	10/06/1884			Y	
Steigewald, William	30	Germany	Y	Bremen	New York	05/16/1889	10/11/1895			Y	
Steigl, Michael	40	Bavaria	Y	Hamburg	New York	07/02/1853	10/09/1854	6	80	N	
Steigl, Michael	40	Bavaria	Y	Hamburg	New York	07/02/1853	10/09/1853	11	83	N	
Steigleder, Andrew	??	Bavaria	Y	?	?	?	10/12/1868			Y	
Steiglider,	48	Bavaria	N	Havre	New York	10/12/1865	?			Y	
Steiler, Joseph	26	Germany	Y	Hamburg	New York	04/01/1886	10/06/1886			Y	
Steimann, Frank	44	Germany	Y	Hamburg	New York	10/11/1881	02/12/1891			Y	
Steimar, Matthias	41	Germany	Y	?	?	11/01/1893	11/01/1894			Y	
Stein, Alexander	40	Germany	Y	?	Cincinnati?	04/09/1880	04/06/1885			Y	
Stein, Anton	29	Germany	Y	Bremen	Baltimore	03/31/1880	12/11/1888			Y	
Stein, Charles	28	Germany	Y	Hamburg	New York	12/15/1887	12/12/1890			Y	
Stein, Frank	24	Bavaria	Y	London	New York	10/22/1854	12/03/1855	13	276	N	
Stein, George	23	Germany	Y	Antwerp	New York	10/13/1881	03/30/1886			Y	
Stein, Gottfried	27	Bavaria	Y	Bremen	New York	07/07/1852	07/09/1855	11	357	N	
Stein, Gregorius	42	Bavaria	Y	Havre	New Orleans	11/25/1845	08/30/1848	22	281	N	
Stein, Isaac	27	Germany	Y	Amsterdam	New York	04/06/1891	05/13/1896			Y	
Stein, Jacob	32	Baden	Y	Havre	New York	07/04/1849	05/20/1852	25	49	N	
Stein, Joseph C.	33	Germany	Y	Antwerp	Rochester	06/12/1871	05/17/1883			Y	
Stein, Michael	22	Baden	Y	Havre	New York	06/29/1849	09/15/1852	25	532	N	
Stein, Valentine	34	Bavaria	Y	Havre	New York	10/04/1847	10/20/1852	5	32	N	
Stein, William	41	Holland	Y	Bremen	Baltimore	09/19/1883	04/09/1886			Y	

CITIZENSHIP RECORDS

APPLICANT	AGE	COUNTRY OF ORIGIN	DEC	DEPART PORT	ENTRY PORT	ARRIVE DATE	DEC DATE	VOL	PG.	FLD	NAT DATE
Steinau, Joseph	61	Bavaria	Y	Rotterdam	New Orleans	04/01/1845	08/01/1851	4	67	N	
Steinauer, Nicholas	??	Switzerland	Y	Havre	New York	08/04/1850	03/25/1851	3	354	N	
Steinbach, August	27	Germany	Y	Antwerp	New York	08/14/1895	10/02/1895			Y	
Steinbach, Leo	43	Germany	Y	Bremen	New York	09/06/1887	10/26/1888			Y	
Steinbach, Martin	23	Germany	Y	Antwerp	Philadelphia	05/09/1890	01/23/1893			Y	
Steinbauer, Charles	21	Germany	Y	?	?	?	07/19/1882			Y	
Steinbauer, William	22	Bavaria	Y	Havre	New York	11/05/1852	11/20/1852	13	265	N	
Steinbeck, Arnold	33	Germany	Y	Havre	New York	08/21/1873	09/07/1880			Y	
Steinbeck, Julius	26	Saxe Weimar	Y	Bremen	Baltimore	06/15/1861	03/31/1862	18	290	N	
Steinberg, August	39	Prussia	Y	Bremen	New Orleans	12/25/1857	12/08/1858	17	385	N	
Steinberger, Lewis	28	Austria	Y	Hamburg	New York	11/17/1876	10/13/1884			Y	
Steinborn, Otto	29	Germany	Y	Hamburg	New York	03/03/1883	08/11/1887			Y	
Steindel, George	29	Bavaria	Y	Bremen	Baltimore	02/??/1848	12/??/1850	2	402	N	
Steindinger, Mathias	29	Wuerttenberg	Y	Havre	New Orleans	05/15/1848	02/12/1849	23	69	N	
Steindl, Josef	??	Austria	Y	?	?	?	09/10/1890			Y	
Steinemann, Fritz	28	Oldenberg	Y	Bremen	Baltimore	09/27/1853	11/01/1854			Y	10/01/1858
Steinemann, George	36	Wuertemberg	Y	Havre	New York	06/28/1853	02/18/1856	26	95	N	
Steiner, Adam	27	Bavaria	Y	Havre	New York	06/20/1849	12/21/1852	5	439	N	
Steiner, Daniel	28	Hesse Darmsta	Y	London	New York	09/10/1849	09/07/1852	25	399	N	
Steiner, George	36	Austria	Y	Bremen	New York	05/29/1859	08/18/1860	27	298	N	
Steiner, Henry	32	Bavaria	Y	Havre	New Orleans	11/20/1851	03/10/1852	24	282	N	
Steiner, Jacob	45	Bavaria	Y	Havre	New Orleans	07/02/1852	10/01/1856	14	89	N	
Steiner, Phillip Jacob	??	Bavaria	Y	Havre	New York	??/19/1848	03/27/1851	3	360	N	
Steinfeld, Arnold	26	Oldenburg	Y	Bremen	New Orleans	11/27/1849	12/06/1852	5	380	N	
Steinfeldt, Henry	68	Germany	Y	Rotterdam	New York	02/25/1874	09/04/1895			Y	
Steinfels, Meyer	34	Hesse Darmsta	Y	Havre	New York	08/05/1851	05/31/1856	14	273	N	
Steinfelz, Lewis	35	Hesse Darmsta	Y	Bremen	Baltimore	08/??/1846	05/21/1859	17	420	N	
Steingroeber, Henry	22	Prussia	Y	Bremen	Baltimore	05/02/1849	04/05/1852	24	366	N	
Steingruber, Herman	29	Saxony	Y	Bremen	Philadelphia	07/23/1855	11/02/1855	13	148	N	
Steinhardt, Henry	56	Germany	Y	Bremen	Baltimore	05/05/1883	11/12/1886			Y	
Steinhart, Adolf	27	Germany	Y	Havre	New York	08/23/1880	09/20/1882			Y	
Steinhauer, Bernard	??	Germany	Y	?	?	?	02/18/1884			Y	
Steinhauer, Martin	29	Germany	Y	Bremen	New York	05/22/1882	05/14/1886			Y	
Steinhausen, John J.	25	Bavaria	Y	Hamburg	Buffalo	07/20/1848	01/27/1851	2	528	N	
Steinhauser, John	26	Wuertemberg	Y	Liverpool	New York	06/14/1853	03/24/1856	26	251	N	
Steinheim, Fredrick	48	Germany	Y	Bremen	Baltimore	04/??/1878	10/09/1896			Y	
Steinius, Christian	41	Germany	Y	Antwerp	New York	09/01/1883	10/29/1887			Y	
Steinkamp, August	39	Germany	N	Bremen	New York	11/??/1867	?			Y	
Steinkamp, Bernard	46	Germany	Y	Bremen	?	09/21/1893	10/23/1896			Y	
Steinkamp, Henry	33	Hanover	Y	Bremen	Baltimore	11/28/1847	03/05/1851	3	204	N	
Steinkamp, John Frederic	23	Hanover	Y	Bremen	Baltimore	01/01/1847	10/05/1848	22	425	N	
Steinkamp, William	22	Hanover	Y	Bremen	Baltimore	10/11/1857	10/08/1860	27	415	N	
Steinke, Ernest	??	Germany	Y	?	?	?	03/19/1892			Y	
Steinke, George (Steinec	48	Germany	Y	Hanover	New York	09/15/1864	10/26/1895			Y	
Steinke, Gerhard Lambert	44	Hanover	Y	Bremen	New Orleans	10/28/1852	03/18/1856	26	225	N	
Steinkopf, Henry	??	Germany	N	?	?	?	?			Y	
Steinkuhle, Charles	21	Germany	Y	Bremen	New York	06/26/1890	10/26/1893			Y	
Steinmann, Christ	25	Germany	Y	Bremen	Baltimore	03/28/1880	10/17/1887			Y	
Steinmann, Henry	24	Germany	Y	Bremen	Baltimore	03/29/1880	09/19/1881			Y	
Steinmetz, Peter	57	France	N	Havre	New York	07/01/1858	?			Y	
Steinmetz, Philipp	28	Germany	Y	Bremen	New York	10/16/1882	03/29/1887			Y	
Steins, Fred	23	Germany	Y	Rotterdam	New York	05/18/1882	01/22/1884			Y	
Steinwart, Henry	68	Germany	N	Hamburg	New York	06/22/1852	?			Y	
Steinwart, Ludwig	21	Hanover	Y	Hamburg	New York	04/02/1854	09/13/1855	12	23	N	
Steitz, Adam	4	Germany	N	?	New York	00/00/1871				Y	10/17/1888
Stella, Puzza	44	Italy	Y	Palermo	New York	11/25/1882	09/12/1900			Y	
Stellfeld, Theodore	28	Germany	Y	Rotterdam	New York	08/22/1891	09/26/1894			Y	
Stellmann, Heinrich	29	Germany	Y	Bremen	Baltimore	04/16/1884	10/22/1889	19	246	N	
Stellwag, Sebastian	54	Bavaria	Y	Bremen	Baltimore	11/11/1851	10/09/1854	6	55	N	

CITIZENSHIP RECORDS

APPLICANT	AGE	COUNTRY OF ORIGIN	DEC	DEPART PORT	ENTRY PORT	ARRIVE DATE	DEC DATE	VOL	PG.	FLD	NAT DATE
Stellwag, Sebastian	54	Bavaria	Y	Bremen	Baltimore	11/11/1851	10/09/1854	11	56	N	
Steltenkamp, Franz	34	Hanover	Y	Bremen	Baltimore	12/17/1853	02/24/1858	16	340	N	
Steltenkamp, Theodore	38	Hanover	Y	Bremen	New York	04/01/1852	04/09/1856	26	482	N	
Steltenkamp, Theodore	38	Hanover	Y	Bremen	New York	04/01/1852	04/09/1856			Y	09/28/1858
Steltenpohl, John	24	Germany	Y	Bremen	Baltimore	11/19/1883	11/12/1887			Y	
Stelzer, Henry	38	Germany	Y	Bremen	Baltimore	06/04/1884	08/23/1886			Y	
Stelzig, John Rudolph	9	Germany	N	?	New York	00/00/1874				Y	10/23/1888
Stemann, George (Steinma	24	Germany	Y	Amsterdam	New York	05/25/1880	01/05/1884			Y	
Stemann, Joseph	16	Germany	N	?	Baltimore	00/00/1882				Y	10/24/1887
Stemmer, Adjutus	30	Germany	Y	Bremen	New York	05/02/1888	09/25/1890			Y	
Stemmer, Andreas	52	Germany	Y	Hamburg	New York	05/16/1880	11/11/1889			Y	
Stemmer, George	58	Germany	Y	Hamburg	New York	05/16/1880	11/11/1889			Y	
Stemmer, Peter	30	Prussia	Y	Bremen	New Orleans	12/16/1850	03/09/1853	7	314	N	
Stemmer, Renig	29	Baden	Y	Havre	New York	06/??/1853	04/02/1855	11	209	N	
Stemmermann, August Chris	30	Hanover	Y	Bremen	New York	04/24/1850	03/21/1853	7	363	N	
Stendenbach, Gerhard	40	Germany	Y	?	Baltimore	05/20/1880	11/30/1880			Y	
Stenger, Ferdinand	28	Germany	Y	Bremen	New York	02/24/1883	08/??/1883			Y	
Stenger, John Adam	26	Bavaria	Y	Bremen	New York	07/02/1857	07/28/1860	27	238	N	
Stenger, Martin	43	Germany	Y	Antwerp	New York	05/18/1872	07/31/1882			Y	
Stentz, Leonhardt	33	Germany	Y	Bremen	Baltimore	07/11/1881	09/17/1888			Y	
Stenzel, Franz	39	Prussia	Y	Bremen	New York	11/14/1854	08/08/1860	27	256	N	
Stenzel, Otto	31	Mecklenburg S	Y	Bremen	New York	05/13/1854	05/26/1854	9	426	N	
Stenzel, Otto	31	Mecklenburg S	Y	Bremen	New York	05/13/1854	05/26/1854	10	9	N	
Stephan, Andrew	29	Baden	Y	Havre	New York	07/02/1848	06/03/1852	25	181	N	
Stephan, Benedict	29	Baden	Y	Havre	New York	11/19/1849	04/12/1852	24	454	N	
Stephan, Charles	28	Baden	Y	Havre	New York	11/19/1849	04/12/1852	24	455	N	
Stephan, Cromer	21	France	Y	Havre	New York	08/01/1853	03/03/1856	26	148	N	
Stephan, George	29	Germany	Y	Antwerp	New York	01/10/1882	09/16/1887			N	
Stephan, Gustav	26	Baden	Y	Havre	New York	11/12/1849	10/09/1854	6	79	N	
Stephan, Gustav	26	Baden	Y	Havre	New York	11/12/1849	10/09/1854	11	82	N	
Stephan, Gustav	51	Germany	Y	Hamburg	New York	10/24/1886	10/03/1900			Y	
Stephan, Henry	21	France	Y	Havre	New Orleans	01/02/1846	01/31/1849	1	550	N	
Stephan, J. A.	68	Germany	N	Germany	New York	05/??/1847	07/02/1849	28	287	N	07/07/1852
Stephan, Julius	44	Germany	Y	Bremen	New York	03/11/1884	04/09/1887			Y	10/19/1892
Stephan, Karl	42	Germany	Y	Antwerp	Philadelphia	09/01/1881	12/26/1883			Y	
Stephany, Julius	48	Germany	N	Havre	New York	11/??/1852	?			Y	
Stephens, John C.	41	Ireland	Y	Belfast	New York	05/14/1850	01/06/1851	2	461	N	
Steppe, Henry	31	Germany	Y	Bremen	Baltimore	08/24/1873	08/10/1877			Y	
Steren, John George	36	Hanover	Y	Bremen	Baltimore	11/24/1850	10/10/1854	6	239	N	
Stermann, Joseph	28	Germany	Y	Amsterdam	New York	07/12/1882	12/08/1888			Y	
Stern, Adolph	??	Hungary	Y	?	New York	08/??/1864	11/02/1868			Y	
Stern, Arthur	??	Austria	Y	?	?	?	08/22/1889			Y	10/23/1893
Stern, Charles	48	Germany	N	Hamburg	New York	09/11/1872	?			Y	
Stern, Edward	22	Russia	Y	Hamburg	New York	07/01/1881	08/09/1881			Y	
Stern, John Henry	24	Hanover	Y	Bremen	New ?	01/01/1846	10/21/1851	4	359	N	
Stern, Lewis	24	Oldenburg	Y	Havre	New York	12/25/1847	03/10/1851	3	267	N	
Stern, Martin	36	Austria	Y	Bremen	New York	11/04/1857	01/23/1862	18	251	N	
Stern, Simon	34	Baden	Y	Havre	New York	05/11/1854	10/08/1860	27	456	N	
Sternagel, Charles	26	Germany	Y	Hamburg	Boston	08/29/1880	03/15/1889			Y	
Sternberg, Jacob	41	Russia	Y	Hamburg	New York	06/28/1881	05/15/1883	28	94	N	
Sternberg, Jacob	36	Russia	Y	Hamburg	New York	06/28/1881	05/15/1883			Y	
Sterne, Samuel	30	Russia	Y	Liverpool	New York	05/23/1895	04/23/1897			Y	
Sterritt, David B.	45	Scotland	Y	Liverpool	Baltimore	07/??/1815	10/01/1856	14	127	N	
Sterzer, Frederick	46	Germany	Y	Bremen	New York	10/24/1884	10/27/1890			Y	
Stetter, Lawrence	28	Wuerttemberg	Y	Havre	New York	06/15/1848	10/??/1848	22	512	N	
Steube, Jacob	33	Hesse Cassel	Y	Bremen	Baltimore	05/24/1857	05/21/1859	17	421	N	
Steuer, John	28	Bavaria	Y	Bremen	New York	12/25/1855	05/20/1856	26	504	N	
Steuer, Matheus	36	Prussia	Y	Antwerp	New York	05/25/1851	05/30/1854	9	456	N	
Steuer, Matheus	36	Prussia	Y	Antwerp	New York	05/25/1851	05/30/1854	10	39	N	

CITIZENSHIP RECORDS

APPLICANT	AGE	COUNTRY OF ORIGIN	DEC	DEPART PORT	ENTRY PORT	ARRIVE DATE	DEC DATE	VOL	PG.	FLD	NAT DATE
Steuernagel, Michael	34	Bavaria	Y	Rotterdam	New York	08/03/1854	10/01/1856	14	77	N	
Steurer, Joseph	25	Nassau	Y	Antwerp	New York	09/26/1858	11/15/1858	17	329	N	
Steutermann, Mathias	23	Hanover	Y	Bremen	New York	06/29/1856	09/09/1857	15	248	N	
Steven, Clemens	34	Baden	Y	Havre	New Orleans	05/04/1843	01/22/1849	1	491	N	
Stevens, Henry Charles J	27	England	Y	Southampton	New York	10/29/1853	11/10/1857	16	6	N	
Stevenson, James	36	Canada	Y	Toronto	Cincinnati	10/10/1859	06/24/1861	18	197	N	
Stewardson, John	29	England	Y	Liverpool	New York	11/01/1837	12/15/1851	4	522	N	
Stewart, James	30	Ireland	Y	Liverpool	New York	04/05/1854	02/10/1857	15	8	N	
Stewart, John	30	Ireland	Y	Greenock	Cleveland	08/09/1851	12/10/1855	13	302	N	
Stewart, William	30	Ireland	Y	Liverpool	New York	03/29/1852	10/06/1856	14	185	N	
Stewe, ? Joseph	??	Oldenburg	Y	?	New Orleans	??/20/18??	10/26/1850	2	307	N	
Stibane, Karl	29	Germany	Y	Bremen	New York	06/12/1879	06/12/1884			Y	
Stibinsky, August	33	Prussia	Y	Bremen	New York	11/23/1854	07/09/1855	11	368	N	
Stichheim, John Ernst	32	Hanover	Y	Hamburg	New York	08/19/1852	10/02/1854	12	304	N	
Stichnath, Christoph	26	Germany	Y	Bremen	New York	06/08/1885	01/29/1894			Y	
Sticht, Charles	60	Germany	Y	Bremen	New York	05/29/1887	07/15/1896			Y	
Sticht, Henry	30	Germany	Y	Bremen	New York	05/25/1887	04/17/1891			Y	
Stickerling, Christopher	31	Saxony	Y	Hamburg	New York	10/??/1847	12/31/1849	23	449	N	
Stickforth, Frederick	37	Hanover	Y	Bremen	Baltimore	11/04/1851	02/16/1858	16	310	N	
Stickheim, John Ernst	32	Hanover	Y	Hamburg	New York	08/19/1852	10/02/1854	10	365	N	
Stickler, Joseph	59	Germany	N	Bremen	Baltimore	09/18/1848	?			Y	
Stickom, William	??	Prussia	Y	Bremen	Baltimore	??/30/1848	08/??/1851	4	175	N	
Stiebey, Emil	36	France	Y	Havre	New York	07/24/1884	02/21/1893			Y	
Stiefel, Christian Gottl	42	Wurttemberg	Y	Havre	New York	09/24/1852	09/30/1854	10	328	N	
Stiefel, Christian Gottl	42	Wurttemberg	Y	Havre	New York	09/24/1852	09/30/1854	12	267	N	
Stiefel, John Jacob	31	Switzerland	Y	Havre	New Orleans	04/17/1856	09/18/1858	16	171	N	
Stiefvater, Theodor	30	Germany	Y	Havre	New York	04/??/1880	09/22/1886			Y	
Stiegeler, Anton	28	Baden	Y	Havre	New York	06/22/1846	04/02/1852	24	352	N	
Stiegelmeyer, Frederick	24	Hanover	Y	Bremen	Baltimore	10/01/1852	10/10/1857	15	388	N	
Stiegelschmitt, Matthias	25	Germany	Y	Bremen	Boston	08/01/1886	01/16/1890			Y	
Stiegler, Peter	40	Germany	Y	Bremen	New York	08/14/1880	06/04/1891			Y	
Stienbeck, Henry	23	Hanover	Y	Bremen	New Orleans	11/24/1855	03/04/1858	16	368	N	
Stiener, Mike	30	Austria (Hung	Y	Bremen	New York	01/06/1893	01/21/1896			Y	
Stienken, Bernard	22	Germany	Y	Amsterdam	New York	09/11/1881	08/19/1884			Y	
Stienker, Henry	63	Germany	Y	Bremen	Baltimore	07/29/1873	10/23/1886	19	72	N	
Stienker, Henry	63	Germany	Y	Bremen	Baltimore	07/29/1873	10/23/1886			Y	
Stiens, John H.	25	Germany	Y	Bremen	New York	03/28/1881	03/25/1884			Y	
Stier, John W.	22	Wurttemberg	Y	Bremen	New York	07/12/1869	07/18/1872	18	506	N	
Stierle, Michael	59	Germany	Y	Hamburg	New York	08/??/1865	08/19/1884			Y	
Stiess, Carl	49	Germany	Y	Bremen	New York	11/22/1888	10/30/1900			Y	
Stifler, Theodor	??	Austria	Y	?	New York	08/??/1891	11/01/1892			Y	
Stigger, John	53	Germany	Y	Bremen	New York	05/03/1872	09/01/1898			Y	
Stiles, Barry	32	Ireland	Y	Canada	Fort Covingt	07/08/1840	03/29/1850	2	286	N	
Stiley, John	48	Germany	Y	Havre	New York	07/27/1884	05/05/1890			Y	
Stille, Ernst	22	Prussia	Y	Bremen	New Orleans	06/07/1854	12/28/1857	16	271	N	
Stimming, Theodore	26	Prussia	Y	Hamburg	New York	08/01/1852	09/20/1855	13	77	N	
Stindt, Meinhard	47	Germany	Y	Hamburg	New York	07/15/1885	10/26/1895			Y	
Sting, Eugen C.	22	Germany	Y	Bremen	New York	07/24/1890	01/29/1895			Y	
Stirber, Adam	25	Kurhessen	Y	Havre	New York	05/12/1851	10/09/1854	6	157	N	
Stiritz, Jacob Gottfried	21	Wurttemberg	Y	Havre	New York	06/27/1854	10/03/1856	14	172	N	
Stirnkorb, Charles	26	Germany	Y	Rotterdam	New York	04/17/1881	10/05/1883			Y	
Stirnkorb, George	36	Wurttemberg	Y	Liverpool	New York	03/28/1852	01/30/1857	14	519	N	
Stirnweiss, John	44	Bavaria	Y	Havre	New Orleans	11/17/1852	11/13/1858	17	326	N	
Stitt, Wilson	??	Great Britain	Y	?	?	?	04/28/1888			Y	
Stober, Wilhelm	38	Baden	Y	Havre	New York	05/27/1849	02/16/1853	7	169	N	
Stock, Bernard	22	Hanover	Y	Bremen	New York	09/20/1868	11/01/1871	18	437	N	
Stock, Bernard	37	Germany	N	Bremen	Baltimore	08/20/1872	?			Y	
Stock, Charles A.	1	Germany	N	?	New York	00/00/1866				Y	10/15/1888
Stock, Frederick William	30	Prussia	Y	Bremen	Baltimore	09/10/1855	01/29/1856	13	515	N	

CITIZENSHIP RECORDS

APPLICANT	AGE	COUNTRY OF ORIGIN	DEC	DEPART PORT	ENTRY PORT	ARRIVE DATE	DEC DATE	VOL	PG.	FLD	NAT DATE
Stock, Henry	29	Hanover	Y	Bremen	Baltimore	10/01/1853	10/06/1856	14	202	N	
Stock, John	??	Germany	Y	?	Baltimore	01/??/1880	11/07/1881			Y	
Stocker, Andreas	37	Germany	Y	?	New York	??/??/1865	10/11/1880			Y	
Stocker, Henry	52	Prussia	Y	Bremen	New Orleans	10/28/1842	09/05/1860	27	338	N	
Stocker, Martin	48	Austria	Y	Bremen	Hoboken	08/31/1880	09/27/1887			Y	
Stocker, William	39	Germany	Y	Bremen	Baltimore	04/09/1870	10/09/1880			Y	0
Stockholer, Thomas	25	Ireland	Y	Dublin	New York	07/07/1848	07/12/1851	3	525	N	
Stockhove, Frederick	25	Hanover	Y	Bremen	Baltimore	12/31/1846	10/07/1848	22	481	N	
Stockman, John	25	Ireland	Y	Liverpool	New York	05/01/1851	03/24/1856	26	288	N	
Stockmann, Bernard	24	Germany	Y	Bremen	Baltimore	04/13/1889	05/04/1892			Y	
Stockmann, Friedrich Wil	38	Germany	Y	Bremen	New York	06/05/1880	06/03/1881			Y	
Stockmann, Valentin	46	Switzerland	Y	Havre	New York	07/23/1882	06/29/1888			Y	
Stockmeyer, Henry	33	Germany	Y	Amsterdam	New York	07/14/1891	07/29/1897			Y	
Stoebel, Frank	24	Prussia	Y	Bremen	New Orleans	11/01/1849	05/25/1854	8	531	N	
Stoeber, Franz	35	Germany	Y	Bremen	New York	05/01/1882	10/25/1886			Y	
Stoeckel, Anton	28	Germany	Y	Havre	New York	06/02/1887	10/07/1892			Y	
Stoecker, Henry	??	Prussia	Y	Bremen	New York	??/14/1848	12/16/1850	2	368	N	
Stoeckle, Albert	20	Germany	Y	Amsterdam	New York	09/24/1881	03/31/1883			Y	
Stoeckle, Fidel	30	Hohenzollern	Y	Havre	New York	08/27/1854	03/04/1862	18	269	N	
Stoeckle, Jacob	26	Germany	Y	Bremen	New York	09/25/1884	10/25/1892			Y	
Stoeckle, Jacob	36	Switzerland	Y	?	New York	??/??/1883	10/24/1890			Y	
Stoehe, John	32	Bavaria	Y	Bremen	New York	05/04/1846	08/30/1848	22	280	N	
Stoehr, John Bernard	??	Hesse Darmsta	Y	Havre	New York	07/28/1845	10/06/1848	22	457	N	
Stoehr, Joseph	29	Germany	Y	Bremen	New York	05/16/1879	11/03/1884			Y	
Stoermer, Adam	25	Kurhessen	Y	Havre	New York	05/12/1851	10/09/1854	10	160	N	
Stoes, George Henry	29	Hanover	Y	Bremen	Baltimore	10/08/1848	02/21/1849	23	243	N	
Stoessel, Bernhard	30	Switzerland	Y	Havre	New York	06/04/1883	09/06/1886			Y	
Stoeve, John Conrad	23	Hanover	Y	Bremen	Baltimore	11/08/1847	09/13/1848	22	340	N	
Stoewer, Henry Diedrich	23	Hanover	Y	Bremen	New Orleans	12/07/1849	03/25/1851	3	336	N	
Stoezer, Remig	22	Baden	Y	Havre	New York	10/28/1856	11/02/1857	15	513	N	
Stoffel, John	48	Germany	N	Havre	New York	??/??/1848	?			Y	
Stoffregen, Heinrich	21	Hanover	Y	Bremen	Baltimore	07/04/1857	07/30/1860			Y	
Stoffregen, Heinrich	21	Hanover	Y	Bremen	Baltimore	07/04/1857	07/31/1860	27	242	N	
Stoffregen, William	25	Hanover	Y	Bremen	Baltimore	10/01/1854	02/23/1857	15	48	N	
Stohrer, Lorenz	27	Wurttemberg	Y	Liverpool	New York	07/??/1852	09/21/1855	13	103	N	
Stokes, James	52	Ireland	Y	Queenstown	New York	10/??/1879	09/09/1884			Y	
Stolkfung, Louis	21	Prussia	Y	Bremen	New York	07/10/1857	10/08/1860	27	446	N	
Stoll, Dionis	23	Wuertemberg	Y	Havre	New York	06/04/1853	03/24/1856	26	250	N	
Stoll, John	55	Wuertemberg	Y	Havre	New York	09/24/1854	03/24/1856	26	252	N	
Stoll, Nicholas	22	Prussia	Y	Antwerp	New York	08/14/1849	07/09/1851	3	517	N	
Stolle, Albert	62	Germany	Y	Bremen	New York	09/07/1875	10/29/1890			Y	
Stolle, Frank	36	Saxony	Y	Hamburg	New York	05/03/1849	04/12/1852	24	465	N	
Stolle, Gerhard Henry	35	Oldenburg	Y	Bremen	New Orleans	11/27/1847	04/02/1852	24	354	N	
Stolle, John	36	Germany	Y	Hamburg	New York	03/22/1881	10/26/1888	19	179	N	
Stolle, John	36	Germany	Y	Hamburg	New York	03/22/1881	10/26/1888			Y	
Stolle, John Henry	40	Germany	Y	Hamburg	New York	04/11/1886	08/16/1888			Y	
Stollz, Jacob	31	Bavaria	Y	Havre	New Orleans	12/19/1852	05/01/1854	8	326	N	
Stolting, Henry	30	Lippe Detwold	Y	Bremen	New Orleans	12/25/1853	08/20/1860	27	310	N	
Stolz, Adam	23	Germany	Y	Amsterdam	New York	07/28/1891	10/06/1896			Y	
Stolz, Carl	29	Germany	Y	Bremen	Baltimore	04/17/1883	09/22/1891			Y	
Stolz, Herman	38	Wurttemberg	Y	Bremen	New York	01/??/1850	12/??/1850	2	426	N	
Stolz, Jacob	23	Bavaria	Y	Havre	New Orleans	11/12/1852	10/06/1856	14	220	N	
Stolz, Johann	20	Germany	Y	Bremen	New York	07/19/1887	03/05/1889			Y	
Stolz, Joseph	33	Bavaria	Y	Havre	New York	10/07/1855	03/05/1858	16	375	N	
Stolz, Simon	34	Nassau	Y	Antwerp	New York	05/05/1851	02/14/1853	7	152	N	
Stolze, John	34	Germany	N	Bremen	Baltimore	09/13/1872	07/??/1876	28	76	N	10/??/1878
Stommel, Frederick	42	Prussia	Y	Bremen	New Orleans	05/01/1849	04/28/1854	8	283	N	
Stommel, Frederick	42	Prussia	Y	Bremen	New Orleans	05/01/1849	04/28/1854	9	154	N	
Stomps, Joseph	27	Prussia	Y	London	New York	08/02/1846	02/14/1849	23	93	N	

CITIZENSHIP RECORDS

APPLICANT	AGE	COUNTRY OF ORIGIN	DEC	DEPART PORT	ENTRY PORT	ARRIVE DATE	DEC DATE	VOL	PG.	FLD	NAT DATE
Stone, James	23	Ireland	Y	Liverpool	New York	11/06/1848	03/29/1853	7	452	N	
Stone, Joseph	22	England	Y	London	New York	02/06/1852	04/09/1856	26	478	N	
Stone, Patrick	30	Ireland	Y	Dublin	New Orleans	03/09/1849	03/08/1851	3	212	N	
Stone, William	23	England	Y	London	New York	02/06/1852	04/09/1856	26	477	N	
Stoneham, Walter	26	Canada	Y	Samia	Detroit	04/05/1886	03/28/1889			Y	
Stoppel, George	36	Wurttemberg	Y	Havre	New York	??/01/1848	02/06/1850	2	43	N	
Stoppel, Joseph	36	Wuerttemberg	Y	Liverpool	New York	08/20/1846	02/05/1849	23	24	N	
Stoppelkamp, Henry	30	Prussia	Y	Bremen	Philadelphia	?	10/10/1854	11	207	N	
Stoppelkamp, Henry	31	Germany	Y	Bremen	Baltimore	08/28/1882	10/24/1896			Y	
Stopper, Hieronimus	22	Wurttemberg	Y	Havre	New York	12/02/1853	09/18/1855	13	66	N	
Stopplekamp, Henry	30	Prussia	Y	Bremen	Philadelphia	10/21/1853	10/10/1854	6	204	N	
Storch, Cornelius	27	Germany	Y	Bremen	New York	06/05/1880	09/22/1881			Y	
Storch, William	23	Germany	Y	Bremen	New York	09/17/1879	11/01/1881			Y	
Stordeur, Ernst	33	Germany	Y	Bremen	New York	02/13/1881	03/23/1882			Y	
Stordeur, Henry	76	Germany	N	Bremen	Baltimore	11/01/1834	??/??/1836	28	46	N	??/??/1838
Stordeur, Henry	22	Germany	N	Bremen	Baltimore	11/01/1834	00/00/1836			Y	00/00/1838
Storey, Wilson	66	Ireland	Y	Belfast	New York	09/??/1880	11/03/1884			Y	
Stork, Charles	33	Germany	N	Antwerp	New York	01/19/1871	?			Y	
Stork, William	24	Prussia	Y	Bremen	New York	11/07/1857	10/19/1860	27	511	N	
Storm, Frederick	22	Germany	Y	?	Baltimore	05/00/1881	10/21/1884			Y	
Storr, Paul	25	Bavaria	Y	Bremen	New York	07/24/1845	01/17/1849	1	445	N	
Stors, George	32	Wurttemberg	Y	Antwerp	New York	08/16/1851	10/30/1858	17	5	N	
Stortz, Christian	32	Wuerttemberg	Y	Antwerp	New York	06/28/1847	05/31/1852	25	168	N	
Storz, John	46	Germany	Y	Havre	New York	07/20/1881	07/05/1883			Y	
Storz, Karl	44	Germany	Y	Bremen	New York	04/02/1886	04/04/1894			Y	
Stothfang, F. H.	21	Germany	Y	Bremen	Baltimore	10/27/1881	09/08/1884			Y	
Stott, Mathias	30	Germany	Y	Hamburg	New York	03/20/1883	05/03/1886			Y	
Stotze, John	18	Germany	N	Bremen	Baltimore	09/13/1872	07/00/1876			Y	10/00/1878
Stouder, Henry	24	Prussia	Y	Bremen	Baltimore	12/14/1849	03/28/1853	7	449	N	
Stout, John	17	Germany	N	?	New York	00/00/1882				Y	12/31/1888
Stover, Frank	1	Germany	N	?	Baltimore	00/00/1868				Y	10/27/1888
Stover, Julius	??	Germany	Y	?	?	?	11/03/1884			Y	
Stoy, Edward	33	Germany	Y	Bremen	New York	06/11/1883	04/09/1887			Y	
Stoy, Lorenz	31	Germany	Y	Bremen	New York	03/03/1884	04/15/1888			Y	
Strack, George Lewis	36	Hesse Darmsta	Y	Bremen	New Orleans	12/23/1852	09/13/1855	13	14	N	
Strack, Leonhard	34	Germany	Y	Antwerp	Philadelphia	10/19/1889	08/27/1894			Y	
Strack, William	39	Germany	Y	Hamburg	New York	06/15/1871	11/27/1886			Y	
Stradtner, John L.	24	Bavaria	Y	Havre	New York	07/26/1866	12/27/1867			Y	
Straehle, Frederick	39	Wurttemberg	Y	Havre	New York	09/15/1848	05/25/1854	8	515	N	
Straerkhoff, John Henry	33	Oldenburg	Y	Bremen	New Orleans	10/27/1845	08/07/1848	22	61	N	
Strahle, Frederick	39	Wurttemberg	Y	Havre	New York	09/15/1848	05/25/1854	9	389	N	
Strahley, Frederick	72	Germany	N	Havre	New York	09/15/1848	?			Y	
Strallo, Guisseppa	40	Italy	Y	Naples	New York	04/01/1881	07/29/1892			Y	
Strang, Benno	24	Bavaria	Y	London	New York	07/02/1849	06/09/1852	25	218	N	
Strang, Edward	28	Bavaria	Y	Havre	New York	07/04/1850	06/09/1852	25	219	N	
Strasse, C. Vorder	23	Germany	Y	Bremen	New York	05/04/1881	07/05/1884			Y	
Strassel, Michael	25	Bavaria	Y	Havre	New Orleans	06/02/1848	02/13/1849	23	83	N	
Strassen, Michael	32	Germany	Y	Bremen	New York	04/??/1873	10/09/1876			Y	
Strasser, John George	42	Wurttemberg	Y	Antwerp	New York	07/01/1848	03/08/1853	7	311	N	
Stratemeyer, Adolph	49	Germany	N	Germany	Baltimore	05/10/1866	?			Y	
Strathmann, Henry	33	Germany	Y	Bremen	Baltimore	04/28/1888	10/27/1893			Y	
Stratman, Conrad	28	Germany	Y	?	New York	??/??/1882	03/17/1900			Y	
Stratmann, Theodore	27	Germany	Y	Bremen	New York	10/21/1883	01/14/1888			Y	
Straub, Charles	24	Germany	Y	Havre	New York	02/21/1881	04/18/1881			Y	
Straub, George Michael	26	Bavaria	Y	Havre	New York	04/13/1852	10/18/1852	5	5	N	
Straub, Sebastian	33	France	Y	Havre	New Orleans	04/20/1853	03/08/1856	26	172	N	
Straub, Theodore	45	Germany	N	Liverpool	New York	08/09/1863	?			Y	
Straub, William Fred	41	Wurttemberg	Y	Hamburg	Galveston	10/??/1847	08/??/1851	4	172	N	
Strauch, Adolph	35	Prussia	Y	Bremen	Galveston	11/05/1851	12/18/1857	16	232	N	

CITIZENSHIP RECORDS

APPLICANT	AGE	COUNTRY OF ORIGIN	DEC	DEPART PORT	ENTRY PORT	ARRIVE DATE	DEC DATE	VOL	PG.	FLD	NAT DATE
Strauch, John	32	Hesse Darmsta	Y	Bremen	New York	08/07/1854	10/07/1856	14	253	N	
Straukamp, Gerhard Henry	63	Hanover	Y	Bremen	New Orleans	11/05/1846	07/01/1851	3	472	N	
Straus, A.	24	Russia	Y	?	New York	08/20/1884	04/05/1890			Y	
Straus, Elias	26	Russia	Y	Hamburg	New York	06/11/1882	02/15/1883			Y	
Straus, Henry	25	Bavaria	Y	Bremen	New York	08/15/1848	06/07/1852	25	195	N	
Straus, Henry	64	Germany	N	Bremen	New York	08/??/1846	?	28	338	N	10/??/1850
Straus, Henry	18	Germany	N	Bremen	New York	08/00/1846				Y	10/00/1850
Straus, John	29	Wurttemberg	Y	Bremen	New Orleans	10/28/1845	01/11/1849	1	393	N	
Straus, Morris G.	22	Germany	Y	Hamburg	New York	11/02/1880	10/22/1884			Y	
Straus, Moses	44	Germany	N	Bremen	New York	09/??/1867	?			Y	
Strause, Matthias	26	Baden	Y	Southampton	New York	03/12/1862	08/28/1862	18	415	N	
Strauss, Leopold	33	Germany	Y	Bremen	New York	11/17/1888	10/26/1899			Y	
Strauss, Maurice	26	Germany	Y	Antwerp	New York	08/25/1882	06/05/1888			Y	
Strauss, Raphael	27	Bavaria	Y	Bremen	New York	09/10/18??	09/19/1857	15	290	N	
Strauss, Seligman	27	Baden	Y	Havre	New York	06/27/1848	09/15/1852	25	524	N	
Straussel, Balthazar	28	France	Y	Havre	New York	01/10/1858	03/07/1860	27	121	N	
Strauthmann, Bernhard	23	Germany	Y	Bremen	Baltimore	10/22/1883	08/18/1888			Y	
Strautmann, Frederick	42	Hanover	Y	Bremen	New York	08/11/1847	04/05/1852	24	394	N	
Strebbemann, Johann Bern	37	Germany	Y	Bremen	New York	11/17/1878	07/07/1888			Y	
Strebel, Heinrich	24	Germany	Y	Rotterdam	New York	07/02/1892	01/35/1896			Y	
Strecker, Charles Willia	39	Hanover	Y	Bremen	New York	08/??/1855	02/23/1861	18	117	N	
Streibich, Balthaser	32	Baden	Y	Havre	New York	10/08/1846	01/22/1853	7	51	N	
Streibich, Michael	23	Baden	Y	Havre	New Orleans	12/20/1848	04/02/1852	24	355	N	
Streicher, Alois	21	Germany	Y	Bremen	New York	08/23/1871	05/10/1873			Y	
Streicher, Frederick	30	Germany	Y	Bremen	Baltimore	10/02/1887	11/01/1893			Y	
Streicher, Joseph	45	Germany	Y	Bremen	New York	10/01/1882	03/12/1889			Y	
Streiff, Leonhard	29	Switzerland	Y	Havre	New Orleans	03/18/1851	09/27/1854	10	260	N	
Streiff, Leonhard	29	Switzerland	Y	Havre	New Orleans	03/18/1851	09/27/1854	12	199	N	
Streile, Ignatz	52	Baden	Y	Havre	New Orleans	02/26/1855	07/21/1862	18	378	N	
Streit, John	39	Germany	Y	Hamburg	New York	03/21/1883	10/15/1888			Y	8
Streithorst, Herman	22	Germany	Y	Bremen	New York	06/??/1880	02/12/1883			Y	
Strempefel, Wilibald	25	Bavaria	Y	Bremen	New York	05/01/1852	05/12/1854	8	428	N	
Strempefel, Wilibald	25	Bavaria	Y	Bremen	New York	05/01/1852	05/12/1854	9	301	N	
Streng, Andreas M.	62	Germany	N	London	New York	07/03/1849	?			Y	
Streng, George	29	Wurttemberg	Y	Havre	New York	07/20/1850	08/15/1855	11	432	N	
Streng, John Fred	39	Germany	N	Bremen	New York	08/??/1866	?			Y	
Strenske, John	54	Germany	Y	Bremen	New York	04/13/1880	05/07/1890			Y	
Stressmann, Gottlieb	42	Prussia	Y	Hamburg	New York	10/26/1850	09/06/1852	25	369	N	
Streule, Daniel	53	Baden	Y	Havre	New York	12/02/1847	05/08/1854	9	266	N	
Streutker, John Henry	55	Hanover	Y	Bremen	New Orleans	??/20/18??	01/??/1850	2	17	N	
Stricker, Joseph	20	Germany	Y	Bremen	Baltimore	07/29/1880	07/25/1881			Y	
Striedelmeier, Heinrich	29	Germany	Y	Bremen	Baltimore	10/08/1882	10/12/1885			Y	
Strieker, Charles	30	Oldenburg	Y	Bremen	Baltimore	11/01/1848	03/08/1852	24	253	N	
Striet, Joseph	26	Germany	Y	Rotterdam	New York	05/24/1883	10/13/1885			Y	
Striethorst, William	31	Germany	Y	Bremen	New York	10/29/1885	03/30/1892			Y	
Strietmann, Henry	29	Prussia	Y	Bremen	Baltimore	05/08/1854	01/11/1860	27	50	N	
Strietmann, Herman Henry	23	Hanover	Y	Bremen	New Orleans	12/25/1846	01/17/1849	1	453	N	
Strietmann, J. F.	64	Germany	N	Bremen	New Orleans	11/03/1848	?			Y	
Strife, Thomas	29	Switzerland	Y	Havre	New Orleans	06/10/1844	08/02/1848	22	44	N	
Striffeler, George	50	Wurttemberg	Y	Antwerp	New York	04/20/1848	04/17/1854	9	42	N	
Striffler, George	50	Wurttemberg	Y	Antwerp	New York	04/20/1848	04/17/1854	8	171	N	
Stringer, Francis B.	28	England	Y	Toronto	Niagara	07/05/1891	09/26/1896			Y	
Stripp, John	69	Germany	Y	Hamburg	New York	??/??/1866	10/18/1883			Y	
Strobbe, John Henry	30	Hanover	Y	Bremen	Baltimore	06/28/1841	11/21/1848	1	360	N	
Strobel, Frank	24	Prussia	Y	Bremen	New Orleans	11/01/1849	05/25/1854	9	405	N	
Strobel, Gottlob	21	Wuertemberg	Y	Havre	New York	04/01/1854	04/07/1856	26	459	N	
Strobel, John	29	Germany	Y	Bremen	New York	03/10/1883	01/31/1887			Y	
Strobel, L. A.	47	Bavaria	N	Havre	New York	12/16/1853	?			Y	
Strobel, Leonhard	26	Baden	Y	Havre	New Orleans	02/28/1847	01/16/1849	1	437	N	

CITIZENSHIP RECORDS

APPLICANT	AGE	COUNTRY OF ORIGIN	DEC	DEPART PORT	ENTRY PORT	ARRIVE DATE	DEC DATE	VOL	PG.	FLD	NAT DATE
Stroebel, Daniel	30	Germany	Y	Bremen	New York	11/11/1899	06/10/1901			Y	
Stroehle, George	27	Wuertemberg	Y	Liverpool	New York	10/22/1853	03/10/1856	26	175	N	
Stroehle, John	40	Wuerttemberg	Y	Havre	New York	09/11/1856	08/15/1860	27	273	N	
Stroehle, William	??	Germany	Y	Rotterdam	New York	05/01/1881	11/12/1889			Y	
Stroemer, Carl	53	Germany	Y	Bremen	New York	04/27/1868	11/02/1889			Y	
Stroer, Bernard	28	Prussia	Y	Bremen	New York	06/01/1854	07/26/1858	16	529	N	
Stroesner, George	28	Bavaria	Y	Hamburg	Buffalo	08/11/1847	03/18/1850	2	208	N	
Stroh, Nicholas	36	Baden	Y	Havre	New Orleans	04/09/1846	12/07/1852	5	390	N	
Strohbach, George	23	Baden	Y	Bremen	New York	08/11/1867	03/10/1869			Y	04/21/1890
Strohmeier, Gottlieb	47	Wurttemberg	Y	Havre	New York	10/12/1856	02/08/1858	16	85	N	
Strohmeier, Sebastian	27	Baden	Y	Havre	New York	10/27/1845	01/14/1850	23	498	N	
Strohmenger, John Bernar	23	Bavaria	Y	Bremen	Baltimore	11/13/1857	12/17/1857	16	228	N	
Strohn, John	29	Prussia	Y	Havre	New York	06/28/1848	06/18/1851	3	401	N	
Strohofer, John	34	Germany	Y	Bremen	New York	10/13/1884	11/05/1889			Y	
Strolkamp, Engelberth	29	Prussia	Y	Bremen	New York	06/10/1849	04/15/1852	24	506	N	
Strom, Mathias	37	Germany	Y	Bremen	New York	07/01/1880	06/22/1888			Y	
Strootmann, John	35	Germany	Y	Bremen	Baltimore	06/11/1890	10/25/1900			Y	
Stroschen, William	25	Germany	Y	Antwerp	New York	11/05/1881	03/28/1888			Y	
Stross, William	28	Germany	Y	Antwerp	Philadelphia	08/15/1883	09/15/1886			Y	
Stroth, Herman Inder	24	Germany	Y	Antwerp	New York	09/12/1883	11/27/1885			Y	
Strotmann, Frederick	58	Germany	Y	Bremen	Baltimore	08/30/1871	10/29/1884			Y	
Strotmann, Henry	34	Prussia	Y	Bremen	New Orleans	12/06/1848	04/12/1852	24	462	N	
Strottkamp, Bernard	26	Hanover	Y	Bremen	New Orleans	11/20/1857	04/02/1862	18	294	N	
Strout, Franz	28	Bavaria	Y	Havre	New Orleans	04/23/1847	02/??/1850	2	78	N	
Strubbe, Wilhelm Herman	??	Germany	Y	?	?	?	03/28/1888			Y	
Strubberg, Conrad	38	Hanover	Y	Bremen	New York	05/??/1844	04/20/1855	11	275	N	
Strube, Daniel	53	Baden	Y	Havre	New York	12/02/1847	05/08/1854	8	393	N	
Struebbe, Frank	23	Hanover	Y	Bremen	New Orleans	06/20/1849	04/12/1852	24	453	N	
Struebbe, Joseph	24	Hanover	Y	Bremen	New York	08/01/1854	11/01/1858	17	242	N	
Strueber, Ludwig	40	Germany	Y	Hamburg	New York	05/11/1893	11/01/1897			Y	
Struever, William	31	Germany	Y	Hamburg	New York	07/24/1892	07/26/1895			Y	
Struke, John C.	??	Germany	Y	?	?	?	11/02/1888			Y	
Strumpler, Henry William	30	Hanover	Y	Bremen	Baltimore	07/19/1849	03/03/1852	24	225	N	
Strunk, Henry	38	Oldenburg	Y	Bremen	New Orleans	11/13/1847	09/06/1852	25	371	N	
Strunlak, Franz	39	Austria	Y	Bremen	New York	08/20/1894	11/04/1897			Y	
Strybel, John	31	Germany	Y	Bremen	New York	03/30/1872	03/25/1881			Y	
Strybel, Michael	27	Germany	Y	Bremen	Baltimore	05/06/1880	03/25/1881			Y	
Stual, Garrett	32	Hanover	Y	Rotterdam	New York	07/02/1850	11/15/1852	6	412	N	
Stubbe, Bernard	21	Hanover	Y	Bremen	New York	09/01/1854	11/05/1856	14	494	N	
Stubbemann, Siegmund	29	Germany	Y	Bremen	Baltimore	08/20/1882	10/03/1884			Y	
Stubbs, Matthew	33	England	Y	Hull	New York	06/01/1841	02/14/1851	3	133	N	
Stubenrauch, Andrew	30	Bavaria	Y	Havre	New Orleans	01/01/1855	12/21/1857	16	239	N	
Stuber, Charles	??	Switzerland	Y	?	?	?	10/29/1885			Y	
Stubler, Gustav	24	Wurttemberg	Y	Hamburg	New York	07/15/1852	10/04/1854	12	352	N	
Stubmann, Christian	35	Hanover	Y	Bremen	Baltimore	04/29/1849	08/08/1851	4	102	N	
Stucker, William	25	Baden	Y	Havre	New York	05/14/1853	01/10/1856	13	444	N	
Stuckmeier, Ernst	30	Prussia	Y	Bremen	Baltimore	11/07/1858	10/01/1860	27	394	N	
Stuckwisch, Gerhard Henr	40	Hanover	Y	Bremen	Baltimore	10/15/1854	10/01/1860	27	392	N	
Stucky, Fritz	26	Germany	Y	?	New York	??/??/1886	10/30/1890			Y	
Studer, Henry	29	Germany	Y	Havre	New York	03/01/1884	07/31/1889			Y	
Studier, Carl	36	Prussia	Y	Bremen	New York	09/30/1853	09/22/1854	10	162	N	
Studier, Carl	36	Prussia	Y	Bremen	New York	09/30/1853	09/22/1854	12	101	N	
Studt, John Henry	21	Hanover	Y	Bremen	Baltimore	10/28/1853	08/17/1855	11	445	N	
Studt, William	34	Hanover	Y	Bremen	Baltimore	10/07/1853	02/03/1857	14	532	N	
Stuebler, Gustav	24	Wurttemberg	Y	Hamburg	New York	07/15/1852	10/04/1854	10	413	N	
Stuehrmann, Herman H.	34	Germany	Y	Bremen	New York	02/09/1892	11/01/1900			Y	
Stueve, John Henry	33	Oldenburg	Y	Bremen	New Orleans	11/12/1848	09/13/1852	25	466	N	
Stufefampe, William	33	Hanover	Y	Bremen	New York	06/27/1849	08/13/1847	4	128	N	
Stuhlberg, Morris	27	Russia	Y	Bremen	Baltimore	08/18/1888	07/10/1894			Y	

CITIZENSHIP RECORDS

APPLICANT	AGE	COUNTRY OF ORIGIN	DEC	DEPART PORT	ENTRY PORT	ARRIVE DATE	DEC DATE	VOL	PG.	FLD	NAT DATE
Stuhlfauth, Christopher	28	Bavaria	Y	Havre	New York	07/04/1853	05/08/1854	8	396	N	
Stuhlfauth, Christopher	28	Bavaria	Y	Havre	New York	07/04/1853	05/08/1854	9	269	N	
Stuhlman, Otto	39	Germany	Y	Antwerp	New York	09/17/1891	10/17/1896			Y	
Stuhlmiller, Joseph	32	Bavaria	Y	Bremen	Baltimore	09/17/1846	05/12/1852	25	8	N	
Stuhlmueller, Ig.	24	Germany	Y	Hamburg	New York	05/23/1881	07/02/1883			Y	
Stuhlreyer, Anton	55	Germany	Y	Antwerp	New York	08/12/1885	10/08/1890			Y	
Stukenborg, Charles	15	Germany	N	?	New York	00/00/1882				Y	10/20/1888
Stulz, Jacob	31	Bavaria	Y	Havre	New Orleans	12/19/1852	05/01/1854	9	199	N	
Stuminski, Albert	45	Germany	Y	Bremen	Baltimore	04/01/1885	03/19/1889			Y	
Stuminski, Andreas	21	Poland	Y	Antwerp	New York	07/05/1886	08/21/1888			Y	
Stuminski, Walenty	35	Germany	Y	Antwerp	New York	04/26/1884	02/14/1888			Y	
Stump, Conrad	25	Kurhassen	Y	Havre	New York	07/28/1845	08/10/1848	22	89	N	
Stump, John William	39	Prussia	Y	Bremen	Baltimore	06/02/1846	07/31/1848	22	14	N	
Stumpe, Casper Henry	27	Hanover	Y	Bremen	New Orleans	12/15/1853	10/01/1856	14	80	N	
Stumpf, John	34	Prussia	Y	Bremen	Baltimore	08/10/1847	03/04/1851	3	218	N	
Stumpp, Gottfried	22	Wuertemberg	Y	Havre	New York	10/09/1853	02/07/1856	26	61	N	
Stunkel, William	47	Germany	Y	Bremen	New York	11/15/1864	02/18/1884			Y	
Stuntebeck, Henry	28	Oldenburg	Y	Bremen	New Orleans	11/01/1845	05/25/1854	9	421	N	
Stuntebeck, Henry	28	Oldenburg	Y	Bremen	New Orleans	11/01/1845	05/25/1854	10	4	N	
Stuntebeck, Herman Henry	31	Oldenburg	Y	Bremen	Baltimore	05/16/1849	10/09/1854	11	163	N	
Stuntebeck, Hermann Henr	31	Oldenburg	Y	Bremen	Baltimore	05/16/1849	10/09/1854	6	160	N	
Stuntebeck, John Henry	35	Oldenburg	Y	Bremen	New Orleans	01/02/1853	10/09/1854	6	181	N	
Stuntebeck, John Henry	35	Oldenburg	Y	Bremen	New Orleans	01/02/1852	10/09/1854	11	184	N	
Stuntebeck, Markus A.	27	Germany	Y	Bremen	Baltimore	10/01/1883	06/03/1886			Y	
Stupperman, Bernard Henr	37	Hanover	Y	Bremen	New Orleans	02/27/1848	04/01/1853	7	482	N	
Sturel, Gerrat	32	Hanover	Y	Rotterdam	New York	07/02/1850	11/15/1852	5	288	N	
Sturenberg, Joseph	28	Oldenburg	Y	Bremen	New Orleans	12/??/1851	12/27/1855	13	371	N	
Sturm, Joseph	51	Germany	N	Havre	New York	11/??/1849	?			Y	
Sturm, Joseph Leonhard	24	Germany	N	Havre	New York	03/04/1867	?			Y	
Sturow, Charles	28	Prussia	Y	Bremen	Baltimore	10/02/1853	08/20/1855	11	460	N	
Sturwold, Henry	30	Oldenburg	Y	bremen	New York	10/18/1850	07/21/1862	18	377	N	
Stute, Herman Henrich	22	Hanover	Y	Bremen	Baltimore	08/08/1846	10/03/1848	22	414	N	
Stuth, John	??	Germany	Y	?	New York	04/??/1891	04/27/1892			Y	
Stutz, Daniel	39	Switzerland	Y	Havre	New Orleans	11/08/1854	10/23/1857	15	484	N	
Stutzman, Valentine	49	Germany	N	Havre	New York	09/27/1861	?			Y	
Stuvenberg, F.	26	Germany	Y	Bremen	New York	05/03/1882	11/01/1883			Y	
Stych, John	30	Germany	Y	Hamburg	New York	05/01/1883	10/29/1887			Y	
Sudbrink, Fred	30	Germany	Y	Bremen	New York	06/15/1885	07/14/1890			Y	
Sudhoff, Anton	42	Germany	Y	Antwerp	New York	12/07/1879	07/08/1881			Y	
Suding, Frank	26	Oldenburg	Y	Bremen	New Orleans	05/01/1849	04/17/1854	8	181	N	
Suding, Herman H.	28	Oldenburg	Y	Bremen	New Orleans	12/21/1845	11/01/1852	6	276	N	
Sudmeier, Henry	??	Hanover	Y	?	Baltimore	07/??/18??	11/05/1856	14	471	N	
Suedbecke, William	24	Oldenburg	Y	Bremen	New York	02/01/1849	12/26/1851	24	17	N	
Suedhoff, Rudolph	32	Germany	Y	Hamburg	New York	03/22/1892	10/13/1892			Y	
Suenderhans, Anton	44	Prussia	Y	Rotterdam	Philadelphia	08/12/1847	07/12/1855	11	378	N	
Suenneberg, Frank	41	Germany	Y	Bremen	New York	08/11/1882	10/26/1889			Y	
Suer, Bernard	23	Germany	Y	Bremen	Baltimore	04/01/1875	09/28/1880			Y	
Suerlieneim, Joseph	40	Hanover	Y	Bremen	New Orleans	12/10/1848	04/05/1852	24	404	N	
Suess, Carl E.	47	Germany	Y	Bremen	New York	04/23/1883	05/25/1885			Y	
Suessmann, Louis	34	Hanover	Y	Liverpool	New York	06/27/1853	09/10/1855	11	531	N	
Suesz, John	28	Germany	Y	Bremen	Baltimore	06/24/1882	06/18/1885			Y	
Suetkamp, Theodore	22	Oldenburg	Y	Bremen	Baltimore	09/30/1846	02/14/1849	23	97	N	
Suettmann, Henry	39	Germany	Y	Bremen	New York	10/03/1885	10/27/1894	21	74	N	
Suettmann, Henry	39	Germany	Y	Bremen	New York	10/03/1885	10/27/1894			Y	
Suffa, George	41	Germany	Y	Bremen	Baltimore	11/14/1879	10/14/1896			Y	
Suffert, Gottlob	28	Saxe Weimar E	Y	Bremen	New York	07/04/1848	09/27/1854	10	275	N	
Suffert, Gottlob	28	Saxe Weimar E	Y	Bremen	New York	07/04/1848	09/27/1854	12	214	N	
Sugarman, Jacob	59	Holland	N	Amsterdam	New York	10/??/1848	?			Y	
Sugenheim, Jacob	31	Bavaria	Y	Havre	New York	11/05/1853	08/28/1862	18	416	N	

CITIZENSHIP RECORDS

APPLICANT	AGE	COUNTRY OF ORIGIN	DEC	DEPART PORT	ENTRY PORT	ARRIVE DATE	DEC DATE	VOL	PG.	FLD	NAT DATE
Suhm, Joseph	29	Germany	Y	Havre	New York	04/07/1880	05/18/1885			Y	
Suhn, Frank	52	Germany	N	Bremen	New York	08/12/1864	?			Y	
Suhr, Elert G.D.	23	Oldenburg	Y	Bremerhafen	New Orleans	06/22/1856	02/09/1861	18	94	N	
Suhr, Henry	26	Hanover	Y	Bremen	New York	08/01/1854	10/02/1856	14	146	N	
Suhr, Jacob	37	France	Y	Havre	New Orleans	07/20/1839	02/16/1852	24	112	N	
Suhre, John Conrad	22	Hanover	Y	Bremen	New Orleans	12/01/1851	10/09/1854	6	185	N	
Suhre, John Conrad	22	Hanover	Y	Bremen	New Orleans	12/01/1851	10/09/1854	11	188	N	
Suhrheinrich, Adolph	23	Prussia	Y	Bremen	New Orleans	12/??/1847	12/13/1850	2	360	N	
Suhrland, Henry B.J.	54	Hamburg	Y	Hamburg	New Orleans	12/11/1847	10/12/1848	1	162	N	
Sukman, Bernard	28	Hanover	Y	Bremen	New Orleans	12/31/1850	04/17/1854	8	173	N	
Sulivan, Daniel	35	Ireland	Y	Cork	Boston	??/01/1839	02/20/1850	2	106	N	
Sullivan, Cornelius	23	Ireland	Y	Cork	New York	08/01/1849	11/16/1855	13	227	N	
Sullivan, Cornelius	24	Ireland	Y	Liverpool	Portsmouth	07/20/1838	10/04/1858	17	42	N	
Sullivan, Daniel J.	??	Great Britain	Y	?	?	?	10/01/1894			Y	
Sullivan, Dennis	27	Ireland	Y	Liverpool	New York	04/15/1841	??/??/1852	5	286	N	
Sullivan, Dennis	27	Ireland	Y	Liverpool	New York	04/15/1841	??/??/1852	6	410	N	
Sullivan, Fergus	48	England	Y	Liverpool	New York	10/05/1881	10/22/1896			Y	
Sullivan, Henry	22	Ireland	Y	Liverpool	Boston	07/??/1847	10/??/1849	23	271	N	
Sullivan, James	45	Ireland	Y	London	New York	09/02/1843	01/03/1853	5	499	N	
Sullivan, James	25	Ireland	Y	Queenstown	New York	08/01/1888	03/06/1890			Y	
Sullivan, James	56	Ireland	N	Ireland	New York	05/12/1862	?			Y	
Sullivan, Jerehmiah	28	Ireland	Y	Liverpool	Boston	05/??/1844	03/10/1853	7	321	N	
Sullivan, Jeremiah	30	Ireland	Y	Cork	New Orleans	12/28/1849	07/21/1851	4	18	N	
Sullivan, Jeremiah	25	Ireland	Y	Canada	Burlington	10/04/1847	10/20/1851	4	337	N	
Sullivan, Jeremiah	40	Ireland	Y	London	New York	01/21/1854	11/09/1857	15	549	N	
Sullivan, Jeremiah	23	Ireland	Y	Liverpool	New Orleans	02/??/1852	03/02/1858	16	357	N	
Sullivan, John	34	Ireland	Y	Cork	New York	06/01/1848	04/20/1850	3	5	N	
Sullivan, John	28	Ireland	Y	Liverpool	Boston	04/01/1847	11/02/1852	5	191	N	
Sullivan, John	22	Ireland	Y	Limerick	Buffalo	11/15/1849	01/04/1853	5	511	N	
Sullivan, John	28	Ireland	Y	Liverpool	Boston	04/01/1847	11/02/1852	6	317	N	
Sullivan, John	23	Ireland	Y	Liverpool	New Orleans	01/27/1848	02/19/1853	7	186	N	
Sullivan, John	28	Ireland	Y	Baltimore	Boston	09/04/1846	06/05/1854	10	77	N	
Sullivan, John	28	Ireland	Y	Baltimore	Boston	09/04/1846	06/05/1854	12	14	N	
Sullivan, John	32	Ireland	Y	Liverpool	Buffalo	09/??/1854	10/22/1858	17	91	N	
Sullivan, John	30	Ireland	Y	Queenstown	Boston	11/10/1870	10/15/1880			Y	
Sullivan, John	??	Great Britain	Y	?	?	?	08/30/1889			Y	
Sullivan, John R.	3	Ireland	N	?	Detroit	00/00/1870				Y	10/27/1888
Sullivan, Michael	36	Ireland	Y	Canada	Watertown	08/01/1833	03/05/1850	2	157	N	
Sullivan, Michael	??	?	Y	London	New ?	09/??/1851	11/01/1852	5	110	N	
Sullivan, Michael	35	Ireland	Y	Liverpool	New York	06/15/1847	02/10/1858	16	100	N	
Sullivan, Michael	60	Ireland	N	?	New York	??/??/1847	?			Y	
Sullivan, Owen	65	Ireland	N	Liverpool	Buffalo	06/??/1846	?			Y	
Sullivan, Patrick	33	Ireland	Y	Liverpool	Boston	05/15/1850	05/17/1854	8	454	N	
Sullivan, Patrick	33	Ireland	Y	Liverpool	New Orleans	06/17/1850	05/17/1854	9	327	N	
Sullivan, Patrick	25	Ireland	Y	Liverpool	Boston	05/14/1855	08/02/1856	14	312	N	
Sullivan, Patrick	25	Ireland	Y	Cork	New York	05/05/1852	03/11/1858	16	395	N	
Sullivan, Patrick	17	Ireland	N	?	New York	00/00/1850				Y	11/03/1888
Sullivan, Patrick	34	Ireland	Y	Queenstown	Boston	05/00/1875	12/17/1885			Y	
Sullivan, Thomas	26	Ireland	Y	Liverpool	New York	10/14/1850	02/01/1853	7	97	N	
Sullivan, Thomas	21	Ireland	Y	Liverpool	New Orleans	01/25/1849	02/17/1852	24	130	N	
Sullivan, Timothy	22	Ireland	Y	Liverpool	New York	04/01/1856	11/19/1857	16	36	N	
Sullivan, Timothy	24	Ireland	Y	Queenstown	New York	03/24/1893	10/22/1896			Y	
Sullivan, Timothy	27	Ireland	Y	Cork	Boston	05/03/1844	02/10/1852	24	84	N	
Sullivan, Timothy	27	Ireland	Y	Liverpool	New Orleans	04/02/1849	02/10/1852	24	88	N	
Sullivan, William	23	Ireland	Y	Tralee	New York	09/25/1856	10/05/1857	15	354	N	
Sullivan, William	22	Ireland	Y	Queenstown	New York	04/26/1890	11/16/1893			Y	
Sulman, Anton	28	Germany	Y	Bremen	Baltimore	01/27/1878	10/08/1880			Y	
Summe, Henry	26	Hanover	Y	Bremen	New Orleans	01/??/1846	08/??/1851	4	176	N	
Summerer, Frank	29	Baden	Y	Havre	New Orleans	??/01/1846	10/??/1849	23	278	N	

CITIZENSHIP RECORDS

APPLICANT	AGE	COUNTRY OF ORIGIN	DEC	DEPART PORT	ENTRY PORT	ARRIVE DATE	DEC DATE	VOL	PG.	FLD	NAT DATE
Summers, George	49	England	Y	New Castle	New York	12/23/1882	10/23/1900			Y	
Summers, James	59	Ireland	Y	New Ross	Quabsch	08/08/1858	10/04/1858	17	45	N	
Sunderbrunch, Henry Wm.	29	Hanover	Y	Bremen	New Orleans	11/25/1847	12/31/1852	5	482	N	
Sunderer, Anton	30	Baden	Y	Havre	New York	07/04/1847	10/09/1854	6	158	N	
Sunderman, Herman Henry	22	Prussia	Y	Bremen	New Orleans	12/25/1847	10/??/1848	1	24	N	
Sunderman, William	57	Germany	Y	Hamburg	New York	05/??/1848	10/11/1880			Y	
Sundermann, Bernard	46	Germany	Y	Bremen	New York	04/26/1866	11/08/1887			Y	
Sundermann, Fred	28	Germany	Y	Rotterdam	New York	07/27/1883	03/24/1888			Y	
Sundermann, Henry	33	Prussia	Y	Bremen	Baltimore	11/03/1842	06/05/1852	25	210	N	
Sundermann, John H.	40	Germany	Y	Bremen	New York	06/01/1866	10/29/1887			Y	
Sundermann, Joseph	43	Germany	Y	Bremen	Baltimore	04/21/1873	06/27/1888			Y	
Sundermeier, Christoph H	26	Hanover	Y	Bremen	New York	09/30/1853	10/22/1857	15	472	N	
Sunneberg, Bernard	17	Germany	N	?	New York	00/00/1882				Y	10/27/1888
Suppult, John	23	Wurttemberg	Y	London	New York	10/26/1848	12/19/1851	4	529	N	
Suptus, Henry William	28	Hanover	Y	Hamburg	New York	08/23/1855	10/05/1857	15	355	N	
Surenbrock, Herman Henry	24	Prussia	Y	Bremen	Baltimore	05/13/1854	11/07/1855	13	182	N	
Surkamp, Frederick	32	Hanover	Y	Bremen	New Orleans	12/25/1857	03/04/1858	16	371	N	
Surkamp, Henry	21	Hanover	Y	Bremen	Baltimore	04/30/1854	03/25/1856	26	322	N	
Surkemp, Joseph	22	Hanover	Y	Bremen	Baltimore	05/04/1855	03/04/1858	16	370	N	
Surmann, Hermann H.	70	Germany	Y	Bremen	Baltimore	12/08/1887	02/05/1894			Y	
Surrey, Joseph	26	Germany	Y	Stettin	New York	09/17/1887	04/02/1888			Y	
Suslow, Max	34	Russia	Y	Bremen	Baltimore	08/02/1892	10/14/1896			Y	
Suslow, Solomon	50	Russia	Y	Bremen	New York	06/05/1892	10/29/1895			Y	
Suss, John	38	Switzerland	Y	Havre	New York	04/01/1885	10/25/1900			Y	
Suss, Max	17	Germany	N	?	New York	00/00/1883				Y	11/03/1888
Sussdorff, Hugo	??	Germany	Y	?	?	?	12/14/1892			Y	
Susselin, Joseph	26	Germany	Y	Havre	New York	01/07/1874	01/10/1880			Y	
Sussmann, August	49	Germany	Y	Antwerp	New York	12/14/1879	03/16/1883	28	178	N	
Sussmann, August	44	Germany	Y	Antwerp	New York	12/14/1879	03/ /1883			N	
Sutcliff, Joseph	48	England	Y	Liverpool	Philadelphia	01/12/1860	03/31/1891	19	326	N	
Suter, Jacob	26	Switzerland	Y	Havre	New York	03/01/1883	05/27/1889			Y	
Suthe, Clemens	27	Prussia	Y	Bremen	Baltimore	05/30/1846	07/31/1848	22	15	N	
Sutherland, Alexander	28	Scotland	Y	Glasgow	New York	03/21/1883	08/21/1888			Y	
Sutherland, Alexander	47	Scotland	Y	?	Boston	02/19/1887	05/07/1888			Y	
Sutherland, James	17	Scotland	N	?	Boston	00/00/1880				Y	10/27/1888
Suthoff, Henry	27	Hanover	Y	Bremen	Baltimore	07/04/1858	07/15/1861	18	207	N	
Suthotmar, Henry	35	Prussia	Y	Bremen	Baltimore	12/08/1853	05/01/1854	8	317	N	
Suthotmar, Henry	35	Prussia	Y	Bremen	Baltimore	12/08/1853	05/01/1854	9	190	N	
Sutter, Adolph	24	Baden	Y	Havre	New York	01/20/1849	05/02/1850	3	40	N	
Sutter, Frederick	27	Baden	Y	Liverpool	New York	07/14/1852	11/26/1855	13	254	N	
Sutter, Henry	24	Germany	Y	?	New York	??/??/1882	06/30/1884			Y	
Sutterer, Anton	30	Baden	Y	Havre	New York	07/04/1847	10/09/1854	11	161	N	
Sutthoff, G. Herman	45	Germany	Y	Bremen	Baltimore	05/07/1869	04/27/1886			Y	
Suttner, George	26	Bavaria	Y	Bremen	Baltimore	07/04/1852	09/27/1854	10	276	N	
Suttner, George	26	Bavaria	Y	Bremen	Baltimore	07/04/1852	09/27/1854	12	215	N	
Sutton, William	42	Ireland	Y	Liverpool	Philadelphia	07/25/1849	08/02/1856	14	310	N	
Sutz, Charles	29	Germany	Y	Bremen	Baltimore	10/17/1888	08/25/1890			Y	
Sutz, Louis	28	Germany	Y	Bremen	New York	11/18/1880	09/27/1890			Y	
Swab, John C.	??	Germany	Y	?	?	?	08/01/1893			Y	
Swahlen, John	80	Switzerland	N	Havre	New Orleans	12/12/1832	??/??/1838	28	252	N	08/??/1841
Swain, John	40	Ireland	Y	Liverpool	Philadelphia	10/25/1847	11/02/1852	5	187	N	
Swain, John	40	Ireland	Y	Liverpool	Philadelphia	10/25/1847	11/02/1852	6	313	N	
Swanovsky, Peter	26	Russia	Y	Hamburg	New York	10/??/1869	07/02/1873			Y	
Swanson, Olaf	??	Sweden/Norway	Y	?	?	?	01/22/1891			Y	
Swartz, Samuel	27	Bavaria	Y	Havre	New York	08/28/1848	04/08/1852	24	420	N	
Swedorf, Frederick	36	Hamburg	Y	Hamburg	New Orleans	06/01/1847	01/06/1851	2	451	N	
Sweeney, Charles	25	Ireland	Y	Liverpool	New York	10/19/1882	11/19/1889	19	278	N	
Sweeney, Charles	25	Ireland	Y	Liverpool	New York	10/19/1882	11/19/1889			Y	
Sweeney, James	23	Ireland	Y	Londonderry	New York	05/30/1889	08/25/1891			Y	

CITIZENSHIP RECORDS

APPLICANT	AGE	COUNTRY OF ORIGIN	DEC	DEPART PORT	ENTRY PORT	ARRIVE DATE	DEC DATE	VOL	PG.	FLD	NAT DATE
Sweeney, James	30	Ireland	Y	Liverpool	Philadelphia	07/14/1850	10/15/1860	27	494	N	
Sweeney, Martin	24	Ireland	Y	Liverpool	Boston	11/??/1848	12/??/1850	2	424	N	
Sweeney, Morgan	32	Ireland	Y	Liverpool	Boston	07/04/1847	11/01/1858	17	221	N	
Sweeney, Morris	40	Ireland	Y	Liverpool	New Orleans	03/18/1852	10/07/1856	14	252	N	
Sweeney, Patrick	29	Ireland	Y	Queenstown	New York	03/??/1870	10/12/1880			Y	
Sweeney, Thomas	23	Ireland	Y	Dublin	New Orleans	01/31/1850	03/22/1853	7	371	N	
Sweeney, Thomas	27	Ireland	Y	?	New York	??/??/1876	10/10/1882			Y	
Sweeny, Cornelius	24	Ireland	Y	Liverpool	New York	05/20/1849	01/27/1851	2	531	N	
Sweeny, Miles	29	Ireland	Y	Liverpool	Boston	11/15/1848	07/12/1851	3	527	N	
Sweeny, Terry	21	Ireland	Y	Liverpool	New Orleans	02/15/1850	02/20/1851	3	147	N	
Sweeny, Thomas	24	Ireland	Y	Liverpool	New Orleans	03/04/1851	03/01/1852	24	187	N	
Sweeny, William	21	Ireland	Y	Dublin	New Orleans	01/31/1850	03/07/1853	7	289	N	
Sweetman, William	24	Ireland	Y	Dublin	New York	05/01/1849	03/15/1852	24	298	N	
Swift, Thomas	46	England	Y	Liverpool	New Orleans	05/06/1850	04/04/1856	26	439	N	
Swift, William Taylor	39	England	Y	London	New York	07/23/1881	11/02/1889			Y	
Swin, Jeremiah	23	Ireland	Y	Liverpool	New York	08/22/1850	10/20/1851	4	343	N	
Switzer, John George	23	Wurttemberg	Y	Rotterdam	New York	06/06/1852	11/20/1852	5	316	N	
Switzer, Nicholas	26	Bavaria	Y	London	New York	??/24/1846	11/21/1849	23	359	N	
Swyer, Patrick	27	Ireland	Y	Limerick	New York	05/02/1847	04/17/1852	24	523	N	
Sybilla, Franz Carl Otto	33	Germany	Y	?	?	11/03/1881	02/05/1883			Y	
Sydekum, Carl H.G.	22	Germany	Y	Bremen	New York	05/14/1889	06/04/1890			Y	
Sygulka, Paul	31	Germany	Y	Hamburg	New York	??/??/1871	04/04/1881			Y	
Sykes, Samuel	24	Prussia	Y	Liverpool	New York	08/18/1848	03/14/1850	2	198	N	
Sykora, John	33	Bohemia	Y	Hamburg	New York	05/??/1880	03/11/1889			Y	
Symon, William Henry	16	Wales	N	?	New York	00/00/1880				Y	10/18/1888
Syndikus, Nick	36	Germany	Y	Antwerp	New York	04/16/1890	01/13/1894			Y	
Synnott, Michael	26	Ireland	Y	Liverpool	Baltimore	03/22/1848	10/22/1858	17	96	N	
Szczypkowski, Peter	55	Germany	Y	Hamburg	New York	04/25/1881	03/02/1894			Y	
Taaffe, William	22	Ireland	Y	Dublin	Buffalo	06/??/1854	08/28/1857	15	197	N	
Tabachink, Aaron	34	Russia	Y	Hamburg	Philadelphia	07/12/1882	09/28/1887			Y	
Tabeling, Heinrich	26	Oldenburg	Y	Bremen	Baltimore	11/03/1854	10/07/1856	14	250	N	
Tachter, Abraham	35	Russia	Y	?	?	?	04/03/1896			Y	
Taeuber, Henry	31	Germany	Y	Bremen	New York	12/24/1882	07/16/1889			Y	
Tafel, Albert	22	Wurttemberg	Y	Bremen	New York	07/07/1858	07/08/8151	3	509	N	
Tahse, William	50	Germany	Y	Bremen	Galveston	12/??/1871	12/07/1885			Y	
Taint, John	32	Germany	Y	Bremen	New York	03/21/1891	04/04/1891			Y	
Tait, John	27	Scotland	Y	Glasgow	New York	03/17/1881	10/13/1884			Y	
Tallen, William	41	Germany	N	Rotterdam	New York	04/??/1869	?			Y	
Tammen, George F. H.	32	Germany	Y	Bremen	Baltimore	05/27/1885	04/18/1895			Y	
Tannenberg, Carl A.	26	Germany	Y	Bremen	New York	08/??/1884	02/17/1887			Y	
Tanner, Charles J.	16	England	N	?	Detroit	00/00/1880				Y	08/24/1887
Tansy, Michael	38	Ireland	Y	Liverpool	New Orleans	06/11/1850	09/23/18??	10	175	N	
Tape, William	50	Germany	N	Bremen	New York	06/10/1862	?			Y	
Taphorn, Gerhard	25	Oldenburg	Y	Bremen	New Orleans	12/11/1848	11/01/1852	5	176	N	
Taphorn, Gerhard	25	Oldenburg	Y	Bremen	New Orleas	12/11/1848	11/01/1852	6	302	N	
Taphorn, Gerhard Henry	23	Oldenburg	Y	Bremen	New Orleans	05/24/1850	04/25/1853	8	110	N	
Taphorn, Henry	38	Germany	Y	Bremen	Baltimore	05/26/1882	11/21/1889			Y	
Tapke, George H.	55	Hanover	Y	Bremen	New Orleans	??/22/18??	04/04/1853	7	506	N	
Tapke, William	24	Oldenburg	Y	Bremen	New Orleans	11/18/1851	09/17/1855	13	40	N	
Tapking, John	24	Hanover	Y	Bremen	New Orleans	10/20/1846	10/12/1848	1	175	N	
Tappehorn, Gustavus H.	43	Germany	Y	Bremen	New York	10/??/1864	09/20/1884			Y	
Tarp, Bernhard Henry	34	Prussia	Y	Bremen	New Orleans	11/30/1852	01/31/1856	13	526	N	
Tarrants, Nicholas	24	Ireland	Y	Liverpool	New Orleans	12/??/1850	06/12/1852	25	244	N	
Tarstiege, Anthony	25	Prussia	Y	Bremen	Baltimore	05/30/1848	02/01/1849	23	13	N	
Taschner, Peter	30	Germany	Y	Hamburg	New York	09/31/1891	10/06/1892			Y	
Taske, Christian	42	Prussia	Y	Bremen	New Orleans	12/16/1852	02/01/1856	13	531	N	
Tatgenhorst, Carl	35	Germanu	Y	Bremen	New York	08/12/1875	08/21/1883			Y	
Tatgenhorst, Carl	30	Hanover	Y	Bremen	New Orleans	11/22/1847	07/31/1848	22	27	N	
Taube, Henry	??	Germany	N	?	?	02/09/1882				Y	10/27/1892

CITIZENSHIP RECORDS

APPLICANT	AGE	COUNTRY OF ORIGIN	DEC	DEPART PORT	ENTRY PORT	ARRIVE DATE	DEC DATE	VOL	PG.	FLD	NAT DATE
Taube, Paul	31	Germany	Y	Bremen	New York	10/28/1882	10/30/1882			Y	
Taubner, Carl Heinrich	53	Germany	Y	Hamburg	New York	05/31/1883	03/05/1888			Y	
Tausch, Mathias	28	Germany	Y	Bremen	Baltimore	05/21/1881	04/22/1885			Y	
Tavel, Abram	31	Russia	Y	Hamburg	New York	07/15/1887	12/19/1891			Y	
Taxis, Otto	21	Wuerttemberg	Y	Havre	New York	05/22/1859	04/13/1860	27	151	N	
Taye, Naclav	37	Austria	Y	Hamburg	New York	09/25/1887	10/06/1894			Y	
Taylor, Frederick Darnle	??	England	Y	?	?	?	07/19/1889			Y	
Taylor, George	45	England	Y	Liverpool	New York	11/15/1859	09/02/1885			Y	
Taylor, John	30	Ireland	Y	Sligo	New Orleans	08/26/1850	12/25/1851	24	4	N	
Taylor, John	37	England	Y	Liverpool	New Orleans	03/26/1841	06/02/1852	25	175	N	
Taylor, Joseph	45	England	Y	Liverpool	New York	??/??/1867	03/08/1888			Y	
Taylor, Joshua	??	England	Y	Liverpool	New York	12/31/1856	01/01/1861	18	38	N	
Taylor, Luke	24	Ireland	Y	Sligo	New Orleans	05/10/1848	12/25/1851	24	3	N	
Taylor, Michael	45	Ireland	N	Liverpool	New York	05/25/1868	?			Y	
Tebbe, Bernard	23	Germany	Y	Bremen	Baltimore	06/03/1886	12/11/1888			Y	
Tebbe, Heinrich	53	Germany	Y	Bremen	Baltimore	05/01/1885	11/26/1888			Y	
Tebbe, Henry	??	Germany	Y	?	?	?	08/08/1887			Y	
Tebbe, Ignatz	21	Hanover	Y	Bremen	Baltimore	05/04/1854	04/04/1856	26	434	N	
Tebben, Johann Joseph	27	Germany	Y	Bremen	Baltimore	07/27/1882	10/13/1885			Y	
Tebben, John	30	Germany	Y	Bremen	Baltimore	06/02/1884	11/13/1888			Y	
Tebben, William	34	Germany	Y	Bremen	Baltimore	06/02/1883	02/08/1888			Y	
Tebbenhoff, J. D.	33	Prussia	Y	Hamburg	New York	02/13/1857	10/07/1868			Y	
Tebbing, Gerhard Henry	27	Hanover	Y	Bremen	New Orleans	11/18/1847	04/29/1850	3	19	N	
Teckemeier, Ernst	36	Prussia	Y	Bremen	New Orleans	11/24/1850	10/05/1854	12	397	N	
Teckmeier, Ernst	36	Prussia	Y	Bremen	New Orleans	11/24/1850	10/05/1854	10	458	N	
Tedeschi, Cesare	31	Italy	Y	Havre	New York	11/01/1884	04/02/1890			Y	
Tedeschi, Isidoro	32	Italy	Y	Havre	New York	07/20/1893	08/14/1894			Y	
Tedesco, Ignazio	31	Italy	Y	Palermo	New York	03/17/1884	10/23/1893			Y	
Tedtmann, Henry	28	Hanover	Y	Bremen	New Orleans	05/03/1849	05/24/1854	8	501	N	
Tedtmann, Henry	28	Hanover	Y	Bremen	New Orleans	05/03/1849	05/24/1854	9	375	N	
Teedman, Martin (Taedtma	24	Hanover	Y	Bremen	New Orleans	05/18/1848	08/21/1848	22	218	N	
Teehan, Timothy	??	England	Y	?	?	?	10/03/1876			Y	
Teemann, Frederick Henry	39	Hanover	Y	Bremen	New Orleans	11/15/1847	07/01/1851	3	475	N	
Teepe, Henry	30	Germany	Y	Bremen	Baltimore	10/21/1884	03/08/1887			Y	
Teevens, Patrick	30	Ireland	N	Liverpool	New York	03/??/1872	?			Y	
Tefhaus, Herman	31	Germany	Y	Liverpool	New York	05/11/1884	11/01/1884			Y	
Tegan, Henry Joseph	28	Ireland	Y	Queenstown	New York	06/09/1891	02/10/1897			Y	
Tegeder, Henry	27	Hanover	Y	Bremen	Baltimore	05/??/1846	12/26/1850	2	399	N	
Tegel, Joseph	38	Austria	Y	Bremen	New York	09/28/1882	10/04/1890			Y	
Tegeler, August	35	Germany	Y	Bremen	Baltimore	05/19/1881	02/09/1893			Y	
Tegeler, Henry	25	Germany	Y	Bremen	New York	05/24/1881	07/05/1881			Y	
Tegeler, Henry	27	Germany	Y	Bremen	Baltimore	06/15/1873	04/03/1879			Y	
Tegeler, Wilhelm	33	Germany	Y	Rotterdam	New York	05/10/1893	05/27/1900			Y	
Tegenkamp, Bernard Henry	44	Germany	Y	Bremen	Baltimore	03/31/1888	04/01/1891			Y	
Tegtmeier, Frederick	32	Prussia	Y	Bremen	New Orleans	06/27/1851	10/03/1854	12	337	N	
Tehan, Daniel	29	Ireland	Y	?	New York	??/??/1885	10/09/1890			Y	
Teichmann, August	31	Saxony	Y	Hamburg	New York	08/14/1854	12/24/1855	13	358	N	
Teichmann, Casper	31	Bavaria	Y	Antwerp	New York	11/09/1849	??/19/1853	7	41	N	
Teiler, Benedick	46	Switzerland	Y	Havre	New York	05/13/1854	10/29/1858	17	180	N	
Teismann, Clemens August	40	Germany	Y	Rotterdam	New York	06/14/1871	10/23/1889			Y	
Teitz, Bernhard	??	Germany	Y	?	?	?	09/06/1888			Y	
Tekulve, John B.	??	Prussia	Y	?	?	?	10/08/1872			Y	
Telford, Alexander	??	Great Britain	Y	?	?	?	02/18/1891			Y	
Telford, John	42	Ireland	Y	Liverpool	New York	04/17/1882	04/??/1883	28	384	N	
Telford, John	32	Ireland	Y	Liverpool	New York	04/17/1882	04/00/1883			Y	
Telford, John	32	Ireland	Y	Liverpool	New York	04/17/1882	04/00/1883			Y	
Telford, Thomas	40	Ireland	Y	Queenstown	Philadelphia	02/??/1874	10/23/1886			Y	
Telge, Theodore	42	Germany	Y	?	?	?	07/26/1884			Y	
Telgkamp, Heinrich	25	Germany	Y	Bremen	New York	11/03/1890	10/30/1895			Y	

CITIZENSHIP RECORDS

APPLICANT	AGE	COUNTRY OF ORIGIN	DEC	DEPART PORT	ENTRY PORT	ARRIVE DATE	DEC DATE	VOL	PG.	FLD	NAT DATE
Tell, William	52	Germany	Y	Bremen	New York	07/06/1867	02/20/1891			Y	
Tellmann, John H.	33	Germany	Y	Bremen	New York	03/07/1893	10/25/1904			Y	
Tellmann, William	30	Prussia	Y	Bremen	New Orleans	12/25/1847	12/22/1851	4	544	N	
Temmen, Herman	32	Germany	Y	Bremen	Baltimore	08/24/1887	02/21/1891			Y	
Temmer, Anthony	40	Hanover	Y	Bremen	New Orleans	01/24/1846	02/02/1849	23	14	N	
Temming, Joseph	30	Prussia	Y	Liverpool	New Orleans	10/22/1854	08/15/1860	27	272	N	
Tempel, Charles	32	Prussia	Y	Bremen	New York	05/27/1854	12/08/1857	16	205	N	
Tempest, Michael	24	England	Y	Liverpool	New York	09/05/1847	03/18/1850	2	215	N	
Templeton, Nicholas Jose	34	Ireland	Y	Canada	Rochester	04/26/1847	04/25/1853	8	112	N	
Ten Bokum, Herman	21	Holland	Y	Bremen	Baltimore	08/31/1888	12/31/1891			Y	02/19/1894
Tenbrink, Clemens (Tembe	60	Germany	Y	Bremen	New York	10/12/1886	10/13/1896			Y	
Tenbrink, Herman	43	Germany	N	Bremen	Baltimore	10/??/1865	?			Y	
Tenbrunsel, Herman	30	Germany	Y	Rotterdam	New York	07/07/1873	09/02/1884			Y	
Tendam, Adolph	30	Germany	Y	Antwerp	New York	05/30/1882	04/18/1889			Y	
Tenforth, Bernard	??	Germany	N	?	?	11/08/1880				Y	10/14/1892
Tenhave, John Henry	37	Holland	Y	Rotterdam	New York	06/07/1846	08/07/1848	22	68	N	
Tenhundfeld, G.H.	72	Germany	Y	Bremen	New Orleans	12/??/1856	10/09/1880			Y	
Tenkotl, Bernard	28	Prussia	Y	Bremen	Baltimore	05/17/1869	02/24/1872	18	558	N	
Tennenbaum, Jacob	28	Russia	Y	Hamburg	New York	07/01/1886	05/31/1893			Y	
Tenner, Louis	26	Germany	Y	Bremen	New York	04/23/1892	10/10/1894			Y	
Tenngen, Patrick	25	Ireland	Y	Liverpool	New York	12/05/1844	06/12/1852	25	242	N	
Tennison, Mark	22	England	Y	Canada	Buffalo	07/01/1849	03/28/1853	7	441	N	
Tenoever, John H.	17	Holland	N	?	New York	00/00/1881				Y	10/29/1887
Tensey, Patrick	24	Ireland	Y	Liverpool	New York	04/17/1848	05/19/1852	25	43	N	
Teobold, Conrad	24	Bavaria	Y	Havre	New Orleans	11/17/1850	01/22/1856	13	495	N	
Tepe, Bernard	27	Hanover	Y	Bremen	New Orleans	02/04/1852	11/27/1852	5	353	N	
Tepe, Clemens	49	Germany	Y	Bremen	Baltimore	06/13/1891	07/17/1895			Y	
Tepe, Reinhart	25	Hanover	Y	Bremen	New Orleans	12/18/1850	11/27/1852	5	352	N	
Terbeck, Joseph	27	Prussia	Y	Rotterdam	New York	05/24/1854	08/05/1856	14	351	N	
Terhaer, John Henry	28	Hanover	Y	Bremen	Baltimore	11/08/1854	08/05/1856	14	348	N	
Terheggen, Ernst	24	Germany	Y	Antwerp	New York	10/22/1881	08/15/1882			Y	
Termath, Heinrich	23	Prussia	Y	Bremen	New York	10/08/1854	12/06/1859	17	495	N	
Terry, John	40	Ireland	Y	Kilresch	New York	08/04/1847	05/04/1854	9	239	N	
Tessendorff, August	32	Germany	Y	Hamburg	New York	05/07/1881	11/07/1887			Y	
Tessing, Paul	25	Prussia	Y	Bremen	New York	05/17/1859	12/28/1859	17	532	N	
Teufel, Michael	35	Germany	Y	Bremen	New York	03/28/1873	03/07/1883			Y	
Teupe, Joseph	30	Germany	Y	Bremen	New York	11/08/1881	11/20/1885			Y	
Teuscher, Peter	??	Germany	Y	?	?	01/??/1881	01/15/1884			Y	
Teutenberg, Caspar	39	Germany	Y	Bremen	New York	10/18/1874	04/30/1887			Y	
Tewes, Gerhard Henry	27	Prussia	Y	Bremen	New York	06/13/1853	11/03/1858	17	267	N	
Tewes, William	48	Hanover	Y	Bremen	New Orleans	12/15/1856	02/17/1857	15	25	N	
Textor, J. George	28	Wurttemberg	Y	Bremen	New York	05/25/1854	05/29/1862	18	344	N	
Tezlaf, August	24	Prussia	Y	Bremen	New York	12/25/1853	10/02/1856	14	161	N	
Thaenges, George Ludwig	28	Hesse Darmsta	Y	Liverpool	New York	06/18/1852	09/30/1856	14	70	N	
Thale, Heinrich	24	Germany	Y	Rotterdam	New York	11/21/1885	10/17/1888			Y	
Thalmann, Joseph	??	Germany	Y	?	?	?	11/25/1892			Y	
Thamann, Bernard	26	Germany	Y	Bremen	New York	12/01/1889	02/17/1893			Y	
Thamer, Henry	??	Germany	Y	?	?	11/??/1872	10/29/1884			Y	
Thaubald, John	??	Bavaria	Y	Hamburg	New York	06/04/1847	03/??/1851	3	227	N	
Thedieck, Bernard	30	Hanover	Y	Bremen	New York	09/15/1855	10/08/1860	27	447	N	
Thedieck, Diederich	42	Hanover	Y	Bremen	New Orleans	12/06/1838	10/10/1857	15	387	N	
Theil, Frank	29	Germany	Y	Antwerp	New York	09/25/1885	10/14/1887			Y	
Theil, Wilhelm	44	Hungary	Y	Bremen	New York	04/27/1900	06/01/1903			Y	
Theile, Henry	25	Hanover	Y	Bremen	Baltimore	06/10/1845	10/13/1851	4	233	N	
Theilmann, John	27	Germany	Y	Bremen	New York	11/01/1889	10/29/1892			Y	
Theis, George	??	Oldenburg	Y	Bremen	New York	??/07/1849	12/09/1850	2	352	N	
Theis, Helen M.	50	Germany	Y	Bremen	Baltimore	11/01/1864	11/13/1897			Y	
Theis, John	??	Oldenburg	Y	Havre	New York	??/11/1847	12/09/1850	2	349	N	
Theis, John	28	Germany	Y	Hamburg	New York	04/24/1881	04/06/1886			Y	

CITIZENSHIP RECORDS

APPLICANT	AGE	COUNTRY OF ORIGIN	DEC	DEPART PORT	ENTRY PORT	ARRIVE DATE	DEC DATE	VOL	PG.	FLD	NAT DATE
Theisinger, Nicolas	22	Bavaria	Y	Havre	New York	10/04/1847	09/10/1852	25	438	N	
Theiss, Friedrich	47	Germany	N	Havre	New York	12/01/1865	?			Y	
Theissen, August	25	Prussia	Y	Bremen	New Orleans	05/20/1849	04/04/1853	8	28	N	
Themann, Frank	24	Germany	Y	Bremen	New York	09/08/1883	03/13/1888			Y	
Theobald, Daniel	28	Bavaria	Y	Havre	New Orleans	01/??/1854	09/13/1855	13	20	N	
Theobald, John	34	Bavaria	Y	Havre	New York	05/31/1856	09/26/1857	15	328	N	
Theobald, John	31	Bavaria	Y	Havre	New Orleans	04/22/1855	11/16/1858	17	337	N	
Theobald, John	36	Bavaria	Y	Havre	New York	05/31/1856	09/07/1860	27	346	N	
Theobald, Kark	75	Germany	N	Havre	New York	05/06/1857	?			Y	
Theobald, Phillip	29	Bavaria	Y	Rotterdam	Boston	11/01/1845	08/29/1848	22	275	N	
Thera, Adam	22	Bavaria	Y	Bremen	Erie	10/??/1851	05/17/1854	8	459	N	
Thera, Adam	22	Bavaria	Y	Bremen	Erie	10/??/1851	05/17/1854	9	332	N	
Thera, John	27	Bavaria	Y	Bremen	New York	08/16/1851	05/17/1854	8	458	N	
Thera, John	27	Bavaria	Y	Bremen	New York	08/16/1851	05/17/1854	9	339	N	
Theriault, Vital	46	Canada	Y	?	Boston	09/22/1886	01/02/1891			Y	
Therrey, John	40	Ireland	Y	Kilresch	New York	08/04/1847	05/04/1854	8	366	N	
Thesen, Peter	??	Germany	Y	?	?	?	06/23/1882			Y	
Thesing, Casper	??	Germany	N	?	?	08/30/1873				Y	10/28/1892
Theulker, Fred	57	Germany	Y	Bremen	Baltimore	08/02/1883	01/05/1895			Y	
Theulker, Fred W.	36	Germany	Y	Bremen	New York	08/17/1882	01/05/1895			Y	
Thewes, John	26	Prussia	Y	Antwerp	New York	06/22/1847	02/09/1849	23	36	N	
They, Friedrich	30	Hanover	Y	Hamburg	New Orleans	11/01/1850	05/27/1852	25	120	N	
Thiedemann, William	26	Hanover	Y	Bremen	New Orleans	11/17/1854	12/31/1855	13	407	N	
Thiel, Herman	26	Germany	Y	Bremen	Baltimore	11/13/1881	05/01/1883			Y	
Thiel, Louis	27	Germany	Y	Bremen	New York	02/22/1885	02/03/1887			Y	
Thiele, Hermann	40	Germany	Y	Hamburg	Boston	04/10/1897	10/24/1900			Y	
Thielen, Casper	23	Prussia	Y	Antwerp	New York	07/04/1849	02/17/1851	3	136	N	
Thiem, Christian E.	20	Prussia	N	Prussia	New York	06/00/1849	04/00/1850			Y	09/00/1854
Thiemann, Herman Henry	32	Hanover	Y	Bremen	New Orleans	11/10/1845	10/11/1848	1	112	N	
Thiemann, John Henry	26	Hanover	Y	Bremen	New Orleans	07/15/1852	11/03/1852	5	223	N	
Thiemann, Theodor	28	Germany	Y	Hamburg	New York	03/25/1888	10/16/1891			Y	
Thieme, Christ. E.	23	Prussia	Y	Hamburg	New York	08/18/1849	03/04/1852	24	233	N	
Thiemer, William	22	Germany	Y	Bremen	Baltimore	08/01/1879	04/09/1880			Y	
Thien, L. Henry	33	Hanover	Y	Bremen	New Orleans	12/18/1847	01/??/1850	23	522	N	
Thier, George	28	Germany	Y	Amsterdam	New York	04/07/1883	10/17/1890	19	289	N	
Thier, George	28	Germany	Y	Amsterdam	New York	04/07/1883	10/17/1890			Y	
Thierauf, George	23	Germany	Y	Antwerp	New York	10/01/1893	03/16/1894			Y	
Thiergartner, Mattheus	29	Germany	Y	Bremen	New York	10/24/1883	10/10/1888			Y	
Thiersch, Ferdinand J.	32	Germany	Y	Hamburg	New York	07/07/1884	03/25/1887			Y	
Thiersch, Gustav	34	Germany	Y	Bremen	New YOork	08/29/1890	05/08/1893			Y	
Thies, Joseph	28	Germany	Y	Bremen	New York	10/19/1881	07/08/1889			Y	
Thies, Louis	23	Germany	Y	Hamburg	New York	09/01/1882	10/10/1887			Y	
Thiessen, Peter Wilhelm	30	Germany	Y	Hamburg	New York	05/26/1885	03/19/1888			Y	
Thoben, Henry	27	Germany	Y	Bremen	New York	06/01/1881	11/17/1884			Y	
Thoben, Wilhelm	54	Germany	Y	Bremen	New York	12/11/1867	09/14/1877			Y	
Thoben, Wilhelm	54	Germany	N	Bremen	New York	12/11/1867	?			Y	
Thole, Bernard Henry	48	Prussia	Y	Bremen	New York	11/08/1868	02/20/1872	18	556	N	
Thole, John Henry	26	Hanover	Y	Bremen	New Orleans	07/13/1847	10/14/1848	1	212	N	
Thole, John Theodore	31	Oldenburg	Y	Bremen	New Orleans	11/01/1847	09/03/1852	25	348	N	
Thole, Joseph	30	Holland	Y	Bremen	New Orleans	07/04/1844	11/01/1852	5	86	N	
Tholen, F.D.	27	Hanover	Y	Bremen	New Orleans	11/19/1852	10/30/1858	17	190	N	
Thoma, Augustus	25	Baden	Y	Havre	New Orleans	04/21/1849	02/23/1853	7	221	N	
Thoma, Sebastian	27	Baden	Y	Liverpool	New York	06/01/1853	04/03/1856	26	421	N	
Thoman, Anton	35	Baden	Y	Havre	New Orleans	05/12/1852	04/20/1854	8	218	N	
Thoman, Anton	35	Baden	Y	Havre	New Orleans	05/12/1852	04/20/1854	9	89	N	
Thomann, John B.	38	Germany	N	Bremen	New York	11/07/1867	?			Y	
Thomann, William	25	Germany	Y	Bremen	New York	10/05/1882	02/03/1886			Y	
Thomas, Barnard	36	Prussia	Y	London	New York	10/04/1847	04/29/1854	9	159	N	
Thomas, Bernard	36	Prussia	Y	London	New York	10/04/1847	04/29/1854	8	287	N	

CITIZENSHIP RECORDS

APPLICANT	AGE	COUNTRY OF ORIGIN	DEC	DEPART PORT	ENTRY PORT	ARRIVE DATE	DEC DATE	VOL	PG.	FLD	NAT DATE
Thomas, George	53	England	Y	Ginnsburg	New York	11/04/1886	04/01/1896			Y	
Thomas, George Stephen	31	England	Y	London	New York	09/03/1850	06/17/1852	25	284	N	
Thomas, Herman	26	Germany	Y	Amsterdam	New York	05/22/1882	08/07/1889			Y	
Thomas, Jacob	36	Germany	Y	Antwerp	New York	09/20/1881	02/24/1885			Y	
Thomas, James	22	Wales	Y	?	New York	06/28/1894	12/31/1894			Y	
Thomas, John	36	France	Y	Havre	New Orleans	12/04/1849	11/19/1852	5	308	N	
Thomas, Joseph	27	England	Y	Liverpool	New Orleans	02/16/1849	05/31/1852	25	163	N	
Thomas, Martin	37	Germany	Y	Bremen	Baltimore	05/18/1877	05/23/1889			Y	
Thomas, Mathias	60	Germany	Y	Bremen	Baltimore	08/19/1885	10/21/1890			Y	
Thomas, Patrick	29	Ireland	Y	Killala	Calais	08/16/1845	11/01/1852	5	116	N	
Thomas, Thomas	??	Wales	Y	?	?	07/??/1838	10/19/1840			Y	10/30/1844
Thomas, William	25	Wales	Y	Liverpool	New York	09/02/1849	04/04/1853	7	533	N	
Thomas, William	20	England	Y	?	New York	09/06/1880	09/29/1880			Y	
Thompson, Andrew	50	Norway	Y	Goteborg	New York	09/18/1837	10/02/1848	1	40	N	
Thompson, Charles	55	England	Y	Liverpool	Baltimore	07/21/1830	10/19/1852	5	21	N	
Thompson, George	??	England	N	Liverpool	Boston	09/01/1838	?	28	224	N	11/06/1848
Thompson, George (Thomso	33	Scotland	Y	Glasgow	New York	09/18/1855	02/06/1860	27	89	N	
Thompson, John	58	England	Y	Liverpool	Baltimore	07/21/1830	10/19/1852	5	22	N	
Thompson, Michael	29	Ireland	Y	Liverpool	Boston	04/02/1848	03/28/1850	2	274	N	
Thompson, Robert	28	Ireland	Y	Belfast	New York	06/01/1886	11/02/1888			Y	
Thompson, Robert	38	England	Y	?	New York	??/??/1880	12/17/1881			Y	
Thompson, William	32	Ireland	Y	Liverpool	New Orleans	04/26/1850	07/07/1855	11	349	N	
Thompson, William Claud	45	England	Y	Liverpool	New York	10/26/1882	03/17/1891	19	315	N	
Thomsen, Karl	38	Germany	Y	Havre	New York	01/19/1882	08/06/1884			Y	
Thomson, Sydney H.	24	England	Y	Liverpool	New York	08/11/1882	10/04/1886			Y	
Thon, George M.	37	Germany	Y	Hamburg	New York	08/??/1879	05/05/1886			Y	
Thon, Joseph	19	Austria	Y	Hamburg	Boston	09/05/1886	01/10/1887			Y	
Thon, S.	21	Austria	Y	Hamburg	New York	06/15/1881	03/10/1884			Y	
Thor, Adam	22	Bavaria	Y	Havre	New Orleans	07/03/1852	10/07/1854	6	48	N	
Thor, Adam	22	Bavaria	Y	Havre	New Orleans	07/03/1852	10/07/1854	11	49	N	
Thormann, Barney	22	Germany	Y	Hamburg	New York	09/09/1881	02/25/1884			Y	
Thorner, Max	31	Germany	Y	Bremen	New York	06/28/1885	02/04/1891			Y	
Thorp, George	37	Ireland	Y	Dublin	New York	05/31/1858	05/20/1861	18	170	N	
Thorstel, George C.	30	Norway	Y	Christian Sa	New York	05/26/1850	03/??/1851	3	303	N	
Thorwarth, George	23	Germany	Y	Havre	New York	07/02/1881	10/09/1882			Y	
Threm, John Nicholas	24	Prussia	Y	Havre	New York	04/01/1848	06/19/1851	3	415	N	
Thronle, Thomas	36	Baden	Y	Havre	New York	04/05/1861	06/30/1862	18	366	N	
Thrumble, John	26	Ireland	N	Liverpool	New York	10/14/1876	?			Y	
Thrumble, Michael	33	Ireland	Y	Liverpool	New York	06/15/1885	05/21/1898			Y	
Thuenemann, Harry A.	31	Germany	Y	Bremen	New York	10/13/1883	10/12/1896			Y	
Thuenemann, Henry	35	Germany	Y	Bremen	Baltimore	09/13/1884	01/21/1891			Y	
Thuenemann, Henry	35	Germany	Y	Bremen	New York	05/22/1883	10/29/1890			Y	
Thuenemann, John Bernard	36	Hanover	Y	Bremen	New Orleans	12/02/1851	11/01/1858	17	240	N	
Thuerling, Joseph	34	Bavaria	Y	Bremen	New York	12/08/1852	08/22/1855	11	480	N	
Thuerwaechter, John	34	Bavaria	Y	Havre	New York	02/21/1849	12/13/1852	5	411	N	
Thuesing, B.	46	Germany	Y	Hamburg	New York	08/30/1881	10/20/1886			Y	
Thumann, August	23	Germany	Y	Amsterdam	New York	09/27/1888	01/02/1891			Y	
Thumann, Henry	24	Germany	Y	Amsterdam	New York	05/13/1883	08/28/1886			Y	
Thumann, Robert	36	Germany	Y	Hamburg	New York	09/23/1880	07/05/1882			Y	
Thumer, Henry	42	Germany	Y	Bremen	Baltimore	07/02/1881	03/21/1891	19	317	N	
Thumm, Charles	23	Wurttemberg	Y	Antwerp	New York	10/01/1848	03/28/1853	7	438	N	
Thuner, Henry	42	Germany	Y	Bremen	Baltimore	07/02/1881	03/21/1891			Y	
Thunert, Melchior	50	Germany	Y	Bremen	New York	08/27/1867	10/10/1881			Y	
Thuran, Paul	28	Germany	Y	Bremen	Baltimore	07/27/1893	11/01/1893			Y	
Thurmbuehler, Clements	56	Germany	N	Bremen	New York	06/26/1869	?			Y	
Thurn, Anton	41	Germany	Y	Bremen	New York	03/29/1867	03/11/1885			Y	
Thurnherr, Michael	??	Germany	Y	?	?	?	07/19/1892			Y	
Thye, Theodore	35	Germany	Y	Bremen	New York	10/13/1881	10/29/1897			Y	
Thyen, John	29	Germany	Y	Bremen	New York	03/24/1887	10/03/1893			Y	

CITIZENSHIP RECORDS

APPLICANT	AGE	COUNTRY OF ORIGIN	DEC	DEPART PORT	ENTRY PORT	ARRIVE DATE	DEC DATE	VOL	PG.	FLD	NAT DATE
Tiebermann, Richard	62	Germany	N	Hamburg	New York	05/01/1849	?			Y	
Tieck, Paul	35	Germany	Y	Havre	New York	10/12/1882	04/10/1886			Y	
Tiefermann, P. Conrad	22	Germany	Y	Bremen	Baltimore	07/27/1880	11/01/1882			Y	
Tieke, Frederick Henry	23	Hanover	Y	Bremen	New Orleans	10/23/1849	09/07/1852	25	388	N	
Tieke, Henry	21	Lohn	Y	Bremen	New Orleans	03/15/1849	06/28/1851	3	461	N	
Tieken, Fred	26	Hanover	Y	Bremen	New York	09/21/1845	01/07/1850	23	466	N	
Tieken, Gerhard George	47	Prussia	Y	Bremen	Baltimore	11/04/1848	04/18/1853	8	81	N	
Tieman, Henry	28	Germany	Y	Bremen	New York	08/20/1881	04/07/1882			Y	
Tieman, John	26	Ireland	Y	Dublin	New York	09/29/1884	08/30/1888			Y	
Tieman, John Henry	26	Hanover	Y	Bremen	New Orleans	07/15/1852	11/03/1852	6	339	N	
Tiemann, Augsut Fredk. W	30	Hanover	Y	Bremen	New York	10/16/1845	10/11/1848	1	126	N	
Tiemann, Fritz	37	Prussia	Y	Bremen	New Orleans	10/24/1856	09/03/1860	27	325	N	
Tiemann, John	38	Hanover	Y	Bremen	Baltimore	06/24/1841	10/23/1851	4	377	N	
Tiemann, John Henry	30	Hanover	Y	Bremen	Baltimore	11/01/1854	02/09/1858	16	91	N	
Tiemann, Joseph	76	Germany	N	Bremen	Baltimore	07/??/1835	??/??/1837	28	126	N	11/??/1840
Tiemann, William	39	Prussia	Y	Bremen	New York	09/25/1851	10/09/1854	6	183	N	
Tiemann, William	39	Prussia	Y	Bremen	New York	08/25/1851	10/09/1854	11	186	N	
Tiemann, William	32	Hanover	Y	Bremen	New Orleans	??/24/1849	04/28/1855	11	322	N	
Tiemann, William	24	Germany	Y	Bremen	New York	08/26/1886	10/23/1890			Y	
Tiemeier, Henry	22	Hanover	Y	Bremen	New Orleans	11/01/1849	11/01/1852	5	101	N	
Tiemeier, William	27	Hanover	Y	Bremen	Baltimore	11/25/1848	09/06/1852	25	361	N	
Tiemeyer, Ernst	24	Germany	Y	Bremen	New York	02/06/1887	12/21/1893			Y	
Tiemeyer, Herman	49	Germany	Y	Bremen	New York	04/12/1892	10/24/1896			Y	
Tiemeyer, Hermann	24	Germany	Y	Bremen	New York	10/30/1888	12/11/1889			Y	
Tierney, Martin	28	Ireland	Y	Liverpool	New York	08/19/1846	11/24/1848	1	384	N	
Tierney, Martin	53	Ireland	Y	London	New York	08/31/1883	10/23/1888			Y	
Tierney, Patrick	28	Ireland	Y	Liverpool	New York	03/08/1853	07/11/1859	17	463	N	
Tierney, Thomas	35	Ireland	Y	Queenstown	New York	10/12/1887	10/25/1889			Y	
Tierney, Thomas	32	Ireland	Y	Queenstown	New York	03/25/1882	10/29/1888			Y	
Tierny, Lawrence	22	Ireland	Y	Liverpool	New York	05/04/1847	08/12/1851	4	115	N	
Tieste, August	38	Brunswick	Y	Bremen	New York	07/09/1847	01/13/1849	1	413	N	
Tighe, Edward	25	Ireland	Y	Dublin	New York	07/24/1848	11/03/1851	4	484	N	
Tighe, Michael	28	Ireland	Y	Liverpool	New York	05/26/1852	05/21/1859	17	423	N	
Tighe, Thomas	32	Ireland	Y	Queenstown	New York	05/22/1890	10/21/1898			Y	
Tigrist, Hippolyte	??	Germany	Y	?	?	?	09/14/1891			Y	
Tigue, Dominick	53	Ireland	N	Queenstown	New York	08/??/1868	?			Y	
Tillner, Ernst W.	33	Saxony	Y	Bremen	New Orleans	11/05/1849	09/06/1852	25	364	N	
Tilney, Robert	28	England	Y	Liverpool	New York	09/12/1845	10/02/1854	10	345	N	
Tilney, Robert	28	England	Y	Liverpool	New York	09/12/1845	10/02/1854	12	284	N	
Timan, Garrit John	22	Holland	Y	Bremen	New York	07/15/1851	10/09/1854	6	76	N	
Timm, Edward	30	Germany	Y	Hamburg	New York	05/15/1886	06/03/1891			Y	
Timmer, Bernard	23	Prussia	Y	Bremen	New Orleans	12/20/1845	10/??/1848	22	463	N	
Timmerding, Frank	38	Germany	N	Bremen	Baltimore	07/11/1869	?			Y	
Timmermann, Hermann	24	Hanover	Y	Bremen	Baltimore	12/01/1857	06/02/1859	17	451	N	
Timmermann, John Frederi	29	Oldenburg	Y	Bremen	Baltimore	10/12/1846	10/04/1848	1	54	N	
Timmers, Bernard	21	Germany	Y	Rotterdam	New York	09/04/1880	10/10/1883			Y	
Timmich, Gustav	34	Germany	Y	Stettin	Philadelphia	?	02/21/1887			Y	
Timmins, Charles	27	Ireland	Y	Dublin	Philadelphia	03/23/1852	04/15/1852	24	513	N	
Timmins, William	39	Ireland	N	Queenstown	New York	06/30/1873				Y	03/26/1892
Timner, Bernard	24	Hanover	Y	Bremen	Baltimore	05/28/1859	07/16/1860	27	222	N	
Timon, Patrick	27	Ireland	Y	Liverpool	New York	09/27/1890	12/10/1895			Y	
Timperley, Henry	33	England	Y	Liverpool	New Orleans	05/01/1849	06/17/1852	25	283	N	
Tinger, John	33	Hanover	Y	Bremen	Baltimore	05/??/1844	10/08/1860	27	436	N	
Tinker, Frederick	36	England	Y	Liverpool	New Orleans	11/??/1844	12/??/1850	2	422	N	
Tinley, Charles	23	Ireland	Y	Liverpool	New Orleans	04/??/1849	03/25/1851	3	329	N	
Tinley, William	??	Ireland	Y	Liverpool	New Orleans	04/04/1849	03/25/1851	3	330	N	
Tinnemeier, William	22	Hanover	Y	Bremen	Baltimore	08/04/1851	04/27/1854	8	274	N	
Tinnemeyer, William	22	Hanover	Y	Bremen	Baltimore	08/04/1851	04/27/1854	9	145	N	
Tinschert, Frank	25	Germany	Y	Hamburg	New York	05/01/1881	06/02/1884			Y	

CITIZENSHIP RECORDS

APPLICANT	AGE	COUNTRY OF ORIGIN	DEC	DEPART PORT	ENTRY PORT	ARRIVE DATE	DEC DATE	VOL	PG.	FLD	NAT DATE
Tischler, Robert	42	Prussia	Y	Rotterdam	Baltimore	08/??/1848	10/21/1851	4	360	N	
Tishler, Sam	43	Russia	Y	Bremen	Baltimore	12/17/1888	12/17/1894			Y	
Tittel, Joseph	25	Germany	Y	Havre	New York	06/11/1883	10/27/1884			Y	
Tittel, Robert	24	Germany	Y	Havre	New York	11/07/1884	09/21/1887			Y	
Titz, William	??	Prussia	Y	?	?	?	10/24/1892			Y	
Tivennen, Thomas	27	Ireland	Y	Liverpool	New York	03/14/1889	01/12/1894			Y	
Toal, Henry	37	Ireland	Y	Liverpool	New York	07/04/1853	10/06/1854	10	513	N	
Toal, Henry	37	Ireland	Y	Liverpool	New York	07/04/1843	10/06/1854	12	452	N	
Tobaben, Peter	43	Germany	Y	Hamburg	New York	06/02/1891	10/10/1898			Y	
Tobbe, Bernard	54	Germany	Y	Bremen	New York	04/26/1864	03/29/1889	19	227	N	
Tobbee, Barney	36	Germany	Y	Havre	New York	12/10/1866	10/11/1880			Y	
Tobben, Gerhard	21	Oldenburg	Y	Bremen	New York	05/12/1859	11/01/1860	27	521	N	
Toben, T.	31	Oldenburg	Y	Bremen	New York	05/01/1847	01/23/1851	2	521	N	
Tobergle, Christian	41	Germany	Y	Bremen	Baltimore	05/15/1882	07/11/1885			Y	
Tobergte, Bernhard	19	Germany	Y	Rotterdam	New York	02/18/1892	03/01/1892			Y	
Tobergte, Henry	30	Germany	Y	Bremen	Baltimore	09/23/1891	10/17/1891			Y	
Tobes, Jacob	40	Russia	Y	Hamburg	Detroit	07/21/1890	07/19/1893			Y	
Tobias, Henry	44	Prussia	Y	Hamburg	New York	01/15/1848	08/27/1862	18	403	N	
Tobiessen, Emanuel	??	Sweden/Norway	Y	?	?	?	12/17/1900			Y	
Tobin, John	48	Ireland	N	Queenstown	New York	11/18/1864	?			Y	
Tobin, Lawrence	36	Ireland	Y	Liverpool	New Orleans	12/18/1849	02/18/1853	7	178	N	
Tobin, Richard	42	Ireland	N	Queenstown	New York	06/??/1866	?			Y	
Tobin, William, Jr.	24	Ireland	Y	Cork	Philadelphia	07/04/1852	11/07/1857	15	544	N	
Tobler, Edward	??	Switzerland	Y	?	?	02/10/1883	01/12/1885			Y	
Tocher, ?	??	?	Y	?	?	??/02/18??	10/28/1850	2	314	N	
Todd, John	??	Great Britain	Y	?	?	?	09/26/1887			Y	
Todd, Robert	44	Ireland	Y	Belfast	New York	05/??/1858	10/07/1884			Y	
Todenwarth, George	25	Germany	Y	Bremen	New Orleans	06/25/1853	06/29/1860	27	17	N	
Todt, Charles Selmar	24	Saxony	Y	Bremen	New York	10/24/1853	09/12/1855	13	9	N	
Todtenbier, Charles	22	Hesse Cassel	Y	Bremen	New York	05/08/1852	03/24/1856	26	285	N	
Toedt, Henry	31	Germany	Y	Hamburg	New York	10/30/1870	09/03/1880			Y	
Toeniges, Friederick	29	Hanover	Y	Bremen	New York	10/03/1843	01/23/1849	1	497	N	
Toepfer, Andreas	28	Germany	Y	Bremen	Baltimore	12/29/1892	04/06/1897			Y	
Toepfer, Ignatz	32	Germany	N	Bremen	New York	02/20/1882	?			Y	
Toepfer, Johann	29	Germany	Y	Bremen	New York	03/13/1885	09/19/1889				
Toepfer, John	26	Germany	Y	Bremen	New York	11/03/1887	07/03/1890				
Toepke, William	25	Germany	Y	Bremen	New York	10/01/1878	08/16/1884			Y	
Toering, Henry	23	Hanover	Y	Bremen	New Orleans	12/??/1848	11/01/1851	4	460	N	
Toerner, Herman Henry	27	Hanover	Y	Bremen	New York	01/03/1857	11/11/1858	17	320	N	
Toerner, Theodore	28	Prussia	Y	London	New Orleans	12/12/1848	07/28/1851	4	46	N	
Toher, Michael	26	Ireland	Y	Liverpool	New Orleans	05/22/1848	08/12/1851	4	118	N	
Tokarski, Valentine	50	Germany	Y	Hamburg	New York	12/24/1880	03/20/1903			Y	
Tolan, Anthony	32	Ireland	Y	Liverpool	New Orleans	05/10/1847	11/03/1852	4	211	N	
Tolan, Anthony	32	Ireland	Y	Liverpool	New Orleans	05/10/1847	11/03/1852	6	337	N	
Tolan, John	??	Great Britain	Y	?	?	?	12/10/1889			Y	
Tolan, Patrick	31	Ireland	Y	Liverpool	New York	10/14/1846	02/08/1853	7	129	N	
Toliosero, Martin	57	Austria	Y	Marseilles	Charleston	09/30/1851	05/19/1852	25	40	N	
Tolke, Joseph	23	Germany	Y	Bremen	Baltimore	10/26/1882	11/02/1886			Y	
Tolle, John August	28	Lippe Detmold	Y	Bremerhafen	Baltimore	07/??/1858	01/10/1861	18	52	N	
Tollheifs, Albert Julius	35	Germany	Y	Bremen	New York	03/01/1880	09/30/1882			Y	
Tomamichel, John A.	28	Switzerland	Y	Havre	New Orleans	09/01/1851	07/15/1862	18	375	N	
Toman, James	30	England	Y	Liverpool	New York	08/26/1879	10/28/1886	19	92	N	
Tomassini, Charles	26	Italy	Y	Havre	New York	11/28/1846	10/09/1854	11	125	N	
Tombraegel, Joseph	25	Oldenburg	Y	Bremen	New Orleans	12/25/1850	05/01/1854	8	332	N	
Tombragel, Joseph	25	Oldenburg	Y	Bremen	New Orleans	12/25/1850	05/01/1854	9	205	N	
Tomen, James	39	England	Y	Liverpool	New York	08/26/1879	10/28/1886			Y	
Tomkins, Thomas H.	32	England	Y	Liverpool	New Orleans	11/10/1845	11/13/1848	1	267	N	
Tommassin, Charles	26	Italy	Y	Havre	New York	11/28/1846	10/09/1854	6	122	N	
Tondorf, Peter	34	Germany	Y	Rotterdam	New York	06/01/1882	11/11/1885			Y	09/04/1888

390

CITIZENSHIP RECORDS

APPLICANT	AGE	COUNTRY OF ORIGIN	DEC	DEPART PORT	ENTRY PORT	ARRIVE DATE	DEC DATE	VOL	PG.	FLD	NAT DATE
Tonfes, Bernard	34	Oldenburg	Y	Bremen	New Orleans	12/01/1854	12/28/1857	16	267	N	
Tonjes, Clem	34	Germany	Y	Antwerp	New York	05/15/1879	10/29/1892			Y	
Tonnies, Owe	31	Germany	Y	Hamburg	Philadelphia	05/01/1891	06/22/1903			Y	
Tonsmeyer, Frederick	19	Germany	Y	Bremen	Baltimore	10/19/1881	04/10/1882			Y	
Toohig, Patrick	23	Ireland	Y	Liverpool	Buffalo	09/01/1851	10/06/1854	10	515	N	
Toohig, Patrick	23	Ireland	Y	Liverpool	Buffalo	09/01/1851	10/06/1854	12	454	N	
Toole, James	23	Ireland	Y	Liverpool	New York	06/01/1849	04/30/1850	3	35	N	
Toole, Peter	25	Ireland	Y	Liverpool	New York	06/??/1849	10/??/1849	23	275	N	
Topf, Ottomar	23	Schwarzburg S	Y	Bremen	New York	06/15/1853	09/20/1854	10	133	N	
Toph, Ottomar	23	Schwarzburg S	Y	Bremen	New York	06/15/1853	09/20/1854	12	72	N	
Topmoller, Joseph Melchi	26	Germany	Y	Bremen	New York	09/18/1880	07/21/1881			Y	
Torbeck, Gerhard	40	Germany	Y	Amsterdam	New York	03/24/1881	03/15/1892			Y	
Torbeck, Henry	24	Germany	Y	Bremen	New York	10/13/1884	01/13/1885			Y	
Torchia, Gregorio	36	Italy	Y	Naples	New York	05/21/1883	08/13/1888			Y	
Torner, F. H.	41	Germany	Y	Bremen	Baltimore	03/04/1882	03/25/1885			Y	
Torpy, Michael	26	Ireland	Y	Liverpool	New Orleans	02/06/1849	04/04/1853	7	516	N	
Torronto, Michael	29	Ireland	Y	Liverpool	Charleston	11/05/1852	11/01/1858	17	230	N	
Touff, Goetzel (Jacob?)	41	Russia	Y	Antwerp	New York	02/14/1887	08/06/1889			Y	10/28/1892
Touff, Louis E.	??	Russia	N	?	?	02/15/1887				Y	10/13/1892
Touges, William	30	Prussia	Y	Bremen	New Orleans	12/23/1847	02/11/1852	24	97	N	
Touhil, Dennis	25	Ireland	Y	Liverpool	Philadelphia	04/21/1848	09/29/1854	10	303	N	
Touhil, Dennis	25	Ireland	Y	Liverpool	Philadelphia	04/21/1848	09/29/1854	12	242	N	
Toundrow, John S.	32	England	Y	London	New Orleans	03/04/1845	03/08/1851	3	209	N	
Trabach, Nicol	52	Prussia	Y	Bremen	New York	01/13/1854	09/26/1857	15	326	N	
Traber, William	29	Germany	Y	Havre	New York	07/01/1881	10/02/1890			Y	
Tracey, Jeremiah	65	Ireland	N	Liverpool	New Orleans	02/??/1852	?			Y	
Tracy, David	24	Ireland	Y	Liverpool	New York	01/01/1856	01/27/1857	14	511	N	
Tracy, James	63	Ireland	N	Liverpool	New York	03/12/1854	?			Y	
Tracy, William	42	Ireland	Y	Liverpool	New York	05/14/1850	02/02/1857	14	531	N	
Traestel, George	36	Bavaria	Y	Bremen	New Orleans	10/30/1854	03/13/1858	16	397	N	
Trager, Victor	??	Austria	N	?	?	01/20/1886	10/17/1892			Y	
Trageser, George	47	Germany	N	London	New York	??/??/1852	?			Y	
Tragsailer, Joseph	24	Austria	Y	Liverpool	New York	03/02/1860	07/03/1860	27	200	N	
Trainer, Edward H.	50	Ireland	N	?	?	?	?	28	49	N	10/??/1864
Trainer, Martin	23	Ireland	Y	Liverpool	New York	05/12/1883	09/28/1886	19	45	N	
Trampe, Henry	23	Hanover	Y	Bremen	New York	10/17/1859	10/08/1860	27	433	N	
Trampler, John Gottlieb	41	Germany	Y	Bremen	New York	07/13/1882	05/24/1890			Y	
Tranel, John H.	39	Hanover	Y	Bremen	New Orleans	11/21/1848	03/08/1850	2	172	N	
Transbir, Morris	39	Bavaria	Y	London	New York	??/10/1847	01/07/1850	23	472	N	
Trant, Carl	26	Germany	Y	Antwerp	New York	10/11/1883	11/08/1889			Y	
Trantveller, Charles	25	Switzerland	Y	Havre	New York	10/25/1854	04/16/1860	27	161	N	
Trapp, John	28	Bavaria	Y	Bremen	New York	12/21/1853	09/25/1858	16	133	N	
Trapp, Martin	49	Germany	N	Bremen	Baltimore	04/??/1874	?			Y	
Trapp, Wendel	42	Germany	Y	Rotterdam	New York	03/10/1876	06/09/1884			Y	
Trarop, John	27	Prussia	Y	Hamburg	New York	12/05/1856	10/10/1860	27	480	N	
Traub, Frank	26	Germany	Y	Havre	New York	09/01/1881	09/02/1887			Y	
Traub, Fred	55	Germany	Y	Antwerp	New York	09/18/1884	11/07/1900			Y	
Traub, Louis	26	France	Y	Antwerp	New York	12/27/1882	06/24/1886			Y	
Trauth, Jacob	29	Germany	Y	Bremen	New York	05/14/1891	10/03/1892			Y	
Trautman, Conrad	30	Hesse Darmsta	Y	Havre	New York	07/20/1851	05/12/1854	9	305	N	
Trautman, Louis	28	Bavaria	Y	Havre	New Orleans	12/08/1847	05/06/1854	8	384	N	
Trautmann, Conrad	30	Hesse Darmsta	Y	Havre	New York	07/20/1851	05/12/1854	8	432	N	
Trautwein, Frederick	42	Wuerttemberg	Y	Antwerp	New Orleans	12/04/1848	06/15/1852	25	274	N	
Traynor, Michael	30	Ireland	Y	Liverpool	New Orleans	12/14/1848	02/17/1852	24	132	N	
Trebs, Charles	29	Germany	Y	Bremen	Baltimore	12/05/1879	03/26/1888			Y	
Trefz, Christian	43	Germany	Y	Bremen	New York	12/08/1874	04/26/1894			Y	
Trefzgar, August	39	Germany	Y	Havre	New York	02/16/1882	03/03/1885			Y	
Trefzgen, Alois	28	Baden	Y	Antwerp	New York	10/17/1853	07/10/1855	11	370	N	
Trefzger, Fridolin	34	Baden	Y	Antwerp	New York	05/18/1854	10/10/1854	6	209	N	

CITIZENSHIP RECORDS

APPLICANT	AGE	COUNTRY OF ORIGIN	DEC	DEPART PORT	ENTRY PORT	ARRIVE DATE	DEC DATE	VOL	PG.	FLD	NAT DATE
Trefzger, Fridolin	34	Baden	Y	Antwerp	New York	05/18/1854	10/10/1854	11	212	N	
Trefzger, Joseph	23	Germany	Y	Havre	New York	06/16/1881	02/13/1882			Y	
Trekauskas, Wincentas	36	Russia	Y	Bremen	New York	05/19/1887	04/14/1893			Y	
Treking, H. C.	31	Germany	Y	Bremen	Baltimore	04/07/1878	02/09/1882			Y	
Tremel, George	30	Bavaria	Y	Bremen	Baltimore	08/04/1852	03/25/1856	26	320	N	
Trempel, Matheus	31	Bavaria	Y	Bremen	New York	05/26/1854	10/03/1854	10	401	N	
Tremple, Matheus	31	Bavaria	Y	Bremen	New York	05/26/1854	10/03/1854	12	340	N	
Trenk, Emil	28	Germany	Y	Stettine	New York	07/30/1889	10/23/1891			Y	
Trenkamp, John Henry	58	Oldenburg	Y	Bremen	Baltimore	10/30/1855	11/13/1858	17	324	N	
Trentmann, Henry	21	Hanover	Y	Bremen	Baltimore	05/30/1854	03/31/1856	26	384	N	
Trentmann, Louis	21	Hanover	Y	Bremen	Baltimore	06/01/1856	12/07/1857	16	204	N	
Tressler, Reinhard (Dres	33	Germany	Y	?	New York	??/??/1887	10/09/1890			Y	
Trestel, George	65	Germany	N	Bremen	New Orleans	12/??/1854	?			Y	
Triar, Jacob	39	Wurttemberg	Y	Havre	New York	05/14/1840	10/13/1848	1	185	N	
Trick, Adolph	21	Baden	Y	Havre	New York	04/10/1854	04/11/1856	26	485	N	
Trick, John Jacob	22	Wurttemberg	Y	Liverpool	New York	07/18/1852	10/10/1854	6	234	N	
Tricker, Michael	24	Ireland	Y	Liverpool	New Orleans	01/04/1847	10/14/1851	4	273	N	
Tricklin, Bernard	28	Prussia	Y	Bremen	New York	08/15/1847	04/04/1853	8	49	N	
Trieschmann, Carl F.	28	Germany	Y	Bremen	New York	05/31/1881	01/12/1891			Y	
Trigg, Joseph	39	England	Y	Liverpool	New York	10/11/1887	10/16/1893			Y	
Trimble, John George	28	Ireland	Y	Liverpool	?	?	09/09/1857	15	249	N	
Trimble, Patrick	28	Ireland	Y	Liverpool	New Orleans	01/06/1846	11/21/1848	1	355	N	
Trimborn, August	24	Germany	Y	Antwerp	New York	03/02/1890	09/19/1894			Y	
Trimpe, Henry	48	Oldenburg	Y	Bremen	New Orleans	03/??/1850	11/09/1857	15	545	N	
Trink, Leonard	38	Baden	Y	Havre	New Orleans	05/14/1852	10/29/1858	17	183	N	
Trinkle, August	32	Wurttemberg	Y	Havre	New York	02/26/1868	08/26/1872	18	515	N	
Trinkuth, Henry	39	Prussia	Y	Bremen	New York	05/??/1846	12/21/1850	2	383	N	
Trippel, Franz	33	Germany	Y	Havre	New York	06/20/1880	04/19/1889			Y	
Trippel, Leo	53	Germany	Y	Antwerp	Philadelphia	08/16/1880	08/30/1886			Y	
Trippel, Robert	36	Germany	Y	Havre	New York	10/01/1883	07/09/1890			Y	
Tritscheler, Martin	28	Germany	Y	Bremen	New York	08/02/1889	04/19/1892			Y	
Tritschler, Joseph	34	Germany	Y	Antwerp	New York	11/01/1888	06/04/1891			Y	
Troeger, Andreas	35	Bavaria	Y	Bremen	Baltimore	05/15/1851	10/09/1854	11	159	N	
Troehler, Rudolph	38	Switzerland	Y	Bordeaux	New York	01/18/1886	02/07/1890			Y	
Troescher, John	50	Germany	Y	Hamburg	New York	06/??/1881	03/05/1886			Y	
Troester, Joseph	21	Alsace	Y	Havre	New York	09/12/1872	11/07/1872	18	539	N	
Troger, John	25	Bavaria	Y	Bremen	New York	08/12/1851	06/09/1854	10	112	N	
Troger, John	25	Bavaria	Y	Bremen	New York	08/12/1851	06/09/1854	12	49	N	
Troschle, William	22	Wurttemberg	Y	Havre	New York	08/20/1858	12/30/1859	17	538	N	
Trost, Henry	50	Germany	Y	Hamburg	New York	06/20/1870	04/20/1896			Y	
Trost, Waldrin	46	Bavaria	Y	Bremen	New York	07/04/1854	10/09/1860	27	469	N	
Trott, Michael	??	Germany	Y	?	?	?	10/26/1875			Y	
Trousdale, Joseph	26	England	Y	Liverpool	New York	10/06/1844	11/18/1848	1	319	N	
Troutman, Louis	28	Bavaria	Y	Havre	New Orleans	12/08/1847	05/06/1854	9	257	N	
Troutwein, Henry	??	Germany	Y	?	?	?	03/30/1897			Y	
Troy, Michael	34	Ireland	Y	Queenstown	New York	05/16/1880	10/23/1886	19	75	N	
Troy, Timothy	30	Ireland	Y	Liverpool	New Orleans	06/??/1847	02/03/1851	3	84	N	
Truetzschler, August	90	Germany	Y	Saxony	Baltimore	03/21/1882	02/01/1884			Y	
Trummer, Leonhard	25	Germany	Y	Antwerp	New York	07/29/1900	11/05/1900			Y	
Trupo, Frank	34	Italy	Y	?	?	02/12/1882	04/16/1894			Y	
Trzeciak, Jacob	45	Germany	Y	Bremen	Baltimore	02/09/1888	09/21/1894			Y	
Tschan, Emil	32	Switzerland	Y	Havre	New York	05/18/1887	04/30/1892			Y	
Tschanz, Rudolph	33	Switzerland	Y	Havre	New York	05/14/1884	10/12/1891			Y	
Tschira, Herman	23	Baden	Y	Bremen	Baltimore	09/26/1869	10/10/1872	18	533	N	
Tschopp, Wilhelm	35	Switzerland	Y	Havre	New York	09/17/1880	09/30/1891			Y	
Tschudi, Edwin	27	Switzerland	Y	Havre	New York	07/??/1866	10/02/1868			Y	
Tsopiano, Malto	43	Sardina	Y	Havre	New York	07/14/1841	11/03/1851	4	467	N	
Tuchauer, John	45	Bavaria	Y	Bremen	New Orleans	10/31/1844	11/15/1848	1	298	N	
Tuchocki, Bromislaus	44	Germany	Y	Hamburg	Baltimore	04/05/1892	07/21/1897			Y	

CITIZENSHIP RECORDS

APPLICANT	AGE	COUNTRY OF ORIGIN	DEC	DEPART PORT	ENTRY PORT	ARRIVE DATE	DEC DATE	VOL	PG.	FLD	NAT DATE
Tucker, Michael	30	Ireland	Y	Liverpool	New Orleans	04/23/1846	09/29/1848	22	362	N	
Tuckett, James E.	42	England	Y	Liverpool	Philadelphia	03/11/1882	04/28/1892			Y	
Tuding, John Gerhard	22	Hanover	Y	Bremen	New Orleans	11/28/1849	01/17/1853	7	38	N	
Tuechter, Eberhart	35	Prussia	Y	Bremen	New York	06/10/1847	01/??/1850	23	477	N	
Tuechter, Rudolph	50	Prussia	Y	Bremen	Baltimore	10/28/1855	10/29/1858	17	169	N	
Tuemler, Heinrich	24	Prussia	Y	Bremen	New Orleans	12/25/1852	09/29/1854	10	307	N	
Tuerck, Michael	48	Germany	Y	Bremen	New York	05/13/1880	11/01/1897			Y	
Tuergens, Joseph	28	Prussia	Y	Bremen	New York	04/22/1850	10/10/1854	10	204	N	
Tueting, William	22	Germany	Y	?	Baltimore	??/??/1881	11/26/1887			Y	
Tuff, Joseph	32	Ireland	Y	Belfast	New York	08/07/1850	05/08/1854	8	400	N	
Tuff, Joseph	32	Ireland	Y	Belfast	New York	08/07/1850	05/08/1854	9	273	N	
Tuffensdam, Charles	23	Wurttemberg	Y	Bremen	New York	05/17/1854	12/14/1857	16	222	N	
Tufner, Wendelin	25	Wurttemberg	Y	London	New York	10/16/1848	10/16/1851	4	209	N	
Tulley, John	21	Ireland	Y	Liverpool	New York	08/08/1848	08/04/1851	4	81	N	
Tumler, Henry	24	Prussia	Y	Bremen	New Orleans	12/25/1852	09/29/1854	12	246	N	
Tunemann, Henry	33	Prussia	Y	Bremen	Baltimore	10/27/1850	10/21/1854	10	353	N	
Tunemann, Henry	33	Prussia	Y	Bremen	Baltimore	10/27/1850	10/02/1854	12	292	N	
Tunstull, William	29	England	Y	Jamacia	New York	08/15/1847	03/08/1852	24	263	N	
Tuohy, John	38	Ireland	Y	Limerick	New York	07/??/1851	08/??/1851	4	182	N	
Tuohy, John	22	Ireland	Y	Cape Good Ho	Boston	03/12/1852	12/20/1852	5	428	N	
Turayski, Peter	21	Prussia	Y	Hamburg	New York	01/15/1854	02/06/1856	26	55	N	
Turner, Edward	22	Prussia	Y	Bremen	Baltimore	10/20/1851	09/23/1854	10	187	N	
Turner, Edward	22	Prussia	Y	Bremen	Baltimore	10/20/1851	09/23/1854	12	126	N	
Turner, Ernst	33	Germany	Y	?	Baltimore	04/21/1884	12/18/1886			Y	
Turner, James	35	Ireland	Y	Londonderry	Philadelphia	09/08/1844	02/01/1849	23	5	N	
Turpain, Henry	37	France	Y	Havre	New York	02/26/1889	04/07/1890			Y	
Tuschner, Peter	29	Germany	Y	Rotterdam	New York	04/06/1881	10/03/1885			Y	
Tutty, William	40	Ireland	Y	Dublin	New York	05/20/1848	08/15/1851	4	131	N	
Tuve, Julius	37	Germany	N	Bremen	New York	04/02/1878	?			Y	
Twachtmann, William	30	Germany	Y	Bremen	New York	04/01/1867	04/14/1873			Y	
Twalbeck, Henry	35	Hanover	Y	Bremen	Baltimore	??/02/1845	12/31/1850	2	434	N	
Twedy, Robert	48	Scotland	Y	Glasgow	Fairbury	07/09/1885	01/06/1890			Y	
Twehur, Joseph	57	Germany	N	Rotterdam	New Orleans	09/??/1846	?	28	64	N	10/??/1853
Twells, William	55	England	Y	Liverpool	New York	08/??/1865	02/15/1887			Y	
Twickler, Bernard	33	Germany	Y	Bremen	Baltimore	02/??/1884	03/??/1884	28	358	N	
Twickler, Bernard	25	Germany	Y	Bremen	Balt./New Yo	02/00/1884	03/00/1884			Y	
Twohig, Jeremiah	24	Ireland	Y	Liverpool	New Orleans	06/24/1847	11/01/1852	5	164	N	
Twohig, Jeremiah	24	Ireland	Y	Liverpool	New Orleans	06/26/1847	11/01/1852	6	290	N	
Tyler, Henry	29	England	Y	London	New York	09/15/1882	10/22/1889			Y	
Tynan, James	26	Ireland	Y	Liverpool	Boston	05/12/1856	07/21/1860	27	232	N	
Tyx, Casimir	32	Germany	Y	Hamburg	New York	03/29/1884	02/19/1889			Y	
Uchtmann, Bernard	25	Germany	Y	Bremen	Baltimore	05/20/1880	12/28/1882			Y	
Uchtmann, F. H.	24	Germany	N	Bremen	Baltimore	09/21/1873	?			Y	
Uchtmann, Henry	27	Prussia	Y	Bremen	New Orleans	11/17/1847	08/06/1851	4	91	N	
Uderstadt, Charles	21	Prussia	Y	Bremerhafen	Baltimore	08/??/1858	01/07/1861	18	46	N	
Uderstadt, H.E.	49	Prussia	Y	Bremerhafen	New Orleans	??/20/1857	01/07/1861	18	44	N	
Uedry, Joseph	34	Baden	Y	Havre	New Orleans	02/20/1856	03/25/1858	16	450	N	
Uehl, Joseph	25	Baden	Y	Havre	New York	10/02/1849	11/03/1852	6	334	N	
Uehlein, F. Xavier	27	Germany	Y	Havre	New York	10/05/1879	03/30/1883			Y	
Uehlin, John	32	Baden	Y	Havre	New Orleans	04/10/1852	08/17/1855	11	450	N	
Uetrecht, Adolf Gustav	24	Germany	Y	Bremen	Baltimore	06/30/1882	10/16/1882			Y	
Uetrecht, Christian	27	Prussia	Y	Bremen	New York	10/01/1852	09/28/1857	15	331	N	
Uetsch, John Peter	32	Prussia	Y	Antwerp	New York	08/25/1848	02/28/1851	3	180	N	
Uettwiller, Augustin	??	Germany	Y	?	?	?	10/15/1894			Y	
Uffmann, John Henry	36	Prussia	Y	Bremen	New Orleans	11/17/1854	09/10/1857	15	255	N	
Uhe, Victor	29	Germany	Y	Bremen	Baltimore	05/31/1882	06/14/1886			Y	
Uhele, Phillip	50	Baden	Y	Havre	New York	04/05/1848	02/22/1851	3	152	N	
Uhl, Andreas	28	Bavaria	Y	Havre	New York	05/01/1848	03/02/1852	24	215	N	
Uhl, Christian	23	Baden	Y	Havre	New York	10/04/1849	11/01/1851	4	453	N	

CITIZENSHIP RECORDS

APPLICANT	AGE	COUNTRY OF ORIGIN	DEC	DEPART PORT	ENTRY PORT	ARRIVE DATE	DEC DATE	VOL	PG.	FLD	NAT DATE
Uhl, John	24	Bavaria	Y	Havre	New York	05/01/18??	12/20/1851	4	536	N	
Uhl, Joseph	25	Baden	Y	Havre	New York	10/02/1849	11/03/1852	5	208	N	
Uhlenberg, Herman	26	Germany	Y	Bremen	New York	05/16/1891	06/27/1893			Y	
Uhlenbrock, W.	23	Germany	Y	Bremen	Baltimore	08/08/1883	04/26/1887			Y	
Uhlenhake, Joseph	42	Germany	Y	Hamburg	Baltimore	05/15/1872	04/07/1883			Y	
Uhlig, Carl Theodor	56	Germany	Y	Antwerp	New York	12/10/1889	02/06/1892			Y	
Uhlig, F. Robert	41	Germany	Y	Bremen	New York	03/15/1882	06/21/1898			Y	
Uhlman, Herman	29	Germany	Y	Bremen	New York	02/10/1887	03/14/1892			Y	
Uhlmann, Mathias	23	Hanover	Y	Bremen	New Orleans	06/25/1849	05/18/1852	25	37	N	
Uhrig, Louis	37	Germany	N	Germany	New York	08/??/1867	?			Y	
Uhrmacher, John	56	Prussia	N	Bremen	New York	??/??/1854	?			Y	
Ulhorn, Herman A.	40	Germany	N	Bremen	New York	11/15/1867	?	28	299	N	09/??/1881
Ulland, Hermann	30	Germany	Y	Amsterdam	New York	01/01/1886	02/07/1889			Y	
Ullrich, Frank	28	Germany	Y	Bremen	New York	06/10/1893	08/24/1897			Y	
Ulluke, Gregor	30	Germany	Y	Bremen	New York	09/16/1887	04/01/1893	19	419	N	
Ulluke, Gregor	30	Germany	Y	Bremen	New York	09/16/1887	04/01/1893			Y	
Ulm,, Philip	47	Germany	N	Bremen	New York	03/??/1873	??/??/1873	28	430	N	10/25/1897
Ulman, Adolph	46	Germany	N	Antwerp	Portland	04/30/1868	?			Y	
Ulmer, Conrad	27	Wurttemberg	Y	Havre	New York	04/29/1856	08/27/1862	18	408	N	
Ulmer, John Frederick	25	Wuerttemberg	Y	Rotterdam	New York	??/04/1848	11/22/1849	23	361	N	
Ulmer, Michael	30	Wuerttemberg	Y	Liverpool	New York	08/01/1852	04/04/1856	26	436	N	
Ulmschneider, Max	30	Germany	Y	Havre	New York	08/02/1886	08/21/1893			Y	
Ulrich, Adolph	27	Hanover	Y	Bremen	New York	04/28/1851	10/04/1858	17	49	N	
Ulrich, Anton	??	Switzerland	Y	?	?	?	05/26/1894			Y	
Ulrich, Charles	31	France	Y	Havre	New York	06/08/1852	03/27/1856	26	355	N	
Ultsch, Kasper	30	Germany	Y	Antwerp	New York	06/03/1881	11/06/1886			Y	
Umbach, Joseph Henry	29	Wuerttemberg	Y	Havre	New York	??/16/1847	11/13/1849	23	339	N	
Umberg, Frank	24	Switzerland	Y	?	New York	08/08/1891	10/29/1892			Y	
Umfeid, Charles Theodore	30	Wuerttemberg	Y	Havre	New York	06/12/1853	05/08/1860	27	186	N	
Umgelter, Fred	27	Germany	Y	Antwerp	New York	02/26/1881	03/27/1888			Y	
Umhalt, Julius	30	Denmark	Y	Liverpool	New York	08/01/1857	05/30/1859	17	437	N	
Ummethun, Gerhard Willia	23	Hanover	Y	Bremen	Baltimore	12/20/1853	08/21/1855	11	467	N	
Undarstadt, August	21	Prussia	Y	Bremen	New York	09/21/1858	05/09/1859	17	406	N	
Unertl, Andreas	41	Bavaria	Y	Bremen	New York	09/??/1848	11/??/1849	23	334	N	
Unger, Anton	25	Austria	Y	Bremen	Baltimore	04/10/1882	08/18/1885			Y	
Unger, Fritz	27	Germany	Y	Bremen	New York	02/02/1890	09/12/1895			Y	
Unger, Hayman	32	Germany	Y	Hamburg	New York	05/15/1892	07/11/1896			Y	
Unger, John	39	Bavaria	Y	Havre	New Orleans	11/15/1846	09/10/1855	11	522	N	
Unger, John	30	Germany	Y	Bremen	New York	04/30/1878	08/23/1882			Y	
Unger, John	30	Germany	N	Bremen	New York	04/30/1878	?			Y	
Unger, Joseph	29	Austria	Y	Bremen	New York	10/20/1895	10/18/1899			Y	
Unger, Julius	34	Austria	Y	Bremen	New York	02/25/1890	10/18/1893			Y	
Unger, Thomas	35	Austria	Y	Bremen	Baltimore	05/31/1866	10/14/1882			Y	
Ungethuem, Ernst L.	31	Germany	Y	Hamburg	New York	04/13/1881	02/19/1883			Y	
Ungruhe, Carl	23	Germany	Y	Hamburg	New York	03/30/1888	08/31/1892			Y	
Unkraut, Bernard	29	Oldenburg	Y	Bremen	Galveston	01/05/1847	04/05/1852	24	384	N	
Unkraut, Herman	33	Oldenburg	Y	Bremen	Baltimore	08/15/1844	08/19/1848	22	208	N	
Unkraut, William	56	Germany	Y	Bremen	New York	05/??/1868	09/05/1887			Y	
Unmusig, Joseph	36	Baden	Y	London	New York	08/??/1853	09/20/1855	13	76	N	
Unnewehr, Frederick	24	Hanover	Y	Bremen	Baltimore	11/08/1847	11/15/1848	1	303	N	
Unser, Herman G.	31	Germany	Y	Bremen	Baltimore	05/17/1883	02/12/1891			Y	
Unsling, Nicholas	40	Bavaria	Y	Havre	New York	08/??/1846	10/29/1850	2	330	N	
Unsser, John Gottlieb	28	Wurttemberg	Y	Havre	New York	12/22/1851	09/21/18??	15	295	N	
Untied, Nicholas	33	Prussia	Y	Bremen	Baltimore	06/13/1860	10/08/1860	27	419	N	
Uphoff, George	24	Germany	Y	Amsterdam	New York	08/09/1881	05/26/1887			Y	
Uphous, Bernard	25	Prussia	Y	Liverpool	New Orleans	12/28/1848	03/26/1853	7	403	N	
Upkaus, Henry	25	Hanover	Y	Bremen	New Orleans	12/20/1843	10/05/1848	22	436	N	
Upping, Heinrich	29	Germany	Y	Rotterdam	Jersey City	04/29/1887	06/02/1890			Y	
Uprichard, George	51	Ireland	Y	Liverpool	New York	09/06/1848	02/16/1852	24	116	N	

CITIZENSHIP RECORDS

APPLICANT	AGE	COUNTRY OF ORIGIN	DEC	DEPART PORT	ENTRY PORT	ARRIVE DATE	DEC DATE	VOL	PG.	FLD	NAT DATE
Uptmoor, Henry	32	Germany	Y	Bremen	Baltimore	08/23/1883	10/28/1887			Y	
Urbahn, Joshua	25	Prussia	Y	Bremen	New York	05/01/1849	01/30/1850	2	13	N	
Urban, Albert	40	Russia	Y	Hamburg	New York	08/20/1879	08/29/1894			Y	
Urban, Franz	30	Austria	Y	Bremen	New York	05/30/1881	06/13/1887			Y	
Urbanski, John	35	Germany	Y	Bremen	Baltimore	09/17/1883	03/01/1894			Y	
Urbin, Thomas	??	Germany	Y	?	?	?	10/05/1886			Y	
Urlage, Arnold	33	Oldenburg	Y	Bremen	New Orleans	10/20/1846	10/14/1848	1	219	N	
Urlage, Henry	48	Oldenburg	Y	Bremen	New Orleans	10/28/1845	10/14/1848	1	222	N	
Urler, Ludwig	??	Prussia	Y	Bremen	Baltimore	09/27/1847	06/10/1852	25	227	N	
Urmacher, John	32	Prussia	Y	Bremen	New York	10/13/1854	10/29/1858	17	170	N	
Usborne, H. J.	42	England	N	Liverpool	Quebec	09/27/1857	?			Y	
Uth, Franz	23	Germany	Y	Rotterdam	New York	11/16/1881	11/10/1884			Y	
Utheel, Henry	40	Germany	N	Bremen	New York	04/20/1873	?			Y	
Vagifhauser, John	39	Baden	Y	Bremen	Baltimore	04/30/1857	05/25/1861	18	179	N	
Vahl, William	29	Prussia	Y	Hamburg	New Orleans	11/15/1857	12/01/1858	17	368	N	
Vahlsing, Conrad	40	Prussia	Y	Bremen	New Orleans	??/14/1845	01/02/1850	23	457	N	
Vale, Mike	??	Wales	N	?	?	07/26/1868				Y	10/20/1892
Valensky, Nathan	48	Russia	Y	Bremen	Baltimore	11/23/1891	01/08/1900			Y	
Valentin, Karl	21	Germany	Y	Rotterdam	New York	01/05/1892	04/06/1894			Y	
Valentine, John	54	Germany	N	Bremen	New York	12/??/1851	?			Y	
Valken, Adrian G.	34	Holland	Y	Amsterdam	New York	06/18/1881	10/24/1888			Y	
Van Agthoven, Anthony	36	Holland	Y	Rotterdam	New Orleans	01/15/1848	11/20/1857	16	39	N	
Van Dokkum, John Joseph	40	France	Y	Havre	New York	10/19/1849	09/26/1854	12	178	N	
Van Dokkum, Louis Aime	30	France	Y	Havre	New York	10/19/1849	09/26/1854	12	179	N	
Van Driel, Cornelius	36	Holland	Y	Havre	New Orleans	07/01/1852	04/05/1856	26	445	N	
Van Erp, Adrian	31	Holland	Y	Amsterdam	New York	05/12/1884	10/27/1892	19	394	N	
Van Erp, Adrian	31	Holland	Y	Amsterdam	New York	05/12/1884	10/27/1892			Y	
Van Groeninger, U. J. K.	21	Holland	Y	Amsterdam	New York	03/24/1857	10/08/1860	27	438	N	
Van Gulpen, Louis J.	26	Germany	Y	Havre	New York	04/12/1882	04/13/1885			Y	
Van Harxsen, Everet John	28	Holland	Y	New Diepe	Baltimore	10/15/1853	12/10/1855	13	301	N	
Van Hekke, Leendert	??	Netherlands	Y	?	?	?	11/02/1891			Y	
Van Hertum, William	44	Holland	Y	Antwerp	New York	05/07/1857	11/21/1859	17	477	N	
Van Kooten, Herman	26	Holland	Y	Liverpool	New York	06/01/1853	01/04/1856	13	423	N	
Van Krevel, John	54	Holland	Y	Liverpool	New York	06/05/1865	09/09/1897			Y	
Van Nes, Johannes	38	Germany	Y	Bremen	New York	06/??/1864	05/10/1882			Y	
Van Stroke, Henry	22	Hanover	Y	Bremen	Baltimore	06/01/1853	10/02/1856	14	144	N	
Van Vooren, J. B.	34	Holland	Y	Antwerp	New York	06/09/1893	10/01/1897			Y	
Van West, Abram	66	Holland	Y	Amsterdam	New York	10/09/1851	11/07/1893			Y	
Van Worman, George Robin	45	Canada	Y	Brantford	Detroit	??/??/1880	11/07/1900			Y	
Van de Nienwenhuysen, Ge	34	Holland	Y	Amsterdam	New York	05/21/1881	12/28/1885			Y	
Van den Driessche, Charl	35	Belgium	Y	Antwerp	New York	10/??/1842	09/12/1854	13	12	N	
Van der Kolh, Anton	??	Holland	Y	?	?	?	04/12/1895			Y	
Van der Meulen, John	24	Germany	Y	Bremen	Baltimore	03/27/1887	11/26/1887			Y	
Van der Mey, John	??	Netherlands	Y	?	?	?	04/28/1888			Y	
Van, John Lee	65	Ireland	N	Liverpool	New York	06/??/1847	?	28	427	N	10/02/1856
VanDamme, Francis	26	Holland	Y	Liverpool	New York	07/02/1853	09/27/1858	16	116	N	
Vance, Thomas	??	?	Y	?	Philadelphia	07/05/18??	11/03/1856	14	444	N	
Vancleeff, Hyman	37	Hanover	Y	Hamburg	New York	08/01/1857	09/01/1862	18	433	N	
Vander Molen, Nicholas	??	Netherlands	Y	?	?	?	11/07/1898			Y	
Vanderkiste, Charles Wil	28	England	Y	Canada	Detroit	07/06/1855	07/25/1857	15	130	N	
Vanderpal, Seitre	49	Holland	Y	Amsterdam	New Orleans	12/23/1848	02/15/1849	23	139	N	
Vandervegt, John	30	Holland	Y	Amsterdam	New York	05/29/1855	07/05/1860	27	206	N	
Vanderwalle, Charles	25	Belgium	Y	Antwerp	New York	09/02/1877	10/12/1880			Y	
Vandokkum, John Joseph P	40	France	Y	Havre	New York	10/19/1849	09/26/1854	10	239	N	
Vandokkum, Louis Aime	30	France	Y	Havre	New York	10/19/1849	09/26/1854	10	240	N	
Vanoso, Dominico	52	Italy	Y	Marseilles	New York	06/15/1882	08/08/1892			Y	
Vanseton, Julius	??	Germany	Y	?	?	?	05/07/1894			Y	
Varian, Amos	32	Ireland	Y	Liverpool	Philadelphia	05/01/1853	09/30/1854	12	263	N	
Varian, Amos J.	32	Ireland	Y	Liverpool	Philadelphia	05/01/1853	09/30/1854	10	324	N	

CITIZENSHIP RECORDS

APPLICANT	AGE	COUNTRY OF ORIGIN	DEC	DEPART PORT	ENTRY PORT	ARRIVE DATE	DEC DATE	VOL	PG.	FLD	NAT DATE
Varnau, Heinrich	23	Germany	Y	Bremen	New York	07/19/1881	11/19/1885			Y	
Varnau, Heinrich	27	Germany	Y	Bremen	New York	03/22/1879	09/24/1887			Y	
Varnau, Wilhelm	27	Prussia	Y	Bremen	New Orleans	04/27/1855	02/02/1857	14	523	N	
Varnhorn, Ben (Bernard?)	32	Germany	Y	Bremen	Baltimore	09/02/1883	10/24/1887			Y	
Varnhorn, Bernard	32	Oldenburg	Y	Bremen	Baltimore	11/20/1847	05/06/1850	3	48	N	
Varrelmann, Adolf D.	23	Germany	Y	Bremen	New York	01/15/1884	03/15/1887			Y	
Vaske, Fred. B.	27	Germany	Y	Bremen	New York	04/06/1882	09/23/1885			Y	
Vaske, Henry	40	Germany	Y	Bremen	Baltimore	08/??/1864	10/13/1884			Y	
Vasmer, William	46	Prussia	Y	Bremen	New Orleans	12/24/1852	02/02/1856	26	7	N	
Vater, Louis	31	Germany	N	Rotterdam	New York	08/15/1867	?			Y	
Vatter, Andy	23	Germany	Y	?	?	06/??/1881	12/07/1882			Y	
Vatter, Henry	52	Germany	N	Havre	New Orleans	03/20/1853	?			Y	
Vecker, Frederick Emil L	24	Saxe Meininge	Y	Bremen	New York	11/16/1853	11/16/1858	17	334	N	
Vedder, Charles J.	40	Austria	N	Austria	Cincinnati?	10/25/1863	?			Y	
Veelmann, Theodore	26	Germany	Y	Antwerp	New York	07/04/1888	03/02/1894			Y	
Veeneman, Christian	43	Holland	Y	Rotterdam	New York	05/28/1849	08/15/1851	4	138	N	
Veeneman, John Bernardus	26	Holland	Y	Rotterdam	New York	09/27/1855	09/29/1856	14	425	N	
Veeneman, Yan	26	Holland	Y	New Diep	Baltimore	10/09/1853	09/29/1856	14	25	N	
Veenemanm, Herman M.	23	Holland	Y	Amsterdam	Baltimore	10/06/1853	09/29/1856	14	424	N	
Veenemann, John Henry	64	Holland	Y	Rotterdam	New York	09/27/1855	09/29/1856	14	7	N	
Veerkamp, Bernard	69	Germany	N	Bremen	New York	07/??/1837	10/??/1839	28	66	N	10/??/1842
Vehrkamp, John Gerhard	34	Hanover	Y	Bremen	Baltimore	04/27/1849	08/15/1855	11	434	N	
Veid, Michael	57	Germany	N	Havre	New York	03/05/1847	?			Y	
Veigel, Henry	31	Wuerttemberg	Y	Liverpool	New York	07/18/1856	04/19/1860	27	168	N	
Veigele, William	25	Wurttemberg	Y	Havre	New York	05/16/1848	05/01/1854	8	298	N	
Veigele, William	25	Wurttemberg	Y	Havre	New York	05/10/1848	05/01/1854	9	170	N	
Veit, Philipp	33	Bavaria	Y	Havre	New York	11/??/1847	10/29/1851	4	436	N	
Veith, Jacob	24	Germany	Y	Bremen	Baltimore	05/17/1893	11/05/1898			Y	
Veith, Sigmund	??	Bavaria	Y	Havre	New York	??/10/1849	12/04/1850	2	335	N	
Veitk, Gottlieb	25	Baden	Y	London	New York	07/01/1850	01/20/1852	24	40	N	
Veldman, Henry	48	Holland	Y	Rotterdam	New York	06/23/1846	08/14/1848	22	105	N	
Velte, William	24	Wurttemberg	Y	Bremen	New York	12/21/1855	12/29/1857	16	277	N	
Velten, Anselm	25	Germany	Y	Rotterdam	New York	05/14/1882	08/22/1887			Y	
Velten, John	36	Mecklenburg S	Y	Liverpool	New York	07/??/1851	09/20/1855	13	82	N	
Venditto, Cosmo	40	Italy	Y	Naples	New York	04/15/1883	12/12/1888			Y	
Veneeman, Herman	22	Holland	Y	Rotterdam	New York	09/27/1855	09/29/1856	14	8	N	
Venghaus, William	33	Hanover	Y	Bremen	New Orleans	12/25/1845	10/02/1854	10	361	N	
Venghaus, William	33	Hanover	Y	Bremen	New Orleans	12/25/1845	10/02/1854	12	300	N	
Vennemeier, August	30	Germany	Y	Amsterdam	New York	10/15/1889	11/11/1901			Y	
Vennemeier, J. Henry	24	Germany	Y	Bremen	Baltimore	03/26/1884	09/16/1889			Y	
Venninger, William	24	Baden	Y	Havre	New York	06/??/1849	03/22/1853	7	368	N	
Ventker, John	31	Prussia	Y	Bremen	Baltimore	09/18/1856	01/28/1857	14	517	N	
Ventola, Saverio	38	Italy	Y	Palermo	New Orleans	12/24/1884	02/06/1889			Y	
Verbarg, Carl Diedrich	22	Hanover	Y	Bremen	Baltimore	05/01/1849	12/23/1851	4	549	N	
Verges, August	48	Prussia	Y	Bremen	New York	04/14/1854	05/22/1854	8	491	N	
Verges, August	48	Prussia	Y	Bremen	New York	04/14/1854	05/22/1854	9	365	N	
Verhaegen, William	31	Holland	N	Amsterdam	New York	04/??/1876	?			Y	
Verhage, Henry	57	Germany	N	Bremen	New Orleans	11/??/1851	?			Y	
Verhein, August	29	Schwerin	Y	Hamburg	New York	08/15/1854	03/10/1856	26	177	N	
Verhoever, John Jacob	42	Prussia	Y	Rotterdam	New York	10/12/1848	09/29/1856	14	426	N	
Verkamp, Gerhard Henry	60	Germany	N	Bremen	New Orleans	12/25/1846	?	28	394	N	09/15/1854
Verkamp, J. Bernhard	54	Germany	Y	Bremen	New York	06/11/1866	12/26/1891			Y	
Vernezobre, Edward	48	Prussia	Y	Havre	New Orleans	??/01/1849	12/??/1850	2	417	N	
Versteegene, Peter	28	Prussia	Y	Rotterdam	New York	06/27/1847	01/06/1851	2	468	N	
Verwold, Henry	21	Germany	Y	Bremen	?	06/26/1881	10/31/1884			Y	
Vesay, Luke	24	Ireland	Y	Liverpool	New York	10/25/1847	01/28/1950	2	5	N	
Vesay, Michael	28	Ireland	Y	Liverpool	New York	05/28/1842	01/28/1850	2	4	N	
Veser, Anton	53	Germany	Y	?	New York	??/??/1882	11/04/1884			Y	
Vester, Peter	52	Bavaria	N	Havre	New York	06/05/1854	?			Y	

CITIZENSHIP RECORDS

APPLICANT	AGE	COUNTRY OF ORIGIN	DEC	DEPART PORT	ENTRY PORT	ARRIVE DATE	DEC DATE	VOL	PG.	FLD	NAT DATE
Vestring, H.	30	Germany	Y	Antwerp	New York	09/14/1881	01/07/1887			Y	
Vetter, Casper	32	Wurttemberg	Y	Liverpool	New York	06/14/1852	07/09/1855	11	365	N	
Vetter, George	??	Saxe Meininge	Y	Bremen	New York	??/18/1851	04/16/1855	11	245	N	
Vetter, George	30	Germany	Y	Bremen	Baltimore	05/28/1889	10/13/1892			Y	
Vetter, John	30	Baden	Y	Havre	New Orleans	01/12/1849	10/13/1851	4	219	N	
Vetter, Karl Franz	31	Germany	Y	Bremen	Baltimore	12/23/1891	10/15/1900			Y	
Vetter, Michael	39	Germany	Y	Hamburg	New York	09/18/1883	03/28/1891	19	323	N	
Vetter, Richard	??	Germany	Y	?	?	?	11/09/1886			Y	
Vetter, Wolfgang	23	Germany	Y	Bremen	New York	09/01/1882	11/16/1882			Y	
Vey, August Edmund	27	Saxe Coburg	Y	Bremen	New York	08/??/1848	11/04/1851	4	488	N	
Veysey, Wm. Henry	27	England	Y	Liverpool	New York	10/20/18??	03/07/1853	7	307	N	
Vickers, Patrick	25	Ireland	Y	Liverpool	New York	07/02/1851	08/20/1855	11	462	N	
Victor, Pernet	21	France	Y	Havre	New York	06/20/1861	06/18/1862	18	352	N	
Vidale, John	??	Italy	Y	?	?	?	06/15/1893			Y	
Viehmann, John	34	Germany	Y	Bremen	New York	06/14/1880	10/29/1885			Y	
Viektor, Bernard Diedric	28	Hanover	Y	Bremen	Baltimore	06/12/1844	07/??/1848	22	7	N	
Vielhauer, Fred	19	Germany	Y	Hamburg	New York	05/23/1888	02/28/1891			Y	
Vieoch, Sebastian	30	Baden	Y	Havre	New York	11/06/1851	10/08/1857	15	372	N	
Viergutz, Albert	28	Germany	Y	Stetten	New York	10/13/1881	12/26/1885			Y	
Viergutz, Herman	35	Germany	Y	Bremen	Baltimore	07/18/1883	10/27/1886			Y	
Viering, Christian	29	Waldeck	Y	Bremen	New York	08/14/1854	01/18/1860	27	59	N	
Vieson, Joseph	22	Oldenburg	Y	Bremen	New York	05/03/1858	07/01/1861	18	201	N	
Vieth, Ignatz	33	Hungary	Y	London	New York	03/15/1851	03/03/1852	24	221	N	
Viethorn, Jacob	34	Hanover	Y	Bremen	Baltimore	11/01/1856	01/03/1860	27	21	N	
Vietmeier, Ernst	21	Germany	Y	Bremen	Baltimore	09/21/1881	02/20/1882			Y	
Vigranskey, Isaac	50	Russia	Y	Hamburg	New York	08/16/1880	10/25/1890	19	300	N	
Vigransky, Isaac	50	Russia	Y	Hamburg	New York	08/16/1880	10/25/1890			Y	
Vigranstey, Alech	30	Poland	Y	?	New York	05/26/1883	07/23/1889			Y	
Vile, Thomas	42	England	Y	Liverpool	Philadelphia	03/22/1854	03/15/1858	16	408	N	
Villing, John	22	Germany	Y	Havre	New York	10/18/1891	10/04/1894			Y	
Vincenzo, Le Verde	46	Italy	Y	Palermo	New York	10/17/1888	10/23/1893	21	29	N	
Vinths, John Diederich	39	Hanover	Y	Bremen	Baltimore	08/01/1838	02/09/1852	24	75	N	
Vintrop, David	40	Hanover	Y	Bremen	New Orleans	12/16/1845	10/02/1854	10	344	N	
Vintrop, David	40	Hanover	Y	Bremen	New Orleans	12/16/1845	10/02/1854	12	283	N	
Vinzanz, John	27	Switzerland	Y	Havre	New York	12/09/1851	01/13/1853	7	43	N	
Virigge, John Frederick	50	Hanover	Y	Bremen	New Orleans	12/01/1844	08/07/1848	22	67	N	
Visner, John (Wismer?)	??	Sweden/Norway	Y	?	?	?	12/27/1893			Y	
Vissing, Simon A.	25	Hanover	Y	Bremen	New Orleans	12/02/1849	11/30/1861	18	232	N	
Viughn, Patrick	35	Ireland	Y	Liverpool	New York	03/17/1850	11/02/1860	27	556	N	
Vocke, Deiderick John	24	Hanover	Y	Bremen	Baltimore	06/01/1850	10/09/1854	6	51	N	
Vocke, Diederich John	24	Hanover	Y	Bremen	Baltimore	06/01/1850	10/09/1854	11	52	N	
Vocke, George H.	16	Germany	N	?	New York	00/00/1882				Y	10/28/1887
Voe der Mark, Ruben	26	Prussia	Y	Bremen	Baltimore	12/15/1854	09/12/1860	27	364	N	
Voegtle, Joseph	26	Germany	Y	Havre	New York	10/27/1881	04/04/1887			Y	
Voelckel, Charles	24	Bavaria	Y	Hamburg	New York	06/11/1869	06/04/1872	18	497	N	
Voelckel, Charles	39	Germany	N	Hamburg	New York	06/??/1869	?			Y	
Voelkel, Charles M.	23	Germany	Y	Hamburg	New York	01/19/1891	01/13/1893			Y	
Voelkel, Otto	??	Germany	Y	?	?	?	08/15/1890			Y	
Voelker, George	27	Germany	Y	Bremen	New York	05/09/1891	04/22/1892			Y	
Voelker, Gotfried	28	Bavaria	Y	Havre	New Orleans	04/13/1847	10/06/1854	12	425	N	
Voelker, Gottfried	28	Bavaria	Y	Havre	New Orleans	04/13/1847	10/06/1854	10	486	N	
Voelker, John Phillip	59	Bavaria	Y	Antwerp	New Orleans	01/01/1847	06/03/1852	25	180	N	
Voelker, Martin	32	Bavaria	Y	Rotterdam	New York	07/04/1849	10/18/1851	4	330	N	
Voeller, Charles	27	Germany	Y	Bremen	New York	09/17/1889	10/15/1891			Y	
Voellmecke, Frederick	50	Prussia	Y	Bremen	New York	01/05/1854	09/28/1858	16	108	N	
Voemer, Edward	26	Germany	Y	Bremen	Baltimore	05/26/1882	10/03/1885	19	9	N	
Vofs, Julius	25	Hanover	Y	Bremen	Baltimore	??/15/1848	03/24/1851	3	316	N	
Vogedes, Bernard	34	Prussia	Y	Bremen	New York	09/19/1853	03/17/1856	26	217	N	
Vogel, Adolf	31	Wurttemberg	Y	London	New York	11/04/1851	09/18/1855	13	65	N	

CITIZENSHIP RECORDS

APPLICANT	AGE	COUNTRY OF ORIGIN	DEC	DEPART PORT	ENTRY PORT	ARRIVE DATE	DEC DATE	VOL	PG.	FLD	NAT DATE
Vogel, Adolph	40	Germany	Y	Hamburg	New York	05/02/1881	11/15/1884			Y	
Vogel, Anton	40	Sweden	Y	Havre	New York	06/??/1839	11/??/1849	23	366	N	
Vogel, August	27	Brunswick	Y	Bremen	New York	12/01/1858	03/31/1862	18	293	N	
Vogel, Baltheser	38	Wuerttenberg	Y	Rotterdam	New York	09/11/1851	06/17/1852	25	286	N	
Vogel, Charles	36	Saxe Altenbur	Y	Bremen	New York	07/04/1854	07/31/1861	18	212	N	
Vogel, Charles	25	Bavaria	Y	Hamburg	New York	06/10/1847	02/22/1849	23	254	N	
Vogel, Elias	45	Germany	Y	Havre	New York	04/??/1866	10/??/1870			Y	
Vogel, Elias	45	Germany	N	Havre	New York	04/??/1866	?			Y	
Vogel, Ernst Adolf	51	Germany	Y	Bremen	New York	06/14/1884	07/16/1887			Y	
Vogel, Fred W.	30	Germany	Y	Bremen	New York	04/09/1879	01/28/1886			Y	
Vogel, Henry	34	Germany	Y	Bremen	New York	05/22/1885	10/25/1895			Y	
Vogel, John	32	Hesse Darmsta	Y	Antwerp	New Orleans	09/01/1848	03/25/1851	3	333	N	
Vogel, John	27	Switzerland	Y	Havre	New Orleans	02/07/1849	03/25/1853	7	391	N	
Vogel, John	45	Germany	Y	Antwerp	New York	09/??/1881	08/06/1886			Y	
Vogel, John W. H.	23	Germany	Y	Antwerp	New York	08/27/1893	11/26/1894			Y	
Vogel, Ludwig	25	Waldeck	Y	Bremen	New York	12/12/1853	09/01/1857	15	214	N	
Vogel, Ludwig	24	Baden	Y	London	New York	07/04/1849	05/20/1852	25	70	N	
Vogel, Oscar Adolf	26	Germany	Y	Amsterdam	New York	02/24/1882	07/16/1887			Y	
Vogel, Rudolph	34	Germany	Y	Bremen	New York	09/16/1891	10/19/1893	21	27	N	
Vogel, Vicktor Richard	24	Germany	Y	Bremen	New York	06/14/1884	07/16/1887			Y	
Vogel, Xavier	33	Bavaria	Y	Havre	New Orleans	12/19/1851	01/10/1856	13	441	N	
Vogel, Zacharias	55	Germany	Y	Antwerp	New York	07/14/1882	09/23/1887			Y	
Vogelbach, Fred A.	25	Germany	Y	Havre	New York	06/02/1880	06/01/1885			Y	
Vogele, Franz Xaver	49	Germany	Y	Havre	New York	04/??/1862	10/??/1864			Y	
Vogelgesang, Paul	23	Germany	Y	Antwerp	New York	03/27/1885	09/24/1888			Y	
Vogelpohl, Henry	29	Germany	Y	Bremen	Baltimore	05/18/1892	10/22/1897			Y	
Vogelpohl, John Henry	33	Hanover	Y	Bremen	Baltimore	07/02/1858	01/31/1860	27	84	N	
Vogelsang, John	22	Germany	Y	Bremen	Baltimore	05/31/1882	10/06/1886	19	46	N	
Vogelsang, John	22	Germany	Y	Bremen	Baltimore	05/31/1882	10/06/1886			Y	
Vogelsang, Louis	34	Germany	Y	?	New York	??/??/1881	11/01/1889			Y	
Voges, Gerhard Henry	38	Hanover	Y	Bremen	New Orlean	10/25/1856	03/01/1858	16	352	N	
Vogler, Edward	31	Prussia	Y	Hamburg	New York	09/15/1858	01/22/1862	18	247	N	
Vogt, Andrew	68	Baden	Y	Rotterdam	New York	12/30/1847	08/02/1848	22	47	N	
Vogt, Christopher	32	Saxe Weimar	Y	Hamburg	New York	07/??/1858	02/05/1861	18	89	N	
Vogt, Henry	24	Prussia	Y	Bremen	New York	03/15/1849	06/14/1851	3	377	N	
Vogt, Henry	35	Germany	Y	Liverpool	Philadelphia	06/06/1883	10/04/1893			Y	
Vogt, Herman	27	Oldenburg	Y	Bremen	New Orleans	11/18/1849	09/29/1856	14	37	N	
Vogt, Joseph	25	Baden	Y	Havre	New Orleans	01/29/1852	09/13/1852	25	469	N	
Vogt, Martin	21	France	Y	Havre	New Orleans	02/23/1855	04/27/1857	15	92	N	
Vogt, Richard G.	25	Germany	Y	Bremen	New York	05/15/1882	06/08/1887			Y	
Vogt, William F.	31	Germany	Y	Bremen	New York	06/??/1873	12/20/1886			Y	
Vogth, John (Fogth?)	40	Baden	Y	Havre	New York	10/24/1845	08/10/1848	22	87	N	
Vogtmann, John Hermann	29	Hanover	Y	Bremen	New orleans	11/25/1853	01/08/1856	13	431	N	
Vohs, Herman	25	Prussia	Y	Bremen	New York	09/22/1848	01/05/1850	23	463	N	
Vohseler, Martin	29	Germany	Y	Rotterdam	New York	09/02/1885	04/10/1889			Y	
Voigt, Bernard	24	Hanover	Y	Bremen	New York	12/25/1855	12/26/1857	16	251	N	
Voigt, Casper	??	Bavaria	Y	?	New York	11/01/1851	11/05/1856	14	476	N	
Voigt, Christian Samuel	58	Hesse Darmsta	Y	Havre	New York	09/30/1854	10/06/1857	15	362	N	
Voigt, Godfrey	29	Austria	Y	Bremen	New York	01/04/1843	01/12/1849	1	403	N	
Voigtlander, Ernst	43	Germany	Y	Bremen	Baltimore	09/23/1882	02/11/1886			Y	
Vois, Hisil	22	Romania	Y	Liverpool	New York	08/26/1900	12/28/1900			Y	
Voit, Herman	33	Baden	Y	Havre	New York	06/10/1850	09/04/1852	25	354	N	
Volck, Henry	32	Hesse Darmsta	Y	Havre	New York	09/30/1855	03/11/1856	26	181	N	
Volckmer, John	24	Germany	Y	Rotterdam	Detroit	01/22/1893	09/16/1893			Y	
Volk, Charles	??	?	N	?	?	?	?			Y	
Volk, Phillip	33	Baden	Y	Liverpool	New York	10/02/1852	05/30/1854	9	453	N	
Volk, Phillip	33	Baden	Y	Liverpool	New York	10/02/1852	05/30/1854	10	36	N	
Volk, Thomas	34	Baden	Y	Havre	New York	07/12/1852	09/17/1855	13	43	N	
Volkelt, Charles August W	31	Prussia	Y	Hamburg	New York	12/08/1849	07/12/1851	3	529	N	

CITIZENSHIP RECORDS

APPLICANT	AGE	COUNTRY OF ORIGIN	DEC	DEPART PORT	ENTRY PORT	ARRIVE DATE	DEC DATE	VOL	PG.	FLD	NAT DATE
Volkerding, Joseph	27	Germany	Y	Bremen	New York	05/08/1888	10/18/1892			Y	
Volkert, Matthaens	33	Germany	Y	Bremen	New York	05/22/1884	10/23/1891			Y	
Volkert, Philip	56	Baden	Y	Havre	New York	08/??/1851	11/07/1856	14	503	N	
Volkmar, Joseph	28	Prussia	Y	Bremen	Baltimore	06/13/1853	05/22/1856	26	528	N	
Volkmer, Edward	26	Germany	Y	Bremen	Baltimore	05/26/1882	10/03/1885			Y	
Voll, Jacob	74	Germany	Y	Bremen	New York	07/??/1868	10/??/1868			Y	
Voll, Jacob	74	Germany	N	Bremen	New York	07/??/1868	?			Y	
Voll, Joseph	35	Germany	Y	Bremen	New York	08/29/1880	03/03/1886			Y	
Vollath, George	31	Germany	Y	Bremen	New York	01/16/1882	10/17/1887			Y	
Vollmer, Charles	35	Germany	Y	Bremen	New York	05/01/1880	05/12/1893			Y	
Vollmer, George M.	32	Germany	Y	Antwerp	New York	07/25/1892	02/27/1893			Y	
Vollmer, Henry Jr.	??	Germany	N	?	?	06/00/1869				Y	10/28/1892
Vollmer, Jacob	30	Wurtemberg	Y	London	New York	07/04/1849	09/07/1852	25	401	N	
Vollmer, John	26	Wurttemberg	Y	Havre	New York	10/25/1852	09/13/1855	13	21	N	
Vollmer, Louis	27	Germany	Y	Bremen	New York	09/28/1879	01/18/1887			Y	
Vollmer, Valentine	27	Bavaria	Y	Bremen	New Orleans	05/??/1854	10/26/1858	17	117	N	
Vollmer, Valentine	32	Germany	Y	Havre	New York	05/26/1881	11/26/1886			Y	
Vollweiler, Jacob	26	Germany	Y	Amsterdam	New York	03/18/1881	08/09/1884			Y	
Volmer, Charles Joseph	21	Prussia	Y	Antwerp	New York	08/24/1850	07/11/1851	3	521	N	
Volmer, William	27	Germany	Y	Havre	New York	08/19/1888	09/18/1893			Y	
Volp, Edward	25	Hesse Darmsta	Y	Bremen	New York	05/10/1853	09/13/1855	13	15	N	
Volpert, Frank	28	Bavaria	Y	Bremen	New Orleans	10/12/1847	06/19/1851	3	421	N	
Voltermann, Fred	41	Germany	Y	Bremen	Baltimore	06/02/1885	03/03/1890			Y	
Voltmer, Fritz	27	Germany	Y	Bremen	Baltimore	03/01/1883	08/28/1883			Y	
Voltz, George	??	Baden	Y	Havre	New Orleans	02/27/1847	10/09/1848	22	511	N	
Volz, George	36	Bavaria	Y	Havre	New York	08/18/1854	08/24/1857	15	174	N	
Volz, John	54	Germany	Y	Bremen	New York	05/15/1869	10/19/1893			Y	
Volz, Nicholas	40	Baden	Y	Havre	New Orleans	10/??/1851	09/09/1852	25	431	N	
Vom Steeg, Alex	26	Germany	Y	Antwerp	New York	07/29/1889	08/09/1893			Y	
Vomaux, Auguste	25	France	Y	Havre	New York	05/15/1847	11/05/1852	6	357	N	
Von Amelunxen, Theodore	28	Prussia	Y	Bremen	Baltimore	06/06/1855	12/14/1855	13	313	N	
Von Bargen, Jacob Henry	21	Hamburg	Y	Hamburg	New York	07/17/1851	05/11/1854	8	422	N	
Von Behren, Christian	30	Prussia	Y	Bremen	New York	04/13/1847	04/29/1850	3	25	N	
Von Benin, Karl	??	Germany	Y	?	?	?	07/12/1892			Y	
Von Benken, Joseph	23	Germany	Y	Antwerp	New York	07/05/1900	09/13/1900			Y	
Von Bergen, Jacob Henry	21	Hamburg	Y	Hamburg	New York	07/17/1851	05/11/1854	9	295	N	
Von Bokem, Bernard	21	Hanover	Y	Bremen	New York	05/21/1854	10/01/1856	14	91	N	
Von Brinkhorst, Anthony	27	Holland	Y	Rotterdam	New York	09/13/1852	03/24/1856	26	283	N	
Von Cleeff, Joseph	41	Germany	Y	Bremen	New York	05/21/1865	11/30/1878			Y	
Von Derheide, Joseph	26	Oldenburg	Y	Bremen	Baltimore	05/??/1850	10/13/1857	15	414	N	
Von Gent, Fritz	25	Germany	Y	Antwerp	New York	02/28/1880	10/13/1881			Y	
Von Gluchoroski, Jacob	25	Prussia	Y	Liverpool	New York	10/01/1854	12/19/1855	13	334	N	
Von Hone, Henry	33	Germany	Y	?	Baltimore	??/??/1880	11/03/1884			Y	
Von Horn, Paul A. O.	27	Russia	Y	?	New York	07/11/1891	11/13/1893			Y	
Von Lukowitz, Julius	34	Germany	Y	Hamburg	New York	04/05/1882	04/20/1885			Y	
Von Monderode, John Bodo	31	Prussia	Y	Bremen	New York	10/10/1865	03/02/1872	18	467	N	
Von Muegge, John Fred	28	Germany	Y	?	?	?	10/25/1876			Y	
Von Otte, William	24	Germany	Y	Bremen	Baltimore	09/14/1892	05/14/1896			Y	
Von Pein, John Henry	32	Hanover	Y	Hamburg	New York	09/15/1856	12/26/1857	16	262	N	
Von Pein, Otto	27	Hanover	Y	Hamburg	New York	09/14/1856	12/26/1857	16	250	N	
Von Pelzel, David	27	Holland	Y	Rotterdam	New York	02/23/1881	02/27/1884			Y	
Von Suhrte, Peter Henry	58	Oldenburg	Y	Bremen	New Orleans	12/29/1847	04/04/1853	8	51	N	
Von Wahlde, Herman	21	Germany	Y	Bremen	?	03/17/1866	02/26/1877			Y	
Von Wyk, J.	??	Holland	N	Rotterdam	?	02/20/1868	04/??/1870			Y	
Von de Val, John William	26	Holland	Y	Rotterdam	New York	11/??/1853	10/31/1857	15	507	N	
Von den Benken, Theodor	40	Germany	Y	Bremen	New York	05/10/1890	05/14/1894			Y	
Von der Haar, A.	31	Germany	Y	Bremen	Baltimore	03/22/1882	10/29/1886	19	97	N	
Von der Haar, A.	31	Germany	Y	Bremen	Baltimore	03/22/1882	10/29/1886			Y	
Von der Haar, August	26	Germany	Y	Bremen	Baltimore	11/13/1882	11/01/1884			Y	

CITIZENSHIP RECORDS

APPLICANT	AGE	COUNTRY OF ORIGIN	DEC	DEPART PORT	ENTRY PORT	ARRIVE DATE	DEC DATE	VOL	PG.	FLD	NAT DATE
Von der Haar, F.	21	Germany	Y	Amsterdam	New York	11/04/1881	11/01/1884			Y	
Von der Haar, George	31	Germany	Y	Bremen	New York	09/21/1867	03/08/1879			Y	
Von der Haar, John Gerha	26	Germany	Y	?	?	04/15/1882	02/05/1885			Y	
Von der Haar, Joseph	21	Germany	Y	Amsterdam	New York	04/13/1884	05/19/1887			Y	
Von der Heide, Henry	40	Germany	Y	Bremen	Baltimore	05/21/1881	10/26/1888			Y	
Von der Linden, Corneliu	44	Holland	Y	Rotterdam	Hoboken	04/07/1893	04/27/1894			Y	
Von der Meulen, George	22	Germany	Y	Rotterdam	New York	10/12/1888	10/23/1888			Y	
VonDohre, John H.	41	Germany	N	Bremen	Baltimore	12/24/1871	?			Y	
VonLeelen, Herman	33	Germany	N	Bremen	New York	08/27/1882	?			Y	
VonWiller, Charles S.	39	Switzerland	N	Havre	New York	05/24/1880	?			Y	
Vonan, George	29	Bavaria	Y	Havre	New York	06/10/1858	10/08/1860	27	441	N	
Vonarb, Jules	??	Germany	Y	?	?	?	10/14/1889			Y	
Vonaux, August	25	France	Y	Havre	New York	05/15/1847	11/05/1852	5	231	N	
Vondenbrinke, Theo	31	Germany	Y	Bremen	Baltimore	03/01/1883	11/09/1888			Y	12/15/1891
Vonderheid, Leonard	24	Hesse Darmsta	Y	Havre	New York	10/22/1854	09/20/1858	16	180	N	
Vondermark, Henry	35	Prussia	Y	Bremen	Baltimore	07/04/1848	03/06/1852	24	249	N	
Vonhagen, John	21	Oldenburg	Y	Bremen	New Orleans	11/11/1856	11/07/1857	15	542	N	
Voogt, Friederich	27	Prussia	Y	Bremen	Baltimore	06/20/1845	01/23/1849	1	498	N	
Voos, William	24	Hesse Darmsta	Y	Havre	New York	08/13/1849	12/16/1851	4	528	N	
Voots, Franz Albert	27	Germany	Y	Rotterdam	New York	08/18/1879	07/08/1881			Y	
Vorback, Rudolph	31	Germany	Y	?	New York	??/??/1866	11/10/1875			Y	
Vordenbeumen, Anton	31	Hanover	Y	Bremen	New York	11/01/1850	10/09/1854	6	94	N	
Vordenbeumen, Anton	31	Hanover	Y	Bremen	New York	11/01/1850	10/09/1854	11	97	N	
Vorhagen, Joseph	57	Germany	N	Bremen	Baltimore	10/03/1858	?			Y	
Vorhauser, Carl	??	Austria	Y	?	?	?	02/26/1876			Y	
Vorlander, Ewald	22	Prussia	Y	Bremen	New Orleans	12/23/1848	02/09/1849	23	127	N	
Vorlander, Theodore	23	Prussia	Y	Bremen	New Orleans	12/23/1848	02/09/1849	23	124	N	
Vornberger, Anton	51	Germany	Y	Antwerp	New York	07/01/1882	01/23/1890			Y	
Vorndieke, Heinrich	27	Germany	Y	Bremen	Baltimore	08/27/1884	11/13/1888			Y	
Vorndran, George	32	Germany	Y	Hamburg	New York	09/11/1891	05/12/1898			Y	
Vornlocher, Peter	40	Germany	Y	Bremen	New York	10/31/1885	01/23/1888			Y	
Vorwarck, John	??	Oldenburg	Y	Bremen	Baltimore	09/06/18??	10/09/1848	1	90	N	
Vorwerk, Franz Heinrich	??	Germany	Y	?	?	?	04/14/1882			Y	
Voskoetter, Herman	25	Prussia	Y	Bremen	New York	06/29/1854	12/29/1855	13	386	N	
Vosmeier, August	34	Prussia	Y	Bremen	New York	01/07/1854	04/06/1858	16	500	N	
Voss, August	??	Germany	Y	?	?	?	04/24/1894			Y	
Voss, Fred	31	Germany	Y	Bremen	Baltimoree	09/21/1881	10/19/1888			Y	
Voss, Friedrich	23	Hanover	Y	Bremen	New Orleans	05/01/1849	06/07/1852	25	201	N	
Voss, George	60	Hanover	Y	Bremen	New Orleans	12/25/1841	10/11/1848	1	141	N	
Voss, Heinrich	27	Hanover	Y	Bremen	New Orleans	01/30/1851	09/15/1852	25	509	N	
Voss, Henry	39	Prussia	Y	Bremen	Baltimore	10/10/1846	02/14/1849	23	105	N	
Voss, John	25	Germany	Y	Bremen	New York	07/15/1884	09/05/1887			Y	
Voss, John Frederick	32	Hanover	Y	Bremen	New Orleans	10/15/1851	02/26/1858	16	343	N	
Vossing, Jacob	30	Prussia	Y	Bremen	New York	07/01/1853	05/02/1858	17	391	N	
Vossler, Otho Henry	61	Wuerttemberg	N	Liverpool	Philadelphia	09/21/1849	02/08/1851	28	264	N	10/05/1854
Vossler, Otto Henry	24	Wurttemberg	Y	Liverpool	Philadelphia	09/21/1849	02/08/1851	3	106	N	
Vossmer, William	21	Hanover	Y	Bremen	Baltimore	09/23/1855	02/11/1858	16	304	N	
Voswinkle, John Wiegand	33	Prussia	Y	Rotterdam	New York	11/23/1844	02/19/1849	23	219	N	
Votel, Herman	38	Germany	Y	Liverpool	New York	11/29/1866	10/10/1885			Y	
Votel, John Gerhard	25	Hanover	Y	Bremen	New Orleans	05/31/1847	08/15/1851	4	147	N	
Vrenegor, John	31	Germany	Y	Amsterdam	New York	05/27/1882	06/18/1889			Y	
Vrielink, Herman	33	Holland	Y	Rotterdam	Baltimore	05/04/1848	08/15/1848	22	126	N	
Vulhop, Joseph	41	Germany	Y	Bremen	Baltimore	09/11/1884	11/01/1889			Y	
Waack, George Samuel The	46	Prussia	Y	Hamburg	New York	05/26/1850	04/23/1853	8	130	N	
Waag, Fred	46	Germany	Y	Rotterdam	New York	07/24/1881	09/23/1886			Y	
Waas, Henry	28	Hesse Darmsta	Y	Havre	New Orleans	12/02/1848	04/12/1852	24	442	N	
Waaser, Charles	33	Germany	Y	Antwerp	New York	06/20/1887	12/14/1898			Y	
Wachanthal, W.	40	Germany	Y	Hamburg	New York	05/01/1880	11/05/1884			Y	
Wachsman, Henry	??	Geermany	Y	?	?	08/19/1881	03/24/1883			Y	

CITIZENSHIP RECORDS

APPLICANT	AGE	COUNTRY OF ORIGIN	DEC	DEPART PORT	ENTRY PORT	ARRIVE DATE	DEC DATE	VOL	PG.	FLD	NAT DATE
Wachsmann, August	34	Prussia	Y	Hamburg	New York	11/05/1856	05/07/1860	27	180	N	
Wachsmuth, Carl	24	Germany	Y	Hamburg	Boston	09/14/1882	01/24/1885			Y	
Wachsmuth, Frederick	28	Hanover	Y	Bremen	Baltimore	10/07/1851	11/12/1852	5	273	N	
Wachsmuth, Frederick	28	Hanover	Y	Bremen	Baltimore	10/07/1851	11/11/1852	6	397	N	
Wachsmutte, Frederick	23	Brunswick	Y	Bremen	Baltimore	10/03/1846	01/30/1849	1	544	N	
Wacht, Adam	30	Hesse Darmsta	Y	Antwerp	New York	08/17/18??	10/13/1851	4	264	N	
Wacht, Jean	32	Germany	Y	Havre	New York	09/07/1885	05/09/1889			Y	
Wachtel, Aron	23	Germany	Y	?	?	08/18/1883	07/08/1885			Y	
Wachtel, Hehle	42	Germany	Y	Hamburg	New York	07/10/1866	10/25/1881			Y	
Wachtel, Moses	21	Saxony	Y	Bremen	New York	10/07/1854	12/04/1855	13	285	N	
Wachtendorf, Frederick	23	Oldenburg	Y	Bremen	New York	06/07/1852	05/21/1856	26	518	N	
Wachtendorf, George	21	Hanover	Y	Bremen	Baltimore	08/31/1846	01/??/1850	23	503	N	
Wachter, Casper	36	Germany	Y	Hamburg	New York	07/16/1873	04/03/1886			Y	
Wachter, Christ.	25	Saxony	Y	Hamburg	Buffalo	07/06/1848	09/14/1852	25	494	N	
Wachter, Henry	26	Bavaria	Y	Bremen	Baltimore	11/08/1847	03/25/1851	3	346	N	
Wachtler, Herman	30	Saxony	Y	Hamburg	New York	10/??/1855	12/27/1855	13	375	N	
Wack, Michael	50	Germany	N	Liverpool	New York	05/16/1872	?			Y	
Wacker, Bernhard	29	Baden	Y	Rotterdam	New York	10/01/1851	06/05/1854	10	65	N	
Wacker, Bernhard	29	Baden	Y	Rotterdam	New York	10/01/1851	06/05/1854	12	2	N	
Wacker, Charles	26	France	Y	Havre	New Orleans	06/17/1849	09/24/1856	14	259	N	
Wacker, Charles	72	France	N	Havre	New Orleans	06/??/1849	??/??/1851	28	451	N	09/27/1858
Wacker, George	28	Germany	Y	Hamburg	New York	12/16/1881	04/22/1885			Y	
Wacker, John	34	Wurttemberg	Y	Havre	New York	06/??/1854	09/24/1855	13	131	N	
Wacker, Ludwig	23	Bavaria	Y	Havre	New York	04/16/1853	01/09/1856	13	435	N	
Wade, John	22	Ireland	Y	Liverpool	New Orleans	12/25/1850	10/03/1854	10	395	N	
Wade, John	22	Ireland	Y	Liverpool	New Orleans	12/25/1850	10/03/1854	12	334	N	
Wade, Patrick	47	Ireland	N	Queenstown	New York	05/16/1865	?			Y	
Wade, Robert	25	Ireland	Y	Liverpool	New Orleans	??/21/1847	11/??/1849	23	315	N	
Wadowsky, Wilhelm	44	Germany	Y	Hamburg	New York	03/14/1881	05/28/1894			Y	
Waechli, Gottfried	34	Switzerland	Y	Havre	New York	09/??/1869	09/26/1885			Y	
Waehler, John	29	Germany	Y	Bremen	New York	03/22/1880	11/17/1884			Y	
Waerther, John	24	Germany	Y	Bremen	New York	10/26/1881	03/13/1886			Y	
Waffenschmidt, John	49	Germany	Y	Havre	New York	08/14/1881	09/17/1883			Y	
Waffenschmidt, William	22	Germany	Y	Havre	New York	11/03/1882	12/06/1886			Y	
Waffler, Richard	29	Germany	Y	Bremen	Baltimore	06/22/1892	09/10/1892	19	352	N	
Wagemacker, Henry	50	Hanover	Y	Bremen	New Orleans	12/25/1845	10/05/1854	10	456	N	
Wagemacker, Henry	50	Hanover	Y	Bremen	New Orleans	12/25/1845	10/05/1854	12	395	N	
Wagener, Henry	29	Hanover	Y	Bremen	Baltimore	08/26/1844	02/20/1849	23	232	N	
Wager, George	40	Wurttemberg	Y	Havre	New York	07/01/1854	10/25/1855	13	138	N	
Waginger, Otto	22	Germany	Y	Bremen	Baltimore	06/14/1890	12/09/1892			Y	
Wagner, Adam	42	Germany	Y	Antwerp	New York	04/28/1883	10/26/1888	19	180	N	
Wagner, Adam	42	Germany	Y	Antwerp	New York	04/28/1883	10/26/1888			Y	
Wagner, Carl G.	??	Germany	Y	?	?	?	02/27/1884			Y	
Wagner, Charles	33	Baden	Y	Antwerp	New York	02/22/1848	04/10/1860	27	139	N	
Wagner, Christ	32	Germany	Y	Havre	New York	08/16/1882	10/19/1894			Y	
Wagner, Christian	25	Germany	Y	Bremen	Baltimore	10/27/1882	03/13/1885			Y	
Wagner, Christoph	38	Germany	Y	Bremen	Baltimore	06/18/1881	?			Y	
Wagner, Conrad	26	Kurhessen	Y	Bremen	Baltimore	05/30/1849	04/14/1853	8	62	N	
Wagner, Conrad	28	Kurhessen	Y	Bremen	Baltimore	06/21/1853	07/18/1855	11	405	N	
Wagner, Emil	22	Kurhessen	Y	Bremen	New York	06/30/1855	10/30/1858	17	200	N	
Wagner, Francis	27	Prussia	Y	Bremen	New Orleans	11/29/1855	02/05/1857	14	539	N	
Wagner, Franz	27	Germany	Y	Havre	New York	10/24/1883	03/13/1884			Y	
Wagner, Franz	32	Germany	Y	Bremen	New York	04/11/1866	06/08/1882			Y	
Wagner, Frederick	47	Germany	Y	Bremen	Baltimore	12/23/1872	02/02/1880			Y	
Wagner, Friedlieb	22	Hesse Cassel	Y	Southampton	New York	12/24/1854	12/05/1857	16	70	N	
Wagner, George	32	Germany	Y	Bremen	New York	09/11/1882	08/13/1888			Y	
Wagner, George	27	Germany	Y	Antwerp	New York	10/05/1882	10/12/1882			Y	
Wagner, George	27	Germany	N	Antwerp	New York	10/05/1882	?			Y	
Wagner, George	31	Bavaria	Y	Bremen	Baltimore	05/15/1858	08/18/1860	27	296	N	

CITIZENSHIP RECORDS

APPLICANT	AGE	COUNTRY OF ORIGIN	DEC	DEPART PORT	ENTRY PORT	ARRIVE DATE	DEC DATE	VOL	PG.	FLD	NAT DATE
Wagner, John	27	Prussia	Y	Antwerp	New York	09/27/1852	11/08/1855	13	192	N	
Wagner, John	41	France	Y	Havre	New York	04/23/1854	02/02/1858	16	73	N	
Wagner, John	34	Germany	Y	Antwerp	New York	10/21/1886	10/24/1889			Y	
Wagner, John	26	Germany	Y	Antwerp	New York	05/07/1887	05/29/1891			Y	
Wagner, John	37	Germany	N	Bremen	Baltimore	12/??/1871	?			Y	
Wagner, John	23	Bavaria	Y	Havre	New Orleans	03/01/1847	02/13/1849	23	80	N	
Wagner, John Emil	35	Nassau	Y	Havre	New York	09/04/1851	03/18/1856	26	224	N	
Wagner, Julius	32	Saxony	Y	Bremen	New York	09/20/1852	08/31/1857	15	208	N	
Wagner, Mathias	28	France	Y	Havre	New Orleans	01/02/1847	02/19/1849	23	170	N	
Wagner, Mathias	26	Bavaria	Y	Bremen	New York	08/14/1853	03/25/1856	26	305	N	
Wagner, Matthias	52	Germany	Y	Liverpool	New York	04/18/1881	01/15/1891			Y	
Wagner, Michael	24	Bavaria	Y	Havre	New York	??/16/1849	01/31/1851	3	69	N	
Wagner, Michael	38	Germany	Y	Bremen	Baltimore	07/07/1881	03/19/1890			Y	
Wagner, Nicholas	26	Germany	Y	Antwerp	New York	04/29/1886	08/18/1888			Y	
Wagner, Nicholas	23	Bavaria	Y	Havre	New York	04/08/1849	04/13/1852	24	498	N	
Wagner, Paul	23	Germany	Y	Bremen	Baltimore	08/06/1890	03/10/1891			Y	
Wagner, Peter	42	Wurttemberg	Y	Havre	New York	10/24/1852	07/21/1855	11	413	N	
Wagner, Philipp	36	Germany	Y	Bremen	Baltimore	07/02/1881	04/10/1883			Y	
Wagner, Phillip	34	Nassau	Y	Antwerp	New Orleans	09/14/1854	09/30/1856	14	47	N	
Wagner, Theodore	31	Baden	Y	Havre	New York	10/11/1848	11/24/1852	5	337	N	
Wagoner, Herman	31	Prussia	Y	Hamburg	New York	01/23/1873	10/09/1876			Y	
Wagoner, John	29	Prussia	Y	Bremen	New York	04/19/1855	03/24/1860	27	137	N	
Wagschal, Frederick	23	Bremen	Y	Bremen	New York	11/12/1852	05/09/1854	8	403	N	
Wagschal, Frederick	23	Bremen	Y	Bremen	Leister	11/12/1852	05/09/1854	9	276	N	
Waherle, Martin	35	Baden	Y	Havre	New York	12/01/1854	10/26/1858	17	115	N	
Wahking, Henry	59	Prussia	N	Bremen	New Orleans	06/15/1851	02/08/1855	28	197	N	03/10/1857
Wahl, B. Eugene	52	Germany	Y	Bremen	Baltimore	05/08/1881	12/08/1883			Y	
Wahl, Charles	28	Baden	Y	London	New York	06/11/1849	06/19/1852	25	293	N	
Wahl, Gottlieb	27	Wurttemberg	Y	Rotterdam	New York	10/04/1850	10/18/1852	5	14	N	
Wahl, Jacob	43	Germany	Y	Havre	New York	08/??/1861	04/07/1879			Y	
Wahl, John	37	Baden	Y	Havre	New York	11/09/1852	02/15/1856	26	87	N	
Wahl, Phillip	28	Germany	Y	Havre	New York	09/26/1887	05/15/1893			Y	
Wahlbrink, Clements	34	Germany	N	Bremen	Baltimore	06/15/1873	?			Y	
Wahlbrink, John Adolph	28	Prussia	Y	Bremen	New Orleans	12/24/1851	11/05/1855	13	164	N	
Wahle, Ferdinand	38	Germany	Y	Bremen	New York	05/01/1883	08/04/1891			Y	
Wahle, Theodore	32	Prussia	Y	Bremen	Galveston	12/02/1849	01/05/1853	5	517	N	
Wahler, Frederick	30	Bavaria	Y	Bremen	Baltimore	07/29/1858	05/03/1861	18	154	N	
Wahler, John	35	Bavaria	Y	Havre	New York	10/20/1854	05/03/1861	18	153	N	
Wahlicht, Anton	30	Germany	Y	Bremen	Baltimore	06/06/1884	03/24/1887			Y	
Wahrenberger, Adam	46	Switzerland	Y	Havre	New Orleans	01/01/1852	06/14/1852	25	254	N	
Waight, Thomas	34	England	Y	Liverpool	New York	05/11/1850	03/07/1853	7	295	N	
Wainer, Borec	28	Russia	Y	Hamburg	New York	11/29/1890	03/14/1891			Y	
Wais, Peter	44	Bavaria	Y	Hamburg	New York	05/15/1852	11/12/1858	17	322	N	
Waiss, Charles Christian	26	Wurttemberg	Y	Havre	New York	10/02/1850	06/30/1857	15	118	N	
Waixner, Valentine	67	Germany	N	Antwerp	Baltimore	06/13/1847	?			Y	
Wakefield, George	29	England	Y	Liverpool	Boston	07/12/1849	04/04/1861	18	130	N	
Walber, Peter Paul	31	Prussia	Y	Havre	New Orleans	02/17/1852	04/03/1862	18	296	N	
Walburg, Christian	46	Prussia	Y	Bremen	Baltimore	12/08/1845	08/15/1848	22	160	N	
Walch, Albert	35	Germany	N	Havre	New York	10/??/1872	?			Y	
Wald, Marks D.	23	Poland	Y	London	New York	08/17/1853	09/27/1856	14	409	N	
Waldau, Wilhelm Gustav	45	Saxony	Y	Hamburg	New York	09/28/1852	11/12/1855	13	205	N	
Waldbott, Sigmund	28	Germany	Y	Bremen	New York	04/07/1890	07/29/1893			Y	
Waldeck, Charles	28	Belgium	Y	Liverpool	New York	05/18/1855	07/19/1862	18	376	N	
Walder, John	25	Ireland	Y	Liverpool	New Orleans	04/17/1850	09/03/1852	25	347	N	
Walderich, Jacob Frederi	31	Wurttemberg	Y	Antwerp	New York	07/26/1849	08/29/1857	15	200	N	
Waldhaus, Andreas	32	Germany	Y	Havre	New York	06/28/1881	12/30/1884			Y	
Waldher, Ludwig	30	Germany	Y	Bremen	New York	05/12/1883	10/18/1887			Y	
Waldkoenig, Jacob	37	Germany	Y	Antwerp	New York	05/09/1889	10/14/1890			Y	
Waldman, Max	33	Austria	Y	Bremen	New York	06/15/1882	10/26/1895			Y	

CITIZENSHIP RECORDS

APPLICANT	AGE	COUNTRY OF ORIGIN	DEC	DEPART PORT	ENTRY PORT	ARRIVE DATE	DEC DATE	VOL	PG.	FLD	NAT DATE
Waldmann, George	36	Germany	Y	Bremen	New York	06/17/1889	05/19/1893			Y	
Waldmann, Paul	28	Germany	Y	Antwerp	New York	06/06/1885	02/19/1890			Y	
Waldschmidt, Alexander	27	Prussia	Y	Havre	New York	10/13/1848	02/24/1851	3	162	N	
Walerius, Mathias	??	Prussia	Y	Antwerp	New York	06/17/18??	11/05/1856	14	497	N	
Walesinski, Stanislaw	23	Prussia	Y	Liverpool	New York	06/24/1853	12/18/1855	13	331	N	
Walfle, Jacob	34	Baden	Y	Havre	New Orleans	03/12/1854	95/23/1861	18	177	N	
Waligorski, Lorenz	42	Germany	Y	Bremen	Baltimore	04/27/1888	03/17/1894			Y	
Walin, Moses	??	Russia	Y	?	?	?	11/19/1894			Y	
Waling, John	30	Ireland	Y	Liverpool	New York	10/??/1853	09/20/1858	16	185	N	
Walk, John	32	Germany	Y	Bremen	Baltimore	04/01/1887	08/19/1892			Y	
Walk, Simon	30	Bavaria	Y	Havre	New Orleans	12/??/1853	09/22/1855	13	125	N	
Walkenhart, Frank	33	Hanover	Y	Bremerhafen	Baltimore	10/??/1857	01/25/1861	18	70	N	
Walkenhorst, Caspar Henr	33	Hanover	Y	Bremen	Baltimore	10/23/1854	03/08/1858	16	379	N	
Walkenhorst, Joseph	35	Prussia	Y	Bremen	New York	07/04/1856	04/03/1862	18	297	N	
Walker, David	26	Wurttemberg	Y	Antwerp	New York	08/17/1847	02/24/1851	3	163	N	
Walker, Edward P.	30	England	Y	Liverpool	New York	01/29/1883	08/16/1889			Y	
Walker, James S.	55	England	Y	?	New York	??/??/1870	11/08/1887			Y	
Walker, John	44	England	Y	Liverpool	Augdrnsburg?	04/15/1886	10/22/1895			Y	
Walker, William	36	Scotland	Y	Glasgow	New York	11/17/1855	10/20/1858	17	71	N	
Walker, William	23	Scotland	Y	Greenock	New York	07/02/1854	04/02/1856	26	418	N	
Wall, James	27	Ireland	Y	Liverpool	New Orleans	05/16/1849	06/16/1852	25	279	N	
Wall, Thomas	28	Ireland	Y	Liverpool	New York	05/05/1852	10/16/1857	15	433	N	
Wall, William	40	Ireland	Y	Canada	Boston	09/13/1841	10/16/1851	4	311	N	
Wallace, Alexander	26	Scotland	Y	Greenock	New York	08/01/1850	04/17/1854	9	1	N	
Wallace, David	24	Scotland	Y	Greenock	New York	07/19/1852	04/17/1854	9	2	N	
Wallace, Hugh	55	Ireland	Y	Belfast	New York	05/05/1849	10/09/1854	6	144	N	
Wallace, Hugh	55	Ireland	Y	Belfast	New York	05/05/1849	10/09/1854	11	147	N	
Wallace, James	26	Ireland	Y	Liverpool	New York	05/01/1850	05/01/1854	8	321	N	
Wallace, James	26	Ireland	Y	Liverpool	New York	05/01/1850	05/01/1854	9	194	N	
Wallace, Patrick	40	Ireland	Y	Cork	New York	06/15/1848	10/13/1851	4	252	N	
Wallace, Robert	51	Ireland	Y	Liverpool	New York	12/??/1848	12/??/1850	2	433	N	
Wallace, Robert	23	Ireland	Y	Liverpool	Philadelphia	04/10/1846	03/31/1853	7	471	N	
Wallgnann, Nicolaus	24	Prussia	Y	Havre	New Orleans	11/15/1852	09/13/1854	13	22	N	
Wallis, John	53	Ireland	Y	Cork	New York	05/30/1849	04/17/1852	24	519	N	
Walls, Ulrich	48	Bavaria	Y	Bremen	Baltimore	07/22/1853	09/27/1858	16	124	N	
Walo, Casper	39	Bavaria	Y	Havre	New Orleans	11/??/1846	10/28/1851	4	424	N	
Walsdorf, Charles	44	Germany	Y	Bremen	Baltimore	02/27/1880	12/16/1884			Y	
Walser, John	54	Germany	N	Antwerp	New York	05/??/1848	?			Y	
Walsh, James	31	Ireland	Y	Liverpool	New York	04/??/1849	09/07/1852	25	397	N	
Walsh, John	30	Ireland	Y	Cork	Boston	08/08/1846	10/13/1851	4	259	N	
Walsh, John	34	Ireland	Y	Cork	New Orleans	04/04/1852	04/25/1853	8	116	N	
Walsh, John	28	Ireland	Y	Queenstown	New York	06/03/1886	06/15/1896			Y	
Walsh, John	43	Ireland	Y	Liverpool	New York	09/??/1872	10/16/1890			Y	
Walsh, John	30	Ireland	Y	Liverpool	Ogdensburg	12/22/1847	03/02/1852	24	220	N	
Walsh, John	32	Ireland	Y	Liverpool	Baltimore	12/25/1848	04/30/1852	24	527	N	
Walsh, Lawrence	28	Ireland	Y	Dublin	New York	04/14/1858	10/08/1860	27	434	N	
Walsh, Luke	41	Ireland	Y	Liverpool	New Orleans	03/25/1849	04/05/1852	24	382	N	
Walsh, Maurice	24	Ireland	Y	Queenstown	New York	05/05/1884	09/20/1888			Y	
Walsh, Maurice	36	England	N	London	Niagra Falls	09/??/1870	?			Y	
Walsh, Michael	25	Ireland	Y	Liverpool	New York	06/15/1853	06/12/1854	10	119	N	
Walsh, Michael	25	Ireland	Y	Liverpool	New York	05/15/1853	06/12/1854	12	56	N	
Walsh, Michael	27	Ireland	Y	Liverpool	Baltimore	09/24/1851	02/02/1857	14	525	N	
Walsh, Michael	23	Ireland	Y	Liverpool	New York	05/03/1850	04/12/1858	16	463	N	
Walsh, Patrick	21	Ireland	Y	?	?	?	11/02/1887			Y	
Walsh, Patrick	22	Ireland	Y	Liverpool	New York	05/??/1882	05/??/1882			Y	
Walsh, Patrick	35	Ireland	N	Liverpool	New York	05/??/1882	?			Y	
Walsh, Philip	28	Ireland	Y	Liverpool	New York	06/01/1849	12/28/1852	5	461	N	
Walsh, Thomas	23	Ireland	Y	Cork	New York	10/12/1851	04/25/1853	8	122	N	
Walsh, Thomas	23	Ireland	Y	Liverpool	New Orleans	05/03/1852	01/26/1856	13	510	N	

CITIZENSHIP RECORDS

APPLICANT	AGE	COUNTRY OF ORIGIN	DEC	DEPART PORT	ENTRY PORT	ARRIVE DATE	DEC DATE	VOL	PG.	FLD	NAT DATE
Walsh, Thomas	32	Ireland	Y	Canada	Ogdensburg	10/22/1849	04/05/1852	24	389	N	
Walsh, Thomas	31	Ireland	Y	?	New York	05/06/1872	10/18/1882			Y	
Walsh, William	35	Ireland	Y	London	New York	08/03/1852	04/23/1853	8	100	N	
Walsh, William	49	Ireland	N	Ennis	Canada	07/??/1848	?			Y	
Waltemate, August(Walthe	29	Switzerland	Y	Bremen	New York	12/01/1880	10/21/1882			Y	
Walter, Anthony	26	France	Y	Havre	New Orleans	01/01/1852	03/17/1856	26	214	N	
Walter, Benjamin	39	Baden	Y	Havre	New Orleans	02/19/1849	12/31/1855	13	403	N	
Walter, Bernard (Waller?	30	France	Y	Havre	New York	07/03/1840	08/17/1848	22	193	N	
Walter, Christoph	34	Prussia	Y	Bremen	New York	11/01/1857	05/23/1859	17	426	N	
Walter, Frank	26	Germany	Y	Havre	New York	05/14/1886	04/15/1892			Y	
Walter, Frederick Willia	23	Hanover	Y	Bremen	Baltimore	11/23/1853	12/15/1855	13	314	N	
Walter, George	42	Baden	Y	Rotterdam	New York	02/01/1855	01/22/1856	13	489	N	
Walter, Isidor	40	Germany	Y	Bremen	New York	06/29/1868	10/10/1882			Y	
Walter, Joe	22	Germany	Y	Bremen	Baltimore	08/21/1893	12/28/1897			Y	
Walter, Karl (Charles?)	38	Germany	Y	Rotterdam	New York	03/27/1881	02/27/1891			Y	
Walter, Markus	25	Germany	Y	Hamburg	New York	06/03/1881	12/08/1882			Y	
Walter, Martin	28	Bavaria	Y	Havre	New York	07/15/1848	06/19/1851	3	413	N	
Walter, Martin	36	Germany	Y	Havre	New York	03/15/1880	02/25/1889			Y	
Walter, Pietrich	29	Germany	N	?	?	??/??/1871	?			Y	
Walter, Samuel	24	Germany	Y	Havre	New York	04/05/1882	03/17/1887			Y	
Walter, Theodore	49	Germany	Y	Antwerp	Philadelphia	05/26/1879	05/26/1894			Y	
Walter, Wilhelm	26	Germany	Y	Bremen	New York	04/16/1889	10/25/1889			Y	
Walter, Wilhelm	25	Germany	Y	Bremen	New York	08/25/1892	07/13/1893			Y	
Walters, George	29	Hanover	Y	Bremen	Baltimore	04/26/1847	05/20/1852	25	65	N	
Walters, John	45	Ireland	Y	Liverpool	New Orleans	12/22/1848	04/24/1861	18	145	N	
Walters, John	30	Wales	Y	Liverpool	New York	10/20/1879	03/30/1886			Y	
Walthard, Frederic	32	Switzerland	Y	Havre	New York	06/02/1890	06/02/1900			Y	
Walther, August	23	Prussia	Y	Bremen	New York	09/30/1853	04/07/1858	16	504	N	
Walther, Frederick Willi	52	Prussia	Y	Bremen	New York	01/16/1851	02/25/1856	26	126	N	
Walther, Henry	28	Germany	Y	Havre	New York	09/10/1890	05/06/1892			Y	
Walther, Mathias	31	Baden	Y	Antwerp	New York	06/??/1854	02/27/1858	16	344	N	
Walther, Max B.	32	Germany	Y	Hamburg	New York	07/02/1891	11/13/1900			Y	
Walther, Richard	34	Germany	Y	Hamburg	New York	09/20/1883	07/10/1884			Y	
Waltmann, Bernard	31	Prussia	Y	Bremen	New York	06/08/1850	10/16/1851	4	313	N	
Waltner, Adolph	33	Austria	Y	?	New York	??/??/1877	10/08/1884			Y	
Walton, Philip	??	Canada	N	?	?	05/05/1873				Y	10/28/1892
Waltring, Bernard	42	Germany	Y	Bremen	New York	08/22/1881	06/??/1882	28	388	N	
Waltz, John	51	Germany	N	Havre	New York	12/06/1861	?			Y	
Walz, John George	25	Wurttemberg	Y	Havre	New York	04/18/1851	02/14/1853	7	159	N	
Walz, John George	55	Wurttemberg	Y	Liverpool	New York	05/01/1852	02/14/1853	7	160	N	
Walz, Joseph	23	Hohenzollern	Y	Havre	New York	07/??/1849	10/24/1851	4	394	N	
Walz, Louis	26	Germany	Y	Havre	New York	10/29/1889	09/18/1894			Y	
Wambold, Louis	24	Germany	Y	Bremen	New York	06/21/1881	06/01/1885			Y	
Wandstrat, Joseph	??	Germany	N	?	?	01/04/1886				Y	10/27/1892
Wanger, Kasper	35	Austria	Y	Rotterdam	New York	04/16/1891	12/04/1893			Y	
Wanke, Bernard	32	Oldenburg	Y	Bremen	New Orleans	12/01/1852	10/06/1859	17	475	N	
Wanner, August W.	28	Wurttemberg	Y	Havre	New Orleans	02/11/1852	04/19/1853	8	87	N	
Wanner, Ernst	25	Germany	Y	Hamburg	New York	02/11/1881	03/23/1885			Y	
Wanner, John George	21	Wurttemberg	Y	Antwerp	New York	01/01/1855	04/03/1858	16	484	N	
Wanning, John	45	Germany	Y	Bremen	New York	05/04/1871	10/06/1880			Y	
Wanstroth, Diederich	46	Oldenburg	Y	Bremen	Baltimore	07/24/1835	10/12/1857	15	397	N	
Warburg, Bernard	24	Hanover	Y	Bremen	New Orleans	12/17/1845	08/23/1848	22	240	N	
Ward, Frank	26	Ireland	Y	Queenstown	New York	05/29/1882	06/30/1887			Y	
Ward, James	??	Ireland	Y	Liverpool	New York	04/08/18??	10/11/1848	1	104	N	
Ward, James	26	England	Y	Liverpool	New Orleans	04/20/1848	03/12/1851	3	259	N	
Ward, James	27	Ireland	Y	Belfast	New York	03/??/1882	10/07/1885	19	16	N	
Ward, James	27	Ireland	Y	Belfast	New York	03/??/1882	10/07/1885			Y	
Ward, James P.	22	England	Y	Liverpool	New York	06/25/1848	03/03/1851	3	196	N	
Ward, John	35	Ireland	Y	Galway	New York	06/18/1848	04/18/1854	8	203	N	

404

CITIZENSHIP RECORDS

APPLICANT	AGE	COUNTRY OF ORIGIN	DEC	DEPART PORT	ENTRY PORT	ARRIVE DATE	DEC DATE	VOL	PG.	FLD	NAT DATE
Ward, John	35	Ireland	Y	Galway	New York	06/18/1848	04/18/1854	9	74	N	
Ward, Patrick	62	Ireland	N	Hull	Buffalo	06/30/1865	?			Y	
Ward, Patrick	30	Ireland	Y	Liverpool	New York	06/27/1848	02/19/1852	24	141	N	
Ward, Peter	29	Ireland	Y	Liverpool	New Orleans	11/15/1851	10/20/1858	17	79	N	
Warflinger, John	32	Austria	Y	Amsterdam	New York	09/16/1882	06/06/1884			Y	
Wark, Jacob	28	Geermany	Y	?	?	?	07/19/1882			Y	
Wark, Thomas	33	Ireland	Y	Londonderry	Wilmington	06/??/1843	11/??/1849	23	300	N	
Warmer, Jos.	26	Germany	Y	Hamburg	New York	01/15/1891	03/05/1894	21	61	N	
Warndorff, Arnold	70	Germany	Y	Bremen	New York	05/10/1885	10/19/1894			Y	
Warndorff, Bernard	24	Germany	Y	Bremen	New York	05/09/1885	11/04/1889	19	275	N	
Warndorff, Bernard	24	Germany	Y	Bremen	New York	05/09/1885	11/04/1889			Y	
Warnecke, Carl	31	Germany	Y	Hamburg	New York	09/25/1881	03/12/1890			Y	
Warnecke, Charles	60	Germany	N	Schleswig	New York	09/??/1881	10/??/1881	28	480	N	10/??/1886
Warnecke, Charles	21	Germany	N	?	New York	09/00/1881	10/00/1881			Y	10/00/1886
Warneke, Charles	??	Hanover	Y	Bremen	Baltimore	08/06/18??	10/09/1848	1	63	N	
Warner, Christian	21	Prussia	Y	Bremen	Baltimore	10/26/1856	05/23/1859	17	425	N	
Warning, Henry	40	Hanover	Y	Bremen	New Orleans	10/15/1853	09/27/1858	16	126	N	
Warning, John	33	Mecklenburg S	Y	Hamburg	New York	04/01/1852	06/05/1856	14	295	N	
Warnking, Henry	31	Hanover	Y	Bremen	New Orleans	12/19/1846	09/29/1854	10	313	N	
Warnking, Henry	31	Hanover	Y	Bremen	New Orleans	12/19/1846	09/29/1854	12	252	N	
Warnock, Archibald	35	Ireland	Y	Liverpool	New York	05/26/1842	10/05/1848	22	442	N	
Warnock, William James	40	Ireland	Y	Liverpool	New Orleans	03/11/1844	12/16/1852	5	421	N	
Warren, Jeremiah	37	Ireland	Y	Cork	East Port	04/12/1837	10/28/1851	4	429	N	
Warscthacki, Abraham	22	Poland	Y	Liverpool	New York	09/01/1855	04/13/1860	27	153	N	
Warwood, Thomas	35	England	Y	Liverpool	New York	07/??/1850	03/25/1853	7	394	N	
Washauser, Conrad	40	Germany	N	Hamburg	New York	08/30/1873	?			Y	
Waske, Joseph	24	Oldenburg	Y	Bremen	Baltimore	09/??/1845	12/??/1849	23	401	N	
Wasmer, Sebastian	47	Baden	Y	Havre	New York	08/20/1834	01/22/1849	1	484	N	
Wasmuth, John L.	28	Prussia	Y	Hamburg	New York	04/??/1851	03/24/1853	7	377	N	
Wasseman, Samuel	??	Russia	Y	?	?	?	08/11/1892			Y	
Wassenberg, Henry	27	Germany	Y	Bremen	Baltimore	06/14/1884	10/29/1892	19	403	N	
Wasserfuhr, Reinhard	54	Germany	Y	Antwerp	New York	10/24/1879	03/25/1891			Y	
Wassler, Alfons	24	Germany	Y	Havre	New York	11/05/1899	02/13/1902			Y	
Wassler, Eugen	21	Germany	Y	Havre	New York	11/01/1890	09/06/1893			Y	
Wassman, Sebastian	28	Bavaria	Y	Havre	New York	07/28/1851	07/23/1855	11	415	N	
Watermann, Astley	23	England	Y	Plymouth	Niagra Falls	??/01/1857	01/08/1861	18	47	N	
Watermann, Henry	27	Wurttemberg	Y	Havre	New York	08/01/1851	08/17/1857	15	150	N	
Waters, Richard	29	Wales	Y	Liverpool	Port Huron	05/27/1885	10/31/1888	19	206	N	
Wates, Joseph	36	England	Y	Liverpool	New Orleans	07/03/1848	10/02/1848	22	391	N	
Watkins, David	26	England	Y	Liverpool	New York	11/11/1857	08/05/1859	17	466	N	
Watson, James	28	Scotland	Y	Glasgow	New York	04/15/1887	08/12/1895			Y	
Watson, John	32	Ireland	Y	Dublin	New York	09/28/1885	09/05/1889			Y	
Watson, John W.	29	England	Y	Liverpool	New York	06/18/1880	01/29/1886			Y	
Watson, Robert	28	England	Y	Liverpool	New York	06/12/1893	06/18/1895			Y	
Watson, Robert H.	27	Canada	Y	?	?	10/16/1886	06/15/1892			Y	
Watt, Richard	46	Scotland	Y	Queenstown	Lewistown	08/31/1854	08/29/1857	15	198	N	
Watt, William	25	Ireland	Y	Montreal	Sandusky	06/29/1850	10/05/1854	10	439	N	
Watt, William	25	Ireland	Y	Montreal	Sandusky	06/26/1850	10/05/1854	12	378	N	
Watzki, Paul	28	Germany	Y	Havre	New York	03/28/1892	07/15/1895			Y	
Waubnitz, Daniel	38	Baden	Y	Havre	New York	04/01/1844	11/18/1858	17	341	N	
Wauligmann, August	26	Germany	Y	Bremen	New York	05/15/1881	10/24/1888	19	176	N	
Wauligmann, August	26	Germany	Y	Bremen	New York	05/15/1881	10/24/1888			Y	
Waun, John	29	Ireland	Y	Bombay	Providence	10/31/1854	09/20/1858	16	156	N	
Wavra, Franz	24	Germany	Y	Bremen	New York	05/01/1887	05/20/1889			Y	
Wawer, John	37	Hesse Cassel	Y	Bremen	Baltimore	08/26/1839	01/14/1856	13	469	N	
Way, Joseph Francis	60	England	Y	Liverpool	New York	07/30/1852	09/21/1857	15	296	N	
Waywood, Joseph	??	Germany	Y	Bremen	Baltimore	10/25/1889	10/31/1890			Y	
Weabeck, Ludwig	41	Waldeck	Y	Bremen	Baltimore	06/11/1847	07/15/1851	3	540	N	
Weank, John	48	Holland	Y	Bremen	New York	06/18/1859	08/03/1860	27	245	N	

CITIZENSHIP RECORDS

APPLICANT	AGE	COUNTRY OF ORIGIN	DEC	DEPART PORT	ENTRY PORT	ARRIVE DATE	DEC DATE	VOL	PG.	FLD	NAT DATE
Weaver, Christian	48	Bavaria	Y	Havre	New Orleans	12/20/1847	08/14/1848	22	102	N	
Weaver, Frank	29	Hanover	Y	Bremen	New Orleans	02/07/1845	10/14/1851	4	289	N	
Weaver, Frank	27	Oldenburg	Y	Bremen	New Orleans	12/??/1845	11/??/1849	23	356	N	
Webb, William	25	Ireland	Y	Dublin	New York	07/01/1850	01/12/1853	7	12	N	
Webber, Henry	28	Hanover	Y	Bremen	New York	12/29/1846	01/25/1849	1	517	N	
Webber, Peter	33	Prussia	Y	Havre	New York	05/01/1851	05/01/1854	9	212	N	
Weber, Adam	30	Prussia	Y	Antwerp	New York	04/01/1852	10/05/1857	15	353	N	
Weber, Adam	25	Germany	Y	Antwerp	New York	11/02/1881	12/29/1884				Y
Weber, Adam	27	Germany	Y	Bremen	New York	07/10/1886	10/17/1894				Y
Weber, Adam	33	Bavaria	Y	London	New York	05/01/1849	05/19/1852	25	39	N	
Weber, Albert	21	Bavaria	Y	Havre	New York	01/10/1855	02/21/1857	15	46	N	
Weber, Alfred A.	??	Prussia	Y	?	?	?	04/03/1886				Y
Weber, Alois	22	Baden	Y	Antwerp	New York	09/29/1854	05/20/1856	26	510	N	
Weber, Anton	??	Germany	Y	?	?	?	08/09/1892				Y
Weber, Bernard	32	Oldenburg	Y	Bremen	New Orleans	01/01/1849	04/26/1854	8	269	N	
Weber, Bernard	32	Oldenburg	Y	Bremen	New Orleans	01/01/1849	04/26/1854	9	140	N	
Weber, Bernard	40	Germany	Y	Bremen	New York	07/16/1881	10/26/1896				Y
Weber, C.	??	Bavaria	Y	Antwerp	New Orleans	??/26/1848	12/10/1850	2	355		Y
Weber, C. H. William	43	Germany	N	Bremen	New York	10/15/1866	?				Y
Weber, Casper	??	Germany	Y	?	?	?	02/15/1883				Y
Weber, Charles J.	26	Germany	Y	Hamburg	New York	06/16/1880	09/28/1885				Y
Weber, Christian	26	Bavaria	Y	Havre	New Orleans	03/29/1846	10/02/1848	1	4	N	
Weber, Christian	38	Wurttemberg	Y	Rotterdam	New York	10/01/1849	10/18/1852	5	15	N	
Weber, Christian	31	Baden	Y	Havre	New York	05/28/1851	06/01/1854	9	473	N	
Weber, Christian	31	Baden	Y	Havre	New York	05/28/1851	06/01/1854	10	56	N	
Weber, Conrad	23	Bavaria	Y	Havre	New York	06/01/1848	01/31/1851	3	74	N	
Weber, Conrad	31	Bavaria	Y	Bremen	New York	06/01/1848	10/10/1854	6	223	N	
Weber, Conrad	31	Bavaria	Y	Bremen	New York	06/01/1848	10/10/1854	11	226	N	
Weber, Diedrich	35	Hanover	Y	Bremen	New Orleans	12/16/1841	11/22/1848	1	369	N	
Weber, Eberhard	35	Germany	Y	Bremen	New York	03/09/1866	10/09/1882				Y
Weber, Eberhard	49	Germany	N	Bremen	New York	03/08/1866	?				Y
Weber, Ernest Gustav	32	Germany	Y	Bremen	Baltimore	08/14/1892	05/27/1893				Y
Weber, Ernst	30	Prussia	Y	Bremen	Baltimore	06/29/1860	07/03/1860	27	199	N	
Weber, Frank	40	Bavaria	Y	Havre	New Orleans	10/17/1847	10/15/1851	4	295	N	
Weber, Franz	23	Prussia	Y	Bremen	New Orleans	11/01/1851	06/19/1852	25	295	N	
Weber, Frederick	23	Bavaria	Y	Havre	New York	?	11/19/1849	23	351	N	
Weber, Friedrich	27	Bavaria	Y	Havre	New York	07/17/1866	03/11/1872	18	471	N	
Weber, George	36	Bavaria	Y	Bremen	New York	08/13/1849	03/29/1850	2	283	N	
Weber, George	29	France	Y	Havre	New Orleans	01/20/1854	12/07/1858	17	382	N	
Weber, George Henry	22	Bremen	Y	Bremen	New York	05/08/1852	09/25/1854	10	190	N	
Weber, George Henry	22	Bremen	Y	Bremen	New York	05/08/1852	09/25/1854	12	129	N	
Weber, Gerlach	55	Prussia	Y	Bremen	New York	06/04/1848	03/04/1850	2	152	N	
Weber, Gregor	27	Germany	Y	Antwerp	New York	02/14/1887	06/01/1889				Y
Weber, Henry	37	Germany	Y	Bremen	New York	06/09/1883	01/14/1887				Y
Weber, Henry	34	Hanover	Y	Bremen	New Orleans	04/11/1846	04/13/1852	24	493	N	
Weber, Henry	29	Nassau	Y	London	New York	06/13/1853	03/24/1856	26	282	N	
Weber, Joachim Everhard	47	Germany	Y	Bremen	New York	01/02/1897	01/31/1901				Y
Weber, John	21	Luxembourg	Y	Antwerp	New York	05/06/1852	10/20/1852	5	26	N	
Weber, John	23	Prussia	Y	Antwerp	New York	05/04/1852	05/04/1854	8	363	N	
Weber, John	23	Prussia	Y	Antwerp	New York	05/04/1852	05/04/1854	9	236	N	
Weber, John	51	Switzerland	Y	Antwerp	New York	08/28/1853	08/27/1855	11	491	N	
Weber, John	30	Hanover	Y	Bremen	Baltimore	11/02/1853	02/09/1858	16	92	N	
Weber, John	49	Bavaria	Y	Bremen	New York	07/03/1858	10/30/1858	17	208	N	
Weber, John	48	Bohemia, Aust	Y	Bremen	Baltimore	05/16/1856	09/05/1872	18	518	N	
Weber, John	29	Bavaria	Y	Bremen	New York	07/01/1870	12/28/1872	18	545	N	
Weber, John	30	Germany	Y	Bremen	Baltimore	04/27/1893	03/02/1896				Y
Weber, John	26	Germany	Y	Havre	New York	01/25/1888	02/15/1892				Y
Weber, John	34	Germany	Y	?	?	??/??/1889	11/05/1894				Y
Weber, John	62	Austria	Y	Bremen	New York	10/26/1893	10/29/1894				Y

CITIZENSHIP RECORDS

APPLICANT	AGE	COUNTRY OF ORIGIN	DEC	DEPART PORT	ENTRY PORT	ARRIVE DATE	DEC DATE	VOL	PG.	FLD	NAT DATE
Weber, John	32	Germany	Y	Bremen	Baltimore	07/04/1887	07/18/1895			Y	
Weber, John	30	Bavaria	Y	Havre	New Orleans	11/11/1853	02/12/1856	26	73	N	
Weber, John	36	Prussia	Y	Havre	New York	06/17/1853	04/09/1856	26	480	N	
Weber, John A.	25	Bavaria	Y	Bremen	Baltimore	05/18/1847	02/12/1849	23	70	N	
Weber, John B.	72	France	N	Havre	New York	11/27/1853	?			Y	
Weber, John George	37	Bavaria	Y	Bremen	New York	??/30/1848	02/05/1850	2	39	N	
Weber, John George	52	Prussia	Y	Havre	New Orleans	05/15/1849	07/19/1855	11	411	N	
Weber, John Henry	32	Hanover	Y	Bremen	New York	02/20/1849	05/01/1854	8	291	N	
Weber, John Henry	32	Hanover	Y	Bremen	New York	02/20/1849	05/01/1854	9	163	N	
Weber, Joseph	26	Germany	Y	Antwerp	Boston	11/01/1881	09/05/1887			Y	
Weber, Joseph	37	Switzerland	Y	Havre	New York	01/01/1873	12/12/1881			Y	
Weber, Joseph	28	Hanover	Y	Bremen	New York	09/30/1846	10/04/1848	22	419	N	
Weber, Karl	46	Germany	Y	Bremen	New York	10/18/1865	10/31/1888			Y	
Weber, Louis	23	Germany	Y	Antwerp	New York	08/02/1884	09/05/1887			Y	
Weber, M. Anton	25	Germany	Y	Bremen	New York	11/24/1887	09/22/1890			Y	
Weber, Martin	35	Austria	Y	Antwerp	New York	07/01/1869	03/25/1885			Y	
Weber, Michael	32	Bavaria	Y	Havre	New York	11/18/1851	10/28/1858	17	163	N	
Weber, Otto	23	Germany	Y	Havre	New York	10/25/1888	10/25/1893			Y	
Weber, Peter	33	Prussia	Y	Havre	New York	05/01/1851	05/01/1854	8	339	N	
Weber, Peter	??	Germany	Y	?	?	?	04/12/1889			Y	
Weber, Peter	48	Germany	Y	Bremen	New York	08/18/1884	03/24/1894			Y	
Weber, Philip	27	Bavaria	Y	Bremen	New York	06/19/1869	12/28/1872	18	544	N	
Weber, Philip	50	Germany	Y	Bremen	New York	06/24/1871	07/10/1890			Y	
Weber, Philipp	24	Bavaria	Y	Havre	New York	12/18/1850	09/11/1852	25	450	N	
Weber, Phillip	39	Germany	Y	Bremen	New York	05/18/1888	05/14/1894			Y	
Weber, Rudolph	38	Switzerland	Y	Havre	New York	10/14/1856	02/12/1861	18	96	N	
Weber, Severin	35	Germany	Y	Elsas	New York	05/23/1872	10/13/1884			Y	
Weber, Theodore	25	Germany	Y	Bremen	Baltimore	06/04/1876	10/11/1882			Y	
Weber, Valentine	25	Bavaria	Y	Havre	New York	01/07/1850	12/27/1852	5	447	N	
Weber, Wilhelm	49	Germany	Y	Bremen	New York	11/12/1880	11/05/1888	19	221	N	
Weber, Wilhelm	49	Germany	Y	Bremen	New York	11/12/1880	11/05/1888			Y	
Weber, William	24	Hanover	Y	Bremen	Philadelphia	05/07/1846	10/16/1848	1	246	N	
Weber, William	37	Hanover	Y	Bremen	New Orleans	07/15/1846	02/15/1849	23	134	N	
Webold, Heinrich	30	Hanover	Y	Bremen	New Orleans	11/18/1854	01/16/1860	27	54	N	
Webster, John W.	25	Scotland	Y	?	?	10/12/1880	11/06/1885			Y	
Webzenback, Adam	44	Bavaria	Y	Havre	New York	08/29/1853	10/09/1854	6	186	N	
Weckenbrock, Bernard	43	Germany	Y	Bremen	Baltimore	06/15/1865	10/22/1888			Y	
Weddigen, C. A.	22	Germany	Y	?	New York	10/15/1886	05/10/1890			Y	
Wedeck, Peter	??	Hesse Darmsta	Y	Havre	New Orleans	??/28/1847	12/??/1850	2	431	N	
Wedeking, Wilhelm	31	Germany	Y	Hamburg	Philadelphia	11/01/1881	11/01/1882			Y	
Weedfeild, William Stern	23	Denmark	Y	Hamburg	New York	04/31/1860	01/02/1861	18	40	N	
Weefers, Heinrich	33	Germany	Y	Amsterdam	Jersey City	09/08/1888	10/13/1891			Y	
Wege, Ernst H. H.	30	Germany	Y	Bremen	Baltimore	09/18/1888	10/03/1891			Y	
Wegelin, Frederick	23	Bavaria	Y	Havre	New York	10/15/1857	07/03/1860	27	202	N	
Wegener, Adolph	36	Prussia	Y	Hamburg	Buffalo	08/27/1852	09/06/1852	25	374	N	
Wegener, Heinrich	38	Germany	Y	Bremen	New York	05/25/1864	10/17/1878			Y	
Wegener, Henry	34	Prussia	Y	Bremen	New Orleans	01/23/1850	09/06/1852	25	375	N	
Wegener, Philip	30	Prussia	Y	Bremen	New Orleans	06/26/1852	04/02/1856	26	406	N	
Weger, August	28	Prussia	Y	Antwerp	New York	05/12/1848	01/30/1851	3	64	N	
Wegert, Karl Robert	38	Germany	Y	Hamburg	New York	02/11/1881	11/04/1891			Y	
Weghorst, Charles	??	Germany	N	?	?	06/22/1885				Y	10/27/1892
Weghorst, Gerhard Henry	25	Hanover	Y	Bremen	Baltimore	05/04/1854	11/26/1855	13	252	N	
Weglage, George	24	Germany	Y	Amsterdam	New York	10/11/1886	07/10/1889			Y	
Weglage, Henry	47	Hanover	N	Bremen	New York	09/??/1862	?			Y	
Wegloge, Henry	30	Hanover	Y	Bremen	New York	09/01/1848	04/05/1852	24	370	N	
Wegman, Henry	30	Switzerland	Y	Havre	New York	09/14/1857	06/30/1860	27	18	N	
Wegmann, Frank	23	Oldenburg	Y	Bremen	New York	07/02/1849	11/01/1852	5	125	N	
Wegmann, Franz	23	Oldenburg	Y	Bremen	New York	07/02/1849	10/01/1852	6	251	N	
Wegmann, Frederick	29	Prussia	Y	Antwerp	New York	06/11/1854	03/10/1856	26	179	N	

CITIZENSHIP RECORDS

APPLICANT	AGE	COUNTRY OF ORIGIN	DEC	DEPART PORT	ENTRY PORT	ARRIVE DATE	DEC DATE	VOL	PG.	FLD	NAT DATE
Wegmann, William	40	Germany	Y	Rotterdam	New York	08/22/1880	09/26/1883			Y	
Wegnich, Joseph	26	Alsace	Y	Havre	New York	05/19/1868	01/06/1872	18	451	N	
Wehage, George	26	Germany	Y	Bremen	New York	09/??/1874	10/11/1880			Y	
Wehage, Herman	29	Oldenburg	Y	Bremen	New Orleans	11/10/1847	02/04/1851	3	97	N	
Wehberg, Bernhard	29	Hanover	Y	Rotterdam	New York	06/28/1848	05/31/1852	25	156	N	
Wehberg, Max	28	Germany	Y	Rotterdam	New York	09/03/1891	03/01/1897			Y	
Wehe, John George	36	Baden	Y	London	New York	05/??/1846	02/10/1852	24	85	N	
Wehking, Fred	24	Prussia	Y	Bremen	Baltimore	06/09/1857	11/02/1860	27	551	N	
Wehling, Modestus	??	Germany	Y	?	?	?	10/25/1881			Y	
Wehmeier, George	34	Germany	Y	Bremen	Baltimore	04/10/1882	01/04/1887			Y	
Wehmeier, William	33	Prussia	Y	Bremen	New Orleans	12/26/1851	07/25/1855	11	430	N	
Wehre, Henry	33	Oldenburg	Y	Bremen	New Orleans	11/02/1849	04/17/1854	9	18	N	
Wehrenberg, Henry	50	Germany	Y	Bremen	New York	09/26/1873	04/29/1892			Y	
Wehrfritz, Lorenz	29	Germany	Y	Hamburg	New York	03/21/1884	01/28/1890			Y	
Wehring, Adam	51	Alsace	Y	Havre	New York	06/10/1869	07/22/1872	18	507	N	
Wehrkamp, Bernard	29	Prussia	Y	Bremen	New Orleans	05/15/1849	02/11/1851	3	119	N	
Wehrle, Achaz	21	Baden	Y	Havre	New Orleans	05/26/1854	10/09/1854	6	78	N	
Wehrle, Achaz	21	Baden	Y	Havre	New Orleans	05/26/1854	10/09/1854	11	81	N	
Wehrle, Anton	45	Baden	Y	Liverpool	New York	10/02/1854	08/27/1862	18	410	N	
Wehrle, Joseph	23	Baden	Y	Havre	New York	10/13/1852	07/23/1855	11	422	N	
Wehrle, Valentine	26	Baden	Y	Havre	New Orleans	04/16/1852	10/09/1854	6	117	N	
Wehrle, Valentine	26	Baden	Y	Havre	New Orleans	04/16/1852	10/09/1854	11	120	N	
Wehrmann, Henry	15	Germany	N	?	New York	00/00/1881				Y	11/05/1887
Wehrmeyer, Herman	28	Germany	Y	Bremen	Baltimore	10/08/1881	11/01/1888			Y	
Wehrung, Jacques	34	France	Y	Havre	New Orleans	??/14/1849	01/30/1851	2	542	N	
Weibel, Gottlieb	28	Switzerland	Y	Havre	New York	04/12/1880	07/03/1888			Y	
Weibel, Henry	35	Baden	Y	Havre	New York	05/01/1847	04/17/1854	9	14	N	
Weibert, Andrew	22	Bavaria	Y	Bremen	New York	07/01/1854	03/08/1858	16	378	N	
Weibker, Joseph	27	Germany	Y	Rotterdam	New York	05/14/1891	10/12/1896			Y	
Weiboldt, Joseph	38	Hanover	Y	Bremerhafen	New Orleans	12/??/1852	02/06/1858	18	91	N	
Weich, Christ	27	Germany	Y	Bremen	New York	02/08/1882	09/08/1886			Y	
Weich, Joseph	22	Bavaria	Y	Hamburg	New York	06/22/1848	01/19/1849	1	467	N	
Weiche, Franz Ernst	23	Prussia	Y	Bremen	New Orleans	06/13/1857	04/13/1861	18	108	N	
Weichlein, Casper	30	Bavaria	Y	London	New York	09/??/1852	05/17/1854	9	335	N	
Weichman, John William	27	Prussia	Y	Havre	New York	09/??/1848	12/??/1849	23	403	N	
Weichmann, Michael	??	Baden	Y	Havre	New Orleans	04/08/18??	10/09/1848	1	61	N	
Weick, Jacob	38	Germany	Y	Rotterdam	New York	06/02/1866	03/31/1877			Y	
Weickart, John	27	Baden	Y	Havre	New York	11/22/1845	01/02/1856	13	419	N	
Weickner, Ferdinand	30	Baden	Y	Havre	New York	02/10/1848	06/08/1852	25	206	N	
Weideman, George	26	Frankfurt	Y	Havre	New York	07/10/1848	02/05/1849	23	29	N	
Weidemann, Gottlieb	51	Prussia	Y	Bremen	New York	06/03/1848	02/11/1853	7	141	N	
Weidenbach, John Philip	24	Bavaria	Y	Havre	New York	12/25/1853	03/24/1856	26	276	N	
Weidenbacher, Fritz	31	Germany	Y	Hamburg	New York	02/27/1882	05/21/1886			Y	
Weidenbacher, George	27	Germany	Y	Bremen	New York	02/30/1891	10/27/1893			Y	
Weidgenant, William	28	Baden	Y	Havre	New York	10/22/1852	03/31/1856	26	391	N	
Weidinger, John	32	Bavaria	Y	Bremen	Baltimore	10/18/1851	05/18/1854	8	469	N	
Weidinger, John	32	Bavaria	Y	Bremen	Baltimore	10/18/1851	05/18/1854	9	343	N	
Weidl, Ignaz	48	Germany	Y	Hamburg	New York	11/14/1884	12/28/1888			Y	
Weidlich, William	28	Germany	Y	Hamburg	New York	07/15/1876	09/27/1883			Y	
Weidmann, Ferdinand	25	Baden	Y	Havre	New York	11/05/1852	09/25/1854	12	162	N	
Weidner, August	23	Reuss	Y	Bremen	New York	05/01/1854	10/27/1858	17	128	N	
Weidner, Charles	60	Germany	N	Havre	New York	11/??/1849	?			Y	
Weidner, George	??	Germany	Y	?	?	?	06/10/1889			Y	
Weier, Joseph	47	Germany	N	Bremen	New York	08/25/1866	?			Y	
Weierich, Caspar	26	Germany	Y	Rotterdam	New York	12/03/1888	09/20/1893			Y	
Weiermann, John	23	Bavaria	Y	Rotterdam	New York	08/08/1854	03/25/1856	26	326	N	
Weifenbach, Peter	30	Germany	Y	Bremen	New York	04/14/1883	10/13/1894			Y	
Weigand, Frank	41	Germany	Y	Bremen	New York	05/07/1890	08/27/1892			Y	
Weigand, George Adam	28	Kurhessen	Y	Bremen	New York	08/16/1846	11/20/1848	1	352	N	

CITIZENSHIP RECORDS

APPLICANT	AGE	COUNTRY OF ORIGIN	DEC	DEPART PORT	ENTRY PORT	ARRIVE DATE	DEC DATE	VOL	PG.	FLD	NAT DATE
Weigand, Johann Joseph	29	Germany	Y	Bremen	New York	06/16/1893	12/28/1895			Y	
Weigel, George	27	Bavaria	Y	Bremen	Philadelphia	06/29/1859	07/02/1862	18	368	N	
Weigel, Martin	58	Germany	Y	Amsterdam	New York	10/14/1882	11/07/1887			Y	
Weiger, Pius	28	Germany	Y	Bremen	New York	08/30/1881	03/28/1884			Y	
Weighouse, Joseph	28	Oldenburg	Y	Amsterdam	New York	11/15/1842	08/22/1848	22	224	N	
Weightman, Matthew	22	England	Y	Liverpool	New York	07/??/1853	05/02/1854	8	350	N	
Weiglein, Casper	30	Bavaria	Y	London	New York	09/??/1852	05/17/1854	8	461	N	
Weigmann, Joseph	38	Hanover	Y	Bremen	Baltimore	06/02/1845	11/18/1860	27	529	N	
Weihe, Herman	59	Germany	Y	Bremen	New York	06/12/1853	10/03/1883			Y	
Weiher, Joseph	24	Germany	Y	Hamburg	New York	01/27/1879	10/22/1881			Y	
Weik, Jacob	23	Germany	Y	Bremen	Baltimore	04/01/1887	03/14/1889			Y	
Weik, Paul	32	Baden	Y	Antwerp	New Orleans	02/13/1847	02/17/1852	24	129	N	
Weil, Abraham	30	Germany	Y	South Hampto	New York	11/08/1880	08/15/1882			Y	
Weil, David	24	Poland	Y	London	New Orleans	01/15/1847	02/19/1850	2	101	N	
Weil, Frederick	23	Bavaria	Y	Havre	New York	10/29/1854	10/29/1858	17	179	N	
Weil, Henry	25	Hesse Darmsta	Y	Antwerp	New York	04/19/1850	05/14/1852	25	21	N	
Weil, Isaac	26	Bavaria	Y	Havre	New Orleans	04/14/1855	06/04/1861	18	184	N	
Weil, Jacob	23	Bavaria	Y	Havre	New Orleans	05/19/1850	05/30/1854	9	464	N	
Weil, Jacob	23	Bavaria	Y	Havre	New Orleans	05/19/1850	05/31/1854	10	47	N	
Weil, Leopold H.	??	Germany	Y	?	?	09/??/1889	01/19/1891			Y	
Weil, Nicholas	29	Baden	Y	Havre	New Orleans	10/23/1858	07/07/1860	27	210	N	
Weil, Samuel	21	France	Y	Havre	New Orleans	01/01/1847	11/17/1848	1	308	N	
Weil, Valentine	21	Baden	Y	Antwerp	New York	02/09/1855	02/21/1857	15	44	N	
Weiland, S.	27	Russia	Y	Hamburg	New York	12/??/1878	04/06/1885			Y	
Weiler, Fritz	32	Germany	Y	?	New York	05/01/1869	04/15/1882			Y	
Weiler, Martin	23	Wurttemberg	Y	Havre	New Orleans	02/02/1853	10/20/1857	15	466	N	
Weilig, Bernard	33	Prussia	Y	Bremen	New Orleans	05/01/1849	06/10/1852	25	315	N	
Weill, Jonas	35	France	Y	Havre	New York	06/18/1886	11/02/1891			Y	
Weils, Henry	28	Schwartzburg	Y	Hamburg	Baltimore	02/??/1853	02/09/1857	15	1	N	
Weiman, John	55	Mecklenburg S	Y	Hamburg	New York	12/??/1852	03/20/1856	26	235	N	
Weimann, Frederick	40	Kurhessen	Y	Bremen	Baltimore	05/29/1854	09/07/1860	27	345	N	
Weimann, Peter Gottlieb	62	Germany	N	Havre	New York	11/16/1853	?			Y	
Weimar, George	33	Hesse Cassel	Y	Bremen	Baltimore	05/27/1847	02/12/1849	23	57	N	
Weimar, Jacob	22	Prussia	Y	London	New York	01/21/1854	02/23/1856	26	120	N	
Weimer, Michael	32	France	Y	Havre	New York	06/19/1848	03/08/1852	24	259	N	
Weinanz, George	27	Bavaria	Y	Havre	New Orleans	12/15/1845	02/26/1850	2	131	N	
Weinard, Jacob	28	Germany	Y	Antwerp	New York	07/26/1890	09/25/1895			Y	
Weinberg, Jacob	42	Hanover	Y	Bremen	Baltimore	10/25/1849	10/10/1854	6	203	N	
Weinberg, Jacob	42	Hanover	Y	Bremen	Baltimore	10/25/1849	10/10/1854	11	206	N	
Weinberg, Louis	39	Germany	Y	Bremen	New York	02/17/1872	04/26/1886			Y	
Weinberg, Louis	40	Russia	Y	Hamburg	New York	06/15/1888	10/12/1892			Y	
Weinbrecht, Leopold	42	Germany	Y	Bremen	New York	12/25/1887	05/17/1893			Y	
Weinewith, Henry	22	Prussia	Y	Bremen	Baltimore	05/04/1854	08/26/1857	15	190	N	
Weinewuth, Bernard	26	Germany	Y	Bremen	Baltimore	05/21/1881	07/17/1883			Y	
Weingand, Wilhelm	24	Germany	Y	Bremen	New York	04/07/1890	02/11/1892			Y	
Weingarter, George Jacob	23	Bavaria	Y	Havre	New York	11/10/1852	08/20/1855	11	461	N	
Weingartner, Christopher	25	Germany	Y	Hamburg	New York	10/12/1880	01/03/1882			Y	
Weingartner, Joseph	21	Germany	Y	Havre	New York	04/28/1883	10/02/1886			Y	
Weingertner, Philip	35	Hesse Darnsta	Y	?	?	?	11/18/1854			Y	
Weinhard, Henry	24	Wurttemberg	Y	Liverpool	New York	06/15/1851	05/01/1854	8	328	N	
Weinhard, Henry	24	Wurttemberg	Y	Liverpool	New York	06/15/1851	05/01/1854	9	201	N	
Weinherin, Henry	33	Germany	Y	Antwerp	Philadelphia	08/30/1886	09/17/1896			Y	
Weinig, Frank	54	Germany	N	Havre	New York	04/20/1867	?			Y	
Weininger, Heinrich	25	Germany	Y	Bremen	New York	12/01/1891	09/07/1893			Y	
Weinkauf, Charles Edward	29	Prussia	Y	Bremen	Baltimore	08/08/1857	11/27/1858	17	359	N	
Weinkaug, John August	37	Prussia	Y	Bremen	Baltimore	07/25/1858	11/27/1858	17	361	N	
Weinle, Christian	??	Germany	Y	?	?	?	01/15/1883			Y	
Weinman, Gottlieb	26	Wurttemberg	Y	Havre	New York	12/24/1852	05/24/1854	8	506	N	
Weinman, Gottlieb	26	Wurttemberg	Y	Havre	New York	12/24/1852	05/24/1854	9	360	N	

CITIZENSHIP RECORDS

APPLICANT	AGE	COUNTRY OF ORIGIN	DEC	DEPART PORT	ENTRY PORT	ARRIVE DATE	DEC DATE	VOL	PG.	FLD	NAT DATE
Weinmann, John	33	Baden	Y	Havre	New York	11/13/1849	10/20/1851	4	355	N	
Weinstein, Andy	43	Germany	N	Havre	New York	06/30/1870	?			Y	
Weinstein, Joseph	32	Turkey	Y	?	?	?	10/22/1892			Y	
Weinstraub, Louis	38	Russia	Y	Hamburg	New York	09/16/1887	10/04/1894			Y	
Weintz, Robert	40	Hesse Darmsta	Y	Havre	New York	05/02/1859	04/21/1862	18	321	N	
Weir, John	33	Scotland	Y	Glasgow	New York	07/20/1848	07/16/1855	11	395	N	
Weir, William	49	Scotland	Y	Glasgow	New York	01/16/1888	07/03/1899			Y	
Weirich, Anton	32	Germany	Y	Bremen	New York	11/01/1887	11/29/1893			Y	
Weis, Conrad	22	Hesse Darmsta	Y	Rotterdam	New York	07/04/1850	04/11/1853	8	53	N	
Weis, Ernst	31	Baden	Y	Liverpool	Buffalo	01/05/1854	12/16/1859	17	507	N	
Weis, Frederick	32	Schaunberg Li	Y	Bremen	New York	08/25/1855	10/24/1857	15	486	N	
Weis, Isidore	27	Austria	Y	Hamburg	Philadelphia	06/03/1882	10/08/1887			Y	
Weis, Jacob	25	Germany	Y	Bremen	Baltimore	05/20/1884	10/11/1889			Y	
Weis, John	28	Bavaria	Y	Liverpool	New York	06/02/1853	09/25/1854	10	199	N	
Weis, John	38	Bavaria	Y	Liverpool	New York	06/02/1853	09/25/1854	12	138	N	
Weis, Max	??	Austria	N	?	?	07/12/1886				Y	10/13/1892
Weis, Max C.	44	Germany	Y	Havre	New York	07/21/1881	06/14/1884			Y	
Weisbecher, Tobias	28	Baden	Y	Havre	New Orleans	10/16/1858	11/24/1859	17	480	N	
Weisberg, David	74	Russia	Y	Kiev	New York	06/30/1882	10/22/1888			Y	
Weisberg, Jacob	28	Russia	Y	Hamburg	New York	07/15/1881	10/26/1888			Y	
Weisbrod, George	26	Germany	Y	Havre	New York	12/02/1881	05/22/1882			Y	
Weisbrod, Heinrich	39	Bavaria	Y	Bremen	New Orleans	11/04/1857	11/01/1860	27	517	N	
Weisbrod, Philipp	24	Germany	Y	Bremen	New York	04/01/1881	05/22/1882			Y	
Weisbrodt, Henry	40	Germany	Y	Antwerp	Philadelphia	08/02/1881	10/25/1889	19	258	N	
Weisbrodt, Henry	40	Germany	Y	Antwerp	Philadelphia	08/02/1881	10/25/1889			Y	
Weise, F. Albin	29	Germany	Y	Bremen	New York	03/14/1890	03/26/1894			Y	
Weise, Ferdinand	34	Germany	Y	Rotterdam	New Orleans	11/15/1891	04/13/1894			Y	
Weisel, Henry	25	Hesse Darmsta	Y	Havre	New York	05/25/1853	10/27/1858	17	126	N	
Weisenbath, Somon	30	France	Y	Havre	New Orleans	06/02/1840	10/11/1848	1	108	N	
Weishaar, Ignaz	37	Germany	Y	Antwerp	New York	03/04/1881	04/07/1887			Y	
Weishaupt, Michael	28	Bavaria	Y	Havre	New York	11/22/1857	08/31/1860	27	320	N	
Weisinger, Andrew	42	Bavaria	Y	Antwerp	New York	08/27/1844	08/03/1848	22	53	N	
Weiskopf, Carl	27	Bavaria	Y	Havre	New York	01/07/1852	10/05/1854	10	464	N	
Weiskopf, Carl	27	Bavaria	Y	Havre	New York	01/07/1852	10/05/1854	12	403	N	
Weiskopf, Henry	22	Bavaria	Y	Havre	New York	08/06/1852	10/07/1854	10	521	N	
Weiskopf, Henry	22	Bavaria	Y	Havre	New York	08/06/1852	10/07/1854	12	460	N	
Weisman, Peisa	30	Roumania	Y	Rotterdam	New York	08/25/1900	12/26/1901			Y	
Weismuller, Deterich	25	Germany	Y	Hamburg	New York	07/17/1882	04/06/1885			Y	
Weiss, Andrew	26	Switzerland	Y	Havre	New York	07/04/1850	01/20/1853	7	69	N	
Weiss, Benjamin	32	Austria	Y	Bremen	New York	11/28/1888	03/26/1895			Y	
Weiss, Christian	36	Germany	Y	Havre	New York	05/21/1888	10/20/1893			Y	
Weiss, Frank	36	Germany	Y	Bremen	New York	09/26/1885	01/03/1891			Y	
Weiss, Frederick	30	Wurttemberg	Y	Havre	New York	07/04/1852	10/09/1854	11	139	N	
Weiss, George	45	Germany	Y	Bremen	New York	04/14/1883	02/09/1886			Y	
Weiss, Henry Gottleib	26	Lippe Schauen	Y	Bremen	New York	01/01/1850	05/08/1854	9	268	N	
Weiss, Henry Gottlieb	26	Lippe Schauen	Y	Bremen	New Orleans	01/01/1850	05/08/1854	8	395	N	
Weiss, John	32	Wurttemberg	Y	Havre	New York	09/10/1854	09/24/1858	16	143	N	
Weiss, John	30	Germany	Y	Hamburg	New York	03/02/1882	03/13/1884			Y	
Weiss, John	41	Germany	Y	Bremen	New York	08/??/1873	10/??/1875			Y	
Weiss, John Peter	31	France	Y	Havre	New York	10/01/1846	10/09/1854	6	182	N	
Weiss, John Peter	31	France	Y	Havre	New York	10/04/1846	10/09/1854	11	185	N	
Weiss, Joseph	28	Oldenburg	Y	Bremen	New York	11/01/1847	11/20/1848	1	349	N	
Weiss, Joseph	35	Germany	Y	Havre	New York	12/22/1887	12/04/1895			Y	
Weiss, Joseph	31	Germany	Y	Bremen	Baltimore	05/18/1883	12/05/1887			Y	
Weiss, Karl	46	Germany	N	Havre	New York	03/19/1867	?			Y	
Weiss, Paul	27	Germany	Y	Bremen	New York	05/19/1887	10/11/1889	19	236	N	
Weiss, Paul	27	Germany	Y	Bremen	New York	05/19/1887	10/11/1889			Y	
Weiss, Philip	36	France	Y	Havre	New York	04/22/1853	03/15/1856	26	205	N	
Weiss, Rudolf	39	Germany	Y	Bremen	Baltimore	07/11/1881	07/23/1887			Y	

CITIZENSHIP RECORDS

APPLICANT	AGE	COUNTRY OF ORIGIN	DEC	DEPART PORT	ENTRY PORT	ARRIVE DATE	DEC DATE	VOL	PG.	FLD	NAT DATE
Weiss, Seraphin	25	Switzerland	Y	Antwerp	New York	12/06/1854	04/04/1856	26	431	N	
Weissbach, Henry F.J.	30	Germany	Y	Antwerp	Philadelphia	07/12/1880	08/14/1882			Y	
Weisse, Adam	37	Germany	Y	Havre	New York	09/28/1872	03/21/1889			Y	
Weissenberger, August	30	Baden	Y	Havre	New York	06/23/1845	03/25/1850	2	256	N	
Weisshaar, Anton	??	Germany	Y	?	?	?	07/10/1890			Y	
Weissmann, George	54	Germany	Y	Bremen	New York	07/02/1867	10/29/1888			Y	
Weist, Adolph	??	Germany	Y	?	?	?	03/21/1887			Y	
Weist, John	47	Bavaria	Y	Bremen	Baltimore	05/02/1847	12/05/1859	17	492	N	
Weisz, Emil	33	Austria	Y	Antwerp	New York	05/19/1891	04/14/1894			Y	
Weiszmann, John (Weissma	56	Germany	Y	Havre	New York	02/11/1882	07/10/1885			Y	
Weiten, Nicholas	??	Germany	Y	?	New York	09/??/1885	04/02/1887			Y	
Weitheimer, Aaron	53	Hesse Darmsta	Y	Antwerp	New York	07/04/1849	10/10/1854	6	240	N	
Weitlauf, John Adam	25	Bavaria	Y	Havre	New Orleans	11/18/1853	11/05/1855	13	161	N	
Weitzel, Charles	52	Germany	N	Bremen	New York	02/31/1861	?			Y	
Weitzel, Charles	31	Hesse Darmsta	Y	Havre	New York	01/24/1852	03/17/1860	27	127	N	
Weitzel, George	25	Hanover	Y	Bremen	Baltimore	07/25/1848	04/05/1852	24	369	N	
Weitzel, John	52	Hesse Darmsta	Y	Antwerp	New York	07/08/1848	06/13/1851	3	375	N	
Weitzel, John	33	Germany	Y	Amsterdam	New York	09/05/1884	04/09/1888			Y	
Weitzel, Peter	33	Germany	Y	Antwerp	New York	06/13/1888	03/13/1894			Y	
Weitzel, Peter	23	Kuhrhassen	Y	Bremen	New York	06/01/1848	02/09/1849	23	37	N	
Weitzenberg, Theodore	22	Saxony	Y	Hamburg	New York	06/01/1849	12/18/1852	5	425	N	
Wekamp, Henry	24	Hanover	Y	Bremen	New Orleans	05/27/1849	05/20/1852	25	58	N	
Wekerle, Sebastian	36	Germany	Y	Havre	New York	03/01/1880	09/07/1880			Y	
Weking, William	23	Prussia	Y	Bremen	New Orleans	12/16/1852	02/25/1856	26	127	N	
Welage, Joseph	30	Wurttemberg	Y	Bremen	New Orleans	12/02/1853	10/01/1856	14	119	N	
Welbrock, Ferdinand	48	Oldenburg	N	Bremen	Baltimore	??/??/1857	?			Y	
Welch, Carl	37	Prussia	Y	Hamburg	New York	05/02/1849	04/02/1853	7	496	N	
Welch, Edward	29	Ireland	Y	Liverpool	New Orleans	01/13/1851	10/15/1851	4	297	N	
Welch, Michael	??	Ireland	Y	Liverpool	New Orleans	12/10/1848	01/05/1861	18	43	N	
Welch, Patrick	40	Ireland	Y	Liverpool	New York	09/04/1881	10/22/1889			Y	
Welland, Henry	48	England	Y	?	?	?	10/31/1871			Y	
Wellendorf, Henry	21	Germany	Y	Bremen	Baltimore	07/22/1885	11/02/1888			Y	
Weller, George	23	Germany	Y	Bremen	New York	10/04/1892	06/21/1893			Y	
Weller, Gerlach	55	Nassau	Y	Antwerp	New York	06/12/1855	04/11/1860	27	146	N	
Weller, John	26	Prussia	Y	Antwerp	New York	03/04/1853	03/03/1856	26	146	N	
Weller, William	30	Germany	Y	Bremen	Baltimore	06/03/1880	10/13/1885			Y	
Weller, William	23	Prussia	Y	Antwerp	New York	03/04/1852	03/03/1856	26	147	N	
Wellerding, Herman	37	Germany	Y	Bremen	New York	05/30/1881	10/24/1888			Y	
Welleureiter, Charles	23	Baden	Y	Havre	New Orleans	11/09/1852	10/01/1856	14	110	N	
Welling, George	24	Prussia	Y	Bremen	New Orleans	11/10/1847	01/29/1849	1	539	N	
Welling, George	22	Germany	Y	Rotterdam	New York	05/24/1889	05/26/1892			Y	
Welling, Gerhard Herman	29	Hanover	Y	Bremen	Baltimore	05/31/1848	02/19/1849	23	208	N	
Welling, John	41	Germany	N	Bremen	New York	05/20/1864	?			Y	
Welling, John Henry	29	Hanover	Y	Bremen	New Orleans	01/19/1850	01/23/1851	2	523	N	
Welling, Raimundus	33	Hanover	Y	Bremen	New Orleans	11/01/1857	07/26/1858	16	525	N	
Wellingergof, John Frede	32	Hanover	Y	Bremen	Baltimore	07/04/1858	04/08/1862	18	310	N	
Wellinghoff, Henry	23	Germany	Y	Bremen	Baltimore	08/15/1888	03/09/1893			Y	
Wellinghoff, Joseph	28	Hanover	Y	Bremen	New Orleans	01/01/1844	09/12/1848	22	333	N	
Wellman, W.	25	Prussia	Y	Bremerhafen	Baltimore	05/19/1859	01/30/1861	18	79	N	
Wellmann, Geo	55	Germany	Y	Bremen	Baltimore	09/16/1885	11/03/1888	19	215	N	
Wellmann, George	55	Germany	Y	Bremen	Baltimore	09/16/1885	11/03/1888			Y	
Wellmann, Henry	25	Hanover	Y	Bremen	New Orleans	11/??/1847	01/06/1851	2	460	N	
Wellmann, Henry	40	Germany	Y	Bremen	New York	09/26/1866	10/24/1888			Y	
Wellmann, Henry	26	Germany	Y	Bremen	New York	08/29/1885	10/30/1893			Y	
Wellmink, Heinrich	27	Hanover	Y	Bremen	New Orleans	05/18/1852	09/17/1855	13	51	N	
Wellmuth, William	25	Prussia	Y	Rotterdam	New York	06/25/1852	04/17/1854	8	180	N	
Wellner, Ernst	28	Lippe	Y	Bremen	New Orleans	01/01/1848	10/02/1848	1	33	N	
Wellner, Henry	33	Prussia	Y	Bremen	New Orleans	05/12/1848	10/14/1851	4	266	N	
Wellner, Ludwig	22	Lippe Dettmol	Y	Bremerhafen	Baltimore	10/10/1857	01/10/1861	18	49	N	

CITIZENSHIP RECORDS

APPLICANT	AGE	COUNTRY OF ORIGIN	DEC	DEPART PORT	ENTRY PORT	ARRIVE DATE	DEC DATE	VOL	PG.	FLD	NAT DATE
Welofsky, Isaac	45	Russia	N	Kiev	Philadelphia	09/??/1872	?			Y	
Welp, Frank	37	Germany	Y	Bremen	Baltimore	08/24/1891	08/14/1893			Y	
Welp, G. Joseph	39	Germany	Y	Rotterdam	New York	03/24/1871	10/17/1885	19	26	N	
Welp, Gerhard Hermann	33	Hanover	Y	Bremen	Baltimore	11/02/1857	06/19/1862	18	354	N	
Welp, Henry	33	Germany	Y	Bremen	Baltimore	08/31/1882	10/25/1888			Y	
Welp, Joe	27	Germany	Y	Bremen	Baltimore	04/25/1889	12/29/1892			Y	
Welsch, Gustav	42	Germany	Y	Bremen	New York	07/09/1876	07/31/1886			Y	
Welsch, John Leonard	31	Bavaria	Y	Liverpool	New York	06/09/1854	03/19/1858	16	424	N	
Welscher, John	21	Germany	Y	Bremen	Baltimore	03/28/1888	11/07/1890			Y	
Welsh, Anthony	43	Ireland	Y	Liverpool	New Orleans	04/28/1848	10/09/1854	6	101	N	
Welsh, Anthony	42	Ireland	Y	Liverpool	New Orleans	04/28/1848	10/09/1854	11	104	N	
Welsh, David	68	Ireland	Y	Liverpool	New Orleans	01/03/1849	04/02/1853	7	505	N	
Welsh, John	24	Ireland	Y	Liverpool	New Orleans	11/01/1850	10/09/1854	6	195	N	
Welsh, John	25	Ireland	Y	Liverpool	New Orleans	11/01/1850	10/09/1854	11	198	N	
Welsh, John	29	Ireland	Y	Queenstown	New York	09/30/1887	09/24/1892			Y	
Welsh, John	22	Ireland	Y	Glasgow	New York	04/??/1847	01/??/1850	23	532	N	
Welsh, Martin	23	Ireland	Y	Liverpool	New York	11/14/1863	10/06/1866			Y	
Welsh, Michael	31	Ireland	Y	Cork	New York	04/04/1852	11/30/1857	16	56	N	
Welsh, Patrick	35	Ireland	Y	Liverpool	New Orleans	02/01/1850	10/29/1852	5	55	N	
Welsh, Patrick	26	Ireland	Y	Queenstown	New York	09/12/1889	11/05/1894			Y	
Welsh, Peter	50	Ireland	Y	Queenstown	New York	10/07/1889	03/02/1893			Y	
Welsh, Richard	52	Ireland	N	Liverpool	New Orleans	??/??/1850	?	28	83	N	??/??/1860
Welsh, Thomas	30	Ireland	Y	Liverpool	New Orleans	06/17/1850	05/17/1854	8	455	N	
Welsh, Thomas	30	Ireland	Y	Liverpool	New Orleans	06/17/1850	05/17/1854	9	328	N	
Welsh, Thomas	31	Ireland	Y	Liverpool	New Orleans	11/07/1848	12/27/1851	24	22	N	
Welsh, William	51	Ireland	Y	Liverpool	New York	11/03/1853	11/05/1860	18	23	N	
Welte, Albert	40	Switzerland	Y	Havre	New York	10/20/1879	10/28/1898			Y	
Welter, Joseph	52	Germany	N	Bremen	New Orleans	06/05/1860	?			Y	
Welton, John	25	Ireland	Y	Liverpool	New York	04/??/1854	08/24/1857	15	176	N	
Weltz, Charles	25	Bavaria	Y	Havre	New York	10/06/1855	03/25/1858	16	447	N	
Welzbach, Adam	44	Bavaria	Y	Havre	New York	08/27/1853	10/09/1854	11	189	N	
Wemert, John B.	44	France	Y	Havre	New York	11/11/1849	11/12/1852	5	275	N	
Wempe, Clemens A.	23	Oldenburg	Y	Bremen	Baltimore	??/??/1848	10/24/1850	2	298	N	
Wempe, Franz	42	Germany	N	Bremen	Baltimore	11/02/1866	?			Y	
Wempie, Henry	25	Oldenburg	Y	Bremen	Baltimore	07/24/1855	10/30/1858	17	12	N	
Wendering, Theodor	31	Germany	Y	Bremen	Baltimore	03/25/1887	12/17/1892			Y	
Wenderoth, John	??	Kurhessen	Y	Bremen	New York	??/03/18??	03/??/1850	2	285	N	
Wendland, Christian L.	39	Hanover	Y	Bremen	Baltimore	05/28/1848	03/02/1852	24	213	N	
Wendland, Emil	??	Germany	Y	?	?	?	04/21/1893			Y	
Wendlandt, George	30	Hanover	Y	Bremen	Baltimore	02/19/1853	05/22/1856	26	525	N	
Wendling, Emile	30	Germany	Y	Havre	New York	05/17/1896	10/31/1903			Y	
Wendling, Jacob	29	Baden	Y	Havre	New York	06/20/1854	01/24/1856	13	505	N	
Wendt, Gerhard Frederick	23	Prussia	Y	Bremen	New Orleans	04/27/1854	03/05/1857	15	64	N	
Wendt, Henry	51	Germany	Y	Hamburg	New York	03/04/1880	09/08/1885			Y	
Wendt, Herman H.	32	Germany	Y	Bremen	New York	06/01/1881	12/29/1890			Y	
Wendt, William	25	Germany	Y	Hamburg	New York	03/03/1883	09/08/1885			Y	
Wendt, William	23	Germany	Y	Amsterdam	New York	09/27/1889	10/20/1892			Y	
Wendt, William	24	Germany	Y	Bremen	New York	08/29/1888	12/21/1893			Y	
Wendum, Abraham Samuel	??	Austria	Y	?	?	?	11/28/1892			Y	
Wenger, Johann	25	Germany	Y	Bremen	New York	05/18/1885	06/15/1888			Y	
Wenger, Johann	54	Germany	Y	Bremen	New York	06/21/1883	12/19/1887			Y	
Wengert, Joseph	36	Germany	Y	Havre	New York	03/27/1883	10/11/1888			Y	
Weninger, John	33	Germany	Y	Rotterdam	New York	08/07/1883	03/01/1892			Y	
Wenke, Daniel	28	Germany	Y	Bremen	New York	05/27/1879	03/07/1888			Y	
Wenke, John	30	Kurhessen	Y	Bremen	New York	10/??/1852	03/28/1853	7	446	N	
Wenkel, August	35	Germany	Y	Bremen	Baltimore	09/21/1894	03/29/1900			Y	
Wenkel, John Gerhard	28	Hanover	Y	Rotterdam	New York	07/??/1849	03/25/1851	3	343	N	
Wennemer, Bernard Anthon	34	Prussia	Y	Bremen	Baltimore	11/01/1854	10/10/1857	15	386	N	
Wenner, Michael	26	France	Y	Havre	New York	04/14/1853	09/20/1855	13	85	N	

CITIZENSHIP RECORDS

APPLICANT	AGE	COUNTRY OF ORIGIN	DEC	DEPART PORT	ENTRY PORT	ARRIVE DATE	DEC DATE	VOL	PG.	FLD	NAT DATE
Wenning, Bernard	25	Prussia	Y	Bremen	Baltimore	04/25/1847	09/15/1852	25	517	N	
Wenning, Gerhard	28	Prussia	Y	Bremen	Baltimore	05/14/1849	09/15/1852	25	521	N	
Wenning, Max	??	Germany	Y	?	?	?	10/11/1894			Y	
Wenstrup, Joseph	22	Oldenburg	Y	Bremen	Baltimore	07/06/1845	08/23/1848	22	241	N	
Wente, Clemens	22	Oldenburg	Y	Bremen	Baltimore	09/01/1845	08/15/1848	22	145	N	
Wenthurst, Henry	27	Prussia	Y	Bremen	New Orleans	12/23/1851	03/28/1853	7	415	N	
Wentzel, Heinrich	31	Germany	Y	Bremen	Baltimore	06/23/1892	11/12/1892			Y	
Wentzel, Henry	23	Hesse Darmsta	Y	Antwerp	New Orleans	05/??/1847	12/??/1850	2	409	N	
Wentzel, Joseph	??	Germany	N	?	?		09/02/1880			Y	10/28/1892
Wentzler, Charles	43	Wurttemberg	Y	Havre	New York	12/29/1847	01/28/1850	2	1	N	
Wenz, Adam	31	Hesse Darmsta	Y	Havre	New York	08/08/1853	11/05/1860	18	16	N	
Wenz, Hartman	21	Germany	Y	Antwerp	New York	10/02/1881	12/04/1884			Y	
Wenzel, Adam	38	Bohemia	Y	Bremen	Baltimore	08/04/1857	09/10/1860	27	349	N	
Wenzel, Albert	32	Germany	Y	Bremen	Philadelphia	01/31/1899	09/10/1904			Y	
Wenzel, Henry	34	Hanover	Y	Hamburg	New York	05/16/1855	05/14/1859	17	411	N	
Wenzel, Joseph	50	Germany	Y	Bremen	Baltimore	05/??/1873	08/28/1884			Y	
Wenzel, Joseph	50	Germany	Y	Bremen	New Orleans	12/15/1854	11/01/1858	17	243	N	
Werbeck, Bernard	30	Prussia	Y	Bremen	Hamburg	07/16/1881	05/10/1883	28	172	N	
Werber, Louis	30	Austria	Y	Hamburg	New York						
Werdmann, Gerhard	27	Germany	Y	Bremen	Baltimore	05/07/1875	06/08/1882			Y	
Werdmoeller, Andrew	31	Prussia	Y	Bremen	Baltimore	05/02/1849	04/05/1852	24	367	N	
Wergo, William	24	Wurttemberg	Y	Liverpool	New York	08/04/1845	10/21/1858	17	87	N	
Weri, Frank	33	Oldenburg	Y	Bremen	New Orleans	06/10/1849	10/13/1857	15	415	N	
Werich, Henry	38	Oldenburg	Y	Bremen	New Orleans	11/02/1849	04/17/1854	8	147	N	
Werkirman, Jacob	38	France	Y	Havre	New Orleans	12/26/1846	08/15/1848	22	169	N	
Werle, Joseph	35	Prussia	Y	Antwerp	New Orleans	06/26/1847	01/18/1853	7	39	N	
Werling, Herman	24	Prussia	Y	Bremen	New Orleans	02/23/1851	04/17/1854	8	166	N	
Werling, Herman	24	Prussia	Y	Bremen	New Orleans	01/23/1851	04/17/1854	9	37	N	
Wermal, Charles	82	Germany	N	Havre	New Orleans	02/??/1838	??/??/1840	28	3	N	??/??/1843
Wermal, Charles	33	Germany	N	Havre	New Orleans	02/00/1838	00/00/1840			Y	00/00/1843
Wermeling, John Theodore	31	Hanover	Y	Bremen	Baltimore	12/01/1854	09/27/1857	15	330	N	
Werner, Adolh	30	Germany	Y	Havre	New York	11/22/1882	02/01/1887	19	112	N	
Werner, Albert	28	Germany	Y	Havre	New York	01/26/1888	02/10/1892			Y	
Werner, Bernard	27	Germany	Y	Bremen	Baltimore	07/01/1880	10/05/1883			Y	
Werner, Bernhard	40	Hanover	Y	Bremen	New York	06/27/1858	08/28/1862	18	419	N	
Werner, Carl	30	Austria	Y	Havre	New York	07/08/1854	09/23/18??	10	171	N	
Werner, Carl	30	Austria	Y	Havre	New York	07/08/1854	09/23/1854	12	110	N	
Werner, Christoph	23	Hesse Darmsta	Y	Amsterdam	Baltimore	05/28/1847	01/19/1849	1	461	N	
Werner, Connrad	23	Germany	Y	Havre	New York	09/07/1881	03/10/1883			Y	
Werner, Ernest	29	Germany	Y	Bologne	New York	05/12/1891	12/31/1895			Y	
Werner, Fred William	??	Germany	Y	?	?	?	12/09/1881			Y	
Werner, Frederick	37	Prussia	Y	Havre	New York	07/02/1842	10/11/1848	1	133	N	
Werner, Heinrich	24	Germany	Y	Antwerp	New York	05/18/1883	04/12/1886			Y	
Werner, Henry	37	Austria	Y	Liverpool	New York	12/29/1888	02/18/1898			Y	
Werner, Henry	??	Germany	Y	?	?	?	05/10/1893			Y	
Werner, John Jacob	42	Bavaria	Y	Havre	New Orleans	12/??/1845	03/27/1851	3	361	N	
Werner, John W.	22	Germany	Y	Bremen	New York	04/28/1883	02/24/1887			Y	
Werner, Michael	??	Bavaria	Y	Hamburg	New York	07/12/1843	10/14/1848	1	226	N	
Werner, Nicholas	34	Bavaria	Y	Havre	New York	11/26/1847	01/10/1853	5	536	N	
Werner, Peter	28	Prussia	Y	Liverpool	New York	05/06/1849	11/09/1855	13	200	N	
Werner, Sigmund Rudolf	30	Germany	Y	Bremen	New York	06/19/1884	03/16/1889			Y	
Wernert, John B.	44	France	Y	Havre	New York	11/11/1849	11/12/1852	6	399	N	
Wernery, Heinrich	29	Germany	Y	Amsterdam	Baltimore	11/28/1885	11/01/1887	19	124	N	
Wernery, Heinrich	29	Germany	Y	Amsterdam	Baltimore	11/28/1885	11/01/1887				
Wernigs, Phillip Jacob	40	Bavaria	Y	Antwerp	New Orleans	05/15/1847	05/27/1852	25	119	N	
Werning, August	38	Germany	Y	Bremen	Baltmore	07/01/1880	12/21/1885	19	27	N	
Werning, Gerhard	27	Prussia	Y	Bremen	New York	05/04/1848	04/08/1856	26	474	N	
Werning, John Herman Hen	32	Hanover	Y	Bremen	New Orleans	09/??/1844	10/21/1851	4	365	N	
Werning, Joseph	36	Germany	Y	Hamburg	New York	10/03/1871	10/30/1886	19	99	N	
Werning, Joseph	27	Germany	Y	Rotterdam	New York	06/10/1892	03/31/1897			Y	

CITIZENSHIP RECORDS

APPLICANT	AGE	COUNTRY OF ORIGIN	DEC	DEPART PORT	ENTRY PORT	ARRIVE DATE	DEC DATE	VOL	PG.	FLD	NAT DATE
Wernke, Bernard	30	Hanover	Y	Bremen	Baltimore	05/??/1848	10/31/1851	4	446	N	
Wernke, Henry	33	Germany	Y	Bremen	Baltimore	10/26/1888	02/12/1894			Y	
Wernke, Hermann	22	Germany	Y	Amsterdam	New York	04/25/1884	05/10/1888			Y	
Wernke, Joseph	25	Germany	Y	Amsterdam	New York	08/26/1882	08/15/1885			Y	
Wernke, William	21	Hanover	Y	Bremen	New Orleans	11/??/1847	10/??/1849	23	285	N	
Wernz, Fred	21	Germany	Y	Amsterdam	New York	08/28/1882	03/12/1884			Y	
Wernz, Mathew	26	Wurttemberg	Y	Havre	New York	08/16/1853	10/17/1857	15	442	N	
Werpup, Henry	29	Hanover	Y	Bremen	Baltimore	05/25/1854	11/02/1855	13	149	N	
Werrmann, Charles August	30	Germany	Y	?	New York	09/29/1881	10/11/1885			Y	
Wersel, Nicolaus	44	Holland	Y	Rio Janeiro	New York	08/01/1851	09/06/1852	25	366	N	
Wersman, William	22	Wurttemberg	Y	Havre	New Orleans	05/11/1851	08/08/1851	4	103	N	
Wertenberger, Anton	34	Germany	Y	Hamburg	New York	03/30/1887	05/20/1891			Y	
Werth, Charles	28	Germany	Y	Bremen	New York	03/14/1886	11/17/1894			Y	
Wertsch, Frederick	35	Hesse Darmsta	Y	Havre	New York	11/??/1857	12/31/1860	18	34	N	
Wertz, Adam	29	Bavaria	Y	Havre	New Orleans	08/20/1847	02/19/1849	23	198	N	
Wertz, Casper	23	Switzerland	Y	Havre	New Orleans	02/15/1848	08/07/1848	22	73	N	
Wertz, Henry	40	Germany	Y	Havre	New Orleans						
Wesdorp, John	26	Holland	Y	Antwerp	New York	05/17/1884	10/14/1891			Y	
Wesemann, William	22	Lippe Detmold	Y	Rotterdam	New Orleans	01/25/1854	09/30/1856	14	54	N	
Wesener, Albert	26	Prussia	Y	Bremen	Baltimore	05/21/1856	11/01/1858	17	248	N	
Wesler, Frank	60	Germany	N	Bremen	New York	10/03/1846	10/14/1848	1	221	N	
Wesling, William	25	Prussia	Y	Bremen	Baltimore	08/??/1846	?			Y	
Wesmann, Bernold	23	Oldenburg	Y	Bremen	Baltimore	08/04/1848	11/01/1851	4	451	N	
Wesner, Jacob	25	France	Y	Bremen	Baltimore	05/12/1848	05/25/1852	25	106	N	
Wesolowski, Paul	31	Germany	Y	Havre	New Orleans	12/26/1850	04/20/1854	8	222	N	
Wesp, Francis	32	Bohemia, Aust	Y	Havre	New York	04/01/1882	10/31/1888				
Wessel, August P.	28	Germany	Y	Bremen	Baltimore	11/06/1866	04/01/1872	18	483	N	
Wessel, B.	22	Germany	Y	Amsterdam	New York	09/11/1883	05/15/1890			Y	
Wessel, Bernard	22	Oldenburg	Y	Bremen	Baltimore	06/24/1882	12/05/1884			Y	
Wessel, Bernard	73	Germany	Y	Bremen	New York	10/18/1850	10/25/1855	13	141	N	
Wessel, Bernard	73	Germany	Y	Bremen	New York	09/14/1865	10/29/1888	19	198	N	
Wessel, Bernard P.	34	Germany	N	Bremen	New York	09/14/1865	10/29/1888			Y	
Wessel, Bernhard	39	Germany	Y	Bremen	New York	07/07/1873	?			Y	
Wessel, C. Henry William	47	Germany	Y	Bremen	Baltimore	05/23/1879	06/08/1889			Y	
Wessel, Christian	22	Hesse Cassel	Y	Bremen	New York	10/08/1876	11/14/1898			Y	
Wessel, D.T.	18	Hanover	Y	Bremen	New York	05/03/1854	02/04/1856	26	29	N	
Wessel, Frederick	28	Germany	Y	Bremen	New Orleans	11/20/1855	10/04/1858	17	31	N	
Wessel, Henry	43	Germany	N	Bremen	Baltimore	10/09/1881	11/06/1888			Y	
Wessel, Henry	28	Prussia	Y	Bremen	Baltimore	06/??/1860	?			Y	
Wessel, Henry H.L.	25	Germany	Y	Bremen	Baltimore	10/03/1844	08/28/1848	22	257	N	
Wessel, Herman	25	Oldenburg	Y	Bremen	Baltimore	04/16/1886	12/31/1888			Y	
Wessel, Herman	23	Germany	Y	Bremen	New Orleans	11/20/1849	07/24/1851	4	32	N	
Wessel, John	??	Germany	N	Antwerp	Philadelphia	04/17/1885	10/01/1887			Y	
Wessel, Joseph	30	Germany	Y	?	?	06/22/1886				Y	10/08/1892
Wessel, William Frederic	45	Germany	Y	Bremen	Baltimore	09/01/1883	07/26/1889			Y	
Wesseler, William	22	Hanover	Y	Bremen	New York	09/05/1884	08/15/1887			Y	
Wesseling, Gerhard Henry	33	Hanover	Y	Bremen	Baltimore	07/05/1857	09/12/1860	27	363	N	
Wesselmann, Caspar	27	Prussia	Y	Bremen	New Orleans	10/27/1852	10/26/1855	13	137	N	
Wesselmann, Henry	23	Prussia	Y	Bremen	Baltimore	10/24/1856	07/20/1858	16	513	N	
Wesselmann, John Arnold	36	Oldenburg	Y	Bremen	Baltimore	08/08/1853	08/04/1856	14	330	N	
Wessels, Conrad	25	Germany	Y	Bremen	Baltimore	07/01/1844	10/02/1848	22	379	N	
Wessels, Heinrich	40	Prussia	Y	Bremen	Baltimore	08/04/1881	08/15/1884			Y	
Wessels, Henry	40	Prussia	Y	Bremen	New Orleans	05/18/1849	10/10/1854	6	237	N	
Wessels, Henry	40	Prussia	Y	Bremen	New Orleans	05/01/1849	10/10/1854	11	240	N	
Wessels, Johann	62	Germany	Y	Bremen	New Orleans	05/01/1849	10/10/1855	11	356	N	
Wessels, John Henry	49	Germany	N	Bremen	Baltimore	07/??/1880	10/18/1888			Y	
Wessels, William	31	Germany	Y	Bremen	New York	08/21/1859	08/??/1861	28	120	N	10/05/1868
Wessinger, Jacob	27	Germany	Y	Bremen	Baltimore	04/05/1882	10/21/1889			Y	
Wessling, John Gerhard	26	Hanover	Y	Bremen	New Orleans	06/03/1880	09/02/1885			Y	
						11/29/1852	05/16/1854	8	450	N	

CITIZENSHIP RECORDS

APPLICANT	AGE	COUNTRY OF ORIGIN	DEC	DEPART PORT	ENTRY PORT	ARRIVE DATE	DEC DATE	VOL	PG.	FLD	NAT DATE
Wessling, John Gerhard	26	Hanover	Y	Bremen	New Orleans	11/29/1852	05/16/1854	9	323	N	
Wessling, John Herman	23	Hanover	Y	Bremen	New Orleans	11/29/1852	05/16/1854	8	451	N	
Wessling, John Herman	23	Hanover	Y	Bremen	New Orleans	11/29/1852	05/16/1854	9	324	N	
Wessmeier, Henry William	29	Hanover	Y	Bremen	Baltimore	10/27/1849	11/01/1852	5	118	N	
Wessner, Jacob	25	France	Y	Havre	New Orleans	12/26/1850	04/20/1854	9	93	N	
West, Noah	27	England	Y	Liverpool	New York	09/29/1847	05/11/1854	8	427	N	
West, Noah	27	England	Y	Liverpool	New York	09/29/1847	05/11/1854	9	300	N	
Westemeier, Henry	23	Germany	Y	Bremen	New York	09/01/1881	04/03/1882			Y	
Westendorf, Bernard	24	Hanover	Y	Bremen	Baltimore	10/24/1853	10/26/1855	13	135	N	
Westendorf, Franz	29	Germany	Y	Bremen	New York	05/03/1885	10/31/1888			Y	
Westendorf, Henry	23	Hanover	Y	Bremen	New Orleans	11/15/1854	11/01/1858	17	251	N	
Westendorf, Henry	20	Germany	Y	Bremen	Baltimore	09/01/1889	03/28/1890			Y	
Westendorf, Herman	34	Germany	Y	Bremen	Baltimore	08/26/1881	10/25/1888			Y	
Westendorf, Phillip	??	Hanover	Y	Bremen	New Orleans	12/29/18??	10/11/1848	1	149	N	
Westenkamp, Henry	27	Bavaria	Y	London	New York	11/20/1857	08/18/1860	27	295	N	
Westerbeke, Clemens	23	Hanover	Y	Bremen	New Orleans	12/08/1851	10/09/1854	6	107	N	
Westerbeke, Clemens	23	Hanover	Y	Bremen	New Orleans	12/08/1851	10/09/1854	11	110	N	
Westerfeld, Albert	27	Germany	Y	Bremen	New York	10/12/1881	09/14/1885			Y	
Westerhoff, Joseph	28	Prussia	Y	Bremen	New Orleans	05/04/1849	06/19/1851	3	411	N	
Westerkamp, Henry	27	Germany	Y	Bremen	Baltimore	05/24/1889	10/28/1892			Y	
Westerman, Florenz	28	Prussia	Y	Bremen	Baltimore	04/29/1848	10/20/1851	4	353	N	
Westerman, Henry	25	Germany	Y	?	?	07/24/1872	10/20/1896			Y	
Westermann, Edward	35	Germany	Y	Bremen	New York	07/??/1881	11/13/1886			Y	
Westermann, Frederick	30	Prussia	Y	Bremen	Baltimore	12/24/1846	10/03/1848	22	405	N	
Westermann, Frederick	22	Prussia	Y	Bremen	New York	10/01/1857	02/29/1860	27	115	N	
Westermann, Herman	29	Hanover	Y	Bremen	New Orleans	11/28/1848	12/12/1851	4	509	N	
Westermann, Martin	26	Hanover	Y	Bremen	New York	09/25/1866	05/03/18??	17	541	N	
Westermann, Theodore	23	Hanover	Y	Bremen	Baltimore	09/20/1848	12/12/1851	4	510	N	
Westermann, Wilhelm	56	Germany	N	Bremen	New York	12/??/1845	?			Y	
Westermeyer, Frederick	30	Germany	Y	Bremen	Baltimore	07/01/1882	10/26/1887			Y	
Westermeyer, Herman	45	Germany	Y	Bremen	?	??/??/1868	10/26/1887			Y	
Westfal, Nicholas	27	Prussia	Y	London	New York	05/16/1846	11/13/1848	1	254	N	
Westhoff, Arnold	31	Prussia	Y	Bremen	New Orleans	12/23/1848	04/27/1850	3	15	N	
Westhorn, Lambert	24	Baden	Y	Havre	New Orleans	04/30/1854	10/01/1856	14	108	N	
Weston, Bartholomew	32	England	Y	Liverpool	New Orleans	05/28/1849	03/20/1851	3	238	N	
Weston, James William	51	England	Y	London	New York	12/30/1882	08/06/1895			Y	
Westphal, August Ferdina	42	Prussia	Y	Hamburg	New York	07/01/1854	03/20/1856	26	237	N	
Westrich, Charles	30	Bavaria	Y	Havre	New Orleans	06/??/1847	04/27/1855	11	313	N	
Westwood, John	38	England	Y	Liverpool	New York	03/05/1849	03/08/1851	3	210	N	
Wete, John (Witte?)	44	Prussia	Y	Bremen	New Orleans	11/19/1844	08/15/1848	22	176	N	
Wetenkamp, Henry	29	Hanover	Y	Bremen	New Orleans	05/02/1849	05/20/1852	25	75	N	
Wettar, F. Joseph	45	France	N	Havre	New York	08/31/1870	?			Y	
Wetterer, Severin	39	Germany	Y	Havre	New York	08/21/1867	10/08/1883			Y	
Wetternacht, Charles	48	Germany	Y	Havre	New York	10/12/1873	09/13/1892			Y	
Wettle, Amand	55	Germany	N	Bremen	New York	12/??/1869	?			Y	
Wettstein, Alfred	22	Switzerland	Y	Havre	New York	03/09/1887	04/07/1890			Y	
Wetzel, Emanuel	33	Germany	Y	Havre	New York	08/31/1880	10/24/1888			Y	
Wetzel, Fridolin	32	Baden	Y	Havre	New York	12/15/1853	08/27/1862	18	404	N	
Wetzstein, Max B.	23	Kurhessen	Y	Havre	New York	09/30/1849	07/09/1855	11	361	N	
Wetzstein, Meier	19	Germany	Y	Bremen	New York	08/30/1879	02/13/1880			Y	
Wexler, Sam	16	Russia	N	?	Philadelphia	00/00/1882				Y	10/24/1887
Weyand, Nicholas, Jr.	24	Bavaria	Y	Havre	New York	05/10/1850	10/06/1856	14	228	N	
Weydemann, Heinrich	28	Hanover	Y	Bremen	Baltimore	09/08/1857	06/01/1859	17	444	N	
Weydmann, Johannes	24	Germany	Y	Bremen	New York	12/21/1888	10/29/1891			Y	
Weyer, Martin	35	Prussia	Y	Bremen	New York	07/26/1857	10/25/1858	17	102	N	
Weyl, Gottlieb	33	Germany	Y	Hamburg	New York	08/19/1881	10/21/1891			Y	
Weyl, Gustav	40	Germany	Y	Hamburg	New York	03/12/1881	01/15/1889			Y	
Weymann, John	22	Germany	Y	Bremen	New York	08/27/1882	09/01/1885			Y	
Weymar, John	23	Prussia	Y	Havre	New Orleans	05/29/1852	02/11/1853	7	144	N	

CITIZENSHIP RECORDS

APPLICANT	AGE	COUNTRY OF ORIGIN	DEC	DEPART PORT	ENTRY PORT	ARRIVE DATE	DEC DATE	VOL	PG.	FLD	NAT DATE
Weymar, Philip	22	Prussia	Y	Havre	New Orleans	06/29/1852	02/11/1853	7	145	N	
Weyser, Bernhard Friedri	45	Germany	Y	Hamburg	Philadelphia	08/16/1886	04/16/1889			Y	
Whalen, Martin	59	Ireland	N	Galway	Canada	05/??/1846	?			Y	
Whallon, John	30	Ireland	Y	Montreal	Buffalo	08/15/1844	10/02/1848	1	39	N	
Whelan, James	36	Ireland	Y	Liverpool	New York	08/08/1848	02/25/1851	3	171	N	
Whelan, John	31	Ireland	Y	Liverpool	New York	08/07/1853	02/09/1857	15	3	N	
Whelan, Lawrence	25	Ireland	Y	Liverpool	New York	03/28/1852	07/14/1855	11	386	N	
Whelan, Martin	??	Ireland	N	?	?	?	?			Y	
Whelan, Patrick	26	Ireland	Y	Liverpool	New Orleans	03/10/1851	03/30/1857	15	106	N	
Whelan, Richard	23	Ireland	Y	Liverpool	New York	10/05/1849	04/04/1853	8	8	N	
Whelan, Thomas	26	Ireland	Y	Liverpool	Baltimore	04/04/1880	11/10/1884			Y	
Whelen, Patrick	24	Ireland	Y	Liverpool	New Orleans	10/19/1849	02/21/1852	24	148	N	
Wherty, Daniel	30	Ireland	Y	Toronto	Cincinnati	03/22/1859	04/22/1862	18	328	N	
Whitaker, James	??	Great Britain	Y	?	?	?	04/13/1883			Y	
Whitaker, Samuel H.	25	England	Y	Liverpool	New York	09/13/1846	07/23/1855	11	420	N	
Whitaker, Thomas	33	England	Y	Liverpool	New Orleans	05/26/1849	03/10/1851	3	244	N	
White, Andreas	25	Tuscany	Y	Leghorn	New York	09/22/1851	11/20/1857	16	37	N	
White, Arthur	43	England	Y	Liverpool	New York	02/23/1884	01/12/1894			Y	
White, Barney	25	Ireland	Y	Liverpool	New Orleans	04/14/1851	05/13/1854	8	439	N	
White, Barney	25	Ireland	Y	Liverpool	New Orleans	04/14/1851	05/13/1854	9	312	N	
White, Edmond (Edward?)	25	Ireland	Y	Liverpool	Vermont	07/07/1847	03/09/1852	24	276	N	
White, Edward	35	Ireland	Y	Canada	New York	??/07/1839	11/07/1849	23	324	N	
White, Herman	37	Austria	Y	Bremen	New York	08/24/1876	06/06/1882			Y	
White, Isral	37	Russia	Y	Amsterdam	New York	04/17/1890	10/19/1897			Y	
White, James	31	Ireland	Y	Liverpool	New Orleans	04/18/1847	02/14/1850	2	74	N	
White, James	29	Ireland	Y	Dublin	New York	03/02/1852	08/10/1859	17	471	N	
White, James D.	25	England	Y	Liverpool	Portland	02/??/1871	05/04/1876			Y	
White, John	20	Ireland	Y	Liverpool	New York	03/07/1849	02/21/1853	7	204	N	
White, John	27	Ireland	Y	Liverpool	New York	06/22/1849	05/13/1854	8	438	N	
White, John	27	Ireland	Y	Liverpool	New York	06/22/1849	05/13/1854	9	311	N	
White, John	25	Ireland	Y	Queenstown	New York	03/27/1892	03/29/1898			Y	
White, Laurence	36	Bavaria	Y	Bremen	New Orleans	11/11/1852	04/06/1853			Y	
White, Martin	??	Ireland	Y	Dublin	New York	??/17/1848	08/??/1851	4	183	N	
White, Martin	26	Ireland	Y	Liverpool	New York	11/10/1850	12/26/1851	24	8	N	
White, Matthew	25	Ireland	Y	Liverpool	New Orleans	04/22/1850	12/31/1852	5	480	N	
White, Michael	47	Ireland	N	Liverpool	New York	07/??/1860	?			Y	
White, Patrick	36	Ireland	Y	Liverpool	New Orleans	07/03/1848	06/10/1852	25	221	N	
White, Thomas	43	England	Y	Liverpool	Philadelphia	03/21/1852	01/14/1856	13	463	N	
White, Timothy	36	Ireland	Y	Cork	Boston	07/??/1847	03/17/1853	7	344	N	
White, William	26	Ireland	Y	Liverpool	New York	06/06/1847	04/01/1853	7	483	N	
White, William	44	England	Y	?	?	?	09/21/1894			Y	
White, William	35	Ireland	Y	Liverpool	New Orleans	05/??/1849	12/??/1849	23	387	N	
White, William C.	52	Ireland	N	Liverpool	Philadelphia	06/??/1843	?			Y	
Whiting, Richard Ross	29	Canada	Y	Niagra Falls	Watertown, N	03/25/1892	06/24/1901			Y	
Whiting, William A.	28	Canada	Y	?	?	?	09/15/1896			Y	
Whitney, Joseph	23	Ireland	Y	Waterford	New York	07/31/1851	02/18/1856	26	99	N	
Whitsill, Richard Edward	22	Ireland	Y	Dublin	New Orleans	03/??/1849	10/22/1851	4	374	N	
Whittaker, George	41	England	Y	Liverpool	New Orleans	09/??/1849	12/??/1849	23	395	N	
Whittington, Rowland J.	36	England	Y	Liverpool	New York	07/10/1847	03/10/1851	3	231	N	
Whittmann, Nicholas A.	32	France	Y	Havre	New York	10/10/1847	10/30/1852	5	81	N	
Whitworth, James	45	England	Y	Liverpool	New York	09/08/1871	10/04/1888			Y	
Wibbeler, Heinrich	48	Germany	Y	Bremen	New York	07/20/1866	10/26/1887			Y	
Wibbeling, Joseph	23	Germany	Y	Amsterdam	New York	05/01/1881	08/15/1883			Y	
Wibben, Bernard Herman	31	Hanover	Y	Bremen	Baltimore	07/06/1845	02/09/1852	24	78	N	
Wibben, Gerard	27	Hanover	Y	Bremen	New Orleans	11/18/1848	06/19/1851	3	404	N	
Wibben, Herman	27	Hanover	Y	Bremen	Baltimore	05/09/1858	11/01/1860	27	539	N	
Wibiral, Julius	36	Austria	Y	Hamburg	New York	10/27/1888	09/11/1893			Y	
Wichard, John	33	Hanover	Y	Bremen	New Orleans	06/13/1850	10/07/1854	10	525	N	
Wichard, John P.	33	Hanover	Y	Bremen	New Orleans	06/13/1850	10/07/1854	12	464	N	

CITIZENSHIP RECORDS

APPLICANT	AGE	COUNTRY OF ORIGIN	DEC	DEPART PORT	ENTRY PORT	ARRIVE DATE	DEC DATE	VOL	PG.	FLD	NAT DATE
Wichers, William	25	Germany	Y	Bremen	New York	07/02/1869	07/06/1875			Y	
Wichmann, Heinrich	31	Saxony	Y	Bremen	Baltimore	11/28/1850	09/01/1862	18	431	N	
Wichmann, William	38	Germany	Y	Bremen	New York	07/18/1885	06/11/1888			Y	
Wickart, Balthaser	23	Switzerland	Y	Liverpool	New York	06/20/1852	08/27/1855	11	499	N	
Wickenbrick, Bernard	43	Germany	Y	Bremen	Baltimore	06/15/1865	10/22/1888	19	158	N	
Wicker, Vinzenz	24	Wurttemberg	Y	Havre	New York	12/16/1853	10/10/1854	6	225	N	
Wicker, Vinzenz	24	Wurttemberg	Y	Havre	New York	12/16/1853	10/10/1854	11	228	N	
Wickfeldt, Henry	28	Germany	Y	Bremen	New York	04/21/1882	12/26/1885			Y	
Wickler, John	48	Germany	N	Bremen	New York	05/??/1850	?			Y	
Wickman, Henry	28	Oldenburg	Y	Bremen	New Orleans	04/01/1849	01/10/1853	7	4	N	
Widdel, Henry August	22	Hanover	Y	Bremen	New Orleans	11/29/1854	02/02/1856	13	538	N	
Wides, Thomas	25	Russia	Y	?	?	?	10/20/1888			Y	
Widikson, John	29	Sweden	Y	Guttenberg	New York	06/15/1884	11/07/1888			Y	
Widman, Peter	25	Baden	Y	Havre	New York	??/10/1852	04/17/1855	11	264	N	
Widman, William	23	Wurttemberg	Y	Havre	New York	05/01/1847	02/22/1851	3	157	N	
Widmann, Ferdinand	25	Baden	Y	Havre	New York	11/05/1852	09/25/1854	10	223	N	
Widmann, Ludwig	26	Germany	Y	Bremen	New York	10/15/1888	10/07/1890			Y	
Widmer, George	52	Germany	Y	Amsterdam	New York	05/27/1880	10/01/1883			Y	
Widmer, Joseph	??	Switzerland	Y	?	?	?	09/10/1894			Y	
Wiechelman, F. A.	30	Oldenburg	Y	Bremen	Baltimore	06/10/1845	09/01/1848	22	289	N	
Wiechering, Louis	32	Germany	Y	Bremen	New York	04/28/1883	01/14/1888			Y	
Wiechers, F.	28	Germany	Y	Hamburg	New York	03/03/1883	08/04/1885			Y	
Wiechert, Frederick	28	Hanover	Y	Bremen	Baltimore	10/09/1854	12/29/1857	16	276	N	
Wiechmann, Joseph	48	Germany	Y	Bremen	Baltimore	08/28/1881	12/08/1886			Y	
Wiedemann, August	29	Germany	Y	Havre	New York	10/10/1890	01/11/1897			Y	
Wiedemann, Charles F.	31	Germany	Y	Havre	New York	01/26/1882	02/05/1887			Y	
Wiedemann, William	27	Germany	Y	Havre	New York	01/26/1882	05/21/1888			Y	
Wiedemer, Otto	41	Germany	Y	Havre	New York	12/13/1878	04/21/1890			Y	
Wiedenbein, Heinrich	29	Germany	Y	Bremen	Baltimore	05/28/1886	05/24/1888			Y	
Wiedenbein, William	23	Germany	Y	Hamburg	New York	05/05/1885	01/02/1886			Y	
Wiedenweber, William	22	Germany	Y	Bremen	Baltimore	10/07/1880	10/02/1884			Y	
Wiederecht, Elias	50	Kurhessen	Y	Bremen	New Orleans	12/25/1850	09/17/1855	13	53	N	
Wiederkehr, Joseph	24	Switzerland	Y	Havre	New York	12/03/1881	12/29/1883			Y	
Wiederstein, Ludwig	31	Prussia	Y	Liverpool	New York	07/05/1854	03/02/1858	16	356	N	
Wiedersum, Philipp	22	Hesse Darmsta	Y	Bremen	New Orleans	02/09/1849	11/07/1851	4	498	N	
Wieding, Jacob	34	Germany	Y	Amsterdam	New York	03/10/1892	03/20/1900			Y	
Wiegand, Frank	??	Germany	N	?	?	10/00/1881				Y	10/26/1892
Wiegand, John	33	Germany	Y	Antwerp	New York	12/31/1887	09/11/1895			Y	
Wiegand, Louis	32	Hanover	Y	Bremen	New York	07/17/1857	03/20/1862	18	274	N	
Wiegand, Louis	??	Germany	Y	Antwerp	New York	04/24/1885	10/07/1890			Y	
Wiegand, Peter	27	Germany	Y	Rotterdam	New York	??/??/1879	06/01/1886			Y	
Wiegand, Wendel	35	Hesse Darmsta	Y	Antwerp	New York	09/23/1852	12/29/1855	13	398	N	
Wiegart, William	36	Hanover	Y	Bremen	Baltimore	10/08/1856	05/29/1862	18	341	N	
Wiegel, Joseph	66	Germany	N	Bremen	Baltimore	08/29/1873	?			Y	
Wieger, Adolph	26	Brunswick	Y	Hamburg	New York	06/26/1854	10/09/1854	6	92	N	
Wieger, Adolph	26	Brunswick	Y	Brunswick	New York	06/26/1854	10/09/1854	11	95	N	
Wieger, William	27	Brunswick	Y	Hamburg	New York	06/26/1854	10/09/1854	6	93	N	
Wieger, William	27	Brunswick	Y	Hamburg	New York	06/26/1854	10/09/1854	11	96	N	
Wiegers, Henry	28	Holland	Y	Bremen	New Orleans	06/11/1857	02/11/1860	27	103	N	
Wiegmann, Barney	35	Hanover	Y	Bremen	Baltimore	10/20/1846	10/20/1851	4	336	N	
Wiegmann, Frederick	21	Hanover	Y	Bremen	Baltimore	05/24/1854	03/05/1857	15	66	N	
Wiegmann, Henry	36	Hanover	Y	Bremen	New Orleans	12/19/1847	10/09/1854	6	105	N	
Wiegmann, Henry	36	Hanover	Y	Bremen	New Orleans	12/19/1847	10/09/1854	11	108	N	
Wiegmann, Henry	36	Hanover	Y	Bremen	New Orleans	01/18/1854	10/20/1858	17	82	N	
Wiehmann, Gerhard	45	Hanover	Y	Bremen	Philadelphia	10/22/1889	10/27/1890			Y	
Wieland, Anton	24	Germany	Y	Antwerp	New York	08/24/1888	10/27/1890			Y	
Wieland, George	30	Germany	Y	Antwerp	Philadelphia	10/24/1889	03/16/1892			Y	
Wieland, Joseph	23	Germany	Y	Havre	New York	11/06/1882	10/26/1888			Y	
Wieland, Lukas	26	Germany	Y	Antwerp	New York	05/13/1893	07/27/1896			Y	
Wieland, Otto	43	Germany	Y	Antwerp							

CITIZENSHIP RECORDS

APPLICANT	AGE	COUNTRY OF ORIGIN	DEC	DEPART PORT	ENTRY PORT	ARRIVE DATE	DEC DATE	VOL	PG.	FLD	NAT DATE
Wieland, Paul	22	Germany	Y	Liegnitz	New York	05/16/1890	11/01/1894			Y	
Wieland, Richard	34	Germany	Y	Bremen	New York	03/01/1894	06/30/1900			Y	
Wielenberg, John Herman	30	Oldenburg	Y	Bremen	New York	05/02/1851	05/25/1854	8	526	N	
Wielenberg, John Herman	30	Oldenburg	Y	Bremen	New York	05/02/1851	05/25/1854	9	400	N	
Wielenborg, John Henry	48	Oldenburg	Y	Bremen	Baltimore	09/30/1850	08/15/1860	27	291	N	
Wielent, Henry	50	Germany	N	Bremen	New York	10/??/1851	?			Y	
Wielert, Christian	60	Hanover	Y	Bremen	New York	10/18/1851	08/26/1862	18	399	N	
Wieling, Richard John	42	Holland	Y	Amsterdam	New York	09/20/1890	12/26/1893			Y	
Wielinga, Peter	23	Holland	Y	Rotterdam	New York	09/25/1871	06/01/1872	18	503	N	
Wielink, John	35	Holland	Y	Rotterdam	New York	10/14/1848	11/11/1852	5	272	N	
Wielink, John	35	Holland	Y	Rotterdam	New York	10/14/1848	11/11/1852	6	396	N	
Wiemann, Bernhard	23	Prussia	Y	Bremen	New Orleans	12/10/1848	12/20/1851	4	542	N	
Wiemeyer, William	36	Germany	Y	Antwerp	New York	11/20/1880	05/10/1888			Y	
Wienecke, Fred	28	Germany	Y	Bremen	New York	07/24/1886	11/09/1887			Y	
Wieneke, Anton	23	Germany	Y	?	?	?	06/16/1892			Y	
Wiens, John	40	Prussia	Y	Hamburg	New York	06/01/1853	10/22/1857	15	479	N	
Wierling, Bernard	32	Prussia	Y	Antwerp	New York	07/16/1857	05/08/1861	18	162	N	
Wiermel, Michael	24	Bavaria	Y	Havre	New York	05/31/1849	05/11/1854	9	297	N	
Wiers, Henry	30	Prussia	Y	Bremen	New Orleans	12/??/1846	12/15/1852	5	419	N	
Wiersching, John P. G.	29	Saxony	Y	Bremen	Philadelphia	08/20/1840	10/07/1848	22	472	N	
Wierwille, Heinrich	58	Germany	Y	Bremen	Baltimore	06/17/1867	05/14/1894			Y	
Wiese, Arnold	27	Germany	Y	Bremen	New York	04/27/1881	01/16/1884			Y	
Wiese, David	27	Prussia	Y	Bremerhafen	New Orleans	05/06/1860	01/10/1861	18	51	N	
Wiese, John	24	Germany	Y	Bremen	New York	04/27/1881	01/16/1884			Y	
Wiesemann, August	59	Germany	Y	Hamburg	New York	11/26/1881	11/25/1884			Y	
Wiesen, John	32	Bavaria	Y	Bremen	New Orleans	09/12/1845	??/??/1852	25	257	N	
Wiesen, Salamon	25	Austria	Y	Hamburg	New York	02/23/1891	03/22/1894	21	65	N	
Wiesen, Soloman	25	Austria	Y	Hamburg	New York	02/23/1891	03/22/1894			Y	
Wieser, George	47	Germany	Y	Bremen	Baltimore	04/29/1891	10/11/1900			Y	
Wieser, John	58	Baden	Y	Havre	New Orleans	12/25/1852	11/01/1858	17	246	N	
Wieser, Joseph	??	Germany	Y	?	New York	06/??/1888	10/29/1888			Y	
Wiesinger, August	??	Germany	N	?	?	09/13/1887				Y	10/28/1892
Wiesmann, George	38	Germany	Y	Bremen	Baltimore	04/15/1883	02/23/1889			Y	
Wiesner, Robert	33	Germany	Y	Bremen	New York	08/22/1882	08/29/1885			Y	
Wiest, Frank	40	Germany	Y	Bremen	New York	09/05/1873	11/03/1884			Y	
Wiesz, Frederick	30	Wurttemberg	Y	Havre	New York	07/04/1852	10/09/1854	6	136	N	
Wietfeldt, Frederick	44	Hanover	Y	Bremen	New York	06/12/1852	09/10/1855	11	517	N	
Wietfeldt, William	31	Germany	Y	Bremen	New York	08/04/1882	02/26/1887			Y	
Wiethoff, Ernst	27	Prussia	Y	Bremen	Baltimore	05/01/1857	01/30/1860	27	77	N	
Wietkamper, Joseph	27	Prussia	Y	Bremen	New Orleans	12/10/1850	05/29/1852	25	128	N	
Wietlisbach, E.	30	Switzerland	Y	Havre	New York	05/??/1879	01/20/1885			Y	
Wiewel, Bernard	31	Prussia	Y	Bremen	Baltimore	05/26/1859	11/03/1860	18	8	N	
Wiewerig, John Henry	31	Oldenburg	Y	Amsterdam	Baltimore	09/17/1844	08/18/1848	22	207	N	
Wiezorkowski, Adolph	??	Germany	Y	?	?	?	04/26/1878			Y	
Wigand, Philip	58	Germany	N	Antwerp	New York	10/11/1852	?			Y	
Wigbels, Bernard	25	Hanover	Y	Bremen	Baltimore	05/09/1858	11/01/1860	27	535	N	
Wigel, Andrew	27	Bavaria	Y	Hamburg	New York	11/04/1844	10/13/1848	1	195	N	
Wiggeringloh, Bernard	32	Prussia	Y	Antwerp	New Orleans	12/23/1853	10/28/1858	17	148	N	
Wiggers, H. Louis	26	Hanover	Y	Bremen	New Orleans	06/29/1848	02/15/1849	23	135	N	
Wiggers, Henry	51	Hanover	N	Bremen	New York	11/??/1853	?	28	278	N	09/28/1860
Wighaus, Theodore	21	Hanover	Y	Bremen	New Orleans	12/25/1851	12/21/1857	16	237	N	
Wihlein, Adam	37	Baden	Y	Antwerp	New York	02/23/1852	04/10/1856	26	483	N	
Wilb, John	42	Switzerland	Y	Havre	New York	06/28/1852	03/26/1856	26	349	N	
Wilberding, Frank	23	Oldenburg	Y	Bremen	New Orleans	11/25/1850	06/13/1854	10	129	N	
Wilberding, Frank	23	Oldenburg	Y	Bremen	New Orleans	11/25/1850	06/13/1854	12	66	N	
Wilberding, Joseph	23	Germany	Y	Bremen	Baltimore	06/05/1882	11/03/1886			Y	
Wilbers, G.	24	Germany	Y	Amsterdam	New York	11/05/1882	01/18/1884			Y	
Wilbers, Henry	22	Germany	Y	Bremen	Baltimore	06/18/1882	04/19/1886			Y	
Wilcke, John	30	Hanover	Y	Bremen	Baltimore	07/04/1854	10/08/1857	15	377	N	

CITIZENSHIP RECORDS

APPLICANT	AGE	COUNTRY OF ORIGIN	DEC	DEPART PORT	ENTRY PORT	ARRIVE DATE	DEC DATE	VOL	PG.	FLD	NAT DATE
Wilcox, Richard	27	England	Y	London	New York	11/16/1852	02/02/1856	13	535	N	
Wilcox, Thomas	35	England	Y	Liverpool	Philadelphia	08/13/1856	04/22/1861	18	141	N	
Wilcumm, Bernardt	30	Kurhessen	Y	Bremen	New York	05/??/1851	03/28/1853	7	442	N	
Wild, Anton	26	Germany	Y	Havre	New York	03/05/1894	06/01/1896			Y	
Wilde, George	27	Germany	Y	Bremen	New York	07/04/1881	03/28/1884			Y	
Wilde, Henry	30	Germany	Y	Bremen	Baltimore	09/02/1876	02/02/1882			Y	
Wilde, J.	28	Germany	Y	Rotterdam	New York	10/22/1876	04/03/1882			Y	
Wildenhaus, Bernard	36	Prussia	Y	Bremen	New Orleans	12/28/1843	08/15/1848	22	128	N	
Wilder, Alfred James	31	England	Y	Liverpool	New York	10/12/1888	11/21/1898			Y	
Wildhaber, John	42	Switzerland	Y	Havre	New York	05/12/1882	10/26/1901			Y	
Wilds, Christian	40	Hesse Cassel	Y	London	New York	10/??/1854	11/06/1856	14	498	N	
Wildt, Christian	36	Hanover	Y	Hamburg	New York	09/20/1852	10/18/1852	5	11	N	
Wildt, Frederick Jr.	36	Germany	Y	?	New York	??/??/1872	10/21/1885			Y	
Wildt, Michael	48	Wurttemberg	Y	London	New Orleans	09/24/1852	10/05/1854	10	451	N	
Wildt, Michael	48	Wurttemberg	Y	London	New Orleans	09/24/1852	10/05/1854	12	390	N	
Wile, Henry	24	Bavaria	Y	Havre	New York	07/03/1848	03/06/1852	24	244	N	
Wiley, Benjamin	26	Wurttemberg	Y	Havre	New York	09/10/1855	09/29/1856	14	4	N	
Wilharm, Charles Frederi	22	Mecklenburg	Y	Bremen	New Orleans	05/29/1852	05/27/1854	9	433	N	
Wilhelm, Eduard	21	Germany	Y	Antwerp	New York	09/28/1891	12/26/1894	21	77	N	
Wilhelm, Edward	21	Germany	Y	Antwerp	New York	09/23/1891	12/26/1894			Y	
Wilhelm, Eugene	22	Germany	Y	Rotterdam	New York	05/21/1880	07/21/1884			Y	
Wilhelm, Gustave	44	Germany	Y	Rotterdam	New York	01/??/1871	12/14/1885			Y	
Wilhelm, Jacob	40	Prussia	Y	Antwerp	New York	04/18/1849	11/25/1858	17	355	N	
Wilhelm, Martin	38	France	Y	Havre	New York	07/??/1847	01/02/1856	13	414	N	
Wilhelmy, Louis H.	41	Prussia	N	Bremen	New York	09/30/1865	?			Y	
Wilhelmy, William C.	??	Germany	Y	?	?	?	11/03/1888			Y	
Wilisch, Franz B.O.	40	Germany	Y	Bremen	New York	12/04/1882	06/21/1884			Y	
Wilka, August	22	Hanover	Y	Bremen	New Orleans	05/15/1854	10/04/1858	17	46	N	
Wilkarm, Charles Frederi	22	Mecklenburg	Y	Bremen	New Orleans	05/29/1852	05/27/1854	10	16	N	
Wilke, Ferdinand	32	Oldenburg	Y	Bremen	New Orleans	01/01/1847	02/19/1849	23	195	N	
Wilke, Frank	33	Oldenburg	Y	Bremen	Baltimore	05/08/1848	03/12/1852	24	292	N	
Wilke, Henry	28	Germany	Y	Amsterdam	New York	10/07/1886	01/13/1892			Y	
Wilke, Herman	25	Prussia	Y	Bremen	New Orleans	11/18/1852	09/21/1854	10	146	N	
Wilke, Herman	25	Prussia	Y	Bremen	New Orleans	11/18/1852	09/21/1854	12	85	N	
Wilke, Herman H.	44	Hanover	Y	Bremen	Baltimore	11/08/1845	10/11/1848	1	122	N	
Wilke, John Henry	53	Germany	Y	Bremen	Baltimore	03/30/1890	02/08/1894			Y	
Wilke, John Henry	21	Hanover	Y	Bremen	Baltimore	05/29/1848	03/03/1852	24	226	N	
Wilke, Wilhelm	21	Germany	Y	Bremen	New York	04/03/1881	11/02/1881			Y	
Wilkemeier, Herman	23	Hanover	Y	Bremen	Baltimore	04/17/1846	10/12/1848	1	173	N	
Wilken, Anthony	23	Hanover	Y	Bremen	New Orleans	12/26/1846	10/07/1848	22	494	N	
Wilken, Frank	35	Germany	Y	Bremen	New York	07/19/1881	03/21/1891	19	316	N	
Wilken, Frank	35	Germany	Y	Bremen	New York	07/19/1884	03/21/1891			Y	
Wilken, John Barney	25	Germany	Y	Bremen	New York	03/16/1889	06/13/1891			Y	
Wilken, Lambert	40	Germany	Y	?	Baltimore	??/??/1890	04/03/1896			Y	
Wilken, William W.	23	Hanover	Y	Bremen	New Orleans	05/01/1849	05/20/1852	25	63	N	
Wilkening, Henry	36	Hanover	Y	Bremen	New Orleans	11/04/1850	12/24/1851	24	2	N	
Wilkens, Bernhard	28	Germany	Y	Bremen	New York	10/27/1889	11/04/1895			Y	
Wilkens, Henry	33	Hanover	Y	Bremen	New Orleans	01/??/1841	06/09/1852	25	216	N	
Wilkens, J. Henry	19	Germany	Y	Hamburg	New York	06/20/1874	10/10/1874			Y	
Wilker, ?	??	Hanover	Y	?	?	??/01/18??	10/29/1850	2	326	N	
Wilker, Adam	36	Hanover	Y	Bremen	Baltimore	03/16/1847	10/18/1851	4	323	N	
Wilker, Wilhelm	35	Hanover	Y	Bremen	New Orleans	12/05/1853	09/27/1856	14	420	N	
Wilking, Wilhelm	??	Germany	N	?	?	06/00/1885				Y	10/29/1892
Wilkins, James	27	England	Y	Liverpool	New York	10/23/1887	11/23/1893			Y	
Wilkowsky, Julius	40	Russia	Y	Bremen	New York	08/01/1886	10/16/1895			Y	
Will, Adam	29	Bavaria	Y	Havre	New York	05/28/1851	11/15/1852	5	277	N	
Will, Adam	29	Bavaria	Y	Havre	New York	05/28/1851	11/15/1852	6	401	N	
Will, George	72	Germany	Y	Bremen	New York	08/15/1900	08/19/1903			Y	
Will, John	51	Germany	N	Havre	New York	08/??/1867	?			Y	

CITIZENSHIP RECORDS

APPLICANT	AGE	COUNTRY OF ORIGIN	DEC	DEPART PORT	ENTRY PORT	ARRIVE DATE	DEC DATE	VOL	PG.	FLD	NAT DATE
Will, Valentine	29	Bavaria	Y	Havre	New Orleans	02/01/1845	08/07/1848	22	72	N	
Will, Valentine	55	Bavaria	Y	Havre	New York	06/01/1845	10/05/1848	22	443	N	
Will, Willie	30	Germany	Y	?	New York	09/21/1889	04/02/1895			Y	
Wille, August	25	Mecklenburg S	Y	Hamburg	New York	11/09/1851	11/01/1852	5	138	N	
Wille, August	25	Mecklenburg S	Y	Hamburg	New York	11/09/1851	11/01/1852	6	264	N	
Wille, Gerhard	30	Oldenburg	Y	Bremen	New York	05/01/1849	10/25/1851	4	401	N	
Willeke, John	49	Prussia	N	Bremen	Baltimore	06/25/1861	?			Y	
Willeke, William	44	Prussia	Y	Bremen	New York	05/05/1852	11/01/1852	5	178	N	
Willeke, William	44	Prussia	Y	Bremen	New York	05/50/1852	11/01/1852	6	304	N	
Willen, William	35	Germany	N	Amsterdam	New York	05/??/1869	?			Y	
Willenborg, W.	33	Germany	Y	Hamburg	New York	08/02/1882	01/02/1885			Y	
Willenbrinck, Henry	30	Oldenburg	Y	Bremen	New Orleans	10/12/1852	10/09/1854	6	61	N	
Willenbrink, Bernard Ant	23	Oldenburg	Y	Bremen	New Orleans	05/01/1849	06/14/1852	25	256	N	
Willenbrink, Henry	30	Oldenburg	Y	Bremen	New Orleans	10/12/1852	10/09/1854	11	62	N	
Willer, Henry	22	Germany	Y	Bremen	New York	09/29/1886	10/25/1889			Y	
Willer, Henry	30	Germany	Y	Bremen	Baltimore	08/27/1881	05/16/1893			Y	
Willer, Henry	39	Hanover	Y	Bremen	New Orleans	11/10/1847	06/14/1852	25	250	N	
Willering, Louis	21	Germany	Y	Bremen	New York	07/28/1890	08/10/1892			Y	
Willet, Jacob	39	Prussia	Y	Antwerp	New York	09/23/1851	10/10/1854	6	206	N	
Willet, Jacob	39	Prussia	Y	Antwerp	New York	09/23/1851	10/10/1854	11	209	N	
Willi, Albert	26	Switzerland	Y	Havre	New York	02/20/1887	10/24/1889			Y	
Willi, Theodore	??	Switzerland	Y	Havre	New Orleans	03/27/1854	06/15/1861	18	194	N	
William, Michael	35	Bavaria	Y	London	Buffalo	07/24/1847	07/30/1851	3	550	N	
Williams, Charles	31	England	Y	Liverpool	New York	01/31/1888	11/05/1889			Y	
Williams, David S.	29	Wales	Y	Liverpool	New York	08/29/1846	02/24/1851	3	160	N	
Williams, Edward Hawkin	40	England	Y	London	New York	03/??/1872	10/17/1881			Y	09/25/1884
Williams, Edward Vincent	??	Ireland	Y	?	?	?	03/05/1891			Y	
Williams, Francis	27	Luxembourg	Y	Antwerp	New York	12/16/1852	09/29/1858	16	182	N	
Williams, Francis	28	England	Y	Liverpool	New York	06/22/1885	10/31/1893			Y	
Williams, Frederick	41	England	Y	London	New York	08/17/1889	10/12/1893			Y	
Williams, Henry	42	England	Y	Liverpool	New York	03/31/1880	10/20/1892			Y	
Williams, Hugh	32	Wales	Y	Liverpool	New York	06/??/1853	01/26/1857	14	474	N	
Williams, James P.	27	Scotland	Y	Glasgow	New York	06/25/1846	01/21/1852	24	51	N	
Williams, John	37	Ireland	Y	Liverpool	New York	04/06/1840	11/23/1859	17	479	N	
Williams, John	55	Wales	Y	Liverpool	New York	10/27/1857	01/12/1861	18	55	N	
Williams, Joseph	29	Ireland	Y	Liverpool	Baltimore	05/15/1843	10/12/1848	1	167	N	
Williams, Joseph	68	England	Y	Canada	Lewiston	07/??/1838	11/27/1852	5	349	N	
Williams, Nicholas Thoma	24	Ireland	Y	Havre	New Orleans	05/01/1849	03/09/1853	7	315	N	
Williams, Robert Edward	24	North Wales (	Y	Liverpool	New York	04/03/1883	01/12/1887			Y	
Williams, Samuel (Emanue	32	Ireland	Y	London	New York	??/16/1847	11/07/1849	23	326	N	
Williams, Thomas	39	England	Y	Liverpool	Portland	02/20/1862	04/05/1880			Y	
Williams, Thomas	??	England	Y	?	?	09/26/1881	04/05/1893			Y	
Williams, Thomas	23	Wales	Y	Liverpool	New York	06/24/1849	03/03/1852	24	228	N	
Williams, Thomas Lloyd	50	Wales	Y	Liverpool	Philadelphia	09/28/1878	11/09/1894			Y	
Williams, Victor	32	Sweden	Y	Goteborg	New Bedford	08/25/1836	07/21/1851	4	14	N	
Williams, William	35	England	Y	Liverpool	New York	05/19/1850	01/11/1853	7	9	N	
Williams, William E.	55	Wales	Y	Liverpool	New York	08/15/1860	04/01/1885	19	5	N	
Williams, William E.	55	Wales	Y	Liverpool	New York	08/15/1860	04/01/1885			Y	
Williams, William J.	23	Ireland	Y	Liverpool	New York	06/06/1856	03/23/1858	16	437	N	
Williams, William P.	52	England	Y	Liverpool	New York	11/19/1865	10/19/1896			Y	
Williams, William V.	32	England	Y	Liverpool	New York	01/20/1883	10/09/1888	19	143	N	
Williams, William W.	29	Wales	Y	Liverpool	Philadelphia	06/11/1848	01/31/1851	3	72	N	
Williamson, James	34	Ireland	Y	Liverpool	New York	03/12/1853	03/31/1853	7	473	N	
Williamson, Robert	29	Ireland	Y	Belfast	New York	01/??/1846	09/26/1854	10	242	N	
Williamson, Robert	29	Ireland	Y	Belfast	New York	01/??/1846	09/26/1854	12	181	N	
Williamson, William	21	Ireland	Y	Liverpool	Philadelphia	12/04/1853	03/04/1857	15	61	N	
Williamson, William	40	Ireland	Y	Greenock	Buffalo	11/01/1846	11/04/1857	15	532	N	
Williamson, William	24	Scotland	Y	?	?	?	04/18/1893			Y	
Willie, George	36	Germany	Y	Rotterdam	Boston	01/24/1880	11/27/1889			Y	

CITIZENSHIP RECORDS

APPLICANT	AGE	COUNTRY OF ORIGIN	DEC	DEPART PORT	ENTRY PORT	ARRIVE DATE	DEC DATE	VOL	PG.	FLD	NAT DATE
Willie, John	33	Norway	Y	Andell	New Orleans	02/01/1849	02/09/1852	24	74	N	
Willies, Henry William	24	Hanover	Y	Bremen	New Orleans	06/20/1849	07/14/1851	3	534	N	
Willig, Frederick	40	Germany	Y	Rotterdam	New York	06/01/1880	05/23/1889	19	251	N	
Willig, Frederick	40	Germany	Y	Rotterdam	New York	06/01/1880	10/23/1889			Y	
Willig, Jacob	38	Germany	Y	Antwerp	New York	02/17/1887	03/24/1891			Y	
Willig, John	33	Baden	Y	Havre	New York	05/28/1854	09/25/1858	16	137	N	
Willig, Severin	30	Germany	Y	Bremen	New York	03/05/1884	08/15/1889			Y	
Willinbog, Johan	68	Oldenburg	Y	Bremen	Baltimore	08/15/1884	10/12/1893	21	3	N	
Willing, Casper Henry	26	Hanover	Y	Bremen	Baltimore	11/12/1845	10/02/1848	1	29	N	
Willinger, Bernard	22	France	Y	Havre	New York	09/04/1853	09/24/1856	14	358	N	
Willis, Walter	23	England	Y	Liverpool	New York	11/17/1888	05/02/1893			Y	
Willkomm, Joseph	45	Germany	N	Bremen	New York	06/??/1879	?			Y	
Willkommen, William	31	Hanover	Y	Bremen	New Orleans	10/09/8152	12/31/1855	13	400	N	
Willmann, Frederick	27	Hanover	Y	Bremen	Baltimore	09/20/1852	04/05/1856	26	449	N	
Willmann, John Henry	24	Hanover	Y	Bremen	Baltimore	12/24/1849	04/04/1853	8	14	N	
Willmann, Martin	28	Hanover	Y	Bremen	New Orleans	12/14/1845	10/11/1848	1	128	N	
Willmes, Herman Henry	34	Hanover	Y	Bremen	New Orleans	??/08/1845	10/09/1848	1	81	N	
Willmes, John Bernard	??	Hanover	Y	Bremen	New Orleans	01/18/18??	10/09/1948	1	72	N	
Willmes, William	21	Prussia	Y	Antwerp	New York	08/07/1853	08/15/1855	11	435	N	
Willmhoff, Henry	37	Germany	Y	Bremen	New York	05/18/1872	10/25/1888			Y	
Willner, Anton	19	Germany	Y	?	?	07/13/1886	08/02/1890			Y	
Wilmer, Herman	22	Hanover	Y	Bremen	New Orleans	12/08/1852	09/27/1854	10	274	N	
Wilmer, Herman	22	Hanover	Y	Bremen	New Orleans	12/08/1852	09/27/1854	12	213	N	
Wilmers, Frank	29	Prussia	Y	Bremen	Baltimore	05/30/1848	06/26/1851	3	459	N	
Wilmes, George	27	Hanover	Y	Bremen	New Orleans	01/02/1847	02/01/1851	3	78	N	
Wilmes, Herman	39	Germany	Y	Bremen	Baltimore	09/20/1879	10/16/1896			Y	
Wilmes, Hubert	30	Prussia	Y	Liverpool	New York	05/30/1853	?	11	55	N	
Wilmes, Hulbert	30	Prussia	Y	Liverpool	New York	05/30/1853	10/09/1854	6	54	N	
Wilmes, Rudolph	32	Hanover	Y	Bremen	Baltimore	06/12/1846	06/11/1852	25	237	N	
Wilmes, Theodore	28	Prussia	Y	Bremen	New Orleans	11/09/1848	04/12/1852	24	468	N	
Wilming, G. Henry	27	Prussia	Y	London	New Orleans	12/??/1848	11/01/1851	4	456	N	
Wilp, Henry	25	Germany	Y	Bremen	New York	04/30/1881	05/03/1883			Y	
Wilp, John	21	Germany	Y	Bremen	New York	09/18/1881	05/03/1883			Y	
Wilpert, Joseph Anton	43	Switzerland	Y	Antwerp	New York	08/10/1853	09/25/1856	14	381	N	
Wilson, Alex	31	Scotland	Y	Leith	Buffalo	06/10/1838	02/07/1850	2	50	N	
Wilson, David A.	??	Great Britain	Y	?	?	?	10/03/1895			Y	
Wilson, James	39	Scotland	Y	Leith	Buffalo	??/10/1838	02/07/1850	2	49	N	
Wilson, John	40	Ireland	Y	Cork	New York	05/01/1842	01/30/1851	3	62	N	
Wilson, John	29	Ireland	Y	Londonderry	Philadelphia	05/07/1847	07/21/1851	4	15	N	
Wilson, John	34	England	Y	?	New York	??/??/1880	09/04/1883			Y	
Wilson, John	73	Ireland	N	Londonderry	Philadelphia	05/01/1848	??/??/1848	28	390	N	06/??/1854
Wilson, Joseph James	44	England	Y	Liverpool	New York	05/07/1885	02/29/1888			Y	
Wilson, Philip	38	England	Y	Liverpool	New York	08/31/1855	10/01/1856	14	116	N	
Wilson, William	39	Scotland	Y	Glasgow	Chicago	05/05/1882	01/22/1886			Y	
Wilson, William A.	40	England	Y	Liverpool	Boston	05/08/1883	11/04/1890			Y	
Wilz, Johann	34	Bavaria	Y	?	New York	11/28/1854	09/11/1860			Y	
Wilz, Michael	43	Germany	Y	Liverpool	New Orleans	07/12/1874	03/21/1892			Y	
Wilzbach, Adam	31	Bavaria	Y	Havre	New Orleans	10/??/1851	10/06/1856	14	198	N	
Wimberg, George	??	Germany	N	?	?	07/18/1887				Y	10/26/1892
Wimmer, Fred	58	Germany	Y	Antwerp	New York	05/20/1880	11/12/1890			Y	
Wimmer, Frederick	27	Saxe Weimar	Y	Bremen	New Orleans	11/09/1852	01/31/1857	14	522	N	
Wimmer, William	28	Saxony	Y	Bremen	New Orleans	11/29/1849	12/02/1852	5	371	N	
Wimsey, John T.	25	Ireland	Y	Liverpool	Buffalo	03/27/1882	10/27/1886	19	90	N	
Wimsey, Mathew	26	Ireland	Y	Canada	Vermont	07/03/1847	04/05/1852	24	390	N	
Winberg, Isaac	30	Sweden	Y	Gifle	Boston	08/28/1855	02/06/1856	26	56	N	
Winckel, Denck	43	Hanover	Y	Bremen	New Orleans	05/02/1846	11/13/1855	13	216	N	
Winckler, Fred	37	Saxony	Y	Bremen	New Orleans	12/20/1848	07/24/1851	4	34	N	
Winckler, John	54	Austria	Y	Hamburg	New York	06/27/1854	10/05/1857	15	351	N	
Wind, Herman H.	29	Germany	Y	?	New York	??/??/1873	10/08/1881			Y	

CITIZENSHIP RECORDS

APPLICANT	AGE	COUNTRY OF ORIGIN	DEC	DEPART PORT	ENTRY PORT	ARRIVE DATE	DEC DATE	VOL	PG.	FLD	NAT DATE
Windau, William	33	Germany	Y	Bremen	New York	04/22/1884	11/03/1887			Y	
Windels, Gerhard	28	Germany	Y	Bremen	New York	10/15/1883	12/02/1886			Y	
Winder, Fidel	34	Austria	Y	Havre	New York	11/09/1853	01/27/1853	7	76	N	
Winderhalter, Ferdinand	24	Baden	Y	London	New York	05/31/1851	05/30/1854	9	457	N	
Winderhalter, Ferdinand	24	Baden	Y	London	New York	05/31/1851	05/30/1854	10	40	N	
Windgassen, Albert	26	Germany	Y	Antwerp	New York	06/18/1881	11/13/1884			Y	
Windgassen, Edward	59	Germany	N	Bremen	New York	10/??/1854	?			Y	
Windheim, William	48	Germany	Y	Bremen	New York	05/09/1884	11/23/1887			Y	
Windholtz, Joseph	42	Germany	Y	?	New York	03/06/1883	05/01/1884			Y	
Windhor, Anton	63	Germany	N	Hamburg	New York	04/19/1851	?			Y	
Windhorn, Christ	26	Germany	Y	Bremen	Baltimore	06/16/1887	10/17/1892			Y	
Windhorst, Christ	29	Germany	Y	Bremen	Baltimore	05/02/1883	05/12/1886			Y	
Windhorst, Frederick	28	Hanover	Y	Bremen	Baltimore	06/08/1842	03/22/1851	3	306	N	
Windisch, Friederick	26	Germany	Y	Bremen	New York	08/27/1882	10/02/1884			Y	
Windisch, John	21	Germany	Y	Bremen	Baltimore	08/19/1882	10/07/1882			Y	
Windlebacker, Nicholas	33	Germany	Y	Havre	New York	06/26/1887	04/16/1894			Y	
Windmeyer, Gerhard	35	Prussia	Y	Bremen	New York	03/22/1848	07/05/1851	3	494	N	
Windmoeller, William	29	Germany	Y	Bremen	New York	06/19/1882	01/28/1885			Y	
Windmoller, Frederick	36	Prussia	Y	Bremen	Baltimore	12/09/1857	04/02/1861	18	127	N	
Windoffer, William	23	Prussia	Y	Bremen	Baltimore	11/04/1848	11/06/1852	5	246	N	
Windoffer, William	23	Prussia	Y	Bremen	Baltimore	11/04/1848	11/06/1852	6	370	N	
Windolph, Franz	27	Germany	Y	Bremen	New York	05/04/1888	10/24/1889			Y	
Windschiegl, Joseph	35	Germany	Y	Bremen	New York	05/14/1884	10/29/1892			Y	
Windschiegle, Joseph	35	Germany	Y	Bremen	New York	05/14/1884	10/29/1892	19	400	N	
Windshiegl, John	27	Germany	Y	Bremen	New York	05/12/1883	11/02/1891			Y	
Wingerter, Andrew	??	Prussia	Y	?	?	?	04/04/1888			Y	
Wink, Herman	42	Germany	Y	Antwerp	New York	07/01/1882	09/05/1893			Y	
Wink, Jacob	24	Germany	Y	Antwerp	New York	06/19/1882	09/21/1885			Y	
Winkelbeck, Martin	23	Bavaria	Y	Havre	New Orleans	03/14/1855	10/01/1856	14	124	N	
Winkeler, Simon M.	48	Austria	N	Hamburg	New York	11/01/1876	?				
Winkelhorst, John	30	Prussia	Y	Amsterdam	Baltimore	10/10/1853	03/25/1856	26	324	N	
Winkeljohann, August	23	Hanover	Y	Bremen	Baltimore	05/01/1853	10/28/1858	17	152	N	
Winkeljohann, Bernard	23	Germany	Y	Bremen	Baltimore	08/19/1889	10/27/1892			Y	
Winkeljohann, Mathias	57	Germany	Y	Bremen	?	08/19/1889	10/27/1892			Y	
Winkelman, George	25	Oldenburg	Y	Bremen	Baltimore	10/18/1845	10/11/1848	1	131	N	
Winkelman, Herman H.	28	Hanover	Y	Bremen	Baltimore	06/06/1845	07/29/1848	22	8	N	
Winkelmann, Christian	30	Prussia	Y	Bremen	New Orleans	11/02/1853	03/07/1854	14	74	N	
Winkelmann, Henry	56	Germany	N	Bremen	New York	10/??/1862	?			Y	
Winkelmann, William	25	Prussia	Y	Bremen	New York	07/10/1857	09/11/1857	15	256	N	
Winkelmann, William	28	Germany	Y	Bremen	New York	04/22/1888	10/31/1898			Y	
Winkinn, William	21	Prussia	Y	Bremen	New Orleans	09/??/1849	08/??/1851	4	174	N	
Winkler, Charles	35	Bavaria	Y	Havre	New Orleans	12/15/1842	01/15/1853	7	30	N	
Winkler, Jacob	43	Hesse Darmsta	Y	Havre	New Orleans	04/22/1850	04/04/1853	7	507	N	
Winkler, John	28	Austria	Y	Hamburg	New York	11/09/1848	10/06/1854	10	509	N	
Winkler, John	28	Austria	Y	Hamburg	New York	11/09/1848	10/06/1854	12	448	N	
Winkler, John	47	Germany	Y	Rotterdam	New York	06/01/1880	10/13/1886			Y	
Winkler, Mathias	43	Germany	Y	Havre	New York	05/01/1880	04/08/1886			Y	
Winn, Francis	22	Ireland	Y	Liverpool	New Orleans	12/05/1852	01/31/1856	13	530	N	
Winstel, John	24	Bavaria	Y	Havre	New Orleans	06/??/1847	03/22/1853	7	369	N	
Winston, David J.	32	Wales	Y	Liverpool	Philadelphia	11/14/1888	11/02/1892	19	407	N	
Winston, George	79	England	Y	Liverpool	New York	11/01/1852	11/02/1895			Y	
Winter, Andreas	23	Wurttemberg	Y	Havre	New York	05/29/1852	03/25/1853	7	402	N	
Winter, Andreas	25	Germany	Y	Bremen	New York	10/20/1880	10/13/1881			Y	
Winter, Anthony	45	Oldenburg	N	Bremen	Baltimore	05/02/1865	?			Y	
Winter, August	23	Brunswick	Y	Bremen	New Orleans	06/22/1845	07/31/1848	22	17	N	
Winter, Edward	29	Ireland	Y	Liverpool	New York	09/11/1845	09/11/1848	22	318	N	
Winter, Francis	28	Prussia	Y	Bremen	Buffalo	07/18/1855	12/26/1855	13	364	N	
Winter, George	20	Germany	Y	Bremen	New York	05/16/1885	11/12/1889			Y	
Winter, Gerhard Frederic	22	Hanover	Y	Bremen	New York	06/11/1852	09/22/1855	13	113	N	

CITIZENSHIP RECORDS

APPLICANT	AGE	COUNTRY OF ORIGIN	DEC	DEPART PORT	ENTRY PORT	ARRIVE DATE	DEC DATE	VOL	PG.	FLD	NAT DATE
Winter, Henry	31	Germany	Y	Amsterdam	New York	02/02/1891	11/25/1892			Y	
Winter, Michael	28	Ireland	Y	Liverpool	New York	04/03/1846	05/06/1854	8	383	N	
Winter, Michael	28	Ireland	Y	Liverpool	New York	04/03/1846	05/06/1854	9	256	N	
Winterhalter, Conrad	32	Germany	Y	Hamburg	New York	12/24/1872	11/07/1876			Y	
Winterholer, Andreas	??	Wurttemberg	Y	Havre	New York	??/05/1852	04/18/1855	11	271	N	
Winterle, Henry	39	Germany	Y	Bremen	New York	10/20/1881	04/29/1895			Y	
Winterlich, Paul	30	Germany	Y	Bremen	New York	09/30/1890	03/08/1894			Y	
Wintermann, George	39	Hanover	Y	Bremen	New Orleans	11/18/1841	08/08/1848	22	75	N	
Winternheimer, Gustav	39	Germany	Y	Hamburg	New York	11/07/1880	02/12/1883			Y	
Wintle, William	28	England	Y	Liverpool	Whitehall	07/25/1844	02/12/1849	23	71	N	
Wintring, Frank	22	Hanover	Y	Bremen	Baltimore	09/16/1858	08/15/1860	27	286	N	
Winzenred, John	23	Germany	Y	Antwerp	New York	12/02/1880	02/02/1883			Y	
Winzig, Conrad	33	Germany	Y	Antwerp	New York	05/24/1888	01/24/1891			Y	
Wipels, John Henry	35	Holland	Y	Bremen	New Orleans	06/20/1845	08/05/1848	22	58	N	
Wippermann, August	39	Germany	Y	Bremen	New York	05/22/1879	04/11/1891			Y	
Wirbel, Bernard	21	Baden	Y	Havre	New Orleans	05/23/1854	02/15/1856	26	86	N	
Wire, Martin	??	Ireland	Y	?	?	?	10/17/1859			Y	
Wirkmann, John	48	Hanover	Y	Bremen	New York	12/10/1845	10/14/1848	1	211	N	
Wirkner, Anton	51	Austria	Y	Bremen	Baltimore	08/23/1853	09/23/1854	10	182	N	
Wirkner, Anton	51	Austria	Y	Bremen	Baltimore	08/23/1853	09/23/1854	12	121	N	
Wirmel, Jacob	31	Bavaria	Y	Havre	New Orleans	10/22/1846	02/08/1853	7	127	N	
Wirmel, Michael	24	Bavaria	Y	Havre	New York	05/31/1849	05/11/1854	8	424	N	
Wirsch, Franz	30	Switzerland	Y	Havre	New York	05/28/1855	11/10/1858	17	316	N	
Wirsch, Gabriel	21	Switzerland	Y	Havre	New York	07/10/1855	10/14/1857	15	422	N	
Wirth, August	35	Wuerttenburg	Y	Antwerp	New York	09/27/1849	03/01/1852	24	191	N	
Wirth, Friedrich	68	Wuerttenberg	Y	Rotterdam	Baltimore	09/??/1845	08/23/1852	25	327	N	
Wirth, Gustav	23	Germany	Y	Antwerp	New York	07/10/1892	06/27/1896			Y	
Wirth, Henri	??	Switzerland	Y	?	?	?	10/24/1884			Y	
Wirth, John	39	Bavaria	Y	Bremen	New York	11/11/1856	03/22/1858	16	430	N	
Wirth, Paulus	50	Bavaria	Y	Bremen	New York	11/11/1857	04/11/1862	18	314	N	
Wischemeier, Bernard	46	Germany	Y	Bremen	Baltimore	08/??/1865	12/24/1888			Y	
Wischhusen, Martin	30	Germany	Y	Bremen	Baltimore	06/02/1881	02/16/1888			Y	
Wischmeier, Carl	27	Germany	Y	Bremen	Baltimore	04/18/1883	01/05/1886			Y	
Wischmeier, Herman Henry	24	Hanover	Y	Bremen	Baltimore	07/04/1847	02/14/1849	23	106	N	
Wise, Bernard	38	Bavaria	Y	Rotterdam	New York	05/30/1853	09/20/1858	16	157	N	
Wise, John	28	Germany	Y	Hamburg	New York	05/28/1888	12/29/1891			Y	
Wise, Leopold	28	Bavaria	Y	Havre	New York	04/04/1846	03/10/1851	3	228	N	
Wise, M.	38	Russia	Y	Hamburg	New York	11/01/1887	10/19/1896			Y	
Wise, Michael	27	Ireland	Y	Liverpool	New Orleans	02/01/1851	05/10/1854	9	292	N	
Wisler, Joseph	27	Baden	Y	Havre	New Orleans	02/07/1849	04/12/1852	24	443	N	
Wismann, John L.A.	62	Germany	Y	Liverpoool	Baltimore	08/21/1888	10/14/1893			Y	
Wissel, Adam	28	Bavaria	Y	Bremen	Baltimore	10/01/1847	01/12/1849	1	407	N	
Wissel, Joseph	25	Bavaria	Y	Antwerp	New York	03/07/1857	09/19/1857	15	286	N	
Wisseman, John (Wissemei	23	Germany	Y	?	New York	??/??/1882	04/15/1884			Y	
Wisser, Christian	32	Baden	Y	Havre	New York	03/01/1851	05/09/1854	8	401	N	
Wisser, Christian	32	Baden	Y	Havre	New York	03/01/1851	05/09/1854	9	275	N	
Wisshack, Gustavus Adolp	24	Wurttemberg	Y	Havre	New Orleans	06/25/1849	02/04/1853	7	113	N	
Wissler, Leo	29	Germany	Y	Havre	New York	02/23/1883	05/26/1890			Y	
Wissmann, Fritz	40	Germany	Y	Bremen	Baltimore	10/22/1868	10/03/1885			Y	
Wissmann, Jacob	29	Germany	Y	Havre	New York	06/01/1881	04/28/1890			Y	
Wisz, Benedict	22	Switzerland	Y	Havre	New York	08/01/1857	09/03/1860	27	328	N	
Witcomb, Francis	24	England	Y	London	New York	05/15/1856	07/06/1857	15	127	N	
Witscken, Hermann	30	Germany	Y	Bremen	Baltimore	04/28/1894	11/01/1899			Y	
Witskin, Joseph	29	Germany	Y	Bremen	Baltimore	04/26/1894	10/28/1899			Y	
Witt, Adolf R.	33	Germany	Y	Antwerp	Philadelphia	10/16/1881	10/17/1883			Y	
Witt, August	32	Germany	Y	Bremen	Baltimore	06/07/1888	07/11/1890			Y	
Witt, Emil	26	Germany	Y	Bremen	New York	05/30/1893	03/14/1894			Y	
Witt, Sebastian	24	Prussia	Y	Rotterdam	New York	05/12/1855	10/15/1860	27	501	N	
Witt, William	25	Germany	Y	Hamburg	New York	08/05/1889	01/26/1892			Y	

CITIZENSHIP RECORDS

APPLICANT	AGE	COUNTRY OF ORIGIN	DEC	DEPART PORT	ENTRY PORT	ARRIVE DATE	DEC DATE	VOL	PG.	FLD	NAT DATE
Wittberg, Theodore Westb	29	Prussia	Y	Antwerp	New York	06/18/1844	02/17/1849	23	156	N	
Witte, Casper	28	Hanover	Y	Bremen	Baltimore	11/01/1845	10/05/1848	22	437	N	
Witte, Casper	23	Oldenburg	Y	Bremen	New York	08/01/1854	03/25/1856	26	325	N	
Witte, Charles	24	Prussia	Y	Bremen	New York	05/03/1849	09/15/1852	25	511	N	
Witte, Ferdinand	??	Prussia	Y	?	New York	??/31/18??	10/24/1850	2	288	N	
Witte, Gerhard Phillip	27	Prussia	Y	Bremen	Balitmore	10/03/1846	11/17/1848	1	313	N	
Witte, Henry A.	47	Germany	Y	?	New York	??/??/1865	10/14/1884			Y	
Witte, Henry L.	30	Germany	Y	Rotterdam	New York	04/12/1882	07/05/1884			Y	
Witte, John J.	25	Germany	Y	Rotterdam	New York	04/12/1882	07/05/1884			Y	
Witte, Paul M.T.	30	Germany	Y	Bremen	New York	11/29/1884	09/03/1892			Y	
Witte, William	31	Hanover	Y	Bremen	Baltimore	09/25/1845	01/15/1849	1	420	N	
Witteborg, William	33	Prussia	Y	Bremen	New York	04/21/1848	01/21/1851	2	516	N	
Wittebrock, Gradus	26	Holland	Y	Rotterdam	New York	06/07/1846	08/07/1848	22	70	N	
Wittefelt, Christian	26	Hanover	Y	Bremen	New Orleans	11/20/1851	10/06/1854	10	483	N	
Wittefelt, Christian	26	Hanover	Y	Bremen	New Orleans	11/20/1851	10/06/1854	12	422	N	
Wittefelt, John Rudolph	22	Hanover	Y	Bremen	New Orleans	11/20/1851	10/06/1854	10	484	N	
Wittefelt, John Rudolph	22	Hanover	Y	Bremen	New Orleans	11/20/1851	10/06/1854	12	423	N	
Wittekind, Peter	28	Napan	Y	Rotterdam	New York	06/11/1845	01/07/1851	2	474	N	
Wittekind, Peter	65	Germany	N	Rotterdam	New York	07/??/1846	?			Y	
Wittel, Karl	??	Germany	Y	?	?	?	03/17/1883			Y	
Wittenberg, Emil	??	Germany	Y	?	Boston	04/??/1894	10/20/1894			Y	
Wittenberg, Mathias H. F	53	Prussia	Y	Hamburg	New York	01/29/1852	03/21/1856	26	242	N	
Wittenberg, William	17	Germany	N	?	Philadelphia	00/00/1882				Y	10/27/1888
Witthoff, John Christoph	38	Prussia	Y	Bremen	New Orleans	12/20/1849	01/19/1853	7	42	N	
Witthoff, Moritz	??	Prussia	N	Ginterslohe	New Orleans	12/27/1848	09/08/1854	28	476	N	10/09/1856
Wittich, Julius	28	Germany	Y	Bremen	New York	12/16/1872	03/09/1881			Y	
Wittkaemper, August	22	Prussia	Y	Bremen	Baltimore	10/03/1854	09/01/1857	15	209	N	
Wittkamp, Theodore	50	Prussia	Y	Bremen	Philadelphia	08/07/1845	01/16/1849	1	432	N	
Wittkamp, William	29	Prussia	Y	Bremen	Baltimore	07/11/1855	03/27/1856	26	364	N	
Wittler, Bernard	45	Prussia	Y	Bremen	New York	10/08/1837	09/01/1862	18	430	N	
Wittler, Johann Hubert	43	Germany	N	Hamburg	New York	05/09/1871	?			Y	
Wittler, Joseph	26	Prussia	Y	Bremen	New Orleans	12/08/1849	09/12/1855	13	6	N	
Wittler, Theodore	28	Prussia	Y	Bremen	New Orleans	12/26/1854	09/12/1855	13	5	N	
Wittman, Frank	38	Germany	Y	Havre	New York	10/18/1871	10/08/1883			Y	
Wittmann, Nicholas	35	France	Y	Havre	New Orleans	04/27/1854	10/26/1858	17	111	N	
Wittmann, William	??	Germany	Y	?	?	?	10/06/1876			Y	
Wittrock, B.	25	Germany	Y	Rotterdam	New York	08/17/1884	02/07/1887			Y	
Wittrock, Ernst	32	Prussia	Y	Bremen	New York	06/01/1855	02/04/1856	26	23	N	
Wittrock, Ernst			Y	Bremen	Baltimore	07/16/1880	10/13/1898			Y	
Wittsche, Herman	59	Germany	Y	Havre	New Orleans	08/14/1848	05/29/1852	25	130	N	
Witzens, Peter	46	Bavaria	Y	Havre	New Orleans	04/23/1853	05/24/1854	8	505	N	
Witzigmann, Nicholas	29	Baden	Y	Havre	New Orleans	04/23/1853	05/24/1854	9	379	N	
Witzigmann, Nicolaus	29	Baden	Y	?	New Orleans	02/01/1848	04/12/1852	24	475	N	
Witzleben, Henry K.	30	Holstein	Y	Bremen	New Orleans	12/08/18??	10/09/1848	1	84	N	
Wlecke, Frederick Willia	??	Prussia	Y	Amsterdam	New York	04/01/1881	02/??/1883			Y	
Wloszczynski, Casimier	54	Germany	Y	Amsterdam	New York	04/01/1881	?			Y	
Wloszczynski, Casimir	62	Prussia	N	Amsterdam	New York	04/07/1882	?			Y	
Wloszczynski, Kazimir	59	Germany	N	Stettin	New York	01/01/1891	08/28/1893			Y	
Wloszczywski, Constantin	21	Germany	Y	Bremen	Baltimore	02/22/1876	05/26/1879			Y	
Wnaucek, John	35	Austria	Y	Bremen	New York	08/02/1869	04/30/1878			Y	
Wobbe, Clemens	31	Germany	Y	Bremen	New Orleans	12/25/1850	09/25/1854	12	140	N	
Wobbels, John	36	Hanover	Y	Bremen	Baltimore	04/17/1881	03/09/1885			Y	
Wobst, August	31	Germany	Y	Havre	New York	10/13/1860	07/10/1861	18	205	N	
Wochner, Minrod	35	Baden	Y	Hamburg	New York	08/02/1870	?			Y	
Wodrich, Gotthelf W.	38	Germany	N	Bremen	New Orleans	12/??/1850	09/25/1854	10	201	N	
Woebbels, John	36	Hanover	Y	Bremen	Baltimore	08/12/1886	02/13/1894			Y	
Woebkenberg, Bernard	29	Germany	Y	Bremen	Baltimore	08/27/1884	09/26/1890			Y	
Woebkenberg, Henry	31	Germany	Y	Havre	New Orleans	12/12/1848	02/23/1852	24	154	N	
Woechter, Valentine	24	Bavaria	Y	Bremen	Baltimore	03/02/1882	10/14/1889			Y	
Woeckener, Fritz	31	Germany	Y	Bremen	Baltimore	03/02/1882	10/14/1889			Y	

CITIZENSHIP RECORDS

APPLICANT	AGE	COUNTRY OF ORIGIN	DEC	DEPART PORT	ENTRY PORT	ARRIVE DATE	DEC DATE	VOL	PG.	FLD	NAT DATE
Woeff, Jacob	44	Germany	Y	Antwerp	New York	07/15/1881	06/21/1888			Y	
Woeffradt, Carl E.	59	Prussia	N	Hamburg	New York	06/13/1866	?			Y	
Woehler, Henry	38	Germany	Y	Hamburg	New York	08/??/1879	12/28/1886			Y	
Woehner, John George	34	Saxe Coburg G	Y	Bremen	Baltimore	06/10/1853	07/13/1855	11	382	N	
Woehnker, Fred	26	Oldenburg	Y	Bremen	New Orleans	01/01/1849	02/12/1852	24	103	N	
Woehrle, George	??	Germany	Y	?	?	?	06/23/1882			Y	
Woehrle, Matheus	23	Baden	Y	Havre	New Orleans	12/22/1852	05/30/1854	9	468	N	
Woehrle, Matheus	23	Baden	Y	Havre	New Orleans	12/22/1852	05/31/1854	10	51	N	
Woehrmann, Henry	25	Germany	Y	Bremen	Baltimore	10/14/1891	10/25/1895			Y	
Woelfel, John	29	Bavaria	Y	Bremen	New York	05/21/1856	10/24/1857	15	488	N	
Woelfel, John	27	Germany	Y	Antwerp	New York	06/28/1891	09/21/1893			Y	
Woelfer, August	23	Prussia	Y	Hamburg	New York	10/29/1855	11/02/1858	17	260	N	
Woelfle, Eugene	29	France	Y	Havre	New York	02/03/1888	11/06/1893			Y	
Woelfle, Rudolph	40	Germany	Y	Bremen	New York	01/21/1880	04/??/1882			Y	
Woelkel, David	24	Germany	N	Bremen	New York	02/01/1879	?			Y	
Woellner, Henry	26	Prussia	Y	Bremen	New Orleans	03/26/1844	05/04/1850	3	45	N	
Woeltje, Heinrich	??	Germany	Y	?	?	?	03/28/1892			Y	
Woenbel (Weibel), Henry	35	Baden	Y	Havre	New York	05/01/1847	04/17/1854	8	143	N	
Woenshoffer, Herman	28	Germany	Y	?	?	?	10/12/1892			Y	
Woepkenberg, Henry	37	Germany	Y	Rotterdam	New York	03/02/1884	10/12/1900			Y	
Woerner, Frank	47	Baden	Y	Havre	New Orleans	06/10/1850	03/03/1852	24	222	N	
Woerner, Joseph Constant	45	Germany	Y	Havre	Boston	12/14/1873	10/11/1880			Y	
Woerner, Peter	43	Germany	Y	Hamburg	New York	11/29/1873	04/12/1886			Y	
Woerner, Sigmund	26	Germany	Y	Havre	New York	03/17/1883	06/22/1889			Y	
Woerrlein, Henry	26	Germany	Y	Bremen	New York	05/30/1889	02/16/1893			Y	
Woerst, George Adam	38	Baden	Y	Havre	New Orleans	06/08/1855	11/01/1858	17	247	N	
Woerthurin, Chrisitan	28	Wurttemberg	Y	Havre	New York	08/15/1855	09/29/1856	14	5	N	
Woerthwein, John	28	Wuerttemberg	Y	Antwerp	New York	??/19/1847	12/29/1849	23	440	N	
Woerz, Ignatz	29	Wuertemberg	Y	Havre	New York	06/10/1854	05/26/1856	26	555	N	
Woesner, Jacob	31	Germany	Y	Bremen	Baltimore	07/24/1889	07/11/1891			Y	
Woessner, George	31	Germany	Y	Hamburg	Philadelphia	07/26/1885	09/24/1887			Y	
Woessner, George	37	Germany	Y	Hamburg	New York	04/02/1888	10/28/1892			Y	
Woeste, Bernard	23	Prussia	Y	Bremen	New Orleans	06/01/1852	01/07/1856	13	427	N	
Woeste, Bernhard	37	Germany	N	Bremen	Baltimore	10/??/1868	?			Y	
Woeste, Henry	29	Germany	N	Hamburg	Baltimore	11/??/1862	?			Y	
Woeste, W.	24	Germany	Y	Bremen	Baltimore	09/01/1881	12/31/1883			Y	
Woestefeld, Phillip	30	Hanover	Y	Bremen	New York	08/01/1847	06/15/1848	22	147	N	
Woestemann, Gerhard	31	Hanover	Y	Bremen	New Orleans	12/13/1851	10/01/1857	15	337	N	
Wohl, Rimund	23	Austria	Y	Bremen	New York	05/??/1855	09/22/1855	13	121	N	
Wohler, Frank	28	Prussia	Y	Bremen	New Orleans	01/04/1846	11/14/1848	1	295	N	
Wohlfarht, John	27	Nassau	Y	Liverpool	New York	06/01/1853	04/17/1854	8	168	N	
Wohlfarht, John	27	Nassau	Y	Liverpool	New York	06/01/1853	04/17/1854	9	39	N	
Wohlfarht, John					New York	11/07/1890	12/20/1893			Y	
Wohlkaupt, Hermann	32	Germany	Y	Bremen	New Orleans	01/10/1853	10/09/1854	6	85	N	
Wohlleb, Bandelin	33	Baden	Y	Havre	New Orleans	01/10/1853	10/09/1854	11	88	N	
Wohlleb, Bandelin	33	Baden	Y	Havre	New York	10/01/1888	01/16/1890			Y	
Wohlmann, Albert	32	Germany	Y	Bremen	New York	05/16/1854	10/06/1856	14	242	N	
Wohlwander, Wunnebald	28	Wurttemberg	Y	Havre	Baltimore	12/01/1857	08/15/1860	27	281	N	
Wohnler, S.	27	Hanover	Y	Bremen	New York	09/13/1859	08/20/1862	18	393	N	
Wohrstein, Charles	47	Hohenzollern	Y	Havre	New York	12/31/1886	02/12/1887			Y	
Wohylmann, W.	24	Germany	Y	Antwerp	New York	04/29/1869	12/31/1892			Y	
Woirol, Henry	44	Switzerland	Y	Liverpool	New Orleans	12/28/1845	03/05/1852	24	237	N	
Wolbert, John	41	Hanover	Y	Bremen	Baltimore	10/20/1852	02/24/1853	6	228	N	
Woldkelter, John Frederi	29	Hanover	Y	Bremen	New York	05/12/1869	11/13/1871	18	441	N	
Wolf, Abraham	23	Poland (Russi	Y	Hamburg	New York	05/20/1857	09/12/1860	27	367	N	
Wolf, Alexander	39	Bavaria	Y	Havre	New York	10/13/1881	03/19/1889			Y	
Wolf, Alfred	29	Switzerland	Y	Havre	New York	10/14/1884	04/09/1889			Y	
Wolf, August	34	Germany	Y	Hamburg	New York	08/23/1847	08/22/1848	22	225	N	
Wolf, Benjamin Victor	31	Kurhassen	Y	Havre	New Orleans	12/22/1846	11/16/1848	1	284	N	
Wolf, Christian	26	Bavaria	Y	Havre							

CITIZENSHIP RECORDS

APPLICANT	AGE	COUNTRY OF ORIGIN	DEC	DEPART PORT	ENTRY PORT	ARRIVE DATE	DEC DATE	VOL	PG.	FLD	NAT DATE
Wolf, Christian	24	Bavaria	Y	Havre	New York	10/??/1854	09/17/1855	13	58	N	
Wolf, Daniel	24	Bavaria	Y	Havre	New York	07/27/1851	05/25/1854	8	522	N	
Wolf, Daniel	24	Bavaria	Y	Havre	New York	07/27/1851	05/25/1854	9	396	N	
Wolf, Frederick	25	Wurttemberg	Y	Bremen	New York	08/20/1849	06/05/1854	10	86	N	
Wolf, Frederick	25	Wurttemberg	Y	Bremen	New York	08/20/1849	06/05/1854	12	23	N	
Wolf, Frederick	32	Germany	Y	Havre	New York	03/15/1881	11/21/1881			Y	
Wolf, George	26	Hesse Cassel	Y	Bremen	New York	05/28/1847	02/01/1851	3	75	N	
Wolf, George	33	Germany	Y	Bremen	New York	02/04/1880	10/15/1888	19	149	N	
Wolf, George	33	Germany	Y	Bremen	New York	02/04/1880	10/15/1888			Y	
Wolf, George	34	Hesse Darmsta	Y	Antwerp	New Orleans	11/23/1848	05/19/1852	25	46	N	
Wolf, Harris	43	Russia	Y	Hamburg	New York	05/??/1885	10/12/1896			Y	
Wolf, Heinrich	??	Austria	Y	?	?	?	08/08/1893			Y	
Wolf, Henry	40	Bavaria	Y	Havre	New York	11/24/1851	02/26/1856	26	132	N	
Wolf, Jacob	46	Bavaria	Y	Havre	New York	08/16/1851	10/06/1859	17	476	N	
Wolf, John	46	Prussia	Y	Bremen	Indianola	12/17/1852	12/31/1855	13	402	N	
Wolf, John	29	Germany	Y	Hamburg	New York	07/13/1880	06/24/1882			Y	
Wolf, John	39	Germany	N	Rotterdam	Baltimore	??/??/1871	?			Y	
Wolf, John	30	Germany	Y	Bremen	New York	06/14/1882	03/13/1884			Y	
Wolf, John H.	36	Germany	N	Amsterdam	New York	04/??/1869	?			Y	
Wolf, John Michael	36	Germany	Y	Antwerp	New York	05/26/1880	11/08/1882			Y	
Wolf, Joseph	21	Bavaria	Y	Bremen	New York	02/24/1869	04/29/1872	18	491	N	
Wolf, Karl	29	Germany	Y	Bremen	New York	07/27/1882	04/05/1887			Y	
Wolf, Matthias	22	Prussia	Y	Havre	New Orleans	05/??/1846	12/??/1849	23	425	N	
Wolf, Max	??	Germany	Y	?	?	09/01/1856	04/27/1869			Y	
Wolf, Michael	58	Germany	Y	Hamburg	New York	02/21/1884	07/19/1889			Y	
Wolf, Paul	22	Germany	Y	Antwerp	New York	09/23/1887	06/05/1889			Y	
Wolf, Peter	22	Bavaria	Y	Havre	New York	03/04/1854	09/17/1855	13	57	N	
Wolf, Phillipp	26	Bavaria	Y	Antwerp	New Orleans	01/29/1850	01/15/1851	2	498	N	
Wolf, Robert Gottfried	??	Germany	Y	?	?	?	07/03/1884			Y	
Wolf, Sebastian	42	Germany	Y	Havre	New York	05/25/1843	10/05/1883			Y	
Wolf, Theodore	24	Bavaria	Y	Havre	New York	01/15/1855	03/18/1858	16	420	N	
Wolf, Thomas A.	44	Germany	Y	Bremen	New York	05/11/1883	07/15/1885			Y	
Wolf, Wolf	48	Germany	Y	Hamburg	New York	12/10/1882	02/27/1891			Y	
Wolfenperger, Paul	29	Germany	Y	Hamburg	New York	02/16/1880	10/17/1888			Y	
Wolfers, Fredrick	42	Germany	N	Bremen	New York	09/24/1868	?			Y	
Wolff, Alban	26	Germany	Y	Bremen	New York	09/26/1886	09/09/1889			Y	
Wolff, August	24	Prussia	Y	Bremen	New York	03/26/1852	04/25/1854	8	262	N	
Wolff, August	24	Prussia	Y	Bremen	New York	03/26/1852	04/25/1854	9	133	N	
Wolff, Bernard H.	31	Russia	Y	Liverpool	New York	01/25/1889	12/27/1898			Y	
Wolff, Charles	30	Prussia	Y	Bremen	New Orleans	01/??/1848	11/??/1849	23	304	N	
Wolff, Daniel	36	Wuertemberg	Y	Havre	New York	03/02/1852	02/04/1856	26	37	N	
Wolff, Jacob	44	Germany	Y	Antwerp	New York	07/15/1881	06/21/1888	19	133	N	
Wolff, Mike	28	Hungary	Y	Bremen	New York	02/24/1901	08/18/1902			Y	
Wolfingel, John	24	Wurttemberg	Y	Havre	New York	04/18/1851	02/14/1853	7	157	N	
Wolfram, Albert	28	Germany	Y	Bremen	New York	10/20/1883	04/21/1886			Y	
Wolfram, August	31	Germany	Y	Bremen	New York	05/15/1885	01/03/1893			Y	
Wolfram, Ludwig	55	Germany	Y	Bremen	Baltimore	10/29/1884	02/24/1890			Y	
Wolfram, Xaver	47	Bavaria	Y	Bremen	Baltimore	01/01/1847	03/03/1853	7	264	N	
Wolfrom, Charles	23	Germany	Y	Antwerp	New York	06/21/1882	01/25/1886			Y	
Wolfrum, Henry	28	Germany	Y	Bremen	New York	03/19/1880	10/28/1887			Y	
Wolfrum, Henry T.	25	Germany	Y	Bremen	New York	04/13/1892	11/07/1893			Y	
Wolhing, Henry	43	Hanover	Y	Bremen	Baltimore	06/03/1857	07/21/1860	27	231	N	
Wolinski, Eduard	31	Prussia	Y	Hamburg	New York	03/30/1852	04/20/1854	8	223	N	
Wolinski, Eduard	31	Prussia	Y	Hamburg	New York	03/30/1852	04/20/1854	9	94	N	
Wolke, John Henry	38	Germany	Y	Bremen	Baltimore	09/??/1874	10/13/1884			Y	
Wolke, Theodore	24	Germany	Y	Amsterdam	New York	05/01/1882	07/10/1884			Y	
Wolking, Bernard Joseph	26	Germany	Y	Bremen	New York	08/13/1880	07/31/1882			Y	
Wolking, F. Joh.	17	Germany	N	?	New York	00/00/1882				Y	10/26/1887
Wolking, Heinrich Joseph	31	Oldenburg	Y	Hamburg	New York	05/09/1860	06/11/1862	18	350	N	

CITIZENSHIP RECORDS

APPLICANT	AGE	COUNTRY OF ORIGIN	DEC	DEPART PORT	ENTRY PORT	ARRIVE DATE	DEC DATE	VOL	PG.	FLD	NAT DATE
Wolking, Tony	26	Germany	N	Bremen	New York	05/01/1879	?			Y	
Wollenberg, Henry	20	Canada	Y	Waterloo	Cincinnati?	02/07/1889	11/14/1889			Y	
Wollenweber, August	28	Germany	Y	Hamburg	New York	05/12/1883	03/31/1886			Y	
Wollering, K.	26	Germany	Y	Bremen	Baltimore	09/28/1873	10/08/1880			Y	
Wolpert, Frederick	31	Wuerttenberg	Y	Antwerp	New York	07/19/1846	08/23/1848	22	232	N	
Wolsdorf, H.	25	Germany	Y	Hamburg	New York	03/19/1884	07/02/1887			Y	
Wolter, Andreas Frederic	28	Prussia	Y	Bremen	Baltimore	05/29/1845	01/23/1850	23	537	N	
Wolter, Henry	26	Prussia	Y	Bremen	New York	05/28/1852	12/01/1858	17	369	N	
Wolter, Ludwig	23	Mecklenburg S	Y	Hamburg	New York	09/15/1853	01/26/1857	14	506	N	
Woltering, Henry	35	Germany	Y	Rotterdam	New York	05/08/1884	12/10/1892			Y	
Woltermann, John Gerhard	38	Oldenburg	Y	Bremen	New Orleans	12/08/1852	11/01/1858	17	224	N	
Wolters, Henry	26	Hanover	Y	Bremen	New Orleans	05/04/1843	01/18/1849	1	458	N	
Woltz, J. Fred	51	Canada	Y	Toronto	Detroit	04/05/1890	11/23/1894			Y	
Wonn, John	30	Prussia	Y	Bremen	New York	01/28/1855	01/16/1856	13	472	N	
Wood, James	27	England	Y	Liverpool	New Orleans	01/01/1857	06/14/1861	18	193	N	
Wood, James	52	Ireland	Y	Liverpool	Boston	04/31/1866	10/24/1890			Y	
Wood, Thomas	27	England	Y	Liverpool	New Orleans	01/01/1855	02/09/1858	16	94	N	
Wood, William	25	England	Y	London	New York	06/02/1850	08/28/1855	11	509	N	
Wood, William	33	Scotland	Y	Glasgow	New York	04/13/1888	10/29/1897			Y	
Woodall, Joseph	31	England	Y	Liverpool	New York	03/20/1849	08/02/1851	4	72	N	
Woodburn, Robert	24	Ireland	Y	Liverpool	Philadelphia	05/01/1853	11/22/1858	17	348	N	
Woodhead, Thomas	40	England	Y	Liverpool	New York	04/03/1844	05/17/1852	25	32	N	
Woodley, Charles	54	England	Y	Liverpool	New York	02/17/1861	04/03/1890			Y	
Woodruff, Joseph	21	England	Y	?	?	?	10/14/1882			Y	
Woods, Henry	41	England	Y	London	New Uork	08/24/1859	06/25/1861	18	198	N	
Woods, James	21	Ireland	Y	Liverpool	New York	09/15/1849	03/17/1851	3	290	N	
Woods, John	22	Ireland	Y	Belfast	Quebec	??/09/1848	?	2	73	N	
Woods, Lewis	51	England	Y	Liverpool	New York	04/29/1874	10/26/1896			Y	
Woods, Patrick	24	Ireland	Y	London	New York	06/22/1848	02/01/1850	2	22	N	
Woods, Patrick	55	Ireland	Y	Liverpool	New York	10/29/1880	11/07/1892	19	413	N	
Woods, Patrick	55	Ireland	Y	Liverpool	New York	10/29/1890	11/07/1892			Y	
Woolley, William A.	28	England	Y	Liverpool	New York	09/03/1842	06/21/1852	25	298	N	
Woopreys, William	38	Holland	Y	Rotterdam	New Orleans	12/26/1846	02/18/1852	24	135	N	
Wopperer, Charles	47	Germany	Y	Hamburg	New York	05/21/1871	05/18/1891			Y	
Wopperer, John	30	Germany	Y	Antwerp	New York	04/07/1882	03/30/1883			Y	
Worm, August	??	Denmark	Y	?	?	?	08/15/1890			Y	
Wormser, Benjamin	38	Germany	N	Havre	New York	05/21/1867	?			Y	
Worner, Joseph	26	Germany	Y	Havre	New York	07/16/1880	12/11/1882			Y	
Worth, Charles	23	England	Y	?	New York	05/20/1888	05/23/1891			Y	
Worth, John	47	England	Y	Liverpool	Buffalo	??/??/1859	10/10/1979			Y	
Worthman, John	34	Germany	N	Bremen	New York	12/23/1880	?			Y	
Wortman, Henry	54	Germany	N	Bremen	Quebec	??/??/1837	?			Y	
Wortmann, Gerhard	49	Prussia	Y	Bremen	Baltimore	05/27/1850	06/13/1851	3	369	N	
Woseczek, Ludwig	??	Austria	Y	?	?	?	11/15/1893			Y	
Wostbrook, F.	27	Hanover	Y	Bremen	New York	05/27/1857	06/25/1860	27	3	N	
Wostmann, Henry	26	Hanover	Y	Bremen	New Orleans	06/22/1845	02/15/1849	23	138	N	
Woyke, Gottleib	30	Prussia	Y	Bremen	New Orleans	12/24/1851	05/04/1854	9	243	N	
Woyke, Gottlieb	30	Prussia	Y	Bremen	New Orleans	12/24/1851	05/04/1854	8	370	N	
Wrampelmeier, Frederick	33	Hanover	Y	Bremen	New Orleans	12/07/1848	01/02/1851	2	444	N	
Wrampelmeier, Frederick	33	Germany	Y	Bremen	Baltimore	04/30/1882	11/22/1886			Y	
Wratten, James	48	England	Y	London	New York	08/03/1821	12/24/1850	2	388	N	
Wrede, Bernhard	30	Germany	Y	Bremen	Baltimore	09/22/1880	10/04/1880			Y	
Wrede, Henry	28	Brunswick	Y	Bremen	New Orleans	11/04/1850	08/04/1851	4	85	N	
Wright, Alfred	??	Great Britain	Y	?	?	?	10/25/1876			Y	
Wright, Authur	35	Ireland	Y	Liverpool	Cleveland?	03/01/1882	02/03/1892			Y	
Wright, Charles	32	England	Y	Bristol	New York	05/09/1848	04/04/1853	8	4	N	
Wright, John W.	46	England	N	Liverpool	New York	06/20/1861	?			Y	
Wright, Richard	32	England	Y	Liverpool	New York	03/02/1849	12/02/1852	5	368	N	
Wrin, Michael	30	Ireland	Y	Liverpool	New Orleans	12/10/1848	03/03/1851	3	192	N	

CITIZENSHIP RECORDS

APPLICANT	AGE	COUNTRY OF ORIGIN	DEC	DEPART PORT	ENTRY PORT	ARRIVE DATE	DEC DATE	VOL	PG.	FLD	NAT DATE
Wrubel, Elias F.	44	Russia	Y	Hamburg	New York	12/29/1889	11/04/1896			Y	
Wubbolding, A. Ferdinand	49	Germany	N	Bremen	Baltimore	05/16/1854	?			Y	
Wuchtel, Martin	44	Germany	Y	Bremen	Baltimore	05/18/1873	07/24/1882			Y	
Wuebbold, August	25	Germany	Y	Antwerp	New York	03/27/1884	11/05/1889			Y	
Wuebbold, Herman	24	Germany	Y	Bremen	Baltimore	09/12/1897	02/13/1899			Y	
Wuebker, Anton	27	Germany	Y	Rotterdam	New York	10/18/1893	02/02/1899			Y	
Wueblen, Gerhard Heinric	31	Hanover	Y	Bremen	Baltimore	09/20/1846	02/07/1853	7	123	N	
Wuelker, Fred	26	Hanover	Y	Bremen	Baltimore	11/11/1845	02/19/1849	23	209	N	
Wueller, Henry	33	Prussia	Y	Bremen	New Orleans	11/25/1847	06/19/1851	3	430	N	
Wuellner, August	28	Germany	Y	Bremen	New York	04/24/1885	10/29/1895			Y	
Wuensche, Christopher	29	Saxony	Y	Hamburg	New York	02/17/1849	01/24/1853	7	64	N	
Wuenscher, Henry W.	30	Saxe Weimar	Y	Bremen	New York	09/17/1849	07/22/1851	4	26	N	
Wuerffel, John	24	Germany	Y	Bremen	New York	07/07/1892	10/06/1892			Y	
Wuerling, Gustav	41	France	Y	Havre	New York	11/05/1846	07/02/1851	3	476	N	
Wuertershagen, John	27	Prussia	Y	Rotterdam	Baltimore	08/12/1849	02/04/1851	3	95	N	
Wuerzberger, Anton	31	Bavaria	Y	Havre	New Orleans	11/28/1845	08/15/1848	22	146	N	
Wuest, Conrad	24	Bavaria	Y	Bremen	New York	03/20/1881	11/06/1882			Y	
Wuest, Henry	47	Bavaria	Y	Havre	New York	12/01/1842	09/30/1848	22	368	N	
Wuest, Joseph	33	Switzerland	Y	Havre	New York	03/02/1891	05/01/1896			Y	
Wuest, Oswald	23	Switzerland	Y	Havre	New York	03/01/1891	05/26/1894			Y	
Wuest, Oswald	23	Switzerland	Y	Havre	New York	03/01/1891	05/26/1894			Y	
Wuestmann, Gerhard	30	Germany	Y	Bremen	New York	06/20/1890	04/03/1894			Y	
Wuetherich, Alfred	47	Switzerland	Y	Havre	New York	05/17/1884	12/29/1898			Y	
Wuethrich, John	34	Switzerland	Y	Antwerp	New York	03/15/1891	04/08/1897			Y	
Wulbers, Hermann	38	Germany	N	Rotterdam	New York	08/??/1870	?			Y	
Wuldick, Patrick	38	Ireland	Y	Hamilton NC	Lewiston NY	08/25/1840	08/15/1848	22	136	N	
Wulf, Albert	34	Germany	Y	Hamburg	New York	10/03/1886	10/14/1887			Y	
Wulf, Anton	33	Germany	Y	Bremen	New York	06/16/1888	10/20/1892			Y	
Wulf, Heinrich	45	Germany	Y	Hamburg	New York	04/??/1861	10/29/1887			Y	
Wulf, Herman	30	Germany	Y	Bremen	New York	03/29/1885	10/20/1892			Y	
Wulf, Theodore	24	Germany	Y	Bremen	Baltimore	08/13/1884	06/05/1890			Y	
Wulfekuhle, Gerhard Henr	29	Germany	Y	Bremen	Baltimore	06/11/1881	11/03/1887			Y	
Wulff, Franz	28	Germany	Y	Bremen	Baltimore	07/06/1882	12/23/1884			Y	
Wulfoost, Frederick	25	Hanover	Y	Bremen	New Orleans	11/15/1847	03/23/1853	7	379	N	
Wuller, Henry	30	Prussia	Y	Bremen	New Orleans	12/15/1852	09/12/1855	13	10	N	
Wullkotte, George	27	Germany	Y	Amsterdam	New York	11/04/1892	02/24/1896			Y	
Wullkotte, John	38	Germany	Y	Bremen	New York	05/28/1884	10/25/1894			Y	
Wulsten, Aug	??	Germany	Y	?	?	?	11/04/1884			Y	
Wunder, Christ	42	Germany	Y	Bremen	New York	05/05/1885	10/26/1892			Y	
Wunderlich, Fred	??	Germany	Y	?	?	?	11/05/1888			Y	
Wunderlich, Rudolph	39	Germany	Y	Bremen	Baltimore	09/03/1874	10/10/1889			Y	
Wunderlich, Theodor	28	Germany	Y	Antwerp	Philadelphia	07/13/1882	08/01/1892			Y	
Wunnemann, Bernard	25	Germany	Y	Bremen	New York	11/26/1884	05/20/1889			Y	
Wunnemann, Herman	40	Germany	Y	Bremen	New York	05/10/1884	10/29/1892			Y	
Wunsch, Fred	25	Wurttemberg	Y	Bremen	New York	10/??/1845	10/24/1851	4	388	N	
Wunsch, Henry	44	Germany	Y	Bremen	New York	09/05/1884	07/18/1887			Y	
Wunschel, Fred	31	Germany	Y	Bremen	New York	05/19/1890	10/16/1895			Y	
Wurm, George	22	Austria	Y	?	?	?	12/15/1887			Y	
Wurm, Philipp	22	Germany	Y	Bremen	New York	02/01/1895	07/06/1895			Y	
Wurmstee, Oliver	34	Saxe Weimar	Y	Bremen	New York	08/01/1850	03/28/1853	7	434	N	
Wurst, John	29	Wuerttemberg	Y	Haver	New York	09/27/1847	04/06/1852	24	398	N	
Wurst, William	52	Wuerttemberg	Y	Havre	New York	09/27/1847	04/06/1852	24	397	N	
Wurste, Rochus	34	Bavaria	Y	Havre	New York	06/11/1857	02/19/1862	18	265	N	
Wurster, Christian Frede	27	Wurttemberg	Y	Havre	New York	04/09/1849	04/29/1850	3	31	N	
Wurster, John	24	Wuerttemberg	Y	Havre	New York	06/24/1849	09/04/1852	25	358	N	
Wurster, Philipp	23	Germany	Y	Hamburg	New York	08/25/1880	02/17/1883			Y	
Wurtz, John	32	Germany	Y	Hamburg	New York	07/06/1880	11/22/1880			Y	
Wurz, Joseph	49	Germany	N	Liverpool	New York	09/28/1866	?			Y	
Wurzelbacher, Peter	37	Bavaria	Y	Bremen	Baltimore	07/14/1855	07/21/1858	16	517	N	

CITIZENSHIP RECORDS

APPLICANT	AGE	COUNTRY OF ORIGIN	DEC	DEPART PORT	ENTRY PORT	ARRIVE DATE	DEC DATE	VOL	PG.	FLD	NAT DATE
Wust, Andreas	35	Germany	Y	Bremen	Baltimore	04/07/1880	05/03/1883			Y	
Wust, Frederick Christop	41	Bavaria	Y	Havre	New York	10/12/1855	11/08/1855	13	191	N	
Wust, Henry	31	Bavaria	Y	Havre	New York	07/01/1854	09/29/1856	14	19	N	
Wust, William	??	Bavaria	Y	Havre	New Orleans	11/27/1845	10/05/1848	1	56	N	
Wyenauck, Rudolph	33	Prussia	Y	St. Juan	New Orleans	02/27/1851	01/07/1853	5	531	N	
Wyes, Alphonsa	28	Switzerland	Y	Havre	New York	10/08/1879	10/19/1882			Y	
Wyland, Herman	23	Baden	Y	Havre	New Orleans	05/26/1847	10/13/1848	1	191	N	
Wylie, Matthew Duncan	??	Scotland	Y	?	?	?	09/09/1884			Y	
Wynn, James	35	England	Y	Liverpool	Philadelphia	04/10/1887	06/11/1895			Y	
Wynn, Thomas	24	England	Y	Liverpool	New Orleans	12/18/1845	11/13/1848	1	272	N	
Wyse, Michael	27	Ireland	Y	Liverpool	New Orleans	02/01/1851	05/10/1854	8	419	N	
Wyss, Joseph	24	Switzerland	Y	Havre	New York	07/29/1880	01/06/1882			Y	
Wyttenbach, Christian	44	Switzerland	Y	Havre	New York	08/06/1848	02/19/1849	23	216	N	
Yaeger, Frederick	32	Prussia	Y	Baltimore	Baltimore	12/19/1849	10/09/1854	6	86	N	
Yaeger, Frederick	32	Prussia	Y	Havre	Baltimore	12/19/1849	10/09/1854	11	89	N	
Yaeger, Severin	45	Germany	Y	Antwerp	New York	05/26/1880	05/15/1891			Y	
Yaffe, Jacob	??	Russia	N	?	?	05/09/1887				Y	10/17/1892
Yager, John	28	Switzerland	Y	Havre	New York	08/30/1857	09/29/1860	27	387	N	
Yantman, Gerhard	22	Holland	Y	Bremen	New Orleans	07/15/1851	10/09/1854	11	77	N	
Yates, Alfred	45	England	Y	Liverpool	New York	02/19/1881	05/??/1882	28	184	N	
Yeager, Joseph	30	Baden	Y	Havre	New Orleans	07/09/1849	03/28/1853	7	427	N	
Yeaz, John	23	Hesse Darmsta	Y	Havre	New York	03/??/1856	11/03/1856	14	150	N	
Yensen, Bernard	32	Hanover	Y	Bremen	New Orleans	11/27/1857	10/08/1860	27	445	N	
Yesulis, Powils	35	Russia	Y	Bremen	Baltimore	07/13/1891	07/09/1904			Y	
Yoerger, Louis	24	Baden	Y	Havre	New Orleans	07/??/1847	10/22/1851	4	373	N	
Yoger, John	40	Bavaria	Y	Bremen	New York	12/13/1853	05/07/1859	17	402	N	
Yost, Adolph	27	Prussia	Y	Hamburg	New York	10/01/1860	05/19/1862	18	337	N	
Yost, Henry	25	Bavaria	Y	Havre	New Orleans	10/14/1845	09/09/1848	22	317	N	
Young, Frederick	35	Bavaria	Y	Havre	New Orleans	04/04/1846	10/14/1848	1	214	N	
Young, John	33	Nassau	Y	Liverpool	New York	10/02/1849	10/06/1851	4	205	N	
Young, John	50	Bavaria	Y	Havre	New York	08/28/1846	08/10/1848	22	86	N	
Young, Peter	25	France	Y	Havre	New Orleans	04/??/1850	11/29/1855	13	264	N	
Younger, Thomas	26	Scotland	Y	Liverpool	New York	12/11/1853	11/06/1858	17	283	N	
Yubinsky, Sam	40	Russia	Y	Hamburg	New York	04/36/1890	10/27/1899			Y	
Yung, Daniel	22	Germany	Y	Bremen	New York	08/13/1883	09/24/1886			Y	
Yung, Ignatz	41	Baden	Y	Havre	New Orleans	12/09/1853	10/08/1860	27	448	N	
Yungbluth, Herman	23	Germany	Y	Bremen	New York	11/07/1885	03/27/1891			Y	
Yungeblut, August	25	Germany	Y	Bremen	New York	04/04/1882	03/25/1885			Y	
Yungkunz, John	30	Germany	Y	Bremen	Baltimore	04/10/1881	02/04/1888			Y	
Zabel, Frederick	25	Saxony	Y	Hamburg	New York	05/12/1850	03/04/1853	7	270	N	
Zabke, Julius	35	Germany	Y	Bremen	New York	06/07/1881	03/20/1882			Y	
Zacharias, John	61	Germany	Y	Havre	New York	03/10/1865	10/17/1893			Y	
Zachow, August	35	Germany	Y	Bremen	New York	06/01/1893	01/10/1898			Y	
Zachritz, Henry	22	Bavaria	Y	Havre	New Orleans	06/16/1848	08/08/1851	4	100	N	
Zachritz, Louis	23	Bavaria	Y	Havre	New Orleans	09/01/1853	09/27/1858	16	123	N	
Zahlten, August	37	Prussia	Y	Hamburg	New York	08/05/1852	04/29/1854	8	288	N	
Zahlten, August	37	Prussia	Y	Hamburg	New York	08/05/1852	04/29/1854	9	160	N	
Zahn, Adam	29	Bavaria	Y	Havre	New York	11/04/1850	10/03/1854	10	371	N	
Zahn, Adam	29	Bavaria	Y	Havre	New York	11/04/1850	10/03/1854	12	310	N	
Zahn, Balthaser	48	Hesse Darmsta	Y	Havre	New York	04/16/1851	10/09/1854	6	66	N	
Zahn, Balthaser	48	Hesse Darmsta	Y	Havre	New York	04/16/1851	10/09/1854	11	67	N	
Zahn, Friederich	30	Germany	Y	Antwerp	New York	12/01/1881	07/20/1891			Y	
Zahn, George	35	Germany	Y	Bremen	Baltimore	09/??/1872	10/03/1885			Y	
Zahn, John George	31	Hesse Darmsta	Y	Rotterdam	New Orleans	12/??/1843	12/07/1850	2	344	N	
Zahn, Joseph	46	Germany	Y	Hamburg	Portland	02/01/1867	05/02/1883			Y	
Zahn, Michael	39	Baden	Y	Havre	New Orleans	12/22/1846	05/24/1852	25	94	N	
Zahnd, John	32	Switzerland	Y	Havre	New York	05/24/1866	01/29/1872	18	460	N	
Zahneiss, George Jacob	24	Bavaria	Y	Havre	New York	03/07/1853	03/31/1856	26	378	N	
Zahrt, Albert	25	Oldenburg	Y	Bremen	New York	08/22/1853	02/10/1857	15	14	N	

CITIZENSHIP RECORDS

APPLICANT	AGE	COUNTRY OF ORIGIN	DEC	DEPART PORT	ENTRY PORT	ARRIVE DATE	DEC DATE	VOL	PG.	FLD	NAT DATE
Zalonki, Joseph	24	Russia	Y	Bremen	New York	10/29/1890	10/24/1896			Y	
Zander, Christian, Jr.	24	Mecklenburg S	Y	Hamburg	New York	12/25/1854	06/05/1856	14	296	N	
Zander, Christian, Sr.	48	Mecklenburg S	Y	Hamburg	New York	12/25/1854	06/05/1856	14	297	N	
Zang, George	33	Germany	Y	Hamburg	New York	08/25/1880	10/14/1886			Y	
Zanker, Jacob	23	Bavaria	Y	Bremen	New York	04/15/1853	08/04/1856	14	328	N	
Zankowitz, Charles	28	Russia	Y	Hamburg	New York	05/17/1882	08/21/1893			Y	
Zapf, Emil Edward	28	Germany	Y	?	New York	??/??/1880	05/08/1884			Y	
Zapf, Matthews	42	Germany	Y	Antwerp	?	05/26/1882	10/27/1900			Y	
Zapf, Peter	40	Germany	Y	Havre	New York	06/09/1882	02/14/1885			Y	
Zapf, William	??	Baden	Y	?	?	?	10/26/1883			Y	
Zartmann, Clemens August	48	Germany	Y	Bremen	New York	10/04/1884	10/21/1900			Y	
Zawactsky, Nochim	50	Poland	Y	Hamburg	Boston	05/??/1881	07/08/1890			Y	
Zazycki, Jan	42	Germany	Y	Bremen	Baltimore	09/24/1882	03/02/1894			Y	
Zcinder, Christian	29	Switzerland	Y	Havre	New York	05/18/1847	10/02/1848	1	5	N	
Zeckendorf, Alois	??	Austria	Y	?	?	?	09/29/1893			Y	
Zeff, Abe	30	Poland	Y	Bremen	New York	05/17/1898	11/10/1902			Y	
Zeff, Mendel	37	Poland	Y	Hamburg	New York	08/??/1879	05/25/1888			Y	
Zegal, Lazarus	21	Russia	Y	Bremen	Baltimore	08/15/1887	09/23/1890			Y	
Zegal, Meyer	55	Russia	Y	Hamburg	New York	08/04/1884	09/23/1890			Y	
Zehender, Christian Ludw	22	Wurttemberg	Y	Havre	New York	10/05/1854	07/03/1857	15	123	N	
Zehenni, Nader El	25	Arabia (Turke	Y	Beirut	New York	11/14/1888	08/30/1892			Y	
Zehenni, Tanous El	23	Arabia (Turke	Y	Beirut	New York	11/14/1888	08/30/1892			Y	
Zehler, George	22	Bavaria	Y	Havre	New York	05/31/1852	09/20/1854	10	134	N	
Zehler, George	22	Bavaria	Y	Havre	New York	05/31/1852	09/20/1854	12	73	N	
Zehnder, Frederick	23	Switzerland	Y	Havre	New York	08/06/1848	02/19/1849	23	217	N	
Zehnder, Joseph	23	Germany	Y	Havre	New York	10/20/1890	04/26/1892			Y	
Zehnder, Martin	29	Switzerland	Y	Havre	New York	09/22/1852	04/17/1854	8	179	N	
Zehnder, Martin	29	Switzerland	Y	Havre	New York	09/22/1852	04/17/1854	9	50	N	
Zeiner, John	45	Bavaria	Y	Bremen	Baltimore	06/01/1847	03/18/1851	3	305	N	
Zeisel, Andrew	27	Bavaria	Y	Bremen	Baltimore	05/10/1853	10/07/1854	11	13	N	
Zeiszel, Andrew	27	Bavaria	Y	Bremen	Baltimore	04/10/1853	10/07/1854	6	12	N	
Zelaro, Louis	23	Poland	Y	?	?	?	06/27/1889			Y	
Zelazo, Abraham	26	Russia	Y	Antwerp	New York	09/17/1886	04/01/1890			Y	
Zellekews, Werner	24	Prussia	Y	Antwerp	New York	06/06/1860	08/15/1861	18	215	N	
Zeller, Joseph	??	Germany	Y	?	New York	11/??/1889	03/05/1892			Y	
Zeller, Joseph	52	Germany	Y	Bremen	Baltimore	05/23/1869	10/12/1896			Y	
Zellner, George	31	Bavaria	Y	Bremen	New York	09/04/1849	10/07/1854	6	33	N	
Zellner, George	31	Bavaria	Y	Bremen	New York	09/04/1849	10/07/1854	11	34	N	
Zelly, John	34	Germany	Y	Bremen	New York	04/09/1882	03/30/1885			Y	
Zeltner, John	29	Bavaria	Y	Bremen	Baltimore	07/15/1845	08/28/1848	22	265	N	
Zengeler, John	21	Prussia	Y	Havre	New York	02/08/1852	09/11/1855	11	533	N	
Zens, William	35	Prussia	Y	Antwerp	New York	07/24/1846	10/09/1854	6	139	N	
Zens, William	35	Prussia	Y	Antwerp	New York	07/24/1846	10/09/1854	11	142	N	
Zentner, Franz	42	Hesse Darmsta	Y	Hamburg	Galveston	07/03/1847	01/06/1851	2	463	FLD	
Zepf, Erhard	24	Germany	Y	Havre	New York	06/10/1888	12/08/1890			Y	
Zepf, Louis	37	Germany	Y	Rotterdam	New York	10/13/1873	10/26/1888			Y	
Zepin, Osher	44	Russia	Y	Hamburg	Philadelphia	07/27/1882	07/16/1883			Y	
Zeppenfeld, Frank	34	Prussia	Y	Bremen	New Orleans	12/26/1851	11/17/1852	5	301	N	
Zerrusen, Clemens	22	Oldenburg	Y	Bremen	Baltimore	09/06/1845	10/04/1848	22	418	N	
Zeter, Adam	27	Bavaria	Y	Bremen	New York	06/30/1854	11/02/1857	15	519	N	
Zettel, Ignaz	65	Germany	N	Bremen	New York	11/??/1867	?			Y	
Zettl, Anton	29	Germany	Y	Bremen	New York	04/06/1885	04/05/1890			Y	
Zettler, Sebastian	35	Bavaria	Y	Havre	New Orleans	12/19/1849	12/22/1852	5	438	N	
Zettler, Xaver	56	Baden	Y	Havre	New Orleans	03/05/1853	10/22/1857	15	480	N	
Zetzl, Andrew	28	Germany	Y	Bremen	New York	08/01/1885	08/19/1889			Y	
Zeurr, Jacob	22	Wurttemberg	Y	Bremen	New York	08/22/1856	05/09/1859	17	404	N	
Zeyen, Joseph	23	Luxemburg	Y	Antwerp	New York	11/08/1854	05/22/1856	26	534	N	
Zibold, Richard	28	Germany	N	Bremen	New York	08/25/1880	?			Y	
Zick, Christian	50	Bavaria	Y	Havre	New York	05/05/1857	08/08/1862	18	390	N	

CITIZENSHIP RECORDS

APPLICANT	AGE	COUNTRY OF ORIGIN	DEC	DEPART PORT	ENTRY PORT	ARRIVE DATE	DEC DATE	VOL	PG.	FLD	NAT DATE
Zick, Joseph	21	Bavaria	Y	Havre	New York	05/30/1853	12/18/1855	13	328	N	
Ziechner, Oskar	34	Germany	Y	Bremen	New York	12/04/1880	06/18/1889			Y	
Ziefher, Michael	23	France	Y	Havre	New Orleans	05/08/1847	02/12/1849	23	72	N	
Ziegenbein, Ernst	46	Brunswick	Y	Bremen	New Orleans	10/26/1852	10/09/1854	6	163	N	
Ziegenbein, Ernst	46	Brunswick	Y	Bremen	New Orleans	10/26/1852	10/09/1854	11	166	N	
Ziegenbein, Henry	35	Brunswick	Y	Bremen	Baltimore	09/16/1846	01/15/1850	23	510	N	
Ziegenbusch, William K.	22	Germany	Y	?	New York	05/25/1883	01/22/1886			Y	
Ziegenthaler, Edward	22	Germany	Y	Rotterdam	New York	08/27/1893	08/10/1895			Y	
Ziegenthaler, Jacob	51	Germany	Y	Havre	New York	??/??/1853	03/18/1872	18	473	N	
Ziegler, Adolph	23	Germany	Y	?	New York	??/??/1891	11/03/1894			Y	
Ziegler, Adolph Maximili	33	Germany	Y	Hamburg	New York	08/30/1884	12/26/1884			Y	
Ziegler, Andreas	71	Germany	Y	Bremen	New York	10/11/1883	11/18/1883			Y	
Ziegler, Anton	24	France	Y	Havre	New Orleans	12/24/1850	05/17/1852	25	30	N	
Ziegler, Charles	21	Baden	Y	Havre	New Orleans	04/24/1854	12/26/1855	13	362	N	
Ziegler, Charles	30	Germany	Y	Havre	New York	10/19/1882	10/16/1893			Y	
Ziegler, George	39	Germany	Y	Hamburg	New York	01/28/1878	09/07/1887			Y	
Ziegler, Joseph	34	Bavaria	Y	Havre	New York	05/??/1849	01/20/1853	7	48	N	
Ziegler, Karl	20	Germany	Y	Bremen	New York	07/05/1888	11/11/1891			Y	
Ziegler, Lorenz	38	Hesse Darmsta	Y	London	New York	05/29/1848	05/06/1850	3	58	N	
Ziegler, Ludwig	46	Austria	Y	Havre	New Orleans	02/03/1848	05/21/1852	25	87	N	
Ziegler, Martin	27	Germany	Y	?	?	06/10/1891	03/21/1895			Y	
Ziegler, Martin	28	Baden	Y	Bremen	New York	09/28/1845	10/??/1848	22	420	N	
Ziegler, Peter	25	Germany	Y	Antwerp	New York	05/04/1883	10/29/1888	19	195	N	
Ziegler, Peter	25	Germany	Y	Antwerp	New York	05/04/1883	10/29/1888			Y	
Ziegler, Sebastian	37	France	Y	Havre	New Orleans	10/15/1848	09/28/1854	10	284	N	
Ziegler, Sebastian	37	France	Y	Havre	New Orleans	10/15/1848	09/28/1854	12	223	N	
Ziegler, Wilhelm	41	Germany	Y	Bremen	New York	04/15/1882	09/24/1894			Y	
Zielke, Johann	31	Germany	Y	Antwerp	New York	04/13/1882	06/20/1887			Y	
Zielonka, David	35	Russia	Y	Hamburg	New York	10/20/1880	09/11/1885			Y	
Zier, George	50	Baden	Y	Kehle	New Orleans	04/04/1855	09/27/1858	16	117	N	
Zierer, George	29	Germany	Y	Bremen	New York	09/03/1887	12/09/1890			Y	
Zierer, Herman	31	Germany	Y	Bremen	New York	11/19/1889	10/06/1892	19	354	N	
Zierer, Xavier	31	Germany	Y	Bremen	New York	11/18/1889	10/06/1892			Y	
Zieske, Julius	??	Germany	Y	?	?	04/25/1881	10/17/1889			Y	
Zieverink, John	28	Holland	Y	Amsterdam	New York	08/18/1882	12/11/1889			Y	
Ziller, John C.	28	Bavaria	Y	Bremen	New York	07/13/1847	08/03/1848	22	50	N	
Zillinger, Peter	35	Germany	Y	Rotterdam	New York	01/31/1881	03/02/1885			Y	
Zimerman, Adam	33	Baden	Y	London	New York	05/01/1848	06/11/1852	25	238	N	
Zimmer, Jacob	24	Prussia	Y	London	New York	05/04/1851	09/26/1856	14	387	N	
Zimmer, Joseph	25	Wurttemberg	Y	Havre	New York	11/06/1854	04/09/1858	16	468	N	
Zimmer, Lorenz	??	Baden, German	Y	?	?	?	06/29/1882			Y	
Zimmer, Peter	31	Baden	Y	Havre	New Orleans	04/??/1848	02/25/1856	26	125	N	
Zimmerli, Friedrick	??	Switzerland	Y	?	?	?	09/01/1882			Y	
Zimmerman, Andrew	46	Bavaria	Y	Havre	New Orleans	11/05/1845	06/19/1851	3	419	N	
Zimmerman, Anton	??	(Affidavit On	N	?	?	?	06/20/1898			Y	
Zimmerman, Frank	29	Germany	Y	Bremen	Baltimore	06/12/1893	09/12/1898			Y	
Zimmerman, John	31	Bavaria	Y	Bremen	New York	09/06/1848	07/28/1851	4	57	N	
Zimmerman, John	25	Bavaria	Y	Havre	New York	10/18/1851	10/02/1854	10	357	N	
Zimmerman, Joseph	41	Switzerland	Y	Antwerp	New York	01/19/1867	03/25/1885			Y	
Zimmermann, Anton	??	Austria	Y	?	?	?	08/17/1892			Y	
Zimmermann, Anton	34	Germany	Y	Bremen	Baltimore	04/01/1886	10/06/1896			Y	
Zimmermann, Christian	25	Germany	Y	Antwerp	New York	09/17/1886	06/25/1888			Y	
Zimmermann, Emil	32	Germany	Y	Antwerp	New York	12/09/1880	10/21/1889			Y	
Zimmermann, Ferdinand	28	Germany	Y	Bremen	Baltimore	07/29/1880	11/18/1884			Y	
Zimmermann, Jacob	25	Germany	Y	Bremen	Baltimore	08/16/1882	10/25/1889			Y	
Zimmermann, John	??	Baden	Y	?	New York	??/20/18??	10/25/1850	2	302	N	
Zimmermann, John	33	Hesse Darmsta	Y	Havre	New York	08/07/1848	10/04/1854	10	422	N	
Zimmermann, John	25	Bavaria	Y	Havre	New York	10/18/1851	10/02/1854	12	296	N	
Zimmermann, John	33	Hesse Darmsta	Y	Havre	New York	08/07/1848	10/04/1854	12	361	N	

CITIZENSHIP RECORDS

APPLICANT	AGE	COUNTRY OF ORIGIN	DEC	DEPART PORT	ENTRY PORT	ARRIVE DATE	DEC DATE	VOL	PG.	FLD	NAT DATE
Zimmermann, John	44	Germany	Y	Havre	New York	01/01/1884	11/05/1892	19	410	N	
Zimmermann, John	44	Germany	Y	Havre	New York	01/01/1884	11/05/1892			Y	
Zimmermann, John Henry	26	Hanover	Y	Bremen	New Orleans	05/20/1849	02/09/1852	24	76	N	
Zimmermann, Joseph	27	Germany	Y	Antwerp	New York	10/27/1890	10/16/1896			Y	
Zimmermann, Martin	24	Bavaria	Y	Havre	New York	05/??/1854	09/13/1855	13	18	N	
Zimmermann, Philip J.	57	Germany	N	London	New York	06/28/1850	?			Y	
Zimmermann, Rudolph	43	Bavaria	Y	Havre	New York	10/40/1855	10/30/1858	17	6	N	
Zimmermann, Simon	30	Wurttemberg	Y	Antwerp	New York	10/26/1854	04/05/1858	16	497	N	
Zimmermann, Wilhelm	34	Germany	Y	Amsterdam	New York	08/08/1881	10/25/1881			Y	
Zimpelmann, Henry	28	Germany	Y	Bremen	Baltimore	09/18/1887	09/16/1890			Y	
Zimpfer, Karl	27	Germany	Y	Bremen	New York	08/07/1889	10/26/1895			Y	
Zinck, Emil	25	Germany	Y	Bremen	Baltimore	03/11/1886	10/30/1886			Y	
Zindelbaugh, George Adam	31	Bavaria	Y	Havre	New York	08/27/1846	08/23/1848	22	235	N	
Zingerle, Christoph	42	France	Y	Havre	New York	05/05/1853	10/15/1857	15	431	N	
Zingg, Jacob	24	Switzerland	Y	Antwerp	New York	11/25/1887	10/13/1890			Y	
Zink, Fred	28	Germany	Y	Bremen	Baltimore	09/09/1890	11/01/1893			Y	
Zink, Lawrence	24	Germany	Y	Rotterdam	New York	09/20/1880	12/05/1882			Y	
Zint, George	53	France	Y	Havre	New York	11/28/1845	03/??/1850	2	230	N	
Zint, George	27	France	Y	Havre	New Orleans	12/06/1853	01/02/1858	16	295	N	
Zint, Peter	32	France	Y	Havre	New Orleans	10/22/1852	05/16/1859	17	414	N	
Zinzer, Fred	23	Germany	Y	Havre	New York	06/03/1884	03/24/1887			Y	
Zipper, John	37	Switzerland	Y	Havre	New York	07/02/1849	03/05/1851	3	205	N	
Zirwas, C. H.	26	Germany	Y	Bremen	New York	07/29/1883	10/20/1886			Y	
Zirwas, Emil	30	Germany	Y	Antwerp	New York	04/08/1885	06/08/1891			Y	
Zisenis, Bernhard	39	Hanover	Y	Bremen	New York	09/17/1850	10/06/1856	14	205	N	
Zitt, George F.	29	Germany	Y	?	New York	??/??/1871	10/09/1882			Y	
Zitt, George Frederick	25	Bavaria	Y	Havre	New York	09/16/1857	07/02/1860	27	197	N	
Zitt, Jacob	26	Germany	Y	Antwerp	New York	05/09/1881	09/24/1885			Y	
Zitt, John	29	Germany	Y	Hamburg	New York	03/15/1881	02/28/1887			Y	
Ziverch, Ludwig	32	Bavaria	Y	Bremen	New York	06/29/1854	11/08/1858	17	304	N	
Zivi, Joseph	38	Baden	Y	Havre	New York	08/09/1855	02/19/1857	15	34	N	
Zlinsky, Andrew	??	Austria	Y	?	?	?	07/13/1882			Y	
Zobel, Friederich W.	45	Germany	Y	Bremen	Baltimore	04/10/1881	10/07/1886			Y	
Zobeley, Philip	29	Germany	Y	?	?	?	02/19/1890			Y	
Zobrist, Melschior	32	Switzerland	Y	Havre	New York	06/28/1882	12/07/1885			Y	
Zodrow, Frank	47	Germany	N	Bremen	Baltimore	05/31/1873	?			Y	
Zoellner, Isidor	24	Prussia	Y	Amsterdam	New York	09/23/1851	10/18/1852	5	9	N	
Zoellner, Simon	27	Bavaria	Y	Bremen	Baltimore	04/28/1852	03/21/1856	26	247	N	
Zoerb, Conrad	24	Hesse Darmsta	Y	Bremen	New York	05/29/1855	09/20/1858	16	183	N	
Zohmann, Henry	33	Germany	Y	Amsterdam	New York	01/01/1882	04/01/1893	19	417	N	
Zohn, William	30	Bavaria	Y	Havre	New York	07/10/1851	12/27/1851	24	23	N	
Zoll, Nicholas	27	Germany	Y	Berlin	Baltimore	05/15/1891	10/22/1896			Y	
Zoller, Friedrich	23	Germany	Y	Havre	New York	03/08/1881	06/09/1890			Y	
Zoller, John	52	Austria	Y	Bremen	New York	10/06/1872	04/02/1894			Y	
Zoller, Michael Anton	31	Baden	Y	Havre	New York	05/25/1851	11/20/1855	13	237	N	
Zollers, John A.	26	Germany	Y	Bremen	Baltimore	05/14/1891	11/07/1892			Y	
Zorge, Jost Jacobus	33	Holland	Y	Rotterdam	New York	07/09/1850	09/10/1855	11	523	N	
Zorr, Anton	30	Baden	Y	Havre	New Orleans	07/22/1847	09/09/1852	25	426	N	
Zosel, Paul	31	Germany	Y	Bremen	Baltimore	06/07/1892	06/01/1898			Y	
Zottleder, Joseph	23	Austria	Y	Bremen	New York	11/23/1885	10/17/1887			Y	
Zottmann, Jacob	23	Hesse Darmsta	Y	Havre	New York	12/08/1845	01/29/1849	1	541	N	
Zuber, Adam	62	Germany	Y	Rotterdam	New York	05/25/1882	02/18/1887			Y	
Zuber, David	22	Baden	Y	Haver	New Orleans	??/08/1849	12/26/1849	23	430	N	
Zucker, Frank	62	Germany	N	Liverpool	New York	05/09/1866	?			Y	
Zucker, Louis	27	Germany	Y	?	?	?	10/06/1883			Y	
Zucker, Philip	45	Germany	N	Bremen	New York	12/26/1865	?			Y	
Zuckermann, B.	39	Turkey	Y	Hamburg	New York	12/??/1884	04/23/1889			Y	
Zuercher, J. John	25	Switzerland	Y	Havre	New York	05/19/1887	08/24/1891			Y	
Zuercher, Johann	44	Switzerland	Y	Havre	New York	07/04/1883	03/12/1890			Y	

CITIZENSHIP RECORDS

APPLICANT	AGE	COUNTRY OF ORIGIN	DEC	DEPART PORT	ENTRY PORT	ARRIVE DATE	DEC DATE	VOL	PG.	FLD	NAT DATE
Zuigelter, Henry	34	Germany	Y	Bremen	New York	05/04/1870	08/13/1884			Y	
Zulauf, John	42	Hesse Cassel	Y	Rotterdam	Philadelphia	09/19/1845	09/10/1852	25	445	N	
Zumbil, George	32	France	Y	Havre	New York	10/25/1847	02/21/1853	7	199	N	
Zumdieke, Bernard	27	Hanover	Y	Bremen	New Orleans	11/15/1851	12/29/1855	13	387	N	
Zumkeller, John	30	Baden	Y	London	New York	09/??/1848	03/22/1851	3	307	N	
Zumkeller, Leopold	55	Germany	Y	Bremen	New York	10/15/1871	03/06/1900			Y	
Zumstein, Peter	45	Bavaria	Y	Havre	New York	10/17/1849	01/18/1850	23	521	N	
Zurcher, C.	29	Switzerland	Y	Havre	New York	07/23/1858	11/05/1860	18	15	N	
Zurlage, D.	41	Germany	Y	Bremen	Baltimore	09/21/1881	06/25/1883			Y	
Zurlinn, Philip	35	Hanover	Y	Bremen	Baltimore	06/11/1840	10/28/1851	4	425	N	
Zurloh, Herman	26	Prussia	Y	Bremen	Baltimore	11/11/1854	11/01/1858	17	217	N	
Zurloh, Stephen	46	Prussia	Y	Bremen	New York	10/29/1858	11/02/1858	17	265	N	
Zurweiden, Fred B.	33	Germany	Y	Bremen	Baltimore	07/27/1882	10/23/1891			Y	
Zurwieden, Fred B.	33	Germany	Y	Bremen	Baltimore	07/27/1882	10/23/1891	19	341	N	
Zwanzig, Frank	28	Prussia	Y	Hamburg	New York	08/28/1865	05/24/1872			Y	
Zwecker, Franzx	32	Germany	Y	Hamburg	New York	05/21/1883	04/25/1887			Y	
Zwegart, Jacob	30	Germany	Y	Havre	New York	02/19/1886	06/13/1889			Y	
Zweige, Carl	22	Germany	Y	?	?	?	10/15/1888			Y	
Zweige, Fred	34	Germany	Y	Bremen	Baltimore	10/05/1892	05/03/1894			Y	
Zwick, Emil	35	Prussia	Y	?	?	?	02/14/1882			Y	
Zwick, Johannes	28	Bavaria	Y	Havre	New York	07/10/1859	08/09/1862	18	391	N	
Zwick, John	31	Germany	Y	Amsterdam	New York	12/23/1881	03/30/1885			Y	
Zwick, John Adam	32	Bavaria	Y	Havre	New York	06/04/1854	11/01/1858	17	215	N	
Zwickel, Christian	24	Germany	Y	Rotterdam	New York	10/03/1880	10/07/1882			Y	
Zwilling, Hermann	25	Germany	Y	Hamburg	New York	06/28/1888	04/03/1890			Y	
Zwillinger, Benjamin	22	Austria	Y	Hamburg	Chicago	05/21/1890	04/24/1893			Y	
Zwirsler, John	26	Bavaria	Y	Havre	New York	06/23/1847	07/17/1851	3	546	N	
Zwissler, Conrad	21	Bavaria	Y	Havre	New Orleans	01/18/1854	03/06/1857	15	69	N	
Zwosta, Konrad	33	Germany	Y	Bremen	New York	09/01/1888	11/04/1892			Y	

www.ingramcontent.com/pod-product-compliance
Lightning Source LLC
Chambersburg PA
CBHW081146290426
44108CB00018B/2452